D1302767

McGraw-Hill connect®
BUSINESS STATISTICS

STUDENTS...

Want to get **better grades**? *(Who doesn't?)*

Prefer to do your **homework online**? *(After all, you are online anyway.)*

Need **a better way** to **study** before the big test?

(A little peace of mind is a good thing...)

With **McGraw-Hill's** *Connect® Plus Business Statistics,*

STUDENTS GET:

- **Easy online access** to homework, tests, and quizzes assigned by your instructor.

- **Immediate feedback** on how you're doing. (No more wishing you could call your instructor at 1 a.m.)

- **Quick access** to lectures, practice materials, eBook, and more. (All the material you need to be successful is right at your fingertips.)

- **Guided examples** to help you solve problems **during** the assignment by providing narrated walkthroughs of similar problems.

- **Excel Data Files** embedded within many homework problems. (Launch Excel alongside *Connect* to compute solutions quickly without manually entering data.)

- **LearnSmart** provides you with practice, assessment, and remediation for every concept in the textbook. You learn as you go through the questions, focusing on topics you need to master.

Less managing. More teaching. Greater learning.

INSTRUCTORS...

Would you like your **students** to show up for class **more prepared**?
(Let's face it, class is much more fun if everyone is engaged and prepared...)

Want an **easy way to assign** homework online and track student **progress**?
(Less time grading means more time teaching...)

Want an **instant view** of student or class performance relative to learning objectives? *(No more wondering if students understand...)*

Need to **collect data and generate reports** required for administration or accreditation? *(Say goodbye to manually tracking student learning outcomes...)*

Want to **record and post your lectures** for students to view online?

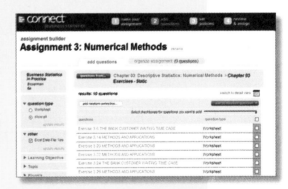

With **McGraw-Hill's *Connect*® Plus Business Statistics,**

INSTRUCTORS GET:

- Simple **assignment management**, allowing you to spend more time teaching.

- **Auto-graded** assignments, quizzes, and tests.

- **Detailed Visual Reporting** where student and section results can be viewed and analyzed.

- Sophisticated **online testing** capability.

- A **filtering and reporting** function that allows you to easily select Excel-based homework problems, as well as assign and report on materials that are correlated to accreditation standards, learning outcomes, and Bloom's taxonomy.

- An easy-to-use **lecture capture** tool.

- The option to **upload course documents** for student access.

Want an online, **searchable version** of your textbook?

Wish your textbook could be **available online** while you're doing your assignments?

Connect® Plus Business Statistics eBook

If you choose to use *Connect® Plus Business Statistics*, you have an affordable and searchable online version of your book integrated with your other online tools.

Connect® Plus Business Statistics eBook offers features like:

- Topic search
- Direct links from assignments
- Adjustable text size
- Jump to page number
- Print by section
- Highlight
- Take notes
- Access instructor highlights/notes

Want to get more **value** from your textbook purchase?

Think learning business statistics should be a bit more **interesting**?

Check out the STUDENT RESOURCES section under the *Connect®* Library tab.

Here you'll find a wealth of resources designed to help you achieve your goals in the course. You'll find things like **quizzes, guided examples, narrated PowerPoints, and Internet activities** to help you study. Every student has different needs, so explore the STUDENT RESOURCES to find the materials best suited to you.

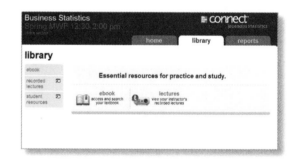

ESSENTIALS OF BUSINESS STATISTICS

ESSENTIALS OF BUSINESS STATISTICS

Communicating with Numbers

Sanjiv Jaggia
*California Polytechnic
State University*

Alison Kelly
Suffolk University

McGraw-Hill Irwin

The McGraw·Hill Companies

McGraw-Hill
Irwin

ESSENTIALS OF BUSINESS STATISTICS: COMMUNICATING WITH NUMBERS

Published by McGraw-Hill/Irwin, a business unit of The McGraw-Hill Companies, Inc., 1221 Avenue of the Americas, New York, NY, 10020. Copyright © 2014 by The McGraw-Hill Companies, Inc. All rights reserved. Printed in the United States of America. No part of this publication may be reproduced or distributed in any form or by any means, or stored in a database or retrieval system, without the prior written consent of The McGraw-Hill Companies, Inc., including, but not limited to, in any network or other electronic storage or transmission, or broadcast for distance learning.

Some ancillaries, including electronic and print components, may not be available to customers outside the United States.

This book is printed on acid-free paper.

3 4 5 6 7 8 9 0 QVS/QVS 1 0 9 8 7 6 5 4

ISBN   978-0-07-802054-4
MHID   0-07-802054-9

Senior Vice President, Products & Markets: *Kurt L. Strand*
Vice President, Content Production & Technology Services: *Kimberly Meriwether David*
Managing Director: *Douglas Reiner*
Senior Brand Manager: *Thomas Hayward*
Executive Director of Development: *Ann Torbert*
Senior Development Editor: *Wanda J. Zeman*
Director of Digital Content: *Doug Ruby*
Senior Marketing Manager: *Heather A. Kazakoff*
Senior Project Manager: *Diane L. Nowaczyk*
Senior Buyer: *Michael R. McCormick*
Lead Designer: *Matthew Baldwin*
Cover Designer: *Matthew Baldwin*
Cover Images: © *Robin Nelson/PhotoEdit*, © *Martin Thomas Photography/Alamy*, © *Car Culture/Corbis*,
          Courtesy of The Home Depot, © *2008 Getty Images/Doug Benc*
Senior Content Licensing Specialist: *Keri Johnson*
Photo Researcher: *Michelle Buhr*
Lead Media Project Manager: *Daryl Horrocks*
Media Project Manager: *Joyce J. Chappetto*
Typeface: *10.5/12 Times LT Std Roman*
Compositor: *MPS Limited*
Printer: *Quad/Graphics*

All credits appearing on page or at the end of the book are considered to be an extension of the copyright page.

Library of Congress Cataloging-in-Publication Data

Jaggia, Sanjiv, 1960-
   Essentials of business statistics : communicating with numbers / Sanjiv Jaggia, Alison Kelly.
      p. cm.
   Includes index.
   ISBN 978-0-07-802054-4 (alk. paper) — ISBN 0-07-802054-9 (alk. paper)
   1. Commercial statistics. I. Hawke, Alison Kelly. II. Title.
HF1017.J343 2014
519.5—dc23
                                                            2012036846

The Internet addresses listed in the text were accurate at the time of publication. The inclusion of a website does not indicate an endorsement by the authors or McGraw-Hill, and McGraw-Hill does not guarantee the accuracy of the information presented at these sites.

www.mhhe.com

Sanjiv Jaggia

Sanjiv Jaggia is a professor of economics and finance at California Polytechnic State University in San Luis Obispo, California. After earning a Ph.D. from Indiana University, Bloomington, in 1990, Dr. Jaggia spent 17 years at Suffolk University, Boston. In 2003 he became a Chartered Financial Analyst (CFA®). Dr. Jaggia's research interests include empirical finance, statistics, and econometrics. He has published extensively in research journals, including the *Journal of Empirical Finance, Review of Economics and Statistics, Journal of Business and Economic Statistics*, and *Journal of Econometrics*. Dr. Jaggia's ability to communicate in the classroom has been acknowledged by several teaching awards. In 2007, he traded one coast for the other and now lives in San Luis Obispo, California, with his wife and daughter. In his spare time, he enjoys cooking, hiking, and listening to a wide range of music.

Alison Kelly

Alison Kelly is a professor of economics at Suffolk University in Boston, Massachusetts. She received her B.A. degree from the College of the Holy Cross in Worcester, Massachusetts; her M.A. degree from the University of Southern California in Los Angeles; and her Ph.D. from Boston College in Chestnut Hill, Massachusetts. Dr. Kelly has published in highly regarded journals such as the *American Journal of Agricultural Economics, Journal of Macroeconomics, Review of Income and Wealth, Applied Financial Economics*, and *Contemporary Economic Policy*. She is a Chartered Financial Analyst (CFA®) and regularly teaches review courses in quantitative methods to candidates preparing to take the CFA exam. Each summer Dr. Kelly also teaches an introductory statistics course at Boston College. She resides in Hamilton, Massachusetts, with her husband and two children.

A unique emphasis on communicating with numbers . . .

Statistics can be a fun and enlightening course for both students and teachers. From our years of experience in the classroom, we have found that an effective way to make statistics interesting is to use timely business applications to which students can relate. If interest can be sparked at the very outset, students may end up learning statistics without realizing they are doing so. By carefully matching timely applications with statistical methods, students learn to appreciate the relevance of business statistics in our world today. We wrote *Essentials of Business Statistics: Communicating with Numbers* because we saw a need for a contemporary, core statistics textbook that sparked student interest and bridged the gap between how statistics is taught and how practitioners think about and apply statistical methods. Throughout the text, the emphasis is on communicating with numbers rather than on number crunching. In every chapter, students are exposed to statistical information conveyed in written form. By incorporating the perspective of professional users, it has been our goal to make the subject matter more relevant and the presentation of material more straightforward for students.

In *Essentials of Business Statistics*, we have incorporated fundamental topics that are applicable for students with various backgrounds and interests. This feature is especially relevant as more and more colleges and universities move toward a one-semester introductory statistics course. The text is intellectually stimulating, practical, and visually attractive, from which students can learn and instructors can teach. Although it is application-oriented, it is also mathematically sound and uses notation that is generally accepted for the topic being covered.

This is probably the **best book** I have seen in terms of explaining concepts.
Brad McDonald, *Northern Illinois University*

The book is **well written, more readable and interesting than most stats texts,** and effective in explaining concepts. The examples and cases are particularly good and effective teaching tools.
Andrew Koch, *James Madison University*

Clarity and brevity are the most important things I look for—this text has both in abundance.
Michael Gordinier, *Washington University, St. Louis*

makes business statistics relevant to students

Key Features

Key to this text's positive reception are six core features around which this text is built.

Integrated Introductory Cases. Realistic introductory cases that students can relate to introduce each chapter topic and form the basis of several examples in the chapters.

Writing with Statistics. Interpreting results and conveying information effectively is critical to effective decision making in a business environment. Students are taught how to take the data, apply it, and convey the information in a meaningful way.

Unique Coverage of Regression Analysis. Relevant coverage of regression without repetition is an important hallmark of this text.

Written as Taught. Topics are presented the way they are taught in class, beginning with the intuition and explanation and concluding with the application.

Integration of Microsoft® Excel. Students are taught to develop an understanding of the concepts and how to derive the calculation; then Excel is used as a tool to perform the cumbersome calculations. In addition, guidelines for using Minitab, SPSS, and JMP are provided in chapter appendices.

Connect Business Statistics. Connect is an online system that gives students the tools they need to be successful in the course. Through guided examples and LearnSmart adaptive study tools, students receive guidance and practice to help them master the topics.

> *I really like the case studies and the **emphasis on writing**. We are making a big effort to incorporate more business writing in our core courses so that meshes well.*
>
> Elizabeth Haran, *Salem State University*

> *For a statistical analyst, your analytical skill is only as good as your communication skill. Writing with statistics **reinforces the importance of communication** and provides students with concrete examples to follow.*
>
> Jun Liu, *Georgia Southern University*

Students learn through real-world cases and business examples . . .

Integrated Introductory Cases

Each chapter opens with a real-life case study that forms the basis for several examples within the chapter. The questions included in the examples create a roadmap for mastering the most important learning outcomes within the chapter. A synopsis of each chapter's introductory case is presented when the last of these examples has been discussed. Instructors of distance learners may find these introductory cases particularly useful.

INTRODUCTORY CASE

Investment Decision

Rebecca Johnson works as an investment counselor at a large bank. Recently, an inexperienced investor asked Johnson about clarifying some differences between two top-performing mutual funds from the last decade: Vanguard's Precious Metals and Mining fund (henceforth, Metals) and Fidelity's Strategic Income fund (henceforth, Income). The investor shows Johnson the return data that he has accessed over the Internet, but the investor has trouble interpreting the data. Table 3.1 shows the return data for these two mutual funds for the years 2000–2009; the data, labeled **Fund_Returns**, can also be found on the text website.

SYNOPSIS OF INTRODUCTORY CASE

Vanguard's Precious Metals and Mining fund (Metals) and Fidelity's Strategic Income fund (Income) were two top-performing mutual funds for the years 2000 through 2009. An analysis of annual return data for these two funds provides important information for any type of investor. Over the past 10 years, the Metals fund posts the higher values for both the mean return and the median return, with values of 24.65% and 33.83%, respectively. When the mean differs dramatically from the median, it is often indicative of extreme values or outliers. Although the mean and the median for the Metals fund do differ by almost 10 percentage points, a boxplot analysis reveals no outliers. The mean return and the median return for the Income fund, on the other hand, are quite comparable at 8.51% and 7.34%, respectively.

*In all of these chapters, **the opening case leads directly into the application questions** that students will have regarding the material. Having a strong and related case will certainly provide more benefit to the student, as context leads to improved learning.*

Alan Chow, *University of South Alabama*

***This is an excellent approach.** The student gradually gets the idea that he can look at a problem—one which might be fairly complex—and break it down into root components. He learns that a little bit of math could go a long way, and even more math is even more beneficial to evaluating the problem.*

Dane Peterson, *Missouri State University*

and build skills to communicate results

Writing with Statistics

One of our most important innovations is the inclusion of a sample report within every chapter (except Chapter 1). Our intent is to show students how to convey statistical information in written form to those who may not know detailed statistical methods. For example, such a report may be needed as input for managerial decision making in sales, marketing, or company planning. Several similar writing exercises are provided at the end of each chapter. Each chapter also includes a synopsis that addresses questions raised from the introductory case. This serves as a shorter writing sample for students. Instructors of large sections may find these reports useful for incorporating writing into their statistics courses.

*Writing with statistics shows that **statistics is more than number crunching.***
Greg Cameron,
Brigham Young University

*These technical writing examples provide a **very useful example of how to take statistics work and turn it into a report** that will be useful to an organization. I will strive to have my students learn from these examples.*
Bruce P. Christensen,
Weber State University

*This is an **excellent approach**.... The ability to translate numerical information into words that others can understand is critical.*
Scott Bailey, *Troy University*

Excellent. Students need to become better writers.
Bob Nauss, *University of Missouri, St. Louis*

WRITING WITH STATISTICS

Gavin Cann listens to two sports analysts quarrel over which statistic is a better predictor of a Major League Baseball team's winning proportion (Win). One argues that the team's batting average (BA) is a better predictor of a team's success since the team with the higher batting average has won approximately 75% of the World Series contests. The other insists that a team's pitching is clearly the main factor in determining a team's winning proportion—the lower a team's earned run average (ERA), the higher the team's winning proportion.

In order to determine if either of these claims is backed by the data, Gavin collects relevant information for the 14 American League (AL) and 16 National League (NL) teams during the regular season of 2010. A portion of the data is shown in Table 12.14; the entire data set, labeled **Baseball**, can be found on the text website.

TABLE 12.14 Winning Proportion, Batting Average, and Earned Run Average in Baseball

Team	League	Win	BA	ERA
Baltimore, Orioles	AL	0.407	0.259	4.59
Boston, Red Sox	AL	0.549	0.268	4.20
⋮	⋮	⋮	⋮	⋮
Washington, Nationals	NL	0.426	0.25	4.13

Source: http://mlb.mlb.com.

Sample Report—Analyzing the Winning Proportion in Baseball

Two sports analysts have conflicting views over how best to predict a Major League Baseball team's winning proportion (Win). One argues that the team's batting average (BA) is a better predictor of a team's success, while the other analyst insists that a team's pitching is the main factor as measured by the pitchers' earned run average (ERA). Three linear regression models are used to analyze a baseball team's winning proportion. The explanatory variables are BA in Model 1, ERA in Model 2, and both BA and ERA in Model 3. A priori, one expects that BA positively influences Win, whereas ERA negatively affects Win. The regression results for the three models are presented in Table 12.A.

TABLE 12.A Model Estimates for the Response Variable Win

Variable	Model 1	Model 2	Model 3
Intercept	−0.2731 (0.3421)	0.9504* (0.0000)	0.1269 (0.4921)
Batting Average	3.0054* (0.0106)	NA	3.2754* (0.0000)
Earned Run Average	NA	−0.1105* (0.0000)	−0.1153* (0.0000)
s_e	0.0614	0.0505	0.0375
R^2	0.2112	0.4656	0.7156
Adjusted R^2	0.1830	0.4465	0.6945
F statistic (p-value)	NA	NA	33.9663* (0.0000)

Notes: Parameter estimates are in the top half of the table with the p-values in parentheses; NA denotes not applicable; * represents significance at the 5% level. The lower part of the table contains goodness-of-fit measures.

Unique coverage and presentation . . .

Unique Coverage of Regression Analysis

We combine simple and multiple regression in one chapter, which we believe is a seamless grouping and eliminates needless repetition. This grouping allows more coverage of regression analysis than the vast majority of *Essentials* texts. This focus reflects the topic's growing use in practice. However, for those instructors who prefer to cover only simple regression, doing so is still an option.

> *By comparing this chapter with other books, I think that this is one of the best explanations about regression I have seen.*
>
> Cecilia Maldonado,
> *Georgia Southwestern State University*

> *The authors have put forth a novel and innovative way to present regression which in and of itself should make instructors take a long and hard look at this book.* **Students should find this book very readable and a good companion for their course.**
>
> Harvey A. Singer, *George Mason University*

Written as Taught

We introduce topics just the way we teach them; that is, the relevant tools follow the opening application. Our roadmap for solving problems is

1. Start with intuition
2. Introduce mathematical rigor, and
3. Produce computer output that confirms results.

We use worked examples throughout the text to illustrate how to apply concepts to solve real-world problems.

> *This is **easy for students to follow** and I do get the feeling . . . the sections are spoken language.*
>
> Zhen Zhu, *University of Central Oklahoma*

that make the content more effective

Integration of Microsoft® Excel

We prefer that students first focus on and absorb the statistical material before replicating their results with a computer. We feel that solving each application manually provides students with a deeper understanding of the relevant concept. However, we recognize that, primarily due to cumbersome calculations or the need for statistical tables, the embedding of computer output is necessary. Microsoft Excel® is the primary software package used in this text and it is integrated within each chapter. We chose Excel over other statistical packages based on reviewer feedback and the fact that students benefit from the added spreadsheet experience. We provide brief guidelines for using Minitab, SPSS, and JMP in chapter appendices; we give more detailed instructions on the text website.

Constructing a Histogram from a Set of Raw Data

A. **FILE** Open the **MV_Houses** data (Table 2.1) from the text website into an Excel spreadsheet.

B. In a column next to the data, enter the values of the upper limits of each class, or in this example, 400, 500, 600, 700, and 800; label this column "Class Limits." The reason for these entries is explained in the next step. The house-price data and the class limits (as well as the resulting frequency distribution and histogram) are shown in Figure 2.10.

FIGURE 2.10 Constructing a histogram from raw data with Excel

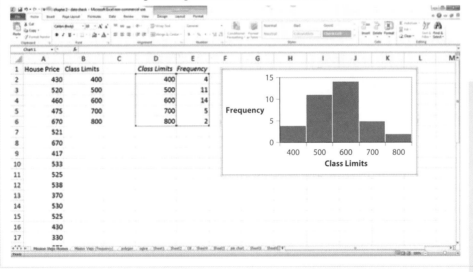

...does a solid job of building the intuition behind the concepts and then adding mathematical rigor to these ideas before finally verifying the results with Excel.

Matthew Dean,
University of
Southern Maine

Real-world exercises and case studies that reinforce the material

Mechanical and Applied Exercises

Chapter exercises are a well-balanced blend of mechanical, computational-type problems followed by more ambitious, interpretive-type problems. We have found that simpler drill problems tend to build students' confidence prior to tackling more difficult applied problems. Moreover, we repeatedly use many data sets—including house prices, rents, stock returns, salaries, and debt—in the text. For instance, students first use these real data to calculate summary measures and then continue on to make statistical inferences with confidence intervals and hypothesis tests and perform regression analysis.

Applied exercises from *The Wall Street Journal, Kiplinger's, Fortune, The New York Times, USA Today;* various websites —Census.gov, Zillow.com, Finance.yahoo.com, ESPN.com; and more.

b. Calculate MAD.

c. Calculate the sample variance and the sample standard deviation.

tions

partment of Transportation (DOT) fields thousands of ...ints about airlines each year. The DOT categorizes and ...omplaints, and then periodically publishes rankings ...ine performance. The following table presents the 2006 ...s for the 10 largest U.S. airlines.

Airline	Complaints*	Airline	Complaints*
Southwest Airlines	1.82	Northwest Airlines	8.84
JetBlue Airways	3.98	Delta Airlines	10.35
Alaska Airlines	5.24	American Airlines	10.87
AirTran Airways	6.24	US Airways	13.59
Continental Airlines	8.83	United Airlines	13.60

Source: Department of Transportation; *per million passengers.

a. Which airline fielded the least amount of complaints? Which airline fielded the most? Calculate the range.

b. Calculate the mean and the median number of complaints for this sample.

c. Calculate the variance and the standard deviation.

31. The monthly closing stock prices (rounded to the nearest dollar) for Starbucks Corp. and Panera Bread Co. for the first six months of 2010 are reported in the following table.

assignment is to analyze the rental market in Ann Arbor, which is home to the University of Michigan. She gathers data on monthly rent for 2011 along with the square footage of 40 homes. A portion of the data is shown in the accompanying table; the entire data set, labeled **AnnArbor_Rental**, can be found on the text website.

Monthly Rent	Square Footage
645	500
675	648
⋮	⋮
2400	2700

Source: http://www.zillow.com.

a. Calculate the mean and the standard deviation for monthly rent.

b. Calculate the mean and the standard deviation for square footage.

c. Which sample data exhibit greater relative dispersion?

33. **FILE** Go to the text website and access the data labeled **Largest_Corporations**. It shows the Fortune 500 rankings of America's largest corporations for 2010. Next to each corporation are its market capitalization (in billions of dollars as of March 26, 2010) and its total return to investors for the year 2009.

a. Calculate the coefficient of variation for market capitalization.

b. Calculate the coefficient of variation for total return.

c. Which sample data exhibit greater relative dispersion?

34. **FILE** Go to the text website and access the data labeled **Census**. It shows, among other variables, median

*I especially like the introductory cases, the **quality of the end-of-section problems**, and the writing examples.*

Dave Leupp, *University of Colorado at Colorado Springs*

Their exercises and problems are excellent!

Erl Sorensen, *Bentley University*

Features that go beyond the typical

Conceptual Review

At the end of each chapter, we provide a conceptual review that provides a more holistic approach to reviewing the material. This section revisits the learning outcomes and provides the most important definitions, interpretations, and formulas.

Conceptual Review

LO 5.1 Distinguish between discrete and continuous random variables.

A **random variable** summarizes outcomes of an experiment with numerical values. A random variable is either discrete or continuous. A **discrete random variable** assumes a countable number of distinct values, whereas a **continuous random variable** is characterized by uncountable values in an interval.

LO 5.2 Describe the probability distribution of a discrete random variable.

The **probability distribution function** of a discrete random variable X is a list of the values of X with the associated probabilities, that is, the list of all possible pairs $(x, P(X = x))$. The **cumulative distribution function** of X is defined as $P(X \leq x)$.

LO 5.3 Calculate and interpret summary measures for a discrete random variable.

For a discrete random variable X with values $x_1, x_2, x_3, \ldots$, which occur with probabilities $P(X = x_i)$, the **expected value** of X is calculated as $E(X) = \mu = \Sigma x_i P(X = x_i)$. We interpret the expected value as the long-run average value of the random variable over infinitely many independent repetitions of an experiment. Measures of dispersion indicate whether the values of X are clustered about μ or widely scattered from μ. The **variance** of X is calculated as $Var(X) = \sigma^2 = \Sigma(x_i - \mu)^2 P(X = x_i)$. The **standard deviation** of X is $SD(X) = \sigma = \sqrt{\sigma^2}$.

Most texts basically list what one should have learned but don't add much to that. You do a good job of reminding the reader of what was covered and what was most important about it.

Andrew Koch, *James Madison University*

*They have gone beyond the typical [summarizing formulas] and I like the structure. This is a **very strong feature** of this text.*

Virginia M. Miori, *St. Joseph's University*

What technology connects students . . .

McGraw-Hill *Connect®* *Business Statistics*

McGraw-Hill *Connect Business Statistics* is an online assignment and assessment solution that connects students with the tools and resources they'll need to achieve success through faster learning, higher retention, and more efficient studying. It provides instructors with tools to quickly select content for assignments according to the topics and learning objectives they want to emphasize.

Online Assignments. *Connect Business Statistics* helps students learn more efficiently by providing practice material and feedback when they are needed. *Connect* grades homework automatically and provides instant feedback on any problems that students are challenged to solve.

Integration of Excel Data Sets. A convenient feature is the inclusion of an Excel data file link in many problems using data files in their calculation. The link allows students to easily launch into Excel, work the problem, and return to *Connect* to key in the answer and receive feedback on their results.

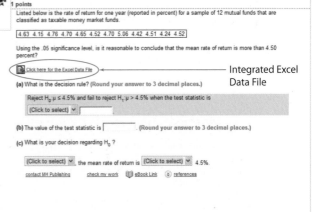

Integrated Excel Data File

Student Resource Library. The *Connect Business Statistics* Student Library is the place for students to access additional resources. The Student Library provides quick access to recorded lectures, practice materials, the eBooks, data files, PowerPoint files, and more.

to success in business statistics?

Guided Examples. These narrated video walkthroughs provide students with step-by-step guidelines for solving selected exercises similar to those contained in the text. The student is given personalized instruction on how to solve a problem by applying the concepts presented in the chapter. The video shows the steps to take to work through an exercise. Students can go through each example multiple times if needed.

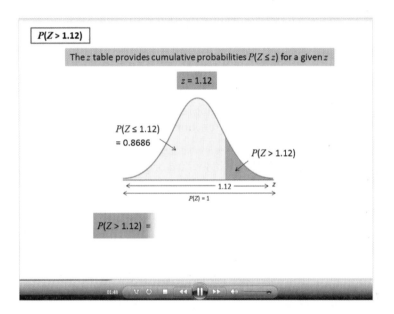

LearnSmart. LearnSmart adaptive self-study technology in *Connect Business Statistics* helps students make the best use of their study time. LearnSmart provides a seamless combination of practice, assessment, and remediation for every concept in the textbook. LearnSmart's intelligent software adapts to students by supplying questions on a new concept when students are ready to learn it. With LearnSmart, students will spend less time on topics they understand and instead focus on the topics they need to master.

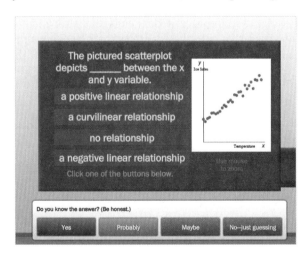

What technology connects students . . .

Simple Assignment Management and Smart Grading. When it comes to studying, time is precious. *Connect Business Statistics* helps students learn more efficiently by providing feedback and practice material when they need it, where they need it. When it comes to teaching, your time also is precious. The grading function enables you to

- Have assignments scored automatically, giving students immediate feedback on their work and the ability to compare their work with correct answers.
- Access and review each response; manually change grades or leave comments for students to review.

Student Reporting. *Connect Business Statistics* keeps instructors informed about how each student, section, and class is performing, allowing for more productive use of lecture and office hours. The progress-tracking function enables you to

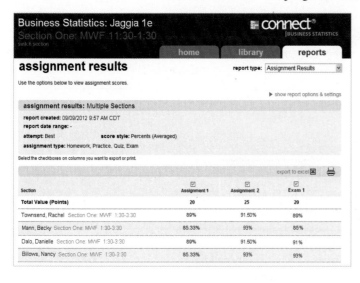

- View scored work immediately and track individual or group performance with assignment and grade reports.
- Access an instant view of student or class performance relative to topic and learning objectives.
- Collect data and generate reports required by many accreditation organizations, such as AACSB.

Instructor Library. The *Connect Business Statistics* Instructor Library is your repository for additional resources to improve student engagement in and out of class. You can select and use any asset that enhances your lecture. The *Connect Business Statistics* Instructor Library includes:

- eBook
- PowerPoint presentations
- Test Bank
- Instructor's Solutions Manual
- Digital Image Library

to success in business statistics?

McGraw-Hill
CONNECT® PLUS
BUSINESS STATISTICS

Connect® Plus Business Statistics includes a seamless integration of an eBook and *Connect Business Statistics,* with rich functionality integrated into the product.

Integrated Media-Rich eBook. An integrated media-rich eBook allows students to access media in context with each chapter. Students can highlight, take notes, and access shared instructor highlights/notes to learn the course material.

Dynamic Links. Dynamic links provide a connection between the problems or questions you assign to your students and the location in the eBook where that problem or question is covered.

Powerful Search Function. A powerful search function pinpoints and connects key concepts in a snap. This state-of-the-art, thoroughly tested system supports you in preparing students for the world that awaits. For more information about *Connect,* go to www.mcgrawhillconnect.com or contact your local McGraw-Hill sales representative.

Tegrity Campus:
Lectures 24/7

Tegrity Campus is integrated in *Connect* to help make your class time available 24/7. With Tegrity, you can capture each one of your lectures in a searchable format for students to review when they study and complete assignments using *Connect.* With a simple one-click start-and-stop process, you can capture everything that is presented to students during your lecture from your computer, including audio. Students can replay any part of any class with easy-to-use browser-based viewing on a PC or Mac.

Educators know that the more students can see, hear, and experience class resources, the better they learn. In fact, studies prove it. With *Tegrity Campus,* students quickly recall key moments by using *Tegrity Campus*'s unique search feature. This search helps students efficiently find what they need, when they need it, across an entire semester of class recordings. Help turn all your students' study time into learning moments immediately supported by your lecture. To learn more about *Tegrity,* watch a two-minute Flash demo at **http://tegritycampus.mhhe.com.**

What software is available with this text?

MegaStat® for Microsoft Excel® 2003, 2007 and 2010 (and Excel: Mac 2011)

CD ISBN: 0077496442 *Note: The CD-ROM is for Windows users only.*

Access Card ISBN: 0077426274 *Note: Best option for both Windows and Mac users.*

MegaStat® by J. B. Orris of Butler University is a full-featured Excel add-in that is available three ways—on CD, through access card packaged with the text, and on the *MegaStat* website at www.mhhe.com/megastat. It works with Excel 2003, 2007, and 2010 (and Excel: Mac 2011). On the website, students have 10 days to successfully download and install *MegaStat* on their local computer. Once installed, *MegaStat* will remain active in Excel with no expiration date or time limitations. The software performs statistical analyses within an Excel workbook. It does basic functions, such as descriptive statistics, frequency distributions, and probability calculations as well as hypothesis testing, ANOVA, and regression. *MegaStat* output is carefully formatted and its ease-of-use features include Auto Expand for quick data selection and Auto Label detect. Since *MegaStat* is easy to use, students can focus on learning statistics without being distracted by the software. *MegaStat* is always available from Excel's main menu. Selecting a menu item pops up a dialog box. Screencam tutorials are included that provide a walkthrough of major business statistics topics. Help files are built in, and an introductory user's manual is also included.

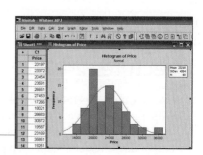

Minitab®

Minitab® Student Version 14 ISBN: 007305237X

Minitab is available to help students solve the business statistics exercises in the text. It can be packaged with any McGraw-Hill business statistics text.

What resources are available for instructors?

Online Learning Center   www.mhhe.com/jkess

The Online Learning Center (OLC) provides the instructor with a complete Instructor's Solutions Manual in Word format, the complete Test Bank in both Word files and computerized EZ Test Online format, Instructor PowerPoint slides, text art files, an introduction to ALEKS®, an introduction to McGraw-Hill *Connect®* Business Statistics, and more.

All test bank questions are available in an EZ Test online. Included are a number of multiple choice, true/false, and short-answer questions and problems. The answers to all questions are given, along with a rating of the level of difficulty, chapter goal the question tests, Bloom's taxonomy question type, and the AACSB knowledge category.

Online Course Management   The **Best** of **Both Worlds**

McGraw-Hill Higher Education and Blackboard have teamed up. What does this mean for you?

1. **Single sign-on.** Now you and your students can access McGraw-Hill's *Connect®* and Create™ right from within your Blackboard course—all with one single sign-on.

2. **Deep integration of content and tools.** You get a single sign-on with *Connect* and Create, and you also get integration of McGraw-Hill content and content engines right into Blackboard. Whether you're choosing a book for your course or building *Connect* assignments, all the tools you need are right where you want them—inside of Blackboard.

3. **One grade book.** Keeping several grade books and manually synchronizing grades into Blackboard is no longer necessary. When a student completes an integrated *Connect* assignment, the grade for that assignment automatically (and instantly) feeds your Blackboard grade center.

4. **A solution for everyone.** Whether your institution is already using Blackboard or you just want to try Blackboard on your own, we have a solution for you. McGraw-Hill and Blackboard can now offer you easy access to industry-leading technology and content, whether your campus hosts it or we do. Be sure to ask your local McGraw-Hill representative for details.

Connect Packaging Options

Connect with LearnSmart 1 Semester Access Card: 0077639499

Connect Plus with LearnSmart 1 Semester Access Card: 0077639502

What resources are available for students?

CourseSmart
ISBN: 0077639537

CourseSmart is a convenient way to find and buy eTextbooks. CourseSmart has the largest selection of eTextbooks available anywhere, offering thousands of the most commonly adopted textbooks from a wide variety of higher-education publishers. CourseSmart eTextbooks are available in one standard online reader with full text search, notes and highlighting, and e-mail tools for sharing notes between classmates. Visit **www.CourseSmart.com** for more information on ordering.

ALEKS

ALEKS is an assessment and learning program that provides individualized instruction in Business Statistics, Business Math, and Accounting. Available online in partnership with McGraw-Hill/Irwin, ALEKS interacts with students much like a skilled human tutor, with the ability to assess precisely a student's knowledge and provide instruction on the exact topics the student is most ready to learn. By providing topics to meet individual students' needs, allowing students to move between explanation and practice, correcting and analyzing errors, and defining terms, ALEKS helps students to master course content quickly and easily.

ALEKS also includes an instructor module with powerful, assignment-driven features and extensive content flexibility. ALEKS simplifies course management and allows instructors to spend less time with administrative tasks and more time directing student learning. To learn more about ALEKS, visit **www.aleks.com**.

Online Learning Center www.mhhe.com/jkess

The Online Learning Center (OLC) provides students with the following content:

- Quizzes—self-grading to access knowledge of the material
- PowerPoints—gives an overview of the chapter content
- Data Files—import into Excel for quick calculation and analysis
- Appendixes—quick lookup when the text isn't available

Assurance of Accuracy

Dear Colleague,

As textbook authors, and, more importantly, as instructors of business statistics, we recognize the great importance placed on accuracy. With this in mind, we have taken the following steps to ensure that *Essentials of Business Statistics: Communicating with Numbers* is error-free:

1. We received detailed feedback from over 150 instructor reviews, starting with first draft manuscript through the final draft submitted to the publisher. Each review contributed in significant ways to the accuracy of the content.

2. We personally class-tested the manuscript with our students in various drafts, continually improving the accuracy of the material.

3. Each of us wrote, reviewed, and carefully checked all of the end-of-chapter material.

4. A developmental editor went through each sentence to ensure that our language was as clear as possible.

5. Multiple accuracy checkers reviewed each chapter and its accompanying end-of-chapter material—once when the final manuscript was submitted to the publisher, and again when our final formatted pages were completed.

6. A copyeditor checked the grammar of the final manuscript.

7. A proofreader reviewed each page to ensure no errors remained.

8. Our Solutions Manual and Test Bank were reviewed by multiple independent accuracy checkers.

Given the steps taken above, we have the utmost confidence that you and your students will have a great experience using *Essentials of Business Statistics: Communicating with Numbers*.

CONTACT INFORMATION We would be grateful to hear from any and all users of this text and its supplements. Send your comments and suggestions to sjaggia@calpoly.edu or akelly@suffolk.edu.

Sincerely,

Sanjiv Jaggia   *Alison Kelly*

ACKNOWLEDGMENTS

We could not have developed our approach to teaching business statistics in isolation. Many thanks go to a multitude of people for helping us make our idea come to fruition. First and foremost, we would like to thank our families and friends for their support, feedback, and patience throughout what has been an arduous, but rewarding, project. We are especially grateful to Chandrika, Minori, John, Megan, and Matthew for bearing with us on a daily basis.

We are indebted to Jerzy Kamburowski (University of Toledo) for his outstanding accuracy check of the textbook and the Solutions Manual and for his guidance on mathematical precision. We would also like to thank Alan Cannon (University of Texas—Arlington), Samuel Frame (Cal Poly, San Luis Obispo), Harvey A. Singer (George Mason University), Wendi Sun (Suffolk University), and Zhaowie Wang (Suffolk University) for their valuable contributions to the ancilliaries.

The editorial staff of McGraw-Hill/Irwin are deserving of our gratitude for their guidance throughout this project, especially Wanda Zeman, Thomas Hayward, Diane Nowaczyk, Michael McCormick, Matt Baldwin, Keri Johnson, and Daryl Horrocks.

Reviewers

The text has benefited immensely from reviewers' helpful suggestions, keen insights, and constructive criticisms. We are very grateful to the following professors for taking the time to provide valuable feedback throughout the development process:

John Affisco
Hofstra University

Mehdi Afiat
College of Southern Nevada

Mohammad Ahmadi
University of Tennessee–Chattanooga

Sung Ahn
Washington State University

Mohammad Ahsanullah
Rider University

Imam Alam
University of Northern Iowa

Mostafa Aminzadeh
Towson University

Ardavan Asef-Vaziri
California State University

Scott Bailey
Troy University

Jayanta Bandyopadhyay
Central Michigan University

Samir Barman
University of Oklahoma

Douglas Barrett
University of North Alabama

John Beyers
University of Maryland

Arnab Bisi
Purdue University–West Lafayette

Randy Boan
Aims Community College

Matthew Bognar
University of Iowa

Juan Cabrera
Ramapo College of New Jersey

Scott Callan
Bentley University

Gregory Cameron
Brigham Young University

Kathleen Campbell
St. Joseph's University

Michael Cervetti
University of Memphis

Samathy Chandrashekar
Salisbury University

Gary Huaite Chao
University of Pennsylvania–Kutztown

Sangit Chatterjee
Northeastern University

Anna Chernobai
Syracuse University

Alan Chesen
Wright State University

Juyan Cho
Colorado State University—Pueblo

Alan Chow
University of South Alabama

Bruce Christensen
Weber State University

Howard Clayton
Auburn University

Robert Collins
Marquette University

M. Halim Dalgin
Kutztown University

Tom Davis
University of Dayton

Matthew Dean
University of Maine

Jason Delaney
University of Arkansas–Little Rock

Ferdinand DiFurio
Tennessee Tech University

Matt Dobra
UMUC

Luca Donno
University of Miami

Joan Donohue
University of South Carolina

David Doorn
  University of Minnesota
James Dunne
  University of Dayton
Mike Easley
  University of New Orleans
Erick Elder
  University of Arkansas–Little Rock
Ashraf ElHoubi
  Lamar University
Grace Esimai
  University of Texas–Arlington
Soheila Fardanesh
  Towson University
Carol Flannery
  University of Texas—Dallas
Sydney Fletcher
  Mississippi Gulf Coast Community College
Andrew Flight
  Portland State University
Priya Francisco
  Purdue University
Vickie Fry
  Westmoreland County Community College
Ed Gallo
  Sinclair Community College
Glenn Gilbreath
  Virginia Commonwealth University
Robert Gillette
  University of Kentucky
Xiaoning Gilliam
  Texas Tech University
Mark Gius
  Quinnipiac University
Malcolm Gold
  Saint Mary's University of Minnesota
Michael Gordinier
  Washington University
Don Gren
  Salt Lake Community College
Deborah Gougeon
  University of Scranton
Robert Hammond
  North Carolina State University
Jim Han
  Florida Atlantic University
Elizabeth Haran
  Salem State University
Edward Hartono
  University of Alabama—Huntsville

Clifford Hawley
  West Virginia University
Paul Hong
  University of Toledo
Ping-Hung Hsieh
  Oregon State University
Marc Isaacson
  Augsburg College
Mohammad Jamal
  Northern Virginia Community College
Robin James
  Harper College
Molly Jensen
  University of Arkansas
Craig Johnson
  Brigham Young University–Idaho
Janine Sanders Jones
  University of St. Thomas
Vivian Jones
  Bethune-Cookman University
Jerzy Kamburowski
  University of Toledo
Howard Kaplon
  Towson University
Krishna Kasibhatla
  North Carolina A&T State University
Mohammad Kazemi
  University of North Carolina—Charlotte
Ken Kelley
  University of Notre Dame
Lara Khansa
  Virginia Tech
Ronald Klimberg
  St. Joseph's University
Andrew Koch
  James Madison University
Subhash Kochar
  Portland State University
Brandon Koford
  Weber University
Randy Kolb
  St. Cloud State University
Vadim Kutsyy
  San Jose State University
Francis Laatsch
  University of Southern Mississippi
David Larson
  University of South Alabama
John Lawrence
  California State University–Fullerton

Shari Lawrence
  Nicholls State University
Radu Lazar
  University of Maryland
David Leupp
  University of Colorado–Colorado Springs
Carel Ligeon
  Auburn University–Montgomery
Carin Lightner
  North Carolina A&T State University
Constance Lightner
  Fayetteville State University
Scott Lindsey
  Dixie State College of Utah
Ken Linna
  Auburn University—Montgomery
Jun Liu
  Georgia Southern University
Chung-Ping Loh
  University of North Florida
Salvador Lopez
  University of West Georgia
John Loucks
  St. Edward's University
Cecilia Maldonado
  Georgia Southwestern State University
Farooq Malik
  University of Southern Mississippi
Ken Mayer
  University of Nebraska—Omaha
Bradley McDonald
  Northern Illinois University
Elaine McGivern
  Duquesne University
John McKenzie
  Babson University
Norbert Michel
  Nicholls State University
John Miller
  Sam Houston State University
Virginia Miori
  St. Joseph's University
Prakash Mirchandani
  University of Pittsburgh
Jason Molitierno
  Sacred Heart University
Joseph Mollick
  Texas A&M University–Corpus Christi

James Moran
Oregon State University

Khosrow Moshirvaziri
California State University–Long Beach

Tariq Mughal
University of Utah

Patricia Mullins
University of Wisconsin–Madison

Kusum Mundra
Rutgers University–Newark

Anthony Narsing
Macon State College

Robert Nauss
University of Missouri–St. Louis

Satish Nayak
University of Missouri–St. Louis

Thang Nguyen
California State University–Long Beach

Mohammad Oskoorouchi
California State University–San Marcos

Barb Osyk
University of Akron

Scott Paulsen
Illinois Central College

James Payne
Calhoun Community College

Norman Pence
Metropolitan State College of Denver

Dane Peterson
Missouri State University

Joseph Petry
University of Illinois–Urbana/Champaign

Courtney Pham
Missouri State University

Martha Pilcher
University of Washington

Cathy Poliak
University of Wisconsin–Milwaukee

Simcha Pollack
St. John's University

Hamid Pourmohammadi
California State University–Dominguez Hills

Tammy Prater
Alabama State University

Manying Qiu
Virginia State University

Troy Quast
Sam Houston State University

Michael Racer
University of Memphis

Srikant Raghavan
Lawrence Technological University

Bharatendra Rai
University of Massachusetts–Dartmouth

Tony Ratcliffe
James Madison University

Bruce Reinig
San Diego State University

Darlene Riedemann
Eastern Illinois University

David Roach
Arkansas Tech University

Carolyn Rochelle
East Tennessee State University

Alfredo Romero
North Carolina A&T State University

Ann Rothermel
University of Akron

Jeff Rummel
Emory University

Deborah Rumsey
The Ohio State University

Stephen Russell
Weber State University

William Rybolt
Babson College

Fati Salimian
Salisbury University

Fatollah Salimian
Perdue School of Business

Samuel Sarri
College of Southern Nevada

Jim Schmidt
University of Nebraska–Lincoln

Patrick Scholten
Bentley University

Bonnie Schroeder
Ohio State University

Pali Sen
University of North Florida

Donald Sexton
Columbia University

Vijay Shah
West Virginia University—Parkersburg

Dmitriy Shaltayev
Christopher Newport University

Soheil Sibdari
University of Massachusetts–Dartmouth

Prodosh Simlai
University of North Dakota

Harvey Singer
George Mason University

Harry Sink
North Carolina A&T State University

Don Skousen
Salt Lake Community College

Robert Smidt
California Polytechnic State University

Gary Smith
Florida State University

Antoinette Somers
Wayne State University

Ryan Songstad
Augustana College

Erland Sorensen
Bentley University

Arun Kumar Srinivasan
Indiana University–Southeast

Scott Stevens
James Madison University

Alicia Strandberg
Temple University

Linda Sturges
Suny Maritime College

Bedassa Tadesse
University of Minnesota

Pandu Tadikamalta
University of Pittsburgh

Roberto Duncan Tarabay
University of Wisconsin–Madison

Faye Teer
James Madison University

Deborah Tesch
Xavier University

Patrick Thompson
University of Florida

Satish Thosar
University of Redlands

Ricardo Tovar-Silos
Lamar University

Quoc Hung Tran
Bridgewater State University

Elzbieta Trybus
California State University–Northridge

Fan Tseng
University of Alabama–Huntsville

Silvanus Udoka
  *North Carolina A&T State
  University*
Shawn Ulrick
  Georgetown University
Bulent Uyar
  University of Northern Iowa
Ahmad Vakil
  Tobin College of Business
Raja Velu
  Syracuse University
Holly Verhasselt
  University of Houston–Victoria
Rachel Webb
  Portland State University
Kyle Wells
  Dixie State College
Alan Wheeler
  *University of
  Missouri–St. Louis*

Mary Whiteside
  *University of
  Texas–Arlington*
Blake Whitten
  University of Iowa
Rick Wing
  *San Francisco State
  University*
Jan Wolcott
  Wichita State University
Rongning Wu
  Baruch College
John Yarber
  *Northeast Mississippi
  Community College*
Mark Zaporowski
  Canisius College
Ali Zargar
  San Jose State University

Dewit Zerom
  *California State
  University*
Eugene Zhang
  *Midwestern State
  University*
Ye Zhang
  *Indiana University-Purdue
  University–Indianapolis*
Yi Zhang
  *California State
  University–Fullerton*
Yulin Zhang
  San Jose State University
Wencang Zhou
  Baruch College
Zhen Zhu
  *University of Central
  Oklahoma*

CONTENTS

Walkthrough   vi

CHAPTER 1

Statistics and Data   2

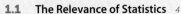

Introductory Case: Tween Survey   3

1.1   The Relevance of Statistics   4

1.2   What Is Statistics?   5
The Need for Sampling   6
Types of Data   6
Getting Started on the Web   7

1.3   Variables and Scales of Measurement   8
The Nominal Scale   9
The Ordinal Scale   10
The Interval Scale   12
The Ratio Scale   12

Synopsis of Introductory Case   13

Conceptual Review   14

CHAPTER 2

Tabular and Graphical Methods   16

Introductory Case: House Prices in Southern California   17

2.1   Summarizing Qualitative Data   18
Visualizing Frequency Distributions for Qualitative Data   20
Using Excel to Construct a Pie Chart   21
Using Excel to Construct a Bar Chart   22
Cautionary Comments When Constructing or Interpreting Charts or Graphs   23

2.2   Summarizing Quantitative Data   26
Guidelines for Constructing a Frequency Distribution   27
Visualizing Frequency Distributions for Quantitative Data   31
Using Excel to Construct a Histogram   32

Synopsis of Introductory Case   37

2.3   Stem-and-Leaf Diagrams   42

2.4   Scatterplots   44
Using Excel to Construct a Scatterplot   45

Writing with Statistics   47

Sample Report—Gas Prices across the United States   47

Conceptual Review   49

Additional Exercises and Case Studies   49
Case Studies   52

Appendix 2.1   Guidelines for Other Software Packages   54

CHAPTER 3

Numerical Descriptive Measures   58

Introductory Case: Investment Decision   59

3.1   Measures of Central Location   60
The Mean   60
The Median   62
The Mode   63
Using Excel to Calculate Measures of Central Location   64

3.2   Percentiles and Box Plots   69
Calculating the pth Percentile   69
Constructing and Interpreting a Box Plot   70

3.3   Measures of Dispersion   73
Range   73
The Mean Absolute Deviation   74
The Variance and the Standard Deviation   74
The Coefficient of Variation   76
Using Excel to Calculate Measures of Dispersion   76

Synopsis of Introductory Case   77

3.4   Mean-Variance Analysis and the Sharpe Ratio   79

3.5   Analysis of Relative Location   81
Chebyshev's Theorem   81
The Empirical Rule   82
z-Scores   83

3.6   Summarizing Grouped Data   85

3.7   Covariance and Correlation   88
Using Excel to Calculate Covariance and the Correlation Coefficient   90

Writing with Statistics   92

Sample Report—Analyzing Speed Limits   92

Conceptual Review   93

Additional Exercises and Case Studies   95
Case Studies   97

Appendix 3.1   Guidelines for Other Software Packages   98

CHAPTER 4

Introduction to Probability   100

Introductory Case: Sportswear Brands   101

4.1   Fundamental Probability Concepts   102
Events   102
Assigning Probabilities   105

4.2   Rules of Probability   109
The Complement Rule   109
The Addition Rule   110

Conditional Probability *112*
Independent and Dependent Events *113*
The Multiplication Rule *114*

4.3 Contingency Tables and Probabilities *118*

Synopsis of Introductory Case *121*

4.4 The Total Probability Rule and Bayes' Theorem *123*
The Total Probability Rule *123*
Bayes' Theorem *126*

Writing with Statistics *130*

Sample Report—Linking Cause of Death with the Method of Losing Weight *130*

Conceptual Review *131*

Additional Exercises and Case Studies *133*
Case Studies *135*

CHAPTER 5

Discrete Probability Distributions *138*

Introductory Case: Available Staff for Probable Customers *139*

5.1 Random Variables and Discrete Probability Distributions *140*
The Discrete Probability Distribution *141*

5.2 Expected Value, Variance, and Standard Deviation *145*
Expected Value *146*
Variance and Standard Deviation *146*
Risk Neutrality and Risk Aversion *147*

5.3 The Binomial Distribution *150*
Using Excel to Obtain Binomial Probabilities *155*

5.4 The Poisson Distribution *158*
Using Excel to Obtain Poisson Probabilities *160*

Synopsis of Introductory Case *161*

5.5 The Hypergeometric Distribution *163*
Using Excel to Obtain Hypergeometric Probabilities *165*

Writing with Statistics *166*

Sample Report—Comparison of Salary Plans *167*

Conceptual Review *168*

Additional Exercises and Case Studies *169*
Case Studies *170*

Appendix 5.1 Guidelines for Other Software Packages *172*

CHAPTER 6

Continuous Probability Distributions *174*

Introductory Case: Demand for Salmon *175*

6.1 Continuous Random Variables and the Uniform Distribution *176*
The Continuous Uniform Distribution *177*

6.2 The Normal Distribution *180*
Characteristics of the Normal Distribution *180*
The Standard Normal Variable *182*
Finding a Probability for a Given *z* Value *182*
Finding a *z* Value for a Given Probability *185*
Revisiting the Empirical Rule *186*

6.3 Solving Problems with Normal Distributions *189*
The Transformation of Normal Random Variables *189*
The Inverse Transformation *191*
Using Excel for the Normal Distribution *193*
A Note on the Normal Approximation of the Binomial Distribution *193*

Synopsis of Introductory Case *194*

6.4 The Exponential Distribution *197*
Using Excel for the Exponential Distribution *199*

Writing with Statistics *201*

Sample Report—Absolute Grading versus Relative Grading *201*

Conceptual Review *202*

Additional Exercises and Case Studies *203*
Case Studies *205*

Appendix 6.1 Guidelines for Other Software Packages *207*

CHAPTER 7

Sampling and Sampling Distributions *210*

Introductory Case: Marketing Iced Coffee *211*

7.1 Sampling *212*
Classic Case of a "Bad" Sample: The *Literary Digest* Debacle of 1936 *212*
Sampling Methods *213*
The Special Election to Fill Ted Kennedy's Senate Seat *215*

7.2 The Sampling Distribution of the Sample Mean *217*
The Expected Value and the Standard Error of the Sample Mean *218*
Sampling from a Normal Population *219*
The Central Limit Theorem *220*

7.3 The Sampling Distribution of the Sample Proportion *224*
The Expected Value and the Standard Error of the Sample Proportion *224*

Synopsis of Introductory Case *227*

7.4 The Finite Population Correction Factor *228*

7.5 Statistical Quality Control *231*
Control Charts *232*
Using Excel to Create a Control Chart *235*

Writing with Statistics *237*

Sample Report—Customer Wait Time *238*

Conceptual Review *239*

Additional Exercises and Case Studies *240*
Case Studies *243*

Appendix 7.1 **Derivation of the Mean and the Variance for $\bar{X}$ and $\bar{P}$** 244

Appendix 7.2 **Guidelines for Other Software Packages** 244

CHAPTER 8

Interval Estimation 246

Introductory Case: Fuel Usage of "Ultra-Green" Cars 247

8.1 **Confidence Interval for the Population Mean When σ Is Known** 248
Constructing a Confidence Interval for μ When σ Is Known 249
The Width of a Confidence Interval 251
Using Excel to Construct a Confidence Interval for μ When σ Is Known 253

8.2 **Confidence Interval for the Population Mean When σ Is Unknown** 255
The t Distribution 255
Constructing a Confidence Interval for μ When σ Is Unknown 258
Using Excel to Construct a Confidence Interval for μ When σ Is Unknown 259

8.3 **Confidence Interval for the Population Proportion** 262

8.4 **Selecting the Required Sample Size** 265
Selecting n to Estimate μ 265
Selecting n to Estimate p 266

Synopsis of Introductory Case 267

Writing with Statistics 269

Sample Report—Weekly Stock Performance: Home Depot vs. Lowe's 270

Conceptual Review 270

Additional Exercises and Case Studies 272
Case Studies 274

Appendix 8.1 **Guidelines for Other Software Packages** 276

CHAPTER 9

Hypothesis Testing 278

Introductory Case: Undergraduate Study Habits 279

9.1 **Introduction to Hypothesis Testing** 280
The Decision to "Reject" or "Not Reject" the Null Hypothesis 280
Defining the Null and the Alternative Hypotheses 281
Type I and Type II Errors 283

9.2 **Hypothesis Test of the Population Mean When σ Is Known** 285
The p-Value Approach 286
The Critical Value Approach 290

Confidence Intervals and Two-Tailed Hypothesis Tests 293
Using Excel to Test μ When σ Is Known 294
One Last Remark 295

9.3 **Hypothesis Test of the Population Mean When σ Is Unknown** 297
Using Excel to Test μ When σ Is Unknown 299

Synopsis of Introductory Case 300

9.4 **Hypothesis Test of the Population Proportion** 303

Writing with Statistics 308

Sample Report—Income Inequality in the United States 308

Conceptual Review 309

Additional Exercises and Case Studies 311
Case Studies 313

Appendix 9.1 **Guidelines for Other Software Packages** 315

CHAPTER 10

Comparisons Involving Means 316

Introductory Case: Effectiveness of Mandatory Caloric Postings 317

10.1 **Inference Concerning the Difference between Two Means** 318
Confidence Interval for $\mu_1 - \mu_2$ 318
Hypothesis Test for $\mu_1 - \mu_2$ 320
Using Excel for Testing Hypotheses about $\mu_1 - \mu_2$ 322

10.2 **Inference Concerning Mean Differences** 327
Recognizing a Matched-Pairs Experiment 328
Confidence Interval for μ_D 328
Hypothesis Test for μ_D 329
Using Excel for Testing Hypotheses about μ_D 330

Synopsis of Introductory Case 332

10.3 **Inference Concerning Differences among Many Means** 334
The F Distribution 335
One-Way ANOVA Test 336
Using Excel for One-Way ANOVA Test 340

Writing with Statistics 344

Sample Report—Evaluating Traffic Congestion by City 345

Conceptual Review 345

Additional Exercises and Case Studies 346
Case Studies 349

Appendix 10.1 **Guidelines for Other Software Packages** 350

CHAPTER 11

Comparisons Involving Proportions 352

Introductory Case: Sportswear Brands 353

11.1 Inference Concerning the Difference between Two Proportions 354
Confidence Interval for $p_1 - p_2$ 354
Hypothesis Test for $p_1 - p_2$ 355

11.2 Goodness-of-Fit Test for a Multinomial Experiment 359
Using Excel to Calculate p-Values 363

11.3 Chi-Square Test for Independence 366
Calculating Expected Frequencies 367

Synopsis of Introductory Case 370

Writing with Statistics 372

Sample Report—Online Dating Preferences 372

Conceptual Review 373

Additional Exercises and Case Studies 374
Case Studies 376

Appendix 11.1 Guidelines for Other Software Packages 378

CHAPTER 12

Basics of Regression Analysis 380

Introductory Case: Consumer Debt Payments 381

12.1 The Simple Linear Regression Model 382
Determining the Sample Regression Equation 383
Using Excel to Construct a Scatterplot and a Trendline 384
Using Excel to Find the Sample Regression Equation 386

12.2 The Multiple Linear Regression Model 389
Determining the Sample Regression Equation 390

12.3 Goodness-of-Fit Measures 393
The Standard Error of the Estimate 394
The Coefficient of Determination R^2 396
The Adjusted R^2 398

12.4 Tests of Significance 401
Tests of Individual Significance 401
Test of Joint Significance 406
Reporting Regression Results 407

Synopsis of Introductory Case 408

Writing with Statistics 412

Sample Report—Analyzing the Winning Proportion in Baseball 412

Conceptual Review 413

Additional Exercises and Case Studies 415
Case Studies 417

Appendix 12.1 Guidelines for Other Software Packages 418

CHAPTER 13

More on Regression Analysis 420

Introductory Case: Is There Evidence of Wage Discrimination? 421

13.1 Dummy Variables 422
Qualitative Variables with Two Categories 422
Qualitative Variables with Multiple Categories 425

Synopsis of Introductory Case 428

13.2 Interval Estimates for the Response Variable 431

13.3 Model Assumptions and Common Violations 436
Common Violation 1: Nonlinear Patterns 438
Common Violation 2: Multicollinearity 439
Common Violation 3: Changing Variability 440
Common Violation 4: Correlated Observations 442
Common Violation 5: Excluded Variables 443
Summary 444

Writing with Statistics 445

Sample Report—Baseball Salaries 446

Conceptual Review 447

Additional Exercises and Case Studies 448
Case Studies 451

Appendix 13.1 Guidelines for Other Software Packages 454

APPENDIXES

APPENDIX A   Tables 456
APPENDIX B   Answers to Even-Numbered Exercises 466

Glossary 503
Photo Credits 508
Index 509

ESSENTIALS OF
BUSINESS STATISTICS

1

Statistics and Data

CHAPTER

LEARNING OBJECTIVES

After reading
this chapter
you should
be able to:

LO **1.1**   Describe the importance of statistics.

LO **1.2**   Differentiate between descriptive statistics and inferential statistics.

LO **1.3**   Explain the need for sampling and discuss various data types.

LO **1.4**   Describe variables and various types of measurement scales.

Every day we are bombarded with data and claims. The analysis of data and the conclusions made from data are part of the field of statistics. A proper understanding of statistics is essential in understanding more of the real world around us, including business, finance, health, social interactions—just about any area of contemporary human activity. In this first chapter, we will differentiate between sound statistical conclusions and questionable conclusions. We will also introduce some important terms, which are referenced throughout the text, that will help us describe different aspects of statistics and their practical importance. You are probably familiar with some of these terms already, from reading or hearing about opinion polls, surveys, and the all-pervasive product ads. Our goal is to place what you already know about these uses of statistics within a framework that we then use for explaining where they came from and what they really mean. A major portion of this chapter is also devoted to the discussion of variables and various types of measurement scales. As we will see in later chapters, we need to distinguish between different variables and measurement scales in order to choose the appropriate statistical methods for analyzing data.

Tween Survey

Luke McCaffrey owns a ski resort two hours outside Boston, Massachusetts, and is in need of a new marketing manager. He is a fairly tough interviewer and believes that the person in this position should have a basic understanding of data fundamentals, including some background with statistical methods. Luke is particularly interested in serving the needs of the "tween" population (children aged 8 to 12 years old). He believes that tween spending power has grown over the past few years, and he wants their skiing experience to be memorable so that they want to return. At the end of last year's ski season, Luke asked 20 tweens four specific questions.

Q1. On your car drive to the resort, which radio station was playing?

Q2. On a scale of 1 to 4, rate the quality of the food at the resort (where 1 is poor, 2 is fair, 3 is good, and 4 is excellent).

Q3. Presently, the main dining area closes at 3:00 pm. What time do you think it should close?

Q4. How much of your *own* money did you spend at the lodge today?

The responses to these questions are shown in Table 1.1; these data are also found on the text website and are labeled **Tween_Survey**.

TABLE 1.1 Tween Responses to Skylark Valley Resort Survey FILE

Tween	Q1	Q2	Q3	Q4	Tween	Q1	Q2	Q3	Q4
1	JAMN94.5	4	5:00 pm	20	11	JAMN94.5	3	3:00 pm	0
2	MIX104.1	2	5:00 pm	10	12	JAMN94.5	4	4:00 pm	5
3	KISS108	2	4:30 pm	10	13	KISS108	2	4:30 pm	5
4	JAMN94.5	3	4:00 pm	0	14	KISS108	2	5:00 pm	10
5	KISS108	1	3:30 pm	0	15	KISS108	3	4:00 pm	5
6	JAMN94.5	1	6:00 pm	25	16	JAMN94.5	3	6:00 pm	20
7	KISS108	2	6:00 pm	15	17	KISS108	2	5:00 pm	15
8	KISS108	3	5:00 pm	10	18	MIX104.1	4	6:00 pm	15
9	KISS108	2	4:30 pm	10	19	KISS108	1	5:00 pm	25
10	KISS108	3	4:30 pm	20	20	KISS108	2	4:30 pm	10

Luke asks each job applicant to use the information to:

1. Classify the tween responses into the appropriate measurement scale.
2. Compare and contrast the type of information that can be extracted from each measurement scale.
3. Given the results of the survey, provide management with suggestions for improvement.

A synopsis from the job applicant with the best answers is provided at the end of Section 1.3.

1.1 The Relevance of Statistics

LO **1.1**

Describe the
importance
of statistics.

In order to make intelligent decisions in a world full of uncertainty, we all have to understand statistics—the language of data. Unfortunately, many people avoid learning statistics because they believe (incorrectly!) that statistics simply deals with incomprehensible formulas and tedious calculations, and that it has no use in real life. This type of thinking is far from the truth because we encounter statistics *every day* in real life. We must understand statistics or risk making uninformed decisions and costly mistakes. While it is true that statistics incorporates formulas and calculations, it is logical reasoning that dictates how the data are collected, the calculations implemented, and the results communicated. A knowledge of statistics also provides the necessary tools to differentiate between sound statistical conclusions and questionable conclusions drawn from an insufficient number of data points, "bad" data points, incomplete data points, or just misinformation. Consider the following examples.

Example 1. After Washington, DC, had record amounts of snow in the winter of 2010, the headline of a newspaper stated, "What global warming?"

Problem with conclusion: The existence or nonexistence of climate change cannot be based on one year's worth of data. Instead, we must examine long-term trends and analyze decades' worth of data.

Example 2. A gambler predicts that his next roll of the dice will be a lucky 7 because he did not get that outcome on the last three rolls.

Problem with conclusion: As we will see later in the text when we discuss probability, the probability of rolling a 7 stays constant with each roll of the dice. It does not become more likely if it did not appear on the last roll or, in fact, any number of preceding rolls.

Example 3. On January 10, 2010, nine days prior to a special election to fill the U.S. Senate seat that was vacated due to the death of Ted Kennedy, a *Boston Globe* poll gave the Democratic candidate Martha Coakley a 15-point lead over the Republican candidate Scott Brown. On January 19, 2010, Brown won 52% of the vote compared to Coakley's 47% and became a U.S. senator for Massachusetts.

Problem with conclusion: Critics accused the *Globe*, which had endorsed Coakley, of purposely running a bad poll to discourage voters from coming out for Brown. In reality, by the time the *Globe* released the poll, it contained old information from January 2–6, 2010. Even more problematic was that the poll included people who said that they were unlikely to vote!

Example 4. Starbucks Corp., the world's largest coffee-shop operator, reported that sales at stores open at least a year climbed 4% at home and abroad in the quarter ended December 27, 2009. Chief Financial Officer Troy Alstead said that "the U.S. is back in a good track and the international business has similarly picked up. . . . Traffic is really coming back. It's a good sign for what we're going to see for the rest of the year" (http://www.bloomberg.com, January 20, 2010).

Problem with conclusion: In order to calculate same-store sales growth, which compares how much each store in the chain is selling compared with a year ago, we remove stores that have closed. Given that Starbucks closed more than 800 stores over the past few years to counter large sales declines, it is likely that the sales increases in many of the stores were caused by traffic from nearby, recently closed stores. In this case, same-store sales growth may overstate the overall health of Starbucks.

Example 5. Researchers at the University of Pennsylvania Medical Center found that infants who sleep with a nightlight are much more likely to develop myopia later in life (*Nature*, May 1999).

Problem with conclusion: This example appears to commit the *correlation-to-causation fallacy*. Even if two variables are highly correlated, one does not necessarily cause the other. *Spurious correlation* can make two variables appear closely related when no causal relation exists. Spurious correlation between two variables is not based on any demonstrable relationship, but rather on a relation that arises in the data solely because each of those variables is related to some third variable. In a follow-up study, researchers at The Ohio State University found no link between infants who sleep with a nightlight and the development of myopia (*Nature*, March 2000). They did, however, find strong links between parental myopia and the development of child myopia, and between parental myopia and the parents' use of a nightlight in their children's room. So the cause of both conditions (the use of a nightlight and the development of child myopia) is parental myopia.

Note the diversity of the sources of these examples—the environment, psychology, polling, business, and health. We could easily include others, from sports, sociology, the physical sciences, and elsewhere. Data and data interpretation show up in virtually every facet of life, sometimes spuriously. All of the above examples basically misuse data to add credibility to an argument. A solid understanding of statistics provides you with tools to react intelligently to information that you read or hear.

1.2 What Is Statistics?

In the broadest sense, we can define the study of statistics as the methodology of extracting useful information from a data set. Three steps are essential for doing good statistics. First, we have to find the right data, which are both complete and lacking any misrepresentation. Second, we must use the appropriate statistical tools, depending on the data at hand. Finally, an important ingredient of a well-executed statistical analysis is to clearly communicate numerical information into written language.

LO **1.2**

Differentiate between descriptive statistics and inferential statistics.

We generally divide the study of statistics into two branches: descriptive statistics and inferential statistics. **Descriptive statistics** refers to the summary of important aspects of a data set. This includes collecting data, organizing the data, and then presenting the data in the forms of charts and tables. In addition, we often calculate numerical measures that summarize, for instance, the data's typical value and the data's variability. Today, the techniques encountered in descriptive statistics account for the most visible application of statistics—the abundance of quantitative information that is collected and published in our society every day. The unemployment rate, the president's approval rating, the Dow Jones Industrial Average, batting averages, the crime rate, and the divorce rate are but a few of the many "statistics" that can be found in a reputable newspaper on a frequent, if not daily, basis. Yet, despite the familiarity of descriptive statistics, these methods represent only a minor portion of the body of statistical applications.

The phenomenal growth in statistics is mainly in the field called inferential statistics. Generally, **inferential statistics** refers to drawing conclusions about a large set of data—called a **population**—based on a smaller set of **sample** data. A population is defined as all members of a specified group (not necessarily people), whereas a sample is a subset of that particular population. In most statistical applications we must rely on sample data in order to make inferences about various characteristics of the population. For example, a 2010 survey of 1,208 registered voters by a USA TODAY/Gallup Poll found that President Obama's job performance was viewed favorably by only 41% of those polled, his lowest rating in a USA TODAY/Gallup Poll since he took office in January 2009 (*USA TODAY*, August 3, 2010). Researchers use this sample result, called a **sample statistic**, in an attempt to estimate the corresponding unknown **population parameter**. In this case, the parameter of interest is the percentage of *all* registered voters that view the president's job performance favorably. It is generally not feasible to obtain population data and calculate the relevant parameter directly due to prohibitive costs and/or practicality, as discussed next.

POPULATION VERSUS SAMPLE

A **population** consists of all items of interest in a statistical problem. A **sample** is a subset of the population. We analyze sample data and calculate a **sample statistic** to make inferences about the unknown **population parameter**.

The Need for Sampling

LO **1.3**

Explain the need for sampling and discuss various data types.

A major portion of inferential statistics is concerned with the problem of estimating population parameters or testing hypotheses about such parameters. If we have access to data that encompass the entire population, then we would know the values of the parameters. Generally, however, we are unable to use population data for two main reasons.

- **Obtaining information on the entire population is expensive**. Consider how the monthly unemployment rate in the United States is calculated by the Bureau of Labor Statistics (BLS). Is it reasonable to assume that the BLS counts every unemployed person each month? The answer is a resounding NO! In order to do this, every home in the country would have to be contacted. Given that there are over 150 million individuals in the labor force, not only would this process cost too much, it would take an inordinate amount of time. Instead, the BLS conducts a monthly sample survey of about 60,000 households to measure the extent of unemployment in the United States.

- **It is impossible to examine every member of the population**. Suppose we are interested in the average length of life of a Duracell© AAA battery. If we tested the duration of each Duracell© AAA battery, then in the end, all batteries would be dead and the answer to the original question would be useless.

Types of Data

Sample data are generally collected in one of two ways. **Cross-sectional data** refers to data collected by recording a characteristic of many subjects at the same point in time, or without regard to differences in time. Subjects might include individuals, households, firms, industries, regions, and countries. The tween data presented in Table 1.1 in the introductory case is an example of cross-sectional data because it contains tween responses to four questions at the end of the ski season. It is unlikely that all 20 tweens took the questionnaire at exactly the same time, but the differences in time are of no relevance in this example. Other examples of cross-sectional data include the recorded scores of students in a class, the sale prices of single-family homes sold last month, the current price of gasoline in different states in the United States, and the starting salaries of recent business graduates from The Ohio State University.

Time series data refers to data collected by recording a characteristic of a subject over several time periods. Time series can include daily, weekly, monthly, quarterly, or annual observations. Examples of time series data include the monthly sales of cars at a dealership in 2010, the daily price of IBM stock in the first quarter of 2012, the weekly exchange rate between the U.S. dollar and the euro, and the annual growth rate of India in the last decade. Figure 1.1 shows a plot of the real (inflation-adjusted) GDP growth rate of the United States from 1980 through 2010. The average growth rate for this period is 2.7%, yet the plot indicates a great deal of variability in the series. It exhibits a wavelike movement, spiking downward in 2008 due to the economic recession before rebounding in 2010.

Figure 1.1 Real GDP growth rate from 1980 through 2010

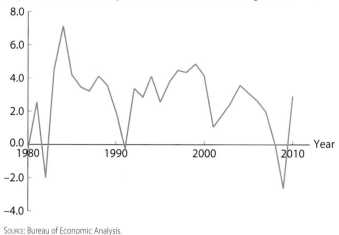

Source: Bureau of Economic Analysis.

Cross-sectional data contain values of a characteristic of many subjects at the same point or approximately the same point in time. **Time series data** contain values of a characteristic of a subject over time.

Getting Started on the Web

As you can imagine, there is an abundance of data on the Internet. We accessed much of the data in this text by simply using a search engine like Google. These search engines often directed us to the same data-providing sites. For instance, the U.S. federal government publishes a great deal of economic and business data. The Bureau of Economic Analysis (BEA), the Bureau of Labor Statistics (BLS), the Federal Reserve Economic Data (FRED), and the U.S. Census Bureau provide data on inflation, unemployment, gross domestic product (GDP), and much more. Zillow.com is a real estate site that supplies data such as recent home sales, monthly rent, and mortgage rates. Finance.yahoo.com is a financial site that lists data such as stock prices, mutual fund performance, and international market data. *The Wall Street Journal*, *The New York Times*, *USA Today, The Economist*, and *Fortune* are all reputable publications that provide all sorts of data. Finally, espn.com offers comprehensive sports data on both professional and college teams. We list these sites in Table 1.2 and summarize *some* of the data that are available.

TABLE 1.2 Select Internet Data Sites

Internet Site	Select Data Availability
Bureau of Economic Analysis (BEA)	National and regional data on gross domestic product (GDP) and personal income, international data on trade in goods and services.
Bureau of Labor Statistics (BLS)	Inflation rates, unemployment rates, employment, pay and benefits, spending and time use, productivity.
Federal Reserve Economic Data (FRED)	Banking, business/fiscal data, exchange rates, reserves, monetary base.
U.S. Census Bureau	Economic indicators, foreign trade, health insurance, housing, sector-specific data.
zillow.com	Recent home sales, home characteristics, monthly rent, mortgage rates.
finance.yahoo.com	Historical stock prices, mutual fund performance, international market data.
The New York Times, USA Today, The Wall Street Journal, The Economist, and *Fortune*	Poverty, crime, obesity, and plenty of business-related data.
espn.com	Professional and college teams' scores, rankings, standings, individual player statistics.

EXERCISES 1.2

1. It came as a big surprise when Apple's touch screen iPhone 4, considered by many to be the best smartphone ever, was found to have a problem (*The New York Times*, June 24, 2010). Users complained of weak reception, and sometimes even dropped calls, when they cradled the phone in their hands in a particular way. A quick survey at a local store found that 2% of iPhone 4 users experienced this reception problem.
   a. Describe the relevant population.
   b. Does 2% denote the population parameter or the sample statistic?

2. Many people regard video games as an obsession for youngsters, but, in fact, the average age of a video game player is 35 years (Reuters.com, August 21, 2009). Is the value 35 likely the actual or the estimated average age of the population? Explain.

3. An accounting professor wants to know the average GPA of the students enrolled in her class. She looks up information on Blackboard about the students enrolled in her class and computes the average GPA as 3.29.
   a. Describe the relevant population.
   b. Does the value 3.29 represent the population parameter or the sample statistic?

4. Business graduates in the United States with a marketing concentration earn high salaries. According to the Bureau of Labor Statistics, the average annual salary for marketing managers was $104,400 in 2007.
   a. What is the relevant population?
   b. Do you think the average salary of $104,400 was computed from the population? Explain.

5. Recent research suggests that depression significantly increases the risk of developing dementia later in life (*BBC News*, July 6, 2010). In a study involving 949 elderly persons, it was reported that 22% of those who had depression went on to develop dementia, compared to only 17% of those who did not have depression.
   a. Describe the relevant population and the sample.
   b. Do the numbers 22% and 17% represent the population parameters or the sample statistics?

6. Go to http://www.finance.yahoo.com/ to get a current stock quote for Google, Inc. (ticker symbol = GOOG). Then, click on historical prices to record the monthly adjusted close price of Google stock in 2010. Create a table that uses this information. What type of data do these numbers represent? Comment on the data.

7. Ask 20 of your friends whether they live in a dormitory, a rental unit, or other form of accommodation. Also find out their approximate monthly lodging expenses. Create a table that uses this information. What type of data do these numbers represent? Comment on the data.

8. Go to http://www.zillow.com/ and find the sale price data of 20 single-family homes sold in Las Vegas, Nevada, in the last 30 days. You must include in the data set the sale price, the number of bedrooms, the square footage, and the age of the house. What type of data do these numbers represent? Comment on the data.

9. The Federal Reserve Bank of St. Louis is a good source for downloading economic data. Go to http://research.stlouisfed.org/fred2/ to extract quarterly data on gross private saving (GPSAVE) from 2008 to 2011 (16 observations). Create a table that uses this information. Plot the data over time and comment on the savings trend in the United States.

10. Another good source of data is the U.S. Census Bureau. Go to http://www.census.gov/ and extract the most recent median household income for Alabama, Arizona, California, Florida, Georgia, Indiana, Iowa, Maine, Massachusetts, Minnesota, Mississippi, New Mexico, North Dakota, and Washington. What type of data do these numbers represent? Comment on the regional differences in income.

1.3 Variables and Scales of Measurement

LO **1.4**

Describe variables and various types of measurement scales.

When we conduct a statistical investigation, we invariably focus on people, objects, or events with particular characteristics. When a characteristic of interest differs in kind or degree among various observations, then the characteristic can be termed a **variable**. We further categorize a variable as either qualitative or quantitative. For a **qualitative variable**, we use labels or names to identify the distinguishing characteristic of each observation. For instance, the 2010 Census asked each respondent to indicate gender on the form. Each respondent chose either male or female. Gender is a qualitative variable. Other examples of qualitative variables include race, profession, type of business, the manufacturer of a car, and so on.

A variable that assumes meaningful numerical values is called a **quantitative variable**. Quantitative variables, in turn, are either discrete or continuous. A **discrete variable** assumes a countable number of values. Consider the number of children in a family or the number of points scored in a basketball game. We may observe values such as 3 children in a family or 90 points being scored in a basketball game, but we will not observe 1.3 children or 92.5 scored points. The values that a discrete variable assumes need not be whole numbers. For example, the price of a stock for a particular firm is a discrete variable. The stock price may take on a value of $20.37 or $20.38, but it cannot take on a value between these two points. Finally, a discrete variable may assume an infinite number of values, but these values are countable, that is, they can be presented as a sequence x_1, x_2, x_3, and so on. The number of cars that cross the Golden Gate Bridge on a Saturday is a discrete variable. Theoretically, this variable assumes the values 0, 1, 2, . . .

A **continuous variable** is characterized by uncountable values that are within a certain interval. Weight, height, time, and investment return are all examples of continuous variables. For example, an unlimited number of values occur between the weights of 100 and 101 pounds, such as 100.3, 100.625, 100.8342, and so on. In practice, however, continuous variables may be measured in discrete values. We may report a newborn's weight (a continuous variable) in discrete terms as 6 pounds 10 ounces and another newborn's weight in similar discrete terms as 6 pounds 11 ounces.

QUALITATIVE VARIABLES VERSUS QUANTITATIVE VARIABLES

A **variable** is the general characteristic being observed on a set of people, objects, or events, where each observation varies in kind or degree. Labels or names are used to categorize the distinguishing characteristics of a **qualitative variable**; eventually, these attributes may be coded into numbers for purposes of data processing. A **quantitative variable** assumes meaningful numerical values, and can be further categorized as either **discrete** or **continuous**. The possible values for a discrete variable may be counted, whereas a continuous variable can take on any value within an interval.

In order to choose the appropriate statistical methods for summarizing and analyzing data, we need to distinguish between different measurement scales. All data measurements can be classified into one of four major categories: nominal, ordinal, interval, and ratio. Nominal and ordinal scales are used for qualitative variables, whereas interval and ratio scales are used for quantitative variables. We discuss these scales in ascending order of sophistication.

The Nominal Scale

The **nominal scale** represents the least sophisticated level of measurement. If we are presented with nominal data, all we can do is categorize or group the data. The values in the data set differ merely by name or label. Consider the following example.

Each company listed in Table 1.3 is a member of the Dow Jones Industrial Average (DJIA). The DJIA is a stock market index that shows how 30 large, publicly owned companies based in the United States have traded during a standard trading session in the stock market. Table 1.3 also shows where stocks of these companies are traded: on either the National Association of Securities Dealers Automated Quotations (Nasdaq) or the New York Stock Exchange (NYSE). These data are classified as nominal scale since we are simply able to group or categorize them. Specifically, only three stocks are traded on Nasdaq, whereas the remaining 27 are traded on the NYSE.

Often we substitute *numbers* for the particular qualitative characteristic or trait that we are grouping. One reason why we do this is for ease of exposition; always referring to the National Association of Securities Dealers Automated Quotations, or even Nasdaq, becomes awkward and unwieldy. In addition, as we will see later in the text, computer statistical analysis is greatly facilitated by using numbers instead of names. For example, we might use the number 0 to show that a company's

TABLE 1.3 Companies of the DJIA and Exchange Where Stock Is Traded

Company	Exchange	Company	Exchange
3M (MMM)	NYSE	Intel (INTC)	Nasdaq
Alcoa (AA)	NYSE	IBM (IBM)	NYSE
American Express (AXP)	NYSE	Johnson & Johnson (JNJ)	NYSE
AT&T (T)	NYSE	JPMorgan Chase (JPM)	NYSE
Bank of America (BAC)	NYSE	Kraft Foods (KFT)	NYSE
Boeing (BA)	NYSE	McDonald's (MCD)	NYSE
Caterpillar (CAT)	NYSE	Merck (MRK)	NYSE
Chevron Corp. (CVX)	NYSE	Microsoft (MSFT)	Nasdaq
Cisco Systems (CSCO)	Nasdaq	Pfizer (PFE)	NYSE
Coca-Cola (KO)	NYSE	Procter & Gamble (PG)	NYSE
DuPont (DD)	NYSE	Travelers (TRV)	NYSE
ExxonMobil (XOM)	NYSE	United Tech. Corp. (UTX)	NYSE
General Electric (GE)	NYSE	Verizon Comm. (VZ)	NYSE
Hewlett-Packard (HPQ)	NYSE	Walmart (WMT)	NYSE
Home Depot (HD)	NYSE	Walt Disney (DIS)	NYSE

SOURCE: http://www.finance.yahoo.com, as of August 31, 2012.

stock is traded on Nasdaq and the number 1 to show that a company's stock is traded on NYSE. In tabular form:

Exchange	Number of Companies Trading on Exchange
0	3
1	27

The Ordinal Scale

Compared to the nominal scale, the **ordinal scale** reflects a stronger level of measurement. With ordinal data we are able to both *categorize* and *rank* the data with respect to some characteristic or trait. The weakness with ordinal data is that we cannot interpret the difference between the ranked values because the actual numbers used are arbitrary. For example, suppose you are asked to classify the service at a particular hotel as excellent, good, fair, or poor. A standard way to record the ratings is

Excellent	4	Fair	2
Good	3	Poor	1

Here the value attached to excellent (4) is higher than the value attached to good (3), indicating that the response of excellent is preferred to good. However, another representation of the ratings might be

Excellent	100	Fair	70
Good	80	Poor	40

Excellent still receives a higher value than good, but now the difference between the two categories is 20 (100 − 80), as compared to a difference of 1 (4 − 3) when we use the first classification. In other words, *differences between categories are meaningless with ordinal data.* (We also should note that we could reverse the ordering so that, for instance, excellent equals 40 and poor equals 100; this renumbering would not change the nature of the data.)

EXAMPLE 1.1

In the introductory case, four questions were posed to tweens. The first question (Q1) asked tweens to name the radio station that they listened to on the ride to the resort, and the second question (Q2) asked tweens to rate the food quality at the resort on a scale of 1 to 4. The tweens' responses to these questions are shown in Table 1.1 in the introductory case.

a. What is the scale of measurement of the radio station data?

b. How are the data based on the ratings of the food quality similar to the radio station data? How are the data different?

c. Summarize the tweens' responses to Q1 and Q2 in tabular form. How can the resort use the information from these responses?

SOLUTION:

a. When asked which radio station played on the car ride to the resort, tweens responded with one of the following answers: JAMN94.5, MIX104.1, or KISS108. These are nominal data—the values in the data differ merely in name or label.

b. Since we can both categorize and rank the food quality data, we classify these responses as ordinal data. Ordinal data are similar to nominal data in the sense that we can categorize the data. The main difference between ordinal and nominal data is that the categories of ordinal data are ranked. A rating of 4 is better than a rating of 3. With the radio station data, we cannot say that KISS108 is ranked higher than MIX104.1; some tweens may argue otherwise, but we simply categorize nominal data without ranking.

c. With respect to the radio station data (Q1), we can assign 1 to JAMN94.5, 2 to MIX104.1, and 3 to KISS108. Counting the responses that fall into each category, we find that six tweens listened to 1, two listened to 2, and 12 listened to 3, or in tabular form:

Radio Station	Number of Tweens Listening to Radio Station
1	6
2	2
3	12

Twelve of the 20 tweens, or 60%, listened to KISS108. This information could prove useful to the management of the resort as they make decisions as to where to allocate their advertising dollars. If the resort could only choose to advertise at one radio station, it would appear that KISS108 would be the wise choice.

Given the food quality responses (Q2), we find that three of the tweens rated food quality with a 4, six tweens rated food quality with a 3, eight tweens rated food quality with a 2, and three tweens rated food quality with a 1. In tabular form:

Rating	Number of Tweens
4	3
3	6
2	8
1	3

The food quality results may be of concern to management. Just as many tweens rated the food quality as excellent as compared to poor. Moreover, the majority $[(8 + 3)/20 = 55\%]$ felt that the food was, at best, fair. Perhaps a more extensive survey that focuses solely on food quality would reveal the reason for their apparent dissatisfaction.

As mentioned earlier, nominal and ordinal scales are used for *qualitative variables*. Values corresponding to a qualitative variable are typically expressed in words but are coded into numbers for purposes of data processing. When summarizing the results of a qualitative variable, we typically count the number or calculate the percentage of persons or objects that fall into each possible category. With a qualitative variable, we are unable to perform meaningful arithmetic operations, such as adding and subtracting.

The Interval Scale

With data on an **interval scale**, not only can we categorize and rank the data, but we are also assured that the differences between scale values are meaningful. Thus, the arithmetic operations of addition and subtraction are meaningful. The Fahrenheit scale for temperatures is an example of an interval scale. Not only is 60 degrees hotter than 50 degrees, but the same difference of 10 degrees exists as between 90 and 80 degrees Fahrenheit.

The main drawback of data on an interval scale is that the value of zero is arbitrarily chosen; the zero point of an interval scale does not reflect a complete absence of what is being measured. No specific meaning is attached to zero degrees Fahrenheit other than to say it is 10 degrees colder than 10 degrees Fahrenheit. With an arbitrary zero point, meaningful ratios cannot be constructed. For instance, it is senseless to say that 80 degrees is twice as hot as 40 degrees; in other words, the ratio 80/40 has no meaning.

The Ratio Scale

The **ratio scale** represents the strongest level of measurement. Ratio data have all the characteristics of interval data as well as a *true zero* point, which allows us to interpret the ratios of values. A ratio scale is used to measure many types of data in business analysis. Variables such as sales, profits, and inventory levels are expressed as ratio data. A meaningful zero allows us to state, for example, that profits for firm A are double those of firm B. Measurements such as weight, time, and distance are also measured on a ratio scale since zero is meaningful.

Unlike qualitative data, arithmetic operations are valid on interval- and ratio-scaled values. In later chapters, we will calculate summary measures for the typical value and variability of quantitative variables; we cannot calculate these measures if the variable is qualitative in nature.

EXAMPLE 1.2

In the last two questions from the introductory case's survey (Q3 and Q4), the 20 tweens were asked: "What time should the main dining area close?" and "How much of your *own* money did you spend at the lodge today?" Their responses appear in Table 1.1 in the introductory case.

a. How are the time data classified? In what ways do the time data differ from ordinal data? What is a potential weakness of this measurement scale?

b. What is the measurement scale of the money data? Why is it considered the strongest form of data?

c. In what ways is the information from Q3 and Q4 useful for the resort?

SOLUTION:

a. Clock time responses, such as 3:00 pm and 3:30 pm, or 5:30 pm and 6:00 pm, are on an interval scale. Interval data are a stronger measurement scale than ordinal data because differences between interval-scaled values are meaningful. In this particular example, we can say that 3:30 pm is 30 minutes later than 3:00 pm and 6:00 pm is 30 minutes later than 5:30 pm. The weakness with interval data is that the value of zero is arbitrary. Here, with the clock time responses, we have no apparent zero point; however, we could always arbitrarily define a zero point, say, at 12:00 am. Thus, although differences are comparable with interval data, ratios are meaningless due to the arbitrariness of the zero point. In other words, it is senseless to form the ratio 6:00 pm/3:00 pm and conclude that 6:00 pm is twice as long a time period as 3:00 pm.

b. Since the tweens' responses are in dollar amounts, this is ratio data. The ratio scale is the strongest form of data because we can categorize and rank values as well as calculate meaningful differences. Moreover, since there is a natural zero point, valid ratios can also be calculated. For example, the data show that three tweens spent $20. These tweens spent four times as much as the three tweens that spent $5 ($20/$5 = 4).

c. A review of the clock time responses (Q3) in Table 1.1 shows that the vast majority of the tweens would like the dining area to remain open later. In fact, only one tween feels that the dining area should close at 3:00 pm. An inspection of the money responses (Q4) in Table 1.1 indicates that only three of the 20 tweens did not spend any of his/her own money. This is very important information. It does appear that the discretionary spending of this age group is significant. The resort would be wise to cater to some of their preferences.

SYNOPSIS OF INTRODUCTORY CASE

A preliminary survey of tween preferences conducted by the management of a ski resort two hours outside Boston, Massachusetts, revealed some interesting information.

- Tweens were first asked to name the radio station that they listened to on the way to the resort. Even though their responses are in the form of nominal data, the least sophisticated form of measurement, useful information can still be extracted from it. For instance, the responses show that 60% of the tweens listened to KISS108. If the resort wishes to contact tweens using this medium, it may want to direct its advertising dollars to this station.

- Next, the tweens were asked to rate the food quality at the resort on a scale of 1 to 4 (where 1 is poor, 2 is fair, 3 is good, and 4 is excellent). Their responses to food quality were ordinal in nature; that is, the responses can be categorized and ranked. The survey results with respect to food quality are disturbing. The majority of the tweens, 55% (11/20), felt that the food was, at best, fair. A more extensive study focusing on food quality appears necessary.

- Tweens were then asked what time the main dining area should close, given a present closing time of 3:00 pm. Their clock-time responses reflect the interval scale. The interval scale is stronger than the nominal and ordinal scales, implying that more can be extracted from the data than mere percentages; however, data on the interval scale have an arbitrary zero point, so meaningful ratios cannot be constructed. The data suggest that the vast majority of the tweens (19 out of 20) would like the dining area to remain open later.

- Finally, the tweens were asked to report the amount of their *own* money they spent at the lodge. Responses in dollar amounts reflect the ratio scale, the strongest form of measurement. The ratio scale has all the characteristics of the interval scale, but valid ratios can also be calculated. The resort is likely pleased with the responses to the last question since 17 of the 20 tweens spent their own money at the lodge. The answers to the last question appear to support the belief that tween spending is growing.

11. Which of the following variables are qualitative and which are quantitative? If the variable is quantitative, then specify whether the variable is discrete or continuous.
    a. Points scored in a football game.
    b. Racial composition of a high school classroom.
    c. Heights of 15-year-olds.

12. Which of the following variables are qualitative and which are quantitative? If the variable is quantitative, then specify whether the variable is discrete or continuous.
    a. Colors of cars in a mall parking lot.
    b. Time it takes each student to complete a final exam.
    c. The number of patrons who frequent a restaurant.

13. In each of the following scenarios, define the type of measurement scale.
    a. A kindergarten teacher marks whether each student is a boy or a girl.
    b. A ski resort records the daily temperature during the month of January.
    c. A restaurant surveys its customers about the quality of its waiting staff on a scale of 1 to 4, where 1 is poor and 4 is excellent.

14. In each of the following scenarios, define the type of measurement scale.
    a. An investor collects data on the weekly closing price of gold throughout a year.
    b. An analyst assigns a sample of bond issues to one of the following credit ratings, given in descending order of credit quality (increasing probability of default): AAA, AA, BBB, BB, CC, D.
    c. The dean of the business school at a local university categorizes students by major (i.e., accounting, finance, marketing, etc.) to help in determining class offerings in the future.

15. In each of the following scenarios, define the type of measurement scale.
    a. A meteorologist records the amount of monthly rainfall over the past year.
    b. A sociologist notes the birth year of 50 individuals.
    c. An investor monitors the daily stock price of BP following the 2010 oil disaster in the Gulf of Mexico.

16. A professor records the majors of her 30 students as follows:

Accounting	Economics	Undecided	Finance	Management
Management	Finance	Marketing	Economics	Management
Marketing	Finance	Marketing	Accounting	Finance
Finance	Undecided	Management	Undecided	Economics
Economics	Accounting	Management	Undecided	Economics
Accounting	Economics	Management	Accounting	Economics

    a. What is the measurement scale of these data?
    b. Summarize the results in tabular form.
    c. What information can be extracted from the data?

17. FILE The accompanying table shows a portion of the 30 companies that comprise the Dow Jones Industrial Average (DJIA); the full data set can be found on the text website and is labeled **DOW_Characteristics**. The second column shows the year that the company joined the DJIA (Year). The third column shows each company's Morningstar rating (Rating). (Five stars is the best rating that a company can receive, indicating that the company's stock price is undervalued and thus a very good buy. One star is the worst rating a company can be given, implying that the stock price is overvalued and a bad buy.) Finally, the fourth column shows each company's stock price as of June 30, 2010 (Stock Price).

Company	Year	Rating	Stock Price
3M (MMM)	1976	*****	$78.99
Alcoa (AA)	1959	****	10.03
⋮	⋮	⋮	⋮
Walt Disney (DIS)	1991	***	31.50

Source: Morningstar ratings retrieved from http://www.morningstar.com on June 30, 2010; stock prices retrieved from http://www.finance.yahoo.com.

    a. What is the measurement scale of the Year data? What are the strengths of this type of data? What are the weaknesses?
    b. What is the measurement scale of Morningstar's star-based rating system? Summarize Morningstar's star-based rating system for the companies in tabular form. Let 5 denote *****, 4 denote ****, and so on. What information can be extracted from these data?
    c. What is the measurement scale of the Stock Price data? What are its strengths?

Conceptual Review

LO **1.1** **Describe the importance of statistics.**

A proper understanding of statistical ideas and concepts helps us understand more of the real world around us, including issues in business, finance, health, and social interactions. We must understand statistics or risk making bad decisions and costly mistakes. A knowledge of statistics also provides the necessary tools to differentiate between sound statistical conclusions and questionable conclusions drawn from an insufficient number of data points, "bad" data points, incomplete data points, or just misinformation.

LO 1.2 Differentiate between descriptive statistics and inferential statistics.

The study of statistics is generally divided into two branches: descriptive statistics and inferential statistics. **Descriptive statistics** refers to the summary of a data set in the form of tables, graphs, or the calculation of numerical measures. **Inferential statistics** refers to extracting useful information from a **sample** to draw conclusions about a **population**.

A **population** consists of the complete collection of items with the characteristic we wish to understand. A **sample** is a subset of the population of interest.

LO 1.3 Explain the need for sampling and discuss various data types.

In general, we use sample data rather than population data for two main reasons: (1) obtaining information on the entire population is expensive and/or (2) it is impossible to examine every item of the population.

Cross-sectional data contain values of a characteristic of many subjects at the same point in time or without regard to differences in time. **Time series data** contain values of a characteristic of a subject over time.

LO 1.4 Describe variables and various types of measurement scales.

A variable is categorized as either qualitative or quantitative. For a **qualitative variable**, we use labels or names to identify the distinguishing characteristic of each observation. A **quantitative variable** assumes meaningful numerical values and can be further categorized as either **discrete** or **continuous**. A discrete variable assumes a countable number of values, whereas a continuous variable can take on any value within an interval.

All data measurements can be classified into one of four major categories.

- The **nominal scale** represents the least sophisticated level of measurement. The values in nominal data differ merely by name or label, and the values are then simply categorized or grouped by name.

- The values of data on an **ordinal scale** can be categorized *and* ranked; however, differences between the ranked values are meaningless.

- The **interval scale** is a stronger measurement scale as compared to nominal and ordinal scales. Values on the interval scale can be categorized and ranked, and differences between scale values are meaningful. The main drawback of the interval scale is that the value of zero is arbitrarily chosen; this implies that ratios constructed from interval-scaled values bear no significance.

- The **ratio scale** represents the strongest level of measurement. Ratio data have all the characteristics of interval data as well as a true zero point; thus, as its name implies, meaningful ratios can be calculated with values on the ratio scale.

Nominal and ordinal scales are used for qualitative variables. When summarizing the results of qualitative data, we typically count the number or calculate the percentage of persons or objects that fall into each possible category. Interval and ratio scales are used for quantitative variables. Unlike qualitative variables, arithmetic operations are valid on quantitative variables.

2

CHAPTER

Tabular and Graphical Methods

LEARNING OBJECTIVES

After reading this chapter you should be able to:

LO **2.1** Summarize qualitative data by forming frequency distributions.

LO **2.2** Construct and interpret pie charts and bar charts.

LO **2.3** Summarize quantitative data by forming frequency distributions.

LO **2.4** Construct and interpret histograms, polygons, and ogives.

LO **2.5** Construct and interpret a stem-and-leaf diagram.

LO **2.6** Construct and interpret a scatterplot.

People often have difficulty processing information provided by data in its raw form. A useful way of interpreting data effectively is to condense the data with some kind of visual or numerical summary. In this chapter we present several tabular and graphical tools that can help us organize and present data. We first deal with qualitative data by constructing frequency distributions. We can visualize these frequency distributions by constructing pie charts and bar charts. For quantitative data, we again make frequency distributions. In addition to giving us an overall picture of where the data tend to cluster, frequency distributions using quantitative data also show us how the data are spread out from the lowest value to the highest value. For visual representations of quantitative data, we examine histograms, polygons, ogives, and stem-and-leaf diagrams. Finally, we show how to construct a scatterplot, which graphically depicts the relationship between two quantitative variables. We will find that a scatterplot is a very useful tool when conducting correlation and regression analysis, topics discussed in depth later in the text.

House Prices in Southern California

Mission Viejo, a city located in Southern California, was named the safest city in California and the third-safest city in the nation (CQPress.com, November 23, 2009). Matthew Edwards, a relocation specialist for a real estate firm in Mission Viejo, often relays this piece of information to clients unfamiliar with the many benefits that the city offers. Recently, a client from Seattle, Washington, asked Matthew for a summary of recent sales. The client is particularly interested in the availability of houses in the $500,000 range. Table 2.1 shows the sale price for 36 single-family houses in Mission Viejo during June 2010; the data are also available on the text website and are labeled **MV_Houses**.

TABLE 2.1 Recent Sale Price of Houses in Mission Viejo, CA, for June 2010 (data in $1000s)

$430	670	530	521	669	445
520	417	525	350	660	412
460	533	430	399	702	735
475	525	330	560	540	537
670	538	575	440	460	630
521	370	555	425	588	430

Source: http://www.zillow.com.

Matthew wants to use the sample information to:

1. Make summary statements concerning the range of house prices.
2. Comment on where house prices tend to cluster.
3. Calculate appropriate percentages in order to compare house prices in Mission Viejo, California, to those in Seattle, Washington.

A synopsis of this case is provided at the end of Section 2.2.

2.1 Summarizing Qualitative Data

LO **2.1**

Summarize qualitative data by forming frequency distributions.

As we discussed in Chapter 1, nominal and ordinal data are types of qualitative data. Nominal data typically consist of observations that represent labels or names; information related to gender or race are examples. Nominal data are considered the least sophisticated form of data since all we can do with the data is categorize it. Ordinal data are stronger in the sense that we can categorize and order the data. Examples of ordinal data include the ratings of a product or a professor, where 1 represents the worst and 4 represents the best. In order to organize qualitative data, it is often useful to construct a frequency distribution.

FREQUENCY DISTRIBUTION FOR QUALITATIVE DATA

A **frequency distribution** for qualitative data groups data into categories and records the number of observations that fall into each category.

To illustrate the construction of a frequency distribution with nominal data, Table 2.2 shows the weather for the month of February (2010) in Seattle, Washington.

TABLE 2.2 Seattle Weather, February 2010

Sunday	Monday	Tuesday	Wednesday	Thursday	Friday	Saturday
	1 Rainy	2 Rainy	3 Rainy	4 Rainy	5 Rainy	6 Rainy
7 Rainy	8 Rainy	9 Cloudy	10 Rainy	11 Rainy	12 Rainy	13 Rainy
14 Rainy	15 Rainy	16 Rainy	17 Sunny	18 Sunny	19 Sunny	20 Sunny
21 Sunny	22 Sunny	23 Rainy	24 Rainy	25 Rainy	26 Rainy	27 Rainy
28 Sunny						

SOURCE: www.wunderground.com.

We first note that the weather in Seattle is categorized as cloudy, rainy, or sunny. The first column in Table 2.3 lists these categories. Initially, we use a "tally" column to record the number of days that fall into each category. Since the first eight days of February were rainy days, we place the first eight tally marks in the rainy category; the ninth day of February was cloudy, so we place one tally mark in the cloudy category, and so on. Finally, we convert each category's total tally count into its respective numerical value in the frequency column. Since only one tally mark appears in the cloudy category, we record the value 1 as its frequency. Note that if we sum the frequency column, we obtain the sample size. A frequency distribution in its final form does not include the tally column.

TABLE 2.3 Frequency Distribution for Seattle Weather, February 2010

Weather	Tally	Frequency
Cloudy	I	1
Rainy	⊞⊞⊞⊞	20
Sunny	⊞ II	7
		Total = 28 days

From the frequency distribution, we can now readily observe that the most common type of day in February was rainy since this type of day occurs with the highest frequency. In many applications we want to compare data sets that differ in size. For example, we might want to compare the weather in February to the weather in March. However, February has 28 days (except during a leap year) and March has 31 days. In this instance, we would convert the frequency distribution to a **relative frequency distribution**. We calculate each category's relative frequency by dividing the respective category's frequency by the total number of observations. The sum of the relative frequencies should equal one, or a value very close to one due to rounding.

Table 2.4 shows the frequency distribution in Table 2.3 converted into a relative frequency distribution. In addition, we also show the relative frequency distribution for the month of March. March had 3 cloudy days, 18 rainy days, and 10 sunny days. Each of these frequencies was then divided by 31, the number of days in the month of March.

TABLE 2.4 Relative Frequency Distribution for Seattle Weather

Weather	February 2010: Relative Frequency	March 2010: Relative Frequency
Cloudy	1/28 = 0.036	3/31 = 0.097
Rainy	20/28 = 0.714	18/31 = 0.581
Sunny	7/28 = 0.250	10/31 = 0.323
	Total = 1	Total = 1 (subject to rounding)

Source: www.wunderground.com.

We can easily convert relative frequencies into percentages by multiplying by 100. For instance, the percent of cloudy days in February and March equals 3.6% and 9.7%, respectively. From the relative frequency distribution, we can now conclude that the weather in Seattle in both February and March was predominantly rainy. However, the weather in March was a bit nicer in that approximately 32% of the days were sunny, as opposed to only 25% of the days in February.

CALCULATING RELATIVE AND PERCENT FREQUENCIES

The **relative frequency** of each category equals the proportion (fraction) of observations in each category. A category's relative frequency is calculated by dividing the frequency by the total number of observations. The sum of the relative frequencies should equal one.

The **percent frequency** is the percent (%) of observations in a category; it equals the relative frequency of the category multiplied by 100.

EXAMPLE 2.1

In Adidas's Online Annual Report 2009, net sales were reported in four regions of the world for the years 2000 and 2009, as shown in Table 2.5. Convert each region's net sales to its respective proportion for that year. Have the proportions of Adidas's net sales in each region remained the same over this 10-year period? Explain.

TABLE 2.5 Adidas's Net Sales by Region (in millions of euros, €)

Region	2000	2009
Europe	2,860	4,384
North America	1,906	2,360
Asia	875	2,614
Latin America	171	1,006
	Total = 5,812	Total = 10,364

SOLUTION: Over the 10-year period, Adidas's total net sales have almost doubled. However, it appears that the increase in net sales within each region has varied dramatically. In order to calculate the proportions of Adidas's net sales for each region, we take each region's net sales and divide by the year's total sales, as shown in Table 2.6.

TABLE 2.6 Proportion of Adidas's Net Sales by Region

Region	2000	2009
Europe	2,860/5,812 = 0.492	4,384/10,364 = 0.423
North America	1,906/5,812 = 0.328	2,360/10,364 = 0.228
Asia	875/5,812 = 0.151	2,614/10,364 = 0.252
Latin America	171/5,812 = 0.029	1,006/10,364 = 0.097
	Total = 1	Total = 1

Once we convert the data to proportions, we see significant changes in the proportion of net sales allocated to each region. In 2009, Europe still has the highest percentage of net sales at 42.3%; however, this percentage has fallen over the 10-year period. A large decline took place in the percentage of net sales in North America, from 32.8% to 22.8%, compared to significant increases in the percentages of net sales in Asia, from 15.1% to 25.2%, and in Latin America, from 2.9% to 9.7%. In short, there has been considerable movement in the percentage of Adidas's net sales allocated to each region over the 10-year period. This type of information can help Adidas when making important marketing decisions.

Visualizing Frequency Distributions for Qualitative Data

LO **2.2**

Construct and interpret pie charts and bar charts.

We can visualize the information found in frequency distributions by constructing various graphs. Graphical representations often portray the data more dramatically, as well as simplify interpretation. A **pie chart** and a **bar chart** are two widely used pictorial representations of qualitative data.

> **GRAPHICAL DISPLAY OF QUALITATIVE DATA: PIE CHARTS**
>
> A **pie chart** is a segmented circle whose segments portray the relative frequencies of the categories of some qualitative variable.

In order to construct a pie chart, first draw a circle. Then cut the circle into slices, or sectors, such that each sector is proportional to the size of the category you wish to display. For instance, Table 2.6 shows that Europe accounted for 49.2% of Adidas's net sales in 2000. Since a circle contains 360 degrees, the portion of the circle representing Europe encompasses $0.492 \times 360 = 177.1$ degrees; thus, almost half of the circle should reflect Europe's contribution to sales. Similar calculations for the other three regions in 2000 yield:

North America: $0.328 \times 360 = 118.1$ degrees

Asia: $0.151 \times 360 = 54.4$ degrees

Latin America: $0.029 \times 360 = 10.4$ degrees

The same methodology can be used to calculate each region's contribution to net sales for the year 2009. Figure 2.1 shows the resulting pie charts.

FIGURE 2.1
Pie charts for Adidas's net sales.

(a) Adidas's net sales by region, 2000   (b) Adidas's net sales by region, 2009

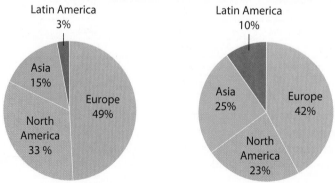

Using Excel to Construct a Pie Chart

Excel offers various options for displaying a pie chart. To replicate the pie chart in Figure 2.1a, follow these steps:

A. `FILE` Open the *Adidas_Sales* data (Table 2.5) from the text website into an Excel spreadsheet.

B. Select the categorical names and respective frequencies from the year 2000. Leave out the heading (top row); see Figure 2.2 below.

C. From the menu choose **Insert > Pie > 2-D Pie** and choose the graph on the top left.

D. In order to give the pie chart category names and their respective percentages, from the menu choose **Layout > Data Labels > More Data Label Options**. Under *Label Options*, deselect "Value" and select "Category Name" and "Percentage."

FIGURE 2.2 Constructing a pie chart with Excel

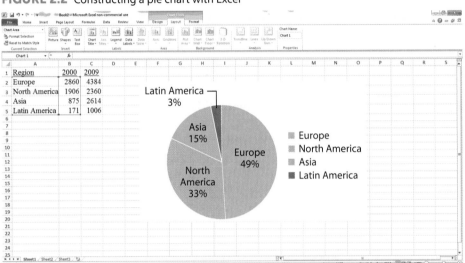

Another way to graphically depict qualitative data is to construct a **bar chart**.

> ## GRAPHICAL DISPLAY OF QUALITATIVE DATA: BAR CHARTS
>
> A **bar chart** depicts the frequency or the relative frequency for each category of the qualitative variable as a series of horizontal or vertical bars, the lengths of which are proportional to the values that are to be depicted.

We first discuss a vertical bar chart, sometimes referred to as a column chart. Here, we place each category on the horizontal axis and mark the vertical axis with an appropriate range of values for either frequency or relative frequency. The height of each bar is equal to the frequency or the relative frequency of the corresponding category. Typically, we leave space between categories to improve clarity.

Figure 2.3 shows a relative frequency bar chart for the Adidas net sales example. It is particularly useful because we can group net sales by region, emphasizing the rise in the proportion of sales in Asia and Latin America versus the fall in the proportion of sales in Europe and North America over the 10-year period.

Using Excel to Construct a Bar Chart

FIGURE 2.3 The proportion of Adidas' net sales in four regions, 2000 versus 2009

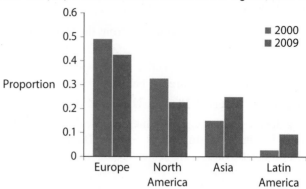

Excel provides many options for showing a bar chart. To replicate the bar chart in Figure 2.3, follow these steps:

A. **FILE** Open the ***Prop_Adidas_Sales*** data (Table 2.6) from the text website into an Excel spreadsheet.

B. Select the categorical names and respective relative frequencies for the years 2000 and 2009. Leave out the heading (top row); see Figure 2.4.

C. Choose **Insert > Column > 2-D Column**. From the options given, choose the graph on the top left. (This will create a vertical bar chart. If you want to construct a horizontal bar chart, choose **Insert > Bar > 2-D Bar**.)

D. In the legend to the right of the bar chart, Excel labels the data for the year 2000 as "Series 1" and the data for the year 2009 as "Series 2" by default. In order to edit the legend, select the legend and choose **Design > Select Data**. From the *Legend Entries*, select "Series 1," then select *Edit*, and under *Series Name*, type the new name of 2000. Follow the same steps to rename "Series 2" to 2009.

FIGURE 2.4 Constructing a bar chart with Excel

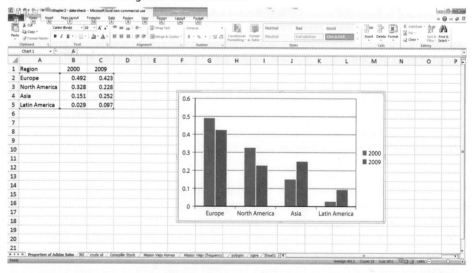

For a horizontal bar chart, we simply place each category on the vertical axis and mark the horizontal axis with an appropriate range of values for either frequency or relative frequency. For example, a recent poll asked more than 1,000 Americans: "When traveling in a non-English-speaking country, which word or phrase is it most important to know in that country's language?" (Source: *Vanity Fair*, January 2, 2012). Figure 2.5 shows the results of the poll. The phrase "Thank you" earned the largest percentage of votes (38%). Fortunately, only 1% of Americans believed that the phrase "Where is McDonald's?" was

FIGURE 2.5 Results to question: "When traveling in a non-English-speaking country, which word or phrase is it most important to know in that country's language?"

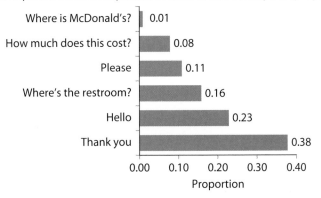

of vital importance. The proportions in Figure 2.5 do not sum to one because we exclude those that responded with uncommon words or phrases.

Cautionary Comments When Constructing or Interpreting Charts or Graphs

As with many of the statistical methods that we examine throughout this text, the possibility exists for unintentional, as well as purposeful, distortions of graphical information. As a careful researcher, you should follow these basic guidelines:

- The simplest graph should be used for a given set of data. Strive for clarity and avoid unnecessary adornments.
- Axes should be clearly marked with the numbers of their respective scales; each axis should be labeled.
- The scale on the vertical axis should begin at zero. Moreover, the vertical axis should not be given a very high value as an upper limit. In these instances, the data may appear compressed so that an increase (or decrease) of the data is not as apparent as it perhaps should be. Conversely, the axis should not be stretched so that an increase (or decrease) of the data appears more pronounced than warranted. For example, Figure 2.6(a) plots the daily price for a barrel of crude oil for the first quarter of 2011 (the data labeled **Crude_Oil** are available on the text website). Due to Middle East unrest, the price of crude oil rose from a low of $83.13 per barrel to a high of $106.19 per barrel, or approximately 28% $\left(= \frac{106.19 - 83.13}{83.13} \right)$. However, since Figure 2.6(a) uses a high value as an upper limit on the vertical axis ($325), the rise in price appears dampened. Figure 2.6(b) charts the daily closing stock price for Johnson & Johnson (JNJ) for the week of April 4, 2011 (the data labeled **JNJ** are available on the text website). It is true that the stock price declined over the week

FILE

FILE

FIGURE 2.6 Misleading scales on vertical axes

(a) Vertical axis with high upper limit

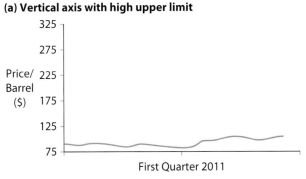

Source: U.S. Energy Information Administration.

(b) Stretched vertical axis

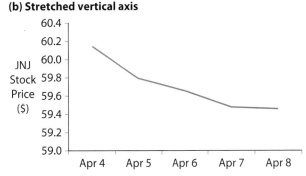

Source: http://www.finance.yahoo.com.

from a high of $60.15 to a low of $59.46; this amounts to a $0.69 decrease or an approximate 1% decline. However, since the vertical axis is stretched, the drop in stock price appears more dramatic.

- When creating a bar chart, each bar should be of the same width. Differing bar widths create distortions. The same principle holds in the next section when we discuss histograms.

EXERCISES 2.1

1. A local restaurant is committed to providing its patrons with the best dining experience possible. On a recent survey, the restaurant asked patrons to rate the quality of their entrées. The responses ranged from 1 to 5, where 1 indicated a disappointing entrée and 5 indicated an exceptional entrée. The results of the survey are as follows:

3	5	4	4	3	2	3	3	2	5	5	5
5	3	3	2	1	4	5	5	4	2	5	5
5	4	4	3	1	5	2	1	5	4	4	4

a. Construct frequency and relative frequency distributions that summarize the survey's results.

b. Are patrons generally satisfied with the quality of their entrées? Explain.

2. First-time patients at North Shore Family Practice are required to fill out a questionnaire that gives the doctor an overall idea of each patient's health. The first question is: "In general, what is the quality of your health?" The patient chooses Excellent, Good, Fair, or Poor. Over the past month, the responses to this question from first-time patients were:

Fair	Good	Fair	Excellent
Good	Good	Good	Poor
Excellent	Excellent	Poor	Good
Fair	Good	Good	Good
Good	Poor	Fair	Excellent
Excellent	Good	Good	Good

a. Construct frequency and relative frequency distributions that summarize the responses to the questionnaire.

b. What is the most common response to the questionnaire? How would you characterize the health of first-time patients at this medical practice?

3. A survey asked chief executives at leading U.S. firms the following question: "Where do you expect the U.S. economy to be 12 months from now?" A representative sample of their responses appears below:

Same	Same	Same	Better	Worse
Same	Same	Better	Same	Worse
Same	Better	Same	Better	Same
Worse	Same	Same	Same	Worse
Same	Same	Same	Better	Same

a. Construct frequency and relative frequency distributions that summarize the responses to the survey. Where did most chief executives expect the U.S. economy to be in 12 months?

b. Use Excel to construct a pie chart and a bar chart to summarize your results.

4. AccuWeather.com reported the following weather delays at these major U.S. airline hubs for July 21, 2010:

City	Delay	City	Delay
Atlanta	PM Delays	Mpls./St. Paul	None
Chicago	None	New York	All Day Delays
Dallas/Ft. Worth	None	Orlando	None
Denver	All Day Delays	Philadelphia	All Day Delays
Detroit	AM Delays	Phoenix	None
Houston	All Day Delays	Salt Lake City	None
Las Vegas	All Day Delays	San Francisco	AM Delays
Los Angeles	AM Delays	Seattle	None
Miami	AM Delays	Washington	All Day Delays

a. Construct frequency and relative frequency distributions that summarize the delays at major U.S. hubs. What was the most common type of delay? Explain.

b. Use Excel to construct a pie chart and a bar chart to summarize your results.

5. Fifty pro-football rookies were rated on a scale of 1 to 5, based on performance at a training camp as well as on past performance. A ranking of 1 indicated a poor prospect whereas a ranking of 5 indicated an excellent prospect. The following frequency distribution was constructed.

Rating	Frequency
1	4
2	10
3	14
4	18
5	4

a. How many of the rookies received a rating of 4 or better? How many of the rookies received a rating of 2 or worse?

b. Construct the corresponding relative frequency distribution. What percent received a rating of 5?

c. Construct a bar chart for these data.

6. A recent survey asked 5,324 individuals: "What's most important to you when choosing where to live?" The

responses are shown in the following relative frequency distribution.

Response	Relative Frequency
Good jobs	0.37
Affordable homes	0.15
Top schools	0.11
Low crime	0.23
Things to do	0.14

Copyright © 2010 Turner, Inc. Used with permission.

a. Construct the corresponding frequency distribution. How many of the respondents chose "low crime" as the most important criterion when choosing where to live?

b. Construct a bar chart for the frequency distribution found in part a.

7. What is the perfect summer trip? A National Geographic Kids survey (*AAA Horizons*, April 2007) asked this question to 316 children ages 8 to 14. Their responses are given in the following frequency distribution.

Top Vacation Choice	Frequency
Cruises	140
Beaches	68
Amusement Parks	68
Big Cities	20
Lakes	12
Summer Camp	8

a. Construct a relative frequency distribution. What percentage of the responses cited "Cruises" as the perfect summer trip?

b. Construct a bar chart for these data.

8. The following table lists U.S. revenue (in $ billions) of the major car-rental companies.

Car-Rental Company	Revenue in 2009
Enterprise	$10.7
Hertz	4.7
Avis Budget	4.0
Dollar Thrifty	1.5
Other	1.0

Source: *The Wall Street Journal*, July 30, 2010.

a. Construct a relative frequency distribution.

b. Hertz accounted for what percentage of sales?

c. Use Excel to construct a pie chart for these data.

9. A survey conducted by CBS News asked 829 respondents which of the following events will happen first. The responses are summarized in the following table:

Cure for cancer found	40%
End of dependence on oil	27%
Signs of life in outer space	12%
Peace in Middle East	8%
Other	6%
None will happen	7%

Source: *Vanity Fair*, December 2009.

a. Use Excel to construct a pie chart and a bar chart for these data.

b. How many people think that a cure for cancer will be found first?

10. A 2010 poll conducted by NBC asked respondents who would win Super Bowl XLV in 2011. The responses by 20,825 people are summarized in the following table.

Team	Number of Votes
Atlanta Falcons	4,040
New Orleans Saints	1,880
Houston Texans	1,791
Dallas Cowboys	1,631
Minnesota Vikings	1,438
Indianapolis Colts	1,149
Pittsburgh Steelers	1,141
New England Patriots	1,095
Green Bay Packers	1,076
Others	

a. How many responses were for "Others"?

b. The Green Bay Packers won Super Bowl XLV, defeating the Pittsburgh Steelers by the score of 31–25. What proportion of respondents felt that the Green Bay Packers would win?

c. Construct a bar chart for these data using relative frequencies.

11. In a recent USA TODAY/Gallup Poll, respondents favored Barack Obama over Mitt Romney in terms of likeability, 60% to 30% (*Los Angeles Times*, July 28, 2012). The following bar chart summarizes the responses.

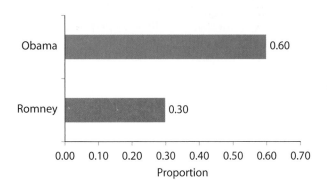

a. What percentage of respondents favored neither Obama nor Romney in terms of likeability?

b. Suppose this survey was based on 500 respondents. How many respondents favored Obama over Romney?

12. A recent survey of 992 people asked: In which professional sport—football, boxing, hockey, or martial arts—is an athlete most likely to sustain an injury that will affect the athlete after he or she retires? (*Vanity Fair*, January 29, 2012.) The following pie chart summarizes the responses.

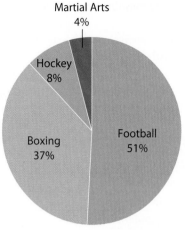

Martial Arts 4%

Hockey 8%

Boxing 37%

Football 51%

Copyright © 2012 Conde Nast. Used with permission.

a. According to this survey, in which sport was an athlete most likely to sustain an injury with lifelong consequences? In which sport was an athlete least likely to sustain an injury with lifelong consequences?

b. How many respondents believed that professional hockey players were most likely to sustain an injury with lifelong consequences?

13. The accompanying figure plots the monthly stock price of Caterpillar, Inc., from July 2009 through March 2011. The stock has experienced tremendous growth over this time period, almost tripling in price. Does the figure reflect this growth? If not, why not?

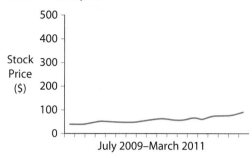

14. Annual sales at a small pharmaceutical firm have been rather stagnant over the most recent five-year period, exhibiting only 1.2% growth over this time frame. A research analyst prepares the accompanying graph for inclusion in a sales report.

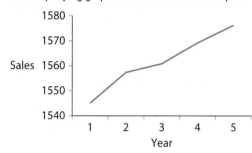

Does this graph accurately reflect what has happened to sales over the last five years? If not, why not?

2.2 Summarizing Quantitative Data

LO 2.3

Summarize quantitative data by forming frequency distributions.

With quantitative data, each observation represents a meaningful amount or count. The number of patents held by pharmaceutical firms (count) and household incomes (amount) are examples of quantitative data. Although different in nature from qualitative data, we still use frequency distributions to summarize quantitative data.

Before discussing the mechanics of constructing a frequency distribution, we find it useful to first examine one in its final form, using the house-price data from Table 2.1. We converted the raw data (the actual values) from Table 2.1 into a frequency distribution with five intervals or **classes**, each of width 100, as shown in Table 2.7. We see, for instance, that four houses sold in the first class, where prices ranged from $300,000 up to $400,000. The data are more manageable using a frequency distribution, but some detail is lost because we no longer see the actual values.

TABLE 2.7 Frequency Distribution for House-Price Data

Class (in $1000s)	Frequency
300 up to 400	4
400 up to 500	11
500 up to 600	14
600 up to 700	5
700 up to 800	2
	Total = 36

EXAMPLE 2.2

Based on the frequency distribution in Table 2.7, what is the price range over this time period? Over what price range did the majority of the houses sell?

SOLUTION: The frequency distribution shows that house prices ranged from $300,000 up to $800,000 over this time period. The most houses (14) sold in the $500,000 up to $600,000 range. Note that only four houses sold in the lowest price range and only two houses sold at the highest price range.

It turns out that reading and understanding a frequency distribution is actually easier than forming one. When we constructed a frequency distribution with qualitative data, the raw data could be categorized in a well-defined way. With quantitative data, we must make certain decisions about the number of classes, as well as the width of each class. We do not apply concrete rules when we define the classes in Table 2.7; however, we are able to follow several guidelines.

Guidelines for Constructing a Frequency Distribution

- *Classes are mutually exclusive.* In other words, classes do not overlap. Each observation falls into one, and only one, class. For instance, suppose a value of 400 appeared in Table 2.1. Given the class divisions in Table 2.7, we would have included this observation in the second class interval. Mathematically, the second class interval is expressed as $400 \le \text{Price} < 500$. Alternatively, we can define the second interval as $400 < \text{Price} \le 500$, in which case the value 400 is included in the previous class interval. In short, no matter the specification of the classes, the observation is included in only one of the classes.

- *Classes are exhaustive.* The total number of classes covers the entire sample (or population). In Table 2.7, if we had left off the last class, 700 up to 800, then we would be omitting two observations from the sample.

- *The total number of classes in a frequency distribution usually ranges from 5 to 20.* Smaller data sets tend to have fewer classes than larger data sets. Recall that the goal of constructing a frequency distribution is to summarize the data in a form that accurately depicts the group as a whole. If we have too many classes, then this advantage of the frequency distribution is lost. For instance, suppose we create a frequency distribution for the house-price data with 17 classes, each of width 25, as shown in Table 2.8.

    Technically, this is a valid frequency distribution, but the summarization advantage of the frequency distribution is lost because there are too many class intervals. Similarly, if the frequency distribution has too few classes, then considerable accuracy and detail are lost. Consider a frequency distribution of the house-price data with three classes, each of width 150, as shown in Table 2.9.

TABLE 2.8 Too Many Classes in a Distribution

Class (in $1000s)	Frequency
325 up to 350	2
350 up to 375	1
375 up to 400	1
400 up to 425	3
425 up to 450	5
450 up to 475	3
475 up to 500	0
500 up to 525	5
525 up to 550	5
550 up to 575	3
575 up to 600	1
600 up to 625	0
625 up to 650	1
650 up to 675	4
675 up to 700	0
700 up to 725	1
725 up to 750	1
	Total = 36

TABLE 2.9 Too Few Classes in a Distribution

Class (in $1000s)	Frequency
300 up to 450	12
450 up to 600	17
600 up to 750	7
	Total = 36

Again, this is a valid frequency distribution. However, we cannot tell whether the 17 houses that sold for $450,000 up to $600,000 fall closer to the price of $450,000, fall closer to the price of $600,000, or are evenly spread within the interval. With only three classes in the frequency distribution, too much detail is lost.

- Once we choose the number of classes for a raw data set, we can then *approximate the width of each class* by using the formula

$$\frac{\text{Largest value} - \text{Smallest value}}{\text{Number of classes}}.$$

Generally, the width of each class is the same for each class interval. If the class width varied, comparisons between the numbers of observations in different intervals would be misleading. Moreover, it is preferable to define class limits that are easy to recognize and interpret.

Suppose we conclude, as we do in Table 2.7, that we should have five classes in the frequency distribution for the house-price data. Applying the class-width formula with the largest value of 735 and the smallest value of 330 (from Table 2.1) yields $\frac{735 - 330}{5} = 81$. Table 2.10 shows the frequency distribution with five classes and a class width of 81.

TABLE 2.10 Cumbersome Class Width in a Distribution

Class (in $1000s)	Frequency
330 up to 411	4
411 up to 492	11
492 up to 573	12
573 up to 654	3
654 up to 735	6
	Total = 36

Again, this is a valid frequency distribution, but it proves unwieldy. Recall that one major goal in forming a frequency distribution is to provide more clarity in interpreting the data. Grouping the data in this manner actually makes analyzing the data more difficult. In order to facilitate interpretation of the frequency distribution, it is best to define class limits with ease of recognition in mind. To this end, and as initially shown in Table 2.7, we set the lower limit of the first class at 300 (rather than 330) and obtain the remaining class limits by successively adding 100 (rather than 81).

Once we have clearly defined the classes for a particular data set, the next step is to count and record the number of data points that fall into each class. As we did with the construction of a qualitative frequency distribution, we usually include a tally column to aid in counting (see Table 2.11), but then we remove this column in the final presentation of the frequency distribution. For instance, in Table 2.1, the first data point, 430, falls in the second class, so we place a tally mark in the second class; the next value of 520 falls in the third class, so we place a tally mark in the third class, and so on. The frequency column shows the numerical value of the respective tally count. Since four tally marks appear in the first class, we record the value 4 as its frequency—the number of observations that fall into the first class. One way to ensure that we have included all the data points in the frequency distribution is to sum the frequency column. This sum should always equal the population or sample size.

TABLE 2.11 Constructing Frequency Distributions for the House-Price Data

Class (in $1000s)	Tally	Frequency	Cumulative Frequency
300 up to 400	IIII	4	4
400 up to 500	HHH HHH I	11	4 + 11 = 15
500 up to 600	HHH HHH IIII	14	4 + 11 + 14 = 29
600 up to 700	HHH	5	4 + 11 + 14 + 5 = 34
700 up to 800	II	2	4 + 11 + 14 + 5 + 1 = 36
		Total = 36	

A frequency distribution indicates how many observations (in this case house prices) fall within some range. However, we might want to know how many observations fall below the upper limit of a particular class. In these cases, our needs are better served with a cumulative frequency distribution.

The last column of Table 2.11 shows values for cumulative frequency. The cumulative frequency of the first class is the same as the frequency of the first class, that is, the value 4. However, the interpretation is different. With respect to the frequency column, the value 4 tells us that four of the houses sold in the $300,000 up to $400,000 range. For the cumulative frequency column, the value 4 tells us that four of the houses sold for less than $400,000. To obtain the cumulative frequency for the second class, we add its frequency, 11, with the preceding frequency, 4, and obtain 15. This tells us that 15 of the houses sold for less than $500,000. We solve for the cumulative frequencies of the remaining classes in a like manner. Note that the cumulative frequency of the last class is equal to the sample size of 36. This indicates that all 36 houses sold for less than $800,000.

FREQUENCY AND CUMULATIVE FREQUENCY DISTRIBUTIONS FOR QUANTITATIVE DATA

For quantitative data, a **frequency distribution** groups data into intervals called **classes** and records the number of observations that falls into each class.

A **cumulative frequency distribution** records the number of observations that falls below the upper limit of each class.

EXAMPLE 2.3

Using Table 2.11, how many of the houses sold in the $500,000 up to $600,000 range? How many of the houses sold for less than $600,000?

SOLUTION: From the frequency distribution, we find that 14 houses sold in the $500,000 up to $600,000 range. In order to find the number of houses that sold for less than $600,000, we use the cumulative frequency distribution. We readily observe that 29 of the houses sold for less than $600,000.

Suppose we want to compare house prices in Mission Viejo, California, to house prices in another region of the United States. Just as for qualitative data, when making comparisons between two quantitative data sets—especially if the data sets differ in size—a relative frequency distribution tends to provide more meaningful information as compared to a frequency distribution.

The second column of Table 2.12 shows the construction of a relative frequency distribution from the frequency distribution in Table 2.11. We take each class's frequency and divide by the total number of observations. For instance, we observed four houses that sold in the lowest range of $300,000 up to $400,000. We take the class frequency of 4 and divide by the sample size, 36, and obtain 0.11. Equivalently, we can say 11% of the houses sold in this price range. We make similar calculations for each class and note that when we sum the column of relative frequencies, we should get a value of one (or, due to rounding, a number very close to one).

TABLE 2.12 Constructing Relative Frequency Distributions for House-Price Data

Class (in $1000s)	Relative Frequency	Cumulative Relative Frequency
300 up to 400	4/36 = 0.11	0.11
400 up to 500	11/36 = 0.31	0.11 + 0.31 = 0.42
500 up to 600	14/36 = 0.39	0.11 + 0.31 + 0.39 = 0.81
600 up to 700	5/36 = 0.14	0.11 + 0.31 + 0.39 + 0.14 = 0.95
700 up to 800	2/36 = 0.06	0.11 + 0.31 + 0.39 + 0.17 + 0.06 ≈ 1
	Total = 1 (subject to rounding)	

The last column of Table 2.12 shows the cumulative relative frequency. The cumulative relative frequency for a particular class indicates the proportion (fraction) of the observations that falls below the upper limit of that particular class. We can calculate the cumulative relative frequency of each class in one of two ways: (1) we can sum successive relative frequencies or (2) we can divide each class's cumulative frequency by the sample size. In Table 2.12 we show the first way. The value for the first class is the same as the value for its relative frequency, that is, 0.11. For the second class we add 0.31 to 0.11 and obtain 0.42; this value indicates that 42% of the house prices were less than $500,000. We continue calculating cumulative relative frequencies in this manner until we reach the last class. Here, we get the value one, which means that 100% of the houses sold for less than $800,000.

RELATIVE AND CUMULATIVE RELATIVE FREQUENCY DISTRIBUTIONS

For quantitative data, a **relative frequency distribution** identifies the proportion (or the fraction) of observations that falls into each class, that is,

$$\text{Class relative frequency} = \frac{\text{Class frequency}}{\text{Total number of observations}}.$$

A **cumulative relative frequency distribution** records the proportion (or the fraction) of observations that fall below the upper limit of each class.

EXAMPLE 2.4

Using Table 2.12, what percent of the houses sold for at least $500,000 but not more than $600,000? What percent of the houses sold for less than $600,000? What percent of the houses sold for $600,000 or more?

SOLUTION: The relative frequency distribution indicates that 39% of the houses sold for at least $500,000 but not more than $600,000. Further, the cumulative relative frequency distribution indicates that 81% of the houses sold for less than $600,000. This result implies that 19% sold for $600,000 or more.

Visualizing Frequency Distributions for Quantitative Data

Histograms and **polygons** are graphical depictions of frequency and relative frequency distributions. The advantage of a visual display is that we can quickly see where most of the observations tend to cluster, as well as the spread and shape of the data. For instance, histograms and polygons may reveal whether or not the distribution is symmetrically shaped.

LO **2.4**

Construct and interpret histograms, polygons, and ogives.

GRAPHICAL DISPLAY OF QUANTITATIVE DATA: HISTOGRAMS

A **histogram** is a series of rectangles where the width and height of each rectangle represent the class width and frequency (or relative frequency) of the respective class.

For quantitative data, a histogram is essentially the counterpart to the vertical bar chart we use for qualitative data. When constructing a histogram, we mark off the class limits along the horizontal axis. The height of each bar represents either the frequency or the relative frequency for each class. No gaps appear between the interval limits. Figure 2.7 shows a histogram for the frequency distribution of house prices shown in Table 2.7. A casual inspection of the histogram reveals that the selling price of houses in this sample ranged from $300,000 to $800,000; however, most house prices fell in the $500,000 to $600,000 range.

FIGURE 2.7 Frequency histogram for house prices

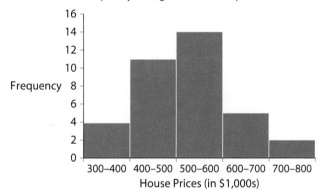

The only difference between a frequency histogram and a relative frequency histogram is the unit of measurement on the vertical axis. For the frequency histogram, we use the frequency of each class to represent the height; for the relative frequency histogram we use the proportion (or the fraction) of each class to represent the height. In a relative frequency histogram, the area of any rectangle is proportional to the relative frequency of observations falling into that class. Figure 2.8 shows the relative frequency histogram for house prices.

FIGURE 2.8 Relative frequency histogram for house prices

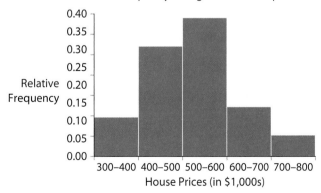

In general, the shape of most data distributions can be categorized as either symmetric or skewed. A symmetric distribution is one that is a mirror image of itself on both sides of its center. That is, the location of values below the center correspond to those above the center. As we will see in later chapters, the smoothed histogram for many data sets approximates a bell-shaped curve, which is indicative of the well-known normal distribution. If the distribution is not symmetric, then it is either positively skewed or negatively skewed.

FIGURE 2.9 Histograms with differing shapes

(a) Symmetric distribution   **(b) Positively skewed distribution**   **(c) Negatively skewed distribution**

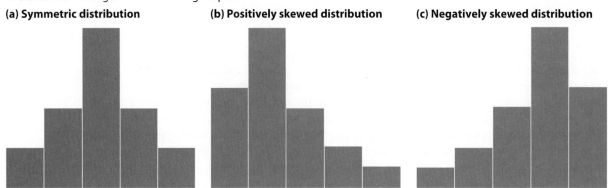

The histogram in Figure 2.9(a) shows a symmetric distribution. If the edges were smoothed, this histogram would approximate the bell-shaped normal distribution. In Figure 2.9(b), the histogram shows a positively skewed, or skewed to the right, distribution with a long tail extending to the right. This attribute reflects the presence of a small number of relatively large values. Finally, the histogram in Figure 2.9(c) indicates a negatively skewed, or skewed to the left, distribution since it has a long tail extending off to the left. Data that follow a negatively skewed distribution have a small number of relatively small values.

Though not nearly as skewed as the data exhibited in Figure 2.9(b), the house-price data in Figure 2.8 exhibit slight positive skew. This is the result of a few, relatively expensive homes in the city. It is common for distributions of house prices and incomes to exhibit positive skewness.

Using Excel to Construct a Histogram

In general, Excel offers two different ways to construct a histogram, depending on whether we have access to the raw data or the frequency distribution. In either case, we need to have the classes clearly defined. We will first construct a histogram for house prices using the raw data from Table 2.1, and then show a histogram for the house prices from the frequency distribution from Table 2.7.

Constructing a Histogram from a Set of Raw Data

A. FILE Open the ***MV_Houses*** data (Table 2.1) from the text website into an Excel spreadsheet.

B. In a column next to the data, enter the values of the upper limits of each class, or in this example, 400, 500, 600, 700, and 800; label this column "Class Limits." The reason for these entries is explained in the next step. The house-price data and the class limits (as well as the resulting frequency distribution and histogram) are shown in Figure 2.10.

FIGURE 2.10 Constructing a histogram from raw data with Excel

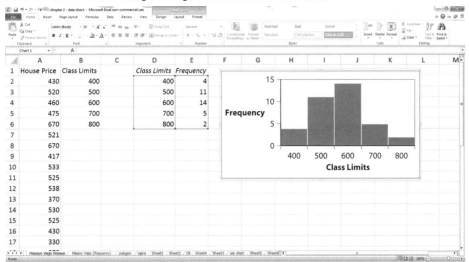

C. From the menu choose **Data** > **Data Analysis** > **Histogram** > **OK**. (*Note:* If you do not see the **Data Analysis** option under **Data**, you must *add in* this option. From the menu choose **File** > **Options** > **Add-Ins** and choose **Go** at the bottom of the dialog box. Select the box to the left of **Analysis Toolpak**, and then click **OK**. If you have installed this option properly, you should now see **Data Analysis** under **Data**.)

D. In the *Histogram* dialog box (see Figure 2.11), under *Input Range*, select the data. Excel uses the term "bins" for the class limits. If we leave the *Bin Range* box empty, Excel creates evenly distributed intervals using the minimum and maximum values of the input range as end points. This methodology is rarely satisfactory. In order to construct a histogram that is more informative, we use the upper limit of each class as the bin values. Under *Bin Range*, we select the *Class Limits* data. (Check the *Labels* box if you have included the names House Price and Class Limits as part of the selection.) Under *Output Options* we choose **Chart Output**, then click **OK**.

FIGURE 2.11 Excel's dialog box for a histogram

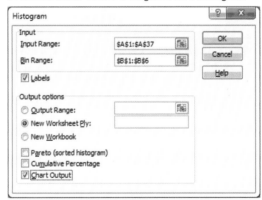

E. Since Excel leaves spaces between the rectangles, we right-click on any of the rectangles, choose **Format Data Series** and change the *Gap Width* to 0, then choose **Close**. In the event that the given class limits do not include all the data points, Excel automatically adds another interval labeled "More" to the resulting frequency distribution and histogram. Since we observe zero observations in this interval for this example, we delete this interval for expositional purposes. Excel also defines its classes by excluding the value of the lower limit and including the value of the upper class limit for each interval. For example, if the value 400 appeared in the house-price data, Excel would have accounted for this observation in the first class. If any upper-limit value appeared in the house-price data, we would have adjusted the class limits in the *Bin Range* to 399, 499, etc., so that Excel's frequency distribution and histogram would be consistent with those that we constructed in Table 2.11 and Figure 2.7. Further formatting regarding colors, axes, grids, etc. can be done by selecting **Layout** from the menu.

Constructing a Histogram from a Frequency Distribution

Suppose we do not have the raw data for house prices, but we have the frequency distribution reported in Table 2.7.

A. **FILE** Open the **MV_Frequency** data (Table 2.7) from the text website into an Excel spreadsheet.

B. Select the classes and respective frequencies. See Figure 2.12 below.

C. From the menu choose **Insert > Column > 2-D Column** and choose the graph on the top left.

D. In order to remove the spaces between the rectangles, right-click on any of the rectangles, choose **Format Data Series** and change the *Gap Width* to 0, then choose **Close**.

E. Further formatting regarding colors, axes, grids, etc. can be done by selecting **Layout** from the menu.

FIGURE 2.12 Constructing a histogram from a frequency distribution with Excel

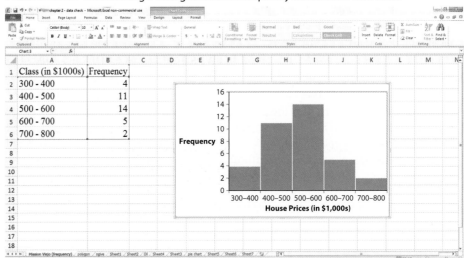

A **polygon** provides another convenient way of depicting a frequency distribution. It too gives a general idea of the shape of a distribution. Like the histogram, we place either the frequency or the relative frequency of the distribution on the *y*-axis, and the upper and lower limits of each class on the *x*-axis. We plot the midpoint of each class with its corresponding frequency or relative frequency. We then connect neighboring points with a straight line.

> **GRAPHICAL DISPLAY OF QUANTITATIVE DATA: POLYGONS**
>
> A **polygon** connects a series of neighboring points where each point represents the midpoint of a particular class and its associated frequency or relative frequency.

If we choose to construct a polygon for the house-price data, we first calculate the midpoint of each interval; thus, the midpoint for the first interval is $\frac{300 + 400}{2} = 350$ and similarly, the midpoints for the remaining intervals are 450, 550, 650, and 750. We treat each midpoint as the *x*-coordinate and the respective frequency (or relative frequency) as the *y*-coordinate. After plotting the points, we connect neighboring points. In order to close off the graph at each end, we add one interval below the lowest interval (so, 200 up to 300 with midpoint 250) and one interval above the highest interval (so, 800 up to 900 with midpoint 850) and assign each of these classes zero frequencies. Table 2.13 shows the relevant coordinates for plotting a polygon using the house-price data. We chose to use relative frequency to represent the *y*-coordinate.

TABLE 2.13 Coordinates for Plotting Relative Frequency Polygon

Classes	x-coordinate (midpoint)	y-coordinate (relative frequency)
(Lower end)	250	0
300–400	350	0.11
400–500	450	0.31
500–600	550	0.39
600–700	650	0.14
700–800	750	0.06
(Upper end)	850	0

Figure 2.13 plots a relative frequency polygon for the house-price data. Here the distribution appears to approximate the bell-shaped distribution discussed earlier. Only a careful inspection of the right tail suggests that the data are slightly positively skewed.

FIGURE 2.13 Polygon for the house-price data

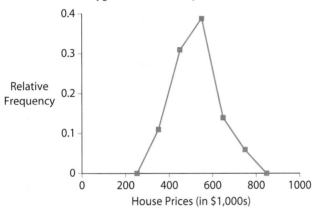

Using Excel to Construct a Polygon

A. To construct a polygon, input the appropriate x- and y-coordinates into an Excel spreadsheet. We use the data from Table 2.13.

B. Select the x- and the y-coordinates (as shown in Figure 2.14) and choose **Insert > Scatter**. Select the box at the middle right.

C. Further formatting regarding colors, axes, grids, etc. can be done by selecting **Layout** from the menu.

FIGURE 2.14 Constructing a polygon with Excel

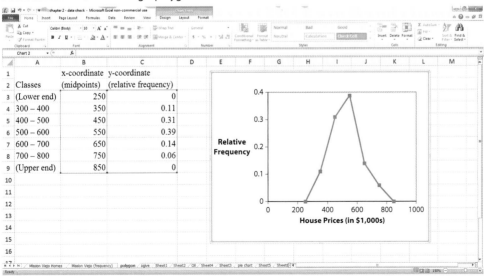

In many instances, we might want to convey information by plotting an ogive (pronounced "ojive").

GRAPHICAL DISPLAY OF QUANTITATIVE DATA: OGIVES

An **ogive** is a graph that plots the cumulative frequency or the cumulative relative frequency of each class against the upper limit of the corresponding class.

An ogive differs from a polygon in that we use the upper limit of each class as the x-coordinate and the cumulative frequency or cumulative relative frequency of the corresponding class as the y-coordinate. After plotting the points, we connect neighboring points. Lastly, we close the ogive only at the lower end by intersecting the x-axis at the lower limit of the first class. Table 2.14 shows the relevant coordinates for plotting an ogive using the house-price data. We choose to use cumulative relative frequency as the y-coordinate. The use of cumulative frequency would not change the shape of the ogive, just the unit of measurement on the y-axis.

TABLE 2.14 Coordinates for the ogive for the house-price data

Classes	x-coordinate (upper limit)	y-coordinate (cumulative relative frequency)
(Lower end)	300	0
300–400	400	0.11
400–500	500	0.42
500–600	600	0.81
600–700	700	0.95
700–800	800	1

Figure 2.15 plots the ogive for the house-price data. In general, we can use an ogive to approximate the proportion of values that are less than a specified value on the horizontal axis. Consider an application to the house-price data in Example 2.5.

FIGURE 2.15 Ogive for the house-price data

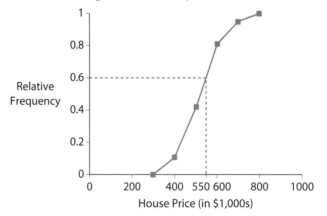

EXAMPLE 2.5

Using Figure 2.15, approximate the percentage of houses that sold for less than $550,000.

SOLUTION: Draw a vertical line that starts at 550 and intersects the ogive. Then follow the line to the vertical axis and read the value. You can conclude that approximately 60% of the houses sold for less than $550,000.

Using Excel to Construct an Ogive

A. To construct an ogive, input the appropriate x- and y-coordinates into an Excel spreadsheet. We use the data from Table 2.14.

B. Select the x- and the y-coordinates (as shown in Figure 2.16) and choose **Insert > Scatter**. Select the box at the middle right.

C. Further formatting regarding colors, axes, grids, etc. can be done by selecting **Layout** from the menu.

FIGURE 2.16 Constructing an ogive with Excel

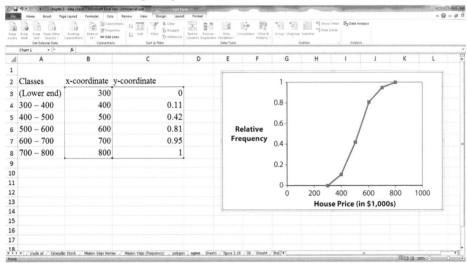

SYNOPSIS OF INTRODUCTORY CASE

During June 2010, Matthew Edwards reviewed the selling prices of 36 home sales in Mission Viejo, California, for a client from Seattle, Washington. After constructing various frequency distributions, he is able to make the following summary conclusions. House prices ranged from $300,000 up to $800,000 over this time period. Most of the houses (14) sold in the $500,000 up to $600,000 range, which is, more or less, the client's price range. Twenty-nine of the houses sold for less than $600,000. Converting the data into percentages so the client can make comparisons with home sales in the Seattle area, Matthew found that 39% of the houses sold for $500,000 up to $600,000. Further, 81% of the houses sold for less than $600,000, which implies that 19% sold for $600,000 or more.

EXERCISES 2.2

Mechanics

15. Consider the following data set:

4	10	8	7	6	10	11	14	13	14
3	9	8	5	7	6	10	3	11	11
8	8	4	5	5	12	12	3	8	8

   a. Construct a frequency distribution using classes of 3 up to 5, 5 up to 7, etc.
   b. Construct relative frequency, cumulative frequency, and cumulative relative frequency distributions.
   c. How many of the observations are at least 7 but less than 9? How many of the observations are less than 9?
   d. What percent of the observations are at least 7 but less than 9? What percent of the observations are less than 9?
   e. Graph a relative frequency histogram.
   f. Graph an ogive.

16. Consider the following data set:

4	10	8	7	6	10	11	14	13	14
3	9	8	5	7	6	10	3	11	11
8	8	4	5	5	12	12	3	8	8
10	−9	28	14	−5	9	11	5	8	−3
33	−4	2	3	22	25	5	29	26	0
−8	−5	0	15	−4	35	21	15	19	23
4	6	−2	12	24	36	15	3	−5	2

   a. Construct a frequency distribution using classes of −10 up to 0, 0 up to 10, etc. How many of the observations are at least 10 but less than 20?
   b. Construct a relative frequency distribution and a cumulative relative frequency distribution. What percent of the observations are at least 10 but less than 20? What percent of the observations are less than 20?
   c. Graph a relative frequency polygon. Is the distribution symmetric? If not, then how is it skewed?

17. Consider the following frequency distribution:

Class	Frequency
10 up to 20	12
20 up to 30	15
30 up to 40	25
40 up to 50	4

   a. Construct a relative frequency distribution. Graph a relative frequency histogram.
   b. Construct a cumulative frequency distribution and a cumulative relative frequency distribution.
   c. What percent of the observations are at least 30 but less than 40? What percent of the observations are less than 40?

18. Consider the following frequency distribution:

Class	Frequency
1000 up to 1100	2
1100 up to 1200	7
1200 up to 1300	3
1300 up to 1400	4

   a. Construct a relative frequency distribution. What percent of the observations are at least 1100 but less than 1200?
   b. Construct a cumulative frequency distribution and a cumulative relative frequency distribution. How many of the observations are less than 1300?
   c. Graph a frequency histogram.

19. Consider the following cumulative frequency distribution:

Class	Cumulative Frequency
15 up to 25	30
25 up to 35	50
35 up to 45	120
45 up to 55	130

   a. Construct a frequency distribution. How many observations are at least 35 but less than 45?
   b. Graph a frequency histogram.
   c. What percent of the observations are less than 45?

20. Consider the following relative frequency distribution:

Class	Relative Frequency
−20 up to −10	0.04
−10 up to 0	0.28
0 up to 10	0.26
10 up to 20	0.22
20 up to 30	0.20

   a. Suppose this relative frequency distribution is based on a sample of 50 observations. Construct a frequency distribution. How many of the observations are at least −10 but less than 0?
   b. Construct a cumulative frequency distribution. How many of the observations are less than 20?
   c. Graph a relative frequency polygon.

21. Consider the following cumulative relative frequency distribution.

Class	Cumulative Relative Frequency
150 up to 200	0.10
200 up to 250	0.35
250 up to 300	0.70
300 up to 350	1

   a. Construct a relative frequency distribution. What percent of the observations are at least 250 but less than 300?
   b. Graph an ogive.

Applications

22. *Kiplinger's* (August 2007) lists the assets (in billions of $) for the 20 largest stock mutual funds (ranked by size) as follows:

$99.8	49.7	86.3	109.2	56.9
88.2	44.1	58.8	176.7	49.9
61.4	128.8	53.6	95.2	92.5
55.0	96.5	45.3	73.0	70.9

a. Construct a frequency distribution using classes of 40 up to 70, 70 up to 100, etc.

b. Construct the relative frequency distribution, the cumulative frequency distribution, and the cumulative relative frequency distribution.

c. How many of the funds had assets of at least $100 but less than $130 (in billions)? How many of the funds had assets less than $160 (in billions)?

d. What percent of the funds had assets of at least $70 but less than $100 (in billions)? What percent of the funds had assets less than $130 (in billions)?

e. Construct a histogram. Comment on the shape of the distribution.

23. The number of text messages sent by 25 13-year-olds over the past month was as follows:

630	516	892	643	627	510	937	909	654
817	760	715	605	975	888	912	952	701
744	793	852	504	562	670	685		

a. Construct a frequency distribution using classes of 500 up to 600, 600 up to 700, etc.

b. Construct the relative frequency distribution, the cumulative frequency distribution, and the cumulative relative frequency distribution.

c. How many of the 13-year-olds sent at least 600 but less than 700 text messages? How many sent less than 800 text messages?

d. What percent of the 13-year-olds sent at least 500 but less than 600 text messages? What percent of the 13-year-olds sent less than 700 text messages?

e. Construct a polygon. Comment on the shape of the distribution.

24. AccuWeather.com listed the following high temperatures (in degrees Fahrenheit) for 33 European cities on July 21, 2010.

75	92	81	85	90	73	94	95	81	64	85
62	84	85	81	86	90	79	74	90	91	95
88	87	81	73	76	86	90	83	75	92	83

a. Construct a frequency distribution using classes of 60 up to 70, 70 up to 80, etc.

b. Construct the relative frequency, the cumulative frequency, and the cumulative relative frequency distributions.

c. How many of the cities had high temperatures less than 80°?

d. What percent of the cities had high temperatures of at least 80° but less than 90°? What percent of the cities had high temperatures less 90°?

e. Construct a polygon. Comment on the shape of the distribution.

25. Fifty cities provided information on vacancy rates (in percent) in local apartments in the following frequency distribution.

Vacancy Rate (in percent)	Frequency
0 up to 3	5
3 up to 6	10
6 up to 9	20
9 up to 12	10
12 up to 15	5

a. Construct the corresponding relative frequency distribution, cumulative frequency distribution, and cumulative relative frequency distribution.

b. How many of the cities had a vacancy rate less than 12%? What percent of the cities had a vacancy rate of at least 6% but less than 9%? What percent of the cities had a vacancy rate of less than 9%?

c. Construct a histogram. Comment on the shape of the distribution.

26. The following relative frequency distribution summarizes the ages of women who had a child in the last year.

Ages	Relative Frequency
15 up to 20	0.10
20 up to 25	0.25
25 up to 30	0.28
30 up to 35	0.24
35 up to 40	0.11
40 up to 45	0.02

SOURCE: *The Statistical Abstract of the United States, 2010.*

a. Assume the relative frequency distribution is based on a sample of 2,000 women. Construct the corresponding frequency distribution, cumulative frequency distribution, and cumulative relative frequency distribution.

b. What percent of the women were at least 25 but less than 30 years old? What percent of the women were younger than 35 years old?

c. Construct a relative frequency polygon. Comment on the shape of the distribution.

d. Construct an ogive. Using the graph, approximate the age of the middle 50% of the distribution.

27. The manager of a nightclub near a local university recorded the ages of the last 100 guests in the following cumulative frequency distribution.

Ages	Cumulative Frequency
18 up to 22	45
22 up to 26	70
26 up to 30	85
30 up to 34	96
34 up to 38	100

a. Construct the corresponding frequency, relative frequency, and cumulative relative frequency distributions.

b. How many of the guests were at least 26 but less than 30 years old? What percent of the guests were at least 22 but less than 26 years old? What percent of the guests were younger than 34 years old? What percent were 34 years or older?

c. Construct a histogram. Comment on the shape of the distribution.

28. The following relative frequency histogram summarizes the median household income for the 50 states in the United States (*U.S. Census*, 2010).

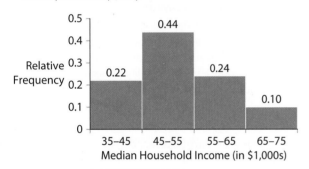

a. Is the distribution symmetric? If not, is it positively or negatively skewed?

b. What percentage of the states had median household income between $45,000 and $55,000?

c. What percentage of the states had median household income between $35,000 and $55,000?

29. The following ogive summarizes the median household income for the 50 states in the United States (*U.S. Census*, 2010).

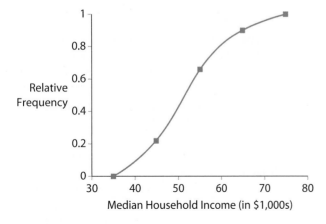

a. Approximate the percentage of states with median household income less than $50,000.

b. Approximate the percentage of states with median household income more than $60,000.

30. The following histogram summarizes Apple Inc.'s monthly stock price for the years 2007 through 2011 (http://finance.yahoo.com, data retrieved April 20, 2012).

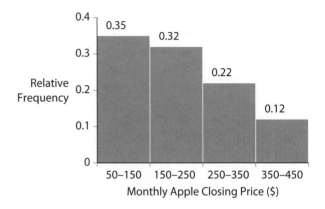

a. Is the distribution symmetric? If not, is it positively or negatively skewed?

b. Over this five-year period, approximate the minimum monthly stock price and the maximum monthly stock price.

c. Over this five-year period, which class had the highest relative frequency.

31. The following histogram summarizes the salaries (in $1,000,000s) for the 30 highest-paid players in the National Basketball Association (NBA) for the 2012 season (www.nba.com, data retrieved March 2012).

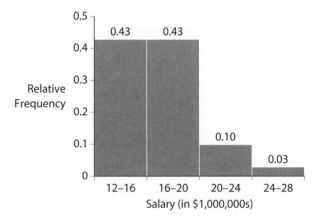

a. Is the distribution symmetric? If not, is it positively or negatively skewed?

b. How many NBA players earned between $20,000,000 and $24,000,000?

c. Approximately how many NBA players earned between $12,000,000 and $20,000,000?

32. The following ogive summarizes the salary (in $1,000,000s) for the 30 highest-paid players in the National Basketball

Association (NBA) for the 2012 season (www.nba.com, data retrieved March 2012).

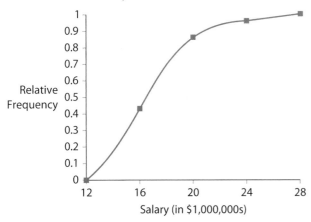

Salary (in $1,000,000s)

a. Approximate the percentage of salaries that were less than $18,000,000.
b. Approximate the number of salaries that were more than $14,000,000.

33. **FILE** The following table lists a portion of the average math SAT scores for each state for the year 2009. The entire data set, labeled **Math_SAT**, can be found on the text website.

State	SAT
Alabama	552
Alaska	516
⋮	⋮
Wyoming	568

Source: www.collegeboard.com.

a. Construct a frequency distribution and histogram using classes of 450 to 500, 501 to 550, etc. Comment on the shape of the distribution. How many of the states had scores between 551 and 600?
b. Construct the relative frequency, the cumulative frequency, and the cumulative relative frequency distributions.
c. How many of the states had math SAT scores of 550 or less?
d. What percent of the states had math SAT scores between 551 and 600? What percent of the states had mean SAT scores of 550 or less?

34. **FILE** The accompanying table shows a portion of median house values for the 50 states as reported by the U.S. Census Bureau in 2010. The entire data set, labeled **Census**, can be found on the text website.

State	House Value
Alabama	$117,600
Alaska	229,100
⋮	⋮
Wyoming	174,000

a. Construct a frequency distribution and histogram for the median house values. Use six classes with upper limits of $100,000, $200,000, etc.

b. Is the distribution symmetric? If not, is it positively or negatively skewed?
c. Which class interval had the highest frequency?
d. What percentage of the states had median house values between $300,000 and $400,000?
e. How many of the states had median house values less than $300,000?

35. **FILE** The accompanying table shows a portion of the average price for a gallon of gas for the 50 states during April 2012. The entire data set, labeled **Gas_Prices_2012**, can be found on the text website.

State	Price per Gallon
Alabama	$4.36
Alaska	3.79
⋮	⋮
Wyoming	3.63

Source: www.AAA.com, data retrieved April 16, 2012.

a. Construct a frequency distribution and histogram for the average gas prices. Use six classes with upper limits of $3.70, $3.90, etc.
b. Is the distribution symmetric? If not, is it positively or negatively skewed?
c. Which class interval had the highest frequency?
d. Given your results from (a), construct an ogive. Approximate the percentage of states that had average gas prices of $3.90 or less. Approximate the number of states that had average gas prices greater than $3.90.

36. **FILE** For the first three months of 2012, the stock market put up its best first-quarter performance in over a decade (Money.cnn.com, April 9, 2012). The accompanying table shows a portion of the daily price index for the Dow Jones Industrial Average (DJIA) over this period. The entire data set, labeled **DJIA_2012**, can be found on the text website.

Day	DJIA Price Index
January 3, 2012	12,397
January 4, 2012	12,418
⋮	⋮
March 31, 2012	13,212

Source: www.AAA.com, data retrieved April 20, 2012.

a. Construct a frequency distribution and histogram for the DJIA price index. Use five classes with upper limits of 12,500, 12,750, etc. On how many days during this quarter was the DJIA less than 12,500?
b. Construct a relative frequency polygon. Is the distribution symmetric? If not, is it positively or negatively skewed?
c. Construct an ogive. Approximate the percentage of days that the DJIA was less than 13,000.

2.3 Stem-and-Leaf Diagrams

John Tukey (1915–2000), a well-known statistician, provided another visual method for displaying quantitative data. A **stem-and-leaf diagram** is often a preliminary step when analyzing a data set. It is useful in that it gives an overall picture of where the data are centered and how the data are dispersed from the center.

> ### GRAPHICAL DISPLAY OF QUANTITATIVE DATA: STEM-AND-LEAF DIAGRAMS
>
> A **stem-and-leaf diagram** is constructed by separating each value of a data set into two parts: a *stem*, which consists of the leftmost digits, and a *leaf*, which consists of the last digit.

The best way to explain a stem-and-leaf diagram is to show an example.

EXAMPLE 2.6

Table 2.15 shows the ages of the 25 wealthiest people in the world in 2010; these data labeled **Wealthiest_People** are also available on the text website. Construct and interpret a stem-and-leaf diagram.

TABLE 2.15 Wealthiest People in the World, 2010

Name	Age	Name	Age
Carlos Slim Helu	70	Li Ka-shing	81
William Gates III	54	Jim Walton	62
Warren Buffet	79	Alice Walton	60
Mukesh Ambani	52	Liliane Bettencourt	87
Lakshmi Mittal	59	S. Robson Walton	66
Lawrence Ellison	65	Prince Alwaleed Alsaud	54
Bernard Arnault	61	David Thomson	52
Eike Batista	53	Michael Otto	66
Amancio Ortega	74	Lee Shau Kee	82
Karl Albrecht	90	Michael Bloomberg	68
Ingvar Kamprad	83	Sergey Brin	36
Christy Walton	55	Charles Koch	74
Stefan Persson	62		

Reprinted by permission of Forbes Media LLC © 2011.

SOLUTION: For each age we first decide that the number in the tens spot will denote the stem, thus leaving the number in the ones spot as the leaf. We then identify the lowest and highest values in the data set. Sergey Brin is the youngest member of this group at 36 years of age (stem: 3, leaf: 6) and Karl Albrecht is the oldest at 90 years of age (stem: 9, leaf: 0). These values give us the first and last values in the stem. This means our stems will be 3, 4, 5, 6, 7, 8, and 9, as shown in Panel A of Table 2.16.

TABLE 2.16 Constructing a Stem-and-Leaf Diagram for Example 2.6

Panel A		Panel B		Panel C	
Stem	Leaf	Stem	Leaf	Stem	Leaf
3		3	6	3	6
4		4		4	
5		5	4 2 9 3 5 4 2	5	2 2 3 4 4 5 9
6		6	5 1 2 2 0 6 6 8	6	0 1 2 2 5 6 6 8
7	0	7	0 9 4 4	7	0 4 4 9
8		8	3 1 7 2	8	1 2 3 7
9		9	0	9	0

We then begin with the wealthiest man in the world, Carlos Slim Helu, whose age of 70 gives us a stem of 7 and a leaf of 0. We place a 0 in the row corresponding to a stem of 7, as shown in Panel A of Table 2.16. We continue this process with all the other ages and obtain the values in Panel B. Finally, in Panel C we arrange each individual leaf row in ascending order; this is the stem-and-leaf diagram in its final form.

The stem-and-leaf diagram (Panel C) presents the original 25 values in a more organized form. From the diagram we can readily observe that the ages range from 36 to 90. Wealthy individuals in their sixties make up the greatest group in the sample with eight members, while those in their fifties place a close second, accounting for seven members. We also note that the distribution is not perfectly symmetric. A stem-and-leaf diagram is similar to a histogram turned on its side with the added benefit of retaining the original values.

Mechanics

37. Consider the following data set:

| 5.4 | 4.6 | 3.5 | 2.8 | 2.6 | 5.5 | 5.5 | 2.3 | 3.2 | 4.2 |
| 4.0 | 3.0 | 3.6 | 4.5 | 4.7 | 4.2 | 3.3 | 3.2 | 4.2 | 3.4 |

Construct a stem-and-leaf diagram. Is the distribution symmetric? Explain.

38. Consider the following data set:

| −64 | −52 | −73 | −82 | −85 | −80 | −79 | −65 | −50 | −71 |
| −80 | −85 | −75 | −65 | −77 | −87 | −72 | −83 | −73 | −80 |

Construct a stem-and-leaf diagram. Is the distribution symmetric? Explain.

Applications

39. A sample of patients arriving at Overbrook Hospital's emergency room recorded the following body temperature readings over the weekend:

| 100.4 | 99.6 | 101.5 | 99.8 | 102.1 | 101.2 | 102.3 | 101.2 | 102.2 | 102.4 |
| 101.6 | 101.5 | 99.7 | 102.0 | 101.0 | 102.5 | 100.5 | 101.3 | 101.2 | 102.2 |

Construct and interpret a stem-and-leaf diagram.

40. Suppose the following high temperatures were recorded for major cities in the contiguous United States for a day in July.

84	92	96	91	96	94	93	82	81	76
90	95	84	90	84	98	94	90	83	78
88	96	106	78	92	98	91	84	80	94
94	93	107	87	77	99	94	73	74	92

Construct and interpret a stem-and-leaf diagram.

41. A police officer is concerned with excessive speeds on a portion of Interstate 90 with a posted speed limit of 65 miles per hour. Using his radar gun, he records the following speeds for 25 cars and trucks:

66	72	73	82	80	81	79	65	70	71
80	75	75	65	67	67	72	73	73	80
81	78	71	70	70

Construct a stem-and-leaf diagram. Are the officer's concerns warranted?

42. Spain was the winner of the 2010 World Cup, beating the Netherlands by a score of 1–0. The ages of the players from both teams were as follows:

Spain									
29	25	23	30	32	25	29	30	26	29
21	28	24	21	27	22	25	21	23	24
Netherlands									
27	22	26	30	35	33	29	25	27	25
35	27	27	26	23	25	23	24	26	39

Construct a stem-and-leaf diagram for each country. Comment on similarities and differences between the two data sets.

2.4 Scatterplots

All of the tabular and graphical tools presented thus far have focused on describing one variable. However, in many instances we are interested in the relationship between two variables. People in virtually every discipline examine how one variable may systematically influence another variable. Consider, for instance, how

- Incomes vary with education.
- Sales vary with advertising expenditures.
- Stock prices vary with corporate profits.
- Crop yields vary with the use of fertilizer.
- Cholesterol levels vary with dietary intake.
- Weight varies with exercise.

SCATTERPLOTS

A **scatterplot** is a graphical tool that helps in determining whether or not two quantitative variables are related in some systematic way. Each point in the diagram represents a pair of known or observed values of the two variables.

When constructing a scatterplot, we generally refer to one of the variables as x and represent it on the horizontal axis and the other variable as y and represent it on the vertical axis. We then plot each pairing: (x_1, y_1), (x_2, y_2), etc. Once the data are plotted, the graph may reveal that

- A linear relationship exists between the two variables;
- A curvilinear relationship exists between the two variables; or
- No relationship exists between the two variables.

For example, Figure 2.17(a) shows points on a scatterplot clustered together along a line with a positive slope; we infer that the two variables have a positive linear relationship. Part (b) depicts a positive curvilinear relationship; as x increases, y tends to increase at an increasing rate. The points in part (c) are scattered with no apparent pattern; thus, there is no relationship between the two variables.

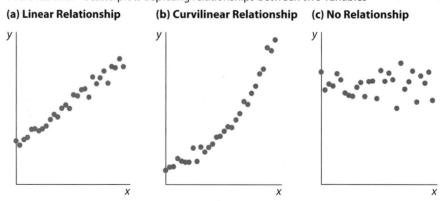

FIGURE 2.17 Scatterplots depicting relationships between two variables

(a) Linear Relationship   **(b) Curvilinear Relationship**   **(c) No Relationship**

In order to illustrate a scatterplot, consider the following example.

EXAMPLE 2.7

A social scientist wants to analyze the relationship between educational attainment and income. He collects the data shown in Table 2.17, where Education refers to years of higher education and Income is the individual's annual income in thousands of dollars. Construct and interpret a scatterplot.

TABLE 2.17 Education and Salary for Eight Individuals

Individual	Education	Income
1	3	45
2	4	56
3	6	85
4	2	35
5	5	55
6	4	48
7	8	100
8	0	38

SOLUTION: We let x and y denote Education and Income, respectively. We plot the first individual's pairing as (3, 45), the second individual's pairing as (4, 56), and so on. The graph should resemble Figure 2.18.

FIGURE 2.18 Scatterplot of Education versus Income

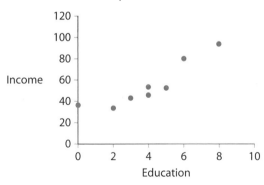

As expected, we observe a positive relationship between the two variables; that is, when Education increases, Income tends to increase.

Using Excel to Construct a Scatterplot

A. To construct a scatterplot, input the appropriate x- and y-coordinates into an Excel spreadsheet. Here we use the data from Example 2.7.

B. As shown in Figure 2.19, select the x- and y-coordinates and choose **Insert** > **Scatter**. Select the graph at the top left.

FIGURE 2.19
Constructing a scatterplot with Excel

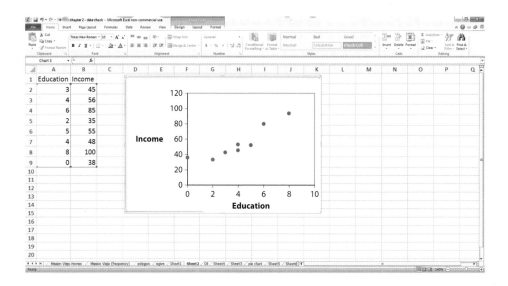

EXERCISES 2.4

Mechanics

43. Construct a scatterplot with the following data. Categorize the relationship between *x* and *y*.

x	3	7	12	5	6
y	22	10	5	14	12

44. Construct a scatterplot with the following data. Does a linear relationship exist between *x* and *y*?

x	10	4	6	3	7
y	3	2	6	6	4

45. Construct a scatterplot with the following data. Categorize the relationship between *x* and *y*.

x	1	2	3	4	5	6	7	8
y	22	20	18	10	5	4	3	2

Applications

46. A statistics instructor wants to examine whether a relationship exists between the hours a student spends studying for the final exam (Hours) and a student's grade on the final exam (Grade). She takes a sample of eight students.

Hours	8	2	3	8	10	15	25	5
Grade	75	47	50	80	85	88	93	55

Construct a scatterplot. What conclusions can you draw from the scatterplot?

47. A recent study offers evidence that the more weight a woman gains during pregnancy, the higher the risk of having a high-birth-weight baby, defined as at least 8 pounds, 13 ounces, or 4 kilograms (*The Wall Street Journal*, August 5, 2010). High-birth-weight babies are more likely to be obese in adulthood. The weight gain (in kilograms) of eight mothers and the birth weight of their newborns (in kilograms) are recorded in the accompanying table.

Mother's Weight Gain	Newborn's Birth Weight
18	4.0
7	2.5
8	3.0
22	4.5
21	4.0
9	3.5
8	3.0
10	3.5

Construct a scatterplot. Do the results support the findings of the study?

48. In order to diversify risk, investors are often encouraged to invest in assets whose returns have either a negative relationship or no relationship. The annual return data on two assets is shown below.

Return A	Return B
−20%	8%
−5	5
18	−1
15	−2
−12	2

Construct a scatterplot. For diversity purposes, would the investor be wise to include these assets in her portfolio? Explain.

49. In an attempt to determine whether a relationship exists between the price of a home and the number of days it takes

to sell the home, a real estate agent collects data on the recent sales of eight homes.

Price (in $1,000s)	Days to Sell Home
265	136
225	125
160	120
325	140
430	145
515	150
180	122
423	145

Construct a scatterplot. What can the realtor conclude?

WRITING WITH STATISTICS

The tabular and graphical tools introduced in this chapter are the starting point for most studies and reports that involve statistics. They can help you organize data so you can see patterns and trends in the data, which can then be analyzed by the methods described in later chapters of this book. In this section, we present an example of using tabular and graphical methods in a sample report. Each of the remaining chapters contains a sample report incorporating the concepts developed in that respective chapter.

Camilla Walford is a newly hired journalist for a national newspaper. One of her first tasks is to analyze gas prices in the United States during the week of the Fourth of July holiday. She collects average gas prices for the 48 contiguous states and the District of Columbia (DC), a portion of which is shown in Table 2.18. The entire data set, labeled **Gas_Prices_2010**, can be found on the text website.

TABLE 2.18 U.S. Gas Prices, July 2, 2010

State	Average Price ($ per gallon)
Alabama	$2.59
Arkansas	2.60
⋮	⋮
Wyoming	2.77

SOURCE: AAA's Daily Fuel Gauge Report, July 2, 2010.

Camilla wants to use the sample information to:

1. Construct frequency distributions to summarize the data.
2. Make summary statements concerning gas prices.
3. Convey the information from the distributions into graphical form.

Historically, in the United States, many people choose to take some time off during the Fourth of July holiday period and travel to the beach, the lake, or the mountains. The roads tend to be heavily traveled, making the cost of gas a concern. The following report provides an analysis of gas prices across the nation over this holiday period.

The analysis focuses on the average gas price for the 48 contiguous states and the District of Columbia (henceforth, referenced as 49 states for ease of exposition). The range of gas prices is from a low of $2.52 per gallon (South Carolina) to a high of $3.15 per gallon (California). To find out how gas prices are distributed between these extremes, the data have been organized into several frequency distributions as shown in Table 2.A. For instance, most states (17 of the 49) have an average gas price between $2.70 and $2.80 per gallon. Equivalently, looking at the relative frequency column, 35%

Sample Report—Gas Prices across the United States

of the states have an average price in this range. The cumulative frequency column indicates that 35 states have an average price less than $2.80 per gallon. Finally, the last column shows that the average price in 72% of the states (approximately three-quarters of the sample) is less than $2.80 per gallon.

TABLE 2.A Frequency Distributions for Gas Prices in the United States, July 2, 2010

Average Price ($ per gallon)	Frequency	Relative Frequency	Cumulative Frequency	Cumulative Relative Frequency
2.50 up to 2.60	5	0.10	5	0.10
2.60 up to 2.70	13	0.27	18	0.37
2.70 up to 2.80	17	0.35	35	0.72
2.80 up to 2.90	8	0.16	43	0.88
2.90 up to 3.00	4	0.08	47	0.96
3.00 up to 3.10	1	0.02	48	0.98
3.10 up to 3.20	1	0.02	49	1.00
	Sample Size = 49			

FIGURE 2.A Histogram of average gas prices nationwide

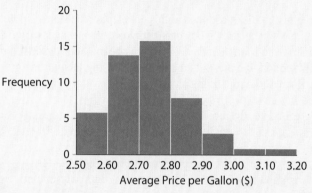

Figure 2.A shows a histogram for gas prices, which graphs the frequency distribution from Table 2.A. This graph reinforces the fact that the average price of gas nationwide is between $2.50 and $3.20 per gallon. Moreover, gas prices are positively skewed since the distribution runs off to the right; only two states (California and Washington) have gas prices that are more than $3.00 per gallon.

Another useful visual representation of the data is an ogive, shown in Figure 2.B. The ogive graphs the cumulative relative frequency distribution from Table 2.A. The ogive is useful for approximating the "middle" price. If we draw a horizontal line to the ogive at the 0.5 relative frequency mark, it intersects the plot at a point corresponding on the horizontal axis to a "middle price" of approximately $2.75. This indicates that gas stations in approximately half of the states charged below this price and half charged above it.

FIGURE 2.B Ogive of average gas prices nationwide

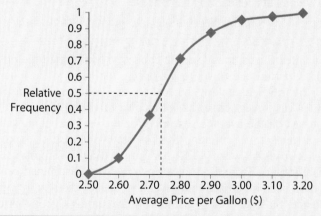

Conceptual Review

LO 2.1 Summarize qualitative data by forming frequency distributions.

For **qualitative data**, a **frequency distribution** groups data into categories and records the number of observations that fall into each category. A **relative frequency distribution** shows the proportion (or the fraction) of observations in each category.

LO 2.2 Construct and interpret pie charts and bar charts.

Graphically, we can show a frequency distribution for qualitative data by constructing a **pie chart** or a **bar chart**. A pie chart is a segmented circle that clearly portrays the sectors of some qualitative variable. A **bar chart** depicts the frequency or the relative frequency for each category of the qualitative variable as a series of horizontal or vertical bars, the lengths of which are proportional to the values that are to be depicted.

LO 2.3 Summarize quantitative data by forming frequency distributions.

For quantitative data, a **frequency distribution** groups data into intervals called **classes**, and records the number of observations that falls into each class. A **cumulative frequency distribution** records the number of observations that falls below the upper limit of each class. A **relative frequency distribution** identifies the proportion (or the fraction) of observations that falls into each class. A **cumulative relative frequency distribution** shows the proportion (or the fraction) of observations that falls below the upper limit of each class.

LO 2.4 Construct and interpret histograms, polygons, and ogives.

Histograms and **polygons** are graphical representations of frequency or relative frequency distributions. A casual inspection of these graphs reveals where most of the observations tend to cluster, as well as the general shape and spread of the data. An **ogive** is a graphical representation of a cumulative frequency or cumulative relative frequency distribution.

LO 2.5 Construct and interpret a stem-and-leaf diagram.

A **stem-and-leaf diagram** is another visual method of displaying quantitative data. It is constructed by separating each value of a data set into a *stem*, which consists of the leftmost digits, and a *leaf*, which consists of the last digit. Like histograms and polygons, stem-and-leaf diagrams give an overall picture of where the data are centered and how the data are dispersed from the center.

LO 2.6 Construct and interpret a scatterplot.

A **scatterplot** is a graphical tool that helps in determining whether or not two quantitative variables are related in some systematic way. Each point in the diagram represents a pair of observed values of the two variables.

Additional Exercises and Case Studies

Exercises

50. A 2003 survey by the Centers for Disease Control and Prevention concluded that smoking is forbidden in nearly 75% of U.S. households (*Boston Globe*, May 25, 2007). The survey gathered responses from at least 900 households in each state. When residents of Utah were asked whether or not smoking was allowed in their households, a representative sample of responses was as follows:

No	No	No	No	No	No	Yes	No	No	No
No	Yes	No	No	No	No	No	No	No	No

When a similar survey was taken in Kentucky, a representative sample of responses was as follows:

No	No	Yes	No	Yes	No	Yes	Yes	No	No
No	Yes	Yes	No	Yes	No	No	Yes	Yes	No

a. Construct a relative frequency distribution that summarizes the responses of residents from Utah and Kentucky. Comment on the results.

b. Construct a bar chart that summarizes the results for each state.

51. Patrons at a local restaurant were asked to rate their recent experience at the restaurant with respect to its advertised atmosphere of upbeat, comfortable, and clean. Possible responses included Outstanding, Good, OK, and Please Get Help. The following table shows the responses of 28 patrons:

Please Get Help	OK	Please Get Help	Please Get Help
OK	OK	Please Get Help	Please Get Help
Please Get Help	OK	Please Get Help	Good
Please Get Help	Good	Good	Good
Please Get Help	OK	Please Get Help	OK
Good	Good	Please Get Help	Good
Please Get Help	OK	Please Get Help	Good

a. Construct a relative frequency distribution that summarizes the responses of the patrons. Briefly summarize your findings. What recommendations would you make to the owner of the restaurant?

b. Use Excel to construct a pie chart and a bar chart for these data.

52. A survey conducted by CBS News asked parents about the professions they would want their children to pursue. The results are summarized in the following table.

Profession	Parents' Preference
Doctor, banker, lawyer, or president	65%
Internet mogul	13
Humanitarian-aid worker	6
Athlete	9
Movie star, rock star	2
Other	5

Source: *Vanity Fair*, December 2009.

a. Use Excel to construct a pie chart and a bar chart for these data.

b. How many parents wanted their children to become athletes if the above results were based on 550 responses?

53. The one-year return (in %) for 24 mutual funds is as follows:

−14.5	−5.0	−3.7	2.5	−7.9	−11.2
4.8	−16.8	9.0	6.5	8.2	5.3
−12.2	15.9	18.2	25.4	3.4	−1.4
5.5	−4.2	−0.5	6.0	−2.4	10.5

a. Construct a frequency distribution using classes of −20 up to −10, −10 up to 0, etc.

b. Construct the relative frequency, the cumulative frequency, and the cumulative relative frequency distributions.

c. How many of the funds had returns of at least 0% but less than 10%? How many of the funds had returns of 10% or more?

d. What percentage of the funds had returns of at least 10% but less than 20%? What percent of the funds had returns less than 20%?

54. *The Statistical Abstract of the United States, 2010* provided the following frequency distribution of the number of people who live below the poverty level by region.

Region	Number of People (in 1,000s)
Northeast	6,166
Midwest	7,237
South	15,501
West	8,372

a. Construct a relative frequency distribution. What percentage of people who live below the poverty level live in the Midwest?

b. Use Excel to construct a pie chart and a bar chart for these data.

55. *Money* magazine (January 2007) reported that an average of 77 million adults in the United States make financial resolutions at the beginning of a new year. Consider the following frequency distribution, which reports the top financial resolutions of 1,026 Americans (MONEY/ICR poll conducted November 8–12, 2006).

Financial Resolution	Frequency
Saving more	328
Paying down debt	257
Making more income	154
Spending less	133
Investing more	103
Saving for a large purchase	41
Don't know	10

a. Construct a relative frequency distribution for these data. What percentage of the respondents indicated that paying down debt was their top financial resolution?

b. Construct a bar chart.

56. A recent poll of 3,057 individuals asked: "What's the longest vacation you plan to take this summer?" The following relative frequency distribution summarizes the results.

Response	Relative Frequency
A few days	0.21
A few long weekends	0.18
One week	0.36
Two weeks	0.25

a. Construct a frequency distribution of these data. How many people are going to take a one-week vacation this summer?

b. Use Excel to construct a pie chart.

57. A survey conducted by CBS News asked 1,026 respondents: "What would you do with an unexpected tax refund?" The responses are summarized in the following table.

Pay off debts	47%
Put it in the bank	30%
Spend it	11%
I never get a refund	10%
Other	2%

Copyright © CBS News Archives. Used with permission.

a. Construct a bar chart for these data.

b. How many people will spend the tax refund?

58. The following table lists the U.S. sales (in $ millions) of prescription drugs used to treat seizure disorders.

Drug	Sales in 2006
Topamax	$1,825.4
Lamictal	1,684.3
Depakote	770.4
Lyrica	727.8
Keppra	710.5

Source: The Wall Street Journal, July 13, 2007.

a. Construct a relative frequency distribution.

b. For what percentage of sales did Lamictal account?

c. Use Excel to construct a pie chart.

59. The manager at a water park constructed the following frequency distribution to summarize attendance in July and August.

Attendance	Frequency
1,000 up to 1,250	5
1,250 up to 1,500	6
1,500 up to 1,750	10
1,750 up to 2,000	20
2,000 up to 2,250	15
2,250 up to 2,500	4

a. Construct the corresponding relative frequency, cumulative frequency, and cumulative relative frequency distributions.

b. What is the most likely attendance range? How many times was attendance less than 2,000 people?

c. What percentage of the time was attendance at least 1,750 but less than 2,000 people? What percentage of the time was attendance less than 1,750 people? What percentage of the time was attendance 1,750 or more?

d. Construct a histogram. Comment on the shape of the distribution.

60. A researcher conducts a mileage economy test involving 80 cars. The frequency distribution describing average miles per gallon (mpg) appears in the following table.

Average mpg	Frequency
15 up to 20	15
20 up to 25	30
25 up to 30	15
30 up to 35	10
35 up to 40	7
40 up to 45	3

a. Construct the corresponding relative frequency, cumulative frequency, and cumulative relative frequency distributions.

b. How many of the cars got less than 30 mpg? What percentage of the cars got at least 20 but less than 25 mpg? What percentage of the cars got less than 35 mpg? What percent got 35 mpg or more?

c. Construct a histogram. Comment on the shape of the distribution.

61. The Wall Street Journal (August 28, 2006) asked its readers: "Ideally, how many days a week, if any, would you work from home?" The following relative frequency distribution summarizes the responses from 3,478 readers.

Days Working from Home	Relative Frequency
0	0.12
1	0.18
2	0.30
3	0.15
4	0.07
5	0.19

Use Excel to construct a pie chart and a bar chart to summarize the data.

62. FILE The accompanying table lists a portion of the ages and net worth of the wealthiest people in America; the complete data set can be found on the text website and is labeled *Wealthiest_Americans*.

Name	Age	Net Worth ($ billions)
William Gates III	53	50.0
Warren Buffet	79	40.0
⋮	⋮	⋮
Philip Knight	71	9.5

Source: Forbes, Special Report, September 2009.

a. What percentage of the wealthiest people in America had net worth more than $20 billion?

b. What percentage of the wealthiest people in America had net worth between $10 billion and $20 billion?

c. Construct a stem-and-leaf diagram on age. Comment on the shape of the distribution and how it compares with Table 2.16.

63. FILE The price-to-earnings growth ratio, or PEG ratio, is the market's valuation of a company relative to its earnings

prospects. A PEG ratio of 1 indicates that the stock's price is in line with growth expectations. A PEG ratio less than 1 suggests that the stock of the company is undervalued (typical of value stocks), whereas a PEG ratio greater than 1 suggests the stock is overvalued (typical of growth stocks). The accompanying table shows a portion of PEG ratios of companies listed on the Dow Jones Industrial Average; the entire data set, labeled **DOW_PEG**, can be found on the text website.

Company	PEG Ratio
3M (MMM)	1.4
Alcoa (AA)	0.9
⋮	⋮
Walt Disney (DIS)	1.2

Source: www.finance.yahoo, data retrieved April 13, 2011.

Construct a stem-and-leaf diagram on the PEG ratio. Interpret your findings.

64. The following table lists the sale price and type of 20 recently sold houses in New Jersey.

Price	Type	Price	Type
$305,000	Ranch	$568,000	Colonial
$450,000	Colonial	$385,000	Other
$389,000	Contemporary	$310,000	Contemporary
$525,000	Other	$450,000	Colonial
$300,000	Ranch	$400,000	Other
$330,000	Contemporary	$359,000	Ranch
$355,000	Contemporary	$379,000	Ranch
$405,000	Colonial	$509,000	Colonial
$365,000	Ranch	$435,000	Colonial
$415,000	Ranch	$510,000	Other

a. Construct a frequency distribution on types of houses sold in New Jersey. Interpret your findings.

b. Construct a frequency distribution for house price using classes of $300,000 up to $350,000, $350,000 up to $400,000, etc.

c. Use a histogram and an ogive to summarize the data.

65. A manager of a local retail store analyzes the relationship between Advertising (in $100s) and Sales (in $1,000s) by reviewing the store's data for the previous six months. Construct a scatterplot and comment on whether or not a relationship exists.

Advertising (in $100s)	Sales (in $1,000s)
20	15
25	18
30	20
22	16
27	19
26	20

66. The following table lists the National Basketball Association's (NBA's) leading scorers, their average minutes per game (MPG), and their average points per game (PPG) for 2008:

Player	MPG	PPG
D. Wade	38.6	30.2
L. James	37.7	28.4
K. Bryant	36.1	26.8
D. Nowitzki	37.3	25.9
D. Granger	36.2	25.8
K. Durant	39.0	25.3
C. Paul	38.5	22.8
C. Anthony	34.5	22.8
C. Bosh	38.0	22.7
B. Roy	37.2	22.6

Source: www.espn.com.

Construct and interpret a scatterplot of PPG against MPG. Does a relationship exist between the two variables?

CASE STUDIES

Case Study 2.1

In its 2000 and 2009 Annual Reports, Nike, Inc., reported the following net revenues, in millions of dollars, in four distinct regions of the world:

Data for Case Study 2.1 Net Revenue of Nike in 2000 and 2009

Region	2000	2009
U.S. Region	$4,732.1	$6,542.9
EMEA Region[a]	2,350.9	5,512.2
Asia Pacific Region	955.1	3,322.0
Americas Region	550.2	1,284.7
	Total = 8,588.3	Total = 16,661.8

[a]EMEA Region consists of Europe, the Middle East, and Africa.

In a report, use the sample information to:

1. Convert each region's net revenues to its respective proportion for that year. Have the proportions of Nike's net sales in each region remained the same over this 10-year period? Discuss any trends that you see.
2. Compare and contrast your findings concerning Nike's net revenues with those of Adidas, found in Table 2.6. What similarities and differences do you detect?

Case Study 2.2

When reviewing the overall strength of a particular firm, financial analysts typically examine the net profit margin. This statistic is generally calculated as the ratio of a firm's net profit after taxes (net income) to its revenue, expressed as a percentage. For example, a 20% net profit margin means that a firm has a net income of $0.20 for each dollar of sales. A net profit margin can even be negative if the firm has a negative net income. In general, the higher the net profit margin, the more effective the firm is at converting revenue into actual profit. The net profit margin serves as a good way of comparing firms in the same industry, since such firms generally are subject to the same business conditions. However, financial analysts also use the net profit margin to compare firms in different industries in order to gauge which firms are relatively more profitable. The accompanying table shows a portion of net profit margins for a sample of clothing retailers; the entire data set, labeled *Net_Profit_Margins*, can be found on the text website.

Data for Case Study 2.2 Net Profit Margin for Clothing Retailers

Firm	Net Profit Margin (in percent)	FILE
Abercrombie & Fitch	1.58	
Aéropostale	10.64	
⋮	⋮	
Wet Seal	16.15	

SOURCE: www.finance.yahoo.com, data retrieved July 2010.

In a report, use the sample information to:

1. Provide a brief definition of net profit margin and explain why it is an important statistic.
2. Construct appropriate tables (frequency distribution, relative frequency distribution, etc.) and graphs that summarize the clothing industry's net profit margin.
3. Discuss where the data tend to cluster and how the data are spread from the lowest value to the highest value.
4. Comment on the net profit margin of the clothing industry, as compared to the beverage industry's net profit margin of approximately 10.9% (Source: biz.yahoo, July 2010).

Case Study 2.3

The following table lists a portion of U.S. life expectancy (in years) for the 50 states; the entire data set, labeled *Life_Expectancy*, can be found on the text website.

Data for Case Study 2.3 Life Expectancy by State, 2010–2011

Rank	State	Life Expectancy (in years)	FILE
1	Hawaii	81.5	
2	Minnesota	80.9	
⋮	⋮	⋮	
50	Mississippi	74.8	

SOURCE: en.wikipedia.org/wiki/List_of_U.S._states_by_life_expectancy, data retrieved April 25, 2012.

In a report, use the sample information to:

1. Construct appropriate tables (frequency distribution, relative frequency distribution, etc.) and graphs to summarize life expectancy in the United States. Use 75, 76.5, etc. for the upper limits of the classes for the distributions.
2. Discuss where the data tend to cluster and how the data are spread from the lowest value to the highest value.
3. Comment on the shape of the distribution.

Appendix 2.1 Guidelines for Other Software Packages

The following section provides brief commands for specific software packages: Minitab, SPSS, and JMP. More detailed instructions can be found on the text website.

MINITAB

Pie Chart

A. (Replicating Figure 2.1) Copy and paste the *Adidas_Sales* data from the text website into a Minitab spreadsheet.

B. From the menu choose **Graph > Pie Chart**. Select **Chart values from a table**, select Region as the **Categorical variable**, and 2000 and 2009 as the **Summary variables**.

C. Choose **Labels**. Select **Titles/Footnotes** and enter Adidas's Net Sales by Region. Then select **Slice Labels** and select **Category name** and **Percent**. Click **OK**.

D. Choose **Multiple Graphs** and then select **On the same graph**.

Bar Chart

A. (Replicating Figure 2.3) Copy and paste the *Prop_Adidas_Sales* data from the text website into a Minitab spreadsheet.

B. From the menu choose **Graph > Bar Chart**. From **Bars Represent** select **Values from a Table**, and from **Two-way Table** select **Cluster**. Click **OK**.

C. In the *Bar Chart—Two-Way Table—Cluster* dialog box, select 2000 and 2009 as **Graph variables**. Select Region as **Row labels**. Under **Table Arrangement**, choose **Rows are outermost categories and columns are innermost**.

Histogram

From Raw Data:

A. (Replicating Figure 2.7) Copy and paste the *MV_Houses* data from the text website into a Minitab spreadsheet.

B. From the menu choose **Graph > Histogram > Simple**. Click **OK**.

C. Select House Price as **Graph Variables**. Click **OK**.

D. Double-click x axis and select **Edit Scale**. Under **Major Tick Positions** choose **Position of Ticks** and enter 300 400 500 600 700 800. Under **Scale Range**, unclick **Auto** for *Minimum* and enter 300. Then unclick **Auto** for *Maximum* and enter 800. Select the **Binning** tab. Under **Interval Type**, select **Cutpoint**. Under **Interval Definition**, select **Midpoint/Cutpoint Definitions** and enter 300 400 500 600 700 800.

From a Frequency Distribution:

A. (Replicating Figure 2.7) Copy and paste the *MV_Frequency* data from the text website into a Minitab spreadsheet.

B. From the menu choose **Graph > Bar Chart**. From **Bars Represent** select **A function of a variable**, and from **One Y** select **Simple**. Click **OK**.

C. Under **Function** select **Sum**. Select Frequency as **Graph variables** and Class (in $1,000s) as **Row labels**. Click **OK**.

D. Double-click x axis. Under **Space Between Scale Categories**, uncheck **Gap between Cluster** and enter 0.

Polygon

A. (Replicating Figure 2.13) Input the x- and y-coordinates from Table 2.13 into a Minitab spreadsheet.

B. From the menu choose **Graph > Scatterplot > With Connect Line**. Click **OK**.

C. Select y-coordinate as **Y variables** and x-coordinate as **X variables**.

● Ogive

A. (Replicating Figure 2.15) Input the *x*- and *y*-coordinates from Table 2.14 into a Minitab spreadsheet.

B. From the menu choose **Graph > Scatterplot > With Connect Line**. Click **OK**.

C. Select y-coordinate as **Y variables** and x-coordinate as **X variables**.

Scatterplot

A. (Replicating Figure 2.18) Input the Education and Income data from Example 2.7 into a Minitab spreadsheet.

B. From the menu choose **Graph > Scatterplot > Simple**. Click **OK**.

C. Select Income as **Y variables** and Education as **X variables**.

SPSS

Pie Chart

A. (Replicating Figure 2.1) Copy and paste the *Adidas_Sales* data from the text website into an SPSS spreadsheet.

B. From the menu choose **Graphs > Legacy Dialogs > Pie**. Choose **Values of individual cases**. Click **Define**.

C. Select Year2000 as **Slices Represent**. Under **Slices Labels**, select Region as **Variable**. Click **OK**.

D. Double-click on the graph to open **Chart Editor**, and then choose **Elements > Show Data Labels**. Under *Display* dialog box, select Percent and Region.

● Bar Chart

A. (Replicating Figure 2.3) Copy and paste the *Prop_Adidas_Sales* data from the text website into an SPSS spreadsheet.

B. From the menu choose **Graphs > Legacy Dialogs > Bar**. Choose **Clustered**. Under **Data in Chart Are**, choose **Values of individual cases**. Click **Define**.

C. Select Year2000 and Year2009 as **Bars Represent**. Under **Category Labels**, select Region as **Variable**.

Histogram

A. (Replicating Figure 2.7) Copy and paste the *MV_Houses* data from the text website into an SPSS spreadsheet.

B. From the menu choose **Graphs > Legacy Dialogs > Histogram**. In the *Histogram* dialog box choose HousePrice as **Variable**. Then click **OK**.

C. In the **Output** window, double-click on the graph to open **Chart Editor**, and then choose **Edit > Select Y Axis**. Under **Range**, enter 0 as **Minimum**, 15 as **Maximum**, and 5 as **Major Increment**. Then click **Apply**.

D. Double-click on the bars. In the **Properties** window, under **Binning**, choose **X Axis > Custom > Interval width**. Enter 100 as interval width.

Polygon

A. (Replicating Figure 2.13) Input the *x*- and *y*-coordinates from Table 2.13 into an SPSS spreadsheet.

● B. From the menu choose **Graphs > Legacy Dialogs > Scatter/Dot**. Choose **Simple Scatter** and then click **Define**.

C. Select y as **Y Axis** and x as **X Axis**. Then click **OK**.

D. Double-click on the graph to open **Chart Editor**, right-click on the graph, and then choose **Add Interpolation Line**. Under the **Line Type**, choose **Straight**.

Ogive

A. (Replicating Figure 2.15) Input the *x*- and *y*-coordinates from Table 2.14 into an SPSS spreadsheet.

B. From the menu choose **Graphs > Legacy Dialogs > Scatter/Dot**. Choose **Simple Scatter**. Then click **Define**.

C. Select y as **Y Axis** and x as **X Axis**. Then click **OK**.

D. Double-click on the graph to open **Chart Editor**, right-click on the graph, and then choose **Add Interpolation Line**. Under the **Line Type**, choose **Straight**. Then click **Apply**.

E. In **Chart Editor**, choose **Edit > Select X Axis**. Under **Scale**, enter 300 as **Minimum**, 800 as **Maximum**, 100 as **Major Increment**, and 300 as **Origin**.

Scatterplot

A. (Replicating Figure 2.18) Input the Education and Income data from Example 2.7 into an SPSS spreadsheet.

B. From the menu choose **Graphs > Legacy Dialogs > Scatter/Dot**. Choose **Simple Scatter**. Then click **Define**.

C. Select Income as **Y Axis** and Education as **X Axis**. Click **OK**.

D. Double-click on the graph to open **Chart Editor**, choose **Edit > Select X Axis**. Under **Scale**, enter 0 as **Minimum**, 10 as **Maximum**, and 2 as **Major Increment**. Click **Apply**.

E. In **Chart Editor**, choose **Edit > Select Y Axis**. Under **Range**, enter 0 as **Minimum**, 120 as **Maximum**, and 20 as **Major Increment**.

JMP

Pie Chart

A. (Replicating Figure 2.1) Copy and paste the ***Adidas_Sales*** data from the text website into a JMP spreadsheet.

B. From the menu choose **Graph > Chart**. Under **Select Columns**, select Region as **Categories, X, Levels**. Under **Options**, choose **Pie Chart**. Under **Select columns**, select 2000, then select **Statistics**, and choose **% of Total (2000)**.

Bar Chart

A. (Replicating Figure 2.3) Copy and import the ***Prop_Adidas_Sales*** data from the text website into a JMP spreadsheet.

B. From the menu choose **Graph > Chart**. Under **Select Columns**, select Region as **Categories, X, Levels**. Under **Options**, choose **Bar Chart**. Under **Select Columns**, select 2000 and 2009, and then under **Statistics** choose **Data**.

Histogram

A. (Replicating Figure 2.7) Copy and paste the ***MV_Houses*** data from the text website into a JMP spreadsheet.

B. From the menu choose **Analyze > Distribution**. Under **Select Columns**, select House Price, then under **Cast Selected Columns into Roles**, select **Y, columns**. Click **OK**.

C. Right-click on the *y* axis and select **Axis Settings**. For **Minimum**, enter 300; for **Maximum** enter 800; and for **Increment**, enter 100.

Polygon

A. (Replicating Figure 2.13) Input the *x*- and *y*-coordinates from Table 2.13 into a JMP spreadsheet.

B. From the menu choose **Graph > Overlay Plot**. Select y-coordinate as **Y** and x-coordinate as **X**. Then click **OK**.

C. In the **Output** window, drag the pull-down list by clicking the red triangle next to the title **Overlay Plot**. Select **Y Options > Connect Points**.

Ogive

A. (Replicating Figure 2.15) Input the *x*- and *y*-coordinates from Table 2.14 into a JMP spreadsheet.

B. From the menu choose **Graph > Overlay Plot**. In the *Overlay Plot* dialog box, select y-coordinate as **Y** and x-coordinate as **X**. Click **OK**.

C. In the **Output** window, drag the pull-down list by clicking the red triangle next to the title **Overlay Plot**. Select **Y Options > Connect Points**.

Scatterplot

A. (Replicating Figure 2.18) Input the Education and Income data from Example 2.7 into a JMP spreadsheet.

B. From the menu choose **Graph > Overlay Plot**. Select Income as **Y** and Education as **X**.

3 Numerical Descriptive Measures

●

LEARNING OBJECTIVES

After reading this chapter you should be able to:

LO **3.1** Calculate and interpret the mean, the median, and the mode.

LO **3.2** Calculate and interpret percentiles and a box plot.

LO **3.3** Calculate and interpret the range, the mean absolute deviation, the variance, the standard deviation, and the coefficient of variation.

LO **3.4** Explain mean-variance analysis and the Sharpe ratio.

LO **3.5** Apply Chebyshev's theorem, the empirical rule, and z-scores.

LO **3.6** Calculate the mean and the variance for grouped data.

LO **3.7** Calculate and interpret the covariance and the correlation coefficient.

●

In Chapter 2 we learned how to summarize data by using tables and graphs so that we can extract meaningful information. In this chapter we focus on numerical descriptive measures. These measures provide precise, objectively determined values that are easy to calculate, interpret, and compare with one another. We first calculate several measures of central location, which attempt to find a typical or central value for the data. In addition to analyzing the center, we need to know how the data vary around the center. Measures of dispersion gauge the underlying variability of the data. We use measures of central location and dispersion to introduce some popular applications, including the Sharpe ratio and the empirical rule. Finally, we discuss measures that examine the linear relationship between two variables. These measures assess whether two variables have a positive linear relationship, a negative linear relationship, or no linear relationship.

●

Investment Decision

Rebecca Johnson works as an investment counselor at a large bank. Recently, an inexperienced investor asked Johnson about clarifying some differences between two top-performing mutual funds from the last decade: Vanguard's Precious Metals and Mining fund (henceforth, Metals) and Fidelity's Strategic Income fund (henceforth, Income). The investor shows Johnson the return data that he has accessed over the Internet, but the investor has trouble interpreting the data. Table 3.1 shows the return data for these two mutual funds for the years 2000–2009; the data, labeled **Fund_Returns**, can also be found on the text website.

TABLE 3.1 Returns (in percent) for the Metals and the Income Funds, 2000–2009

FILE

Year	Metals	Income	Year	Metals	Income
2000	−7.34	4.07	2005	43.79	3.12
2001	18.33	6.52	2006	34.30	8.15
2002	33.35	9.38	2007	36.13	5.44
2003	59.45	18.62	2008	−56.02	−11.37
2004	8.09	9.44	2009	76.46	31.77

Source: http://www.finance.yahoo.com.

Rebecca would like to use the above sample information to:

1. Determine the typical return of the mutual funds.
2. Evaluate the investment risk of the mutual funds.

A synopsis of this case is provided at the end of Section 3.3.

3.1 Measures of Central Location

LO 3.1

Calculate and interpret the mean, the median, and the mode.

The term *central location* relates to the way quantitative data tend to cluster around some middle or central value. Measures of central location attempt to find a typical or central value that describes the data. Examples include finding a typical value that describes the return on an investment, the number of defects in a production process, the salary of a business graduate, the rental price in a neighborhood, the number of customers at a local convenience store, and so on.

The Mean

The **arithmetic mean** is the primary measure of central location. Generally, we refer to the arithmetic mean as simply the **mean** or the **average**. In order to calculate the mean of a data set, we simply add up the values of all the data points and divide by the number of data points in the population or sample.

EXAMPLE 3.1

Let's use the data in Table 3.1 in the introductory case to calculate and interpret the mean return of the Metals fund and the mean return of the Income fund.

SOLUTION: Let's start with the mean return for the Metals fund. We first add all the returns and then divide by the number of returns as follows:

$$\text{Metals fund mean return} = \frac{-7.34 + 18.33 + \cdots + 76.46}{10} = \frac{246.54}{10} = 24.65\%.$$

Similarly, we calculate the mean return for the Income fund as:

$$\text{Income fund mean return} = \frac{4.07 + 6.52 + \cdots + 31.77}{10} = \frac{85.14}{10} = 8.51\%.$$

Thus, over the 10-year period 2000–2009, the mean return for the Metals fund was greater than the mean return for the Income fund, or equivalently, $24.65\% > 8.51\%$. These means represent typical annual returns resulting from a one-year investment.

All of us have calculated a mean before. What might be new for some of us is the notation used to express the mean as a formula. For instance, when calculating the mean return for the Metals fund, we let $x_1 = -7.34$, $x_2 = 18.33$, and so on, and let n represent the number of observations in the sample. So our calculation for the mean can be written as

$$\text{Mean} = \frac{x_1 + x_2 + \cdots + x_{10}}{n}.$$

The mean of the sample is referred to as $\bar{x}$ (pronounced x-bar). Also, we can denote the numerator of this formula using summation notation, which yields the following compact formula for the **sample mean**: $\bar{x} = \frac{\Sigma x_i}{n}$. We should also point out that if we had all the return data for this mutual fund, instead of just the data for the past 10 years, then we would have been able to calculate the **population mean** μ as $\mu = \frac{\Sigma x_i}{N}$, where μ is the Greek letter mu (pronounced as "mew") and N is the number of observations in the population.

THE MEAN

For sample values $x_1, x_2, \ldots, x_n$, the **sample mean** $\bar{x}$ is computed as

$$\bar{x} = \frac{\Sigma x_i}{n}.$$

For population values $x_1, x_2, \ldots, x_N$, the **population mean** μ is computed as

$$\mu = \frac{\Sigma x_i}{N}.$$

The calculation method is identical for the sample mean and the population mean except that the sample mean uses n observations and the population mean uses N observations, where $n < N$. We refer to the population mean as a **parameter** and the sample mean as a **statistic**. Since the population mean is generally unknown, we often use the sample mean to estimate the population mean.

The mean is used extensively in statistics. However, it can give a misleading description of the center of the distribution in the presence of extremely small or large values.

The mean is the most commonly used measure of central location. One weakness of this measure is that it is unduly influenced by **outliers**, that is, extremely small or large values.

Example 3.2 highlights the main weakness of the mean.

EXAMPLE 3.2

Seven people work at Acetech, a small technology firm in Seattle. Their salaries over the past year are listed in Table 3.2. Compute the mean salary for this firm and discuss whether it accurately indicates a typical value.

TABLE 3.2 Salaries of Employees at Acetech

Title	Salary
Administrative Assistant	$ 40,000
Research Assistant	40,000
Computer Programmer	65,000
Senior Research Associate	90,000
Senior Sales Associate	145,000
Chief Financial Officer	150,000
President (and owner)	550,000

SOLUTION: Since all employees of Acetech are included, we calculate the population mean as:

$$\mu = \frac{\Sigma x_i}{N} = \frac{40{,}000 + 40{,}000 + \cdots + 550{,}000}{7} = \$154{,}286.$$

It is true that the mean salary for this firm is $154,286, but this value does not reflect the typical salary at this firm. In fact, six of the seven employees earn less than $154,286. This example highlights the main weakness of the mean, that is, it is very sensitive to extreme observations (extremely large or extremely small values), or outliers.

The Median

Since the mean can be affected by outliers, we often also calculate the **median** as a measure of central location. The median is the middle value of a data set. It divides the data in half; an equal number of observations lie above and below the median. Many government publications and other data sources publish both the mean and the median in order to accurately portray a data set's typical value. If the values of the mean and the median differ significantly, then it is likely that the data set contains outliers. For instance, in 2007 the U.S. Census Bureau determined that the median income for American households was $46,326, whereas the mean income was $63,344. It is well documented that a small number of households in the United States have income considerably higher than the typical American household income. As a result, these top-earning households influence the mean by pushing its value significantly above the value of the median.

THE MEDIAN

The **median** is the middle value of a data set. We arrange the data in ascending (smallest to largest) order and calculate the median as

- The middle value if the number of observations is odd, or
- The average of the two middle values if the number of observations is even.

The median is especially useful when outliers are present.

EXAMPLE 3.3

Use the data in Table 3.2 to calculate the median salary of employees at Acetech.

SOLUTION: In Table 3.2, the data are already arranged in ascending order. We reproduce the salaries along with their relative positions.

Position:	1	2	3	4	5	6	7
Value:	$40,000	40,000	65,000	90,000	145,000	150,000	550,000

Given seven salaries, the median occupies the 4th position. Thus, the median is $90,000. Three salaries are less than $90,000 and three salaries are greater than $90,000. As compared to the mean income of $154,286, the median in this case better reflects the typical salary.

EXAMPLE 3.4

Use the data in Table 3.1 in the introductory case to calculate and interpret the median returns for the Metals and the Income funds.

SOLUTION: Let's start with the median return for the Metals fund. We first arrange the data in ascending order:

Position:	1	2	3	4	5	6	7	8	9	10
Value:	−56.02	−7.34	8.09	18.33	33.35	34.30	36.13	43.79	59.45	76.46

Given 10 observations, the median is the average of the values in the 5th and 6th positions. These values are 33.35 and 34.30, so the median is $\frac{33.35 + 34.30}{2} = 33.83\%$. Over the period 2000–2009, the Metals fund had a median return of 33.83%, which indicates that 5 years had returns less than 33.83% and 5 years had returns greater than 33.83%. A comparison of the median return (33.83%) and the mean return (24.65%) reveals a mean that is less than the median by almost 10 percentage points, which indicates that the Metals data may possibly be affected by very small or large values; we will discuss the detection of outliers later. Thus, in order to give a more transparent description of a data's center, it is wise to report both the mean and the median.

Similarly, we can find the median for the Income fund as 7.34%. In this case, the median return of 7.34% does not appear to deviate drastically from the mean return of 8.51%. This is not surprising since a casual inspection reveals that the relative magnitude of very small or large values is weaker in the Income fund data.

Note that the mean and the median suggest that a typical annual return for the Metals fund is much higher than that for the Income fund. Then why would anyone want to invest in the Income fund? We will come back to this question later in this chapter, when we explore the risk associated with these funds.

The Mode

The **mode** of a data set is the value that occurs most frequently. A data set can have more than one mode, or even no mode. For instance, if we try to calculate the mode return for either the Metals fund or the Income fund in Table 3.1, we see that no value in either fund occurs more than once. Thus, there is no mode value for either fund. If a data set has one mode, then we say it is unimodal. If two or more modes exist, then the data set is multimodal; it is common to call it bimodal in the case of two modes. Generally, the mode's value as a measure of central location tends to diminish with data sets that have more than three modes.

THE MODE

The **mode** is the most frequently occurring value in a data set. A data set may have no mode or more than one mode.

EXAMPLE 3.5

Use the data in Table 3.2 to calculate the modal salary of employees at Acetech.

SOLUTION: The salary $40,000 is earned by two employees. Every other salary occurs just once. So $40,000 is the modal salary. Just because a value occurs with the most frequency does not guarantee that it best reflects the center of the data. It is true that the modal salary at Acetech is $40,000, but most employees earn considerably more than this amount.

In the preceding examples we used measures of central location to describe quantitative data. However, in many instances we want to summarize qualitative data, where the mode is the only meaningful measure of central location.

EXAMPLE 3.6

Kenneth Forbes is a manager at the University of Wisconsin campus bookstore. There has been a recent surge in the sale of women's sweatshirts, which are available in three sizes: Small (S), Medium (M), and Large (L). Kenneth notes that the campus bookstore sold 10 sweatshirts over the weekend in the following sizes:

| S | L | L | M | S | L | M | L | L | M |

Comment on the data set and use the appropriate measure of central location that best reflects the typical size of a sweatshirt.

SOLUTION: This data set is an example of qualitative data. Here, the mode is the only relevant measure of central location. The modal size is L since it appears 5 times as compared to S and M, which appear 2 and 3 times, respectively. Often, when examining issues relating to the demand for a product, such as replenishing stock, the mode tends to be the most relevant measure of central location.

Using Excel to Calculate Measures of Central Location

In general, Excel offers a couple of ways to calculate most of the descriptive measures that we discuss in this chapter.

Excel's Formula Option

Excel provides built-in formulas for virtually every summary measure that we may need. To illustrate, we follow these steps to calculate the mean for the Metals fund.

A. Open the data labeled ***Fund_Returns*** (Table 3.1) from the text website into an Excel spreadsheet and select an empty cell.

B. From the menu choose **Formulas > Insert Function**. In the *Insert Function* dialog box, choose **Statistical** under *Select a Category*. Here you will see a list of all the relevant summary measures that Excel calculates.

C. Since we want to calculate the mean return for the Metals fund, under *Select a Function* choose **AVERAGE**. Click **OK**.

D. See Figure 3.1. In the *Average* dialog box, click on the box to the right of *Number 1* and then select the Metals data. Click **OK**. You should see the value 24.65, which equals the value that we calculated manually. In order to calculate the median and the mode, we repeat these steps, but we choose MEDIAN and MODE as the functions instead of AVERAGE.

Once you get familiar with Excel's function names, an easier way to perform these calculations is to select an empty cell in the spreadsheet and input '=Function Name(array)', where you replace Function Name with Excel's syntax for that particular function and select the relevant data for the array or input the cell designations. For example, when calculating the mean for the Metals fund, we input '=AVERAGE(B2:B11)'; the data for the Metals return data are occupying cells B2 through B11 on the spreadsheet. After choosing <Enter>, Excel returns the function result in the cell. When introducing new functions later in this chapter and other chapters, we will follow this format.

FIGURE 3.1 Excel's AVERAGE dialog box

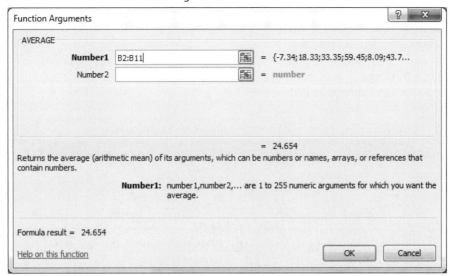

Excel's Data Analysis Toolpak Option

Another way to obtain values for the mean, the median, and the mode is to use Excel's Data Analysis Toolpak option. One advantage of this option is that it provides numerous summary measures using a single command. Again, we illustrate this option using the data from the introductory case.

A. Open the data labeled **Fund_Returns** (Table 3.1) from the text website into an Excel spreadsheet.

B. From the menu choose **Data > Data Analysis > Descriptive Statistics > OK**. (Note: As mentioned in Chapter 2, if you do not see **Data Analysis** under **Data**, you must *Add-in* the Analysis Toolpak option.)

C. See Figure 3.2. In the *Descriptive Statistics* dialog box, click on the box next to *Input Range*, then select the data. If you included the fund names when you high-lighted the data, make sure you click on the option next to *Labels in First Row*. Click the box in front of *Summary Statistics*. Then click **OK**.

FIGURE 3.2 Excel's Descriptive Statistics dialog box

D. Table 3.3 presents the Excel output. If the output is difficult to read, highlight the data and choose **Home** > **Format** > **Column** > **Autofit Selection**. As noted earlier, Excel provides numerous summary measures; we have put the measures of central location in boldface. (Measures of dispersion are also in boldface; we analyze these measures in more detail shortly.) Note that Excel reports the mode as #N/A, which means 'no value is available'; this is consistent with our finding that no value in the data appeared more than once.

TABLE 3.3 Excel Output Using Descriptive Statistics Dialog Box

Metals		Income	
Mean	**24.654**	**Mean**	**8.514**
Standard Error	11.7414004	Standard Error	3.4997715
Median	**33.825**	**Median**	**7.335**
Mode	**#N/A**	Mode	**#N/A**
Standard Deviation	**37.1295681**	**Standard Deviation**	**11.067249**
Sample Variance	**1378.60483**	**Sample Variance**	**122.484**
Kurtosis	1.668701	Kurtosis	2.3615757
Skewness	−1.0076169	Skewness	0.5602496
Range	**132.48**	**Range**	**43.14**
Minimum	−56.02	Minimum	−11.37
Maximum	76.46	Maximum	31.77
Sum	246.54	Sum	85.14
Count	10	Count	10

In Chapter 2, we used histograms to discuss **symmetry** and **skewness**. Recall that the distribution is symmetric if one side of the histogram is a mirror image of the other side. For a symmetric and unimodal distribution, the mean, the median, and the mode are equal. In business applications, it is common to encounter data that are skewed. The mean is usually greater than the median when the data are positively skewed and less than the median when the data are negatively skewed. We would also like to comment on the numerical measure of skewness that Excel reports, even though we will not discuss its calculation. A skewness coefficient of zero indicates the data values are relatively evenly distributed on both sides of the mean. A positive skewness coefficient implies that extreme values are concentrated in the right tail of the distribution, pulling the mean up, relative to the median and the bulk of values lie to the left of the mean. Similarly, a negative skewness coefficient implies that extreme values are concentrated in the left tail of the distribution, pulling the mean down, relative to the median and the bulk of values lie to the right of the mean. We find that the returns are negatively skewed (Skewness = −1.0076) for the Metals fund and positively skewed (Skewness = 0.5602) for the Income fund.

So far we have focused on applications where each observation in the data contributed equally to the mean. The **weighted mean** is relevant when some observations contribute more than others. For example, a student is often evaluated on the basis of the weighted mean since the score on the final exam is typically worth more than the score on the midterm.

THE WEIGHTED MEAN

Let $w_1, w_2, \ldots, w_n$ denote the weights of the sample observations $x_1, x_2, \ldots, x_n$ such that $w_1 + w_2 + \cdots + w_n = 1$. The **weighted mean** for the sample is computed as

$$\bar{x} = \Sigma w_i x_i.$$

The weighted mean for the population is computed similarly.

EXAMPLE 3.7

A student scores 60 on Exam 1, 70 on Exam 2, and 80 on Exam 3. What is the student's average score for the course if Exams 1, 2, and 3 are worth 25%, 25%, and 50% of the grade, respectively?

SOLUTION: We define the weights as $w_1 = 0.25$, $w_2 = 0.25$, and $w_3 = 0.50$. We compute the average score as $\bar{x} = \Sigma w_i x_i = 0.25(60) + 0.25(70) + 0.50(80) = 72.50$. Note that the unweighted mean is only 70 as it does not incorporate the higher weight given to the score on Exam 3.

EXERCISES 3.1

Mechanics

1. Given the following observations from a sample, calculate the mean, the median, and the mode.

8	10	9	12	12

2. Given the following observations from a sample, calculate the mean, the median, and the mode.

−4	0	−6	1	−3	−4

3. Given the following observations from a population, calculate the mean, the median, and the mode.

150	257	55	110	110	43	201	125	55

4. Given the following observations from a population, calculate the mean, the median, and the mode.

20	15	25	20	10	15	25	20	15

Applications

5. At a small firm in Boston, seven employees were asked to report their one-way commute time (in minutes) into the city. Their responses were.

20	35	90	45	40	35	50

   a. How long was the shortest commute? The longest commute?
   b. Calculate the mean, the median, and the mode.

6. In order to get an idea on current buying trends, a real estate agent collects data on 10 recent house sales in the area. Specifically, she notes the number of bedrooms in each house as follows:

3	4	3	3	5	2	4	2	5	6

   a. Calculate the mean, the median, and the mode.
   b. Which measure of central location best reflects the typical value with respect to the number of bedrooms in recent house sales?

7. The following table shows the 10 highest-paid chief executive officers of the last decade.

Name	Firm	Compensation (in millions)
Lawrence Ellison	Oracle	$1,835.7
Barry Diller	IAC, Expedia	1,142.9
Ray Irani	Occidental Petroleum	857.1
Steve Jobs	Apple	748.8
Richard Fairbank	Capital One	568.5
Angelo Mozilo	Countrywide	528.6
Eugene Isenberg	Nabors Industries	518.0
Terry Semel	Yahoo	489.6
Henry Silverman	Cendant	481.2
William McGuire	UnitedHealth Group	469.3

SOURCE: *The Wall Street Journal*, July 27, 2010.

   a. Calculate the mean compensation for the 10 highest-paid chief executive officers.
   b. Does the mean accurately reflect the center of the data? Explain.

8. An investor bought common stock of Microsoft Corporation on three occasions at the following prices.

Date	Price Per Share	Number of Shares
January 2009	$19.58	70
July 2009	$24.06	80
December 2009	$29.54	50

   Calculate the average price per share at which the investor bought these shares.

9. You score 90 on the midterm, 60 on the final, and 80 on the class project. What is your average score if the midterm is worth 30%, the final is worth 50%, and the class project is worth 20%?

10. An investor bought common stock of Dell Inc. on three occasions at the following prices.

Date	Price Per Share
January 2009	$10.34
July 2009	$13.98
December 2009	$14.02

a. What is the average price per share if the investor had bought 100 shares in January, 60 in July, and 40 in December?

b. What is the average price per share if the investor had bought 40 shares in January, 60 in July, and 100 in December?

11. **FILE** The following table shows Fortune 500's rankings of America's 10 largest corporations for 2010. Next to each corporation is its market capitalization (in billions of dollars as of March 26, 2010) and its total return to investors for the year 2009. These data, labeled **Largest_Corporations**, are also available on the text website.

Company	Mkt. Cap. (in $ billions)	Total Return
Walmart	$209	−2.7%
Exxon Mobil	314	−12.6
Chevron	149	8.1
General Electric	196	−0.4
Bank of America	180	7.3
ConocoPhillips	78	2.9
AT&T	155	4.8
Ford Motor	47	336.7
JP Morgan Chase	188	19.9
Hewlett-Packard	125	43.1

Source: http://money.cnn.com, May 3, 2010.

a. Calculate the mean and the median for market capitalization.

b. Calculate the mean and the median for total return.

c. For each variable (market capitalization and total return), comment on which measure better reflects central location.

12. **FILE** One important statistic in baseball is a pitcher's earned run average, or ERA. This number represents the average number of earned runs given up by the pitcher per nine innings. The following table lists a portion of the ERAs for pitchers playing for the New York Yankees and the Baltimore Orioles as of July 22, 2010; the complete data, labeled **ERA**, are available on the text website.

New York Yankees	ERA	Baltimore Orioles	ERA
Sabathia	3.13	Guthrie	4.58
Pettitte	2.88	Millwood	5.77
⋮	⋮	⋮	⋮

Source: http://www.mlb.com.

a. Calculate the mean and the median ERAs for the New York Yankees.

b. Calculate the mean and the median ERAs for the Baltimore Orioles.

c. Based solely on your calculations above, which team is likely to have the better winning record? Explain.

13. **FILE** The following table shows a portion of the sale price (in $1,000s) for 36 homes sold in Mission Viejo, CA, during June 2010; the entire data set, labeled **MV_Houses**, can be found on the text website.

Number	Sale Price (in $1,000s)
1	$430
2	520
⋮	⋮
36	430

Calculate the mean, the median, and the mode.

14. **FILE** The accompanying table shows a portion of the average price for a gallon of gas for the 50 states during entire data set. The entire data set, labeled **Gas_Prices_2012**, is available on the text website.

State	Price per Gallon
Alabama	$4.36
Alaska	3.79
⋮	⋮
Wyoming	3.63

Source: http://AAA.com, data retrieved April 16, 2012.

Find the mean, the median, and the mode for the price per gallon.

15. **FILE** The following table lists a portion of U.S. life expectancy (in years) for the 50 states; the entire data set, labeled **Life_Expectancy**, can be found on the text website.

Rank	State	Life Expectancy (in years)
1	Hawaii	81.5
2	Alaska	80.9
⋮	⋮	⋮
50	Mississippi	74.8

Source: http://en.wikipedia.org/wiki/List_of_U.S._states_by_life_expectancy, data retrieved April 25, 2012.

Find the mean, the median, and the mode of life expectancy.

3.2 Percentiles and Box Plots

As discussed earlier, the median is a measure of central location that divides the data in half; that is, half of the data points fall below the median and half fall above that value. The median is also called the 50th percentile. In many instances, we are interested in a **percentile** other than the 50th percentile. Here we discuss calculating and interpreting percentiles. Generally, percentiles are calculated for large data sets; for ease of exposition, we show their use with small data sets. In addition, we construct a box plot, which is, more or less, a visual representation of particular percentiles. It also helps us identify outliers and skewness in the data.

LO **3.2**

Calculate and interpret percentiles and a box plot.

Percentiles provide detailed information about how data are spread over the interval from the smallest value to the largest value. You have probably been exposed to percentiles. For example, the SAT is the most widely used test in the undergraduate admissions process. Scores on the math portion of the SAT range from 200 to 800. Suppose you obtained a raw score of 650 on this section of the test. It may not be readily apparent how you did relative to other students that took the same test. However, if you know that the raw score corresponds to the 75th percentile, then you know that approximately 75% of students had scores lower than your score and approximately 25% of students had scores higher than your score.

PERCENTILES

In general, the *p*th **percentile** divides a data set into two parts:

- Approximately *p* percent of the observations have values less than the *p*th percentile;

- Approximately $(100 - p)$ percent of the observations have values greater than the *p*th percentile.

Calculating the *p*th Percentile

A. First arrange the data in ascending (smallest to largest) order.

B. Locate the approximate position of the percentile by calculating L_p:

$$L_p = (n + 1)\frac{p}{100},$$

where L_p indicates the location of the desired *p*th percentile and *n* is the sample size. For the population percentile, replace *n* by *N*. For example, we set $p = 50$ for the median as it is the 50th percentile.

C. Once you find the value for L_p, observe whether or not L_p is an integer:

- If L_p is an integer, then L_p denotes the location of the *p*th percentile. For instance, if L_{20} is equal to 2, then the 20th percentile is equal to the second observation in the ordered data set.

- If L_p is not an integer, we need to interpolate between two observations to approximate the desired percentile. So if L_{20} is equal to 2.25, then we need to interpolate 25% of the distance between the second and third observations in order to find the 20th percentile.

EXAMPLE 3.8

Consider the information presented in the introductory case of this chapter. Calculate and interpret the 25th and the 75th percentiles for the Metals fund.

SOLUTION: The first step is to arrange the data in ascending order:

Position:	1	2	3	4	5	6	7	8	9	10
Value:	−56.02	−7.34	8.09	18.33	33.35	34.30	36.13	43.79	59.45	76.46

For the 25th percentile: $L_{25} = (n + 1)\frac{p}{100} = (10 + 1)\frac{25}{100} = 2.75$. So, the 25th percentile is located 75% of the distance between the second and third observations; it is calculated as

$$-7.34 + 0.75(8.09 - (-7.34)) = -7.34 + 11.57 = 4.23.$$

Thus, 25% of the returns were less than 4.23% and 75% of the returns were greater than 4.23%.

For the 75th percentile: $L_{75} = (n + 1)\frac{p}{100} = (10 + 1)\frac{75}{100} = 8.25$. So, the 75th percentile is located 25% of the distance between the eighth and ninth observations; it is calculated as

$$43.79 + 0.25(59.45 - 43.79) = 43.79 + 3.92 = 47.71.$$

Thus, 75% of the returns were less than 47.71% and 25% of the returns were greater than 47.71%.

Earlier we calculated the median or the 50th percentile for the Metals fund and obtained a value of 33.83%. When we calculate the 25th, the 50th, and the 75th percentiles for a data set, we have effectively divided the data into four equal parts, or quarters. Thus, the 25th percentile is also referred to as the first quartile (Q1), the 50th percentile is referred to as the second quartile (Q2), and the 75th percentile is referred to as the third quartile (Q3).

Constructing and Interpreting a Box Plot

A **box plot**, also referred to as a box-and-whisker plot, is a convenient way to graphically display the minimum value (Min), the quartiles (Q1, Q2, and Q3), and the maximum value (Max) of a data set. Using our results from the Metals fund, Table 3.4 summarizes the five values that we will plot:

TABLE 3.4 Summary Values for the Metals Fund

Min	Q1	Q2	Q3	Max
−56.02%	4.23%	33.83%	47.71%	76.46%

The values in Table 3.4 are often referred to as the five-number summary for the data set. Box plots are particularly useful when comparing similar information gathered at another place or time. They also are used as an effective tool for identifying outliers and skewness. In Section 3.1 we discussed that the mean is unduly influenced by outliers. Sometimes outliers may indicate bad data due to incorrectly recorded observations or incorrectly included observations in the data set. In such cases, the relevant observations should be corrected or simply deleted from the data set. Alternatively, outliers may just be due to random variations, in which case the relevant observations should remain in the data set. In any event, it is important to be able to identify potential outliers so that one can take corrective actions, if needed.

In order to construct a box plot, we follow these steps.

A. Plot the five-number summary values in ascending order on the horizontal axis.

B. Draw a box encompassing the first and third quartiles.

C. Draw a dashed vertical line in the box at the median.

D. To determine if a given observation is an outlier, first calculate the difference between Q3 and Q1. This difference is called the **interquartile range** or IQR. Therefore, the length of the box is equal to the IQR and the span of the box contains the middle half of the data. Draw a line ("whisker") that extends from Q1 to the minimum data value that is not farther than $1.5 \times$ IQR from Q1. Similarly, draw a line that extends from Q3 to the maximum data value that is not farther than $1.5 \times$ IQR from Q3.

E. Use an asterisk to indicate points that are farther than $1.5 \times$ IQR from the box. These points are considered outliers.

Consider the box plot in Figure 3.3 for illustration. In the figure, the left whisker extends from Q1 to Min since Min is not farther than $1.5 \times$ IQR from Q1. The right whisker, on the other hand, does not extend from Q3 to Max since there is an observation that is farther than $1.5 \times$ IQR from Q3. The asterisk on the right indicates this observation is considered an outlier.

Box plots are also used to informally gauge the shape of the distribution. Symmetry is implied if the median is in the center of the box and the left and right whiskers are equidistant from their respective quartiles. If the median is left of center and the right whisker is longer than the left whisker, then the distribution is positively skewed. Similarly, if the median is right of center and the left whisker is longer than the right whisker, then the distribution is negatively skewed. From Figure 3.3, we note that the median is located to the left of center and the right whisker is longer than the left whisker. This indicates that the underlying distribution is positively skewed.

FIGURE 3.3 A sample box plot

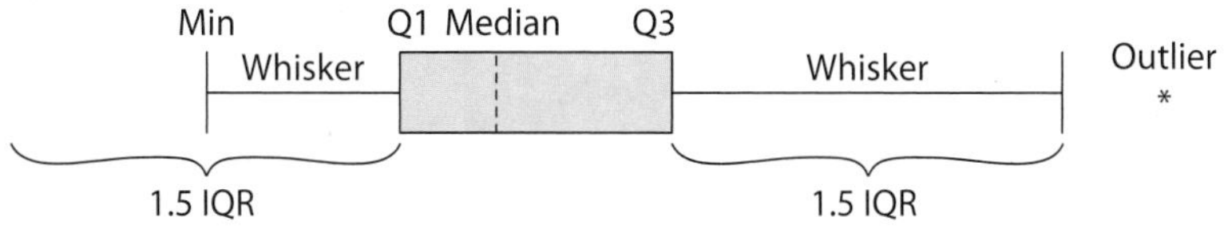

EXAMPLE 3.9

Use the information presented in the introductory case of this chapter to construct and interpret the box plot for the Metals fund.

SOLUTION: Based on the information in Table 3.4, we calculate the IQR as the difference between Q3 and Q1, or $47.71\% - 4.23\% = 43.48\%$. We then calculate $1.5 \times$ IQR, or $1.5 \times 43.48\% = 65.22\%$. The distance between Q1 and the smallest value, $4.23 - (-56.02\%) = 60.25\%$, is within the limit of 65.22%; thus, the line will extend to the minimum value of -56.02% on the left side of the box plot (see Figure 3.4). Similarly, the distance between the largest value and Q3, $76.46\% - 47.71\% = 28.75$, is also well within the limit of 65.22%; here the line will extend to the right up to the maximum value of 76.46%. Given the criteria for constructing a box plot, there are no outliers in this data set.

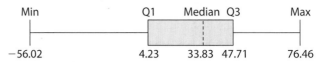

FIGURE 3.4 Box plot for the Metals Fund

| Min | Q1 | Median | Q3 | Max |

−56.02   4.23   33.83 47.71   76.46

From this box plot we can quickly grasp several points concerning the distribution of returns for the Metals fund. First, returns range from −56.02% to 76.46%, with about half being less than 33.83% and half being greater than 33.83%. We make two further observations: (1) the median is off-center within the box, being located to the right of center, and (2) the left whisker is longer than the right whisker. This suggests that the distribution is negatively skewed.

EXERCISES 3.2

Mechanics

16. Calculate the 20th, 50th, and 80th percentiles for the following data set:

| 120 | 215 | 187 | 343 | 268 | 196 | 312 |

17. Calculate the 20th, 40th, and 70th percentiles for the following data set:

| −300 | −257 | −325 | −234 | −297 | −362 | −255 |

18. Consider the following box plot.

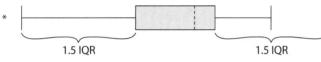

1.5 IQR   1.5 IQR

a. Does the above box plot indicate possible outliers in the data?
b. Comment on the skewness of the underlying distribution.

19. Consider the following box plot.

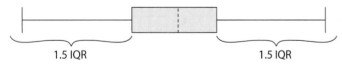

1.5 IQR   1.5 IQR

a. Does the above box plot indicate possible outliers in the data?
b. Comment on the skewness of the underlying distribution.

20. Consider the following data set:

| 12 | 9 | 27 | 15 | 58 | 35 | 21 | 32 | 22 |

a. Calculate and interpret the 25th, 50th, and 75th percentiles.
b. Construct a box plot. Are there any outliers?

21. Consider the following data set:

| 0.04 | 0.10 | −0.05 | −0.02 | 0.08 | 0.15 | −0.09 |

a. Calculate and interpret the 25th, 50th, and 75th percentiles.
b. Construct a box plot. Are there any outliers?

Applications

22. Scores on the final in a statistics class are as follows.

| 75 | 25 | 75 | 62 | 80 | 85 | 80 | 99 | 90 | 60 |
| 86 | 92 | 40 | 74 | 72 | 65 | 87 | 70 | 85 | 70 |

a. Calculate and interpret the 25th, 50th, and 75th percentiles.
b. Construct a box plot. Are there any outliers? Is the distribution symmetric? If not, comment on its skewness.

23. Consider the return data (in percent) for the Income fund in Table 3.1.

a. Calculate and interpret the 25th, 50th, and 75th percentiles.
b. Construct a box plot. Are there any outliers?
c. Is the distribution symmetric? If not, comment on its skewness.

24. **FILE** A price-earnings ratio or P/E ratio is calculated as a firm's share price compared to the income or profit earned by the firm per share. Generally, a high P/E ratio suggests that investors are expecting higher earnings growth in the future compared to companies with a lower P/E ratio. The accompanying table shows a portion of companies that comprise the Dow Jones Industrial Average (DJIA) and their P/E ratios as of May 17, 2012 (at the time data were retrieved, the P/E ratio for one firm on the DJIA, Bank of America, was not available). The entire data set, labeled **PE_Ratio**, can be found on the text website.

Company	P/E Ratio
3M (MMM)	14
Alcoa (AA)	24
⋮	⋮
Walt Disney (DIS)	14

a. Calculate and interpret the 25th, 50th, and 75th percentiles.

b. Construct a box plot. Are there any outliers? Is the distribution symmetric? If not, comment on its skewness.

25. **FILE** The accompanying table shows a portion of median household income (Income) and median house value (House Value) for the 50 states in 2010. The entire data set, labeled **Census**, can be found on the text website.

State	Income	House Value
Alabama	$42,081	$117,600
Alaska	66,521	229,100
⋮	⋮	⋮
Wyoming	53,802	174,000

Source: 2010 U.S. Census.

a. Construct a box plot for household income and use it to identify outliers, if any, and comment on skewness.
b. Construct a box plot for median house value and use it to identify outliers, if any, and comment on skewness.
c. Are you surprised by the above results?

3.3 Measures of Dispersion

In Section 3.1, we focused on measures of central location, in an attempt to find a typical or central value that describes the data. It is also important to analyze how the data vary around the center. Recall that over the 10-year period 2000–2009, the average returns for the Metals and Income funds were 24.65% and 8.51%, respectively. As an investor you might ask why anyone would put money in the Income fund when, on average, this fund has a lower return. The answer to this question will become readily apparent once we analyze measures of variability or dispersion.

Table 3.5 shows each fund's minimum and maximum returns, as well as each fund's average return, over this time period. Note that the average return for the Income fund is relatively closer to its minimum and maximum returns as compared to the Metals fund. The comparison of the funds illustrates that the average is not sufficient when summarizing a data set; that is, it fails to describe the underlying variability of the data.

LO **3.3**

Calculate and interpret the range, the mean absolute deviation, the variance, the standard deviation, and the coefficient of variation.

TABLE 3.5 Select Measures for the Metal and Income Funds, 2000–2009

	Minimum Return	Average Return	Maximum Return
Metals fund	−56.02%	24.65%	76.46%
Income fund	−11.37%	8.51%	31.77%

We now discuss several measures of dispersion that gauge the variability of a data set. Each measure is a numerical value that equals zero if all data values are identical, and increases as data values become more diverse.

Range

The **range** is the simplest measure of dispersion; it is the difference between the maximum (Max) and the minimum (Min) values in a data set.

$$\textbf{Range} = \text{Max} - \text{Min}.$$

EXAMPLE 3.10

Use the data in Table 3.5 to calculate the range for the Metals and the Income funds.

SOLUTION:

Metals fund: $76.46\% - (-56.02\%) = 132.48\%$

Income fund: $31.77\% - (-11.37\%) = 43.14\%$

The Metals fund has the higher value for the range, indicating that it has more dispersion with respect to its minimum and maximum values.

The range is not considered a good measure of dispersion because it focuses solely on the extreme values and ignores every other observation in the data set. While the interquartile range, IQR = Q3 − Q1, discussed in Section 3.2, does not depend on the extreme values, this measure still does not incorporate all the data.

The Mean Absolute Deviation

A good measure of dispersion should consider differences of all observations from the mean. If we simply average all differences from the mean, the positives and the negatives will cancel out, even though they both contribute to dispersion, and the resulting average will equal zero. The **mean absolute deviation** (MAD) is an average of the absolute differences between the observations and the mean.

THE MEAN ABSOLUTE DEVIATION (MAD)

For sample values, $x_1, x_2, \ldots, x_n$, the **sample MAD** is computed as

$$\text{Sample MAD} = \frac{\Sigma |x_i - \bar{x}|}{n}.$$

For population values, $x_1, x_2, \ldots, x_N$, the **population MAD** is computed as

$$\text{Population MAD} = \frac{\Sigma |x_i - \mu|}{N}.$$

EXAMPLE 3.11

Use the data in Table 3.1 to calculate MAD for the Metals and the Income funds.

SOLUTION: We first compute MAD for the Metals fund. The second column in Table 3.6 shows differences from the sample mean, $\bar{x} = 24.65$. As mentioned above, the sum of these differences equals zero (or a number very close to zero due to rounding). The third column shows the absolute value of each deviation from the mean. Summing these values yields the numerator for the MAD formula.

TABLE 3.6 MAD Calculations for the Metals Fund

x_i	$x_i - \bar{x}$	$|x_i - \bar{x}|$
−7.34	−7.34 − 24.65 = −31.99	31.99
18.33	18.33 − 24.65 = −6.32	6.32
⋮	⋮	⋮
76.46	76.46 − 24.65 = 51.81	51.81
	Total = 0 (subject to rounding)	Total = 271.12

For the Metals fund: $\text{MAD} = \frac{\Sigma |x_i - \bar{x}|}{n} = \frac{271.12}{10} = 27.11.$

Similar calculations for the Income fund yield: $\text{MAD} = \frac{\Sigma |x_i - \bar{x}|}{n} = \frac{70.30}{10} = 7.03.$

The Income fund has a smaller value for MAD than the Metals fund, again indicating a less dispersed data set.

The Variance and the Standard Deviation

The **variance** and the **standard deviation** are the two most widely used measures of dispersion. Instead of calculating the average of the absolute differences from the mean, as in MAD, we calculate the average of the squared differences from the mean. The squaring of differences from the mean emphasizes larger differences more than smaller ones; MAD weighs large and small differences equally.

The variance is defined as the average of the squared differences between the observations and the mean. The formula for the variance differs depending on whether we have a sample or a population. We also note that variance squares the original units of measurement. In order to return to the original units of measurement, we take the positive square root of variance, which gives us the standard deviation.

THE VARIANCE AND THE STANDARD DEVIATION

For sample values $x_1, x_2, \ldots, x_n$, the **sample variance** s^2 and the **sample standard deviation** s are computed as

$$s^2 = \frac{\Sigma(x_i - \bar{x})^2}{n - 1} \qquad \text{and} \qquad s = \sqrt{s^2}.$$

For population values $x_1, x_2, \ldots, x_N$, the **population variance** σ^2 (the Greek letter sigma, squared) and the **population standard deviation** σ are computed as

$$\sigma^2 = \frac{\Sigma(x_i - \mu)^2}{N} \qquad \text{and} \qquad \sigma = \sqrt{\sigma^2}.$$

Note: The sample variance uses $n - 1$ rather than n in the denominator; the reason is discussed in Chapter 8.

EXAMPLE 3.12

Use the data in Table 3.1 to calculate the sample variance and the sample standard deviation for the Metals and the Income funds. Express the answers in the correct units of measurement.

SOLUTION: We will show the calculations for the Metals fund with the mean return of 24.65 percent. The second column in Table 3.7 shows each return less the mean. The third column shows the square of each deviation from the mean. Summing these values yields the numerator for the sample variance formula.

TABLE 3.7 Sample Variance Calculation for the Metals Fund

x_i	$x_i - \bar{x}$	$(x_i - \bar{x})^2$
-7.34	$-7.34 - 24.65 = -31.99$	$(-31.99)^2 = 1{,}023.36$
18.33	$18.33 - 24.65 = -6.32$	$(-6.32)^2 = 39.94$
$\vdots$	$\vdots$	$\vdots$
76.46	$76.46 - 24.65 = 51.81$	$(51.81)^2 = 2{,}684.28$
	Total $= 0$ (subject to rounding)	Total $= 12{,}407.44$

For the Metals fund: $s^2 = \dfrac{\Sigma(x_i - \bar{x})^2}{n - 1} = \dfrac{12{,}407.44}{10 - 1} = 1{,}378.60(\%)^2$. Note that the units of measurement are squared. The sample standard deviation is $s = \sqrt{1{,}378.60} = 37.13(\%)$.

Similar calculations for the Income fund yield

$$s^2 = \frac{\Sigma(x_i - \bar{x})^2}{n - 1} = \frac{1{,}102.34}{10 - 1} = 122.48(\%)^2 \text{ and } s = \sqrt{122.48} = 11.07(\%).$$

Based on all measures of dispersion discussed thus far, we can conclude that the Income fund is less dispersed than the Metals fund. With financial data, standard deviation tends to be the most common measure of risk. Therefore the investment risk of the Income fund is lower than that of the Metals fund.

The Coefficient of Variation

In some instances, analysis entails comparing the variability of two or more data sets that have different means or units of measurement. The **coefficient of variation (CV)** serves as a relative measure of dispersion and adjusts for differences in the magnitudes of the means. Calculated by dividing a data set's standard deviation by its mean, CV is a unitless measure that allows for direct comparisons of mean-adjusted dispersion across different data sets.

THE COEFFICIENT OF VARIATION (CV)

$$\text{Sample CV} = \frac{s}{\bar{x}}$$

$$\text{Population CV} = \frac{\sigma}{\mu}$$

EXAMPLE 3.13

Calculate and interpret the coefficient of variation for the Metals and Income funds.

SOLUTION: We use the sample means and the standard deviations computed earlier.

$$\text{For the Metals fund: } CV = \frac{s}{\bar{x}} = \frac{37.13\%}{24.65\%} = 1.51.$$

$$\text{For the Income fund: } CV = \frac{s}{\bar{x}} = \frac{11.07\%}{8.51\%} = 1.30.$$

Since 1.51 is greater than 1.30, we can conclude that the data for the Metals fund have more relative dispersion than the Income fund.

Using Excel to Calculate Measures of Dispersion

Excel's Formula Option

As discussed in Section 3.1, Excel provides built-in formulas for most summary measures. Table 3.8 shows each measure of dispersion that we discussed and its corresponding Function Name in Excel. For example, in order to calculate the standard deviation for the Metals fund, we open the **_Fund_Returns_** data from the text website. We find an empty cell and insert ′=STDEV.S(B2:B11)′ and then choose **\<Enter\>**. Excel returns a value of 37.13, which matches the value that we calculated by hand.

TABLE 3.8 Excel's Functions for Measures of Dispersion

Measure of Dispersion	Excel Function Name
Range	=MAX(array) − MIN(array)
Mean Absolute Deviation	=AVEDEV(array)
Sample Variance	=VAR.S(array)
Sample Standard Deviation	=STDEV.S(array)
Population Variance	=VAR.P(array)
Population Standard Deviation	=STDEV.P(array)
Coefficient of Variation (Sample)	=STDEV.S(array)/AVERAGE(array)
Coefficient of Variation (Population)	=STDEV.P(array)/AVERAGE(array)

Excel's Data Analysis Toolpak Option

In Section 3.1 we also discussed using Excel's Data Analysis Toolpak option, **Data > Data Analysis > Descriptive Statistics**, for calculating summary measures. For measures of variability, Excel treats the data as a sample and calculates the range, the sample variance, and the sample standard deviation. These values for the Metals and Income funds are shown in boldface in Table 3.3.

SYNOPSIS OF INTRODUCTORY CASE

Vanguard's Precious Metals and Mining fund (Metals) and Fidelity's Strategic Income fund (Income) were two top-performing mutual funds for the years 2000 through 2009. An analysis of annual return data for these two funds provides important information for any type of investor. Over the past 10 years, the Metals fund posts the higher values for both the mean return and the median return, with values of 24.65% and 33.83%, respectively. When the mean differs dramatically from the median, it is often indicative of extreme values or outliers. Although the mean and the median for the Metals fund do differ by almost 10 percentage points, a boxplot analysis reveals no outliers. The mean return and the median return for the Income fund, on the other hand, are quite comparable at 8.51% and 7.34%, respectively.

While measures of central location typically represent the reward of investing, these measures do not incorporate the risk of investing. Standard deviation tends to be the most common measure of risk with financial data. Since the standard deviation for the Metals fund is substantially greater than the standard deviation for the Income fund (37.13% > 11.07%), the Metals fund is likelier to have returns far above as well as far below its mean. Also, the coefficient of variation—a relative measure of dispersion—for the Metals fund is greater than the coefficient of variation for the Income fund. These two measures of dispersion indicate that the Metals fund is the riskier investment. These funds provide credence to the theory that funds with higher average returns often carry higher risk.

EXERCISES 3.3

Mechanics

26. Consider the following population data:

34	42	12	10	22

a. Calculate the range.
b. Calculate MAD.
c. Calculate the population variance.
d. Calculate the population standard deviation.

27. Consider the following population data:

0	−4	2	−8	10

a. Calculate the range.
b. Calculate MAD.
c. Calculate the population variance.
d. Calculate the population standard deviation.

28. Consider the following sample data:

40	48	32	52	38	42

   a. Calculate the range.
   b. Calculate MAD.
   c. Calculate the sample variance.
   d. Calculate the sample standard deviation.

29. Consider the following sample data:

−10	12	−8	−2	−6	8

   a. Calculate the range.
   b. Calculate MAD.
   c. Calculate the sample variance and the sample standard deviation.

Applications

30. The Department of Transportation (DOT) fields thousands of complaints about airlines each year. The DOT categorizes and tallies complaints, and then periodically publishes rankings of airline performance. The following table presents the 2006 results for the 10 largest U.S. airlines.

Airline	Complaints*	Airline	Complaints*
Southwest Airlines	1.82	Northwest Airlines	8.84
JetBlue Airways	3.98	Delta Airlines	10.35
Alaska Airlines	5.24	American Airlines	10.87
AirTran Airways	6.24	US Airways	13.59
Continental Airlines	8.83	United Airlines	13.60

Source: Department of Transportation; *per million passengers.

   a. Which airline fielded the least amount of complaints? Which airline fielded the most? Calculate the range.
   b. Calculate the mean and the median number of complaints for this sample.
   c. Calculate the variance and the standard deviation.

31. The monthly closing stock prices (rounded to the nearest dollar) for Starbucks Corp. and Panera Bread Co. for the first six months of 2010 are reported in the following table.

Month	Starbucks Corp.	Panera Bread Co.
January 2010	$22	$71
February 2010	23	73
March 2010	24	76
April 2010	26	78
May 2010	26	81
June 2010	24	75

Source: http://www.finance.yahoo.com.

   a. Calculate the sample variance and the sample standard deviation for each firm's stock price.
   b. Which firm's stock price had greater variability as measured by the standard deviation?
   c. Which firm's stock price had the greater relative dispersion?

32. **FILE** While the housing market is in recession and is not likely to emerge anytime soon, real estate investment in college towns continues to promise good returns (*The Wall Street Journal*, September 24, 2010). Marcela Treisman works for an investment firm in Michigan. Her assignment is to analyze the rental market in Ann Arbor, which is home to the University of Michigan. She gathers data on monthly rent for 2011 along with the square footage of 40 homes. A portion of the data is shown in the accompanying table; the entire data set, labeled ***AnnArbor_Rental***, can be found on the text website.

Monthly Rent	Square Footage
645	500
675	648
⋮	⋮
2400	2700

Source: http://www.zillow.com.

   a. Calculate the mean and the standard deviation for monthly rent.
   b. Calculate the mean and the standard deviation for square footage.
   c. Which sample data exhibit greater relative dispersion?

33. **FILE** Go to the text website and access the data labeled ***Largest_Corporations***. It shows the Fortune 500 rankings of America's largest corporations for 2010. Next to each corporation are its market capitalization (in billions of dollars as of March 26, 2010) and its total return to investors for the year 2009.

   a. Calculate the coefficient of variation for market capitalization.
   b. Calculate the coefficient of variation for total return.
   c. Which sample data exhibit greater relative dispersion?

34. **FILE** Go to the text website and access the data labeled ***Census***. It shows, among other variables, median household income and median house value for the 50 states.

   a. Compute and discuss the range of household income and house value.
   b. Compute the sample MAD and the sample standard deviation of household income and house value.
   c. Discuss why we cannot directly compare the sample MAD and the standard deviations of the two data sets.

3.4 Mean-Variance Analysis and the Sharpe Ratio

In the introduction to Section 3.3, we asked why any rational investor would invest in the Income fund over the Metals fund since the average return for the Income fund over the 2000–2009 period was approximately 9%, whereas the average return for the Metals fund was close to 25%. It turns out that investments with higher returns also carry higher risk. Investments include financial assets such as stocks, bonds, and mutual funds. The average return represents an investor's reward, whereas variance, or equivalently standard deviation, corresponds to risk. That is, the higher the average associated with the return on a particular stock, bond, or mutual fund, the higher is the reward. Similarly, the higher the variance, the higher is the level of risk.

According to mean-variance analysis, we can measure performance of any risky asset solely on the basis of the average and the variance of its returns.

LO **3.4**

Explain mean-variance analysis and the Sharpe ratio.

MEAN-VARIANCE ANALYSIS

Mean-variance analysis postulates that we measure the performance of an asset by its rate of return and evaluate this rate of return in terms of its reward (mean) and risk (variance). In general, investments with higher average returns are also associated with higher risk.

Consider Table 3.9, which summarizes the mean and variance for the Metals and Income funds.

TABLE 3.9 Mean-Variance Analysis of Two Mutual Funds, 2000–2009

Fund	Mean Return	Variance
Metals fund	24.65%	1,378.61(%)^2
Income fund	8.51%	122.48(%)^2

It is true that the Metals fund provided an investor with a higher reward over the 10-year period, but this same investor encountered considerable risk compared to an investor who invested in the Income fund. Table 3.9 shows that the variance of the Metals fund $(1,378.61(\%)^2)$ is significantly greater than the variance of the Income fund $(122.48(\%)^2)$. If we look back at Table 3.1 and focus on the Metals fund, we see returns far above the average return of 24.65% (for example, 59.45% and 76.46%), but also returns far below the average return of 24.65% (for example, -7.34% and -56.02%). Repeating this same analysis for the Income fund, the returns are far closer to the average return of 8.51%; thus, the Income fund provided a lower return, but also far less risk.

A discussion of mean-variance analysis seems almost incomplete without mention of the **Sharpe ratio**. Nobel Laureate William Sharpe developed what he originally referred to as the "reward-to-variability" ratio. However, academics and finance professionals prefer to call it the "Sharpe ratio." The Sharpe ratio is used to characterize how well the return of an asset compensates for the risk that the investor takes. Investors are often advised to pick investments that have high Sharpe ratios.

The Sharpe ratio is defined with the reward specified in terms of the population mean and the variability specified in terms of the population variance. However, we often compute the Sharpe ratio in terms of the sample mean and sample variance, where the return is usually expressed as a percent and not a decimal.

THE SHARPE RATIO

The **Sharpe ratio** measures the extra reward per unit of risk. The Sharpe ratio for an investment I is computed as:

$$\frac{\bar{x}_I - \bar{R}_f}{s_I}$$

where $\bar{x}_I$ is the mean return for the investment, $\bar{R}_f$ is the mean return for a risk-free asset such as a Treasury bill (T-bill), and s_I is the standard deviation for the investment.

The numerator of the Sharpe ratio measures the extra reward that investors receive for the added risk taken—this difference is often called excess return. The higher the Sharpe ratio, the better the investment compensates its investors for risk.

EXAMPLE 3.14

Calculate and interpret the Sharpe ratios for the Metals and Income funds given that the return on a 1-year T-bill is 2%.

SOLUTION: Since the return on a 1-year T-bill is 2%, $\bar{R}_f = 2$. Plugging in the values of the relevant means and standard deviations into the Sharpe ratio yields:

$$\text{Sharpe ratio for the Metals fund: } \frac{\bar{x}_I - \bar{R}_f}{s_I} = \frac{24.65 - 2}{37.13} = 0.61.$$

$$\text{Sharpe ratio for the Income fund: } \frac{\bar{x}_I - \bar{R}_f}{s_I} = \frac{8.51 - 2}{11.07} = 0.59.$$

We had earlier shown that the Metals fund had a higher return, which is good, along with a higher variance, which is bad. We can use the Sharpe ratio to make a valid comparison between the funds. The Metals fund provides the higher Sharpe ratio than the Income fund (0.61 > 0.59); therefore, the Metals fund offered more reward per unit of risk compared to the Income fund.

EXERCISES 3.4

Mechanics

35. Consider the following data for two investments, A and B:

Investment A:	$\bar{x} = 8$ and $s = 5$
Investment B:	$\bar{x} = 10$ and $s = 7$

a. Which investment provides the higher return? Which investment provides less risk? Explain.

b. Given a risk-free rate of 2%, calculate the Sharpe ratio for each investment. Which investment provides the higher reward per unit of risk? Explain.

36. Consider the following data for two investments, A and B:

Investment A:	$\bar{x} = 10$ and $s = 5$
Investment B:	$\bar{x} = 15$ and $s = 10$

a. Which investment provides the higher return? Which investment provides less risk? Explain.

b. Given a risk-free rate of 1.4%, calculate the Sharpe ratio for each investment. Which investment provides the higher reward per unit of risk? Explain.

37. Consider the following returns for two investments, A and B, over the past four years:

Investment 1:	2%	8%	−4%	6%
Investment 2:	6%	12%	−8%	10%

a. Which investment provides the higher return?

b. Which investment provides less risk?

c. Given a risk-free rate of 1.2%, calculate the Sharpe ratio for each investment. Which investment has performed better? Explain.

Applications

38. The following table shows the annual returns (in percent) and summary measures for the Vanguard Energy Fund and the Vanguard Health Care Fund from 2005 through 2009.

Year	Energy	Health Care
2005	44.60	15.41
2006	19.68	10.87
2007	37.00	4.43
2008	−42.87	−18.45
2009	38.36	20.96
	$\bar{x}_{Energy} = 19.35$	$\bar{x}_{Health} = 6.64$
	$s_{Energy} = 35.99$	$s_{Health} = 15.28$

Source: http://www.finance.yahoo.com.

a. Which fund had the higher average return?

b. Which fund was riskier over this time period?

c. Given a risk-free rate of 3%, which fund has the higher Sharpe ratio? What does this ratio imply?

39. The following table shows the annual returns (in percent) for the Fidelity Latin America Fund and the Fidelity Canada Fund from 2005 through 2009.

Year	Latin America	Canada
2005	55.17	27.89
2006	44.33	15.04
2007	43.71	35.02
2008	−54.64	−42.64
2009	91.60	39.63

Source: http://www.finance.yahoo.com.

a. Which fund had the higher average return?
b. Which fund was riskier over this time period?
c. Given a risk-free rate of 3%, which fund has the higher Sharpe ratio? What does this ratio imply?

40. [FILE] The accompanying table shows a portion of the annual return (in percent) for the Fidelity Select Technology Fund and Fidelity Select Energy Fund from 2000 through 2011. The entire data set, labeled **Fidelity_Select**, can be found on the text website.

Year	Technology	Energy
2000	−24.31	30.47
2001	−38.55	−12.49
⋮	⋮	⋮
2011	−12.21	−8.76

Source: http://www.finance.com.

a. Compare the sample mean and the sample standard deviation of the two fund returns.
b. Use a risk-free rate of 2% to compare the Sharpe ratios of the two funds.

3.5 Analysis of Relative Location

The mean and the standard deviation are the most extensively used measures of central location and dispersion, respectively. Unlike the mean, it is not easy to interpret the standard deviation intuitively. All we can say is that a low value of standard deviation indicates that the data points are close to the mean, while a high standard deviation indicates that the data are spread out. In this section we will use Chebyshev's theorem and the empirical rule to make precise statements regarding the percentage of data values that fall within a specified number of standard deviations from the mean. We will also compute z-scores where we use the mean and the standard deviation to measure the relative location of a value within a data set; z-scores are also used to detect outliers.

LO **3.5**

Apply Chebyshev's theorem, the empirical rule, and **z**-scores.

Chebyshev's Theorem

As we will see in more detail in later chapters, it is important to be able to use the standard deviation to make statements about the proportion of observations that fall within certain intervals. Fortunately, a Russian mathematician named Pavroty Chebyshev (1821–1894) found bounds for the proportion of the data that lie within a specified number of standard deviations from the mean.

CHEBYSHEV'S THEOREM

For any data set, the proportion of observations that lie within k standard deviations from the mean is at least $1 - 1/k^2$, where k is any number greater than 1.

This theorem holds both for a sample and for a population. For example, it implies that at least 0.75, or 75%, of the observations fall within $k = 2$ standard deviations from the mean. Similarly, at least 0.89, or 89%, of the observations fall within $k = 3$ standard deviations from the mean.

EXAMPLE 3.15

A large lecture class has 280 students. The professor has announced that the mean score on an exam is 74 with a standard deviation of 8. At least how many students scored within 58 and 90?

SOLUTION: The score 58 is two standard deviations below the mean ($\bar{x} - 2s = 74 - (2 \times 8) = 58$), while the score 90 is two standard deviations above the mean ($\bar{x} + 2s = 74 + (2 \times 8) = 90$). Using Chebyshev's theorem and $k = 2$, we have $1 - 1/2^2 = 0.75$. In other words, Chebyshev's theorem asserts that at least 75% of the scores will fall within 58 and 90. Therefore, at least 75% of 280 students, or $0.75(280) = 210$ students, scored within 58 and 90.

The main advantage of Chebyshev's theorem is that it applies to all data sets, regardless of the shape of the distribution. However, it results in conservative bounds for the percentage of observations falling in a particular interval. The actual percentage of observations lying in the interval may in fact be much larger.

The Empirical Rule

If we know that our data are drawn from a relatively symmetric and bell-shaped distribution—perhaps by a visual inspection of its histogram—then we can make more precise statements about the percentage of observations that fall within certain intervals. Symmetry and bell-shape are characteristics of the normal distribution, a topic that we discuss in Chapter 6. The normal distribution is often used as an approximation for many real-world applications. The **empirical rule** is illustrated in Figure 3.5. It provides the approximate percentage of observations that fall within 1, 2, or 3 standard deviations from the mean.

FIGURE 3.5 Graphical description of the empirical rule

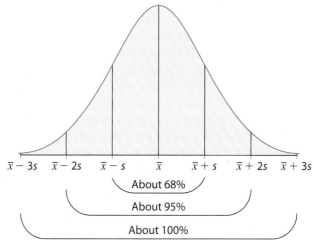

THE EMPIRICAL RULE

Given a sample mean $\bar{x}$, a sample standard deviation s, and a relatively symmetric and bell-shaped distribution:

- Approximately 68% of all observations fall in the interval $\bar{x} \pm s$,
- Approximately 95% of all observations fall in the interval $\bar{x} \pm 2s$, and
- Almost all observations fall in the interval $\bar{x} \pm 3s$.

EXAMPLE 3.16

Let's revisit Example 3.15 regarding a large lecture class with 280 students with a mean score of 74 and a standard deviation of 8. Assume that the distribution is symmetric and bell-shaped.

a. Approximately how many students scored within 58 and 90?

b. Approximately how many students scored more than 90?

SOLUTION:

a. As shown in Example 3.15, the score 58 is two standard deviations below the mean while the score 90 is two standard deviations above the mean. The empirical rule states that approximately 95% of the observations fall within two standard deviations of the mean. Therefore about 95% of 280 students, or $0.95(280) = 266$ students, scored within 58 and 90.

b. We know that the score 90 is two standard deviations above the mean. Since approximately 95% of the observations fall within two standard deviations of the mean, we can infer that 5% of the observations fall outside the interval. Therefore, about half of 5%, or 2.5%, of 280 students scored above 90. Equivalently, about 7 students (0.025×280) scored above 90 on the exam. If the professor uses a cutoff score above 90 for an A, then only seven students in the class are expected to get an A.

The main difference between Chebyshev's theorem and the empirical rule is that Chebyshev's theorem applies to all data sets whereas the empirical rule is appropriate when the distribution is symmetric and bell-shaped. In the above two examples, while Chebyshev's theorem asserts that at least 75% of the students scored between 58 and 90, we are able to make a more precise statement with the empirical rule that suggests that about 95% of the students scored between 58 and 90. It is preferable to use the empirical rule if the histogram or other visual and numerical measures suggest a symmetric and bell-shaped distribution.

z-Scores

It is often instructive to use the mean and the standard deviation to find the relative location of values within a data set. Suppose a student gets a score of 90 on her accounting exam and 90 on her marketing exam. While the student's scores are identical in both classes, her relative position in these classes may be quite different. What if the mean score was different in the classes? Even with the same mean scores, what if the standard deviation was different in the classes? Both the mean and the standard deviation are needed to find the relative position of this student in both classes.

We use the **z-score** to find the relative position of a sample value within the data set by dividing the deviation of the sample value from the mean by the standard deviation.

z-score

A z-score is computed as

$$z = \frac{x - \bar{x}}{s}$$

where x is a sample value and $\bar{x}$ and s are the sample mean and the sample standard deviation, respectively.

A z-score is a unitless measure since its numerator and the denominator have the same units, which cancel out with each other. It measures the distance of a given sample value from the mean in standard deviations. For example a z-score of 2 implies that the given sample value is 2 standard deviations above the mean. Similarly, a z-score of -1.5 implies that the given sample value is 1.5 standard deviations below the mean. Converting sample data into z-scores is also called **standardizing** the data.

EXAMPLE 3.17

The mean and the standard deviation of scores on an accounting exam are 74 and 8, respectively. The mean and standard deviation of scores on a marketing exam are 78 and 10, respectively. Find the z-score of a student who scores 90 in both classes.

SOLUTION: The z-score in the accounting class is $z = \dfrac{90 - 74}{8} = 2$. Similarly, the z-score in the marketing class is $z = \dfrac{90 - 78}{10} = 1.2$. Therefore, the student has fared relatively better in accounting since she is two standard deviations above the mean as compared to marketing where she is only 1.2 standard deviations above the mean.

In Section 3.2, we used box plots as an effective tool to identify outliers. If the data are relatively symmetric and bell-shaped, we can also use z-scores to detect outliers. Since almost all observations fall within three standard deviations of the mean, it is common to treat an observation as an outlier if its z-score is more than 3 or less than -3. Such observations must be reviewed to determine if they should remain in the data set.

EXAMPLE 3.18

Consider the information presented in the introductory case of this chapter. Use z-scores to determine if there are outliers in the Metals fund data.

SOLUTION: The smallest and the largest observations in the data set are -56.02 and 76.46, respectively. The z-score for the smallest observation is $z = \dfrac{-56.02 - 24.65}{37.13} = -2.17$ and the z-score for the largest observation is $z = \dfrac{76.46 - 24.65}{37.13} = 1.40$. Since the absolute value of both z-scores is less than 3, we conclude that there are no outliers in the Metals fund data, assuming that the distribution is relatively symmetric and bell-shaped. This result is consistent with our earlier analysis with the box plot.

EXERCISES 3.5

Mechanics

41. A data set has a mean of 80 and a standard deviation of 5.
    a. Using Chebyshev's theorem, what percentage of the observations fall between 70 and 90?
    b. Using Chebyshev's theorem, what percentage of the observations fall between 65 and 95?

42. A data set has a mean of 1500 and a standard deviation of 100.
    a. Using Chebyshev's theorem, what percentage of the observations fall between 1300 and 1700?
    b. Using Chebyshev's theorem, what percentage of the observations fall between 1100 and 1900?

43. A data set has a mean of 500 and a standard deviation of 25.
    a. Using Chebyshev's theorem, find the interval that encompasses at least 75% of the data.

    b. Using Chebyshev's theorem, find the interval that encompasses at least 89% of the data.

44. Data are drawn from a bell-shaped distribution with a mean of 20 and a standard deviation of 2.
    a. What percentage of the observations fall between 18 and 22?
    b. What percentage of the observations fall between 16 and 24?
    c. What percentage of the observations are less than 16?

45. Consider a bell-shaped distribution with a mean of 750 and a standard deviation of 50. There are 500 observations in the data set.
    a. What percentage of the observations are less than 700?
    b. Approximately how many observations are less than 700?

46. Data are drawn from a bell-shaped distribution with a mean of 25 and a standard deviation of 4. There are 1,000 observations in the data set.

a. What percentage of the observations are less than 33?

b. Approximately how many observations are less than 33?

47. Data are drawn from a bell-shaped distribution with a mean of 5 and a standard deviation of 2.5.

   a. What percentage of the observations are positive?

   b. What percentage of the observations are not positive?

48. Data with 250 observations are drawn from a bell-shaped distribution with a mean of 50 and a standard deviation of 12. Approximately how many observations are more than 74?

49. Consider a sample with six observations of 6, 9, 12, 10, 9, and 8. Compute the z-scores for each sample observation.

50. Consider a sample with 10 observations of $-3, 8, 4, 2, -4,$ 15, 6, 0, -4, and 5. Use z-scores to determine if there are any outliers in the data; assume a bell-shaped distribution.

Applications

51. A sample of the salaries of assistant professors on the business faculty at a local university revealed a mean income of $72,000 with a standard deviation of $3,000.

   a. Using Chebyshev's theorem, what percentage of the faculty earns at least $66,000 but no more than $78,000?

   b. Using Chebyshev's theorem, what percentage of the faculty earns at least $63,000 but no more than $81,000?

52. The historical returns on a portfolio had an average return of 8 percent and a standard deviation of 12 percent. Assume that returns on this portfolio follow a bell-shaped distribution.

   a. What percentage of returns were greater than 20 percent?

   b. What percentage of returns were below –16 percent?

53. It is often assumed that IQ scores follow a bell-shaped distribution with a mean of 100 and a standard deviation of 16.

   a. What percentage of scores are between 84 and 116?

   b. What percentage of scores are less than 68?

   c. What percentage of scores are more than 116?

54. An investment strategy has an expected return of 8 percent and a standard deviation of 6 percent. Assume investment returns are bell shaped.

   a. How likely is it to earn a return between 2 percent and 14 percent?

   b. How likely is it to earn a return greater than 14 percent?

   c. How likely is it to earn a return below –4 percent?

55. Average talk time between charges of a given cell phone is advertised as 4 hours. Let the standard deviation be 0.8 hour.

   a. Use Chebyshev's theorem to approximate the proportion of cell phones that will have talk time between 2.4 hours and 5.6 hours.

   b. Assume a bell-shaped distribution to approximate the proportion of cell phones that will have talk time between 2.4 hours and 5.6 hours.

56. FILE Go to the text website and access the data labeled **Census**. It shows, among other variables, median household income and median house value for the 50 states in 2010. Assume that income and house value data are bell-shaped.

   a. Use z-scores to determine if there are any outliers in the household income data.

   b. Use z-scores to determine if there are any outliers in the house value data.

57. FILE Go to the text website and access the data labeled **Fidelity_Select**. It shows the annual return (in percent) for the Fidelity Select Technology Fund and the Fidelity Select Energy Fund from 2000 through 2011. Assume that the return data are bell-shaped.

   a. Use z-scores to determine if there are any outliers in the technology return data.

   b. Use z-scores to determine if there are any outliers in the energy return data.

3.6 Summarizing Grouped Data

The mean and the variance are the most widely used descriptive measures in statistics. However, the formulas in Sections 3.1 and 3.3 apply to ungrouped or raw data. In many instances we access data that are in the form of a frequency distribution or grouped data. This is especially true of secondary data, such as data we obtain from government publications. When data are grouped or aggregated, the formulas for the mean and the variance must be modified.

LO **3.6**

Calculate the mean and the variance for grouped data.

CALCULATING THE MEAN AND THE VARIANCE FOR A FREQUENCY DISTRIBUTION

Sample:

Mean: $\bar{x} = \dfrac{\Sigma m_i f_i}{n}$

Variance: $s^2 = \dfrac{\Sigma(m_i - \bar{x})^2 f_i}{n - 1}$

Population:

Mean: $\mu = \dfrac{\Sigma m_i f_i}{N}$

Variance: $\sigma^2 = \dfrac{\Sigma(m_i - \mu)^2 f_i}{N}$,

where m_i and f_i are the midpoint and the frequency of the ith class, respectively. The standard deviation is the positive square root of the variance.

In these formulas, we actually use the concept of the weighted mean because the relative frequency f_i/n can be treated as a weight for the midpoint m_i. We also note that by aggregating, some of the data information is lost. Therefore, unlike in the case of raw data, we can only compute approximate values of the summary measures with grouped data.

EXAMPLE 3.19

Recall the frequency distribution of house prices that we constructed in Chapter 2.

Class (in $1000s)	Frequency
300 up to 400	4
400 up to 500	11
500 up to 600	14
600 up to 700	5
700 up to 800	2

a. Calculate the average house price.

b. Calculate the sample variance and the sample standard deviation.

SOLUTION: Table 3.10 shows the frequency f_i and the midpoint m_i for each class in the second and third columns, respectively.

TABLE 3.10 The Sample Mean and the Sample Variance Calculation for Grouped Data

Class (in $1,000s)	f_i	m_i	$m_i f_i$	$(m_i - \bar{x})^2 f_i$
300 up to 400	4	350	1,400	$(350 - 522)^2 \times 4 = 118{,}336$
400 up to 500	11	450	4,950	$(450 - 522)^2 \times 11 = 57{,}024$
500 up to 600	14	550	7,700	$(550 - 522)^2 \times 14 = 10{,}976$
600 up to 700	5	650	3,250	$(650 - 522)^2 \times 5 = 81{,}920$
700 up to 800	2	750	1,500	$(750 - 522)^2 \times 2 = 103{,}968$
Total	36		18,800	372,224

a. For the mean, we multiply each class's midpoint by its respective frequency, as shown in the fourth column of Table 3.10. Finally, we sum the fourth column and divide by the sample size. Or,

$$\bar{x} = \frac{\Sigma m_i f_i}{n} = \frac{18{,}800}{36} = 522.$$ The average house price is thus $522,000.

b. For the sample variance, we first calculate the sum of the weighted squared differences from the mean. The fifth column in Table 3.10 shows the appropriate calculations for each class. Summing the values in the fifth column yields the numerator for the variance formula. Thus, we calculate the variance as:

$$s^2 = \frac{\Sigma(m_i - \bar{x})^2 f_i}{n - 1} = \frac{372{,}224}{36 - 1} = 10{,}635(\$)^2.$$

The standard deviation is simply the positive square root of the sample variance, or $s = \sqrt{10{,}635} = 103.13(\$)$. The standard deviation is $103.13.

Many times the data from secondary sources are distributed in the form of a relative frequency distribution rather than a frequency distribution. In order to use the formulas for the mean and variance for grouped data, first convert the relative frequency distribution into a frequency distribution, as discussed in Section 2.2 of Chapter 2.

Mechanics

58. Consider the following frequency distribution.

Class	Frequency
2 up to 4	20
4 up to 6	60
6 up to 8	80
8 up to 10	20

a. Calculate the population mean.
b. Calculate the population variance and the population standard deviation.

59. Consider the following frequency distribution.

Class	Frequency
50 up to 60	10
60 up to 70	15
70 up to 80	8
80 up to 100	2

a. Calculate the sample mean.
b. Calculate the sample variance and the sample standard deviation.

60. The following relative frequency distribution was constructed from a population of 200. Calculate the population mean, the population variance, and the population standard deviation.

Class	Relative Frequency
−20 up to −10	0.35
−10 up to 0	0.25
0 up to 10	0.40
10 up to 20	0.05

61. The following relative frequency distribution was constructed from a sample of 50. Calculate the sample mean, the sample variance, and the sample standard deviation.

Class	Relative Frequency
0 up to 2	0.34
2 up to 4	0.20
4 up to 6	0.40
6 up to 8	0.06

Applications

62. Fifty cities provided information on vacancy rates (in percent) for local apartments in the following frequency distribution.

Vacancy Rate (in percent)	Frequency
0 up to 3	5
3 up to 6	5
6 up to 9	10
9 up to 12	20
12 up to 15	10

a. Calculate the average vacancy rate.
b. Calculate the variance and the standard deviation for this sample.

63. A local hospital provided the following frequency distribution summarizing the weights of babies delivered over the month of January.

Weight (in pounds)	Number of Babies
2 up to 4	3
4 up to 6	8
6 up to 8	25
8 up to 10	30
10 up to 12	4

a. Calculate the mean weight.
b. Calculate the variance and the standard deviation for this sample.

64. A researcher conducts a mileage economy test involving 80 cars. The frequency distribution describing average miles per gallon (mpg) appears in the accompanying frequency distribution.

Average MPG	Frequency
15 up to 20	15
20 up to 25	30
25 up to 30	15
30 up to 35	10
35 up to 40	7
40 up to 45	3

a. Calculate the mean mpg.
b. Calculate the variance and the standard deviation.

65. The Boston Security Analysts Society, Inc. (BSAS) is a nonprofit association that serves as a forum for the exchange of ideas for the investment community. Suppose the ages of its members are based on the following frequency distribution.

Age	Frequency
21–31	11
32–42	44
43–53	26
54–64	7

   a. Calculate the mean age.
   b. Calculate the sample variance and the sample standard deviation.

66. The National Sporting Goods Association (NSGA) conducted a survey of the ages of people that purchased athletic footwear in 2009. The ages are summarized in the following relative frequency distribution.

Age of Purchaser	Percent
Under 14 years old	19
14 to 17 years old	6
18 to 24 years old	10
25 to 34 years old	13
35 to 44 years old	14
45 to 64 years old	25
65 years old and over	13

Suppose the survey was based on 100 individuals. Calculate the average age of this distribution. Calculate the sample standard deviation. Use 10 as the midpoint of the first class and 75 as the midpoint of the last class.

3.7 Covariance and Correlation

LO **3.7**

Calculate and interpret the covariance and the correlation coefficient.

In Chapter 2, we introduced the idea of a scatterplot to visually assess whether two variables had some type of linear relationship. In this section we present two numerical measures that quantify the direction and strength of a particular relationship between two variables, x and y.

An objective numerical measure that reveals the direction of the linear relationship between two variables is called the **covariance**. We use s_{xy} to refer to a sample covariance and σ_{xy} to refer to a population covariance.

THE COVARIANCE

For values $(x_1, y_1), (x_2, y_2), \ldots, (x_n, y_n)$, the **sample covariance** s_{xy} is computed as

$$s_{xy} = \frac{\Sigma(x_i - \bar{x})(y_i - \bar{y})}{n - 1}.$$

For values $(x_1, y_1), (x_2, y_2), \ldots, (x_N, y_N)$, the **population covariance** σ_{xy} is computed as

$$\sigma_{xy} = \frac{\Sigma(x_i - \mu_x)(y_i - \mu_y)}{N}.$$

Note: As in the case of the sample variance, the sample covariance uses $n - 1$ rather than n in the denominator.

- A positive value of covariance indicates a positive linear relationship between the two variables; on average, if x is above its mean, then y tends to be above its mean, and vice versa.

- A negative value of covariance indicates a negative linear relationship between the two variables; on average, if x is above its mean, then y tends to be below its mean, and vice versa.

- The covariance is zero if y and x have no linear relationship.

The covariance, like the variance earlier, is difficult to interpret because it is sensitive to the units of measurement. That is, the covariance between two variables might be 100 and the covariance between another two variables might be 1,000; yet all we can conclude is that both sets of variables are positively related. We cannot comment on the strength of the relationships. An easier measure to interpret is the **correlation coefficient**; it describes both the direction and strength of the linear relationship between x and y. We use r_{xy} to refer to a sample correlation coefficient and ρ_{xy} (the Greek letter rho) to refer to a population correlation coefficient.

THE CORRELATION COEFFICIENT

The **sample correlation coefficient** is computed as $r_{xy} = \dfrac{s_{xy}}{s_x s_y}$, and the **population correlation coefficient** is computed as $\rho_{xy} = \dfrac{\sigma_{xy}}{\sigma_x \sigma_y}$.

The correlation coefficient is unit free since the units in the numerator cancel with those in the denominator. The value of the correlation coefficient falls between −1 and 1. A perfect positive relationship exists if it equals 1, and a perfect negative relationship exists if it equals −1. Other values for the correlation coefficient must be interpreted with reference to −1, 0, or 1. For instance, a correlation coefficient equal to −0.80 indicates a strong negative relationship, whereas a correlation coefficient equal to 0.12 indicates a weak positive relationship.

EXAMPLE 3.20

Calculate the covariance and the correlation coefficient for the Metals (x) and Income (y) funds. Interpret these values. Recall that $\bar{x} = 24.65$, $s_x = 37.13$, $\bar{y} = 8.51$, and $s_y = 11.07$.

SOLUTION: As a first step, Figure 3.6 shows a scatterplot of the return data for the Metals and Income funds. It appears that there is a positive linear relationship between the two fund returns.

FIGURE 3.6 Scatterplot of return data for the Metals and Income funds

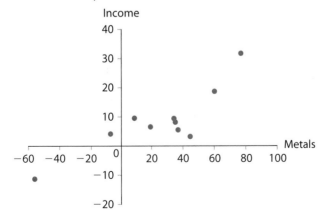

Table 3.11 shows the return data for each fund in the first two columns. The third column shows the product of differences from the mean.

Summing the values in the third column yields the numerator for the covariance formula. Thus, we calculate the covariance as:

$$s_{xy} = \frac{\Sigma(x_i - \bar{x})(y_i - \bar{y})}{n - 1} = \frac{3,165.55}{10 - 1} = 351.73.$$

TABLE 3.11 Covariance Calculation for the Metals and Income Funds

x_i	y_i	$(x_i - \bar{x})(y_i - \bar{y})$
−7.34	4.07	$(-7.34 - 24.65)(4.07 - 8.51) = 142.04$
18.33	6.52	$(18.33 - 24.65)(6.52 - 8.51) = 12.58$
⋮	⋮	⋮
76.46	31.77	$(76.46 - 24.65)(31.77 - 8.51) = 1{,}205.10$
		Total = 3,165.55

The covariance of 351.73 indicates that the variables have a positive linear relationship. In other words, on average, when one fund's return is above its mean, the other fund's return is above its mean, and vice versa. The covariance is used to compute the correlation coefficient as:

$$r_{xy} = \frac{s_{xy}}{s_x s_y} = \frac{351.73}{(37.13)(11.07)} = 0.86.$$

The correlation coefficient of 0.86 indicates a strong positive linear relationship. In order to diversify the risk in an investor's portfolio, an investor is often advised to invest in assets (such as stocks, bonds, and mutual funds) whose returns are not strongly correlated. If asset returns are not strongly correlated, then if one investment does poorly, the other may still do well.

Using Excel to Calculate Covariance and the Correlation Coefficient

Excel provides formulas for the covariance and the correlation coefficient. Table 3.12 shows Excel's function names for these descriptive measures. For example, in order to calculate the sample covariance between the Metals fund and the Income fund, we open the ***Fund_Returns*** data from the text website. We find an empty cell and insert '=COVAR.S(B2:B11,C2:C11)'; note that the data for the Metals fund are sitting in cells B2 through B11 (array1) and the data for the Income fund are sitting in cells C2 through C11 (array2). After choosing **<Enter>**, Excel returns a value of 351.73, which matches the value that we calculated by hand.

TABLE 3.12 Excel's Functions for the Covariance and the Correlation Coefficient

Measure of Dispersion	Excel Function Name
Sample Covariance	=COVARIANCE.S(array1,array2)
Population Covariance	=COVARIANCE.P(array1,array2)
Correlation Coefficient	=CORREL(array1,array2)

EXERCISES 3.7

Mechanics

67. Consider the following sample data:

x	12	18	20	22	25
y	15	20	25	22	27

a. Calculate the covariance between the variables.
b. Calculate and interpret the correlation coefficient.

68. Consider the following sample data:

x	−2	0	3	4	7
y	−2	−3	−8	−9	−10

a. Calculate the covariance between the variables.
b. Calculate and interpret the correlation coefficient.

Applications

69. The following table shows the annual returns (in percent) for T-Rowe Price's Value and International Stock funds for the time period 2005–2009.

Year	Value Fund	International Fund
2005	6.30	16.27
2006	19.75	19.26
2007	0.75	13.43
2008	−39.76	−48.02
2009	37.15	52.20

a. Calculate and interpret the covariance between the returns.
b. Calculate and interpret the correlation coefficient.

70. In an attempt to determine whether a linear relationship exists between the price of a home and the number of days it takes to sell the home, a real estate agent collected the following data from recent sales in his city.

Price (in $1,000s)	Days to Sell Home	Price (in $1,000s)	Days to Sell Home
265	136	430	145
225	125	515	121
160	120	180	122
325	140	423	145

a. Calculate the covariance. What kind of linear relationship exists?
b. Calculate the correlation coefficient. Comment on the strength of the linear relationship.

71. The director of graduate admissions at a local university is analyzing the relationship between scores on the Graduate Record Examination (GRE) and subsequent performance in graduate school, as measured by a student's grade point average (GPA). She uses a sample of 10 students who graduated within the past five years.

GRE	GPA
1500	3.4
1400	3.5
1000	3.0
1050	2.9
1100	3.0
1250	3.3
800	2.7
850	2.8
950	3.2
1350	3.3

a. Calculate and interpret the covariance.
b. Calculate and interpret the correlation coefficient. Does an applicant's GRE score seem to be a good indicator of subsequent performance in graduate school?

72. A social scientist wants to analyze the relationship between educational attainment and salary. He collects the following sample of data where Education refers to years of higher education and Salary is the person's annual salary in thousands of dollars.

Education	3	4	6	2	5	4	8	0
Salary	40	53	60	35	55	50	80	35

a. Calculate the covariance. What kind of linear relationship exists?
b. Calculate the correlation coefficient. Comment on the strength of the linear relationship.

73. FILE Go to the text website and access the data labeled **Census**.
a. Compute and interpret the correlation coefficient of household income and house value.
b. Compute and interpret the correlation coefficient of household income and the percentage of the residents who are foreign born.
c. Compute and interpret the correlation coefficient of household income and the percentage of the residents who are without a high school diploma.

74. FILE Many attempts have been made to relate happiness with various factors. One such study relates happiness with age and finds that holding everything else constant, people are least happy when they are in their mid-40s (*The Economist*, December 16, 2010). Consider the following table for data on a respondent's age and his/her perception of well-being on a scale from 0 to 100. A portion of the data is presented below; the entire data set, labeled **Happiness_Age**, can be found on the text website.

Age	Happiness
49	62
51	66
⋮	⋮
69	72

a. Calculate and interpret the sample correlation coefficient between age and happiness.
b. Construct a scatterplot to point out a flaw with the above correlation analysis.

Many environmental groups and politicians are suggesting a return to the federal 55-mile-per-hour (mph) speed limit on America's highways. They argue that not only will a lower national speed limit reduce greenhouse emissions, it will also increase traffic safety.

Cameron Grinnell believes that a lower speed limit will not increase traffic safety. He believes that traffic safety is based on the variability of the speeds with which people are driving, rather than the average speed. The person who drives 20 mph below the pace of traffic is often as much a safety menace as the speeder. Cameron gathers the speeds of 40 cars from a highway with a speed limit of 55 mph (Highway 1) and the speeds of 40 cars from a highway with a speed limit of 65 mph (Highway 2). A portion of the data is shown in Table 3.13; the entire data set, labeled **Highway_Speeds**, can be found on the text website.

TABLE 3.13 Speed of Cars from Highway 1 and Highway 2

FILE	Highway 1 (55-mph limit)	Highway 2 (65-mph limit)
	60	70
	55	65
	⋮	⋮
	52	65

Cameron would like to use the above sample information to:

1. Compute and interpret the typical speed on these highways.
2. Compute and interpret the variability of speed on these highways.
3. Discuss if the reduction in the speed limit to 55 mph would increase safety on the highways.

Sample Report— Analyzing Speed Limits

Recently, many concerned citizens have lobbied for a return to the federal 55-mile-per-hour (mph) speed limit on America's highways. The reduction may lower gas emissions and save consumers on gasoline costs, but whether it will increase traffic safety is not clear. Many researchers believe that traffic safety is based on the variability of the speed rather than the average speed with which people are driving—the more variability in speed, the more dangerous the roads. Is there less variability in speed on a highway with a 55-mph speed limit as opposed to a 65-mph speed limit?

To compare average speeds, as well as the variability of speeds on highways, the speeds of 40 cars were recorded on a highway with a 55-mph speed limit (Highway 1) and on a highway with a 65-mph speed limit (Highway 2). Table 3.A shows the most relevant descriptive measures for the analysis.

TABLE 3.A Summary Measures for Highway 1 and Highway 2

	Highway 1 (55-mph speed limit)	Highway 2 (65-mph speed limit)
Mean	57	66
Median	56	66
Mode	50	70
Minimum	45	60
Maximum	74	70
Standard deviation	7.0	3.0
Coefficient of variation	0.12	0.05
Number of cars	40	40

The average speed of a car on Highway 1 was 57 mph, as opposed to 66 mph on Highway 2. On Highway 1, half of the 40 cars drove faster than 56 mph and half drove slower than 56 mph, as measured by the median; the median for Highway 2 was 66 mph. The mode shows that the most common speeds on Highway 1 and Highway 2 were 50 mph and 70 mph, respectively. Based on each measure of central location, Highway 2 experiences higher speeds as compared to Highway 1.

While measures of central location typically represent where the data cluster, these measures do not relay information about the variability in the data. Given the minimum and maximum speeds of 45 mph and 74 mph, respectively, the range of speeds is 29 mph for Highway 1 as compared to a range of just 10 mph for Highway 2. Generally, standard deviation is a more credible measure of dispersion, since range is based entirely on the minimum and the maximum values. The standard deviation for Highway 1 is substantially greater than the standard deviation for Highway 2 (7.0 mph > 3.0 mph). Therefore, the speeds on Highway 1 are more variable than the speeds on Highway 2. Even adjusting for differences in the magnitudes of the means by calculating the coefficient of variation, the speeds on Highway 1 are still more dispersed than on Highway 2 (0.12 > 0.05).

On average, it is true that the speeds on Highway 2 are higher than the speeds on Highway 1; however, the variability of speeds is greater on Highway 1. If traffic safety improves when the variability of speeds declines, then the data suggest that a return to a federal 55-mph speed limit may not enhance the well-being of highway travelers.

Conceptual Review

Calculate and interpret the mean, the median, and the mode.

The mean (average) is the most widely used measure of central location. The **sample mean** and the **population mean** are computed as $\bar{x} = \frac{\Sigma x_i}{n}$ and $\mu = \frac{\Sigma x_i}{N}$, respectively. One weakness of the mean is that it is unduly influenced by **outliers**—extremely small or large values.

The **median** is the middle value of a data set and is especially useful when outliers are present. We arrange the data in ascending (smallest to largest) order and find the median as the middle value if the number of observations is odd, or the average of the two middle values if the number of observations is even.

The **mode** is the value in the data set that occurs with the most frequency. A data set may have no mode or more than one mode. If the data are qualitative, then the mode is the only meaningful measure of central location.

3.2 Calculate and interpret percentiles and a box plot.

Percentiles provide detailed information about how the data are spread over the interval from the smallest value to the largest value. In general, the pth percentile divides the data set into two parts, where approximately p percent of the observations have values less than the pth percentile and the rest have values greater than the pth percentile. The 25th percentile is also referred to as the first quartile (Q1), the 50th percentile is referred to as the second quartile (Q2), and the 75th percentile is referred to as the third quartile (Q3).

A **box plot** displays the five-number summary (the minimum value, Q1, Q2, Q3, and the maximum value) for the data set. Box plots are particularly useful when comparing similar information gathered at another place or time. They are also used as an effective tool for identifying outliers and skewness.

LO 3.3 **Calculate and interpret the range, the mean absolute deviation, the variance, the standard deviation, and the coefficient of variation.**

The **range** is the difference between the maximum and the minimum values in a data set.

The **mean absolute deviation** (MAD) is an average of the absolute differences between the observations and the mean of a data set. The sample MAD and the population MAD are computed as $\text{MAD} = \frac{\Sigma |x_i - \bar{x}|}{n}$ and $\text{MAD} = \frac{\Sigma |x_i - \mu|}{N}$, respectively.

The **variance** and the **standard deviation**, which are based on squared differences from the mean, are the two most widely used measures of dispersion. The sample variance s^2 and the sample standard deviation s are computed as $s^2 = \frac{\Sigma (x_i - \bar{x})^2}{n - 1}$ and $s = \sqrt{s^2}$, respectively. The population variance σ^2 and the population standard deviation σ are computed as $\sigma^2 = \frac{\Sigma (x_i - \mu)^2}{N}$ and $\sigma = \sqrt{\sigma^2}$, respectively. Variance squares the original units of measurement; by calculating the standard deviation, we return to the original units of measurement.

The **coefficient of variation CV** is a relative measure of dispersion. The CV allows comparisons of variability between data sets with different means or different units of measurement. The sample CV and the population CV are computed as $\text{CV} = \frac{s}{\bar{x}}$ and $\text{CV} = \frac{\sigma}{\mu}$, respectively.

LO 3.4 **Explain mean-variance analysis and the Sharpe ratio.**

Mean-variance analysis postulates that we measure the performance of an asset by its rate of return and evaluate this rate of return in terms of its reward (mean) and risk (variance). In general, investments with higher average returns are also associated with higher risk.

The **Sharpe ratio** measures extra reward per unit of risk. The Sharpe ratio for an investment I is computed as $\frac{\bar{x}_I - \bar{R}_f}{s_I}$, where $\bar{R}_f$ denotes the return on a risk-free asset. The higher the Sharpe ratio, the better the investment compensates its investors for risk.

LO 3.5 **Apply Chebyshev's theorem, the empirical rule, and z-scores.**

Chebyshev's theorem dictates that for any data set, the proportion of observations that lie within k standard deviations from the mean will be at least $1 - 1/k^2$, where k is any number greater than 1.

Given a sample mean $\bar{x}$, a sample standard deviation s, and a bell-shaped distribution, the **empirical rule** dictates that

- Approximately 68% of all observations fall in the interval $\bar{x} \pm s$,

- Approximately 95% of all observations fall in the interval $\bar{x} \pm 2s$, and

- Almost all observations fall in the interval $\bar{x} \pm 3s$.

A **z-score**, calculated as $(x - \bar{x})/s$, measures the relative location of the sample value x; it is also used to detect outliers.

LO 3.6 **Calculate the mean and the variance for grouped data.**

When analyzing **grouped data**, the formulas for the mean and the variance are modified as follows:

- The sample mean and the population mean are computed as $\bar{x} = \frac{\Sigma m_i f_i}{n}$ and $\mu = \frac{\Sigma m_i f_i}{N}$, respectively.

- The sample variance and the population variance are computed as $s^2 = \frac{\Sigma (m_i - \bar{x})^2 f_i}{n - 1}$ and $\sigma^2 = \frac{\Sigma (m_i - \mu)^2 f_i}{N}$, respectively. As always the standard deviation is calculated as the positive square root of the variance.

The **covariance** and the **correlation coefficient** are measures that assess the direction and strength of a linear relationship between two variables, x and y.

The sample covariance s_{xy} and the population covariance σ_{xy} are computed as $s_{xy} = \dfrac{\Sigma(x_i - \bar{x})(y_i - \bar{y})}{n - 1}$ and $\sigma_{xy} = \dfrac{\Sigma(x_i - \mu_x)(y_i - \mu_y)}{N}$, respectively.

The sample correlation coefficient r_{xy} and the population correlation coefficient ρ_{xy} are computed as $r_{xy} = \dfrac{s_{xy}}{s_x s_y}$ and $\rho_{xy} = \dfrac{\sigma_{xy}}{\sigma_x \sigma_y}$, respectively.

Additional Exercises and Case Studies

75. Annual growth rates for individual firms in the toy industry tend to fluctuate dramatically, depending on consumers' tastes and current fads. Consider the following growth rates (in percent) for two companies in this industry, Hasbro and Mattel.

Year	2005	2006	2007	2008	2009
Hasbro	3.0	2.1	21.8	4.8	1.2
Mattel	1.5	9.1	5.7	−0.1	−8.2

SOURCE: Annual Reports for Hasbro, Inc., and Mattel Inc.

a. Use the standard deviation to evaluate the variability for each firm.
b. Which company's growth rate had greater variability?

76. The following table lists the sales (in millions of dollars) of the top Italian restaurant chains in 2009.

Restaurant	Sales (millions)
Olive Garden	$3,300
Carrabba's Italian Grill	629
Romano's Macaroni Grill	583
Maggiano's	366
Carino's Italian Grill	356
Buca di Beppo	220
Bertucci's	210

SOURCE: *The Boston Globe*, July 31, 2010.

Calculate the mean, the median, and the mode. Which measure of central tendency best reflects typical sales? Explain.

77. The following table shows the annual returns (in percent) for Fidelity's Electronic and Utilities funds.

Year	Electronic	Utilities
2005	13.23	9.36
2006	1.97	32.33
2007	2.77	21.03
2008	−50.00	−35.21
2009	81.65	14.71

SOURCE: http://www.finance.yahoo.com.

a. Calculate the sample mean, the sample variance, and the sample standard deviation for each fund.

b. Which fund had the higher average return?
c. Which fund was riskier over this time period? Use both the standard deviation and the coefficient of variation in your explanation.
d. Given a risk-free rate of 4%, which fund has the higher Sharpe ratio? What does this ratio imply?

78. Monthly stock prices for two competing firms are as follows.

Month	Firm A	Firm B
January	$28	$21
February	31	24
March	32	24
April	35	27
May	34	25
June	28	20

a. Calculate the sample mean, the sample variance, and the sample standard deviation for each firm's stock price.
b. Which firm had the higher stock price over the time period?
c. Which firm's stock price had greater variability as measured by the standard deviation? Which firm's stock price had the greater relative dispersion?

79. The manager at a water park constructed the following frequency distribution to summarize attendance for 60 days in July and August.

Attendance	Frequency
1,000 up to 1,250	5
1,250 up to 1,500	6
1,500 up to 1,750	10
1,750 up to 2,000	20
2,000 up to 2,250	15
2,250 up to 2,500	4

a. Calculate the mean attendance.
b. Calculate the variance and the standard deviation.

80. The National Sporting Goods Association (NSGA) conducted a survey of the ages of individuals that purchased skateboarding footwear. The ages of this survey are summarized in the following relative frequency distribution.

Age of User	Percent
Under 14 years old	35
14 to 17 years old	41
18 to 24 years old	15
25 to 34 years old	4
35 to 44 years old	4
45 to 64 years old	1

Suppose the survey was based on a sample of 200 individuals. Calculate the mean and the standard deviation of the age of individuals that purchased skateboarding shoes. Use 10 as the midpoint of the first class.

81. The following table shows the annual returns (in percent) for two of Putnam's mutual funds: the Voyager Growth Fund and the George Putnam Fund of Boston.

Year	Growth Fund	Fund of Boston
2002	−26.43	−8.42
2003	24.71	17.40
2004	4.80	8.32
2005	5.50	4.04
2006	5.23	12.25

Source: http://www.finance.yahoo.com.

a. Calculate and interpret the covariance.
b. Calculate the correlation coefficient. Comment on the strength of the linear relationship.

82. A manager of a local retail store analyzes the relationship between advertising and sales by reviewing the store's data for the previous six months.

Advertising (in $100s)	Sales (in $1,000s)
20	15
25	18
30	20
22	16
27	19
26	20

a. Calculate the mean of advertising and the mean of sales.
b. Calculate the standard deviation of advertising and the standard deviation of sales.
c. Calculate and interpret the covariance between advertising and sales.
d. Calculate and interpret the correlation coefficient.

83. FILE An economist wishes to summarize sample data from 26 metropolitan areas in the United States. The following table lists a portion of each area's 2010–2011 median income as well as the monthly unemployment rate and average consumer debt for August 2010; the entire data set, labeled **Debt_Payments,** can be found on the text website.

Metropolitan Area	Income (in $1,000s)	Unemployment	Debt
Washington, D.C.	$103.50	6.3%	$1,285
Seattle	81.70	8.5	1,135
⋮	⋮	⋮	⋮
Pittsburgh	63.00	8.3	763

Source: eFannieMae.com reports 2010–2011 area median incomes; www.bls.gov gives monthly unemployment rates for August 2010; Experian.com collected average monthly consumer debt payments in August 2010 and published the data in November 2010.

Use Excel to compute the summary measures of income, the monthly unemployment rate, and average consumer debt. Interpret these summary measures.

84. FILE American football is the highest paying sport on a per-game basis. Given that the quarterback is considered the most important player on an NFL team, he is typically well-compensated. Consider a portion of the following quarterback salary data in 2009; the entire data set, labeled **Quarterback_Salaries**, can be found on the text website.

Name	Salary (in $ millions)
Philip Rivers	25.5566
Jay Cutler	22.0441
⋮	⋮
Tony Romo	0.6260

Source: http://www.nfl.com.

a. Use Excel to compute and interpret the mean and the median salary of a quarterback.
b. Use Excel to compute and interpret the range and the standard deviation of quarterback salaries.

85. FILE The accompanying table shows a portion of the number of cases of car thefts for the 50 states during 2010. The entire data set, labeled **Car_Theft**, can be found on the text website.

State	Car Theft
Alabama	658
Alaska	280
⋮	⋮
Wyoming	84

Source: http://www.fbi.gov.

a. Calculate the mean, the median, and the mode of the number of car thefts.
b. Use z-scores to determine if there are any outliers in the data. Are you surprised by the result?

86. FILE The accompanying table shows a portion of the average price for a gallon of gas for the 50 states during April 2012. The entire data set, labeled **Gas_Prices_2012**, can be found on the text website.

State	Price per Gallon
Alabama	$4.36
Alaska	3.79
⋮	⋮
Wyoming	3.63

Source: http://AAA.com, data retrieved April 16, 2012.

a. Construct a box plot for the gasoline price and use it to identify outliers, if any.

b. Confirm your analysis by using z-scores to determine if there are any outliers in the gasoline price.

87. FILE The accompanying table shows a portion of the number of cases of crime related to gambling (Gambling) and offenses against the family and children (Family Abuse) for the 50 states in the United States during 2010. The entire data set, labeled **Gambling**, can be found on the text website.

State	Gambling	Family Abuse
Alabama	47	1,022
Alaska	10	315
⋮	⋮	⋮
Wyoming	0	194

Source: http://www.fbi.gov.

a. Construct a box plot for gambling and use it to identify outliers, if any.

b. Construct a box plot for abuse and use it to identify outliers, if any.

c. Calculate and interpret the sample correlation coefficient between gambling and family abuse.

CASE STUDIES

Case Study 3.1

An article in *The Wall Street Journal* (July 11, 2008) outlined a number of reasons as to why the 16 teams in Major League Baseball's National League (NL) are inferior to the 14 teams in the American League (AL). One reason for the imbalance pointed to the disparity in opening-day payrolls: the average AL payroll is greater than the NL average. A portion of the data showing opening-day payroll for each team is shown in the accompanying table; the entire data set, labeled **MLB_Salaries**, can be found on the text website.

Data for Case Study 3.1 Major League Baseball's Opening-Day Payrolls, 2010

American League	Payroll	National League	Payroll
New York Yankees	$206,333,389	Chicago Cubs	$146,609,000
Boston Red Sox	162,447,333	Philadelphia Phillies	141,928,379
⋮	⋮	⋮	⋮

Source: http://www.bizofbaseball.com.

In a report, use the sample information to:

1. Discuss the mean and the median of AL and NL opening-day salaries and comment on skewness.

2. Compare the range and the standard deviation of AL and NL opening-day salaries.

3. Use these summary measures to comment on the findings in *The Wall Street Journal*.

Case Study 3.2

Five years after graduating from college, Lucia Li feels that she is finally ready to invest some of her earnings. She has eliminated her credit card debt and has established an emergency fund. Her parents have been pleased with the performance of their mutual fund investments with Janus Capital Group. She has narrowed her search down to two mutual funds:

The Janus Balanced Fund: This "core" fund consists of stocks and bonds and its goal is diversification. It has historically produced solid long-term returns through different market cycles.

The Janus Overseas Fund: This fund invests in overseas companies based on their individual merits instead of their geography or industry sector.

The following table reports the annual returns (in percent) of these two funds over the past 10 years; these data, labeled **Janus_Funds**, are also available on the text website.

Data for Case Study 3.2 Returns (in percent) for Janus Funds

FILE

Year	Janus Balanced Fund	Janus Overseas Fund	Year	Janus Balanced Fund	Janus Overseas Fund
2000	−2.16	−18.57	2005	7.75	32.39
2001	−5.04	−23.11	2006	10.56	47.21
2002	−6.56	−23.89	2007	10.15	27.76
2003	13.74	36.79	2008	−15.22	−52.75
2004	8.71	18.58	2009	24.28	78.12

SOURCE: http://www.finance.yahoo.com.

In a report, use the sample information to:

1. Calculate measures of central location to describe the similarities and the differences in these two funds' returns.
2. Calculate measures of dispersion to assess the risk of each fund.
3. Calculate and interpret measures of correlation between the two funds.

Case Study 3.3

Due to a crisis in subprime lending, obtaining a mortgage has become difficult even for people with solid credit. In a report by the Associated Press (August 25, 2007), sales of existing homes fell for a 5th consecutive month, while home prices dropped for a record 12th month in July 2007. Mayan Horowitz, a research analyst for QuantExperts, wishes to study how the mortgage crunch has impacted the once-booming market of Florida. He collects data on the sale prices (in $1,000s) of 25 single-family homes in Fort Myers, Florida, in January 2007 and collects another sample in July 2007. For a valid comparison, he samples only three-bedroom homes, each with 1,500 square feet or less of space on a lot size of 10,000 square feet or less. A portion of the data is shown in the accompanying table; the entire data set, labeled **Fort_Myers_Sales**, can be found on the text website.

Data for Case Study 3.3 Home Prices (in $1,000s) in January 2007 and July 2007

FILE

Number	January	July
1	$100	$136
2	190	235
⋮	⋮	⋮
25	200	180

SOURCE: http://www.zillow.com.

In a report, use the sample information to:

1. Compare the mean, the median, and the mode in each of the two sample periods.
2. Compare the standard deviation and the coefficient of variation in each of the two sample periods.
3. Discuss significant changes in the housing market in Fort Myers over the 6-month period.

Appendix 3.1 Guidelines for Other Software Packages

The following section provides brief commands for specific software packages: Minitab, SPSS, and JMP. More detailed instructions can be found on the text website.

MINITAB

Calculating Summary Measures

A. (Replicating Table 3.3) Copy and paste the **Fund_Returns** data from the text website into a Minitab spreadsheet.

B. From the menu choose **Stat > Basic Statistics > Display Descriptive Statistics**. Then select Metals and Income as **Variables**. Click **Statistics**.

C. Choose the summary measures that you wish to calculate, such as **Mean, Standard deviation**, etc.

Constructing a Box Plot

A. (Replicating Figure 3.3) Copy and paste the ***Fund_Returns*** data from the text website into a Minitab spreadsheet.

B. From the menu choose **Graph > Boxplot > One Y–Simple**. Then click **OK**.

C. Choose Metals as **Graph variables**. Click **Data View**. Choose **Interquartile range box**, **Outlier symbols**, **Individual symbols**, and **Median connect line**. Click **OK**.

D. Click **Scale** and select the **Transpose value and category scales** box.

Calculating the Covariance and the Correlation Coefficient

A. (Replicating Example 3.20) Copy and paste the ***Fund_Returns*** data from the text website into a Minitab spreadsheet.

B. From the menu choose **Stat > Basic Statistics > Covariance** (choose **Correlation** to calculate the correlation coefficient). Then select Metals and Income as **Variables**.

SPSS

Calculating Summary Measures

A. (Replicating Table 3.3) Copy and paste the ***Fund_Returns*** data from the text website into an SPSS spreadsheet.

B. From the menu choose **Analyze > Descriptive Statistics > Descriptives**. Choose Metals and Income as **Variable(s)**. Click **Options**. Choose the summary measures that you wish to calculate, such as **Mean, Std. deviation**, etc.

Calculating the Covariance and the Correlation Coefficient

A. (Replicating Example 3.20) Copy and paste the ***Fund_Returns*** data from the text website into an SPSS spreadsheet.

B. From the menu choose **Analyze > Correlate > Bivariate**. Then choose Metals and Income as **Variable(s)**. Click **Options**. Choose **Cross-product deviations and covariances**.

JMP

Calculating Summary Measures and Constructing a Box Plot

A. (Replicating Table 3.3 and Figure 3.3) Copy and paste the ***Fund_Returns*** data from the text website into a JMP spreadsheet.

B. From the menu choose **Analyze > Distribution**. Under **Select Columns**, choose Metals and Income as **Y, Columns**.

Calculating the Covariance and the Correlation Coefficient

A. (Replicating Example 3.20) Copy and paste the ***Fund_Returns*** data from the text website into a JMP spreadsheet.

B. From the menu choose **Analyze > Multivariate**. Choose Metals and Income as **Y, Columns**. Click **OK**.

C. Click the red triangle beside **Multivariate**. Select **Covariance Matrix**.

4 Introduction to Probability

LEARNING OBJECTIVES

After reading this chapter you should be able to:

LO **4.1** Describe fundamental probability concepts.

LO **4.2** Formulate and explain subjective, empirical, and classical probabilities.

LO **4.3** Calculate and interpret the probability of the complement of an event and the probability that at least one of two events will occur.

LO **4.4** Calculate and interpret a conditional probability and apply the multiplication rule.

LO **4.5** Distinguish between independent and dependent events.

LO **4.6** Calculate and interpret probabilities from a contingency table.

LO **4.7** Apply the total probability rule and Bayes' theorem.

Every day we make choices about issues in the presence of uncertainty. Uncertainty describes a situation where a variety of events are possible. Usually, we either implicitly or explicitly assign probabilities to these events and plan or act accordingly. For instance, we read the paper, watch the news, or check the Internet to determine the likelihood of rain and whether we should carry an umbrella. Retailers strengthen their sales force before the end-of-year holiday season in anticipation of an increase in shoppers. The Federal Reserve cuts interest rates when it believes the economy is at risk for weak growth and raises interest rates when it feels that inflation is the greater risk. By figuring out the chances of various events, we are better prepared to make the more desirable choices. This chapter presents the essential probability tools needed to frame and address many real-world issues involving uncertainty. Probability theory turns out to be the very foundation for statistical inference, and numerous concepts introduced in this chapter are essential for understanding later chapters.

Sportswear Brands

Annabel Gonzalez is chief retail analyst at Longmeadow Consultants, a marketing firm. One aspect of her job is to track sports-apparel sales and uncover any particular trends that may be unfolding in the industry. Recently, she has been following Under Armour, Inc., the pioneer in the compression-gear market. Compression garments are meant to keep moisture away from a wearer's body during athletic activities in warm and cool weather. Under Armour has experienced exponential growth since the firm went public in November 2005. However, Nike, Inc., and Adidas Group, with 18% and 10% market shares, respectively, have aggressively entered the compression-gear market (*The Wall Street Journal*, October 23, 2007).

As part of her analysis, Annabel would first like to examine whether the age of the customer matters when buying compression clothing. Her initial feeling is that the Under Armour brand attracts a younger customer, whereas the more established companies, Nike and Adidas, draw an older clientele. She believes this information is relevant to advertisers and retailers in the sporting-goods industry as well as to some in the financial community. She collects data on 600 recent purchases in the compression-gear market. She cross-classifies the data by age group and brand name, as shown in Table 4.1.

TABLE 4.1 Purchases of Compression Garments Based on Age and Brand Name

| Age Group | Brand Name | | |
	Under Armour	Nike	Adidas
Under 35 years	174	132	90
35 years and older	54	72	78

Annabel wants to use the sample information to:

1. Calculate and interpret relevant probabilities concerning brand name and age.
2. Determine whether the appeal of the Under Armour brand is mostly to younger customers.

A synopsis of this case is provided at the end of Section 4.3.

4.1 Fundamental Probability Concepts

Since many choices we make involve some degree of uncertainty, we are better prepared for the eventual outcome if we can use probabilities to describe which events are likely and which are unlikely.

> A **probability** is a numerical value that measures the likelihood that an event occurs. This value is between zero and one, where a value of zero indicates *impossible* events and a value of one indicates *definite* events.

In order to define an event and assign the appropriate probability to it, it is useful to first establish some terminology and impose some structure on the situation.

An **experiment** is a process that leads to one of several possible outcomes. The diversity of the outcomes of an experiment is due to the uncertainty of the real world. When you purchase a new computer, there is no guarantee as to how long it will last before any repair work is needed. It may need repair in the first year, in the second year, or after two years. You can think of this as an experiment because the actual outcome will be determined only over time. Other examples of an experiment include whether a roll of a fair die will result in a value of 1, 2, 3, 4, 5, or 6; whether the toss of a coin results in heads or tails; whether a project is finished early, on time, or late; whether the economy will improve, stay the same, or deteriorate; whether a ball game will end in a win, loss, or tie.

A **sample space**, denoted by S, of an experiment contains all possible outcomes of the experiment. For example, suppose the sample space representing the letter grade in a course is given by $S = \{A, B, C, D, F\}$. If the teacher also gives out an I (incomplete) grade, then S is not valid because all outcomes of the experiment are not included in S. The sample space for an experiment need not be unique. For example, in the above experiment, we can also define the sample space with just P (pass) and F (fail) outcomes, that is, $S = \{P, F\}$.

> An **experiment** is a process that leads to one of several possible outcomes. A **sample space**, denoted S, of an experiment contains all possible outcomes of the experiment.

EXAMPLE 4.1

A snowboarder competing in the Winter Olympic Games is trying to assess her probability of earning a medal in her event, the ladies' halfpipe. Construct the appropriate sample space.

SOLUTION: The athlete's attempt to predict her chances of earning a medal is an experiment because, until the Winter Games occur, the outcome is unknown. We formalize an experiment by constructing its sample space. The athlete's competition has four possible outcomes: gold medal, silver medal, bronze medal, and no medal. We formally write the sample space as $S = \{$gold, silver, bronze, no medal$\}$.

Events

An **event** is a subset of the sample space. A simple event consists of just one of the possible outcomes of an experiment. Getting an A in a course is an example of a simple event. An event may also contain several outcomes of an experiment. For example, we can define an event as getting a passing grade in a course; this event is formed by the subset of outcomes A, B, C, and D.

An **event** is any subset of outcomes of the experiment. It is called a simple event if it contains a single outcome.

Let us define two events from Example 4.1, where one event represents "earning a medal" and the other denotes "failing to earn a medal." These events are **exhaustive** because they include all outcomes in the sample space. In the earlier grade-distribution example, the events of getting grades A and B are not exhaustive events because they do not include many feasible grades in the sample space. However, the events P and F, defined as pass and fail, respectively, are exhaustive.

Another important probability concept concerns **mutually exclusive** events. For two mutually exclusive events, the occurrence of one event precludes the occurrence of the other. Suppose we define the two events "at least earning a silver medal" (outcomes of gold and silver) and "at most earning a silver medal" (outcomes of silver, bronze, no medal). These two events are exhaustive because no outcome of the experiment is omitted. However, in this case, the events are not mutually exclusive because the outcome "silver" appears in both events. Going back to the grade-distribution example, while the events of getting grades A and B are not exhaustive, they are mutually exclusive, since you cannot possibly get an A as well as a B in the same course. However, getting grades P and F are mutually exclusive and exhaustive. Similarly, the events defined as "at least earning a silver medal" and "at most earning a bronze medal" are mutually exclusive and exhaustive.

Events are **exhaustive** if all possible outcomes of an experiment belong to the events.

Events are **mutually exclusive** if they do not share any common outcome of an experiment.

For any experiment, we can define events based on one or more outcomes of the experiment and also combine events to form new events. The **union** of two events, denoted $A \cup B$, is the event consisting of all outcomes in A or B. A useful way to illustrate these concepts is through the use of a Venn diagram, named after the British mathematician John Venn (1834–1923). Figure 4.1 shows a Venn diagram where the rectangle represents the sample space S and the two circles represent events A and B. The union $A \cup B$ is the portion in the Venn diagram that is included in either A or B.

FIGURE 4.1 The union of two events, $A \cup B$

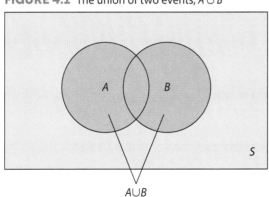

$A \cup B$

The **intersection** of two events, denoted $A \cap B$, is the event consisting of all outcomes in A and B. Figure 4.2 depicts the intersection of two events A and B. The intersection $A \cap B$ is the portion in the Venn diagram that is included in both A and B.

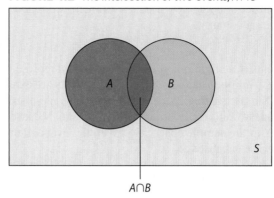

FIGURE 4.2 The intersection of two events, $A \cap B$

$A \cap B$

The **complement** of event A, denoted A^c, is the event consisting of all outcomes in the sample space S that are not in A. In Figure 4.3, A^c is everything in S that is not included in A.

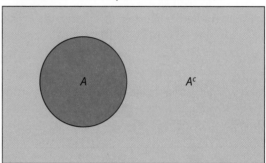

FIGURE 4.3 The complement of an event, A^c

COMBINING EVENTS

- The **union** of two events, denoted $A \cup B$, is the event consisting of all outcomes in A or B.
- The **intersection** of two events, denoted $A \cap B$, is the event consisting of all outcomes in A and B.
- The **complement** of event A, denoted A^c, is the event consisting of all outcomes in the sample space S that are not in A.

EXAMPLE 4.2

Recall that the snowboarder's sample space from Example 4.1 is defined as $S = \{\text{gold, silver, bronze, no medal}\}$. Now suppose the snowboarder defines the following three events:

- $A = \{\text{gold, silver, bronze}\}$, that is, event A denotes earning a medal;
- $B = \{\text{silver, bronze, no medal}\}$, that is, event B denotes earning at most a silver medal; and
- $C = \{\text{no medal}\}$, that is, event C denotes failing to earn a medal.

a. Find $A \cup B$ and $B \cup C$.
b. Find $A \cap B$ and $A \cap C$.
c. Find B^c.

SOLUTION:

a. The union of A and B denotes all outcomes common to A or B; here, the event $A \cup B = \{$gold, silver, bronze, no medal$\}$. Note that there is no double counting of the outcomes "silver" or "bronze" in $A \cup B$. Similarly, we have the event $B \cup C = \{$silver, bronze, no medal$\}$.

b. The intersection of A and B denotes all outcomes common to A and B; here, the event $A \cap B = \{$silver, bronze$\}$. The event $A \cap C = \varnothing$, where $\varnothing$ denotes the null (empty) set; no common outcomes appear in both A and C.

c. The complement of B denotes all outcomes in S that are not in B; here, the event $B^c = \{$gold$\}$.

Assigning Probabilities

LO **4.2**

Formulate and explain subjective, empirical, and classical probabilities.

Now that we have described a valid sample space and the various ways in which we can define events from that sample space, we are ready to assign probabilities. When we arrive at a probability, we generally are able to categorize the probability as a *subjective probability*, an *empirical probability*, or a *classical probability*. Regardless of the method used, there are two defining properties of probability.

> **THE TWO DEFINING PROPERTIES OF PROBABILITY**
>
> 1. The probability of any event A is a value between 0 and 1, that is, $0 \le P(A) \le 1$.
>
> 2. The sum of the probabilities of any list of mutually exclusive and exhaustive events equals 1.

Suppose the snowboarder from Example 4.1 believes that there is a 10% chance that she will earn a gold medal, a 15% chance that she will earn a silver medal, a 20% chance that she will earn a bronze medal, and a 55% chance that she will fail to earn a medal. She has assigned a **subjective probability** to each of the simple events. She made a personal assessment of these probabilities without referencing any data.

The snowboarder believes that the most likely outcome is failing to earn a medal since she gives that outcome the greatest chance of occurring at 55%. When formally writing out the probability that an event occurs, we generally construct a probability statement. Here, the probability statement might take the form: $P(\{$no medal$\}) = 0.55$, where $P(\text{"event"})$ represents the probability that a given event occurs. Table 4.2 summarizes these events and their respective subjective probabilities. Note that here the events are mutually exclusive and exhaustive.

TABLE 4.2 Snowboarder's Subjective Probabilities

Event	Probability
Gold	0.10
Silver	0.15
Bronze	0.20
No medal	0.55

Reading from the table we can readily see, for instance, that she assesses that there is a 15% chance that she will earn a silver medal, or $P(\{$silver$\}) = 0.15$. We should note that all the probabilities are between the values of zero and one, and they add up to one, thus meeting the defining properties of probability.

Suppose the snowboarder wants to calculate the probability of earning a medal. In Example 4.2 we defined "earning a medal" as event A, so the probability statement takes the form $P(A)$. We calculate this probability by summing the probabilities of the outcomes in A, or equivalently,

$$P(A) = P(\{\text{gold}\}) + P(\{\text{silver}\}) + P(\{\text{bronze}\}) = 0.10 + 0.15 + 0.20 = 0.45.$$

EXAMPLE 4.3

Given the events in Example 4.2 and the probabilities in Table 4.2, calculate the following probabilities.

a. $P(B \cup C)$

b. $P(A \cap C)$

c. $P(B^c)$

SOLUTION:

a. The probability that event B or event C occurs is

$$P(B \cup C) = P(\{silver\}) + P(\{bronze\}) + P(\{no\ medal\})$$
$$= 0.15 + 0.20 + 0.55 = 0.90.$$

b. The probability that event A and event C occur is

$$P(A \cap C) = 0;\ \text{recall that there are no common outcomes in } A \text{ and } C.$$

c. The probability that the complement of B occurs is

$$P(B^c) = P(\{gold\}) = 0.10.$$

In many instances we calculate probabilities by referencing data based on the observed outcomes of an experiment. The **empirical probability** of an event is the observed relative frequency with which an event occurs. The experiment must be repeated a large number of times for empirical probabilities to be accurate.

EXAMPLE 4.4

The frequency distribution in Table 4.3 summarizes the ages of the richest 400 Americans. Suppose we randomly select one of these individuals.

a. What is the probability that the individual is at least 50 but less than 60 years old?

b. What is the probability that the individual is younger than 60 years old?

c. What is the probability that the individual is at least 80 years old?

TABLE 4.3 Frequency Distribution of Ages of 400 Richest Americans

Ages	Frequency
30 up to 40	7
40 up to 50	47
50 up to 60	90
60 up to 70	109
70 up to 80	93
80 up to 90	45
90 up to 100	9

Source: http://www.forbes.com.

SOLUTION: In Table 4.3a, we first label each outcome with letter notation; for instance, the outcome "30 up to 40" is denoted as event A. Next we calculate the relative frequency of each event and use the relative frequency to denote the probability of the event.

TABLE 4.3a Relative Frequency Distribution of Ages of 400 Richest Americans

Ages	Event	Frequency	Relative Frequency
30 up to 40	A	7	7/400 = 0.0175
40 up to 50	B	47	0.1175
50 up to 60	C	90	0.2250
60 up to 70	D	109	0.2725
70 up to 80	E	93	0.2325
80 up to 90	F	45	0.1125
90 up to 100	G	9	0.0225

a. The probability that an individual is at least 50 but less than 60 years old is

$$P(C) = \frac{90}{400} = 0.225.$$

b. The probability that an individual is younger than 60 years old is

$$P(A \cup B \cup C) = \frac{7 + 47 + 90}{400} = 0.360.$$

c. The probability that an individual is at least 80 years old is

$$P(F \cup G) = \frac{45 + 9}{400} = 0.135.$$

In a more narrow range of well-defined problems, we can sometimes deduce probabilities by reasoning about the problem. The resulting probability is a **classical probability**. Classical probabilities are often used in games of chance. They are based on the assumption that all outcomes of an experiment are equally likely. Therefore, the classical probability of an event is computed as the number of outcomes belonging to the event divided by the total number of outcomes.

EXAMPLE 4.5

Suppose our experiment consists of rolling a six-sided die. Then we can define the appropriate sample space as $S = \{1, 2, 3, 4, 5, 6\}$.

a. What is the probability that we roll a 2?
b. What is the probability that we roll a 2 or 5?
c. What is the probability that we roll an even number?

SOLUTION: Here we recognize that each outcome is equally likely. So with 6 possible outcomes, each outcome has a 1/6 chance of occurring.

a. The probability that we roll a 2, $P(\{2\})$, is thus 1/6.
b. The probability that we roll a 2 or 5, $P(\{2\}) + P(\{5\})$, is $1/6 + 1/6 = 1/3$.
c. The probability that we roll an even number, $P(\{2\}) + P(\{4\}) + P(\{6\})$, is $1/6 + 1/6 + 1/6 = 1/2$.

According to a famous **law of large numbers**, the empirical probability approaches the classical probability if the experiment is run a very large number of times. Consider, for example, flipping a fair coin 10 times. It is possible that the heads may not show up exactly 5 times and, therefore, the relative frequency may not be 0.5. However, if we flip the fair coin a very large number of times, the heads will show up approximately 1/2 of the time.

EXERCISES 4.1

Mechanics

1. Determine whether the following probabilities are best categorized as subjective, empirical, or classical probabilities.
   a. Before flipping a fair coin, Sunil assesses that he has a 50% chance of obtaining tails.
   b. At the beginning of the semester, John believes he has a 90% chance of receiving straight A's.
   c. A political reporter announces that there is a 40% chance that the next person to come out of the conference room will be a Republican, since there are 60 Republicans and 90 Democrats in the room.

2. A sample space S yields five equally likely events, A, B, C, D, and E.
   a. Find $P(D)$.
   b. Find $P(B^c)$.
   c. Find $P(A \cup C \cup E)$.

3. You roll a die with the sample space $S = \{1, 2, 3, 4, 5, 6\}$. You define A as $\{1, 2, 3\}$, B as $\{1, 2, 3, 5, 6\}$, C as $\{4, 6\}$, and D as $\{4, 5, 6\}$. Determine which of the following events are exhaustive and/or mutually exclusive.
   a. A and B
   b. A and C
   c. A and D
   d. B and C

4. A sample space, S, yields four simple events, A, B, C, and D, such that $P(A) = 0.35$, $P(B) = 0.10$, and $P(C) = 0.25$.
   a. Find $P(D)$.
   b. Find $P(C^c)$.
   c. Find $P(A \cup B)$.

Applications

5. Jane Peterson has taken Amtrak to travel from New York to Washington, DC, on six occasions, of which three times the train was late. Therefore, Jane tells her friends that the probability that this train will arrive on time is 0.50. Would you label this probability as empirical or classical? Why would this probability not be accurate?

6. Survey data, based on 65,000 mobile phone subscribers, shows that 44% of the subscribers use smartphones (*Forbes*, December 15, 2011). Based on this information, you infer that the probability that a mobile phone subscriber uses a smartphone is 0.44. Would you consider this probability estimate accurate? Is it a subjective, empirical, or classical probability?

7. Consider the following scenarios to determine if the mentioned combination of attributes represents a union or an intersection.
   a. A marketing firm is looking for a candidate with a business degree and at least five years of work experience.
   b. A family has decided to purchase Toyota or Honda.

8. Consider the following scenarios to determine if the mentioned combination of attributes represents a union or an intersection.
   a. There are two courses that seem interesting to you, and you would be happy if you can take at least one of them.
   b. There are two courses that seem interesting to you, and you would be happy if you can take both of them.

9. You apply for a position at two firms. Let event A represent the outcome of getting an offer from the first firm and event B represent the outcome of getting an offer from the second firm.
   a. Explain why events A and B are not exhaustive.
   b. Explain why events A and B are not mutually exclusive.

10. An alarming number of U.S. adults are either overweight or obese. The distinction between overweight and obese is made on the basis of body mass index (BMI), expressed as weight/height^2. An adult is considered overweight if the BMI is 25 or more but less than 30. An obese adult will have a BMI of 30 or greater. According to a January 2012 article in the *Journal of the American Medical Association*, 33.1% of the adult population in the United States is overweight and 35.7% is obese. Use this information to answer the following questions.
    a. What is the probability that a randomly selected adult is either overweight or obese?
    b. What is the probability that a randomly selected adult is neither overweight nor obese?
    c. Are the events "overweight" and "obese" exhaustive?
    d. Are the events "overweight" and "obese" mutually exclusive?

11. Many communities are finding it more and more difficult to fill municipal positions such as town administrators, finance directors, and treasurers. The following table shows the percentage of municipal managers by age group in the United States for the years 1971 and 2006.

Age	1971	2006
Under 30	26%	1%
30 to 40	45%	12%
41 to 50	21%	28%
51 to 60	5%	48%
Over 60	3%	11%

Source: *The International City-County Management Association.*

   a. In 1971, what was the probability that a municipal manager was 40 years old or younger? In 2006, what was the probability that a municipal manager was 40 years old or younger?
   b. In 1971, what was the probability that a municipal manager was 51 years old or older? In 2006, what was the probability that a municipal manager was 51 years old or older?
   c. What trends in ages can you detect from municipal managers in 1971 versus municipal managers in 2006?

12. At four community health centers on Cape Cod, Massachusetts, 15,164 patients were asked to respond to questions designed to detect depression (*The Boston Globe*, June 11, 2008). The survey produced the following results.

Diagnosis	Number
Mild	3,257
Moderate	1,546
Moderately Severe	975
Severe	773
No Depression	8,613

a. What is the probability that a randomly selected patient suffered from mild depression?

b. What is the probability that a randomly selected patient did not suffer from depression?

c. What is the probability that a randomly selected patient suffered from moderately severe to severe depression?

d. Given that the national figure for moderately severe to severe depression is approximately 6.7%, does it appear that there is a higher rate of depression in this summer resort community? Explain.

4.2 Rules of Probability

Once we have determined the probabilities of simple events, we have various rules to calculate the probabilities of more complex events.

LO **4.3**

Calculate and interpret the probability of the complement of an event and the probability that at least one of two events will occur.

The Complement Rule

The complement rule follows from one of the defining properties of probability: The sum of probabilities assigned to simple events in a sample space must equal one. Note that since S is a collection of all possible outcomes of the experiment (nothing else can happen), $P(S) = 1$. Let's revisit the sample space that we constructed when we rolled a six-sided die: $S = \{1, 2, 3, 4, 5, 6\}$. Suppose event A is defined as an even-numbered outcome or $A = \{2, 4, 6\}$. We then know that the complement of A, A^c, is the set consisting of $\{1, 3, 5\}$. Moreover, we can deduce that $P(A) = 1/2$ and $P(A^c) = 1/2$, so $P(A) + P(A^c) = 1$. Rearranging this equation, we obtain the complement rule: $P(A^c) = 1 - P(A)$.

> **THE COMPLEMENT RULE**
>
> The **complement rule** states that the probability of the complement of an event, $P(A^c)$, is equal to one minus the probability of the event, that is, $P(A^c) = 1 - P(A)$.

The complement rule is quite straightforward and rather simple, but it is widely used and powerful.

EXAMPLE 4.6

According to the 2010 U.S. Census, 37% of women ages 25 to 34 have earned at least a college degree as compared with 30% of men in the same age group.

a. What is the probability that a randomly selected woman between the ages of 25 to 34 does not have a college degree?

b. What is the probability that a randomly selected man between the ages of 25 to 34 does not have a college degree?

SOLUTION:

a. Let's define A as the event that a randomly selected woman between the ages of 25 and 34 has a college degree; thus $P(A) = 0.37$. In this problem we are interested in the complement of A. So $P(A^c) = 1 - P(A) = 1 - 0.37 = 0.63$.

b. Similarly, we define B as the event that a randomly selected man between the ages of 25 to 34 has a college degree, so $P(B) = 0.30$. Thus, $P(B^c) = 1 - P(B) = 1 - 0.30 = 0.70$.

The Addition Rule

The addition rule allows us to find the probability of the union of two events. Suppose we want to find the probability that either A occurs or B occurs, so in probability terms, $P(A \cup B)$. We reproduce the Venn diagram, used earlier in Figure 4.1, to help in exposition. Figure 4.4 shows a sample space S with the two events A and B. Recall that the union, $A \cup B$, is the portion in the Venn diagram that is included in either A or B. The intersection, $A \cap B$, is the portion in the Venn diagram that is included in both A and B.

FIGURE 4.4 Finding the probability of the union, $P(A \cup B)$

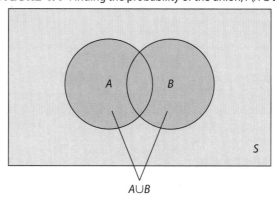

$A \cup B$

If we try to obtain $P(A \cup B)$ by simply summing $P(A)$ with $P(B)$, then we overstate the probability because we double-count the probability of the intersection of A and B, $P(A \cap B)$. When implementing the addition rule, we sum $P(A)$ and $P(B)$ and then subtract $P(A \cap B)$ from this sum.

THE ADDITION RULE

The **addition rule** states that the probability that A or B occurs, or that at least one of these events occurs, is equal to the probability that A occurs, plus the probability that B occurs, minus the probability that both A and B occur, or equivalently,

$$P(A \cup B) = P(A) + P(B) - P(A \cap B).$$

EXAMPLE 4.7

Anthony feels that he has a 75% chance of getting an A in Statistics and a 55% chance of getting an A in Managerial Economics. He also believes he has a 40% chance of getting an A in both classes.

a. What is the probability that he gets an A in at least one of these courses?

b. What is the probability that he does not get an A in either of these courses?

SOLUTION:

a. Let $P(A_S)$ correspond to the probability of getting an A in Statistics and $P(A_M)$ correspond to the probability of getting an A in Managerial Economics. Thus, $P(A_S) = 0.75$ and $P(A_M) = 0.55$. In addition, there is a 40% chance that Anthony gets an A in both classes, that is, $P(A_S \cap A_M) = 0.40$. In order to find the probability that he receives an A in at least one of these courses, we calculate:

$$P(A_S \cup A_M) = P(A_S) + P(A_M) - P(A_S \cap A_M) = 0.75 + 0.55 - 0.40 = 0.90.$$

b. The probability that he does not receive an A in either of these two courses is actually the complement of the union of the two events, that is, $P((A_S \cup A_M)^c)$. We calculated the union in part a, so using the complement rule we have

$$P((A_S \cup A_M)^c) = 1 - P(A_S \cup A_M) = 1 - 0.90 = 0.10.$$

An alternative expression that correctly captures the required probability is $P((A_S \cup A_M)^c) = P(A_S^c \cap A_M^c)$. A common mistake is to calculate the probability as $P((A_S \cap A_M)^c) = 1 - P(A_S \cap A_M) = 1 - 0.40 = 0.60$, which simply indicates that there is a 60% chance that Anthony will not get an A in both courses. This is clearly not the required probability that Anthony does not get an A in either course.

The Addition Rule for Mutually Exclusive Events

As mentioned earlier, mutually exclusive events do not share any outcome of an experiment. Figure 4.5 shows the Venn diagram for two mutually exclusive events; note that the circles do not intersect.

FIGURE 4.5 Mutually exclusive events

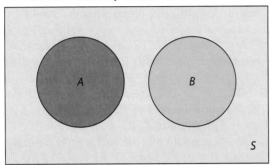

For mutually exclusive events A and B, the probability of their intersection is zero, that is, $P(A \cap B) = 0$. We need not concern ourselves with double-counting, and, therefore, the probability of the union is simply the sum of the two probabilities.

> **THE ADDITION RULE FOR MUTUALLY EXCLUSIVE EVENTS**
>
> If A and B are mutually exclusive events, then $P(A \cap B) = 0$ and, therefore, the addition rule simplifies to $P(A \cup B) = P(A) + P(B)$.

EXAMPLE 4.8

Samantha Greene, a college senior, contemplates her future immediately after graduation. She thinks there is a 25% chance that she will join the Peace Corps and teach English in Madagascar for the next few years. Alternatively, she believes there is a 35% chance that she will enroll in a full-time law school program in the United States.

a. What is the probability that she joins the Peace Corps or enrolls in law school?

b. What is the probability that she does not choose either of these options?

SOLUTION:

a. We can write the probability that Samantha joins the Peace Corps as $P(A) = 0.25$ and the probability that she enrolls in law school as $P(B) = 0.35$. Immediately after college, Samantha cannot choose both of these options. This implies that these events are mutually exclusive, so $P(A \cap B) = 0$. Thus, when solving for the probability that Samantha joins the Peace Corps or enrolls in law school, $P(A \cup B)$, we can simply sum $P(A)$ and $P(B)$: $P(A \cup B) = P(A) + P(B) = 0.25 + 0.35 = 0.60$.

b. In order to find the probability that she does not choose either of these options, we need to recognize that this probability is the complement of the union of the two events, that is, $P((A \cup B)^c)$. Therefore, using the complement rule, we have

$$P((A \cup B)^c) = 1 - P(A \cup B) = 1 - 0.60 = 0.40.$$

LO **4.4**

Calculate and interpret a conditional probability and apply the multiplication rule.

Conditional Probability

In business applications, the probability of interest is often a conditional probability. Examples include the probability that the housing market will improve conditional on the Federal Reserve taking remedial actions; the probability of making a six-figure salary conditional on getting an MBA; the probability that a company's stock price will go up conditional on higher-than-expected profits; the probability that sales will improve conditional on the firm launching a new innovative product.

Let's use an example to illustrate the concept of conditional probability. Suppose the probability that a recent business college graduate finds a suitable job is 0.80. The probability of finding a suitable job is 0.90 if the recent business college graduate has prior work experience. This type of probability is called a **conditional probability**, where the probability of an event is conditional on the occurrence of another event. If A represents "finding a job" and B represents "prior work experience," then $P(A) = 0.80$ and the conditional probability is denoted as $P(A|B) = 0.90$. The vertical mark | means "given that" and the conditional probability is typically read as "the probability of A given B." In the above example, the probability of finding a suitable job increases from 0.80 to 0.90 when conditioned on prior work experience. In general, the conditional probability, $P(A|B)$, is greater than the **unconditional probability**, $P(A)$, if B exerts a positive influence on A. Similarly, $P(A|B)$ is less than $P(A)$ when B exerts a negative influence on A. Finally, if B exerts no influence on A, then $P(A|B)$ equals $P(A)$.

As we will see later, it is important that we write the event that has already occurred after the vertical mark, since in most instances $P(A|B) \neq P(B|A)$. In the above example $P(B|A)$ would represent the probability of prior work experience conditional on having found a job.

We again rely on the Venn diagram in Figure 4.6 to explain the conditional probability.

FIGURE 4.6 Finding the conditional probability, $P(A|B)$

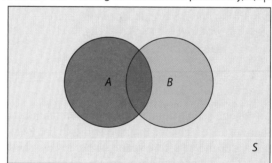

Since $P(A|B)$ represents the probability of A conditional on B (B has occurred), the original sample space S reduces to B. The conditional probability $P(A|B)$ is based on the portion of A that is included in B. It is derived as the ratio of the probability of the intersection of A and B to the probability of B.

CALCULATING A CONDITIONAL PROBABILITY

Given two events A and B, each with a positive probability of occurring, the probability that A occurs given that B has occurred (A conditioned on B) is equal to $P(A|B) = \frac{P(A \cap B)}{P(B)}$. Similarly, the probability that B occurs given that A has occurred (B conditioned on A) is equal to $P(B|A) = \frac{P(A \cap B)}{P(A)}$.

EXAMPLE 4.9

Economic globalization is defined as the integration of national economies into the international economy through trade, foreign direct investment, capital flows, migration, and the spread of technology. Although globalization is generally viewed favorably, it also increases the vulnerability of a country to economic conditions of the other country. An economist predicts a 60% chance that country A will perform poorly and a 25% chance that country B will perform poorly. There is also a 16% chance that both countries will perform poorly.

a. What is the probability that country A performs poorly given that country B performs poorly?

b. What is the probability that country B performs poorly given that country A performs poorly?

c. Interpret your findings.

SOLUTION: We first write down the available information in probability terms. Defining A as "country A performing poorly" and B as "country B performing poorly," we have the following information: $P(A) = 0.60$, $P(B) = 0.25$, and $P(A \cap B) = 0.16$.

a. $P(A|B) = \dfrac{P(A \cap B)}{P(B)} = \dfrac{0.16}{0.25} = 0.64.$

b. $P(B|A) = \dfrac{P(A \cap B)}{P(A)} = \dfrac{0.16}{0.60} = 0.27.$

c. It appears that globalization has definitely made these countries vulnerable to the economic woes of the other country. The probability that country A performs poorly increases from 60% to 64% when country B has performed poorly. Similarly, the probability that country B performs poorly increases from 25% to 27% when conditioned on country A performing poorly.

Independent and Dependent Events

LO **4.5**

Distinguish between independent and dependent events.

Of particular interest to researchers is whether or not two events influence one another. Two events are **independent** if the occurrence of one event does not affect the probability of the occurrence of the other event. Let's revisit the earlier example where the probability of finding a job is 0.80 and the probability of finding a job given prior work experience is 0.90. Prior work experience exerts a positive influence on finding a job because the conditional probability, $P(A|B) = 0.90$, exceeds the unconditional probability, $P(A) = 0.80$. Now consider the probability of finding a job given that your neighbor has bought a red car. Obviously, your neighbor's decision to buy a red car has no influence on your probability of finding a job, which remains at 0.80.

Events are considered **dependent** if the occurrence of one is related to the probability of the occurrence of the other. We generally test for the independence of two events by comparing the conditional probability of one event, for instance $P(A|B)$, to its unconditional probability, $P(A)$. If these two probabilities are the same, we say that the two events, A and B, are independent; if the probabilities differ, the two events are dependent.

INDEPENDENT VERSUS DEPENDENT EVENTS

Two events, A and B, are **independent** if $P(A|B) = P(A)$ or, equivalently, $P(B|A) = P(B)$. Otherwise, the events are **dependent**.

EXAMPLE 4.10

Suppose that for a given year there is a 2% chance that your desktop computer will crash and a 6% chance that your laptop computer will crash. Moreover, there is a 0.12% chance that both computers will crash. Is the reliability of the two computers independent of each other?

SOLUTION: Let event D represent the outcome that your desktop crashes and event L represent the outcome that your laptop crashes. Therefore, $P(D) = 0.02$, $P(L) = 0.06$, and $P(D \cap L) = 0.0012$. The reliability of the two computers is independent because

$$P(D|L) = \frac{P(D \cap L)}{P(L)} = \frac{0.0012}{0.06} = 0.02 = P(D).$$

In other words, if your laptop crashes, it does not alter the probability that your desktop also crashes. Equivalently,

$$P(L|D) = \frac{P(D \cap L)}{P(D)} = \frac{0.0012}{0.02} = 0.06 = P(L).$$

The Multiplication Rule

In some situations, we are interested in finding the probability that two events, A and B, both occur, that is, $P(A \cap B)$. In order to obtain this probability, we can rearrange the formula for conditional probability to derive $P(A \cap B)$. For instance, from $P(A|B) = \frac{P(A \cap B)}{P(B)}$, we can easily derive $P(A \cap B) = P(A|B)P(B)$. Similarly, from $P(B|A) = \frac{P(A \cap B)}{P(A)}$, we derive $P(A \cap B) = P(B|A)P(A)$. Since we calculate the product of two probabilities to find $P(A \cap B)$, we refer to it as the **multiplication rule** for probabilities.

THE MULTIPLICATION RULE

The **multiplication rule** states that the probability that A and B both occur is equal to the probability that A occurs given that B has occurred times the probability that B occurs, that is, $P(A \cap B) = P(A|B)P(B)$. Equivalently, we can also arrive at this probability as $P(A \cap B) = P(B|A)P(A)$.

EXAMPLE 4.11

A stockbroker knows from past experience that the probability that a client owns stocks is 0.60 and the probability that a client owns bonds is 0.50. The probability that the client owns bonds if he/she already owns stocks is 0.55.

a. What is the probability that the client owns both of these securities?
b. Given that the client owns bonds, what is the probability that the client owns stocks?

SOLUTION:

a. Let A correspond to the event that a client owns stocks and B correspond to the event that a client owns bonds. Thus, the unconditional probabilities that the client owns stocks and that the client owns bonds are $P(A) = 0.60$ and $P(B) = 0.50$, respectively. The conditional probability that the client owns bonds given that he/she owns stocks is $P(B|A) = 0.55$. We calculate the probability that the client owns both of these securities as $P(A \cap B) = P(B|A)P(A) = 0.55 \times 0.60 = 0.33$.

b. We need to calculate the conditional probability that the client owns stocks given that he/she owns bonds, or $P(A|B)$. Using the formula for conditional probability and the answer from part a, we find $P(A|B) = \frac{P(A \cap B)}{P(B)} = \frac{0.33}{0.50} = 0.66$.

The Multiplication Rule for Independent Events

We know that two events, A and B, are independent if $P(A|B) = P(A)$. With independent events, the multiplication rule $P(A \cap B) = P(A|B)P(B)$ simplifies to $P(A \cap B) = P(A)P(B)$. We can use this rule to determine whether or not two events are independent. That is, two events are independent if the probability $P(A \cap B)$ equals the product of their unconditional probabilities, $P(A)P(B)$. In Example 4.10, we were given the probabilities $P(D) = 0.02$, $P(L) = 0.06$, and $P(D \cap L) = 0.0012$. Consistent with the earlier result, events D and L are independent because $P(D \cap L) = 0.0012$ equals $P(D)P(L) = 0.02 \times 0.06 = 0.0012$.

THE MULTIPLICATION RULE FOR INDEPENDENT EVENTS

The **multiplication rule for independent events** states that the probability of A and B equals the product of the unconditional probabilities of A and B, that is, $P(A \cap B) = P(A)P(B)$.

EXAMPLE 4.12

The probability of passing the Level 1 CFA (Chartered Financial Analyst) exam is 0.50 for John Campbell and 0.80 for Linda Lee. The prospect of John's passing the exam is completely unrelated to Linda's success on the exam.

a. What is the probability that both John and Linda pass the exam?

b. What is the probability that at least one of them passes the exam?

SOLUTION:

We can write the unconditional probabilities that John passes the exam and that Linda passes the exam as $P(J) = 0.50$ and $P(L) = 0.80$, respectively.

a. Since we are told that John's chances of passing the exam are not influenced by Linda's success at the exam, we can conclude that these events are independent, so $P(J) = P(J|L) = 0.50$ and $P(L) = P(L|J) = 0.80$. Thus, when solving for the probability that both John and Linda pass the exam, we calculate the product of the unconditional probabilities, so $P(J \cap L) = P(J) \times P(L) = 0.50 \times 0.80 = 0.40$.

b. We calculate the probability that at least one of them passes the exam as:
$P(J \cup L) = P(J) + P(L) - P(J \cap L) = 0.50 + 0.80 - 0.40 = 0.90$.

EXERCISES 4.2

Mechanics

13. Let $P(A) = 0.65$, $P(B) = 0.30$, and $P(A|B) = 0.45$.
    a. Calculate $P(A \cap B)$.
    b. Calculate $P(A \cup B)$.
    c. Calculate $P(B|A)$.

14. Let $P(A) = 0.55$, $P(B) = 0.30$, and $P(A \cap B) = 0.10$.
    a. Calculate $P(A|B)$.
    b. Calculate $P(A \cup B)$.
    c. Calculate $P((A \cup B)^c)$.

15. Let A and B be mutually exclusive with $P(A) = 0.25$ and $P(B) = 0.30$.
    a. Calculate $P(A \cap B)$.
    b. Calculate $P(A \cup B)$.
    c. Calculate $P(A|B)$.

16. Let A and B be independent with $P(A) = 0.40$ and $P(B) = 0.50$.
    a. Calculate $P(A \cap B)$.
    b. Calculate $P((A \cup B)^c)$.
    c. Calculate $P(A|B)$.

17. Let $P(A) = 0.65$, $P(B) = 0.30$, and $P(A|B) = 0.45$.
    a. Are A and B independent events? Explain.
    b. Are A and B mutually exclusive events? Explain.
    c. What is the probability that neither A nor B takes place?

18. Let $P(A) = 0.15$, $P(B) = 0.10$, and $P(A \cap B) = 0.05$.
    a. Are A and B independent events? Explain.
    b. Are A and B mutually exclusive events? Explain.
    c. What is the probability that neither A nor B takes place?

19. Consider the following probabilities: $P(A) = 0.25$, $P(B^c) = 0.40$, and $P(A \cap B) = 0.08$. Find:
   a. $P(B)$
   b. $P(A|B)$
   c. $P(B|A)$

20. Consider the following probabilities: $P(A^c) = 0.30$, $P(B) = 0.60$, and $P(A \cap B^c) = 0.24$. Find:
   a. $P(A|B^c)$
   b. $P(B^c|A)$
   c. Are A and B independent events? Explain.

21. Consider the following probabilities: $P(A) = 0.40$, $P(B) = 0.50$, and $P(A^c \cap B^c) = 0.24$. Find:
   a. $P(A^c|B^c)$
   b. $P(A^c \cup B^c)$
   c. $P(A \cup B)$

Applications

22. Survey data, based on 65,000 mobile phone subscribers, shows that 44% of the subscribers use smartphones (*Forbes*, December 15, 2011). Moreover, 51% of smartphone users are women.
   a. Find the probability that a mobile phone subscriber is a woman who uses a smartphone.
   b. Find the probability that a mobile phone subscriber is a man who uses a smartphone.

23. Twenty percent of students in a college ever go to their professor during office hours. Of those who go, 30% seek minor clarification and 70% seek major clarification.
   a. What is the probability that a student goes to the professor during her office hours for a minor clarification?
   b. What is the probability that a student goes to the professor during her office hours for a major clarification?

24. The probabilities that stock A will rise in price is 0.40 and that stock B will rise in price is 0.60. Further, if stock B rises in price, the probability that stock A will also rise in price is 0.80.
   a. What is the probability that at least one of the stocks will rise in price?
   b. Are events A and B mutually exclusive? Explain.
   c. Are events A and B independent? Explain.

25. Despite government bailouts and stimulus money, unemployment in the United States had not decreased significantly as economists had expected (*US News and World Report*, July 2, 2010). Many analysts predicted only an 18% chance of a reduction in U.S. unemployment. However, if Europe slipped back into a recession, the probability of a reduction in U.S. unemployment would drop to 0.06.
   a. What is the probability that there is not a reduction in U.S. unemployment?
   b. Assume there is an 8% chance that Europe slips back into a recession. What is the probability that there is not a reduction in U.S. unemployment and that Europe slips into a recession?

26. Dr. Miriam Johnson has been teaching accounting for over 20 years. From her experience she knows that 60% of her students do homework regularly. Moreover, 95% of the students who do their homework regularly generally pass the course. She also knows that 85% of her students pass the course.
   a. What is the probability that a student will do homework regularly and also pass the course?
   b. What is the probability that a student will neither do homework regularly nor will pass the course?
   c. Are the events "pass the course" and "do homework regularly" mutually exclusive? Explain.
   d. Are the events "pass the course" and "do homework regularly" independent? Explain.

27. Records show that 5% of all college students are foreign students who also smoke. It is also known that 50% of all foreign college students smoke. What percent of the students at this university are foreign?

28. An analyst estimates that the probability of default on a seven-year AA-rated bond is 0.06, while that on a seven-year A-rated bond is 0.13. The probability that they will both default is 0.04.
   a. What is the probability that at least one of the bonds defaults?
   b. What is the probability that neither the seven-year AA-rated bond nor the seven-year A-rated bond defaults?
   c. Given that the seven-year AA-rated bond defaults, what is the probability that the seven-year A-rated bond also defaults?

29. In general, shopping online is supposed to be more convenient than going to stores. However, according to a recent Harris Interactive poll, 87% of people have experienced problems with an online transaction (*The Wall Street Journal*, October 2, 2007). Forty-two percent of people who experienced a problem abandoned the transaction or switched to a competitor's website. Fifty-three percent of people who experienced problems contacted customer-service representatives.
   a. What percentage of people did not experience problems with an online transaction?
   b. What percentage of people experienced problems with an online transaction and abandoned the transaction or switched to a competitor's website?
   c. What percentage of people experienced problems with an online transaction and contacted customer-service representatives?

30. Mike Danes has been delayed in going to the annual sales event at one of his favorite apparel stores. His friend has just texted him that there are only 20 shirts left, of which 8 are in size M, 10 in size L, and 2 in size XL. Also 3 of the shirts are white, 5 are blue, and the remaining are of mixed colors. Mike is interested in getting a white or a blue shirt in size L. Define the events $A =$ Getting a white or a blue shirt and $B =$ Getting a shirt in size L.
   a. Find $P(A)$, $P(A^c)$, and $P(B)$.
   b. Are the events A and B mutually exclusive and exhaustive? Explain.
   c. Would you describe Mike's preference by the events $A \cup B$ or $A \cap B$?

31. A manufacturing firm just received a shipment of 20 assembly parts, of slightly varied sizes, from a vendor. The manager knows that there are only 15 parts in the shipment that would be suitable. He examines these parts one at a time.

    a. Find the probability that the first part is suitable.

    b. If the first part is suitable, find the probability that the second part is also suitable.

    c. If the first part is suitable, find the probability that the second part is not suitable.

32. Despite the repeated effort by the government to reform how Wall Street pays its executives, some of the nation's biggest banks are continuing to pay out bonuses nearly as large as those in the best years before the crisis (*The Washington Post*, January 15, 2010). It is known that 10 out of 15 members of the board of directors of a company were in favor of the bonus. Suppose two members were randomly selected by the media.

    a. What is the probability that both of them were in favor of the bonus?

    b. What is the probability that neither of them was in favor of the bonus?

33. Apple products have become a household name in America with 51 percent of all households owning at least one Apple product (*CNN*, March 19, 2012). The likelihood of owning an Apple product is 61 percent for households with kids and 48 percent for households without kids. Suppose there are 1,200 households in a representative community of which 820 are with kids and the rest are without kids.

    a. Are the events "household with kids" and "household without kids" mutually exclusive and exhaustive? Explain.

    b. What is the probability that a household is without kids?

    c. What is the probability that a household is with kids and owns an Apple product?

    d. What is the probability that a household is without kids and does not own an Apple product?

34. According to the Census's Population Survey, the percentage of children with two parents at home is the highest for Asians and lowest for blacks (*USA TODAY*, February 26, 2009). It is reported that 85% of Asian, 78% of white, 70% of Hispanic, and 38% of black children have two parents at home. Suppose there are 500 students in a representative school of which 280 are white, 50 are Asian, 100 are Hispanic, and 70 are black.

    a. Are the events "Asians" and "black" mutually exclusive and exhaustive? Explain.

    b. What is the probability that a given child is not white?

    c. What is the probability that a child is white and has both parents at home?

    d. What is the probability that a child is Asian and does not have both parents at home?

35. Christine Wong has asked Dave and Mike to help her move into a new apartment on Sunday morning. She has asked them both in case one of them does not show up. From past experience, Christine knows that there is a 40% chance that Dave will not show up and a 30% chance that Mike will not

show up. Dave and Mike do not know each other and their decisions can be assumed to be independent.

    a. What is the probability that both Dave and Mike will show up?

    b. What is the probability that at least one of them will show up?

    c. What is the probability that neither Dave nor Mike will show up?

36. According to a recent survey by two United Nations agencies and a nongovernmental organization, two in every three women in the Indian capital of New Delhi are likely to face some form of sexual harassment in a year (*BBC World News*, July 9, 2010). The study also reports that women who use public transportation are especially vulnerable. Suppose the corresponding probability of harassment for women who use public transportation is 0.82. It is also known that 28% of women use public transportation.

    a. What is the probability that a woman takes public transportation and also faces sexual harassment?

    b. If a woman is sexually harassed, what is the probability that she had taken public transportation?

37. Since the fall of 2008, millions of Americans have lost jobs due to the economic meltdown. A recent study shows that unemployment has not impacted white-collar and blue-collar workers equally (*Newsweek*, April 20, 2009). According to the Bureau of Labor Statistics report, while the national unemployment rate is 8.5%, it is only 4.3% for those with a college degree. It is fair to assume that 27% of people in the labor force are college educated. You have just heard that another worker in a large firm has been laid off. What is the probability that the worker is college educated?

38. A recent study challenges the media narrative that foreclosures are dangerously widespread (*New York Times*, March 2, 2009). According to this study, 62% of all foreclosures were centered in only four states, namely, Arizona, California, Florida, and Nevada. The national average rate of foreclosures in 2008 was 0.79%. What percent of the homes in the United States were foreclosed in 2008 and also centered in Arizona, California, Florida, or Nevada?

39. According to results from the Spine Patient Outcomes Research Trial, or SPORT, surgery for a painful, common back condition resulted in significantly reduced back pain and better physical function than treatment with drugs and physical therapy (*The Wall Street Journal*, February 21, 2008). SPORT followed 803 patients, of whom 398 ended up getting surgery. After two years, of those who had surgery, 63% said they had a major improvement in their condition, compared with 29% among those who received nonsurgical treatment.

    a. What is the probability that a patient had surgery? What is the probability that a patient did not have surgery?

    b. What is the probability that a patient had surgery and experienced a major improvement in his or her condition?

    c. What is the probability that a patient received nonsurgical treatment and experienced a major improvement in his or her condition?

4.3 Contingency Tables and Probabilities

LO **4.6**

Calculate
and interpret
probabilities
from a
contingency
table.

We learned in Chapter 2 that, when organizing qualitative data, it is often useful to construct a frequency distribution. A frequency distribution is a useful tool when we want to sort one variable at a time. However, in many instances we want to examine or compare two qualitative variables. On these occasions, a **contingency table** proves very useful. Contingency tables are widely used in marketing and biomedical research, as well as in the social sciences.

> **A CONTINGENCY TABLE**
>
> A **contingency table** generally shows frequencies for two qualitative (categorical) variables, x and y, where each cell represents a mutually exclusive combination of the pair of x and y values.

Table 4.4, first presented in the introductory case study of this chapter, is an example of a contingency table where the qualitative variables of interest, x and y, are Age Group and Brand Name, respectively. Age Group has two possible categories: (1) under 35 years and (2) 35 years and older; Brand Name, has three possible categories: (1) Under Armour, (2) Nike, and (3) Adidas.

TABLE 4.4 Purchases of Compression Garments Based on Age and Brand Name

Age Group	Brand Name		
	Under Armour	Nike	Adidas
Under 35 years	174	132	90
35 years and older	54	72	78

Each cell in Table 4.4 represents a frequency; for example, there are 174 customers under the age of 35 who purchase an Under Armour product, whereas there are 54 customers at least 35 years old who purchase an Under Armour product. Recall that we estimate an empirical probability by calculating the relative frequency of the occurrence of the event. To make calculating these probabilities less cumbersome, it is often useful to denote each event with letter notation and calculate totals for each column and row as shown in Table 4.4a.

TABLE 4.4a A Contingency Table Labeled Using Event Notation

Age Group	Brand Name			Total
	B_1	B_2	B_3	
A	174	132	90	396
A^c	54	72	78	204
Total	228	204	168	600

Thus, let events A and A^c correspond to "under 35 years" and "35 years and older," respectively; similarly, let events B_1, B_2, and B_3 correspond to "Under Armour," "Nike," and "Adidas," respectively. In addition, after calculating row totals, it is now easier to recognize that 396 of the customers are under 35 years old and 204 of the customers are at least 35 years old. Similarly, column totals indicate that 228 customers purchase Under Armour, 204 purchase Nike, and 168 purchase Adidas. Finally, the frequency corresponding to the cell in the last column and the last row is 600. This value represents the sample size, that is, the total number of customers in the sample. We arrive at this value by either summing the values in the last column (396 + 204) or summing the values in the last row (228 + 204 + 168).

The following example illustrates how to calculate probabilities when the data are presented in the form of a contingency table.

EXAMPLE 4.13

Using the information in Table 4.4a, answer the following questions.

a. What is the probability that a randomly selected customer is younger than 35 years old?

b. What is the probability that a randomly selected customer purchases an Under Armour garment?

c. What is the probability that a customer is younger than 35 years old and purchases an Under Armour garment?

d. What is the probability that a customer is either younger than 35 years old or purchases an Under Armour garment?

e. What is the probability that a customer is under 35 years of age, given that the customer purchases an Under Armour garment?

SOLUTION:

a. $P(A) = \frac{396}{600} = 0.66$; there is a 66% chance that a randomly selected customer is less than 35 years old.

b. $P(B_1) = \frac{228}{600} = 0.38$; there is a 38% chance that a randomly selected customer purchases an Under Armour garment.

c. $P(A \cap B_1) = \frac{174}{600} = 0.29$; there is a 29% chance that a randomly selected customer is younger than 35 years old and purchases an Under Armour garment.

d. $P(A \cup B_1) = \frac{174 + 132 + 90 + 54}{600} = \frac{450}{600} = 0.75$; there is a 75% chance that a randomly selected customer is either younger than 35 years old or purchases an Under Armour garment. Alternatively, we can use the addition rule to solve this problem as $P(A \cup B_1) = P(A) + P(B_1) - P(A \cap B_1) = 0.66 + 0.38 - 0.29 = 0.75$.

e. We wish to calculate the conditional probability, $P(A|B_1)$. When the information is in the form of a contingency table, calculating a conditional probability is rather straightforward. We are given the information that the customer purchases an Under Armour garment, so the sample space shrinks from 600 customers to 228 customers. We can ignore all customers that make Nike or Adidas purchases, or all outcomes in events B_2 and B_3. Thus, of the 228 customers who make an Under Armour purchase, 174 of them are under 35 years of age. Therefore, the probability that a customer is under 35 years of age given that the customer makes an Under Armour purchase is calculated as $P(A|B_1) = \frac{174}{228} = 0.76$. Alternatively, we can use the conditional probability formula to solve the problem as $P(A|B_1) = \frac{P(A \cap B_1)}{P(B_1)} = \frac{174/600}{228/600} = \frac{174}{228} = 0.76$.

Arguably, a more convenient way of calculating relevant probabilities is to convert the contingency table to a **joint probability table**. The frequency in each cell is divided by the number of outcomes in the sample space, which in this example is 600 customers. Table 4.4b shows the results.

TABLE 4.4b Converting a Contingency Table to a Joint Probability Table

Age Group	Brand Name			Total
	B_1	B_2	B_3	
A	0.29	0.22	0.15	0.66
A^c	0.09	0.12	0.13	0.34
Total	0.38	0.34	0.28	1.00

The values in the interior of the table represent the probabilities of the intersection of two events, also referred to as **joint probabilities**. For instance, the probability that a randomly selected person is under 35 years of age and makes an Under Armour purchase, denoted $P(A \cap B_1)$, is 0.29. Similarly, we can readily read from this table that 12% of the customers purchase a Nike garment and are at least 35 years old, or $P(A^c \cap B_2) = 0.12$.

The values in the margins of Table 4.4b represent unconditional probabilities. These probabilities are also referred to as **marginal probabilities**. For example, the probability that a randomly selected customer is under 35 years of age, $P(A)$, is simply 0.66. Also, the probability of purchasing a Nike garment, $P(B_2)$, is 0.34.

Note that the conditional probability is basically the ratio of a joint probability to an unconditional probability. Since $P(A|B_1) = \frac{P(A \cap B_1)}{P(B_1)}$, the numerator is the joint probability, $P(A \cap B_1)$, and the denominator is the unconditional probability, $P(B_1)$. Let's refer back to the probability that we calculated earlier; that is, the probability that a customer is under 35 years of age, given that the customer purchases an Under Armour product. This conditional probability is easily computed as $P(A|B_1) = \frac{P(A \cap B_1)}{P(B_1)} = \frac{0.29}{0.38} = 0.76$.

EXAMPLE 4.14

Given the information in Table 4.4b, what is the probability that a customer purchases an Under Armour product, given that the customer is under 35 years of age?

SOLUTION: Now we are solving for $P(B_1|A)$. So

$$P(B_1|A) = \frac{P(A \cap B_1)}{P(A)} = \frac{0.29}{0.66} = 0.44.$$

Note that $P(B_1|A) = 0.44 \neq P(A|B_1) = 0.76$.

EXAMPLE 4.15

Determine whether the events "under 35 years old" and "Under Armour" are independent.

SOLUTION: In order to determine whether two events are independent, we compare an event's conditional probability to its unconditional probability; that is, events A and B are independent if $P(A|B) = P(A)$. In the Under Armour example, we have already found that $P(A|B_1) = 0.76$. In other words, there is a 76% chance that a customer is under 35 years old given that the customer purchases an Under Armour product. We compare this conditional probability to its unconditional probability, $P(A) = 0.66$. Since these probabilities differ, the events "under 35 years old" and "Under Armour" are not independent events. We could have compared $P(B_1|A)$ to $P(B_1)$ and found that $0.44 \neq 0.38$, which leads us to the same conclusion that the events are dependent. As discussed in the preceding section, an alternative approach is to compare the joint probability with the product of the two unconditional probabilities. Events are independent if $P(A \cap B_1) = P(A)P(B_1)$. In the above example, $P(A \cap B_1) = 0.29$ does not equal $P(A)P(B_1) = 0.66 \times 0.38 = 0.25$, so the two events are not independent.

It is important to note that the conclusions about independence, such as the one made in Example 4.15, are informal since they are based on empirical probabilities computed from given sample information. In the above example, these probabilities will change if a different sample of 600 customers is used. Formal tests of independence are discussed in Chapter 11.

SYNOPSIS OF INTRODUCTORY CASE

After careful analysis of the contingency table representing customer purchases of compression garments based on age and brand name, several interesting remarks can be made. From a sample of 600 customers, it appears that the majority of the customers who purchase these products tend to be younger: 66% of the customers were younger than 35 years old, whereas 34% were at least 35 years old. It is true that more customers chose to purchase Under Armour garments (with 38% of purchases) as compared to Nike or Adidas garments (with 34% and 28% of purchases, respectively). However, given that Under Armour was the pioneer in the compression-gear market, this company should be concerned with the competition posed by Nike and Adidas. Further inspection of the contingency table reveals that if a customer was under 35 years old, the chances of the customer purchasing an Under Armour garment rises to about 44%. This result indicates that the age of a customer seems to influence the brand name purchased. In other words, 38% of the customers choose to buy Under Armour products, but as soon as the attention is confined to those customers who are under 35 years old, the likelihood of a purchase from Under Armour rises to about 44%. The information that the Under Armour brand appeals to younger customers is relevant not only for Under Armour and how the firm may focus its advertising efforts, but also to competitors and retailers in the compression garment market.

EXERCISES 4.3

Mechanics

40. Consider the following contingency table.

	B	Bᶜ
A	26	34
Aᶜ	14	26

a. Convert the contingency table into a joint probability table.
b. What is the probability that A occurs?
c. What is the probability that A and B occur?
d. Given that B has occurred, what is the probability that A occurs?
e. Given that Aᶜ has occurred, what is the probability that B occurs?
f. Are A and B mutually exclusive events? Explain.
g. Are A and B independent events? Explain.

41. Consider the following joint probability table.

	B_1	B_2	B_3	B_4
A	0.09	0.22	0.15	0.20
Aᶜ	0.03	0.10	0.09	0.12

a. What is the probability that A occurs?
b. What is the probability that B_2 occurs?
c. What is the probability that A^c and B_4 occur?
d. What is the probability that A or B_3 occurs?

e. Given that B_2 has occurred, what is the probability that A occurs?
f. Given that A has occurred, what is the probability that B_4 occurs?

Applications

42. According to an online survey by Harris Interactive for job site CareerBuilder.com, more than half of IT (information technology) workers say they have fallen asleep at work (*InformationWeek*, September 27, 2007). Sixty-four percent of government workers admitted to falling asleep on the job. Consider the following contingency table that is representative of the survey results.

	Job Category	
	IT	Government
Slept on the Job?	Professional	Professional
Yes	155	256
No	145	144

a. Convert the contingency table into a joint probability table.
b. What is the probability that a randomly selected worker is an IT professional?
c. What is the probability that a randomly selected worker slept on the job?
d. If a randomly selected worker slept on the job, what is the probability that he/she is an IT professional?

e. If a randomly selected worker is a government professional, what is the probability that he/she slept on the job?

f. Are the events "IT Professional" and "Slept on the Job" independent? Explain using probabilities.

43. A recent poll asked 16- to 21-year-olds whether or not they are likely to serve in the U.S. military. The following table, cross-classified by gender and race, reports the percentage of those polled who responded that they are likely or very likely to serve in the active-duty military.

Gender	Race		
	Hispanic	Black	White
Male	33.5%	20.5%	16.5%
Female	14.5%	10.5%	4.5%

Source: Defense Human Resources Activity telephone poll of 3,228 Americans conducted October through December 2005.

a. What is the probability that a randomly selected respondent is female?

b. What is the probability that a randomly selected respondent is Hispanic?

c. Given that a respondent is female, what is the probability that she is Hispanic?

d. Given that a respondent is white, what is the probability that the respondent is male?

e. Are the events "Male" and "White" independent? Explain using probabilities.

44. A recent report suggests that business majors spend the least amount of time on course work than all other college students (*The New York Times*, November 17, 2011). A provost of a university decides to conduct a survey where students are asked if they study hard, defined by spending at least 20 hours per week on course work. Of 120 business majors included in the survey, 20 said that they studied hard as compared to 48 out of 150 nonbusiness majors who said that they studied hard.

a. Construct a contingency table that shows the frequencies for the qualitative variables Major (business or nonbusiness) and Study Hard (yes or no).

b. Find the probability that a business major spends less than 20 hours per week on course work.

c. What is the probability that a student studies hard?

d. If a student spends at least 20 hours on course work, what is the probability that he/she is a business major? What is the corresponding probability that he/she is a nonbusiness major?

45. According to a Michigan State University researcher, Americans are becoming increasingly polarized on issues pertaining to the environment. (*http://news.msu.edu*, April 19, 2011). It is reported that 70% of Democrats see signs of global warming as compared to only 29% of Republicans who feel the same. Suppose the survey was based on 400 Democrats and 400 Republicans.

a. Construct a contingency table that shows frequencies for the qualitative variables Political Affiliation (Democrat or Republican) and Global Warming (yes or no).

b. Find the probability that a Republican sees signs of global warming.

c. Find the probability that a person does not see signs of global warming.

d. If a person sees signs of global warming, what is the probability that this person is a Democrat?

46. Merck & Co. conducted a study to test the promise of its experimental AIDS vaccine (*The Boston Globe*, September 22, 2007). Volunteers in the study were all free of the human immunodeficiency virus (HIV), which causes AIDS, at the start of the study, but all were at high risk for getting the virus. Volunteers were given either the vaccine or a dummy shot; 24 of 741 volunteers who got the vaccine became infected with HIV, whereas 21 of 762 volunteers who got the dummy shot became infected with HIV. The following table summarizes the results of the study.

	Vaccinated	Dummy Shot
Infected	24	21
Not Infected	717	741

a. Convert the contingency table into a joint probability table.

b. What is the probability that a randomly selected volunteer got vaccinated?

c. What is the probability that a randomly selected volunteer became infected with the HIV virus?

d. If the randomly selected volunteer was vaccinated, what is the probability that he/she got infected?

e. Are the events "Vaccinated" and "Infected" independent? Explain using probabilities. Given your answer, is it surprising that Merck & Co. ended enrollment and vaccination of volunteers in the study? Explain.

47. More and more households are struggling to pay utility bills given a shaky economy and high heating costs (*The Wall Street Journal*, February 14, 2008). Particularly hard hit are households with homes heated with propane or heating oil. Many of these households are spending twice as much to stay warm this winter compared to those who heat with natural gas or electricity. A representative sample of 500 households was taken to investigate if the type of heating influences whether or not a household is delinquent in paying its utility bill. The following table reports the results.

Delinquent in Payment?	Type of Heating			
	Natural Gas	Electricity	Heating Oil	Propane
Yes	50	20	15	10
No	240	130	20	15

a. What is the probability that a randomly selected household uses heating oil?

b. What is the probability that a randomly selected household is delinquent in paying its utility bill?

c. What is the probability that a randomly selected household uses heating oil and is delinquent in paying its utility bill?

d. Given that a household uses heating oil, what is the probability that it is delinquent in paying its utility bill?

e. Given that a household is delinquent in paying its utility bill, what is the probability that the household uses electricity?

f. Are the events "Heating Oil" and "Delinquent in Payment" independent? Explain using probabilities.

48. The research team at a leading perfume company is trying to test the market for its newly introduced perfume. In particular the team wishes to look for gender and international differences in the preference for this perfume. They sample 2,500 people internationally and each person in the sample is asked to try the new perfume and list his/her preference. The following table reports the results.

Preference	Gender	America	Europe	Asia
Like it	Men	210	150	120
	Women	370	310	180
Don't like it	Men	290	150	80
	Women	330	190	120

a. What is the probability that a randomly selected man likes the perfume?

b. What is the probability that a randomly selected Asian likes the perfume?

c. What is the probability that a randomly selected European woman does not like the perfume?

d. What is the probability that a randomly selected American man does not like the perfume?

e. Are the events "Men" and "Like Perfume" independent in (i) America, (ii) Europe, (iii) Asia? Explain using probabilities.

f. Internationally, are the events "Men" and "Like Perfume" independent? Explain using probabilities.

4.4 The Total Probability Rule and Bayes' Theorem

In this section we present two important rules in probability theory: the total probability rule and Bayes' theorem. The **total probability rule** is a useful tool for breaking the computation of a probability into distinct cases. **Bayes' theorem** uses this rule to update a probability of an event that has been affected by a new piece of evidence.

LO **4.7**

Apply the total probability rule and Bayes' theorem.

The Total Probability Rule

Sometimes the unconditional probability of an event is not readily apparent from the given information. The total probability rule expresses the unconditional probability of an event in terms of joint or conditional probabilities. Let $P(A)$ denote the unconditional probability of an event of interest. We can express $P(A)$ as the sum of probabilities of the intersections of A with some mutually exclusive and exhaustive events corresponding to an experiment. For instance, consider event B and its complement B^c. Figure 4.7 shows the sample space partitioned entirely into these two mutually exclusive and exhaustive events. The circle, representing event A, consists entirely of its intersections with B and B^c. According to the total probability rule, $P(A)$ equals the sum of $P(A \cap B)$ and $P(A \cap B^c)$.

FIGURE 4.7 The total probability rule: $P(A) = P(A \cap B) + P(A \cap B^c)$

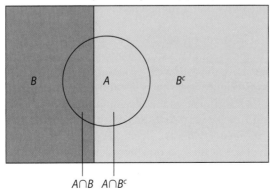

$A \cap B$ $A \cap B^c$

Oftentimes the joint probabilities needed to compute the total probability are not explicitly specified. Therefore, we use the multiplication rule to derive these probabilities from the conditional probabilities as $P(A \cap B) = P(A|B)P(B)$ and $P(A \cap B^c) = P(A|B^c)P(B^c)$.

THE TOTAL PROBABILITY RULE CONDITIONAL ON TWO EVENTS

The **total probability rule** expresses the unconditional probability of an event, A, in terms of probabilities of the intersection of A with any mutually exclusive and exhaustive events. The total probability rule based on two events, B and B^c, is

$$P(A) = P(A \cap B) + P(A \cap B^c),$$

or equivalently,

$$P(A) = P(A|B)P(B) + P(A|B^c)P(B^c).$$

An intuitive way to express the total probability rule is with the help of a **probability tree**. Whenever an experiment can be broken down into stages, with a different aspect of the result observed at each stage, we can use a probability tree to represent the various possible sequences of observations. We also use an alternative tabular method for computing the unconditional probability $P(A)$. The following example illustrates the mechanics of a probability tree and the tabular method.

EXAMPLE 4.16

Even though a certain statistics professor does not require attendance as part of a student's overall grade, she has noticed that those who regularly attend class have a higher tendency to get a final grade of A. The professor calculates that there is an 80% chance that a student attends class regularly. Moreover, given that a student attends class regularly, there is a 35% chance that the student receives an A grade; however, if a student does not attend class regularly, there is only a 5% chance of an A grade. Use this information to answer the following questions.

a. What is the probability that a student does not attend class regularly?

b. What is the probability that a student attends class regularly and receives an A grade?

c. What is the probability that a student does not attend class regularly and receives an A grade?

d. What is the probability that a student receives an A grade?

SOLUTION: We first let A correspond to the event that a student receives an A grade and R correspond to the event that a student attends class regularly. From the above information, we then have the following probabilities: $P(R) = 0.80$, $P(A|R) = 0.35$, and $P(A|R^c) = 0.05$. Figure 4.8 shows a probability tree that consists of nodes (junctions) and branches (lines) where the initial node O is called the origin. The branches emanating from O represent the possible outcomes that may occur at the first stage. Thus, at stage 1 we have events R and R^c originating from O. These events become the nodes at the second stage. The sum of the probabilities coming from any particular node is equal to one.

FIGURE 4.8 Probability tree for class attendance and final grade in statistics.

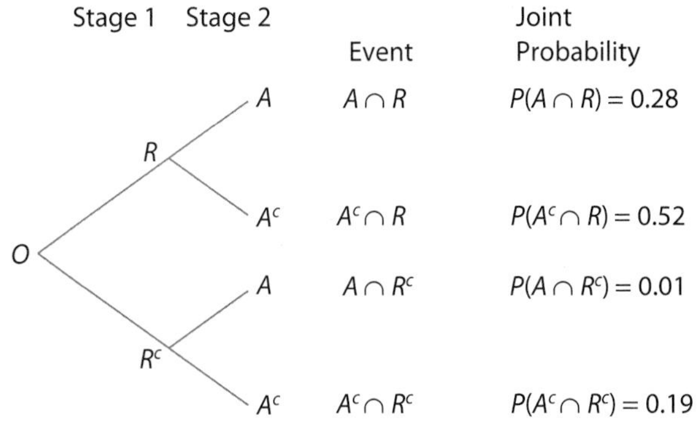

a. Using the complement rule, if we know that there is an 80% chance that a student attends class regularly, $P(R) = 0.80$, then the probability that a student does not attend class regularly is found as $P(R^c) = 1 - P(R) = 1 - 0.80 = 0.20$.

In order to arrive at a subsequent stage, and deduce the corresponding probabilities, we use the information obtained from the previous stage. For instance, given that a student attends class regularly, there is a 35% chance that the student receives an A grade, that is, $P(A|R) = 0.35$. Given that a student regularly attends class, the likelihood of not receiving an A grade is 65% because $P(A^c|R) = 1 - P(A|R) = 0.65$. Similarly, given $P(A|R^c) = 0.05$, we compute $P(A^c|R^c) = 1 - P(A|R^c) = 1 - 0.05 = 0.95$. Any path through branches of the tree from the origin to a terminal node defines the intersection of the earlier two events. Thus, following the top branches, we arrive at the event $A \cap R$, meaning that a student attends class regularly and receives an A grade. The probability of this event is the product of the probabilities attached to the branches forming that path; here we are simply applying the multiplication rule. Now we are prepared to answer parts b and c.

b. Multiplying the probabilities attached to the top branches we obtain $P(A \cap R) = P(A|R)P(R) = 0.35 \times 0.80 = 0.28$; there is a 28% chance that a student attends class regularly and receives an A grade.

c. In order to find the probability that a student does not attend class regularly and receives an A grade, we compute $P(A \cap R^c) = P(A|R^c)P(R^c) = 0.05 \times 0.20 = 0.01$.

d. The unconditional probability that a student receives an A grade, $P(A)$, is not explicitly given in Example 4.16. However, we can sum the relevant joint probabilities in parts b and c to obtain this unconditional probability:

$$P(A) = P(A \cap R) + P(A \cap R^c) = 0.28 + 0.01 = 0.29.$$

An alternative method uses a tabular representation of probabilities. Table 4.5 contains all relevant probabilities that are directly or indirectly specified in Example 4.16.

TABLE 4.5 Tabular Method for Computing $P(A)$

Unconditional Probability	Conditional Probability	Joint Probability
$P(R) = 0.80$	$P(A|R) = 0.35$	$P(A \cap R) = P(A|R) P(R) = 0.28$
$P(R^c) = 0.20$	$P(A|R^c) = 0.05$	$P(A \cap R^c) = P(A|R^c) P(R^c) = 0.01$
$P(R) + P(R^c) = 1$		$P(A) = P(A \cap R) + P(A \cap R^c) = 0.29$

As we saw earlier, each joint probability is computed as a product of its conditional probability and the corresponding unconditional probability; that is, $P(A \cap R) = P(A|R)P(R) = 0.35 \times 0.80 = 0.28$. Similarly, $P(A \cap R^c) = P(A|R^c)P(R^c) = 0.05 \times 0.20 = 0.01$. Therefore, $P(A) = P(A \cap R) + P(A \cap R^c) = 0.29$.

Bayes' Theorem

The total probability rule is also needed to derive Bayes' theorem, developed by the Reverend Thomas Bayes (1702–1761). Bayes' theorem is a procedure for updating probabilities based on new information. The original probability is an unconditional probability called a **prior probability** in the sense that it reflects only what we know now before the arrival of any new information. On the basis of new information, we update the prior probability to arrive at a conditional probability called a **posterior probability**.

Suppose we know that 99% of the individuals who take a lie detector test tell the truth. Therefore, the prior probability of telling the truth is 0.99. Suppose an individual takes the lie detector test and the results indicate that the individual lied. Bayes' theorem updates a prior probability to compute a posterior probability, which in the above example is essentially a conditional probability based on the information that the lie detector has detected a lie.

Let $P(B)$ denote the prior probability and $P(B|A)$ the posterior probability. Note that the posterior probability is conditional on event A, representing new information. Recall the conditional probability formula from Section 4.2:

$$P(B|A) = \frac{P(A \cap B)}{P(A)}.$$

In some instances we may have to evaluate $P(B|A)$, but we do not have explicit information on $P(A \cap B)$ or $P(A)$. However, given information on $P(B)$, $P(A|B)$ and $P(A|B^c)$, we can use the total probability rule and the multiplication rule to find $P(B|A)$ as follows:

$$P(B|A) = \frac{P(A \cap B)}{P(A)} = \frac{P(A \cap B)}{P(A \cap B) + P(A \cap B^c)} = \frac{P(A|B)P(B)}{P(A|B)P(B) + P(A|B^c)P(B^c)}.$$

BAYES' THEOREM

The posterior probability $P(B|A)$ can be found using the information on the prior probability $P(B)$ along with the conditional probabilities $P(A|B)$ and $P(A|B^c)$ as:

$$P(B|A) = \frac{P(A \cap B)}{P(A)} = \frac{P(A \cap B)}{P(A \cap B) + P(A \cap B^c)} = \frac{P(A|B)P(B)}{P(A|B)P(B) + P(A|B^c)P(B^c)}.$$

In the above formula, we have used Bayes' theorem to update the prior probability $P(B)$ to the posterior probability $P(B|A)$. Equivalently, we can use Bayes' theorem to update the prior probability $P(A)$ to derive the posterior probability $P(A|B)$ by interchanging the events A and B in the above formula.

EXAMPLE 4.17

In a lie-detector test, an individual is asked to answer a series of questions while connected to a polygraph (lie detector). This instrument measures and records several physiological responses of the individual on the basis that false answers will produce distinctive measurements. Assume that 99% of the individuals who go in for a polygraph test tell the truth. These tests are considered to be 95% reliable. In other words, there is a 95% chance that the test will detect a lie if an individual actually lies. Let there also be a 0.5% chance that the test erroneously detects a lie even when the individual is telling the truth. An individual has just taken a polygraph test and the test has detected a lie. What is the probability that the individual was actually telling the truth?

SOLUTION: First we define some events and their associated probabilities. Let D and T correspond to the events that the polygraph detects a lie and that an individual is telling the truth, respectively. We are given that $P(T) = 0.99$, implying that $P(T^c) = 1 - 0.99 = 0.01$. In addition, we formulate $P(D|T^c) = 0.95$ and $P(D|T) = 0.005$. We need to find $P(T|D)$ when we are not explicitly given $P(D \cap T)$ and $P(D)$. We can use Bayes' theorem to find:

$$P(T|D) = \frac{P(D \cap T)}{P(D)} = \frac{P(D \cap T)}{P(D \cap T) + P(D \cap T^c)} = \frac{P(D|T)P(T)}{P(D|T)P(T) + P(D|T^c)P(T^c)}.$$

Although we can use this formula to solve the problem directly, it is often easier to solve it systematically with the help of the following table.

TABLE 4.6 Computing Posterior Probabilities for Example 4.17

Prior Probability	Conditional Probability	Joint Probability	Posterior Probability
$P(T) = 0.99$	$P(D|T) = 0.005$	$P(D \cap T) = 0.00495$	$P(T|D) = 0.34256$
$P(T^c) = 0.01$	$P(D|T^c) = 0.95$	$P(D \cap T^c) = 0.00950$	$P(T^c|D) = 0.65744$
$P(T) + P(T^c) = 1$		$P(D) = 0.01445$	$P(T|D) + P(T^c|D) = 1$

The first column presents prior probabilities and the second column shows related conditional probabilities. We first compute the denominator of Bayes' theorem by using the total probability rule, $P(D) = P(D \cap T) + P(D \cap T^c)$. Joint probabilities are calculated as products of conditional probabilities with their corresponding prior probabilities. For instance, in Table 4.6, in order to obtain $P(D \cap T)$, we multiply $P(D|T)$ with $P(T)$, which yields $P(D \cap T) = 0.005 \times 0.99 = 0.00495$. Similarly, we find $P(D \cap T^c) = 0.95 \times 0.01 = 0.00950$. Thus, according to the total probability rule, $P(D) = 0.00495 + 0.00950 = 0.01445$. Finally, $P(T|D) = \frac{P(D \cap T)}{P(D \cap T) + P(D \cap T^c)} = \frac{0.00495}{0.01445} = 0.34256$. The prior probability of an individual telling the truth is 0.99. However, given the new information that the polygraph detected the individual telling a lie, the posterior probability of this individual telling the truth is now revised downward to 0.34256.

So far we have used the total probability rule as well as Bayes' theorem based on two mutually exclusive and exhaustive events, namely, B and B^c. We can easily extend the analysis to include n mutually exclusive and exhaustive events, $B_1, B_2, \ldots, B_n$.

EXTENSIONS OF THE TOTAL PROBABILITY RULE AND BAYES' THEOREM

If $B_1, B_2, \ldots B_n$ represent n mutually exclusive and exhaustive events, then the **total probability rule** extends to:

$$P(A) = P(A \cap B_1) + P(A \cap B_2) + \cdots + P(A \cap B_n),$$

or equivalently,

$$P(A) = P(A|B_1)P(B_1) + P(A|B_2)P(B_2) + \cdots + P(A|B_n)P(B_n).$$

Similarly, **Bayes' theorem,** for any $i = 1, 2, \ldots, n$, extends to:

$$P(B_i|A) = \frac{P(A \cap B_i)}{P(A \cap B_1) + P(A \cap B_2) + \cdots + P(A \cap B_n)},$$

or equivalently,

$$P(B_i|A) = \frac{P(A|B_i)P(B_i)}{P(A|B_1)P(B_1) + P(A|B_2)P(B_2) + \cdots + P(A|B_n)P(B_n)}.$$

EXAMPLE 4.18

Scott Myers is a security analyst for a telecommunications firm called Webtalk. Although he is optimistic about the firm's future, he is concerned that its stock price will be considerably affected by the condition of credit flow in the economy. He believes that the probability is 0.20 that credit flow will improve significantly, 0.50 that it will improve only marginally, and 0.30 that it will not improve at all. He also estimates that the probability that the stock price of Webtalk will go up is 0.90 with significant improvement in credit flow in the economy, 0.40 with marginal improvement in credit flow in the economy, and 0.10 with no improvement in credit flow in the economy.

a. Based on Scott's estimates, what is the probability that the stock price of Webtalk goes up?

b. If we know that the stock price of Webtalk has gone up, what is the probability that credit flow in the economy has improved significantly?

SOLUTION: As always, we first define the relevant events and their associated probabilities. Let S, M, and N denote significant, marginal, and no improvement in credit flow, respectively. Then $P(S) = 0.20$, $P(M) = 0.50$, and $P(N) = 0.30$. In addition, if we allow G to denote an increase in stock price, we formulate $P(G|S) = 0.90$, $P(G|M) = 0.40$, and $P(G|N) = 0.10$. We need to calculate $P(G)$ in part a and $P(S|G)$ in part b. Table 4.7 aids in assigning probabilities.

TABLE 4.7 Computing Posterior Probabilities for Example 4.18

Prior Probability	Conditional Probability	Joint Probability	Posterior Probability
$P(S) = 0.20$	$P(G|S) = 0.90$	$P(G \cap S) = 0.18$	$P(S|G) = 0.4390$
$P(M) = 0.50$	$P(G|M) = 0.40$	$P(G \cap M) = 0.20$	$P(M|G) = 0.4878$
$P(N) = 0.30$	$P(G|N) = 0.10$	$P(G \cap N) = 0.03$	$P(N|G) = 0.0732$
$P(S) + P(M) + P(N) = 1$		$P(G) = 0.41$	$P(S|G) + P(M|G) + P(N|G) = 1$

a. In order to calculate $P(G)$, we use the total probability rule, $P(G) = P(G \cap S) + P(G \cap M) + P(G \cap N)$. The joint probabilities are calculated as a product of conditional probabilities with their corresponding prior probabilities. For instance, in Table 4.7, $P(G \cap S) = P(G|S)P(S) = 0.90 \times 0.20 = 0.18$. Therefore, the probability that the stock price of Webtalk goes up equals $P(G) = 0.18 + 0.20 + 0.03 = 0.41$.

b. According to Bayes' theorem, $P(S|G) = \dfrac{P(G \cap S)}{P(G)} = \dfrac{P(G \cap S)}{P(G \cap S) + P(G \cap M) + P(G \cap N)}$. We use the total probability rule in the denominator to find $P(G) = 0.18 + 0.20 + 0.03 = 0.41$. Therefore, $P(S|G) = \dfrac{P(G \cap S)}{P(G)} = \dfrac{0.18}{0.41} = 0.4390$. Note that the prior probability of a significant improvement in credit flow is revised upward from 0.20 to a posterior probability of 0.4390.

EXERCISES 4.4

Mechanics

49. Let $P(A) = 0.70$, $P(B|A) = 0.55$, and $P(B|A^c) = 0.10$. Use a probability tree to calculate the following probabilities:

a. $P(A^c)$

b. $P(A \cap B)$ and $P(A^c \cap B)$

c. $P(B)$

d. $P(A|B)$

50. Let $P(B) = 0.60$, $P(A|B) = 0.80$, and $P(A|B^c) = 0.10$. Calculate the following probabilities:

a. $P(B^c)$

b. $P(A \cap B)$ and $P(A \cap B^c)$

c. $P(A)$

d. $P(B|A)$

51. Complete the following probability table.

Prior Probability	Conditional Probability	Joint Probability	Posterior Probability
$P(B) = 0.85$	$P(A\mid B) = 0.05$	$P(A \cap B) =$	$P(B\mid A) =$
$P(B^c) =$	$P(A\mid B^c) = 0.80$	$P(A \cap B^c) =$	$P(B^c\mid A) =$
Total $=$		$P(A) =$	Total $=$

52. Let a sample space be partitioned into three mutually exclusive and exhaustive events, B_1, B_2, and B_3. Complete the following probability table.

Prior Probabilities	Conditional Probabilities	Joint Probabilities	Posterior Probabilities
$P(B_1) = 0.10$	$P(A\mid B_1) = 0.40$	$P(A \cap B_1) =$	$P(B_1\mid A) =$
$P(B_2) =$	$P(A\mid B_2) = 0.60$	$P(A \cap B_2) =$	$P(B_2\mid A) =$
$P(B_3) = 0.30$	$P(A\mid B_3) = 0.80$	$P(A \cap B_3) =$	$P(B_3\mid A) =$
Total $=$		$P(A) =$	Total $=$

Applications

53. Christine has always been weak in mathematics. Based on her performance prior to the final exam in Calculus, there is a 40% chance that she will fail the course if she does not have a tutor. With a tutor, her probability of failing decreases to 10%. There is only a 50% chance that she will find a tutor at such short notice.
    a. What is the probability that Christine fails the course?
    b. Christine ends up failing the course. What is the probability that she had found a tutor?

54. An analyst expects that 20% of all publicly traded companies will experience a decline in earnings next year. The analyst has developed a ratio to help forecast this decline. If the company is headed for a decline, there is a 70% chance that this ratio will be negative. If the company is not headed for a decline, there is a 15% chance that the ratio will be negative. The analyst randomly selects a company and its ratio is negative. What is the posterior probability that the company will experience a decline?

55. The State Police are trying to crack down on speeding on a particular portion of the Massachusetts Turnpike. To aid in this pursuit, they have purchased a new radar gun that promises greater consistency and reliability. Specifically, the gun advertises $\pm$ one-mile-per-hour accuracy 98% of the time; that is, there is a 0.98 probability that the gun will detect a speeder, if the driver is actually speeding. Assume there is a 1% chance that the gun erroneously detects a speeder even when the driver is below the speed limit. Suppose that 95% of the drivers drive below the speed limit on this stretch of the Massachusetts Turnpike.
    a. What is the probability that the gun detects speeding and the driver was speeding?
    b. What is the probability that the gun detects speeding and the driver was not speeding?
    c. Suppose the police stop a driver because the gun detects speeding. What is the probability that the driver was actually driving below the speed limit?

56. According to a recent study, cell phones are the main medium for teenagers to stay connected with friends and family (*CNN*,

March 19, 2012). It is estimated that 90% of older teens (aged 14 to 17) and 60% of younger teens (aged 12 to 13) own a cell phone. Suppose 70 percent of all teens are older teens.
    a. What is the implied probability that a teen owns a cell phone?
    b. Given that a teen owns a cell phone, what is the probability that he/she is an older teen?
    c. Given that the teen owns a cell phone, what is the probability that he/she is a younger teen?

57. According to data from the *National Health and Nutrition Examination Survey*, 33% of white, 49.6% of black, 43% of Hispanic, and 8.9% of Asian women are obese. In a representative town, 48% of women are white, 19% are black, 26% are Hispanic, and the remaining 7% are Asian.
    a. Find the probability that a given woman in this town is obese.
    b. Given that a woman is obese, what is the probability that she is white?
    c. Given that a woman is obese, what is the probability that she is black?
    d. Given that a woman is obese, what is the probability that she is Asian?

58. A crucial game of the Los Angeles Lakers basketball team depends on the health of their key player. According to his doctor's report, there is a 40% chance that he will be fully fit to play, a 30% chance that he will be somewhat fit to play, and a 30% chance that he will not be able to play at all. The coach has estimated the chances of winning at 80% if the player is fully fit, 60% if he is somewhat fit, and 40% if he is unable to play.
    a. What is the probability that the Lakers will win the game?
    b. You have just heard that the Lakers won the game. What is the probability that the key player had been fully fit to play in the game?

59. An analyst thinks that next year there is a 20% chance that the world economy will be good, a 50% chance that it will be neutral, and a 30% chance that it will be poor. She also predicts probabilities that the performance of a start-up firm, Creative Ideas, will be good, neutral, or poor for each of the economic states of the world economy. The following table presents probabilities for three states of the world economy and the corresponding conditional probabilities for Creative Ideas.

State of the World Economy	Probability of Economic State	Performance of Creative Ideas	Conditional Probability of Creative Ideas
Good	0.20	Good	0.60
		Neutral	0.30
		Poor	0.10
Neutral	0.50	Good	0.40
		Neutral	0.30
		Poor	0.30
Poor	0.30	Good	0.20
		Neutral	0.30
		Poor	0.50

a. What is the probability that the performance of the world economy will be neutral and that of creative ideas will be poor?

b. What is the probability that the performance of Creative Ideas will be poor?

c. The performance of Creative Ideas was poor. What is the probability that the performance of the world economy had also been poor?

WRITING WITH STATISTICS

A University of Utah study examined 7,925 severely obese adults who had gastric bypass surgery and an identical number of people who did not have the surgery (*The Boston Globe*, August 23, 2007). The study wanted to investigate whether or not losing weight through stomach surgery prolonged the lives of severely obese patients, thereby reducing their deaths from heart disease, cancer, and diabetes.

Over the course of the study, 534 of the participants died. Of those who died, the cause of death was classified as either a disease death (such as heart disease, cancer, and diabetes) or a nondisease death (such as suicide or accident). Lawrence Plummer, a research analyst, is handed Table 4.8, which summarizes the study's findings:

TABLE 4.8 Deaths Cross-Classified by Cause and Method of Losing Weight

	Method of Losing Weight	
Cause of Death	No Surgery	Surgery
Death from Disease	285	150
Death from Nondisease	36	63

Lawrence wants to use the sample information to:

1. Calculate and interpret relevant probabilities for the cause of death and the method of losing weight.

2. Determine whether the events "Death from Disease" and "No Surgery" are independent.

Sample Report— Linking Cause of Death with the Method of Losing Weight

Numerous studies have documented the health risks posed to severely obese people—those people who are at least 100 pounds overweight. Severely obese people, for instance, typically suffer from high blood pressure and are more likely to develop diabetes. A University of Utah study examined whether the manner in which a severely obese person lost weight influenced a person's longevity. The study followed 7,925 patients who had stomach surgery and an identical number who did not have the surgery. Of particular interest in this report are the 534 participants who died over the course of the study.

The deceased participants were cross-classified by the method in which they lost weight and by the cause of their death. The possible outcomes for the method of losing weight were either "no surgery" or "surgery," and the possible outcomes for the cause of death were either "disease death" (such as heart disease, cancer, or diabetes) or a "nondisease death" (such as suicide or accident). Table 4.A shows the joint probability table.

TABLE 4.A Joint Probability Table of Deaths Cross-Classified by Cause and Method of Losing Weight

Cause of Death	Method of Losing Weight		Total
	No Surgery	Surgery	
Death from Disease	0.53	0.28	0.81
Death from Nondisease	0.07	0.12	0.19
Total	0.60	0.40	1.00

The unconditional probabilities reveal that 0.60 of the deceased participants in the study did not have surgery, while 0.40 of those who died had opted for the stomach surgery. Of the 534 participants that died, the vast majority, 0.81, died from disease, whereas the cause of death for the remainder was from a nondisease cause.

Joint probabilities reveal that the probability that a deceased participant had no surgery and died from disease was 0.53; yet the probability that a deceased participant had surgery and died from disease was only 0.28. Using the unconditional probabilities and the joint probabilities, it is possible to calculate conditional probabilities. For example, given that a participant's cause of death was from disease, the probability that the participant did not have surgery was 0.65 (= 0.53/0.81). Similarly, of those participants who opted for no surgery, the likelihood that their death was from disease was 0.88 (= 0.53/0.60).

A comparison of the conditional probabilities with the unconditional probabilities can reveal whether or not the events "Death from Disease" and "No Surgery" are independent. For instance, there is an 81% chance that a randomly selected obese person dies from disease. However, given that an obese person chooses to lose weight without surgery, the likelihood that he/she dies from disease jumps to 88%. Thus, this initial research appears to suggest that a participant's cause of death is associated with his/her method of losing weight.

Conceptual Review

4.1 Describe fundamental probability concepts.

In order to assign the appropriate probability to an uncertain event, it is useful to establish some terminology. An **experiment** is a process that leads to one of several possible outcomes. A **sample space**, denoted S, of an experiment contains all possible outcomes of the experiment. An **event** is any subset of outcomes of an experiment, and is called a simple event if it contains a single outcome. Events are **exhaustive** if all possible outcomes of an experiment belong to the events. Events are **mutually exclusive** if they do not share any common outcome of an experiment.

A **probability** is a numerical value that measures the likelihood that an event occurs. It assumes a value between zero and one where a value zero indicates an impossible event and a value one indicates a definite event. The **two defining properties of a probability** are (1) the probability of any event A is a value between 0 and 1, $0 \leq P(A) \leq 1$, and (2) the sum of the probabilities of any list of mutually exclusive and exhaustive events equals 1.

4.2 Formulate and explain subjective, empirical, and classical probabilities.

A **subjective** probability is calculated by drawing on personal and subjective judgment. An **empirical probability** is calculated as a relative frequency of occurrence. A **classical probability** is based on logical analysis rather than on observation or personal judgment.

LO 4.3 | Calculate and interpret the probability of the complement of an event and the probability that at least one of two events will occur.

Rules of probability allow us to calculate the probabilities of more complex events. The **complement rule** states that the probability of the complement of an event can be found by subtracting the probability of the event from one: $P(A^c) = 1 - P(A)$. We calculate the probability that at least one of two events occurs by using the **addition rule**: $P(A \cup B) = P(A) + P(B) - P(A \cap B)$. Since $P(A \cap B) = 0$ for mutually exclusive events, the addition rule then simplifies in these instances to $P(A \cup B) = P(A) + P(B)$.

LO 4.4 | Calculate and interpret a conditional probability and the multiplication rule.

The probability of event A, denoted $P(A)$, is an **unconditional probability**. It is the probability that A occurs without any additional information. The probability that A occurs given that B has already occurred, denoted $P(A|B)$, is a **conditional probability**. A conditional probability is computed as $P(A|B) = \frac{P(A \cap B)}{P(B)}$. We rearrange the conditional probability formula to arrive at the **multiplication rule**. When using this rule we find the probability that two events, A and B, both occur, that is, $P(A \cap B) = P(A|B)P(B) = P(B|A)P(A)$.

LO 4.5 | Distinguish between independent and dependent events.

Two events, A and B, are **independent** if $P(A|B) = P(A)$, or if $P(B|A) = P(B)$. Otherwise, the events are **dependent**. For independent events, the multiplication rule simplifies to $P(A \cap B) = P(A)P(B)$.

LO 4.6 | Calculate and interpret probabilities from a contingency table.

A **contingency table** generally shows frequencies for two qualitative (categorical) variables, x and y, where each cell represents a mutually exclusive combination of x-y values. Empirical probabilities are easily calculated as the relative frequency of the occurrence of the event.

LO 4.7 | Apply the total probability rule and Bayes' theorem.

The **total probability rule** expresses the unconditional probability of an event A in terms of probabilities of the intersection of A with two mutually exclusive and exhaustive events, B and B^c:

$$P(A) = P(A \cap B) + P(A \cap B^c) = P(A|B)P(B) + P(A|B^c)P(B^c).$$

We can extend the above rule where the sample space is partitioned into n mutually exclusive and exhaustive events, $B_1, B_2, \ldots, B_n$. The total probability rule is:

$$P(A) = P(A \cap B_1) + P(A \cap B_2) + \cdots + P(A \cap B_n), \text{ or equivalently,}$$

$$P(A) = P(A|B_1)P(B_1) + P(A|B_2)P(B_2) + \cdots + P(A|B_n)P(B_n).$$

Bayes' theorem provides a procedure for updating probabilities based on new information. Let $P(B)$ be the prior probability and $P(B|A)$ be the posterior probability based on new information provided by A. Then:

$$P(B|A) = \frac{P(A \cap B)}{P(A \cap B) + P(A \cap B^c)} = \frac{P(A|B)P(B)}{P(A|B)P(B) + P(A|B^c)P(B^c)}.$$

For the extended case, Bayes' theorem, for any $i = 1, 2, \ldots, n$, is:

$$P(B_i|A) = \frac{P(A \cap B_i)}{P(A \cap B_1) + P(A \cap B_2) + \cdots + P(A \cap B_n)}, \text{ or}$$

$$\text{equivalently, } P(B_i|A) = \frac{P(A|B_i)P(B_i)}{P(A|B_1)P(B_1) + P(A|B_2)P(B_2) + \cdots + P(A|B_n)P(B_n)}.$$

Additional Exercises and Case Studies

60. According to a global survey of 4,400 parents of children between the ages of 14 to 17, 44% of parents spy on their teen's Facebook account (http://msnbc.com, April 25, 2012). Assume that American parents account for 10% of all parents of teens with Facebook accounts, of which 60% spy on their teen's Facebook account. Suppose a parent is randomly selected, and the following events are defined: A = selecting an American parent and B = selecting a spying parent.
    a. Based on the above information, what are the probabilities that can be established? Would you label them as subjective, empirical, or classical?
    b. Are the events A and B mutually exclusive and/or exhaustive? Explain.
    c. Are the events A and B independent? Explain.
    d. What is the probability of selecting an American parent given that she/he is a spying parent?

61. According to a recent study, cell phones, especially text messaging, is the main medium for teenagers to stay connected with friends and family (CNN, March 19, 2012). It is found that only 23% of teens don't own a cell phone. Of those who own a cell phone, only one in four uses a smartphone. What proportion of all teenagers use a smartphone?

62. Henry Chow is a stockbroker working for Merrill Lynch. He knows from past experience that there is a 70% chance that his new client will want to include U.S. equity in her portfolio and a 50% chance that she will want to include foreign equity. There is also a 40% chance that she will want to include both U.S. equity and foreign equity in her portfolio.
    a. What is the probability that the client will want to include U.S. equity if she already has foreign equity in her portfolio?
    b. What is the probability that the client decides to include neither U.S. equity nor foreign equity in her portfolio?

63. The following frequency distribution shows the ages of India's 40 richest individuals. One of these individuals is selected at random.

Ages	Frequency
30 up to 40	3
40 up to 50	8
50 up to 60	15
60 up to 70	9
70 up to 80	5

Source: http://www.forbes.com.

    a. What is the probability that the individual is between 50 and 60 years of age?
    b. What is the probability that the individual is younger than 50 years of age?
    c. What is the probability that the individual is at least 60 years of age?

64. Anthony Papantonis, owner of Nauset Construction, is bidding on two projects, A and B. The probability that he wins project A is 0.40 and the probability that he wins project B is 0.25. Winning Project A and winning Project B are independent events.
    a. What is the probability that he wins project A or project B?
    b. What is the probability that he does not win either project?

65. Since the fall of 2008, millions of Americans have lost jobs due to the economic meltdown. A recent study shows that unemployment has not impacted males and females in the same way (Newsweek, April 20, 2009). According to a Bureau of Labor Statistics report, 8.5% of those who are eligible to work are unemployed. The unemployment rate is 8.8% for eligible men and only 7.0% for eligible women. Suppose 52% of the eligible workforce in the U.S. consists of men.
    a. You have just heard that another worker in a large firm has been laid off. What is the probability that this worker is a man?
    b. You have just heard that another worker in a large firm has been laid off. What is the probability that this worker is a woman?

66. How much you smile in your younger days can predict your later success in marriage (http://msnbc.com, April 16, 2009). The analysis is based on the success rate in marriage of people over age 65 and their smiles when they were only 10 years old. Researchers found that only 11% of the biggest smilers had been divorced, while 31% of the biggest frowners had experienced a broken marriage.
    a. Suppose it is known that 2% of the people are the biggest smilers at age 10 and divorced in later years. What percent of people are the biggest smilers?
    b. If 25% of people are considered to be the biggest frowners, calculate the probability that a person is the biggest frowner at age 10 and divorced later in life.

67. A professor of management has heard that eight students in his class of 40 have landed an internship for the summer. Suppose he runs into two of his students in the corridor.
    a. Find the probability that neither of these students has landed an internship.
    b. Find the probability that both of these students have landed an internship.

68. Wooden boxes are commonly used for the packaging and transportation of mangoes. A convenience store in Morganville, New Jersey, regularly buys mangoes from a wholesale dealer. For every shipment, the manager randomly inspects two mangoes from a box containing 20 mangoes for damages due to transportation. Suppose the chosen box contains exactly 3 damaged mangoes.
    a. Find the probability that the first mango is not damaged.

b. Find the probability that none of the mangoes is damaged.

c. Find the probability that both mangoes are damaged.

69. According to the CGMA Economic Index, which measures executive sentiment across the world, 18% of all respondents expressed optimism about the global economy (http://www.aicpa.org, March 29, 2012). Moreover, 22% of the respondents from the United States and 9% from Asia felt optimistic about the global economy.

a. What is the probability that an Asian respondent is not optimistic about the global economy?

b. If 28% of all respondents are from the United States, what is the probability that a respondent is from the United States and is optimistic about the global economy?

c. Suppose 22% of all respondents are from Asia. If a respondent feels optimistic about the global economy, what is the probability that the respondent is from Asia?

70. At a local bar in a small Midwestern town, beer and wine are the only two alcoholic options. The manager noted that of all male customers who visited over the weekend, 150 ordered beer, 40 ordered wine, and 20 asked for soft drinks. Of female customers, 38 ordered beer, 20 ordered wine, and 12 asked for soft drinks.

a. Construct a contingency table that shows frequencies for the qualitative variables Gender (male or female) and Drink Choice (beer, wine, or soft drink).

b. Find the probability that a customer orders wine.

c. What is the probability that a male customer orders wine?

d. Are the events "Wine" and "Male" independent? Explain using probabilities.

71. It has generally been believed that it is not feasible for men and women to be just friends (*The New York Times*, April 12, 2012). Others argue that this belief may not be true anymore since gone are the days when men worked and women stayed at home and the only way they could get together was for romance. In a recent survey, 186 heterosexual college students were asked if it was feasible for men and women to be just friends. Thirty-two percent of females and 57% of males reported that it was not feasible for men and women to be just friends. Suppose the study consisted of 100 female and 86 male students.

a. Construct a contingency table that shows frequencies for the qualitative variables Gender (men or women) and Feasible (yes or no).

b. Find the probability that a student believes that men and women can be friends.

c. If a student believes that men and women can be friends, what is the probability that this student is a male? Find the corresponding probability that this student is a female.

72. A recent study in the *Journal of the American Medical Association* (February 20, 2008) found that patients who go into cardiac arrest while in the hospital are more likely to

die if it happens after 11 pm. The study investigated 58,593 cardiac arrests that occurred during the day or evening. Of those, 11,604 survived to leave the hospital. There were 28,155 cardiac arrests during the shift that began at 11 pm, commonly referred to as the graveyard shift. Of those, 4,139 survived for discharge. The following contingency table summarizes the results of the study.

	Survived for Discharge	Did not Survive for Discharge	
Day or Evening Shift	11,604	46,989	58,593
Graveyard Shift	4,139	24,016	28,155
	15,743	71,005	86,748

a. What is the probability that a randomly selected patient experienced cardiac arrest during the graveyard shift?

b. What is the probability that a randomly selected patient survived for discharge?

c. Given that a randomly selected patient experienced cardiac arrest during the graveyard shift, what is the probability the patient survived for discharge?

d. Given that a randomly selected patient survived for discharge, what is the probability the patient experienced cardiac arrest during the graveyard shift?

e. Are the events "Survived for Discharge" and "Graveyard Shift" independent? Explain using probabilities. Given your answer, what type of recommendations might you give to hospitals?

73. It has been reported that women end up unhappier than men later in life, even though they start out happier (*Yahoo News*, August 1, 2008). Early in life, women are more likely to fulfill their family life and financial aspirations, leading to greater overall happiness. However, men report a higher satisfaction with their financial situation and family life, and are thus happier than women in later life. Suppose the results of the survey of 300 men and 300 women are presented in the following table.

Response to the question "Are you satisfied with your financial and family life?"

Response by Women	Age		
	20 to 35	35 to 50	Over 50
Yes	73	36	32
No	67	54	38

Response by Men	Age		
	20 to 35	35 to 50	Over 50
Yes	58	34	38
No	92	46	32

a. What is the probability that a randomly selected woman is satisfied with her financial and family life?

b. What is the probability that a randomly selected man is satisfied with his financial and family life?

c. For women, are the events "Yes" and "20 to 35" independent? Explain using probabilities.

d. For men, are the events "Yes" and "20 to 35" independent? Explain using probabilities.

74. An analyst predicts that there is a 40% chance that the U.S. economy will perform well. If the U.S. economy performs well, then there is an 80% chance that Asian countries will also perform well. On the other hand, if the U.S. economy performs poorly, the probability of Asian countries performing well goes down to 0.30.

a. What is the probability that both the U.S. economy and the Asian countries will perform well?

b. What is the unconditional probability that the Asian countries will perform well?

c. What is the probability that the U.S. economy will perform well, given that the Asian countries perform well?

75. Apparently, depression significantly increases the risk of developing dementia later in life (*BBC News,* July 6, 2010). In a recent study it was reported that 22% of those who had depression went on to develop dementia, compared to only 17% of those who did not have depression. Suppose 10% of all people suffer from depression.

a. What is the probability of a person developing dementia?

b. If a person has developed dementia, what is the probability that the person suffered from depression earlier in life?

76. According to data from the *National Health and Nutrition Examination Survey,* 36.5% of adult women and 26.6% of adult men are at a healthy weight. Suppose 50.52% of the adult population consists of women.

a. What proportion of adults is at a healthy weight?

b. If an adult is at a healthy weight, what is the probability that the adult is a woman?

c. If an adult is at a healthy weight, what is the probability that the adult is a man?

77. Suppose that 60% of the students do homework regularly. It is also known that 80% of students who had been doing homework regularly, end up doing well in the course (get a grade of A or B). Only 20% of students who had not been doing homework regularly, end up doing well in the course.

a. What is the probability that a student does well in the course?

b. Given that the student did well in the course, what is the probability that the student had been doing homework regularly?

78. According to the Census's Population Survey, the percentage of children with two parents at home is the highest for Asians and lowest for blacks (*USA TODAY,* February 26, 2009). It is reported that 85% of Asian children have two parents at home versus 78% of white, 70% of Hispanic, and 38% of black. Suppose there are 500 students in a representative school of which 280 are white, 50 are Asian, 100 are Hispanic, and 70 are black.

a. What is the probability that a child has both parents at home?

b. If both parents are at home, what is the probability the child is Asian?

c. If both parents are at home, what is the probability the child is black?

CASE STUDIES

Case Study 4.1

Ever since the introduction of New Coke failed miserably in the 1980s, most food and beverage companies have been cautious about changing the taste or formula of their signature offerings. In an attempt to attract more business, Starbucks recently introduced a new milder brew, Pike Place Roast, as its main drip coffee at the majority of its locations nationwide. The idea was to offer a more approachable cup of coffee with a smoother finish. However, the strategy also downplayed the company's more established robust roasts; initially, the milder brew was the only option for customers after noon. Suppose on a recent afternoon, 100 customers were asked whether or not they would return in the near future for another cup of Pike Place Roast. The following contingency table (cross-classified by type of customer and whether or not the customer will return) lists the results:

Data for Case Study 4.1

	Customer Type	
Return in Near Future?	First-time Customer	Established Customer
Yes	35	10
No	5	50

In a report, use the sample information to:

1. Calculate and interpret unconditional probabilities.

2. Calculate the probability that a customer will return given that the customer is an established customer.

3. Determine whether the events "Customer will Return" and "Established Customer" are independent. Shortly after the introduction of Pike Place Roast, Starbucks decided to offer its bolder brew again in the afternoon at many of its locations. Do your results support Starbucks' decision? Explain.

Case Study 4.2

It is common to ignore the thyroid gland of women during pregnancy (*New York Times*, April 13, 2009). This gland makes hormones that govern metabolism, helping to regulate body weight, heart rate, and a host of other factors. If the thyroid malfunctions, it can produce too little or too much of these hormones. Hypothyroidism, caused by an untreated underactive thyroid in pregnant women, carries the risk of impaired intelligence in the child. According to one research study, 62 out of 25,216 pregnant women were identified with hypothyroidism. Nineteen percent of the children born to women with an untreated underactive thyroid had an I.Q. of 85 or lower, compared with only 5% of those whose mothers had a healthy thyroid. It was also reported that if mothers have their hypothyroidism treated, their children's intelligence would not be impaired.

In a report, use the sample information to:

1. Find the likelihood that a woman suffers from hypothyroidism during pregnancy and later has a child with an I.Q. of 85 or lower.

2. Determine the number of children in a sample of 100,000 that are likely to have an I.Q. of 85 or lower if the thyroid gland of pregnant women is ignored.

3. Compare and comment on your answer to part b with the corresponding number if all pregnant women are tested and treated for hypothyroidism.

Case Study 4.3

Enacted in 1998, the Children's Online Privacy Protection Act requires firms to obtain parental consent before tracking the information and the online movement of children; however, the act applies to those children ages 12 and under. Teenagers are often oblivious to the consequences of sharing their lives online. Data reapers create huge libraries of digital profiles and sell these profiles to advertisers, who use it to detect trends and micro-target their ads back to teens. For example, a teen searching online for ways to lose weight could become enticed by an ad for dietary supplements, fed into his/her network by tracking cookies. As a preliminary step in gauging the magnitude of teen usage of social networking sites, an economist surveys 200 teen girls and 200 teen boys. Of teen girls, 166 use social networking sites; of teen boys, 156 use social networking sites.

In a report, use the sample information to:

1. Construct a contingency table that shows frequencies for the qualitative variables Gender (male or female) and Use of Social Networking Sites (Yes or No).

2. What is the probability that a teen uses social networking sites?

3. What is the probability that a teen girl uses a social networking site?

4. A bill before Congress would like to extend the Children's Online Privacy Protection Act to apply to 15-year-olds. In addition, the bill would also ban Internet companies from sending targeted advertising to children under 16 and give these children and their parents the ability to delete their digital footprint and profile with an "eraser button" (*The Boston Globe*, May 20, 2012). Given the probabilities that you calculated with respect to teen usage of social networking sites, do you think that this legislation is necessary? Explain.

Case Study 4.4

In 2008, it appeared that rising gas prices had made Californians less resistant to offshore drilling. A Field Poll survey showed that a higher proportion of Californians supported the idea of drilling for oil or natural gas along the state's coast than in 2005 (*The Wall Street Journal*, July 17, 2008). Assume that random drilling for oil only succeeds 5% of the time.

An oil company has just announced that it has discovered new technology for detecting oil. The technology is 80% reliable. That is, if there is oil, the technology will signal "oil" 80% of the time. Let there also be a 1% chance that the technology erroneously detects oil, when in fact no oil exists.

In a report, use the above information to:

1. Prepare a table that shows the relevant probabilities.
2. Find the probability that, on a recent expedition, oil actually existed but the technology detected "no oil" in the area.

5

Discrete Probability Distributions

CHAPTER

LEARNING OBJECTIVES

After reading this chapter you should be able to:

LO 5.1 Distinguish between discrete and continuous random variables.

LO 5.2 Describe the probability distribution of a discrete random variable.

LO 5.3 Calculate and interpret summary measures for a discrete random variable.

LO 5.4 Describe the binomial distribution and compute relevant probabilities.

LO 5.5 Describe the Poisson distribution and compute relevant probabilities.

LO 5.6 Describe the hypergeometric distribution and compute relevant probabilities.

In this chapter we extend our discussion about probability by introducing the concept of a random variable. A random variable summarizes the results of an experiment in terms of numerical values. It can be classified as discrete or continuous depending on the range of values that it assumes. A discrete random variable assumes a countable number of distinct values, whereas a continuous random variable is characterized by uncountable values. In this chapter, we focus on discrete random variables. Examples include the number of credit cards carried by consumers, the number of foreclosures in a sample of 100 households, and the number of cars lined up at a toll booth. Once we define the range of possible values that a random variable assumes, we use a probability distribution to compute the probabilities associated with these different values. We also calculate summary measures for a random variable, including its mean, variance, and standard deviation. Finally, we discuss three widely used discrete probability distributions: the binomial, the Poisson, and the hypergeometric distributions.

Available Staff for Probable Customers

In addition to its previous plan to shut 100 stores, Starbucks announced plans in 2008 to close 500 more U.S. locations (*The Wall Street Journal*, July 9, 2008). Executives claimed that a weak economy and higher gas and food prices led to a drop in domestic store traffic. Others speculate that Starbucks' rapid expansion produced a saturated market. The locations that will close are not profitable, are not expected to be profitable, and/or are located near an existing company-operated Starbucks.

Anne Jones, a manager at a local Starbucks, has been reassured by headquarters that her store will remain open. She is concerned about how other nearby closings might affect business at her store. Anne knows that a typical Starbucks customer visits the chain between 15 and 18 times a month, making it among the nation's most frequented retailers. She believes that her loyal Starbucks customers, along with displaced customers, will average 18 visits to the store over a 30-day month. To decide staffing needs, Anne knows that she needs a solid understanding about the probability distribution of customer arrivals. If too many employees are ready to serve customers, some employees will be idle, which is costly to the store. However, if not enough employees are available to meet demand, this could result in losing angry customers who choose not to wait for service.

Anne wants to use the above information to:

1. Calculate the expected number of visits from a typical Starbucks customer in a specified time period.

2. Calculate the probability that a typical Starbucks customer visits the chain a certain number of times in a specified time period.

A synopsis of this case is provided at the end of Section 5.4.

5.1 Random Variables and Discrete Probability Distributions

We often have to make important decisions in the face of uncertainty. For example, a car dealership has to determine the number of cars to hold on its lot when the actual demand for cars is unknown. Similarly, an investor has to select a portfolio when the actual outcomes of investment returns are not known. This uncertainty is captured by what we call a **random variable**. A random variable summarizes outcomes of an experiment with numerical values.

> A **random variable** is a function that assigns numerical values to the outcomes of an experiment.

We generally use the letter X to denote a random variable. A **discrete random variable** assumes a countable number of distinct values such as x_1, x_2, x_3 and so on. It may assume either a finite number of values or an infinite sequence of values. A **continuous random variable**, on the other hand, is characterized by uncountable values. In other words, a continuous random variable can take on any value within an interval or collection of intervals.

> A **discrete random variable** assumes a countable number of distinct values, whereas a **continuous random variable** is characterized by uncountable values of an interval.

Recall from Chapter 4, the sample space S is a set of all outcomes of an experiment. Whenever some numerical values are assigned to these outcomes, a random variable X can be defined. Consider the following experiments, and some examples of discrete random variables (with their possible values shown) that are associated with the experiments:

Experiment 1. Rolling a six-sided die; $S = \{1, 2, 3, 4, 5, 6\}$.
Let X = Win \$10 if odd number, lose \$10 if even number; possible values: $\{-10,10\}$
Let X = Win \$10 if number less than 3, lose \$10 if number more than 4; possible values = $\{-10,0,10\}$

Experiment 2. Two shirts are selected from the production line and each can be defective (D) or nondefective (N); $S = \{(D,D), (D,N), (N,D), (N,N)\}$.
Let X = the number of defective shirts; possible values = $\{0, 1, 2\}$
Let X = the proportion of defective shirts; possible values = $\{0, 1/2, 1\}$

Experiment 3. Reviewing a single mortgage application and deciding whether the client gets approved (A) or denied (D); $S = \{A, D\}$.
Let X = 1 for A and 0 for D; possible values = $\{0,1\}$
Let X = 1 for A and -1 for D; possible values = $\{-1, 1\}$

Experiment 4. Reviewing multiple mortgage applications and, for each client, deciding whether the client gets approved (A) or denied (D); S = the set of all possible infinite sequences whose elements are A or D.
Let X = the number of approvals; possible values = $\{0, 1, 2, 3, \ldots\}$
Let X = the squared number of approvals; possible values = $\{0, 1, 4, 9, \ldots\}$

The random variables defined for Experiments 1, 2, and 3 have a finite and countable number of values, while the two random variables defined for Experiment 4 have an infinite but countable number of values.

Sometimes, we can define a random variable *directly* by identifying its values with some numerical outcomes. For example, we may be interested in the number of students who get financial aid out of the 100 students who applied. Then the set of possible values of the random variable, equivalent to the sample space, is {0, 1, . . . , 100}. In a similar way, we can define a discrete random variable with an infinite number of values that it may take. For example, consider the number of cars that cross the Brooklyn Bridge between 9:00 am and 10:00 am on a Monday morning. Here the discrete random variable takes an infinite but countable number of values from {0, 1, 2, . . .}. Note that we cannot specify an upper bound on the observed number of cars.

Although, we explore discrete random variables in this chapter, random variables can also be continuous. For example, the time taken by a student to complete a 60-minute exam may assume any value between 0 and 60 minutes. Thus, the set of such values is uncountable; that is, it is impossible to put all real numbers from the interval [0, 60] in a sequence. Here, the random variable is continuous because the outcomes are uncountable. Some students may think that time in the above example is countable in seconds; however, this is not the case once we consider fractions of a second. We will discuss the details of continuous random variables in the next chapter.

The Discrete Probability Distribution

LO **5.2**

Describe the probability distribution of a discrete random variable.

Every random variable is associated with a **probability distribution** that describes it completely. It is common to define discrete random variables in terms of their **probability mass function** and continuous random variables in terms of their **probability density function**. Both variables can also be defined in terms of their **cumulative distribution function**.

> The **probability mass function** of a discrete random variable X is a list of the values of X with the associated probabilities, that is, the list of all possible pairs $(x, P(X = x))$.
> The **cumulative distribution function** of X is defined as $P(X \leq x)$.

For convenience, we will use terms like "probability distribution" and "distribution" for the probability mass function. We will do the same in the next chapter for the probability density function. In both chapters, we will use "cumulative probability distribution" for the cumulative distribution function.

We can view a discrete probability distribution in several ways, including tabular, algebraic, and graphical forms. Example 5.1 shows one of two tabular forms. In general, we can construct a table in two different ways. The first approach directly specifies the probability that the random variable assumes a specific value.

EXAMPLE 5.1

Refer back to Experiment 1 of rolling a fair six-sided die, with the random variable defined as the number rolled. Present the probability distribution in a tabular form.

SOLUTION: A probability distribution for rolling a six-sided die is shown in Table 5.1.

TABLE 5.1 Probability Distribution for Example 5.1

x	1	2	3	4	5	6
P(X = x)	1/6	1/6	1/6	1/6	1/6	1/6

From Table 5.1, we can deduce, for instance, that $P(X = 5)$ equals 1/6. For that matter, the probability that X assumes any of the six possible values is 1/6.

The probability distribution defined in Example 5.1 illustrates two components of all discrete probability distributions.

TWO KEY PROPERTIES OF DISCRETE PROBABILITY DISTRIBUTIONS

- The probability of each value x is a value between 0 and 1, or equivalently, $0 \leq P(X = x) \leq 1$.
- The sum of the probabilities equals 1. In other words, $\Sigma P(X = x_i) = 1$ where the sum extends over all values x of X.

The second tabular view of a probability distribution is based on the cumulative probability distribution.

The cumulative probability distribution is convenient when we are interested in finding the probability over a range of values rather than a specific value. For the random variable defined in Example 5.1, the cumulative probability distribution is shown in Table 5.2.

TABLE 5.2 Cumulative Probability Distribution for Example 5.1

x	1	2	3	4	5	6
$P(X \leq x)$	1/6	2/6	3/6	4/6	5/6	6/6

If we are interested in finding the probability of rolling a four or less, $P(X \leq 4)$, we see from the cumulative probability distribution that this probability is 4/6. With the earlier probability representation, we would add up the probabilities to compute $P(X \leq 4)$ as

$$P(X = 1) + P(X = 2) + P(X = 3) + P(X = 4) = 1/6 + 1/6 + 1/6 + 1/6 = 4/6.$$

At the same time, we can use the cumulative probability distribution to find the probability that the random variable assumes a specific value. For example, $P(X = 3)$ can be found as $P(X \leq 3) - P(X \leq 2) = 3/6 - 2/6 = 1/6$.

In many instances we can express a probability distribution by applying an algebraic formula. A formula representation of the probability distribution of the random variable defined in Example 5.1 is:

$$P(X = x) = \begin{cases} 1/6 & \text{if } x = 1, 2, 3, 4, 5, 6 \\ 0 & \text{otherwise.} \end{cases}$$

Thus, from the formula we can ascertain that $P(X = 5) = 1/6$ and $P(X = 7) = 0$.

In order to graphically depict a probability distribution, we place all values x of X on the horizontal axis and the associated probabilities $P(X = x)$ on the vertical axis. We then draw a line segment that emerges from each x and ends where its height equals $P(X = x)$. Figure 5.1 graphically illustrates the probability distribution of the random variable defined in Example 5.1.

FIGURE 5.1 Probability distribution when rolling a six-sided die

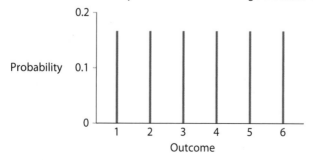

The probability distribution in Figure 5.1 is an example of a **discrete uniform distribution**, which has the following characteristics:

- The distribution has a finite number of specified values.
- Each value is equally likely.
- The distribution is symmetric.

EXAMPLE 5.2

The number of homes that a Realtor sells over a one-month period has the probability distribution shown in Table 5.3.

TABLE 5.3 Probability Distribution for the Number of Houses Sold

Number of Houses Sold	Probability
0	0.30
1	0.50
2	0.15
3	0.05

a. Is this a valid probability distribution?

b. What is the probability that the Realtor does not sell any houses in a one-month period?

c. What is the probability that the Realtor sells at most one house in a one-month period?

d. What is the probability that the Realtor sells at least two houses in a one-month period?

e. Graphically depict the probability distribution and comment on its symmetry/skewness.

SOLUTION:

a. We first note that the random variable X denotes the number of houses that the Realtor sells over a one-month period. This variable assumes the values 0 through 3. The probability distribution is valid because it satisfies the following two conditions: (1) all probabilities fall between 0 and 1, and (2) the probabilities sum to 1 (0.30 + 0.50 + 0.15 + 0.05 = 1).

b. In order to find the probability that the Realtor does not sell any houses in a one-month period, we first write the question using the appropriate probability statement notation. We find $P(X = 0) = 0.30$.

c. We express the appropriate probability statement and then sum the respective probabilities: $P(X \leq 1) = P(X = 0) + P(X = 1) = 0.30 + 0.50 = 0.80$.

d. We again write the probability statement and then sum the respective probabilities: $P(X \geq 2) = P(X = 2) + P(X = 3) = 0.15 + 0.05 = 0.20$.

Note that since the sum of the probabilities over all values of X equals 1, we can also find the above probability as $P(X \geq 2) = 1 - P(X \leq 1) = 1 - 0.80 = 0.20$.

e. The graph in Figure 5.2 shows that the distribution is not symmetric; rather, it is positively skewed. There are small chances of selling two or three houses in a one-month period. The most likely outcome by far is selling one house over a one-month period, with a probability of 0.50.

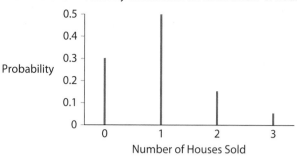

FIGURE 5.2 Probability distribution for the number of houses sold

EXERCISES 5.1

Mechanics

1. Consider the following discrete probability distribution.

x	15	22	34	40
$P(X = x)$	0.14	0.40	0.26	0.20

a. Is this a valid probability distribution? Explain.
b. Graphically depict this probability distribution.
c. What is the probability that the random variable X is less than 40?
d. What is the probability that the random variable X is between 10 and 30?
e. What is the probability that the random variable X is greater than 20?

2. Consider the following discrete probability distribution.

x	−25	−15	10	20
$P(X = x)$	0.35	0.10		0.10

a. Complete the probability distribution.
b. Graphically depict the probability distribution and comment on the symmetry of the distribution.
c. What is the probability that the random variable X is negative?
d. What is the probability that the random variable X is greater than −20?
e. What is the probability that the random variable X is less than 20?

3. Consider the following cumulative probability distribution.

x	0	1	2	3	4	5
$P(X \le x)$	0.15	0.35	0.52	0.78	0.84	1

a. Calculate $P(X \le 3)$.
b. Calculate $P(X = 3)$.
c. Calculate $P(2 \le X \le 4)$.

4. Consider the following cumulative probability distribution.

x	−25	0	25	50
$P(X \le x)$	0.25	0.50	0.75	1

a. Calculate $P(X \le 0)$.
b. Calculate $P(X = 50)$.
c. Is this a discrete uniform distribution? Explain.

Applications

5. Identify the possible values of the following random variables. Which of the random variables are discrete?
   a. The numerical grade a student receives in a course.
   b. The grade point average of a student.
   c. The salary of an employee, defined in figures (4 figure, 5 figure, etc.).
   d. The salary of an employee defined in dollars.

6. Identify the possible values of the following random variables. Which of the random variables are discrete?
   a. The advertised size of a round Domino's pizza.
   b. The actual size of a round Domino's pizza.
   c. The number of daily visitors to Yosemite National Park.
   d. The age of a visitor to Yosemite National Park.

7. India is the second most populous country in the world, with a population of over 1 billion people. Although the government has offered various incentives for population control, some argue that the birth rate, especially in rural India, is still too high to be sustainable. A demographer assumes the following probability distribution of the household size in India.

Household Size	Probability
1	0.05
2	0.09
3	0.12
4	0.24
5	0.25
6	0.12
7	0.07
8	0.06

a. What is the probability that there are less than 5 members in a household in India?

b. What is the probability that there are 5 or more members in a household in India?

c. What is the probability that the number of members in a household in India is strictly between 3 and 6?

d. Graphically depict this probability distribution and comment on its symmetry.

8. A financial analyst creates the following probability distribution for the performance of an equity income mutual fund.

Performance	Numerical Score	Probability
Very poor	1	0.14
Poor	2	0.43
Neutral	3	0.22
Good	4	0.16
Very good	5	0.05

a. Comment on the optimism or pessimism depicted in the analyst's estimates.

b. Convert the above probability distribution to a cumulative probability distribution.

c. What is the probability that this mutual fund will do at least good?

9. A basketball player is fouled while attempting to make a basket and receives two free throws. The opposing coach believes there is a 55% chance that the player will miss both shots, a 25% chance that he will make one of the shots, and a 20% chance that he will make both shots.

a. Construct the appropriate probability distribution.

b. What is the probability that he makes no more than one of the shots?

c. What is the probability that he makes at least one of the shots?

10. In early 2010, leading U.S. stock markets tumbled more than 2.5% as U.S. consumer confidence fell to its lowest level since August 2009 (*BBC News,* July 16, 2010). Given fresh economic data, an economist believes there is a 35% chance that consumer confidence will fall below 62 and only a 25% chance that it will rise above 65. The economist defines the confidence score as 1 if consumer confidence is below 62, 2 if it is between 62 and 65, and 3 if it is above 65.

a. According to the economist, what is the probability that the confidence score is 2?

b. According to the economist, what is the probability that the confidence score is not 1?

11. Professor Sanchez has been teaching Principles of Economics for over 25 years. He uses the following scale for grading.

Grade	Numerical Score	Probability
A	4	0.10
B	3	0.30
C	2	0.40
D	1	0.10
F	0	0.10

a. Depict the above probability distribution graphically. Comment on whether or not the probability distribution is symmetric.

b. Convert the above probability distribution to a cumulative probability distribution.

c. What is the probability of earning at least a B in Professor Sanchez's course?

d. What is the probability of passing Professor Sanchez's course?

12. Jane Wormley is a professor of management at a university. She expects to be able to use her grant money to fund up to two students for research assistance. While she realizes that there is a 5% chance that she may not be able to fund any student, there is an 80% chance that she will be able to fund two students.

a. What is the probability that Jane will fund one student?

b. Construct a cumulative probability distribution of the random variable defined as the number of students that Jane will be able to fund.

13. Fifty percent of the customers who go to Sears Auto Center for tires buy four tires and 30% buy two tires. Moreover, 18% buy fewer than two tires, with 5% buying none.

a. What is the probability that a customer buys three tires?

b. Construct a cumulative probability distribution for the number of tires bought.

5.2 Expected Value, Variance, and Standard Deviation

The analysis of probability distributions is useful because it allows us to calculate various probabilities associated with the different values that the random variable assumes. In addition, it helps us calculate summary measures for a random variable. These summary measures include the mean, the variance, and the standard deviation.

LO **5.3**

Calculate and interpret summary measures for a discrete random variable.

Expected Value

One of the most important probabilistic concepts in statistics is that of the **expected value**, also referred to as the **population mean**. The expected value of the discrete random variable X, denoted by $E(X)$ or simply μ, is a weighted average of all possible values of X. Before we present its formula, we would like to point out that the expected value of a random variable should not be confused with its most probable value. As we will see later, the expected value is, in general, not even one of the possible values of the random variable. We can think of the expected value as the long-run average value of the random variable over infinitely many independent repetitions of an experiment. Consider a simple experiment with a fair coin, where you win $10 if it is heads and lose $10 if it is tails. If you flip the coin many times, the expected gain is $0, which is neither of the two possible values, namely $10 or $-$10.

> **EXPECTED VALUE OF A DISCRETE RANDOM VARIABLE**
>
> For a discrete random variable X with values x_1, x_2, x_3, . . . , which occur with probabilities $P(X = x_i)$, the **expected value** of X is calculated as
>
> $$E(X) = \mu = \Sigma x_i P(X = x_i).$$

Variance and Standard Deviation

The mean μ of the random variable X provides us with a measure of the central location of the distribution of X, but it does not give us information on how the various values are dispersed from μ. We need a measure that indicates whether the values of X are clustered about μ or widely scattered from μ.

> **VARIANCE AND STANDARD DEVIATION OF A DISCRETE RANDOM VARIABLE**
>
> For a discrete random variable X with values x_1, x_2, x_3, . . . , which occur with probabilities $P(X = x_i)$, the **variance** of X is calculated as
>
> $$Var(X) = \sigma^2 = \Sigma (x_i - \mu)^2 P(X = x_i).$$
>
> The **standard deviation** of X is $SD(X) = \sigma = \sqrt{\sigma^2}$.

EXAMPLE 5.3

Brad Williams is the owner of a large car dealership in Chicago. Brad decides to construct an incentive compensation program that equitably and consistently compensates employees on the basis of their performance. He offers an annual bonus of $10,000 for superior performance, $6,000 for good performance, $3,000 for fair performance, and $0 for poor performance. Based on prior records, he expects an employee to perform at superior, good, fair, and poor performance levels with probabilities 0.15, 0.25, 0.40, and 0.20, respectively. Table 5.4 lists the bonus amount, performance type, and the corresponding probabilities.

TABLE 5.4 Probability Distribution for Compensation Program

Bonus (in $1,000s)	Performance Type	Probability
$10	Superior	0.15
6	Good	0.25
3	Fair	0.40
0	Poor	0.20

a. Calculate the expected value of the annual bonus amount.

b. Calculate the variance and the standard deviation of the annual bonus amount.

c. What is the total annual amount that Brad can expect to pay in bonuses if he has 25 employees?

SOLUTION:

a. Let the random variable X denote the bonus amount (in $1,000s) for an employee. The first and second columns of Table 5.5 show the probability distribution of X. The calculations of the mean are provided in the third column. We weigh each outcome by its respective probability, $x_i P(X = x_i)$, and then sum these weighted values. Thus, as shown at the bottom of the third column, $E(X) = \mu = \Sigma x_i P(X = x_i) = 4.2$, or $4,200. Note that the expected value is not one of the possible values of X; that is, none of the employees will earn a bonus of $4,200. This outcome reinforces the interpretation of expected value as a long-run average.

TABLE 5.5 Calculations for Example 5.3

Value, x_i	Probability, $P(X = x_i)$	Weighted Value, $x_i P(X = x_i)$	Weighted Squared Deviation, $(x_i - \mu)^2 P(X = x_i)$
10	0.15	$10 \times 0.15 = 1.5$	$(10 - 4.2)^2 \times 0.15 = 5.05$
6	0.25	$6 \times 0.25 = 1.5$	$(6 - 4.2)^2 \times 0.25 = 0.81$
3	0.40	$3 \times 0.40 = 1.2$	$(3 - 4.2)^2 \times 0.40 = 0.58$
0	0.20	$0 \times 0.20 = 0$	$(0 - 4.2)^2 \times 0.20 = 3.53$
		Total $= 4.2$	Total $= 9.97$

b. The last column of Table 5.5 shows the calculation for the variance. We first calculate each x_i's squared difference from the mean $(x_i - \mu)^2$, weigh each value by the appropriate probability, $(x_i - \mu)^2 P(X = x_i)$, and then sum these weighted squared differences. Thus, as shown at the bottom of the last column, $Var(X) = \sigma^2 = \Sigma (x_i - \mu)^2 P(X = x_i) = 9.97$, or 9.97 (in ($1,000s)^2$). The standard deviation is the positive square root of the variance, $SD(X) = \sigma = \sqrt{9.97} = 3.158$, or $3,158.

c. Note that the expected bonus of an employee is $4,200. Since Brad has 25 employees, he can expect to pay $4,200 \times 25 = $105,000 in bonuses.

Risk Neutrality and Risk Aversion

An important concept in economics, finance, and psychology relates to the behavior of consumers under uncertainty. Consumers are said to be **risk neutral** if they are indifferent to risk and care only about their expected gains. They are said to be **risk averse** if they care about risk and, if confronted with two choices with the same expected gains, they prefer the one with lower risk. In other words, a risk averse consumer will take a risk only if it entails a suitable compensation. Consider a seemingly fair gamble where you flip a coin and get $10 if it is heads and lose $10 if it is tails, resulting in an expected gain of zero ($10 \times 0.5 - 10 \times 0.5 = 0$). A risk-neutral consumer is indifferent about participating in this gamble. For a risk-averse consumer, the pain associated with losing $10 is more than the pleasure of winning $10. Therefore, the consumer will not want to participate in this seemingly fair gamble because there is no reward to compensate for the risk. Example 5.4 expands on this type of consumer behavior.

A **risk-neutral consumer** completely ignores risk and makes his/her decisions solely on the basis of expected gains. A **risk-averse consumer** demands a positive expected gain as compensation for taking risk. This compensation increases with the level of risk taken and the degree of risk aversion. Finally, a **risk loving consumer** may be willing to take a risk even if the expected gain is negative.

EXAMPLE 5.4

You have a choice of receiving $1,000 in cash or receiving a beautiful painting from your grandmother. The actual value of the painting is uncertain. You are told that the painting has a 20% chance of being worth $2,000, a 50% chance of being worth $1,000, and a 30% chance of being worth $500. What should you do?

SOLUTION: Let the random variable X represent the worth of the painting. Given the above information, we define the probability distribution as shown in Table 5.6.

TABLE 5.6 Probability Distribution for the Value of the Painting

x	P(X = x)
$2,000	0.20
1,000	0.50
500	0.30

We calculate the expected value as

$$E(X) = \Sigma x_i P(X = x_i) = \$2,000 \times 0.20 + \$1,000 \times 0.50 + \$500 \times 0.30$$
$$= \$1,050.$$

Since the expected value of the painting is more than $1,000, it may appear that the right choice is to pick the painting over $1,000 in cash. This choice, however, is based entirely on the expected value of the painting, paying no attention to risk. While the expected value of $1,050 is more than $1,000, the painting entails some risk. For instance, there is a 30% chance that it may be worth only $500. Therefore, a risk-neutral consumer will take the painting because its expected value exceeds the risk-free cash value of $1,000. This consumer is not concerned with risk. A risk lover will be thrilled to take the painting. For a risk-averse consumer, however, the decision is not clear-cut. It depends on the risk involved in picking the painting and how much he/she wants to be compensated for this risk. Further details are beyond the scope of this book.

EXERCISES 5.2

Mechanics

14. Calculate the mean, the variance, and the standard deviation of the following discrete probability distribution.

x	5	10	15	20
P(X = x)	0.35	0.30	0.20	0.15

15. Calculate the mean, the variance, and the standard deviation of the following discrete probability distribution.

x	−23	−17	−9	−3
P(X = x)	0.50	0.25	0.15	0.10

Applications

16. The number of homes that a Realtor sells over a one-month period has the following probability distribution.

Number of Houses Sold	Probability
0	0.30
1	0.50
2	0.15
3	0.05

a. On average, how many houses is the Realtor expected to sell over a one-month period?

b. What is the standard deviation of this probability distribution?

17. A marketing firm is considering making up to three new hires. Given its specific needs, the management feels that there is a 60% chance of hiring at least two candidates. There is only a 5% chance that it will not make any hires and a 10% chance that it will make all three hires.

a. What is the probability that the firm will make at least one hire?

b. Find the expected value and the standard deviation of the number of hires.

18. An analyst has developed the following probability distribution of the rate of return for a common stock.

Scenario	Probability	Rate of Return
1	0.30	−5%
2	0.45	0%
3	0.25	10%

a. Calculate the expected rate of return.

b. Calculate the variance and the standard deviation of this probability distribution.

19. Organizers of an outdoor summer concert in Toronto are concerned about the weather conditions on the day of the concert. They will make a profit of $25,000 on a clear day and $10,000 on a cloudy day. They will make a loss of $5,000 if it rains. The weather channel has predicted a 60% chance of rain on the day of the concert. Calculate the expected profit from the concert if the likelihood is 10% that it will be sunny and 30% that it will be cloudy.

20. Mark Underwood is a professor of Economics at Indiana University. He has been teaching Principles of Economics for over 25 years. Professor Underwood uses the following scale for grading.

Grade	Probability
A	0.10
B	0.30
C	0.40
D	0.10
F	0.10

Calculate the expected numerical grade in Professor Underwood's class using 4.0 for A, 3.0 for B, etc.

21. The manager of a publishing company plans to give a $20,000 bonus to the top 15 percent, $10,000 to the next 30 percent, and $5,000 to the next 10 percent of sales representatives. If the publishing company has a total of 200 sales representatives, what is the expected bonus that the company will pay?

22. An electronics store sells additional warranties on its Blu-ray players. Twenty percent of the buyers buy the limited warranty for $25 and 5% buy the extended warranty for $60. What is the expected revenue for the store if it sells 120 players?

23. You are considering buying insurance for your new laptop computer, which you have recently bought for $1,500. The insurance premium for three years is $80. Over the three-year period there is an 8% chance that your laptop computer will require work worth $400, a 3% chance that it will require work worth $800, and a 2% chance that it will completely break down with a scrap value of $100. Should you buy the insurance? (Assume risk neutrality.)

24. Four years ago, Victor Consuelo purchased a very reliable automobile (as rated by a reputable consumer advocacy publication). His warranty has just expired, but the manufacturer has just offered him a 5-year, bumper-to-bumper warranty extension. The warranty costs $3,400. Consuelo constructs the following probability distribution with respect to anticipated costs if he chooses not to purchase the extended warranty.

Cost (in $)	Probability
1,000	0.25
2,000	0.45
5,000	0.20
10,000	0.10

a. Calculate Victor's expected cost.

b. Given your answer in part a, should Victor purchase the extended warranty? (Assume risk neutrality.) Explain.

25. An investor considers investing $10,000 in the stock market. He believes that the probability is 0.30 that the economy will improve, 0.40 that it will stay the same, and 0.30 that it will deteriorate. Further, if the economy improves, he expects his investment to grow to $15,000, but it can also go down to $8,000 if the economy deteriorates. If the economy stays the same, his investment will stay at $10,000.

a. What is the expected value of his investment?

b. What should the investor do if he is risk neutral?

c. Is the decision clear-cut if he is risk averse? Explain.

26. You are considering two mutual funds for your investment. The possible returns for the funds are dependent on the state of the economy and are given in the accompanying table.

State of the Economy	Fund 1	Fund 2
Good	20%	40%
Fair	10%	20%
Poor	−10%	−40%

You believe that the likelihood is 20% that the economy will be good, 50% that it will be fair, and 30% that it will be poor.

a. Find the expected value and the standard deviation of returns for Fund 1.

b. Find the expected value and the standard deviation of returns for Fund 2.

c. Which fund will you pick if you are risk averse? Explain.

27. Investment advisors recommend risk reduction through international diversification. International investing allows you to take advantage of the potential for growth in foreign economies, particularly in emerging markets. Janice Wong is considering investment in either Europe or Asia. She has studied these markets and believes that both markets will be influenced by the U.S. economy, which has a 20% chance for being good, a 50% chance for being fair, and a 30% chance for being poor. Probability distributions of the returns for these markets are given in the accompanying table.

State of the U.S. Economy	Returns in Europe	Returns in Asia
Good	10%	18%
Fair	6%	10%
Poor	−6%	−12%

a. Find the expected value and the standard deviation of returns in Europe and Asia.

b. What will Janice pick as an investment if she is risk neutral?

c. Discuss Janice's decision if she is risk averse.

5.3 The Binomial Distribution

LO 5.4

Describe the binomial distribution and compute relevant probabilities.

Different types of experiments generate different probability distributions. In the next three sections, we discuss three special cases: the binomial, the Poisson, and the hypergeometric probability distributions. Here we focus on the binomial distribution. Before we can discuss the binomial distribution, we first must ensure that the experiment satisfies the conditions of a **Bernoulli process**, which is a particular type of experiment named after the person who first described it, the Swiss mathematician James Bernoulli (1654–1705).

> A **Bernoulli process** consists of a series of n independent and identical trials of an experiment such that on each trial:
> - There are only two possible outcomes, conventionally labeled success and failure; and
> - Each time the trial is repeated, the probabilities of success and failure remain the same.

We use p to denote the probability of success, and therefore $1 - p$ is the probability of failure.

A **binomial random variable** is defined as the number of successes achieved in the n trials of a Bernoulli process. The possible values of a binomial random variable include $0, 1, \ldots, n$. Many experiments fit the conditions of a Bernoulli process. For instance:

- A bank grants or denies a loan to a mortgage applicant.
- A consumer either uses or does not use a credit card.
- An employee travels or does not travel by public transportation.
- A life insurance policy holder dies or does not die.
- A drug is either effective or ineffective.
- A college graduate applies or does not apply to graduate school.

Our goal is to attach probabilities to various outcomes of a Bernoulli process. The result is a **binomial probability distribution**, or simply, a **binomial distribution**.

> A **binomial random variable** X is defined as the number of successes achieved in the n trials of a Bernoulli process. A **binomial distribution** shows the probabilities associated with the possible values of X.

We will eventually arrive at a general formula that helps us derive a binomial distribution. First, however, we will use a specific example and construct a **probability tree** in order to illustrate the possible outcomes and their associated probabilities.

EXAMPLE 5.5

From past experience, a manager of an upscale shoe store knows that 85% of her customers will use a credit card when making purchases. Suppose three customers are in line to make a purchase.

a. Does this example satisfy the conditions of a Bernoulli process?

b. Construct a probability tree.

c. Using the probability tree, derive the binomial probability distribution.

SOLUTION:

a. This example satisfies the conditions of a Bernoulli process because a customer either uses a credit card (labeled success), with an 85% likelihood, or does not use a credit card (labeled failure), with a 15% likelihood. Moreover, given a large number of customers, these probabilities of success and failure do not change from customer to customer.

b. Recall from Chapter 4 that we can use a probability tree whenever an experiment can be broken down into stages. Here we can view each stage as a trial. The probability tree for Example 5.5 is shown in Figure 5.3. We let S denote the outcome that a customer uses a credit card and F denote the outcome that a customer does not use a credit card. Starting from the unlabeled node on the left, customer 1 has an 85% chance of using a credit card and a 15% chance of not using one. The branches emanating from customer 1 denote conditional probabilities of customer 2 using a credit card, given whether or not customer 1 used a credit card. However, since we assume that the trials of a Bernoulli process are independent, the conditional probability of the branch outcome's occurring is the same as its unconditional probability. In other words, customer 2 has an 85% chance of using a credit card and a 15% chance of not using one regardless of what customer 1 uses. The same holds for the probabilities for customer 3. The fourth column shows that there are eight possible events at the end of the probability tree. We are able to obtain relevant probabilities by using the multiplication rule for independent events. For instance, following the top branches throughout the probability tree, we calculate the probability that all three customers use a credit card as $(0.85)(0.85)(0.85) = 0.614$. The probabilities for the remaining events are found in a similar manner.

c. Since we are not interested in identifying the particular customer who uses a credit card, but rather the number of customers who use a credit card, we can combine events with the same number of successes, using the addition rule for mutually exclusive events. For instance, in order to find the probability that one customer uses a credit card, we add the probabilities that correspond to the outcome $x = 1$ (see shaded areas in table): $0.019 + 0.019 + 0.019 = 0.057$. Similarly, we calculate the remaining probabilities corresponding to the other values

FIGURE 5.3 Probability tree for Example 5.5

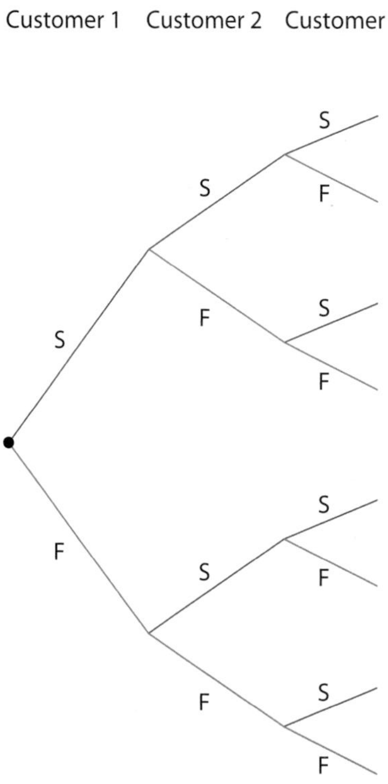

| | | | | Customers using | |
| Customer 1 | Customer 2 | Customer 3 | Events | credit card, x | Probabilities |

Events	x	Probabilities
SSS	3	(0.85)(0.85)(0.85) = 0.614
SSF	2	(0.85)(0.85)(0.15) = 0.108
SFS	2	(0.85)(0.15)(0.85) = 0.108
SFF	1	(0.85)(0.15)(0.15) = 0.019
FSS	2	(0.15)(0.85)(0.85) = 0.108
FSF	1	(0.15)(0.85)(0.15) = 0.019
FFS	1	(0.15)(0.15)(0.85) = 0.019
FFF	0	(0.15)(0.15)(0.15) = 0.003

of X and construct the probability distribution shown in Table 5.7. Note that in many solved problems, the probabilities do not add up to 1 due to rounding.

TABLE 5.7 Binomial Probabilities for Example 5.5

x	$P(X = x)$
0	0.003
1	0.057
2	0.324
3	0.614
	Total = 1 (subject to rounding)

Fortunately we do not have to construct a probability tree each time we want to construct a binomial distribution. We can use the following formula for calculating probabilities associated with a binomial random variable.

THE BINOMIAL DISTRIBUTION

For a **binomial random variable** X, the probability of x successes in n Bernoulli trials is

$$P(X = x) = \binom{n}{x}p^x(1 - p)^{n - x} = \frac{n!}{x!(n - x)!}p^x(1 - p)^{n - x}$$

for $x = 0, 1, 2, \ldots, n$. By definition, $0! = 1$.

The formula consists of two parts:

- The first term, $\binom{n}{x} = \frac{n!}{x!(n-x)!}$, tells us how many sequences with x successes and $n-x$ failures are possible in n trials. We refer to it as the binomial coefficient, which is really the familiar combination formula used to find the number of ways to choose x objects from a total of n objects, where the order in which the x objects are listed *does not matter*. For instance, in order to calculate the number of sequences that contain exactly 1 credit card user in 3 trials, we substitute $x = 1$ and $n = 3$ into the formula and calculate $\binom{n}{x} = \frac{n!}{x!(n-x)!} = \frac{3!}{1!(3-1)!} = \frac{3 \times 2 \times 1}{(1) \times (2 \times 1)} = 3$. So there are three sequences having exactly 1 success—we can verify this result with Figure 5.3.

- The second part of the equation, $p^x(1-p)^{n-x}$, represents the probability of any particular sequence with x successes and $n-x$ failures. For example, we can obtain the probability of 1 success in 3 trials from rows 4, 6, or 7 on the last column of the probability tree as (see shaded areas):

$$\left.\begin{array}{l} \text{row 4: } 0.85 \times 0.15 \times 0.15 \\ \text{row 6: } 0.15 \times 0.85 \times 0.15 \\ \text{row 7: } 0.15 \times 0.15 \times 0.85 \end{array}\right\} \quad \text{or} \quad (0.85)^1 \times (0.15)^2 = 0.019$$

In other words, each sequence consisting of 1 success in 3 trials has a 1.9% chance of occurring.

In order to obtain the overall probability of getting 1 success in 3 trials, we then multiply the binomial coefficient by the probability of obtaining the particular sequence, or here, $3 \times 0.019 = 0.057$. This is precisely the probability that we found for $P(X = 1)$ using the probability tree.

Moreover, we could use the formulas shown in Section 5.2 to calculate the expected value, the variance, and the standard deviation of any binomial random variable. Fortunately, for the binomial distribution, these formulas simplify to $E(X) = np$, $Var(X) = np(1-p)$, and $SD(X) = \sqrt{np(1-p)}$. The simplified formula for expected value is rather intuitive in that if we know the probability of success p of an experiment and we repeat the experiment n times, then on average, we expect np successes.

EXPECTED VALUE, VARIANCE, AND STANDARD DEVIATION OF A BINOMIAL RANDOM VARIABLE

If X is a binomial random variable, then

$$E(X) = \mu = np,$$
$$Var(X) = \sigma^2 = np(1-p), \text{ and}$$
$$SD(X) = \sigma = \sqrt{np(1-p)}.$$

For instance, for the binomial probability distribution assumed in Example 5.5, we can derive the expected value with the earlier general formula as

$$E(X) = \Sigma x_i P(X = x_i) = (0 \times 0.003) + (1 \times 0.057) + (2 \times 0.324) + (3 \times 0.614) = 2.55.$$

However, an easier way is to use $E(X) = np$ and thus calculate the expected value as $3 \times 0.85 = 2.55$. Similarly, the variance can be easily calculated as

$$Var(X) = np(1-p) = 3 \times 0.85 \times 0.15 = 0.38.$$

EXAMPLE 5.6

In the United States, about 30% of adults have four-year college degrees (*The Wall Street Journal*, April 26, 2012). Suppose five adults are randomly selected.

a. What is the probability that none of the adults has a college degree?

b. What is the probability that no more than two of the adults have a college degree?

c. What is the probability that at least two of the adults have a college degree?

d. Calculate the expected value, the variance, and the standard deviation of this binomial distribution.

e. Graphically depict the probability distribution and comment on its symmetry/skewness.

SOLUTION: First, this problem satisfies the conditions for a Bernoulli process with a random selection of five adults, $n = 5$. Here, an adult either has a college degree, with probability $p = 0.30$, or does not have a college degree, with probability $1 - p = 1 - 0.30 = 0.70$. Given a large number of adults, it fulfills the requirement that the probability that an adult has a college degree stays the same from adult to adult.

a. In order to find the probability that none of the adults has a college degree, we let $x = 0$ and find

$$P(X = 0) = \frac{5!}{0!(5 - 0)!} \times (0.30)^0 \times (0.70)^{5-0}$$

$$= \frac{5 \times 4 \times \cdots \times 1}{(1) \times (5 \times 4 \times \cdots \times 1)} \times 1 \times (0.70)^5 = 1 \times 1 \times 0.1681$$

$$= 0.1681.$$

In other words, there is a 16.81% chance that none of the adults has a college degree.

b. The phrase "no more than two workers" leads to the following probability statement:

$$P(X \le 2) = P(X = 0) + P(X = 1) + P(X = 2).$$

We have already found $P(X = 0)$ from part a. So we now compute $P(X = 1)$ and $P(X = 2)$:

$$P(X = 1) = \frac{5!}{1!(5 - 1)!} \times (0.30)^1 \times (0.70)^{5-1} = 0.3602$$

$$P(X = 2) = \frac{5!}{2!(5 - 2)!} \times (0.30)^2 \times (0.70)^{5-2} = 0.3087$$

Next we sum the three relevant probabilities and obtain $P(X \le 2) = 0.1681 + 0.3602 + 0.3087 = 0.8370$. From a random sample of five adults, there is an 83.7% likelihood that no more than two of them will have a college degree.

c. The phrase "at least two workers" leads to the following probability statement:

$$P(X \ge 2) = P(X = 2) + P(X = 3) + P(X = 4) + P(X = 5).$$

We can solve this problem by calculating and then summing each of the four probabilities, from $P(X = 2)$ to $P(X = 5)$. A simpler method uses one of the key properties of a probability distribution, which states that the sum of the probabilities over all values of X equals 1. Therefore, $P(X \ge 2)$ can be written as $1 - [P(X = 0) + P(X = 1)]$. We have already calculated $P(X = 0)$ and $P(X = 1)$ from parts a and b, so

$$P(X \ge 2) = 1 - [P(X = 0) + P(X = 1)] = 1 - (0.1681 + 0.3602) = 0.4717.$$

d. We use the simplified formulas to calculate the mean, the variance, and the standard deviation as

$E(X) = np = 5 \times 0.30 = 1.5$ adults,

$Var(X) = \sigma^2 = np(1-p) = 5 \times 0.30 \times 0.70 = 1.05 (\text{adults})^2$, and

$SD(X) = \sigma = \sqrt{np(1-p)} = \sqrt{1.05} = 1.02$ adults.

e. Before we graph this distribution, we first show the complete binomial distribution for Example 5.6 in Table 5.8.

TABLE 5.8 Binomial Distribution with $n = 5$ and $p = 0.30$

x	P(X = x)
0	0.1681
1	0.3602
2	0.3087
3	0.1323
4	0.0284
5	0.0024

This binomial distribution is graphically depicted in Figure 5.4. When randomly selecting five adults, the most likely outcome is that exactly one adult will have a college degree. The distribution is not symmetric; rather, it is positively skewed. In later chapters, we will learn that the binomial distribution is approximately symmetric when the sample size n is large.

FIGURE 5.4 Binomial distribution with $n = 5$ and $p = 0.30$

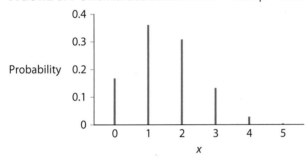

Using Excel to Obtain Binomial Probabilities

As you may have noticed, at times it is somewhat tedious and cumbersome to solve binomial distribution problems using the formulas. This issue becomes even more pronounced when we encounter large values for n and we wish to determine probabilities where X assumes a wide range of values. Some textbooks include probability tables to help with the calculations for important discrete probability distributions. We will rely on Excel to find cumbersome binomial probabilities. Consider the following problem.

EXAMPLE 5.7

In 2007 approximately 4.7% of the households in the Detroit metropolitan area were in some stage of foreclosure, the highest foreclosure rate in the nation (*The Associated Press*, February 13, 2008). Suppose 100 mortgage-holding households in the Detroit area were sampled.

a. What is the probability that exactly 5 of these households were in some stage of foreclosure?

b. What is the probability that no more than 5 of these households were in some stage of foreclosure?

c. What is the probability that more than 5 households were in some stage of foreclosure?

SOLUTION:

a. It is possible to use the binomial formula and solve this problem as $P(X = 5) = \frac{100!}{5!95!} \times (0.047)^5 \times (0.953)^{95}$, but we would quickly find the arithmetic quite unwieldy. Fortunately, we can use Excel's BINOM.DIST function to calculate this probability. In general, we find an empty cell and insert '=BINOM.DIST(x, n, p, 0 or 1)', where x is the number of successes in n trials, n is the number of trials, and p is the probability of success. For the last argument in the function, if we enter 0, then we are prompting Excel to return the probability of a specific value, $P(X = x)$; if we enter 1, then we are prompting Excel to return a cumulative probability $P(X \le x)$. In this example, we input '=BINOM. DIST(5, 100, 0.047, 0)'. After choosing <**Enter**>, Excel returns a value of 0.1783; thus, $P(X = 5) = 0.1783$.

b. We write the probability that no more than 5 of these households are in some stage of foreclosure as $P(X \le 5)$. Here, we input '=BINOM.DIST(5, 100, 0.047, 1)'. Excel returns the probability 0.6697; thus, $P(X \le 5) = 0.6697$.

c. The probability that more than five households are in some stage of foreclosure is written as $P(X > 5)$. Using the information in part b, we find this as $P(X > 5) = 1 - P(X \le 5) = 1 - 0.6697 = 0.3303$.

EXERCISES 5.3

Mechanics

28. Assume that X is a binomial random variable with $n = 5$ and $p = 0.35$. Calculate the following probabilities.
   a. $P(X = 0)$
   b. $P(X = 1)$
   c. $P(X \le 1)$

29. Assume that X is a binomial random variable with $n = 6$ and $p = 0.68$. Calculate the following probabilities.
   a. $P(X = 5)$
   b. $P(X = 4)$
   c. $P(X \ge 4)$

30. Assume that X is a binomial random variable with $n = 8$ and $p = 0.32$. Calculate the following probabilities.
   a. $P(3 < X < 5)$
   b. $P(3 < X \le 5)$
   c. $P(3 \le X \le 5)$

31. Let the probability of success on a Bernoulli trial be 0.30. In five Bernoulli trials, what is the probability that there will be (a) 4 failures, (b) more than the expected number of failures?

32. (Use computer) Let X represent a binomial random variable with $n = 150$ and $p = 0.36$. Find the following probabilities.
   a. $P(X \le 50)$
   b. $P(X = 40)$

   c. $P(X > 60)$
   d. $P(X \ge 55)$

33. (Use computer) Let X represent a binomial random variable with $n = 200$ and $p = 0.77$. Find the following probabilities.
   a. $P(X \le 150)$
   b. $P(X > 160)$
   c. $P(155 \le X \le 165)$
   d. $P(X = 160)$

Applications

34. According to a report from the Center for Studying Health System Change, 20% of Americans delay or go without medical care because of concerns about cost (*The Wall Street Journal*, June 26, 2008). Suppose eight individuals are randomly selected.
   a. What is the probability that none will delay or go without medical care?
   b. What is the probability that no more than two will delay or go without medical care?
   c. What is the probability that at least seven will delay or go without medical care?
   d. What is the expected number of individuals who will delay or go without medical care?
   e. Calculate the variance and the standard deviation for this probability distribution.

35. At a local community college, 40% of students who enter the college as freshmen go on to graduate. Ten freshmen are randomly selected.
    a. What is the probability that none of them graduates from the local college?
    b. What is the probability that at most nine will graduate from the local college?
    c. What is the expected number that will graduate?

36. The percentage of Americans who have confidence in U.S. banks dropped to 23% in June 2010, which is far below the pre-recession level of 41% reported in June 2007 (gallup.com).
    a. What is the probability that fewer than half of 10 Americans in 2010 have confidence in U.S. banks?
    b. What would have been the corresponding probability in 2007?

37. In recent analyses of Census figures, one in four American counties has passed or is approaching the tipping point where black, Hispanic, and Asian children constitute a majority of the under-20 population (*New York Times*, August 6, 2008). Racial and ethnic minorities now account for 43% of Americans under 20.
    a. What is the expected number of under-20 whites in a random sample of 5,000 Americans? What is the corresponding standard deviation?
    b. What is the expected number of racial and ethnic minorities in a random sample of 5,000 under-20 Americans? What is the corresponding standard deviation?
    c. If you randomly sample six American counties, what is the probability that for the under-20 population, whites have a clear majority in all of the counties?

38. Approximately 76% of baby boomers aged 43 to 61 are still in the workforce (*The Boston Globe*, July 10, 2008). Six baby boomers are selected at random.
    a. What is the probability that exactly one of the baby boomers is still in the workforce?
    b. What is the probability that at least five of the baby boomers are still in the workforce?
    c. What is the probability that less than two of the baby boomers are still in the workforce?
    d. What is the probability that more than the expected number of the baby boomers are still in the workforce?

39. Sikhism, a religion founded in the 15th century in India, is going through turmoil due to a rapid decline in the number of Sikh youths who wear turbans (*Washington Post,* March 29, 2009). The tedious task of combing and tying up long hair and a desire to assimilate has led to approximately 25% of Sikh youths giving up the turban.
    a. What is the probability that exactly two in a random sample of five Sikh youths wear a turban?
    b. What is the probability that two or more in a random sample of five Sikh youths wear a turban?
    c. What is the probability that more than the expected number of Sikh youths wear a turban in a random sample of five Sikh youths?

    d. What is the probability that more than the expected number of Sikh youths wear a turban in a random sample of 10 Sikh youths?

40. According to the U.S. Census, roughly half of all marriages in the United States end in divorce. Researchers from leading universities have shown that the emotions aroused by one person's divorce can transfer like a virus, making divorce contagious (*CNN,* June 10, 2010). A splitup between immediate friends increases a person's own chances of getting divorced from 36% to 63%, an increase of 75%. Use these findings to answer the following questions.
    a. Compute the probability that more than half of four randomly selected marriages will end in divorce.
    b. Redo part a if it is known that the couple's immediate friends have split up.
    c. Redo part a if it is known that none of the couple's immediate friends has split up.

41. Sixty percent of a firm's employees are men. Suppose four of the firm's employees are randomly selected.
    a. What is more likely, finding three men and one woman or two men and two women?
    b. Do you obtain the same answer as in part a if 70% of the firm's employees had been men?

42. The principal of an architecture firm tells her client that there is at least a 50% chance of having an acceptable design by the end of the week. She knows that there is only a 25% chance that any one designer would be able to do so by the end of the week.
    a. Would she be correct in her statement to the client if she asks two of her designers to work on the design, independently?
    b. If not, what if she asks three of her designers to work on the design, independently?

43. (Use computer) Suppose 40% of recent college graduates plan on pursuing a graduate degree. Fifteen recent college graduates are randomly selected.
    a. What is the probability that no more than four of the college graduates plan to pursue a graduate degree?
    b. What is the probability that exactly seven of the college graduates plan to pursue a graduate degree?
    c. What is the probability that at least six but no more than nine of the college graduates plan to pursue a graduate degree?

44. (Use computer) At the University of Notre Dame Mendoza College of Business, 40% of the students seeking a master's degree specialize in finance (*Kiplinger's Personal Finance*, March 2009). Twenty master's degree students are randomly selected.
    a. What is the probability that exactly 10 of the students specialize in finance?
    b. What is the probability that no more than 10 of the students specialize in finance?
    c. What is the probability that at least 15 of the students specialize in finance?

45. (Use computer) The Washington, D.C., region has one of the fastest-growing foreclosure rates in the nation, as 15,613 homes went into foreclosure during the one-year period ending in February 2008 (*The Washington Post*, June 19, 2008). Over the past year, the number of foreclosures per 10,000 is 131 for the Washington area, while it is 87 nationally. In other words, the foreclosure rate is 1.31% for the Washington area and 0.87% for the nation. Assume that the foreclosure rates remain stable.

a. What is the probability that in a given year, fewer than 2 out of 100 houses in the Washington area will go up for foreclosure?

b. What is the probability that in a given year, fewer than 2 out of 100 houses in the nation will go up for foreclosure?

c. Comment on the above findings.

5.4 The Poisson Distribution

LO **5.5**

Describe the Poisson distribution and compute relevant probabilities.

Another important discrete probability distribution is the **Poisson distribution**, named after the French mathematician Simeon Poisson (1781–1849). It is particularly useful in problems that deal with finding the number of occurences of a certain event over time or space, where space refers to area or region.

> A **Poisson random variable** counts the number of occurrences of a certain event over a given interval of time or space.

For simplicity, we call these occurences "successes." We first must ensure that our experiment satisfies the conditions of a **Poisson process**.

> An experiment satisfies a **Poisson process** if:
> - The number of successes within a specified time or space interval equals any integer between zero and infinity.
> - The number of successes counted in nonoverlapping intervals are independent.
> - The probability that success occurs in any interval is the same for all intervals of equal size and is proportional to the size of the interval.

For a Poisson process, we define the number of successes achieved in a specified time or space interval as a Poisson random variable. Like the Bernoulli process, many experiments fit the conditions of a Poisson process. Consider the following examples of Poisson random variables categorized by those relating to time and those relating to space.

Examples of Poisson Random Variables with Respect to Time

- The number of cars that cross the Brooklyn Bridge between 9:00 am and 10:00 am on a Monday morning.
- The number of customers that use a McDonald's drive-thru in a day.
- The number of bankruptcies that are filed in a month.
- The number of homicides that occur in a year.

Examples of Poisson Random Variables with Respect to Space

- The number of defects in a 50-yard roll of fabric.
- The number of schools of fish in 100 square miles.
- The number of leaks in a specified stretch of a pipeline.
- The number of bacteria in a specified culture.

We use the following formula for calculating probabilities associated with a Poisson random variable.

THE POISSON DISTRIBUTION

For a **Poisson random variable** X, the probability of x successes over a given interval of time or space is

$$P(X = x) = \frac{e^{-\mu}\mu^x}{x!},$$

for $x = 0, 1, 2, \ldots$, where μ is the mean number of successes and $e \approx 2.718$ is the base of the natural logarithm.

As with the binomial random variable, we have simplified formulas to calculate the variance and the standard deviation of a Poisson random variable. An interesting fact is that the mean of the Poisson random variable is equal to the variance.

EXPECTED VALUE, VARIANCE, AND STANDARD DEVIATION OF A POISSON RANDOM VARIABLE

If X is a Poisson random variable, then

$$E(X) = \mu,$$
$$Var(X) = \sigma^2 = \mu, \quad \text{and}$$
$$SD(X) = \sigma = \sqrt{\mu}.$$

EXAMPLE 5.8

We can now address questions first posed by Anne Jones in the introductory case of this chapter. Recall that Anne is concerned about staffing needs at the Starbucks that she manages. She has specific questions about the probability distribution of customer arrivals at her store. Anne believes that the typical Starbucks customer averages 18 visits to the store over a 30-day month. She has the following questions:

a. How many visits should Anne expect in a 5-day period from a typical Starbucks customer?

b. What is the probability that a customer visits the chain five times in a 5-day period?

c. What is the probability that a customer visits the chain no more than two times in a 5-day period?

d. What is the probability that a customer visits the chain at least three times in a 5-day period?

SOLUTION: In applications of the Poisson distribution, we first determine the mean number of successes in the relevant time or space interval. We use the Poisson process condition that the probability that success occurs in any interval is the same for all intervals of equal size and is proportional to the size of the interval. Here, the relevant mean will be based on the rate of 18 visits over a 30-day month.

a. Given the rate of 18 visits over a 30-day month, we can write the mean for the 30-day period as $\mu_{30} = 18$. For this problem, we compute the proportional mean for a 5-day period as $\mu_5 = 3$ because $\frac{18 \text{ visits}}{30 \text{ days}} = \frac{3 \text{ visits}}{5 \text{ days}}$.
In other words, on average, a typical Starbucks customer visits the store three times over a 5-day period.

b. In order to find the probability that a customer visits the chain five times in a 5-day period, we calculate

$$P(X = 5) = \frac{e^{-3}3^5}{5!} = \frac{(0.0498)(243)}{120} = 0.1008.$$

c. For the probability that a customer visits the chain no more than two times in a 5-day period, we express the appropriate probability statement as $P(X \le 2)$. Since this probability is equivalent to $P(X = 0) + P(X = 1) + P(X = 2)$, we first must calculate these individual probabilities and then find the sum:

$$P(X = 0) = \frac{e^{-3}3^0}{0!} = \frac{(0.0498)(1)}{1} = 0.0498,$$

$$P(X = 1) = \frac{e^{-3}3^1}{1!} = \frac{(0.0498)(3)}{1} = 0.1494, \quad \text{and}$$

$$P(X = 2) = \frac{e^{-3}3^2}{2!} = \frac{(0.0498)(9)}{2} = 0.2241.$$

Thus, $P(X \le 2) = 0.0498 + 0.1494 + 0.2241 = 0.4233$. There is approximately a 42% chance that a customer visits the chain no more than two times in a 5-day period.

d. We write the probability that a customer visits at least three times in a 5-day period as $P(X \ge 3)$. Initially, we might attempt to solve this problem by evaluating $P(X \ge 3) = P(X = 3) + P(X = 4) + P(X = 5) + \cdots$. However, given the infinite number of possible values, we cannot solve a Poisson problem this way. Here, we find $P(X \ge 3)$ as $1 - [P(X = 0) + P(X = 1) + P(X = 2)]$. Based on the probabilities in part c, we have $P(X \ge 3) = 1 - [0.0498 + 0.1494 + 0.2241] = 1 - 0.4233 = 0.5767$. Thus, there is about a 58% chance that a customer will frequent the chain at least three times in a 5-day period.

Figure 5.5 graphs the Poisson distribution $P(X = x)$ with $\mu = 3$, for x ranging from 0 to 8. The most likely outcomes are when x equals 2 and x equals 3, and the distribution is positively skewed. Remember that, theoretically, the values that the Poisson random variable assumes are infinitely countable, but the probabilities approach zero beyond those shown here.

FIGURE 5.5 Poisson distribution with $\mu = 3$

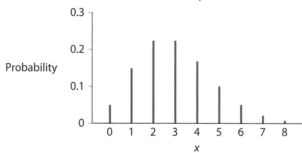

Using Excel to Obtain Poisson Probabilities

Like the binomial formula, the manual use of the Poisson formula can become quite cumbersome, especially when the values of x and μ become large. Excel again proves useful when calculating Poisson probabilities, as the next example shows.

EXAMPLE 5.9

Last year, even as a recession gripped the country, 114 microbreweries and brewpubs opened in the United States (*The Wall Street Journal*, March 18, 2009). Assume this number represents an average and remains constant over time. Find the following probabilities with Excel.

a. What is the probability that no more than 100 microbreweries or brewpubs open in a given year?

b. What is the probability that exactly 115 microbreweries or brewpubs open in a given year?

SOLUTION:

a. We wish to determine the probability that no more than 100 microbreweries or brewpubs open in a given year, that is, $P(X \leq 100)$. We use Excel's POISSON.DIST function to calculate this probability. In general, to find $P(X = x)$, we find an empty cell and insert '=POISSON.DIST(x, μ, 0 or 1)', where x is the number of successes over some interval and μ is the mean over that interval. As similarly defined for Excel's binomial function, the term 0 will prompt Excel to return the probability of a specific value, $P(X = x)$, whereas 1 prompts Excel to return the cumulative probability $P(X \leq x)$. In this example, we input '=POISSON.DIST(100, 114, 1)'. Excel returns a value of 0.1012; thus, $P(X \leq 100) = 0.1012$. There is about a 10% chance that no more than 100 microbreweries or brewpubs will open in any given year.

b. Here we wish to find $P(X = 115)$, that is, the probability that exactly 115 microbreweries or brewpubs open in any given year. We input '=POISSON.DIST(115, 114, 0)' and Excel returns 0.0370. Thus, there is a 3.7% chance that exactly 115 microbreweries or brewpubs will open in any given year.

SYNOPSIS OF INTRODUCTORY CASE

Anne Jones, the manager of a Starbucks store, is concerned about how other nearby store closings might affect foot traffic at her store. A solid understanding of the likelihood of customer arrivals is necessary before she can make further statistical inference. Historical data allow her to assume that a typical Starbucks customer averages 18 visits to a Starbucks store over a 30-day month. With this information and the knowledge that she can model customer arrivals using the Poisson distribution, she deduces that a typical customer averages three visits in a 5-day period. The likelihood that a typical customer frequents her store five times in a 5-day period is approximately 10%. Moreover, there is approximately a 42% chance that a typical customer goes to Starbucks no more than two times, while the chances that this customer visits the chain at least three times is approximately 58%. These preliminary probabilities will prove vital as Anne plans her future staffing needs.

Mechanics

46. Assume that X is a Poisson random variable with $\mu = 1.5$. Calculate the following probabilities.
    a. $P(X = 1)$
    b. $P(X = 2)$
    c. $P(X \geq 2)$

47. Assume that X is a Poisson random variable with $\mu = 4$. Calculate the following probabilities.
    a. $P(X = 4)$
    b. $P(X = 2)$
    c. $P(X \leq 1)$

48. Let the mean success rate of a Poisson process be 8 successes per hour.
    a. Find the expected number of successes in a half-hour period.
    b. Find the probability of at least 2 successes in a given half-hour period.

c. Find the expected number of successes in a two-hour period.
d. Find the probability of 10 successes in a given two-hour period.

49. (Use computer) Assume that X is a Poisson random variable with $\mu = 15$. Calculate the following probabilities.
    a. $P(X \leq 10)$
    b. $P(X = 13)$
    c. $P(X > 15)$
    d. $P(12 \leq X \leq 18)$

50. (Use computer) Assume that X is a Poisson random variable with $\mu = 20$. Calculate the following probabilities.
    a. $P(X < 14)$
    b. $P(X \geq 20)$
    c. $P(X = 25)$
    d. $P(18 \leq X \leq 23)$

Applications

51. Which of the following probabilities are likely to be found using a Poisson distribution?
    a. The probability that there will be six leaks in a specified stretch of a pipeline.
    b. The probability that at least 10 students in a class of 40 will land a job right after graduation.
    c. The probability that at least 50 families will visit the Acadia National Park over the weekend.
    d. The probability that no customer will show up in the next five minutes.

52. Which of the following are likely to represent Poisson random variables?
    a. The number of violent crimes in New York over a six-week period.
    b. The number of customers of a bank manager who will default.
    c. The number of scratches on a 2-by-1-foot portion of a large wooden table.
    d. The number of patients of a doctor for whom the drug will be effective.

53. On average, there are 12 potholes per mile on a particular stretch of the state highway. Suppose the potholes are distributed evenly on the highway.
    a. Find the probability of finding fewer than two potholes in a quarter-mile stretch of the highway.
    b. Find the probability of finding more than one pothole in a quarter-mile stretch of the highway.

54. A textile manufacturing process finds that on average, 2 flaws occur per every 50 yards of material produced.
    a. What is the probability of exactly 2 flaws in a 50-yard piece of material?
    b. What is the probability of no more than 2 flaws in a 50-yard piece of material?
    c. What is the probability of no flaws in a 25-yard piece of material?

55. A tollbooth operator has observed that cars arrive randomly at an average rate of 360 cars per hour.
    a. Find the probability that 2 cars arrive during a specified one-minute period.
    b. Find the probability that at least 2 cars arrive during a specified one-minute period.
    c. Find the probability that 40 cars arrive between 10:00 am and 10:10 am.

56. Airline travelers should be ready to be more flexible as airlines once again cancel thousands of flights this summer. The Coalition for Airline Passengers Rights, Health, and Safety averages 400 calls a day to help stranded travelers deal with airlines (http://seattlepi.com, July 10, 2008). Suppose the hotline is staffed for 16 hours a day.
    a. Calculate the average number of calls in a one-hour interval; 30-minute interval; 15-minute interval.
    b. What is the probability of exactly 6 calls in a 15-minute interval?
    c. What is the probability of no calls in a 15-minute interval?
    d. What is the probability of at least 2 calls in a 15-minute interval?

57. Motorists arrive at a Gulf gas station at the rate of two per minute during morning hours.
    a. What is the probability that more than two motorists will arrive at the Gulf gas station during a one-minute interval in the morning?
    b. What is the probability that exactly six motorists will arrive at the Gulf gas station during a five-minute interval in the morning?
    c. How many motorists can an employee expect in her three-hour morning shift?

58. According to a recent government report, the aging of the U.S. population is translating into many more visits to doctors' offices and hospitals (*USA Today,* August 7, 2008). It is estimated that an average person makes four visits a year to doctors' offices and hospitals.
    a. What are the mean and the standard deviation of an average person's number of monthly visits to doctors' offices and hospitals?
    b. What is the probability that an average person does not make any monthly visits to doctors' offices and hospitals?
    c. What is the probability that an average person makes at least one monthly visit to doctors' offices and hospitals?

59. (Use computer) On average, 400 people a year are struck by lightning in the United States (*The Boston Globe,* July 21, 2008).
    a. What is the probability that at most 425 people are struck by lightning in a year?
    b. What is the probability that at least 375 people are struck by lightning in a year?

60. (Use computer) In the fiscal year that ended September 30, 2008, there were 24,584 age-discrimination claims filed with the Equal Employment Opportunity Commission, an increase of 29% from the previous year (*The Wall Street Journal,* March 7–8, 2009). Assume there were 260 working days in the fiscal year for which a worker could file a claim.
    a. Calculate the average number of claims filed on a working day.
    b. What is the probability that exactly 100 claims were filed on a working day?
    c. What is the probability that no more than 100 claims were filed on a working day?

61. (Use computer) According to Nielsen, the average teenager sends 3,339 texts per month (*CNN,* October 15, 2010).
    a. Find the probability that an average teenager sends more than 1,000 texts per week.
    b. Find the probability that an average teenager sends fewer than 500 texts per week.

5.5 The Hypergeometric Distribution

In Section 5.3 we defined a binomial random variable X as the number of successes in the n trials of a Bernoulli process. The trials, according to a Bernoulli process, are independent and the probability of success does not change from trial to trial. The **hypergeometric distribution** is appropriate in applications where we cannot assume the trials are independent.

Consider a box full of production items, of which 10% are known to be defective. Let success be labeled as the draw of a defective item. The probability of success may not be the same from trial to trial; it will depend on the size of the population and whether the sampling was done with or without replacement. Suppose the box consists of 20 items of which 10%, or 2, are defective. The probability of success in the first draw is $0.10\,(= 2/20)$. However, the probability of success in subsequent draws will depend on the outcome of the first draw. For example, if the first item was defective, the probability of success in the second draw will be $0.0526\,(= 1/19)$, while if the first item was not defective, the probability of success in the second draw will be $0.1053\,(= 2/19)$. Therefore, the binomial distribution is not appropriate because the trials are not independent and the probability of success changes from trial to trial.

LO **5.6**

Describe the hypergeometric distribution and compute relevant probabilities.

> We use the **hypergeometric distribution** in place of the binomial distribution when we are sampling **without replacement** from a population whose size N is not significantly larger than the sample size n.

In the above example, we assumed sampling without replacement; in other words, after an item is drawn, it is not put back in the box for subsequent draws. The binomial distribution would be appropriate if we sample with replacement since, in that case, for each draw there will be 20 items of which 2 are defective, resulting in an unchanging probability of success. Moreover, the dependence of the trials can be ignored if the population size is very large relative to the sample size. For instance, if the box consists of 10,000 items of which 10%, or 1,000, are defective, then the probability of success in the second draw will be either 999/9,999 or 1,000/9,999, which are both approximately equal to 0.10.

THE HYPERGEOMETRIC DISTRIBUTION

For a **hypergeometric random variable X**, the probability of x successes in a random selection of n items is

$$P(X = x) = \frac{\binom{S}{x}\binom{N-S}{n-x}}{\binom{N}{n}},$$

for $x = 0, 1, 2, \ldots, n$ if $n \le S$ or $x = 0, 1, 2, \ldots, S$ if $n > S$, where N denotes the number of items in the population of which S are successes.

The formula consists of three parts:

- The first term in the numerator, $\binom{S}{x} = \frac{S!}{x!(S-x)!}$, represents the number of ways x successes can be selected from S successes in the population.
- The second term in the numerator, $\binom{N-S}{n-x} = \frac{(N-S)!}{(n-x)!(N-S-n+x)!}$, represents the number of ways $(n-x)$ failures can be selected from $(N-S)$ failures in the population.
- The denominator, $\binom{N}{n} = \frac{N!}{n!(N-n)!}$, represents the number of ways a sample of size n can be selected from the population of size N.

As with the binomial and Poisson distributions, simplified formulas can be used to calculate the mean, the variance, and the standard deviation of a hypergeometric random variable.

EXPECTED VALUE, VARIANCE, AND STANDARD DEVIATION OF A HYPERGEOMETRIC RANDOM VARIABLE

If X is a hypergeometric random variable, then

$$E(X) = \mu = n\left(\frac{S}{N}\right),$$

$$Var(X) = \sigma^2 = n\left(\frac{S}{N}\right)\left(1 - \frac{S}{N}\right)\left(\frac{N-n}{N-1}\right), \quad \text{and}$$

$$SD(X) = \sigma = \sqrt{n\left(\frac{S}{N}\right)\left(1 - \frac{S}{N}\right)\left(\frac{N-n}{N-1}\right)}.$$

EXAMPLE 5.10

Wooden boxes are commonly used for the packaging and transportation of mangoes. A convenience store in Morganville, New Jersey, regularly buys mangoes from a wholesale dealer. For every shipment, the manager randomly inspects five mangoes from a box containing 20 mangoes for damages due to transportation. Suppose the chosen box contains exactly two damaged mangoes.

a. What is the probability that one out of five mangoes used in the inspection is damaged?

b. If the manager decides to reject the shipment if one or more mangoes are damaged, what is the probability that the shipment will be rejected?

c. Calculate the expected value, the variance, and the standard deviation of the number of damaged mangoes used in the inspection.

SOLUTION: The hypergeometric distribution is appropriate because the probability of finding a damaged mango changes from draw to draw (sampling is without replacement and the population size N is not significantly more than the sample size n). We use the following values to answer the questions: $N = 20$, $n = 5$, $S = 2$.

a. The probability that one out of five mangoes is damaged is $P(X = 1)$. We calculate

$$P(X = 1) = \frac{\binom{2}{1}\binom{20-2}{5-1}}{\binom{20}{5}} = \frac{\left(\frac{2!}{1!1!}\right)\left(\frac{18!}{4!14!}\right)}{\left(\frac{20!}{5!15!}\right)} = \frac{(2)(3060)}{15,504} = 0.3947.$$

Therefore, the likelihood that exactly one out of five mangoes is damaged is 39.47%.

b. In order to find the probability that one or more mangoes are damaged, we need to calculate $P(X \geq 1)$. We note that $P(X \geq 1) = 1 - P(X = 0)$ where

$$P(X = 0) = \frac{\binom{2}{0}\binom{20-2}{5-0}}{\binom{20}{5}} = \frac{\left(\frac{2!}{0!2!}\right)\left(\frac{18!}{5!13!}\right)}{\left(\frac{20!}{5!15!}\right)} = \frac{(1)(8568)}{15504} = 0.5526.$$

Therefore, the probability that the shipment will be rejected equals $P(X \geq 1) = 1 - P(X = 0) = 1 - 0.5526 = 0.4474$.

c. We use the simplified formulas to obtain the mean, the variance, and the standard deviation as

$$E(X) = n\left(\frac{S}{N}\right) = 5\left(\frac{2}{20}\right) = 0.50,$$

$$Var(X) = n\left(\frac{S}{N}\right)\left(1 - \frac{S}{N}\right)\left(\frac{N-n}{N-1}\right) = 5\left(\frac{2}{20}\right)\left(1 - \frac{2}{20}\right)\left(\frac{20-5}{20-1}\right) = 0.3553, \text{ and}$$

$$SD(X) = \sqrt{0.3553} = 0.5960.$$

Using Excel to Obtain Hypergeometric Probabilities

Since it is tedious to solve hypergeometric distribution problems using the formula, we typically use Excel's HYPGEOM.DIST function to aid in the calculations. In general, to find $P(X = x)$, we find an empty cell and insert '=HYPGEOM.DIST(x, n, S, N, 0 or 1)', where x is the number of successes in the sample, n is the sample size, S is the number of successes in the population, and N is the population size. As noted in Sections 5.3 and 5.4, entering the term 0 returns $P(X = x)$, whereas entering the term 1 returns $P(X \le x)$. In Example 5.10a, we input '=HYPGEOM.DIST(1, 5, 2, 20, 0)'. Excel returns a value of 0.3947; thus, $P(X = 1) = 0.3947$, which is the value that we calculated manually.

Mechanics

62. Assume that X is a hypergeometric random variable with $N = 25$, $S = 3$, and $n = 4$. Calculate the following probabilities.
    a. $P(X = 0)$
    b. $P(X = 1)$
    c. $P(X \le 1)$

63. Assume that X is a hypergeometric random variable with $N = 15$, $S = 4$, and $n = 3$. Calculate the following probabilities.
    a. $P(X = 1)$
    b. $P(X = 2)$
    c. $P(X \ge 2)$

64. Compute the probability of no success in a random sample of three items obtained from a population of 12 items that contains two successes. What are the expected number and the standard deviation of the number of successes from the sample?

65. (Use computer) Assume that X is a hypergeometric random variable with $N = 50$, $S = 20$, and $n = 5$. Calculate the following probabilities.
    a. $P(X = 2)$
    b. $P(X \ge 2)$
    c. $P(X \le 3)$

66. (Use computer) Compute the probability of at least eight successes in a random sample of 20 items obtained from a population of 100 items that contains 25 successes. What are the expected number and the standard deviation of the number of successes?

Applications

67 Suppose you have an urn of ten marbles, of which five are red and five are green. If you draw two marbles from this urn, what is the probability that both marbles are red? What is the probability that at least one of the marbles is red?

68. A professor of management has heard that eight students in his class of 40 have landed an internship for the summer. Suppose he runs into three of his students in the corridor.
    a. Find the probability that none of these students has landed an internship.

b. Find the probability that at least one of these students has landed an internship.

69. Despite the repeated effort by the government to reform how Wall Street pays its executives, some of the nation's biggest banks are continuing to pay out bonuses nearly as large as those in the best years before the crisis (*The Washington Post*, January 15, 2010). It is known that ten out of 15 members of the board of directors of a company were in favor of a bonus. Suppose three members were randomly selected by the media.
    a. What is the probability that all of them were in favor of a bonus?
    b. What is the probability that at least two members were in favor of a bonus?

70. Many programming teams work independently at a large software company. The management has been putting pressure on these teams to finish a project on time. The company currently has 18 large programming projects, of which only 12 are likely to finish on time. Suppose the manager decides to randomly supervise three such projects.
    a. What is the probability that all three are likely to finish on time?
    b. What is the probability that at least two are likely to finish on time?

71. David Barnes and his fiancée Valerie Shah are visiting Hawaii. There are 20 guests registered for orientation. It is announced that 12 randomly selected registered guests will receive a free lesson of the Tahitian dance.
    a. What is the probability that both David and Valerie get picked for the Tahitian dance lesson?
    b. What is the probability that neither of them gets picked for the Tahitian dance lesson?

72. The National Science Foundation is fielding applications for grants to study climate change. Twenty universities apply for a grant, and only four of them will be awarded. If Syracuse University and Auburn University are among the 20 applicants, what is the probability that these two universities will receive a grant? Assume that the selection is made randomly.

73. (Use computer) A committee of 40 members consists of 24 men and 16 women. A subcommittee consisting of ten randomly selected members will be formed.

    a. What are the expected number of men and women in the subcommittee?

    b. What is the probability that at least half of the members in the subcommittee will be women?

74. (Use computer) Powerball is a jackpot game with a grand prize starting at $20 million and often rolling over into the hundreds of millions. In 2006, the jackpot was $365 million. The winner may choose to receive the jackpot prize paid over 29 years or as a lump-sum payment. For $1 the player selects six numbers for the base game of Powerball. There are two independent stages of the game. Five balls are randomly drawn from 59 consecutively numbered white balls. Moreover, one ball, called the Powerball, is randomly drawn from 39 consecutively numbered red balls. To be a winner, the numbers selected by the player must match the numbers on the randomly drawn white balls as well as the Powerball.

    a. What is the probability that the player is able to match the numbers of two out of five randomly drawn white balls?

    b. What is the probability that the player is able to match the numbers of all five randomly drawn white balls?

    c. What is the probability that the player is able to match the Powerball for a randomly drawn red ball?

    d. What is the probability of winning the jackpot? [*Hint: Remember that the two stages of drawing white and red balls are independent.*]

WRITING WITH STATISTICS

Senior executives at Skyhigh Construction, Inc., participate in a pick-your-salary plan. They choose salaries in a range between $125,000 and $150,000. By choosing a lower salary, an executive has an opportunity to make a larger bonus. If Skyhigh does not generate an operating profit during the year, then no bonuses are paid. Skyhigh has just hired two new senior executives, Allen Grossman and Felicia Arroyo. Each must decide whether to choose *Option* 1: a base pay of $125,000 with a possibility of a large bonus or *Option* 2: a base pay of $150,000 with a possibility of a bonus, but the bonus would be one-half of the bonus under Option 1.

    Grossman, 44 years old, is married with two young children. He bought his home at the height of the market and has a rather large monthly mortgage payment. Arroyo, 32 years old, just completed her M.B.A. at a prestigious Ivy League university. She is single and has no student loans due to a timely inheritance upon entering graduate school. Arroyo just moved to the area so she has decided to rent an apartment for at least one year. Given their personal profiles, inherent perceptions of risk, and subjective views of the economy, Grossman and Arroyo construct their individual probability distributions with respect to bonus outcomes shown in Table 5.9.

TABLE 5.9 Grossman's and Arroyo's Probability Distributions

Bonus (in $)	Probability	
	Grossman	Arroyo
0	0.35	0.20
50,000	0.45	0.25
100,000	0.10	0.35
150,000	0.10	0.20

Jordan Lake, an independent human resource specialist, is asked to summarize the payment plans with respect to each executive's probability distribution.

Jordan would like to use the above probability distributions to

1. Compute expected values to evaluate payment plans for Grossman and Arroyo.
2. Help Grossman and Arroyo decide whether to choose Option 1 or Option 2 for his/her compensation package.

Sample Report— Comparison of Salary Plans

Skyhigh Construction, Inc., has just hired two new senior executives, Allen Grossman and Felicia Arroyo, to oversee planned expansion of operations. As senior executives, they participate in a pick-your-salary plan. Each executive is given two options for compensation:

Option 1: A base pay of $125,000 with a possibility of a large bonus.

Option 2: A base pay of $150,000 with a possibility of a bonus, but the bonus would be one-half of the bonus under Option 1.

Grossman and Arroyo understand that if the firm does not generate an operating profit in the fiscal year, then no bonuses are paid. Each executive has constructed a probability distribution given his/her personal background, underlying risk preferences, and subjective view of the economy.

Given the probability distributions and with the aid of expected values, the following analysis will attempt to choose the best option for each executive. Grossman, a married father with two young children, believes that Table 5.A best reflects his bonus payment expectations.

TABLE 5.A Calculating Grossman's Expected Bonus

Bonus (in $)	Probability	Weighted Value, $x_i P(x_i)$
0	0.35	$0 \times 0.35 = 0$
50,000	0.45	$50,000 \times 0.45 = 22,500$
100,000	0.10	$100,000 \times 0.10 = 10,000$
150,000	0.10	$150,000 \times 0.10 = 15,000$
		Total = $47,500

Expected bonus, $E(X)$, is calculated as a weighted average of all possible bonus values and is shown at the bottom of the third column of Table 5.A. Grossman's expected bonus is $47,500. Using this value for his bonus, his salary options are

Option 1: $125,000 + $47,500 = $172,500

Option 2: $150,000 + (1/2 \times $47,500) = $173,750

Grossman should choose *Option 2* as his salary plan.

Arroyo is single with few financial constraints. Table 5.B shows the expected value of her bonus given her probability distribution.

TABLE 5.B Calculating Arroyo's Expected Bonus

Bonus (in $)	Probability	Weighted Value, $x_i P(x_i)$
0	0.20	$0 \times 0.20 = 0$
50,000	0.25	$50,000 \times 0.25 = 12,500$
100,000	0.35	$100,000 \times 0.35 = 35,000$
150,000	0.20	$150,000 \times 0.20 = 30,000$
		Total = $77,500

Arroyo's expected bonus amounts to $77,500. Thus, her salary options are

Option 1: $125,000 + $77,500 = $202,500

Option 2: $150,000 + (1/2 \times $77,500) = $188,750

Arroyo should choose *Option 1* as her salary plan.

Conceptual Review

LO 5.1 | **Distinguish between discrete and continuous random variables.**

A **random variable** summarizes outcomes of an experiment with numerical values. A random variable is either discrete or continuous. A **discrete random variable** assumes a countable number of distinct values, whereas a **continuous random variable** is characterized by uncountable values in an interval.

LO 5.2 | **Describe the probability distribution of a discrete random variable.**

The **probability distribution function** of a discrete random variable X is a list of the values of X with the associated probabilities, that is, the list of all possible pairs $(x, P(X = x))$. The **cumulative distribution function** of X is defined as $P(X \le x)$.

LO 5.3 | **Calculate and interpret summary measures for a discrete random variable.**

For a discrete random variable X with values $x_1, x_2, x_3, \ldots$, which occur with probabilities $P(X = x_i)$, the **expected value** of X is calculated as $E(X) = \mu = \Sigma x_i P(X = x_i)$. We interpret the expected value as the long-run average value of the random variable over infinitely many independent repetitions of an experiment. Measures of dispersion indicate whether the values of X are clustered about μ or widely scattered from μ. The **variance** of X is calculated as $Var(X) = \sigma^2 = \Sigma(x_i - \mu)^2 P(X = x_i)$. The **standard deviation** of X is $SD(X) = \sigma = \sqrt{\sigma^2}$.

A **risk-neutral consumer** completely ignores risk and makes his/her decisions solely on the basis of expected gains. A **risk-averse consumer** demands a positive expected gain as compensation for taking risk. This compensation increases with the level of risk taken and the degree of risk aversion. Finally, a **risk-loving consumer** may be willing to take a risk even if the expected gain is negative.

LO 5.4 | **Describe the binomial distribution and compute relevant probabilities.**

A **Bernoulli process** is a series of n independent and identical trials of an experiment such that on each trial there are only two possible outcomes, conventionally labeled "success" and "failure." The probabilities of success and failure, denoted p and $1 - p$, remain constant from trial to trial.

For a **binomial random variable** X, the probability of x successes in n Bernoulli trials is $P(X = x) = \binom{n}{x} p^x (1 - p)^{n-x} = \frac{n!}{x!(n - x)!} p^x (1 - p)^{n-x}$ for $x = 0, 1, 2, \ldots, n$.

The **expected value**, the **variance**, and the **standard deviation** of a binomial random variable are $E(X) = np$, $Var(X) = \sigma^2 = np(1 - p)$, and $SD(X) = \sigma = \sqrt{np(1 - p)}$, respectively.

LO 5.5 | **Describe the Poisson distribution and compute relevant probabilities.**

A **Poisson random variable** counts the number of occurrences of a certain event over a given interval of time or space. For simplicity, we call these occurrences "successes." For a Poisson random variable X, the probability of x successes over a given interval of time or space is $P(X = x) = \frac{e^{-\mu} \mu^x}{x!}$ for $x = 0, 1, 2, \ldots$, where μ is the mean number of successes and $e \approx 2.718$ is the base of the natural logarithm. The **expected value**, the **variance**, and the **standard deviation** of a Poisson distribution are $E(X) = \mu$, $Var(X) = \sigma^2 = \mu$, and $SD(X) = \sigma = \sqrt{\mu}$, respectively.

LO 5.6 | **Describe the hypergeometric distribution and compute relevant probabilities.**

The hypergeometric distribution is appropriate in applications where the trials are not independent and the probability of success changes from trial to trial. We use it in place of the binomial distribution when we are **sampling without replacement** from a population whose size N is not significantly larger than the sample size n. For a **hyper-geometric random variable** X, the probability of x successes in a random selection of n items is $P(X = x) = \dfrac{\binom{S}{x}\binom{N-S}{n-x}}{\binom{N}{n}}$ for $x = 0, 1, 2, \ldots, n$ if $n \leq S$ or $x = 0, 1, 2, \ldots, S$ if $n > S$, where N denotes the number of items in the population of which S are successes. The **expected value**, the **variance**, and the **standard deviation** of a hypergeometric distribution are $E(X) = n\left(\frac{S}{N}\right)$, $Var(X) = \sigma^2 = n\left(\frac{S}{N}\right)\left(1 - \frac{S}{N}\right)\left(\frac{N-n}{N-1}\right)$, and $SD(X) = \sigma = \sqrt{n\left(\frac{S}{N}\right)\left(1 - \frac{S}{N}\right)\left(\frac{N-n}{N-1}\right)}$, respectively.

Additional Exercises and Case Studies

75. Facing the worst economic climate since the dot-com bust in the early 2000s, high-tech companies in the United States search for investment opportunities with cautious optimism (*USA TODAY*, February 17, 2009). Suppose the investment team at Microsoft is considering an innovative start-up project. According to its estimates, Microsoft can make a profit of $5 million if the project is very successful and $2 million if it is somewhat successful. It also stands to lose $4 million if the project fails. Calculate the expected profit or loss for Microsoft if the probabilities that the project is very successful and somewhat successful are 0.10 and 0.40, respectively, with the remaining amount being the failure probability.

76. An analyst developed the following probability distribution for the rate of return for a common stock.

Scenario	Probability	Rate of Return
1	0.25	−15%
2	0.35	5%
3	0.40	10%

   a. Calculate the expected rate of return.
   b. Calculate the variance and the standard deviation of this probability distribution.

77. A professor uses a relative scale for grading. She announces that 60% of the students will get at least a B, with 15% getting A's. Also, 5% will get a D and another 5% will get an F. Assume that no incompletes are given in the course. Let Score be defined by 4 for A, 3 for B, 2 for C, 1 for D, and 0 for F.
   a. Find the probability that a student gets a B.
   b. Find the probability that a student gets at least a C.
   c. Compute the expected value and the standard deviation of Score.

78. Fifty percent of the customers who go to Sears Auto Center for tires buy four tires and 30% buy two tires. Moreover, 18% buy fewer than two tires, with 5% buying none.
   a. Find the expected value and the standard deviation of the number of tires a customer buys.
   b. If Sears Auto Center makes a $15 profit on every tire it sells, what is its expected profit if it services 120 customers?

79. Rent-to-own (RTO) stores allow consumers immediate access to merchandise in exchange for a series of weekly or monthly payments. The agreement is for a fixed time period. At the same time, the customer has the flexibility to terminate the contract by returning the merchandise. Suppose the RTO store makes a $200 profit on appliances when the customer ends up owning the merchandise by making all payments. It makes a $20 profit when the customer returns the product and a loss of $600 when the customer defaults. Let the return and default probabilities be 0.60 and 0.05, respectively.
   a. Construct a probability distribution for the profit per appliance.
   b. What is the expected profit for a store that sells 200 rent-to-own contracts?

80. Forty-four percent of consumers with credit cards carry balances from month to month (http://bankrate.com, February 20, 2007). Four consumers with credit cards are randomly selected.
   a. What is the probability that all consumers carry a credit card balance?
   b. What is the probability that fewer than two consumers carry a credit card balance?
   c. Calculate the expected value, the variance, and the standard deviation of this binomial distribution.

81. According to the Department of Transportation, 27% of domestic flights were delayed in 2007 (*Money*, May 2008). At New York's John F. Kennedy Airport, five flights are randomly selected.
   a. What is the probability that all five flights are delayed?
   b. What is the probability that all five are on time?

82. Apple products have become a household name in America with 51% of all households owning at least one Apple product (*CNN*, March 19, 2012).
   a. What is the probability that two in a random sample of four households own an Apple product?
   b. What is the probability that all four in a random sample of four households own an Apple product?
   c. In a random sample of 100 households, find the expected value and the standard deviation of the number of households that own an Apple product.

83. (Use computer) Twenty percent of U.S. mortgages are "underwater" (*The Boston Globe*, March 5, 2009). A mortgage is considered underwater if the value of the home is less than what is owed on the mortgage. Suppose 100 mortgage holders are randomly selected.

    a. What is the probability that exactly 15 of the mortgages are underwater?

    b. What is the probability that more than 20 of the mortgages are underwater?

    c. What is the probability that at least 25 of the mortgages are underwater?

84. (Use computer) According to a survey by consulting firm Watson Wyatt, approximately 19% of employers have eliminated perks or plan to do so in the next year (*Kiplinger's Personal Finance*, February 2009). Suppose 30 employers are randomly selected.

    a. What is the probability that exactly ten of the employers have eliminated or plan to eliminate perks?

    b. What is the probability that at least ten employers, but no more than 20 employers, have eliminated or plan to eliminate perks?

    c. What is the probability that at most eight employers have eliminated or plan to eliminate perks?

85. Studies have shown that bats can consume an average of ten mosquitoes per minute (berkshiremuseum.org).

    a. Calculate the average number of mosquitoes that a bat consumes in a 30-second interval.

    b. What is the probability that a bat consumes four mosquitoes in a 30-second interval?

    c. What is the probability that a bat does not consume any mosquitoes in a 30-second interval?

    d. What is the probability that a bat consumes at least one mosquito in a 30-second interval?

86. (Use computer) Despite the fact that home prices seem affordable and mortgage rates are at historic lows, real estate agents say they are showing more homes, but not selling more (*The Boston Globe*, March 7, 2009). A real estate company estimates that an average of five people show up at an open house to view a property. There is going to be an open house on Sunday.

    a. What is the probability that at least five people will show up to view the property?

    b. What is the probability that fewer than five people will show up to view the property?

87. (Use computer) The police have estimated that there are twelve major accidents per day on a particular 10-mile stretch of a national highway. Suppose the incidence of accidents is evenly distributed in this 10-mile stretch of the highway.

    a. Find the probability that there will be fewer than eight major accidents in this 10-mile stretch of the highway.

    b. Find the probability that there will be more than two accidents in a 1-mile stretch of this highway.

88. Suppose you draw three cards, without replacement, from a deck of well shuffled cards. Remember that each deck consists of 52 cards, with 13 each of spades, hearts, clubs, and diamonds.

    a. What is the probability that you draw all spades?

    b. What is the probability that you draw two or fewer spades?

    c. What is the probability that you draw all spades or hearts?

89. A professor has learned that three students in her class of 20 will cheat on the exam. She decides to focus her attention on four randomly chosen students during the exam.

    a. What is the probability that she finds at least one of the students cheating?

    b. What is the probability that she finds at least one of the students cheating if she focuses on six randomly chosen students?

90. (Use computer) Many U.S. households still do not have Internet access. Suppose 20 out of 80 households in a small southern town do not have Internet access. A company that provides high-speed Internet has recently entered the market. As part of the marketing campaign, the company decides to randomly select ten households and offer them free laptops along with a brochure that describes their services. The aim is to build goodwill and, with a free laptop, tempt nonusers into getting Internet access.

    a. What is the probability that six laptop recipients do not have Internet access?

    b. What is the probability that at least five laptop recipients do not have Internet access?

    c. What is the probability that two or fewer laptop recipients do not have Internet access?

    d. What is the expected number of laptop recipients who do not have Internet access?

CASE STUDIES

Case Study 5.1

An extended warranty is a prolonged warranty offered to consumers by the warranty administrator, the retailer, or the manufacturer. A recent report in *The New York Times* (November 23, 2009) suggests that 20.4% of laptops fail over three years. Roberto D'Angelo is interested in an extended warranty for his laptop. A good extended warranty is being offered at Compuvest.com for $74. It will cover any repair job that his laptop may need in the next three years. Based on his research, he determines that the likelihood of a repair job in the next three years is 13% for a minor repair, 8% for a major repair, and 3% for a catastrophic repair. The extended warranty will save him $80 for a minor repair, $320 for a major repair, and $500 for a catastrophic repair. These results are summarized in the following probability distribution.

Data for Case Study 5.1 Probability Distribution for Repair Cost

Type of Repair	Probability	Repair Cost
None	0.76	$0
Minor	0.13	$80
Major	0.08	$320
Catastrophic	0.03	$500

In a report, use the above information to

1. Calculate and interpret the expected value of the repair cost.
2. Analyze the expected gain or loss for a consumer who buys the above extended warranty.
3. Determine what kind of a consumer (risk neutral, risk averse, or both) will buy this extended warranty.

Case Study 5.2

According to figures released by the New York City government, smoking among New York City teenagers is on a decline, continuing a trend that began more than a decade ago (*The New York Times*, January 2, 2008). According to the New York City Youth Risk Behavior Survey, the teenage smoking rate dropped to 8.5% in 2007 from about 17.6% in 2001 and 23% in 1997. City officials attribute the lower smoking rate to factors including a cigarette tax increase, a ban on workplace smoking, and television and subway ads that graphically depict tobacco-related illnesses.

In a report, use the above information to

1. Calculate the probability that at least one in a group of 10 New York City teenagers smoked in 2007.
2. Calculate the probability that at least one in a group of 10 New York City teenagers smoked in 2001.
3. Calculate the probability that at least one in a group of 10 New York City teenagers smoked in 1997.
4. Comment on the smoking trend between 1997 and 2007.

Case Study 5.3

Disturbing news regarding Scottish police concerns the number of crashes involving vehicles on operational duties (*BBC News*, March 10, 2008). Statistics showed that Scottish forces' vehicles had been involved in traffic accidents at the rate of 1,000 per year. The statistics included vehicles involved in 999 calls (the equivalent of 911 in the United States) and pursuits. Fire service and ambulance vehicles were not included in the figures.

In a report, use the above information to

1. Calculate and interpret the expected number of traffic accidents per day involving vehicles on operational duties.
2. Use this expected value to construct the probability distribution table that lists the probability of 0, 1, 2, ... , 10 traffic accidents per day. Graph this distribution and summarize your findings.

Appendix 5.1 Guidelines for Other Software Packages

The following section provides brief commands for specific software packages: Minitab, SPSS, and JMP. More detailed instructions can be found on the text website.

MINITAB

The Binomial Distribution

A. (Replicating Example 5.7a) From the menu choose **Calc>Probability Distributions > Binomial**.

B. Select **Probability** since we are finding $P(X = 5)$. (For cumulative probabilities, select **Cumulative probability**.) Enter 100 as the **Number of trials** and 0.047 as the **Event probability**. Select **Input constant** and enter the value 5.

The Poisson Distribution

A. (Replicating Example 5.9a) From the menu choose **Calc>Probability Distributions>Poisson**.

B. Select **Cumulative probability** since we are finding $P(X \le 100)$. (For calculating $P(X = x)$, select **Probability**.) Enter 114 for the **Mean**. Select **Input constant** and enter the value 100.

The Hypergeometric Distribution

A. (Replicating Example 5.10a) From the menu choose **Calc>Probability Distributions>Hypergeometric**.

B. Select **Probability** since we are finding $P(X = 1)$. (For cumulative probabilities, select **Cumulative probability**.) Enter 20 for the **Population size(N)**, 2 for **Event count in population(M)**, and 5 for the **Sample size(n)**. Select **Input constant** and enter 1.

SPSS

The Binomial Distribution

A. (Replicating Example 5.7a) From the menu choose **Transform>Compute Variable**. Note: In order to access the commands, SPSS must "view" data on the spreadsheet. For this purpose, we enter a value of zero in the top left cell.

B. Type pdfbinomial as **Target Variable**. Since we are calculating $P(X = 5)$, under **Function group** select **PDF & Noncentral PDF**, and under **Functions and Special Variables**, double-click on **Pdf.Binom**. (For cumulative probabilities, under **Function group** select **CDF & Noncentral CDF**, and under **Functions and Special Variables** double-click on **Cdf.Binom**.) In the **Numeric Expression** box, enter 5 for **quant**, 100 for **n**, and 0.047 for **prob**.

The Poisson Distribution

A. (Replicating Example 5.9a) From the menu choose **Transform>Compute Variable**.

B. Type cdfpoisson as **Target Variable**. Since we are calculating $P(X \le 100)$, under **Function group** select **CDF & Noncentral CDF**, and under **Functions and Special Variables**, double-click on **Pdf.Poisson**. (For calculating $P(X = x)$, under **Function group** select **PDF & Noncentral PDF**, and under **Functions and Special Variables** double-click on **Pdf.Poisson**.) In the *Numeric Expression* box, enter 100 for **quant** and 114 for **Mean**.

The Hypergeometric Distribution

A. (Replicating Example 5.10a) From the menu choose **Transform>Compute Variable**.

B. Type pdfhyper as **Target Variable**. Since we are calculating $P(X = 1)$, under **Function group** select **PDF & Noncentral PDF**, and under **Functions and Special Variables**, double-click on **Pdf.Hyper**. (For cumulative probabilities, under **Function group** select **CDF & Noncentral CDF**, and under **Functions and Special Variables** double-click on **Cdf.Hyper**.) In the *Numeric Expression* box, enter 1 for **quant**, 20 for **total**, 5 for **sample**, and 2 for **hits**.

JMP

The Binomial Distribution

A. (Replicating Example 5.7a) Right-click on the header at the top of the column in the spreadsheet view. Under **Functions (grouped)**, choose **Discrete Probability>Binomial Probability**. (Select **Binomial Distribution** for cumulative probabilities.) Note: In order to see the calculated probability on the spreadsheet view, JMP must "view" data on the spreadsheet. For this purpose, we enter a value of zero in the first cell of the column.

B. Enter 0.047 for **p**, 100 for **n**, and 5 for **k**.

The Poisson Distribution

A. (Replicating Example 5.9a) Right-click on the header at the top of the column in the spreadsheet view. Under **Functions (grouped)**, choose **Discrete Probability>Poisson Distribution**. (For calculating $P(X = x)$, select **Poisson Probability**.)

B. Enter 114 for **lambda** and 100 for **k**.

The Hypergeometric Distribution

A. (Replicating Example 5.10a) Right-click on the header at the top of the column in the spreadsheet view. Under **Functions (grouped)**, choose **Discrete Probability>Hypergeometric Probability**. (For cumulative probabilities, select **Hypergeometric Distribution**).

B. Enter 20 for **N**, 2 for **K**, 5 for **n**, and 1 for **x**.

6 Continuous Probability Distributions

C H A P T E R

LEARNING OBJECTIVES

After reading this chapter you should be able to:

LO **6.1** Describe a continuous random variable.

LO **6.2** Calculate and interpret probabilities for a random variable that follows the continuous uniform distribution.

LO **6.3** Explain the characteristics of the normal distribution.

LO **6.4** Use the standard normal table (z table).

LO **6.5** Calculate and interpret probabilities for a random variable that follows the normal distribution.

LO **6.6** Calculate and interpret probabilities for a random variable that follows the exponential distribution.

In the preceding chapter, we defined a random variable and discussed its numerical values. We then classified the random variable as a discrete or a continuous random variable, depending on the range of numerical values that it can assume. A discrete random variable assumes a countable number of distinct values, such as the number of houses that a Realtor sells in a month, the number of foreclosures in a sample of 100 households, and the number of cars lined up at a toll booth. A continuous random variable, on the other hand, is characterized by uncountable values because it can take on any value within an interval. Examples of a continuous random variable include the investment return on a mutual fund, the waiting time at a toll booth, and the amount of soda in a cup. In all of these examples, it is impossible to list all possible values of the random variable. In this chapter we focus our attention on continuous random variables. Most of this chapter is devoted to the discussion of the normal distribution, which is the most extensively used continuous probability distribution and is the cornerstone of statistical inference. Other important continuous distributions discussed are the continuous uniform and the exponential distributions.

Demand for Salmon

Akiko Hamaguchi is the manager of a small sushi restaurant called Little Ginza in Phoenix, Arizona. As part of her job, Akiko has to purchase salmon every day for the restaurant. For the sake of freshness, it is important that she buys the right amount of salmon daily. Buying too much may result in wastage and buying too little may disappoint some customers on high-demand days.

Akiko has estimated that the daily consumption of salmon is normally distributed with a mean of 12 pounds and a standard deviation of 3.2 pounds. She has always bought 20 pounds of salmon every day. Lately, she has been criticized by the owners because this amount of salmon was too often resulting in wastage. As part of cost cutting, Akiko is considering a new strategy. She will buy salmon that is sufficient to meet the daily demand of customers on 90% of the days.

Akiko wants to use the above information to:

1. Calculate the proportion of days that demand for salmon at Little Ginza was above her earlier purchase of 20 pounds.

2. Calculate the proportion of days that demand for salmon at Little Ginza was below 15 pounds.

3. Determine the amount of salmon that should be bought daily so that it meets demand on 90% of the days.

   A synopsis of this case is provided at the end of Section 6.3.

6.1 Continuous Random Variables and the Uniform Distribution

LO **6.1**

Describe a continuous random variable.

As discussed in Chapter 5, a discrete random variable X assumes a countable number of distinct values such as x_1, x_2, x_3, and so on. A **continuous random variable**, on the other hand, is characterized by uncountable values because it can take on any value within an interval. Unlike the case of a discrete random variable, we cannot describe the possible values of a continuous random variable X with a list $x_1, x_2, \ldots$ because the outcome $(x_1 + x_2)/2$, not in the list, might also be possible. Consider, for example, a continuous random variable defined by the amount of time a student takes to finish the exam. Here, it is impossible to put in a sequence all possible values of the random variable.

For a discrete random variable, we can compute the probability that it assumes a particular value x, or written as a probability statement, $P(X = x)$. For instance, for a binomial random variable, we can calculate the probability of exactly one success in n trials, that is, $P(X = 1)$. We cannot make this calculation with a continuous random variable. The probability that a continuous random variable assumes a particular value x is zero, that is, $P(X = x) = 0$. This occurs because we cannot assign a nonzero probability to each of the uncountable values and still have the probabilities sum to one. Thus, for a continuous random variable it is only meaningful to calculate the probability that the value of the random variable falls within some specified interval. Therefore, for a continuous random variable, $P(a \le X \le b) = P(a < X < b) = P(a \le X < b) = P(a < X \le b)$ since $P(X = a)$ and $P(X = b)$ are both zero.

For a continuous random variable, the counterpart to the probability mass function is called the **probability density function**, denoted by $f(x)$. As mentioned in Chapter 5, in this book we often use the term "probability distribution" to refer to both functions. The graph of $f(x)$ approximates the relative frequency polygon for the population. Unlike the discrete probability distribution, $f(x)$ does not provide probabilities directly. The probability that the variable assumes a value within an interval, say $P(a \le X \le b)$, is defined as the area under $f(x)$ between points a and b. Moreover, the entire area under $f(x)$ over all values of x must equal one; this is equivalent to the fact that, for discrete random variables, the probabilities add up to one.

THE PROBABILITY DENSITY FUNCTION

The probability density function $f(x)$ of a continuous random variable X has the following properties:

- $f(x) \ge 0$ for all possible values x of X, and
- the area under $f(x)$ over all values of x equals one.

As in the case of discrete random variables, we can use the **cumulative distribution function**, denoted by $F(x)$, to compute probabilities for continuous random variables. For a value x of the random variable X, $F(x) = P(X \le x)$ is simply the area under the probability density function up to the value x.

THE CUMULATIVE DISTRIBUTION FUNCTION

For any value x of the random variable X, the cumulative distribution function $F(x)$ is defined as

$$F(x) = P(X \le x).$$

If you are familiar with calculus, then you will recognize that this cumulative probability is the integral of $f(u)$ for values less than or equal to x. Similarly, $P(a \le X \le b) = F(b) - F(a)$ is the integral of $f(u)$ between points a and b. Fortunately, we do not necessarily need the knowledge of integral calculus to compute probabilities for the continuous random variables discussed in this text.

The Continuous Uniform Distribution

LO **6.2**

Calculate and interpret probabilities for a random variable that follows the continuous uniform distribution.

One of the simplest continuous probability distributions is called the **continuous uniform distribution**. This distribution is appropriate when the underlying random variable has an equally likely chance of assuming a value within a specified range. Examples of uniformly distributed random variables include the delivery time of an appliance, the flight time between cities, and the waiting time for a campus bus. Any specified range for each of the above random variables can be assumed to be equally probable.

Suppose you are informed that your new refrigerator will be delivered between 2:00 pm and 3:00 pm. Let the random variable X denote the delivery time of your refrigerator. This variable is bounded below by 2:00 pm and above by 3:00 pm for a total range of 60 minutes. It is reasonable to infer that the probability of delivery between 2:00 pm and 2:30 pm equals 0.50 ($=30/60$), as does the probability of delivery between 2:30 pm and 3:00 pm. Similarly, the probability of delivery in any 15-minute interval equals 0.25 ($=15/60$), and so on.

Figure 6.1 depicts the probability density function of the continuous uniform random variable. The values a and b on the horizontal axis represent its lower and upper limits, respectively. The continuous uniform distribution is symmetric around its mean μ, computed as $\frac{a+b}{2}$. In the refrigerator delivery example, the mean is $\mu = \frac{2+3}{2} = 2.5$, implying that you expect the delivery at 2:30 pm. The standard deviation σ of a continuous uniform variable equals $\sqrt{(b-a)^2/12}$.

FIGURE 6.1 Continuous uniform probability density function

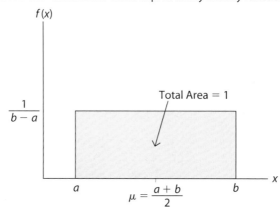

It is important to emphasize that the height of the probability density function does not directly represent a probability. As mentioned earlier, for all continuous random variables, it is the area under $f(x)$ that corresponds to probability. For the continuous uniform distribution, the probability is essentially the area of a rectangle, which is the base times the height. Therefore, the probability is easily computed by multiplying the length of a specified interval (base) with $f(x) = \frac{1}{b-a}$ (height).

THE CONTINUOUS UNIFORM DISTRIBUTION

A random variable X follows the **continuous uniform distribution** if its probability density function is

$$f(x) = \begin{cases} \dfrac{1}{b-a} & \text{for } a \le x \le b, \text{ and} \\ 0 & \text{for } x < a \text{ or } x > b, \end{cases}$$

where a and b represent the lower and upper limits of values, respectively, that the random variable assumes.

The expected value and the standard deviation of X are computed as

$$E(X) = \mu = \frac{a+b}{2} \quad \text{and} \quad SD(X) = \sigma = \sqrt{(b-a)^2/12}.$$

EXAMPLE 6.1

A manager of a local drugstore is projecting next month's sales for a particular cosmetic line. She knows from historical data that sales follow a continuous uniform distribution with a lower limit of $2,500 and an upper limit of $5,000.

a. What are the mean and the standard deviation of this continuous uniform distribution?

b. What is the probability that sales exceed $4,000?

c. What is the probability that sales are between $3,200 and $3,800?

SOLUTION:

a. With a value for the lower limit of $a = \$2,500$ and a value for the upper limit of $b = \$5,000$, we calculate the mean and the standard deviation of this continuous uniform distribution as

$$\mu = \frac{a + b}{2} = \frac{\$2,500 + \$5,000}{2} = \$3,750, \text{ and}$$

$$\sigma = \sqrt{(b - a)^2/12} = \sqrt{(5,000 - 2,500)^2/12} = \$721.69.$$

b. We find $P(X > 4,000)$, which is the area between $4,000 and $5,000, as shown in Figure 6.2. The base of the rectangle equals $5,000 - 4,000 = 1,000$ and the height equals $\frac{1}{5,000 - 2,500} = 0.0004$. Thus $P(X > 4,000) = 1,000 \times 0.0004 = 0.40$.

FIGURE 6.2 Area to the right of 4,000 (Example 6.1b)

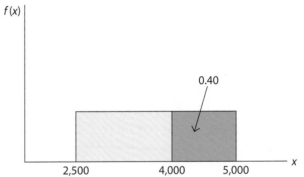

c. We find $P(3,200 \leq X \leq 3,800)$. Using the same methodology as in part b, we multiply the base times the height of the rectangle, as shown in Figure 6.3. Therefore, we obtain the probability as $(3,800 - 3,200) \times 0.0004 = 0.24$.

FIGURE 6.3 Area between 3,200 and 3,800 (Example 6.1c)

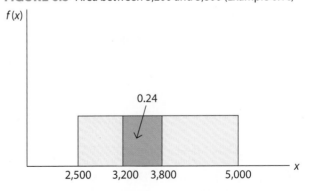

Mechanics

1. The cumulative probabilities for a continuous random variable X are $P(X \le 10) = 0.42$ and $P(X \le 20) = 0.66$. Calculate the following probabilities.
   a. $P(X > 10)$
   b. $P(X > 20)$
   c. $P(10 < X < 20)$

2. For a continuous random variable X with an upper bound of 4, $P(0 \le X \le 2.5) = 0.54$ and $P(2.5 \le X \le 4) = 0.16$. Calculate the following probabilities.
   a. $P(X < 0)$
   b. $P(X > 2.5)$
   c. $P(0 \le X \le 4)$

3. For a continuous random variable X, $P(20 \le X \le 40) = 0.15$ and $P(X > 40) = 0.16$. Calculate the following probabilities.
   a. $P(X < 40)$
   b. $P(X < 20)$
   c. $P(X = 40)$

4. A random variable X follows the continuous uniform distribution with a lower bound of 5 and an upper bound of 35.
   a. What is the height of the density function $f(x)$?
   b. What are the mean and the standard deviation of the distribution?
   c. Calculate $P(X > 10)$.

5. A random variable X follows the continuous uniform distribution with a lower bound of -2 and an upper bound of 4.
   a. What is the height of the density function $f(x)$?
   b. What are the mean and the standard deviation of the distribution?
   c. Calculate $P(X \le -1)$.

6. A random variable X follows the continuous uniform distribution with a lower limit of 10 and an upper limit of 30.
   a. Calculate the mean and the standard deviation of the distribution.
   b. What is the probability that X is greater than 22?
   c. What is the probability that X is between 15 and 23?

7. A random variable X follows the uniform distribution with a lower limit of 750 and an upper limit of 800.
   a. Calculate the mean and the standard deviation of this distribution.
   b. What is the probability that X is less than 770?

Applications

8. Suppose the average price of electricity for a New England customer follows the continuous uniform distribution with a lower bound of 12 cents per kilowatt-hour and an upper bound of 20 cents per kilowatt-hour.
   a. Calculate the average price of electricity for a New England customer.
   b. What is the probability that a New England customer pays less than 15.5 cents per kilowatt-hour?
   c. A local carnival is not able to operate its rides if the average price of electricity is more than 14 cents per kilowatt-hour. What is the probability that the carnival will need to close?

9. The arrival time of an elevator in a 12-story dormitory is equally likely at any time range during the next 4 minutes.
   a. Calculate the expected arrival time.
   b. What is the probability that an elevator arrives in less than 1½ minutes?
   c. What is the probability that the wait for an elevator is more than 1½ minutes?

10. The Netherlands is one of the world leaders in the production and sale of tulips. Suppose the heights of the tulips in the greenhouse of Rotterdam's Fantastic Flora follow a continuous uniform distribution with a lower bound of 7 inches and an upper bound of 16 inches. You have come to the greenhouse to select a bouquet of tulips, but only tulips with a height greater than 10 inches may be selected. What is the probability that a randomly selected tulip is tall enough to pick?

11. The scheduled arrival time for a daily flight from Boston to New York is 9:25 am. Historical data show that the arrival time follows the continuous uniform distribution with an early arrival time of 9:15 am and a late arrival time of 9:55 am.
    a. Calculate the mean and the standard deviation of the distribution.
    b. What is the probability that a flight arrives late (later than 9:25 am)?

12. You were informed at the nursery that your peach tree will definitely bloom sometime between March 18 and March 30. Assume that the bloom times follow a uniform distribution between these specified dates.
    a. What is the probability that the tree does not bloom until March 25?
    b. What is the probability that the tree will bloom by March 20?

13. You have been informed that the assessor will visit your home sometime between 10:00 am and 12:00 pm. It is reasonable to assume that his visitation time is uniformly distributed over the specified two-hour interval. Suppose you have to run a quick errand at 10:00 am.
    a. If it takes 15 minutes to run the errand, what is the probability that you will be back before the assessor visits?
    b. If it takes 30 minutes to run the errand, what is the probability that you will be back before the assessor visits?

6.2 The Normal Distribution

The **normal probability distribution**, or simply the **normal distribution**, is the familiar **bell-shaped distribution**. It is also referred to as the Gaussian distribution.[1] The normal distribution is the most extensively used probability distribution in statistical work. One reason for this common use is that the normal distribution closely approximates the probability distribution of a wide range of random variables of interest. Examples of random variables that closely follow a normal distribution include

- Heights and weights of newborn babies
- Scores on the SAT
- Cumulative debt of college graduates
- Advertising expenditure of firms
- Rate of return on an investment

Whenever possible, it is instructive to analyze the underlying data to determine if the normal distribution is appropriate for a given application. There are various ways to do that including inspecting histograms (Chapter 2) and boxplots (Chapter 3) for symmetry and bell shape. In this chapter we simply assume that the random variable in question is normally distributed and focus on finding probabilities associated with this type of random variable. The computation of these probabilities is easy and direct. Another important function of the normal distribution is that it serves as the cornerstone of statistical inference. Recall from Chapter 1 that the study of statistics is divided into two branches: Descriptive Statistics and Inferential Statistics. Statistical inference is generally based on the assumption of the normal distribution and serves as the major topic in the remainder of this text.

LO **6.3**

Explain the characteristics of the normal distribution.

Characteristics of the Normal Distribution

- The normal distribution is **symmetric** around its mean, that is, one side of the mean is just the mirror image of the other side. In other words, the mean, the median, and the mode are all equal for a normally distributed random variable.
- The normal distribution is **completely described by two parameters**—the population mean μ and the population variance σ^2. The population mean describes the central location and the population variance describes the dispersion of the distribution.
- The normal distribution is **asymptotic** in the sense that the tails get closer and closer to the horizontal axis but never touch it. Thus, theoretically, a normal random variable can assume any value between minus infinity and plus infinity.

The following definition mathematically expresses the probability density function of the normal distribution.

THE NORMAL DISTRIBUTION

A random variable X with mean μ and variance σ^2 follows the normal distribution if its probability density function is

$$f(x) = \frac{1}{\sigma\sqrt{2\pi}} \exp\left(-\frac{(x - \mu)^2}{2\sigma^2}\right)$$

where π equals approximately 3.14159 and $\exp(w) = e^w$ is the exponential function where $e \approx 2.718$ is the base of the natural logarithm.

A graph depicting the normal probability density function is often referred to as the **normal curve** or the **bell curve**. The following example relates the normal curve to the location and the dispersion of the normally distributed random variable.

---

[1]The discovery of the normal (Gaussian) distribution is often credited to Carl Friedrich Gauss (1777–1855), even though some attribute the credit to De Moivre (1667–1754), who had earlier discovered it in the context of simplifying the binomial distribution calculations.

EXAMPLE 6.2

Suppose we know that the ages of employees in Industries A, B, and C are normally distributed. We are given the following information on the relevant parameters:

Industry A	Industry B	Industry C
$\mu = 42$ years	$\mu = 36$ years	$\mu = 42$ years
$\sigma = 5$ years	$\sigma = 5$ years	$\sigma = 8$ years

Graphically compare the ages of employees in Industry A with Industry B. Repeat the comparison for Industry A with Industry C.

SOLUTION: Figure 6.4 illustrates the difference in location given that the mean age of employees of Industry A is greater than that of Industry B. Both distributions show the same dispersion since the standard deviation is the same. Figure 6.5 compares the dispersion given that the standard deviation of age in Industry A is less than that of Industry C. Here, the peak of Industry A is higher than the peak of Industry C, reflecting the fact that an employee's age is likelier to be closer to the mean age in Industry A. These graphs also serve to point out that we can capture the entire distribution of any normally distributed random variable based on its mean and variance (or standard deviation).

FIGURE 6.4 Normal probability density function for two values of μ along with $\sigma = 5$

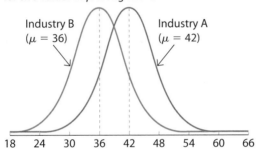

FIGURE 6.5 Normal probability density function for two values of σ along with $\mu = 42$

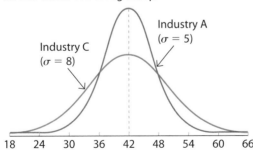

We generally use the cumulative distribution function $F(x)$ to compute probabilities for a normally distributed random variable, where $F(x) = P(X \leq x)$ is simply the area under $f(x)$ up to the value x. As mentioned earlier, we do not necessarily need the knowledge of integral calculus to compute probabilities for the normal distribution. Instead, we rely on a table to find probabilities. We can also compute probabilities with Excel and other statistical packages. The specifics of how to use the table are delineated next.

The Standard Normal Variable

The **standard normal distribution** is a special case of the normal distribution with a mean equal to zero and a standard deviation (or variance) equal to one. Using the letter Z to denote a random variable with the standard normal distribution, we have $E(Z) = 0$ and $SD(Z) = 1$. As usual, we use the lowercase letter z to denote the value that the random variable Z may assume.

The value z is actually the z-score that we discussed in Chapter 3. It measures the number of standard deviations a given value is away from the mean. For example, a z-score of 2 implies that the given value is 2 standard deviations above the mean. Similarly, a z-score of -1.5 implies that the given value is 1.5 standard deviations below the mean. As mentioned in Chapter 3, converting values into z-scores is called standardizing the data.

In this section we focus on solving problems related to the standard normal distribution. In the next section, we will show that any normal distribution is equivalent to the standard normal distribution when the unit of measurement is changed to measure standard deviations from the mean. Therefore, while most real-world normally distributed variables are not standard normal, we can always transform (standardize) them into standard normal to compute the relevant probabilities.

All introductory statistics texts include a **standard normal table**, also referred to as the ***z* table**, that provide areas (probabilities) under the z curve. However, the format of these tables is sometimes different. In this book the z table provides cumulative probabilities $P(Z \le z)$; this table appears on two pages in Appendix A and is labeled Table 1. The left-hand page provides cumulative probabilities for z values less than or equal to zero. The right-hand page shows cumulative probabilities for z values greater than or equal to zero. Given the symmetry of the normal distribution and the fact that the area under the entire curve is one, other probabilities can be easily computed.

STANDARD NORMAL DISTRIBUTION

The standard normal random variable Z is a normal random variable with $E(Z) = 0$ and $SD(Z) = 1$. The z table provides cumulative probabilities $P(Z \le z)$ for positive and for negative values of z.

Figure 6.6 represents the standard normal distribution (z distribution). Since the random variable Z is symmetric around its mean of zero, $P(Z < 0) = P(Z > 0) = 0.5$. As is the case with all continuous random variables, we can also write the probabilities as $P(Z \le 0) = P(Z \ge 0) = 0.5$.

FIGURE 6.6 Standard normal probability density function

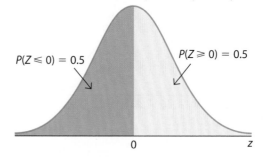

$P(Z \le 0) = 0.5$ $P(Z \ge 0) = 0.5$

0   z

Finding a Probability for a Given *z* Value

As mentioned earlier, the z table provides cumulative probabilities $P(Z \le z)$ for a given z. Consider, for example, a cumulative probability $P(Z \le 1.52)$. Since $z = 1.52$ is positive, we can look up this probability from the right-hand page of the z table; Table 6.1 shows a portion of the table.

TABLE 6.1 Portion of the Right-Hand Page of the z Table

z	0.00	0.01	0.02
0.0	0.5000	0.5040	↓
0.1	0.5398	0.5438	↓
⋮	⋮	⋮	⋮
1.5	→	→	0.9357

The first column of the table, denoted as the z column, shows values of z up to the tenth decimal point, while the first row of the table, denoted as the z row, shows hundredths values. Thus, for z = 1.52, we match 1.5 on the z column with 0.02 on the z row to find a corresponding probability of 0.9357. The arrows in Table 6.1 indicate that $P(Z \le 1.52) = 0.9357$.

In Figure 6.7, the cumulative probability corresponding to z = 1.52 is highlighted. Note that $P(Z \le 1.52) = 0.9357$ represents the area under the z curve to the left of 1.52. Therefore, the area to the right of 1.52 can be computed as $P(Z > 1.52) = 1 - P(Z \le 1.52) = 1 - 0.9357 = 0.0643$. Note that since $P(Z > 1.52) = P(Z < -1.52)$, an alternative way to find the probability of 0.0643 is to use the left-hand page of the z table as discussed next.

FIGURE 6.7 Cumulative probability with respect to z = 1.52

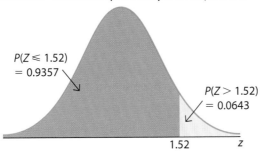

Suppose we want to find $P(Z \le -1.96)$. Since z is a negative value, we can look up this probability from the left-hand page of the z table; Table 6.2 shows a portion of the table with arrows indicating that $P(Z \le -1.96) = 0.0250$. Figure 6.8 highlights the corresponding probability. As before, the area to the right of −1.96 can be computed as $P(Z > -1.96) = 1 - P(Z \le -1.96) = 1 - 0.0250 = 0.9750$. Note that since $P(Z > -1.96) = P(Z < 1.96)$, an alternative way is to use the right-hand page of the z table to find the probability as 0.9750.

TABLE 6.2 Portion of the Left-Hand Page of z Table

z	0.00	0.01	0.02	0.03	0.04	0.05	0.06
−3.9	0.0000	0.0000	0.0000	0.0000	0.0000	0.0000	↓
−3.8	0.0001	0.0001	0.0001	0.0001	0.0001	0.0001	↓
⋮	⋮	⋮	⋮	⋮	⋮	⋮	⋮
−1.9	→	→	→	→	→	→	0.0250

FIGURE 6.8 Cumulative probability with respect to z = −1.96

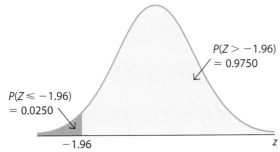

EXAMPLE 6.3

Find the following probabilities for the standard normal random variable Z.

a. $P(0 \leq Z \leq 1.96)$
b. $P(1.52 \leq Z \leq 1.96)$
c. $P(-1.52 \leq Z \leq 1.96)$
d. $P(Z > 4)$

SOLUTION: It always helps to start by highlighting the relevant probability in the z graph.

a. As shown in Figure 6.9, the area between 0 and 1.96 is equivalent to the area to the left of 1.96 minus the area to the left of 0. Therefore, $P(0 \leq Z \leq 1.96) = P(Z \leq 1.96) - P(Z < 0) = 0.9750 - 0.50 = 0.4750$.

FIGURE 6.9 Finding the probability between 0 and 1.96

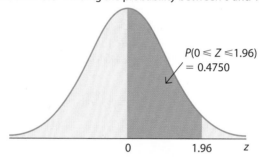

b. As in part a and shown in Figure 6.10, $P(1.52 \leq Z \leq 1.96) = P(Z \leq 1.96) - P(Z < 1.52) = 0.9750 - 0.9357 = 0.0393$.

FIGURE 6.10 Finding the probability between 1.52 and 1.96

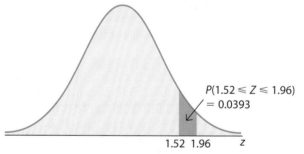

c. From Figure 6.11, $P(-1.52 \leq Z \leq 1.96) = P(Z \leq 1.96) - P(Z < -1.52) = 0.9750 - 0.0643 = 0.9107$.

FIGURE 6.11 Finding the probability between -1.52 and 1.96

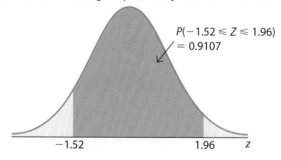

d. $P(Z > 4) = 1 - P(Z \leq 4)$. However, the z table only goes up to 3.99 with $P(Z \leq 3.99) = 1.0$ (approximately). In fact, for any z value greater than 3.90, it is acceptable to treat $P(Z \leq z) = 1.0$. Therefore, $P(Z > 4) = 1 - P(Z \leq 4) = 1 - 1 = 0$.

Finding a z Value for a Given Probability

So far we have computed probabilities for given z values. Now we will evaluate z values for given probabilities.

EXAMPLE 6.4

For the standard normal variable Z, find the z values that satisfy the following probability statements.

a. $P(Z \leq z) = 0.6808$
b. $P(Z \leq z) = 0.90$
c. $P(Z \leq z) = 0.0643$
d. $P(Z > z) = 0.0212$
e. $P(-z \leq Z \leq z) = 0.95$

SOLUTION: As mentioned earlier, it is useful to draw a graph to set up a problem. Recall too that the z table lists z values along with the corresponding cumulative probabilities. Noncumulative probabilities can be evaluated using symmetry.

a. Since the probability is already in a cumulative format, that is, $P(Z \leq z) = 0.6808$, we simply look up 0.6808 from the body of the table (right-hand side) to find the corresponding z value from the row/column of z. Table 6.3 shows the relevant portion of the z table and Figure 6.12 depicts the corresponding area. Therefore, $z = 0.47$.

TABLE 6.3 Portion of the z Table for Example 6.4a

z	0.00	0.01	0.02	0.03	0.04	0.05	0.06	0.07
0.0	0.5000	0.5040	0.5080	0.5120	0.5160	0.5199	0.5239	↑
0.1	0.5398	0.5438	0.5478	0.5517	0.5557	0.5596	0.5636	↑
⋮	⋮	⋮	⋮	⋮	⋮	⋮	⋮	⋮
0.4	←	←	←	←	←	←	←	0.6808

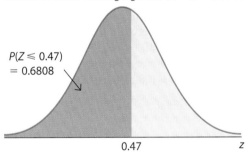

FIGURE 6.12 Finding z given $P(Z \leq z) = 0.6808$

$P(Z \leq 0.47)$
$= 0.6808$

0.47   z

b. When deriving z for $P(Z \leq z) = 0.90$, we find that the z table (right-hand side) does not contain the cumulative probability 0.90. In such cases, we use the closest cumulative probability to solve the problem. Therefore, z is approximately equal to 1.28, which corresponds to a cumulative probability of 0.8997. Figure 6.13 shows this result graphically.

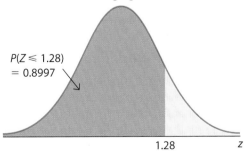

FIGURE 6.13 Finding z given $P(Z \leq z) = 0.90$

$P(Z \leq 1.28)$
$= 0.8997$

1.28   z

c. As shown in Figure 6.14, the z value that solves $P(Z \le z) = 0.0643$ must be negative because the probability to its left is only 0.0643 (less than 0.50). We look up the cumulative probability 0.0643 in the table (left-hand side) to get $z = -1.52$.

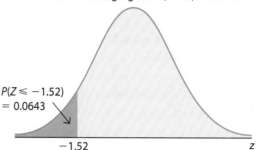

FIGURE 6.14 Finding z given $P(Z \le z) = 0.0643$

$P(Z \le -1.52)$
$= 0.0643$

-1.52

z

d. We have to find a z value such that the probability to the right of this value is 0.0212. Since the table states cumulative probabilities, we look up $P(Z \le z) = 1 - 0.0212 = 0.9788$ in the table (right-hand side) to get $z = 2.03$. Figure 6.15 shows the results.

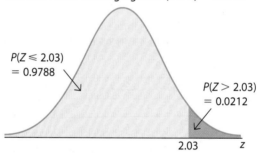

FIGURE 6.15 Finding z given $P(Z > z) = 0.0212$

$P(Z \le 2.03)$
$= 0.9788$

$P(Z > 2.03)$
$= 0.0212$

2.03

z

e. Since we know that the total area under the curve equals one, and we want to find $-z$ and z such that the area between the two values equals 0.95, we can conclude that the area in either tail is 0.025, that is, $P(Z < -z) = 0.025$ and $P(Z > z) = 0.025$. Figure 6.16 shows these results. We then use the cumulative probability, $P(Z \le z) = 0.95 + 0.025 = 0.975$, to find $z = 1.96$.

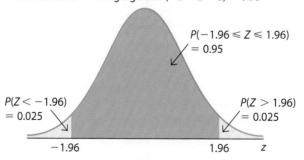

FIGURE 6.16 Finding z given $P(-z \le Z \le z) = 0.95$

$P(-1.96 \le Z \le 1.96)$
$= 0.95$

$P(Z < -1.96)$
$= 0.025$

$P(Z > 1.96)$
$= 0.025$

-1.96

1.96

z

Revisiting the Empirical Rule

In Chapter 3, we used the empirical rule to approximate the percentage of values that fall within 1, 2, or 3 standard deviations of the mean. Approximate percentages are appropriate for many real-world applications where the normal distribution is used only as an approximation. For normally distributed random variables, we can find the exact percentages.

The empirical rule for normal distributions is shown in Figure 6.17. Given a normal random variable X with mean μ and standard deviation σ:

- 68.26% of the values fall within 1 standard deviation of the mean, that is, $P(\mu - \sigma \leq X \leq \mu + \sigma) = 0.6826$,
- 95.44% of the values fall within 2 standard deviations of the mean, that is, $P(\mu - 2\sigma \leq X \leq \mu + 2\sigma) = 0.9544$, and
- 99.73% of the values fall within 3 standard deviations of the mean, that is, $P(\mu - 3\sigma \leq X \leq \mu + 3\sigma) = 0.9973$.

FIGURE 6.17 Graphical description of the empirical rule

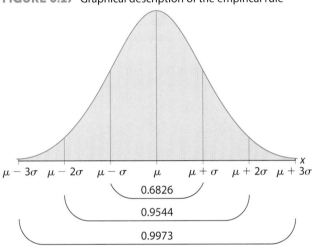

For the standard normal variable Z, $P(-1 \leq Z \leq 1)$ refers to the probability within 1 standard deviation of the mean since $\mu = 0$ and $\sigma = 1$. From the z table, we can show that $P(-1 \leq Z \leq 1)$ equals $P(Z \leq 1) - P(Z < -1) = 0.8413 - 0.1587 = 0.6826$. Therefore, the exact probability that Z falls within 1 standard deviation of the mean is 0.6826. Similarly, the exact probabilities that Z falls within 2 and 3 standard deviations of the mean are $P(-2 \leq Z \leq 2) = 0.9544$ and $P(-3 \leq Z \leq 3) = 0.9973$, respectively.

EXAMPLE 6.5

An investment strategy has an expected return of 4% and a standard deviation of 6%. Assume that investment returns are normally distributed.

a. What is the probability of earning a return greater than 10%?

b. What is the probability of earning a return less than −8%?

SOLUTION: We use the empirical rule for normal distributions with $\mu = 4$ and $\sigma = 6$ to solve these questions.

a. A return of 10% is one standard deviation above the mean because $10 = 4 + 6$. Since 68.26% of observations fall within one standard deviation of the mean, 31.74% (100% − 68.26%) of the observations are outside the range. Using symmetry, we conclude that 15.87% (half of 31.74%) of the observations are greater than 10% (see Figure 6.18).

FIGURE 6.18 Finding $P(X > 10)$

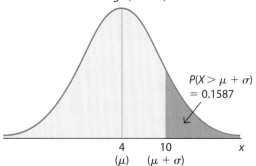

$P(X > \mu + \sigma)$
$= 0.1587$

4   10
(μ) $(\mu + \sigma)$ X

b. A return of -8% is two standard deviations below the mean, or $-8 = 4 - (2 \times 6)$. Since 95.44% of the observations fall within two standard deviations of the mean, only 2.28% (half of 4.56%) are below -8% (see Figure 6.19).

FIGURE 6.19 Finding $P(X < -8)$

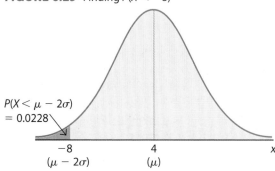

$P(X < \mu - 2\sigma)$
$= 0.0228$

-8 4
$(\mu - 2\sigma)$ (μ) X

EXERCISES 6.2

Mechanics

14. Find the following probabilities based on the standard normal variable Z.
    a. $P(Z > 1.32)$
    b. $P(Z \le -1.32)$
    c. $P(1.32 \le Z \le 2.37)$
    d. $P(-1.32 \le Z \le 2.37)$

15. Find the following probabilities based on the standard normal variable Z.
    a. $P(Z > 0.74)$
    b. $P(Z \le -1.92)$
    c. $P(0 \le Z \le 1.62)$
    d. $P(-0.90 \le Z \le 2.94)$

16. Find the following probabilities based on the standard normal variable Z.
    a. $P(-0.67 \le Z \le -0.23)$
    b. $P(0 \le Z \le 1.96)$
    c. $P(-1.28 \le Z \le 0)$
    d. $P(Z > 4.2)$

17. Find the following z values for the standard normal variable Z.
    a. $P(Z \le z) = 0.9744$
    b. $P(Z > z) = 0.8389$
    c. $P(-z \le Z \le z) = 0.95$
    d. $P(0 \le Z \le z) = 0.3315$

18. Find the following z values for the standard normal variable Z.
    a. $P(Z \le z) = 0.1020$
    b. $P(z \le Z \le 0) = 0.1772$
    c. $P(Z > z) = 0.9929$
    d. $P(0.40 \le Z \le z) = 0.3368$

Applications

19. The historical returns on a balanced portfolio have had an average return of 8% and a standard deviation of 12%. Assume that returns on this portfolio follow a normal distribution. Use the empirical rule for normal distributions to answer the following questions.
    a. What percentage of returns were greater than 20%?
    b. What percentage of returns were below -16%?

20. Assume that IQ scores follow a normal distribution with a mean of 100 and a standard deviation of 16. Use the empirical rule for normal distributions to answer the following questions.
    a. What percentage of people score between 84 and 116?
    b. What percentage of people score less than 68?

21. The average rent in a city is $1,500 per month with a standard deviation of $250. Assume rent follows the normal distribution. Use the empirical rule for normal distributions to answer the following questions.
    a. What percentage of rents are between $1,250 and $1,750?
    b. What percentage of rents are less than $1,250?
    c. What percentage of rents are greater than $2,000?

22. A professional basketball team averages 80 points per game with a standard deviation of 10 points. Assume points per game follow the normal distribution. Use the empirical rule for normal distributions to answer the following questions.
    a. What percentage of scores are between 60 and 100 points?
    b. What percentage of scores are more than 100 points? If there are 82 games in a regular season, in how many games will the team score more than 100 points?

6.3 Solving Problems with Normal Distributions

In the preceding section, we found probabilities for the standard normal distribution, which is a normal distribution with mean zero and standard deviation one. For other normal distributions, we found probabilities using the empirical rule. However, in many applications, the underlying distribution is not standard normal and the interval for computing a probability cannot be expressed within one, two, or three standard deviations of the mean. In this section we examine problems in these situations.

LO **6.5**

Calculate and interpret probabilities for a random variable that follows the normal distribution.

The Transformation of Normal Random Variables

The importance of the standard normal distribution arises from the fact that any normal random variable can be transformed into the standard normal random variable to derive the relevant probabilities. In other words, any normally distributed random variable X with mean μ and standard deviation σ can be transformed (standardized) into the standard normal variable Z with mean zero and standard deviation one. We transform X into Z by subtracting from X its mean and dividing by its standard deviation.

THE STANDARD TRANSFORMATION: CONVERTING X INTO Z

Any normally distributed random variable X with mean μ and standard deviation σ can be transformed into the standard normal random variable Z as

$$Z = \frac{X - \mu}{\sigma}.$$

This standard transformation implies that any value x of X has a corresponding value z of Z given by

$$z = \frac{x - \mu}{\sigma}.$$

As illustrated in Figure 6.20, if the x value is at the mean, that is, $x = \mu$, then the corresponding z value is $z = \frac{\mu - \mu}{\sigma} = 0$. Therefore, by construction, $E(Z) = 0$ and $SD(Z) = 1$. Similarly, if the x value is at one standard deviation above the mean, that is, $x = \mu + \sigma$, then the corresponding z value is $z = \frac{\mu + \sigma - \mu}{\sigma} = 1$.

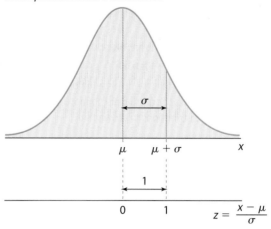

EXAMPLE 6.6

Scores on a management aptitude exam are normally distributed with a mean of 72 and a standard deviation of 8.

a. What is the probability that a randomly selected manager will score above 60?

b. What is the probability that a randomly selected manager will score between 68 and 84?

SOLUTION: Let X represent scores with $\mu = 72$ and $\sigma = 8$. We will use the standard transformation $z = \frac{x - \mu}{\sigma}$ to solve these problems.

a. The probability that a manager scores above 60 is $P(X > 60)$. Figure 6.21 shows the probability as the shaded area to the right of 60. We derive $P(X > 60) =$ $P\left(Z > \frac{60 - 72}{8}\right) = P(Z > -1.5)$. Since $P(Z > -1.5) = 1 - P(Z \leq -1.5)$, we look up -1.50 in the z table (left-hand side) to get this probability as $1 - 0.0668 = 0.9332$.

FIGURE 6.21 Finding $P(X > 60)$

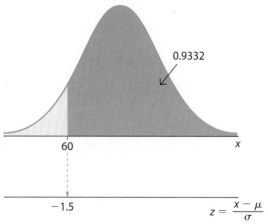

b. Here, we find $P(68 \leq X \leq 84)$. The shaded area in Figure 6.22 shows this probability. We derive $P(68 \leq X \leq 84) = P\left(\frac{68 - 72}{8} \leq Z \leq \frac{84 - 72}{8}\right) = P(-0.5 \leq Z \leq 1.5)$. We compute this probability using the z table as $P(Z \leq 1.5) - P(Z < -0.5) = 0.9332 - 0.3085 = 0.6247$.

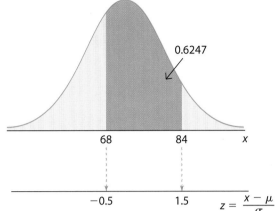

FIGURE 6.22 Finding $P(68 \leq X \leq 84)$

0.6247

68   84 x

-0.5 1.5

$z = \dfrac{x - \mu}{\sigma}$

The Inverse Transformation

So far we have used the standard transformation to compute probabilities for given x values. We can use the **inverse transformation**, $x = \mu + z\sigma$, to compute x values for given probabilities.

> **THE INVERSE TRANSFORMATION: CONVERTING Z INTO X**
>
> The standard normal variable Z can be transformed to the normally distributed random variable X with mean μ and standard deviation σ as $X = \mu + Z\sigma$.
>
> Therefore, any value z of Z has a corresponding value x of X given by $x = \mu + z\sigma$.

EXAMPLE 6.7

Scores on a management aptitude examination are normally distributed with a mean of 72 and a standard deviation of 8.

a. What is the lowest score that will place a manager in the top 10% (90th percentile) of the distribution?

b. What is the highest score that will place a manager in the bottom 25% (25th percentile) of the distribution?

SOLUTION: Let X represent scores on a management aptitude examination with $\mu = 72$ and $\sigma = 8$. We will use the inverse transformation $x = \mu + z\sigma$ to solve these problems.

a. The 90th percentile is a numerical value x such that $P(X < x) = 0.90$. We look up 0.90 (or the closest value to 0.90) in the z table (right-hand side) to get $z = 1.28$ and use the inverse transformation to find $x = 72 + 1.28(8) = 82.24$. Therefore, a score of 82.24 or higher will place a manager in the top 10% of the distribution (see Figure 6.23).

FIGURE 6.23 Finding x given P(X < x) = 0.90

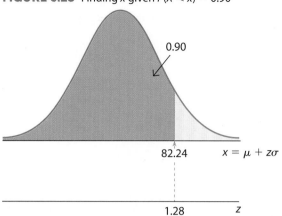

b. We find x such that $P(X < x) = 0.25$. Using the z table (left-hand side), we solve for the corresponding z value that satisfies $P(Z < z) = 0.25$ as -0.67. We then find $x = 72 - 0.67(8) = 66.64$. Therefore, a score of 66.64 or lower will place a manager in the bottom 25% of the distribution (see Figure 6.24).

FIGURE 6.24 Finding x given P(X < x) = 0.25

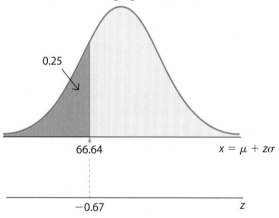

EXAMPLE 6.8

We can now answer the questions first posed by Akiko Hamaguchi in the introductory case of this chapter. Recall that Akiko would like to buy the right amount of salmon for daily consumption at Little Ginza. Akiko has estimated that the daily consumption of salmon is normally distributed with a mean of 12 pounds and a standard deviation of 3.2 pounds. She wants to answer the following questions:

a. What proportion of days was the demand at Little Ginza above her earlier purchase of 20 pounds?

b. What proportion of days was the demand at Little Ginza below 15 pounds?

c. How much salmon should she buy so that it meets customer demand on 90% of the days?

SOLUTION: Let X denote customer demand for salmon at the restaurant. We know that X is normally distributed with $\mu = 12$ and $\sigma = 3.2$.

a. $P(X > 20) = P\left(Z > \dfrac{20 - 12}{3.2}\right) = P(Z > 2.50) = 1 - 0.9938 = 0.0062.$

b. $P(X < 15) = P\left(Z < \dfrac{15 - 12}{3.2}\right) = P(Z < 0.94) = 0.8264.$

c. In order to compute the required amount of salmon, we solve for x in $P(X \leq x) = 0.90$. Since $P(X \leq x) = 0.90$ is equivalent to $P(Z \leq z) = 0.90$, we first derive $z = 1.28$. Given $x = \mu + z\sigma$, we find $x = 12 + 1.28(3.2) = 16.10$. Therefore, Akiko should buy 16.10 pounds of salmon daily to ensure that customer demand is met on 90% of the days.

Using Excel for the Normal Distribution

The Standard Transformation

We can easily find normal probabilities using Excel's NORM.DIST function. In general, in order to find $P(X \leq x)$, we input '=NORM.DIST(x, μ, σ, 1)', where x is the value for which we want to evaluate the cumulative normal probability, μ is the mean of the distribution, σ is the standard deviation of the distribution, and 1 is prompting Excel to return a cumulative probability. If we enter 0 as the fourth argument, Excel returns the height of the normal probability distribution at the point x. This feature is particularly useful if we want to plot the normal curve. Let's revisit Example 6.8a, where we want to find $P(X > 20)$. We know that the data are normally distributed with a mean of 12 and a standard deviation of 3.2. We input '=NORM.DIST(20, 12, 3.2, 1)'. Excel returns a cumulative probability of 0.9938, which means that $P(X \leq 20) = 0.9938$. Since we want to find $P(X > 20)$, we compute $1 - 0.9938 = 0.0062$.

The Inverse Transformation

We can use Excel's NORM.INV function if we want to find a particular x value for a given cumulative probability. In general, we input 'NORM.INV(*probability*, μ, σ)', where *probability* is the given cumulative probability, μ is the mean of the distribution, and σ is the standard deviation of the distribution. Let's revisit Example 6.8c, where we want to find x such that $P(X \leq x) = 0.90$. We input '=NORM.INV(0.90, 12, 3.2)'. Excel returns the value 16.10. As we found manually in that exercise, 16.10 pounds of salmon are needed to meet customer demand on 90% of the days.

We also note here that Excel has related formulas if we assume $\mu = 0$ and $\sigma = 1$; that is, the variable has already been standardized. The formula NORM.S.DIST finds $P(Z \leq z)$ and NORM.S.INV finds a particular z value for a given cumulative probability. For example, to find $P(Z \leq 1.52)$, we input '=NORM.S.DIST(1.52, 1)' and Excel returns 0.9357—this is the same probability that we found in Section 6.2 when we used the z table (Figure 6.7). Similarly, to find the z value such that $P(Z \leq z) = 0.6808$ (Example 6.4a), we input '=NORM.S.INV(0.6808)' and Excel returns 0.47, or equivalently, $z = 0.47$. We will find these functions quite useful when solving problems in later chapters.

A Note on the Normal Approximation of the Binomial Distribution

Recall from Chapter 5 that it is tedious to compute binomial probabilities with the formula when we encounter large values for n. As it turns out, with large values for n, the binomial distribution can be approximated by the normal distribution. Based on this normal distribution approximation, with mean $\mu = np$ and standard deviation $\sigma = \sqrt{npq}$, we can use the z table to compute relevant binomial probabilities. Some researchers believe that the discovery of the normal distribution in the 18th century was due to the need to simplify the binomial probability calculations. The popularity of this method, however, has been greatly reduced by the advent of computers. As we learned in Chapter 5, it is easy to compute exact binomial probabilities with Excel; thus, there is no reason to approximate. The normal distribution approximation, however, is extremely important when making an inference for the population proportion p, which is a key parameter of the binomial distribution. In later chapters, we will study the details of this approximation and how it is used for making inferences.

Akiko Hamaguchi is a manager at a small sushi restaurant called Little Ginza in Phoenix, Arizona. She is aware of the importance of purchasing the right amount of salmon daily. While purchasing too much salmon results in wastage, purchasing too little can disappoint customers who may choose not to frequent the restaurant in the future. In the past, she has always bought 20 pounds of salmon daily. A careful analysis of her purchasing habits and customer demand reveals that Akiko is buying too much salmon. The probability that the demand for salmon would exceed 20 pounds is very small at 0.0062. Even a purchase of 15 pounds satisfies customer demand on 82.64% of the days. In order to execute her new strategy of meeting daily demand of customers on 90% of the days, Akiko should purchase approximately 16 pounds of salmon daily.

EXERCISES 6.3

Mechanics

23. Let X be normally distributed with mean $\mu = 10$ and standard deviation $\sigma = 6$.
    a. Find $P(X \leq 0)$.
    b. Find $P(X > 2)$.
    c. Find $P(4 \leq X \leq 10)$.
    d. Find $P(6 \leq X \leq 14)$.

24. Let X be normally distributed with mean $\mu = 10$ and standard deviation $\sigma = 4$.
    a. Find $P(X \leq 0)$.
    b. Find $P(X > 2)$.
    c. Find $P(4 \leq X \leq 10)$.
    d. Find $P(6 \leq X \leq 14)$.

25. Let X be normally distributed with mean $\mu = 120$ and standard deviation $\sigma = 20$.
    a. Find $P(X \leq 86)$.
    b. Find $P(80 \leq X \leq 100)$.
    c. Find x such that $P(X \leq x) = 0.40$.
    d. Find x such that $P(X > x) = 0.90$.

26. Let X be normally distributed with mean $\mu = 2.5$ and standard deviation $\sigma = 2$.
    a. Find $P(X > 7.6)$.
    b. Find $P(7.4 \leq X \leq 10.6)$.
    c. Find x such that $P(X > x) = 0.025$.
    d. Find x such that $P(x \leq X \leq 2.5) = 0.4943$.

27. Let X be normally distributed with mean $\mu = 2500$ and standard deviation $\sigma = 800$.
    a. Find x such that $P(X \leq x) = 0.9382$.
    b. Find x such that $P(X > x) = 0.025$.
    c. Find x such that $P(2500 \leq X \leq x) = 0.1217$.
    d. Find x such that $P(X \leq x) = 0.4840$.

28. The random variable X is normally distributed. Also, it is known that $P(X > 150) = 0.10$.

    a. Find the population mean μ if the population standard deviation $\sigma = 15$.
    b. Find the population mean μ if the population standard deviation $\sigma = 25$.
    c. Find the population standard deviation σ if the population mean $\mu = 136$.
    d. Find the population standard deviation σ if the population mean $\mu = 128$.

29. (Use Excel) Let X be normally distributed with $\mu = 254$ and $\sigma = 11$. In addition to providing the answer, state the relevant Excel commands.
    a. Find $P(X \leq 266)$.
    b. Find $P(250 < X < 270)$.
    c. Find x such that $P(X \leq x) = 0.33$.
    d. Find x such that $P(X > x) = 0.33$.

30. (Use Excel) Let X be normally distributed with $\mu = -15$ and $\sigma = 9$. In addition to providing the answer, state the relevant Excel commands.
    a. Find $P(X > -12)$.
    b. Find $P(0 \leq X \leq 5)$.
    c. Find x such that $P(X \leq x) = 0.25$.
    d. Find x such that $P(X > x) = 0.25$.

Applications

31. The average high school teacher annual salary is $43,000 (Payscale.com, August 20, 2010). Let teacher salary be normally distributed with a standard deviation of $18,000.
    a. What percentage of high school teachers make between $40,000 and $50,000?
    b. What percentage of high school teachers make more than $80,000?

32. Americans are increasingly skimping on their sleep (*National Geographic News*, February 24, 2005). A health expert believes that American adults sleep an average of 6.2 hours on weekdays with a standard deviation of 1.2 hours. To

answer the following questions, assume that sleep time on weekdays is normally distributed.

a. What percentage of American adults sleep more than 8 hours on weekdays?

b. What percentage of American adults sleep less than 6 hours on weekdays?

c. What percentage of American adults sleep between 6 and 8 hours on weekdays?

33. The weight of turkeys is normally distributed with a mean of 22 pounds and a standard deviation of 5 pounds.

a. Find the probability that a randomly selected turkey weighs between 20 and 26 pounds.

b. Find the probability that a randomly selected turkey weighs less than 12 pounds.

34. Suppose that the miles-per-gallon (mpg) rating of passenger cars is a normally distributed random variable with a mean and a standard deviation of 33.8 mpg and 3.5 mpg, respectively.

a. What is the probability that a randomly selected passenger car gets at least 40 mpg?

b. What is the probability that a randomly selected passenger car gets between 30 and 35 mpg?

c. An automobile manufacturer wants to build a new passenger car with an mpg rating that improves upon 99 percent of existing cars. What is the minimum mpg that would achieve this goal?

35. According to the company's website, the top 25% of the candidates who take the entrance test will be called for an interview. You have just been called for an interview. The reported mean and standard deviation of the test scores are 68 and 8, respectively. What is the possible range for your test score if you assume that the scores are normally distributed?

36. A financial advisor informs a client that the expected return on a portfolio is 8 percent with a standard deviation of 12 percent. There is a 25% chance that the return would be negative and a 15% chance that the return would be above 16 percent. If the advisor is right about her assessment, is it reasonable to assume that the underlying return distribution is normal?

37. A packaging system fills boxes to an average weight of 18 ounces with a standard deviation of 0.2 ounce. It is reasonable to assume that the weights are normally distributed. Calculate the 1st, 2nd, and 3rd quartiles of the box weight.

38. According to the Bureau of Labor Statistics, it takes an average of 22 weeks for someone over 55 to find a new job, compared with 16 weeks for younger workers (*The Wall Street Journal*, September 2, 2008). Assume that the probability distributions are normal and that the standard deviation is 2 weeks for both distributions.

a. What is the probability that it takes a worker over the age of 55 more than 19 weeks to find a job?

b. What is the probability that it takes a younger worker more than 19 weeks to find a job?

c. What is the probability that it takes a worker over the age of 55 between 23 and 25 weeks to find a job?

d. What is the probability that it takes a younger worker between 23 and 25 weeks to find a job?

39. Loans that are 60 days or more past due are considered seriously delinquent. The Mortgage Bankers Association reported that the rate of seriously delinquent loans has an average of 9.1% (*The Wall Street Journal*, August 26, 2010). Let the rate of seriously delinquent loans follow a normal distribution with a standard deviation of 0.80%.

a. What is the probability that the proportion of seriously delinquent loans has a rate above 8%?

b. What is the probability that the proportion of seriously delinquent loans has a rate between 9.5% and 10.5%?

40. The time required to assemble an electronic component is normally distributed with a mean and a standard deviation of 16 minutes and 8 minutes, respectively.

a. Find the probability that a randomly picked assembly takes between 10 and 20 minutes.

b. It is unusual for the assembly time to be above 24 minutes or below 6 minutes. What proportion of assembly times fall in these unusual categories?

41. Recent research suggests that Americans make an average of 10 phone calls per day (*CNN*, August 26, 2010). Let the number of calls be normally distributed with a standard deviation of 3 calls.

a. What is the probability that an average American makes between 4 and 12 calls per day?

b. What is the probability that an average American makes more than 6 calls per day?

c. What is the probability that an average American makes more than 16 calls per day?

42. The manager of a night club in Boston stated that 95% of the customers are between the ages of 22 and 28 years. If the age of customers is normally distributed with a mean of 25 years, calculate its standard deviation.

43. The average college student graduated with $27,200 in debt (*The Boston Globe*, May 27, 2012). Let debt among recent college graduates be normally distributed with a standard deviation of $7,000.

a. What is the probability that a recent college graduate has debt of less than $25,000?

b. What is the probability that a recent college graduate has debt of more than $30,000?

c. What is the amount of debt that places a recent college graduate in the bottom 10% in terms of debt?

d. What is the amount of debt that places a recent college graduate in the top 15% in terms of debt?

44. Scores on a marketing exam are known to be normally distributed with mean and standard deviation of 60 and 20, respectively.

a. Find the probability that a randomly selected student scores between 50 and 80.

b. Find the probability that a randomly selected student scores between 20 and 40.

c. The syllabus suggests that the top 15% of the students will get an A in the course. What is the minimum score required to get an A?

d. What is the passing score if 10% of the students will fail the course?

45. Average talk time between charges of a cell phone is advertised as 4 hours. Assume that talk time is normally distributed with a standard deviation of 0.8 hour.

a. Find the probability that talk time between charges for a randomly selected cell phone is below 3.5 hours.

b. Find the probability that talk time between charges for a randomly selected cell phone is either more than 4.5 hours or below 3.5 hours.

c. Twenty-five percent of the time, talk time between charges is below the 1st quartile value. What is this value?

46. A young investment manager tells his client that the probability of making a positive return with his suggested portfolio is 90%. If it is known that returns are normally distributed with a mean of 5.6%, what is the risk, measured by standard deviation, that this investment manager assumes in his calculation?

47. A construction company in Naples, Florida, is struggling to sell condominiums. In order to attract buyers, the company has made numerous price reductions and better financing offers. Although condominiums were once listed for $300,000, the company believes that it will be able to get an average sale price of $210,000. Let the price of these condominiums in the next quarter be normally distributed with a standard deviation of $15,000.

a. What is the probability that the condominium will sell at a price (i) below $200,000?, (ii) above $240,000?

b. The company is also trying to sell an artist's condo. Potential buyers will find the unusual features of this condo either pleasing or objectionable. The manager expects the average sale price of this condo to be the same as others at $210,000, but with a higher standard deviation of $20,000. What is the probability that this condo will sell at a price (i) below $200,000?, (ii) above $240,000?

48. You are considering the risk-return profile of two mutual funds for investment. The relatively risky fund promises an expected return of 8% with a standard deviation of 14%. The relatively less risky fund promises an expected return and standard deviation of 4% and 5%, respectively. Assume that the returns are approximately normally distributed.

a. Which mutual fund will you pick if your objective is to minimize the probability of earning a negative return?

b. Which mutual fund will you pick if your objective is to maximize the probability of earning a return above 8%?

49. First introduced in Los Angeles, the concept of Korean style tacos sold from a catering truck has been gaining popularity nationally (*The New York Times,* July 27, 2010). This taco is an interesting mix of corn tortillas with Korean-style beef, garnished with onion, cilantro and a hash of chili-soy-dressed lettuce. Suppose one such taco truck operates in

the Detroit area. The owners have estimated that the daily consumption of beef is normally distributed with a mean of 24 pounds and a standard deviation of 6 pounds. While purchasing too much beef results in wastage, purchasing too little can disappoint customers.

a. Determine the amount of beef the owners should buy so that it meets demand on 80 percent of the days.

b. How much should the owners buy if they want to meet demand on 95 percent of the days?

50. A new car battery is sold with a two-year warranty whereby the owner gets the battery replaced free of cost if it breaks down during the warranty period. Suppose an auto store makes a net profit of $20 on batteries that stay trouble-free during the warranty period; it makes a net loss of $10 on batteries that break down. The life of batteries is known to be normally distributed with a mean and a standard deviation of 40 and 16 months, respectively.

a. What is the probability that a battery will break down during the warranty period?

b. What is the expected profit of the auto store on a battery?

c. What is the expected monthly profit on batteries if the auto store sells an average of 500 batteries a month?

51. (Use Excel) While Massachusetts is no California when it comes to sun, the solar energy industry is flourishing in this state (*The Boston Globe,* May 27, 2012). The state's capital, Boston, averages 211.7 sunny days per year. Assume that the number of sunny days follows a normal distribution with a standard deviation of 20 days. In addition to providing the answer, state the relevant Excel commands.

a. What is the probability that Boston has less than 200 sunny days in a given year?

b. Los Angeles averages 266.5 sunny days per year. What is the probability that Boston has at least as many sunny days as Los Angeles?

c. Suppose a dismal year in Boston is one where the number of sunny days is in the bottom 10% for that year. At most, how many sunny days must occur annually for it to be a dismal year in Boston?

d. In 2012, Boston experienced unusually warm, dry, and sunny weather. Suppose this occurs only 1% of the time. What is the minimum number of sunny days that would satisfy the criteria for being an unusually warm, dry, and sunny year in Boston?

52. (Use Excel) A certain brand of refrigerators has a length of life that is normally distributed with a mean and a standard deviation of 15 years and 2 years, respectively. In addition to providing the answer, state the relevant Excel commands.

a. What is the probability a refrigerator will last less than 6.5 years?

b. What is the probability that a refrigerator will last more than 23 years?

c. What length of life should the retailer advertise for these refrigerators so that only 3% of the refrigerators fail before the advertised length of life?

6.4 The Exponential Distribution

As discussed earlier, the normal distribution is the most extensively used probability distribution in statistical work. One reason that this occurs is because the normal distribution accurately describes numerous random variables of interest. However, there are applications where other continuous distributions are more appropriate.

A useful nonsymmetric continuous probability distribution is the **exponential distribution**. The exponential distribution is related to the Poisson distribution, even though the Poisson distribution deals with discrete random variables. Recall from Chapter 5 that the Poisson random variable counts the number of occurrences of an event over a given interval of time or space. For instance, the Poisson distribution is used to calculate the likelihood of a specified number of cars arriving at a McDonald's drive-thru over a particular time period or the likelihood of a specified number of defects in a 50-yard roll of fabric. Sometimes we are less interested in the *number* of occurrences over a given interval of time or space, but rather in the time that has elapsed or space encountered *between* such occurrences. For instance, we might be interested in the length of time that elapses between car arrivals at the McDonald's drive-thru or the distance between defects in a 50-yard roll of fabric. We use the exponential distribution for describing these times or distances. The exponential random variable is nonnegative; that is, the underlying variable X is defined for $x \geq 0$.

In order to better understand the connection between the Poisson and the exponential distributions, consider the introductory case of Chapter 5 where Anne was concerned about staffing needs at the Starbucks that she managed. Recall that Anne believed that the typical Starbucks customer averaged 18 visits to the store over a 30-day period. The Poisson random variable appropriately captures the number of visits, with the expected value (mean), over a 30-day period, as

$$\mu_{\text{Poisson}} = 18.$$

Since the number of visits follows the Poisson distribution, the time between visits has an exponential distribution. In addition, given the expected number of 18 visits over a 30-day month, the expected time between visits is derived as

$$\mu_{\text{Exponential}} = \frac{30}{18} = 1.67.$$

It is common to define the exponential probability distribution in terms of its *rate parameter* λ (the Greek letter lambda), which is the inverse of its mean. In the above example,

$$\lambda = \frac{1}{\mu} = \frac{1}{1.67} = 0.60.$$

We can think of the mean of the exponential distribution as the average time between arrivals, whereas the rate parameter measures the average number of arrivals per unit of time. Note that the rate parameter is the same as the mean of the Poisson distribution, when defined per unit of time. For a Poisson process, the mean of 18 visits over a 30-day period is equivalent to a mean of $18/30 = 0.60$ per day, which is the same as the rate parameter λ.

THE EXPONENTIAL DISTRIBUTION

A random variable X follows the **exponential distribution** if its probability density function is

$$f(x) = \lambda e^{-\lambda x} \quad \text{for } x \geq 0,$$

where λ is a rate parameter and $e \approx 2.718$ is the base of the natural logarithm.

The mean and the standard deviation of X are equal: $E(X) = SD(X) = \frac{1}{\lambda}$. For $x \geq 0$, the **cumulative distribution function** of X is

$$P(X \leq x) = 1 - e^{-\lambda x}.$$

Therefore, $P(X > x) = 1 - P(X \leq x) = e^{-\lambda x}$.

LO **6.6**

Calculate and interpret probabilities for a random variable that follows the exponential distribution.

The curves in Figure 6.25 show the shapes of the exponential probability density function based on various values of the rate parameter λ.

FIGURE 6.25 Exponential probability density function for various values of λ

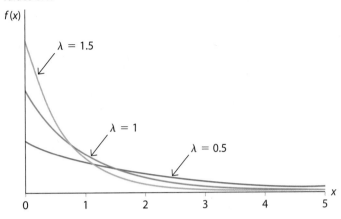

EXAMPLE 6.9

Let the time between e-mail messages during work hours be exponentially distributed with a mean of 25 minutes.

a. Calculate the rate parameter λ.

b. What is the probability that you do not get an e-mail for more than one hour?

c. What is the probability that you get an e-mail within 10 minutes?

SOLUTION:

a. Since the mean $E(X)$ equals $\frac{1}{\lambda}$, we compute $\lambda = \frac{1}{E(X)} = \frac{1}{25} = 0.04$.

b. The probability that you do not get an e-mail for more than an hour is $P(X > 60)$. We use $P(X > x) = 1 - P(X \le x) = e^{-\lambda x}$ to compute $P(X > 60) = e^{-0.04(60)} = e^{-2.40} = 0.0907$. The probability of not getting an e-mail for more than one hour is 0.0907. Figure 6.26 highlights this probability.

FIGURE 6.26 Finding $P(X > 60)$ (Example 6.9b)

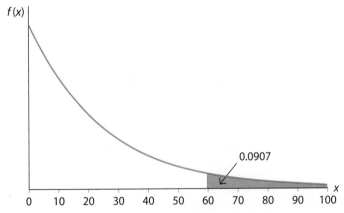

c. Here, $P(X \le 10) = 1 - e^{-0.04(10)} = 1 - 0.6703 = 0.3297$. The probability of getting an e-mail within 10 minutes is 0.3297. Figure 6.27 highlights this probability.

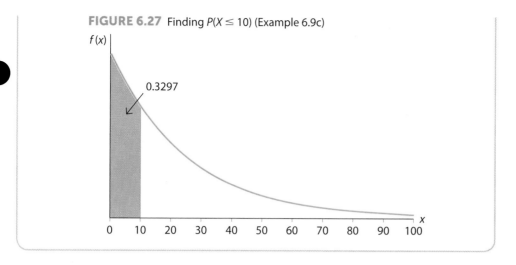

FIGURE 6.27 Finding $P(X \le 10)$ (Example 6.9c)

The exponential distribution is also used in modeling lifetimes or failure times. For example, an electric bulb with a rated life of 1,000 hours is expected to fail after about 1,000 hours of use. However, the bulb may burn out either before or after 1,000 hours. Thus, the lifetime of an electric bulb is a random variable with an expected value of 1,000. A noted feature of the exponential distribution is that it is "memoryless," thus implying a constant failure rate. In the electric bulb example, it implies that the probability that the bulb will burn out on a given day is independent of whether the bulb has already been used for 10, 100, or 1,000 hours.

Using Excel for the Exponential Distribution

We can find exponential probabilities using Excel's EXPON.DIST function. In general, in order to find $P(X \le x)$, we input '=EXPON.DIST$(x, \lambda, 1)$', where x is the value for which we want to evaluate the cumulative probability, λ is the rate parameter, and 1 is prompting Excel to return a cumulative probability. If we enter 0 as the third argument, Excel returns the height of the exponential distribution at the point x. This option is useful if we want to plot the exponential distribution. Let's revisit Example 6.9b where we want to find $P(X > 60)$. We input '=EXPON.DIST$(60, 0.04, 1)$'. Excel returns a cumulative probability of 0.9093. Since we want to find $P(X > 60)$, we compute $1 - 0.9093 = 0.0907$.

EXERCISES 6.4

Mechanics

53. Assume a Poisson random variable has a mean of 6 successes over a 120-minute period.
    a. Find the mean of the random variable, defined by the time between successes.
    b. What is the rate parameter of the appropriate exponential distribution?
    c. Find the probability that the time to success will be more than 60 minutes.

54. Assume a Poisson random variable has a mean of four arrivals over a 10-minute interval.
    a. What is the mean of the random variable, defined by the time between arrivals?
    b. Find the probability that the next arrival would be within the mean time.

c. Find the probability that the next arrival would be between one and two minutes.

55. A random variable X is exponentially distributed with a mean of 0.1.
    a. What is the rate parameter λ? What is the standard deviation of X?
    b. Compute $P(X > 0.20)$.
    c. Compute $P(0.10 \le X \le 0.20)$.

56. A random variable X is exponentially distributed with an expected value of 25.
    a. What is the rate parameter λ? What is the standard deviation of X?
    b. Compute $P(20 \le X \le 30)$.
    c. Compute $P(15 \le X \le 35)$.

57. A random variable X is exponentially distributed with a probability density function of $f(x) = 5e^{-5x}$. Calculate the mean and the standard deviation of X.

58. (Use Excel) Let X be exponentially distributed with $\lambda = 0.5$. In addition to providing the answer, state the relevant Excel commands.
    a. $P(X \le 1)$
    b. $P(2 < X < 4)$
    c. $P(X > 10)$

59. (Use Excel) Let X be exponentially distributed with $\mu = 1.25$. In addition to providing the answer, state the relevant Excel commands.
    a. $P(X < 2.3)$
    b. $P(1.5 \le X \le 5.5)$
    c. $P(X > 7)$

Applications

60. Studies have shown that bats can consume an average of 10 mosquitoes per minute (http://berkshiremuseum.org). Assume that the number of mosquitoes consumed per minute follows a Poison distribution.
    a. What is the mean time between eating mosquitoes?
    b. Find the probability that the time between eating mosquitoes is more than 15 seconds.
    c. Find the probability that the time between eating mosquitoes is between 15 and 20 seconds.

61. According to *Daily Mail* (February 28, 2012), there was an average of one complaint every 12 seconds against Britain's biggest banks in 2011. It is reasonable to assume that the time between complaints is exponentially distributed.
    a. What is the mean time between complaints?
    b. What is the probability that the next complaint will take less than the mean time?
    c. What is the probability that the next complaint will take between 5 and 10 seconds?

62. A tollbooth operator has observed that cars arrive randomly at an average rate of 360 cars per hour.
    a. What is the mean time between car arrivals at this tollbooth?
    b. What is the probability that the next car will arrive within ten seconds?

63. Customers make purchases at a convenience store, on average, every six minutes. It is fair to assume that the time between customer purchases is exponentially distributed. Jack operates the cash register at this store.
    a. What is the rate parameter λ? What is the standard deviation of this distribution?
    b. Jack wants to take a five-minute break. He believes that if he goes right after he has serviced a customer, he will

lower the probability of someone showing up during his five-minute break. Is he right in this belief?
    c. What is the probability that a customer will show up in less than five minutes?
    d. What is the probability that nobody shows up for over half an hour?

64. When crossing the Golden Gate Bridge, traveling into San Francisco, all drivers must pay a toll. Suppose the amount of time (in minutes) drivers wait in line to pay the toll follows an exponential distribution with a probability density function of $f(x) = 0.2e^{-0.2x}$.
    a. What is the mean waiting time that drivers face when entering San Francisco via the Golden Gate Bridge?
    b. What is the probability that a driver spends more than the average time to pay the toll?
    c. What is the probability that a driver spends more than 10 minutes to pay the toll?
    d. What is the probability that a driver spends between 4 and 6 minutes to pay the toll?

65. A hospital administrator worries about the possible loss of electric power as a result of a power blackout. The hospital, of course, has a standby generator, but it too is subject to failure, having a mean time between failures of 500 hours. It is reasonable to assume that the time between failures is exponentially distributed.
    a. What is the probability that the standby generator fails during the next 24-hour blackout?
    b. Suppose the hospital owns two standby generators that work independently of one another. What is the probability that both generators fail during the next 24-hour blackout?

66. (Use Excel) On average, the state police catch eight speeders per hour at a certain location on Interstate I-90. Assume that the number of speeders per hour follows the Poisson distribution. In addition to providing the answer, state the relevant Excel commands.
    a. What is the probability that the state police wait less than 10 minutes for the next speeder?
    b. What is the probability that state police wait between 15 and 20 minutes for the next speeder?
    c. What is the probability that state police wait more than 25 minutes for the next speeder?

67. (Use Excel) Motorists arrive at a Gulf station at the rate of two per minute during morning hours. Assume that the arrival of motorists at the station follows a Poisson distribution. In addition to providing the answer, state the relevant Excel commands.
    a. What is the probability that the next car's arrival is in less than one minute?
    b. What is the probability that the next car's arrival is in more than five minutes?

WRITING WITH STATISTICS

Professor Lang is a professor of Economics at Salem State University. She has been teaching a course in Principles of Economics for over 25 years. Professor Lang has never graded on a curve since she believes that relative grading may unduly penalize (benefit) a good (poor) student in an unusually strong (weak) class. She always uses an absolute scale for making grades, as shown in the two left columns of Table 6.4.

TABLE 6.4 Grading Scales with Absolute Grading versus Relative Grading

Absolute Grading		Relative Grading	
Grade	Score	Grade	Probability
A	92 and above	A	0.10
B	78 up to 92	B	0.35
C	64 up to 78	C	0.40
D	58 up to 64	D	0.10
F	Below 58	F	0.05

A colleague of Professor Lang's has convinced her to move to relative grading, since it corrects for unanticipated problems. Professor Lang decides to experiment with grading based on the relative scale as shown in the two right columns of Table 6.4. Using this relative grading scheme, the top 10% of students will get As, the next 35% Bs, and so on. Based on her years of teaching experience, Professor Lang believes that the scores in her course follow a normal distribution with a mean of 78.6 and a standard deviation of 12.4.

Professor Lang wants to use the above information to:

1. Calculate probabilities based on the absolute scale. Compare these probabilities to the relative scale.

2. Calculate the range of scores for various grades based on the relative scale. Compare these ranges to the absolute scale.

3. Determine which grading scale makes it harder to get higher grades.

Sample Report— Absolute Grading versus Relative Grading

Many teachers would confess that grading is one of the most difficult tasks of their profession. Two common grading systems used in higher education are relative and absolute. Relative grading systems are norm referenced or curve based, in which a grade is based on the student's relative position in class. Absolute grading systems, on the other hand, are criterion referenced, in which a grade is related to the student's absolute performance in class. In short, with absolute grading, the student's score is compared to a predetermined scale whereas with relative grading, the score is compared to the scores of other students in the class.

Let X represent the grade in Professor Lang's class, which is normally distributed with a mean of 78.6 and a standard deviation of 12.4. This information is used to derive the grade probabilities based on the absolute scale. For instance, the probability of receiving an A is derived as $P(X \geq 92) = P(Z \geq 1.08) = 0.14$. Other probabilities, derived similarly, are presented in Table 6.A.

TABLE 6.A Probabilities Based on Absolute Scale and Relative Scale

Grade	Probability Based on Absolute Scale	Probability Based on Relative Scale
A	0.14	0.10
B	0.38	0.35
C	0.36	0.40
D	0.07	0.10
F	0.05	0.05

The second column of Table 6.A shows that 14% of students are expected to receive As, 38% Bs, and so on. Although these numbers are generally consistent with the relative scale shown in the third column of Table 6.A, it appears that the relative scale makes it harder for students to get higher grades. For instance, 14% get As with the absolute scale compared to only 10% with the relative scale.

Alternatively, we can compare the two grading methods on the basis of the range of scores for various grades. The second column of Table 6.B restates the range of scores based on absolute grading. In order to obtain the range of scores based on relative grading, it is once again necessary to apply concepts from the normal distribution. For instance, the minimum score required to earn an A with relative grading is derived by solving for x in $P(X \geq x) = 0.10$. Since $P(X \geq x) = 0.10$ is equivalent to $P(Z \geq z) = 0.10$, it follows that $z = 1.28$. Inserting the proper values of the mean, the standard deviation, and z into $x = \mu + z\sigma$ yields a value of x equal to 94.47. Ranges for other grades, derived similarly, are presented in the third column of Table 6.B.

TABLE 6.B Range of Scores with Absolute Grading versus Relative Grading

Grade	Range of Scores Based on Absolute Grading	Range of Scores Based on Relative Grading
A	92 and above	94.47 and above
B	78 up to 92	80.21 up to 94.47
C	64 up to 78	65.70 up to 80.21
D	58 up to 64	58.20 up to 65.70
F	Below 58	Below 58.20

Once again comparing the results in Table 6.B, the use of the relative scale makes it harder for students to get higher grades in Professor Lang's courses. For instance, in order to receive an A with relative grading, a student must have a score of at least 94.47 versus a score of at least 92 with absolute grading. Both absolute and relative grading methods have their merits and teachers often make the decision on the basis of their teaching philosophy. However, if Professor Lang wants to keep the grades consistent with her earlier absolute scale, she should base her relative scale on the probabilities computed in the second column of Table 6.A.

Conceptual Review

LO **6.1**   **Describe a continuous random variable.**

A **continuous random variable** is characterized by uncountable values because it can take on any value within an interval. The probability that a continuous random variable X assumes a particular value x is zero, that is, $P(X = x) = 0$. Thus, for a continuous random variable, we calculate the probability within a specified interval. Moreover, the following equalities hold: $P(a \leq X \leq b) = P(a < X < b) = P(a \leq X < b) = P(a < X \leq b)$.

The **probability density function** $f(x)$ of a continuous random variable X is nonnegative and the entire area under this function equals one. The probability $P(a \leq X \leq b)$ is the area under $f(x)$ between points a and b.

For any value x of the random variable X, the **cumulative distribution function** $F(x)$ is defined as $F(x) = P(X \leq x)$.

Calculate and interpret probabilities for a random variable that follows the continuous uniform distribution.

The **continuous uniform distribution** describes a random variable that has an equally likely chance of assuming a value within a specified range. The probability is essentially the area of a rectangle, which is the base times the height, that is, the length of a specified interval times the probability density function $f(x) = \frac{1}{b-a}$, where a and b are the lower and upper bounds of the interval, respectively.

Explain the characteristics of the normal distribution.

The **normal distribution** is the most extensively used continuous probability distribution and is the cornerstone of statistical inference. It is the familiar bell-shaped distribution, which is symmetric around the mean, that is, one side of the mean is just the mirror image of the other side. The normal distribution is completely described by two parameters: the population mean μ and the population variance σ^2.

The **standard normal distribution**, also referred to as the z **distribution**, is a special case of the normal distribution, with mean zero and standard deviation (or variance) one.

Use the standard normal table (z table).

The **standard normal table**, also called the z **table**, provides **cumulative probabilities** $P(Z \le z)$; this table appears on two pages in Table 1 of Appendix A. The left-hand page provides cumulative probabilities for z values less than or equal to zero. The right-hand page shows cumulative probabilities for z values greater than or equal to zero. We also use the table to compute z values for given cumulative probabilities.

Calculate and interpret probabilities for a random variable that follows the normal distribution.

Any normally distributed random variable X with mean μ and standard deviation σ can be transformed into the standard normal random variable Z as $Z = \frac{X - \mu}{\sigma}$. This standard transformation implies that any value x of X has a corresponding value z of Z given by $z = \frac{x - \mu}{\sigma}$.

The standard normal variable Z can be transformed to the normally distributed random variable X with mean μ and standard deviation σ as $X = \mu + Z\sigma$. This inverse transformation implies that any value z of Z has a corresponding value x of X given by $x = \mu + z\sigma$.

Calculate and interpret probabilities for a random variable that follows the exponential distribution.

A useful nonsymmetric continuous probability distribution is the **exponential distribution**. A random variable X follows the exponential distribution if its probability density function is $f(x) = \lambda e^{-\lambda x}$ for $x \ge 0$, where λ is a rate parameter and $e \approx 2.718$ is the base of the natural logarithm. The mean and the standard deviation of the distribution are both equal to $1/\lambda$. For $x \ge 0$, the **cumulative probability** is computed as $P(X \le x) = 1 - e^{-\lambda x}$.

Additional Exercises and Case Studies

Exercises

68. A florist makes deliveries between 1:00 pm and 5:00 pm daily. Assume delivery times follow the continuous uniform distribution.

    a. Calculate the mean and the variance of this distribution.

    b. Determine the percentage of deliveries that are made after 4:00 pm.

    c. Determine the percentage of deliveries that are made prior to 2:30 pm.

69. A worker at a landscape design center uses a machine to fill bags with potting soil. Assume that the quantity put in each bag follows the continuous uniform distribution with low and high filling weights of 10 pounds and 12 pounds, respectively.

    a. Calculate the expected value and the standard deviation of this distribution.

b. Find the probability that the weight of a randomly selected bag is no more than 11 pounds.

c. Find the probability that the weight of a randomly selected bag is at least 10.5 pounds.

70. The revised guidelines from the National High Blood Pressure Education Program define normal blood pressure as readings below 120/80 millimeters of mercury (*The New York Times*, May 14, 2003). Prehypertension is suspected when the top number (systolic) is between 120 and 139 or when the bottom number (diastolic) is between 80 and 90. A recent survey reported that the mean systolic reading of Canadians is 125 with a standard deviation of 17 and the mean diastolic reading is 79 with a standard deviation of 10. Assume that diastolic as well as systolic readings are normally distributed.

a. What proportion of Canadians are suffering from prehypertension caused by high diastolic readings?

b. What proportion of Canadians are suffering from prehypertension caused by high systolic readings?

71. U.S. consumers are increasingly viewing debit cards as a convenient substitute for cash and checks. The average amount spent annually on a debit card is $7,790 (*Kiplinger's*, August 2007). Assume that the average amount spent on a debit card is normally distributed with a standard deviation of $500.

a. A consumer advocate comments that the majority of consumers spend over $8,000 on a debit card. Find a flaw in this statement.

b. Compute the 25th percentile of the amount spent on a debit card.

c. Compute the 75th percentile of the amount spent on a debit card.

d. What is the interquartile range of this distribution?

72. On St. Patrick's Day, men spend an average of $43.87 while women spend an average of $29.54 (*USA TODAY*, March 17, 2009). Assume the standard deviations of spending for men and women are $3 and $11, respectively, and that both distributions are normally distributed.

a. What is the probability that men spend over $50 on St. Patrick's Day?

b. What is the probability that women spend over $50 on St. Patrick's Day?

c. Are men or women more likely to spend over $50 on St. Patrick's Day?

73. Lisa Mendes and Brad Lee work in the sales department of an AT&T Wireless Store. Lisa has been signing in an average of 48 new cell phone customers every month with a standard deviation of 22, while Brad signs in an average of 56 new customers with a standard deviation of 17. The store manager offers both Lisa and Brad a $100 incentive bonus if they can sign in more than 100 new customers in a month. Assume a normal distribution to answer the following questions.

a. What is the probability that Lisa will earn the $100 incentive bonus?

b. What is the probability that Brad will earn the $100 incentive bonus?

c. Are you surprised by the results? Explain.

74. The car speeds on a certain stretch of the interstate highway I-95 are known to be normally distributed with a mean of 72 and a standard deviation of 15. You have just heard a policeman comment that about 3% of the drivers drive at extremely dangerous speeds. What range of speeds is he referring to?

75. The average household income in a community is known to be $80,000. Also, 20% of the households have an income below $60,000 and anoher 20% have income above $90,000. Is it reasonable to use the normal distribution to model the household income in this community?

76. The length of components produced by a company is normally distributed with a mean of 6 cm and a standard deviation of 0.02 cm. Calculate the 1st, 2nd, and 3rd quartiles of the component length.

77. Entrance to a prestigious MBA program in India is determined by a national test where only the top 10% of the examinees are admitted to the program. Suppose it is known that the scores on this test are normally distributed with a mean of 420 and a standard deviation of 80. Parul Monga is trying desperately to get into this program. What is the minimum score that she must earn to get admitted?

78. A new water filtration system is sold with a 10-year warranty that includes all parts and repairs. Suppose the life of this water filtration system is normally distributed with mean and standard deviation of 16 and 5 years, respectively.

a. What is the probability that the water filtration system will require a repair during the warranty period?

b. Suppose the water filtration firm makes a $300 profit for every new system it installs. This profit, however, is reduced to $50 if the system requires repair during the warranty period. Find the expected profit of the firm if it installs 1,000 new water filtration systems.

79. (Use Excel) Suppose that the average IQ score is normally distributed with a mean of 100 and a standard deviation of 16. In addition to providing the answer, state the relevant Excel commands.

a. What is the probability a randomly selected person will have an IQ score of less than 80?

b. What is the probability that a randomly selected person will have an IQ score greater than 125?

c. What minimum IQ score does a person have to achieve to be in the top 2.5% of IQ scores?

80. (Use Excel) Suppose that the annual household income in a small midwestern community is normally distributed with a mean of $55,000 and a standard deviation of $4,500. In addition to providing the answer, state the relevant Excel commands.
    a. What is the probability that a randomly selected household will have an income between $50,000 and $65,000?
    b. What is the probability that a randomly selected household will have an income of more than $70,000?
    c. What minimum income does a household in this community have to earn in order to be in the top 5 percent?
    d. What maximum income does a household in this community have to earn to be in the bottom 40 percent?

81. On a particularly busy section of the Garden State Parkway in New Jersey, police use radar guns to detect speeders. Assume the time that elapses between successive speeders is exponentially distributed with a mean of 15 minutes.
    a. Calculate the rate parameter λ.
    b. What is the probability of a waiting time less than 10 minutes between successive speeders?
    c. What is the probability of a waiting time in excess of 25 minutes between successive speeders?

82. According to the Federal Bureau of Investigation, there is a violent crime in the United States every 22 seconds (*ABC News*, September 25, 2007). Assume that the time between successive violent crimes is exponentially distributed.
    a. What is the probability that there is a violent crime in the United States in the next one minute?
    b. If there has not been a violent crime in the previous minute, what is the probability that there will be a violent crime in the subsequent minute?

83. In a local law office, jobs to a printer are sent at a rate of 8 jobs per hour. Suppose that the number of jobs sent to a printer follows the Poisson distribution.
    a. What is the expected time between successive jobs?
    b. What is the probability that the next job will be sent within five minutes?

84. Disturbing news regarding Scottish police concerns the number of crashes involving vehicles on operational duties (*BBC News*, March 10, 2008). Statistics showed that Scottish forces' vehicles had been involved in traffic accidents at the rate of 1,000 per year. Suppose the number of crashes involving vehicles on operational duties follows a Poisson distribution.
    a. What is the average number of days between successive crashes?
    b. What is the rate parameter of the appropriate exponential distribution?
    c. What is the probability that the next vehicle will crash within a day?

85. A large technology firm receives an average of 12 new job applications every 10 days for positions that are not even advertised. Suppose the number of job applications received follows a Poisson distribution.
    a. What is the average number of days between successive job applications?
    b. What is the probability that the next job application is received within a day?
    c. What is the probability that the next job application is received between 1 and 2 days?

86. (Use Excel) The mileage (in 1,000s of miles) that car owners get with a certain kind of radial tire is a random variable having an exponential distribution with a mean of 50. In addition to providing the answer, state the relevant Excel commands.
    a. What is the probability that a tire will last at most 40,000 miles?
    b. What is the probability that a tire will last at least 65,000 miles?
    c. What is the probability that a tire will last between 70,000 and 80,000 miles?

87. (Use Excel) On average, a certain kind of kitchen appliance requires repairs once every four years. Assume that the times between repairs are exponentially distributed. In addition to providing the answer, state the relevant Excel commands.
    a. What is the probability that the appliance will work no more than three years without requiring repairs?
    b. What is the probability that the appliance will work at least six years without requiring repairs?

CASE STUDIES

Case Study 6.1

Body mass index (BMI) is a reliable indicator of body fat for most children and teens. BMI is calculated from a child's weight and height and is used as an easy-to-perform method of screening for weight categories that may lead to health problems. For children and teens, BMI is age- and sex-specific and is often referred to as BMI-for-age.

The Centers for Disease Control and Prevention (CDC) reports BMI-for-age growth charts for girls as well as boys to obtain a percentile ranking. Percentiles are the most commonly used indicator to assess the size and growth patterns of individual children in the United States.

The following table provides weight status categories and the corresponding percentiles and BMI ranges for 10-year-old boys in the United States.

Weight Status Category	Percentile Range	BMI Range
Underweight	Less than 5th	Less than 14.2
Healthy Weight	Between 5th and 85th	Between 14.2 and 19.4
Overweight	Between 85th and 95th	Between 19.4 and 22.2
Obese	More than 95th	More than 22.2

Health officials of a midwestern town are concerned about the weight of children in their town. For example, they believe that the BMI of their 10-year-old boys is normally distributed with mean 19.2 and standard deviation 2.6.

In a report, use the sample information to:

1. Compute the proportion of 10-year-old boys in this town that are in the various weight status categories given the BMI ranges.
2. Discuss whether the concern of health officials is justified.

Case Study 6.2

In the introductory case of Chapter 3 we discussed Vanguard's Precious Metals and Mining fund (Metals) and Fidelity's Strategic Income fund (Income), which were two top-performing mutual funds for the years 2000 through 2009. An analysis of annual return data for these two funds provided important information for any type of investor. Over the past 10 years, the Metals fund posted a mean return of 24.65% with a standard deviation of 37.13%. On the other hand, the mean and the standard deviation of return for the Income fund were 8.51% and 11.07%, respectively. It is reasonable to assume that the returns of the Metals and the Income funds are both normally distributed, where the means and the standard deviations are derived from the 10-year sample period.

In a report, use the sample information to compare and contrast the Metals and Income funds from the perspective of an investor whose objective is to:

1. Minimize the probability of earning a negative return.
2. Maximize the probability of earning a return between 0% and 10%.
3. Maximize the probability of earning a return greater than 10%.

Case Study 6.3

A variety of packaging solutions exist for products that must be kept within a specific temperature range. A cold chain distribution is a temperature-controlled supply chain. An unbroken cold chain is an uninterrupted series of storage and distribution activities that maintain a given temperature range. Cold chains are particularly useful in the food and pharmaceutical industries. A common suggested temperature range for a cold chain distribution in pharmaceutical industries is between 2 and 8 degrees Celsius.

Gopal Vasudeva works in the packaging branch of Merck & Co. He is in charge of analyzing a new package that the company has developed. With repeated trials, Gopal has determined that the mean temperature that this package is able to maintain during its use is 5.6°C with a standard deviation of 1.2°C. Assume that the temperature is normally distributed.

In a report, use the sample information to:

1. Calculate and interpret the probability that temperature goes (a) below 2°C and (b) above 8°C.
2. Calculate and interpret the 5th and the 95th percentiles of the temperature that the package maintains.

Appendix 6.1 Guidelines for Other Software Packages

The following section provides brief commands for specific software packages: Minitab, SPSS, and JMP. More detailed instructions can be found on the text website.

MINITAB

The Uniform Distribution

A. (Replicating Example 6.1b) From the menu choose **Calc > Probability Distributions > Uniform**.

B. Choose **Cumulative probability**. Enter 2500 as the **Lower endpoint** and 5000 as the **Upper endpoint**. Then select **Input constant** and enter 4000. Since Minitab returns a cumulative probability, we calculate $1 - P(X \le 4000)$.

The Normal Distribution

The Normal Transformation

A. (Replicating Example 6.8a) From the menu choose **Calc > Probability Distributions > Normal**.

B. Choose **Cumulative probability**. Enter 12 for the **Mean** and 3.2 for the **Standard deviation**. Select **Input constant** and enter 20. Since Minitab returns a cumulative probability, we calculate $1 - P(X \le 20)$.

The Inverse Transformation

A. (Replicating Example 6.8c) From the menu choose **Calc > Probability Distributions > Normal**.

B. Choose **Inverse cumulative probability**. Enter 12 for the **Mean** and 3.2 for the **Standard deviation**. Select **Input constant** and enter 0.90.

The Exponential Distribution

A. (Replicating Example 6.9b) Choose **Calc > Probability Distributions > Exponential**.

B. Choose **Cumulative probability**. Enter 25 for **Scale** (since Scale $= E(X) = 25$) and 0.0 for **Threshold**. Select **Input constant** and enter 60. Since Minitab returns a cumulative probability, we calculate $1 - P(X \le 60)$.

SPSS

The Uniform Distribution

A. (Replicating Example 6.1b) From the menu choose **Transform > Compute Variable**. Note: In order to access the commands, SPSS must "view" data on the spreadsheet. For this purpose, we enter a value of zero in the top left cell.

B. In the *Compute Variable* window, type cdfuniform as **Target Variable**. Under **Function group**, select **CDF & Noncentral CDF** and under **Functions and Special Variables**, double-click on **Cdf.Uniform**. In the *Numeric Expression* box, enter 4000 for **quant**, 2500 for **min**, and 5000 for **max**. Since SPSS returns a cumulative probability, we calculate $1 - P(X \leq 4000)$.

The Normal Distribution
The Normal Transformation

A. (Replicating Example 6.8a) From the menu choose **Transform > Compute Variable**.

B. In the *Compute Variable* window, type cdfnorm as **Target Variable**. Under **Function group**, select **CDF & Noncentral CDF** and under **Functions and Special Variables**, double-click on **Cdf.Normal**. In the *Numeric Expression* box, enter 20 for **quant**, 12 for **mean**, and 3.2 for **stddev**. Since SPSS returns a cumulative probability, we calculate $1 - P(X \leq 20)$.

The Inverse Transformation

A. (Replicating Example 6.8c) From the menu choose **Transform > Compute Variable**.

B. In the *Compute Variable* window, type invnorm as **Target Variable**. Under **Function group**, select **Inverse DF** and under **Functions and Special Variables**, double-click on **Idf.Normal**. In the *Numeric Expression* box, enter 0.9 for **prob**, 12 for **mean**, and 3.2 for **stddev**.

The Exponential Distribution

A. (Replicating Example 6.9b) From the menu choose **Transform > Compute Variable**.

B. In the *Compute Variable* window, type cdfexp as **Target Variable**. Under **Function group**, select **CDF & Noncentral CDF** and under **Functions and Special Variables**, double-click on **Cdf.Exp**. In the *Numeric Expression* box, enter 60 for **quant** and 0.04 for **scale**. Since SPSS returns a cumulative probability, we calculate $1 - P(X \leq 60)$.

JMP

The Normal Distribution
The Normal Transformation

A. (Replicating Example 6.8a) Right-click on the header at the top of the column in the spreadsheet view. Under **Functions (grouped)**, choose **Probability > Normal Probability**. Note: In order to see the calculated probability on the spreadsheet view, JMP must "view" data on the spreadsheet. For this purpose, we enter a value of zero in the first cell of the column.

B. Put the insertion marker on the box for **x** and click the insert button (shown as a caret ^ with the mathematical operations) until you see **mean** and **std dev** next to **x**. Enter 20 for **x**, 12 for **mean**, and 3.2 for **std dev**. Since JMP returns a cumulative probability, we calculate $1 - P(X \leq 20)$.

The Inverse Transformation

A. (Replicating Example 6.8c) Right-click on the header at the top of the column in the spreadsheet view. Under **Functions (grouped)**, choose **Probability > Normal Quantile**.

B. Put the insertion marker on the box for **p** and click the insert button (shown as a caret ^ with the mathematical operations) until you see **mean** and **std dev** next to **p**. Enter 0.90 for **p**, 12 for **mean**, and 3.2 for **std dev**.

The Exponential Distribution

A. (Replicating Example 6.9b) Right-click on the header at the top of the column in the spreadsheet view. Under **Functions (grouped)**, choose **Probability > Weibull Distribution**. (The exponential distribution is a special case of the Weibull distribution when the shape parameter, see next step, equals 1.)

B. Put the insertion marker on the box for **x** and click the insert button (shown as a caret ^ with the mathematical operations) until you see **shape** and **scale** next to **x**. Enter 60 for **x**, 1 for **shape**, and 25 for **scale**. Since JMP returns a cumulative probability, we calculate $1 - P(X \leq 60)$.

7
Sampling and Sampling Distributions

LEARNING OBJECTIVES

After reading this chapter you should be able to:

LO **7.1** Explain common sample biases.

LO **7.2** Describe various sampling methods.

LO **7.3** Describe the sampling distribution of the sample mean.

LO **7.4** Explain the importance of the central limit theorem.

LO **7.5** Describe the sampling distribution of the sample proportion.

LO **7.6** Use a finite population correction factor.

LO **7.7** Construct and interpret control charts for quantitative and qualitative data.

In the last few chapters we had information on the population parameters, such as the population proportion and the population mean, for the analysis of discrete and continuous random variables. In many instances we do not have information on the parameters, so we make statistical inferences on the basis of sample statistics. The credibility of any statistical inference depends on the quality of the sample on which it is based. In this chapter we discuss various ways to draw a good sample and also highlight cases in which the sample misrepresents the population. It is important to note that any given statistical problem involves only one population, but many possible samples from which a statistic can be derived. Therefore, while the population parameter is a constant, the sample statistic is a random variable whose value depends on the choice of the random sample. We will discuss how to evaluate the properties of sample statistics. In particular, we will study the probability distributions of the sample mean and the sample proportion based on simple random sampling. Finally, we will use these distributions to construct control charts, which are popular statistical tools for monitoring and improving quality.

Marketing Iced Coffee

Although hot coffee is still Americans' drink of choice, the market share of iced coffee is growing steadily. Thirty percent of coffee drinkers had at least one iced, frozen, or blended coffee drink in 2009, up from 28% in 2008 (*The Boston Globe*, April 6, 2010). In response to this growing change in taste, the coffee chains have ramped up their offerings: Starbucks recently introduced an upgraded Frappuccino; Dunkin' Donuts launched a new iced dark roast; and McDonald's unveiled new blended coffee iced drinks and smoothies.

In order to capitalize on this trend, Starbucks advertised a Happy Hour from May 7 through May 16 whereby customers enjoyed a half-price Frappuccino beverage between 3 pm and 5 pm (http://starbucks.com). Anne Jones, a manager at a local Starbucks (see the Chapter 5 introductory case), wonders how this marketing campaign has affected her business. She knows that women and teenage girls comprise the majority of the iced-coffee market, since they are willing to spend more on indulgences. In fact, Anne reviews her records prior to the promotion and finds that 43% of iced-coffee customers were women and 21% were teenage girls. She also finds that customers spent an average of $4.18 on iced coffee with a standard deviation of $0.84.

One month after the marketing period ends, Anne surveys 50 of her iced-coffee customers and finds that they had spent an average of $4.26. In addition, 23 (46%) of the customers were women and 17 (34%) were teenage girls. Anne wants to determine if the marketing campaign has had a lingering effect on the amount of money customers spend on iced coffee and on the proportion of customers who are women and teenage girls. Anne wonders if Starbucks would have gotten such business if it had chosen not to pursue the marketing campaign.

Anne wants to use the above survey information to:

1. Calculate the probability that customers spend an average of $4.26 or more on iced coffee.

2. Calculate the probability that 46% or more of iced-coffee customers are women.

3. Calculate the probability that 34% or more of iced-coffee customers are teenage girls.

A synopsis of this case is provided at the end of Section 7.3.

7.1 Sampling

A major portion of statistics is concerned with statistical inference, where we examine the problem of estimating population parameters or testing hypotheses about such parameters. Recall that a population consists of all items of interest in the statistical problem. If we had access to data that encompass the entire population, then the values of the parameters would be known and no statistical inference would be needed. Since it is generally not feasible to gather data on an entire population, we use a subset of the population, or a sample, and use this information to make statistical inference. We can think of a census and survey data as representative of population and sample data, respectively. While a census captures almost everyone in the country, a survey captures a small number of people who fit a particular category. We regularly use survey data to analyze government and business activities.

> **POPULATION VERSUS SAMPLE**
>
> A **population** consists of all items of interest in a statistical problem, whereas a **sample** is a subset of the population. We use a calculated **sample statistic**, or simply **statistic**, to make inferences about the unknown population **parameter**.

LO 7.1
Explain common sample biases.

In later chapters we explore estimation and hypothesis testing, which are based on sample information. It is important to note that no matter how sophisticated the statistical methods are, the credibility of statistical inference depends on the quality of the sample on which it is based. A primary requisite for a "good" sample is that it be **representative** of the population we are trying to describe. When the information from a sample is not typical of information in the population in a systematic way, we say that **bias** has occurred.

> **Bias** refers to the tendency of a sample statistic to systematically over- or underestimate a population parameter. It is often caused by samples that are not representative of the population.

Classic Case of a "Bad" Sample: The *Literary Digest* Debacle of 1936

In theory, drawing conclusions about a population based on a good sample sounds logical; however, in practice, what constitutes a "good" sample? Unfortunately, there are many ways to collect a "bad" sample. One way is to inadvertently pick a sample that represents only a portion of the population. The *Literary Digest*'s attempt to predict the 1936 presidential election is a classic example of an embarrassingly inaccurate poll.

In 1932 and amid the Great Depression, Herbert Hoover was voted out of the White House and Franklin Delano Roosevelt (FDR) was elected the 32nd president of the United States. Although FDR's attempts to end the Great Depression within four years were largely unsuccessful, he retained the general public's faith. In 1936, FDR ran for reelection against Alf Landon, the governor of Kansas and the Republican nominee. The *Literary Digest,* an influential, general-interest weekly magazine, wanted to predict the next U.S. president, as it had done successfully five times before.

After conducting the largest poll in history, the *Literary Digest* predicted a landslide victory for Alf Landon: 57% of the vote to FDR's 43%. Moreover, the *Literary Digest* claimed that its prediction would be within a fraction of 1% of the actual vote. Instead, FDR won in a landslide: 62% to 38%. So what went wrong?

The *Literary Digest* sent postcards to 10 million people (one-quarter of the voting population at the time) and received responses from 2.4 million people. The response rate of 24% (2.4 million/10 million) might seem low to some, but in reality it is a reasonable response rate given this type of polling. What was atypical of the poll is the manner in which the *Literary Digest* obtained the respondents' names. The *Literary Digest* randomly sampled its own subscriber list, club membership rosters, telephone directories, and automobile registration rolls. This sample reflected predominantly middle- and upper-class people; that is, the vast majority of those polled were wealthier people who were more inclined to vote for the Republican candidate. Back in the 1930s, owning a phone, for instance, was far from universal. Only 11 million residential phones were in service in 1936 and these homes were disproportionately well-to-do and in favor of Landon. The sampling methodology employed by the *Literary Digest* suffered from **selection bias**. Selection bias occurs when portions of the population are underrepresented in the sample. FDR's support came from lower-income classes whose opinion was not reflected in the poll. The sample, unfortunately, misrepresented the general electorate.

> **Selection bias** refers to a systematic underrepresentation of certain groups from consideration for the sample.

What should the *Literary Digest* have done differently? At a minimum, most would agree that names should have been obtained from voter registration lists rather than telephone directory lists and car registrations.

In addition to selection bias, the *Literary Digest* survey also had a great deal of **nonresponse bias**. This occurs when those responding to a survey or poll differ systematically from the nonrespondents. In the survey, a larger percentage of educated people mailed back the questionnaires. During that time period, the more educated tended to come from affluent families that again favored the Republican candidate. Problems with nonresponse bias persist today. Most people do not want to spend time carefully reading and responding to polls conducted by mail. Only those who care a great deal about an election or a particular issue take the time to read the instructions, fill out the questionnaire, and mail it back. Those who do respond may be atypical of the population as a whole.

> **Nonresponse bias** refers to a systematic difference in preferences between respondents and nonrespondents to a survey or a poll.

The most effective way to deal with nonresponse bias is to reduce nonresponse rates. Paying attention to survey design, wording, and ordering of the questions can increase the response rate. Sometimes, rather than sending out a very large number of surveys, it may be preferable to use a smaller representative sample for which the response rate is likely to be high.

It turns out that someone did accurately predict the 1936 presidential election. From a sample of 50,000 with a response rate of 10% (5,000 respondents), a young pollster named George Gallup predicted that Roosevelt would win 56% of the vote to Landon's 44%. Despite using a far smaller sample with a lower response rate, it was far more *representative* of the true voting population. Gallup later founded the Gallup Organization, one of the leading polling companies of all times.

Sampling Methods

As mentioned earlier, a primary requisite for a "good" sample is that it be representative of the population you are trying to describe. The basic type of sample that can be used to draw statistically sound conclusions about a population is a **simple random sample**.

LO **7.2**

Describe various sampling methods.

SIMPLE RANDOM SAMPLE

A **simple random sample** is a sample of n observations that has the same probability of being selected from the population as any other sample of n observations. Most statistical methods presume simple random samples.

EXAMPLE 7.1

A recent analysis shows a dramatic decline in studying time among today's college students (*The Boston Globe*, July 4, 2010). In 1961, students invested 24 hours per week in their academic pursuits, whereas today's students study an average of 14 hours per week. A dean at a large university in California wonders if this trend is reflective of the students at her university. The university has 20,000 students and the dean would like a sample of 100. Use Excel to generate a simple random sample of 100 students.

SOLUTION: We can use Excel's RANDBETWEEN function to generate random integers within some interval. In general, we input '=RANDBETWEEN(Bottom, Top)', Bottom and Top refer to the smallest and largest integers, respectively, that Excel might return. In order to randomly select a student from a list of 20,000 students, we input '=RANDBETWEEN(1, 20000)'. Suppose Excel returns the value 6,319. The dean can then choose the 6,319th student from the list. In order to generate the remaining 99 random numbers, we can select the cell with the value 6,319, drag it down 99 cells, and then from the menu choose **Home > Fill > Down**.

While a simple random sample is the most commonly used sampling method, in some situations other sampling methods have an advantage over simple random samples. Two alternative methods for forming a sample are stratified random sampling and cluster sampling.

Political pollsters often employ **stratified random sampling** in an attempt to ensure that each area of the country, each ethnic group, each religious group, and so forth, is appropriately represented in the sample. With stratified random sampling, the population is divided into groups (strata) based on one or more classification criteria. Simple random samples are then drawn from each stratum in sizes proportional to the relative size of each stratum in the population. These samples are then pooled.

STRATIFIED RANDOM SAMPLING

In stratified random sampling, the population is first divided up into mutually exclusive and collectively exhaustive groups, called *strata*. A stratified sample includes randomly selected observations from each stratum. The number of observations per stratum is proportional to the stratum's size in the population. The data for each stratum are eventually pooled.

Stratified random sampling has two advantages. First, it guarantees that the population subdivisions of interest are represented in the sample. Second, the estimates of parameters produced from stratified random sampling have greater precision than estimates obtained from simple random sampling.

Even stratified random sampling, however, can fall short with its predictive ability. One of the nagging mysteries of the 2008 Democratic presidential primaries was: Why were the polls so wrong in New Hampshire? All nine major polling groups predicted that

Barack Obama would beat Hillary Clinton in the New Hampshire primary by an average of 8.3 percentage points. When the votes were counted, Clinton won by 2.6%. Several factors contributed to the wrong prediction by the polling industry. First, pollsters over-estimated the turnout of young voters, who overwhelmingly favored Obama in exit polls but did not surge to vote as they had in the Iowa caucus. Second, Clinton's campaign made a decision to target women Democrats, especially single women. This focus did not pay off in Iowa, but it did in New Hampshire. Finally, on the eve of the primary, a woman in Portsmouth asked Clinton: "How do you do it?" Clinton's teary response was powerful and warm. Voters, who rarely saw Clinton in such an emotional moment, found her response humanizing and appealing. Most polls had stopped phoning voters over the weekend, too soon to catch the likely voter shift.

Cluster sampling is another method for forming a representative sample. A cluster sample is formed by dividing the population into groups (clusters), such as geographic areas, and then selecting a sample of the groups for the analysis. The technique works best when most of the variation in the population is within the groups and not between the groups. In such instances, a cluster is a miniversion of the population.

CLUSTER SAMPLING

In cluster sampling, the population is first divided up into mutually exclusive and collectively exhaustive groups, called *clusters*. A cluster sample includes observations from randomly selected clusters.

In general, cluster sampling is cheaper as compared to other sampling methods. However, for a given sample size, it provides less precision than either simple random sampling or stratified sampling. Cluster sampling is useful in applications where the population is concentrated in natural clusters such as city blocks, schools, and other geographic areas. It is especially attractive when constructing a complete list of the population members is difficult and/or costly. For example, since it may not be possible to create a full list of customers that go to Walmart, we can form a sample that includes customers only from selected stores.

STRATIFIED VERSUS CLUSTER SAMPLING

In stratified sampling, the sample consists of observations from each group, whereas in cluster sampling, the sample consists of observations from the selected groups. Stratified sampling is preferred when the objective is to increase precision and cluster sampling is preferred when the objective is to reduce costs.

The Special Election to Fill Ted Kennedy's Senate Seat

On January 19, 2010, Scott Brown, the Republican candidate, beat Martha Coakley, the Democratic candidate, in a special election to fill the U.S. Senate seat for Massachusetts that had been vacated with the death of Senator Ted Kennedy. Given that Kennedy, the "Liberal Lion," had held the seat for over 40 years, the election was one of the biggest upsets in Massachusetts' political history. Nine days prior to the election, a *Boston Globe* poll gave Coakley, the state's attorney general, a 15-point lead over Brown. Critics accused the *Globe*, which had endorsed Coakley, of purposely running a bad poll to discourage voters from coming out for Brown. In reality, by the time the *Globe* released the poll, it contained old information from January 2–6. In addition, the *Globe* partnered with the University of New Hampshire for the poll, and unfortunately included people in the poll who said that they were unlikely to vote! Eighty years after the *Literary Digest* fiasco, pollsters are still making predictions based on samples with a great deal of selection bias.

The first poll that foretold Brown's stunning victory over Coakley was released by Suffolk University on January 14. The poll had Brown ahead by 50% to Coakley's 46%, approximately one percentage point off the Election Day results (52% to 47%). How did Suffolk University arrive at its findings? It conducted a statewide poll and, in addition, implemented a form of cluster sampling. As mentioned earlier, the technique works best when most of the variation in the population is within the groups and not between the groups. The pollsters from Suffolk University selected three bellwethers, or towns that would indicate the way that the state would vote. In choosing the bellwethers, the pollsters spent enormous amounts of time examining the results of similar elections over many years. Figure 7.1 shows a map of Massachusetts and the three bellwethers: Gardner, Fitchburg, and Peabody. The statewide poll and the results from the bellwethers were reported separately but yielded the same results.

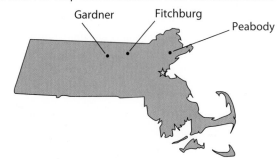

FIGURE 7.1 Map of Massachusetts with three bellwethers (towns)

In practice, it is extremely difficult to obtain a truly random sample that is representative of the underlying population. As researchers, we need to be aware of the population from which the sample was selected and then limit our conclusions to that population. For the remainder of the text, we assume that the sample data are void of "human error"; that is, we have sampled from the correct population (no selection bias); we have no response bias; and we have collected, analyzed, and reported the data properly.

EXERCISES 7.1

1. In 2010, Apple introduced the iPad, a tablet-style computer that its former CEO Steve Jobs called a "a truly magical and revolutionary product" (*CNN*, January 28, 2010). Suppose you are put in charge of determining the age profile of people who purchased the iPad in the United States. Explain in detail the following sampling strategies that you could use to select a representative sample.
   a. Simple random sampling
   b. Stratified random sampling
   c. Cluster sampling

2. A marketing firm opens a small booth at a local mall over the weekend, where shoppers are asked how much money they spent at the food court. The objective is to determine the average monthly expenditure of shoppers at the food court. Has the marketing firm committed any sampling bias? Discuss.

3. Natalie Min is a business student in the Haas School of Business at Berkeley. She wishes to pursue an MBA from Berkeley and wants to know the profile of other students who are likely to apply to the Berkeley MBA program. In particular, she wants to know the GPA of students with whom she might be competing. She randomly surveys

40 students from her accounting class for the analysis. Discuss in detail whether or not Natalie's analysis is based on a representative sample.

4. Vons, a large supermarket in Grover Beach, California, is considering extending its store hours from 7:00 am to midnight, seven days a week, to 6:00 am to midnight. Discuss the sampling bias in the following sampling strategies:
   a. Mail a prepaid envelope to randomly selected residents in the Grover Beach area, asking for their preference for the store hours.
   b. Ask the customers who frequent the store in the morning if they would prefer an earlier opening time.
   c. Place an ad in the local newspaper, requesting people to submit their preference for store hours on the store's website.

5. In the previous question regarding Vons's store hours, explain how you can obtain a representative sample based on the following sampling strategies:
   a. Simple random sampling.
   b. Stratified random sampling.
   c. Cluster sampling.

7.2 The Sampling Distribution of the Sample Mean

As mentioned earlier, we are generally interested in the characteristics of a population. For instance, a student is interested in the average starting salary (population mean) of business graduates. Similarly, a banker is interested in the default probability (population proportion) of mortgage holders. Recall that the population mean and the population proportion are parameters that describe quantitative and qualitative data, respectively. Since it is cumbersome or impossible to analyze the entire population, we generally make inferences about the characteristics of the population on the basis of a random sample drawn from the population.

It is important to note that there is only one population, but many possible samples of a given size can be drawn from the population. Therefore, a population parameter is a constant, even though its value may be unknown. A statistic, on the other hand, is a random variable whose value depends on the particular sample that is randomly drawn from the population.

> A **parameter** is a **constant**, although its value may be unknown. A **statistic**, such as the sample mean or the sample proportion, is a **random variable** whose value depends on the chosen random sample.

Consider the starting salary of business graduates as the variable of interest. If you decide to make inferences about the population mean salary on the basis of a random draw of 38 recent business graduates, then the sample mean $\overline{X}$ is the relevant statistic. Note that the value of $\overline{X}$ will change if you choose a different random sample of 38 business graduates. In other words, $\overline{X}$ is a random variable whose value depends on the chosen random sample. The sample mean is commonly referred to as the estimator of the population mean.

ESTIMATOR AND ESTIMATE

When a statistic is used to estimate a parameter, it is referred to as an **estimator**. A particular value of the estimator is called an **estimate**.

It is common to refer to an estimator as a **point estimator** because it provides a single value—*a point*—as an estimate of the unknown population parameter. Similarly, an estimate is also called a **point estimate**.

In the above example, the sample mean $\overline{X}$ is the estimator of the mean starting salary of business graduates. If the average derived from a specific sample is $54,000, then $\bar{x} = 54,000$ is the estimate of the population mean. Similarly, if the variable of interest is the default probability of mortgage holders, then the sample proportion of defaults, denoted by $\overline{P}$, from a random sample of 80 mortgage holders is the estimator of the population proportion. If 10 out of 80 mortgage holders in a given sample default, then $\bar{p} = 10/80 = 0.125$ is the estimate of the population proportion.

In this section we will focus on the probability distribution of the sample mean $\overline{X}$, which is commonly referred to as the **sampling distribution** of $\overline{X}$. Since $\overline{X}$ is a random variable, its sampling distribution is simply the probability distribution derived from all possible samples of a given size from the population. Consider, for example, a mean derived from a sample of n observations. Another mean can similarly be derived from a different sample of n observations. If we repeat this process a very large number of times, then the frequency distribution of the sample means can be thought of as its sampling distribution. In particular, we will discuss the expected value and the standard deviation of the sample mean. We will also study the conditions under which the sampling distribution of the sample mean is normally distributed.

LO 7.3

Describe the sampling
distribution of the
sample mean.

The Expected Value and the Standard Error of the Sample Mean

Let the random variable X represent a certain characteristic of a population under study, with an expected value, $E(X) = \mu$, and a variance, $Var(X) = \sigma^2$. Let the sample mean $\overline{X}$ be based on a random sample of n observations from this population. It is easy to derive the expected value and the variance of $\overline{X}$ (see Appendix 7.1 at the end of the chapter for the derivations).

The **expected value** of $\overline{X}$ is the same as the expected value of the individual observation, that is, $E(\overline{X}) = E(X) = \mu$. In other words, if we were to sample repeatedly from a given population, the average value of the sample means will equal the population mean from the underlying population. This is an important property of an estimator, called unbiasedness, that holds irrespective of whether the sample mean is based on a small or a large sample. An estimator is **unbiased** if its expected value equals the population parameter.

THE EXPECTED VALUE OF THE SAMPLE MEAN

The **expected value** of the sample mean $\overline{X}$ equals the population mean, or $E(\overline{X}) = \mu$. In other words, the sample mean is an **unbiased** estimator of the population mean.

It is important to note that we estimate the population mean on the basis of one sample. The above result shows that we are not systematically under- or overestimating the population parameter.

The **variance** of $\overline{X}$ is equal to $Var(\overline{X}) = \frac{\sigma^2}{n}$. In other words, if we were to sample repeatedly from a given population, the variance of the sample mean will equal the variance of the individual observation, drawn from the underlying population, divided by the sample size. Note that $Var(\overline{X})$ is smaller than the variance of X, which is equal to $Var(X) = \sigma^2$. This is an intuitive result, suggesting that the variability between sample means is less than the variability between observations. Since each sample is likely to contain both high and low observations, the highs and lows cancel one another, making the variance of X-bar smaller than the variance of X. As usual, the **standard deviation** of $\overline{X}$ is calculated as the positive square root of the variance. However, in order to distinguish the variability between samples from the variability between individual observations, we refer to the standard deviation of $\overline{X}$ as the **standard error of the sample mean** computed as $se(\overline{X}) = \frac{\sigma}{\sqrt{n}}$.

THE STANDARD ERROR OF THE SAMPLE MEAN

The standard deviation of the sample mean $\overline{X}$ is referred to as the **standard error of the sample mean**. It equals the population standard deviation divided by the square root of the sample size, that is, $se(\overline{X}) = \frac{\sigma}{\sqrt{n}}$.

As discussed in Chapter 8, the exact standard error of an estimator is often not known, and therefore, must be estimated from the given sample data. For convenience, we use 'se' to denote both the exact and the estimated standard error of an estimator.

EXAMPLE 7.2

The chefs at a local pizza chain in Cambria, California, strive to maintain the suggested size of their 16-inch pizzas. Despite their best efforts, they are unable to make every pizza exactly 16 inches in diameter. The manager has determined that the size of the pizzas is normally distributed with a mean of 16 inches and a standard deviation of 0.8 inch.

a. What are the expected value and the standard error of the sample mean derived from a random sample of 2 pizzas?

b. What are the expected value and the standard error of the sample mean derived from a random sample of 4 pizzas?

c. Compare the expected value and the standard error of the sample mean with those of an individual pizza.

SOLUTION: We know that the population mean $\mu = 16$ and the population standard deviation $\sigma = 0.8$. We use $E(\overline{X}) = \mu$ and $se(\overline{X}) = \frac{\sigma}{\sqrt{n}}$ to calculate the following results.

a. With the sample size $n = 2$, $E(\overline{X}) = 16$ and $se(\overline{X}) = \frac{0.8}{\sqrt{2}} = 0.57$.

b. With the sample size $n = 4$, $E(\overline{X}) = 16$ and $se(\overline{X}) = \frac{0.8}{\sqrt{4}} = 0.40$.

c. The expected value of the sample mean for both sample sizes is identical to the expected value of the individual pizza. However, the standard error of the sample mean with $n = 4$ is lower than the one with $n = 2$. For both sample sizes, the standard error of the sample mean is lower than the standard deviation of the individual pizza. This result confirms that averaging reduces variability.

Sampling from a Normal Population

An important feature of the sampling distribution of the sample mean $\overline{X}$ is that, irrespective of the sample size n, $\overline{X}$ is normally distributed if the population X from which the sample is drawn is normal. In other words, if X is normal with expected value μ and standard deviation σ, then $\overline{X}$ is also normal with expected value μ and standard error $\sigma/\sqrt{n}$.

SAMPLING FROM A NORMAL POPULATION

For any sample size n, the sampling distribution of $\overline{X}$ is **normal** if the population X from which the sample is drawn is normally distributed.

If $\overline{X}$ is normal, we can transform it into a **standard normal random variable** as:

$$Z = \frac{\overline{X} - E(\overline{X})}{se(\overline{X})} = \frac{\overline{X} - \mu}{\sigma/\sqrt{n}}.$$

Therefore, any value $\bar{x}$ on $\overline{X}$ has a corresponding value z on Z given by $z = \frac{\bar{x} - \mu}{\sigma/\sqrt{n}}$.

EXAMPLE 7.3

Use the information in Example 7.2 to answer the following questions:

a. What is the probability that a randomly selected pizza is less than 15.5 inches?

b. What is the probability that 2 randomly selected pizzas average less than 15.5 inches?

c. What is the probability that 4 randomly selected pizzas average less than 15.5 inches?

d. Comment on the computed probabilities.

SOLUTION: Since the population is normally distributed, the sampling distribution of the sample mean is also normal. Figure 7.2 depicts the shapes of the three distributions based on the population mean $\mu = 16$ and the population standard deviation $\sigma = 0.8$.

FIGURE 7.2 Normal distribution of the sample mean

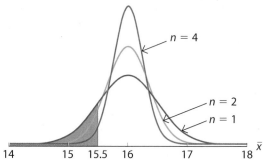

Note that when the sample size $n = 1$, the sample mean $\bar{x}$ is the same as the individual observation x.

a. We use the standard transformation to derive $P(X < 15.5) = P\left(Z < \frac{15.5 - 16}{0.8}\right) = P(Z < -0.63) = 0.2643$. There is a 26.43% chance that an individual pizza is less than 15.5 inches.

b. Here we use the standard transformation to derive $P(\bar{X} < 15.5) = P\left(Z < \frac{15.5 - 16}{0.8/\sqrt{2}}\right) = P(Z < -0.88) = 0.1894$. In a random sample of 2 pizzas, there is an 18.94% chance that the average size is less than 15.5 inches.

c. Again we find $P(\bar{X} < 15.5)$, but now $n = 4$. Therefore, $P(\bar{X} < 15.5) = P\left(Z < \frac{15.5 - 16}{0.8/\sqrt{4}}\right) = P(Z < -1.25) = 0.1056$. In a random sample of 4 pizzas, there is a 10.56% chance that the average size is less than 15.5 inches.

d. The probability that the average size is under 15.5 inches, for 4 randomly selected pizzas, is less than half of that for an individual pizza. This is due to the fact that while X and $\bar{X}$ have the same expected value of 16, the variance of $\bar{X}$ is less than that of X.

LO 7.4 The Central Limit Theorem

Explain the importance of the central limit theorem.

For making statistical inferences, it is essential that the sampling distribution of $\bar{X}$ is normally distributed. So far we have only considered the case where $\bar{X}$ is normally distributed because the population X from which the sample is drawn is normal. What if the underlying population is not normal? Here we present the **central limit theorem (CLT)**, which perhaps is the most remarkable result of probability theory. The CLT states that the sum or the average of a large number of independent observations from the same underlying distribution has an approximate normal distribution. The approximation steadily improves as the number of observations increases. In other words, irrespective of whether or not the population X is normal, the sample mean $\bar{X}$ computed from a random sample of size n will be approximately normally distributed as long as n is sufficiently large.

THE CENTRAL LIMIT THEOREM FOR THE SAMPLE MEAN

For any population X with expected value μ and standard deviation σ, the sampling distribution of $\bar{X}$ will be **approximately normal if the sample size n is sufficiently large**. As a general guideline, the normal distribution approximation is justified when $n \geq 30$.

As before, if $\bar{X}$ is approximately normal, then we can transform it to $Z = \frac{\bar{X} - \mu}{\sigma/\sqrt{n}}$.

Figure 7.2, discussed in Example 7.3, is not representative of the CLT principle because for a normal population, the sampling distribution of $\overline{X}$ is normal irrespective of the sample size. Figures 7.3 and 7.4, however, illustrate the CLT by using random samples of various sizes drawn from nonnormal populations. The relative frequency polygon of $\overline{X}$, which essentially represents its distribution, is generated from repeated draws (computer simulations) from the continuous uniform distribution (Figure 7.3) and the exponential distribution (Figure 7.4). Both of these nonnormal distributions were discussed in Chapter 6.

FIGURE 7.3 Sampling distribution of $\overline{X}$ when the population has a uniform distribution

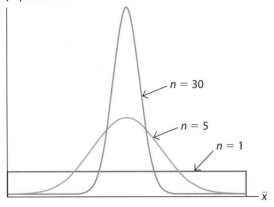

FIGURE 7.4 Sampling distribution of $\overline{X}$ when the population has an exponential distribution

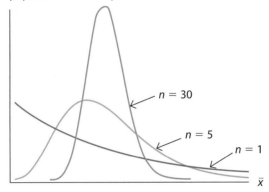

Note that when the sample size $n = 1$, the sample mean is the same as the individual observation (population) with the familiar uniform and exponential shapes. With $n = 5$, the sampling distribution of $\overline{X}$ begins to resemble the shape of the normal distribution. With $n = 30$, the shapes of the sampling distribution of $\overline{X}$ are approximately normal with the uniform as well as the exponential population distributions. The CLT can similarly be illustrated with other distributions of the population. How large a sample is necessary for normal convergence depends on the magnitude of the departure of the population from normality. As mentioned above, practitioners often use the normal distribution approximation when $n \geq 30$.

EXAMPLE 7.4

Consider the information presented in the introductory case of this chapter. Recall that Anne wants to determine if the marketing campaign has had a lingering effect on the amount of money customers spend on iced coffee. Before the campaign, customers spent an average of $4.18 on iced coffee with a standard deviation of $0.84. Anne reports that the average amount, based on 50 customers sampled after the campaign, is $4.26. She wants to calculate the probability that customers spend an average of $4.26 or more on iced coffee.

SOLUTION: If Starbucks did not pursue the marketing campaign, spending on iced coffee would still have mean $\mu = 4.18$ and standard deviation $\sigma = 0.84$. Anne needs to calculate the probability that the sample mean is at least 4.26, that is, $P(\bar{X} \geq 4.26)$. The population from which the sample is drawn is not known to be normal. However, since $n \geq 30$, from the central limit theorem, we know that $\bar{X}$ is approximately normal. Therefore, as shown in Figure 7.5, $P(\bar{X} \geq 4.26) = P\left(Z \geq \frac{4.26 - 4.18}{0.84/\sqrt{50}}\right) = P(Z \geq 0.67) = 1 - 0.7486 = 0.2514$. It is quite plausible (probability $= 0.2514$) that in a sample of 50 customers, the sample mean is $4.26 or more even if Starbucks did not pursue the marketing campaign.

FIGURE 7.5 Finding $P(\bar{X} \geq 4.26)$

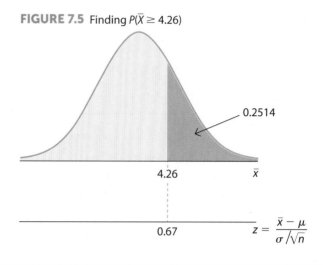

EXERCISES 7.2

Mechanics

6. A random sample is drawn from a normally distributed population with mean $\mu = 12$ and standard deviation $\sigma = 1.5$.
   a. Comment on the sampling distribution of the sample mean with $n = 20$ and $n = 40$.
   b. Can you use the standard normal distribution to calculate the probability that the sample mean is less than 12.5 for both sample sizes?
   c. Report the probability if you answered yes to the previous question for either sample size.

7. A random sample is drawn from a population with mean $\mu = 66$ and standard deviation $\sigma = 5.5$.
   a. Comment on the sampling distribution of the sample mean with $n = 16$ and $n = 36$.
   b. Can you use the standard normal distribution to calculate the probability that the sample mean falls between 66 and 68 for both sample sizes?
   c. Report the probability if you answered yes to the previous question for either sample size.

8. A random sample of size $n = 100$ is taken from a population with mean $\mu = 80$ and standard deviation $\sigma = 14$.
   a. Calculate the expected value and the standard error for the sampling distribution of the sample mean.
   b. What is the probability that the sample mean falls between 77 and 85?
   c. What is the probability that the sample mean is greater than 84?

9. A random sample of size $n = 50$ is taken from a population with mean $\mu = -9.5$ and standard deviation $\sigma = 2$.
   a. Calculate the expected value and the standard error for the sampling distribution of the sample mean.
   b. What is the probability that the sample mean is less than -10?
   c. What is the probability that the sample mean falls between -10 and -9?

Applications

10. According to a recent survey, high school girls average 100 text messages daily (*The Boston Globe*, April 21, 2010). Assume the population standard deviation is 20 text messages. Suppose a random sample of 50 high school girls is taken.
    a. What is the probability that the sample mean is more than 105?
    b. What is the probability that the sample mean is less than 95?
    c. What is the probability that the sample mean is between 95 and 105?

11. Beer bottles are filled so that they contain an average of 330 ml of beer in each bottle. Suppose that the amount of beer in a bottle is normally distributed with a standard deviation of 4 ml.
    a. What is the probability that a randomly selected bottle will have less than 325 ml of beer?
    b. What is the probability that a randomly selected 6-pack of beer will have a mean amount less than 325 ml?
    c. What is the probability that a randomly selected 12-pack of beer will have a mean amount less than 325 ml?
    d. Comment on the sample size and the corresponding probabilities.

12. Despite its nutritional value, seafood is only a tiny part of the American diet, with the average American eating just 16 pounds of seafood per year. Janice and Nina both work in the seafood industry and they decide to create their own random samples and document the average seafood diet in their sample. Let the standard deviation of the American seafood diet be 7 pounds.
    a. Janice samples 42 Americans and finds an average seafood consumption of 18 pounds. How likely is it to get an average of 18 pounds or more if she had a representative sample?
    b. Nina samples 90 Americans and finds an average seafood consumption of 17.5 pounds. How likely is it to get an average of 17.5 pounds or more if she had a representative sample?
    c. Which of the two women is likely to have used a more representative sample? Explain.

13. The weight of people in a small town in Missouri is known to be normally distributed with a mean of 180 pounds and a standard deviation of 28 pounds. On a raft that takes people across the river, a sign states, "Maximum capacity 3,200 pounds or 16 persons." What is the probability that a random sample of 16 persons will exceed the weight limit of 3,200 pounds?

14. The weight of turkeys is known to be normally distributed with a mean of 22 pounds and a standard deviation of 5 pounds.
    a. Discuss the sampling distribution of the sample mean based on a random draw of 16 turkeys.
    b. Find the probability that the mean weight of 16 randomly selected turkeys is more than 25 pounds.
    c. Find the probability that the mean weight of 16 randomly selected turkeys is between 18 and 24 pounds.

15. A small hair salon in Denver, Colorado, averages about 30 customers on weekdays with a standard deviation of 6. It is safe to assume that the underlying distribution is normal. In an attempt to increase the number of weekday customers, the manager offers a $2 discount on 5 consecutive weekdays. She reports that her strategy has worked since the sample mean of customers during this 5 weekday period jumps to 35.
    a. How unusual would it be to get a sample average of 35 or more customers if the manager had not offered the discount?
    b. Do you feel confident that the manager's discount strategy has worked? Explain.

16. Last year, the typical college student graduated with $27,200 in debt (*The Boston Globe,* May 27, 2012). Let debt among recent college graduates be normally distributed with a standard deviation of $7,000.
    a. What is the probability that the average debt of four recent college graduates is more than $25,000?
    b. What is the probability that the average debt of four recent college graduates is more than $30,000?

17. Forty families gathered for a fund-raising event. Suppose the individual contribution for each family is normally distributed with a mean and a standard deviation of $115 and $35, respectively. The organizers would call this event a success if the total contributions exceed $5,000. What is the probability that this fund-raising event is a success?

18. A doctor is getting sued for malpractice by four of her former patients. It is believed that the amount that each patient will sue her for is normally distributed with a mean of $800,000 and a standard deviation of $250,000.
    a. What is the probability that a given patient sues the doctor for more than $1,000,000?
    b. If the four patients sue the doctor independently, what is the probability that the total amount they sue for is over $4,000,000?

19. Suppose that the miles-per-gallon (mpg) rating of passenger cars is a normally distributed random variable with a mean and a standard deviation of 33.8 and 3.5 mpg, respectively.
    a. What is the probability that a randomly selected passenger car gets more than 35 mpg?
    b. What is the probability that the average mpg of four randomly selected passenger cars is more than 35 mpg?
    c. If four passenger cars are randomly selected, what is the probability that all of the passenger cars get more than 35 mpg?

20. Suppose that IQ scores are normally distributed with a mean of 100 and a standard deviation of 16.
    a. What is the probability that a randomly selected person will have an IQ score of less than 90?
    b. What is the probability that the average IQ score of four randomly selected people is less than 90?
    c. If four people are randomly selected, what is the probability that all of them have an IQ score of less than 90?

7.3 The Sampling Distribution of the Sample Proportion

LO **7.5**

Describe the sampling distribution of the sample proportion.

Our discussion thus far has focused on the population mean, but many business, socio-economic, and political matters are concerned with the population proportion. For instance, a banker is interested in the default probability of mortgage holders; a superintendent may note the proportion of students suffering from the flu when determining whether to keep school open; an incumbent up for reelection cares about the proportion of constituents that will ultimately cast a vote for him/her. In all of these examples, the parameter of interest is the population proportion p. However, analogous to our discussion concerning the mean, we almost always make inferences about the population proportion on the basis of sample data. Here, the relevant statistic (estimator) is the sample proportion, $\overline{P}$; a particular value (estimate) is denoted by $\overline{p}$. Since $\overline{P}$ is a random variable, we need to discuss its sampling distribution.

The Expected Value and the Standard Error of the Sample Proportion

We first introduced the population proportion p in Chapter 5, when we discussed the binomial distribution. It turns out that the sampling distribution of $\overline{P}$ is closely related to the binomial distribution. Recall that the binomial distribution describes the number of successes X in n independent trials where p is the probability of success on one particular trial; thus, $\overline{P} = \frac{X}{n}$ is the total number of successes X divided by the sample size n. We can derive the **expected value** and the **variance** of the sampling distribution of $\overline{P}$ as $E(\overline{P}) = p$ and $Var(\overline{P}) = \frac{p(1-p)}{n}$, respectively. (See Appendix 7.1 at the end of the chapter for the derivations.) Note that since $E(\overline{P}) = p$, it implies that $\overline{P}$ is an unbiased estimator of p. Analogous to our discussion in the last section, we refer to the standard deviation of the sample proportion as the **standard error of the sample proportion**, that is, $se(\overline{P}) = \sqrt{\frac{p(1-p)}{n}}$.

EXPECTED VALUE AND STANDARD ERROR OF THE SAMPLE PROPORTION

The expected value of $\overline{P}$ equals $E(\overline{P}) = p$.

The standard error of $\overline{P}$ equals $se(\overline{P}) = \sqrt{\frac{p(1-p)}{n}}$.

EXAMPLE 7.5

Many people apply for jobs to serve as paramedics or firefighters, yet they cannot complete basic physical fitness standards. A recent study found that 77% of all candidates for paramedic and firefighter positions were overweight or obese (*Obesity*, March 19, 2009).

a. What are the expected value and the standard error of the sample proportion derived from a random sample of 100 candidates for paramedic or firefighter positions?

b. What are the expected value and the standard error of the sample proportion derived from a random sample of 200 candidates for paramedic or firefighter positions?

c. Comment on the value of the standard error as the sample size gets larger.

SOLUTION: Given that $p = 0.77$, we can derive the expected value and the standard error of $\overline{P}$ as follows.

a. With $n = 100$, $E(\overline{P}) = 0.77$ and $se(\overline{P}) = \sqrt{\dfrac{p(1-p)}{n}} = \sqrt{\dfrac{0.77(1-0.77)}{100}} = 0.042$.

b. With $n = 200$, $E(\overline{P}) = 0.77$ and $se(\overline{P}) = \sqrt{\dfrac{p(1-p)}{n}} = \sqrt{\dfrac{0.77(1-0.77)}{200}} = 0.030$.

c. As in the case of the sample mean, while the expected value of the sample proportion is unaffected by the sample size, the standard error of the sample proportion is reduced as the sample size increases.

In this text, we make statistical inferences about the population proportion only when the sampling distribution of $\overline{P}$ is approximately normal. From the CLT stated in Section 7.2, we can conclude that $\overline{P}$ is approximately normally distributed when the sample size is sufficiently large.

THE CENTRAL LIMIT THEOREM FOR THE SAMPLE PROPORTION

For any population proportion p, the sampling distribution of $\overline{P}$ is **approximately normal if the sample size n is sufficiently large**. As a general guideline, the normal distribution approximation is justified when $np \geq 5$ and $n(1 - p) \geq 5$.

If $\overline{P}$ is normal, we can transform it into the **standard normal random variable** as

$$Z = \frac{\overline{P} - E(\overline{P})}{se(\overline{P})} = \frac{\overline{P} - p}{\sqrt{\dfrac{p(1-p)}{n}}}.$$

Therefore, any value $\bar{p}$ on $\overline{P}$ has a corresponding value z on Z given by

$$z = \frac{\bar{p} - p}{\sqrt{\dfrac{p(1-p)}{n}}}.$$

According to the CLT, the sampling distribution of $\overline{P}$ approaches the normal distribution as the sample size increases. However, as the population proportion deviates from $p = 0.50$, we need a larger sample size for the approximation. We illustrate these results by generating the sampling distribution of $\overline{P}$ from repeated draws from a population with various values of the population proportion and sample sizes. As in the case of $\overline{X}$, we use the relative frequency polygon to represent the distribution of $\overline{P}$. The simulated sampling distribution of $\overline{P}$ is based on the population proportion $p = 0.10$ (Figure 7.6) and $p = 0.30$ (Figure 7.7).

FIGURE 7.6 Sampling distribution of $\overline{P}$ when the population proportion is $p = 0.10$

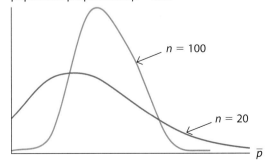

$n = 100$

$n = 20$

$\bar{p}$

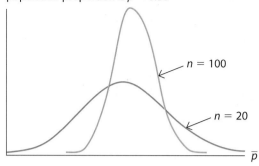

FIGURE 7.7 Sampling distribution of $\bar{P}$ when the population proportion is $p = 0.30$

When $p = 0.10$, the sampling distribution of $\bar{P}$ does not resemble the shape of the normal distribution with $n = 20$ since the approximation condition $np \geq 5$ and $n(1 - p) \geq 5$ is not satisfied. However, the curve becomes close to normal with $n = 100$. When $p = 0.30$, the shape of the sampling distribution of $\bar{P}$ is approximately normal since the approximation condition is satisfied with both sample sizes. In empirical work, it is common to work with large survey data, and as a result, the normal distribution approximation is justified.

EXAMPLE 7.6

Consider the information presented in the introductory case of this chapter. Recall that Anne Jones wants to determine if the marketing campaign has had a lingering effect on the proportion of customers who are women and teenage girls. Prior to the campaign, 43% of the customers were women and 21% were teenage girls. Based on a random sample of 50 customers after the campaign, these proportions increase to 46% for women and 34% for teenage girls. Anne has the following questions.

a. If Starbucks chose not to pursue the marketing campaign, how likely is it that 46% or more of iced-coffee customers are women?

b. If Starbucks chose not to pursue the marketing campaign, how likely is it that 34% or more of iced-coffee customers are teenage girls?

SOLUTION: If Starbucks had not pursued the marketing campaign, the proportion of customers would still be $p = 0.43$ for women and $p = 0.21$ for teenage girls. With $n = 50$, the normal approximation of the sample proportion is justified for both population proportions.

a. As shown in Figure 7.8, we use the standard transformation to derive $P(\bar{P} \geq 0.46) = P\left(Z \geq \frac{0.46 - 0.43}{\sqrt{\frac{0.43(1 - 0.43)}{50}}}\right) = P(Z \geq 0.43) = 1 - 0.6664 = 0.3336.$

FIGURE 7.8 Finding $P(\bar{P} \geq 0.46)$

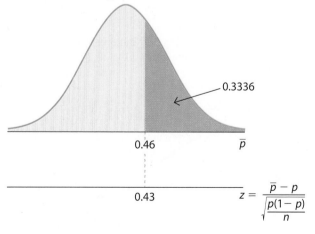

With a likelihood of 33.36%, it is quite plausible that the proportion of iced coffee purchased by women is at least 0.46 even if Starbucks did not pursue the marketing campaign.

b. Here, as shown in Figure 7.9, we find $P(\overline{P} \geq 0.34) = P\left(Z \geq \dfrac{0.34 - 0.21}{\sqrt{\frac{0.21(1 - 0.21)}{50}}}\right) = P(Z \geq 2.26) = 1 - 0.9881 = 0.0119$.

FIGURE 7.9 Finding $P(\overline{P} \geq 0.34)$

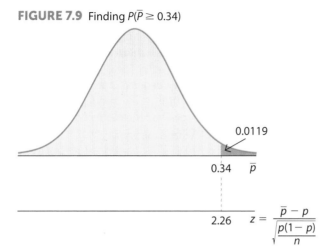

0.0119

0.34 $\overline{p}$

2.26 $z = \dfrac{\overline{p} - p}{\sqrt{\dfrac{p(1 - p)}{n}}}$

With only a 1.19% chance, it is unlikely that the proportion of iced coffee purchased by teenage girls is at least 0.34 if Starbucks did not pursue the marketing campaign.

Therefore, Anne can use this sample information to infer that the increase in the proportion of iced-coffee sales to women may not necessarily be due to the marketing campaign. However, the marketing campaign seems to have been successful in increasing the proportion of iced-coffee sales to teenage girls.

SYNOPSIS OF INTRODUCTORY CASE

Iced coffee, traditionally a warm-weather and warm-region drink, has broadened its appeal over the years. According to a May 13, 2010 report in *Bloomberg Businessweek*, the number of servings of iced coffee surged from 300 million in 2001 to 1.2 billion in 2009. Large corporations have taken notice and have engaged in various strategies to capitalize on the growing trend. Starbucks, for instance, recently promoted a happy hour where customers paid half-price for a Frappuccino beverage between 3:00 pm and 5:00 pm for a 10-day period in May. One month after the marketing period ended, Anne Jones, the manager at a local Starbucks, surveys 50 of her customers. She reports an increase in spending in the sample, as well as an
increase in the proportion of customers who are women and teenage girls. Anne wants to determine if the increase is due to chance or due to the marketing campaign. Based on an analysis with probabilities, Anne finds that higher spending in a sample of 50 customers is plausible even if Starbucks had not pursued the marketing campaign. Using a similar analysis with proportions, she infers that while the marketing campaign may not have necessarily increased the proportion of women customers, it seems to have attracted more teenage girls. The findings are consistent with current market research, which has shown that teenage girls have substantial income of their own to spend and often purchase items that are perceived as indulgences.

EXERCISES 7.3

Mechanics

21. Consider a population proportion $p = 0.68$.
    a. Calculate the expected value and the standard error of $\bar{P}$ with $n = 20$. Is it appropriate to use the normal distribution approximation for $\bar{P}$? Explain.
    b. Calculate the expected value and the standard error of $\bar{P}$ with $n = 50$. Is it appropriate to use the normal distribution approximation for $\bar{P}$? Explain.

22. Consider a population proportion $p = 0.12$.
    a. Discuss the sampling distribution of the sample proportion with $n = 20$ and $n = 50$.
    b. Can you use the normal approximation to calculate the probability that the sample proportion is between 0.10 and 0.12 for both sample sizes?
    c. Report the probabilities if you answered yes to the previous question.

23. A random sample of size $n = 200$ is taken from a population with population proportion $p = 0.75$.
    a. Calculate the expected value and the standard error for the sampling distribution of the sample proportion.
    b. What is the probability that the sample proportion is between 0.70 and 0.80?
    c. What is the probability that the sample proportion is less than 0.70?

Applications

24. A recent study by Allstate Insurance Co. finds that 82% of teenagers have used cell phones while driving (*The Wall Street Journal*, May 5, 2010). Suppose a random sample of 100 teen drivers is taken.
    a. Discuss the sampling distribution of the sample proportion.
    b. What is the probability that the sample proportion is less than 0.80?
    c. What is the probability that the sample proportion is within ±0.02 of the population proportion?

25. According to a recent FCC survey, one in six cell phone users has experienced "bill shock" from unexpectedly high cell phone bills (*Tech Daily Dose*, May 26, 2010).
    a. Discuss the sampling distribution of the sample proportion based on a sample of 200 cell phone

users. Is it appropriate to use the normal distribution approximation for the sample proportion?
    b. What is the probability that more than 20% of cell phone users in the sample have experienced "bill shock"?

26. A car manufacturer is concerned about poor customer satisfaction at one of its dealerships. The management decides to evaluate the satisfaction surveys of its next 40 customers. The dealer will be fined if the number of customers who report favorably is between 22 and 26. The dealership will be dissolved if fewer than 22 customers report favorably. It is known that 70% of the dealer's customers report favorably on satisfaction surveys.
    a. What is the probability that the dealer will be fined?
    b. What is the probability that the dealership will be dissolved?

27. Europeans are increasingly upset at their leaders for making deep budget cuts to many social programs that are becoming too expensive to sustain. For instance, the popularity of then President Nicolas Sarkozy of France plummeted in 2010, giving him an approval rating of just 26% (*The Wall Street Journal*, July 2, 2010).
    a. What is the probability that fewer than 60 of 200 French people gave President Sarkozy a favorable rating?
    b. What is the probability that more than 150 of 200 French people gave President Sarkozy an *unfavorable* rating?

28. At a new exhibit in the Museum of Science, people are asked to choose between 50 or 100 random draws from a machine. The machine is known to have 60 green balls and 40 red balls. After each draw, the color of the ball is noted and the ball is put back for the next draw. You win a prize if more than 70% of the draws result in a green ball. Would you choose 50 or 100 draws for the game? Explain.

29. After years of rapid growth, illegal immigration into the United States has declined, perhaps owing to the recession and increased border enforcement by the United States (*Los Angeles Times*, September 1, 2010). While its share has declined, California still accounts for 23% of the nation's estimated 11.1 million undocumented immigrants.
    a. In a sample of 50 illegal immigrants, what is the probability that more than 20% live in California?
    b. In a sample of 200 illegal immigrants, what is the probability that more than 20% live in California?
    c. Comment on the reason for the difference between the computed probabilities in parts a and b.

7.4 The Finite Population Correction Factor

LO **7.6**

Use a finite population correction factor.

One of the implicit assumptions we have made thus far is that the sample size n is much smaller than the population size N. In many applications, the size of the population is not even known. For instance, we do not have information on the total number of pizzas made at a local pizza chain in Cambria (Examples 7.2 and 7.3) or the total number of customers at the local Starbucks store (Examples 7.4 and 7.6). If the population size is known and is relatively small (finite), then it is preferable to use a correction factor in the standard error of the estimators, which accounts for the added precision gained by sampling a larger percentage of the population. As a general guideline, we use the finite factor correction when the sample constitutes at least 5% of the population, that is, $n \geq 0.05N$.

THE FINITE POPULATION CORRECTION FACTOR FOR THE SAMPLE MEAN

We use the **finite population correction factor** to reduce the sampling variation of $\overline{X}$. The resulting standard error is $se(\overline{X}) = \frac{\sigma}{\sqrt{n}}\left(\sqrt{\frac{N-n}{N-1}}\right)$. The transformation of $\overline{X}$ to Z is made accordingly.

Note that the correction factor is always less than one; when N is large relative to n, the correction factor is close to one and the difference between the formulas with and without the correction is negligible.

EXAMPLE 7.7

A large introductory marketing class has 340 students. The class is divided up into groups for the final course project. Connie is in a group of 34 students. These students had averaged 72 on the midterm, when the class as a whole had an average score of 73 with a standard deviation of 10.

a. Calculate the expected value and the standard error of the sample mean based on a random sample of 34 students.

b. How likely is it that a random sample of 34 students will average 72 or lower?

SOLUTION: The population mean is $\mu = 73$ and the population standard deviation is $\sigma = 10$.

a. The expected value of the sample mean is $E(\overline{X}) = \mu = 73$. We use the finite population correction factor because the sample size $n = 34$ is more than 5% of the population size $N = 340$. Therefore, the standard error of the sample mean is $se(\overline{X}) = \frac{\sigma}{\sqrt{n}}\left(\sqrt{\frac{N-n}{N-1}}\right) = \frac{10}{\sqrt{34}}\left(\sqrt{\frac{340-34}{340-1}}\right) = 1.63$.
Note that without the correction factor, the standard error would be higher at $se(\overline{X}) = \frac{\sigma}{\sqrt{n}} = \frac{10}{\sqrt{34}} = 1.71$.

b. We use the standard transformation to find $P(\overline{X} \leq 72) = P\left(Z \leq \frac{72-73}{1.63}\right) = P(Z \leq -0.61) = 0.2709$.
That is, the likelihood of 34 students averaging 72 or lower is 27.09%.

We can use a similar finite population correction factor for a sample proportion when the sample size is at least 5% of the population size.

THE FINITE POPULATION CORRECTION FACTOR FOR THE SAMPLE PROPORTION

We use the **finite population correction factor** to reduce the sampling variation of the sample proportion $\overline{P}$. The resulting standard error of $\overline{P}$ is $se(\overline{P}) = \sqrt{\frac{p(1-p)}{n}}\left(\sqrt{\frac{N-n}{N-1}}\right)$. The transformation of $\overline{P}$ to Z is made accordingly.

EXAMPLE 7.8

The home ownership rate during 2009 declined to approximately 67% and is now comparable to the rate in early 2000 (*U.S. Census Bureau News*, February 2, 2010). A random sample of 80 households is taken from a small island community with 1,000 households. The home ownership rate on the island is equivalent to the national home ownership rate of 67%.

a. Calculate the expected value and the standard error for the sampling distribution of the sample proportion. Is it necessary to apply the finite population correction factor? Explain.

b. What is the probability that the sample proportion is within 0.02 of the population proportion?

SOLUTION:

a. We must apply the finite population correction factor because the sample size $n = 80$ is at least 5% of the population size $N = 1000$. Therefore, $E(\overline{P}) = p = 0.67$ and

$$se(\overline{P}) = \sqrt{\frac{p(1-p)}{n}}\left(\sqrt{\frac{N-n}{N-1}}\right) = \sqrt{\frac{0.67(1-0.67)}{80}}\left(\sqrt{\frac{1,000-80}{1,000-1}}\right) = 0.0505.$$

b. The probability that the sample proportion is within 0.02 of the population proportion is $P(0.65 \leq \overline{P} \leq 0.69)$. Applying the standard transformation, we find that $P(0.65 \leq \overline{P} \leq 0.69) = P\left(\frac{0.65 - 0.67}{0.0505} \leq Z \leq \frac{0.69 - 0.67}{0.0505}\right) = P(-0.40 \leq Z \leq 0.40) = 0.6554 - 0.3446 = 0.3108$. The likelihood that the home ownership rate is within 0.02 of the population proportion is 31.08%.

EXERCISES 7.4

Mechanics

30. A random sample of size $n = 100$ is taken from a population of size $N = 2,500$ with mean $\mu = -45$ and variance $\sigma^2 = 81$.

    a. Is it necessary to apply the finite population correction factor? Explain. Calculate the expected value and the standard error of the sample mean.

    b. What is the probability that the sample mean is between -47 and -43?

    c. What is the probability that the sample mean is greater than -44?

31. A random sample of size $n = 70$ is taken from a finite population of size $N = 500$ with mean $\mu = 220$ and variance $\sigma^2 = 324$.

    a. Is it necessary to apply the finite population correction factor? Explain. Calculate the expected value and the standard error of the sample mean.

    b. What is the probability that the sample mean is less than 210?

    c. What is the probability that the sample mean lies between 215 and 230?

32. A random sample of size $n = 100$ is taken from a population of size $N = 3,000$ with a population proportion of $p = 0.34$.

    a. Is it necessary to apply the finite population correction factor? Explain. Calculate the expected value and the standard error of the sample proportion.

    b. What is the probability that the sample proportion is greater than 0.37?

33. A random sample of size $n = 80$ is taken from a population of size $N = 600$ with a population proportion $p = 0.46$.

    a. Is it necessary to apply the finite population correction factor? Explain. Calculate the expected value and the standard error of the sample proportion.

    b. What is the probability that the sample mean is less than 0.40?

Applications

34. The issues surrounding the levels and structure of executive compensation have gained added prominence in the wake of the financial crisis that erupted in the fall of 2008. Based on the 2006 compensation data obtained from the Securities and Exchange Commission (SEC) website, it was determined that the mean and the standard deviation of compensation for the 500 highest paid CEOs in publicly traded U.S. companies are $10.32 million and $9.78 million, respectively. An analyst randomly chooses 32 CEO compensations for 2006.

    a. Is it necessary to apply the finite population correction factor? Explain.

b. Is the sampling distribution of the sample mean approximately normally distributed? Explain.

c. Calculate the expected value and the standard error of the sample mean.

d. What is the probability that the sample mean is more than $12 million?

35. Suppose in the previous question that the analyst had randomly chosen 12 CEO compensations for 2006.

a. Is it necessary to apply the finite population correction factor? Explain.

b. Is the sampling distribution of the sample mean approximately normally distributed? Explain.

c. Calculate the expected value and the standard error of the sample mean.

d. Can you use the normal approximation to calculate the probability that the sample mean is more than $12 million? Explain.

36. Given the recent economic downturn, only 60% in a graduating class of 250 will find employment in the first round of a job search. You have 20 friends who have recently graduated.

a. Discuss the sampling distribution of the sample proportion of your friends who will find employment in the first round of a job search.

b. What is the probability that less than 50% of your friends will find employment in the first round of a job search?

37. A recent study finds that companies are setting aside a large chunk of their IT spending for green technology projects (*BusinessWeek,* March 5, 2009). Two out of three of the large companies surveyed by Deloitte said they have at least 5% of their IT budget earmarked for green IT projects. Suppose that the survey was based on 1,000 large companies. What is the probability that more than 75 of 120 large companies will have at least 5% of their IT expenditure earmarked for green IT projects?

7.5 Statistical Quality Control

Now more than ever, a successful firm must focus on the quality of the products and services it offers. Global competition, technological advances, and consumer expectations are all factors contributing to the quest for quality. In order to ensure the production of high-quality goods and services, a successful firm implements some form of quality control. In this section we give a brief overview of the field of **statistical quality control**.

LO **7.7**

Construct and interpret control charts for quantitative and qualitative data.

> **Statistical quality control** involves statistical techniques used to develop and maintain a firm's ability to produce high-quality goods and services.

In general, two approaches are used for statistical quality control. A firm uses **acceptance sampling** if it produces a product (or offers a service) and at the completion of the production process, the firm then inspects a portion of the products. If a particular product does not conform to certain specifications, then it is either discarded or repaired. The problems with this approach to quality control are, first, it is costly to discard or repair a product. Second, the detection of all defective products is not guaranteed. Defective products may be delivered to customers, thus damaging the firm's reputation.

A preferred approach to quality control is the **detection approach**. A firm using the detection approach inspects the production process and determines at which point the production process does not conform to specifications. The goal is to determine whether the production process should be continued or adjusted before a large number of defects are produced. In this section we focus on the detection approach to quality control.

In general, no two products or services are identical. In any production process, variation in the quality of the end product is inevitable. Two types of variation occur. **Chance variation** is caused by a number of randomly occurring events that are part of the production process. This type of variation is not generally considered under the control of the individual worker or machine. For example, suppose a machine fills one-gallon jugs of milk. It is unlikely that the filling weight of each jug is exactly 128 ounces. Very slight differences in the production process lead to minor differences in the weights of one jug to the next. Chance variation is expected and is not a source of alarm in the production process so long as its magnitude is tolerable and the end product meets acceptable specifications.

The other source of variation is referred to as **assignable variation**. This type of variation in the production process is caused by specific events or factors that can usually be identified and eliminated. Suppose in the milk example that the machine is "drifting" out of alignment. This causes the machine to overfill each jug—a costly expense for the firm. Similarly, it is bad for the firm in terms of its reputation, if the machine begins to underfill each jug. The firm wants to identify and correct these types of variations in the production process.

Control Charts

Walter A. Shewhart, a researcher at Bell Telephone Laboratories during the 1920s, is often credited as being the first to apply statistics to improve the quality of output. He developed the **control chart**—a tool used to monitor the behavior of a production process.

THE CONTROL CHART

The most commonly used statistical tool in quality control is the **control chart**, a plot of calculated statistics of the production process over time. If the calculated statistics fall in an expected range, then the production process is in control. If the calculated statistics reveal an undesirable trend, then adjustment of the production process is likely necessary.

We can construct a number of different control charts where each differs by either the variable of interest and/or the type of data that are available. For quantitative data, examples of control charts include

- The $\bar{x}$ **chart**, which monitors the *central tendency* of a production process, and
- The R **chart** and the s **chart**, which monitor the *variability* of a production process.

For qualitative data, examples of control charts include

- The $\bar{p}$ **chart**, which monitors the *proportion* of defectives (or some other characteristic) in a production process,
- The c **chart**, which monitors the *count* of defects per item, such as the number of blemishes on a sampled piece of furniture.

In general, all of these control charts (and others that we have not mentioned) have the following characteristics:

1. A control chart plots the sample estimates, such as $\bar{x}$ or $\bar{p}$. So as more and more samples are taken, the resulting control chart provides one type of safeguard when assessing if the production process is operating within predetermined guidelines.

2. All sample estimates are plotted with reference to a **centerline**. The centerline represents the variable's expected value when the production process is in control.

3. In addition to the centerline, all control charts include an **upper control limit** and a **lower control limit**. These limits indicate excessive deviation above (upper control limit) or below (lower control limit) the expected value of the variable of interest. A control chart is valid only if the sampling distribution of the relevant estimator is (approximately) normal. Under this assumption, the control limits are generally set at three standard deviations from the centerline. As we observed in Chapter 6, the area under the normal curve that corresponds to ± 3 standard deviations from the expected value is 0.9973. Thus, there is only

a $1 - 0.9973 = 0.0027$ chance that the sample estimates will fall outside the limit boundaries. In general, we define the upper and lower control limits as follows:

Upper Control Limit (UCL): Expected Value + (3 × Standard Error)

Lower Control Limit (LCL): Expected Value − (3 × Standard Error)

If the sample estimates fall randomly within the upper and lower control limits, then the production process is deemed in control. Any sample estimate that falls above the upper control limit or below the lower control limit is considered evidence that the production process is out of control and should be adjusted. In addition, any type of patterns within the control limits may suggest possible problems with the process. One indication of a process that is potentially heading out of control is unusually long runs above or below the centerline. Another possible problem is any evidence of a trend within the control limits.

In the next example we focus on quantitative data and illustrate the $\bar{x}$ chart. We then turn to qualitative data and construct the $\bar{p}$ chart.

EXAMPLE 7.9

A firm that produces one-gallon jugs of milk wants to ensure that the machine is operating properly. Every two hours, the company samples 25 jugs and calculates the following sample mean filling weights (in ounces):

128.7	128.4	128.0	127.8	127.5	126.9

Assume that when the machine is operating properly, $\mu = 128$ and $\sigma = 2$, and that filling weights follow the normal distribution. Can the firm conclude that the machine is operating properly? Should the firm have any concerns with respect to this machine?

SOLUTION: Here the firm is interested in monitoring the population mean. To answer these questions, we construct an $\bar{x}$ chart. As mentioned earlier, this chart relies on the normal distribution for the sampling distribution of the estimator $\bar{X}$. Recall that if we are sampling from a normal population, then $\bar{X}$ is normally distributed even for small sample sizes. In this example, we are told that filling weights follow the normal distribution, a common assumption in the literature on quality control.

For the $\bar{x}$ chart, the centerline is the mean when the process is in control. Here, we are given that $\mu = 128$. We then calculate the upper and lower control limits as plus and minus three standard deviations from the mean:

Upper Control Limit, UCL: $\quad \mu + 3\dfrac{\sigma}{\sqrt{n}} = 128 + 3\dfrac{2}{\sqrt{25}} = 129.2$

Lower Control Limit, LCL: $\mu - 3\dfrac{\sigma}{\sqrt{n}} = 128 - 3\dfrac{2}{\sqrt{25}} = 126.8$

Figure 7.10 shows the centerline and the control limits as well as the sample means for Example 7.9.

All of the sample means fall within the upper control and the lower control limits, which indicates, at least initially, that the production process is in control. However, the sample means should be randomly spread between these limits; there should be no pattern. In this example, there is clearly a downward trend in the sample means. It appears as though the machine is beginning to underfill the one-gallon jugs. So even though none of the sample means lies beyond the control limits, the production process is likely veering out of control and the firm would be wise to inspect the machine sooner rather than later.

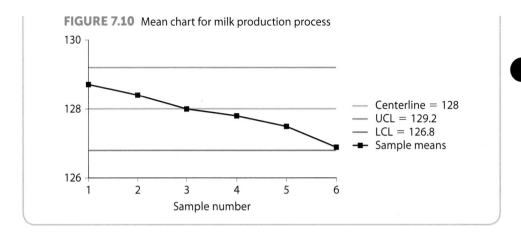

FIGURE 7.10 Mean chart for milk production process

Centerline = 128
UCL = 129.2
LCL = 126.8
Sample means

A firm may be interested in the stability of the proportion of its goods or services possessing a certain attribute or characteristic. For example, most firms strive to produce high-quality goods (or services) and thus hope to keep the proportion of defects at a minimum. When a production process is to be assessed based on sample proportions—here, the proportion of defects—then a $\bar{p}$ chart proves quite useful. Since the primary purpose of the $\bar{p}$ chart is to track the proportion of defects in a production process, it is also referred to as a fraction defective chart or a percent defective chart. Consider the next example.

EXAMPLE 7.10

A production process has a 5% defective rate. A quality inspector takes 6 samples of $n = 500$. The following sample proportions are obtained:

| 0.065 | 0.075 | 0.082 | 0.086 | 0.090 | 0.092 |

a. Construct a $\bar{p}$ chart. Plot the sample proportions on the $\bar{p}$ chart.
b. Is the production process in control? Explain.

SOLUTION:

a. The $\bar{p}$ chart relies on the central limit theorem for the normal approximation for the sampling distribution of the sample proportion $\bar{P}$. Recall that so long as np and $n(1 - p)$ are greater than or equal to five, then the sampling distribution of $\bar{P}$ is approximately normally distributed. This condition is satisfied in Example 7.10. Since the expected proportion of defects is equal to 0.05, we set the centerline at $p = 0.05$. We then calculate the upper control limit and lower control limit as follows:

$$\text{UCL: } p + 3\sqrt{\frac{p(1 - p)}{n}} = 0.05 + 3\sqrt{\frac{0.05(1 - 0.05)}{500}} = 0.079$$

$$\text{LCL: } p - 3\sqrt{\frac{p(1 - p)}{n}} = 0.05 - 3\sqrt{\frac{0.05(1 - 0.05)}{500}} = 0.021$$

We note that if UCL is a value greater than one, then we reset UCL to one in the control chart. Similarly, if the LCL is a negative value, we reset LCL to zero in the control chart.

Plotting the values for the centerline, UCL, and LCL, as well as the sample proportions, yields Figure 7.11.

b. Four of the most recent sample proportions fall above the upper control limit. This provides evidence that the process is out of control and needs adjustment.

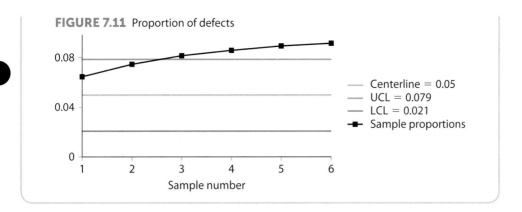

FIGURE 7.11 Proportion of defects

— Centerline = 0.05
— UCL = 0.079
— LCL = 0.021
-■- Sample proportions

Using Excel to Create a Control Chart

Even though Excel does not have a built-in function to create a control chart, it is still relatively easy to construct one. The added step when using Excel is that if we are not given values for the centerline, UCL, LCL, and the sample means, then we have to calculate these values first—other software packages do these calculations for us. We will replicate Figure 7.10 using the values that we have calculated (or were given) in Example 7.9.

- Enter Headings for the Centerline, UCL, LCL, and Sample Mean as shown in the first row of the Excel spreadsheet in Figure 7.12.
- Enter the relevant values under each of the headings. For columns with many repeated values (Centerline, UCL, and LCL), it is useful to select the respective value, drag it down a certain number of cells, and then from the menu choose **Home > Fill > Down**. For instance, for the Centerline value of 128, select 128, drag the cursor down five more cells (since we want it repeated six times), and choose **Home > Fill > Down**.
- After all the data have been entered into the spreadsheet, select all the data with the headings and choose **Insert > Line > 2-D Line** (choose the option on the top left). Figure 7.12 shows the embedded control chart.
- Formatting regarding colors, axes, grids, etc. can be done by selecting **Layout** from the menu.

In order to construct a $\bar{p}$ chart using Excel, you would follow the same steps as those outlined above for the $\bar{x}$ chart.

FIGURE 7.12 Using Excel to create a control chart

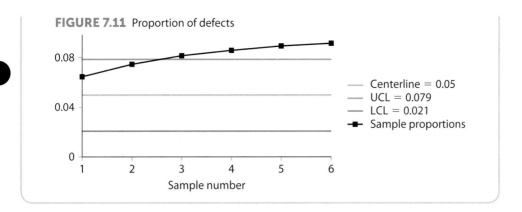

EXERCISES 7.5

Mechanics

38. Consider a normally distributed population with mean $\mu = 80$ and standard deviation $\sigma = 14$.
    a. Construct the centerline and the upper and lower control limits for the $\bar{x}$ chart if samples of size 5 are used.
    b. Repeat the analysis with samples of size 10.
    c. Discuss the effect of the sample size on the control limits.

39. Random samples of size $n = 25$ are taken from a normally distributed population with mean $\mu = 20$ and standard deviation $\sigma = 10$.
    a. Construct the centerline and the upper and lower control limits for the $\bar{x}$ chart.
    b. Suppose six samples of size 25 produced the following sample means: 18, 16, 19, 24, 28, and 30. Plot these values on the $\bar{x}$ chart.
    c. Are any points outside the control limits? Does it appear that the process is under control? Explain.

40. Random samples of size $n = 36$ are taken from a population with mean $\mu = 150$ and standard deviation $\sigma = 42$.
    a. Construct the centerline and the upper and lower control limits for the $\bar{x}$ chart.
    b. Suppose five samples of size 36 produced the following sample means: 133, 142, 150, 165, and 169. Plot these values on the $\bar{x}$ chart.
    c. Are any points outside the control limits? Does it appear that the process is under control? Explain.

41. Random samples of size $n = 250$ are taken from a population with $p = 0.04$.
    a. Construct the centerline and the upper and lower control limits for the $\bar{p}$ chart.
    b. Repeat the analysis with $n = 150$.
    c. Discuss the effect of the sample size on the control limits.

42. Random samples of size $n = 400$ are taken from a population with $p = 0.10$.
    a. Construct the centerline and the upper and lower control limits for the $\bar{p}$ chart.
    b. Suppose six samples of size 400 produced the following sample proportions: 0.06, 0.11, 0.09, 0.08, 0.14, and 0.16. Plot these values on the $\bar{p}$ chart.
    c. Is the production process under control? Explain.

43. Random samples of size $n = 500$ are taken from a population with $p = 0.34$.
    a. Construct the centerline and the upper and lower control limits for the $\bar{p}$ chart.
    b. Suppose six samples of size 500 produced the following sample proportions: 0.28, 0.30, 0.33, 0.34, 0.37, and 0.39. Plot these values on the $\bar{p}$ chart.
    c. Are any points outside the control limits? Does it appear that the process is under control? Explain.

Applications

44. A production process is designed to fill boxes with an average of 14 ounces of cereal. The population of filling weights is normally distributed with a standard deviation of 2 ounces. Inspectors take periodic samples of 10 boxes. The following sample means are obtained.

13.7	14.2	13.9	14.1	14.3	13.9

    a. Construct an $\bar{x}$ chart. Plot the sample means on the $\bar{x}$ chart.
    b. Can the firm conclude that the production process is operating properly? Explain.

45. Major League Baseball Rule 1.09 states that "the baseball shall weigh not less than 5 or more than 5¼ ounces" (http://www.mlb.com). Use these values as the lower and the upper control limits, respectively. Assume the centerline equals 5.125 ounces. Periodic samples of 50 baseballs produce the following sample means:

5.05	5.10	5.15	5.20	5.22	5.24

    a. Construct an $\bar{x}$ chart. Plot the sample means on the $\bar{x}$ chart.
    b. Are any points outside the control limits? Does it appear that the process is under control? Explain.

46. FILE Fast bowling, also known as pace bowling, is an important component of the bowling attack in the sport of cricket. The objective is to bowl at a high speed and make the ball turn in the air and off the ground so that it becomes difficult for the batsman to hit it cleanly. Kalwant Singh is a budding Indian cricketer in a special bowling camp. While his coach is happy with Kalwant's average bowling speed, he feels that Kalwant lacks consistency. He records his bowling speed on the next four overs, where each over consists of six balls; the data, labeled **Cricket**, are also available on the text website.

Over 1	Over 2	Over 3	Over 4
96.8	99.2	88.4	98.4
99.5	100.2	97.8	91.4
88.8	90.1	82.8	85.5
81.9	98.7	91.2	87.6
100.1	96.4	94.2	90.3
96.8	98.8	89.8	85.9

    It is fair to assume that Kalwant's bowling speed is normally distributed with a mean and a standard deviation of 94 miles and 2.8 miles per hour, respectively.
    a. Construct the centerline and the upper and lower control limits for the $\bar{x}$ chart. Plot the average speed of Kalwant's four overs on the $\bar{x}$ chart.

b. Is there any pattern in Kalwant's bowling that justifies his coach's concerns that he is not consistent in bowling? Explain.

47. A firm produces computer chips for personal computers. From past experience, the firm knows that 4% of the chips are defective. The firm collects a sample of the first 500 chips manufactured at 1:00 pm for the past two weeks. The following sample proportions are obtained:

0.044	0.052	0.060	0.036	0.028	0.042	0.034	0.054	0.048	0.025

a. Construct a $\bar{p}$ chart. Plot the sample proportions on the $\bar{p}$ chart.
b. Can the firm conclude that the process is operating properly?

48. A manufacturing process produces steel rods in batches of 1,000. The firm believes that the percent of defective items generated by this process is 5%.
a. Construct the centerline and the upper and lower control limits for the $\bar{p}$ chart.
b. An engineer inspects the next batch of 1,000 steel rods and finds that 6.2% are defective. Is the manufacturing process under control? Explain.

49. The college admissions office at a local university usually admits 750 students and knows from previous experience that 25% of these students choose not to enroll at the university.

a. Construct the centerline and the upper and lower control limits for the $\bar{p}$ chart.
b. Assume that this year the university admits 750 students and 240 choose not to enroll at the university. Should the university be concerned? Explain.

50. Following customer complaints about the quality of service, Dell stopped routing corporate customers to a technical support call center in Bangalore, India (*USA TODAY*, November 24, 2003). Suppose Dell's decision to direct customers to call centers outside of India was based on consumer complaints in the last six months. Let the number of complaints per month for 80 randomly selected customers be given below.

Month	Number of Complaints
1	20
2	12
3	24
4	14
5	25
6	22

a. Construct the centerline and the upper and lower control limits for the $\bar{p}$ chart if management allows a 15% complaint rate.
b. Can you justify Dell's decision to direct customers to call centers outside of India?

WRITING WITH STATISTICS

Barbara Dwyer, the manager at Lux Hotel, makes every effort to ensure that customers attempting to make phone reservations wait an average of only 60 seconds to speak with a reservations specialist. She knows that this is likely to be the customer's first impression of the hotel and she wants the initial interaction to be a positive one. Since the hotel accepts phone reservations 24 hours a day, Barbara wonders if this quality service is consistently maintained throughout the day. She takes six samples of $n = 4$ calls during each of four shifts over one 24-hour period and records the wait time of each call. A portion of the data, in seconds, is presented in Table 7.1; the complete data, labeled **Lux_Hotel**, are available on the text website.

Barbara assumes that wait times are normally distributed with a mean and standard deviation of 60 seconds and 30 seconds, respectively. She wants to use the sample information to:

1. Prepare a control chart for wait times.
2. Use the control chart to determine whether quality service is consistently maintained throughout the day.

TABLE 7.1 Wait times for phone reservations

Shift	Sample	Wait Time (in seconds)				Sample Mean, $\bar{x}$
Shift 1:	1	67	48	52	71	60
12:00 am–6:00 am	2	57	68	60	66	63
	3	37	41	60	41	45
	4	83	59	49	66	64
	5	82	63	64	83	73
	6	87	53	66	69	69
⋮	⋮	⋮	⋮	⋮	⋮	⋮
Shift 4:	19	6	11	8	9	9
6:00 pm–12:00 am	20	10	8	10	9	9
	21	11	7	14	7	10
	22	8	9	9	12	10
	23	9	12	9	14	11
	24	5	8	15	11	10

Sample Report— Customer Wait Time

When a potential customer phones Lux Hotel, it is imperative for the reservations special-ist to set a tone that relays the high standard of service that the customer will receive if he/she chooses to stay at the Lux. For this reason, management at the Lux strives to minimize the time that elapses before a potential customer speaks with a reservations specialist; however, management also recognizes the need to use its resources wisely. If too many reservations specialists are on duty, then resources are wasted due to idle time; yet if too few reservations specialists are on duty, the result might mean angry first-time customers or, worse, lost customers. In order to ensure customer satisfaction as well as an efficient use of resources, a study is conducted to determine whether a typical customer waits an aver-age of 60 seconds to speak with a reservations specialist. Before data are collected, a con-trol chart is constructed. The upper control limit (UCL) and the lower control limit (LCL) are set three standard deviations from the desired average of 60 seconds. In Figure 7.A, the desired average of 60 seconds is denoted as the centerline and the upper and lower control limits amount to 105 seconds and 15 seconds $\left(\mu \pm 3\frac{\sigma}{\sqrt{n}} = 60 \pm 3\frac{30}{\sqrt{4}} = 60 \pm 45 \right)$, respectively. The reservation process is deemed under control if the sample means fall randomly within the upper and lower control limits; otherwise the process is out of con-trol and adjustments should be made.

FIGURE 7.A Sample mean wait times

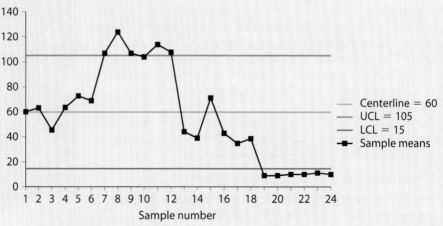

During each of four shifts, six samples of $n = 4$ calls are randomly selected over one 24-hour period and the average wait time of each sample is recorded. All six sample means from the first shift (1st shift: 12:00 am–6:00 am, sample numbers one through six) fall within the control limits, indicating that the reservation process is in control. However, five sample means from the second shift (2nd shift: 6:00 am–12:00 pm, sample numbers seven through 12) lie above the upper control limit. Customers calling during the second shift are waiting too long before they speak with a specialist. In terms of quality standards, this is unacceptable from the hotel's perspective. All six sample means from the third shift fall within the control limits (3rd shift: 12:00 pm–6:00 pm, sample numbers 13 through 18), yet all sample means for the fourth shift fall below the lower control limit (4th shift: 6:00 pm–12:00 am, sample numbers 19 through 24). Customers are waiting for very short periods of time to speak with a reservations specialist, but reservations specialists may have too much idle time. Perhaps one solution is to shift some reservations specialists from shift four to shift two.

Conceptual Review

LO 7.1 Explain common sample biases.

A sampling **bias** occurs when the information from a sample is not typical of that in the population in a systematic way. It is often caused by samples that are not representative of the population. **Selection bias** refers to a systematic underrepresentation of certain groups from consideration for the sample. **Nonresponse bias** refers to a systematic difference in preferences between respondents and nonrespondents to a survey or a poll.

LO 7.2 Describe various sampling methods.

A **simple random sample** is a sample of n observations that has the same probability of being selected from the population as any other sample of n observations. Most statistical methods presume simple random samples.

A **stratified random sample** is formed when the population is divided into groups (strata) based on one or more classification criteria. A stratified random sample includes randomly selected observations from each stratum. The number of observations per stratum is proportional to the stratum's size in the population. The data for each stratum are eventually pooled. A **cluster sample** is formed when the population is divided into groups (clusters) based on geographic areas. Whereas a stratified random sample consists of elements from each group, a cluster sample includes observations from randomly selected clusters. Stratified random sampling is preferred when the objective is to **increase precision** and cluster sampling is preferred when the objective is to **reduce costs**.

LO 7.3 Describe the sampling distribution of the sample mean.

A particular characteristic of a population, such as the mean or the proportion, is called a **parameter**, which is a constant even though its value may be unknown. A **statistic**, such as the sample mean or the sample proportion, is a **random variable** whose value depends on the chosen random sample. When a statistic is used to estimate a parameter, it is referred to as an **estimator**. A particular value of the estimator is called an **estimate**.

Since the statistic $\bar{X}$ is a random variable, its sampling distribution is the probability distribution of sample means derived from all possible samples of a given size from the population. The **expected value** of the sample mean $\bar{X}$ equals $E(\bar{X}) = \mu$ and the standard deviation, commonly referred to as the **standard error**, equals $se(\bar{X}) = \frac{\sigma}{\sqrt{n}}$. For any sample size, the sampling distribution of $\bar{X}$ is normal if the **population is normally distributed**.

A normally distributed $\overline{X}$ can be transformed into a **standard normal random variable** as $Z = \frac{\overline{X} - \mu}{\sigma/\sqrt{n}}$. Therefore, any value $\overline{x}$ on $\overline{X}$ has a corresponding value z on Z given by $z = \frac{\overline{x} - \mu}{\sigma/\sqrt{n}}$.

LO 7.4 **Explain the importance of the central limit theorem.**

The **central limit theorem** (**CLT**) is used when the random sample is drawn from a nonnormal population. It states that for any population X with expected value μ and standard deviation σ, the sampling distribution of $\overline{X}$ is approximately normal if the sample size n **is sufficiently large**. As a general guideline, the normal distribution approximation is justified when $n \geq 30$.

LO 7.5 **Describe the sampling distribution of the sample proportion.**

The **expected value** and the **standard error** of the sample proportion $\overline{P}$ are $E(\overline{P}) = p$ and $se(\overline{P}) = \sqrt{\frac{p(1-p)}{n}}$. From the CLT, we can conclude that for any population proportion p, the sampling distribution of $\overline{P}$ is approximately normal if the sample size n **is sufficiently large**. As a general guideline, the normal distribution approximation is justified when $np \geq 5$ and $n(1 - p) \geq 5$. If we assume $\overline{P}$ to be normal, it can be transformed into a standard normal random variable as $Z = \frac{\overline{P} - p}{\sqrt{\frac{p(1-p)}{n}}}$. Therefore, any value $\overline{p}$ on $\overline{P}$ has a corresponding value z on Z given by $z = \frac{\overline{p} - p}{\sqrt{\frac{p(1-p)}{n}}}$.

LO 7.6 **Use a finite population correction factor.**

If the population size is relatively small (finite) and its value is known, then it is preferable to use the correction factor in the standard error of the estimators. As a general guideline, we use the finite correction factor when the sample constitutes at least 5% of the population, that is, $n \geq 0.05N$. With the correction factor, $se(\overline{X}) = \frac{\sigma}{\sqrt{n}}\left(\sqrt{\frac{N-n}{N-1}}\right)$ and $se(\overline{P}) = \sqrt{\frac{p(1-p)}{n}}\left(\sqrt{\frac{N-n}{N-1}}\right)$. The transformation to Z is made accordingly.

LO 7.7 **Construct and interpret control charts for quantitative and qualitative data.**

Statistical quality control involves statistical techniques used to develop and maintain a firm's ability to produce high-quality goods and services. The most commonly used statistical tool in quality control is the **control chart**. A control chart specifies a centerline as well as an upper control limit (UCL) and a lower control limit (LCL). In general, the UCL and the LCL are set within three standard deviations of the centerline.

The upper and lower control limits for the $\overline{x}$ **chart** are defined as $\mu + 3\frac{\sigma}{\sqrt{n}}$ and $\mu - 3\frac{\sigma}{\sqrt{n}}$, respectively. For the $\overline{p}$ **chart**, these limits are defined as $p + 3\sqrt{\frac{p(1-p)}{n}}$ and $p - 3\sqrt{\frac{p(1-p)}{n}}$, respectively. In general, if the sample means or the sample proportions fall within the control limits, then the process is under control; otherwise it is out of control and adjustment is necessary. However, even if these sample estimates fall within the control limits, they must be randomly spread between the limits. If there is a trend or unusually long runs above or below the centerline, then the process may be veering out of control.

Additional Exercises and Case Studies

51. A seminal study conducted by scientists at the University of Illinois found evidence of improved memory and reasoning for those who took three vigorous 40-minute walks a week over six months (*Newsweek*, June 28–July 5, 2010). As an assistant manager working for a public health institute based in Florida, you would like to estimate the proportion of adults in Miami, Florida, who follow such a walking regimen. Discuss the sampling bias

in the following strategies where people are asked if they walk regularly:

a. Randomly selected adult beachgoers in Miami.

b. Randomly selected Miami residents who are requested to disclose the information in prepaid envelopes.

c. Randomly selected Miami residents who are requested to disclose the information on the firm's website.

d. Randomly selected adult patients at all hospitals in Miami.

52. In the previous question regarding walking regimens of the residents of Miami, explain how you can obtain a representative sample based on the following sampling strategies:

a. Simple random sampling.

b. Stratified random sampling.

c. Cluster sampling.

53. According to the Bureau of Labor Statistics it takes an average of 22 weeks for someone over 55 to find a new job, compared with 16 weeks for younger workers (*The Wall Street Journal*, September 2, 2008). Assume that the probability distributions are normal and that the standard deviation is 2 weeks for both distributions.

a. What is the probability that 8 workers over the age of 55 take an average of more than 20 weeks to find a job?

b. What is the probability that 20 younger workers average less than 15 weeks to find a job?

54. While starting salaries have fallen for college graduates in many of the top hiring fields, there is some good news for business undergraduates with concentrations in accounting and finance (*Bloomberg Businessweek,* July 1, 2010). According to the National Association of Colleges and Employers' Summer 2010 Salary Survey, accounting graduates commanded the second highest salary at $50,402, followed by finance graduates at $49,703. Let the standard deviation for accounting and finance graduates be $6,000 and $10,000, respectively.

a. What is the probability that 100 randomly selected accounting graduates will average more than $52,000 in salary?

b. What is the probability that 100 randomly selected finance graduates will average more than $52,000 in salary?

c. Comment on the above probabilities.

55. An automatic machine in a manufacturing process is operating properly if the length of an important subcomponent is normally distributed with a mean $\mu = 80$ cm and a standard deviation $\sigma = 2$ cm.

a. Find the probability that the length of one randomly selected unit is less than 79 cm.

b. Find the probability that the average length of 10 randomly selected units is less than 79 cm.

c. Find the probability that the average length of 30 randomly selected units is less than 79 cm.

56. Trader Joe's is a privately held chain of specialty grocery stores in the United States. Starting out as a small chain of convenience stores, it has expanded to over 340 stores as of June 2010 (http://Traderjoe.com). It has developed a reputation as a unique grocery store selling products such as gourmet foods, beer and wine, bread, nuts, cereal, and coffee. One of their best-selling nuts is Raw California Almonds, which are priced at $4.49 for 16 ounces. Since it is impossible to pack exactly 16 ounces in each packet, a researcher has determined that the weight of almonds in each packet is normally distributed with a mean and a standard deviation equal to 16.01 ounces and 0.08 ounces, respectively.

a. Discuss the sampling distribution of the sample mean based on any given sample size.

b. Find the probability that a random sample of 20 bags of almonds will average less than 16 ounces.

c. Suppose your cereal recipe calls for no less than 48 ounces of almonds. What is the probability that three packets of almonds will meet your requirement?

57. Georgia residents spent an average of $470.73 on the lottery in 2010, or 1% of their personal income (http://www.msn.com, May 23, 2012). Suppose the amount spent on the lottery follows a normal distribution with a standard deviation of $50.

a. What is the probability that a randomly selected Georgian spent more than $500 on the lottery?

b. If four Georgians are randomly selected, what is the probability that the average amount spent on the lottery was more than $500?

c. If four Georgians are randomly selected, what is the probability that all of them spent more than $500 on the lottery?

58. Data from the Bureau of Labor Statistics' Consumer Expenditure Survey (CE) show that annual expenditures for cellular phone services per consumer unit increased from $210 in 2001 to $608 in 2007. Let the standard deviation of annual cellular expenditure be $48 in 2001 and $132 in 2007.

a. What is the probability that the average annual expenditure of 100 cellular customers in 2001 exceeded $200?

b. What is the probability that the average annual expenditure of 100 cellular customers in 2007 exceeded $600?

59. According to a recent report, scientists in New England say they have identified a set of genetic variants that predicts extreme longevity with 77% accuracy (*New York Times,* July 1, 2010). Assume 150 patients decide to get their genome sequenced.

a. If the claim by scientists is accurate, what is the probability that more than 120 patients will get a correct diagnosis for extreme longevity?

b. If the claim by scientists is accurate, what is the probability that fewer than 70% of the patients will get a correct diagnosis for extreme longevity?

60. American workers are increasingly planning to delay retirement (*US News & World Report*, June 30, 2010). According to a Pew Research Center comprehensive survey, 35% of employed adults of age 62 and older say they have pushed back their retirement date.

   a. What is the probability that in a sample of 100 employed adults of age 62 and older, more than 40% have pushed back their retirement date?

   b. What is the probability that in a sample of 200 employed adults of age 62 and older, more than 40% have pushed back their retirement date?

   c. Comment on the difference between the two estimated probabilities.

61. Presidential job approval is the most-watched statistic in American politics. According to the June 2010 NBC/*Wall Street Journal* public opinion poll, president Barack Obama had reached his lowest approval rating since taking office in January of 2009. The poll showed that 48% of people disapproved of the job Obama was doing as president of the United States, while only 45% approved. Experts attributed the drop in approval ratings to a poor economy and the government's reaction to the massive oil spill in the Gulf of Mexico. Use the June 2010 approval and disapproval ratings to answer the following questions.

   a. What is the probability that President Obama gets a majority support in a random sample of 50 Americans?

   b. What is the probability that President Obama gets a majority disapproval in a random sample of 50 Americans?

62. The producer of a particular brand of soup claims that its sodium content is 50% less than that of its competitor. The food label states that the sodium content measures 410 milligrams per serving. Assume the population of sodium content is normally distributed with a standard deviation of 25 milligrams. Inspectors take periodic samples of 25 cans and measure the sodium content. The following sample means are obtained.

405	412	399	420	430	428

   a. Construct an $\bar{x}$ chart. Plot the sample means on the $\bar{x}$ chart.

   b. Can the inspectors conclude that the producer is advertising the sodium content accurately? Explain.

63. **FILE** A variety of packaging solutions exist for products that must be kept within a specific temperature range. Cold chain distribution is particularly useful in the food and pharmaceutical industries. A packaging company strives to maintain a constant temperature for its packages. It is believed that the temperature of its packages follows a normal distribution with a mean of 5 degrees Celsius and a standard deviation of 0.3 degree

Celsius. Inspectors take weekly samples for 5 weeks of eight randomly selected boxes and report the following temperatures in degrees Celsius. A portion of the data is given below; the complete data, labeled **Packaging**, are available on the text website.

Week 1	Week 2	Week 3	Week 4	Week 5
3.98	5.52	5.79	3.98	5.14
4.99	5.52	6.42	5.79	6.25
⋮	⋮	⋮	⋮	⋮
4.95	4.95	5.44	5.95	4.28

   a. Construct an $\bar{x}$ chart for quality control. Plot the five weekly sample means on the $\bar{x}$ chart.

   b. Are any points outside the control limits? Does it appear that the process is in control? Explain.

64. Acceptance sampling is an important quality control technique, where a batch of data is tested to determine if the proportion of units having a particular attribute exceeds a given percentage. Suppose that 10% of produced items are known to be nonconforming. Every week a batch of items is evaluated and the production machines are adjusted if the proportion of nonconforming items exceeds 15%.

   a. What is the probability that the production machines will be adjusted if the batch consists of 50 items?

   b. What is the probability that the production machines will be adjusted if the batch consists of 100 items?

65. In the previous question, suppose that the management decides to use a $\bar{p}$ chart for the analysis. As noted earlier, 10% of produced items are known to be nonconforming. The firm analyzes a batch of production items for 6 weeks and computes the following percentages of nonconforming items.

Week	Nonconforming Percentage
1	5.5%
2	13.1%
3	16.8%
4	13.6%
5	19.8%
6	2.0%

   a. Suppose weekly batches consisted of 50 items. Construct a $\bar{p}$ chart and determine if the machine needs adjustment in any of the weeks.

   b. Suppose weekly batches consisted of 100 items. Construct a $\bar{p}$ chart and determine if the machine needs adjustment in any of the weeks.

Case Study 7.1

The significant decline of savings in the United States from the 1970s and 1980s to the 1990s and 2000s has been widely discussed by economists (http://money.cnn.com, June 30, 2010). According to the Bureau of Economic Analysis, the savings rate of American households, defined as a percentage of the disposable personal income, was 4.20% in 2009. The reported savings rate is not uniform across the country. A public policy institute conducts two of its own surveys to compute the savings rate in the Midwest. In the first survey, a sample of 160 households is taken and the average savings rate is found to be 4.48%. Another sample of 40 households finds an average savings rate of 4.60%. Assume that the population standard deviation is 1.4%.

In a report, use the above information to:

1. Compute the probability of obtaining a sample mean that is at least as high as the one computed in each of the two surveys.
2. Use these probabilities to decide which of the two samples is likely to be more representative of the United States as a whole.

Case Study 7.2

According to a report, college graduates in 2010 were likely to face better job prospects than 2009 graduates (*New York Times,* May 24, 2010). Many employers who might have been pessimistic at the start of the 2009–2010 academic year were making more offers than expected. Despite the improvement in job prospects, the Bureau of Labor Statistics reported that the current jobless rate for college graduates under age 25 was still 8%. For high school graduates under age 25 who did not enroll in college, the current jobless rate was 24.5%. Cindy Chan works in the sales department of a trendy apparel company and has recently been relocated to a small town in Iowa. She finds that there are a total of 220 college graduates and 140 high school graduates under age 25 who live in this town. Cindy wants to gauge the demand for her products by the number of youths in this town who are employed.

In a report, use the above information to:

1. Compute the expected number of college and high school graduates who are employed.
2. Report the probabilities that at least 200 college graduates and at least 100 high school graduates under age 25 are employed.

Case Study 7.3

Hockey pucks used by the National Hockey League (NHL) and other professional leagues weigh an average of 163 grams (5.75 ounces). A quality inspector monitors the manufacturing process for hockey pucks. She takes eight samples of $n = 10$. Measured in grams, the weights appear in the table below. It is believed that puck weights are normally distributed, and when the production process is in control, $\mu = 163$ and $\sigma = 7.5$. A portion of the data, measured in grams, is shown in the accompanying table; the complete data, labeled ***Hockey_Puck***, are available on the text website.

Data for Case Study 7.3 Hockey Puck Weights (in grams)

#1	#2	#3	#4	#5	#6	#7	#8
162.2	165.8	156.4	165.3	168.6	167.0	186.8	178.3
159.8	166.2	156.4	173.3	175.8	171.4	160.4	163.0
⋮	⋮	⋮	⋮	⋮	⋮	⋮	⋮
160.3	160.6	152.2	166.4	168.2	168.4	176.8	171.3

In a report, use the above information to:

1. Prepare a control chart that specifies a centerline as well as an upper control limit (UCL) and a lower control limit (LCL).
2. Use the control chart to determine whether the process is in control.

Appendix 7.1 Derivation of the Mean and the Variance for $\bar{X}$ and $\bar{P}$

$\bar{X}$

Let the expected value and the variance of the population X be denoted by $E(X) = \mu$ and $Var(X) = \sigma^2$, respectively. The sample mean $\bar{X}$ based on a random draw of n observations, $X_1, X_2, \ldots, X_n$, from the population is computed as $\bar{X} = \frac{X_1 + X_2 + \cdots + X_n}{n}$.

We use the properties of the sum of random variables to derive

$$E(\bar{X}) = E\left(\frac{X_1 + X_2 + \cdots + X_n}{n}\right) = \frac{E(X_1) + E(X_2) + \cdots + E(X_n)}{n}$$

$$= \frac{\mu + \mu + \cdots + \mu}{n} = \frac{n\mu}{n} = \mu.$$

Since the sample mean is based on n independent draws from the population, the covariance terms drop out and the variance of the sample mean is thus derived as:

$$Var(\bar{X}) = Var\left(\frac{X_1 + X_2 + \cdots + X_n}{n}\right) = \frac{1}{n^2} Var(X_1 + X_2 + \cdots + X_n)$$

$$= \frac{1}{n^2}(Var(X_1) + Var(X_2) + \cdots + Var(X_n))$$

$$= \frac{\sigma^2 + \sigma^2 + \cdots + \sigma^2}{n^2} = \frac{n\sigma^2}{n^2} = \frac{\sigma^2}{n}.$$

$\bar{P}$

Let X be a binomial random variable representing the number of successes in n trials. Recall from Chapter 5 that $E(X) = np$ and $Var(X) = np(1 - p)$ where p is the probability of success. For the sample proportion $\bar{P} = \frac{X}{n}$,

$$E(\bar{P}) = E\left(\frac{X}{n}\right) = \frac{E(X)}{n} = \frac{np}{n} = p, \quad \text{and}$$

$$Var(\bar{P}) = Var\left(\frac{X}{n}\right) = \frac{Var(X)}{n^2} = \frac{np(1 - p)}{n^2} = \frac{p(1 - p)}{n}.$$

Appendix 7.2 Guidelines for Other Software Packages

The following section provides brief commands for specific software packages: Minitab, SPSS, and JMP. More detailed instructions can be found on the text website.

MINITAB

Generating a Random Sample

A. (Replicating Example 7.1) From the menu choose **Calc > Random Data > Integer**.
B. Enter 100 as the **Number of rows of data to generate**; enter C1 for **Store in column**; enter 1 for **Minimum value** and 20000 as **Maximum value**.

Constructing an $\bar{x}$ Chart

A. (Replicating Figure 7.A) First stack all wait times in C1. In C2 indicate how the data are grouped; for instance, the first four observations are given the value 1; the next four observations, the value 2, and so on.

B. From the menu choose **Stat > Control Charts > Variables Charts for Subgroups > Xbar**.

C. Choose **All observations for a chart are in one column**, and in box directly under this one, select C1. For **Subgroup sizes** select C2.

D. Select **Xbar Options** and enter 60 for **Mean** and 30 for **Standard deviation**.

SPSS

Constructing an $\bar{x}$ Chart

A. (Replicating Figure 7.A) First stack all wait times in C1. In C2 indicate how the data are grouped; for instance, the first four observations are given the value 1; the next four observations, the value 2, and so on.

B. From the menu select **Analyze > Quality Control > Control Charts > X-bar, R, s**.

C. Select C1 as **Process Measurement** and select C2 as **Subgroups labeled by**.

JMP

Generating a Random Sample

A. (Replicating Example 7.1) Right-click on the header at the top of the column in the spreadsheet view. Under **Functions (grouped)**, choose **Random > Random Integer**.

B. Enter 20000 for **n1**.

Constructing the $\bar{x}$ Chart

A. (Replicating Figure 7.A) First stack all wait times in Column 1. From the menu choose **Graph > Control Chart**.

B. Select **Xbar** and under **Parameters** select **KSigma** and enter 3. Select Column 1 for **Process**. Under **Sample Size**, select **Sample Size Constant** and enter 4. Select **Specify Stats**. Enter 30 for **Sigma** and 60 for **Mean(measure)**.

Interval Estimation

C H A P T E R

LEARNING OBJECTIVES

After reading
this chapter
you should
be able to:

LO **8.1** Explain an interval estimator.

LO **8.2** Calculate a confidence interval for the population mean when the population
standard deviation is known.

LO **8.3** Describe the factors that influence the width of a confidence interval.

LO **8.4** Discuss features of the *t* distribution.

LO **8.5** Calculate a confidence interval for the population mean when the population
standard deviation is not known.

LO **8.6** Calculate a confidence interval for the population proportion.

LO **8.7** Select a sample size to estimate the population mean and the population
proportion.

In earlier chapters we made a distinction between the population parameters, such as the population mean and the population proportion, and the corresponding sample statistics. The sample statistics are used to make statistical inferences regarding the unknown values of the population parameters. In general, two basic methodologies emerge from the inferential branch of statistics: estimation and hypothesis testing. As discussed in Chapter 7, a point estimator uses sample data to produce a single value as an estimate of the unknown population parameter of interest. A confidence interval, on the other hand, produces a range of values that estimate the unknown population parameter. In this chapter, we develop and interpret confidence intervals for the population mean and the population proportion. Since obtaining a sample is one of the first steps in making statistical inferences, we also learn how an appropriate sample size is determined in order to achieve a certain level of precision in the estimates.

Fuel Usage of "Ultra-Green" Cars

A car manufacturer advertises that its new "ultra-green" car obtains an average of 100 miles per gallon (mpg) and, based on its fuel emissions, is one of the few cars that earns an A+ rating from the Environmental Protection Agency. Jared Beane, an analyst at Pinnacle Research, records the mpg for a sample of 25 "ultra-green" cars after the cars were driven equal distances under identical conditions. Table 8.1 shows each car's mpg; these data, labeled **MPG**, are also available on the text website.

TABLE 8.1 MPG for a Sample of 25 "Ultra-Green" Cars

97	117	93	79	97
87	78	83	94	96
102	98	82	96	113
113	111	90	101	99
112	89	92	96	98

Jared has already used tabular and graphical methods to summarize the data in his report. He would like to make statistical inferences regarding key population parameters. In particular, he wants to use the above sample information to:

1. Estimate the mean mpg of all ultra-green cars with 90% confidence.
2. Estimate the proportion of all ultra-green cars that obtain over 100 mpg with 90% confidence.
3. Determine the sample size that will enable him to achieve a specified level of precision in his mean and proportion estimates.

A synopsis of this case is provided at the end of Section 8.4.

8.1 Confidence Interval for the Population Mean When σ Is Known

Recall that a population consists of all items of interest in a statistical problem, whereas a sample is a subset of the population. Given sample data, we use the sample statistics to make inferences about the unknown population parameters, such as the population mean and the population proportion. Two basic methodologies emerge from the inferential branch of statistics: estimation and hypothesis testing. Although the sample statistics are based on a portion of the population, they contain useful information to estimate the population parameters and to conduct tests regarding the population parameters. In this chapter we focus on estimation.

As discussed in Chapter 7, when a statistic is used to estimate a parameter, it is referred to as a point estimator, or simply an estimator. A particular value of the estimator is called a point estimate or an estimate. Recall that the sample mean $\overline{X}$ is the estimator of the population mean μ and the sample proportion $\overline{P}$ is the estimator of the population proportion p. Let us consider the introductory case where Jared Beane records the mpg for a sample of 25 ultra-green cars. We use the sample information in Table 8.1 to compute the mean mpg of the cars as $\bar{x} = 96.52$ mpg. Similarly, since Jared is also interested in the proportion of these cars that get an mpg greater than 100 and seven of the cars in the sample satisfied this criterion, we compute the relevant sample proportion as $\bar{p} = 7/25 = 0.28$. Therefore, our estimate of the mean mpg of all ultra-green cars is 96.52 mpg and our estimate of the proportion of all ultra-green cars with mpg greater than 100 is 0.28.

It is important to note that the above estimates are based on a sample of 25 cars and, therefore, are likely to vary between samples. For instance, the values will change if another sample of 25 cars is used. What Jared really wishes to estimate are the mean and proportion (parameters) of all ultra-green cars (population), not just those comprising the sample. We now examine how we can extract useful information from a single sample to make inferences about these population parameters.

So far we have only discussed point estimators. Often it is more informative to provide a range of values—an **interval**—rather than a single point estimate of the unknown population parameter. This range of values is called a **confidence interval**, also referred to as an **interval estimate**, for the population parameter.

CONFIDENCE INTERVAL

A **confidence interval** provides a range of values that, with a certain level of confidence, contains the population parameter of interest.

In order to construct a confidence interval for the population mean μ or the population proportion p, it is essential that the sampling distributions of $\overline{X}$ and $\overline{P}$ follow, or approximately follow, a normal distribution. Other methods that do not require the normality condition are not discussed in this text. Recall from Chapter 7 that $\overline{X}$ follows a normal distribution when the underlying population is normally distributed; this result holds irrespective of the sample size n. If the underlying population is not normally distributed, then by the central limit theorem, the sampling distribution of $\overline{X}$ will be approximately normal if the sample size is sufficiently large, that is, when $n \geq 30$. Similarly, the sampling distribution of $\overline{P}$ is approximately normal if the sample size is sufficiently large, that is, when $np \geq 5$ and $n(1 - p) \geq 5$.

The main ingredient for developing a confidence interval is the sampling distribution of the underlying statistic. The sampling distribution of $\overline{X}$, for example, describes how the sample mean varies between samples. Recall that the variability between samples is measured by the standard error of $\overline{X}$. If the standard error is small, it implies that the sample means are not only close to one another, they are also close to the unknown population mean μ.

A confidence interval is generally associated with a **margin of error** that accounts for the standard error of the estimator and the desired confidence level of the interval. For estimating the population mean and the population proportion, the sampling distribution of the underlying statistic is approximately normal. The symmetry implied by the normal distribution allows us to construct a confidence interval by adding and subtracting the same margin of error to the point estimate.

It is common to construct a confidence interval as: Point estimate ± Margin of error.

An analogy to a simple weather example is instructive. If you feel that the outside temperature is about 50 degrees, then perhaps you can, with a certain level of confidence, suggest that the actual temperature is between 40 and 60 degrees. In this example, 50 degrees is analogous to a point estimate of the actual temperature and 10 degrees is the margin of error that is added to and subtracted from this point estimate.

We know from the introductory case study that the point estimate of the population mean mpg of all ultra-green cars is 96.52 mpg; that is, $\bar{x} = 96.52$. We can construct a confidence interval by using the point estimate as a base to which we add and subtract the margin of error.

Constructing a Confidence Interval for μ When σ Is Known

LO 8.2

Calculate a confidence interval for the population mean when the population standard deviation is known.

Let us construct a 95% confidence interval for μ. As mentioned earlier, in order to construct this interval, the sampling distribution of $\bar{X}$ must be normal. Consider the standard normal random variable Z. Using the symmetry of Z, we can compute $P(Z > 1.96) = P(Z < -1.96) = 0.025$; see Figure 8.1. Remember that $z = 1.96$ is easily determined from the z table given the probability of 0.025 in the upper tail of the distribution. Therefore, we formulate the probability statement $P(-1.96 \leq Z \leq 1.96) = 0.95$.

FIGURE 8.1 Graphical depiction of $P(Z < -1.96) = 0.025$ and $P(Z > 1.96) = 0.025$

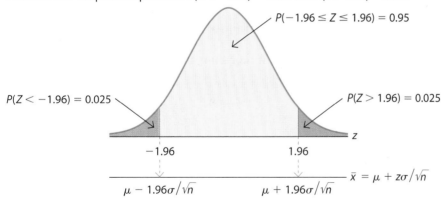

Since $Z = \frac{\bar{X} - \mu}{\sigma/\sqrt{n}}$, for a normal $\bar{X}$ with mean μ and standard error $\sigma/\sqrt{n}$, we get

$$P\left(-1.96 \leq \frac{\bar{X} - \mu}{\sigma/\sqrt{n}} \leq 1.96\right) = 0.95.$$

Finally, we multiply by $\sigma/\sqrt{n}$ and add μ to obtain

$$P\left(\mu - 1.96\sigma/\sqrt{n} \leq \bar{X} \leq \mu + 1.96\sigma/\sqrt{n}\right) = 0.95.$$

This equation (see also the lower portion of Figure 8.1) implies that there is a 0.95 probability that the sample mean $\bar{X}$ will fall between $\mu - 1.96\sigma/\sqrt{n}$ and $\mu + 1.96\sigma/\sqrt{n}$, that is, within the interval $\mu \pm 1.96\sigma/\sqrt{n}$. If samples of size n are drawn repeatedly from a given population, 95% of the computed sample means, $\bar{x}$'s, will fall within the interval and the remaining 5% will fall outside the interval.

We do not know the population mean μ, and therefore cannot determine if a particular $\bar{x}$ falls within the interval or not. However, we do know that $\bar{x}$ will fall within the interval $\mu \pm 1.96\sigma/\sqrt{n}$ if and only if μ falls within the interval $\bar{x} \pm 1.96\sigma/\sqrt{n}$. This will happen 95% of the time given how the interval is constructed. Therefore, we call the interval $\bar{x} \pm 1.96\sigma/\sqrt{n}$ a 95% confidence interval for the population mean, where $1.96\,\sigma/\sqrt{n}$ is its margin of error.

Confidence intervals are often misinterpreted; you need to exercise care in characterizing them. For instance, the above 95% confidence interval does *not* imply that the probability that μ falls in the confidence interval is 0.95. Remember that μ is a constant, although its value is not known. It either falls in the interval (probability equals one) or does not fall in the interval (probability equals zero). The randomness comes from $\bar{X}$, not μ, since many possible sample means can be derived from a population. Therefore, it is incorrect to say that the probability that μ falls in the $\bar{x} \pm 1.96\sigma/\sqrt{n}$ interval is 0.95. A 95% confidence interval simply implies that if numerous samples of size n are drawn from a given population, then 95% of the intervals formed by the above procedure (formula) will contain μ. Keep in mind that we only use a single sample to derive the estimates. Since there are many possible samples, we will be right 95% of the time, thus giving us 95% confidence.

INTERPRETING A 95% CONFIDENCE INTERVAL

Technically, a 95% confidence interval for the population mean μ implies that for 95% of the samples, the procedure (formula) produces an interval that contains μ. Informally, we can report with 95% confidence that μ lies in the given interval. It is not correct to say that there is a 95% chance that μ lies in the given interval.

EXAMPLE 8.1

A sample of 25 cereal boxes of Granola Crunch, a generic brand of cereal, yields a mean weight of 1.02 pounds of cereal per box. Construct a 95% confidence interval for the mean weight of all cereal boxes. Assume that the weight is normally distributed with a population standard deviation of 0.03 pound.

SOLUTION: Note that the normality condition of $\bar{X}$ is satisfied since the underlying population is normally distributed. A 95% confidence interval for the population mean is computed as

$$\bar{x} \pm 1.96\frac{\sigma}{\sqrt{n}} = 1.02 \pm 1.96\frac{0.03}{\sqrt{25}} = 1.02 \pm 0.012.$$

With 95% confidence, we can report that the mean weight of all cereal boxes falls between 1.008 and 1.032 pounds.

While it is common to report a 95% confidence interval, in theory we can construct an interval of any level of confidence ranging from 0 to 100%. Let's now extend the analysis to include intervals of any confidence level. Let the Greek letter α (alpha) denote the allowable probability of error that in Chapter 9 will define the so-called significance level. This is the probability that the estimation procedure will generate an interval that does not contain μ. The **confidence coefficient** $(1 - \alpha)$ is interpreted similarly. The probability of error α and the confidence level are related as

- Confidence coefficient $= 1 - \alpha$, and
- Confidence level $= 100(1 - \alpha)\%$.

For example, a confidence coefficient of 0.95 implies that the probability of error α equals $1 - 0.95 = 0.05$ and the confidence level equals $100(1 - 0.05)\% = 95\%$. Similarly, for a 90% confidence interval, $\alpha = 1 - 0.90 = 0.10$. The following statement generalizes the construction of a confidence interval for μ when σ is known.

CONFIDENCE INTERVAL FOR μ WHEN σ IS KNOWN

A $100(1 - \alpha)\%$ confidence interval for the population mean μ when the population standard deviation σ is known is computed as

$$\bar{x} \pm z_{\alpha/2}\frac{\sigma}{\sqrt{n}} \quad \text{or} \quad \left[\bar{x} - z_{\alpha/2}\frac{\sigma}{\sqrt{n}}, \bar{x} + z_{\alpha/2}\frac{\sigma}{\sqrt{n}}\right].$$

This formula is valid only if $\bar{X}$ (approximately) follows a normal distribution.

The notation $z_{\alpha/2}$ is the z value associated with the probability of $\alpha/2$ in the upper tail of the standard normal probability distribution. In other words, if Z is a standard normal random variable and α is any probability, then $z_{\alpha/2}$ represents a z value such that the area under the z curve to the right of $z_{\alpha/2}$ is $\alpha/2$, that is, $P(Z \geq z_{\alpha/2}) = \alpha/2$. Figure 8.2 depicts the notation $z_{\alpha/2}$.

FIGURE 8.2 Graphical depiction of the notation $z_{\alpha/2}$

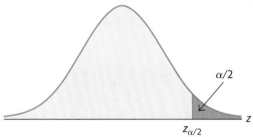

As discussed earlier, for a 95% confidence interval, $\alpha = 0.05$ and $\alpha/2 = 0.025$. Therefore, $z_{\alpha/2} = z_{0.025} = 1.96$. Similarly, using the z table or Excel's function NORM.S.INV, we can derive the following:

- For a 90% confidence interval, $\alpha = 0.10$, $\alpha/2 = 0.05$, and $z_{\alpha/2} = z_{0.05} = 1.645$.
- For a 99% confidence interval, $\alpha = 0.01$, $\alpha/2 = 0.005$, and $z_{\alpha/2} = z_{0.005} = 2.576$.

The Width of a Confidence Interval

LO **8.3**

The margin of error used in the computation of the confidence interval for the population mean, when the population standard deviation is known, is $z_{\alpha/2}\frac{\sigma}{\sqrt{n}}$. Since we are basically adding and subtracting this quantity from $\bar{x}$, the width of the confidence interval is two times the margin of error. In Example 8.1, the margin of error for a 95% confidence interval is 0.012 and the width of the interval is $1.032 - 1.008 = 2(0.012) = 0.024$. Now let's examine how the width of a confidence interval is influenced by various factors.

Describe the factors that influence the width of a confidence interval.

I. For a given confidence level $100(1 - \alpha)\%$ and sample size n, the larger the population standard deviation σ, the wider the confidence interval.

EXAMPLE 8.1b
Let the standard deviation of the population in Example 8.1 be 0.05 instead of 0.03. Compute a 95% confidence interval based on the same sample information.

SOLUTION: We use the same formula as before, but we substitute 0.05 for the standard deviation instead of 0.03:

$$1.02 \pm 1.96\frac{0.05}{\sqrt{25}} = 1.02 \pm 0.020.$$

The width has increased from 0.024 to $2(0.020) = 0.040$.

II. For a given confidence level $100(1 - \alpha)\%$ and population standard deviation σ, the smaller the sample size n, the wider the confidence interval.

EXAMPLE 8.1c

Instead of 25 observations, let the sample in Example 8.1 be based on 16 observations. Compute a 95% confidence interval using the same sample mean of 1.02 pounds and the same population standard deviation of 0.03.

SOLUTION: Again we use the same formula as before, but this time we substitute 16 for n instead of 25:

$$1.02 \pm 1.96 \frac{0.03}{\sqrt{16}} = 1.02 \pm 0.015.$$

The width has increased from 0.024 to $2(0.015) = 0.030$.

III. For a given sample size n and population standard deviation σ, the greater the confidence level $100(1 - \alpha)\%$, the wider the confidence interval.

EXAMPLE 8.1d

Compute a 99%, instead of a 95%, confidence interval based on the information in Example 8.1.

SOLUTION: Now we use the same formula and substitute the value 2.576 for $z_{\alpha/2}$ instead of 1.96:

$$1.02 \pm 2.576 \frac{0.03}{\sqrt{25}} = 1.02 \pm 0.015.$$

The width has increased from 0.024 to $2(0.015) = 0.030$.

The precision is directly linked with the width of the confidence interval—the wider the interval, the lower is its precision. Continuing with the weather analogy, a temperature estimate of 40 to 80 degrees is imprecise because the interval is too wide to be of value. We lose precision when the sample does not reveal a great deal about the population, resulting in a wide confidence interval. Examples 8.1b and 8.1c suggest that the estimate will be less precise if the variability of the underlying population is high (σ is high) or a small segment of the population is sampled (n is small). Example 8.1d relates the width with the confidence level. For a given sample information, the only way we can gain confidence is by making the interval wider. If you are 95% confident that the outside temperature is between 40 and 60, then you can increase your confidence level to 99% only by using a wider range, say between 35 and 65. This result also helps us understand the difference between precision (width of the interval) and the confidence level. There is a trade-off between the amount of confidence we have in an interval and its width.

EXAMPLE 8.2

IQ tests are designed to yield scores that are approximately normally distributed. A reporter is interested in estimating the average IQ of employees in a large high-tech firm in California. She gathers the IQ information on 22 employees of this firm and records the sample mean IQ as 106. She assumes that the population standard deviation is 15.

a. Compute 90% and 99% confidence intervals for the average IQ in this firm.

b. Use these results to infer if the mean IQ in this firm is significantly different from the national average of 100.

SOLUTION:

a. For a 90% confidence interval, $z_{\alpha/2} = z_{0.05} = 1.645$. Similarly, for a 99% confidence interval, $z_{\alpha/2} = z_{0.005} = 2.576$.

The 90% confidence interval is $106 \pm 1.645 \frac{15}{\sqrt{22}} = 106 \pm 5.26$.

The 99% confidence interval is $106 \pm 2.576 \frac{15}{\sqrt{22}} = 106 \pm 8.24$.

Note that the 99% interval is wider than the 90% interval.

b. With 90% confidence, the reporter can infer that the average IQ of this firm's employees differs from the national average, since the value 100 falls outside the 90% confidence interval, [100.74, 111.26]. However, she cannot infer the same result with 99% confidence, since the wider range of the interval, [97.76, 114.24], includes the value 100. We will study the link between estimation and testing in more detail in the next chapter.

Using Excel to Construct a Confidence Interval for μ When σ Is Known

We can use Excel's functions to construct a confidence interval. These functions are particularly useful with large data sets. Consider the following example.

EXAMPLE 8.3

Table 8.2 lists a portion of the weights (in grams) for a sample of 80 hockey pucks; the complete data set can be found on the text website, labeled **Hockey_Pucks**. Construct the 92% confidence interval for the population mean weight assuming that the population standard deviation is 7.5 grams.

TABLE 8.2 Hockey Puck Weights, $n = 80$

FILE

Weight (in grams)
162.2
159.8
⋮
171.3

SOLUTION: We need to compute $\bar{x} \pm z_{\alpha/2} \frac{\sigma}{\sqrt{n}}$. We are given $\sigma = 7.5$ and $n = 80$. In order to find $\bar{x}$, we open **Hockey_Pucks**, find an empty cell, and calculate the sample mean by inputting '=AVERAGE(A2:A81)'; Excel returns 166.71. For a 92% confidence interval, $\alpha = 0.08$, so we need to find $z_{\alpha/2} = z_{0.04}$. Excel's NORM.S.INV function finds a particular z value for a given cumulative probability. Since we want the z value such that the area under the z curve to the right of $z_{0.04}$ is 0.04, we insert '=NORM.S.INV(0.96)'. Excel returns 1.751 or, equivalently, $z_{0.04} = 1.751$. Inserting these values into the formula and simplifying yields: $166.71 \pm 1.751 \frac{7.5}{\sqrt{80}} = 166.71 \pm 1.47$. With 92% confidence, we conclude that the mean weight of all hockey pucks falls between 165.24 and 168.18 grams.

EXERCISES 8.1

Mechanics

1. Find $z_{\alpha/2}$ for each of the following confidence levels used in estimating the population mean.
   a. 90%
   b. 98%
   c. 88%

2. Find $z_{\alpha/2}$ for each of the following confidence levels used in estimating the population mean.
   a. 89%
   b. 92%
   c. 96%

3. A simple random sample of 25 observations is derived from a normally distributed population with a known standard deviation of 8.2.
   a. Is the condition that $\bar{X}$ is normally distributed satisfied? Explain.
   b. Compute the margin of error with 80% confidence.
   c. Compute the margin of error with 90% confidence.
   d. Which of the two margins of error will lead to a wider interval?

4. Consider a population with a known standard deviation of 26.8. In order to compute an interval estimate for the population mean, a sample of 64 observations is drawn.
   a. Is the condition that $\bar{X}$ is normally distributed satisfied? Explain.
   b. Compute the margin of error at a 95% confidence level.
   c. Compute the margin of error at a 95% confidence level based on a larger sample of 225 observations.
   d. Which of the two margins of error will lead to a wider confidence interval?

5. Discuss the factors that influence the margin of error of the confidence interval for the population mean. What can a practitioner do to reduce the margin of error?

Applications

6. The average life expectancy for Bostonians is 78.1 years (*The Boston Globe*, August 16, 2010). Assume that this average was based on a sample of 50 Bostonians and that the population standard deviation is 4.5 years.
   a. What is the point estimate of the population mean?
   b. At 90% confidence, what is the margin of error?
   c. Construct the 90% confidence interval for the population average life expectancy of Bostonians.

7. In order to estimate the mean 30-year fixed mortgage rate for a home loan in the United States, a random sample of 28 recent loans is taken. The average calculated from this sample is 5.25%. It can be assumed that 30-year fixed mortgage rates are normally distributed with a standard deviation of 0.50%. Compute 90% and 99% confidence intervals for the population mean 30-year fixed mortgage rate.

8. An article in the *National Geographic News* ("U.S. Racking Up Huge Sleep Debt," February 24, 2005) argues that Americans are increasingly skimping on their sleep. A researcher in a small midwestern town wants to estimate the mean weekday sleep time of its adult residents. He takes a random sample of 80 adult residents and records their weekday mean sleep time as 6.4 hours. Assume that the population standard deviation is fairly stable at 1.8 hours.
   a. Calculate the 95% confidence interval for the population mean weekday sleep time of all adult residents of this midwestern town.
   b. Can we conclude with 95% confidence that the mean sleep time of all adult residents in this midwestern town is not 7 hours?

9. A family is relocating from St. Louis, Missouri, to California. Due to an increasing inventory of houses in St. Louis, it is taking longer than before to sell a house. The wife is concerned and wants to know when it is optimal to put their house on the market. They ask their Realtor friend for help and she informs them that the last 26 houses that sold in their neighborhood took an average time of 218 days to sell. The Realtor also tells them that based on her prior experience, the population standard deviation is 72 days.
   a. What assumption regarding the population is necessary for making an interval estimate for the population mean?
   b. Construct the 90% confidence interval for the mean sale time for all homes in the neighborhood.

10. U.S. consumers are increasingly viewing debit cards as a convenient substitute for cash and checks. The average amount spent annually on a debit card is $7,790 (*Kiplinger's*, August 2007). Assume that this average was based on a sample of 100 consumers and that the population standard deviation is $500.
    a. At 99% confidence, what is the margin of error?
    b. Construct the 99% confidence interval for the population mean amount spent annually on a debit card.

11. Suppose a 95% confidence interval for the mean salary of college graduates in a town in Mississippi is given by [$36,080, $43,920]. The population standard deviation used for the analysis is known to be $12,000.
    a. What is the point estimator of the mean salary of all college graduates in this town?
    b. Determine the sample size used for the analysis.

12. A manager is interested in estimating the mean time (in minutes) required to complete a job. His assistant uses a sample of 100 observations to report the confidence interval as [14.355, 17.645]. The population standard deviation is known to be equal to 10 minutes.
    a. Find the sample mean time used to compute the confidence interval.
    b. Determine the confidence level used for the analysis.

13. **FILE** A study reports that recent college graduates from New Hampshire face the highest average debt of $31,048 (*The Boston Globe*, May 27, 2012). A researcher from Connecticut wants to determine how recent undergraduates from that state fare. He collects data on debt from 40 recent undergraduates. A portion of the data is shown below; the complete data set, labeled **CT_Undergrad_Debt**, can be found on the text website. Assume that the population standard deviation is $5,000.

Debt
87
86
⋮
86

a. Use Excel to construct the 95% confidence interval for the mean debt of all undergraduates from Connecticut.

b. Use the 95% confidence interval to determine if the debt of Connecticut undergraduates differs from that of New Hampshire undergraduates.

14. **FILE** An economist wants to estimate the mean hourly wage of all workers. She collects data on 50 hourly wage earners. A portion of the data is shown in the accompanying table; the complete data set, labeled **Hourly_Wage**, can be found on the text website. Assume that the population standard deviation is $6. Construct and interpret 90% and 99% confidence intervals for the mean hourly wage of all workers.

Hourly Wage (in $)
37.85
21.72
⋮
24.18

15. **FILE** A safety officer is concerned about speeds on a certain section of the New Jersey Turnpike. He records the speeds of 40 cars on a Saturday afternoon. The accompanying table shows a portion of the results; the complete data set, labeled **Highway_Speeds**, can be found on the text website. Assume that the population standard deviation is 5 mph. Construct the 95% confidence interval for the mean speed of all cars on that section of the turnpike. Are the safety officer's concerns valid if the speed limit is 55 mph? Explain.

Highway Speeds (mph)
70
65
⋮
65

8.2 Confidence Interval for the Population Mean When σ Is Unknown

So far we have considered confidence intervals for the population mean where the population standard deviation σ is known. In reality, σ is rarely known. Recall from Chapter 3 that the population variance and the population standard deviation are calculated as $\sigma^2 = \frac{\Sigma(x_i - \mu)^2}{N}$ and $\sigma = \sqrt{\sigma^2}$, respectively. It is highly unlikely that σ is known when μ is not. However, there are instances when the population standard deviation is considered fairly stable and, therefore, can be determined from prior experience. In these cases the population standard deviation is treated as known.

Recall that the margin of error in a confidence interval depends on the standard error of the estimator and the desired confidence level. With σ unknown, the standard error of $\bar{X}$, given by $\sigma/\sqrt{n}$, can be conveniently estimated by $s/\sqrt{n}$, where s denotes the sample standard deviation. Recall from Chapter 7 that, for convenience, we denote this estimate of the standard error of $\bar{X}$ also by $se(\bar{X}) = s/\sqrt{n}$.

The *t* Distribution

LO **8.4**

As discussed earlier, in order to derive a confidence interval for μ, it is essential that $\bar{X}$ be normally distributed. A normally distributed $\bar{X}$ is standardized as $Z = \frac{\bar{X} - \mu}{\sigma/\sqrt{n}}$ where Z follows the z distribution. Another standardized statistic, which uses the estimator S in place of σ, is computed as $T = \frac{\bar{X} - \mu}{S/\sqrt{n}}$. The random variable T follows the Student's t distribution, more commonly known as the t distribution.[1]

Discuss features of the *t* distribution.

[1]William S. Gossett (1876–1937) published his research concerning the t distribution under the pen name "Student" because his employer, the Guinness Brewery, did not allow employees to publish their research results.

THE *t* DISTRIBUTION

If a random sample of size n is taken from a normal population with a finite variance, then the statistic $T = \dfrac{\bar{X} - \mu}{S/\sqrt{n}}$ follows the t distribution with $(n - 1)$ degrees of freedom, df.

The t distribution is actually a family of distributions, which are similar to the z distribution in that they are all bell-shaped and symmetric around zero. However, all t distributions have slightly broader tails than the z distribution. Each t distribution is identified by the **degrees of freedom**, or simply df. The degrees of freedom determine the extent of the broadness of the tails of the distribution; the fewer the degrees of freedom, the broader the tails. Since the t distribution is defined by the degrees of freedom, it is common to refer to it as the t_{df} distribution.

Specifically, the degrees of freedom refer to the number of independent pieces of information that go into the calculation of a given statistic and, in this sense, can be "freely chosen." Consider the number of independent observations that enter into the calculation of the sample mean. If it is known that $\bar{x} = 20$, $n = 4$, and three of the observations have values of $x_1 = 16$, $x_2 = 24$, and $x_3 = 18$, then there is no choice but for the fourth observation to have a value of 22. In other words, three degrees of freedom are involved in computing $\bar{x} = 20$ if $n = 4$; in effect, one degree of freedom is lost.

Summary of the t_{df} Distribution

- Like the z distribution, the t_{df} distribution is bell-shaped and symmetric around 0 with asymptotic tails (the tails get closer and closer to the horizontal axis but never touch it).
- The t_{df} distribution has slightly broader tails than the z distribution.
- The t_{df} distribution consists of a family of distributions where the actual shape of each one depends on the degrees of freedom df. As df increases, the t_{df} distribution becomes similar to the z distribution; it is identical to the z distribution when df approaches infinity.

From Figure 8.3 we note that the tails of the t_2 and t_5 distributions are broader than the tails of the t_{50} distribution. For instance, for t_2 and t_5, the area exceeding a value of 3, or $P(T_{df} > 3)$, is greater than that for t_{50}. In addition, the t_{50} resembles the z distribution.

FIGURE 8.3 The t_{df} distribution with various degrees of freedom

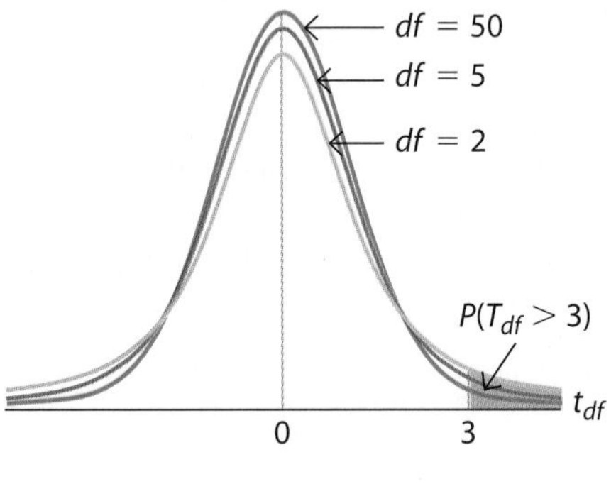

Locating t_{df} Values and Probabilities

Table 8.3 lists t_{df} values for selected upper-tail probabilities and degrees of freedom df. Table 2 of Appendix A provides a more complete table. Since the t_{df} distribution is a family of distributions identified by the df parameter, the t table is not as comprehensive as the z table. It only lists probabilities corresponding to a limited number of values. Also, unlike the cumulative probabilities in the z table, the t table provides the probabilities in the upper tail of the distribution.

TABLE 8.3 Portion of the *t* Table

df	\multicolumn{5}{c}{Area in Upper Tail, α}
	0.10	0.05	0.025	0.01	0.005
1	3.078	6.314	12.706	31.821	63.657
⋮	⋮	⋮	⋮	⋮	⋮
10	1.372	**1.812**	2.228	2.764	3.169
⋮	⋮	⋮	⋮	⋮	⋮
∞	1.282	1.645	1.960	2.326	2.576

We use the notation $t_{\alpha,df}$ to denote a value such that the area in the upper tail equals α for a given *df*. In other words, for a random variable T_{df}, the notation $t_{\alpha,df}$ represents a value such that $P(T_{df} \geq t_{\alpha,df}) = \alpha$. Similarly, $t_{\alpha/2,df}$ represents a value such that $P(T_{df} \geq t_{\alpha/2,df}) = \alpha/2$. Figure 8.4 illustrates the notation.

FIGURE 8.4 Graphical depiction of $P(T_{df} \geq t_{\alpha,df}) = \alpha$

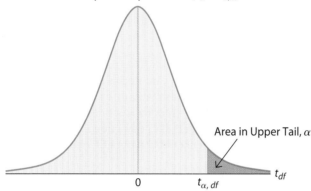

Area in Upper Tail, α

t_{df}

0 $t_{\alpha, df}$

When determining the value $t_{\alpha,df}$, we need two pieces of information: (a) the sample size *n*, or analogously, $df = n - 1$, and (b) α. For instance, suppose we want to find the value $t_{\alpha,df}$ with $\alpha = 0.05$ and $df = 10$, that is, $t_{0.05,10}$. Using Table 8.3, we look at the first column labeled *df* and find the row 10. We then continue along this row until we reach the column $\alpha = 0.05$. The value 1.812 suggests that $P(T_{10} \leq 1.812) = 0.05$. Due to the symmetry of the *t* distribution, we also get $P(T_{10} \leq -1.812) = 0.05$. Figure 8.5 shows these results graphically. Also, since the area under the entire t_{df} distribution sums to one, we deduce that $P(T_{10} < 1.812) = 1 - 0.05 = 0.95$, which also equals $P(T_{10} > -1.812)$.

FIGURE 8.5 Graph of the probability $\alpha = 0.05$ on both sides of T_{10}

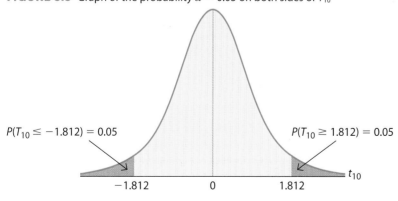

$P(T_{10} \leq -1.812) = 0.05$

$P(T_{10} \geq 1.812) = 0.05$

t_{10}

-1.812 0 1.812

Sometimes the exact probability cannot be determined from the *t* table. For example, given $df = 10$, the exact probability $P(T_{10} \geq 1.562)$ is not included in the table. However, this probability is between 0.05 and 0.10 because the value 1.562 falls between 1.372 and 1.812. Similarly, $P(T_{10} < 1.562)$ is between 0.90 and 0.95. We can use Excel and other statistical packages to find exact probabilities.

EXAMPLE 8.4

Compute $t_{\alpha,df}$ for $\alpha = 0.025$ using 2, 5, and 50 degrees of freedom.

SOLUTION:

- For $df = 2$, $t_{0.025,2} = 4.303$.
- For $df = 5$, $t_{0.025,5} = 2.571$.
- For $df = 50$, $t_{0.025,50} = 2.009$.

Note that the t_{df} values change with the degrees of freedom. Moreover, as df increases, the t_{df} distribution begins to resemble the z distribution. In fact with $df = \infty$, $t_{0.025,\infty} = 1.96$, which is identical to the corresponding z value; recall that $P(Z \geq 1.96) = P(Z > 1.96) = 0.025$.

LO **8.5**

Calculate a confidence interval for the population mean when the population standard deviation is not known.

Constructing a Confidence Interval for μ When σ Is Unknown

We can never stress enough the importance of the requirement that $\overline{X}$ follows a normal distribution in estimating the population mean. Recall that $\overline{X}$ follows the normal distribution when the underlying population is normally distributed or when the sample size is sufficiently large ($n \geq 30$). We still construct the confidence interval for μ as: Point estimate $\pm$ Margin of error. However, when the population standard deviation is unknown, we now use the t_{df} distribution to calculate the margin of error.

CONFIDENCE INTERVAL FOR μ WHEN σ IS NOT KNOWN

A $100(1 - \alpha)\%$ confidence interval for the population mean μ when the population standard deviation σ is not known is computed as

$$\overline{x} \pm t_{\alpha/2,df} \frac{s}{\sqrt{n}} \quad \text{or} \quad \left[\overline{x} - t_{\alpha/2,df} \frac{s}{\sqrt{n}}, \overline{x} + t_{\alpha/2,df} \frac{s}{\sqrt{n}} \right],$$

where s is the sample standard deviation. This formula is valid only if $\overline{X}$ (approximately) follows a normal distribution.

As before, $100(1 - \alpha)\%$ is the confidence level and $t_{\alpha/2,df}$ is the t_{df} value associated with the probability $\alpha/2$ in the upper tail of the distribution with $df = n - 1$. In other words, $P(T_{df} > t_{\alpha/2,df}) = \alpha/2$. It is important to note that uncertainty is increased when we estimate the population standard deviation with the sample standard deviation, making the confidence interval wider, especially for smaller samples. This is appropriately captured by the wider tail of the $t_{\alpha/2}$ distribution.

EXAMPLE 8.5

In the introductory case of this chapter, Jared Beane wants to estimate the mean mpg of all ultra-green cars. Table 8.1 lists the mpg of a sample of 25 cars. Use this information to construct a 90% confidence interval for the population mean. Assume that mpg follows a normal distribution.

SOLUTION: The condition that $\overline{X}$ follows a normal distribution is satisfied since we assumed that mpg is normally distributed. Thus, we construct the confidence interval as $\overline{x} \pm t_{\alpha/2,df} \frac{s}{\sqrt{n}}$. This is a classic example where a statistician has access only to sample data. Since the population standard deviation is not known, the sample standard deviation has to be computed from the sample. From the sample data in Table 8.1, we find that $\bar{x} = \frac{\Sigma x_i}{n} = \frac{2413}{25} = 96.52$ mpg and $s = \sqrt{\frac{\Sigma(x_i - \bar{x})^2}{n-1}} = \sqrt{\frac{2746.24}{25-1}} = 10.70$; alternatively, we can use Excel to find these values. For a 90% confidence interval, $\alpha = 0.10$, $\alpha/2 = 0.05$, and given $n = 25$, $df = 25 - 1 = 24$. Thus, $t_{0.05,24} = 1.711$.

A 90% confidence interval for μ is computed as

$$\bar{x} \pm t_{\alpha/2,df} \frac{s}{\sqrt{n}} = 96.52 \pm 1.711 \frac{10.70}{\sqrt{25}} = 96.52 \pm 3.66.$$

Thus, Jared concludes with 90% confidence that the average mpg of all ultra-green cars is between 92.86 mpg and 100.18 mpg. Note that the manufacturer's claim that the ultra-green car will average 100 mpg cannot be rejected by the sample data since the value 100 falls within the 90% confidence interval.

Using Excel to Construct a Confidence Interval for μ When σ Is Unknown

Again we find that Excel's functions are quite useful when constructing confidence intervals. Consider the following example.

EXAMPLE 8.6

A recent article found that Massachusetts residents spent an average of $860.70 on the lottery in 2010 (http://www.businessweek.com, March 14, 2012). In order to verify the results, a researcher at a Boston think tank surveys 100 Massachusetts residents and asks them about their annual expenditures on the lottery. Table 8.4 shows a portion of the results; the complete data set can be found on the text website, labeled **Lottery**. Construct a 95% confidence interval for the average annual expenditures on the lottery for all Massachusetts residents. Do the results dispute the article's claim? Explain.

TABLE 8.4 Massachusetts Residents' Annual Lottery Expenditures, $n = 100$

FILE	Annual Lottery Expenditures (in $)
	790
	594
	⋮
	759

SOLUTION: We need to compute $\bar{x} \pm t_{\alpha/2,df} \frac{s}{\sqrt{n}}$. The only value that is readily available is $n = 100$. In order to find $\bar{x}$ and s, we open **Lottery**, find empty cells, and input '=AVERAGE(A2:A101)' and '=STDEV.S(A2:A101)', respectively; Excel returns a sample mean of 841.94 and a sample standard deviation of 217.15. For a 95% confidence interval with $\alpha = 0.05$ and $df = n - 1 = 100 - 1 = 99$, we need to find $t_{\alpha/2,df} = t_{0.025,99}$. Excel's T.INV function finds a particular t_{df} value for a given cumulative probability. Since we want $t_{0.025,99}$ such that the area under the t_{99} curve to the right of $t_{0.025,99}$ is 0.025, we insert '=T.INV(0.975,99).' Excel returns 1.984. Excel also provides another extremely similar function, '=TINV(α,df)' that directly computes $t_{\alpha/2,df}$. For example, '=TINV(0.05,99)' also returns 1.984. Inserting the values returned by Excel into the formula and simplifying yields: $841.94 \pm 1.984 \frac{217.15}{\sqrt{100}} = 841.94 \pm 43.08$. With 95% confidence, we conclude that the average annual expenditures on the lottery for all Massachusetts residents fall between $798.86 and $885.02. The results do not dispute the article's claim since the interval includes the article's reported mean value of $860.70.

EXERCISES 8.2

Mechanics

16. Find $t_{\alpha,df}$ from the following information.
    a. $\alpha = 0.025$ and $df = 12$
    b. $\alpha = 0.10$ and $df = 12$
    c. $\alpha = 0.025$ and $df = 25$
    d. $\alpha = 0.10$ and $df = 25$

17. We use the t distribution for the statistical inference of the population mean when the underlying population standard deviation is not known. Under the assumption that the population is normally distributed, find $t_{\alpha/2,df}$ for the following scenarios.
    a. A 90% confidence level and a sample of 28 observations.
    b. A 95% confidence level and a sample of 28 observations.
    c. A 90% confidence level and a sample of 15 observations.
    d. A 95% confidence level and a sample of 15 observations.

18. A random sample of 24 observations is used to estimate the population mean. The sample mean and the sample standard deviation are calculated as 104.6 and 28.8, respectively. Assume that the population is normally distributed.
    a. Construct the 90% confidence interval for the population mean.
    b. Construct the 99% confidence interval for the population mean.
    c. Use your answers to discuss the impact of the confidence level on the width of the interval.

19. Consider a normal population with an unknown population standard deviation. A random sample results in $\bar{x} = 48.68$ and $s^2 = 33.64$.
    a. Compute the 95% confidence interval for μ if $\bar{x}$ and s^2 were obtained from a sample of 16 observations.
    b. Compute the 95% confidence interval for μ if $\bar{x}$ and s^2 were obtained from a sample of 25 observations.
    c. Use your answers to discuss the impact of the sample size on the width of the interval.

20. Let the following sample of 8 observations be drawn from a normal population with unknown mean and standard deviation: 22, 18, 14, 25, 17, 28, 15, 21.
    a. Calculate the sample mean and the sample standard deviation.
    b. Construct the 80% confidence interval for the population mean.
    c. Construct the 90% confidence interval for the population mean.
    d. What happens to the margin of error as the confidence level increases from 80% to 90%?

Applications

21. A random sample of eight drugstores shows the following prices (in $) of a popular pain reliever:

3.50	4.00	2.00	3.00	2.50	3.50	2.50	3.00

Assume the normal distribution for the underlying population to construct the 90% confidence interval for the population mean.

22. As reported by tradingeconomics.com on September 2, 2012, the unemployment rates (in %) in major economies around the world are as follows:

Country	Unemployment Rate (in %)
Australia	5.2
China	4.1
France	10.0
Germany	6.8
India	3.8
United Kingdom	8.0
United States	8.3

a. Calculate the margin of error used in the 95% confidence level for the population mean. Explain the assumption made for the analysis.
b. How can we reduce the margin of error for the 95% confidence interval?

23. A popular weight loss program claims that with its recommended healthy diet regimen, users lose significant weight within a month. In order to estimate the mean weight loss of all customers, a nutritionist takes a sample of 18 dieters and records their weight loss one month after joining the program. He computes the sample mean and the standard deviation of weight loss as 12.5 pounds and 9.2 pounds, respectively. He believes that weight loss is likely to be normally distributed.
    a. Calculate the margin of error with 95% confidence.
    b. Compute the 95% confidence interval for the population mean.

24. The manager of The Cheesecake Factory in Boston reports that on six randomly selected weekdays, the number of customers served was 120, 130, 100, 205, 185, and 220. She believes that the number of customers served on weekdays follows a normal distribution. Construct the 90% confidence interval for the average number of customers served on weekdays.

25. According to a recent survey, high school girls average 100 text messages daily (The Boston Globe, April 21, 2010). Assume that the survey was based on a random sample of 36 high school girls. The sample standard deviation is computed as 10 text messages daily.
    a. Calculate the margin of error with 99% confidence.
    b. What is the 99% confidence interval for the population mean texts that all high school girls send daily?

26. The Chartered Financial Analyst (CFA®) designation is fast becoming a requirement for serious investment professionals. Although it requires a successful completion of three levels of grueling exams, it also entails promising careers with lucrative salaries. A student of finance is curious about the average salary of a CFA® charterholder. He takes a random

sample of 36 recent charterholders and computes a mean salary of $158,000 with a standard deviation of $36,000. Use this sample information to determine the 95% confidence interval for the average salary of a CFA® charterholder.

27. The *Sudoku* puzzle has recently become very popular all over the world. It is based on a 9×9 grid and the challenge is to fill in the grid so that every row, every column, and every 3×3 box contains the digits 1 through 9. A researcher is interested in estimating the average time taken by a college student to solve the puzzle. He takes a random sample of 8 college students and records their solving times as 14, 7, 17, 20, 18, 15, 19, 28 minutes.

   a. Construct the 99% confidence interval for the average time taken by a college student to solve a *Sudoku* puzzle.

   b. What assumption is necessary to make this inference?

28. Executive compensation has risen dramatically compared to the rising levels of an average worker's wage over the years. Sarah is an MBA student who decides to use her statistical skills to estimate the mean CEO compensation in 2010 for all large companies in the United States. She takes a random sample of six CEO compensations.

Firm	Compensation (in $ millions)
Intel	8.20
Coca-Cola	2.76
Wells Fargo	6.57
Caterpillar	3.88
McDonald's	6.56
U.S. Bancorp	4.10

Source: http://finance.yahoo.com.

   a. How will Sarah use the above information to provide the 90% confidence interval for the mean CEO compensation of all large companies in the United States?

   b. What assumption did Sarah make for deriving the interval estimate?

   c. How can Sarah reduce the margin of error reported in the above interval estimate?

29. A price-earnings ratio or P/E ratio is calculated as a firm's share price compared to the income or profit earned by the firm per share. Generally, a high P/E ratio suggests that investors are expecting higher earnings growth in the future compared to companies with a lower P/E ratio. The following table shows the P/E ratios for a sample of firms in the footwear industry:

Firm	P/E Ratio
Brown Shoe Co., Inc.	26
CROCS, Inc.	13
DSW, Inc.	21
Foot Locker, Inc.	16
Nike, Inc.	21

Source: http://biz.yahoo.com, data retrieved September 2, 2012.

Let these ratios represent a random sample drawn from a normally distributed population. Construct the 90% confidence interval for the mean P/E ratio for the entire footwear industry.

30. The monthly closing stock prices (rounded to the nearest dollar) for Panera Bread Co. for the first six months of 2010 are reported in the following table.

Month	Closing Stock Price
January 2010	$71
February 2010	73
March 2010	76
April 2010	78
May 2010	81
June 2010	75

Source: http://finance.yahoo.com.

   a. Calculate the sample mean and the sample standard deviation.

   b. Compute the 90% confidence interval for the mean stock price of Panera Bread Co., assuming that the stock price is normally distributed.

   c. What happens to the margin of error if a higher confidence level is used for the interval estimate?

31. The following table shows the annual returns (in percent) for Fidelity's Electronic and Utilities funds.

Year	Electronic	Utilities
2005	13.23%	9.36%
2006	1.97	32.33
2007	2.77	21.03
2008	−50.55	−35.21
2009	81.65	14.71

Source: http://finance.yahoo.com.

   a. Derive 99% confidence intervals for the mean return of Fidelity's Electronic and Utilities funds.

   b. What did you have to assume to make the above inferences?

32. Suppose the 90% confidence interval for the mean SAT scores of applicants at a business college is given by [1690, 1810]. This confidence interval uses the sample mean and the sample standard deviation based on 25 observations. What are the sample mean and the sample standard deviation used for the interval?

33. A teacher wants to estimate the mean time (in minutes) students take to go from one classroom to the next. His research assistant uses the sample time of 36 students to report the confidence interval as [8.20, 9.80].

   a. Find the sample mean time used to compute the confidence interval.

   b. Determine the confidence level if the sample standard deviation used for the interval is 2.365.

34. In order to lure female customers, a new clothing store offers free gourmet coffee and pastry to its customers. The average daily revenue over the past five-week period has been

$1,080 with a standard deviation of $260. Use this sample information to construct the 95% confidence interval for the average daily revenue. The store manager believes that the coffee and pastry strategy would lead to an average daily revenue of $1,200. Use the above 95% interval to determine if the manager is wrong.

35. FILE Many of today's leading companies, including Google, Microsoft, and Facebook, are based on technologies developed within universities. Lisa Fisher is a business school professor who believes that a university's research expenditure in $ millions (Research) and the age of its technology transfer office in years (Duration) are major factors that enhance innovation. She wants to know what the average values are for the Research and the Duration variables. She collects data from 143 universities on these variables for the academic year 2008. A portion of the data is shown below; the complete data set, labeled **Startups**, can be found on the text website.

Research ($ millions)	Duration
$145.52	23
$237.52	23
⋮	⋮
$154.38	9

Source: Association of University Managers and National Science Foundation.

a. Construct and interpret the 95% confidence interval for the mean research expenditure of all universities.

b. Construct and interpret the 95% confidence interval for the mean duration of all universities.

36. FILE An associate dean of a university wishes to compare the mean on the standardized final exams in microeconomics and macroeconomics. He has access to a random sample of 40 scores from each of these two courses. A portion of the data is shown below; the complete data set, labeled **Economics**, can be found on the text website.

Micro	Macro
85	48
78	79
⋮	⋮
75	74

a. Use Excel to construct 95% confidence intervals for the mean score in microeconomics and the mean score in macroeconomics.

b. Explain why the widths of the two intervals are different.

37. FILE For decades, people have believed that boys are innately more capable than girls in math. In other words, due to the intrinsic differences in brains, boys are better suited for doing math than girls. Recent research challenges this stereotype, arguing that gender differences in math performance have more to do with culture than innate aptitude. Others argue, however, that while the average may be the same, there is more variability in math ability for boys than girls, resulting in some boys with soaring math skills. A portion of the data on math scores of boys and girls is shown below; the complete data set, labeled **Math_Scores**, can be found on the text website.

Boys	Girls
74	83
89	76
⋮	⋮
66	74

a. Use Excel to construct 95% confidence intervals for the mean scores of boys and the mean scores of girls. Explain your assumptions.

b. Explain why the widths of the two intervals are different.

38. FILE A recent study found that consumers are making average monthly debt payments of $983 (Experian.com, November 11, 2010). The accompanying table shows a portion of average debt payments for 26 metropolitan areas. The complete data set, labeled **Debt_Payments**, can be found on the text website. Use Excel to construct 90% and 95% confidence intervals for the population mean. Comment on the width of the interval.

City	Debt Payments
Washington, D.C.	$1,285
Seattle	1,135
⋮	⋮
Pittsburgh	763

Source: http://www.Experian.com, November 11, 2010.

8.3 Confidence Interval for the Population Proportion

LO **8.6**

Calculate a confidence interval for the population proportion.

Sometimes the parameter of interest describes a population that is qualitative rather than quantitative. Recall that while the population mean μ and population variance σ^2 describe quantitative data, the population proportion p is the essential descriptive measure when the data type is qualitative. The parameter p represents the proportion of successes in the population, where success is defined by a particular outcome. Examples of population proportions include the proportion of women students at a university, the proportion of defective items in a manufacturing process, and the default probability on a mortgage loan.

As in the case of the population mean, we estimate the population proportion on the basis of its sample counterpart. In particular, we use the sample proportion $\bar{P}$ as the point estimator of the population proportion p. Also, although the sampling distribution of $\bar{P}$ is based on a binomial distribution, we can approximate it by a normal distribution for large samples, according to the central limit theorem. This approximation is valid when the sample size n is such that $np \geq 5$ and $n(1 - p) \geq 5$.

Using the normal approximation for $\bar{P}$ with $E(\bar{P}) = p$ and $se(\bar{P}) = \sqrt{p(1-p)/n}$, analogous to the derivation of the confidence interval for the population mean, a $100(1 - \alpha)\%$ confidence interval for the population proportion is

$$\bar{p} \pm z_{\alpha/2}\sqrt{\frac{p(1-p)}{n}} \quad \text{or} \quad \left[\bar{p} - z_{\alpha/2}\sqrt{\frac{p(1-p)}{n}}, \bar{p} + z_{\alpha/2}\sqrt{\frac{p(1-p)}{n}}\right].$$

This confidence interval is theoretically sound; however, it cannot be implemented because it uses p in the derivation, which is unknown. Since we always use large samples for the normal distribution approximation, we can also conveniently replace p with its estimate $\bar{p}$ in the construction of the interval. Therefore, for $\sqrt{\frac{p(1-p)}{n}}$, we substitute $\sqrt{\frac{\bar{p}(1-\bar{p})}{n}}$. This substitution yields a feasible confidence interval for the population proportion.

CONFIDENCE INTERVAL FOR p

A $100(1 - \alpha)\%$ confidence interval for the population proportion p is computed as

$$\bar{p} \pm z_{\alpha/2}\sqrt{\frac{\bar{p}(1-\bar{p})}{n}} \quad \text{or} \quad \left[\bar{p} - z_{\alpha/2}\sqrt{\frac{\bar{p}(1-\bar{p})}{n}}, \bar{p} + z_{\alpha/2}\sqrt{\frac{\bar{p}(1-\bar{p})}{n}}\right]$$

This formula is valid only if $\bar{P}$ (approximately) follows a normal distribution.

The normality condition is evaluated at the sample proportion $\bar{p}$. In other words, for constructing a confidence interval for the population proportion p, we require that $n\bar{p} \geq 5$ and $n(1 - \bar{p}) \geq 5$.

EXAMPLE 8.7

In the introductory case of this chapter, Jared Beane wants to estimate the proportion of all ultra-green cars that obtain over 100 mpg. Use the information in Table 8.1 to construct 90% and 99% confidence intervals for the population proportion.

SOLUTION: As shown in Table 8.1, seven of the 25 cars obtain over 100 mpg; thus the point estimate of the population proportion is $\bar{p} = 7/25 = 0.28$. Note that the normality condition is satisfied since $np \geq 5$ and $n(1 - p) \geq 5$, where p is evaluated at $\bar{p} = 0.28$. With a 90% confidence level, $\alpha/2 = 0.10/2 = 0.05$; thus we find $z_{\alpha/2} = z_{0.05} = 1.645$. Substituting the appropriate values into $\bar{p} \pm z_{\alpha/2}\sqrt{\frac{\bar{p}(1-\bar{p})}{n}}$ yields

$$0.28 \pm 1.645\sqrt{\frac{0.28(1 - 0.28)}{25}} = 0.28 \pm 0.148.$$

With 90% confidence, Jared reports that the percentage of cars that obtain over 100 mpg is between 13.2% and 42.8%.

If Jared had wanted a 99% confidence level, we would use $\alpha/2 = 0.01/2 = 0.005$ and $z_{\alpha/2} = z_{0.005} = 2.576$ to obtain

$$0.28 \pm 2.576\sqrt{\frac{0.28(1 - 0.28)}{25}} = 0.28 \pm 0.231.$$

At a higher confidence level of 99%, the interval for the percentage of cars that obtain over 100 mpg becomes 4.9% to 51.1%. Given the current sample size of 25 cars, Jared can gain confidence (from 90% to 99%) at the expense of precision, as the corresponding margin of error increases from 0.148 to 0.231.

EXERCISES 8.3

Mechanics

39. A random sample of 100 observations results in 40 successes.
    a. What is the point estimate for the population proportion of successes?
    b. Construct the 90% confidence interval for the population proportion.
    c. Construct the 99% confidence interval for the population proportion.

40. A random sample of 80 observations results in 50 successes.
    a. Construct the 95% confidence interval for the population proportion of successes.
    b. Construct the 95% confidence interval for the population proportion of failures.

41. Assume $\bar{p} = 0.6$ in a sample of size $n = 50$.
    a. Construct the 95% confidence interval for the population proportion.
    b. What happens to the margin of error if the above sample proportion is based on $n = 200$ instead of $n = 50$?

42. A sample of 80 results in 30 successes.
    a. Calculate the point estimate for the population proportion of successes.
    b. Construct 90% and 99% confidence intervals for the population proportion.
    c. Can we conclude at 90% confidence that the population proportion differs from 0.5?
    d. Can we conclude at 99% confidence that the population proportion differs from 0.5?

43. In a sample of 30 observations the number of successes equals 18.
    a. Construct the 88% confidence interval for the population proportion of successes.
    b. Construct the 98% confidence interval for the population proportion of successes.
    c. What happens to the margin of error as you move from an 88% confidence interval to a 98% confidence interval?

Applications

44. A survey of 1,026 people asked: "What would you do with an unexpected tax refund?" Forty-seven percent responded that they would pay off debts (*Vanity Fair*, June 2010).
    a. At 95% confidence, what is the margin of error?
    b. Construct the 95% confidence interval for the population proportion of people who would pay off debts with an unexpected tax refund.

45. A recent poll of 1,079 adults finds that 51% of Americans support Arizona's stringent new immigration enforcement law, even though it may lead to racial profiling (*New York Times/CBS News*, April 28–May 2, 2010). Use the sample information to compute the 95% confidence interval for the population parameter of interest.

46. An economist reports that 560 out of a sample of 1,200 middle-income American households actively participate in the stock market.
    a. Construct the 90% confidence interval for the proportion of middle-income Americans who actively participate in the stock market.
    b. Can we conclude that the proportion of middle-income Americans who actively participate in the stock market is not 50%?

47. In a CNNMoney.com poll conducted on July 13, 2010, a sample of 5,324 Americans were asked about what matters most to them in a place to live. Thirty-seven percent of the respondents felt job opportunities matter most.
    a. Construct the 90% confidence interval for the proportion of Americans who feel that good job opportunities matter most in a place to live.
    b. Construct the 99% confidence interval for the proportion of Americans who feel that good job opportunities matter most in a place to live.
    c. Which of the above two intervals has a higher margin of error? Explain why.

48. In a recent poll of 760 homeowners in the United States, one in five homeowners reports having a home equity loan that he or she is currently paying off. Using a confidence coefficient of 0.90, derive an interval estimate for the proportion of all homeowners in the United States that hold a home equity loan.

49. In an *NBC News/Wall Street Journal* poll of 1,000 American adults conducted August 5–9, 2010, 44% of respondents approved of the job that Barack Obama was doing in handling the economy.
    a. Compute the 90% confidence interval for the proportion of Americans who approved of Barack Obama's handling of the economy.
    b. What is the resulting margin of error?
    c. Compute the margin of error associated with a 99% confidence level.

50. Obesity is generally defined as 30 or more pounds over a healthy weight. A recent study of obesity reports 27.5% of a random sample of 400 adults in the United States to be obese.
    a. Use this sample information to compute the 90% confidence interval for the adult obesity rate in the United States.
    b. Is it reasonable to conclude with 90% confidence that the adult obesity rate in the United States differs from 30%?

51. An accounting professor is notorious for being stingy in giving out good letter grades. In a large section of 140 students in the fall semester, she gave out only 5% As, 23% Bs, 42% Cs, and 30% Ds and Fs. Assuming that this was

a representative class, compute the 95% confidence interval of the probability of getting at least a B from this professor.

52. A recent survey asked 5,324 individuals: What's most important to you when choosing where to live? The responses are shown by the following frequency distribution.

Response	Frequency
Good jobs	1,969
Affordable homes	799
Top schools	586
Low crime	1,225
Things to do	745

Source: CNNMoney.com, July 13, 2010.

a. Calculate the margin of error used in the 95% confidence level for the population proportion of those who believe that low crime is most important.

b. Calculate the margin of error used in the 95% confidence level for the population proportion of those who believe that good jobs or affordable homes are most important.

c. Explain why the margins of error in parts a and b are different.

53. A survey conducted by CBS News asked 1,026 respondents: "What would you do with an unexpected tax refund?" The responses are summarized in the following table.

Response	Frequency
Pay off debts	482
Put it in the bank	308
Spend it	112
I never get a refund	103
Other	21

Source: Vanity Fair, June 2010.

a. Construct the 90% confidence interval for the population proportion of those who would put the tax refund in the bank.

b. Construct the 90% confidence interval for the population proportion of those who never get a refund.

54. One in five 18-year-old Americans has not graduated from high school (The Wall Street Journal, April 19, 2007). A mayor of a northeastern city comments that its residents do not have the same graduation rate as the rest of the country. An analyst from the Department of Education decides to test the mayor's claim. In particular, she draws a random sample of 80 18-year-olds in the city and finds that 20 of them have not graduated from high school.

a. Compute the point estimate for the proportion of 18-year-olds who have graduated from high school in this city.

b. Use this point estimate to derive the 95% confidence interval for the population proportion.

c. Can the mayor's comment be justified at 95% confidence?

8.4 Selecting the Required Sample Size

So far we have discussed how a confidence interval provides useful information on an unknown population parameter. We compute the confidence interval by adding and subtracting the margin of error to/from the point estimate. If the margin of error is very large, the confidence interval becomes too wide to be of much value. For instance, little useful information can be gained from a confidence interval that suggests that the average annual starting salary of a business graduate is between $16,000 and $64,000. Similarly, an interval estimate that 10% to 60% of business students pursue an MBA is not very informative.

Statisticians like precision in their interval estimates, which is implied by a low margin of error. If we are able to increase the size of the sample, the larger n reduces the margin of error for the interval estimates. Although a larger sample size improves precision, it also entails the added cost in terms of time and money. Before getting into data collection, it is important that we first decide on the sample size that is adequate for what we wish to accomplish. In this section, we examine the required sample size, for a desired margin of error, in the confidence intervals for the population mean μ and the population proportion p. In order to be conservative, we always round up non-integer values of the required sample size.

LO 8.7

Select a sample size to estimate the population mean and the population proportion.

Selecting n to Estimate μ

Consider a confidence interval for μ with a known population standard deviation σ. In addition, let E denote the desired margin of error. In other words, you do not want the sample mean to deviate from the population mean by more than E, for a given level of confidence. Since $E = z_{\alpha/2} \frac{\sigma}{\sqrt{n}}$, we rearrange this equation to derive the formula for the required sample size as $n = \left(\frac{z_{\alpha/2}\sigma}{E} \right)^2$. The sample size can be computed if we specify the population standard deviation σ, the value of $z_{\alpha/2}$ based on the confidence level $100(1 - \alpha)\%$, and the desired margin of error E.

This formula is based on a knowledge of σ. However, in most cases σ is not known and, therefore, has to be estimated. Note that the sample standard deviation s cannot be used as an estimate for σ because s can be computed only after a sample of size n has been selected. In such cases, we replace σ with its reasonable estimate $\hat{\sigma}$.

THE REQUIRED SAMPLE SIZE WHEN ESTIMATING THE POPULATION MEAN

For a desired margin of error E, the minimum sample size n required to estimate a $100(1 - \alpha)\%$ confidence interval for the population mean μ is

$$n = \left(\frac{z_{\alpha/2}\hat{\sigma}}{E} \right)^2,$$

where $\hat{\sigma}$ is a reasonable estimate of σ in the planning stage.

If σ is known, we replace $\hat{\sigma}$ with σ. Sometimes we use the sample standard deviation from a preselected sample as $\hat{\sigma}$ in the planning stage. Another choice for $\hat{\sigma}$ is to use an estimate of the population standard deviation from prior studies. Finally, if the lowest and highest possible values of the population are available, a rough approximation for the population standard deviation is given by $\hat{\sigma} = \text{range}/4$.

EXAMPLE 8.8

Let us revisit Example 8.5, where Jared Beane wants to construct the 90% confidence interval for the mean mpg of all ultra-green cars. Suppose Jared would like to constrain the margin of error to within 2 mpg. Further, Jared knows that the lowest mpg in the population is 76 mpg, whereas the highest is 118 mpg. How large a sample does Jared need to compute the 90% confidence interval for the population mean?

SOLUTION: For a 90% confidence level, Jared computes $z_{\alpha/2} = z_{0.05} = 1.645$. He estimates the population standard deviation as $\hat{\sigma} = \text{range}/4 = (118 - 76)/4 = 10.50$. Given $E = 2$, the required sample size is

$$n = \left(\frac{z_{\alpha/2}\hat{\sigma}}{E} \right)^2 = \left(\frac{1.645 \times 10.50}{2} \right)^2 = 74.58,$$

which is rounded up to 75. Therefore, Jared needs a random sample of at least 75 ultra-green cars to provide a more precise interval estimate of the mean mpg.

Selecting n to Estimate p

The margin of error E for the confidence interval for the population proportion p is $E = z_{\alpha/2}\sqrt{\frac{\bar{p}(1 - \bar{p})}{n}}$, where $\bar{p}$ represents the sample proportion. By rearranging, we derive the formula for the required sample size as $n = \left(\frac{z_{\alpha/2}}{E} \right)^2 \bar{p}(1 - \bar{p})$. Note that this formula is not feasible because it uses $\bar{p}$, which cannot be computed unless a sample of size n has already been selected. We replace $\bar{p}$ with a reasonable estimate $\hat{p}$ of the population proportion p.

THE REQUIRED SAMPLE SIZE WHEN ESTIMATING THE POPULATION PROPORTION

For a desired margin of error E, the minimum sample size n required to estimate a $100(1 - \alpha)\%$ confidence interval for the population proportion p is

$$n = \left(\frac{z_{\alpha/2}}{E}\right)^2 \hat{p}(1 - \hat{p}),$$

where $\hat{p}$ is a reasonable estimate of p in the planning stage.

Sometimes we use the sample proportion from a preselected sample as $\hat{p}$ in the planning stage. Once the optimal sample size is determined, the final sample is selected for estimating the population proportion. Another choice for $\hat{p}$ is to use an estimate of the population proportion from prior studies. If no other reasonable estimate of the population proportion is available, we can use $\hat{p} = 0.5$ as a conservative estimate to derive the optimal sample size; note that the required sample is the largest when $\hat{p} = 0.5$.

EXAMPLE 8.9

Let us revisit Example 8.7, where Jared Beane wants to construct the 90% confidence interval for the proportion of all ultra-green cars that obtain over 100 mpg. Jared does not want the margin of error to be more than 0.10. How large a sample does Jared need for his analysis of the population proportion?

SOLUTION: For a 90% confidence level, Jared computes $z_{\alpha/2} = z_{0.05} = 1.645$. Since no estimate for the population proportion is readily available, Jared uses a conservative estimate of $\hat{p} = 0.50$. Given $E = 0.10$, the required sample size is

$$n = \left(\frac{z_{\alpha/2}}{E}\right)^2 \hat{p}(1 - \hat{p}) = \left(\frac{1.645}{0.10}\right)^2 0.50(1 - 0.50) = 67.65,$$

which is rounded up to 68. Therefore, Jared needs to find another random sample of at least 68 ultra-green cars to provide a more precise interval estimate for the proportion of all ultra-green cars that obtain over 100 mpg.

SYNOPSIS OF INTRODUCTORY CASE

Jared Beane, an analyst at a research firm, prepares to write a report on the new ultra-green car that boasts an average of 100 mpg. Based on a sample of 25 cars, Jared reports with 90% confidence that the average mpg of all ultra-green cars is between 92.86 mpg and 100.18 mpg. Jared also constructs the 90% confidence interval for the proportion of cars that obtain more than 100 mpg and obtains an interval estimate of 0.132 to 0.428. Jared wishes to increase the precision of his confidence intervals by reducing the margin of error. If his desired margin of error is 2 mpg for the population mean, he must use a sample of at least 75 cars for the analysis. Jared also wants to reduce the margin of error to 0.10 for the proportion of cars that obtain more than 100 mpg. Using a conservative estimate, he calculates that a sample of at least 68 cars is needed to achieve this goal. Thus, in order to gain precision in the interval estimate for both the mean and the proportion with 90% confidence, Jared's sample must contain at least 75 cars.

EXERCISES 8.4

Mechanics

55. What is the minimum sample size n required to estimate μ with 90% confidence if the desired margin of error is $E = 1.2$? The population standard deviation is estimated as $\hat{\sigma} = 3.5$. What happens to n if the desired margin of error decreases to $E = 0.7$?

56. The lowest and highest observations in a population are 20 and 80, respectively. What is the minimum sample size n required to estimate μ with 80% confidence if the desired margin of error is $E = 2.6$? What happens to n if you decide to estimate μ with 95% confidence?

57. Find the required sample size for estimating the population mean in order to be 95% confident that the sample mean is within 10 units of the population mean. Assume that the population standard deviation is 40.

58. You need to compute a 99% confidence interval for the population mean. How large a sample should you draw to ensure that the sample mean does not deviate from the population mean by more than 1.2? (Use 6.0 as an estimate of the population standard deviation from prior studies.)

59. What is the minimum sample size n required to estimate p with 95% confidence if the desired margin of error $E = 0.08$? The population proportion is estimated as $\hat{p} = 0.36$ from prior studies. What happens to n if the desired margin of error increases to $E = 0.12$?

60. In the planning stage, a sample proportion is estimated as $\hat{p} = 40/50 = 0.80$. Use this information to compute the minimum sample size n required to estimate p with 99% confidence if the desired margin of error $E = 0.12$. What happens to n if you decide to estimate p with 90% confidence?

61. You wish to compute a 95% confidence interval for the population proportion. How large a sample should you draw to ensure that the sample proportion does not deviate from the population proportion by more than 0.06? No prior estimate for the population proportion is available.

Applications

62. An analyst from an energy research institute in California wishes to precisely estimate the 99% confidence interval for the average price of unleaded gasoline in the state. In particular, she does not want the sample mean to deviate from the population mean by more than $0.06. What is the minimum number of gas stations that she should include in her sample if she uses the standard deviation estimate of $0.32, as reported in the popular press?

63. An analyst would like to construct 95% confidence intervals for the mean stock returns in two industries. Industry A is a high-risk industry with a known population standard deviation of 20.6%, whereas Industry B is a lower-risk industry with a known population standard deviation of 12.8%.

    a. What is the minimum sample size required by the analyst if she wants to restrict the margin of error to 4% for Industry A?

    b. What is the minimum sample size required by the analyst if she wants to restrict the margin of error to 4% for Industry B?

    c. Why do the above results differ if they use the same margin of error?

64. The manager of a pizza chain in Albuquerque, New Mexico, wants to determine the average size of their advertised 16-inch pizzas. She takes a random sample of 25 pizzas and records their mean and standard deviation as 16.10 inches and 1.8 inches, respectively. She subsequently computes the 95% confidence interval of the mean size of all pizzas as [15.36, 16.84]. However, she finds this interval to be too broad to implement quality control and decides to reestimate the mean based on a bigger sample. Using the standard deviation estimate of 1.8 from her earlier analysis, how large a sample must she take if she wants the margin of error to be under 0.5 inch?

65. Mortgage lenders often use FICO® scores to check the credit worthiness of consumers applying for real estate loans. In general, FICO scores range from 300 to 850 with higher scores representing a better credit profile. A lender in a midwestern town would like to estimate the mean credit score of its residents. What is the required number of sample FICO scores needed if the lender does not want the margin of error to exceed 20, with 95% confidence?

66. The manager of a newly opened Target store wants to estimate the average expenditure of his customers. From a preselected sample, the standard deviation was determined to be $18. The manager would like to construct the 95% confidence interval for the mean customer expenditure.

    a. Find the appropriate sample size necessary to achieve a margin of error of $5.

    b. Find the appropriate sample size necessary to achieve a margin of error of $3.

67. A budget airline wants to estimate what proportion of customers would consider paying $12 for in-flight wireless access. Given that the airline has no prior knowledge of the proportion, how many customers would it have to sample to ensure a margin of error of no more than 0.05 for a 90% confidence interval?

68. Newscasters wish to estimate the proportion of registered voters who support the incumbent candidate in the mayoral election. In an earlier poll of 240 registered voters, 110 had supported the incumbent candidate. Find the sample size required to construct a 90% confidence interval if newscasters do not want the margin of error to exceed 0.02.

69. A survey by the AARP (*Money*, June 2007) reported that approximately 70% of people in the 50 to 64 age bracket have tried some type of alternative therapy (for instance, acupuncture or the use of nutrition supplements). Assume this survey was based on a sample of 400 people.

    a. Identify the relevant parameter of interest for these qualitative data and compute its point estimate as well as the margin of error with 90% confidence.

b. You decide to redo the analysis with the margin of error reduced to 2%. How large a sample do you need to draw? State your assumptions in computing the required sample size.

70. Subprime lending was big business in the United States in the mid-2000s, when lenders provided mortgages to people with poor credit. However, subsequent increases in interest rates coupled with a drop in home values necessitated many borrowers to default. Suppose a recent report finds that two in five subprime mortgages are likely to default nationally. A research economist is interested in estimating default rates in Illinois with 95% confidence. How large a sample is needed to restrict the margin of error to within 0.06, using the reported national default rate?

71. A student of business is interested in estimating the 99% confidence interval for the proportion of students who bring laptops to campus. He wishes a precise estimate and is willing to draw a large sample that will keep the sample proportion within five percentage points of the population proportion. What is the minimum sample size required by this student, given that no prior estimate of the population proportion is available?

WRITING WITH STATISTICS

Callie Fitzpatrick, a research analyst with an investment firm, has been asked to write a report summarizing the weekly stock performance of Home Depot and Lowe's. Her manager is trying to decide whether or not to include one of these stocks in a client's portfolio and the average stock performance is one of the factors influencing this decision. Callie decides to use descriptive measures to summarize stock returns in her report, as well as provide confidence intervals for the average return for Home Depot and Lowe's. She collects weekly returns for each firm for the first eight months of 2010. A portion of the return data is shown in Table 8.5; the complete data set, labeled **Weekly_Returns**, can be found on the text website.

TABLE 8.5 Weekly Returns (in percent) for Home Depot and Lowe's

FILE Date	Home Depot	Lowe's
1/11/2010	−1.44	−1.59
1/19/2010	−2.98	−3.53
⋮	⋮	⋮
8/30/2010	−2.61	−3.89

SOURCE: http://finance.yahoo.com.

Callie would like to use the sample information to:

1. Summarize weekly returns for Home Depot and Lowe's.
2. Provide confidence intervals for the average weekly returns.
3. Make recommendations for further analysis.

Sample
Report—
Weekly Stock
Performance:
Home Depot
vs. Lowe's

Grim news continues to distress the housing sector. On August 24, 2010, Reuters reported that the sales of previously owned U.S. homes took a record plunge in July to the slowest pace in 15 years. Combine this fact with the continued fallout from the subprime mortgage debacle, a sluggish economy, and high unemployment, and the housing sector appears quite unstable. Have these unfavorable events managed to trickle down and harm the financial performance of Home Depot and Lowe's, the two largest home improvement retailers in the United States?

One way to analyze their financial stability is to observe their stock performance during this period. In order to make valid statements concerning the reward of holding these stocks, weekly return data for each firm were gathered from January through August of 2010. Table 8.A summarizes the important descriptive statistics.

TABLE 8.A Descriptive Statistics for Weekly Returns of Home Depot and Lowe's ($n = 34$)

	Home Depot	Lowe's
Mean	0.00%	−0.33%
Median	0.76%	−0.49%
Minimum	−8.08%	−7.17%
Maximum	5.30%	7.71%
Standard deviation	3.59%	3.83%
Margin of error with 95% confidence	1.25%	1.34%

Over the past 34 weeks, Home Depot posted both a higher average return and median return of 0.00% and 0.76%, respectively. Lowe's return over the same period was negative, whether the central tendency was measured by its mean (−0.33%) or its median (−0.49%). In terms of dispersion, Lowe's return data had the higher standard deviation (3.83% > 3.59%). In terms of descriptive measures, the investment in Home Depot's stock not only provided higher returns, but also was less risky than the investment in Lowe's stock.

Table 8.A also shows the margins of error for 95% confidence intervals for the mean returns. With 95% confidence, the mean return for Home Depot fell in the range [−1.25%, 1.25%], while that for Lowe's fell in the range [−1.67%, 1.01%]. Given that these two intervals overlap, one cannot conclude that Home Depot delivered the higher reward over this period—a conclusion one may have arrived at had only the point estimates been evaluated. It is not possible to recommend one stock over the other for inclusion in a client's portfolio based solely on the mean return performance. Other factors, such as the standard deviation of the returns and the correlation between the stock and the existing portfolio, must be analyzed before this decision can be made.

Conceptual Review

LO **8.1** **Explain an interval estimator.**

The sample mean $\overline{X}$ is the point estimator of the population mean μ and the sample proportion $\overline{P}$ is the point estimator of the population proportion p. Sample values of the point estimators represent the point estimates of the population parameter of interest; $\overline{x}$ and $\overline{p}$ are the point estimates of μ and p, respectively. While a point estimator provides a single value that approximates the unknown parameter, a **confidence interval**, or an **interval estimate**, provides a range of values that, with a certain level of confidence, will contain the population parameter of interest.

Often, we construct a confidence interval as: point estimate ± margin of error. The **margin of error** accounts for the variability of the estimator and the desired confidence level of the interval.

LO 8.2 **Calculate a confidence interval for the population mean when the population standard deviation is known.**

A $100(1 - \alpha)\%$ confidence interval for the population mean μ when the population standard deviation σ is known is computed as $\bar{x} \pm z_{\alpha/2} \frac{\sigma}{\sqrt{n}}$, where $z_{\alpha/2} \frac{\sigma}{\sqrt{n}}$ is the margin of error. This formula is valid only if $\bar{X}$ (approximately) follows a normal distribution.

LO 8.3 **Describe the factors that influence the width of a confidence interval.**

The **precision** of a confidence interval is directly linked with the **width** of the interval: the wider the interval, the lower is its precision. A confidence interval is wider (a) the greater the population standard deviation σ, (b) the smaller the sample size n, and (c) the greater the confidence level.

LO 8.4 **Discuss features of the t distribution.**

The ***t* distribution** is a family of distributions that are similar to the z distribution, in that they are all symmetric and bell-shaped around zero with asymptotic tails. However, the t distribution has broader tails than does the z distribution. Each t distribution is identified by a parameter known as the **degrees of freedom df**. The df determine the extent of broadness—the smaller the df, the broader the tails. Since the t distribution is defined by the degrees of freedom, it is common to refer to it as the t_{df} distribution.

LO 8.5 **Calculate a confidence interval for the population mean when the population standard deviation is not known.**

A $100(1 - \alpha)\%$ confidence interval for the population mean μ when the population standard deviation σ is not known is computed as $\bar{x} \pm t_{\alpha/2,df} \frac{s}{\sqrt{n}}$, where s is the sample standard deviation. This formula is valid only if $\bar{X}$ (approximately) follows a normal distribution.

LO 8.6 **Calculate a confidence interval for the population proportion.**

A $100(1 - \alpha)\%$ confidence interval for the population proportion p is computed as $\bar{p} \pm z_{\alpha/2} \sqrt{\frac{\bar{p}(1 - \bar{p})}{n}}$, where $\bar{p}$ is the sample proportion. This formula is valid only if $\bar{P}$ (approximately) follows a normal distribution.

LO 8.7 **Select a sample size to estimate the population mean and the population proportion.**

For a desired margin of error E, the minimum n required to estimate μ with $100(1 - \alpha)\%$ confidence is $n = \left(\frac{z_{\alpha/2}\hat{\sigma}}{E}\right)^2$, where $\hat{\sigma}$ is a reasonable estimate of σ in the planning stage. If σ is known, we replace $\hat{\sigma}$ with σ. Other choices for $\hat{\sigma}$ include an estimate from a preselected sample, prior studies, or $\hat{\sigma} = $ range$/4$.

For a desired margin of error E, the minimum n required to estimate p with $100(1 - \alpha)\%$ confidence is $n = \left(\frac{z_{\alpha/2}}{E}\right)^2 \hat{p}(1 - \hat{p})$, where $\hat{p}$ is a reasonable estimate of p in the planning stage. Choices for $\hat{p}$ include an estimate from a preselected sample or prior studies; a conservative estimate of $\hat{p} = 0.5$ is used when no other reasonable estimate is available.

Additional Exercises and Case Studies

72. Over a 10-year sample period, the mean return and the standard deviation of annual returns on a portfolio you are analyzing were 10% and 15%, respectively. You assume that returns are normally distributed. Construct the 95% confidence interval for the population mean.

73. A hair salon in Cambridge, Massachusetts, reports that on seven randomly selected weekdays, the number of customers who visited the salon were 40, 30, 28, 22, 36, 16, and 50. It can be assumed that weekday customer visits follow a normal distribution.
    a. Construct the 90% confidence interval for the average number of customers who visit the salon on weekdays.
    b. Construct the 99% confidence interval for the average number of customers who visit the salon on weekdays.
    c. What happens to the width of the interval as the confidence level increases?

74. Recently, six single-family homes in San Luis Obispo County in California sold at the following prices (in $1,000s): $549, $449, $705, $529, $639, $609.
    a. Construct the 95% confidence interval for the mean sale price in San Luis Obispo County.
    b. What assumption have you made when constructing this confidence interval?

75. According to data from the Organization for Economic Cooperation and Development, the average U.S. worker takes 16 days of vacation each year (*The Wall Street Journal*, June 20, 2007). Assume that these data were based on a sample of 225 workers and that the sample standard deviation is 12 days.
    a. Construct the 95% confidence interval for the population mean.
    b. At a 95% confidence level, can we conclude that the average U.S. worker does not take 14 days of vacation each year?

76. A machine that is programmed to package 1.20 pounds of cereal is being tested for its accuracy. In a sample of 36 cereal boxes, the sample mean filling weight is calculated as 1.22 pounds. The population standard deviation is known to be 0.06 pound.
    a. Identify the relevant parameter of interest for these quantitative data and compute its point estimate as well as the margin of error with 95% confidence.
    b. Can we conclude that the packaging machine is operating improperly?
    c. How large a sample must we take if we want the margin of error to be at most 0.01 pound with 95% confidence?

77. The SAT is the most widely used test in the undergraduate admissions process. Scores on the math portion of the SAT are believed to be normally distributed and range from 200 to 800. A researcher from the admissions department at the University of New Hampshire is interested in estimating the mean math SAT scores of the incoming class

with 90% confidence. How large a sample should she take to ensure that the margin of error is below 15?

78. A recent study by Allstate Insurance Co. finds that 82% of teenagers have used cell phones while driving (*The Wall Street Journal*, May 5, 2010). Suppose this study was based on a random sample of 50 teen drivers.
    a. Construct the 99% confidence interval for the proportion of all teenagers that have used cell phones while driving.
    b. What is the margin of error with 99% confidence?

79. The following table shows the annual returns (in percent) for the Vanguard Energy Fund.

Year	Return
2005	44.60
2006	19.68
2007	37.00
2008	−42.87
2009	38.36

Source: http://finance.yahoo.com.

   a. Calculate the point estimate for μ.
   b. Construct the 95% confidence interval for μ.
   c. What assumption did you make when constructing the interval?

80. Students who graduated from college in 2010 owed an average of $25,250 in student loans (*New York Times*, November 2, 2011). An economist wants to determine if average debt has changed. She takes a sample of 40 recent graduates and finds that their average debt was $27,500 with a standard deviation of $9,120. Use a 90% confidence interval to determine if average debt has changed.

81. **FILE** A Realtor wants to estimate the mean price of houses in Mission Viejo, California. She collects a sample of 36 recent house sales, a portion of which is shown in the accompanying table; the complete data set, labeled **MV_Houses**, can be found on the text website. Assume that the population standard deviation is 100 (in $1,000s). Construct and interpret 95% and 98% confidence intervals for the mean price of all houses in Mission Viejo, CA.

Prices (in $1,000s)
430
520
⋮
430

82. **FILE** Residents of Hawaii have the longest life expectancies, averaging 81.48 years (http://www.worldlifeexpectancy .com, data retrieved June 4, 2012). A sociologist collects data on the age at death for 50 recently deceased Michigan residents. A portion of the data is shown in the

accompanying table; the complete data set, labeled **MI_Life_Expectancy**, can be found on the text website. Assume that the population standard deviation is 5 years.

Age at Death
76.4
76.0
⋮
73.6

a. Use Excel to construct the 95% confidence interval for the mean life expectancy of all residents of Michigan.

b. Use the 95% confidence interval to determine if the mean life expectancy of Michigan residents differs from that for Hawaii residents.

83. **FILE** The manager of a minor league baseball team wants to estimate the average fastball speed of two pitchers. He clocks 50 fastballs, in miles per hour, for each pitcher. A portion of the data is shown in the accompanying table; the complete data set, labeled **Fastballs**, can be found on the text website.

Pitcher 1	Pitcher 2
87	82
86	92
⋮	⋮
86	93

a. Use Excel to construct 95% confidence intervals for the mean speed for each pitcher.

b. Explain why the widths of the two intervals are different.

84. **FILE** The new manager of a theater would like to offer discounts to increase the number of tickets sold for shows on Monday and Tuesday evenings. She uses a sample of 30 weeks to record the number of tickets sold on these two days. A portion of the data is shown in the accompanying table; the complete data set, labeled **Theater**, can be found on the text website.

Monday	Tuesday
221	208
187	199
⋮	⋮
194	180

a. Use Excel to compare the margin of error for the 95% confidence intervals for the mean number of tickets sold for shows on Monday and Tuesday evenings.

b. Use Excel to construct the 95% confidence intervals for the mean number of tickets sold for shows on Monday and Tuesday evenings.

c. Determine if the population mean differs from 200 for shows on Monday and Tuesday evenings.

85. **FILE** While the housing market is in the tank and is not likely to emerge anytime soon, real estate investment in college towns continues to promise good returns (*The Wall Street Journal*, September 24, 2010). Marcela Treisman works for an investment firm in Michigan. Her assignment is to analyze the rental market in Ann Arbor, which is home to the University of Michigan. She gathers data on monthly rents for 2011 along with the square footage of 40 homes. A portion of the data is shown in the accompanying table; the complete data set, labeled **Ann Arbor_Rental**, can be found on the text website.

Monthly Rent	Square Footage
645	500
675	648
⋮	⋮
2400	2700

Source: http://www.zillow.com.

a. Use Excel to construct 90% and 95% confidence intervals for the mean rent for all rental homes in Ann Arbor, Michigan.

b. Use Excel to construct 90% and 95% confidence intervals for the mean square footage for all rental homes in Ann Arbor, Michigan.

86. According to a survey of 1,235 businesses by IDC, a market-research concern in Framingham, Massachusetts, 12.1% of sole proprietors are engaging in e-commerce (*The Wall Street Journal*, July 26, 2007).

a. With 95% confidence, what is the margin of error when estimating the proportion of sole proprietors that engage in e-commerce?

b. Construct a 95% confidence interval for the population proportion.

87. A Monster.com poll of 3057 individuals asked: "What's the longest vacation you plan to take this summer?" The following relative frequency distribution summarizes the results.

Response	Relative Frequency
A few days	0.21
A few long weekends	0.18
One week	0.36
Two weeks	0.22

Source: *The Boston Globe*, June 12, 2007.

a. Construct the 95% confidence interval for the proportion of people who plan to take a one-week vacation this summer.

b. Construct the 99% confidence interval for the proportion of people who plan to take a one-week vacation this summer.

c. Which of the two confidence intervals is wider?

88. Linda Barnes has learned from prior studies that one out of five applicants gets admitted to top MBA programs in the country. She wishes to construct her own 90% confidence interval for the acceptance rate in top MBA programs. How large a sample should she take if she does not want the acceptance rate of the sample to deviate from that of the population by more than five percentage points? State your assumptions in computing the required sample size.

89. **FILE** There is a declining interest among teenagers to pursue a career in science and health care (*US News and World Report*, May 23, 2011). Thirty college-bound students in Portland, Oregon, are asked about the field they would like to pursue in college. The choices offered in the questionnaire are science, business, and other. The gender information also is included in the questionnaire. A portion of the data is shown below; the complete data set, labeled *Field_Choice*, can be found on the text website.

Field Choice	Gender
Business	Male
Other	Female
⋮	⋮
Science	Female

a. Compare the 95% confidence interval for the proportion of students who would like to pursue Science with the proportion who would like to pursue Business.
b. Construct and interpret the 90% confidence interval for the proportion of female students who are college bound.

90. **FILE** A recent study examined "sidewalk rage" in an attempt to find insight into anger's origins and offer suggestions for anger-management treatments (*The Wall Street Journal*, February 15, 2011). "Sidewalk ragers" tend to believe that pedestrians should behave in a certain way. One possible strategy for sidewalk ragers is to avoid walkers who are distracted by other activities such as smoking and tourism. Sample data were obtained from 50 pedestrians in Lower Manhattan. It was noted if the pedestrian was smoking (equaled 1 if smoking, 0 otherwise) or was a tourist (equaled 1 if tourist, 0 otherwise). The accompanying table shows a portion of the data; the complete data set, labeled *Pedestrians*, can be found on the text website.

Smoking	Tourist
0	1
0	1
⋮	⋮
0	0

a. Construct and interpret the 95% confidence interval for the proportion of pedestrians in Lower Manhattan who smoke while walking.
b. Construct and interpret the 95% confidence interval for the proportion of pedestrians in Lower Manhattan who are tourists.

91. An economist would like to estimate the 95% confidence interval for the average real estate taxes collected by a small town in California, ravaged by the economic crisis. In a prior analysis, the standard deviation of real estate taxes was reported as $1,580. What is the minimum sample size required by the economist if he wants to restrict the margin of error to $500?

92. An employee of the Bureau of Transportation Statistics has been given the task of estimating the proportion of on-time arrivals of a budget airline. A prior study had estimated this on-time arrival rate as 78.5 percent. What is the minimum number of arrivals this employee must include in the sample to ensure that the margin of error for a 95% confidence interval is no more than 0.05?

93. According to a recent report by the PEW Research Center, 85% of adults under 30 feel optimistic about the economy, but the optimism is shared by only 45% of those who are over 50 (*Newsweek*, September 13, 2010). A research analyst would like to construct 95% confidence intervals for the proportion patterns in various regions of the country. She uses the reported rates by the PEW Research Center to determine the sample size that would restrict the margin of error to within 0.05.

a. How large a sample is required to estimate the proportion of adults under 30 who feel optimistic about the economy?
b. How large a sample is required to estimate the proportion of adults over 50 who feel optimistic about the economy?

CASE STUDIES

Case Study 8.1

Texas is home to more than one million undocumented immigrants and most of them are stuck in low-paying jobs. Meanwhile, the state also suffers from a lack of skilled workers. The Texas Workforce Commission estimates that 133,000 jobs are currently unfilled, many because employers cannot find qualified applicants (*The Boston Globe*, September 29, 2011). Texas was the first state to pass a law that allows children of undocumented immigrants to pay in-state college tuition rates if they have lived in Texas for three years and plan to become permanent residents. The law passed easily back in 2001 because most legislators believed that producing college graduates and keeping them in Texas benefits the business community. In addition, since college graduates earn more money, they also provide the state with more revenue. Carol Capaldo wishes to estimate the mean hourly wage of workers with various levels of education. She collects a sample of the hourly wages of 30 Texas workers with a bachelor's degree or higher, 30 Texas workers with only a high school diploma, and 30 Texas workers who did not finish high school. A portion of the data is shown in the accompanying table; the complete data set, labeled **Texas_Wages**, can be found on the text website.

Data for Case Study 8.1 Hourly Wages of Texas Workers by Education Level (in $)

FILE	Bachelor's Degree or Higher	High School Diploma	No High School Diploma
	$22.50	$12.68	$11.21
	19.57	11.23	8.54
	⋮	⋮	⋮
	21.44	7.47	10.27

In a report, use the above information to:

1. Use descriptive statistics to compare the hourly wages of the three education levels.
2. Construct and interpret 95% confidence intervals for the mean hourly wage at each education level.

Case Study 8.2

The following table presents the returns of two mutual funds offered by the investment giant Fidelity. The *Fidelity Select Automotive Fund* invests primarily in companies engaged in the manufacturing, marketing, or sales of automobiles, trucks, specialty vehicles, parts, tires, and related services. The *Fidelity Gold Fund* invests primarily in companies engaged in exploration, mining, processing, or dealing in gold and, to a lesser degree, in other precious metals and minerals. A portion of the annual return data is shown below; the complete data set, labeled **Fidelity_Returns**, can be found on the text website.

Data for Case Study 8.2 Annual Total Return (%) History

FILE		Annual Total Return (%) History	
	Year	Fidelity Select Automotive Fund	Fidelity Select Gold Fund
	2001	22.82	24.99
	2002	−6.48	64.28
	⋮	⋮	⋮
	2009	122.28	38.00

Source: http://finance.yahoo.com.

In a report, use the above information to:

1. Use descriptive statistics to compare the returns of the mutual funds.
2. Assess reward by constructing and interpreting 95% confidence intervals for the population mean return. What assumption did you make for the interval estimates?

Case Study 8.3

The information gathered from opinion polls and political surveys is becoming so increasingly important for candidates on the campaign trail that it is hard to imagine an election that lacks extensive polling. An NBC News/*Wall Street Journal* survey (August 5–9, 2010) of 1,000 adults asked people's preferences on candidates and issues prior to the midterm 2010 elections. Some of the responses to the survey are shown below, as well as responses from prior surveys. (Copyright © 2010 Dow Jones & Co., Inc.)

Question: In general, do you approve or disapprove of the way Barack Obama is handling the aftermath of the Gulf Coast oil spill in August 2010 (and George W. Bush's handling of Katrina in March 2006)?

	August 2010	March 2006
Approve	50%	36%
Disapprove	38%	53%
Not sure	12%	11%

Question: Which are more important to you in your vote for Congress this November: domestic issues such as the economy, health care, and immigration; or international issues such as Afghanistan, Iran, and terrorism?

	August 2010	September 2006
Domestic issues	73%	43%
International issues	12%	28%
Both equally important	15%	28%

In a report, construct 95% confidence intervals for the relevant population proportions to:

1. Compare the approval rates of President Obama's handling of the Gulf Coast oil spill and President George W. Bush's handling of the Hurricane Katrina crisis.
2. Compare the importance of domestic issues in August 2010 and in September 2006.

Appendix 8.1 Guidelines for Other Software Packages

The following section provides brief commands for specific software packages: Minitab, SPSS, and JMP. More detailed instructions can be found on the text website.

MINITAB

Estimating μ, σ known

A. (Replicating Example 8.3) From the menu choose **Stat > Basic Statistics > 1-Sample Z**.
B. Choose **Samples in columns** and select C1 (Weight). Enter 7.5 for **Standard deviation**.
C. Choose **Options**. Enter 92.0 for **Confidence Level**.

Estimating μ, σ unknown

A. (Replicating Example 8.6) From the menu choose **Stat > Basic Statistics > 1-Sample t**.
B. Choose **Samples in columns** and select C1 (Annual Lottery Expenditures).
C. Choose **Options**. Enter 95.0 for **Confidence Level**.

SPSS

Estimating μ, σ unknown

A. (Replicating Example 8.6) From the menu choose **Analyze > Compare Means > One-Sample T Test**. Select Expenditures as **Test Variables(s)**.
B. Choose **Options**. Enter 95.0 for **Confidence Interval Percentage**.

JMP

Estimating μ, σ known

A. (Replicating Example 8.3) From the menu choose **Analyze > Distribution**.

B. Choose Column 1, then choose **Y, Columns**. Click **OK**.

C. Click on the red triangle in the output window beside Column 1 (or name of variable; here it is Weight) above the histogram. Choose **Confidence Interval** and after **Enter (1-alpha for Confidence level)** enter 0.92. Select **Use known sigma** and enter 7.5.

Estimating μ, σ unknown

A. (Replicating Example 8.6) From the menu choose **Analyze > Distribution**.

B. Choose Column 1, then choose **Y, Columns**. Click **OK**.

C. JMP automatically calculates a 95% confidence interval. For other levels of confidence, click on the red triangle in the output window beside Column 1 (or name of variable; here it is Annual Lottery Expenditures) above the histogram. Choose **Confidence Interval** and specify the confidence level.

9 Hypothesis Testing

CHAPTER

LEARNING OBJECTIVES

After reading
this chapter
you should
be able to:

LO **9.1**   Define the null hypothesis and the alternative hypothesis.

LO **9.2**   Distinguish between Type I and Type II errors.

LO **9.3**   Conduct a hypothesis test using the *p*-value approach.

LO **9.4**   Conduct a hypothesis test using the critical value approach.

LO **9.5**   Differentiate between the test statistics for the population mean.

LO **9.6**   Specify the test statistic for the population proportion.

In Chapter 8, we used confidence intervals to estimate an unknown population parameter of interest. In this chapter, we will focus on the second major area of statistical inference, called hypothesis testing. We use a hypothesis test to challenge the status quo, or some belief about an underlying population parameter, based on sample data. For instance, we may wish to test whether the average age of MBA students in the United States is less than 30 years. Since we do not have access to the ages of all MBA students in the country, we have to perform statistical inference on the basis of limited sample information. Suppose that a sample of 40 MBA students reveals a mean age of 29 years. Although the sample mean is less than 30, it does not guarantee that the mean age of all MBA students in the population is less than 30. We may be able to justify the lower sample mean by pure chance. In this chapter, we will discuss how to determine whether the conclusion from the sample can be deemed real (that is, the mean age of all MBA students is less than 30) or due to chance (that is, the mean age of all MBA students is not less than 30).

Undergraduate Study Habits

Are today's college students studying hard or hardly studying? A recent study asserts that over the past five decades the number of hours that the average college student studies each week has been steadily dropping (*The Boston Globe*, July 4, 2010). In 1961, students invested 24 hours per week in their academic pursuits, whereas today's students study an average of 14 hours per week.

Susan Knight is a dean at a large university in California. She wonders if the study trend is reflective of the students at her university. She randomly selects 35 students and asks their average study time per week (in hours). The responses are shown in Table 9.1; the data set, labeled **Study_Hours**, can also be found on the text website.

TABLE 9.1 Average Hours Studied per Week for a Sample of 35 College Students

25	17	8	14	17	7	11
19	16	9	15	12	17	19
26	14	22	17	14	35	24
11	21	6	20	27	17	6
29	10	10	4	25	13	16

Summary measures: $\bar{x} = 16.37$ hours and $s = 7.22$ hours.

Susan wants to use the sample information to:

1. Determine if the mean study time of students at her university is below the 1961 national average of 24 hours per week.

2. Determine if the mean study time of students at her university differs from today's national average of 14 hours per week.

A synopsis of this case is provided at the end of Section 9.3.

9.1 Introduction to Hypothesis Testing

LO 9.1

Define the null hypothesis and the alternative hypothesis.

Every day people make decisions based on their beliefs about the true state of the world. They hold some things to be true and others to be false, and then act accordingly. For example, an engineer believes that a certain steel cable has a breaking strength of 5,000 pounds or more, and then permits its use at a construction site; a manufacturer believes that a certain process yields capsules that contain precisely 100 milligrams of a drug, and then ships the capsules to a pharmacy; an agronomist believes that a new fertilizer increases soy bean production by more than 30%, and then switches to this new fertilizer; a manager believes that an incoming shipment contains less than 2% of defects, and then accepts the shipment. In these cases, and many more, the formation of these beliefs may have started as a mere conjecture, an informed guess, or a proposition tentatively advanced as possibly true. When people formulate a belief in this way, we refer to it as a hypothesis. Sooner or later, however, every hypothesis eventually confronts evidence that either substantiates or refutes it. Determining the validity of an assumption of this nature is called hypothesis testing.

We use hypothesis testing to resolve conflicts between two competing hypotheses on a particular population parameter of interest. We refer to one hypothesis as the **null hypothesis**, denoted H_0, and the other as the **alternative hypothesis**, denoted H_A. We think of the null hypothesis as corresponding to a presumed default state of nature or status quo. The alternative hypothesis, on the other hand, contradicts the default state or status quo. In other words, only one of the two hypotheses is true and the hypotheses cover all possible values of the population parameter.

NULL HYPOTHESIS VERSUS ALTERNATIVE HYPOTHESIS

When constructing a hypothesis test, we define a **null hypothesis**, denoted H_0, and an **alternative hypothesis**, denoted H_A. We conduct a hypothesis test to determine whether or not sample evidence contradicts H_0.

In statistics we use sample information to make inferences regarding the unknown population parameters of interest. In this chapter our goal is to determine if the null hypothesis can be rejected in favor of the alternative hypothesis. An analogy can be drawn with applications in the medical and legal fields, where we can define the null hypothesis as "an individual is free of a particular disease" or "an accused is innocent." In both cases the verdict is based on limited evidence, which in statistics translates into making a decision based on limited sample information.

The Decision to "Reject" or "Not Reject" the Null Hypothesis

The hypothesis testing procedure enables us to make one of two decisions. If sample evidence is inconsistent with the null hypothesis, we reject the null hypothesis. Conversely, if sample evidence is not inconsistent, then we do not reject the null hypothesis. It is not correct to conclude that "we accept the null hypothesis" because while the sample data may not be inconsistent with the null hypothesis, they do not necessarily prove that the null hypothesis is true.

On the basis of sample information, we either **"reject the null hypothesis"** or **"do not reject the null hypothesis."**

Consider the example just referenced where the null is defined as "an individual is free of a particular disease." Suppose a medical procedure does not detect this disease. On the basis of this limited information, we can only conclude that we are unable to detect the disease (do not reject the null hypothesis). It does not necessarily prove that the person does not have the disease (accept the null hypothesis). Similarly, in the court example where the null hypothesis is defined as "an accused is innocent," we can conclude that the person is guilty (reject the null hypothesis) or that there is not enough evidence to convict (do not reject the null hypothesis).

Defining the Null and the Alternative Hypotheses

As mentioned earlier, we use a hypothesis test to contest the status quo, or some belief about an underlying population parameter, based on sample data. A very crucial step concerns the formulation of the two competing hypotheses, since the conclusion of the test depends on how the hypotheses are stated. As a general guideline, whatever we wish to establish is placed in the alternative hypothesis, whereas the null hypothesis includes the status quo. If we are unable to reject the null hypothesis, then we maintain the status quo or "business as usual." However, if we reject the null hypothesis, this establishes that the evidence supports the alternative hypothesis, which may require that we take some kind of action. For instance, if we reject the null hypothesis that an individual is free of a particular disease, then we conclude that the person is sick, for which treatment may be prescribed. Similarly, if we reject that an accused is innocent, we conclude that the person is guilty and should be suitably punished.

Another requirement in hypothesis testing is that some form of the equality sign appears in the null hypothesis. (The justification for the equality sign will be provided later.) In general, any statement including one of the three signs "=", "≤", or "≥" is valid for the null hypothesis. Given that the alternative hypothesis states the opposite of the null hypothesis, the alternative hypothesis is then specified with a "≠", ">", or "<" sign.

> As a general guideline, we use the alternative hypothesis as a vehicle to establish something new, that is, contest the status quo. In general, the null hypothesis regarding a particular population parameter of interest is specified with one of the following signs: =, ≤, or ≥; the alternative hypothesis is then specified with the corresponding opposite sign: ≠, >, or <.

A hypothesis test can be **one-tailed** or **two-tailed**. A two-tailed test is defined when the alternative hypothesis includes the sign "≠". For example, H_0: $\mu = \mu_0$ versus H_A: $\mu \neq \mu_0$ and H_0: $p = p_0$ versus H_A: $p \neq p_0$ are two-tailed tests, where μ_0 and p_0 represent hypothesized values of the population mean and the population proportion, respectively. If the null hypothesis is rejected, it suggests that the true parameter does not equal the hypothesized value.

A one-tailed test, on the other hand, involves a null hypothesis that can only be rejected on one side of the hypothesized value. For example, consider H_0: $\mu \leq \mu_0$ versus H_A: $\mu > \mu_0$. Here we can reject the null hypothesis only when there is substantial evidence that the population mean is greater than μ_0. It is also referred to as a **right-tailed test** since rejection of the null hypothesis occurs on the right side of the hypothesized mean, that is, if the sample mean $\bar{x}$ is significantly greater than μ_0. Another example is a **left-tailed test**, H_0: $\mu \geq \mu_0$ versus H_A: $\mu < \mu_0$, where the null hypothesis can only be rejected on the left side of the hypothesized mean. One-tailed tests for the population proportion are defined similarly.

> ### ONE-TAILED VERSUS TWO-TAILED HYPOTHESIS TESTS
> Hypothesis tests can be **one-tailed** or **two-tailed**. In a **one-tailed test** we can reject the null hypothesis only on one side of the hypothesized value of the population parameter. In a **two-tailed test**, we can reject the null hypothesis on either side of the hypothesized value of the population parameter.

In general, we follow three steps when formulating the competing hypotheses:

- Identify the relevant population parameter of interest.
- Determine whether it is a one- or a two-tailed test.
- Include some form of the equality sign in the null hypothesis and use the alternative hypothesis to establish a claim.

The following examples highlight one- and two-tailed tests of the population mean and the population proportion. In each example we want to state the appropriate competing hypotheses.

EXAMPLE 9.1

A trade group predicts that back-to-school spending will average $606.40 per family this year. A different economic model is needed if the prediction is wrong. Specify the null and the alternative hypotheses to determine if a different economic model may be needed.

SOLUTION: Given that we are examining average back-to-school spending, the parameter of interest is the population mean. Since we want to be able to determine if the population mean differs from $606.40 ($\mu \neq 606.40$), we need a two-tailed test and formulate the null and alternative hypotheses as

$$H_0: \mu = 606.40$$

$$H_A: \mu \neq 606.40$$

The trade group is advised to use a different economic model if the null hypothesis is rejected.

EXAMPLE 9.2

An advertisement for a popular weight-loss clinic suggests that participants in its new diet program lose, on average, more than 10 pounds. A consumer activist wants to determine if the advertisement's claim is valid. Specify the null and the alternative hypotheses to validate the advertisement's claim.

SOLUTION: The advertisement's claim concerns average weight loss; thus, the parameter of interest is again the population mean. This is an example of a one-tailed test because we want to determine if the mean weight loss is more than 10 pounds ($\mu > 10$). We specify the competing hypotheses as

$$H_0: \mu \leq 10 \text{ pounds}$$

$$H_A: \mu > 10 \text{ pounds}$$

The underlying claim that the mean weight loss is more than 10 pounds is true if our decision is to reject the null hypothesis. Conversely, if we do not reject the null hypothesis, we infer that the claim is not supported by the sample data.

EXAMPLE 9.3

A television research analyst wishes to test a claim that more than 50% of the households will tune in for a TV episode. Specify the null and the alternative hypotheses to test the claim.

SOLUTION: This is an example of a one-tailed test regarding the population proportion p. Given that the analyst wants to determine whether $p > 0.50$, this claim is placed in the alternative hypothesis, whereas the null hypothesis is just its opposite.

$$H_0: p \leq 0.50$$

$$H_A: p > 0.50$$

The claim that more than 50% of the households will tune in for a TV episode is valid only if the null hypothesis is rejected.

EXAMPLE 9.4

It is generally believed that at least 60% of the residents in a small town in Texas are happy with their lives. A sociologist is concerned about the lingering economic crisis and wants to determine whether the crisis has adversely affected the happiness level in this town. Specify the null and the alternative hypotheses to determine if the sociologist's concern is valid.

SOLUTION: This is also a one-tailed test regarding the population proportion p. While the population proportion has been at least 0.60 ($p \geq 0.60$), the sociologist wants to establish that the current population proportion is below 0.60 ($p < 0.60$). Therefore, the hypotheses are formulated as

$$H_0: p \geq 0.60$$
$$H_A: p < 0.60$$

In this case, the sociologist's concern is valid if the null hypothesis is rejected. Nothing new is established if the null hypothesis is not rejected.

Type I and Type II Errors

LO **9.2**

Distinguish between Type I and Type II errors.

Since the decision of a hypothesis test is based on limited sample information, we are bound to make errors. Ideally, we would like to be able to reject the null hypothesis when the null hypothesis is false and not reject the null hypothesis when the null hypothesis is true. However, we may end up rejecting or not rejecting the null hypothesis erroneously. In other words, sometimes we reject the null hypothesis when we should not, or choose not to reject the null hypothesis when we should.

We consider two types of errors in the context of hypothesis testing: a **Type I error** and a **Type II error**. A Type I error is committed when we reject the null hypothesis when the null hypothesis is actually true. On the other hand, a Type II error is made when we do not reject the null hypothesis and the null hypothesis is actually false.

Table 9.2 summarizes the circumstances surrounding Type I and Type II errors. Two correct decisions are possible: not rejecting the null hypothesis when the null hypothesis is true and rejecting the null hypothesis when the null hypothesis is false. Conversely, two incorrect decisions (errors) are also possible: rejecting the null hypothesis when the null hypothesis is true (Type I error) and not rejecting the null hypothesis when the null hypothesis is false (Type II error).

TABLE 9.2 Type I and Type II Errors

Decision	Null hypothesis is true	Null hypothesis is false
Reject the null hypothesis	Type I error	Correct decision
Do not reject the null hypothesis	Correct decision	Type II error

EXAMPLE 9.5

Consider the following hypotheses that relate to the medical example mentioned earlier.

$$H_0: \text{A person is free of a particular disease}$$
$$H_A: \text{A person has a particular disease}$$

Suppose a person takes a medical test that attempts to detect this disease. Discuss the consequences of a Type I error and a Type II error.

SOLUTION: A Type I error occurs when the medical test indicates that the person has the disease (reject H_0), but, in reality, the person is free of the disease. We often refer to this type of result as a false positive. If the medical test shows that the person is free of the disease (do not reject H_0), when the person actually has the disease, then a Type II error occurs. We often call this type of result a false negative. Arguably, the consequences of Type II error in this example are more serious than those of Type I error.

EXAMPLE 9.6

Consider the following competing hypotheses that relate to the court of law.

H_0: An accused person is innocent

H_A: An accused person is guilty

Suppose the accused person is judged by a jury of her peers. Discuss the consequences of a Type I error and a Type II error.

SOLUTION: A Type I error is a verdict that finds that the accused is guilty (reject H_0) when she is actually innocent. A Type II error is due to a verdict that concludes that the accused is innocent (do not reject H_0) when, in reality, she is guilty. In this example, it is not clear which of the two errors is more costly to society.

As noted in Example 9.6, it is not always easy to determine which of the two errors has more serious consequences. For given evidence, there is a trade-off between these errors; by reducing Type I error, we implicitly increase Type II error, and vice versa. The only way we can reduce both errors is by collecting more evidence. Let us denote the probability of a Type I error by α, the probability of a Type II error by β, and the strength of the evidence by the sample size n. Therefore, we can conclude that the only way we can lower both α and β is by increasing n. For a given n, however, we can reduce α only at the expense of a higher β and reduce β only at the expense of a higher α. The optimal choice of α and β depends on the relative cost of these two types of errors, and determining these costs is not always easy. Typically, the decision regarding the optimal use of Type I and Type II errors is made by the management of a firm where the job of a statistician is to conduct the hypothesis test for a chosen value of α.

EXERCISES 9.1

1. Explain why the following hypotheses are not constructed correctly.

   a. $H_0: \mu \leq 10; H_A: \mu \geq 10$
   b. $H_0: \mu \neq 500; H_A: \mu = 500$
   c. $H_0: p \leq 0.40; H_A: p > 0.42$
   d. $H_0: \bar{X} \leq 128; H_A: \bar{X} > 128$

2. Which of the following statements are valid null and alternative hypotheses? If they are invalid hypotheses, explain why.

   a. $H_0: \bar{X} \leq 210; H_A: \bar{X} > 210$
   b. $H_0: \mu = 120; H_A: \mu \neq 120$

   c. $H_0: p \leq 0.24; H_A: p > 0.24$
   d. $H_0: \mu < 252; H_A: \mu > 252$

3. Explain why the following statements are not correct.

   a. "With my methodological approach, I can reduce the Type I error with the given sample information without changing the Type II error."

   b. "I have already decided how much of the Type I error I am going to allow. A bigger sample will not change either the Type I or Type II error."

   c. "I can reduce the Type II error by making it difficult to reject the null hypothesis."

d. "By making it easy to reject the null hypothesis, I am reducing the Type I error."

4. Which of the following statements are correct? Explain if incorrect.

   a. "I accept the null hypothesis since sample evidence is not inconsistent with the null hypothesis."

   b. "Since sample evidence cannot be supported by the null hypothesis, I reject the null hypothesis."

   c. "I can establish a given claim if sample evidence is consistent with the null hypothesis."

   d. "I cannot establish a given claim if the null hypothesis is not rejected."

5. Construct the null and the alternative hypotheses for the following tests:

   a. Test if the mean weight of cereal in a cereal box differs from 18 ounces.

   b. Test if the stock price increases on more than 60% of the trading days.

   c. Test if Americans get an average of less than seven hours of sleep.

6. Define the consequences of Type I and Type II errors for each of the tests considered in the preceding question.

7. Construct the null and the alternative hypotheses for the following claims:

   a. "I am going to get the majority of the votes to win this election."

   b. "I suspect that your 10-inch pizzas are, on average, less than 10 inches in size."

   c. "I will have to fine the company since its tablets do not contain an average of 250 mg of ibuprofen as advertised."

8. Discuss the consequences of Type I and Type II errors for each of the claims considered in the preceding question.

9. A polygraph (lie detector) is an instrument used to determine if the individual is telling the truth. These tests are considered to be 95% reliable. In other words, if an individual lies, there is a 0.95 probability that the test will detect a lie. Let there also be a 0.005 probability that the test erroneously detects a lie even when the individual is actually telling the truth. Consider the null hypothesis, "the individual is telling the truth," to answer the following questions.

   a. What is the probability of Type I error?

   b. What is the probability of Type II error?

   c. Discuss the consequences of Type I and Type II errors.

   d. What is wrong with the statement, "I can prove that the individual is telling the truth on the basis of the polygraph result."

10. The screening process for detecting a rare disease is not perfect. Researchers have developed a blood test that is considered fairly reliable. It gives a positive reaction in 98% of the people who have that disease. However, it erroneously gives a positive reaction in 3% of the people who do not have the disease. Answer the following questions using the null hypothesis as "the individual does not have the disease."

    a. What is the probability of Type I error?

    b. What is the probability of Type II error?

    c. Discuss the consequences of Type I and Type II errors.

    d. What is wrong with the nurse's analysis, "The blood test result has proved that the individual is free of disease."

11. The manager of a large manufacturing firm is considering switching to new and expensive software that promises to significantly reduce its assembly costs. Before purchasing the software, the manager wants to conduct a hypothesis test to determine if the new software does significantly reduce its assembly costs.

    a. Is the manager of the manufacturing firm more concerned about Type I or Type II error? Explain.

    b. Is the software company more concerned about Type I or Type II error? Explain.

12. A consumer group has accused a restaurant for using higher fat content than what is reported on its menu. The group has been asked to conduct a hypothesis test to substantiate its claims.

    a. Is the manager of the restaurant more concerned about Type I or Type II error? Explain.

    b. Is the consumer group more concerned about Type I or Type II error? Explain.

9.2 Hypothesis Test of the Population Mean When σ Is Known

In Chapter 8 we discussed that the population standard deviation σ is rarely known. There are instances when σ is considered fairly stable and, therefore, can be determined from prior experience. In such cases the population standard deviation is treated as known. We use the case of a known population standard deviation to introduce the basic methodology for hypothesis testing, a technique we will use throughout the remainder of the book.

A hypothesis test regarding the population mean μ is based on the sampling distribution of the sample mean $\bar{X}$. In particular, it uses the fact that $E(\bar{X}) = \mu$ and $se(\bar{X}) = \sigma/\sqrt{n}$. Also, in order to implement the test, it is essential that the sampling distribution of $\bar{X}$ is normal. Recall that $\bar{X}$ is normally distributed when the underlying population is normally distributed. If the underlying population is not normally distributed, then, by the central limit theorem, $\bar{X}$ is approximately normally distributed if the sample size is sufficiently large, that is, $n \geq 30$.

The basic principle of hypothesis testing is to first assume that the null hypothesis is true and then determine if sample evidence contradicts this assumption. This principle is analogous to the scenario in the court of law where the null hypothesis is defined as "the individual is innocent" and the decision rule is best described by "innocent until proven guilty."

We follow a four-step procedure when implementing a hypothesis test. We make a distinction between two equivalent methods—the **p-value approach** and the **critical value approach**—for hypothesis testing. The four-step procedure with the two approaches is valid for one-tailed and two-tailed tests regarding the population mean, the population proportion, or any other population parameter of interest.

LO **9.3**

The p-Value Approach

Conduct a hypothesis test using the p-value approach.

Suppose a sociologist wants to establish that the mean retirement age is greater than $67 (\mu > 67)$. It is assumed that retirement age is normally distributed with a known population standard deviation of 9 years $(\sigma = 9)$. We can investigate the sociologist's belief by a test of the population mean where we specify the competing hypotheses as

$$H_0: \mu \leq 67$$
$$H_A: \mu > 67$$

Let a random sample of 25 retirees produce an average retirement age of 71, that is, $\bar{x} = 71$. This sample evidence casts doubt on the validity of the null hypothesis, since the sample mean is greater than the hypothesized value, $\mu_0 = 67$. However, the discrepancy between $\bar{x}$ and μ_0 does not necessarily imply that the null hypothesis is false. Perhaps the discrepancy can be explained by pure chance. It is common to evaluate this discrepancy in terms of the appropriate test statistic.

TEST STATISTIC FOR μ WHEN σ IS KNOWN

The value of the **test statistic** for the hypothesis test of the **population mean μ** when the **population standard deviation σ is known** is computed as $z = \dfrac{\bar{x} - \mu_0}{\sigma/\sqrt{n}}$, where μ_0 is the hypothesized value of the population mean. This formula is valid only if $\bar{X}$ (approximately) follows a normal distribution.

Note that the value of the test statistic z is evaluated at $\mu = \mu_0$, which explains why we need some form of the equality sign in the null hypothesis. Given that the population is normally distributed with a known standard deviation, $\sigma = 9$, we compute the value of the test statistic as $z = \dfrac{\bar{x} - \mu_0}{\sigma/\sqrt{n}} = \dfrac{71 - 67}{9/\sqrt{25}} = 2.22$. Therefore, comparing $\bar{x} = 71$ with 67 is identical to comparing $z = 2.22$ with 0, where 67 and 0 are the means of $\bar{X}$ and Z, respectively.

We now compute the **p-value**, which is the likelihood of obtaining a sample mean that is at least as extreme as the one derived from the given sample, under the assumption that the null hypothesis is true as an equality, that is, $\mu_0 = 67$. Since in this example $\bar{x} = 71$, we define the extreme value as a sample mean of 71 or higher and use the z table to compute the p-value as $P(\bar{X} \geq 71) = P(Z \geq 2.22) = 1 - 0.9868 = 0.0132$. Figure 9.1 shows the computed p-value.

FIGURE 9.1 The *p*-value for a right-tailed test with $z = 2.22$

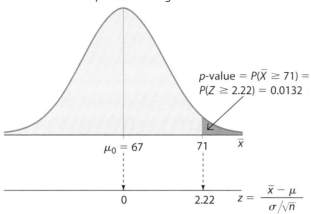

$p\text{-value} = P(\bar{X} \geq 71) =$
$P(Z \geq 2.22) = 0.0132$

$\mu_0 = 67$ 71 $\bar{x}$

0   2.22 $z = \dfrac{\bar{x} - \mu}{\sigma/\sqrt{n}}$

Note that when the null hypothesis is true, there is only a 1.32% chance that the sample mean will be 71 or more. This seems like a very small chance, but is it small enough to allow us to reject the null hypothesis in favor of the alternative hypothesis? Let's see how we define "small enough."

Remember that a Type I error occurs when we reject the null hypothesis when it is actually true. We define the *allowed* probability of making a Type I error as α; we refer to $100\alpha\%$ as the **significance level**. The *p*-value, on the other hand, is referred to as the *observed* probability of making a Type I error. When using the *p*-value approach, **the decision rule is to reject the null hypothesis if the *p*-value $< \alpha$ and not reject the null hypothesis if the *p*-value $\geq \alpha$.**

We generally choose a value for α *before* implementing a hypothesis test; that is, we set the rules of the game before playing. Most hypothesis tests are conducted using a significance level of 1, 5, or 10%, using $\alpha = 0.01, 0.05,$ or 0.10, respectively. For example, $\alpha = 0.05$ means that we allow a 5 percent chance of rejecting a true null hypothesis. We can also interpret these conventional significance levels as follows:

- If we reject a null hypothesis at the 10% significance level ($\alpha = 0.10$), then we have *some evidence* that the null hypothesis is false;

- If we reject a null hypothesis at the 5% significance level ($\alpha = 0.05$), then we have *strong evidence* that the null hypothesis is false; and

- If we reject a null hypothesis at the 1% significance level ($\alpha = 0.01$), then we have *very strong evidence* that the null hypothesis is false.

In our example, given the *p*-value of 0.0132, if we decide to reject the null hypothesis, then there is a 1.32% chance that our decision will be erroneous.

Suppose we had chosen $\alpha = 0.05$ to conduct the above test. Therefore, we reject the null hypothesis because $0.0132 < 0.05$. This means that the sample data support the sociologist's claim that the average retirement age is greater than 67 years old. Individuals may be working past the normal retirement age of 67 either because their savings have been depleted due to the financial crisis and/or because this generation is expected to outlive any previous generation and needs a job to pay the bills. We should note that if α had been set at 0.01, then the findings would have been different. At this smaller significance level, the evidence does not allow us to reject the null hypothesis ($0.0132 > 0.01$). At the 1% significance level, we cannot conclude that the mean retirement age is greater than 67.

In the retirement age example of a right-tailed test, we calculated the *p*-value as $P(Z \geq z)$. Analogously, for a left-tailed test the *p*-value is given by $P(Z \leq z)$. For a two-tailed test, the extreme values exist on both sides of the distribution of the test statistic. Given the symmetry of the z distribution, the *p*-value for a two-tailed test is twice that of the *p*-value for a one-tailed test. It is calculated as $2P(Z \geq z)$ if $z > 0$ or as $2P(Z \leq z)$ if $z < 0$.

THE *p*-VALUE APPROACH

Under the assumption that $\mu = \mu_0$, the *p*-value is the likelihood of observing a sample mean that is at least as extreme as the one derived from the given sample. Its calculation depends on the specification of the alternative hypothesis.

Alternative Hypothesis	*p*-value
$H_A: \mu > \mu_0$	Right-tail probability: $P(Z \geq z)$
$H_A: \mu < \mu_0$	Left-tail probability: $P(Z \leq z)$
$H_A: \mu \neq \mu_0$	Two-tail probability: $2P(Z \geq z)$ if $z > 0$ or $2P(Z \leq z)$ if $z < 0$

The decision rule: Reject H_0 if the *p*-value $< \alpha$.

Figure 9.2 shows the three different scenarios of determining the *p*-value depending on the specification of the competing hypotheses.

FIGURE 9.2 The *p*-values for one- and two-tailed tests

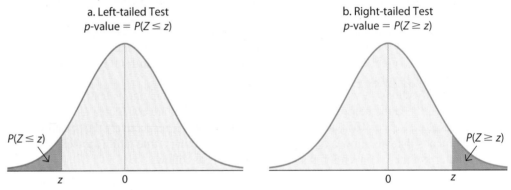

a. Left-tailed Test
p-value = $P(Z \leq z)$

b. Right-tailed Test
p-value = $P(Z \geq z)$

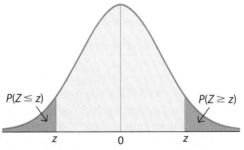

c. Two-tailed Test
If $z < 0$, then *p*-value = $2P(Z \leq z)$
If $z > 0$, then *p*-value = $2P(Z \geq z)$

Figure 9.2a shows the *p*-value for a left-tailed test. Since the appropriate test statistic follows the standard normal distribution, we calculate the *p*-value as $P(Z \leq z)$. When calculating the *p*-value for a right-tailed test (see Figure 9.2b), we find the area to the right of the value of the test statistic z or, equivalently, $P(Z \geq z)$. Figure 9.2c shows the *p*-value for a two-tailed test, calculated as $2P(Z \leq z)$ when $z < 0$ or as $2P(Z \geq z)$ when $z > 0$.

It is important to note that we *cannot* reject H_0 for a right-tailed test if $\bar{x} \leq \mu$, or equivalently, $z \leq 0$. Consider, for example, a right-tailed test with the hypotheses specified as H_0: $\mu \leq 67$ versus $H_A: \mu > 67$. Here, if $\bar{x} = 65$, there is no need for formal testing since we have no discrepancy between the sample mean and the hypothesized value of the population mean. Similarly, we *cannot* reject H_0 for a left-tailed test if $\bar{x} \geq \mu$ or, equivalently, $z \geq 0$. We will now summarize the four-step procedure using the *p*-value approach.

THE FOUR-STEP PROCEDURE USING THE *p*-VALUE APPROACH

Step 1. Specify the null and the alternative hypotheses. We identify the relevant population parameter of interest, determine whether it is a one- or a two-tailed test and, most importantly, include some form of the equality sign in the null hypothesis and place whatever we wish to establish in the alternative hypothesis.

Step 2. Specify the significance level. Before implementing a hypothesis test, we first specify α, which is the *allowed* probability of making a Type I error.

Step 3. Calculate the value of the test statistic and the *p*-value. When the population standard deviation σ is known, the value of the test statistic is $z = \frac{\bar{x} - \mu}{\sigma/\sqrt{n}}$, where μ_0 is the hypothesized value of the population mean. For a right-tailed test, the *p*-value is $P(Z \geq z)$ and for a left-tailed test the *p*-value is $P(Z \leq z)$. For a two-tailed test, the *p*-value is $2P(Z \geq z)$ if $z > 0$ or $2P(Z \leq z)$ if $z < 0$. The *p*-value is also referred to as the *observed* probability of making a Type I error.

Step 4. State the conclusion and interpret results. The decision rule is to reject the null hypothesis when *p*-value $< \alpha$ and not reject the null hypothesis when *p*-value $\geq \alpha$.

EXAMPLE 9.7

A research analyst disputes a trade group's prediction that back-to-school spending will average $606.40 per family this year. She believes that average back-to-school spending will significantly differ from this amount. She decides to conduct a test on the basis of a random sample of 30 households with school-age children. She calculates the sample mean as $622.85. She also believes that back-to-school spending is normally distributed with a population standard deviation of $65. She wants to conduct the test at the 5% significance level.

a. Specify the competing hypotheses in order to test the research analyst's claim.

b. In this hypothesis test, what is the allowed probability of a Type I error?

c. Calculate the value of the test statistic and the *p*-value.

d. At the 5% significance level, does average back-to-school spending differ from $606.40?

SOLUTION:

a. Since we want to determine if the average is different from the predicted value of $606.40, we specify the hypotheses as

$$H_0: \mu = 606.40$$

$$H_A: \mu \neq 606.40$$

b. The allowed probability of a Type I error is equivalent to the significance level of the test, which in this example is given as $\alpha = 0.05$.

c. Note that $\bar{X}$ is normally distributed since it is computed from a random sample drawn from a normal population. Since σ is known, the test statistic follows the standard normal distribution, and its value is

$$z = \frac{\bar{x} - \mu_0}{\sigma/\sqrt{n}} = \frac{622.85 - 606.40}{65/\sqrt{30}} = 1.39.$$

For a two-tailed test with a positive value for the test statistic, we compute the *p*-value as $2P(Z \geq 1.39)$. From the *z* table, we first find $P(Z \geq 1.39) = 1 - 0.9177 = 0.0823$; so the *p*-value $= 2 \times 0.0823 = 0.1646$.

d. The decision rule is to reject the null hypothesis if the *p*-value is less than α. Since $0.1646 > 0.05$, we do not reject H_0. Therefore, at the 5% significance level, we cannot conclude that average back-to-school spending differs from $606.40 per family this year. The sample data do not support the research analyst's claim.

LO **9.4**

Conduct a hypothesis test using the critical value approach.

The Critical Value Approach

We always use sample evidence and the chosen significance level α to conduct hypothesis tests. The *p*-value approach makes the comparison in terms of probabilities. The value of the test statistic is used to compute the *p*-value, which is then compared with α in order to arrive at a decision. As we will see shortly, most statistical software packages report *p*-values, so the *p*-value approach to hypothesis testing tends to be favored by most researchers and practitioners. The critical value approach, on the other hand, makes the comparison directly in terms of the value of the test statistic. This approach is particularly useful when a computer is unavailable and all calculations must be done manually. Some also find the critical value approach more intuitively appealing. Both approaches, however, always lead to the same conclusion.

Earlier, we had used the *p*-value approach to validate a sociologist's claim that the mean retirement age in the United States is greater than 67 at the 5% significance level. In a random sample of 25 retirees, the average retirement age was 71. It was also assumed that retirement age is normally distributed with a population standard deviation of 9 years. With the critical value approach, we still specify the competing hypotheses and calculate the value of the test statistic as we did with the *p*-value approach. In the retirement age example, the competing hypotheses are $H_0: \mu \leq 67$ versus $H_A: \mu > 67$ and the value of the test statistic is $z = \frac{\bar{x} - \mu_0}{\sigma/\sqrt{n}} = \frac{71 - 67}{9/\sqrt{25}} = 2.22$.

The critical value approach specifies a region of values, also called the **rejection region**, such that if the value of the test statistic falls into this region, then we reject the null hypothesis. The **critical value** is a point that separates the rejection region from the nonrejection region. Once again we need to make distinctions between the three types of competing hypotheses. For a right-tailed test, the critical value is z_α, where $P(Z \geq z_\alpha) = \alpha$. The resulting rejection region includes values greater than z_α.

With α known, we can easily find the corresponding z_α from the z table. In the retirement age example with $\alpha = 0.05$, we evaluate $P(Z \geq z_\alpha) = 0.05$ to derive the critical value as $z_\alpha = z_{0.05} = 1.645$. Figure 9.3 shows the critical value as well as the corresponding rejection region of the test.

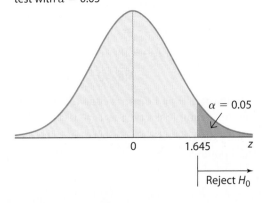

FIGURE 9.3 The critical value for a right-tailed test with $\alpha = 0.05$

As shown in Figure 9.3, the decision rule is to reject H_0 if $z > 1.645$. Since the value of the test statistic, $z = 2.22$, exceeds the critical value, $z_\alpha = 1.645$, we reject the null hypothesis and conclude that the mean age is significantly greater than 67. Thus, we confirm the conclusion reached with the *p*-value approach.

We would like to stress that we always arrive at the same conclusion whether we use the p-value approach or the critical value approach. If z falls in the rejection region, then the p-value must be less than α. Similarly, if z does not fall in the rejection region, then the p-value must be greater than α. Figure 9.4 shows the equivalence of the two results in the retirement age example of a right-tailed test.

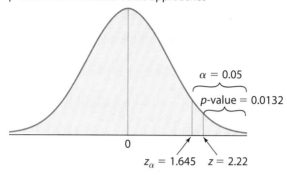

FIGURE 9.4 Equivalent conclusions resulting from the p-value and the critical value approaches

We reject the null hypothesis because the p-value $= 0.0132$ is less than $\alpha = 0.05$, or, equivalently, because $z = 2.22$ is greater than $z_\alpha = 1.645$.

The above example uses a right-tailed test to calculate the critical value as z_α. Given the symmetry of the z distribution around zero, the critical value for a left-tailed test is $-z_\alpha$. For a two-tailed test, we split the significance level in half to determine *two* critical values $-z_{\alpha/2}$ and $z_{\alpha/2}$ where $P(Z \geq z_{\alpha/2}) = \alpha/2$.

THE CRITICAL VALUE APPROACH

The critical value approach specifies a region such that if the value of the test statistic falls into the region, the null hypothesis is rejected. The specification of the competing hypotheses and the significance level determine the critical value(s).

Alternative Hypothesis	Critical Value
$H_A: \mu > \mu_0$	Right-tailed critical value is z_α, where $P(Z \geq z_\alpha) = \alpha$.
$H_A: \mu < \mu_0$	Left-tailed critical value is $-z_\alpha$, where $P(Z \geq z_\alpha) = \alpha$.
$H_A: \mu \neq \mu_0$	Two-tailed critical values $-z_{\alpha/2}$ and $z_{\alpha/2}$, where $P(Z \geq z_{\alpha/2}) = \alpha/2$.

The **decision rule**:

- Reject H_0 if $z > z_\alpha$ for a right-tailed test.
- Reject H_0 if $z < -z_\alpha$ for a left-tailed test.
- Reject H_0 if $z > z_{\alpha/2}$ or $z < -z_{\alpha/2}$.

For a given α, Figure 9.5 shows the three different scenarios of determining the critical value(s) depending on the specification of the competing hypotheses.

Figure 9.5a shows a negative critical value for a left-tailed test where we reject the null hypothesis if $z < -z_\alpha$. Similarly, Figure 9.5b shows a positive critical value for a right-tailed test where we reject the null hypothesis if $z > z_\alpha$. There are two critical values for a two-tailed test, where we reject the null hypothesis when $z < -z_{\alpha/2}$ or when $z > z_{\alpha/2}$ (see Figure 9.5c).

FIGURE 9.5 Critical values for one- and two-tailed tests

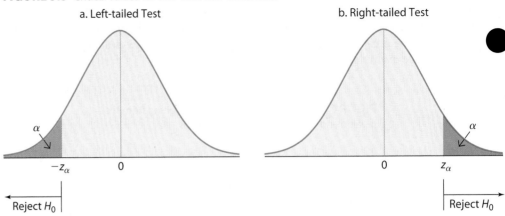

a. Left-tailed Test

b. Right-tailed Test

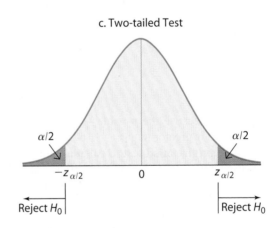

c. Two-tailed Test

We will now summarize the four-step procedure using the critical value approach.

THE FOUR-STEP PROCEDURE USING THE CRITICAL VALUE APPROACH

Step 1. Specify the null and the alternative hypotheses. We identify the relevant parameter of interest, determine whether it is a one- or a two-tailed test, and, most importantly, include some form of the equality sign in the null hypothesis and place whatever we wish to establish in the alternative hypothesis.

Step 2. Specify the significance level and find the critical value(s). We first specify α, which is the *allowed* probability of making a Type I error. When the population standard deviation σ is known, the critical value for a right-tailed test is z_α, where $P(Z \geq z_\alpha) = \alpha$, and the critical value for a left-tailed test is $-z_\alpha$. The critical values for a two-tailed test are $-z_{\alpha/2}$ and $z_{\alpha/2}$, where $P(Z \geq z_{\alpha/2}) = \alpha/2$.

Step 3. Calculate the value of the test statistic. The value of the test statistic is $z = \dfrac{\bar{x} - \mu}{\sigma/\sqrt{n}}$, where μ_0 is the hypothesized value of the population mean.

Step 4. State the conclusion and interpret results. If the value of the test statistic falls in the rejection region, the decision rule is to reject the null hypothesis. So for a right-tailed test, we reject the null hypothesis if $z > z_\alpha$; for a left-tailed test, we reject the null hypothesis if $z < -z_\alpha$; and for a two-tailed test, we reject the null hypothesis if $z > z_{\alpha/2}$ or $z < -z_{\alpha/2}$.

EXAMPLE 9.8

Repeat Example 9.7 using the critical value approach. Recall that a research analyst wishes to determine if average back-to-school spending differs from $606.40. A random sample of 30 households, drawn from a normally distributed population with a standard deviation of $65, results in a sample mean of $622.85. The test is conducted at the 5% significance level.

SOLUTION: The competing hypotheses and the value of the test statistic are the same; that is, $H_0: \mu = 606.40$ versus $H_A: \mu \neq 606.40$ and $z = \frac{\bar{x} - \mu_0}{\sigma/\sqrt{n}} = \frac{622.85 - 606.40}{65/\sqrt{30}} = 1.39$. For a two-tailed test, we split the significance level in half to determine *two* critical values, one on each side of the distribution of the test statistic. Given a 5% level of significance, $\alpha/2 = 0.05/2 = 0.025$ is used to derive $z_{\alpha/2} = z_{0.025}$ as 1.96. Thus, the critical values are -1.96 and 1.96. As shown in Figure 9.6, the decision rule is to reject H_0 if $z > 1.96$ or $z < -1.96$.

FIGURE 9.6 The critical values for a two-tailed test with $\alpha = 0.05$

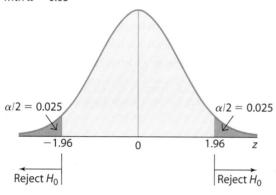

Since $z = 1.39$ does not fall in the rejection region $(-1.96 < 1.39 < 1.96)$, we do not reject the null hypothesis. At the 5% significance level, we cannot conclude that average back-to-school spending differs from $606.40 per family. As always, our conclusion is consistent with that using the *p*-value approach.

Confidence Intervals and Two-Tailed Hypothesis Tests

For a two-tailed hypothesis test, we can also construct a confidence interval to arrive at the conclusion. Given that we conduct the hypothesis test at the α significance level, we can use the sample data to determine a corresponding $100(1 - \alpha)\%$ confidence interval for the population mean μ. If the confidence interval does not contain the hypothesized value of the population mean μ_0, then we reject the null hypothesis. If the confidence interval contains μ_0, then we do not reject the null hypothesis.

IMPLEMENTING A TWO-TAILED TEST USING A CONFIDENCE INTERVAL

The general specification for a $100(1 - \alpha)\%$ confidence interval of the population mean μ when the population standard deviation σ is known is computed as

$$\bar{x} \pm z_{\alpha/2}\frac{\sigma}{\sqrt{n}} \quad \text{or} \quad \left[\bar{x} - z_{\alpha/2}\frac{\sigma}{\sqrt{n}}, \bar{x} + z_{\alpha/2}\frac{\sigma}{\sqrt{n}}\right].$$

Given a hypothesized value of the population mean μ_0, the **decision rule** is

$$\text{Reject } H_0 \text{ if } \mu_0 < \bar{x} - z_{\alpha/2}\frac{\sigma}{\sqrt{n}} \text{ or if } \mu_0 > \bar{x} + z_{\alpha/2}\frac{\sigma}{\sqrt{n}}.$$

EXAMPLE 9.9

Repeat Example 9.8 by constructing a confidence interval for μ.

SOLUTION: We are testing H_0: $\mu = 606.40$ versus H_A: $\mu \neq 606.40$ at the 5% significance level. We use $n = 30$, $\bar{x} = 622.85$, and $\sigma = 65$, along with $\alpha = 0.05$, to determine a 95% confidence interval. We find $z_{\alpha/2} = z_{0.025} = 1.96$ and compute

$$\bar{x} \pm z_{\alpha/2}\frac{\sigma}{\sqrt{n}} = 622.85 \pm 1.96\frac{65}{\sqrt{30}} = 622.85 \pm 23.26,$$

resulting in the interval [599.59, 646.11]. Since the hypothesized value of the population mean $\mu_0 = 606.40$ falls within the 95% confidence interval, we do not reject H_0. Thus, we arrive at the same conclusion as with the p-value and the critical value approaches; that is, the sample data do not support the research analyst's claim that average back-to-school spending differs from \$606.40 per family this year.

As shown above, we use the confidence interval as an alternative method for conducting a two-tailed test. It is possible to adjust the confidence interval to accommodate a one-tailed test, but we do not discuss this adjustment in this text.

Using Excel to Test μ When σ Is Known

Excel provides several functions that simplify the steps of a hypothesis test. Here we discuss one of these functions using the following example.

FILE

EXAMPLE 9.10

A recent report in *The New York Times* (August 7, 2010) suggests that consumers are spending less not only as a response to the economic downturn, but also due to a realization that excessive spending does not make them happier. A researcher wants to use debit card data to contradict the generally held view that the average amount spent annually on a debit card is at least \$8,000. She surveys 20 consumers and asks them how much they spend annually on their debit cards. The results are given below; the data, labeled ***Debit_Spending***, are also available on the text website.

7,960	7,700	7,727	7,704	8,543	7,661	7,767	8,761	7,530	8,128
7,938	7,771	7,272	8,113	7,727	7,697	7,690	8,000	8,079	7,547

It is assumed that the population standard deviation is \$500 and that spending on debit cards is normally distributed. Test the claim at a 1% level of significance.

SOLUTION: The researcher would like to establish that average spending on debit cards is less than \$8,000, or, equivalently, $\mu < 8,000$. Thus, we formulate the hypotheses as

$$H_0: \mu \geq 8,000$$
$$H_A: \mu < 8,000$$

The normality condition of $\bar{X}$ is satisfied since spending on debit cards is assumed to be normally distributed. Also, since the population standard deviation is known, the test statistic is assumed to follow the z distribution. Excel's function Z.TEST returns the p-value for a right-tailed test, or equivalently, $P(Z \geq z)$. For a left-tailed test, as in this example, we simply subtract the value that Excel returns from one. (For a two-tailed test, if the value that Excel returns for $P(Z \geq z)$ is less than 0.50, we multiply this value by 2 to obtain the p-value; if the value that Excel returns is greater than 0.50, we calculate the p-value as $2 \times (1 - P(Z \geq z))$.) In general, this function takes the form '=Z.TEST(*array*, μ_0, σ)', where *array* specifies the cell locations of the relevant data, μ_0 is the hypothesized value of the population mean under the null hypothesis, and σ is the value of the known population standard deviation. In order to solve Example 9.10, we open the **Debit_Spending** data file, find an empty cell, and insert '=Z.TEST(A2:A21, 8000, 500)'. Excel returns the probability of 0.8851, which corresponds to a right-tailed p-value. Subtracting this value from one yields 0.1149, which is the p-value for the left-tailed test.

The hypothesis test is conducted at the 1% significance level. Thus, since 0.1149 is not less than $\alpha = 0.01$, we do not reject the null hypothesis. In other words, at a 1% level of significance, the researcher cannot conclude that annual spending on debit cards is less than $8,000. Perhaps these findings can be reconciled with a report that claims that individuals are shunning their credit cards and using debit cards to avoid incurring more debt (http://Businessweek.com, September 8, 2010).

One Last Remark

An important component of any well-executed statistical analysis is to clearly communicate the results. Thus, it is not sufficient to end the analysis with a conclusion that you reject the null hypothesis or you do not reject the null hypothesis. You must interpret the results, clearly reporting whether or not the claim regarding the population parameter of interest can be justified on the basis of the sample information.

Mechanics

13. Consider the following hypotheses:

$$H_0: \mu \leq 12.6$$
$$H_A: \mu > 12.6$$

A sample of 25 observations yields a sample mean of 13.4. Assume that the sample is drawn from a normal population with a known population standard deviation of 3.2.

a. Calculate the p-value.

b. What is the conclusion if $\alpha = 0.10$?

c. Calculate the p-value if the above sample mean was based on a sample of 100 observations.

d. What is the conclusion if $\alpha = 0.10$?

14. Redo the preceding question using the critical value approach.

15. Consider the following hypotheses:

$$H_0: \mu \geq 150$$
$$H_A: \mu < 150$$

A sample of 80 observations results in a sample mean of 144. The population standard deviation is known to be 28.

a. What is the critical value for the test with $\alpha = 0.01$ and with $\alpha = 0.05$?

b. Does the above sample evidence enable us to reject the null hypothesis at $\alpha = 0.01$?

c. Does the above sample evidence enable us to reject the null hypothesis at $\alpha = 0.05$?

16. Redo the preceding question using the p-value approach.

17. Consider the following hypotheses:

$$H_0: \mu = 1800$$
$$H_A: \mu \neq 1800$$

The population is normally distributed with a population standard deviation of 440. Compute the value of the test statistic and the resulting p-value for each of the following sample results. For each sample, determine if you can reject the null hypothesis at the 10% significance level.

a. $\bar{x} = 1850; n = 110$

b. $\bar{x} = 1850; n = 280$

c. $\bar{x} = 1650; n = 32$

d. $\bar{x} = 1700; n = 32$

18. Consider the following hypotheses:

$$H_0: \mu = 120$$
$$H_A: \mu \neq 120$$

The population is normally distributed with a population standard deviation of 46.

a. Use a 5% level of significance to determine the critical value(s) of the test.

b. What is the conclusion with $\bar{x} = 132$ and $n = 50$?

c. Use a 10% level of significance to determine the critical value(s) of the test.

d. What is the conclusion with $\bar{x} = 108$ and $n = 50$?

19. Consider the following hypothesis test:

$$H_0: \mu \le -5$$
$$H_A: \mu > -5$$

A random sample of 25 observations yields a sample mean of -8. The population standard deviation is 10. Calculate the p-value. What is the conclusion to the test if $\alpha = 0.05$?

20. Consider the following hypothesis test:

$$H_0: \mu \ge 75$$
$$H_A: \mu < 75$$

A random sample of 100 observations yields a sample mean of 80. The population standard deviation is 30. Calculate the p-value. What is the conclusion to the test if $\alpha = 0.10$?

21. Consider the following hypothesis test:

$$H_0: \mu = -100$$
$$H_A: \mu \ne -100$$

A random sample of 36 observations yields a sample mean of -125. The population standard deviation is 42. If $\alpha = 0.01$, find the critical value(s). What is the conclusion to the test?

Applications

22. Customers at Costco spend an average of $130 per trip (*The Wall Street Journal*, October 6, 2010). One of Costco's rivals would like to determine whether its customers spend more per trip. A survey of the receipts of 25 customers found that the sample mean was $135.25. Assume that the population standard deviation is $10.50 and that spending follows a normal distribution.
    a. Specify the appropriate null and alternative hypotheses to test whether average spending at the rival's store is more than $130.
    b. Calculate the value of the test statistic. Calculate the p-value.
    c. At the 5% significance level, what is the conclusion to the test?
    d. Repeat the test using the critical value approach.

23. It is advertised that the average braking distance for a small car traveling at 65 miles per hour equals 120 feet. A transportation researcher wants to determine if the statement made in the advertisement is false. She randomly test drives 36 small cars at 65 miles per hour and records the braking distance. The sample average braking distance is computed as 114 feet. Assume that the population standard deviation is 22 feet.
    a. State the null and the alternative hypotheses for the test.
    b. Calculate the value of the test statistic and the p-value.
    c. Use $\alpha = 0.01$ to determine if the average breaking distance differs from 120 feet.
    d. Repeat the test with the critical value approach.

24. An article in the *National Geographic News* (February 24, 2005) reports that Americans are increasingly skimping on their sleep. A researcher wants to determine if Americans

are sleeping less than the recommended 7 hours of sleep on weekdays. He takes a random sample of 150 Americans and computes the average sleep time of 6.7 hours on weekdays. Assume that the population is normally distributed with a known standard deviation of 2.1 hours.
    a. Use the p-value approach to test the researcher's claim at $\alpha = 0.01$.
    b. Use the critical value approach to test the researcher's claim at $\alpha = 0.01$.

25. In May 2008 CNN reported that sports utility vehicles (SUVs) are plunging toward the "endangered" list. Due to soaring oil prices and environmental concerns, consumers are replacing gas-guzzling vehicles with fuel-efficient smaller cars. As a result, there has been a big drop in the demand for new as well as used SUVs. A sales manager of a used car dealership for SUVs believes that it takes more than 90 days, on average, to sell an SUV. In order to test his claim, he samples 40 recently sold SUVs and finds that it took an average of 95 days to sell an SUV. He believes that the population standard deviation is fairly stable at 20 days.
    a. State the null and the alternative hypotheses for the test.
    b. What is the p-value?
    c. Is the sales manager's claim justifiable at $\alpha = 0.01$?
    d. Repeat the above hypothesis test with the critical value approach.

26. A local bottler in Hawaii wishes to ensure that an average of 16 ounces of passion fruit juice is used to fill each bottle. In order to analyze the accuracy of the bottling process, he takes a random sample of 48 bottles. The mean weight of the passion fruit juice in the sample is 15.80 ounces. Assume that the population standard deviation is 0.8 ounce.
    a. State the null and the alternative hypotheses for the test.
    b. Use the critical value approach to test the bottler's concern at $\alpha = 0.05$.
    c. Make a recommendation to the bottler.

27. **FILE** (Use Excel) A Realtor in Mission Viejo, California, believes that the average price of a house is more than $500 thousand.
    a. State the null and the alternative hypotheses for the test.
    b. Open the **MV_Houses** data from the text website into an Excel spreadsheet (data are in $1,000s). Use the function Z.TEST to calculate the p-value. Assume the population standard deviation is $100 (in $1,000s).
    c. At $\alpha = 0.05$ what is the conclusion to the test? Is the Realtor's claim supported by the data?

28. **FILE** (Use Excel) Access the hourly wage data on the text website (**Hourly_Wage**). An economist wants to test if the average hourly wage is less than $22.
    a. State the null and the alternative hypotheses for the test.
    b. Use the function Z.TEST to calculate the p-value. Assume that the population standard deviation is $6.
    c. At $\alpha = 0.05$ what is the conclusion to the test? Is the average hourly wage less than $22?

29. [FILE] (Use Excel) Access the weekly stock price data for Home Depot on the text website (**Home_Depot**). Assume that returns are normally distributed with a population standard deviation of $3.

   a. State the null and the alternative hypotheses in order to test whether or not the average weekly price differs from $30.

   b. Specify the critical value(s) of the test at the 5% significance level.

   c. Compute the value of the test statistic.

   d. At $\alpha = 0.05$, can you conclude that the average weekly stock price does not equal $30?

30. [FILE] (Use Excel) On average, a college student last year graduated with $27,200 in debt (*The Boston Globe*, May 27, 2012). A researcher collects data on debt from 40 recent undergraduates from Connecticut. The data set, labeled **CT_Undergrad_Debt**, can be found on the text website. Assume that the population standard deviation is $5,000.

   a. The researcher believes that recent undergraduates from Connecticut have more debt than the national average. Specify the competing hypotheses to test this belief.

   b. Specify the critical value(s) of the test at the 10% significance level.

   c. Compute the value of the test statistic.

   d. Do the data support the researcher's claim, at $\alpha = 0.10$?

9.3 Hypothesis Test of the Population Mean When σ Is Unknown

So far we have considered hypothesis tests of the population mean μ under the assumption that the population standard deviation σ is known. As discussed in Chapter 8, in most business applications, σ is not known and we have to replace σ with the sample standard deviation s to estimate the standard error of $\overline{X}$.

LO 9.5

Differentiate between the test statistics for the population mean.

TEST STATISTIC FOR μ WHEN σ IS UNKNOWN

The value of the **test statistic** for the hypothesis test of the **population mean μ** when the **population standard deviation σ is unknown** is computed as $t_{df} = \dfrac{\overline{x} - \mu_0}{s/\sqrt{n}}$, where μ_0 is the hypothesized value of the population mean and the degrees of freedom $df = n-1$. This formula is valid only if $\overline{X}$ (approximately) follows a normal distribution.

The next two examples show how we use the four steps outlined in the previous section for hypothesis testing when we do not know the population standard deviation σ. When conducting this test manually, it turns out that the critical value approach is slightly easier to implement since the exact *p*-value may not be available from the *t* table. So we choose to show this approach first in this section.

EXAMPLE 9.11

In the introductory case to this chapter, the dean at a large university in California wonders if students at her university study less than the 1961 national average of 24 hours per week. She randomly selects 35 students and asks their average study time per week (in hours). From their responses (see Table 9.1) she calculates a sample mean of 16.37 hours and a sample standard deviation of 7.22 hours.

   a. Specify the competing hypotheses to test the dean's concern.

   b. At the 5% significance level, specify the critical value(s).

   c. Calculate the value of the test statistic.

   d. What is the conclusion to the hypothesis test?

SOLUTION:

a. This is an example of a one-tailed test where we would like to determine if the mean hours studied is less than 24, that is, $\mu < 24$. We formulate the competing hypotheses as

$$H_0: \mu \geq 24 \text{ hours}$$
$$H_A: \mu < 24 \text{ hours}$$

b. Recall that for any statistical inference regarding the population mean, it is essential that the sample mean $\overline{X}$ is normally distributed. This condition is satisfied because the sample size is greater than 30, specifically $n = 35$. Since we have a left-tailed test, the critical value is given by $-t_{\alpha,df}$ where $P(T_{df} \geq t_{\alpha,df}) = \alpha$. Referencing the t table with $\alpha = 0.05$ and $df = n - 1 = 34$, we first find $t_{\alpha,df} = t_{0.05,34} = 1.691$. Therefore, the critical value is $-t_{0.05,34} = -1.691$.

c. Given $\overline{x} = 16.37$ and $s = 7.22$, we compute the value of the test statistic as

$$t_{34} = \frac{\overline{x} - \mu_0}{s/\sqrt{n}} = \frac{16.37 - 24}{7.22/\sqrt{35}} = -6.25.$$

d. As shown in Figure 9.7, the decision rule is to reject the null hypothesis if $t_{34} < -1.691$. Since –6.25 is less than –1.691, we reject the null hypothesis. At the 5% significance level, we conclude that average study time at the university is less than the 1961 average of 24 hours per week.

Figure 9.7 The critical value for a left-tailed test with $\alpha = 0.05$ and $df = 34$

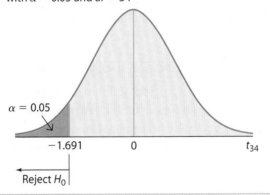

$\alpha = 0.05$

−1.691   0 t_{34}

Reject H_0

EXAMPLE 9.12

As the introductory case to this chapter mentions, recent research finds that today's undergraduates study an average of 14 hours per week. Using the sample data from Table 9.1, the dean would also like to test if the mean study time of students at her university differs from today's national average of 14 hours per week.

a. How should the dean formulate the competing hypotheses for this test?

b. Calculate the value of the test statistic.

c. Approximate the *p*-value.

d. At the 5% significance level, what is the conclusion to this test?

SOLUTION:

a. The dean would like to test if the mean study time of students at her university differs from 14 hours per week. Therefore, we formulate the hypotheses for this two-tailed test as

$$H_0: \mu = 14 \text{ hours}$$
$$H_A: \mu \neq 14 \text{ hours}$$

b. Given $n = 35$, $\bar{x} = 16.37$, and $s = 7.22$, we calculate the value of the test statistic as

$$t_{34} = \frac{\bar{x} - \mu_0}{s/\sqrt{n}} = \frac{16.37 - 14}{7.22/\sqrt{35}} = 1.94.$$

c. Since $t_{34} = 1.94 > 0$, the p-value for a two-tailed test is $2P(T_{34} \geq t_{34})$. Referencing the t table for $df = 34$, we find that the exact probability $P(T_{34} \geq 1.94)$ cannot be determined. Table 9.3 shows a portion of the t table where we see that $t_{34} = 1.94$ lies between 1.691 and 2.032. This means that $P(T_{34} \geq 1.94)$ is strictly between $P(T_{34} \geq 2.032) = 0.025$ and $P(T_{34} \geq 1.691) = 0.05$, that is, $0.025 < P(T_{34} \geq 1.94) < 0.05$. Multiplying this double inequality by 2 results in $0.05 < \text{p-value} < 0.10$. In Example 9.13, show how to use Excel to find exact p-values.

TABLE 9.3 Portion of the t Table

df	0.20	0.10	0.05	0.025	0.01	0.005
	\multicolumn{6}{c}{Area in Upper Tail, α}					
1	1.376	3.078	6.341	12.706	31.821	63.657
⋮	⋮	⋮	⋮	⋮	⋮	⋮	⋮
34	0.852	1.307	1.691	2.032	2.441	2.728

d. Since the p-value satisfies $0.05 < \text{p-value} < 0.10$, it must be greater than $\alpha = 0.05$; we do not reject the null hypothesis. Therefore, the mean study time of students at the university is not significantly different from today's national average of 14 hours per week.

Using Excel to Test μ When σ Is Unknown

Again we find that Excel's functions are quite useful when calculating the value of the test statistic as well as calculating the exact p-value. Consider the following example.

EXAMPLE 9.13

Residents of Hawaii have the longest life expectancies, averaging 81.48 years (http://www.worldlifeexpectancy.com, retrieved June 4, 2012). A sociologist collects data on the age at death for 50 recently deceased Michigan residents. Table 9.4 shows a portion of the data; the complete data set, labeled **MI_Life_Expectancy**, can be found on the text website.

a. The sociologist believes that the life expectancies of Michigan residents are significantly less than those of Hawaii residents. Specify the competing hypotheses to test this belief.

b. Calculate the value of the test statistic and the exact p-value.

c. At the 1% significance level, do the data support the sociologist's belief?

TABLE 9.4 Michigan Residents' Age at Death, $n = 50$

FILE

Age at Death
76.4
76.0
⋮
73.6

SOLUTION:

a. In order to determine whether Michigan residents have shorter life expectancies than Hawaii residents, we set up the following competing hypotheses

$$H_0: \mu \geq 81.48$$
$$H_A: \mu < 81.48$$

b. As we saw in earlier chapters, Excel has all the necessary built-in functions to calculate the value of the test statistic, $t_{df} = \frac{\bar{x} - \mu_0}{s/\sqrt{n}}$. We open **MI_Life_Expectancy**, find an empty cell, and input '=(AVERAGE(A2:A51) − 81.48)/(STDEV.S(A2:A51)/sqrt(50)).' Excel returns a value of −4.75, so $t_{34} = -4.75$.

Excel offers three different functions to find probabilities for the t distribution. The choice of the appropriate function depends on the specification of the competing hypotheses. In order to obtain the p-value for a right-tailed test, we use the function '=T.DIST.RT(t_{df}, df),' where t_{df} is the value of the test statistic and df is the relevant degrees of freedom. The function '=T.DIST(t_{df}, df, 1)' returns the p-value for a left-tailed test, where the argument 1 prompts Excel to return a cumulative probability. The function '=T.DIST.2T($|t_{df}|$, df)' returns the p-value for a two-tailed test, but note that we use the absolute value of the test statistic as the first argument. In order to find the exact
p-value for this example, that is, $P(T_{49} \leq -4.75)$, we input '=T.DIST(−4.75, 49, 1).' Excel returns 9.06×10^{-6}; this indicates that $P(T_{49} \leq -4.75) = 9.06 \times 10^{-6} \approx 0$.

c. Since the p-value is less than 0.01, the null hypothesis is rejected. At the 1% significance level, the data suggest that Michigan residents have shorter life spans than Hawaii residents. These results support the claim of the sociologist.

SYNOPSIS OF INTRODUCTORY CASE

A recent report claims that undergraduates are studying far less today as compared to five decades ago (*The Boston Globe*, July 4, 2010). The report finds that in 1961 students invested 24 hours per week in their academic pursuits, whereas today's students study an average of 14 hours per week. In an attempt to determine whether or not this national trend is present at a large university in California, 35 students are randomly selected and asked their average study time per week (in hours). The sample produces a mean of 16.37 hours with a standard deviation of 7.22 hours. Two hypothesis tests are conducted. The first test examines whether the mean study time of students at this university is below the 1961 national average of 24 hours per week. At the 5% significance level, the sample data suggest that the mean is significantly less than 24 hours per week. The second test investigates whether the mean study time of students at this university differs from today's national average of 14 hours per week. At the 5% significance level, the results suggest that the mean study time is not significantly different from 14 hours per week. Thus, the sample results support the overall findings of the report: undergraduates study, on average, 14 hours per week, far below the 1961 average of 24 hours per week. The present analysis, however, does not explain why that might be the case. For instance, it cannot be determined whether students have just become lazier or if with the advent of the computer, they can access information in less time.

Mechanics

31. Consider the following hypotheses:

$$H_0: \mu \le 210$$
$$H_A: \mu > 210$$

Approximate the p-value for this test based on the following sample information.

a. $\bar{x} = 216; s = 26; n = 40$
b. $\bar{x} = 216; s = 26; n = 80$
c. $\bar{x} = 216; s = 16; n = 40$
d. $\bar{x} = 214; s = 16; n = 40$

32. Which of the sample information in the preceding question enables us to reject the null hypothesis at $\alpha = 0.01$ and at $\alpha = 0.10$?

33. Consider the following hypotheses:

$$H_0: \mu = 12$$
$$H_A: \mu \ne 12$$

Approximate the p-value for this test based on the following sample information.

a. $\bar{x} = 11; s = 3.2; n = 36$
b. $\bar{x} = 13; s = 3.2; n = 36$
c. $\bar{x} = 11; s = 2.8; n = 36$
d. $\bar{x} = 11; s = 2.8; n = 49$

34. Which of the sample information in the preceding question enables us to reject the null hypothesis at $\alpha = 0.01$ and at $\alpha = 0.10$?

35. Determine the critical values for the following tests of the population mean with an unknown population standard deviation. The analysis is based on 18 observations drawn from a normally distributed population at a 1% level of significance.

a. $H_0: \mu \le 52$ versus $H_A: \mu > 52$
b. $H_0: \mu = 9.2$ versus $H_A: \mu \ne 9.2$
c. $H_0: \mu \ge 5.6$ versus $H_A: \mu < 5.6$
d. $H_0: \mu = 10$ versus $H_A: \mu \ne 10$

36. In order to conduct a hypothesis test of the population mean, a random sample of 24 observations is drawn from a normally distributed population. The resulting mean and the standard deviation are calculated as 4.8 and 0.8, respectively. Use the p-value approach to conduct the following tests at $\alpha = 0.05$.

a. $H_0: \mu \le 4.5$ against $H_A: \mu > 4.5$
b. $H_0: \mu = 4.5$ against $H_A: \mu \ne 4.5$

37. Use the critical value approach to conduct the same two tests in the preceding question at $\alpha = 0.05$.

38. In order to test if the population mean differs from 16, you draw a random sample of 32 observations and compute the sample mean and the sample standard deviation as 15.2 and 0.6, respectively. Use (a) the p-value approach and (b) the critical value approach to implement the test at a 1% level of significance.

39. Consider the following hypotheses:

$$H_0: \mu = 8$$
$$H_A: \mu \ne 8$$

The population is normally distributed. A sample produces the following observations:

| 6 | 9 | 8 | 7 | 7 | 11 | 10 |

Use the p-value approach to conduct the test at a 5% level of significance.

40. Consider the following hypotheses:

$$H_0: \mu \ge 100$$
$$H_A: \mu < 100$$

The population is normally distributed. A sample produces the following observations:

| 95 | 99 | 85 | 80 | 98 | 97 |

Use the critical value approach to conduct the test at a 1% level of significance.

Applications

41. A machine that is programmed to package 1.20 pounds of cereal is being tested for its accuracy. In a sample of 36 cereal boxes, the mean and standard deviation are calculated as 1.22 pounds and 0.06 pound, respectively.

a. Set up the null and the alternative hypotheses to determine if the machine is working improperly, that is, it is either underfilling or overfilling the cereal boxes.
b. Calculate the value of the test statistic.
c. Approximate the p-value. At a 5% level of significance, can you conclude that the machine is working improperly? Explain.
d. Repeat the exercise using the critical value approach.

42. The manager of a small convenience store does not want her customers standing in line for too long prior to a purchase. In particular, she is willing to hire an employee for another cash register if the average wait time of the customers is more than five minutes. She randomly observes the wait time (in minutes) of customers during the day as:

| 3.5 | 5.8 | 7.2 | 1.9 | 6.8 | 8.1 | 5.4 |

a. Set up the null and the alternative hypotheses to determine if the manager needs to hire another employee.
b. Calculate the value of the test statistic. What assumption regarding the population is necessary to implement this step?

c. Use the critical value approach to decide whether the manager needs to hire another employee at $\alpha = 0.10$.

d. Repeat the above analysis with the p-value approach.

43. Small, energy-efficient, Internet-centric, new computers are increasingly gaining popularity (*New York Times,* July 20, 2008). These computers, often called netbooks, have scant onboard memory and are intended largely for surfing websites and checking e-mail. Some of the biggest companies are wary of the new breed of computers because their low price could threaten PC makers' already thin profit margins. An analyst comments that the larger companies have a cause for concern since the mean price of these small computers has fallen below $350. She examines six popular brands of these small computers and records their retail prices as:

$322	$269	$373	$412	$299	$389

a. What assumption regarding the distribution of the price of small computers is necessary to test the analyst's claim?

b. Specify the appropriate null and alternative hypotheses to test the analyst's claim.

c. Calculate the value of the test statistic.

d. At the 5% significance level, specify the critical value(s). What is the conclusion to the test? Should the larger computer companies be concerned?

44. A local brewery wishes to ensure that an average of 12 ounces of beer is used to fill each bottle. In order to analyze the accuracy of the bottling process, the bottler takes a random sample of 48 bottles. The sample mean weight and the sample standard deviation of the bottles are 11.80 ounces and 0.8 ounce, respectively.

a. State the null and the alternative hypotheses for the test.

b. Do you need to make any assumption regarding the population for testing?

c. At $\alpha = 0.05$, specify the critical value(s). What is the decision rule?

d. Make a recommendation to the bottler.

45. Based on the average predictions of 47 members of the National Association of Business Economists (NABE), the U.S. gross domestic product (GDP) will expand by 3.2% in 2011 (*The Wall Street Journal,* May 23, 2010). Suppose the sample standard deviation of their predictions was 1%. At a 5% significance level, test if the mean forecast GDP of all NABE members is greater than 3%.

46. A car manufacturer is trying to develop a new sports car. Engineers are hoping that the average amount of time that the car takes to go from 0 to 60 miles per hour is below 6 seconds. The car company tested 12 of the cars and clocked their performance times. Three of the cars clocked in at 5.8 seconds, 5 cars at 5.9 seconds, 3 cars at 6.0 seconds, and 1 car at 6.1 seconds. At a 5% level of significance, test if the new sports car is meeting its goal to go from 0 to 60 miles per hour in less than 6 seconds. Assume a normal distribution for the analysis.

47. In September 2007, U.S. home prices continued to fall at a record pace, and price declines in Los Angeles and Orange counties in California outpaced other major metropolitan areas (*Los Angeles Times,* November 28, 2007). The report was based on the Standard & Poor's/Case-Shiller index that measures the value of single-family homes based on their sales histories. According to this index, the prices in San Diego dropped by an average of 9.6% from a year earlier. Assume that the survey was based on recent sales of 34 houses in San Diego that also resulted in a standard deviation of 5.2%. Can we conclude that the mean drop of all home prices in San Diego is greater than the 7% drop in Los Angeles? Use a 1% level of significance for the analysis.

48. A mortgage specialist would like to analyze the average mortgage rates for Atlanta, Georgia. He studies the following sample APR quotes. These are the annual percentage rates (APR) for 30-year fixed loans. If he is willing to assume that these rates are randomly drawn from a normally distributed population, can he conclude that the mean mortgage rate for the population exceeds 4.2%? Test the hypothesis at a 10% level of significance using (a) the p-value approach and (b) the critical value approach.

Financial Institution	APR
G Squared Financial	4.125%
Best Possible Mortgage	4.250
Hersch Financial Group	4.250
Total Mortgages Services	4.375
Wells Fargo	4.375
Quicken Loans	4.500
Amerisave	4.750

Source: MSN Money.com; data retrieved October 1, 2010.

49. (Use Excel) One of the consequences of the economic meltdown has been a free fall of the stock market's average price/earnings ratio, or P/E ratio (*The Wall Street Journal,* August 30, 2010). Generally, a high P/E ratio suggests that investors are expecting higher earnings growth in the future compared to companies with a lower P/E ratio. An analyst wants to determine if the P/E ratio of firms in the footwear industry is different from the overall average of 14.9. The table below shows the P/E ratios for a sample of seven firms in the footwear industry:

Firm	P/E Ratio
Brown Shoe Co., Inc.	20.54
Collective Brands, Inc.	9.33
Crocs, Inc.	22.63
DSW, Inc.	14.42
Nike, Inc.	18.68
Skechers USA, Inc.	9.35
Timberland Co.	14.93

Source: http://biz.yahoo.com, data retrieved August 23, 2010.

a. State the null and the alternative hypotheses in order to test whether the P/E ratio of firms in the footwear industry differs from the overall average of 14.9.

b. What assumption regarding the population is necessary?

c. Use Excel to calculate the value of the test statistic and the exact p-value.

d. At $\alpha = 0.10$, does the P/E ratio of firms in the footwear industry differ from the overall average of 14.9? Explain.

50. FILE (Use Excel) Access the miles per gallon data (**MPG**) on the text website.

a. State the null and the alternative hypotheses in order to test whether the average MPG differs from 95.

b. Use Excel to calculate the value of the test statistic and the exact p-value.

c. At $\alpha = 0.05$, can you conclude that the average MPG differs from 95?

51. FILE (Use Excel) A recent study found that consumers are making average monthly debt payments of $983 (Experian.com, November 11, 2010). The accompanying table shows a portion of average debt payments for 26 metropolitan areas. The complete data set, labeled **Debt_Payments**, can be found on the text website.

City	Debt Payments
Washington, D.C.	$1,285
Seattle	1,135
⋮	⋮
Pittsburgh	763

Source: http://www.Experian.com, November 11, 2010.

a. State the null and the alternative hypotheses in order to test whether average monthly debt payments are greater than $900.

b. What assumption regarding the population is necessary to implement this step?

c. Use Excel to calculate the value of the test statistic and the exact p-value.

d. At $\alpha = 0.05$, are average monthly debt payments greater than $900? Explain.

52. FILE (Use Excel) A police officer is concerned about speeds on a certain section of Interstate 95. He records the speeds of 40 cars on a Saturday afternoon. The data set, labeled **Highway_Speeds**, can be found on the text website.

a. The speed limit on this portion of Interstate 95 is 65 mph. Specify the competing hypotheses in order to determine if the average speed differs from the speed limit.

b. Specify the critical value(s) of the test at the 1% significance level.

c. Compute the value of the test statistic.

d. At $\alpha = 0.01$, are the officer's concerns warranted? Explain.

53. FILE (Use Excel) A recent article found that Massachusetts residents spent an average of $860.70 on the lottery in 2010, more than three times the U.S. average (http://www.businessweek.com, March 14, 2012). A researcher at a Boston think tank believes that Massachusetts residents spend significantly less than this amount. He surveys 100 Massachusetts residents and asks them about their annual expenditures on the lottery. The data set, labeled **Lottery**, can be found on the text website.

a. Specify the competing hypotheses to test the researcher's claim.

b. Specify the critical value(s) of the test at the 10% significance level.

c. Compute the value of the appropriate test statistic.

d. At the 10% significance level, do the data support the researcher's claim? Explain.

9.4 Hypothesis Test of the Population Proportion

As discussed earlier, sometimes the variable of interest is *qualitative* rather than *quantitative*. While the population mean μ describes quantitative data, the population proportion p is the essential descriptive measure when the data type is qualitative. The parameter p represents the proportion of observations with a particular attribute.

As in the case of the population mean, we estimate the population proportion on the basis of its sample counterpart. In particular, we use the sample proportion $\bar{P}$ to estimate the population proportion p. Recall that although $\bar{P}$ is based on a binomial distribution, it can be approximated by a normal distribution in large samples. This approximation is considered valid when $np \geq 5$ and $n(1 - p) \geq 5$. Since p is not known, we typically test the sample size requirement under the hypothesized value of the population proportion p_0. In most applications, the sample size is large and the normal distribution approximation is justified. However, when the sample size is not deemed large enough, the statistical methods suggested here for inference regarding the population proportion are no longer valid.

LO **9.6**

Specify the test statistic for the population proportion.

Recall from Chapter 7 that the mean and standard error of the sample proportion $\bar{P}$ are given by $E(\bar{P}) = p$ and $se(\bar{P}) = \sqrt{p(1-p)/n}$, respectively. The test statistic for p is defined as follows.

TEST STATISTIC FOR p

The value of the **test statistic** for the hypothesis test of the **population proportion p** is computed as $z = \dfrac{\bar{p} - p_0}{\sqrt{p_0(1 - p_0)/n}}$, where p_0 is the hypothesized value of the population proportion. This formula is valid only if $\bar{P}$ (approximately) follows a normal distribution.

The following examples elaborate on the four-step procedure for a hypothesis test of the population proportion.

EXAMPLE 9.14

A popular weekly magazine asserts that fewer than 40% of households in the United States have changed their lifestyles because of escalating gas prices. A recent survey of 180 households finds that 67 households have made lifestyle changes due to escalating gas prices.

a. Specify the competing hypotheses to test the magazine's claim.

b. Calculate the value of the test statistic and the corresponding p-value.

c. At a 10% level of significance, what is the conclusion to the test?

SOLUTION:

a. We wish to establish that the population proportion is less than 0.40, that is, $p < 0.40$. Thus, we construct the competing hypotheses as

$$H_0: p \geq 0.40$$
$$H_A: p < 0.40$$

b. We first ensure that the normality condition is satisfied. Since both np_0 and $n(1 - p_0)$ exceed 5, the normal approximation is justified. We use the sample proportion, $\bar{p} = 67/180 = 0.3722$, to compute the value of the test statistic as

$$z = \frac{\bar{p} - p_0}{\sqrt{p_0(1 - p_0)/n}} = \frac{0.3722 - 0.40}{\sqrt{0.40(1 - 0.40)/180}} = -0.76.$$

Since this is a left-tailed test of the population proportion, we compute the p-value as $P(Z \leq z) = P(Z \leq -0.76) = 0.2236$. Figure 9.8 shows the value of the test statistic and the corresponding p-value.

FIGURE 9.8 The p-value for a left-tailed test with $z = -0.76$

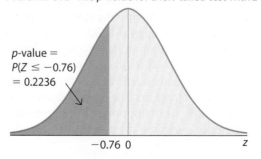

p-value = $P(Z \leq -0.76)$ = 0.2236

-0.76 0 z

c. The p-value of 0.2236 is greater than the chosen $\alpha = 0.10$. Therefore, we do not reject the null hypothesis. This means that the magazine's claim that fewer than 40% of households in the United States have changed their lifestyles because of escalating gas prices is not justified by the sample data. Such a conclusion may be welcomed by firms that have invested in alternative energy.

EXAMPLE 9.15

Nearly one in three children and teens in the United States is obese or overweight (*Health*, October 2010). A health practitioner in the Midwest collects data on 200 children and teens and finds that 84 of them are either obese or overweight.

a. The health practitioner believes that the proportion of obese and overweight children in the Midwest is not representative of the national proportion. Specify the competing hypotheses to test her claim.

b. At the 1% significance level, specify the critical value(s).

c. Calculate the value of the test statistic.

d. Do the sample data support the health practitioner's belief?

SOLUTION:

a. The parameter of interest is again the population proportion p. The health practitioner wants to test if the population proportion of obese or overweight children in the Midwest differs from the national proportion of $1/3 \approx 0.33$. We construct the hypotheses as

$$H_0: p = 0.33$$
$$H_A: p \neq 0.33$$

b. When evaluated at $p_0 = 0.33$ with $n = 200$, the normality requirement that $np \geq 5$ and $n(1 - p) \geq 5$ is easily satisfied. Given a 1% level of significance and a two-tailed test, $\alpha/2 = 0.01/2 = 0.005$ is used to find $z_{\alpha/2} = z_{0.005} = 2.576$. As shown in Figure 9.9, the critical values are -2.576 and 2.576.

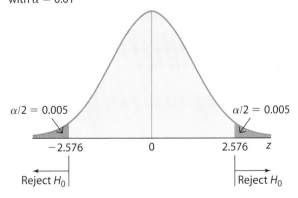

FIGURE 9.9 The critical values for a two-tailed test with $\alpha = 0.01$

$\alpha/2 = 0.005$ $\alpha/2 = 0.005$

-2.576 0   2.576   z

Reject H_0 Reject H_0

c. We use $\bar{p} = 84/200 = 0.42$ to calculate the value of the test statistic as

$$z = \frac{0.42 - 0.33}{\sqrt{0.33(1 - 0.33)/200}} = 2.71.$$

d. The decision rule is to reject H_0 if $z < -2.576$ or if $z > 2.576$. Since the value of the test statistic, $z = 2.71$, is greater than 2.576, the appropriate decision is to reject the null hypothesis. Therefore, at the 1% significance level, the practitioner concludes that the proportion of obese or overweight children in the Midwest is not the same as the national proportion of 0.33. Given that the test statistic fell in the right side of the distribution, the practitioner can conduct further analysis to determine whether or not the proportion of obese or overweight children in the Midwest is significantly greater than the national proportion. If this is the case, the obesity epidemic may be more problematic in the Midwest than elsewhere and may require more educational initiatives to curb its harmful ramifications.

EXERCISES 9.4

Mechanics

54. Consider the following hypotheses:

$$H_0: p \geq 0.38$$
$$H_A: p < 0.38$$

Compute the p-value based on the following sample information.

a. $x = 22; n = 74$
b. $x = 110; n = 300$
c. $\bar{p} = 0.34; n = 50$
d. $\bar{p} = 0.34; n = 400$

55. Which sample information in the preceding question enables us to reject the null hypothesis at $\alpha = 0.01$ and at $\alpha = 0.10$?

56. Consider the following hypotheses:

$$H_0: p = 0.32$$
$$H_A: p \neq 0.32$$

Compute the p-value based on the following sample information

a. $x = 20; n = 66$
b. $x = 100; n = 264$
c. $\bar{p} = 0.40; n = 40$
d. $\bar{p} = 0.38; n = 180$

57. Which sample information in the preceding question enables us to reject the null hypothesis at $\alpha = 0.05$ and at $\alpha = 0.10$?

58. Specify the critical value(s) for the following tests of the population proportion. The analysis is conducted at a 5% level of significance.

a. $H_0: p \leq 0.22; H_A: p > 0.22$
b. $H_0: p = 0.69; H_A: p \neq 0.69$
c. $H_0: p \geq 0.56; H_A: p < 0.56$

59. In order to conduct a hypothesis test of the population proportion, you sample 320 observations that result in 128 successes. Use the p-value approach to conduct the following tests at $\alpha = 0.05$.

a. $H_0: p \geq 0.45; H_A: p < 0.45$
b. $H_0: p = 0.45; H_A: p \neq 0.45$

60. Repeat the preceding exercise using the critical value approach at $\alpha = 0.01$.

61. You would like to determine if the population probability of success differs from 0.70. You find 62 successes in 80 binomial trials. Implement the test at a 1% level of significance.

62. You would like to determine if more than 50% of the observations in a population are below 10. At $\alpha = 0.05$, conduct the test on the basis of the following 20 sample observations:

8	12	5	9	14	11	9	3	7	8
12	6	8	9	2	6	11	4	13	10

Applications

63. A recent study by Allstate Insurance Co. finds that 82% of teenagers have used cell phones while driving (*The Wall Street Journal*, May 5, 2010). In October 2010, Massachusetts enacted a law that forbids cell phone use by drivers under the age of 18. A policy analyst would like to determine whether the law has decreased the proportion of drivers under the age of 18 who use a cell phone.

a. State the null and the alternative hypotheses to test the policy analyst's objective.
b. Suppose a sample of 200 drivers under the age of 18 results in 150 who still use a cell phone while driving. What is the value of the test statistic? What is the p-value?
c. At $\alpha = 0.05$, has the law been effective?
d. Repeat this exercise using the critical value approach with $\alpha = 0.05$.

64. Due to the recent economic downturn, Americans have started raiding their already fragile retirement accounts to endure financial hardships such as unemployment,

medical emergencies, and buying a home (*MSN Money*, July 16, 2008). It is reported that between 1998 and 2004, about 12% of families with 401(k) plans borrowed from them. An economist is concerned that this percentage now exceeds 20%. He randomly surveys 190 households with 401(k) plans and finds that 50 are borrowing against them.

a. Set up the null and the alternative hypotheses to test the economist's concern.

b. Compute the value of the test statistic.

c. Use the *p*-value approach to test if the economist's concern is justifiable at $\alpha = 0.05$.

65. The margarita is one of the most common tequila-based cocktails, made with tequila mixed with Triple Sec and lime or lemon juice, often served with salt on the glass rim. A common ratio for a margarita is 2:1:1, which includes 50% tequila, 25% Triple Sec, and 25% fresh lime or lemon juice. A manager at a local bar is concerned that the bartender uses incorrect proportions in more than 50% of margaritas. He secretly observes the bartender and finds that he used the correct proportions in only 10 out of 30 margaritas. Use the critical value approach to test if the manager's suspicion is justified at $\alpha = 0.05$.

66. A movie production company is releasing a movie with the hopes of many viewers returning to see the movie in the theater for a second time. Their target is to have 30 million viewers, and they want more than 30% of the viewers to return to see the movie again. They show the movie to a test audience of 200 people, and after the movie they asked them if they would see the movie in theaters again. Of the test audience, 68 people said they would see the movie again.

a. At a 5% level of significance, test if more than 30% of the viewers will return to see the movie again.

b. Repeat the analysis at a 10% level of significance.

c. Interpret your results.

67. Recent research commissioned by Vodafone suggests that older workers are the happiest employees (*BBC News*, July 21, 2008). The report documents that 70% of older workers in England feel fulfilled, compared with just 50% of younger workers. A demographer believes that an identical pattern does not exist in Asia. A survey of 120 older workers in Asia finds that 75 feel fulfilled. A similar survey finds that 58% of 210 younger workers feel fulfilled.

a. At a 5% level of significance, test if older workers in Asia feel less fulfilled than their British counterparts.

b. At a 5% level of significance, test if younger workers in Asia feel more fulfilled than their British counterparts.

68. A politician claims that he is supported by a clear majority of voters. In a recent survey, 24 out of 40 randomly

selected voters indicated that they would vote for the politician. Is the politician's claim justifiable at a 5% level of significance?

69. New research shows that many banks are unwittingly training their online customers to take risks with their passwords and other sensitive account information, leaving them more vulnerable to fraud (Yahoo.com, July 23, 2008). Even web-savvy surfers could find themselves the victims of identity theft because they have been conditioned to ignore potential signs about whether the banking site they are visiting is real or a bogus site served up by hackers. Researchers at the University of Michigan found design flaws in 78% of the 214 U.S. financial institution websites they studied. Is the above sample evidence sufficient to conclude that more than three out of four financial institutions that offer online banking facilities are prone to fraud? Use a 5% significance level for the test.

70. The Social Security Administration is not expected to provide any increases in Social Security benefits for the second straight year (*US News & World Report*, October 4, 2010). With increasing medical prices, it is claimed that more than 60% of seniors are likely to make serious adjustments to their lifestyle. Test this claim at a 1% level of significance if in a survey of 140 seniors, 90 reported that they have made serious adjustments to their lifestyle.

71. **FILE** (Use Excel) According to a report on workforce diversity, about 60% of the employees in high-tech firms in Silicon Valley are whites and about 20% are Asians (http://moneycnn.com, November 9, 2011). Women, along with blacks and Hispanics, are highly underrepresented. Just about 30% of all employees are women, with blacks and Hispanics, accounting for only about 15% of the workforce. Tara Jones is a recent college graduate, working for a large high-tech firm in Silicon Valley. She wants to determine if her firm faces the same diversity as in the report. She collects gender and ethnicity information on 50 employees in her firm. A portion of the data is shown in the accompanying table; the complete data set, labeled **Silicon_ Valley**, can be found on the text website.

Gender	Ethnicity
Female	White
Male	White
⋮	⋮
Male	Nonwhite

a. At the 5% level of significance, determine if the proportion of women in Tara's firm is different from 30%.

b. At the 5% level of significance, determine if the proportion of whites in Tara's firm is more than 50%.

WRITING WITH STATISTICS

The Associated Press reports that income inequality is at record levels in the United States (September 28, 2010). Over the years, the rich have become richer while working-class wages have stagnated. A local Latino politician has been vocal regarding his concern about the welfare of Latinos, especially given the recent downturn of the U.S. economy. In various speeches he has stated that the mean salary of Latinos in his county has fallen below the 2008 mean of $49,000. He has also stated that the proportion of Latino households making less than $30,000 has risen above the 2008 level of 20%. Both of his statements are based on income data for 36 Latino households in the county as shown in Table 9.5; the data set, labeled **Latino_Income**, can also be found on the text website.

TABLE 9.5 Representative Sample of Latino Household Incomes in 2010

FILE

22	36	78	103	38	43
62	53	26	28	25	31
62	44	51	38	77	37
29	38	46	52	61	57
20	72	41	73	16	32
52	28	69	27	53	46

Incomes are measured in $1,000s and have been adjusted for inflation.

Trevor Jones is a newspaper reporter who is interested in verifying the concerns of the local politician.

Trevor wants to use the sample information to:

1. Determine if the mean income of Latino households has fallen below the 2008 level of $49,000.

2. Determine if the proportion of Latino households making less than $30,000 has risen above 20%.

Sample Report—Income Inequality in the United States

One of the hotly debated topics in the United States is that of growing income inequality. Market forces such as increased trade and technological advances have made highly skilled and well-educated workers more productive, thus increasing their pay. Institutional forces, such as deregulation, the decline of unions, and the stagnation of the minimum wage, have contributed to income inequality. Arguably, this income inequality has been felt by minorities, especially African Americans and Latinos, since a very high proportion of both groups is working class. The condition has been further exacerbated by the recent economic meltdown.

A sample of 36 Latino households resulted in a mean household income of $46,278 with a standard deviation of $19,524. The sample mean is below the 2008 level of $49,000. In addition, nine Latino households, or 25%, make less than $30,000; the corresponding percentage in 2008 was 20%. Based on these results, a politician concludes that current market conditions continue to negatively impact the welfare of Latinos. However, it is essential to provide statistically significant evidence to substantiate these claims. Toward this end, formal tests of hypotheses regarding the population mean and the population proportion are conducted. The results of the tests are summarized in Table 9.A.

TABLE 9.A Test Statistic Values and p-Values for Hypothesis Tests

Hypotheses	Test Statistic Value	p-Value
$H_0: \mu \geq 49{,}000$ $H_A: \mu < 49{,}000$	$t_{35} = \dfrac{46{,}278 - 49{,}000}{19{,}524/\sqrt{36}} = -0.84$	0.2033
$H_0: p \leq 0.20$ $H_A: p > 0.20$	$z = \dfrac{0.25 - 0.20}{\sqrt{\dfrac{(0.20)(0.80)}{36}}} = 0.75$	0.2266

When testing whether the mean income of Latino households has fallen below the 2008 level of \$49,000, a test statistic value of -0.84 is obtained. Given a p-value of 0.2033, the null hypothesis regarding the population mean, specified in Table 9.A, cannot be rejected at any reasonable level of significance. Similarly, given a p-value of 0.2266, the null hypothesis regarding the population proportion cannot be rejected. Therefore, sample evidence does not support the claims that the mean income of Latino households has fallen below \$49,000 or that the proportion of Latino households making less than \$30,000 has risen above 20%. Perhaps the politician's remarks were based on a cursory look at the sample statistics and not on a thorough statistical analysis of the incomes.

Conceptual Review

LO 9.1 Define the null hypothesis and the alternative hypothesis.

Every hypothesis test contains two competing hypotheses: the **null hypothesis**, denoted H_0, and the **alternative hypothesis**, denoted H_A. We can think of the null hypothesis as corresponding to a presumed default state of nature or status quo, whereas the alternative hypothesis contradicts the default state or status quo.

On the basis of sample information, we either **reject H_0** or **do not reject H_0**.

As a general guideline, whatever we wish to establish is placed in the alternative hypothesis. If we reject the null hypothesis, we are able to conclude that the alternative hypothesis is true.

Hypothesis tests can be **one-tailed** or **two-tailed**. A one-tailed test allows the rejection of the null hypothesis only on one side of the hypothesized value of the population parameter. In a two-tailed test, the null hypothesis can be rejected on both sides of the hypothesized value of the population parameter.

LO 9.2 Distinguish between Type I and Type II errors.

Since the statistical conclusion of a hypothesis test relies on sample data, there are two types of errors that may occur: a **Type I error** or a **Type II error**. A Type I error is committed when we reject the null hypothesis when it is actually true. On the other hand, a Type II error is made when we do not reject the null hypothesis when it is actually false. We denote the probability of a Type I error by α and the probability of a Type II error by β. For a given sample size n, a decrease (increase) in α will increase (decrease) β. However, both α and β will decrease if the sample size n increases.

LO 9.3 Conduct a hypothesis test using the p-value approach.

Every hypothesis test can be implemented by following a four-step procedure. There are two equivalent approaches, namely the **p-value approach** and the **critical value approach**. For the p-value approach, we follow these four steps:

Step 1. Specify the null and the alternative hypotheses. We identify the relevant population parameter of interest, determine whether it is a one- or a two-tailed test and, most importantly, include some form of the equality sign in the null hypothesis and place whatever we wish to establish in the alternative hypothesis.

Step 2. Specify the significance level. Before implementing a hypothesis test, we first specify α, which is the *allowed* probability of making a Type I error.

Step 3. Calculate the value of the test statistic and the *p*-value. We derive the value of the test statistic by converting the estimate of the relevant population parameter into its corresponding standardized value, either z or t_{df}.

The *p*-value is the probability that the test statistic is as extreme as its value computed from the given sample. We can also interpret it as the *observed* probability of making a Type I error. If the test statistic follows the z distribution, then the *p*-value is calculated as

- $P(Z \geq z)$ for a right-tailed test,
- $P(Z \leq z)$ for a left-tailed test, or
- $2P(Z \geq z)$ if $z > 0$ or $2P(Z \leq z)$ if $z < 0$ for a two-tailed test.

Z and z are replaced with T_{df} and t_{df} if the test statistic follows the t_{df} distribution with degrees of freedom $df = n - 1$.

Step 4. State the conclusion and interpret results. The decision rule is to reject the null hypothesis if the *p*-value $< \alpha$, where α is the chosen significance level.

LO **9.4**   **Conduct a hypothesis test using the critical value approach.**

For the critical value approach, we follow these four steps:

Step 1 is the same as the *p*-value approach; that is, we specify the competing hypotheses.

Step 2. Specify the significance level and find the critical value(s). We first specify α, which is the *allowed* probability of making a Type I error. The critical value(s) defines the region of values of the test statistic for which the null hypothesis can be rejected. If the test statistic follows the z distribution, then for a given α, we find the critical value(s) as

- z_α where $P(Z \geq z_\alpha) = \alpha$, for a right-tailed test;
- $-z_\alpha$ where $P(Z \geq z_\alpha) = \alpha$, for a left-tailed test; or
- $-z_{\alpha/2}$ and $z_{\alpha/2}$, where $P(Z \geq z_{\alpha/2}) = \alpha/2$ for a two-tailed test.

Z and z_α are replaced with T_{df} and $t_{\alpha,df}$ if the test statistic follows the t_{df} distribution with $n - 1$ degrees of freedom.

Step 3. Calculate the value of the test statistic. We derive the value of the test statistic by converting the estimate of the relevant population parameter into its corresponding standardized value, either z or t_{df}.

Step 4. State the conclusion and interpret results. The decision rule with the critical value approach is to reject the null hypothesis if the test statistic falls in the rejection region, or,

- For a right-tailed test, reject H_0 if $z > z_\alpha$;
- For a left-tailed test, reject H_0 if $z < -z_\alpha$; or
- For a two-tailed test, reject H_0 if $z < -z_{\alpha/2}$ or if $z > z_{\alpha/2}$.

z is replaced by t_{df} if the assumed test statistic follows the t_{df} distribution with degrees of freedom $df = n - 1$.

LO **9.5**   **Differentiate between the test statistics for the population mean.**

The value of the test statistic for the hypothesis test of the **population mean μ** when the **population standard deviation σ is known** is computed as $z = \frac{\bar{x} - \mu_0}{\sigma/\sqrt{n}}$, where μ_0 is the hypothesized value of the population mean. The value of the test statistic for the hypothesis test of the **population mean μ when the population standard deviation σ is**

unknown is computed as $t_{df} = \dfrac{\bar{x} - \mu_0}{s/\sqrt{n}}$, where μ_0 is the hypothesized value of the population mean and degrees of freedom $df = n - 1$.

LO 9.6 **Specify the test statistic for the population proportion.**

The value of the test statistic for the hypothesis test of the **population proportion** p is computed as $z = \dfrac{\bar{p} - p_o}{\sqrt{p_0(1 - p_0)/n}}$, where p_0 is the hypothesized value of the population proportion.

Additional Exercises and Case Studies

72. A pharmaceutical company has developed a new drug for depression. There is a concern, however, that the drug also raises the blood pressure of its users. A researcher wants to conduct a test to validate this claim. Is the manager of the pharmaceutical company more concerned about Type I or Type II error? Explain.

73. A company has developed a new diet that it claims will lower one's weight by more than 10 pounds. Health officials decide to conduct a test to validate this claim.
    a. Is the manager of the company more concerned about Type I or Type II error? Explain.
    b. Should the consumers be more concerned about Type I or Type II error? Explain.

74. A phone manufacturer wants to compete in the touch screen phone market. He understands that the lead product has a battery life of just 5 hours. The manufacturer claims that while the new touch phone is more expensive, its battery life is more than twice as long as that of the leading product. In order to test the claim, a researcher samples 45 units of the new phone and finds that the sample battery life averages 10.5 hours with a sample standard deviation of 1.8 hours.
    a. Set up the relevant null and the alternative hypotheses.
    b. Compute the value of the test statistic.
    c. Use the critical value approach to test the phone manufacturer's claim at $\alpha = 0.05$.
    d. Repeat the analysis with the p-value approach.

75. An advertisement for a popular weight loss clinic suggests that participants in its new diet program lose, on average, more than 10 pounds. A consumer activist decides to test the authenticity of the claim. She follows the progress of 18 women who recently joined the weight reduction program. She calculates the mean weight loss of these participants as 10.8 pounds with a standard deviation of 2.4 pounds.
    a. Set up the competing hypotheses to test the advertisement's claim.
    b. At the 5% significance level, specify the critical value(s). What is the decision rule?
    c. Calculate the value of the test statistic.
    d. What does the consumer activist conclude?

76. A city council is deciding whether or not to spend additional money to reduce the amount of traffic. The council decides that it will increase the transportation budget if the amount

of waiting time for drivers exceeds 20 minutes. A sample of 32 main roads results in a mean waiting time of 22.08 minutes with a standard deviation of 5.42 minutes. Conduct a hypothesis test at a 1% level of significance to determine whether or not the city should increase its transportation budget.

77. Rates on 30-year fixed mortgages continue to be at historic lows (*Chron Business News*, September 23, 2010). According to Freddie Mac, the average rate for 30-year fixed loans for the week was 4.37%. An economist wants to test if there is any change in the mortgage rates in the following week. She searches for 30-year fixed loans on google.com in the following week and reports the rates offered by seven banks as 4.25%, 4.125%, 4.375%, 4.50%, 4.75%, 4.375%, and 4.875%. Assume that rates are normally distributed.
    a. State the hypotheses to test if the average mortgage rate differs from 4.37%.
    b. Specify the critical value(s) with $\alpha = 0.05$.
    c. What is the value of the test statistic?
    d. At the 5% significance level, does the average mortgage rate differ from 4.37%? Explain.

78. **FILE** (Use Excel) Using data from the past 25 years, an investor wants to test whether the average return of Vanguard's Precious Metals and Mining Fund is greater than 12%. Assume returns are normally distributed with a population standard deviation of 30%.
    a. State the null and the alternative hypotheses for the test.
    b. Open the **Metals** data from the text website into an Excel spreadsheet. Use the function Z.TEST to calculate the p-value.
    c. At $\alpha = 0.05$ what is the conclusion? Is the return on Vanguard's Precious Metals and Mining Fund greater than 12%?

79. **FILE** (Use Excel) An entrepreneur examines monthly sales (in $1,000s) for 40 convenience stores in Rhode Island. Access the convenience store sales data on the text website (**Convenience_Stores**).
    a. State the null and the alternative hypotheses in order to test whether average sales differ from $130,000.
    b. Use Excel to calculate the value of the test statistic and the exact p-value.
    c. At $\alpha = 0.05$ what is your conclusion to the test? Do average sales differ from $130,000?

80. **FILE** (Use Excel) On average, Americans drive 13,500 miles per year (*The Boston Globe,* June 7, 2012). An economist gathers data on the driving habits of 50 residents in the Midwest. The data set, labeled **Midwest_Drivers**, can be found on the text website.

   a. The economist believes that the average number of miles driven annually by Midwesterners is different from the U.S. average. Specify the competing hypotheses to test the economist's claim.

   b. Use Excel to calculate the value of the test statistic and the exact *p*-value.

   c. At the 10% significance level, do the data support the researcher's claim? Explain.

81. **FILE** (Use Excel) The euro-zone crisis continues to wreak havoc on U.S. stock markets (*The Wall Street Journal,* June 8, 2012). A portfolio analyst wonders if the average trading volume on the Dow Jones Industrial Average (DJIA) has increased since the beginning of the year. She gathers data on daily trading volumes for a sample of 30 days. The data set, labeled **DJIA_Volume**, can be found on the text website.

   a. She finds that the average trading volume in the beginning of the year was about 4,000 shares (in millions). Specify the competing hypotheses to test her claim.

   b. Specify the critical value(s) at the 5% significance level.

   c. Compute the value of the test statistic.

   d. At the 5% significance level, does it appear that trading volume has increased since the beginning of the year?

82. A retailer is looking to evaluate its customer service. Management has determined that if the retailer wants to stay competitive, then it will have to have at least a 90% satisfaction rate among its customers. Management will take corrective actions if the satisfaction rate falls below 90%. A survey of 1,200 customers showed that 1,068 were satisfied with their customer service.

   a. State the hypotheses to test if the retailer needs to improve its services.

   b. What is the value of the test statistic?

   c. Compute the *p*-value.

   d. Interpret the results at $\alpha = 0.05$.

83. The lingering economic crisis has cost America trillions of dollars in lost wealth and also has levied a heavy toll on the national psyche (*The Wall Street Journal,* December 21, 2009). According to a recent poll, just 33% of those surveyed said America was headed in the right direction. Suppose this poll was based on a sample of 1,000 people. Does the sample evidence suggest that the proportion of Americans who feel that America is headed in the right direction is below 35%? Use a 5% level of significance for the analysis. What if the sample size was 2,000?

84. A television network is deciding whether or not to give its newest television show a spot during prime viewing time at night. For this to happen, it will have to move one of its most viewed shows to another slot. The network conducts a survey asking its viewers which show they would rather watch. The network will keep its current lineup of shows unless the majority of the customers want to watch the new show. The network receives 827 responses, of which 428 indicate that they would like to see the new show in the lineup.

   a. Set up the hypotheses to test if the television network should give its newest television show a spot during prime viewing time at night.

   b. Compute the value of the test statistic.

   c. Define the rejection region(s) at $\alpha = 0.01$.

   d. What should the television network do?

85. A Pew Research study finds that 23% of Americans use only a cell phone, and no land line, for making phone calls (*The Wall Street Journal*, October 14, 2010). A year later, a researcher samples 200 Americans and finds that 51 of them use only cell phones for making phone calls.

   a. Set up the hypotheses in order to determine whether the proportion of Americans who solely use cell phones to make phone calls differs from 23%.

   b. Compute the value of the test statistic and the corresponding *p*-value.

   c. At $\alpha = 0.05$, are the sample data inconsistent with Pew Research's findings of 2010? What do the sample data suggest?

86. A national survey found that 33% of high school students said they texted or e-mailed while driving (*The Boston Globe,* June 8, 2012). These findings came a day after a Massachusetts teenager was convicted for causing a fatal crash while texting. A researcher wonders whether texting or e-mailing while driving is more prevalent among Massachusetts teens. He surveys 100 teens and 42% of them admitted that they texted or e-mailed while behind the wheel. Can he conclude at the 1% significance level that Massachusetts teens engage in this behavior at a rate greater than the national rate?

87. **FILE** (Use Excel) A recent report suggests that business majors spend the least amount of time on course work than do all other college students (*New York Times,* November 17, 2011). A provost of a university conducts a survey of 50 business and 50 nonbusiness students. Students are asked if they study hard, defined as spending at least 20 hours per week on course work. The response shows "yes" if they study hard or "no" otherwise. A portion of the data is shown in the accompanying table; the complete data set, labeled **Study_Hard**, can be found on the text website.

Business Majors	Nonbusiness Majors
Yes	No
No	Yes
⋮	⋮
Yes	Yes

a. At the 5% level of significance, determine if the proportion of business majors who study hard is less than 20%.

b. At the 5% level of significance, determine if the proportion of nonbusiness majors who study hard is more than 20%.

CASE STUDIES

Case Study 9.1

Harvard University has recently revolutionized its financial aid policies, aimed at easing the financial strain on middle and upper-middle income families (*Newsweek*, August 18–25, 2008). The expected contribution of students who are admitted to Harvard has been greatly reduced. Many other elite private colleges are following suit to compete for top students. The motivation for these policy changes stems from competition from public universities as well as political pressure.

A spokesman from an elite college claims that elite colleges have been very responsive to financial hardships faced by families due to rising costs of education. Now, he says, families with income of $40,000 will have to spend less than $6,500 to send their children to prestigious colleges. Similarly, families with incomes of $80,000 and $120,000 will have to spend less than $20,000 and $35,000, respectively, for their children's education.

Although in general, the cost of attendance has gone down at each family-income level, it still varies by thousands of dollars among prestigious schools. The accompanying table shows information on the cost of attendance by family income for 10 prestigious schools. (The data set, labeled ***Family_Income***, can also be found on the text website.)

Data for Case Study 9.1 Cost of Attendance to Schools by Family Income

| School | Family Income | | |
	$40,000	$80,000	$120,000
Amherst College	$ 5,302	$19,731	$37,558
Bowdoin College	5,502	19,931	37,758
Columbia University	4,500	12,800	36,845
Davidson College	5,702	20,131	37,958
Harvard University	3,700	8,000	16,000
Northwestern University	6,311	26,120	44,146
Pomona College	5,516	19,655	37,283
Princeton University	3,887	11,055	17,792
Univ. of California system	10,306	19,828	25,039
Yale University	4,300	6,048	13,946

Source: *Newsweek*, August 18–25, 2008.

In a report, use the sample information to:

1. Determine whether families with income of $40,000 will have to spend less than $6,500 to send their children to prestigious colleges. (Use $\alpha = 0.05$.)

2. Repeat the hypothesis test from part 1 by testing the spokesman's claims concerning college costs for families with incomes of $80,000 and $120,000, respectively. (Use $\alpha = 0.05$.)

3. Assess the validity of the spokesman's claims.

Case Study 9.2

The effort to reward city students for passing Advanced Placement tests is part of a growing trend nationally and internationally. Financial incentives are offered in order to lift attendance and achievement rates. One such program in Dallas, Texas, offers $100 for every Advanced Placement test on which a student scores a three or higher (Reuters, September 20, 2010). A wealthy entrepreneur decides to experiment with the same idea of rewarding students to enhance performance, but in Chicago. He offers monetary incentives to students at an inner-city high school. Due to this incentive, 122 students take the Advancement Placement tests. Twelve tests are scored at 5, the highest possible score. There are 49 tests with scores of 3 and 4, and 61 tests with failing scores of 1 and 2. Historically, about 100 of these tests are taken at this school each year, where 8% score 5, 38% score 3 and 4, and the remaining are failing scores of 1 and 2.

In a report, use the sample information to:

1. Provide a descriptive analysis of student achievement on Advanced Placement before and after the monetary incentive is offered.

2. Conduct a hypothesis test that determines, at the 5% significance level, whether the monetary incentive has resulted in a higher proportion of scores of 5, the highest possible score.

3. At the 5% significance level, has the monetary incentive decreased the proportion of failing scores of 1 and 2?

4. Assess the effectiveness of monetary incentives in improving student achievement.

Case Study 9.3

The Gallup-Healthways Well-Being Index (http://www.well-beingindex.com) provides an assessment measure of health and well-being of U.S. residents. By collecting periodic data on life evaluation, physical health, emotional health, healthy behavior, work environment, and basic access, this assessment measure is of immense value to researchers in diverse fields such as business, medical sciences, and journalism. The overall composite score, as well as a score in each of the above six categories, is calculated on a scale from 0 to 100, where 100 represents fully realized well-being. In 2009, the overall well-being index score of American residents was reported as 65.9. Let the following table represent the overall well-being score of a random sample of 35 residents in Hawaii. The data set, labeled **Hawaiians**, can also be found on the text website.

Data for Case Study 9.3 Overall Well-being of Hawaiians, $n = 35$

FILE						
20	40	40	100	60	20	40
90	90	60	60	90	90	90
80	100	90	80	80	80	100
70	90	80	100	20	70	90
80	30	80	90	90	80	30

In a report, use the sample information to:

1. Determine whether the well-being score of Hawaiians is more than the national average of 65.9 at the 5% significance level.

2. Determine if fewer than 40% of Hawaiians report a score below 50 at the 5% significance level.

3. Use your results to comment on the well-being of Hawaiians.

Appendix 9.1 Guidelines for Other Software Packages

The following section provides brief commands for specific software packages: Minitab, SPSS, and JMP. More detailed instructions can be found on the text website.

MINITAB

Testing μ, σ known

A. (Replicating Example 9.10) From the menu choose **Stat** > **Basic Statistics** > **1-Sample Z**.

B. Choose **Samples in columns** and select C1 (Debit Spending). Enter 500 for **Standard deviation**. Select **Perform hypothesis test** and enter 8000 for **hypothesized mean**.

C. Choose **Options**. Choose **'less than'** for **Alternative**.

Testing μ, σ unknown

A. (Replicating Example 9.13) From the menu choose **Stat** > **Basic Statistics** > **1-Sample t**.

B. Choose **Samples in columns** and select C1 (Age). Select **Perform hypothesis test** and enter 81.48 for **hypothesized mean**.

C. Choose **Options**. Choose **'less than'** for **Alternative**.

Testing p

A. (Replicating Example 9.14) From the menu choose **Stat** > **Basic Statistics** > **1-Proportion**. Choose **Summarized data** and enter 67 for **Number of events** and 180 for **Number of trials**. Select **Perform hypothesis test** and enter 0.40 for **Hypothesized proportion**.

B. Choose **Options**. Select **'less than'** for **Alternative** and check **Use test and interval based on normal distribution**.

SPSS

Testing μ, σ unknown

(Replicating Example 9.13) From the menu choose **Analyze** > **Compare Means** > **One-Sample T Test**. Select Age as **Test Variables(s)**. Enter 81.48 for **Test Value**.

JMP

Testing μ, σ known

A. (Replicating Example 9.10) From the menu choose **Analyze** > **Distribution**.

B. Choose Column 1 (Debit Spending), then choose **Y**, **Columns**. Click **OK**.

C. Click on the red triangle in the output window beside Column 1 above the histogram. Choose **Test Mean**. After **Specify Hypothesized Mean** enter 8000 and after **Enter true standard deviation to do z-test rather than t test** enter 500.

Testing μ, σ unknown

A. (Replicating Example 9.13) From the menu choose **Analyze** > **Distribution**.

B. Choose Column 1 (Age), then choose **Y**, **Columns**. Click **OK**.

C. Click on the red triangle in the output window beside Column 1 above the histogram. Choose **Test Mean**. After **Specify Hypothesized Mean** enter 81.48.

10

Comparisons Involving Means

LEARNING OBJECTIVES

After reading
this chapter
you should
be able to:

LO 10.1 Make inferences about the difference between two population means based on independent sampling.

LO 10.2 Make inferences about the mean difference based on matched-pairs sampling.

LO 10.3 Discuss features of the *F* distribution.

LO 10.4 Make inferences about the difference between three or more population means using an analysis of variance (ANOVA) test.

In the preceding two chapters, we used estimation and hypothesis testing to analyze the population mean. In this chapter we extend our discussion from the analysis of a single population to the comparison of two or more populations. We first analyze differences between two population means. For instance, an economist may be interested in analyzing the salary difference between male and female employees. In this example, we use independent sampling for the analysis. We will also consider the mean difference of two populations based on matched-pairs sampling. An example would be a consumer group activist wanting to analyze the mean weight difference of customers before and after they enroll in a new diet program. Finally, we use analysis of variance (ANOVA) to test for differences between three or more population means. For instance, we may want to determine whether all brands of small hybrid cars have the same average miles per gallon. ANOVA tests are based on a new distribution called the *F* distribution.

INTRODUCTORY CASE

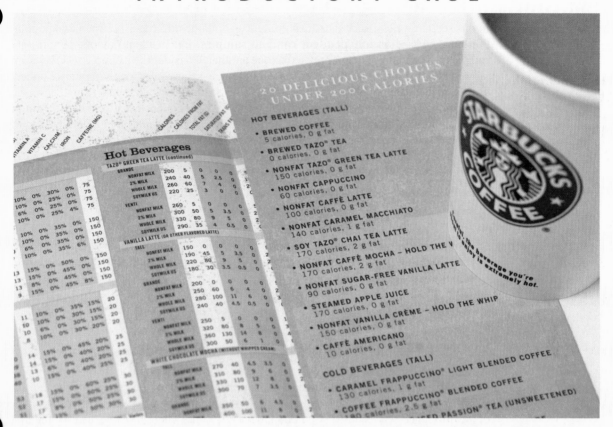

Effectiveness of Mandatory Caloric Postings

The federal health-care law enacted in March 2010 requires chain restaurants with 20 locations or more to post caloric information on their menus. The government wants calorie listings posted to make it easier for consumers to select healthier options. New York City pioneered the requirement of caloric information on menus in 2008, but research has shown mixed results on whether this requirement has prompted consumers to select healthier foods (*The Wall Street Journal*, August 31, 2010). Molly Hosler, a nutritionist in San Mateo, California, would like to study the effects of a recent local menu ordinance requiring caloric postings. She obtains transaction data for 40 Starbucks cardholders around the time that San Mateo implemented the ordinance. The average drink and food calories were recorded for each customer prior to the ordinance and then after the ordinance. Table 10.1 shows a portion of the data; the complete data, stored separately in files **Drink_Calories** and **Food_Calories**, are available on the text website.

TABLE 10.1 Average Caloric Intake Before and After Menu-Labeling Ordinance

	Drink Calories		Food Calories	
Customer	Before	After	Before	After
1	141	142	395	378
2	137	140	404	392
⋮	⋮	⋮	⋮	⋮
40	147	141	406	400

Molly wants to use the sample information to:

1. Determine whether average calories of purchased drinks declined after the passage of the ordinance.
2. Determine whether average calories of purchased food declined after the passage of the ordinance.
3. Assess the implications of caloric postings for Starbucks and other chains.

A synopsis of this case is provided at the end of Section 10.2.

10.1 Inference Concerning the Difference between Two Means

LO **10.1**

Make inferences about the difference between two population means based on independent sampling.

In this section we consider statistical inference about the difference between two population means based on **independent random samples**. Independent random samples are samples that are completely unrelated to one another. Consider the example where we are interested in the difference between male and female salaries. For one sample, we collect data from the male population, while for the other sample we gather data from the female population. The two samples are considered to be independent because the selection of one is in no way influenced by the selection of the other. Similarly, in a comparison of battery lives between Brand A and Brand B, one sample comes from the Brand A population, while the other sample stems from the Brand B population. Again, both samples can be considered to be drawn independently.

INDEPENDENT RANDOM SAMPLES

Two (or more) random samples are considered independent if the process that generates one sample is completely separate from the process that generates the other sample. The samples are clearly delineated.

Confidence Interval for $\mu_1 - \mu_2$

As discussed earlier, we use sample statistics to estimate the population parameter of interest. For example, the sample mean $\overline{X}$ is the point estimator of the population mean μ. In a similar vein, the difference between the two sample means $\overline{X}_1 - \overline{X}_2$ is a point estimator of the difference between two population means $\mu_1 - \mu_2$, where μ_1 is the mean of the first population and μ_2 is the mean of the second population. The values of the sample means $\bar{x}_1$ and $\bar{x}_2$ are computed from two independent random samples with n_1 and n_2 observations, respectively.

Let's first discuss the sampling distribution of $\overline{X}_1 - \overline{X}_2$. As in the case of a single parameter, this estimator is unbiased, that is, $E(\overline{X}_1 - \overline{X}_2) = \mu_1 - \mu_2$. Moreover, recall that the statistical inference regarding the population mean μ is based on the condition that the sample mean $\overline{X}$ is normally distributed. Similarly, for statistical inference regarding $\mu_1 - \mu_2$, it is imperative that the sampling distribution of $\overline{X}_1 - \overline{X}_2$ is normal. Therefore, we generally assume that the two sample means are derived from two independent, normally distributed populations because a linear combination of normally distributed random variables is also normally distributed. If the underlying populations cannot be assumed to be normal, then by the central limit theorem, the sampling distribution of $\overline{X}_1 - \overline{X}_2$ is approximately normal only if both sample sizes are sufficiently large, that is, $n_1 \geq 30$ and $n_2 \geq 30$.

As in the case of a single population mean, we consider two scenarios. If we know the variances of the two populations σ_1^2 and σ_2^2 (or the standard deviations σ_1 and σ_2), we use the z distribution for the statistical inference. A more common case is to use the t_{df} distribution, where the sample variances, s_1^2 and s_2^2, are used in place of the unknown population variances. When σ_1^2 and σ_2^2 are not known, we will examine two cases: (a) they can be assumed equal ($\sigma_1^2 = \sigma_2^2$) or (b) they cannot be assumed equal ($\sigma_1^2 \neq \sigma_2^2$).

The confidence interval for the difference in means is based on the same procedure outlined in Chapter 8. In particular, the formula for the confidence interval will follow the standard format given by: Point estimate $\pm$ Margin of error.

We use sample data to calculate the point estimate of $\mu_1 - \mu_2$ as the difference between the two sample means $\bar{x}_1 - \bar{x}_2$. The margin of error equals the standard error $se(\overline{X}_1 - \overline{X}_2)$ multiplied by $z_{\alpha/2}$ or $t_{\alpha/2,df}$, depending on whether or not the population variances are known.

CONFIDENCE INTERVAL FOR $\mu_1 - \mu_2$

A $100(1 - \alpha)\%$ confidence interval of the difference between two population means $\mu_1 - \mu_2$ is given by

1. $(\bar{x}_1 - \bar{x}_2) \pm z_{\alpha/2}\sqrt{\frac{\sigma_1^2}{n_1} + \frac{\sigma_2^2}{n_2}}$, if the population variances, σ_1^2 and σ_2^2, are known.

2. $(\bar{x}_1 - \bar{x}_2) \pm t_{\alpha/2,df}\sqrt{s_p^2\left(\frac{1}{n_1} + \frac{1}{n_2}\right)}$, if σ_1^2 and σ_2^2 are unknown but assumed equal. A pooled estimate of the common variance is $s_p^2 = \frac{(n_1 - 1)s_1^2 + (n_2 - 1)s_2^2}{n_1 + n_2 - 2}$, where s_1^2 and s_2^2 are the corresponding sample variances and the degrees of freedom $df = n_1 + n_2 - 2$.

3. $(\bar{x}_1 - \bar{x}_2) \pm t_{\alpha/2,df}\sqrt{\frac{s_1^2}{n_1} + \frac{s_2^2}{n_2}}$, if σ_1^2 and σ_2^2 are unknown and cannot be assumed equal. The degrees of freedom $df = \frac{(s_1^2/n_1 + s_2^2/n_2)^2}{(s_1^2/n_1)^2/(n_1 - 1) + (s_2^2/n_2)^2/(n_2 - 1)}$. Since the resultant value for df is rarely an integer, we generally round the value down to obtain the appropriate t value from the t table.

These formulas are valid only if $\bar{X}_1 - \bar{X}_2$ (approximately) follows a normal distribution.

Note that in the case when we construct a confidence interval for $\mu_1 - \mu_2$ where σ_1^2 and σ_2^2 are unknown but assumed equal, we calculate a pooled estimate of the common variance s_p^2. In other words, because the two populations are assumed to have the same population variance, the two sample variances s_1^2 and s_2^2 are simply two separate estimates of this population variance. We estimate the population variance by a *weighted* average of s_1^2 and s_2^2, where the weights applied are their respective degrees of freedom relative to the total number of degrees of freedom. In the case when σ_1^2 and σ_2^2 are unknown and cannot be assumed equal, we cannot calculate a pooled estimate of the population variance.

EXAMPLE 10.1

A consumer advocate analyzes the nicotine content in two brands of cigarettes. A sample of twenty cigarettes of Brand A resulted in an average nicotine content of 1.68 milligrams with a standard deviation of 0.22 milligram; twenty-five cigarettes of Brand B yielded an average nicotine content of 1.95 milligrams with a standard deviation of 0.24 milligram.

Brand A	Brand B
$\bar{x}_1 = 1.68$ mg	$\bar{x}_2 = 1.95$ mg
$s_1 = 0.22$ mg	$s_2 = 0.24$ mg
$n_1 = 20$	$n_2 = 25$

Construct a 95% confidence interval for the difference between the two population means. Nicotine content is assumed to be normally distributed. In addition, the population variances are unknown but assumed equal.

SOLUTION: We wish to construct a confidence interval for $\mu_1 - \mu_2$ where μ_1 is the mean nicotine level for brand A and μ_2 is the mean nicotine level for brand B. Since the population variances are unknown but assumed equal, we use the formula

$$(\bar{x}_1 - \bar{x}_2) \pm t_{\alpha/2,df}\sqrt{s_p^2\left(\frac{1}{n_1} + \frac{1}{n_2}\right)}.$$

We calculate the point estimate $\bar{x}_1 - \bar{x}_2 = 1.68 - 1.95 = -0.27$. In order to find $t_{\alpha/2,df}$, we determine $df = n_1 + n_2 - 2 = 20 + 25 - 2 = 43$. For a 95% confidence interval, $\alpha = 0.05$, so using the t table we find $t_{0.025,43} = 2.017$.

We then calculate the pooled estimate of the population variance as

$$s_p^2 = \frac{(n_1 - 1)s_1^2 + (n_2 - 1)s_2^2}{n_1 + n_2 - 2} = \frac{(20 - 1)(0.22)^2 + (25 - 1)(0.24)^2}{20 + 25 - 2} = 0.0535.$$

Inserting the appropriate values into the formula we have

$$-0.27 \pm 2.017\sqrt{0.0535\left(\frac{1}{20} + \frac{1}{25}\right)} = -0.27 \pm 0.14.$$

In other words, the 95% confidence interval for the difference between the two means ranges from -0.41 to -0.13. Shortly, we will see how to use this interval to conduct a two-tailed hypothesis test.

Hypothesis Test for $\mu_1 - \mu_2$

As always, when we specify the null hypothesis and the alternative hypothesis, it is important that we identify the relevant population parameter of interest, determine whether we conduct a one- or a two-tailed test, and finally include some form of the equality sign in the null hypothesis and use the alternative hypothesis to establish a claim. When conducting hypothesis tests concerning the parameter $\mu_1 - \mu_2$, the competing hypotheses will take one of the following general forms:

Two-Tailed Test	Right-Tailed Test	Left-Tailed Test
$H_0: \mu_1 - \mu_2 = d_0$	$H_0: \mu_1 - \mu_2 \leq d_0$	$H_0: \mu_1 - \mu_2 \geq d_0$
$H_A: \mu_1 - \mu_2 \neq d_0$	$H_A: \mu_1 - \mu_2 > d_0$	$H_A: \mu_1 - \mu_2 < d_0$

In most applications, the hypothesized difference d_0 between two population means μ_1 and μ_2 is zero. In this scenario, a two-tailed test determines whether the two means differ from one another; a right-tailed test determines whether μ_1 is greater than μ_2; and a left-tailed test determines whether μ_1 is less than μ_2.

We can also construct hypotheses where the hypothesized difference d_0 is a value other than zero. For example, if we wish to determine if the mean return of an emerging market fund is more than two percentage points higher than that of a developed market fund, the resulting hypotheses are $H_0: \mu_1 - \mu_2 \leq 2$ versus $H_A: \mu_1 - \mu_2 > 2$.

EXAMPLE 10.2

Revisit Example 10.1.

a. Specify the competing hypotheses in order to determine whether the average nicotine levels differ between Brand A and Brand B.

b. Using the 95% confidence interval, what is the conclusion to the test?

SOLUTION:

a. We want to determine if the average nicotine levels differ between the two brands, or $\mu_1 \neq \mu_2$, so we formulate a two-tailed hypothesis test as

$$H_0: \mu_1 - \mu_2 = 0$$
$$H_A: \mu_1 - \mu_2 \neq 0$$

b. In Example 10.1, we calculated the 95% confidence interval for the difference between the two means as -0.27 ± 0.14, or equivalently, the confidence interval ranges from -0.41 to -0.13. This interval does not contain zero, the value hypothesized under the null hypothesis. This information allows us to reject H_0; the sample data support the conclusion that average nicotine levels between the two brands differ at the 5% significance level.

While it is true that we can use confidence intervals to conduct two-tailed hypothesis tests, the four-step procedure outlined in Chapter 9 can be implemented to conduct one- or two-tailed hypothesis tests. (It is possible to adjust the confidence interval to accommodate a one-tailed test, but we do not discuss this modification.) The only real change in the process is the specification of the test statistic. We convert the point estimate $\bar{x}_1 - \bar{x}_2$ into the values z or t_{df} of the corresponding test statistics by dividing the difference of $(\bar{x}_1 - \bar{x}_2) - d_0$ by the standard error of the estimator $(\overline{X}_1 - \overline{X}_2)$.

TEST STATISTIC FOR TESTING $\mu_1 - \mu_2$

1. If σ_1^2 and σ_2^2 are known, then the value of the test statistic is computed as
$$z = \frac{(\bar{x}_1 - \bar{x}_2) - d_0}{\sqrt{\dfrac{\sigma_1^2}{n_1} + \dfrac{\sigma_2^2}{n_2}}}.$$

2. If σ_1^2 and σ_2^2 are unknown but assumed equal, then the value of the test statistic is computed as $t_{df} = \dfrac{(\bar{x}_1 - \bar{x}_2) - d_0}{\sqrt{s_p^2\left(\dfrac{1}{n_1} + \dfrac{1}{n_2}\right)}}$, where $s_p^2 = \dfrac{(n_1 - 1)s_1^2 + (n_2 - 1)s_2^2}{n_1 + n_2 - 2}$ and $df = n_1 + n_2 - 2$.

3. If σ_1^2 and σ_2^2 are unknown and cannot be assumed equal, then the value of the test statistic is computed as $t_{df} = \dfrac{(\bar{x}_1 - \bar{x}_2) - d_0}{\sqrt{\dfrac{s_1^2}{n_1} + \dfrac{s_2^2}{n_2}}}$, where $df = \dfrac{(s_1^2/n_1 + s_2^2/n_2)^2}{(s_1^2/n_1)^2/(n_1 - 1) + (s_2^2/n_2)^2/(n_2 - 1)}$ is rounded down to the nearest integer.

These formulas are valid only if $\overline{X}_1 - \overline{X}_2$ (approximately) follows a normal distribution.

EXAMPLE 10.3

An economist claims that average weekly food expenditure for households in City 1 is more than the average weekly food expenditure for households in City 2. She surveys 35 households in City 1 and obtains an average weekly food expenditure of $164. A sample of 30 households in City 2 yields an average weekly food expenditure of $159. Prior studies suggest that the population standard deviation for City 1 and City 2 are $12.50 and $9.25, respectively.

City 1	City 2
$\bar{x}_1 = \$164$	$\bar{x}_2 = \$159$
$\sigma_1 = \$12.50$	$\sigma_2 = \$9.25$
$n_1 = 35$	$n_2 = 30$

a. Specify the competing hypotheses to test the economist's claim.

b. Calculate the value of the test statistic and its associated p-value.

c. At the 5% significance level, is the economist's claim supported by the data?

SOLUTION:

a. The relevant parameter of interest is $\mu_1 - \mu_2$, where μ_1 is the mean weekly food expenditure for City 1 and μ_2 is the mean weekly food expenditure for City 2. The economist wishes to determine if the mean weekly food expenditure in City 1 is more than that of City 2, that is, $\mu_1 > \mu_2$. This is an example of a right-tailed test where the appropriate hypotheses are

$$H_0: \mu_1 - \mu_2 \le 0$$
$$H_A: \mu_1 - \mu_2 > 0$$

b. Since the population standard deviations are known, we compute the value of the test statistic as

$$z = \frac{(\bar{x}_1 - \bar{x}_2) - d_0}{\sqrt{\dfrac{\sigma_1^2}{n_1} + \dfrac{\sigma_2^2}{n_2}}} = \frac{(164 - 159) - 0}{\sqrt{\dfrac{(12.50)^2}{35} + \dfrac{(9.25)^2}{30}}} = \frac{5}{2.70} = 1.85.$$

The p-value of the above right-tailed test is computed as p-value $= P(Z \ge 1.85) = 1 - 0.9678 = 0.0322$.

c. We reject the null hypothesis since the p-value of 0.0322 is less than the chosen $\alpha = 0.05$. Therefore, at the 5% significance level, the economist concludes that average weekly food expenditure in City 1 is more than that of City 2.

Using Excel for Testing Hypotheses about $\mu_1 - \mu_2$

Excel provides several options that simplify the steps when conducting a hypothesis test that compares two means. This is especially useful when we are given raw sample data and we first have to compute the sample means and the sample standard deviations for the test. Here, we discuss one of the options under the **Data** tab using the next example.

EXAMPLE 10.4

Table 10.2 shows annual return data for 10 firms in the gold industry and 10 firms in the oil industry; these data, labeled *Gold_Oil*, are also available on the text website. Can we conclude at the 5% significance level that the average returns in the two industries differ? Here we assume that we are sampling from two normal populations and that the population variances are unknown and not equal. The assumption concerning the population variances is reasonable since variance is a common measure of risk when analyzing financial returns; we cannot assume that the risk from investing in the gold industry is the same as the risk from investing in the oil industry.

TABLE 10.2 Annual Returns (in percent)

FILE	Gold	Oil
	6	−3
	15	15
	19	28
	26	18
	2	32
	16	31
	31	15
	14	12
	15	10
	16	15

SOLUTION: We let μ_1 denote the mean return for the gold industry and μ_2 denote the mean return for the oil industry. Since we wish to test whether the mean returns differ, we set up the null and alternative hypotheses as

$$H_0: \mu_1 - \mu_2 = 0$$
$$H_A: \mu_1 - \mu_2 \neq 0$$

Given that we are testing the difference between two means when the population variances are unknown and not equal, we need to calculate $t_{df} = \dfrac{(\bar{x}_1 - \bar{x}_2) - d_0}{\sqrt{\dfrac{s_1^2}{n_1} + \dfrac{s_2^2}{n_2}}}$.

Recall that the calculation for the degrees of freedom for the corresponding test statistic is rather involved. Using one command on Excel, we are provided with the value of the test statistic, the degrees of freedom, and the p-value, as well as the relevant critical values. We follow these steps.

a. Open the **Gold_Oil** data found on the text website.

b. Choose **Data > Data Analysis > t-Test: Two-Sample Assuming Unequal Variances > OK**. (Note: Excel provides two other options when we want to test the difference between two population means from independent samples and we have access to the raw data. If the population variances are known, we can use the option **z-Test: Two-Sample for Means**. If the population variances are unknown but assumed equal, we can use the option **t-Test: Two-Sample Assuming Equal Variances**.)

c. See Figure 10.1. In the *t-Test: Two-Sample Assuming Unequal Variances* dialog box, choose *Variable 1 Range* and select the gold data. Then, choose *Variable 2 Range* and select the oil data. Enter a *Hypothesized Mean Difference* of 0 since $d_0 = 0$, check the *Labels* box if you include Gold and Oil as headings, and enter an α value of 0.05 since the test is conducted at the 5% significance level. Choose an output range and click **OK**.

FIGURE 10.1 Excel's dialog box for *t* test with unequal variances

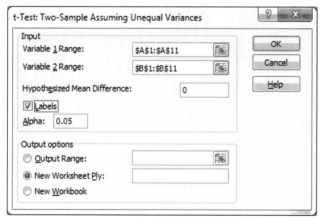

Table 10.3 shows the relevant output.

The output from Excel allows us to conduct the hypothesis test using either the p-value approach or the critical value approach. Given that we have a two-tailed hypothesis test, the relevant p-value is 0.7661 (see **P(T ≤ t) two-tail** in Table 10.3). At the 5% significance level, we cannot reject H_0 since the p-value is greater than 0.05. While average returns in the oil industry seem to slightly outperform average returns in the gold industry ($\bar{x}_2 = 17.3\% > 16.0\% = \bar{x}_1$), the difference is not statistically significant.

TABLE 10.3 Excel's Output for t Test with Unequal Variances

	Gold	Oil
Mean	16	17.3
Variance	70.6667	114.2333
Observations	10	10
Hypothesized Mean Difference	0	
Df	17	
t Stat	**−0.3023**	
P(T ≤ t) one-tail	0.3830	
t Critical one-tail	1.7396	
P(T ≤ t) two-tail	**0.7661**	
t Critical two-tail	**2.1098**	

We now show that we reach the same conclusion concerning the mean return of these two industries using the critical value approach as well as the confidence interval approach. Given $\alpha = 0.05$, the relevant critical values for this two-tailed test are -2.1098 and 2.1098 (see **t Critical two-tail** in Table 10.3). The decision rule is to reject H_0 if $t_{17} > 2.1098$ or $t_{17} < -2.1098$. The value of the test statistic is $t_{17} = -0.3023$ (see **t Stat** in Table 10.3). Since the value of the test statistic is between the two critical values, $-2.1098 < -0.3023 < 2.1098$, we cannot reject the null hypothesis. As always, our conclusion is consistent with that of the p-value approach.

Finally, given the information in Table 10.3, it is also possible to calculate the corresponding 95% confidence interval for $\mu_1 - \mu_2$ as

$$(\bar{x}_1 - \bar{x}_2) \pm t_{\alpha/2,df}\sqrt{\frac{s_1^2}{n_1} + \frac{s_2^2}{n_2}} = (16.0 - 17.3) \pm 2.1098\sqrt{\frac{70.6667}{10} + \frac{114.2333}{10}}$$

$$= -1.3 \pm 9.07$$

That is, the 95% confidence interval for the difference between the two means ranges from -10.37 to 7.77. We note that this interval contains zero, the value hypothesized under the null hypothesis. Using a 95% confidence interval, we again see that the sample data support the conclusion that the population mean returns do not differ at the 5% significance level.

EXERCISES 10.1

Mechanics

1. Consider the following data:

   $$\bar{x}_1 = 25.7 \qquad \bar{x}_2 = 30.6$$
   $$\sigma_1^2 = 98.2 \qquad \sigma_2^2 = 87.4$$
   $$n_1 = 20 \qquad n_2 = 25$$

   a. Construct a 95% confidence interval for the difference between the population means.

   b. Specify the competing hypotheses in order to determine whether or not the population means differ.

   c. Using the confidence interval from part a, can you reject the null hypothesis? Explain.

2. Consider the following data:

   $$\bar{x}_1 = -10.5 \qquad \bar{x}_2 = -16.8$$
   $$s_1^2 = 7.9 \qquad s_2^2 = 9.3$$
   $$n_1 = 15 \qquad n_2 = 20$$

   a. Construct a 95% confidence interval for the difference between the population means. Assume the population variances are unknown but equal.

   b. Specify the competing hypotheses in order to determine whether or not the population means differ.

   c. Using the confidence interval from part a, can you reject the null hypothesis? Explain.

3. Consider the following competing hypotheses and accompanying sample data drawn independently from normally distributed populations.

$$H_0: \mu_1 - \mu_2 = 0$$
$$H_A: \mu_1 - \mu_2 \neq 0$$

$\bar{x}_1 = 57$	$\bar{x}_2 = 63$
$\sigma_1 = 11.5$	$\sigma_2 = 15.2$
$n_1 = 20$	$n_2 = 20$

a. Using the p-value approach, test whether the population means differ at the 5% significance level.

b. Repeat the hypothesis test using the critical value approach.

4. Consider the following competing hypotheses and accompanying sample data. The two populations are known to be normally distributed.

$$H_0: \mu_1 - \mu_2 \leq 0$$
$$H_A: \mu_1 - \mu_2 > 0$$

$\bar{x}_1 = 20.2$	$\bar{x}_2 = 17.5$
$s_1 = 2.5$	$s_2 = 4.4$
$n_1 = 10$	$n_2 = 12$

a. Implement the test at the 5% level under the assumption that the population variances are unknown but equal.

b. Repeat the analysis at the 10% level.

5. Consider the following competing hypotheses and accompanying sample data drawn independently from normally distributed populations.

$$H_0: \mu_1 - \mu_2 \geq 0$$
$$H_A: \mu_1 - \mu_2 < 0$$

$\bar{x}_1 = 249$	$\bar{x}_2 = 272$
$s_1 = 35$	$s_2 = 23$
$n_1 = 10$	$n_2 = 10$

a. Implement the test at the 5% level under the assumption that the population variances are unknown but equal.

b. Implement the test at the 5% level under the assumption that the population variances are unknown and are not equal.

6. Consider the following competing hypotheses and accompanying sample data.

$$H_0: \mu_1 - \mu_2 = 5$$
$$H_A: \mu_1 - \mu_2 \neq 5$$

$\bar{x}_1 = 57$	$\bar{x}_2 = 43$
$s_1 = 21.5$	$s_2 = 15.2$
$n_1 = 22$	$n_2 = 18$

Assume that the populations are normally distributed with unknown but equal variances.

a. Calculate the value of the test statistic.

b. Using the p-value approach, test the above hypotheses at the 5% significance level.

c. Repeat the analysis using the critical value approach.

7. Consider the following sample data drawn independently from normally distributed populations with equal population variances.

Sample 1	Sample 2
12.1	8.9
9.5	10.9
7.3	11.2
10.2	10.6
8.9	9.8
9.8	9.8
7.2	11.2
10.2	12.1

a. Construct the relevant hypotheses to test if the mean of the second population is greater than the mean of the first population.

b. What is the inference of the test at a 1% level of significance?

c. What is the inference of the test at a 10% level of significance?

8. Consider the following sample data drawn independently from normally distributed populations with unequal population variances.

Sample 1	Sample 2
88	98
110	114
102	118
96	128
74	102
120	110

a. Construct the relevant hypothesis to test if the means of the two populations differ.

b. What is the value of the test statistic?

c. Approximate the p-value.

d. What is the inference of the test at a 10% level of significance?

Applications

9. According to a new Health of Boston report, female residents in Boston have a higher average life expectancy as compared to male residents (*The Boston Globe*, August 16, 2010). You collect the following sample data to verify the results of the report. You also use the historical standard deviation of 8.2 years for females and 8.6 years for males.

Female	Male
$\bar{x}_1 = 81.1$ years	$\bar{x}_2 = 74.8$ years
$n_1 = 32$	$n_2 = 32$

a. Set up the hypotheses to test whether the average life expectancy of female Bostonians is higher than that of male Bostonians.

b. Calculate the value of the test statistic and its p-value.

c. At the 10% significance level, what is the conclusion? On average, do female Bostonians live longer than male Bostonians?

d. Repeat the hypothesis test using the critical value approach.

10. A joint project of the U.S. Census Bureau and the National Science Foundation shows that people with a bachelor's degree who transferred from a community college earn less than those who start at a four-year school (*USA TODAY*, March 17, 2009). Previous studies referred to this occurrence as a "community college penalty." Lucille Barnes uses the following information to determine if a similar pattern applies to her university. She believes that the population standard deviation is $4,400 for graduates with an associate degree and $1,500 for graduates with no associate degree.

Bachelor's Degree with Associate Degree	Bachelor's Degree with No Associate Degree
$\bar{x}_1 = \$52,000$	$\bar{x}_2 = \$54,700$
$n_1 = 100$	$n_2 = 100$

a. Set up the hypotheses to test if the report's conclusion also applies to Lucille's university.

b. Calculate the value of the test statistic and its *p*-value.

c. At the 5% significance level, can we conclude that there is a "community college penalty" at Lucille's university?

11. The Chartered Financial Analyst (CFA®) designation is fast becoming a requirement for serious investment professionals. It is an attractive alternative to getting an MBA for students wanting a career in investment. A student of finance is curious to know if a CFA designation is a more lucrative option than an MBA. He collects data on 38 recent CFAs with a mean salary of $138,000 and a standard deviation of $34,000. A sample of 80 MBAs results in a mean salary of $130,000 with a standard deviation of $46,000.

a. Use the *p*-value approach to test if a CFA designation is more lucrative than an MBA at the 5% significance level. Do not assume that the population variances are equal. Make sure to state the competing hypotheses.

b. Repeat the analysis with the critical value approach.

12. David Anderson has been working as a lecturer at Michigan State University for the last three years. He teaches two large sections of introductory accounting every semester. While he uses the same lecture notes in both sections, his students in the first section outperform those in the second section. He believes that students in the first section not only tend to get higher scores, they also tend to have lower variability in scores. David decides to carry out a formal test to validate his hunch regarding the difference in average scores. In a random sample of 18 students in the first section, he computes a mean and a standard deviation of 77.4 and 10.8, respectively. In the second section, a random sample of 14 students results in a mean of 74.1 and a standard deviation of 12.2.

a. Construct the null and the alternative hypotheses to test David's hunch.

b. Compute the value of the test statistic. What assumption regarding the populations is necessary to implement this step?

c. Implement the test at $\alpha = 0.01$ and interpret your results.

13. A phone manufacturer wants to compete in the touch screen phone market. Management understands that the leading product has a less than desirable battery life. They aim to compete with a new touch phone that is guaranteed to have a battery life more than two hours longer than the leading product. A recent sample of 120 units of the leading product provides a mean battery life of 5 hours and 40 minutes with a standard deviation of 30 minutes. A similar analysis of 100 units of the new product results in a mean battery life of 8 hours and 5 minutes and a standard deviation of 55 minutes. It is not reasonable to assume that the population variances of the two products are equal.

a. Set up the hypotheses to test if the new product has a battery life more than two hours longer than the leading product.

b. Implement the test at the 5% significance level using the critical value approach.

14. In May 2008, CNN reported that sports utility vehicles (SUVs) are plunging toward the "endangered" list. Due to soaring oil prices and environmental concerns, consumers are replacing gas-guzzling vehicles with fuel-efficient smaller cars. As a result, there has been a big drop in the demand for new as well as used SUVs. A sales manager of a used car dealership believes that it takes 30 days longer to sell an SUV as compared to a small car. In the last two months, he sold 18 SUVs that took an average of 95 days to sell with a standard deviation of 32 days. He also sold 38 small cars with an average of 48 days to sell and a standard deviation of 24 days.

a. Construct the null and the alternative hypotheses to contradict the manager's claim.

b. Compute the value of the test statistic under the assumption that the variability of selling time for the SUVs and the small cars is the same.

c. Implement the test at $\alpha = 0.10$ and interpret your results.

15. **FILE** (Use Excel) A consumer advocate researches the length of life between two brands of refrigerators, Brand A and Brand B. He collects data (measured in years) on the longevity of 40 refrigerators for Brand A and repeats the sampling for Brand B. The data set, labeled **Refrigerator_Longevity**, can be found on the text website.

a. Specify the competing hypotheses to test whether the average length of life differs between the two brands.

b. Using the appropriate commands in Excel, find the value of the test statistic. Assume that $\sigma_A^2 = 4.4$ and $\sigma_B^2 = 5.2$. What is the *p*-value?

c. At the 5% significance level, what is the conclusion?

16. **FILE** (Use Excel) According to a study published in the *New England Journal of Medicine*, overweight people on low-carbohydrate and Mediterranean diets lost more weight and got greater cardiovascular benefits than people on a conventional low-fat diet (*Boston Globe*, July 17, 2008). A nutritionist wishes to verify these results and documents the weight loss (in pounds) of 30 dieters on the low-carbohydrate and Mediterranean diets and 30 dieters on the low-fat diet. The data set, labeled **Different_Diets**, can be found on the text website.

a. Set up the hypotheses to test the claim that the mean weight loss for those on low-carbohydrate or Mediterranean diets is greater than the mean weight loss for those on a conventional low-fat diet.

b. Using the appropriate commands in Excel, find the value of the test statistic. Assume that the population variances are equal and that the test is conducted at the 5% significance level. Specify the critical value(s) and the decision rule.

c. At the 5% significance level, can the nutritionist conclude that people on low-carbohydrate or Mediterranean diets lost more weight than people on a conventional low-fat diet?

17. **FILE** (Use Excel) Baseball has always been a favorite pastime in America and is rife with statistics and theories. In a recent paper, researchers showed that major league players who have nicknames live 2½ years longer than those without them (*The Wall Street Journal*, July 16, 2009). You do not believe in this result and decide to collect data on the lifespan of 30 baseball players along with a nickname variable that equals 1 if the player had a nickname and 0 otherwise. The accompanying table shows a portion of the data; the complete data set, labeled **Nicknames**, can be found on the text website.

Years	Nickname
74	1
62	1
⋮	⋮
64	0

a. Create two subsamples consisting of players with and without nicknames. Calculate the average longevity for each subsample.

b. Specify the hypotheses to contradict the claim made by researchers at Wayne State University.

c. State the conclusion of the test using a 5% level of significance. Assume the population variances are unknown but equal.

18. **FILE** (Use Excel) As the class of 2012 celebrates the end of college, for many the promise of a college degree has turned to disappointment as they find themselves struggling to find a job (*Financial Times*, June 1, 2012). It is especially disturbing since recent evidence suggests that graduating at bad economic times can impact the person's earning power for a long time. An associate dean at a prestigious college wants to determine if the starting salary of his college graduates has declined from 2008 to 2010. He expects the variance of the salaries to be different between these two years. The accompanying table shows a portion of the salary data for 40 college graduates; the complete data set, labeled **Starting_Salaries**, can be found on the text website.

Salary 2008 ($)	Salary 2010 ($)
35,000	34,000
56,000	62,000
⋮	⋮
47,000	54,000

Use the *p*-value approach, at the 5% significance level, to determine if the mean starting salary has decreased from 2008 to 2010. Describe your steps clearly.

19. **FILE** (Use Excel) Researchers at The Wharton School of Business have found that men and women shop for different reasons. While women enjoy the shopping experience, men are on a mission to get the job done. Men do not shop as frequently, but when they do, they make big purchases like expensive electronics. The accompanying table shows a portion of the amount spent over the weekend by 40 men and 60 women at a local mall; the complete data set, labeled **Spending_Gender**, can be found on the text website. It is reasonable to assume that the population variances are equal.

Spending by Men ($)	Spending by Women ($)
85	90
102	79
⋮	⋮

At the 1% significance level, use the critical value approach to determine if the mean amount spent by men is more than that by women. Describe your steps clearly.

10.2 Inference Concerning Mean Differences

LO **10.2**

Make inferences about the mean difference based on matched-pairs sampling.

One of the crucial assumptions in Section 10.1 concerning differences between two population means is that the samples are drawn independently. As mentioned earlier, two samples are independent if the selection of one is not influenced by the selection of the other. When we want to conduct tests on two population means based on samples that we believe are not independent, we need to employ a different methodology.

A common case of dependent sampling, commonly referred to as **matched-pairs sampling**, is when the samples are paired or matched in some way. Such samples are useful in evaluating strategies because the comparison is made between "apples" and "apples." For instance, an effective way to assess the benefits of a new medical treatment is by evaluating the same patients before and after the treatment. If, however, one group of people is given the treatment and another group is not, then it is not clear if the observed differences are due to the treatment or due to other important differences between the groups.

For matched-pairs sampling, the parameter of interest is referred to as the mean difference μ_D where $D = X_1 - X_2$, and the random variables X_1 and X_2 are matched in a pair. The statistical inference regarding μ_D is based on the estimator $\overline{D}$, representing the sample mean difference. It requires that $X_1 - X_2$ is normally distributed or that the sample size is sufficiently large ($n \geq 30$).

Recognizing a Matched-Pairs Experiment

It is important to be able to determine whether a particular experiment uses independent or matched-pairs sampling. In general, two types of matched-pairs sampling occur:

1. The first type of matched-pairs sample is characterized by a measurement, an intervention of some type, and then another measurement. We generally refer to these experiments as "before" and "after" studies. For example, an operation manager of a production facility wants to determine whether a new workstation layout improves productivity at her plant. She first measures output of employees before the layout change. Then she measures output of the same employees after the change. Another classic before-and-after example concerns weight loss of clients at a diet center. In these examples, the same individual gets sampled before and after the experiment.

2. The second type of matched-pairs sample is characterized by a pairing of observations, where it is not the same individual that gets sampled twice. Suppose an agronomist wishes to switch to an organic fertilizer but is unsure what the effects might be on his crop yield. It is important to the agronomist that the yields be similar. He matches 20 adjacent plots of land using the nonorganic fertilizer on one half of the plot and the organic fertilizer on the other.

In order to recognize a matched-pairs experiment, we watch for a natural pairing between one observation in the first sample and one observation in the second sample. If a natural pairing exists, then the experiment involves matched samples.

Confidence Interval for μ_D

When constructing a confidence interval for the mean difference μ_D, we follow the same general format of point estimate ± margin of error.

CONFIDENCE INTERVAL FOR μ_D

A $100(1 - \alpha)\%$ confidence interval of the mean difference μ_D is given by

$$\bar{d} \pm t_{\alpha/2,df} s_D / \sqrt{n},$$

where $\bar{d}$ and s_D are the mean and the standard deviation, respectively, of the n sample differences and $df = n - 1$. This formula is valid only if $\bar{D}$ (approximately) follows a normal distribution.

In the next example, the values for $\bar{d}$ and s_D are explicitly given; we will outline the calculations when we discuss hypothesis testing.

EXAMPLE 10.5

A manager is interested in improving productivity at a plant by changing the layout of the workstation. She measures the variable representing productivity of 10 workers before the change and again after the change. She calculates the following summary statistics for the sample productivity difference: $\bar{d} = 8.5$, $s_D = 11.38$, and $n = 10$. Construct a 95% confidence interval for the mean difference, assuming that the productivity variable, before and after, is normally distributed.

SOLUTION: In order to construct a 95% confidence interval for the mean difference, we use $\bar{d} \pm t_{\alpha/2,df} s_D / \sqrt{n}$. With $df = n - 1 = 10 - 1 = 9$ and $\alpha = 0.05$, we find $t_{\alpha/2,df} = t_{0.025,9} = 2.262$. Plugging the relevant values into the formula, we calculate $8.5 \pm 2.262(11.38/\sqrt{10}) = 8.5 \pm 8.14$. That is, a 95% confidence interval for the mean difference ranges from 0.36 to 16.64. This represents a fairly wide interval, caused by the high standard deviation s_D of the 10 sample differences.

Hypothesis Test for μ_D

As before, we generally want to test whether the mean difference μ_D is equal to, greater than, or less than a given hypothesized mean difference d_0, or:

Two-Tailed Test	Right-Tailed Test	Left-Tailed Test
$H_0: \mu_D = d_0$	$H_0: \mu_D \le d_0$	$H_0: \mu_D \ge d_0$
$H_A: \mu_D \ne d_0$	$H_A: \mu_D > d_0$	$H_A: \mu_D < d_0$

In practice, the competing hypotheses tend to be based on $d_0 = 0$.

EXAMPLE 10.6

Using the information from Example 10.5, can the manager conclude at the 5% significance level that there has been a change in productivity since the adoption of the new workstation?

SOLUTION: In order to determine whether or not there has been a change in the mean difference, we formulate the null and the alternative hypotheses as

$$H_0: \mu_D = 0$$
$$H_A: \mu_D \ne 0$$

In Example 10.5, we found that a 95% confidence interval for the mean difference ranges from 0.36 to 16.64. Although the interval is very wide, the entire range is above the hypothesized value of zero. Therefore, at the 5% significance level the sample data suggest that the mean difference differs from zero. In other words, there has been a change in productivity due to the different layout in the workstation.

We now examine the four-step procedure to conduct one- or two-tailed hypothesis tests concerning the mean difference. We again convert the sample mean difference into its corresponding t_{df} statistic by dividing the difference between the sample mean difference and the value of the hypothesized mean difference d_0 by the standard error of the estimator.

> **TEST STATISTIC FOR HYPOTHESIS TESTS ABOUT μ_D**
>
> The value of the test statistic for hypothesis tests about the population mean difference μ_D is computed as $t_{df} = \dfrac{\bar{d} - d_0}{s_D/\sqrt{n}}$, where $df = n - 1$, $\bar{d}$ and s_D are the mean and the standard deviation, respectively, of the n sample differences, and d_0 is the hypothesized mean difference. This formula is valid only if $\overline{D}$ (approximately) follows a normal distribution.

FILE

EXAMPLE 10.7

Let's revisit the chapter's introductory case. Recall that a local ordinance requires chain restaurants to post caloric information on their menus. A nutritionist wants to examine whether average drink calories declined at Starbucks after the passage of the ordinance. The nutritionist obtains transaction data for 40 Starbucks cardholders and records their average drink calories prior to the ordinance and then after the ordinance. A portion of the data is shown in Table 10.4. The entire data set, labeled **Drink_Calories**, can be found on the text website. Using the critical value approach, can she conclude at the 5% significance level that the ordinance reduced average drink calories?

SOLUTION: We first note that this is a matched-pairs experiment; specifically, it conforms to a "before" and "after" type of study. Moreover, we want to find out whether average drink calories consumed prior to the ordinance are significantly greater than average drink calories consumed after passage of the ordinance. Thus, we want to test if the mean difference μ_D is greater than zero, where $D = X_1 - X_2$, X_1 denotes drink calories before the ordinance, and X_2 denotes drink calories after the ordinance for a randomly selected Starbuck's customer. We specify the competing hypotheses as

$$H_0: \mu_D \leq 0$$
$$H_A: \mu_D > 0$$

The normality condition for the test is satisfied since the sample size $n \geq 30$. The value of the test statistic is calculated as $t_{df} = \frac{\bar{d} - d_0}{s_D/\sqrt{n}}$ where d_0 equals 0. In order to determine $\bar{d}$ and s_D, we first calculate the difference d_i for each i-th consumer. For instance, consumer 1 consumes 141 calories prior to the ordinance and 142 calories after the ordinance, for a difference of $d_1 = 141 - 142 = -1$. The differences for a portion of the other consumers appear in the fourth column of Table 10.4.

TABLE 10.4 Data and Calculations for Example 10.7, $n = 40$

Customer	Drink Calories Before	Drink Calories After	d_i	$(d_i - \bar{d})^2$
1	141	142	-1	$(-1 - 2.1)^2 = 9.61$
2	137	140	-3	$(-3 - 2.1)^2 = 26.01$
⋮	⋮	⋮	⋮	⋮
40	147	141	6	$(6 - 2.1)^2 = 15.21$
			$\Sigma d_i = 84$	$\Sigma(d_i - \bar{d})^2 = 2{,}593.60$

We obtain the sample mean as

$$\bar{d} = \frac{\Sigma d_i}{n} = \frac{84}{40} = 2.10.$$

Similarly, in the fifth column of Table 10.4, we square the differences between d_i and $\bar{d}$. Summing these squared differences yields the numerator in the formula for the sample variance s_D^2. The denominator is simply $n - 1$, so:

$$s_D^2 = \frac{\Sigma(d_i - \bar{d})^2}{n - 1} = \frac{2{,}593.60}{40 - 1} = 66.50.$$

As usual, the standard deviation is the positive square root of the sample variance, that is, $s_D = \sqrt{66.50} = 8.15$. We compute the value of the t_{df} test statistic with $df = n - 1 = 40 - 1 = 39$ as

$$t_{39} = \frac{\bar{d} - d_0}{s_D/\sqrt{n}} = \frac{2.10 - 0}{8.15/\sqrt{40}} = 1.63.$$

Given a right-tailed hypothesis test with $df = 39$, the relevant critical value with $\alpha = 0.05$ is found as $t_{\alpha,df} = t_{0.05,39} = 1.685$. Thus, the decision rule is to reject H_0 if $t_{39} > 1.685$. Since $t_{39} = 1.63$, we do not reject H_0. At the 5% significance level, we cannot conclude that the posting of nutritional information decreases average drink calories.

We should note that once we have calculated the mean difference and the standard deviation of the mean difference, the hypothesis test essentially reduces to a one-sample t test for the population mean.

Using Excel for Testing Hypotheses about μ_D

Excel provides an option that simplifies the calculations for a hypothesis test concerning μ_D. Example 10.8 illustrates the procedure.

EXAMPLE 10.8

The nutritionist from Example 10.7 also wants to use the data from the 40 Starbucks cardholders in order to determine if the posting of caloric information has reduced the intake of average food calories. This test is also conducted at the 5% significance level.

SOLUTION: We set up the same competing hypotheses as in Example 10.7 since we want to know if food caloric intake was greater before the ordinance as compared to after the ordinance.

$$H_0: \mu_D \le 0$$
$$H_A: \mu_D > 0$$

If we follow these steps, then Excel provides the sample value of the test statistic, the p-value, and the critical value(s).

a. Open the **_Food_Calories_** data found on the text website.

b. Choose **Data > Data Analysis > t-Test: Paired Two Sample for Means > OK.**

c. See Figure 10.2. In the _t-Test: Paired Two Sample for Means_ dialog box, choose _Variable 1 Range_ and select food caloric intake before the ordinance. Choose _Variable 2 Range_ and select food caloric intake after the ordinance. Enter a _Hypothesized Mean Difference_ of 0 since $d_0 = 0$, check the _Labels_ box if you include Before and After as headings, and enter an α value of 0.05 since the test is conducted at the 5% significance level. Choose an output range and click **OK.**

FIGURE 10.2 Excel's dialog box for t test with paired sample

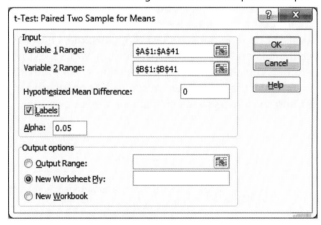

Table 10.5 shows the relevant output.

TABLE 10.5 Excel's Output for t Test with Paired Sample

	Before	After
Mean	400.275	391.475
Variance	49.94808	42.3583
Observations	40	40
Pearson Correlation	0.27080	
Hypothesized Mean Difference	0	
Df	39	
t Stat	**6.7795**	
P(T ≤ t) one-tail	**2.15E-08**	
t Critical one-tail	**1.6849**	
P(T ≤ t) two-tail	4.31E-08	
t Critical two-tail	2.0227	

The output from Excel allows us to conduct the hypothesis test using either the p-value approach or the critical value approach. Given that we have a one-tailed hypothesis test, the relevant p-value is 2.15E-08, that is, virtually zero. At the 5% significance level, we can reject H_0 because the p-value is less than 0.05.

Given degrees of freedom of 39 and $\alpha = 0.05$, the relevant critical value for this one-tailed test is $t_{\alpha,df} = t_{0.05,39} = 1.6849$ (see **t Critical one-tail** in Table 10.5). Since the value of the test statistic is greater than the critical value, $6.7795 > 1.6849$, we reject the null hypothesis. Thus, at the 5% significance level we can conclude that average food caloric intake has declined after the ordinance.

SYNOPSIS OF INTRODUCTORY CASE

In an effort to make it easier for consumers to select healthier options, the government wants chain restaurants to post caloric information on their menus. A nutritionist studies the effects of a recent local menu ordinance requiring caloric postings at a Starbucks in San Mateo, California. She obtains transaction data for 40 Starbucks cardholders and records their average drink and food calories prior to the ordinance and then after the ordinance. Two hypothesis tests are conducted. The first test examines whether drink caloric intake is less since the passage of the ordinance. After conducting a test on the mean difference at the 5% significance level, the nutritionist infers that the ordinance did not prompt consumers to reduce their drink caloric intake. The second test investigates whether food caloric intake is less since the passage of the ordinance. At the 5% significance level, the sample data suggest that consumers have reduced their food caloric intake since the passage of the ordinance. In sum, while the government is trying to ensure that customers process the calorie information as they are ordering, the results are consistent with research that has shown mixed results on whether mandatory caloric postings are prompting consumers to select healthier foods.

EXERCISES 10.2

Mechanics

20. A sample of 20 paired observations generates the following data: $\bar{d} = 1.3$ and $s_D^2 = 2.6$. Assume a normal distribution.

   a. Construct a 90% confidence interval for the mean difference μ_D.

   b. Using the confidence interval, test whether the mean difference differs from zero. Explain.

21. The following table contains information on matched sample values whose differences are normally distributed.

Number	Sample 1	Sample 2
1	18	21
2	12	11
3	21	23
4	22	20
5	16	20
6	14	17
7	17	17
8	18	22

   a. Construct a 95% confidence interval for the mean difference μ_D.

   b. Specify the competing hypotheses in order to test whether the mean difference differs from zero.

   c. Using the confidence interval from part a, are you able to reject H_0? Explain.

22. Consider the following competing hypotheses and accompanying results from matched samples:

$$H_0: \mu_D \geq 0;\ H_A: \mu_D < 0$$
$$\bar{d} = -2.8,\ s_D = 5.7,\ n = 12$$

   a. At the 5% significance level, find the critical value(s).

   b. Calculate the value of the test statistic under the assumption that the sample difference is normally distributed.

   c. What is the conclusion to the hypothesis test?

23. Consider the following competing hypotheses and accompanying results from matched samples:

$$H_0: \mu_D \leq 2;\ H_A: \mu_D > 2$$
$$\bar{d} = 5.6,\ s_D = 6.2,\ n = 10$$

a. Calculate the value of the test statistic and approximate the p-value assuming that the sample difference is normally distributed.

b. Use the 1% significance level to make a conclusion.

24. A sample of 35 paired observations generates the following results: $\bar{d} = 1.2$ and $s_D = 3.8$.

a. Specify the appropriate hypotheses to test if the mean difference is greater than zero.

b. Compute the value of the test statistic and approximate the p-value.

c. At the 5% significance level, can you conclude that the mean difference is greater than zero? Explain.

d. Repeat the hypothesis test using the critical value approach.

25. Consider the following matched samples representing observations before and after an experiment. Assume that the sample differences are normally distributed.

Before	2.5	1.8	1.4	−2.9	1.2	−1.9	−3.1	2.5
After	2.9	3.1	3.9	−1.8	0.2	0.6	−2.5	2.9

a. Construct the competing hypotheses to determine if the experiment increases the magnitude of the observations.

b. Implement the test at a 5% significance level.

c. Do the results change if we implement the test at a 1% significance level?

Applications

26. A manager of an industrial plant asserts that workers on average do not complete a job using Method A in the same amount of time as they would using Method B. Seven workers are randomly selected. Each worker's completion time (in minutes) is recorded by the use of Method A and Method B.

Worker	Method A	Method B
1	15	16
2	21	25
3	16	18
4	18	22
5	19	23
6	22	20
7	20	20

a. Specify the null and alternative hypotheses to test the manager's assertion.

b. Assuming that the completion time difference is normally distributed, calculate the value of the test statistic.

c. At the 10% significance level, specify the critical value(s) and the decision rule.

d. Is the manager's assertion supported by the data?

27. A diet center claims that it has the most effective weight loss program in the region. Its advertisements say, "Participants in our program lose more than 5 pounds within a month." Six clients of this program are weighed on the first day of the diet and then one month later.

Client	Weight on First Day of Diet	Weight One Month Later
1	158	151
2	205	200
3	170	169
4	189	179
5	149	144
6	135	129

a. Specify the null and alternative hypotheses that test the diet center's claim.

b. Assuming that weight loss is normally distributed, calculate the value of the test statistic.

c. Approximate the p-value.

d. At the 5% significance level, do the data support the diet center's claim?

28. A bank employs two appraisers. When approving borrowers for mortgages, it is imperative that the appraisers value the same types of properties consistently. To make sure that this is the case, the bank evaluates six properties that the appraisers had valued recently.

Property	Value from Appraiser 1	Value from Appraiser 2
1	$235,000	$239,000
2	195,000	190,000
3	264,000	271,000
4	315,000	310,000
5	435,000	437,000
6	515,000	525,000

a. Specify the competing hypotheses that determine whether there is any difference between the values estimated by appraiser 1 and appraiser 2.

b. At the 5% significance level, find the critical value(s).

c. Assuming that the value difference is normally distributed, calculate the value of the test statistic.

d. Is there sufficient evidence to conclude that the appraisers are inconsistent in their estimates? Explain.

29. FILE (Use Excel) A recent report criticizes SAT-test-preparation providers for promising big score gains without any hard data to back up such claims (*The Wall Street Journal*, May 20, 2009). Suppose eight college-bound students take a mock SAT, complete a three-month test-prep course, and then take the real SAT. The data set, labeled *Mock_SAT*, can also be found on the text website.

Student	Score on Mock SAT	Score on Real SAT
1	1830	1840
2	1760	1800
3	2000	2010
4	2150	2190
5	1630	1620
6	1840	1960
7	1930	1890
8	1710	1780

a. Specify the competing hypotheses that determine whether completion of the test-prep course increases a student's score on the real SAT.

b. Assuming that the SAT scores difference is normally distributed, calculate the value of the test statistic and its associated p-value.

c. At the 5% significance level, do the sample data support the test-prep providers' claims?

30. FILE (Use Excel) The following table shows the annual returns (in percent) for Fidelity's Select Electronic and Select Utilities mutual funds. The data set, labeled **Electronic_Utilities**, can also be found on the text website.

Year	Electronic	Utilities
2001	−14.23	−21.89
2002	−50.54	−30.40
2003	71.89	26.42
2004	−9.81	24.22
2005	15.75	9.36
2006	0.30	30.08
2007	4.67	18.13
2008	−49.87	−36.00
2009	84.99	14.39

Source: http://www.finance.yahoo.com

a. Set up the hypotheses to test the claim that the mean return for the Electronic mutual fund differs from the mean return for the Utilities mutual fund.

b. Using the appropriate commands in Excel, find the value of the test statistic. What is the p-value?

c. At the 5% significance level, do the mean returns differ?

31. FILE (Use Excel) It is fairly common for people to put on weight when they quit smoking. While a small weight gain is normal, excessive weight gain can create new health concerns that erode the benefits of not smoking. The accompanying table shows a portion of the weight data for 50 women before quitting and six months after quitting; the complete data set, labeled **Smoking_Weight**, are available on the text website.

Weight after Quitting	Weight before Quitting
155	140
142	144
⋮	⋮
147	135

a. Construct and interpret a 95% confidence interval for the mean gain in weight.

b. Use the above confidence interval to determine whether or not the mean gain in weight is 5 pounds.

32. FILE (Use Excel) When faced with a power hitter, many baseball teams utilize a defensive shift. A shift usually involves putting three infielders on one side of second base against pull hitters. Many believe that a power hitter's batting average is lower when he faces a shift defense as compared to when he faces a standard defense. Consider the following batting averages of 10 power hitters over the 2010 and 2011 seasons when they faced a shift defense versus when they faced a standard defense. The data set, labeled **Shift**, can also be found on the text website.

Player	Average When Shift	Average When No Shift
Jack Cust	0.239	0.270
Adam Dunn	0.189	0.230
Prince Fielder	0.150	0.263
Adrian Gonzalez	0.186	0.251
Ryan Howard	0.177	0.317
Brian McCann	0.321	0.250
David Ortiz	0.245	0.232
Carlos Pena	0.243	0.191
Mark Teixeira	0.168	0.182
Jim Thome	0.211	0.205

Source: The Fielding Bible-Volume III, March 2012

a. Specify the competing hypotheses to determine whether the use of the defensive shift lowers a power hitter's batting average.

b. What are the value of the test statistic and the p-value?

c. At the 5% significance level, is the defensive shift effective in lowering a power hitter's batting average?

10.3 Inference Concerning Differences among Many Means

We use an analysis of variance (ANOVA) test to determine if differences exist between the means of three or more populations under independent sampling. This test is actually a generalization of the two-sample *t* test with equal but unknown variances discussed in Section 10.1 The ANOVA test is based on a new distribution, called the **F distribution**.[1] We will first discuss the characteristics of this important distribution before getting into the details of the ANOVA test.

The *F* Distribution

Like the t_{df} distribution, the F distribution is characterized by a family of distributions; however, each distribution depends on *two* degrees of freedom: the numerator degrees of freedom df_1 and the denominator degrees of freedom df_2. It is common to refer to it as the $F_{(df_1,df_2)}$ distribution. The $F_{(df_1,df_2)}$ distribution is positively skewed with values ranging from zero to infinity but becomes increasingly symmetric as df_1 and df_2 increase.

LO **10.3**

Discuss features of the F distribution.

FIGURE 10.3 The $F_{(df_1,df_2)}$ distribution with various degrees of freedom

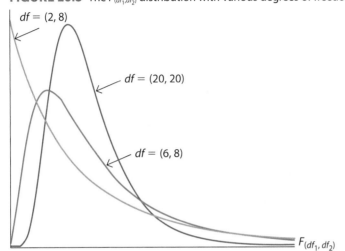

From Figure 10.3 we note that all $F_{(df_1,df_2)}$ distributions are positively skewed, where skewness depends on degrees of freedom, df_1 and df_2. As df_1 and df_2 grow larger, the $F_{(df_1,df_2)}$ distribution becomes less skewed and approaches the normal distribution. For instance, $F_{(20,20)}$ is relatively less skewed and more bell-shaped as compared to $F_{(2,8)}$ or $F_{(6,8)}$.

As with the t_{df} distribution, we use the notation $F_{\alpha,(df_1,df_2)}$ to represent a value such that the area in the right tail of the distribution is α. In other words, $P(F_{(df_1,df_2)} \geq F_{\alpha,(df_1,df_2)}) = \alpha$. Figure 10.4 illustrates the notation $F_{\alpha,(df_1,df_2)}$ used in the F table.

FIGURE 10.4 Graphical depiction of $P(F_{(df_1,df_2)} \geq F_{\alpha,(df_1,df_2)}) = \alpha$

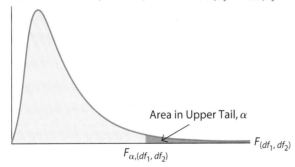

A portion of the right-tail probabilities α and the corresponding $F_{(df_1,df_2)}$ values are given in Table 10.6. Table 4 of Appendix A provides a more complete table.

---

[1]The F distribution is named in honor of Sir Ronald Fisher, who discovered the distribution in 1922.

10.3 Inference Concerning Differences among Many Means | **335**

TABLE 10.6 Portion of the *F* Table

Denominator Degrees of Freedom, df_2	Area in Upper Tail, α	Numerator Degrees of Freedom, df_1		
		6	7	8
6	0.10	3.05	3.01	2.98
	0.05	4.28	4.21	4.15
	0.025	5.82	5.70	5.60
	0.01	8.47	8.26	8.10
7	0.10	2.83	2.78	2.75
	0.05	3.87	3.79	3.73
	0.025	5.12	4.99	4.90
	0.01	7.19	6.99	6.84
8	0.10	2.67	2.62	2.59
	0.05	**3.58**	3.50	3.44
	0.025	4.65	4.53	4.43
	0.01	**6.37**	6.18	6.03

Consider the degrees of freedom given by $df_1 = 6$ and $df_2 = 8$. With $df_1 = 6$ (read from the top row) and $df_2 = 8$ (read from the first column), we can easily determine the area in the right tail as $P(F_{(6,8)} \geq 3.58) = 0.05$ and $P(F_{(6,8)} \geq 6.37) = 0.01$. The *F* table is not very comprehensive and lists probabilities corresponding to a limited number of values in the right tail of the distribution. For instance, the exact probability $P(F_{(6,8)} \geq 3.92)$ cannot be determined from the table and we have to rely on approximate values. All we can say is the area to the right of 3.92 is between 0.025 and 0.05. Shortly, we will use Excel to find exact probabilities.

LO **10.4**

Make inferences about the difference between three or more population means using an analysis of variance (ANOVA) test.

One-Way ANOVA Test

We will discuss a one-way ANOVA test through an example. Sean Cox, a research analyst at an environmental organization, believes that an upswing in the use of public transportation has taken place due to environmental concerns, the volatility of gas prices, and the general economic climate. He is pleased with a recent study, which highlights the average annual cost savings when commuters use public transportation (*Boston Globe*, May 8, 2009). Sean wants to determine whether there are differences in mean cost savings among cities. He focuses on annual cost savings in Boston, New York, San Francisco, and Chicago. The summary statistics for each city are presented in Table 10.7; the raw data used for these summary statistics, labeled ***Public_Transportation***, are available on the text website.

TABLE 10.7 Summary Statistics from Using Public Transportation in Four Cities

FILE	Boston	New York	San Francisco	Chicago
	$\bar{x}_1 = \$12,622$	$\bar{x}_2 = \$12,585$	$\bar{x}_3 = \$11,720$	$\bar{x}_4 = \$10,730$
	$s_1 = \$87.79$	$s_2 = \$80.40$	$s_3 = \$83.96$	$s_4 = \$90.62$
	$n_1 = 5$	$n_2 = 8$	$n_3 = 6$	$n_4 = 5$

A one-way ANOVA test compares population means based on one categorical variable or factor. For instance, in the public transportation example, we want to compare cost savings of using public transportation depending on where an individual resides. We thus delineate cost savings of using public transportation by city (the categorical variable). In general, the one-way ANOVA test is used for testing c population means under the following assumptions:

1. The populations are normally distributed.
2. The population variances are unknown but assumed equal.
3. The samples are selected independently.

In short, each population i, where $i = 1, 2, \ldots, c$, has mean μ_i and a common standard deviation σ where these parameters are unknown. From these populations, we draw independent random samples where the selection of one sample does not affect the selection of another sample. From each sample, we calculate the sample mean $\bar{x}_i$ and the sample standard deviation s_i to implement the test.

Since we wish to test whether or not the mean annual cost savings from using public transportation is the same in Boston, New York, San Francisco, and Chicago, we formulate the following competing hypotheses:

$$H_0: \mu_1 = \mu_2 = \mu_3 = \mu_4$$
$$H_A: \text{Not all population means are equal}$$

Note that H_A does not require that all means must differ from one another. In principle, the sample data may support the rejection of H_0 in favor of H_A even if only two means differ.

When conducting the equality of means test, you might be tempted to set up a series of hypothesis tests, comparing μ_1 and μ_2, then μ_1 and μ_3, and so on, and then use the two-sample t test with equal variances discussed in Section 10.1. However, such an approach is not only cumbersome, but also flawed. In this example, where we evaluate the equality of four means, we would have to compare six combinations of two means at a time. Also, by conducting numerous pairwise comparisons, we inflate the risk of the Type I error α; that is, we increase the risk of incorrectly rejecting the null hypothesis. In other words, if we conduct all six pairwise tests at a 5% level of significance, the resulting significance level for the overall test will be greater than 5%.

Fortunately, the ANOVA technique avoids this problem by providing one test that simultaneously evaluates the equality of several means. In the public transportation example, if the four population means are equal, we would expect the resulting sample means, $\bar{x}_1$, $\bar{x}_2$, $\bar{x}_3$, and $\bar{x}_4$, to be relatively close to one another. Figure 10.5a illustrates the distribution of the sample means if H_0 is true. Here, the relatively small variability in the sample means can be explained by chance. What if the population means differ? Figure 10.5b shows the distributions of the sample means if the sample data support H_A. In this scenario, the sample means are relatively far apart since each sample mean is calculated from a population with a different mean. The resulting variability in the sample means cannot be explained by chance alone.

FIGURE 10.5 The logic of ANOVA

a. Distribution of sample means if H_0 is true

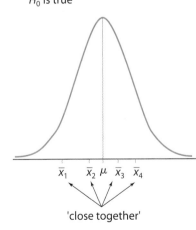

'close together'

b. Distributions of sample means if H_0 is false

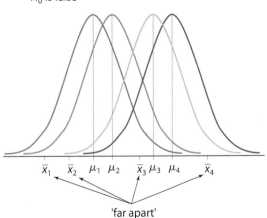

'far apart'

The term 'treatments' is often used to identify the c populations being examined. The practice of referring to different populations as different treatments is due to the fact that many ANOVA applications were originally developed in connection with agricultural experiments where different fertilizers were regarded as different treatments applied to soil. In order to determine if significant differences exist between some of the population means, we develop two independent estimates of the common population variance σ^2.

One estimate can be attributed to inherent differences between the c populations, while the other estimate can be attributed to chance.

1. **Between-Treatments Estimate of σ^2.** One estimate of σ^2 is based on the variability *between* the sample means. This is referred to as **between-treatments variance**, and is denoted by *MSTR*.

2. **Within-Treatments Estimate of σ^2.** The other estimate of σ^2 is based on the variability of the data *within* each sample, that is, the variability due to chance. This estimate is generally called **within-treatments variance**, and is denoted by *MSE*.

If we find that between-treatments variance is significantly greater than within-treatments variance, then we are able to reject the null hypothesis of equal means; this is equivalent to concluding that the ratio of between-treatments variance to within-treatments variance is significantly greater than one.

Between-Treatments Estimate of σ^2

Between-treatments variance is based on a weighted sum of squared differences between the sample means and the overall mean of the data set, referred to as the **grand mean** and denoted as $\bar{\bar{x}}$. We compute the grand mean by summing all observations in the data set and dividing by the total number of observations.

Each squared difference of a sample mean from the grand mean $(\bar{x}_i - \bar{\bar{x}})^2$ is multiplied by the respective sample size for each treatment n_i. After summing the weighted squared differences, we arrive at a value called the **sum of squares due to treatments** or *SSTR*. When we average a sum of squares over its respective degrees of freedom, we obtain the mean sum of squares. Dividing *SSTR* by $c - 1$ yields the **mean square for treatments** or *MSTR*.

CALCULATIONS FOR THE BETWEEN-TREATMENTS ESTIMATE FOR σ^2

The **grand mean** $\bar{\bar{x}}$ is calculated as $\bar{\bar{x}} = \dfrac{\sum\limits_{i=1}^{c} \sum\limits_{j=1}^{n_i} x_{ij}}{n_T}$, where $n_T = \sum\limits_{i=1}^{c} n_i$ is the total sample size.

The **sum of squares due to treatments** *SSTR* is calculated as $SSTR = \sum\limits_{i=1}^{c} n_i(\bar{x}_i - \bar{\bar{x}})^2$.

The **mean square for treatments** *MSTR* is calculated as $MSTR = \dfrac{SSTR}{c-1}$.

The calculations for $\bar{\bar{x}}$, *SSTR*, and *MSTR* for the public transportation example are as follows:

$$\bar{\bar{x}} = \frac{\sum\limits_{j=1}^{c} \sum\limits_{i=1}^{n_j} x_{ij}}{n_T} = \frac{12{,}500 + 12{,}640 + \cdots + 10{,}740}{24} = \$11{,}990.$$

$$\begin{aligned} SSTR = \sum_{i=1}^{c} n_i(\bar{x}_i - \bar{\bar{x}})^2 &= 5(12{,}622 - 11{,}990)^2 + 8(12{,}585 - 11{,}990)^2 \\ &\quad + 6(11{,}720 - 11{,}990)^2 + 5(10{,}730 - 11{,}990)^2 \\ &= 13{,}204{,}720. \end{aligned}$$

$$MSTR = \frac{SSTR}{c-1} = \frac{13{,}204{,}720}{4-1} = 4{,}401{,}573.$$

Within-Treatments Estimate of σ^2

We just calculated a value of *MSTR* equal to 4,401,573. Is this value of *MSTR* large enough to indicate that the population means differ? To answer this question we compare *MSTR* to the variability that we expect due to chance. We first calculate the **sum of squares due to errors**, denoted as *SSE*. *SSE* provides a measure of the degree of variability that exists even if all population means are the same. We calculate *SSE* as a weighted sum of the sample variances of each treatment, and the **mean square error** *MSE* by dividing *SSE* by its respective degrees of freedom, $df = n_T - c$.

CALCULATIONS FOR WITHIN-TREATMENTS ESTIMATE FOR σ^2

The **error sum of squares** *SSE* is calculated as $SSE = \sum_{i=1}^{c} (n_i - 1)s_i^2$.

The **mean square error** *MSE* is calculated as $MSE = \frac{SSE}{n_T - c}$.

The values of *SSE* and *MSE* for the public transportation example are calculated as follows:

$$SSE = \sum_{i=1}^{c} (n_i - 1)s_i^2$$
$$= (5 - 1)(87.79)^2 + (8 - 1)(80.40)^2 + (6 - 1)(83.96)^2 + (5 - 1)(90.62)^2$$
$$= 144{,}172.$$
$$MSE = \frac{SSE}{n_T - c} = \frac{144{,}172}{24 - 4} = 7{,}209.$$

As mentioned earlier, if the ratio of the between-treatments variance to the within-treatments variance is significantly greater than one, then this finding provides evidence for rejecting the null hypothesis of equal population means. Equivalently, if this ratio is not significantly greater than one, then we are not able to reject this null hypothesis in favor of the alternative hypothesis. We use this ratio to develop the ANOVA test.

TEST STATISTIC FOR A ONE-WAY ANOVA TEST

The value of the **test statistic** for the hypothesis test of the equality of the population means using one-way ANOVA is computed as $F_{(df_1, df_2)} = \frac{MSTR}{MSE}$, where $df_1 = c - 1$, $df_2 = n_T - c$, and n_T is the total sample size. *MSTR* is the between-treatments variance and *MSE* is the within-treatments variance where these values are based on independent samples drawn from c normally distributed populations with a common variance σ^2.

ANOVA tests are always specified as right-tailed tests.

We are now in a position to conduct a four-step hypothesis test for the public transportation example. Given $MSTR = 4{,}401{,}573$, $MSE = 7{,}209$, $df_1 = c - 1 = 4 - 1 = 3$, and $df_2 = n_T - c = 24 - 4 = 20$, we compute the value of the test statistic as

$$F_{(3,20)} = \frac{MSTR}{MSE} = \frac{4{,}401{,}573}{7{,}209} = 610.57.$$

Since the ANOVA test is a right-tailed test, the critical value with $\alpha = 0.05$, $df_1 = 3$, and $df_2 = 20$ is found from the F table as $F_{\alpha,(df_1,df_2)} = F_{0.05,(3,20)} = 3.10$; we show a portion of the F table in Table 10.8. Hence, the decision rule is to reject H_0 if $F_{(3,20)} > 3.10$.

TABLE 10.8 Portion of the F table

Denominator Degrees of Freedom, df_2	Area in Upper Tail	Numerator Degrees of Freedom, df_1		
		1	2	3
20	0.10	2.97	2.59	2.38
	0.05	4.35	3.49	**3.10**
	0.025	5.87	4.46	3.86
	0.01	8.10	5.85	4.94

We reject the null hypothesis because the value of the test statistic falls in the rejection region (610.57 is greater than 3.10). Therefore, we conclude that the mean cost savings from using public transportation are not the same for each city.

The One-Way ANOVA Table

Most software packages summarize the ANOVA calculations in a table. The general format of the ANOVA table is presented in Table 10.9.

TABLE 10.9 General Format of a One-way ANOVA Table

Source of Variation	SS	df	MS	F
Between Groups	SSTR	$c - 1$	MSTR	$F_{(df_1, df_2)} = \dfrac{MSTR}{MSE}$
Within Groups	SSE	$n_T - c$	MSE	
Total	SST	$n_T - 1$		

We should also note that **total sum of squares** SST is equal to the sum of the squared differences of each observation from the grand mean. This is equivalent to summing $SSTR$ with SSE; that is, $SST = SSTR + SSE$.

Using Excel for One-Way ANOVA Test

Fortunately, Excel provides the value of the $F_{(df_1, df_2)}$ test statistic, the critical value, as well as the precise p-value for a one-way ANOVA problem. In order to solve the public transportation example using Excel, we follow these steps.

A. **FILE** Open the **Public_Transportation** data found on the text website.

B. Choose **Data > Data Analysis > ANOVA: Single Factor**.

C. In the *ANOVA: Single Factor* dialog box shown in Figure 10.6, choose the box next to *Input range* and then select all the data, including the city names. Check the *Labels* box. If testing at a significance level other than 5%, insert the relevant α value in the box next to *Alpha*. Choose an output range and click **OK**.

FIGURE 10.6 Excel's ANOVA: Single Factor dialog box

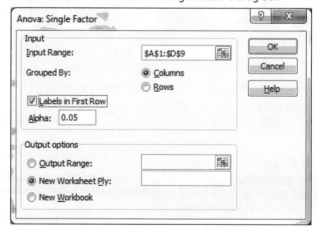

In addition to the ANOVA table, Excel provides descriptive statistics for the sample data. Table 10.10 shows the results. You should verify that all of the hand calculations match the values produced by Excel. Any differences between the hand calculations and the computer-generated results are due to rounding.

TABLE 10.10 Excel-Produced ANOVA Results for Public Transportation Example

SUMMARY					
Groups	**Count**	**Sum**	**Average**	**Variance**	
Boston	5	63110	12622	7707.5	
New York	8	100680	12585	6464.3	
San Francisco	6	70320	11720	7050	
Chicago	5	53650	10730	8212.5	

ANOVA						
Source of Variation	**SS**	**df**	**MS**	**F**	**p-value**	**F crit**
Between Groups	13204720	3	4401573	**610.57**	**7.96E-20**	3.098
Within Groups	144180	20	7209			
Total	13348900	23				

EXAMPLE 10.9

Using the information in Table 10.10, repeat the ANOVA test for the public transportation example using the p-value approach.

SOLUTION: In order to determine whether cost savings in public transportation differ between the four cities, we again specify the competing hypotheses as

$$H_0: \mu_1 = \mu_2 = \mu_3 = \mu_4$$
$$H_A: \text{Not all population means are equal}$$

From Table 10.10, we find that the value of the test statistic is $F_{3,20} = 610.57$. Its corresponding p-value is 7.96×10^{-20}, or, equivalently, $P(F_{3,20} \geq 610.57) \approx 0$. (See the value for the test statistic and the p-value in boldface in Table 10.10.) Since the p-value is less than $\alpha = 0.05$, we reject the null hypothesis and again conclude that the mean cost savings from using public transportation is not the same for each city.

It is important to note that if we reject the null hypothesis, we can only conclude that not all population means are equal. The one-way ANOVA test does not allow us to infer which individual means differ. Therefore, even though the sample mean is the highest for Boston, we cannot conclude that Boston leads other cities in the amount that commuters save by taking public transportation. Further analysis of the difference between paired population means is beyond the scope of this text.

EXERCISES 10.3

Mechanics

33. A random sample of five observations from three normally distributed populations produced the following data:

Treatments		
A	**B**	**C**
22	20	19
25	25	22
27	21	24
24	26	21
22	23	19
$\bar{x}_A = 24$	$\bar{x}_B = 23$	$\bar{x}_C = 21$
$s_A^2 = 4.5$	$s_B^2 = 6.5$	$s_C^2 = 4.5$

a. Calculate the grand mean.
b. Calculate SSTR and MSTR.
c. Calculate SSE and MSE.
d. Specify the competing hypotheses in order to determine whether some differences exist between the population means.
e. Calculate the value of the $F_{(df_1, df_2)}$ test statistic.
f. Using the critical value approach at the 5% significance level, what is the conclusion to the test?

34. Random sampling from four normally distributed populations produced the following data:

	Treatments			
	A	**B**	**C**	**D**
	−11	−8	−8	−12
	−13	−13	−13	−13
	−10	−15	−8	−15
		−12	−13	
			−10	
	$\bar{x}_A = -11.3$	$\bar{x}_B = -12$	$\bar{x}_C = -10.4$	$\bar{x}_D = -13.3$
	$s_A^2 = 2.33$	$s_B^2 = 8.7$	$s_C^2 = 6.3$	$s_D^2 = 2.3$

a. Calculate the grand mean.

b. Calculate SSTR and MSTR.

c. Calculate SSE and MSE.

d. Specify the competing hypotheses in order to determine whether some differences exist between the population means.

e. Calculate the value of the $F_{(df_1, df_2)}$ test statistic.

f. Approximate the p-value.

g. At the 10% significance level, what is the conclusion to the test?

35. Given the following information obtained from three normally distributed populations, construct an ANOVA table and perform an ANOVA test of mean differences at the 1% significance level.

$SSTR = 220.7; SSE = 2,252.2; c = 3; n_1 = n_2 = n_3 = 8$

36. Given the following information obtained from four normally distributed populations, construct an ANOVA table and perform an ANOVA test of mean differences at the 5% significance level.

$SST = 70.47; SSTR = 11.34; c = 4; n_1 = n_2 = n_3 = n_4 = 15$

37. An analysis of variance experiment produced a portion of the accompanying ANOVA table.

Source of Variation	SS	df	MS	F	p-value	F crit
Between Groups	25.08	3	?	?	0.0004	2.725
Within Groups	92.64	76	?			
Total	117.72	79				

a. Fill in the missing statistics in the ANOVA table.

b. Specify the competing hypotheses in order to determine whether some differences exist between the population means.

c. At the 5% significance level, what is the conclusion to the test?

38. An analysis of variance experiment produced a portion of the following ANOVA table.

Source of Variation	SS	df	MS	F	p-value	F crit
Between Groups		5	?	?	?	?
Within Groups	4321.11	54	?			
Total	4869.48	59				

a. Fill in the missing statistics in the ANOVA table.

b. Specify the competing hypotheses in order to determine whether some differences exist between the population means.

c. At the 10% significance level, what is the conclusion to the test?

Applications

39. Asian residents in Boston have the highest average life expectancy of any racial or ethnic group—a decade longer than black residents (*Boston Globe*, August 16, 2010). Suppose sample results indicative of the overall results are as follows.

Asian	**Black**	**Latino**	**White**
$\bar{x}_1 = 83.7$ years	$\bar{x}_2 = 73.5$ years	$\bar{x}_3 = 80.6$ years	$\bar{x}_4 = 79.0$ years
$s_1^2 = 26.3$	$s_2^2 = 27.5$	$s_3^2 = 28.2$	$s_4^2 = 24.8$
$n_1 = 20$	$n_2 = 20$	$n_3 = 20$	$n_4 = 20$

a. Construct an ANOVA table. Assume life expectancies are normally distributed.

b. Specify the competing hypotheses to test whether there are some differences in average life expectancies between the four ethnic groups.

c. At the 5% significance level, what is the conclusion to the test?

40. A well-known conglomerate claims that its detergent "whitens and brightens better than all the rest." In order to compare the cleansing action of the top three brands of detergents, 24 swatches of white cloth were soiled with red wine and grass stains and then washed in front-loading machines with the respective detergents. The following whiteness readings were obtained:

	Detergent		
	1	**2**	**3**
	84	78	87
	79	74	80
	87	81	91
	85	86	77
	94	86	78
	89	89	79
	89	69	77
	83	79	78
	$\bar{x}_1 = 86.3$	$\bar{x}_2 = 80.3$	$\bar{x}_3 = 80.9$
	$s_1^2 = 20.8$	$s_2^2 = 45.1$	$s_3^2 = 27.3$
		$\bar{\bar{x}} = 82.5$	

a. Construct an ANOVA table. Assume whiteness readings are normally distributed.

b. Specify the competing hypotheses to test whether there are some differences in the average whitening effectiveness of the three detergents.

c. At the 5% significance level, what is the conclusion to the test?

41. A recent survey by Genworth Financial Inc., a financial-services company, concludes that the cost of long-term

care in the United States varies significantly, depending on where an individual lives (*The Wall Street Journal*, May 16, 2009). An economist collects data from the five states with the highest annual costs (Alaska, Massachusetts, New Jersey, Rhode Island, and Connecticut) in order to determine if his sample data are consistent with the survey's conclusions. The economist provides the following portion of an ANOVA table:

Source of Variation	SS	df	MS	F	p-value
Between Groups	635.0542	4	?	?	?
Within Groups	253.2192	20	?		
Total	888.2734	24			

a. Complete the ANOVA table. Assume that long-term care costs are normally distributed.

b. Specify the competing hypotheses to test whether some differences exist in the mean long-term care costs in these five states.

c. At the 5% significance level, do mean costs differ?

42. An online survey by the Sporting Goods Manufacturers Association, a trade group of sports retailers and marketers, claimed that household income of recreational athletes varies by sport (*The Wall Street Journal*, August 10, 2009). In order to verify this claim, an economist samples five sports enthusiasts participating in each of six different recreational sports and obtains each enthusiast's income (in $1,000s), as shown in the accompanying table.

Snorkeling	Sailing	Boardsailing/ Windsurfing	Bowling	On-road Triathlon	Off-road Triathlon
90.9	87.6	75.9	79.3	64.5	47.7
86.0	95.0	75.6	75.8	67.2	59.6
93.6	94.6	83.1	79.6	62.8	68.0
98.8	87.2	74.4	78.5	59.2	60.9
98.4	82.5	80.5	73.2	66.5	50.9
$\bar{x}_1 = 93.5$	$\bar{x}_2 = 89.4$	$\bar{x}_3 = 77.9$	$\bar{x}_4 = 77.3$	$\bar{x}_5 = 64.0$	$\bar{x}_6 = 57.4$
$s_1^2 = 28.8$	$s_2^2 = 28.5$	$s_3^2 = 13.8$	$s_4^2 = 7.4$	$s_5^2 = 10.3$	$s_6^2 = 66.4$
		$\bar{\bar{x}} = 76.6$			

a. Specify the competing hypotheses in order to test the association's claim.

b. Create an ANOVA table. Assume incomes are normally distributed.

c. At the 5% significance level, what is the critical value?

d. Do some average incomes differ depending on the recreational sport? Explain.

43. The following Excel output summarizes the results of an analysis of variance experiment in which the treatments were three different hybrid cars and the variable measured was the miles per gallon (mpg) obtained while driving the same route. Assume mpg is normally distributed.

Source of Variation	SS	df	MS	F	p-value	F crit
Between Groups	1034.51	2	517.26	19.86	4.49E-07	3.182
Within Groups	1302.41	50	26.05			
Total	2336.92	52				

At the 5% significance level, can we conclude that average mpg differs between the hybrids? Explain.

44. Do energy bills vary dramatically depending on where you live in the United States? Suppose 25 households from four regions in the United States are sampled. The values for the average annual energy bill are shown in the accompanying table and are consistent with those found by The Department of Energy (*Money*, June 2009). A portion of the ANOVA table is also shown.

Region	West	Northeast	Midwest	South
Average Annual Energy Bill	$1,491	$2,319	$1,768	$1,758

Source of Variation	SS	df	MS	F	p-value
Between Groups	7531769	3	?	?	7.13E-24
Within Groups	3492385	96	?		
Total	11024154	99			

a. Complete the ANOVA table. Assume energy costs are normally distributed.

b. At the 1% significance level, can we conclude that average annual energy bills vary by region?

45. **FILE** (Use Excel) The accompanying table shows a portion of quarterly data on Nike's revenue for the fiscal years 2001 through 2010. Data for Nike's fiscal year refer to the time period from June 1 through May 31. The entire data set, labeled **Nike_Revenues**, can be found on the text website. Assume revenue is normally distributed.

	Quarters Ended			
Year	August 31	November 30	February 28	May 31
2001	2,637	2,199	2,170	2,483
2002	2,614	2,337	2,260	2,682
⋮	⋮	⋮	⋮	⋮
2010	4,799	4,406	4,733	5,077

Source: Annual Reports for Nike, Inc.

Use one-way ANOVA to determine if the data provide enough evidence at the 5% significance level to indicate that there are quarterly differences in Nike's revenue.

46. **FILE** (Use Excel) A statistics instructor wonders whether significant differences exist in her students' final exam scores in her three different sections. She randomly selects the scores from 10 different students in each section. A portion of the data is shown below; the complete data set, labeled **Exam_Scores**, can be found on the text website. Assume exam scores are normally distributed.

Section 1	Section 2	Section 3
85	91	74
68	84	69
⋮	⋮	⋮
74	75	73

Do these data provide enough evidence at the 5% significance level to indicate that there are some differences in final exam scores among these three sections?

47. **FILE** (Use Excel) The accompanying table shows a portion of the number of customers that frequent a restaurant on weekend days over the past 52 weeks. The entire data set, labeled **Patronage**, can be found on the text website.

Fridays	Saturdays	Sundays
391	450	389
362	456	343
⋮	⋮	⋮
443	441	376

At the 5% significance level, can we conclude that the average number of customers that frequent the restaurant differs by weekend day?

48. **FILE** (Use Excel) A human resource specialist wants to determine whether the average job satisfaction score (on a scale of 0 to 100) differs depending on a person's field of employment. She collects scores from 30 employees in three different fields. A portion of the data is shown in the accompanying table. The entire data set, labeled **Job_Satisfaction**, can be found on the text website.

Field 1	Field 2	Field 3
80	76	81
76	73	77
⋮	⋮	⋮
79	67	80

At the 10% significance level, can we conclude that the average job satisfaction differs by field?

WRITING WITH STATISTICS

The Texas Transportation Institute, one of the finest higher-education-affiliated transportation research agencies in the nation, recently published its highly anticipated *2009 Annual Urban Mobility Report* (July 8, 2009). The study finds that the average U.S. driver languished in rush-hour traffic for 36.1 hours, as compared to 12 hours in 1982 when the records begin. This congestion also wasted approximately 2.81 billion gallons in fuel, or roughly three weeks' worth of gas per traveler. John Farnham, a research analyst at an environmental firm, is stunned by some of the report's conclusions. John is asked to conduct an independent study in order to see if differences exist in congestion depending on the city where the traveler drives. He selects 25 travelers from each of the five cities that suffered from the worst congestion. He asks each traveler to approximate the time spent in traffic (in hours) over the last calendar year. Table 10.11 shows a portion of his sample results. The entire data set, labeled **Congestion**, can be found on the text website.

TABLE 10.11 Annual Hours of Delay per Traveler in Five Cities

Los Angeles	Washington, DC	Atlanta	Houston	San Francisco
71	64	60	58	57
60	64	58	56	56
⋮	⋮	⋮	⋮	⋮
68	57	57	59	56

John wants to use the sample information to:

1. Determine whether significant differences exist in congestion, depending on the city where the traveler drives. Assume delay times are normally distributed.
2. Interpret the results.

Does traffic congestion vary by city? *The 2009 Annual Urban Mobility Report* found that traffic congestion, measured by annual hours of delay per traveler, was the worst in Los Angeles; followed by Washington, DC; Atlanta; Houston; and then San Francisco. An independent survey was conducted to verify some of the findings. Twenty-five travelers in each of these cities were asked how many hours they wasted in traffic over the past calendar year. Table 10.A reports the summary statistics. The sample data indicate that Los Angeles residents waste the most time sitting in traffic with an average of 69.2 hours per year. Washington, DC, residents rank a close second, spending an average of 62 hours per year in traffic. Residents in Atlanta, Houston, and San Francisco spend on average 57.0, 56.5, and 55.6 hours per year in traffic.

TABLE 10.A Summary Statistics

Los Angeles	Washington, DC	Atlanta	Houston	San Francisco
$\bar{x}_1 = 69.2$	$\bar{x}_2 = 62.0$	$\bar{x}_3 = 57.0$	$\bar{x}_4 = 56.5$	$\bar{x}_5 = 55.6$
$s_1 = 4.6$	$s_2 = 4.7$	$s_3 = 4.8$	$s_4 = 5.4$	$s_5 = 3.7$
$n_1 = 25$	$n_2 = 25$	$n_3 = 25$	$n_4 = 25$	$n_5 = 25$

A one-way ANOVA test is conducted to test if significant differences in congestion exist in these five worst-congested cities. The value of the test statistic is $F_{4,120} = 37.3$ with a p-value of approximately zero. Therefore, at the 5% level of significance, we reject the null hypothesis of equal means and conclude that traffic congestion does vary by city.

Although the above test allows us to conclude that congestion varies by city, it does not allow us to compare congestion between any two cities. For instance, we cannot conclude that Los Angeles has significantly higher average delays per traveler than San Francisco. Further analysis of the difference between paired population means is advised.

Conceptual Review

LO 10.1 Make inferences about the difference between two population means based on independent sampling.

Independent samples are samples that are completely unrelated to one another.

A $100(1 - \alpha)\%$ **confidence interval for the difference between two population means** $\mu_1 - \mu_2$, based on independent samples, is

- $(\bar{x}_1 - \bar{x}_2) \pm z_{\alpha/2}\sqrt{\dfrac{\sigma_1^2}{n_1} + \dfrac{\sigma_2^2}{n_2}}$, if σ_1^2 and σ_2^2 are known.

- $(\bar{x}_1 - \bar{x}_2) \pm t_{\alpha/2,df}\sqrt{s_p^2\left(\dfrac{1}{n_1} + \dfrac{1}{n_2}\right)}$, if σ_1^2 and σ_2^2 are unknown but assumed equal. The pooled sample variance s_p^2 is $s_p^2 = \dfrac{(n_1 - 1)s_1^2 + (n_2 - 1)s_2^2}{n_1 + n_2 - 2}$ and $df = n_1 + n_2 - 2$.

- $(\bar{x}_1 - \bar{x}_2) \pm t_{\alpha/2,df}\sqrt{\dfrac{s_1^2}{n_1} + \dfrac{s_2^2}{n_2}}$, if σ_1^2 and σ_2^2 are unknown and assumed unequal. The degrees of freedom are calculated as $df = \dfrac{(s_1^2/n_1 + s_2^2/n_2)^2}{(s_1^2/n_1)^2/(n_1 - 1) + (s_2^2/n_2)^2/(n_2 - 1)}$ and are rounded down to the nearest integer.

When conducting **hypothesis tests about the difference between two means** $\mu_1 - \mu_2$, based on independent samples, the value of the **test statistic** is

- $z = \dfrac{(\bar{x}_1 - \bar{x}_2) - d_0}{\sqrt{\dfrac{\sigma_1^2}{n_1} + \dfrac{\sigma_2^2}{n_2}}}$, if σ_1^2 and σ_2^2 are known.

- $t_{df} = \dfrac{(\bar{x}_1 - \bar{x}_2) - d_0}{\sqrt{s_p^2\left(\dfrac{1}{n_1} + \dfrac{1}{n_2}\right)}}$, if σ_1^2 and σ_2^2 are unknown but assumed equal.

- $t_{df} = \dfrac{(\bar{x}_1 - \bar{x}_2) - d_0}{\sqrt{\left(\dfrac{s_1^2}{n_1} + \dfrac{s_2^2}{n_2}\right)}}$, if σ_1^2 and σ_2^2 are unknown and assumed unequal.

The degrees of freedom for the last two tests are the same as the ones defined for the corresponding confidence intervals. The above formulas for estimation and testing are valid only if $\bar{X}_1 - \bar{X}_2$ (approximately) follows a normal distribution.

Make inferences about the mean difference based on matched-pairs sampling.

In general, two types of **matched-pairs sampling** occur. The first type of a matched-pairs sample is characterized by a measurement, an intervention of some type, and then another measurement. We generally refer to these experiments as "before" and "after" studies. The second type of a matched-pairs sample is characterized by a pairing of observations, where it is not the same individual that gets sampled twice.

For matched-pairs sampling, the population parameter of interest is referred to as the mean difference μ_D where $D = X_1 - X_2$, and the random variables X_1 and X_2 are matched in a pair. A $100(1 - \alpha)\%$ **confidence interval for the mean difference** μ_D, based on a matched-pairs sample, is given by $\bar{d} \pm t_{\alpha/2,df} s_D/\sqrt{n}$, where $\bar{d}$ and s_D are the mean and the standard deviation of D, respectively, and $df = n - 1$.

When conducting a **hypothesis test about** μ_D the value of the **test statistic** is calculated as $t_{df} = \dfrac{\bar{d} - d_0}{s_D/\sqrt{n}}$, where d_0 is a hypothesized mean difference.

The above formulas are valid only if $\bar{D}$ (approximately) follows a normal distribution.

Discuss features of the F distribution.

The **F distribution** is characterized by a family of distributions, where each distribution depends on two degrees of freedom: the numerator degrees of freedom df_1 and the denominator degrees of freedom df_2. It is common to refer to it as the $F_{(df_1, df_2)}$ distribution. The distribution is positively skewed with values ranging from zero to infinity but becomes increasingly symmetric as df_1 and df_2 increase.

Make inferences about the difference between three or more population means using an analysis of variance (ANOVA) test.

The **one-way analysis of variance (ANOVA)** test is used to determine if differences exist between the means of three or more populations. These tests are based on the F distribution.

The one-way ANOVA test examines the amount of variability *between* the samples relative to the amount of variability *within* the samples to determine whether or not all population means are equal. The value of the **test statistic** for the hypothesis test of the equality of the c population means is computed as $F_{(df_1, df_2)} = \dfrac{MSTR}{MSE}$, where $df_1 = c - 1$, $df_2 = n_T - c$, and n_T is the total sample size. $MSTR$ and MSE are based on independent samples drawn from c normally distributed populations with a common variance σ^2. The one-way ANOVA test is always specified as a right-tailed test.

Additional Exercises and Case Studies

49. Do men really spend more money on St. Patrick's Day as compared to women? A recent survey found that men spend an average of $43.87 while women spend an average of $29.54 (*USA Today*, March 17, 2009). Assume that these data were based on a sample of 100 men and 100 women and the population standard deviations of spending for men and women are $32 and $25, respectively.

    a. Specify the competing hypotheses to determine whether men spend more money than women spend on St. Patrick's Day.

    b. Calculate the value of the test statistic.

    c. Calculate the p-value.

    d. At the 1% significance level, do men spend more money than women spend on St. Patrick's day? Explain.

50. A new study has found that, on average, 6- to 12-year-old children are spending less time on daily household chores today compared to 1981 levels (*The Wall Street Journal*, August 27,

2008). Suppose two samples representative of the study's results report the following summary statistics for the two periods:

1981 Levels	2008 Levels
$\bar{x}_1 = 30$ minutes	$\bar{x}_2 = 24$ minutes
$s_1 = 4.2$ minutes	$s_1 = 3.9$ minutes
$n_1 = 30$	$n_2 = 30$

    a. Specify the competing hypotheses to test the study's claim that children today spend less time on household chores as compared to children in 1981.

    b. Calculate the value of the test statistic assuming that the unknown population variances are equal.

    c. Approximate the p-value.

    d. At the 5% significance level, do the data support the study's claim? Explain.

    e. Repeat the hypothesis test using the critical value approach.

51. Paige Thomsen is about to graduate from college at a local university in San Francisco. Her options are to look for a job in San Francisco or go home to Denver and search for work there. Recent data suggest that average starting salaries for college graduates is $48,900 in San Francisco and $40,900 in Denver (*Forbes*, June 26, 2008). Suppose these data were based on 100 recent graduates in each city where the population standard deviation is $16,000 in San Francisco and $14,500 in Denver. Determine whether the average starting salary in San Francisco is greater than Denver's average starting salary at the 5% significance level.

52. **FILE** (Use Excel) It is well documented that cholesterol over 200 is a risk factor in developing heart disease for both men and women (http://Livingstrong.com, January 11, 2011). Younger men are known to have higher cholesterol levels than younger women; however, beyond age 55, women are more likely to have higher cholesterol levels. A recent college graduate working at a local blood lab has access to the cholesterol data of 50 men and 50 women in the 20–40 age group. The accompanying table shows a portion of the cholesterol data; the complete data set, labeled **Cholesterol_ Levels**, can be found on the text website.

Men	Women
181	178
199	193
⋮	⋮
190	182

Use the critical value approach, at the 1% significance level, to determine if there are any differences in the mean cholesterol levels for men and women in the age group. It is fair to assume that the population variances for men and women are equal. Describe your steps clearly.

53. **FILE** (Use Excel) It is important for women to gain the right amount of weight during pregnancy by eating a healthy, balanced diet (http://webmd.com). It is recommended that a woman of average weight before pregnancy should gain 25 to 35 pounds during pregnancy. The accompanying table shows a portion of the weight data for 40 women before and after pregnancy; the complete data set, labeled **Pregnancy_ Weight**, can be found on the text website.

Weight after Pregnancy	Weight before Pregnancy
168	114
161	107
⋮	⋮
157	136

a. At the 5% level of significance, determine if the mean weight gain of women due to pregnancy is more than 30 pounds.

b. At the 5% level of significance, determine if the mean weight gain of women due to pregnancy is more than 35 pounds.

54. A farmer is concerned that a change in fertilizer to an organic variant might change his crop yield. He subdivides 6 lots and uses the old fertilizer on one-half of each lot and the new fertilizer on the other half. The following table shows the results.

Lot	Crop Yield Using Old Fertilizer	Crop Yield Using New Fertilizer
1	10	12
2	11	10
3	10	13
4	9	9
5	12	11
6	11	12

a. Specify the competing hypotheses that determine whether there is any difference between the average crop yields from the use of the different fertilizers.

b. Assuming that crop yields are normally distributed, calculate the value of the test statistic.

c. At the 5% significance level, find the critical value(s).

d. Is there sufficient evident to conclude that the crop yields are different? Should the farmer be concerned?

55. **FILE** (Use Excel) The accompanying table shows annual return data from 2001–2009 for Vanguard's Balanced Index and European Stock Index mutual funds. The data set, labeled **Balanced_European**, can also be found on the text website. Assume that returns are normally distributed.

Year	Balanced Index	European Index
2001	−3.02%	−20.30%
2002	−9.52	−17.95
2003	19.87	38.70
2004	9.33	20.86
2005	4.65	9.26
2006	11.02	33.42
2007	6.16	13.82
2008	−22.21	−44.73
2009	20.05	31.91

Source: http://www.finance.yahoo.com

a. Set up the hypotheses to test whether the mean returns of the two funds differ.

b. What are the value of the test statistic and its associated *p*-value given unequal population standard deviations?

c. At the 5% significance level, what is the conclusion?

56. **FILE** (Use Excel) The SAT is required of most students applying for college admission in the United States. This standardized test has gone through many revisions over the years. In 2005, a new writing section was introduced that includes a direct writing measure in the form of an essay. People argue that female students generally do worse on math tests but better on writing tests. Therefore, the new section may help reduce the usual male lead on the overall average SAT score (*Washington Post*, August 30, 2006). Consider the following scores on the writing component of the test of 8 male and 8 female students. The data set, labeled **SAT_Writing**, can also be found on the text website. Assume that scores are normally distributed.

Males	620	570	540	580	590	580	480	620
Females	660	590	540	560	610	590	610	650

a. Construct the null and the alternative hypotheses to test if females outscore males on the writing component of the test.

b. Compute the value of the test statistic. Do not assume that the population variances are equal.

c. Implement the test at $\alpha = 0.01$ and interpret your results.

57. FILE (Use Excel) An engineer wants to determine the effectiveness of a safety program. He collects annual loss of hours due to accidents in 12 plants "before and after" the program was put into operation. The data set, labeled **Safety_Program**, can also be found on the text website.

Plant	Before	After	Plant	Before	After
1	100	98	7	88	90
2	90	88	8	75	70
3	94	90	9	65	62
4	85	86	10	58	60
5	70	67	11	67	60
6	83	80	12	104	98

a. Specify the competing hypotheses that determine whether the safety program was effective.

b. Assuming that the hours differences are normally distributed, calculate the value of the test statistic.

c. At the 5% significance level, calculate the critical value(s).

d. Is there sufficient evident to conclude that the safety program was effective? Explain.

58. A government agency wants to determine whether the average salaries of four various kinds of transportation operators differ. A random sample of five employees in each of the four categories yields the salary data given in the table below:

Average Salaries of Transportation Operators ($1,000s)			
Locomotive Engineer	Truck Driver	Bus Driver	Taxi and Limousine Driver
54.7	40.5	32.4	26.8
53.2	42.7	31.2	27.1
55.1	41.6	30.9	28.3
54.3	40.9	31.8	27.9
51.5	39.2	29.8	29.9
$\bar{x}_1 = 53.76$	$\bar{x}_2 = 40.98$	$\bar{x}_3 = 31.22$	$\bar{x}_4 = 28.00$
$s_1^2 = 2.10$	$s_2^2 = 1.69$	$s_3^2 = 0.96$	$s_4^2 = 1.49$
Grand mean: $\bar{\bar{x}} = 38.49$			

a. Construct an ANOVA table and estimate the p-value.

b. Specify the competing hypotheses in order to determine whether the average salaries of the transportation operators differ.

c. At the 5% significance level, can we conclude that the average salaries of the four transportation operators differ?

59. An economist wants to determine whether average Price/Earnings (P/E) ratios differ for firms in three industries. Independent samples of five firms in each industry show the following results:

Industry A	12.19	12.44	7.28	9.96	10.51	$\bar{x}_A = 10.48$, $s_A^2 = 4.32$
Industry B	14.34	17.80	9.32	14.90	9.41	$\bar{x}_B = 13.15$, $s_B^2 = 13.69$
Industry C	26.38	24.75	16.88	16.87	16.70	$\bar{x}_C = 20.32$, $s_C^2 = 23.30$
			Grand Mean: $\bar{\bar{x}} = 14.65$			

a. Construct an ANOVA table. Assume that P/E ratios are normally distributed.

b. At the 5% significance level, determine whether average P/E ratios differ in the three industries.

60. An employee of a small software company in Minneapolis bikes to work during the summer months. He can travel to work using one of three routes and wonders whether the average commute times (in minutes) differ between the three routes. He obtains the following data after traveling each route for one week.

Route 1	29	30	33	30	32
Route 2	27	32	28	30	29
Route 3	25	27	24	29	26

The following one-way ANOVA results were obtained for $\alpha = 0.01$:

ANOVA						
Source of Variation	SS	df	MS	F	p-value	F crit
Between Groups	54.53	2	27.27	8.099	0.0059	6.93
Within Groups	40.40	12	3.37			
Total	94.93	14				

Assuming that commute times are normally distributed, determine at the 1% significance level whether average commute times differ between the three routes.

61. Before the recession, job-creating cities in the Sunbelt, like Las Vegas, Phoenix, and Orlando, saw their populations, income levels, and housing prices surge. Las Vegas, however, offered something that often eluded these other cities: upward mobility for the working class. For example, hard-working hotel maids were able to prosper during the boom times. According to the Bureau of Labor Statistics (BLS), the average hourly rate for hotel maids was $14.25 in Las Vegas, versus $9.25 in Phoenix and $8.84 in Orlando (*The Wall Street Journal*, July 20, 2009). Suppose the following summary statistics and ANOVA table were produced for $\alpha = 0.05$ from a sample of hourly wages of 25 hotel maids in each city.

SUMMARY		
Groups	Count	Average
Las Vegas	25	13.91
Phoenix	25	8.82
Orlando	25	8.83

ANOVA						
Source of Variation	SS	df	MS	F	p-value	F crit
Between Groups	430.87	2	215.44	202.90	2.58E-30	3.124
Within Groups	76.44	72	1.06			
Total	507.31	74				

At the 5% significance level, do mean hourly rates for hotel maids differ between the three cities? Assume that hourly wages are normally distributed.

62. An accounting professor wants to know if students perform the same on the departmental final exam irrespective of the accounting section they attend. For three sections, he obtains the final exam grades for 20 students. The following Excel output for $\alpha = 0.05$ summarizes a portion of the results.

ANOVA						
Source of Variation	SS	df	MS	F	p-value	F crit
Between Groups	57.39	2	MSTR = ?	$F_{2,57}$ = ?	0.3461	3.159
Within Groups	SSE = ?	57	MSE = ?			
Total	1570.19	59				

a. Find the missing values in the ANOVA table.
b. At the 5% significance level, can you conclude that average grades differ in the accounting sections?

63. FILE (Use Excel) The manager of an SAT review program wonders whether average SAT scores differ depending on the ethnicity of the test taker. Thirty test scores for four ethnicities are collected. A portion of the data is shown in the accompanying table; the entire data set, labeled **SAT_Ethnicity**, can be found on the text website.

White	Black	Asian-American	Mexican-American
1587	1300	1660	1366
1562	1255	1576	1531
⋮	⋮	⋮	⋮
1500	1284	1584	1358

At the 5% significance level, can we conclude that the average SAT scores differ by ethnicity?

64. FILE (Use Excel) An engineer wants to determine whether the average strength of plywood boards (in pounds per square inch) differs depending on the type of glue used. For three types of glue, she measures the strength of 20 plywood boards. A portion of the data is shown in the accompanying table. The entire data set, labeled **Plywood**, can be found on the text website.

Glue 1	Glue 2	Glue 3
38	41	42
34	38	38
⋮	⋮	⋮
38	49	50

At the 5% significance level, can she conclude that the average strength of the plywood boards differs by the type of glue used? Assume that the strength of plywood boards is normally distributed.

CASE STUDIES

Case Study 10.1

Chad Perrone is a financial analyst in Boston studying the annual return data for the health and information technology industries. He randomly samples 20 firms in each industry and notes each firm's annual return. A portion of the data is shown in the accompanying table; the entire data set, labeled **Health_Info**, can be found on the text website.

Data for Case Study 10.1 Annual Returns for Firms in Health and Information Technology Industries

	Health	Information Technology
FILE	10.29%	4.77%
	32.17	1.14
	⋮	⋮
	13.21	22.61

In a report, use the sample information to:

1. Provide descriptive statistics and comment on the reward and risk in each industry.
2. Determine whether the average returns in each industry differ at the 5% significance level. Assume that returns are normally distributed and that the population variances are unequal.

Case Study 10.2

The Speedo LZR Racer Suit is a high-end, body-length swimsuit that was launched on February 13, 2008. When 17 world records fell at the December 2008 European Short Course Championships in Croatia, many believed a modification in the rules surrounding swim-suits was necessary. The FINA Congress, the international governing board for swimming, banned the LZR Racer and all other body-length swimsuits from competition effective January 2010. In a statement to the public, FINA defended its position with the following statement: "FINA wishes to recall the main and core principle that swimming is a sport essentially based on the physical performance of the athlete" (*BBC Sport*, March 14, 2009).

Luke Johnson, a freelance journalist, wonders if the decision made by FINA has statistical backing. He conducts an experiment with the local university's Division I swim team. He times 10 of the swimmers swimming the 50-meter breaststroke in his/her bathing suit and then retests them while wearing the LZR Racer. A portion of the data is shown in the accompanying table. The entire data set, labeled ***LZR_Racer***, can be found on the text website.

FILE Data for Case Study 10.2 50-Meter Breaststroke Times (in seconds)

Swimmer	Time in Bathing Suit	Time in LZR Racer
1	27.64	27.45
2	27.97	28.06
⋮	⋮	⋮
10	38.08	37.93

In a report, use the sample information to:

1. Determine whether the LZR Racer significantly improves swimmers' times at the 5% significance level. Assume that swim time differences are normally distributed.
2. Comment on whether the data appear to support FINA's decision.

Case Study 10.3

Lisa Grattan, a financial analyst for a small investment firm, collects annual stock return data for 10 firms in the energy industry, 13 firms in the retail industry, and 16 firms in the utilities industry. A portion of the data is shown in the accompanying table; the entire data set, labeled ***Industry_Returns***, can be found on the text website.

FILE Data for Case Study 10.3 Annual Stock Returns (in %)

Energy	Retail	Utilities
12.5	6.6	3.5
8.2	7.4	6.4
⋮	⋮	⋮
6.9	7.9	4.3

In a report, use the sample information to:

1. Determine whether significant differences exist in the annual returns for the three industries at the 5% significance level. Assume that returns are normally distributed.
2. Interpret your results.

Appendix 10.1 Guidelines for Other Software Packages

The following section provides brief commands for specific software packages: Minitab, SPSS, and JMP. More detailed instructions can be found on the text website. All three packages have an option to perform a paired-comparisons test. However, it is also possible to conduct this test by finding the differences between the paired items, and then using the one-sample methods of Chapter 9 on the sample differences.

MINITAB

Testing $\mu_1 - \mu_2$

A. (Replicating Example 10.4) From the menu choose **Stat** > **Basic Statistics** > **2-Sample t**. Choose **Samples in different columns** and select Gold for **First** and Oil for **Second**.

B. Choose **Options**. Select '**not equal**' for **Alternative**.

Testing μ_D

A. (Replicating Example 10.8) From the menu choose **Stat** > **Basic Statistics** > **Paired t**. Choose **Samples in columns** and select Before for **First sample** and After for **Second sample**.

B. Choose **Options**. Select '**greater than**' for **Alternative**.

One-Way ANOVA

(Replicating Example 10.9) From the menu choose **Stat** > **ANOVA** > **One-Way (Unstacked)**. Select Boston, NY, SF, and Chicago as **Responses (in separate columns)**.

SPSS

Testing $\mu_1 - \mu_2$

A. (Replicating Example 10.4) Pool all *Gold_Oil* data in one column and label 'Pooled.' In adjacent column (label as 'Group'), denote all Gold values with 0 and all Oil values with 1.

B. From the menu choose **Analyze** > **Compare Means** > **Independent-Samples T Test**.

C. Select **Pooled** as **Test Variable(s)** and **Group** as **Grouping Variable**. Select **Define Groups** and enter 0 for **Group 1** and 1 for **Group 2**.

Testing μ_D

A. (Replicating Example 10.8) From the menu choose **Analyze** > **Compare Means** > **Independent-Samples T Test**.

B. Select Before as **Variable1** and After as **Variable2**.

One-Way ANOVA

A. (Replicating Example 10.9) Pool all *Public_Transportation* data in one column and label 'Pooled.' In adjacent column (label as 'Group'), denote all Boston values with 1, all New York values with 2, etc.

B. From the menu choose **Analyze** > **Compare Means** > **One-Way ANOVA**.

C. Select **Pooled** as **Dependent List** and **Group** as **Factor**.

JMP

Testing $\mu_1 - \mu_2$

A. (Replicating Example 10.4) Pool all *Gold_Oil* data in one column and label 'Pooled.' In adjacent column (label as 'Group' and read as nominal data), denote all Gold values with 0 and all Oil values with 1.

B. From the menu choose **Analyze** > **Fit Y by X**.

C. Select Column 1 (Pooled) as **Y, Response** and Column 2 (Group) as **X, Factor**.

D. Click on the red triangle next to the header that reads **Oneway Analysis of Column 1 by Column 2** and select **t test** (to use a pooled variance, select **Means/Anova/Pooled t**).

Testing μ_D

A. (Replicating Example 9.13) From the menu choose **Analyze** > **Matched Pairs**.

B. Choose Column 1 and Column 2 as **Y, Paired Response**.

One-Way ANOVA

A. (Replicating Example 10.9) Pool all *Public_Transportation* data in one column and label 'Pooled.' In adjacent column (label as 'Group' and read as nominal data), denote all Boston values with 1, all New York values with 2, etc.

B. From the menu choose **Analyze** > **Fit Y by X**.

C. Select Column 1 (Pooled) as **Y, Response** and Column 2 (Group) as **X, Factor**.

D. Click on the red triangle next to the header that reads **Oneway Analysis of Column 1 by Column 2** and select **Means/Anova**.

11

Comparisons Involving Proportions

CHAPTER

LEARNING OBJECTIVES

After reading this chapter you should be able to:

LO 11.1 Make inferences about the difference between two population proportions.

LO 11.2 Discuss features of the χ^2 distribution.

LO 11.3 Conduct a goodness-of-fit test for a multinomial experiment.

LO 11.4 Conduct a test of independence.

In Chapter 10, we used quantitative data to make inferences regarding the means of two or more populations. In this chapter we focus on qualitative data. We will first use the z-test to compare the difference between two population proportions. For instance, marketing executives and advertisers are often interested in the different preferences between males and females when determining where to target advertising dollars. We then introduce χ^2 (chi-square) tests to assess two types of comparison. First, a *goodness-of-fit test* is commonly used with frequency data representing the various outcomes of a qualitative variable. This test basically compares the proportions of three or more populations. For instance, we may want to substantiate a claim that market shares in the automotive industry have changed dramatically over the past 10 years. While we use a goodness-of-fit test to conduct statistical inference on a single qualitative variable, we employ a *test of independence* to compare two qualitative variables. For example, we may want to determine whether a person's gender influences his/her purchase of a product.

Sportswear Brands

In the introductory case to Chapter 4, Annabel Gonzalez, chief retail analyst at a marketing firm, studies the relationship between the brand name of compression garments in the sport-apparel industry and the age of the consumer. Specifically, she wants to know whether the age of the consumer influences the brand name purchased.

Her initial feeling is that the Under Armour brand attracts a younger customer, whereas the more established companies, Nike and Adidas, draw an older clientele. She believes this information is relevant to advertisers and retailers in the sporting-goods industry, as well as to some in the financial community. Suppose she collects data on 600 recent purchases in the compression-gear market. For ease of exposition, the contingency table (cross-classified by age and brand name) from Chapter 4 is reproduced here as Table 11.1.

TABLE 11.1 Purchases of Compression Garments Based on Age and Brand Name

Age Group	Brand Name		
	Under Armour	Nike	Adidas
Under 35 years	174	132	90
35 years or older	54	72	78

Annabel wants to use the above sample information to:

1. Determine whether the two variables (Age Group and Brand Name) are related at the 5% significance level.

2. Discuss how the findings from the test for independence can be used.

A synopsis of this case will be provided at the end of Section 11.3.

11.1 Inference Concerning the Difference between Two Proportions

In the previous chapter we focused on quantitative data, where we compared means of two populations. Now we turn our attention to qualitative data, where we provide statistical inference concerning the difference between two population proportions. This technique has many practical applications. For instance, an investor may want to determine whether the bankruptcy rate is the same for firms in the technology industry as compared to firms in the construction industry. The resulting analysis will help determine the relative risk of investing in these two industries. Or perhaps a marketing executive maintains that the proportion of women who buy a firm's product is significantly greater than the proportion of men who buy the product. If this claim is supported by the data, it provides information as to where the firm should advertise. In another case, a consumer advocacy group may state that the proportion of young adults (aged 18 to 35 years old) who carry health insurance is less than the proportion of older adults (aged 36 years or older). Health and government officials might be particularly interested in this type of information. All of these examples deal with comparing two population proportions. Our parameter of interest is $p_1 - p_2$, where p_1 and p_2 denote the proportions in the first and second populations, respectively. The estimator for the difference between two population proportions is $\overline{P}_1 - \overline{P}_2$.

Confidence Interval for $p_1 - p_2$

Since the population proportions p_1 and p_2 are unknown, we estimate them by $\overline{p}_1$ and $\overline{p}_2$, respectively. The first sample proportion is computed as $\overline{p}_1 = x_1/n_1$ where x_1 denotes the number of successes in n_1 observations drawn from population 1. Similarly, $\overline{p}_2 = x_2/n_2$ is the sample proportion derived from population 2 where x_2 is the number of successes in n_2. The difference $\overline{p}_1 - \overline{p}_2$ is a point estimate of $p_1 - p_2$. Recall from Chapter 7 that the standard errors for the estimators $\overline{P}_1$ and $\overline{P}_2$ are

$se(\overline{P}_1) = \sqrt{\frac{p_1(1-p_1)}{n_1}}$ and $se(\overline{P}_2) = \sqrt{\frac{p_2(1-p_2)}{n_2}}$, respectively. Therefore, for two independently

drawn samples, the standard error, $se(\overline{P}_1 - \overline{P}_2) = \sqrt{\frac{p_1(1-p_1)}{n_1} + \frac{p_2(1-p_2)}{n_2}}$. Since p_1 and p_2 are

unknown, we estimate the standard error by $\sqrt{\frac{\overline{p}_1(1-\overline{p}_1)}{n_1} + \frac{\overline{p}_2(1-\overline{p}_2)}{n_2}}$. Finally, when both

n_1 and n_2 are sufficiently large, the sampling distribution of $\overline{P}_1 - \overline{P}_2$ can be approximated by the normal distribution. We construct a confidence interval for the difference between two population proportions using the following formula.

CONFIDENCE INTERVAL FOR $p_1 - p_2$

A $100(1-\alpha)\%$ confidence interval for the difference between two population proportions $p_1 - p_2$ is given by:

$$(\overline{p}_1 - \overline{p}_2) \pm z_{\alpha/2}\sqrt{\frac{\overline{p}_1(1-\overline{p}_1)}{n_1} + \frac{\overline{p}_2(1-\overline{p}_2)}{n_2}}.$$

As noted, the above formula is valid only when the two samples are sufficiently large; the general guideline is that n_1p_1, $n_1(1-p_1)$, n_2p_2, and $n_2(1-p_2)$ must all be greater than or equal to 5, where p_1 and p_2 are evaluated at $\overline{p}_1$ and $\overline{p}_2$, respectively.

EXAMPLE 11.1

Despite his inexperience and some perception that he is a risky choice, candidate A appears to have gained support among the electorate. Three months ago, in a survey of 120 registered voters, 55 said that they would vote for Candidate A. Today, 41 registered voters in a sample of 80 said that they would vote for Candidate A. Construct a 95% confidence interval for the difference between the two population proportions.

SOLUTION: Let p_1 and p_2 represent the population proportion of the electorate who support the candidate today and three months ago, respectively. In order to calculate a 95% confidence interval for $p_1 - p_2$, we use the formula $(\bar{p}_1 - \bar{p}_2) \pm z_{\alpha/2}\sqrt{\frac{\bar{p}_1(1 - \bar{p}_1)}{n_1} + \frac{\bar{p}_2(1 - \bar{p}_2)}{n_2}}$. We compute the sample proportions as

$$\bar{p}_1 = x_1/n_1 = 41/80 = 0.5125 \quad \text{and} \quad \bar{p}_2 = x_2/n_2 = 55/120 = 0.4583.$$

Note that the normality condition is satisfied because $n_1\bar{p}_1$, $n_1(1 - \bar{p}_1)$, $n_2\bar{p}_2$, and $n_2(1 - \bar{p}_2)$ all exceed 5. For a 95% confidence interval we use the z table to find $z_{\alpha/2} = z_{0.05/2} = z_{0.025} = 1.96$. Substituting the values, we find

$$(0.5125 - 0.4583) \pm 1.96\sqrt{\frac{0.5125(1 - 0.5125)}{80} + \frac{0.4583(1 - 0.4583)}{120}}$$

$$= 0.0542 \pm 0.1412 \text{ or } [-0.0870, 0.1954].$$

With 95% confidence, we can report that the percentage change of support for the candidate is between -8.70% and 19.54%.

Hypothesis Test for $p_1 - p_2$

The null and alternative hypotheses for testing the difference between two population proportions under independent sampling will take one of the following forms:

Two-Tailed Test	Right-Tailed Test	Left-Tailed Test
$H_0: p_1 - p_2 = d_0$	$H_0: p_1 - p_2 \leq d_0$	$H_0: p_1 - p_2 \geq d_0$
$H_A: p_1 - p_2 \neq d_0$	$H_A: p_1 - p_2 > d_0$	$H_A: p_1 - p_2 < d_0$

We use the symbol d_0 to denote a given hypothesized difference between the unknown population proportions p_1 and p_2. In most cases, d_0 is set to zero. For example, when testing if the population proportions differ—that is, if $p_1 \neq p_2$—we use a two-tailed test with the null hypothesis defined as $H_0: p_1 - p_2 = 0$. If, on the other hand, we wish to determine whether or not the proportions differ by some amount, say 20%, we set $d_0 = 0.20$ and define the null hypothesis as $H_0: p_1 - p_2 = 0.20$. One-tailed tests are defined similarly.

EXAMPLE 11.2

Let's revisit Example 11.1. Specify the competing hypotheses in order to determine whether the proportion of those who favor Candidate A has changed over the three-month period. Using the 95% confidence interval, what is the conclusion to the test? Explain.

SOLUTION: In essence, we would like to determine whether $p_1 \neq p_2$, where p_1 and p_2 represent the population proportion of the electorate who support the candidate today and three months ago, respectively. We formulate the competing hypotheses as:

$$H_0: p_1 - p_2 = 0$$
$$H_A: p_1 - p_2 \neq 0$$

In the previous example, we constructed a 95% confidence interval for the difference between the population proportions as $[-0.0870, 0.1954]$. We note that the interval contains zero, the value hypothesized under the null hypothesis. Therefore, we are unable to reject the null hypothesis. In other words, from the given sample data, we cannot conclude at the 5% significance level that the support for candidate A has changed.

We now introduce the standard four-step procedure for conducting one- or two-tailed hypothesis tests concerning the difference between two proportions $p_1 - p_2$. We transform its estimator $\bar{P}_1 - \bar{P}_2$ into a corresponding z statistic by subtracting the hypothesized difference d_0 from this estimator and dividing by the standard error of the estimator $se(\bar{P}_1 - \bar{P}_2)$. When we developed the confidence interval for $p_1 - p_2$ we assumed $se(\bar{P}_1 - \bar{P}_2) = \sqrt{\frac{\bar{p}_1(1 - \bar{p}_1)}{n_1} + \frac{\bar{p}_2(1 - \bar{p}_2)}{n_2}}$. However, if d_0 is zero, that is, $H_0: p_1 = p_2$, both $\bar{p}_1$ and $\bar{p}_2$ are essentially the estimates of the same unknown population proportion. For this reason, the standard error can be improved by computing the pooled estimate $\bar{p} = (x_1 + x_2)/(n_1 + n_2)$ of this proportion, based on a larger sample.

TEST STATISTIC FOR TESTING $p_1 - p_2$

The test statistic is assumed to follow the z distribution.

1. If the hypothesized difference d_0 is zero, then the value of the test statistic is

$$z = \frac{\bar{p}_1 - \bar{p}_2}{\sqrt{\bar{p}(1 - \bar{p})\left(\frac{1}{n_1} + \frac{1}{n_2}\right)}},$$

where $\bar{p}_1 = \frac{x_1}{n_1}, \bar{p}_2 = \frac{x_2}{n_2}$, and $\bar{p} = \frac{x_1 + x_2}{n_1 + n_2} = \frac{n_1\bar{p}_1 + n_2\bar{p}_2}{n_1 + n_2}$.

2. If the hypothesized difference d_0 is not zero, then the value of the test statistic is

$$z = \frac{(\bar{p}_1 - \bar{p}_2) - d_0}{\sqrt{\frac{\bar{p}_1(1 - \bar{p}_1)}{n_1} + \frac{\bar{p}_2(1 - \bar{p}_2)}{n_2}}}.$$

As in the case of the confidence interval, the above formula is valid only when the two samples are sufficiently large.

EXAMPLE 11.3

Recent research by analysts and retailers claims significant gender differences when it comes to online shopping (*The Wall Street Journal*, March 13, 2008). A survey revealed that 5,400 of 6,000 men said they "regularly" or "occasionally" make purchases online, compared with 8,600 of 10,000 women surveyed. At the 5% significance level, test whether the proportion of all men who regularly or occasionally make purchases online is greater than the proportion of all women.

SOLUTION: We use the critical value approach to conduct this test. Let p_1 and p_2 denote the population proportions of men and of women who make online purchases, respectively. We wish to test whether the proportion of men who make purchases online is greater than the proportion of women, that is, $p_1 - p_2 > 0$. Therefore, we construct the competing hypotheses as

$$H_0: p_1 - p_2 \leq 0$$
$$H_A: p_1 - p_2 > 0$$

For a right-tailed test with $\alpha = 0.05$, the appropriate critical value is $z_\alpha = z_{0.05} = 1.645$. Since the hypothesized difference is zero, or $d_0 = 0$, we compute the value of the test statistic as $z = \dfrac{\bar{p}_1 - \bar{p}_2}{\sqrt{\bar{p}(1-\bar{p})\left(\frac{1}{n_1} + \frac{1}{n_2}\right)}}$. We first compute the sample proportions $\bar{p}_1 = x_1/n_1 = 5{,}400/6{,}000 = 0.90$ and $\bar{p}_2 = x_2/n_2 = 8{,}600/10{,}000 = 0.86$. The normality condition is satisfied since $n_1\bar{p}_1$, $n_1(1 - \bar{p}_1)$, $n_2\bar{p}_2$, and $n_2(1 - \bar{p}_2)$ all exceed 5.

Next we calculate $\bar{p} = \dfrac{x_1 + x_2}{n_1 + n_2} = \dfrac{5{,}400 + 8{,}600}{6{,}000 + 10{,}000} = 0.875$. Thus,

$$z = \frac{(0.90 - 0.86)}{\sqrt{0.875(1 - 0.875)\left(\dfrac{1}{6{,}000} + \dfrac{1}{10{,}000}\right)}} = \frac{0.04}{0.0054} = 7.41.$$

The decision rule is to reject H_0 if $z > 1.645$. Since $7.41 > 1.645$, we reject H_0. The proportion of men who shop online either regularly or occasionally is greater than the proportion of women at the 5% significance level. Our results are consistent with the recent decision by so many retailers to redesign their websites to attract and keep male customers.

EXAMPLE 11.4

While we expect relatively expensive wines to have more desirable characteristics than relatively inexpensive wines, people are often confused in their assessment of the quality of wine in a blind test (*New York Times*, December 16, 2010). In a recent experiment at a local winery, the same wine is served to two groups of people but with different price information. In the first group, 60 people are told that they are tasting a $25 wine, of which 48 like the wine. In the second group, only 20 of 50 people like the wine when they are told that it is a $10 wine. The experiment is conducted to determine if the proportion of people who like the wine in the first group is more than 20 percentage points higher than those in the second group. Conduct this test at the 5% significance level using the *p*-value approach.

SOLUTION: Let p_1 and p_2 denote the proportions of people who like the wine in groups 1 and 2, respectively. We want to test if the proportion of people who like the wine in the first group is more than 20 percentage points higher than in the second group. Thus, we construct the competing hypotheses as

$$H_0: p_1 - p_2 \leq 0.20$$
$$H_A: p_1 - p_2 > 0.20$$

We first compute the sample proportions as $\bar{p}_1 = x_1/n_1 = 48/60 = 0.80$ and $\bar{p}_2 = x_2/n_2 = 20/50 = 0.40$ and note that the normality condition is satisfied since $n_1\bar{p}_1$, $n_1(1 - \bar{p}_1)$, $n_2\bar{p}_2$, and $n_2(1 - \bar{p}_2)$ all exceed 5.

Since $d_0 = 0.20$, the value of the test statistic is computed as

$$z = \frac{(\bar{p}_1 - \bar{p}_2) - d_0}{\sqrt{\dfrac{\bar{p}_1(1 - \bar{p}_1)}{n_1} + \dfrac{\bar{p}_2(1 - \bar{p}_2)}{n_2}}} = \frac{(0.80 - 0.40) - 0.20}{\sqrt{\dfrac{0.80(1 - 0.80)}{60} + \dfrac{0.40(1 - 0.40)}{50}}} = 2.31.$$

For this right-tailed test, we compute the *p*-value as $P(Z \geq 2.31) = 1 - 0.9896 = 0.0104$. Since the *p*-value $< \alpha$ ($0.0104 < 0.05$), we reject the null hypothesis. At the 5% significance level, we conclude that the proportion of people who like the wine in the first group is more than 20 percentage points higher than in the second group. Overall, this result is consistent with scientific research, which has demonstrated the power of suggestion and expectations in wine tasting.

EXERCISES 11.1

Mechanics

1. Given $x_1 = 50$, $n_1 = 200$, $x_2 = 70$, $n_2 = 250$, construct a 95% confidence interval for the difference between the population proportions. Is there a difference between the population proportions at the 5% significance level? Explain.

2. Given $\bar{p}_1 = 0.85$, $n_1 = 400$, $\bar{p}_2 = 0.90$, $n_2 = 350$, construct a 90% confidence interval for the difference between the population proportions. Is there a difference between the population proportions at the 10% significance level? Explain.

3. Consider the following competing hypotheses and accompanying sample data.

$$H_0: p_1 - p_2 = 0$$
$$H_A: p_1 - p_2 \neq 0$$

$x_1 = 100$	$x_2 = 172$
$n_1 = 250$	$n_2 = 400$

   a. Calculate the value of the test statistic.
   b. Calculate the p-value.
   c. At the 5% significance level, what is the conclusion to the test? Do the population proportions differ?
   d. Repeat the analysis with the critical value approach.

4. Consider the following competing hypotheses and accompanying sample data.

$$H_0: p_1 - p_2 \geq 0$$
$$H_A: p_1 - p_2 < 0$$

$x_1 = 250$	$x_2 = 275$
$n_1 = 400$	$n_2 = 400$

   a. At the 5% significance level, find the critical value(s).
   b. Calculate the value of the test statistic.
   c. What is the conclusion to the test? Is p_1 significantly less than p_2?

5. Consider the following competing hypotheses and accompanying sample data.

$$H_0: p_1 - p_2 = 0$$
$$H_A: p_1 - p_2 \neq 0$$

$x_1 = 300$	$x_2 = 325$
$n_1 = 600$	$n_2 = 500$

   a. Calculate the value of the test statistic.
   b. Calculate the p-value.
   c. At the 5% significance level, what is the conclusion to the test? Do the population proportions differ?

6. Consider the following competing hypotheses and accompanying sample data.

$$H_0: p_1 - p_2 = 0.20$$
$$H_A: p_1 - p_2 \neq 0.20$$

$x_1 = 150$	$x_2 = 130$
$n_1 = 250$	$n_2 = 400$

   a. Calculate the value of the test statistic.
   b. Calculate the p-value.
   c. At the 5% significance level, what it the conclusion to the test? Can you conclude that the difference between the population proportions differs from 0.20?
   d. Repeat the analysis with the critical value approach.

Applications

7. A recent study claims that girls and boys do not do equally well on math tests taken from the 2nd to 11th grades (*Chicago Tribune*, July 25, 2008). Suppose in a representative sample, 344 of 430 girls and 369 of 450 boys score at proficient or advanced levels on a standardized math test.

   a. Construct a 95% confidence interval for the difference between the population proportions of girls and boys who score at proficient or advanced levels.
   b. Develop the appropriate null and alternative hypotheses to test whether the proportion of girls who score at proficient or advanced levels differs from the proportion of boys.
   c. At the 5% significance level, what is the conclusion to the test? Do the results support the study's claim?

8. According to the Pew report, 14.6% of newly married couples in 2008 reported that their spouse was of another race or ethnicity (*CNNLiving*, June 7, 2010). In a similar survey in 1980, only 6.8% of newlywed couples reported marrying outside their race or ethnicity. Suppose both of these surveys were conducted on 120 newly married couples.

   a. Specify the competing hypotheses to test the claim that there is an increase in the proportion of people who marry outside their race or ethnicity.
   b. Calculate the value of the test statistic and the p-value.
   c. At the 5% level of significance, what is the conclusion to the test?

9. Research by Harvard Medical School experts suggests that boys are more likely than girls to grow out of childhood asthma when they hit their teenage years (*BBC News*, August 15, 2008). Scientists followed over 1,000 children between the ages of 5 and 12, all of whom had mild to moderate asthma. By the age of 18, 14% of the girls and 27% of the boys seemed to have grown out of asthma. Suppose their analysis was based on 500 girls and 500 boys.

   a. Develop the hypotheses to test whether the proportion of boys who grow out of asthma in their teenage years is more than that of girls.
   b. Use the p-value approach to test the assertion in (a) at the 5% significance level.
   c. Does the above experiment suggest that the proportion of boys who grow out of asthma in their teenage years is 0.10 or more than that of girls? Use the critical value approach to test this assertion at the 5% significance level.

10. More people are using social media to network, rather than phone calls or e-mails *(US News & World Report,* October 20, 2010). From an employment perspective, jobseekers are no longer calling up friends for help with job placement, as they can now get help online. In a recent survey of 150 jobseekers, 67 said they used LinkedIn to search for jobs. A similar survey of 140 jobseekers, conducted three years ago, had found that 58 jobseekers had used LinkedIn for their job search. Is there sufficient evidence to suggest that more people are now using LinkedIn to search for jobs as compared to three years ago? Use a 5% level of significance for the analysis.

11. According to a recent report, 32.2% of American adults (aged 20 and older) are obese *(New York Times,* August 15, 2008). Among ethnic groups in general, African-American women are more overweight than Caucasian women, but African-American men are less obese than Caucasian men. Sarah Weber, a recent college graduate, is curious to determine if the same pattern also exists in her hometown on the West Coast. She randomly selects 220 African Americans and 300 Caucasian adults for the analysis. The following table contains the sample information.

Race	Gender	Obese	Not Obese
African Americans	Males	36	94
	Females	35	55
Caucasians	Males	62	118
	Females	31	89

a. Use the *p*-value approach to test if the proportion of obese African-American men is less than the proportion of obese Caucasian men at $\alpha = 0.05$.

b. Use the critical value approach to test if the proportion of obese African-American women is more than the proportion of obese Caucasian women at $\alpha = 0.05$.

c. Use the critical value approach to test if the proportion of obese African Americans differs from the proportion of obese Caucasian adults at the 5% significance level.

12. Only 26% of psychology majors are "satisfied" or "very satisfied" with their career paths as compared to 50% of accounting majors *(The Wall Street Journal,* October 11, 2010). Suppose these results were obtained from a survey of 300 psychology majors and 350 accounting majors.

a. Develop the appropriate null and alternative hypotheses to test whether the proportion of accounting majors satisfied with their career paths differs from psychology majors by more than 20%.

b. Calculate the value of the test statistic and the *p*-value.

c. At the 5% significance level, what is the conclusion?

13. A recent report suggests that business majors spend the least amount on course work than all other college students *(New York Times,* November 17, 2011). A provost of a university decides to conduct a survey where students are asked if they study hard, defined as spending at least 20 hours per week on course work. Of 120 business majors included in the survey, 20 said that they studied hard, as compared to 48 out of 150 nonbusiness majors who said that they studied hard. At the 5% significance level, can we conclude that the proportion of business majors who study hard is less than that of nonmajors? Provide the details.

14. It has generally been believed that it is not feasible for men and women to be just friends *(New York Times,* April 12, 2012). Others argue that this belief may not be true anymore since gone are the days when men worked and women stayed at home and the only way they could get together was for romance. In a recent survey, 186 heterosexual college students were asked if it was feasible for male and female students to be just friends. Thirty-two percent of females and 57% of males reported that it was not feasible for men and women to be just friends. Suppose the study consisted of 100 female and 86 male students. At the 5% significance level, can we conclude that there is a greater than 10 percentage point difference between the proportion of male and female students with this view? Provide the details.

11.2 Goodness-of-Fit Test for a Multinomial Experiment

LO **11.2**

Discuss features of the χ^2 distribution.

There are many instances where we may want to make inferences about the relative sizes of more than two population proportions. For instance, in a heavily concentrated industry consisting of four firms, we may want to determine whether each firm has an equal market share. Or, in a political contest, we may want to determine whether Candidates A, B, and C will receive 70%, 20%, and 10% of the vote, respectively. These tests are based on a new distribution called the χ^2 (**chi-square**) distribution. Like the *t* distribution, the χ^2 distribution is characterized by a family of distributions, where each distribution depends on its particular degrees of freedom *df*. It is common, therefore, to refer to it as the χ^2_{df} distribution.

From Figure 11.1, we note that the χ^2_{df} distributions are positively skewed, where the extent of skewness depends on the degrees of freedom. As the *df* grow larger, the χ^2_{df} distribution approaches the normal distribution. For instance, in Figure 11.1, the χ^2_{20} distribution resembles the shape of the normal distribution.

FIGURE 11.1 The χ^2_{df} distribution with various degrees of freedom

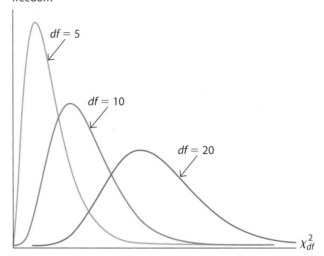

As in the case of the t_{df} distribution, for a χ^2_{df} distributed random variable, we use the notation $\chi^2_{\alpha,df}$ to represent a value such that the area in the right (upper) tail of the distribution is α. In other words, $P(\chi^2_{df} \geq \chi^2_{\alpha,df}) = \alpha$. Figure 11.2 illustrates the notation $\chi^2_{\alpha,df}$, which we use to locate χ^2_{df}-values and probabilities from the χ^2 table.

FIGURE 11.2 Graphical depiction of $P(\chi^2_{df} \geq \chi^2_{\alpha,df}) = \alpha$

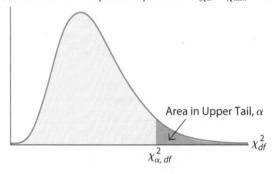

A portion of the right-tail probabilities and the corresponding values of χ^2_{df} distributions is given in Table 11.2. Table 3 of Appendix A provides a more complete χ^2 table.

Suppose we want to find the value $\chi^2_{\alpha,df}$ with $\alpha = 0.05$ and $df = 10$, that is, $\chi^2_{0.05,10}$. Using Table 11.2, we look at the first column labeled df and find the value 10. We then continue along this row until we reach the column $\alpha = 0.05$. Here we see the value $\chi^2_{0.05,10} = 18.307$ such that $P(\chi^2_{10} \geq 18.307) = 0.05$.

TABLE 11.2 Portion of the χ^2 table

	Area in Upper Tail, α									
df	0.995	0.990	0.975	0.950	0.900	0.100	0.050	0.025	0.010	0.005
1	0.000	0.000	0.001	0.004	0.016	2.706	3.841	5.024	6.635	7.879
⋮	⋮	⋮	⋮	⋮	⋮	⋮	⋮	⋮	⋮	⋮
10	2.156	2.558	3.247	3.940	4.865	15.987	**18.307**	20.483	23.209	25.188
⋮	⋮	⋮	⋮	⋮	⋮	⋮	⋮	⋮	⋮	⋮
100	67.328	70.065	74.222	77.929	82.358	118.342	124.342	129.561	135.807	140.170

We will now examine whether two or more population proportions equal each other or some predetermined (hypothesized) set of values. Before conducting this test, we must first ensure that the random experiment satisfies the conditions of a **multinomial experiment**, which is simply a generalization of the Bernoulli process first introduced in Chapter 5.

LO **11.3**

Conduct a goodness-of-fit test for a multinomial experiment.

Recall that a Bernoulli process, also referred to as a binomial experiment, is a series of n independent and identical trials of an experiment, where each trial has only two possible outcomes, conventionally labeled "success" and "failure." For the binomial experiment, we generally denote the probability of success as p and the probability of failure as $1 - p$. Alternatively, we could let p_1 and p_2 represent these probabilities, where $p_1 + p_2 = 1$. Now let us assume that the number of outcomes per trial is k where $k \geq 2$.

A MULTINOMIAL EXPERIMENT

A **multinomial experiment** consists of a series of n independent and identical trials, such that for each trial

- There are k possible outcomes called categories.
- The probability p_i associated with the ith category remains the same.
- The sum of the probabilities is one, that is, $p_1 + p_2 + \cdots + p_k = 1$.

Note that when $k = 2$, the multinomial experiment specializes to a binomial experiment.

Numerous experiments fit the conditions of a multinomial experiment. For instance,

- As compared from the previous day, a stockbroker records whether the price of a stock rises, falls, or stays the same. This example has three possible categories ($k = 3$).
- A consumer rates service at a restaurant as excellent, good, fair, or poor ($k = 4$).
- The admissions office records which of the six business concentrations a student picks ($k = 6$).

When setting up the competing hypotheses for a multinomial experiment, we have essentially two choices. We can set all population proportions equal to the same specific value or, equivalently, equal to one another. For instance, if we want to judge on the basis of sample data whether the proportion of voters who favor four different candidates is the same, the competing hypotheses would take the following form:

$$H_0: p_1 = p_2 = p_3 = p_4 = 0.25$$
$$H_A: \text{Not all population proportions are equal to 0.25.}$$

Note that the hypothesized value under the null hypothesis is 0.25 because the population proportions must sum to one. We can also set each population proportion equal to a different predetermined (hypothesized) value. Suppose we want to determine whether 40% of the voters favor Candidate 1, 30% favor Candidate 2, 20% favor Candidate 3, and 10% favor Candidate 4. The competing hypotheses are formulated as

$$H_0: p_1 = 0.40, p_2 = 0.30, p_3 = 0.20, \text{ and } p_4 = 0.10$$
$$H_A: \text{Not all population proportions equal their hypothesized values.}$$

When conducting a test, we take a random sample and determine whether the sample proportions are close enough to the hypothesized population proportions. For this reason, this type of test is called a **goodness-of-fit test**. Under the usual assumption that the null hypothesis is true, we derive the expected frequencies of the categories in a multinomial experiment and compare them with observed frequencies. The objective is to determine whether we can reject the null hypothesis in favor of the alternative hypothesis. To see how to conduct a goodness-of-fit test, consider the following example.

One year ago, the management at a restaurant chain surveyed its patrons to determine whether changes should be made to the menu. One question on the survey asked patrons to rate the quality of the restaurant's entrées. The percentages of the patrons responding Excellent, Good, Fair, or Poor are listed in the following table:

Excellent	Good	Fair	Poor
15%	30%	45%	10%

Based on responses to the overall survey, management decided to revamp the menu. Recently, the same question concerning the quality of entrées was asked of a random sample of 250 patrons. Their responses are shown below:

Excellent	Good	Fair	Poor
46	83	105	16

At the 5% significance level, we want to determine whether there has been any change in the population proportions calculated one year ago.

Since we want to determine whether the responses of the 250 patrons are consistent with the earlier proportions, we let the earlier population proportions denote the hypothesized proportions for the test. Thus, we use p_1, p_2, p_3, and p_4 to denote the population proportions of those that responded Excellent, Good, Fair, or Poor, respectively, and construct the following competing hypotheses.

H_0: $p_1 = 0.15$, $p_2 = 0.30$, $p_3 = 0.45$, and $p_4 = 0.10$

H_A: Not all population proportions equal their hypothesized values.

The first step in calculating the value of the test statistic is to calculate an expected frequency for each category. That is, we need to estimate the frequencies that we would expect to get if the null hypothesis is true. In general, in order to calculate the expected frequency e_i for category i, we multiply the sample size n by the respective hypothesized value of the population proportion p_i. For example, consider the category Excellent. If H_0 is true, then we expect that 15% ($p_1 = 0.15$) of 250 patrons will find the quality of entrées to be excellent. Therefore, the expected frequency of Excellent responses is 37.5 ($= 250 \times 0.15$), whereas the corresponding observed frequency is 46. Expected frequencies for other responses are found similarly. Ultimately, when computing the value of the test statistic, we compare these expected frequencies to the frequencies we actually observe.

GOODNESS-OF-FIT TEST STATISTIC

For a multinomial experiment with k categories, the value of the test statistic is calculated as

$$\chi^2_{df} = \Sigma \frac{(o_i - e_i)^2}{e_i},$$

where $df = k - 1$ and o_i and $e_i = np_i$ are the observed and expected frequency in the ith category, respectively.

Note: The test is valid so long as the expected frequencies for each category are five or more.

Table 11.3 shows the expected frequency e_i for each category. The condition that each expected frequency e_i must equal five or more is satisfied here. As we will see shortly, sometimes it is necessary to combine data from two or more categories to achieve this result.

TABLE 11.3 Calculation of Expected Frequency for Restaurant Example

	Hypothesized Proportion, p_i	Expected Frequency, $e_i = np_i$
Excellent	0.15	$250 \times 0.15 = 37.5$
Good	0.30	$250 \times 0.30 = 75.0$
Fair	0.45	$250 \times 0.45 = 112.5$
Poor	0.10	$250 \times 0.10 = 25.0$
		$\Sigma e_i = 250$

As a check on the calculations, the sum of the expected frequencies Σe_i must equal the sample size n, which in this example equals 250. Once the expected frequencies are estimated, we are ready to calculate the value of the test statistic.

The χ^2_{df} statistic measures how much the observed frequencies vary (or differ) from the expected frequencies. In particular, χ^2_{df} is computed as the sum of the standardized squared deviations. The smallest value that χ^2_{df} can assume is zero—this occurs when each observed frequency equals its expected frequency. Rejection of the null hypothesis occurs when χ^2_{df} is significantly greater than zero. As a result, these tests of hypotheses regarding multiple population proportions $(p_1, p_2, p_3, \ldots)$ are always implemented as right-tailed tests. However, since the alternative hypothesis states that not all population proportions equal their hypothesized values, rejection of the null hypothesis does not indicate which proportions differ from these values.

In this example, there are four categories ($k = 4$), so, $df = k - 1 = 3$. Since a goodness-of-fit test is a right-tailed test, the critical value with $\alpha = 0.05$ is found from the χ^2 table as $\chi^2_{\alpha,df} = \chi^2_{0.05,3} = 7.815$; we show a portion of the χ^2 table in Table 11.4. The value of the test statistic is calculated as

$$\chi^2_{df} = \chi^2_3 = \Sigma \frac{(o_i - e_i)^2}{e_i}$$

$$= \frac{(46 - 37.5)^2}{37.5} + \frac{(83 - 75)^2}{75} + \frac{(105 - 112.5)^2}{112.5} + \frac{(16 - 25)^2}{25}$$

$$= 1.93 + 0.85 + 0.50 + 3.24 = 6.52.$$

The decision rule is to reject H_0 if $\chi^2_3 > 7.815$. Since $\chi^2_3 = 6.52 < 7.815$, we do not reject H_0. We cannot conclude that the proportions differ from the ones from one year ago at the 5% significance level. Management may find this news disappointing in that the goal of the menu change was to improve customer satisfaction. Responses to other questions on the survey may shed more light on whether the goals of the menu change met or fell short of expectations.

TABLE 11.4 Portion of the χ^2 table

df	\multicolumn{10}{c}{Area in Upper Tail, α}
	0.995	0.990	0.975	0.950	0.900	0.100	0.050	0.025	0.010	0.005
1	0.000	0.000	0.001	0.004	0.016	2.706	3.841	5.024	6.635	7.879
2	0.010	0.020	0.051	0.103	0.211	4.605	5.991	7.378	9.210	10.597
3	0.072	0.115	0.216	0.352	0.584	6.251	**7.815**	9.348	11.345	12.838

Using Excel to Calculate p-Values

As usual, we can conduct the above hypothesis test by using the p-value approach to hypothesis testing rather than the critical value approach, where the p-value is derived as $P(\chi^2_3 \geq 6.52)$. If we refer to Table 11.4, we see that 6.52 falls between 6.251 and 7.815, which allows us to conclude that the p-value is somewhere between 0.05 and 0.10. We can use Excel's CHISQ.DIST.RT function to calculate the exact p-value. In general, to find the right-tailed area under the chi-square distribution, we find an empty cell and input '=CHISQ.DIST.RT (χ^2_{df}, df)', where χ^2_{df} is the value of the test statistic and df are the respective degrees of freedom. In the survey example, we input '=CHISQ.DIST.RT(6.52, 3)'.

Excel returns the probability of 0.0889, which is the p-value. Again, given a significance level of 5%, we are unable to reject the null hypothesis.

EXAMPLE 11.5

Table 11.5 lists the market share in 2010 of the five firms that manufacture a particular product. A marketing analyst wonders whether the market shares have changed since 2010. He surveys 200 customers. The last column of Table 11.5 shows the number of customers who recently purchased the product at each firm.

TABLE 11.5 Market Share of Five Firms

Firm	Market Share in 2010	Number of Recent Customers
1	0.40	70
2	0.32	60
3	0.24	54
4	0.02	10
5	0.02	6

a. Specify the competing hypotheses to test whether the market shares have changed since 2010.

b. Calculate the value of the test statistic.

c. Use $a = 0.05$ to determine if the market shares have changed since 2010.

SOLUTION:

a. Let p_i denote the market share for the ith firm. In order to test whether the market shares have changed since 2010, we *initially* set up the competing hypotheses as

H_0: $p_1 = 0.40$, $p_2 = 0.32$, $p_3 = 0.24$, $p_4 = 0.02$, and $p_5 = 0.02$

H_A: Not all market shares equal their hypothesized values.

b. The value of the test statistic is calculated as $\chi^2_{df} = \Sigma \frac{(o_i - e_i)^2}{e_i}$. The last column of Table 11.5 shows each firm's observed frequency o_i, so before applying the formula, we first calculate each firm's expected frequency e_i.

$$e_1 = 200 \times 0.40 = 80$$
$$e_2 = 200 \times 0.32 = 64$$
$$e_3 = 200 \times 0.24 = 48$$
$$\left.\begin{array}{l} e_4 = 200 \times 0.02 = 4 \\ e_5 = 200 \times 0.02 = 4 \end{array}\right\}8$$

We note that expected frequencies for firms 4 and 5 are less than five. The test is valid so long as the expected frequencies in each category are five or more. In order to achieve this result, we combine the expected frequencies for firms 4 and 5 to obtain a combined frequency of eight ($e_4 + e_5 = 8$). We could have made other combinations, say e_4 with e_1 and e_5 with e_2, but we preferred to maintain a category for the less dominant firms. After making this combination, we now re-specify the competing hypotheses as

H_0: $p_1 = 0.40$, $p_2 = 0.32$, $p_3 = 0.24$, and $p_4 = 0.04$

H_A: Not all market shares equal their hypothesized values.

With $df = k - 1 = 3$, we calculate the value of the test statistic as

$$\chi_3^2 = \Sigma \frac{(o_i - e_i)^2}{e_i} = \frac{(70 - 80)^2}{80} + \frac{(60 - 64)^2}{64} + \frac{(54 - 48)^2}{48} + \frac{(16 - 8)^2}{8}$$

$$= 1.25 + 0.25 + 0.75 + 8 = 10.25.$$

c. Given $\alpha = 0.05$, we find the critical value as $\chi_{0.05,3}^2 = 7.815$. The decision rule is to reject H_0 if $\chi_3^2 > 7.815$. Since 10.25 is greater than 7.815, we reject the null hypothesis and conclude that some market shares changed since 2010.

As mentioned earlier, one limitation of this type of chi-square test is that we cannot tell which proportions differ from their hypothesized values. However, given the divergence between the observed and expected frequencies for the less dominant firms, it appears that they may be making some headway in this industry. Further testing can be conducted to see if this is the case.

EXERCISES 11.2

Mechanics

15. Consider a multinomial experiment with $n = 250$ and $k = 4$. The null hypothesis to be tested is H_0: $p_1 = p_2 = p_3 = p_4 = 0.25$. The observed frequencies resulting from the experiment are

Category	1	2	3	4
Frequency	70	42	72	66

a. Specify the alternative hypothesis.
b. Find the critical value at the 5% significance level.
c. Calculate the value of the test statistic.
d. What is the conclusion to the hypothesis test?

16. Consider a multinomial experiment with $n = 400$ and $k = 3$. The null hypothesis is H_0: $p_1 = 0.60$, $p_2 = 0.25$, and $p_3 = 0.15$. The observed frequencies resulting from the experiment are

Category	1	2	3
Frequency	250	94	56

a. Define the alternative hypothesis.
b. Calculate the value of the test statistic and approximate the p-value for the test.
c. At the 5% significance level, what is the conclusion to the hypothesis test?

17. A multinomial experiment produced the following results:

Category	1	2	3	4	5
Frequency	57	63	70	55	55

Can we conclude at the 1% significance level that the population proportions are not equal?

18. A multinomial experiment produced the following results:

Category	1	2	3
Frequency	128	87	185

At the 1% significance level, can we reject H_0: $p_1 = 0.30$, $p_2 = 0.20$, and $p_3 = 0.50$?

Applications

19. You suspect that an unscrupulous employee at a casino has tampered with a die; that is, he is using a loaded die. In order to test this claim, you roll the die 200 times and obtain the following frequencies:

Category	1	2	3	4	5	6
Frequency	40	35	33	30	33	29

a. Specify the null and alternative hypotheses in order to test your claim.
b. Approximate the p-value.
c. At a 10% significance level, can you conclude that the die is loaded?

20. A study conducted in September and October of 2010 found that fewer than half of employers who hired new college graduates last academic year plan to definitely do so again (The Wall Street Journal, November 29, 2010). Suppose the hiring intentions of the respondents were as follows:

Definitely hire	Likely to hire	Hire uncertain	Will not hire
37%	17%	28%	18%

Six months later, a sample of 500 employers were asked their hiring intentions and gave the following responses:

Definitely hire	Likely to hire	Hire uncertain	Will not hire
170	100	120	110

a. Specify the competing hypotheses to test whether the proportions from the initial study have changed.
b. Find the critical value at the 5% significance level.
c. Calculate the value of the test statistic.
d. What is the conclusion to the hypothesis test? Interpret your results.

21. A rent-to-own (RTO) agreement appeals to low-income and financially distressed consumers. It allows immediate access to merchandise, and by making all payments, the consumer acquires the merchandise. At the same time, goods can be returned at any point without penalty. Suppose a recent study documents that 65% of RTO contracts are returned, 30% are purchased, and the remaining 5% default. In order to test the validity of this claim, an RTO researcher looks at the transaction data of 420 RTO contracts, of which 283 are returned, 109 are purchased, and the rest defaulted.

   a. Set up the competing hypothesis to test whether the return, purchase, and default probabilities of RTO contracts differ from 0.65, 0.30, and 0.05, respectively.

   b. Compute the value of the test statistic.

   c. Conduct the test at the 5% level of significance and interpret the test results.

22. Despite Zimbabwe's shattered economy, with endemic poverty and widespread political strife and repression, thousands of people from overseas still head there every year (*BBC News*, August 27, 2008). Main attractions include the magnificent Victoria Falls, the ruins of Great Zimbabwe, and herds of roaming wildlife. A tourism director claims that Zimbabwe visitors are equally represented by Europe, North America, and the rest of the world. Records show that of the 380 tourists who recently visited Zimbabwe, 135 were from Europe, 126 from North America, and 119 from the rest of the world.

   a. A recent visitor to Zimbabwe believes that the tourism director's claim is wrong. Set up the competing hypotheses such that rejection of the null hypothesis supports the visitor's belief.

   b. Use the critical value approach to conduct the test at a 5% level. Do the sample data support the visitor's belief?

   c. Repeat the analysis with the *p*-value approach.

23. In 2003 *The World Wealth Report* first started publishing market shares of global millionaires (*The Wall Street Journal*, June 25, 2008). At this time, the distribution of the world's people worth $1 million or more was

Region	Percentage of Millionaires
Europe	35.7%
North America	31.4%
Asia Pacific	22.9%
Latin America	4.3%
Middle East	4.3%
Africa	1.4%

Source: *The Wealth Report*, 2003.

A recent sample of 500 global millionaires produces the following results:

Region	Number of Millionaires
Europe	153
North America	163
Asia Pacific	139
Latin America	20
Middle East	20
Africa	5

   a. Test whether the distribution of millionaires today is different from the distribution in 2003 at $\alpha = 0.05$.

   b. Would the conclusion change if we tested it at $\alpha = 0.10$?

24. An Associated Press/GfK Poll shows that 38% of American drivers favor U.S. cars, while 33% prefer Asian brands, with the remaining 29% going for other foreign cars (http://www.msnbc.com, April 21, 2010). This highlights a significant improvement for U.S. automakers, especially when just a few years ago General Motors Co. and Chrysler LLC needed government help just to survive. Perhaps Americans are giving U.S. automakers a closer look due to their buffed-up offerings. A researcher believes that the "buy American" sentiment may also be the result of watching an iconic American industry beaten down amid the Great Recession. He wonders whether the preferences for cars have changed since the Associated Press/GfK Poll. He surveys 200 Americans and finds that the number of respondents in the survey who prefer American, Asian, and other foreign cars are 66, 70, and 64, respectively. At the 5% significance level, can the researcher conclude that preferences have changed since the Associated Press/GfK Poll?

11.3 Chi-Square Test for Independence

LO **11.4**

Conduct a test of independence.

Recall from Chapter 4 that a contingency table is a useful tool when we want to examine or compare two qualitative variables defined on the same population.

CONTINGENCY TABLE

A **contingency table** generally shows frequencies for two qualitative (categorical) variables, *x* and *y*, where each cell of the table represents a mutually exclusive combination of the pair of *x* and *y* values.

In this section, we use the data in a contingency table to conduct a hypothesis test that determines whether the two qualitative variables depend upon one another. Whereas a goodness-of-fit test examines a single qualitative variable, a **test of independence**—also called a **chi-square test of a contingency table**—assesses the relationship between two qualitative variables. Many examples of the use of this test arise, especially in marketing, biomedical research, and courts of law. For instance, a retailer may be trying to determine whether there is a relationship between the age of its clientele and where it chooses to advertise. Doctors might want to investigate whether or not losing weight through stomach surgery can extend the lives of severely obese patients. Or one party in a discrimination lawsuit may be trying to show that gender and promotion are not independent events. All of these examples lend themselves to applications of the hypothesis test discussed in this section.

In the introductory case study, we are presented with a contingency table cross-classified by the variables Age Group and Brand Name. Specifically, we want to determine whether or not the age of a consumer influences his/her decision to buy a garment from Under Armour, Nike, or Adidas. We will conduct this test at the 5% significance level.

In general, the competing hypotheses for a statistical test of independence are formulated such that rejecting the null hypothesis leads to the conclusion that the two qualitative variables are dependent. Formally,

H_0: The two qualitative variables are independent.

H_A: The two qualitative variables are dependent.

Since the criteria upon which we classify the data are Age Group and Brand Name, we write the competing hypotheses as

H_0: Age Group and Brand Name are independent.

H_A: Age Group and Brand Name are dependent.

Table 11.6 reproduces Table 11.1 of the introductory case. The variable Age Group has two possible categories: (1) under 35 years and (2) 35 years or older. The variable Brand Name has three possible categories: (1) Under Armour, (2) Nike, and (3) Adidas. Each cell in this table represents an observed frequency o_{ij} where the subscript ij refers to the ith row and the jth column. Thus, o_{13} refers to the cell in the first row and the third column. Here, $o_{13} = 90$, or, equivalently, 90 customers under 35 years of age purchased an Adidas product.

TABLE 11.6 Purchases of Compression Garments Based on Age and Brand Name

Age Group	Brand Name		
	Under Armour	Nike	Adidas
Under 35 years	174	132	90
35 years or older	54	72	78

We will use the independence assumption postulated under the null hypothesis to derive an expected frequency for each cell from the sample data. In other words, we first estimate values as if no relationship exists between the age of a consumer and the brand name of the clothing purchased. Then we will compare these expected frequencies with the observed values to compute the value of the test statistic.

Calculating Expected Frequencies

For ease of exposition, we first denote each event using algebraic notation. We let events A_1 and A_2 represent "under 35 years" and "35 years or older," respectively; events B_1, B_2, and B_3 stand for Under Armour, Nike, and Adidas, respectively. We then sum the frequencies for each column and row. For instance, the sum of the frequencies for Event A_1 is 396; this is obtained by summing the values in row A_1: 174, 132, and 90. Totals for the other rows and columns are shown in Table 11.7.

TABLE 11.7 Row and Column Totals

Age Group	Brand Name			Row Total
	B_1	B_2	B_3	
A_1	e_{11}	e_{12}	e_{13}	396
A_2	e_{21}	e_{22}	e_{23}	204
Column Total	228	204	168	600

Our goal is to calculate the expected frequency e_{ij} for each cell, where again the subscript ij refers to the ith row and the jth column. Thus, e_{13} refers to the cell in the first row and the third column, or the expected number of customers under 35 years of age who purchase an Adidas product.

Before we can arrive at the expected frequencies, we first calculate marginal row probabilities (the proportion of people under 35 years of age and those 35 years old or older) and marginal column probabilities (the proportion of people purchasing from each brand name). We calculate marginal row (column) probabilities by dividing the row (column) sum by the total sample size:

Marginal Row Probabilities:

$$P(A_1) = \frac{396}{600} \quad \text{and} \quad P(A_2) = \frac{204}{600}$$

Marginal Column Probabilities:

$$P(B_1) = \frac{228}{600}, P(B_2) = \frac{204}{600}, \text{ and } P(B_3) = \frac{168}{600}$$

We can now calculate each cell probability by recalling from Chapter 4 the multiplication rule for independent events. That is, if two events are independent, say events A_1 and B_1 (our assumption under the null hypothesis), then their joint probability is

$$P(A_1 \cap B_1) = P(A_1)P(B_1) = \left(\frac{396}{600}\right)\left(\frac{228}{600}\right) = 0.2508.$$

Multiplying this joint probability by the sample size yields the expected frequency:

$$e_{11} = 600(0.2508) = 150.48.$$

CALCULATING EXPECTED FREQUENCIES FOR A TEST OF INDEPENDENCE

We use the following general formula to calculate the expected frequencies for each cell in a contingency table:

$$e_{ij} = \frac{(\text{Row } i \text{ total})(\text{Column } j \text{ total})}{\text{Sample Size}}.$$

Applying the formula, we calculate all expected frequencies as

$$e_{11} = \frac{(396)(228)}{600} = 150.48 \quad e_{12} = \frac{(396)(204)}{600} = 134.64 \quad e_{13} = \frac{(396)(168)}{600} = 110.88$$

$$e_{21} = \frac{(204)(228)}{600} = 77.52 \quad e_{22} = \frac{(204)(204)}{600} = 69.36 \quad e_{23} = \frac{(204)(168)}{600} = 57.12$$

Table 11.8 shows the expected frequency e_{ij} of each cell. In order to satisfy subsequent assumptions, each expected frequency e_{ij} *must equal five or more*. This condition is satisfied here. As we saw in Example 11.5, it may be necessary to combine two or more rows or columns to achieve this result in other applications.

TABLE 11.8 Expected Frequencies for Contingency Table

Age Group	Brand Name			Row Total
	B_1	B_2	B_3	
A_1	150.48	134.64	110.88	396
A_2	77.52	69.36	57.12	204
Column Total	228	204	168	600

When conducting a test of independence, we calculate the value of the chi-square test statistic χ^2_{df}. Analogous to the discussion in Section 11.2, χ^2_{df} measures how much the observed frequencies vary (or differ) from the expected frequencies. The smallest value that χ^2_{df} can assume is zero—this occurs when each observed frequency equals its expected frequency. Thus, a test of independence is also implemented as a *right-tailed test*.

TEST STATISTIC FOR A TEST OF INDEPENDENCE

For a contingency table with r rows and c columns, the value of the test statistic is calculated as

$$\chi^2_{df} = \sum_i \sum_j \frac{(o_{ij} - e_{ij})^2}{e_{ij}},$$

where $df = (r - 1)(c - 1)$ and o_{ij} and e_{ij} are the observed and the expected frequencies corresponding to the ith row and the jth column, respectively.

Note: This test is valid only when the expected frequencies for each cell are five or more.

With two rows and three columns in the contingency table, degrees of freedom are calculated as $df = (r - 1)(c - 1) = (2 - 1)(3 - 1) = 2$. We apply the formula to compute the value of the test statistic as

$$\chi^2_2 = \frac{(174 - 150.48)^2}{150.48} + \frac{(132 - 134.64)^2}{134.64} + \frac{(90 - 110.88)^2}{110.88}$$
$$+ \frac{(54 - 77.52)^2}{77.52} + \frac{(72 - 69.36)^2}{69.36} + \frac{(78 - 57.12)^2}{57.12}$$
$$= 3.68 + 0.05 + 3.93 + 7.14 + 0.10 + 7.63 = 22.53.$$

Given a significance level of 5% and $df = 2$, we find the critical value as $\chi^2_{\alpha,df} = \chi^2_{0.05,2} = 5.991$. Hence, the decision rule is to reject H_0 if $\chi^2_2 > 5.991$. Since $\chi^2_2 = 22.53 > 5.991$, we reject H_0. At the 5% significance level, we conclude that the two qualitative variables are dependent; that is, there is a relationship between the age of a consumer and the brand name of the apparel purchased.

As usual, we can conduct the above hypothesis test by using the p-value approach to hypothesis testing rather than the critical value approach, where the p-value is derived as $P(\chi^2_2 \geq 22.53)$. As discussed earlier, we can calculate an exact p-value using Excel by invoking '=CHISQ.DIST.RT(22.53, 2)'. Excel returns an almost zero p-value of 1.28×10^{-5}. Again, given a significance level of 5%, we reject the null hypothesis and conclude that Age Group and Brand Name are not independent of one another.

EXAMPLE 11.6

A recent study of gender preferences among car shoppers found that men and women equally favor economy cars (http://www.cargurus.com, February 14, 2011). A marketing analyst doubts these results. He believes that a person's gender influences the decision to purchase an economy car. He collects data on 400 recent car purchases cross-classified by Gender and Car Type (economy car versus noneconomy car). The results are shown in Table 11.9. At the 10% significance level, determine whether the sample data support the marketing analyst's claim.

TABLE 11.9 Car Preferences by Gender

Gender	Car Type		Row Total
	Economy Car	Noneconomy Car	
Female	50	60	110
Male	120	170	290
Column Total	170	230	400

SOLUTION: In order to determine whether an economy car purchase depends on gender, we specify the competing hypotheses as

H_0: Gender and Car Type are independent.

H_A: Gender and Car Type are dependent.

With two rows ($r = 2$) and two columns ($c = 2$) in the contingency table, we compute degrees of freedom as $df = (r - 1)(c - 1) = 1$. Given $\alpha = 0.10$, we find the critical value as $\chi^2_{0.10,1} = 2.706$.

The value of the test statistic for testing independence is calculated as $\chi^2_{df} = \sum_i \sum_j \frac{(o_{ij} - e_{ij})^2}{e_{ij}}$. Table 11.9 provides each cell's observed frequency o_{ij}, so before applying the formula, we first calculate each cell's expected frequency e_{ij}:

$$e_{11} = \frac{(110)(170)}{400} = 46.75 \qquad e_{12} = \frac{(110)(230)}{400} = 63.25$$

$$e_{21} = \frac{(290)(170)}{400} = 123.25 \qquad e_{22} = \frac{(290)(230)}{400} = 166.75$$

We then calculate

$$\chi^2_1 = \frac{(50 - 46.75)^2}{46.75} + \frac{(60 - 63.25)^2}{63.25} + \frac{(120 - 123.25)^2}{123.25} + \frac{(170 - 166.75)^2}{166.75}$$

$$= 0.23 + 0.17 + 0.09 + 0.06 = 0.55.$$

Since $\chi^2_1 = 0.55 < 2.706$, we do not reject the null hypothesis. The sample data do not support the marketing analyst's claim that gender differences exist with respect to the purchase of an economy car.

SYNOPSIS OF INTRODUCTORY CASE

Under Armour pioneered clothing in the compression-gear market. Compression garments are meant to keep moisture away from a wearer's body during athletic activities in warm and cool weather. Under Armour has experienced exponential growth since the firm went public in November 2005 (*USA TODAY*, June 16, 2010); however, Nike and Adidas have aggressively entered the compression-gear market as well. An analysis is conducted to examine whether the age of the customer matters when making a purchase in the compression-gear market. This information is relevant not only for Under Armour and how the firm may focus its advertising efforts, but also to competitors and retailers in this market. Data were collected on 600 recent purchases in the compression-gear market; the data were then cross-classified by age group and brand name. A test of independence was conducted at the 5% significance level. The results suggest that a customer's age and the brand name purchased are related to one another. Given that age influences the brand name purchased, it is not surprising that Under Armour recently signed NFL quarterback Tom Brady (http://cnbc.com, October 6, 2010) to endorse its products, a move likely to attract a younger consumer. Brady had spent most of his career with Nike before breaking away to go with Under Armour.

EXERCISES 11.3

Mechanics

25. Suppose you are conducting a test of independence. Specify the critical value under the following scenarios:
    a. $r = 3, c = 3$, and $\alpha = 0.10$.
    b. $r = 4, c = 5$, and $\alpha = 0.05$.

26. Suppose you are conducting a test of independence. Specify the critical value under the following scenarios:
    a. $r = 5, c = 2$, and $\alpha = 0.025$.
    b. $r = 3, c = 5$, and $\alpha = 0.01$.

27. Given the following contingency table, conduct a test of independence at the 5% significance level using (a) the critical value approach and (b) the p-value approach.

Variable B	Variable A	
	1	2
1	23	47
2	32	53

28. Given the following contingency table, conduct a test of independence at the 1% significance level using (a) the p-value approach and (b) the critical value approach.

Variable B	Variable A			
	1	2	3	4
1	120	112	100	110
2	127	115	120	124
3	118	115	110	124

Applications

29. According to an online survey by Harris Interactive for job site CareerBuilder.com (InformationWeek.com, September 27, 2007), more than half of IT workers say they have fallen asleep at work. Sixty-four percent of government workers admitted to falling asleep on the job. Assume that the following contingency table is representative of the survey results.

Slept on the Job?	Job Category	
	IT Professional	Government Professional
Yes	155	256
No	145	144

a. Specify the competing hypotheses to determine whether sleeping on the job is associated with job category.
b. Compute the value of the test statistic.
c. Approximate the p-value.
d. At the 5% significance level, can you conclude that sleeping on the job depends on job category?

30. A market researcher for an automobile company suspects differences in preferred color between male and female buyers. Advertisements targeted to different groups should take such differences into account, if they exist. The researcher examines the most recent sales information of a particular car that comes in three colors.

Color	Gender of Automobile Buyer	
	Male	Female
Silver	470	280
Black	535	285
Red	495	350

a. Specify the competing hypotheses to determine whether color preference depends on gender.
b. Find the critical value at the 1% significance level.
c. Compute the value of the test statistic.
d. Does your conclusion suggest that the company should target advertisements differently for males versus females? Explain.

31. The following sample data reflect shipments received by a large firm from three different vendors.

Vendor	Defective	Acceptable
1	14	112
2	10	70
3	22	150

a. Specify the competing hypotheses to determine whether quality is associated with the source of the shipments.
b. Conduct the test at a 1% significance level using the critical value approach.
c. Should the firm be concerned about the source of the shipments? Explain.

32. According to a 2008 survey by the Pew Research Center, people in China are highly satisfied with their roaring economy and the direction of their nation (USA TODAY, July 22, 2008). Eighty-six percent of those who were surveyed expressed positive views of the way China is progressing and described the economic situation as good. A political analyst wants to know if this optimism among the Chinese depends on age. In an independent survey of 280 Chinese residents, the respondents are asked how happy they are with the direction that their country is taking. Their responses are tabulated below.

Age	Very Happy	Somewhat Happy	Not Happy
20 up to 40	23	50	18
40 up to 60	51	38	16
60 and above	19	45	20

a. Set up the appropriate hypotheses to test the claim that optimism regarding China's direction depends on the age of the respondent.
b. Use Excel to compute the p-value for the test.
c. At a 1% level of significance, can we infer that optimism among the Chinese is dependent on age?

33. A study by the Massachusetts Community & Banking Council found that blacks, and, to a lesser extent, Latinos, remain largely unable to borrow money at the same interest rate as whites (Boston Globe, February 28, 2008). The following contingency table shows representative data for the city

of Boston, cross-classified by race and type of interest rate received:

Race	Type of Interest Rate on Loan	
	High Interest Rate	Lower Interest Rate
Black	553	480
Latino	265	324
White	491	3701

At the 5% significance level, do the data indicate that the interest rate received on a loan is dependent on race? Provide the details.

34. Founded in February 2004, Facebook is a social utility that helps people communicate with their friends and family. In just six years, Facebook has acquired more than 500 million active users, of which 50% log on to Facebook in any given day. In a survey of 3,000 Facebook users, the designers looked at why Facebook users break up in a relationship (*The Wall Street Journal*, November 27–28, 2010).

Reasons for Breakup	Gender	
	Men	Women
Nonapproval	3%	4%
Distance	21%	16%
Cheating	18%	22%
Lost Interest	28%	26%
Other	30%	32%

Source: Internal survey of 3,000 Facebook users.

Suppose the survey consisted of 1,800 men and 1,200 women. Use the data to determine whether the reasons for breakup depend on gender at the 1% significance level. Provide the details.

WRITING WITH STATISTICS

The recent phenomenon of online dating has made it as likely for would-be couples to meet via e-mail or other virtual matchmaking service as through friends and family (*CNN*, February 6, 2012). Studies that have looked at gender differences in mate selection have found that women put greater emphasis on the race and financial stability of a partner, while men mostly look for physical attractiveness. Recent survey results reported in *USA TODAY* (February 2, 2012) showed that 13% of women and 8% of men want their partner to be of the same ethnic background. The same survey also reported that 36% of women and 13% of men would like to meet someone who makes as much money as they do.

Anka Wilder, working for a small matchmaking service in Cincinnati, Ohio, wants to know if a similar pattern also exists with her customers. She has access to the preferences of 160 women and 120 men customers. In this sample, she finds that 28 women and 12 men customers value their partner to be of the same ethnicity background. Also, 50 women and 10 men value their partner to make as much money as they do.

Anka wants to use this sample information to:

1. Determine whether the proportion of women who value their partner to be of the same ethnic background is significantly greater than that of men.

2. Determine whether the proportion of women who value their partner to make as much money as they do is more than 20 percentage points greater than that of men.

Sample Report— Online Dating Preferences

With the advent of the Internet, there has been a surge in online dating services that connect individuals with similar interests, religious, and cultural backgrounds for personal relationships. In 1992, when the Internet was still in its infancy, less than 1% of Americans met their partners through online dating services. By 2009, about 22% of heterosexual couples and 61% of same-sex couples reported meeting online (*CNN*, February 6, 2012). A recent survey suggested that a higher proportion of women than men would like to meet someone with a similar ethnic background. Also, the difference between the proportion of women and men who would like to meet someone who makes as much money as they do is greater than 20%.

A couple of hypothesis tests were performed to determine if similar gender differences existed for online dating customers in Cincinnati, Ohio. The sample consisted of responses from 160 women and 120 men. The summary of the test results is presented in Table 11.A.

TABLE 11.A Test Statistics and p-values for Hypothesis Tests

Hypotheses	Test Statistic	p-value
$H_0: p_1 - p_2 \leq 0$ $H_A: p_1 - p_2 > 0$	$z = \dfrac{0.175 - 0.10}{\sqrt{0.1429(1 - 0.1429)\left(\dfrac{1}{160} + \dfrac{1}{120}\right)}} = 1.77$	0.0384
$H_0: p_1 - p_2 \leq 0.20$ $H_A: p_1 - p_2 > 0.20$	$z = \dfrac{0.3125 - 0.0833 - 0.20}{\sqrt{\dfrac{0.3125(1 - 0.3125)}{160} + \dfrac{0.0833(1 - 0.0833)}{120}}} = 0.66$	0.2546

First, it was tested if the proportion of women, denoted p_1, who value their partner to be of the same ethnicity is significantly greater than that of men, denoted p_2. It was found that 28 out of 160 women valued this trait, yielding a sample proportion of $\bar{p}_1 = 28/160 = 0.175$; a similar proportion for men was calculated as $\bar{p}_2 = 12/120 = 0.10$. The first row of Table 11.A shows the competing hypotheses, the value of the test statistic, and the p-value for this test. At the 5% significance level, the proportion of women who value the same ethnicity was greater than that of men. In the second test, p_1 and p_2 denoted the proportion of women and men, respectively, who would like their partner to make as much money as they do; here $\bar{p}_1 = 50/160 = 0.3125$ and $\bar{p}_2 = 10/120 = 0.0833$. The second row of Table 11.A shows the competing hypotheses, the value of the test statistic, and the p-value for this test. At the 5% significance level, the proportion of women who value their partner to make as much income as they do is not more than 20 percentage points greater than that of men. Online dating is a relatively new market and any such information is important for individuals looking for relationships as well as for service providers.

Conceptual Review

LO 11.1 **Make inferences about the difference between two population proportions based on independent sampling.**

A $100(1 - \alpha)\%$ **confidence interval for the difference between two population proportions $p_1 - p_2$** is given by $(\bar{p}_1 - \bar{p}_2) \pm z_{\alpha/2}\sqrt{\dfrac{\bar{p}_1(1 - \bar{p}_1)}{n_1} + \dfrac{\bar{p}_2(1 - \bar{p}_2)}{n_2}}$.

When conducting **hypothesis tests about the difference between two population proportions $p_1 - p_2$**, the value of the **test statistic** is calculated as:

- $z = \dfrac{\bar{p}_1 - \bar{p}_2}{\sqrt{\bar{p}(1 - \bar{p})\left(\dfrac{1}{n_1} + \dfrac{1}{n_2}\right)}}$, if the hypothesized difference d_0 between p_1 and p_2 is zero.

  The pooled sample proportion is $\bar{p} = \dfrac{x_1 + x_2}{n_1 + n_2} = \dfrac{n_1\bar{p}_1 + n_2\bar{p}_2}{n_1 + n_2}$.

- $z = \dfrac{(\bar{p}_1 - \bar{p}_2) - d_0}{\sqrt{\dfrac{\bar{p}_1(1 - \bar{p}_1)}{n_1} + \dfrac{\bar{p}_2(1 - \bar{p}_2)}{n_2}}}$, if the hypothesized difference d_0 between p_1 and p_2 is not zero.

LO 11.2 **Discuss features of the χ^2 distribution.**

The χ^2 **distribution** is characterized by a family of distributions, where each distribution depends on its particular degrees of freedom df; thus, it is common to refer to it as the χ^2_{df} distribution. It is positively skewed with values ranging from zero to infinity. As df grow larger, the χ^2_{df} distribution approaches the normal distribution.

Conduct a goodness-of-fit test for a multinomial experiment.

A **multinomial experiment** consists of a series of n independent and identical trials such that on each trial there are k possible outcomes, called categories; the probability p_i associated with the ith category remains the same; and, the sum of the probabilities is one.

A **goodness-of-fit test** is conducted to determine if the population proportions equal some predetermined (hypothesized) values. The value of the **test statistic** is calculated as $\chi^2_{df} = \Sigma \frac{(o_i - e_i)^2}{e_i}$, where $df = k - 1$ and o_i and $e_i = np_i$ are the observed and expected frequencies in the ith category, respectively. The test is valid when the expected frequencies for each category are five or more. This test is always implemented as a right-tailed test.

Conduct a test of independence.

A goodness-of-fit test examines a single qualitative variable, whereas a **test of independence**, also called a **chi-square test of a contingency table**, analyzes the relationship between two qualitative variables defined on the same population. A contingency table shows frequencies for two qualitative variables, x and y, where each cell of the table represents a mutually exclusive combination of the pair of x and y values.

In order to determine whether or not the two variables are related, we again compare observed frequencies with expected frequencies. The expected frequency for each cell is calculated as $e_{ij} = \frac{(\text{Row } i \text{ total})(\text{Column } j \text{ total})}{\text{Sample Size}}$.

The value of the chi-square **test statistic** is calculated as $\chi^2_{df} = \sum_i \sum_j \frac{(o_{ij} - e_{ij})^2}{e_{ij}}$, where o_{ij} and e_{ij} are the observed and expected frequencies corresponding to the ith row and the jth column, respectively. Degrees of freedom are calculated as $(r - 1)(c - 1)$ where r and c refer to the number of rows and columns, respectively, in the contingency table. The test of independence is also implemented as a right-tailed test and is valid when the expected frequencies for each cell are five or more.

Additional Exercises and Case Studies

35. A recent Health of Boston report suggests that 14% of female residents suffer from asthma as opposed to 6% of males (*Boston Globe*, August 16, 2010). Suppose 250 females and 200 males responded to the study.

    a. Develop the appropriate null and alternative hypotheses to test whether the proportion of females suffering from asthma is greater than the proportion of males.

    b. Calculate the value of the test statistic and the *p*-value.

    c. At the 5% significance level, what is the conclusion? Do the data suggest that females suffer more from asthma than males?

36. Depression engulfs millions of Americans every day. A new federal study reported that 10.9% of adults aged 18–24 identified with some level of depression versus 6.8% of adults aged 65 or older (*Boston Globe*, October 18, 2010). Suppose 250 young adults (18–24 years old) and 200 older adults (65 years old and older) responded to the study.

    a. Develop the appropriate null and alternative hypotheses to test whether the proportion of young adults suffering

    from depression is greater than the proportion of older adults suffering from depression.

    b. Calculate the value of the test statistic and the *p*-value.

    c. At the 5% significance level, what is the conclusion? Do the sample data suggest that young adults suffer more from depression than older adults?

37. Fresh numbers from the U.S. Department of Transportation suggest that fewer flights in the U.S. arrive on time than before. The explanations offered for the lackluster performance are understaffed airlines, a high volume of travelers, and overtaxed air traffic control. A transportation analyst is interested in comparing the performance at two major international airports, namely Kennedy International (JFK) in New York and O'Hare International in Chicago. She finds that 70% of the flights were on time at JFK compared with 63% at O'Hare. Suppose these proportions were based on 200 flights at each of these two airports. The analyst believes that the proportion of on-time flights at JFK is more than 5 percentage points higher than that of O'Hare.

a. Develop the competing hypotheses to test the transportation analyst's belief.

b. Compute the value of the test statistic.

c. Use the p-value approach to test the above assertion.

d. Repeat the analysis with the critical value approach.

38. The following table lists the market share of the four firms in a particular industry in 2010 and total sales for each firm in 2011.

Firm	Market Share in 2010	Total Sales in 2011 (in billions of $)
1	0.40	200
2	0.30	180
3	0.20	100
4	0.10	70

a. Specify the competing hypotheses to test whether the market shares in 2011 are consistent with those from 2010.

b. At the 1% significance level, find the critical value.

c. Calculate the value of the test statistic.

d. Do the sample data suggest that the market shares changed from 2010 to 2011?

39. A study suggests that airlines have increased restrictions on cheap fares by raising overnight requirements (*The Wall Street Journal*, August 19, 2008). This would force business travelers to pay more for their flights, since they tend to need the most flexibility and want to be home on weekends. Eight months ago, the overnight stay requirements were as follows:

One night	Two nights	Three nights	Saturday night
37%	17%	28%	18%

A recent sample of 644 flights found the following restrictions:

One night	Two nights	Three nights	Saturday night
117	137	298	92

a. Specify the competing hypotheses to test whether the recent proportions differ from those cited in the study.

b. At the 5% significance level, find the critical value.

c. Calculate the value of the test statistic.

d. What is the conclusion to the hypothesis test? Interpret your results.

40. A local TV station claims that 60% of people support Candidate A, 30% support Candidate B, and 10% support Candidate C. A survey of 500 registered voters is taken. The accompanying table indicates how they are likely to vote.

Candidate A	Candidate B	Candidate C
350	125	25

a. Specify the competing hypotheses to test whether the TV station's claim can be rejected by the data.

b. Use the p-value approach to test the hypothesis at a 1% significance level.

41. Although founded only in 2004, Facebook has more than 500 million active users, of which 50% log on to Facebook on any given day. In a recent survey by Facebook, young users (those born after 1984) were asked about their preference for delivering the news about breaking up a relationship (*The Wall Street Journal*, November 27–28, 2010). One of the shocking results was that only 47% of users preferred to break the news in person. A researcher decides to verify the survey results of Facebook by taking her own sample of 200 young Facebook users. The preference percentages from Facebook and the researcher's survey are presented in the following table.

Delivery Method	Facebook Results	Researcher's Results
In Person	47%	55%
Phone	30%	28%
E-mail	4%	8%
Facebook	5%	3%
Instant Message	14%	6%

At the 5% level of significance, test if the researcher's results are inconsistent with the survey results conducted by Facebook. Provide the details, using the p-value approach.

42. A recent study in the *Journal of the American Medical Association* (February 20, 2008) found that patients who go into cardiac arrest while in the hospital are more likely to die if it happens after 11 pm. The study investigated 58,593 cardiac arrests during the day or evening. Of those, 11,604 survived to leave the hospital. There were 28,155 cardiac arrests during the shift that began at 11 pm, commonly referred to as the graveyard shift. Of those, 4,139 survived for discharge. The following contingency table summarizes the results of the study:

Shift	Survived for Discharge	Did Not Survive for Discharge	Row Total
Day or Evening Shift	11,604	46,989	58,593
Graveyard Shift	4,139	24,016	28,155
Column Total	15,743	71,005	86,748

a. Specify the competing hypotheses to determine whether a patient's survival depends on the time at which he/she experiences cardiac arrest.

b. At a 1% significance level, find the critical value.

c. Calculate the value of the test statistic.

d. What is the conclusion to the test? Is the timing of when a cardiac arrest occurs independent of whether or not the patient survives for discharge? Given your answer, what type of recommendations might you give to hospitals?

43. An analyst is trying to determine whether the prices of certain stocks on the NASDAQ are independent of the industry to which they belong. She examines four industries and classifies the stock prices in these industries into one of three categories (high-priced, average-priced, low-priced).

Stock Price	Industry			
	I	II	III	IV
High	16	8	10	14
Average	18	16	10	12
Low	7	8	4	9

a. Specify the competing hypotheses to determine whether stock price depends on the industry.

b. Calculate the value of the test statistic. Approximate the *p*-value with the table or calculate its exact value with Excel.

c. At a 1% significance level, what can the analyst conclude?

44. Many parents have turned to St. John's wort, a herbal remedy, to treat their children with attention deficit hyperactivity disorder (ADHD). *The Journal of the American Medical Association* (June 11, 2008) recently published an article that explored the herb's effectiveness. Children with ADHD were randomly assigned to take either St. John's wort capsules or placebos. The accompanying contingency table broadly reflects the results found in the study.

	Effect on ADHD	
Treatment	No Change in ADHD	Improvement in ADHD
St. John's wort	12	15
Placebo	14	13

At the 5% significance level, do the data indicate that St. John's wort affects children with ADHD?

45. A recent poll asked 3,228 Americans aged 16 to 21 whether they are likely to serve in the U.S. military. The following table, cross-classified by gender and race, reports those who responded that they are likely or very likely to serve in the active-duty military.

	Race		
Gender	Hispanic	Black	White
Male	1,098	678	549
Female	484	355	64

Source: Defense Human Resources Activity telephone poll of 3228 Americans conducted October through December 2005.

a. State the competing hypotheses to test whether race and gender are dependent when making a choice to serve in the military.

b. Conduct the test using the critical value approach at the 5% significance level.

46. Given a shaky economy and high heating costs, more and more households are struggling to pay utility bills (*The Wall Street Journal*, February, 14, 2008). Particularly hard hit are households with homes heated with propane or heating oil. Many of these households are spending twice as much to stay warm this winter compared to those who heat with natural gas or electricity. A representative sample of 500 households was taken to investigate if the type of heating influences whether or not a household is delinquent in paying its utility bill. The following table reports the results.

	Type of Heating			
Delinquent in Payment?	Natural Gas	Electricity	Heating Oil	Propane
Yes	50	20	15	10
No	240	130	20	15

At the 5% significance level, test whether the type of heating influences a household's delinquency in payment. Interpret your results.

47. According to the Census's Population Survey, the percentage of children with two parents at home is the highest for Asians and lowest for blacks (*USA TODAY*, February 26, 2009). It is reported that 85% of Asian children have two parents at home versus 78% of white, 70% of Hispanic, and 38% of black. Suppose there are 500 students in a representative school of which 280 are white, 50 are Asian, 100 are Hispanic, and 70 are black.

a. Construct a contingency table that shows the frequencies for the qualitative variables Race (Asian, White, Hispanic, or Black) and Both Parents at Home (yes or no).

b. Conduct a test at the 1% significance level to determine whether the variables Race and Both Parents at Home are dependent. Provide the details.

CASE STUDIES

Case Study 11.1

According to a recent study, cell phones are the main medium for teenagers to stay connected with friends and family (*CNN*, March 19, 2012). These days text messaging followed by cell calling have become an integral part of life for teenagers. It is estimated that 90% of older teens (aged 14–17) and 60% of younger teens (aged 12–13) own a cell phone. Moreover, one in four teenagers who owns a cell phone uses a smartphone. Susan Alder works at an AT&T store in the campus town of Ames, Iowa. She has been tasked to determine if the patterns reported in the above study apply to Ames teens. She surveys 120 older teens and 90 younger teens. In her sample, 100 older teens and 48 younger teens own a cell phone. She also finds that 26 older teens and 9 younger teens use a smartphone. In a report use the above information to:

1. Determine at the 5% significance level whether the proportion of older teens who own a cell phone is more than 20 percentage points greater than that of younger teens.

2. Of the teens who own a cell phone, determine at the 5% significance level whether the proportion of older teens that use a smartphone is greater than that of younger teens.

Case Study 11.2

A detailed study of Americans' religious beliefs and practices by the Pew Forum on Religion & Public Life revealed that religion is quite important in an individual's life (*Boston Globe*, June 24, 2008). The second column of the accompanying table reports the proportion of Americans who feel a certain way about religion. The study also concludes that Massachusetts residents are the least likely to say that they are religious. In order to test this claim, assume 400 randomly selected Massachusetts residents are asked about the importance of religion in his/her life. The results of this survey are shown in the last column of the accompanying table.

Data for Case Study 11.2 Importance of Religion, U.S. versus Massachusetts

Importance of Religion	U.S. Results	Responses of Massachusetts Residents
Very important	0.58	160
Somewhat important	0.25	140
Not too important	0.15	96
Don't know	0.02	4

In a report, use the sample information to:

1. Determine whether Massachusetts residents' religious beliefs differ from those based on the United States at a 5% significance level.

2. Discuss whether you would expect to find the same conclusions if you conducted a similar test for the state of Utah or states in the Southern Belt of the United States.

Case Study 11.3

A University of Utah study examined 7,925 severely obese adults who had gastric bypass surgery and an identical number of people who did not have the surgery (*Boston Globe*, August 23, 2007). The study wanted to investigate whether losing weight through stomach surgery prolonged the lives of severely obese patients, thereby reducing their deaths from heart disease, cancer, and diabetes.

Over the course of the study, 534 of the participants died. Of those who died, the cause of death was classified as either a disease death (disease deaths include heart disease, cancer, and diabetes) or a nondisease death (nondisease deaths include suicide or accident). The following contingency table summarizes the study's findings:

Data for Case Study 11.3 Deaths Cross-Classified by Cause and Method of Losing Weight

Cause of Death	Method of Losing Weight	
	No Surgery	Surgery
Death from disease	285	150
Death from nondisease	36	63

In a report, use the sample information to:

1. Determine at the 5% significance level whether the cause of death is related to the method of losing weight.

2. Discuss how the findings of the test used in question 1 might be used by those in the health industry.

Appendix 11.1 Guidelines for Other Software Packages

The following section provides brief commands for specific software packages: Minitab, SPSS, and JMP. More detailed instructions can be found on the text website.

MINITAB

Testing $p_1 - p_2$

A. (Replicating Example 11.3) From the menu choose **Stat > Basic Statistics > 2 Proportions**. Choose **Summarized data**. For **First**, enter 5400 for **Events** and 6000 for **Trials**. For **Second**, enter 8600 for **Events** and 10000 for **Trials**.

B. Choose **Options**. Enter 0 for **Test difference**. Select '**greater than**' for **Alternative**. Select **Use pooled estimate of p for test**.

Goodness-of-Fit Test

A. (Replicating Example 11.5) Input the data from Table 11.5 into the spreadsheet. Remember to combine the data for Firms 4 and 5.

B. From the menu choose **Stat > Tables > Chi-Square Goodness-of-Fit Test (One Variable)**. Choose **Observed counts** and then select Number of Recent Customers. For **Test**, select **Specific proportions** and then select Market Share.

C. Choose **Results**. Select **Display test results**.

Test of Independence

A. (Replicating Example 11.6) Copy the data from Table 11.9 into a Minitab spreadsheet. Do not include the row totals or the column totals.

B. From the menu choose **Stat > Tables > Chi-Square Test (Two Way Table in Worksheet)**. In the *Chi-Square Test* dialog box, select Economy Car and Noneconomy Car for **Columns containing the table**. Click **OK**.

SPSS

Goodness-of-Fit Test

A. (Replicating Example 11.5) In the first column, labeled Share, input codes 1, 2, 3, 4 for the 4 firms (remember that we are combining firms 4 and 5) and in the second column, labeled Number, input the frequencies for the Number of Recent Customers (again, combine the frequencies for firms 4 and 5).

B. From the menu choose **Data > Weight Cases**. Select **Weight cases by** and select **Number** for **Frequency Variable**.

C. From the menu choose **Analyze > Nonparametric Tests > Legacy Dialogs > Chi-Square**. Select Share as **Test Variable List**. Under **Expected Values** select **Values** and **Add** 0.40, 0.32, 0.24, and 0.04.

Test of Independence

A. (Replicating Example 11.6) Label two columns 'Gender' and 'Type'. The first 50 rows are designated as Female for Gender and Economy for Type, the next 60 rows are designated as Female for Gender and Noneconomy for Type, the next 120 rows have Male for Gender and Economy for Type, and the final 170 rows have Male for Gender and Noneconomy for Type.

B. From the menu choose **Analyze > Descriptive Statistics > Crosstabs**. Select Gender for **Row(s)** and Type for **Column(s)**. Choose **Statistics** and select **Chi-Square**.

JMP

Test of Independence

A. (Replicating Example 11.6) Label three columns Gender, Type, and Frequency, respectively. The first two columns are nominal data, whereas the last column is continuous. In the first row enter Female, Economy, and 50; in the second row input Female, Noneconomy, 60; in the third row enter Male, Economy, 120; and in the fourth row, enter Male, Noneconomy, 170.

B. From the menu choose **Analyze—Fit Y by X**. Select Type as **Y, Response**, Gender as **X, Factor**, and Frequency as **Freq**.

12 Basics of Regression Analysis

CHAPTER

LEARNING OBJECTIVES

After reading this chapter you should be able to:

LO **12.1**   Estimate the simple linear regression model and interpret the coefficients.

LO **12.2**   Estimate the multiple linear regression model and interpret the coefficients.

LO **12.3**   Calculate and interpret the standard error of the estimate.

LO **12.4**   Calculate and interpret the coefficient of determination R^2.

LO **12.5**   Differentiate between R^2 and adjusted R^2.

LO **12.6**   Conduct tests of individual significance.

LO **12.7**   Conduct a test of joint significance.

Regression analysis is one of the most important statistical methodologies used in business applications. It is used to examine the relationship between two or more variables. In particular, it captures the impact of one or more variables, called the explanatory variables, on the variable of interest, called the response variable. We first explore the procedures for estimating a simple linear relationship between two variables, commonly referred to as the simple linear regression model. We then extend the simple linear regression model to the case involving several variables, called the multiple linear regression model. Finally, in order to assess how well the estimated model fits the data, we examine goodness-of-fit measures and conduct hypothesis tests. We use goodness-of-fit measures to select the best-fitting linear regression model. We carry out hypothesis tests to determine whether the relationship between the variables, as stated in the linear regression model, is real or due to chance.

INTRODUCTORY CASE

Consumer Debt Payments

A recent study found that American consumers are making average monthly debt payments of $983 (Experian.com, November 11, 2010). However, the study of 26 metropolitan areas reveals quite a bit of variation in debt payments, depending on where the consumer lives. For instance, in Washington, DC, residents pay the most ($1,285 per month), while Pittsburghers pay the least ($763 per month). Madelyn Davis, an economist at a large bank, believes that income differences between cities are the primary reason for the disparate debt payments. For example, the Washington, DC, area's high incomes have likely contributed to its placement at the top of the list. Madelyn also wonders about the likely effect of unemployment on consumer debt payments. On the one hand, higher unemployment rates may reduce consumer debt payments, as consumers forgo making major purchases such as homes and cars. On the other hand, higher unemployment rates may raise consumer debt payments as consumers struggle to pay their bills. In order to analyze the relationship between income, the unemployment rate, and consumer debt payments, Madelyn gathers data from the same 26 metropolitan areas used in the debt payment study. Specifically, she collects each area's 2010–2011 median household income as well as the monthly unemployment rate and average consumer debt for August 2010. Table 12.1 shows a portion of the data; the entire data set, labeled **Debt_Payments**, can be found on the text website.

TABLE 12.1 Income, the Unemployment Rate, and Consumer Debt Payments, 2010–2011

Metropolitan Area	Income (in $1,000s)	Unemployment	Debt
Washington, DC	$103.50	6.3%	$1,285
Seattle	81.70	8.5	1,135
⋮	⋮	⋮	⋮
Pittsburgh	63.00	8.3	763

Source: eFannieMae.com reports 2010–2011 Area Median Household Incomes; bls.com gives monthly unemployment rates for August 2010; Experian.com collected average monthly consumer debt payments in August 2010 and published the data in November 2010.

Madelyn would like to use the sample information in Table 12.1 to:

1. Use regression analysis to make predictions for debt payments for given values of income and the unemployment rate.
2. Use various goodness-of-fit measures to determine the linear regression model that best fits the data.
3. Determine the significance of income and the unemployment rate at the 5% significance level.

A synopsis of this case is provided at the end of Section 12.4.

12.1 The Simple Linear Regression Model

LO **12.1**

Estimate the simple linear regression model and interpret the coefficients.

Regression analysis is one of the most important statistical methodologies used in business applications. It is used to examine the relationship between two or more variables. In the introductory case, Madelyn is interested in examining how income and the unemployment rate might influence debt payments. In another scenario, we may want to predict a firm's sales based on its advertising; estimate an individual's salary based on education and years of experience; predict the selling price of a house on the basis of its size and location; or describe auto sales with respect to consumer income, interest rates, and price discounts. In all of these examples, we can use regression analysis to describe the relationship between the variables of interest.

With regression analysis, we explicitly assume that one variable, called the **response variable**, is influenced by other variables, called the **explanatory variables**. Consequently, we use information on the explanatory variables to predict and/or describe changes in the response variable. Alternative names for the explanatory variables are independent variables, predictor variables, control variables, or regressors, while the response variable is often referred to as the dependent variable, the explained variable, the predicted variable, or the regressand.

No matter the response variable that we choose to examine, we cannot expect to predict its exact value because some omitted explanatory variables may also influence it. If the value of the response variable is uniquely determined by the values of the explanatory variables, we say that the relationship between the variables is **deterministic**. This is often the case in the physical sciences. For example, momentum p is the product of the mass m and velocity v of an object, that is, $p = mv$. In most fields of research, however, we tend to find that the relationship between the explanatory variables and the response variable is **inexact**, due to the omission of relevant factors (sometimes not measurable) that influence the response variable. For instance, debt payments are likely to be influenced by housing costs—a variable that is not included in the introductory case. Similarly, when trying to predict an individual's salary, the individual's natural ability is often omitted since it is extremely difficult, if not impossible, to quantify.

> ### DETERMINISTIC VERSUS INEXACT RELATIONSHIPS
>
> The relationship between the response variable and the explanatory variables is **deterministic** if the value of the response variable is uniquely determined by the explanatory variables; otherwise, the relationship is **inexact**.

Our objective is to develop a mathematical model that captures the relationship between the **response variable y** and the **k explanatory variables $x_1, x_2, \ldots, x_k$**. The model must also account for the randomness that is a part of real life. In order to develop a linear regression model, we start with a deterministic component that approximates the relationship we want to model, and then add a random term to it, making the relationship inexact.

In this section we focus on the **simple linear regression model**, which uses one explanatory variable, denoted x_1, to explain the variability in the response variable, denoted y. For ease of exposition when discussing the simple linear regression model, we often drop the subscript on the explanatory variable and refer to it solely as x. In the next section we extend the simple linear regression model to the **multiple linear regression model**, where more than one explanatory variable is linearly related with the response variable.

A fundamental assumption underlying the simple linear regression model is that the expected value of y lies on a straight line, denoted by $\beta_0 + \beta_1 x$, where β_0 and β_1 (the Greek letters read as betas) are the unknown intercept and slope parameters, respectively. (You have actually seen this relationship before, but you just used different notation. Recall the equation for a line: $y = mx + b$, where b and m are the intercept and the slope, respectively, of the line.)

The expression $\beta_0 + \beta_1 x$ is the deterministic component of the simple linear regression model, which can be thought of as the expected value of y for a given value of x. In other words, conditional on x, $E(y) = \beta_0 + \beta_1 x$. The slope parameter β_1 determines whether the linear relationship between x and $E(y)$ is positive ($\beta_1 > 0$) or negative ($\beta_1 < 0$); $\beta_1 = 0$ indicates that there is no linear relationship. Figure 12.1 shows the deterministic portion of the simple linear regression model for various values of the intercept β_0 and the slope β_1 parameters.

FIGURE 12.1 Various examples of a simple linear regression model

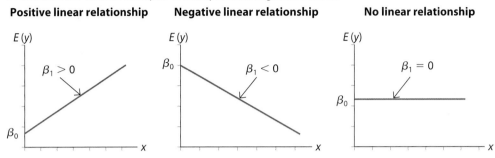

As noted earlier, the actual value y may differ from the expected value $E(y)$. Therefore, we add a random error term ε (the Greek letter read as epsilon) to develop a simple linear regression model.

> **THE SIMPLE LINEAR REGRESSION MODEL**
>
> The simple linear regression model is defined as
>
> $$y = \beta_0 + \beta_1 x + \varepsilon,$$
>
> where y and x are the response variable and the explanatory variable, respectively, and ε is the random error term. The coefficients β_0 and β_1 are the unknown parameters to be estimated.

Determining the Sample Regression Equation

The population parameters β_0 and β_1 used in the simple linear regression model are unknown, and, therefore, must be estimated. As always, we use sample data to estimate the population parameters of interest. Here sample data consist of n pairs of observations on y and x.

Let b_0 and b_1 represent the estimates of β_0 and β_1, respectively. We form the **sample regression equation** as $\hat{y} = b_0 + b_1 x$, where $\hat{y}$ (read as y-hat) is the predicted value of the response variable given a specified value of the explanatory variable x. For a given value of x, the observed and the predicted values of the response variable are likely to be different since many factors besides x influence y. We refer to the difference between the observed and the predicted values of y, that is $y - \hat{y}$, as the **residual** e.

> The **sample regression equation** for the simple linear regression model is denoted as
>
> $$\hat{y} = b_0 + b_1 x,$$
>
> where b_0 and b_1 are the point estimates of β_0 and β_1, respectively.
>
> Since the predictions cannot be totally accurate, the difference between the observed and the predicted values of y represents the **residual** e; that is, $e = y - \hat{y}$.

Before estimating a simple linear regression model, it is useful to visualize the relationship between y and x by constructing a scatterplot. Here, we explicitly place y on the vertical axis and x on the horizontal axis, implying that x influences the variability in y. In Figure 12.2 we use the data from the introductory case to show a scatterplot of debt payments against income. We then superimpose a linear trend line through the points on the scatterplot.

The superimposed line in Figure 12.2 is the sample regression equation, $\hat{y} = b_0 + b_1 x$, where y and x represent debt payments and income, respectively. The upward slope of the line suggests that as income increases, the predicted debt payments also increase. Also, the vertical distance between any data point on the scatterplot and the corresponding point on the line, y and $\hat{y}$, represents the residual, $e = y - \hat{y}$.

FIGURE 12.2 Scatterplot with a superimposed trend line

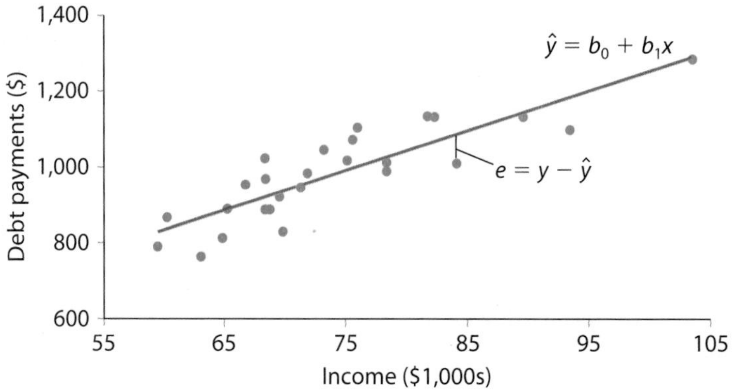

Using Excel to Construct a Scatterplot and a Trendline [FILE]

In order to replicate Figure 12.2 using Excel, we follow these steps.

A. Open the **Debt Payments** data found on the text website. For the purpose of creating a scatterplot of debt payments against income, disregard the column with the unemployment data.

B. Simultaneously select the data for Income and Debt and choose **Insert > Scatter**. Select the graph on the top left.

C. Right-click on the scatter points, choose **Add Trendline**, and then choose **Linear**.

D. Further formatting regarding colors, axes, etc. can be done by selecting **Layout** from the menu.

A common approach to fitting a line to the scatterplot is the **method of least squares**, also referred to as **ordinary least squares (OLS)**. In other words, we use OLS to estimate the parameters β_0 and β_1. OLS estimators have many desirable properties if certain assumptions hold (these assumptions are discussed in the next chapter). The OLS method chooses the line whereby the **sum of squares due to error (residual) SSE** is minimized, where $SSE = \Sigma(y_i - \hat{y}_i)^2 = \Sigma e_i^2$. SSE is the sum of the squared differences between the observed observations y and their predicted values $\hat{y}$, or, equivalently, the sum of the squared distances from the regression equation. Thus, using this distance measure, we say that the OLS method produces the straight line that is "closest" to the data. In the context of Figure 12.2, the superimposed line has been estimated by OLS.

Using calculus, equations have been developed for b_0 and b_1 that satisfy the OLS criterion.

CALCULATING THE COEFFICIENTS b_1 AND b_0

The slope b_1 and the intercept b_0 of the sample regression equation are calculated as

$$b_1 = \frac{\Sigma(x_i - \bar{x})(y_i - \bar{y})}{\Sigma(x_i - \bar{x})^2} \quad \text{and}$$

$$b_0 = \bar{y} - b_1 \bar{x}.$$

It is important to be able to interpret the estimated regression coefficients. As we will see in the following example, it is not always possible to provide an economic interpretation of the intercept estimate b_0; mathematically, however, it represents the predicted value of $\hat{y}$ when x has a value of zero. The slope estimate b_1 represents the change in $\hat{y}$ when x increases by one unit.

EXAMPLE 12.1

Using the data from Table 12.1, let debt payments represent the response variable and income represent the explanatory variable.

a. Calculate and interpret b_1.

b. Calculate and interpret b_0.

c. What is the sample regression equation?

d. Predict debt payments if income is $80,000.

SOLUTION: We use the simple linear regression model, Debt $= \beta_0 + \beta_1$Income $+ \varepsilon$, or simply, $y = \beta_0 + \beta_1 x + \varepsilon$, where y and x represent debt payments and income, respectively.

a. We first find the sample mean of income and debt payments and obtain $\bar{x} = 74.05$ and $\bar{y} = 983.46$ (calculations not shown). In order to obtain b_1, we calculate deviations from the mean for both x and y, as shown in the first two columns of Table 12.2. We then calculate the product of deviations from the mean, as shown in the third column. The sum of the products of the deviations from the mean is the numerator in the formula for b_1; this value is found in the last cell of the third column. The fourth column shows the squared deviations from the mean for x. The sum of these squared deviations, found in the last cell of the fourth column, is the denominator in the formula for b_1.

TABLE 12.2 Calculations for Example 12.1

$x_i - \bar{x}$	$y_i - \bar{y}$	$(x_i - \bar{x})(y_i - \bar{y})$	$(x_i - \bar{x})^2$
$103.50 - 74.05 = 29.45$	$1{,}285 - 983.46 = 301.54$	$(29.45)(301.54) = 8{,}880.35$	$(29.45)^2 = 867.30$
$81.70 - 74.05 = 7.65$	$1{,}135 - 983.46 = 151.54$	$(7.65)(151.54) = 1{,}159.28$	$(7.65)^2 = 58.52$
$\vdots$	$\vdots$	$\vdots$	$\vdots$
$63.00 - 74.05 = -11.05$	$763 - 983.46 = -220.46$	$(-11.05)(-220.46) = 2{,}436.08$	$(-11.05)^2 = 122.10$
		$\Sigma(x_i - \bar{x})(y_i - \bar{y}) = 27{,}979.50$	$\Sigma(x_i - \bar{x})^2 = 2{,}679.75$

Using the summations from the last cells of the last two columns, we compute $b_1 = \dfrac{\Sigma(x_i - \bar{x})(y_i - \bar{y})}{\Sigma(x_i - \bar{x})^2} = \dfrac{27{,}979.50}{2{,}679.75} = 10.44$. As anticipated, the slope is positive, suggesting a positive relationship between income and debt payments. Since income is measured in $1,000s, our interpretation is that if median household income increases by $1,000, then on average, we predict consumer debt payments to increase by b_1, that is, by $10.44.

b. Using $b_1 = 10.44$ and the sample means, $\bar{x} = 74.05$ and $\bar{y} = 983.46$, we obtain an estimate for b_0 as $b_0 = \bar{y} - b_1\bar{x} = 983.46 - 10.44(74.05) = 210.38$. This estimated intercept coefficient of 210.38 suggests that if income equals zero, then predicted debt payments are $210.38. In this particular application, this conclusion makes some sense, since a household with no income still needs to make debt payments for any credit card use, automobile loans, and/or a mortgage. However, we should be careful about predicting y when we use a value for x that is not included in the sample range of x. In the

Debt Payments data set, the lowest and highest values for income (in $1,000s) are $59.40 and $103.50, respectively; plus the scatterplot suggests that a line fits the data well within this range of the explanatory variable. Unless we assume that income and debt payments will maintain the same linear relationship at income values less than $59.40 and more than $103.50, we should refrain from making predictions based on values of the explanatory variable outside the sample range.

c. With $b_0 = 210.38$ and $b_1 = 10.44$, we write the sample regression equation as $\hat{y} = 210.38 + 10.44x$, that is, $\widehat{Debt} = 210.38 + 10.44\text{Income}$.

d. Note that income is measured in $1,000s; therefore if income equals $80,000, we input Income $= 80$ in the sample regression equation and find predicted debt payments as $\widehat{Debt} = 210.38 + 10.44(80) = \$1,045.58$.

Using Excel to Find the Sample Regression Equation

Fortunately, we rarely have to calculate a sample regression equation by hand. Virtually every statistical software package computes the necessary output to construct a sample regression equation. In addition, values of all relevant statistics for assessing the model, discussed shortly, are also included.

EXAMPLE 12.2 FILE

Given the data from Table 12.1, use Excel to reestimate the sample regression equation with debt payments as the response variable and income as the explanatory variable.

SOLUTION:

A. Open the data labeled ***Debt Payments*** found on the text website.

B. Choose **Data** > **Data Analysis** > **Regression** from the menu.

C. See Figure 12.3. In the *Regression* dialog box, click on the box next to *Input Y Range*, then select Debt data, including its heading. For *Input X Range*, select the Income data, including its heading. Check *Labels*, since we are using Debt and Income as headings.

D. Click **OK**.

FIGURE 12.3 Regression dialog box for Example 12.2

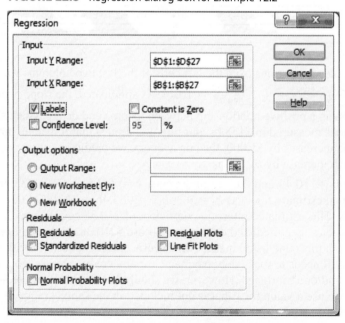

The Excel output is presented in Table 12.3.

TABLE 12.3 Regression Results for Example 12.2

Regression Statistics	
Multiple R	0.8675
R Square	0.7526
Adjusted R Square	0.7423
Standard Error	63.2606
Observations	26

ANOVA					
	df	SS	MS	F	Significance F
Regression	1	292136.9086	292136.9086	72.9996	9.6603E-09
Residual	24	96045.5529	4001.8980		
Total	25	388182.4615			

	Coefficients	Standard Error	t Stat	p-value	Lower 95%	Upper 95%
Intercept	**210.2977**	91.3387	2.3024	0.0303	21.7838	398.8116
Income	**10.4411**	1.2220	8.5440	9.6603E-09	7.9189	12.9633

As Table 12.3 shows, Excel produces quite a bit of statistical information. In order to answer the questions in Example 12.2, we need only the estimated coefficients, which we have put in boldface. We will address the remaining information shortly. The estimates for β_0 and β_1 are $b_0 = 210.2977$ and $b_1 = 10.4411$. The sample regression equation, $\widehat{Debt} = 210.30 + 10.44 Income$, is virtually the same as the one we calculated with the formulas; the intercept estimate is slightly off due to rounding.

EXERCISES 12.1

Mechanics

1. In a simple linear regression, the following information is given:
$$\bar{x} = 34; \bar{y} = 44; \Sigma(x_i - \bar{x})(y_i - \bar{y}) = 1250;$$
$$\Sigma(x_i - \bar{x})^2 = 925$$
   a. Calculate b_1.
   b. Calculate b_0.
   c. What is the sample regression equation? Predict y if x equals 40.

2. In a simple linear regression, the following information is given:
$$\bar{x} = -25; \bar{y} = 56; \Sigma(x_i - \bar{x})(y_i - \bar{y}) = -866;$$
$$\Sigma(x_i - \bar{x})^2 = 711$$
   a. Calculate b_1.
   b. Calculate b_0.
   c. What is the sample regression equation? Predict y if x equals −20.

3. In a simple linear regression, the following sample regression equation is obtained:
$$\hat{y} = 15 + 2.5x.$$
   a. Predict y if x equals 10.
   b. What happens to this prediction if x doubles in value?

4. In a simple linear regression, the following sample regression equation is obtained:
$$\hat{y} = 436 - 17x.$$
   a. Interpret the slope coefficient.
   b. Predict y if x equals −15.

5. Consider the following sample data:

x	12	23	11	23	14	21	18	16
y	28	43	21	40	33	41	37	32

   a. Construct a scatterplot and verify that estimating a simple linear regression model is appropriate in this problem.
   b. Calculate b_1 and b_0. What is the sample regression equation?
   c. Find the predicted value for y if x equals 10, 15, and 20.

6. Consider the following sample data:

x	22	24	27	21	23	14	14	15
y	101	139	250	88	87	14	16	20

   a. Construct a scatterplot and verify that estimating a simple linear regression model is appropriate in this problem.
   b. Calculate b_0 and b_1. What is the sample regression equation?
   c. Find the predicted value for y if x equals 15, 20, and 25.

7. Thirty observations were used to estimate $y = \beta_0 + \beta_1 x + \varepsilon$. A portion of the Excel results is as follows:

	Coefficients	Standard Error	t Stat	p-value
Intercept	41.82	8.58	4.87	3.93E-05
x	0.49	0.10	4.81	4.65E-05

a. What is the point estimate for β_1? Interpret this value.
b. What is the sample regression equation?
c. If $x = 30$, what is $\hat{y}$?

8. Twenty-four observations were used to estimate $y = \beta_0 + \beta_1 x + \varepsilon$. A portion of the Excel results is as follows:

	Coefficients	Standard Error	t Stat	p-value
Intercept	2.25	2.36	0.95	0.3515
x	−0.16	0.30	−0.53	0.6017

a. What is the point estimate for β_1? Interpret this value.
b. What is the sample regression equation?
c. What is the predicted value for y if $x = 2$? If $x = -2$?

Applications

9. The director of graduate admissions at a large university is analyzing the relationship between scores on the math portion of the Graduate Record Examination (GRE) and subsequent performance in graduate school, as measured by a student's grade point average (GPA). She uses a sample of 8 students who graduated within the past five years. The data are as follows:

GRE	700	720	650	750	680	730	740	780
GPA	3.0	3.5	3.2	3.7	3.1	3.9	3.3	3.5

a. Construct a scatterplot placing GRE on the horizontal axis.
b. Find the sample regression equation for the model: $GPA = \beta_0 + \beta_1 GRE + \varepsilon$.
c. What is a student's predicted GPA if he/she scored 710 on the math portion of the GRE?

10. A social scientist would like to analyze the relationship between educational attainment and salary. He collects the following sample data, where Education refers to years of higher education and Salary is the individual's annual salary in thousands of dollars:

Education	3	4	6	2	5	4	8	0
Salary	$40	53	80	42	70	50	110	38

a. Find the sample regression equation for the model: $Salary = \beta_0 + \beta_1 Education + \varepsilon$.
b. Interpret the coefficient for Education.
c. What is the predicted salary for an individual who completed 7 years of higher education?

11. The owner of several used-car dealerships believes that the selling price of a used car can best be predicted using the car's age. He uses data on the recent selling price and age

of 20 used sedans to estimate $Price = \beta_0 + \beta_1 Age + \varepsilon$. A portion of the Excel results is as follows:

	Coefficients	Standard Error	t Stat	P-value
Intercept	21187.94	733.42	28.89	1.56E-16
Age	−1208.25	128.95	−9.37	2.41E-08

a. What is the point estimate for β_1? Interpret this value.
b. What is the sample regression equation?
c. Predict the selling price of a 5-year-old sedan.

12. If a firm spends more on advertising, is it likely to increase sales? Data on annual sales (in $100,000s) and advertising expenditures (in $10,000s) were collected for 20 firms in order to estimate the model $Sales = \beta_0 + \beta_1 Advertising + \varepsilon$. A portion of the Excel results is as follows:

	Coefficients	Standard Error	t Stat	p-value
Intercept	−7.42	1.46	−5.09	7.66E-05
Advertising	0.42	0.05	8.70	7.26E-08

a. Is the sign on the slope as expected? Explain.
b. What is the sample regression equation?
c. Predict the sales for a firm that spends $500,000 annually on advertising.

13. FILE The consumption function captures one of the key relationships in economics that was first developed by John Maynard Keynes. It expresses consumption as a function of disposable income, where disposable income is income after taxes. The table below shows a portion of average U.S. annual consumption and disposable income for the years 1985–2006. The entire data set, labeled *Consumption_Function*, can be found on the text website.

	Consumption	Disposable Income
1985	$23,490	$22,887
1986	23,866	23,172
⋮	⋮	⋮
2006	48,398	58,101

Source: The Statistical Abstract of the United States.

a. Use Excel to estimate the model: $Consumption = \beta_0 + \beta_1 Disposable\ Income + \varepsilon$.
b. What is the sample regression equation?
c. In this model the slope coefficient is called the marginal propensity to consume. Interpret its meaning.
d. What is predicted consumption if disposable income is $57,000?

14. FILE The following table lists Major League Baseball's (MLB's) leading pitchers, their earned run average (ERA), and their salary (in millions of dollars) for 2008. The entire data set, labeled *MLB_Pitchers*, can be found on the text website.

	ERA	Salary (in $ millions)
J. Santana	2.53	17.0
C. Lee	2.54	4.0
T. Lincecum	2.62	0.4
C. Sabathia	2.70	11.0
R. Halladay	2.78	10.0
J. Peavy	2.85	6.5
D. Matsuzaka	2.90	8.3
R. Dempster	2.96	7.3
B. Sheets	3.09	12.1
C. Hamels	3.09	0.5

SOURCE: http://www.ESPN.com.

a. Use Excel to estimate the model: Salary $= \beta_0 + \beta_1 ERA + \varepsilon$ and interpret the coefficient of ERA.
b. Use the estimated model to predict salary for each player, given his ERA. For example, use the sample regression equation to predict the salary for J. Santana with ERA = 2.53.
c. Derive the corresponding residuals and explain why the residuals might be so high.

15. FILE In order to answer the following questions, use the data labeled **Happiness_Age** on the text website.
   a. Use Excel to estimate a simple linear regression model with Happiness as the response variable and Age as the explanatory variable.
   b. Use the estimates to predict Happiness when Age equals 25, 50, and 75.
   c. Construct a scatterplot of Happiness against Age. Discuss why your predictions might not be accurate.

16. FILE The accompanying table shows a portion of the grades that 32 students obtained on the midterm and the final examinations in a course in statistics. The entire data set, labeled **Test_Scores**, can be found on the text website.

Midterm	Final
78	86
97	94
⋮	⋮
47	91

   a. Determine the sample regression equation that enables us to predict a student's final examination grade in this course on the basis of his/her midterm grade.
   b. Predict the final examination grade of a student who received an 80 on the midterm examination.

17. FILE The accompanying table shows a portion of a data set that refers to the size of a home (in square feet) and its property taxes owed by the owner (in $) in an affluent suburb 30 miles outside New York City. The entire data set, labeled **Property_Taxes**, can be found on the text website.

Size (in square feet)	Property Taxes (in $)
2449	21928
2479	17339
⋮	⋮
2864	29235

   a. Determine the sample regression equation that enables us to predict property taxes on the basis of the size of the home.
   b. Interpret the slope coefficient.
   c. Predict the property taxes for a 1500-square-foot home.

12.2 The Multiple Linear Regression Model

The simple linear regression model allows us to analyze the linear relationship between one explanatory variable and the response variable. However, by restricting the number of explanatory variables to one, we sometimes reduce the potential usefulness of the model. In Chapter 13, we will discuss how the OLS estimates can be quite misleading when important explanatory variables are excluded. A **multiple linear regression model** allows us to study how the response variable is influenced by two or more explanatory variables. The choices of the explanatory variables are based on economic theory, intuition, and/or prior research. The multiple linear regression model is a straightforward extension of the simple linear regression model.

LO **12.2**

Estimate the multiple linear regression model and interpret the coefficients.

THE MULTIPLE LINEAR REGRESSION MODEL

The multiple linear regression model is defined as

$$y = \beta_0 + \beta_1 x_1 + \beta_2 x_2 + \cdots + \beta_k x_k + \varepsilon,$$

where y is the response variable, $x_1, x_2, \ldots, x_k$ are the k explanatory variables, and ε is the random error term. The coefficients $\beta_0, \beta_1, \ldots, \beta_k$ are the unknown parameters to be estimated.

The difference between the observed and the predicted values of y represents the residual e; that is, $e = y - \hat{y}$.

Determining the Sample Regression Equation

As in the case of the simple linear regression model, we apply the OLS method that minimizes SSE, where $SSE = \Sigma(y_i - \hat{y}_i)^2 = \Sigma e_i^2$.

> The **sample regression equation** for the multiple linear regression model is denoted as
>
> $$\hat{y} = b_0 + b_1x_1 + b_2x_2 + \cdots + b_kx_k,$$
>
> where $b_0, b_1, \ldots, b_k$ are the point estimates of $\beta_0, \beta_1, \ldots, \beta_k$.

For each explanatory variable x_j ($j = 1, \ldots, k$), the corresponding slope coefficient b_j is the point estimate of β_j. We slightly modify the interpretation of the slope coefficients in the context of a multiple linear regression model. Here b_j measures the change in the predicted value of the response variable $\hat{y}$ given a unit increase in the associated explanatory variable x_j, *holding all other explanatory variables constant*. In other words, it represents the partial influence of x_j on $\hat{y}$.

When we used formulas to estimate the simple linear regression model, we found that the calculations were quite cumbersome. As you might imagine, if we were to estimate the multiple linear regression model by hand, the calculations would become even more tedious. Thus, we rely solely on using statistical packages to estimate a multiple linear regression model.

EXAMPLE 12.3 FILE

In the previous section we analyzed how debt payments are influenced by income, ignoring the possible effect of the unemployment rate.

a. Given the data from Table 12.1, estimate the multiple linear regression model with debt payments as the response variable and income and the unemployment rate as the explanatory variables.

b. Interpret the regression coefficients.

c. Predict debt payments if income is \$80,000 and the unemployment rate is 7.5%.

SOLUTION:

a. We will use Excel to estimate the multiple linear regression model, Debt $= \beta_0 + \beta_1$Income $+ \beta_2$Unemployment $+ \varepsilon$. We follow similar steps as we did when we estimated the simple linear regression model.

- Open the data labeled **Debt Payments** found on the text website.

- Choose **Data** > **Data Analysis** > **Regression** from the menu.

- In the *Regression* dialog box, click on the box next to *Input Y Range*, then select the data for Debt. For *Input X Range, simultaneously* select the data for Income and Unemployment. Select *Labels,* since we are using Debt, Income, and Unemployment as headings.

- Click **OK**.

We show the Excel output in Table 12.4.

TABLE 12.4 Regression Results for Example 12.3

Regression Statistics						
Multiple R	0.8676					
R Square	0.7527					
Adjusted R Square	0.7312					
Standard Error	64.6098					
Observations	26					

ANOVA						
	df	SS	MS	F	Significance F	
Regression	2	292170.8	146085.4	34.99536	1.05E-07	
Residual	23	96011.7	4174.4			
Total	25	388182.5				

	Coefficients	Standard Error	t Stat	p-value	Lower 95%	Upper 95%
Intercept	**198.9956**	156.3619	1.2727	0.2159	−124.464	522.455
Income	**10.5122**	1.4765	7.1120	2.98E-07	7.458	13.567
Unemployment	**0.6186**	6.8679	0.0901	0.9290	−13.589	14.826

Using the boldface estimates, $b_0 = 198.9956$, $b_1 = 10.5122$, and $b_2 = 0.6186$, we derive the sample regression equation as

$$\widehat{Debt} = 199.00 + 10.51 Income + 0.62 Unemployment.$$

b. The regression coefficient of Income is 10.51. Since income is measured in $1,000s, the model suggests that if income increases by $1,000, then debt payments are predicted to increase by $10.51, holding the unemployment rate constant. Similarly, the regression coefficient of Unemployment is 0.62, implying that a one percentage point increase in the unemployment rate leads to a predicted increase in debt payments of $0.62, holding income constant. It seems that the predicted impact of Unemployment, with Income held constant, is rather small. In fact, the influence of the unemployment rate is not even statistically significant at any reasonable level; we will discuss such tests of significance shortly.

c. If income is $80,000 and the unemployment rate is 7.5%, predicted debt payments are

$$\widehat{Debt} = 199.00 + 10.51(80) + 0.62(7.5) = \$1,044.45.$$

EXERCISES 12.2

Mechanics

18. In a multiple regression, the following sample regression equation is obtained:

$$\hat{y} = 152 + 12.9x_1 + 2.7x_2.$$

a. Predict y if x_1 equals 20 and x_2 equals 35.

b. Interpret the slope coefficient of x_1.

19. In a multiple regression, the following sample regression equation is obtained:

$$\hat{y} = -8 + 2.6x_1 - 47.2x_2.$$

a. Predict y if x_1 equals 40 and x_2 equals −10.

b. Interpret the slope coefficient of x_2.

20. Thirty observations were used to estimate $y = \beta_0 + \beta_1 x_1 + \beta_2 x_2 + \varepsilon$. A portion of the Excel results is as follows:

	Coefficients	Standard Error	t Stat	p-value
Intercept	21.97	2.98	7.37	6.31E-08
x_1	30.00	2.23	13.44	1.75E-13
x_2	−1.88	0.27	−6.96	1.75E-07

a. What is the point estimate for β_1? Interpret this value.
b. What is the sample regression equation?
c. If $x_1 = 30$ and $x_2 = 20$, what is $\hat{y}$?

21. Forty observations were used to estimate $y = \beta_0 + \beta_1 x_1 + \beta_2 x_2 + \varepsilon$. A portion of the regression results is shown in the following table.

	Coefficients	Standard Error	t Stat	p-value
Intercept	13.83	2.42	5.71	1.56E-06
x_1	-2.53	0.15	-16.87	5.84E-19
x_2	0.29	0.06	4.83	2.38E-05

a. What is the point estimate for β_1? Interpret this value.
b. What is the sample regression equation?
c. What is the predicted value for y if $x_1 = -9$ and $x_2 = 25$.

Applications

22. On the first day of class, an economics professor administers a test to gauge the math preparedness of her students. She believes that the performance on this math test and the number of hours studied per week on the course are the primary factors that predict a student's score on the final exam. Using data from her class of 60 students, she estimates Final $= \beta_0 + \beta_1$Math $+ \beta_2$Hours $+\varepsilon$. A portion of the regression results is shown in the following table.

	Coefficients	Standard Error	t Stat	p-value
Intercept	40.55	3.37	12.03	2.83E-17
Math	0.25	0.04	6.06	1.14E-07
Hours	4.85	0.57	8.53	9.06E-12

a. What is the slope coefficient of Hours?
b. What is the sample regression equation?
c. What is the predicted final exam score for a student who has a math score of 70 and studies 4 hours per week?

23. Using data from 50 workers, a researcher estimates Wage $= \beta_0 + \beta_1$ Education $+ \beta_2$Experience $+ \beta_3$Age $+ \varepsilon$, where Wage is the hourly wage rate and Education, Experience, and Age are the years of higher education, the years of experience, and the age of the worker, respectively. A portion of the regression results is shown in the following table.

	Coefficients	Standard Error	t Stat	p-value
Intercept	7.87	4.09	1.93	0.0603
Education	1.44	0.34	4.24	0.0001
Experience	0.45	0.14	3.16	0.0028
Age	-0.01	0.08	-0.14	0.8920

a. Interpret the point estimates for β_1 and β_2.
b. What is the sample regression equation?
c. Predict the hourly wage rate for a 30-year-old worker with 4 years of higher education and 3 years of experience.

24. Osteoporosis is a degenerative disease that primarily affects women over the age of 60. A research analyst wants to

forecast sales of StrongBones, a prescription drug for treating this debilitating disease. She uses the model Sales $= \beta_0 + \beta_1$Population $+ \beta_2$Income $+ \varepsilon$, where Sales refers to the sales of StrongBones ($ millions), Population is the number of women over the age of 60 (in millions), and Income is the average income of women over the age of 60 ($1,000s). She collects data on 38 cities across the United States and obtains the following relevant regression results:

	Coefficients	Standard Error	t Stat	p-value
Intercept	10.35	4.02	2.57	0.0199
Population	8.47	2.71	3.12	0.0062
Income	7.62	6.63	1.15	0.2661

a. What is the sample regression equation?
b. Interpret the slope coefficients.
c. Predict sales if a city has 1.5 million women over the age of 60 and their average income is $44,000.

25. A sociologist believes that the crime rate in an area is significantly influenced by the area's poverty rate and median income. Specifically, she hypothesizes crime will increase with poverty and decrease with income. She collects data on the crime rate (crimes per 100,000 residents), the poverty rate (in %), and the median income (in $1,000s) from 41 New England cities. A portion of the regression results is shown in the following table.

	Coefficients	Standard Error	t Stat	p-value
Intercept	-301.62	549.71	-0.55	0.5864
Poverty	53.16	14.22	3.74	0.0006
Income	4.95	8.26	0.60	0.5526

a. Are the signs as expected on the slope coefficients?
b. Interpret the slope coefficient for Poverty.
c. Predict the crime rate in an area with a poverty rate of 20% and a median income of $50,000.

26. FILE A realtor in Arlington, Massachusetts, is analyzing the relationship between the sale price of a home (Price), its square footage (Sqft), the number of bedrooms (Beds), and the number of bathrooms (Baths). She collects data on 36 recent sales in Arlington in the first quarter of 2009 for the analysis. A portion of the data is shown in the accompanying table; the entire data set, labeled **Arlington_Homes**, can be found on the text website.

Price	Sqft	Beds	Baths
840000	2768	4	3.5
822000	2500	4	2.5
⋮	⋮	⋮	⋮
307500	850	1	1

Source: http://Newenglandmoves.com.

a. Estimate the model Price $= \beta_0 + \beta_1$Sqft $+ \beta_2$Beds $+ \beta_3$Baths $+ \varepsilon$.
b. Interpret the slope coefficients.
c. Predict the price of a 2,500-square-foot home with three bedrooms and two bathrooms.

27. **FILE** Education reform is one of the most hotly debated subjects on both state and national policy makers' list of socioeconomic topics. Consider a linear regression model that relates school expenditures and family background to student performance in Massachusetts using 224 school districts. The response variable is the mean score on the MCAS (Massachusetts Comprehensive Assessment System) exam given in May 1998 to 10th-graders. Four explanatory variables are used: (1) STR is the student-to-teacher ratio, (2) TSAL is the average teacher's salary, (3) INC is the median household income, and (4) SGL is the percentage of single family households. A portion of the data is shown in the accompanying table; the entire data set, labeled **MCAS**, can be found on the text website.

Score	STR (%)	TSAL (in $1,000)	INC (in $1,000)	SGL (%)
227.00	19.00	44.01	48.89	4.70
230.67	17.90	40.17	43.91	4.60
⋮	⋮	⋮	⋮	⋮
230.67	19.20	44.79	47.64	5.10

Source: Massachusetts Department of Education and the Census of Population and Housing.

a. For each explanatory variable, discuss whether it is likely to have a positive or negative causal effect on Score.
b. Find the sample regression equation. Are the signs of the slope coefficients as expected?
c. What is the predicted score if STR = 18, TSAL = 50, INC = 60, SGL = 5?
d. What is the predicted score if everything else is the same as in part c except INC = 80?

28. **FILE** American football is the highest paying sport on a per-game basis. The quarterback, considered the most important player on the team, is appropriately compensated. A sports statistician wants to use 2009 data to estimate a multiple linear regression model that links the quarterback's salary with his pass completion percentage (PCT), total touchdowns scored (TD), and his age. A portion of the data is shown in the accompanying table; the entire data set, labeled **Quarterback_Salaries**, can be found on the text website.

Name	Salary (in $ millions)	PCT	TD	Age
Philip Rivers	25.5566	65.2	28	27
Jay Cutler	22.0441	60.5	27	26
⋮	⋮	⋮	⋮	⋮
Tony Romo	0.6260	63.1	26	29

Source: USA Today database for salaries; http://NFL.com for other data.

a. Estimate the model defined as Salary = $\beta_0 + \beta_1$PCT + β_2TD + β_3Age + ε.
b. Are you surprised by the estimated coefficients?
c. Drew Brees earned 12.9895 million dollars in 2009. According to the model, what is his predicted salary given his PCT, TD, and age of 70.6, 34, and 30, respectively?
d. Tom Brady earned 8.0073 million dollars in 2009. According to the model, what is his predicted salary given his PCT, TD, and age of 65.7, 28, and 32, respectively?
e. Compute and interpret the residual salary for Drew Brees and Tom Brady.

29. **FILE** The accompanying table shows a portion of data consisting of the selling price, the age, and the mileage for 20 used sedans. The entire data set, labeled **Car_Prices**, can be found on the text website.

Selling Price	Age	Mileage
13590	6	61485
13775	6	54344
⋮	⋮	⋮
11988	8	42408

a. Determine the sample regression equation that enables us to predict the price of a sedan on the basis of its age and mileage.
b. Interpret the slope coefficient of Age.
c. Predict the selling price of a five-year-old sedan with 65,000 miles.

30. **FILE** The accompanying table shows a portion of data consisting of the rent, the number of bedrooms, the number of bathrooms, and the square footage for 40 apartments in the college town of Ann Arbor, Michigan. The entire data set, labeled **AnnArbor_Rental**, can be found on the text website.

Rent	Bed	Bath	Sqft
645	1	1	500
675	1	1	648
⋮	⋮	⋮	⋮
2400	3	2.5	2700

a. Determine the sample regression equation that enables us to predict the rent of an Ann Arbor apartment on the basis of the number of bedrooms, the number of bathrooms, and the square footage.
b. Interpret the slope coefficient of Bath.
c. Predict the rent for a 1500-square-foot apartment with 2 bedrooms and 1 bathroom.

12.3 Goodness-of-Fit Measures

By simply observing the sample regression equation, we cannot assess how well the explanatory variables explain the variability of the response variable. However, several objective "goodness-of-fit" measures do exist that summarize how well the sample regression equation fits the data. If all the observations lie on the sample regression equation, then we have a perfect fit. Since that almost never happens, we evaluate the models on a relative basis.

We will study three goodness-of-fit measures: the standard error of the estimate, the coefficient of determination, and the adjusted coefficient of determination. The relevant formulas used to derive these measures are applicable for both simple and multiple linear regression models, as long as the model includes the intercept term.

In the first two sections of this chapter, we were interested in predicting consumer debt payments. We analyzed two models. Let Model 1 represent the simple linear regression model, Debt = $\beta_0 + \beta_1$Income + ε, and Model 2 represent the multiple linear regression model, Debt = $\beta_0 + \beta_1$Income + β_2Unemployment + ε. (For ease of exposition, we use the same notation to refer to the coefficients in Models 1 and 2. We note, however, that these coefficients and their estimates may have a different meaning depending on which model we are referencing.)

If you had to choose one of these models to predict debt payments, which model would you choose? It may be that by using more explanatory variables, you can better describe the response variable. However, for a given sample, more is not always better. In order to select the preferred model, we need to examine goodness-of-fit measures.

The Standard Error of the Estimate

LO 12.3

Calculate and interpret the standard error of the estimate.

We first describe goodness-of-fit measures in the context of a simple linear regression model. Figure 12.4 reproduces the scatterplot of debt payments against income, as well as the sample regression line. Recall that the residual e represents the difference between an observed value and the predicted value of the response variable, that is, $e = y - \hat{y}$. If all the data points had fallen on the line, then each residual would be zero; in other words, there would be no dispersion between the observed and the predicted values. Since in practice we rarely, if ever, obtain this result, we evaluate models on the basis of the relative magnitude of the residuals. The sample regression equation provides a good fit when the dispersion of the residuals is relatively small.

FIGURE 12.4 Scatterplot of debt payments y against income x

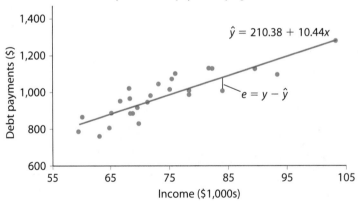

A numerical measure that gauges dispersion from the sample regression equation is the sample variance of the residual, denoted s_e^2. We generally report the standard deviation of the residual, denoted s_e, more commonly referred to as the **standard error of the estimate**. The variance s_e^2 is defined as the average squared difference between y_i and $\hat{y}_i$. The numerator of the formula is the sum of squares due to error, $SSE = \Sigma(y_i - \hat{y}_i)^2 = \Sigma e_i^2$. Dividing SSE by its respective degrees of freedom $n - k - 1$ yields s_e^2, also referred to as the **mean square due to error**, or simply the **mean square error MSE**. Recall that k denotes the number of explanatory variables in the linear regression model; thus, for a simple linear regression model, k equals one. The standard error of the estimate s_e is the positive square root of s_e^2. The less the dispersion, the smaller the s_e, which implies a better fit to the model.

THE STANDARD ERROR OF THE ESTIMATE

The **standard error of the estimate** s_e is calculated as

$$s_e = \sqrt{s_e^2} = \sqrt{MSE} = \sqrt{\frac{SSE}{n-k-1}} = \sqrt{\frac{\Sigma e_i^2}{n-k-1}}.$$

Theoretically, s_e can assume any value between zero and infinity, $0 \le s_e < \infty$. The closer s_e is to zero, the better the model fits.

We would like to point out that for a given sample size n, increasing the number k of the explanatory variables reduces both the numerator (SSE), as well as the denominator ($n-k-1$) in the formula for s_e. The net effect, shown by the value of s_e, allows us to determine if the added explanatory variables improve the usefulness of the model.

EXAMPLE 12.4

Consider the sample data in Table 12.1 and the regression output for Model 1 in Table 12.3. Use the sample regression equation, $\widehat{Debt} = 210.30 + 10.44$ Income, to calculate the standard error of the estimate s_e.

SOLUTION: First, we calculate the variance of the residual s_e^2. Let y and x denote Debt and Income, respectively. The first two columns of Table 12.5 show the values of these variables. The third column shows the predicted values $\hat{y}$ and the fourth column shows the squared residuals, $e^2 = (y-\hat{y})^2$. The sum of the squared residuals, shown in the last cell of the last column, is the familiar SSE and is the numerator in the formula for s_e^2.

TABLE 12.5 Calculations for Example 12.4

y	x	$\hat{y} = 210.30 + 10.44x$	$e^2 = (y-\hat{y})^2$
1285	103.50	$210.30 + 10.44 \times 103.50 = 1290.84$	$(1285 - 1290.84)^2 = 34.11$
1135	81.70	$210.30 + 10.44 \times 81.70 = 1063.25$	$(1135 - 1063.25)^2 = 5148.35$
$\vdots$	$\vdots$	$\vdots$	$\vdots$
763	63.00	$210.30 + 10.44 \times 63.00 = 868.02$	$(763 - 868.02)^2 = 11029.20$
			$\Sigma(y_i - \hat{y}_i)^2 = \Sigma e_i^2 = 96045.72$

Using $SSE = \Sigma e_i^2 = 96{,}045.72$, we determine the variance of the residual s_e^2 as

$$s_e^2 = MSE = \frac{\Sigma e_i^2}{n-k-1} = \frac{96{,}045.72}{26-1-1} = 4{,}001.91.$$

Taking the square root of the variance, we obtain

$$s_e = \sqrt{s_e^2} = \sqrt{4{,}001.91} = 63.26.$$

The standard error of the estimate is measured in the same units of measurement as the response variable. Since debt payments are in dollars, we report s_e as $\$63.26$.

Most of the time we rely on statistical software packages to report s_e. (If s_e is not explicitly given, other statistics like SSE are generally provided, which then greatly facilitate the calculation of s_e.) Excel reports the value for s_e in the regression output section entitled *Regression Statistics*. It is simply referred to as Standard Error. In column 2 of Table 12.6, we report the Excel regression statistics for Model 1. Note that $s_e = 63.26$ is the same as the one calculated above.

TABLE 12.6 Regression Statistics for Model 1 and Model 2

	Model 1	Model 2
Multiple R	0.8675	0.8676
R Square	0.7526	0.7527
Adjusted R Square	0.7423	0.7312
Standard Error	63.26	64.61
Observations	26	26
Regression Equation	$\hat{y} = 210.30 + 10.44x$	$\hat{y} = 199 + 10.51x_1 + 0.62x_2$

Our objective in adding another explanatory variable to the linear regression model is to increase the model's usefulness. In Model 2 we use income x_1 and the unemployment rate x_2 to explain debt payments y. If Model 2 is an improvement over Model 1, then we would expect it to have a smaller standard error of the estimate. Table 12.6 also shows the relevant regression statistics for Model 2. We note that the standard error of the estimate for Model 2, $s_e = \$64.61$, is actually greater than that for Model 1 ($64.61 > 63.26$). In other words, there is less dispersion between the observed values of debt payments and the predicted values of debt payments when we include only one explanatory variable in the model. So far, this suggests that Model 1 provides a better fit for the sample data. In general, we use the standard error of the estimate in conjunction with other measures to judge the overall usefulness of a model.

LO **12.4**

Calculate and interpret the coefficient of determination R^2.

The Coefficient of Determination R^2

In Example 12.4 we calculated $s_e = \$63.26$. It is difficult to interpret this value in isolation. The fact that a value closer to 0 implies a better fit does not allow us to conclude whether or not a value of $63.26 is close to zero. The standard error of the estimate is a useful goodness-of-fit measure when we are comparing various models—the model with the smaller s_e provides the better relative fit. However, it proves less useful when we are assessing a single model. One reason for this is due to the fact that s_e has no predefined upper limit, that is, $0 \le s_e < \infty$. The **coefficient of determination**, commonly referred to as R^2, is another goodness-of-fit measure that is easier to interpret than the standard error of the estimate. As we will see shortly, R^2 has both lower and upper bounds that make its interpretation quite a bit more intuitive.

Like the standard error of the estimate, the coefficient of determination evaluates how well the sample regression equation fits the data. In particular, R^2 quantifies the sample variability in the response variable y that is explained by changes in the explanatory variable(s), that is, by the sample regression equation. It is computed as the ratio of the explained variation of the response variable to its total variation. We generally convert this ratio into a percent by multiplying it by 100. For example, if $R^2 = 0.72$, we say that 72% of the variation in the response variable is explained by the sample regression equation. Other factors, which have not been included in the model, account for the remaining 28% of the sample variation.

We use analysis of variance (ANOVA), in the context of the linear regression model, to derive R^2. We denote the **total variation** in y as $\Sigma(y_i - \bar{y})^2$, which is the numerator in the formula for the variance of y. This value, called the **total sum of squares SST**, can be broken down into two components: **explained** variation and **unexplained** variation. Figure 12.5 illustrates the decomposition of the total variation in y into its two components.

FIGURE 12.5 Total, explained, and unexplained variations in y

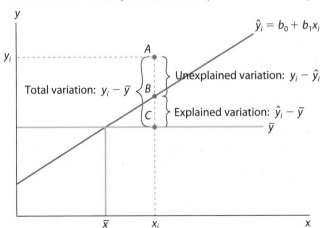

For ease of exposition, we show a scatterplot with all the points removed except one (point A). Point A refers to the observation (x_i, y_i). The blue line represents the estimated regression equation based on the entire sample data; the horizontal and vertical green lines represent the sample means $\bar{y}$ and $\bar{x}$, respectively. The vertical distance (difference) between the data point A and $\bar{y}$ (point C) is the total variation $y_i - \bar{y}$ (distance AC). For each data point, we square these differences and then find their sum—this amounts to $SST = \Sigma(y_i - \bar{y})^2$.

Now, we focus on the difference between the predicted value of the data point $\hat{y}_i$ (point B) and $\bar{y}$. This difference is the explained variation in y (distance BC). Explained variation indicates that the positive difference between $\hat{y}_i$ and $\bar{y}$ occurs because y rises with x and in this case x is above its mean. Squaring all such differences and summing them yields the **sum of squares due to regression, SSR**, where $SSR = \Sigma(\hat{y}_i - \bar{y})^2$.

The difference between the particular observation and its predicted value (distance AB) is the unexplained variation in y. This is the portion of the variation in y that remains unexplained; it is the variation due to random error or chance. Squaring all such differences and summing them yields the familiar sum of squares due to error, $SSE = \Sigma(y_i - \hat{y}_i)^2$.

Thus, the total variation in y can be decomposed into explained and unexplained variation as follows:

$$SST = SSR + SSE.$$

Dividing both sides by SST and rearranging yields:

$$\frac{SSR}{SST} = 1 - \frac{SSE}{SST}.$$

The sides of the above equation show two equivalent formulas for the coefficient of determination R^2. The value of R^2 falls between zero and one, $0 \le R^2 \le 1$. The closer R^2 is to one, the stronger the fit; the closer it is to zero, the weaker the fit.

THE COEFFICIENT OF DETERMINATION R^2

The coefficient of determination R^2 is the proportion of the variation in the response variable that is explained by the sample regression equation. We compute R^2 as

$$R^2 = \frac{SSR}{SST}, \text{ or equivalently, } R^2 = 1 - \frac{SSE}{SST},$$

where $SSR = \Sigma(\hat{y} - \bar{y})^2$, $SSE = \Sigma(y_i - \hat{y}_i)^2$, and $SST = \Sigma(y_i - \bar{y})^2$.

The value of R^2 falls between zero and one; the closer the value is to one, the better the fit.

Most statistical packages, including Excel, provide the calculations for SSR, SSE, and SST in an ANOVA table. The general format of the ANOVA table that accompanies regression output is shown in Table 12.7. We will discuss the values for MSR, MSE, $F_{(df_1, df_2)}$, and the p-value for $F_{(df_1, df_2)}$ in the next section.

TABLE 12.7 General Format of ANOVA Table That Accompanies Regression Results

ANOVA					
	df	SS	MS	F	Significance F
Regression	k	SSR	MSR	$F_{(df_1, df_2)} = \frac{MSR}{MSE}$	p-value for $F_{(df_1, df_2)}$
Residual	$n - k - 1$	SSE	MSE		
Total	$n - 1$	SST			

EXAMPLE 12.5

Calculate and interpret the coefficient of determination R^2 given the sample data in Table 12.1 and the sample regression equation for Model 1: $\widehat{Debt} = 210.30 + 10.44Income$.

SOLUTION: In Example 12.4 we calculated SSE for Model 1 as 96,045.72. Using $R^2 = 1 - SSE/SST$, the only missing part is SST. Given $\bar{y} = 983.46$, we calculate SST as

$$\Sigma(y_i - \bar{y})^2 = (1285 - 983.46)^2 + (1135 - 983.46)^2 + \cdots + (763 - 983.46)^2$$
$$= 388{,}182.46.$$

Therefore,

$$R^2 = 1 - \frac{SSE}{SST} = 1 - \frac{96{,}045.72}{388{,}182.46} = 0.7526.$$

Note that this value matches the Excel estimate shown in Table 12.6. The coefficient of determination R^2 shows that 75.26% of the sample variation in debt payments is explained by changes in income.

Recall that the standard error of the estimate for Model 1 ($s_e = 63.26$) was smaller than that for Model 2 ($s_e = 64.61$), suggesting that Model 1 provides a better fit. Since the coefficient of determination for Model 2 ($R^2 = 0.7527$) is slightly higher than that of Model 1 ($R^2 = 0.7526$), one may think that Model 2 explains more of the variation in debt payments. How do we resolve these apparent conflicting results? It turns out that we cannot use R^2 for model comparison when the competing models do not include the same number of explanatory variables. This occurs because R^2 never decreases as we add more explanatory variables to the model. A popular model selection method in such situations is to choose a model that has the highest adjusted R^2 value.

LO **12.5**

Differentiate between R^2 and adjusted R^2.

The Adjusted R^2

Since R^2 never decreases as we add more explanatory variables to the linear regression model, it is possible to increase its value unintentionally by including a group of explanatory variables that may have no economic or intuitive foundation in the linear regression model. This is true especially when the number of explanatory variables k is large relative to the sample size n. In order to avoid the possibility of R^2 creating a false impression, virtually all software packages include **adjusted R^2**. Unlike R^2, adjusted R^2 explicitly accounts for the sample size n and the number of explanatory variables k. It is common to use adjusted R^2 for model selection because it imposes a penalty for any additional explanatory variable that is included in the analysis.

ADJUSTED R^2

The adjusted coefficient of determination, calculated as adjusted $R^2 = 1 - (1 - R^2)\left(\frac{n-1}{n-k-1}\right)$, is used to compare competing linear regression models with different numbers of explanatory variables; the higher the adjusted R^2, the better the model.

If SSE is substantially greater than zero and k is large compared to n, then adjusted R^2 will differ substantially from R^2. Adjusted R^2 may be negative, if the correlation between the response variable and the explanatory variables is sufficiently low.

We would also like to point out that both the standard error of the estimate and the adjusted R^2 are useful for comparing the linear regression models with different numbers of explanatory variables. Adjusted R^2, however, is the more commonly used criterion for model selection.

EXAMPLE 12.6

Using the regression statistics from Table 12.6, use the value of the adjusted R^2 for model comparison.

SOLUTION: We note from Table 12.6 that Model 1 has an adjusted R^2 of 0.7423, whereas Model 2's value is 0.7312. Therefore, given its higher adjusted R^2, we choose Model 1 to predict debt payments.

EXERCISES 12.3

Mechanics

31. In a simple linear regression based on 25 observations, the following intermediate data are given: $\Sigma(y_i - \hat{y})^2 = 1250$ and $\Sigma(y_i - \bar{y})^2 = 1500$.
    a. Calculate s_e^2 and s_e.
    b. Calculate R^2.

32. In a simple linear regression based on 30 observations, it is found that $SSE = 2540$ and $SST = 13{,}870$.
    a. Calculate s_e^2 and s_e.
    b. Calculate R^2.

33. In a multiple regression with two explanatory variables, the following intermediate data are given: $n = 50$, $\Sigma(y_i - \hat{y})^2 = 35$, and $\Sigma(y_i - \bar{y})^2 = 90$.
    a. Calculate the standard error of the estimate.
    b. Calculate the coefficient of determination R^2.

34. In a multiple regression with four explanatory variables and 100 observations, it is found that $SSR = 4.75$ and $SST = 7.62$.
    a. Calculate the standard error of the estimate.
    b. Calculate the coefficient of determination R^2.
    c. Calculate adjusted R^2.

35. The following ANOVA table was obtained when estimating a simple linear regression model.

ANOVA	df	SS	MS	F	Significance F
Regression	1	81.58	81.58	366.50	1.27E-17
Residual	28	6.23	0.22		
Total	29	87.81			

    a. Calculate the standard error of the estimate.
    b. Calculate the coefficient of determination. Interpret this value.

36. The following ANOVA table was obtained when estimating a simple linear regression model.

ANOVA	df	SS	MS	F	Significance F
Regression	1	75.92	75.92	178.76	1.12E-13
Residual	28	11.89	0.42		
Total	29	87.81			

    a. Calculate s_e.
    b. Calculate and interpret R^2.

37. The following ANOVA table was obtained when estimating a multiple linear regression model.

ANOVA	df	SS	MS	F	Significance F
Regression	2	161478.4	80739.19	11.5854	0.0002
Residual	27	188163.9	6969.03		
Total	29	349642.2			

    a. Calculate the standard error of the estimate.
    b. Calculate and interpret the coefficient of determination.
    c. Calculate the adjusted R^2.

38. The following ANOVA table was obtained when estimating a multiple regression model.

ANOVA	df	SS	MS	F	Significance F
Regression	2	188246.8	94123.4	35.2	9.04E-07
Residual	17	45457.32	2673.96		
Total	19	233704.1			

    a. Calculate the standard error of the estimate.
    b. Calculate and interpret the coefficient of determination.
    c. Calculate the adjusted R^2.

Applications

39. When estimating the selling price of a used sedan as a function of its age using the model Price $= \beta_0 + \beta_1 \text{Age} + \varepsilon$, a researcher gets the following ANOVA results:

ANOVA	df	SS	MS	F	Significance F
Regression	1	199.93	199.93	87.80	2.41E-08
Residual	18	40.99	2.28		
Total	19	240.92			

   a. How many observations did the researcher use?

   b. What is the standard error of the estimate?

   c. Calculate and interpret the coefficient of determination.

40. When estimating the sales of a firm as a function of its advertising expenditures using the model Sales $= \beta_0 + \beta_1 \text{Advertising} + \varepsilon$, an analyst obtains the following ANOVA results:

ANOVA	df	SS	MS	F	Significance F
Regression	1	199.93	199.93	87.80	2.41E-08
Residual	18	40.99	2.28		
Total	19	240.92			

   a. What proportion of the variability in sales is explained by advertising expenditures?

   b. What proportion of the variability in sales is unexplained by advertising expenditures?

41. The director of college admissions at a local university is trying to determine whether a student's high school GPA or SAT score is a better predictor of the student's subsequent college GPA. She formulates two models:

Model 1. College GPA $= \beta_0 + \beta_1 \text{High School GPA} + \varepsilon$

Model 2. College GPA $= \beta_0 + \beta_1 \text{SAT Score} + \varepsilon$

She estimates these models using data from a sample of 10 recent college graduates. A portion of the results are as follows:

ANOVA Results for Model 1					
	df	SS	MS	F	Significance F
Regression	1	1.4415	1.4415	11.5032	0.0095
Residual	8	1.0025	0.1253		
Total	9	2.4440			

ANOVA Results for Model 2					
	df	SS	MS	F	Significance F
Regression	1	1.0699	1.0699	6.2288	0.0372
Residual	8	1.3741	0.1718		
Total	9	2.4440			

   a. Calculate the standard error of the estimate for Model 1 and Model 2.

   b. Calculate the coefficient of determination for Model 1 and Model 2.

   c. Given these two measures, which model is a better fit? Explain.

42. For a sample of 41 New England cities, a sociologist studies the crime rate in each city (crimes per 100,000 residents) as a function of its poverty rate (in %) and its median income (in $1,000s). A portion of the regression results is shown in the following table.

ANOVA	df	SS	MS	F	Significance F
Regression	2	3549788	1774894	16.12513	8.5E-06
Residual	38	4182663	110070.1		
Total	40	7732451			

   a. Calculate the standard error of the estimate.

   b. What proportion of the variability in crime rate is explained by the variability in the explanatory variables? What proportion is unexplained?

43. A financial analyst uses the following model to estimate a firm's stock return: Return $= \beta_0 + \beta_1 \text{P/E} + \beta_2 \text{P/S} + \varepsilon$, where P/E is a firm's price-to-earnings ratio and P/S is a firm's price-to-sales ratio. A portion of the regression results is shown in the following table.

ANOVA	df	SS	MS	F	Significance F
Regression	2	918.746	459.373	2.817	0.0774
Residual	27	4402.786	163.066		
Total	29	5321.532			

   a. Calculate the standard error of the estimate.

   b. Calculate and interpret the coefficient of determination.

   c. Calculate the corresponding adjusted R^2.

44. **FILE** (Use Excel) Access the data **Test_Scores** from the text website.

   a. Estimate a student's final grade as a function of his/her midterm grade.

   b. Find the standard error of the estimate.

   c. Find and interpret the coefficient of determination.

45. **FILE** (Use Excel) Access the data **Property_Taxes** from the text website.

   a. Estimate a home's property taxes as a linear function of the size of the home (measured by its square footage).

   b. What proportion of the variability in property taxes is explained by the home's size?

   c. What proportion of the variability in property taxes is unexplained by the home's size?

46. **FILE** Is it defense or offense that wins football games? Consider the following data, which include a team's winning record (Win), the average number of yards gained, and the average number of yards allowed during the 2009 NFL season. The complete data, labeled **Football**, can be found on the text website.

Team	Win (%)	Yards Gained	Yards Allowed
Arizona Cardinals	62.50	344.40	346.40
Atlanta Falcons	56.30	340.40	348.90
⋮	⋮	⋮	⋮
Washington Redskins	25.00	312.50	319.70

Source: NFL website.

a.   Compare two simple linear regression models, where Model 1 predicts winning percentage based on Yards Gained and Model 2 uses Yards Allowed.

b.   Estimate a multiple linear regression model, Model 3, that applies both Yards Gained and Yards Allowed to forecast winning percentage. Is this model an improvement over the other two models? Explain.

47. [FILE] Executive compensation has risen dramatically beyond the rising levels of an average worker's wage over the years. This has been a hot topic for discussion, especially with the crisis in the financial sector and the controversy over the federal bailout. The government is even considering a cap on high-flying salaries for executives (*New York Times*, February 9, 2009). Consider the following data, which link total compensation of the 455 highest-paid CEOs in 2006 with two performance measures (industry-adjusted return on assets (Adj ROA) and industry-adjusted stock return (Adj Stock Return)) and the firm's size (Total Assets). The entire data set, labeled **Executive_Compensation**, can be found on the text website.

Compensation (in $ millions)	Adj ROA	Adj Stock Return	Total Assets (in $ millions)
16.58	2.53	−0.15	20,917.5
26.92	1.27	0.57	32,659.5
⋮	⋮	⋮	⋮
2.3	0.45	0.75	44,875.0

Source: SEC website and Compustat.

a.   Estimate three simple linear regression models that use Compensation as the response variable with Adj ROA, Adj Stock Return, or Total Assets as the explanatory variable. Which model do you select? Explain.

b.   Estimate multiple linear regression models that use various combinations of two, or all three explanatory variables. Which model do you select? Explain.

12.4 Tests of Significance

In this section, we continue our assessment of the linear regression model by turning our attention to hypothesis tests about the unknown parameters (coefficients) $\beta_0, \beta_1, \ldots, \beta_k$. In particular, we test the slope coefficients both individually and jointly in order to determine whether there is evidence of a linear relationship between the response and the explanatory variables. We must point out that these tests require that the ordinary least squares (OLS) estimators b_j of β_j be normally distributed. This condition is satisfied if the random error ε of the model has a normal distribution. If we cannot assume that ε is normal, then the tests are valid only for large sample sizes. We will discuss the underlying assumptions of the linear regression models in Chapter 13.

Tests of Individual Significance

LO **12.6**

Conduct tests of individual significance.

Consider the following simple linear regression model, which links the response variable y with the explanatory variable x:

$$y = \beta_0 + \beta_1 x + \varepsilon.$$

If the slope coefficient β_1 equals zero, then x basically drops out of the above equation, implying that x does not influence y. In other words, if β_1 equals zero, then there is no linear relationship between x and y. Conversely, if β_1 does not equal zero, then x influences y. We will see shortly that we can easily extend this logic to the multiple linear regression model where the response variable y is linked with k explanatory variables $x_1, x_2, \ldots, x_k$.

Following the hypothesis testing methodology introduced in earlier chapters, we want to test whether the population slope coefficient β_1 is different from, greater than, or less than β_{10} where β_{10} is the hypothesized value of β_1. That is, the competing hypotheses take one of the following forms:

Two-Tailed Test	Right-Tailed Test	Left-Tailed Test
$H_0: \beta_1 = \beta_{10}$	$H_0: \beta_1 \le \beta_{10}$	$H_0: \beta_1 \ge \beta_{10}$
$H_A: \beta_1 \ne \beta_{10}$	$H_A: \beta_1 > \beta_{10}$	$H_A: \beta_1 < \beta_{10}$

When testing whether x significantly influences y, we set $\beta_{10} = 0$ and specify a two-tailed test as $H_0: \beta_1 = 0$ and $H_A: \beta_1 \ne 0$. We could easily specify one-tailed competing hypotheses for a positive linear relationship ($H_0: \beta_1 \le 0$ and $H_A: \beta_1 > 0$) or a negative linear relationship ($H_0: \beta_1 \ge 0$ and $H_A: \beta_1 < 0$).

Although tests of significance are commonly based on $\beta_{10} = 0$, in some situations we might wish to determine whether the slope coefficient differs from a nonzero value. For instance, if we are analyzing the relationship between a student's exam score on the basis of hours studied, we may want to determine if an extra hour of review before the exam will increase a student's score by more than 5 points. Here, we formulate the hypotheses as $H_0: \beta_1 \leq 5$ and $H_A: \beta_1 > 5$, where $\beta_{10} = 5$.

More generally, we use the above logic for specifying the competing hypothesis in a multiple linear regression model with k explanatory variables. For example, the hypotheses for a two-tailed test of significance for an explanatory variable x_j, where $j = 1, 2, \ldots, k$, are specified as $H_0: \beta_j = \beta_{j0}$ and $H_A: \beta_j \neq \beta_{j0}$, where β_{j0} is the hypothesized value of β_j. Finally, although in most applications we are interested in conducting hypothesis tests on the slope coefficient(s), there are instances where we may also be interested in testing the intercept β_0. The testing framework for the intercept remains the same; that is, if we want to test whether the intercept differs from zero, we specify the competing hypotheses as $H_0: \beta_0 = 0$ and $H_A: \beta_0 \neq 0$.

As in all hypothesis tests, the next essential piece of information is how we define the test statistic for the simple as well as the multiple linear regression models.

TEST STATISTIC FOR THE TEST OF INDIVIDUAL SIGNIFICANCE

The test statistic for a **test of individual significance** is assumed to follow the t_{df} distribution with $df = n - k - 1$ and its value is

$$t_{df} = \frac{b_j - \beta_{j0}}{se(b_j)},$$

where n is the sample size, k is the number of explanatory variables, b_j is the point estimate for β_j, $se(b_j)$ is the estimated standard error of the OLS estimator b_j, and β_{j0} is the hypothesized value of β_j. If $\beta_{j0} = 0$, the value of the test statistic reduces to $t_{df} = \frac{b_j}{se(b_j)}$.

EXAMPLE 12.7

Let's revisit Model 1, Debt $= \beta_0 + \beta_1$Income $+ \varepsilon$, estimated with the sample data in Table 12.1. We reproduce a portion of the regression results in Table 12.8. Conduct a hypothesis test to determine whether Income influences Debt at the 5% significance level.

TABLE 12.8 Portion of Regression Results for Model 1: Debt $= \beta_0 + \beta_1$Income $+ \varepsilon$

	Coefficients	Standard Error	t Stat	p-value	Lower 95%	Upper 95%
Intercept	10.2977	91.3387	2.3024	0.0303	21.7838	398.8116
Income	10.4411	1.2220	8.5440	9.6603E-09	7.9189	12.9633

SOLUTION: We use the p-value approach for the test. We set up the following competing hypotheses in order to determine whether Debt and Income have a linear relationship:

$$H_0: \beta_1 = 0$$
$$H_A: \beta_1 \neq 0$$

From Table 12.8, we find that $b_1 = 10.4411$ and $se(b_j) = 1.2220$. In addition, given $n = 26$ and $k = 1$, we find $df = n - k - 1 = 26 - 1 - 1 = 24$. So we calculate the value of the test statistic as $t_{24} = \frac{b_1 - \beta_{10}}{se(b_j)} = \frac{10.4411 - 0}{1.2220} = 8.5443$. From Table 12.8 we see that this calculation may not have been necessary since Excel automatically provides the value of the test statistic (slight difference due to rounding) and its associated p-value.

It is important to note that the Excel reported results are valid only in a standard case where a two-tailed test is implemented to determine if a regression coefficient differs from zero. Here we can use the Excel reported results since the above example represents a standard case; shortly, we will see an application with a non-standard case. As usual, the decision rule is to reject H_0 if the p-value $< \alpha$. Since the p-value of $9.6603 \times 10^{-9} \approx 0 < 0.05 = \alpha$, we reject H_0. At the 5% significance level, there is a linear relationship between Debt and Income; in other words, Income significantly influences Debt.

Using a Confidence Interval to Determine Individual Significance

In earlier chapters we constructed a confidence interval to conduct a two-tailed hypothesis test. When assessing whether the regression coefficient differs from zero, we can apply the same methodology.

CONFIDENCE INTERVAL FOR β_j

The $100(1 - \alpha)\%$ confidence interval of the regression coefficient β_j is computed as

$$b_j \pm t_{\alpha/2,df}se(b_j) \quad \text{or} \quad [b_j - t_{\alpha/2,df}se(b_j), b_j + t_{\alpha/2,df}se(b_j)],$$

where $se(b_j)$ is the estimated standard error of b_j and $df = n - k - 1$.

Excel automatically provides a 95% confidence interval for the regression coefficients; it will provide other levels if prompted. In general, if the confidence interval for the slope coefficient contains the value zero, then the explanatory variable associated with the regression coefficient is not significant. Conversely, if the confidence interval does not contain the value zero, then the explanatory variable associated with the regression coefficient is significant. The next example shows how we can conduct individual significance tests on a multiple linear regression model.

EXAMPLE 12.8

Let's revisit Model 2, Debt $= \beta_0 + \beta_1$Income $+ \beta_2$Unemployment $+ \varepsilon$, estimated with the sample data in Table 12.1. We reproduce a portion of the regression results in Table 12.9. Use the 95% confidence interval to determine whether Unemployment is significant in explaining Debt.

TABLE 12.9 Portion of Regression Results for Model 2:
Debt $= \beta_0 + \beta_1$Income $+\beta_2$Unemployment $+ \varepsilon$

	Coefficients	Standard Error	t Stat	p-value	Lower 95%	Upper 95%
Intercept	198.9956	156.3619	1.2727	0.2159	−124.464	522.455
Income	10.5122	1.4765	7.1120	2.98E-07	7.458	13.567
Unemployment	0.6186	6.8679	0.0901	0.9290	−13.589	14.826

SOLUTION: For testing whether Unemployment significantly influences Debt, we set up the following competing hypotheses:

$$H_0: \beta_2 = 0$$

$$H_A: \beta_2 \neq 0$$

For the 95% confidence interval, $\alpha = 0.05$ and $\alpha/2 = 0.025$. With $n = 26$ and $k = 2$ (there are two explanatory variables in the model), we use $df = 26 - 2 - 1 = 23$ and reference the t table to find $t_{\alpha/2,df} = t_{0.025,23} = 2.069$. From Table 12.9 we find

$b_2 = 0.6186$ and $se(b_2) = 6.8679$, and the 95% confidence interval for the population coefficient β_2 is

$$b_j \pm t_{\alpha/2,df}se(b_j) = 0.6186 \pm 2.069 \times 6.8679 = 0.6186 \pm 14.2097.$$

Thus, the lower and upper limits of the confidence interval are −13.5911 and 14.8283, respectively. Note that Table 12.9 also provides these values (slight differences are due to rounding). Since the 95% confidence interval contains the value zero, we cannot conclude that Unemployment is significant in explaining Debt at $\alpha = 0.05$. Note that we come to this same conclusion using the p-value approach. The p-value when testing the significance of β_2 is 0.9290; this value is greater than $\alpha = 0.05$, indicating that we do not reject H_0: $\beta_2 = 0$. This result is not surprising since the goodness-of-fit measures suggested that Model 1 with only one explanatory variable (Income) provided a better fit for Debt as compared to Model 2 with two explanatory variables (Income and Unemployment).

So far, we have only considered examples of two-tailed tests to determine if a regression coefficient differs from zero. As mentioned earlier, for such standard cases, we can use the computer-generated value of the test statistic as well as the corresponding p-value. For a one-tailed test with $\beta_{j0} = 0$, the value of the test statistic is valid, but the p-value is not. For a one- or two-tailed test to determine if the regression coefficient differs from a nonzero value, both the computer-generated value of the test statistic and the p-value become invalid. These facts are summarized below.

COMPUTER-GENERATED TEST STATISTIC AND THE *P*-VALUE

Excel and virtually all other statistical packages report a value of the test statistic and its associated p-value for a two-tailed test that assesses whether the regression coefficient differs from zero.

- If we specify a one-tailed test, then we need to divide the computer-generated p-value in half.
- If we test whether the coefficient differs from a nonzero value, then we cannot use the value of the computer-generated test statistic and its p-value.

We would also like to point out that for a one-tailed test with $\beta_{j0} = 0$, there are rare instances when the computer generated p-value is invalid. This occurs when the sign of b_j (and the value of the accompanying test statistic) is not inconsistent with the null hypothesis. For example, for a right-tailed test, H_0: $\beta_j \leq 0$ and H_A: $\beta_j > 0$, the null hypothesis cannot be rejected if the estimate b_j (and the value of the accompanying test statistic t_{df}) is negative. Similarly, no further testing is necessary if $b_j > 0$ (and thus $t_{df} > 0$) for a left-tailed test.

A Test for a Nonzero Slope Coefficient

In Examples 12.7 and 12.8, the null hypothesis included a zero value for the slope coefficient, that is, $\beta_{j0} = 0$. We now motivate a test where the hypothesized value is not zero by using a renowned financial application—the capital asset pricing model (CAPM).

Let R represent the return on a stock or portfolio of interest. Given the market return R_M and the risk-free return R_f, the CAPM expresses the risk-adjusted return of an asset, $R - R_f$, as a function of the risk-adjusted market return, $R_M - R_f$. It is common to use the return of the S&P 500 index for R_M and the return on a Treasury bill for R_f. For empirical estimation, it is customary to express the CAPM as

$$R - R_f = \alpha + \beta(R_M - R_f) + \varepsilon.$$

We can rewrite the model as $y = \alpha + \beta x + \varepsilon$, where $y = R - R_f$ and $x = R_M - R_f$. Note that this is essentially a simple linear regression model that uses α and β, in place of the usual β_0 and β_1, to represent the intercept and the slope coefficients, respectively. The slope coefficient β, called the stock's **beta**, measures how sensitive the stock's return is to changes in the level of the overall market. When β equals 1, any change in the market return leads to an identical change in the given stock return. A stock for which β is greater than 1 is considered more "aggressive" or riskier than the market, whereas one for which the value is less than 1 is considered "conservative" or less risky. We also give importance to the intercept coefficient α, called the stock's **alpha**. The CAPM theory predicts α to be zero, and thus a nonzero estimate indicates abnormal returns. Abnormal returns are positive when $\alpha > 0$ and negative when $\alpha < 0$.

EXAMPLE 12.9

Johnson & Johnson (J&J) was founded more than 120 years ago on the premise that doctors and nurses should use sterile products to treat people's wounds. Since that time, J&J products have become staples in most people's homes. Consider the CAPM where the J&J risk-adjusted stock return $R - R_f$ is used as the response variable and the risk-adjusted market return $R_M - R_f$ is used as the explanatory variable. A portion of 60 months of data is shown in Table 12.10; the complete data set, labeled *Johnson_Johnson*, can be found on the text website.

TABLE 12.10 Risk-Adjusted Stock Return of J&J and Market Return

FILE

Date	$R - R_f$	$R_M - R_f$
1/1/2006	−4.59	2.21
2/1/2006	0.39	−0.31
⋮	⋮	⋮
12/1/2010	0.48	2.15

Source: http://finance.yahoo.com and U.S. Treasury.

a. Since consumer staples comprise many of the products sold by J&J, its stock is often considered less risky; that is, people need these products whether the economy is good or bad. At the 5% significance level, is the beta coefficient less than one?

b. At the 5% significance level, are there abnormal returns? In other words, is the alpha coefficient significantly different from zero?

SOLUTION: We use the critical value approach to answer part a and the p-value approach for part b. Using the CAPM notation, we estimate the model $R - R_f = \alpha + \beta(R_M - R_f) + \varepsilon$; the relevant portion of the Excel output is presented in Table 12.11.

TABLE 12.11 Portion of CAPM Regression Results for J&J

	Coefficients	Standard Error	t Stat	p-value
Intercept	0.2666	0.4051	0.6580	0.5131
$R_M - R_f$	0.5844	0.0803	7.2759	0.0000

a. The estimate for the beta coefficient is 0.5844 and its standard error is 0.0803. Interestingly, our estimate is identical to the beta reported in the popular press (http://www.dailyfinance.com, March 4, 2011). In order to determine whether the beta coefficient is significantly less than one, we formulate the hypotheses as

$$H_0: \beta \geq 1$$
$$H_A: \beta < 1$$

Given 60 data points, $df = n - k - 1 = 60 - 1 - 1 = 58$. With $df = 58$ and a 5% significance level, the critical value for a left-tailed test is $-t_{0.05,58} = -1.672$. We cannot use the test statistic value reported in Table 12.10, since the hypothesized value of β is not zero. We calculate the test statistic value as $t_{58} = \frac{0.5844 - 1}{0.0803} = -5.18$. The decision rule is to reject H_0 if $t_{58} < -t_{0.05,58}$. Since $-5.18 < -1.672$, we reject H_0 and conclude that β is significantly less than one; that is, the return on J&J stock is less risky than the return on the market.

b. Abnormal returns exist when α is significantly different from zero. Thus, the competing hypotheses are $H_0: \alpha = 0$ versus $H_A: \alpha \neq 0$. Since it is a standard case, where the hypothesized value of the coefficient is zero, we can use the reported test statistic value of 0.6580 with an associated p-value of 0.5131. Given such a large p-value, we cannot reject H_0 at any reasonable level of significance. Therefore, we cannot conclude that there are abnormal returns for J&J stock.

LO **12.7**

Conduct a test of joint significance.

Test of Joint Significance

So far we have considered tests of individual significance of explanatory variables. For instance, we used a t test to determine whether a household's income (or the unemployment rate) has a statistically significant influence on its debt payments. When we assess a multiple linear regression model, it is also important to conduct a **test of joint significance**. A test of joint significance is often regarded as a test of the overall usefulness of a regression. This test determines whether the explanatory variables $x_1, x_2, \ldots, x_k$ have a joint statistical influence on y.

In the null hypothesis of the test of joint significance, *all* of the slope coefficients are assumed zero. The competing hypotheses for a test of joint significance are specified as

$$H_0: \beta_1 = \beta_2 = \cdots = \beta_k = 0$$
$$H_A: \text{At least one } \beta_j \neq 0.$$

You might be tempted to implement this test by performing a series of tests of individual significance with the t statistic. However, such an option is not appropriate. The test of joint significance determines if at least one of the explanatory variables is significant. Therefore, it is not clear how many explanatory variables must be significant in order to document a joint significance. In addition, recall from the discussion of ANOVA in Chapter 10 that if we conduct many individual tests at a 5% level of significance, the resulting significance level for the test of joint significance will be greater than 5%.

To conduct the test of joint significance, we employ a right-tailed F test. (Recall that the $F_{(df_1,df_2)}$ distribution was introduced in Chapter 10.) The test statistic measures how well the regression equation explains the variability in the response variable. It is defined as the ratio of the **mean square due to regression**, or simply the **mean square regression** *MSR* to the mean square error *MSE*, where $MSR = SSR/k$ and $MSE = SSE/(n - k - 1)$. These values, including the $F_{(df_1,df_2)}$ test statistic value, are provided in the ANOVA portion of the regression results.

TEST STATISTIC FOR THE TEST OF JOINT SIGNIFICANCE

The test statistic for a **test of joint significance** is assumed to follow the $F_{(df_1,df_2)}$ distribution with $df_1 = k$ and $df_2 = n - k - 1$ and its value is

$$F_{(df_1,df_2)} = \frac{SSR/k}{SSE/(n - k - 1)} = \frac{MSR}{MSE},$$

where *MSR* and *MSE* are the mean square regression and the mean square error, respectively.

In general, a large value of $F_{(df_1, df_2)}$ indicates that a large portion of the variability in y is explained by the linear regression model; thus, the model is useful. A small value of $F_{(df_1, df_2)}$ implies that a large portion of the variability in y remains unexplained. In fact, the test of joint significance is sometimes referred to as the test of the significance of R^2. Note that while the test of joint significance is important for a multiple linear regression model, it becomes equivalent to the t test for the simple linear regression model. In fact, in a simple linear regression model, the p-value of the F test is identical to that of the t test; we advise you to verify this fact.

EXAMPLE 12.10

Let's revisit Model 2, Debt $= \beta_0 + \beta_1$Income $+ \beta_2$Unemployment $+ \varepsilon$, estimated with the sample data in Table 12.1. We reproduce the ANOVA portion of the regression results in Table 12.12. Conduct a test to determine if Income and Unemployment are jointly significant in explaining Debt at $\alpha = 0.05$.

TABLE 12.12 ANOVA Portion of Regression Results for Model 2: Debt $= \beta_0 + \beta_1$Income $+ \beta_2$Unemployment $+ \varepsilon$

ANOVA	df	SS	MS	F	Significance F
Regression	2	292170.8	146085.4	34.99536	1.05E-07
Residual	23	96011.7	4174.4		
Total	25	388182.5			

SOLUTION: When testing whether the explanatory variables are jointly significant in explaining Debt, we set up the following competing hypotheses:

$$H_0: \beta_1 = \beta_2 = 0$$
$$H_A: \text{At least one } \beta_j \neq 0.$$

Given $n = 26$ and $k = 2$, we find that $df_1 = k = 2$ and $df_2 = n - k - 1 = 23$. From Table 12.12, we calculate the value of the test statistic as

$$F_{(2,23)} = \frac{MSR}{MSE} = \frac{146085.4}{4174.4} = 34.9955.$$

Note that this value is essentially the same as the one reported by Excel. Given the computer-generated regression output, the easiest way to conduct the test of joint significance is with the p-value approach, since the ANOVA table provides both the value of the test statistic and its associated p-value. The value under the heading *Significance F* is the p-value, that is, $P(F_{(2,23)} \geq 34.99536) = 1.05 \times 10^{-7} \approx 0$. Since the p-value is less than $\alpha = 0.05$, we reject H_0. At the 5% significance level, Income and Unemployment are jointly significant in explaining Debt. The results of the individual significance tests, in Examples 12.7 and 12.8, suggested that only Income (not Unemployment) significantly influenced Debt.

Reporting Regression Results

Regression results are often reported in a "user-friendly" table. Table 12.13 reports the regression results for the two models discussed in this chapter that attempt to explain consumer debt payments. The explanatory variables are Income in Model 1 and Income and Unemployment in Model 2. If we were supplied with only this table, we would be able to compare these models, construct the sample regression equation of the chosen model, and perform a respectable assessment of the model with the statistics provided. Many tables contain a Notes section at the bottom explaining some of the notation. We choose to put the *p*-values in parentheses under all estimated coefficients; however, some researchers place the standard errors of the coefficients or the values of the test statistics in parentheses. Whichever format is chosen, it must be made clear to the reader in the Notes section.

TABLE 12.13 Model Estimates for the Response Variable Debt

Variable	Model 1	Model 2
Intercept	210.2977* (0.0303)	198.9956 (0.2159)
Income	10.4411* (0.0000)	10.5122* (0.0000)
Unemployment	NA	0.6186 (0.9290)
S_e	63.26	64.61
R^2	0.7526	0.7527
Adjusted R^2	0.7423	0.7312
F statistic (*p*-value)	NA	35.00* (0.0000)

NOTES: Parameter estimates are in the top half of the table with the *p*-values in parentheses; NA denotes not applicable; * represents significance at the 5% level. The lower part of the table contains goodness-of-fit measures.

SYNOPSIS OF INTRODUCTORY CASE

A recent study shows substantial variability in consumer debt payments depending on where the consumer resides (Experian.com, November 11, 2010). A possible explanation is that a linear relationship exists between consumer debt payments and an area's median household income. In addition to income, the unemployment rate may also impact consumer debt payments. In order to substantiate these claims, relevant data on 26 metropolitan areas are collected.

Two linear regression models are estimated for the analysis. A simple linear regression model (Model 1), using consumer debt payments as the response variable and median household income as the explanatory variable, is estimated as $\widehat{Debt} = 210.30 + 10.44Income$. For every $1,000 increase in median household income, consumer debt payments are predicted to increase by $10.44. In an attempt to improve upon the prediction, a multiple linear regression model (Model 2) is proposed, where median household income and the unemployment rate are used as explanatory variables. The sample regression equation for Model 2 is $\widehat{Debt} = 199.00 + 10.51Income + 0.62Unemployment$. Given its slope coefficient of only 0.62, the economic impact of the unemployment rate on consumer debt payments, with median household income held fixed, seems extremely weak.

Goodness-of-fit measures confirm that Model 1 provides a better fit than Model 2. The standard error of the estimate is smaller for Model 1, suggesting less dispersion of the data from the sample regression equation. In addition, the adjusted R^2 is higher for Model 1, implying a better fit. Lastly, at the 5% significance level, median household income is significant in explaining consumer debt payments but unemployment is not. Using Model 1 and assuming that an area's median household income is $80,000, consumer debt payments are predicted to be $1,045.50.

Mechanics

48. In a simple linear regression based on 30 observations, it is found that $b_1 = 3.25$ and $se(b_1) = 1.36$. Consider the hypotheses:
$$H_0: \beta_1 = 0 \text{ and } H_A: \beta_1 \neq 0.$$

a. Calculate the value of the test statistic.

b. Approximate the p-value.

c. At the 5% significance level, what is the conclusion? Is the explanatory variable significant?

49. In a simple linear regression based on 25 observations, it is found that $b_1 = 0.5$ and $se(b_1) = 0.3$. Consider the hypotheses:
$$H_0: \beta_1 \leq 0 \text{ and } H_A: \beta_1 > 0.$$

a. At the 5% significance level, find the critical value(s).

b. Calculate the value of the test statistic.

c. What is the conclusion to the test?

50. In a simple linear regression based on 30 observations, it is found that $b_1 = 7.2$ and $se(b_1) = 1.8$. Consider the hypotheses:
$$H_0: \beta_1 \geq 10 \text{ and } H_A: \beta_1 < 10.$$

a. At the 5% significance level, find the critical value(s).

b. Calculate the value of the test statistic.

c. What is the conclusion to the test?

51. Consider the following regression results based on 20 observations.

	Coefficients	Standard Error	t Stat	p-value	Lower 95%	Upper 95%
Intercept	34.2123	4.5665	7.4920	0.0000	24.62	43.81
x_1	0.1223	0.1794	0.6817	0.5041	−0.25	0.50

a. Specify the hypotheses to determine if the intercept differs from zero. Perform this test at the 5% significance level.

b. Construct the 95% confidence interval for the slope coefficient. At the 5% significance level, does the slope differ from zero? Explain.

52. Consider the following regression results based on 40 observations.

	Coefficients	Standard Error	t Stat	p-value	Lower 95%	Upper 95%
Intercept	43.1802	12.6963	3.4010	0.0016	17.48	68.88
x_1	0.9178	0.9350	0.9816	0.3325	−0.97	2.81

a. Specify the hypotheses to determine if the slope differs from minus one.

b. At the 5% significance level, find the critical value(s).

c. Calculate the value of the test statistic.

d. Does the slope differ from minus one? Explain.

53. When estimating a multiple linear regression model based on 30 observations, the following results were obtained.

	Coefficients	Standard Error	t Stat	p-value	Lower 95%	Upper 95%
Intercept	152.27	119.70	1.27	0.2142	−93.34	397.87
x_1	12.91	2.68	4.81	5.06E-05	7.40	18.41
x_2	2.74	2.15	1.28	0.2128	−1.67	7.14

a. Specify the hypotheses to determine whether x_1 is linearly related to y. At the 5% significance level, use the p-value approach to complete the test. Are x_1 and y linearly related?

b. What is the 95% confidence interval for β_2? Using this confidence interval, is x_2 significant in explaining y? Explain.

c. At the 5% significance level, can you conclude that β_1 is less than 20? Show the relevant steps of the appropriate hypothesis test.

54. The following ANOVA table was obtained when estimating a multiple linear regression model.

ANOVA	df	SS	MS	F	Significance F
Regression	2	22016.75	11008.38		0.0228
Residual	17	39286.93	2310.996		
Total	19	61303.68			

a. How many explanatory variables were specified in the model? How many observations were used?

b. Specify the hypotheses to determine whether the explanatory variables are jointly significant.

c. Compute the value of the test statistic.

d. At the 5% significance level, what is the conclusion to the test? Explain.

Applications

55. In order to examine the relationship between the selling price of a used car and its age, an analyst uses data from 20 recent transactions and estimates Price $= \beta_0 + \beta_1 Age + \varepsilon$. A portion of the regression results is shown in the accompanying table.

	Coefficients	Standard Error	t Stat	p-value
Intercept	21187.94	733.42	28.89	1.56E-16
Age	−1208.25	128.95		2.41E-08

a. Specify the competing hypotheses in order to determine whether the selling price of a used car and its age are linearly related.

b. Calculate the value of the test statistic.

c. At the 5% significance level, what is the conclusion to the test? Is the age of a used car significant in explaining its selling price?

d. Conduct a hypothesis test at the 5% significance level in order to determine if β_1 differs from -1000. Show all of the relevant steps.

56. A marketing manager analyzes the relationship between the annual sales of a firm (in \$100,000s) and its advertising expenditures (in \$10,000s). He collects data from 20 firms and estimates Sales $= \beta_0 + \beta_1 Advertising + \varepsilon$. A portion of the regression results is shown in the accompanying table.

	Coefficients	Standard Error	t Stat	p-value
Intercept	−7.42	1.46	−5.09	7.66E-05
Advertising	0.42	0.05		7.26E-08

a. Specify the competing hypotheses in order to determine whether advertising expenditures and sales have a positive linear relationship.

b. Calculate the value of the test statistic. What is the p-value?

c. At the 5% significance level, what is the conclusion to the test? Do advertising expenditures and sales have a positive linear relationship?

57. A recent study on the evolution of mankind shows that, with a few exceptions, world-record holders in the 100-meter dash have progressively gotten bigger over time (*The Wall Street Journal*, July 22, 2009). The following table shows runners who have held the record, along with their record-holding times and heights:

Record Holder/Year	Time (in seconds)	Height (in inches)
Eddie Tolan (1932)	10.30	67
Jesse Owens (1936)	10.20	70
Charles Greene (1968)	9.90	68
Eddie Hart (1972)	9.90	70
Carl Lewis (1991)	9.86	74
Asafa Powell (2007)	9.74	75
Usain Bolt (2008)	9.69	77

A portion of the regression results from estimating Time = $\beta_0 + \beta_1$Height + ε is:

	Coefficients	Standard Error	t Stat	p-value	Lower 95%	Upper 95%
Intercept	13.353	1.1714	11.3990	9.1E-05	10.34	16.36
Height	−0.0477	0.0163		0.0332	−0.09	−0.01

a. Formulate the estimated regression equation.

b. Specify the hypotheses to determine whether Height is linearly related to Time.

c. Calculate the value of the test statistic.

d. At the 5% significance level, is Height significant? Explain.

58. An economist examines the relationship between changes in short-term interest rates and long-term interest rates. He believes that changes in short-term rates are significant in explaining long-term interest rates. He estimates the model Dlong = $\beta_0 + \beta_1$Dshort + ε, where Dlong is the change in the long-term interest rate (10-year Treasury bill) and Dshort is the change in the short-term interest rate (3-month Treasury bill). Monthly data from January 2006 through December 2010 were obtained from the St. Louis Federal Reserve's website. A portion of the regression results is shown below (n = 60):

	Coefficients	Standard Error	t Stat	p-value	Lower 95%	Upper 95%
Intercept	−0.0038	0.0088	−0.4273	0.6708	−0.02	0.01
Dshort	0.0473	0.0168	2.8125	0.0067	0.01	0.08

Use a 5% significance level in order to determine whether there is a linear relationship between Dshort and Dlong.

59. For a sample of 20 New England cities, a sociologist studies the crime rate in each city (crimes per 100,000 residents) as a function of its poverty rate (in %) and its median income (in $1,000s). A portion of the regression results is shown in the accompanying table.

ANOVA	df	SS	MS	F	Significance F
Regression	2	188246.8	94123.4		9.04E-07
Residual	17	45457.32	2673.96		
Total	19	233704.1			

	Coefficients	Standard Error	t Stat	p-value	Lower 95%	Upper 95%
Intercept	−301.62	549.7135	−0.5487	0.5903	−1,461.52	858.28
Poverty	53.1597	14.2198	3.7384	0.0016	23.16	83.16
Income	4.9472	8.2566	0.5992	0.5569	−12.47	22.37

a. Specify the sample regression equation.

b. At the 5% significance level, show whether the poverty rate and the crime rate are linearly related.

c. Construct the 95% confidence interval for the slope coefficient of income. Using the confidence interval, determine whether income is significant in explaining the crime rate at the 5% significance level.

d. At the 5% significance level, are the poverty rate and income jointly significant in explaining the crime rate?

60. A researcher estimates the following model relating the return on a firm's stock as a function of its price-to-earnings ratio and its price-to-sales ratio: Return = $\beta_0 + \beta_1$P/E + β_2P/S + ε. A portion of the regression results is shown in the accompanying table.

ANOVA	df	SS	MS	F	Significance F
Regression	2	918.746	459.3728	2.817095	0.077415
Residual	27	4402.786	163.0661		
Total	29	5321.532			

	Coefficients	Standard Error	t Stat	p-value	Lower 95%	Upper 95%
Intercept	−12.0243	7.886858	−1.5246	0.1390	−28.21	4.16
P/E	0.1459	0.4322	0.3376	0.7383	−0.74	1.03
P/S	5.4417	2.2926	2.3736	0.0250	0.74	10.15

a. Specify the sample regression equation.

b. At the 10% significant level, are P/E and P/S jointly significant? Show the relevant steps of the appropriate hypothesis test.

c. Are both explanatory variables individually significant at the 10% significance level? Show the relevant steps of the appropriate hypothesis tests.

61. Akiko Hamaguchi is a manager at a small sushi restaurant in Phoenix, Arizona. Akiko is concerned that the weak economic environment has hampered foot traffic in her area, thus causing a dramatic decline in sales. In order to offset the decline in sales, she has pursued a strong advertising

campaign. She believes advertising expenditures have a positive influence on sales. To support her claim, Akiko estimates the following linear regression model: Sales $= \beta_0 + \beta_1$Unemployment $+ \beta_2$Advertising $+ \varepsilon$. A portion of the regression results is shown in the accompanying table.

ANOVA	df	SS	MS	F	Significance F
Regression	2	72.6374	36.3187	8.760	0.0034
Residual	14	58.0438	4.1460		
Total	16	130.681			

	Coefficients	Standard Error	t Stat	p-value	Lower 95%	Upper 95%
Intercept	17.5060	3.9817	4.3966	0.0006	8.97	26.05
Unemployment	−0.6879	0.2997	−2.2955	0.0377	−1.33	−0.05
Advertising	0.0266	0.0068	3.9322	0.0015	0.01	0.04

a. At the 5% significance level, test whether the explanatory variables jointly influence sales.

b. At the 1% significance level, test whether the unemployment rate is negatively related with sales.

c. At the 1% significance level, test whether advertising expenditures are positively related with sales.

62. FILE Access the data labeled **Test_Scores** from the text website. Use the information on 32 students to estimate a student's final grade as a linear function of a student's midterm grade. At the 1% significance level, is a student's midterm grade significant in explaining a student's final grade? Show the relevant steps of the test.

63. FILE Access the data labeled **Property_Taxes** from the text website. The data represent the size of a home (in square feet) and its property taxes owed by the owner (in $) in an affluent suburb 30 miles outside New York City. Use the data to estimate a home's property taxes as a linear function of its size. At the 5% significance level, do home size and property taxes have a linear relationship? Show the relevant steps of the test.

64. FILE Caterpillar, Inc. manufactures and sells heavy construction equipment worldwide. The performance of Caterpillar's stock is likely to be strongly influenced by the economy. For instance, during the subprime mortgage crisis, the value of Caterpillar's stock plunged dramatically. Monthly data for Caterpillar's risk-adjusted return and the risk-adjusted market return are collected for a five-year period ($n = 60$). A portion of the data is shown in the accompanying table. The entire data set, labeled **Caterpillar**, can be found on the text website.

Date	$R - R_f$	$R_M - R_f$
1/1/2006	17.66	2.21
2/1/2006	7.27	−0.31
⋮	⋮	⋮
11/1/2010	3.37	2.15

Source: http://finance.yahoo.com and U.S. Treasury.

a. Estimate the CAPM model for Caterpillar, Inc. Show the regression results in a well-formatted table.

b. At the 5% significance level, determine if investment in Caterpillar is riskier than the market (beta significantly greater than 1).

c. At the 5% significance level, is there evidence of abnormal returns?

65. FILE A Realtor examines the factors that influence the price of a house in Arlington, Massachusetts. He collects data on recent house sales (Price) and notes each house's square footage (Sqft) as well as its number of bedrooms (Beds) and number of bathrooms (Baths). A portion of the data is shown in the accompanying table; the entire data set, labeled **Arlington_Homes**, can be found on the text website.

Price	Sqft	Beds	Baths
840000	2768	4	3.5
822000	2500	4	2.5
⋮	⋮	⋮	⋮
307500	850	1	1

a. Estimate: Price $= \beta_0 + \beta_1$Sqft $+ \beta_2$Beds $+ \beta_3$Baths $+ \varepsilon$. Show the regression results in a well-formatted table.

b. At the 5% significance level, are the explanatory variables jointly significant in explaining Price?

c. At the 5% significance level, are all explanatory variables individually significant in explaining Price?

66. FILE On the first day of class, an economics professor administers a test to gauge the math preparedness of her students. She believes that the performance on this math test and the number of hours studied per week on the course are the primary factors that predict a student's score on the final exam. She collects data from 60 students, a portion of which is shown in the accompanying table. The entire data set, labeled **Final_Test**, can be found on the text website.

Final	Math	Hours
94	92	5
74	90	3
⋮	⋮	⋮
63	64	2

a. Specify the sample regression equation that enables us to predict a student's final exam score on the basis of his/her math score and the number of hours studied per week.

b. At the 5% significance level, are a student's math score and the number of hours studied per week jointly significant in explaining a student's final exam score?

c. At the 5% significance level, is each explanatory variable individually significant in explaining a student's final exam score?

Gavin Cann listens to two sports analysts quarrel over which statistic is a better predictor of a Major League Baseball team's winning proportion (Win). One argues that the team's batting average (BA) is a better predictor of a team's success since the team with the higher batting average has won approximately 75% of the World Series contests. The other insists that a team's pitching is clearly the main factor in determining a team's winning proportion—the lower a team's earned run average (ERA), the higher the team's winning proportion.

In order to determine if either of these claims is backed by the data, Gavin collects relevant information for the 14 American League (AL) and 16 National League (NL) teams during the regular season of 2010. A portion of the data is shown in Table 12.14; the entire data set, labeled **Baseball**, can be found on the text website.

TABLE 12.14 Winning Proportion, Batting Average, and Earned Run Average in Baseball

Team	League	Win	BA	ERA
Baltimore, Orioles	AL	0.407	0.259	4.59
Boston, Red Sox	AL	0.549	0.268	4.20
⋮	⋮	⋮	⋮	⋮
Washington, Nationals	NL	0.426	0.25	4.13

Source: http://mlb.mlb.com.

Gavin wants to use this sample information to:

1. Estimate three linear regression models where winning proportion is based on BA (Model 1), ERA (Model 2), and both BA and ERA (Model 3).

2. Use goodness-of-fit measures to determine which of the three models best fits the data.

3. Determine the individual and the joint significance of BA and ERA at the 5% significance level.

Sample Report— Analyzing the Winning Proportion in Baseball

Two sports analysts have conflicting views over how best to predict a Major League Baseball team's winning proportion (Win). One argues that the team's batting average (BA) is a better predictor of a team's success, while the other analyst insists that a team's pitching is the main factor as measured by the pitchers' earned run average (ERA). Three linear regression models are used to analyze a baseball team's winning proportion. The explanatory variables are BA in Model 1, ERA in Model 2, and both BA and ERA in Model 3. A priori, one expects that BA positively influences Win, whereas ERA negatively affects Win. The regression results for the three models are presented in Table 12.A.

TABLE 12.A Model Estimates for the Response Variable Win

Variable	Model 1	Model 2	Model 3
Intercept	−0.2731 (0.3421)	0.9504* (0.0000)	0.1269 (0.4921)
Batting Average	3.0054* (0.0106)	NA	3.2754* (0.0000)
Earned Run Average	NA	−0.1105* (0.0000)	−0.1153* (0.0000)
s_e	0.0614	0.0505	0.0375
R^2	0.2112	0.4656	0.7156
Adjusted R^2	0.1830	0.4465	0.6945
F statistic (p-value)	NA	NA	33.9663* (0.0000)

Notes: Parameter estimates are in the top half of the table with the p-values in parentheses; NA denotes not applicable; * represents significance at the 5% level. The lower part of the table contains goodness-of-fit measures.

If simply choosing between Models 1 and 2 where only one explanatory variable influences Win, then Model 2 with ERA as an explanatory variable appears to provide the better fit since it has a lower standard error of the estimate ($s_e = 0.0505$) and a higher coefficient of determination ($R^2 = 0.4656$). However, Model 3 uses both BA and ERA as explanatory variables and it has the lowest standard error of the estimate ($s_e = 0.0375$) and the highest adjusted R^2 with a value of 0.6945. Thus, Model 3 provides the best overall fit with a sample regression equation of $\widehat{\text{Win}} = 0.13 + 3.28\text{BA} - 0.12\text{ERA}$. As expected, the slope coefficient of BA is positive and the slope coefficient of ERA is negative.

Further testing of Model 3 reveals that the two explanatory variables are jointly as well as individually significant in explaining a team's winning proportion at the 5% significance level. It appears that neither sports analyst is totally right or totally wrong. With an $R^2 = 0.7156$, approximately 72% of the sample variability in the winning proportion is explained by the estimated Model 3. However, 28% of the variability in winning proportion remains unexplained. This is not entirely surprising, since other factors, besides a team's batting average and earned run average, influence a baseball team's winning proportion.

Conceptual Review

LO 12.1 Estimate the simple linear regression model and interpret the coefficients.

Regression analysis explicitly assumes that one variable, called the **response variable**, is influenced by other variables, called the **explanatory variables**.

The **simple linear regression model** uses only one explanatory variable to predict and/or describe change in the response variable. The model is expressed as $y = \beta_0 + \beta_1 x + \varepsilon$, where y and x are the response variable and the explanatory variable, respectively, and ε is the random error term. The coefficients β_0 and β_1 are the unknown parameters to be estimated.

We apply the **ordinary least squares (OLS)** method to find a sample regression equation, $\hat{y} = b_0 + b_1 x$, where $\hat{y}$ is the predicted value of the response variable and b_0 and b_1 are the point estimates of β_0 and β_1, respectively. The estimated slope coefficient b_1 represents the change in $\hat{y}$ when x increases by one unit.

LO 12.2 Estimate the multiple linear regression model and interpret the coefficients.

The **multiple linear regression model** allows more than one explanatory variable to be linearly related with the response variable y. It is defined as $y = \beta_0 + \beta_1 x_1 + \beta_2 x_2 + \cdots + \beta_k x_k + \varepsilon$, where y is the response variable, $x_1, x_2, \ldots, x_k$ are the k explanatory variables, and ε is the random error term. The coefficients $\beta_0, \beta_1, \ldots, \beta_k$ are the unknown parameters to be estimated. We again use the OLS method to arrive at the following sample regression equation: $\hat{y} = b_0 + b_1 x_1 + b_2 x_2 + \cdots + b_k x_k$, where $b_0, b_1, \ldots, b_k$ are the point estimates of $\beta_0, \beta_1, \ldots, \beta_k$, respectively.

For each explanatory variable x_j ($j = 1, \ldots, k$), the corresponding slope coefficient b_j is the estimated regression coefficient. It measures the change in the predicted value of the response variable $\hat{y}$ given a unit increase in the associated explanatory variable x_j, *holding all other explanatory variables constant*. In other words, it represents the partial influence of x_j on $\hat{y}$.

LO 12.3 Calculate and interpret the standard error of the estimate.

The **standard error of the estimate** s_e is calculated as $s_e = \sqrt{s_e^2} = \sqrt{MSE} = \sqrt{\frac{SSE}{n-k-1}} = \sqrt{\frac{\Sigma e_i^2}{n-k-1}}$. Theoretically, s_e can assume any value between zero and infinity, $0 \leq s_e < \infty$;

the closer s_e is to zero, the better the model fits. Since s_e has no predetermined upper limit, it is difficult to interpret the standard error of the estimate in isolation; however, it is a useful goodness-of-fit measure when we are comparing various models that have the same response variable—the model with the smaller s_e provides the better relative fit.

LO 12.4

Calculate and interpret the coefficient of determination R^2.

The **coefficient of determination R^2** is the proportion of the variation in the response variable that is explained by the sample regression equation. It falls between 0 and 1; the closer the value is to 1, the better the model fits. For example, if $R^2 = 0.72$, we say that 72% of the sample variation in y is explained by the estimated model.

We compute the coefficient of determination as $R^2 = \frac{SSR}{SST} = 1 - \frac{SSE}{SST}$, where $SSR = \Sigma(\hat{y} - \bar{y})^2$, $SSE = \Sigma(y_i - \hat{y}_i)^2$, and $SST = \Sigma(y_i - \bar{y})^2$.

LO 12.5

Differentiate between R^2 and adjusted R^2.

Adjusted R^2 adjusts R^2 by accounting for the sample size n and the number of explanatory variables k used in the regression. It is calculated as adjusted $R^2 = 1 - (1 - R^2)\left(\frac{n - 1}{n - k - 1}\right)$. In comparing competing models with different numbers of explanatory variables, the preferred model will have the highest adjusted R^2.

LO 12.6

Conduct tests of individual significance.

A test of individual significance determines whether the explanatory variable x_j has an individual statistically significant influence on y. The test statistic is assumed to follow the t_{df} distribution with $df = n - k - 1$ and its value is $t_{df} = \frac{b_j - \beta_{j0}}{se(b_j)}$, where b_j is the estimate for β_j, $se(b_j)$ is the standard error of the OLS estimator b_j, and β_{j0} is the hypothesized value of β_j. If $\beta_{j0} = 0$, the value of the test statistic reduces to $t_{df} = \frac{b_j}{se(b_j)}$. If H_0 of a two-tailed test is rejected, we conclude that x_j has a statistically significant influence on y.

Excel reports a value of a test statistic and its associated p-value for a two-tailed test that assesses whether the regression coefficient differs from zero, that is, $\beta_j \neq 0$. If we specify a one-tailed test, then we need to divide the computer-generated p-value in half. If we test whether the coefficient differs from a nonzero value, that is, $\beta_{j0} \neq 0$, then we cannot use the value of the computer-generated test statistic and its p-value.

The $100(1 - \alpha)\%$ confidence interval of the regression coefficient β_j is given by $b_j \pm t_{\alpha/2,df}\,se(b_j)$ or $[b_j - t_{\alpha/2,df}\,se(b_j), b_j + t_{\alpha/2,df}\,se(b_j)]$, where $df = n - k - 1$. We can use this confidence interval to conduct a two-tailed hypothesis test.

LO 12.7

Conduct a test of joint significance.

A test of joint significance determines whether the explanatory variables $x_1, x_2, \ldots, x_k$ in a multiple linear regression model have a joint statistically significant influence on y. The test statistic is assumed to follow the $F_{(df_1, df_2)}$ distribution with $df_1 = k$ and $df_2 = n - k - 1$ and its value is $F_{(df_1, df_2)} = \frac{SSR/k}{SSE/(n - k - 1)} = \frac{MSR}{MSE}$, where MSR and MSE are the mean square regression and the mean square error, respectively.

It is implemented as a right-tailed test and if H_0 is rejected, we conclude that $x_1, x_2, \ldots, x_k$ have a statistically significant influence on y.

The ANOVA table from computer output provides both the value of the test statistic and its associated p-value.

Additional Exercises and Case Studies

67. In an attempt to determine whether or not a linear relationship exists between the price of a home (in $1,000s) and the number of days it takes to sell the home, a real estate agent collected data from recent sales in his city and estimated the following model: Price = $\beta_0 + \beta_1$Days + ε. A portion of the results is shown in the accompanying table.

	Coefficients	Standard Error	t Stat	p-value
Intercept	−491.27	156.94	−3.13	0.0203
Days	6.17	1.19	5.19	0.0020

   a. What is the sample regression equation?
   b. Predict the price of a home that has been on the market for 100 days.
   c. Specify the competing hypotheses to determine whether Days is significant in explaining a house's price.
   d. At the 5% significance level, what is the conclusion to the test? Explain.

68. FILE A sociologist wishes to study the relationship between an individual's age and his/her happiness. He interviews 24 individuals and collects data on his/her age and happiness score, measured on a scale from 0 to 100. A portion of the data is shown; the entire data set, labeled **Happiness_Age**, can be found on the text website.

Age	Happiness
49	62
51	66
⋮	⋮
69	72

   Estimate Happiness = $\beta_0 + \beta_1$Age + ε.
   a. What is the sample regression equation?
   b. Predict the happiness score for a 45-year old person.
   c. Interpret the coefficient of determination.
   d. At the 1% significance level, does Age influence Happiness? Show the relevant steps of the hypothesis test.

69. FILE In response to the global financial crisis, Federal Reserve leaders continue to keep the short-run target interest rate near zero. While the Fed controls short-term interest rates, long-term interest rates essentially depend on supply/demand dynamics, as well as longer-term interest rate expectations. Consider the following annualized rates for 3-month Treasury yields and 10-year Treasury yields. The entire data set, labeled **Yields**, can be found on the text website.

Year	3-Month Yield (%)	10-Year Yield (%)
2001	3.47	5.02
2002	1.63	4.61
2003	1.03	4.02
2004	1.40	4.27
2005	3.21	4.29
2006	4.85	4.79
2007	4.47	4.63
2008	1.39	3.67
2009	0.15	3.26
2010	0.14	3.21

Source: Federal Reserve Bank of Dallas.

   a. Construct and interpret a scatterplot of a 10-year treasury yield against a 3-month yield.
   b. Determine the sample regression equation that enables us to predict the 10-year yield on the basis of the 3-month yield.
   c. Interpret the coefficient of determination.
   d. At the 5% significance level, is the 3-month yield significant in explaining the 10-year yield?
   e. Many wonder whether a change in the 3-month yield implies the same change in the 10-year yield. Verify this hypothesis at the 5% significance level.

70. FILE The homeownership rate in the United States was 67.4% in 2009. In order to determine if homeownership is linked with income, 2009 state level data on the homeownership rate (Ownership) and median household income (Income) were collected. A portion of the data is shown below; the entire data set, labeled **Home_Ownership**, can be found on the text website.

State	Income	Ownership
Alabama	$39,980	74.1%
Alaska	$61,604	66.8%
⋮	⋮	⋮
Wyoming	$52,470	73.8%

Source: http://www.census.gov.

   a. Estimate and interpret the model: Ownership = $\beta_0 + \beta_1$Income + ε.
   b. What is the standard error of the estimate?
   c. Interpret the coefficient of determination.

71. FILE The accompanying table gives a portion of data on gold prices, the Consumer Price Index (CPI), and the New York Stock Exchange (NYSE) Index for the United States for the period 1980–2010. The entire data set, labeled **Gold_NYSE**, can be found on the text website.

Year	Gold	CPI	NYSE
1980	614.61	86.3	720.15
1981	459.26	94.0	782.62
⋮	⋮	⋮	⋮
2010	1224.52	218.8	7230.43

Source: Data on gold prices and CPI are from http://www.gold.org, retrieved on June 20, 2012. Data on NYSE are from the *Economic Report of the President*, January 2012, Tables B-95 and B-96.

An investment is supposed to be a hedge against inflation if its price and/or rate of return at least keeps pace with inflation. To test this assumption, suppose you decide to estimate the following models:

$$\text{Gold} = \beta_0 + \beta_1\text{CPI} + \varepsilon$$
$$\text{NYSE} = \beta_0 + \beta_1\text{CPI} + \varepsilon$$

Use goodness-of-fit measures to determine which investment is a better hedge against inflation.

72. [FILE] A research analyst is trying to determine whether a firm's price-earnings (P/E) and price-sales (P/S) ratios can explain the firm's stock performance over the past year. A P/E ratio is calculated as a firm's share price compared to the income or profit earned by the firm per share. Generally, a high P/E ratio suggests that investors are expecting higher earnings growth in the future compared to companies with a lower P/E ratio. The P/S ratio is calculated by dividing a firm's share price by the firm's revenue per share for the trailing 12 months. In short, investors can use the P/S ratio to determine how much they are paying for a dollar of the firm's sales rather than a dollar of its earnings (P/E ratio). In general, the lower the P/S ratio, the more attractive the investment. The accompanying table shows the year-to-date (YTD) returns and the P/E and P/S ratios for a portion of the 30 firms included in the Dow Jones Industrial Average. The entire data set, labeled **Dow_2010**, can be found on the text website.

	YTD return (in %)	P/E ratio	P/S ratio
1. 3M Co.	4.4	14.37	2.41
2. Alcoa Inc.	−4.5	11.01	0.78
⋮	⋮	⋮	⋮
30. Walt Disney Company	16.3	13.94	1.94

SOURCE: The 2010 returns (January 1, 2010–December 31, 2010) were obtained from *The Wall Street Journal*, January 3, 2010; the P/E ratios and the P/S ratios were obtained from http://finance.yahoo.com on January 20, 2011.

a. Estimate: Return $= \beta_0 + \beta_1 P/E + \beta_2 P/S + \varepsilon$. Are the signs on the coefficients as expected? Explain.
b. Interpret the slope coefficient of the P/S ratio.
c. What is the predicted return for a firm with a P/E ratio of 10 and a P/S ratio of 2?
d. What is the standard error of the estimate?
e. Interpret R^2.
f. At the 5% significance level, are the explanatory variables jointly significant?
g. At the 5% significance level, are the explanatory variables individually significant?

73. [FILE] There has been a lot of discussion regarding the relationship between Scholastic Aptitude Test (SAT) scores and test-takers' family income (*New York Times,* August 27, 2009). It is generally believed that the wealthier a student's family, the higher the SAT score. Another commonly used predictor for SAT scores is the student's grade point average (GPA). Consider the following data collected on 24 students. The entire data set, labeled **SAT**, can be found on the text website.

SAT	Income	GPA
1651	47,000	2.79
1581	34,000	2.97
⋮	⋮	⋮
1940	113,000	3.96

a. Estimate three models:
  (i) SAT $= \beta_0 + \beta_1 \text{Income} + \varepsilon$,
  (ii) SAT $= \beta_0 + \beta_1 \text{GPA} + \varepsilon$, and
  (iii) SAT $= \beta_0 + \beta_1 \text{Income} + \beta_2 \text{GPA} + \varepsilon$.
b. Use goodness-of-fit measures to select the best-fitting model.
c. Predict SAT given the mean value of the explanatory variable(s).

74. [FILE] Many of today's leading companies, including Google, Microsoft, and Facebook, are based on technologies developed within universities. Lisa Fisher is a business school professor who would like to analyze university factors that enhance innovation. She collects data on 143 universities in 2008 for a regression where the response variable is the number of startups (Startups), which is used as a measure for innovation. The explanatory variables include the university's research expenditure in $ millions (Research), the number of patents issued (Patents), and the age of its technology transfer office in years (Duration). A portion of the data is shown below; the entire data set, labeled **Startups**, can be found on the text website.

Startups	Research ($ millions)	Patents	Duration
1	$145.52	8	23
1	$237.52	16	23
⋮	⋮	⋮	⋮
1	$154.38	3	9

SOURCE: Association of University Managers and National Science Foundation.

a. Estimate: Startups $= \beta_0 + \beta_1 \text{Research} + \beta_2 \text{Patents} + \beta_3 \text{Duration} + \varepsilon$.
b. Predict the number of startups for a university that spent $120 million on research, issued 8 patents, and has had a technology transfer office for 20 years.
c. How much more research expenditure is needed for the university to have an additional predicted startup, with everything else being the same?

75. [FILE] A researcher interviews 50 employees of a large manufacturer and collects data on each worker's hourly wage (Wage), years of higher education (EDUC), experience (EXPER), and age (AGE). The entire data set, labeled **Hourly_Wage**, can be found on the text website.

a. Estimate: Wage $= \beta_0 + \beta_1 \text{EDUC} + \beta_2 \text{EXPER} + \beta_3 \text{AGE} + \varepsilon$.
b. Are the signs as expected?
c. Interpret the coefficient of EDUC.
d. Interpret the coefficient of determination.
e. Predict the hourly wage of a 40-year-old employee who has 5 years of higher education and 8 years of experience.
f. At the 5% significance level, are the explanatory variables jointly significant?
g. At the 5% significance level, are the explanatory variables individually significant?

76. **FILE** Access the data *AnnArbor_Rental* from the text website. The data represent the rent, the number of bedrooms, the number of bathrooms, and the square footage for 40 apartments in the college town of Ann Arbor, Michigan.

a. Determine the sample regression equation that enables us to predict the rent on the basis of the number of bedrooms, the number of bathrooms, and the square footage.

b. Interpret the coefficient of determination. What percent of the variation in Rent is unexplained by the sample regression equation?

c. At the 5% significance level, are the explanatory variables jointly significant?

d. At the 5% significance level, are the explanatory variables individually significant?

CASE STUDIES

Case Study 12.1

Akiko Hamaguchi, the manager at a small sushi restaurant in Phoenix, Arizona, is concerned that the weak economic environment has hampered foot traffic in her area, thus causing a dramatic decline in sales. Her cousin in San Francisco, Hiroshi Sato, owns a similar restaurant, but he has seemed to prosper during these rough economic times. Hiroshi agrees that higher unemployment rates have likely forced some customers to dine out less frequently, but he maintains an aggressive marketing campaign to thwart this apparent trend. For instance, he advertises in local papers with valuable two-for-one coupons and promotes early-bird specials over the airwaves. Despite the fact that advertising increases overall costs, he believes that this campaign has positively affected sales at his restaurant. In order to support his claim, Hiroshi provides monthly sales data and advertising costs pertaining to his restaurant, as well as the monthly unemployment rate from San Francisco County. A portion of the data is shown in the accompanying table; the entire data set, labeled *Sushi_Restaurant*, can be found on the text website.

Data for Case Study 12.1 Hiroshi's Sales, Advertising Costs, and Unemployment Data

Month	Year	Sales (in $1,000s)	Advertising Costs (in $)	Unemployment Rate* (in percent)
January	2008	27.0	550	4.6
February	2008	24.2	425	4.3
⋮	⋮	⋮	⋮	⋮
May	2009	27.4	550	9.1

SOURCE FOR THE UNEMPLOYMENT RATE DATA: Development Department, State of California, June 2009.

In a report, use the sample information to:

1. Estimate a simple linear regression model, Sales $= \beta_0 + \beta_1$Advertising $+ \varepsilon$ as well as a multiple linear regression model, Sales $= \beta_0 + \beta_1$Advertising $+ \beta_2$Unemployment $+ \varepsilon$.

2. Show that the multiple linear regression model is more appropriate for making predictions.

3. Make predictions for sales with an unemployment rate of 6% and advertising costs of $400 and $600.

Case Study 12.2

Megan Hanson, a Realtor in Brownsburg, Indiana, would like to use estimates from a multiple linear regression model to help prospective sellers determine a reasonable asking price for their homes. She believes that the following four factors influence the asking price (Price) of a house: (1) the square footage of the house (SQFT); (2) the number of bedrooms (Bed); (3) the number of bathrooms (Bath); and (4) the lot size (LTSZ) in acres. She randomly collects online listings for 50 single-family homes. A portion of the data is presented in the accompanying table; the entire data set, labeled *Indiana_RealEstate*, can be found on the text website.

Data for Case Study 12.2 Real Estate Data for Brownsburg, Indiana

FILE

Price	SQFT	Bed	Bath	LTSZ
399,900	5026	4	4.5	0.3
375,000	3200	4	3	5
⋮	⋮	⋮	⋮	⋮
102,900	1938	3	1	0.1

Source: *Indianapolis Star*, February 27, 2008.

In a report, use the sample information to:

1. Provide summary statistics on the asking price, the square footage, the number of bedrooms, the number of bathrooms, and the lot size.

2. Estimate a multiple linear regression model where Price is the response variable and SQFT, Bed, Bath, and LTSZ are the explanatory variables.

3. Interpret the resulting coefficient of determination.

4. Conduct joint and individual significance tests at the 5% significance level.

Case Study 12.3

Apple Inc. has established a unique reputation in the consumer electronics industry with its development of products such as the iPod, the iPhone, and the iPad. As of May 2010, Apple had surpassed Microsoft as the most valuable company in the world (*New York Times*, May 26, 2010). Michael Gomez is a stock analyst and wonders if the return on Apple's stock is best modeled using the CAPM model. He collects five years of monthly data, a portion of which is shown. The entire data set, labeled **Apple**, can be found on the text website.

Data for Case Study 12.3 Apple Return Data, $n = 60$

FILE

Date	$R - R_f$	$R_M - R_f$
1/1/2006	4.70	2.21
2/1/2006	−9.65	−0.31
⋮	⋮	⋮
11/1/2010	1.68	2.15

Source: http://finance.yahoo.com and U.S. Treasury.

In a report, use the sample information to:

1. Estimate CAPM: $R - R_f = \beta_0 + \beta_1(R_M - R_f) + \varepsilon$. Search for Apple's reported Beta on the Web and compare it with your estimate.

2. At the 5% significance level, is the stock return of Apple riskier than that of the market? At the 5% significance level, do abnormal returns exist? Explain.

Appendix 12.1 Guidelines for Other Software Packages

The following section provides brief commands for specific software packages: Minitab, SPSS, and JMP. More detailed instructions can be found on the text website.

MINITAB

Constructing a Scatterplot with Trendline
(Replicating Figure 12.2) From the menu choose **Graph** > **Scatterplot** > **With Regression**. Select Debt as **Y variables** and Income as **X variables**.

Simple Linear Regression

(Replicating Example 12.2) From the menu choose **Stat** > **Regression** > **Regression**. Select Debt as **Response** and Income as **Predictors**.

Multiple Regression

(Replicating Example 12.3) From the menu choose **Stat** > **Regression** > **Regression**. Select Debt as **Response** and Income and Unemployment as **Predictors**.

SPSS

Simple Linear Regression

(Replicating Example 12.2) From the menu choose **Analyze** > **Regression-Linear**. Select Debt as **Dependent** and Income as **Independent(s)**.

Multiple Regression

(Replicating Example 12.3) From the menu choose **Analyze** > **Regression-Linear**. Select Debt as **Dependent** and Income and Unemployment as **Independent(s)**.

JMP

Constructing a Scatterplot with Trendline and Simple Linear Regression

A. (Replicating Figure 12.2 and Example 12.2) From the menu choose **Analyze** > **Fit Y by X**. Select Debt as **Y, Response** and Income as **X, Factor**.

B. Click on the red triangle next to the header that reads **Bivariate Fit of Debt by Income** and select **Fit line**.

Multiple Regression

(Replicating Example 12.3) From the menu choose **Analyze** > **Fit Model**. Under **Pick Role Variables**, select Debt and under **Construct Model Effects**, Select Income and **Unemployment**, and choose **Add**.

13 More on Regression Analysis

CHAPTER

LEARNING OBJECTIVES

After reading this chapter you should be able to:

LO 13.1 Use dummy variables to represent qualitative explanatory variables.

LO 13.2 Test for differences between the categories of a qualitative variable.

LO 13.3 Calculate and interpret confidence intervals and prediction intervals.

LO 13.4 Explain the role of the assumptions on the OLS estimators.

LO 13.5 Describe common violations of the assumptions and offer remedies.

In Chapter 12, we used regression analysis to answer questions such as: How much does an extra year of education contribute to salary? What is the contribution of advertisement expenditures on sales of electronic goods? Is a student's SAT score a good predictor of his/her college GPA? These questions use explanatory variables that are quantitative. There are other important applications that use qualitative explanatory variables representing two or more categories. For instance, we may want answers to questions such as: Do women get paid as much as men for the same work? Are sales of electronic goods higher in the 4th quarter than in the other quarters? Is a student's college GPA influenced by field of study? In this chapter we use dummy variables that capture the various categories of a qualitative variable.

In Chapter 12, we also used the sample regression model to compute the predicted value of the response variable for given values of the explanatory variables. In this chapter, we develop interval estimates for both the individual and expected values of the response variable. Finally, we examine the importance of the assumptions on the statistical properties of the OLS estimators, as well as the validity of the testing procedures. We address common violations to the model assumptions, discuss the consequences when these assumptions are violated, and offer some remedial measures.

INTRODUCTORY CASE

Is There Evidence of Wage Discrimination?

Three female Seton Hall professors recently learned in a court decision that they could pursue their lawsuit alleging that the university paid better salaries to younger instructors and male professors (http://www.nj.com, November 23, 2010). Numerous studies have focused on salary differences between men and women, whites and blacks, and young and old. Mary Schweitzer works in the human resources department at a large liberal arts college. After the Seton Hall news, the college asked her to test for both gender and age discrimination in salaries. Mary gathered information on the annual salaries (in $1,000s) of 42 professors, along with their experience (in years), gender (male or female), and age (under 60 years old or at least 60 years old). A portion of the data is shown in Table 13.1; the entire data set, labeled **Professor_Salary**, can be found on the text website.

TABLE 13.1 Salary and Other Information on 42 Professors

FILE

Individual	Salary (in $1,000s)	Experience (in years)	Gender	Age
1	67.50	14	Male	Under
2	53.51	6	Male	Under
⋮	⋮	⋮	⋮	⋮
42	73.06	35	Female	Over

Mary would like to use the sample information in Table 13.1 to:

1. Determine whether there is evidence of gender discrimination in salaries.
2. Determine whether there is evidence of age discrimination in salaries.

A synopsis of this case is provided in Section 13.1.

13.1 Dummy Variables

Up until now, the explanatory variables used in the regression applications have been **quantitative**; in other words, they assume meaningful numerical values. For example, in the previous chapter we used income and unemployment (both quantitative variables) to explain variations in consumer debt. In empirical work, however, it is common to include some explanatory variables that are **qualitative**. Although qualitative variables can be described by several categories, they are commonly described by only two categories. Examples include gender (male or female), homeownership (own or do not own), shipment (rejected or not rejected), and MBA (yes or no).

> ### QUANTITATIVE VERSUS QUALITATIVE VARIABLES IN REGRESSION
> Explanatory variables employed in a regression can be **quantitative** or **qualitative**. Quantitative variables assume meaningful numerical values, whereas qualitative variables represent categories.

Given the professor salary data in the introductory case, we can estimate the model as $\hat{y} = 48.83 + 1.15x$ where y represents salary (in \$1,000s) and x is the usual quantitative variable, representing experience (in years). The sample regression equation implies that the predicted salary increases by about \$1,150 ($1.15 \times 1,000$) for every year of experience. Arguably, in addition to experience, variations in salary are also caused by qualitative explanatory variables such as gender (male or female) and age (under or over 60 years).

Qualitative Variables with Two Categories

A qualitative variable with two categories can be associated with a **dummy variable**, also referred to as an **indicator variable**. A dummy variable d is defined as a variable that assumes a value of 1 for one of the categories and 0 for the other. For example, in the case of a dummy variable categorizing gender, we can define 1 for males and 0 for females. Alternatively, we can define 1 for females and 0 for males, with no change in inference. Sometimes we define a dummy variable by converting a quantitative variable to a qualitative variable. In the introductory case the qualitative variable age (under or over 60 years) was actually defined from the quantitative variable age. Similarly, in studying teen behavior, we may have access to quantitative information on age, but we can generate a dummy variable that equals 1 for ages between 13 and 19 and 0 otherwise.

> ### A DUMMY VARIABLE
> A **dummy variable** d is defined as a variable that takes on values of 1 or 0. It is commonly used to describe a qualitative variable with two categories.

LO 13.1

Use dummy variables to represent qualitative explanatory variables.

For the sake of simplicity, we will first consider a model containing one quantitative explanatory variable and one dummy variable. As we will see shortly, the model can easily be extended to include additional variables.

Consider the following model:

$$y = \beta_0 + \beta_1 x + \beta_2 d + \varepsilon,$$

where x is a quantitative variable and d is a dummy variable with values of 1 or 0. We can use sample data to estimate the model as

$$\hat{y} = b_0 + b_1 x + b_2 d.$$

For a given x and $d = 1$, we can compute the predicted value as

$$\hat{y} = b_0 + b_1 x + b_2 = (b_0 + b_2) + b_1 x.$$

Similarly, for $d = 0$,

$$\hat{y} = b_0 + b_1 x.$$

Observe that the two regression lines, $\hat{y} = (b_0 + b_2) + b_1 x$ and $\hat{y} = b_0 + x$, have the same slope b_1. Thus, the sample regression equation $\hat{y} = b_0 + b_1 x + b_2 d$ accommodates two parallel lines; that is, the dummy variable d affects the intercept but not the slope. The difference between the intercepts is b_2 when d changes from 0 to 1. Figure 13.1 shows the two regression lines when $b_2 > 0$.

FIGURE 13.1 Using d for an intercept shift

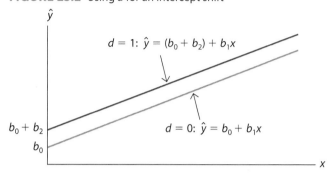

EXAMPLE 13.1
The objective outlined in the introductory case is to determine if there is any gender or age discrimination at a large liberal arts college. Use the data in Table 13.1 to answer the following questions.

a. Estimate $y = \beta_0 + \beta_1 x + \beta_2 d_1 + \beta_3 d_2 + \varepsilon$, where y is the annual salary (in $1,000s) of a professor, x is the number of years of experience, d_1 is a gender dummy variable that equals 1 if the professor is male and 0 otherwise, and d_2 is an age dummy variable that equals 1 if the professor is 60 years of age or older and 0 otherwise.

b. Compute the predicted salary of a 50-year-old male professor with 10 years of experience. Compute the predicted salary of a 50-year-old female professor with 10 years of experience. Discuss the impact of gender on predicted salary.

c. Compute the predicted salary of a 65-year-old female professor with 10 years of experience. Discuss the impact of age on predicted salary.

SOLUTION:

a. To estimate the model in part a, we first convert the qualitative variables in Table 13.1 to their respective gender and age dummy variables, d_1 and d_2. A portion of the converted data is shown in Table 13.2.

TABLE 13.2 Generating d_1 and d_2 from the Data in Table 13.1

y	x	d_1 (Gender)	d_2 (Age)
67.50	14	1	0
53.51	6	1	0
⋮	⋮	⋮	⋮
73.06	35	0	1

Table 13.3 shows the relevant regression results.

TABLE 13.3 Regression Results for Example 13.1

	Coefficients	Standard Error	t Stat	p-value
Intercept	40.61	3.69	11.00	0.00
x	1.13	0.18	6.30	0.00
d_1 (Gender)	13.92	2.87	4.86	0.00
d_2 (Age)	4.34	4.64	0.94	0.36

The estimated model is $\hat{y} = 40.61 + 1.13x + 13.92d_1 + 4.34d_2$.

b. The predicted salary of a 50-year old male professor ($d_1 = 1$ and $d_2 = 0$) with 10 years of experience ($x = 10$) is

$$\hat{y} = 40.61 + 1.13(10) + 13.92(1) + 4.34(0) = 65.83, \text{ that is, } \$65{,}830.$$

The corresponding salary of a 50-year-old female professor ($d_1 = 0$ and $d_2 = 0$) is

$$\hat{y} = 40.61 + 1.13(10) + 13.92(0) + 4.34(0) = 51.91, \text{ that is, } \$51{,}910.$$

The predicted difference in salary between a male and a female professor with 10 years of experience is $13,920 (65,830 − 51,910). This difference can also be inferred from the estimated coefficient 13.92 of the gender dummy variable d_1. Note that the salary difference does not change with experience. For instance, the predicted salary of a 50-year-old male with 20 years of experience is $77,130. The corresponding salary of a 50-year-old female is $63,210, for the same difference of $13,920.

c. For a 65-year-old female professor with 10 years of experience, the predicted salary is

$$\hat{y} = 40.61 + 1.13(10) + 13.92(0) + 4.34(1) = 56.25, \text{ or } 56{,}250.$$

Prior to any statistical testing, it appears that an older female professor earns, on average, $4,340 (56,250 − 51,910) more than a younger female professor with the same experience.

LO **13.2**

Test for differences between the categories of a qualitative variable.

Dummy variables are treated just like other explanatory variables; that is, all statistical tests discussed in Chapter 12 remain valid. In particular, we can examine whether a particular dummy variable is statistically significant by using the standard t test. Here, the statistical significance indicates that the response variable depends on the two categories of the dummy variable.

TESTING THE SIGNIFICANCE OF DUMMY VARIABLES

In a model, $y = \beta_0 + \beta_1 x + \beta_2 d_1 + \beta_3 d_2 + \varepsilon$, we can perform the t test to determine the significance of each dummy variable.

EXAMPLE 13.2

Refer to the regression results in Table 13.3.

a. Determine whether there is a difference in salary depending on gender at the 5% significance level.

b. Determine whether an older professor's salary differs from a younger professor's salary at the 5% significance level.

SOLUTION:

a. In order to test for a salary difference between male and female professors, we set up the hypotheses as $H_0: \beta_2 = 0$ against $H_A: \beta_2 \neq 0$. Given a value of the t_{df} test statistic of 4.86 with a p-value ≈ 0, we reject the null hypothesis and conclude that the gender dummy variable is statistically significant at the 5% level. We conclude that male and female professors do not make the same salary, holding other variables constant.

b. Here the hypotheses take the form $H_0: \beta_3 = 0$ against $H_A: \beta_3 \neq 0$. Given a value of the t_{df} test statistic of 0.94 with a p-value $= 0.36$, we cannot reject the null hypothesis. At the 5% significance level, we cannot conclude that age discrimination exists with respect to a professor's salary.

We now use the adjusted R^2 criterion to select the preferred model for the analysis. Regression results are summarized in Table 13.4.

TABLE 13.4 Summary of Model Estimates

Variable	Model 1	Model 2	Model 3
Intercept	48.83*	39.43*	40.61*
	(0.00)	(0.00)	(0.00)
Experience	1.15*	1.24*	1.13*
	(0.00)	(0.00)	(0.00)
Gender	NA	13.89*	13.92*
		(0.01)	(0.00)
Age	NA	NA	4.34
			(0.36)
Adjusted R^2	0.5358	0.7031	0.7022

Notes: The table contains parameter estimates with p-values in parentheses; NA denotes not applicable; *represents significance at the 5% level; adjusted R^2, reported in the last row, is used for model selection.

Model 1 uses only the quantitative variable, Experience. In addition to Experience, Model 2 includes a dummy variable, Gender and Model 3 includes Experience and two dummy variables, Gender and Age. This raises an important question: which of the above three models should we use for making predictions? As discussed in Chapter 12, we usually rely on adjusted R^2 to compare models with different numbers of explanatory variables. Based on the adjusted R^2 values of the models, reported in the last row of Table 13.4, we select Model 2 as the preferred model because it has the highest adjusted R^2 value of 0.7031. This is consistent with the test results that showed that Gender is significant, but Age is not significant, at the 5% level.

Qualitative Variables with Multiple Categories

So far we have used dummy variables to describe qualitative variables with only two categories, such as gender with males and females. Sometimes, a qualitative variable may be defined by more than two categories. In such cases we use multiple dummy variables to capture all categories. For example, the mode of transportation used to commute may be described by three categories: Public Transportation, Driving Alone, and Car Pooling. We can then define two dummy variables d_1 and d_2, where d_1 equals 1 for Public Transportation, 0 otherwise, and d_2 equals 1 for Driving Alone, 0 otherwise. For this three-category case, we need to define only two dummy variables; Car Pooling is indicated when $d_1 = d_2 = 0$.

Consider the following regression model:

$$y = \beta_0 + \beta_1 x + \beta_2 d_1 + \beta_3 d_2 + \varepsilon,$$

where y represents commuting expenditure, x represents distance to work, and d_1 and d_2 represent the Public Transportation and Driving Alone dummy variables, respectively. We can use sample data to estimate the model as

$$\hat{y} = b_0 + b_1 x + b_2 d_1 + b_3 d_2.$$

For $d_1 = 1$, $d_2 = 0$ (Public Transportation), $\hat{y} = b_0 + b_1 x + b_2 = (b_0 + b_2) + b_1 x$.

For $d_1 = 0$, $d_2 = 1$ (Driving Alone), $\hat{y} = b_0 + b_1 x + b_3 = (b_0 + b_3) + b_1 x$.

For $d_1 = d_2 = 0$ (Car Pooling), $\hat{y} = b_0 + b_1 x$.

Here we use Car Pooling as the reference category in the estimated regression line with the intercept b_0. The intercept changes to $(b_0 + b_2)$ for Public Transportation and $(b_0 + b_3)$ for Driving Alone. Therefore, we account for all three categories with just two dummy variables.

Given the intercept term, we exclude one of the dummy variables from the regression, where the excluded variable represents the reference category against which the others are assessed. If we include as many dummy variables as there are categories, then their sum will equal one. For instance, if we add a third dummy d_3 that equals 1 to denote Car Pooling, then for all observations, $d_1 + d_2 + d_3 = 1$. This creates a problem called perfect multicollinearity, which we will discuss in the last section of this chapter. Such a model cannot be estimated. This situation is sometimes referred to as the **dummy variable trap**.

AVOIDING THE DUMMY VARIABLE TRAP

Assuming that the linear regression model includes an intercept, the number of dummy variables representing a qualitative variable should be **one less than the number of categories** of the variable.

EXAMPLE 13.3

A recent article suggests that Asian-Americans face serious discrimination in the college admissions process (*The New York Times*, February 8, 2012). Specifically, Asian students need higher standardized test scores than white students for college admission. Another report suggests that colleges are eager to recruit Hispanic students who are generally underrepresented in applicant pools (*USA TODAY*, February 8, 2010). A researcher from the Center for Equal Opportunity wants to determine if SAT scores of admitted students at a large state university differed by ethnic background. She collects data on 200 admitted students with their SAT scores and ethnic background. A portion of the data is shown in Table 13.5; the entire data set, labeled **SAT_Ethnicity**, can be found on the text website.

TABLE 13.5 SAT Scores and Ethnic Background; $n = 200$

Individual	SAT	White	Black	Asian	Hispanic
1	1515	1	0	0	0
2	1530	0	0	0	1
⋮	⋮	⋮	⋮	⋮	⋮
200	1614	1	0	0	0

a. Estimate the model $y = \beta_0 + \beta_1 d_1 + \beta_2 d_2 + \beta_3 d_3 + \varepsilon$, where y represents a student's SAT score; d_1 equals 1 if the student is white, 0 otherwise; d_2 equals 1 if the student is black, 0 otherwise; and d_3 equals 1 if the student is Asian, 0 otherwise. Note that the reference category is Hispanics.

b. What is the predicted SAT score for an Asian student? For a Hispanic student?

c. Do SAT scores vary by ethnic background at the 5% significance level? Explain.

SOLUTION:

a. We report the regression results of this model in Table 13.6.

TABLE 13.6 Regression Results for Example 13.3

	Coefficients	Standard Error	t Stat	p-value
Intercept	1388.89	9.36	148.44	0.00
d_1 (White)	201.14	12.91	15.59	0.00
d_2 (Black)	−31.45	22.19	−1.42	0.16
d_3 (Asian)	264.86	17.86	14.83	0.00

b. For an Asian student, we set $d_1 = 0$, $d_2 = 0$, $d_3 = 1$ and calculate $\hat{y} = 1388.89 + 264.86 = 1653.75$. Thus, the predicted SAT score for an Asian student is approximately 1654. The predicted SAT score for a Hispanic student ($d_1 = d_2 = d_3 = 0$) is $\hat{y} = 1388.89$, or approximately 1389.

c. Since the p-values corresponding to d_1 and d_3 are approximately zero, we conclude at the 5% level that the SAT scores of admitted white and Asian students are different from those of Hispanic students. However, with a p-value of 0.16, we cannot conclude that the SAT scores of admitted black and Hispanic students are statistically different.

EXAMPLE 13.4

Use the SAT data in Table 13.5 to reformulate the model to determine, at the 5% level of significance, if the SAT scores of white students are lower than the SAT scores of Asian students. As in Example 13.3, we must consider all ethnic categories for the analysis.

SOLUTION:

We note that the regression results reported in Table 13.6 cannot be used to determine if the SAT scores of white students are lower than the SAT scores of Asian students. In order to conduct the relevant test, we must use either Asians or whites as the reference category against which the other one is assessed. We estimate the model as $y = \beta_0 + \beta_1 d_1 + \beta_2 d_2 + \beta_3 d_3 + \varepsilon$, where d_1 and d_2 are again dummy variables corresponding to the categories of white and black students, respectively, but now d_3 equals 1 if the student is Hispanic; 0 otherwise. Here the reference category is Asian. We report the regression results of this model in Table 13.7.

TABLE 13.7 Regression Results for Example 13.4

	Coefficient	Standard Error	t Stat	p-value
Intercept	1653.75	15.21	108.72	0.00
d_1 (White)	−63.71	17.62	−3.62	0.00
d_2 (Black)	−296.31	25.22	−11.75	0.00
d_3 (Hispanic)	−264.86	17.86	−14.83	0.00

For an Asian student, we set $d_1 = d_2 = d_3 = 0$ to find the predicted SAT score as 1653.75, which is the same as derived earlier. In fact, we can show that all predicted SAT scores are identical to those found in Example 13.3. This shows that the choice of the reference category does not matter for making predictions. The results in Table 13.7, however, can be used to determine if the SAT scores of white students are lower than the SAT scores of Asian students. We specify the hypothesis for a left-tailed test as $H_0: \beta_1 \geq 0$ against $H_A: \beta_1 < 0$ and use the critical value approach for the test. Given $n = 200$ and $k = 3$, we find $df = n - k - 1 = 196$. At $\alpha = 0.05$, we reject the null hypothesis since the value of the test statistic, $t_{196} = -3.62$, is less than the critical value, $-t_{0.05,196} = -1.653$. Therefore, we conclude that the SAT scores of admitted white students are less than the SAT scores of admitted Asian students at the 5% significance level.

SYNOPSIS OF INTRODUCTORY CASE

A recent lawsuit brought against Seton Hall University by three female professors alleges that the university engages in both age and gender discrimination with respect to salaries (http://www.nj.com, November 23, 2010). Another large university wonders if the same can be said about its practices. Information is collected on the annual salaries (in $1,000s) of 42 professors, along with his/her experience (in years), gender (male or female), and age (whether he/she is 60 years old or older). In order to determine if there is gender or age discrimination at this university, a regression model is developed using salary as the response variable and experience, a gender dummy variable, and an age dummy variable as the explanatory variables.

The estimated model reveals that the gender dummy variable is significant, but the age dummy variable is not significant, at the 5% level. In addition, in terms of the adjusted R^2, the model that includes only experience and the gender dummy variable outperforms the models with other combinations of the explanatory variables. According to this preferred model, the estimated salary increases by about $1,240 for every year of experience. For the same level of experience, male professors are predicted to make about $1,390 more than their female counterparts. In sum, the findings suggest that there is gender discrimination at this university, while age discrimination does not seem to be a problem.

EXERCISES 13.1

Mechanics

1. Consider a linear regression model where y represents the response variable, x is a quantitative explanatory variable, and d is a dummy variable. The model is estimated as

$$\hat{y} = 14.8 + 4.4x - 3.8d.$$

   a. Interpret the dummy variable coefficient.
   b. Compute $\hat{y}$ for $x = 3$ and $d = 1$.
   c. Compute $\hat{y}$ for $x = 3$ and $d = 0$.

2. Consider a linear regression model where y represents the response variable and d_1 and d_2 are dummy variables. The model is estimated as $\hat{y} = 160 + 15d_1 + 32d_2$.

   a. Compute $\hat{y}$ for $d_1 = 1$ and $d_2 = 1$.
   b. Compute $\hat{y}$ for $d_1 = 0$ and $d_2 = 0$.

3. Using 50 observations, the following regression output is obtained from estimating $y = \beta_0 + \beta_1 x + \beta_2 d_1 + \beta_3 d_2 + \varepsilon$.

	Coefficients	Standard Error	t Stat	p-value
Intercept	−0.61	0.23	−2.75	0.0074
x	3.12	1.04	3.01	0.0034
d_1	−13.22	15.65	−0.85	0.4006
d_2	5.35	1.25	4.27	0.0000

a. Compute $\hat{y}$ for $x = 250$, $d_1 = 1$, and $d_2 = 0$; then compute $\hat{y}$ for $x = 250$, $d_1 = 0$, and $d_2 = 1$.

b. Interpret d_1 and d_2. Are both dummy variables individually significant at the 5% level? Explain.

Applications

4. An executive researcher wants to better understand the factors that explain differences in salaries for marketing majors. He decides to estimate two models: $y = \beta_0 + \beta_1 d_1 + \varepsilon$ (Model 1) and $y = \beta_0 + \beta_1 d_1 + \beta_2 d_2 + \varepsilon$ (Model 2). Here y represents salary, d_1 is a dummy variable that equals 1 for male employees, and d_2 is a dummy variable that equals 1 for employees with an MBA.
   a. What is the reference group in Model 1?
   b. What is the reference group in Model 2?
   c. In the above models, would it matter if d_1 equaled 1 for female employees?

5. House price y is estimated as a function of the square footage of a house x and a dummy variable d that equals 1 if the house has ocean views. The estimated house price, measured in \$1,000s, is given by $\hat{y} = 118.90 + 0.12x + 52.60d$.
   a. Compute the predicted price of a house with ocean views and square footage of 2,000 and 3,000, respectively.
   b. Compute the predicted price of a house without ocean views and square footage of 2,000 and 3,000, respectively.
   c. Discuss the impact of ocean views on the house price.

6. **FILE** A sociologist is studying the relationship between consumption expenditures y of families in the United States, family income x, and whether or not the family lives in an urban or rural community. She collects data on 50 families, a portion of which is shown in the accompanying table. The entire data set, labeled **Urban_Rural**, can be found on the text website.

Consumption (\$)	Income (\$)	Community
62,336	87,534	Rural
60,076	94,796	Urban
⋮	⋮	⋮
59,055	100,908	Urban

   a. Estimate $y = \beta_0 + \beta_1 x + \beta_2 d + \varepsilon$ where the dummy variable d equals 1 for urban families. Use the estimated model to predict the consumption expenditure of urban families with an income of \$80,000. What is the corresponding consumption expenditure of rural families?
   b. Estimate $y = \beta_0 + \beta_1 x + \beta_2 d + \varepsilon$ where the dummy variable d equals 1 for rural families. Use the estimated model to predict the consumption expenditure of urban families with an income of \$80,000. What is the corresponding consumption expenditure of rural families?
   c. Interpret the results of the above two models.

7. **FILE** One of the theories regarding initial public offering (IPO) pricing is that the initial return y (change from offer to open price) on an IPO depends on the price revision x (change from pre-offer to offer price). Another factor that may influence the initial return is whether or not it is a high-tech firm. Consider the data on 264 IPO firms from January 2001 through September 2004; the entire data set, labeled **IPO_Pricing**, can be found on the text website.

Initial Return (%)	Price Revision (%)	High-Tech?
33.93	7.14	No
18.68	−26.39	No
⋮	⋮	⋮
0.08	−29.41	Yes

Source: http://www.ipohome.com; http://www.nasdaq.com.

   a. Estimate $y = \beta_0 + \beta_1 x + \beta_2 d + \varepsilon$ where the dummy variable d equals 1 for firms that are high-tech. Use the estimated model to predict the initial return of a high-tech firm with a 10% price revision. Find the corresponding predicted return of a firm that is not high-tech.
   b. Estimate $y = \beta_0 + \beta_1 x + \beta_2 d + \varepsilon$ where the dummy variable d equals 1 for firms that are not high-tech. Use the estimated model to predict the initial return of a high-tech firm with a 10% price revision. Find the corresponding predicted return of a firm that is not high-tech.
   c. In the above two models, determine if the dummy variable is significant at the 5% level.

8. According to the *World Health Organization*, obesity has reached epidemic proportions globally. While obesity has generally been linked with chronic disease and disability, researchers argue that it may also affect salaries. In other words, the body mass index (BMI) of an employee is a predictor for salary. (A person is considered overweight if his/her BMI is at least 25 and obese if BMI exceeds 30.) Consider salary data of 30 college-educated men with their respective BMI and their race defined as 1 for white and 0 for nonwhite. A portion of the data is shown in the accompanying table; the entire data set, labeled **BMI_Salary**, can be found on the text website.

Salary (\$1,000)	BMI	Race
34	33	1
34	33	1
⋮	⋮	⋮
45	21	1

   a. Estimate a model for Salary using BMI and Race as the explanatory variables. Determine if BMI influences salary at the 5% level of significance.
   b. What is the estimated salary of a white college-educated worker with a BMI of 30? Compute the corresponding salary of a nonwhite worker.

9. In an attempt to "time the market," a financial analyst studies the quarterly returns of a stock. He uses the model $y = \beta_0 + \beta_1 d_1 + \beta_2 d_2 + \beta_3 d_3 + \varepsilon$ where y is the quarterly return of a stock, d_1 is a dummy variable that equals 1 if quarter 1 and 0 otherwise, d_2 is a dummy variable that equals 1 if quarter 2 and 0 otherwise, and d_3 is a dummy variable that equals 1 if quarter 3 and 0 otherwise. The following table shows a portion of the regression results.

	Coefficients	Standard Error	t Stat	p-value
Intercept	10.62	5.81	1.83	0.08
d_1	−7.26	8.21	−0.88	0.38
d_2	−1.87	8.21	−0.23	0.82
d_3	−9.31	8.21	−1.13	0.27

a. Given that there are four quarters in a year, why doesn't the analyst include a fourth dummy variable in his model? What is the reference category?

b. At the 5% significance level, are the dummy variables individually significant? Explain. Is the analyst able to obtain higher returns depending on the quarter?

c. Explain how you would reformulate the model to determine if the quarterly return is higher in quarter 2 than in quarter 3, still accounting for all quarters.

10. FILE In the United States, baseball has always been a favorite pastime and is rife with statistics and theories. While baseball purists may disagree, to an applied statistician no topic in baseball is too small or hypothesis too unlikely. In a recent paper, researchers at Wayne State University showed that major league players who have nicknames live 2½ years longer than those without them (*The Wall Street Journal*, July 16, 2009). Consider the following portion of data on the lifespan (Years) of a player and a Nickname dummy variable that equals 1 if the player had a nickname and 0 otherwise; the entire data set, labeled **Nicknames**, can be found on the text website.

Years	Nickname
74	1
62	1
⋮	⋮
64	0

a. Create two subsamples, with one consisting of players with a nickname and the other one without a nickname. Calculate the average longevity for each subsample.

b. Estimate a linear regression model of Years on the Nickname dummy variable. Compute the predicted longevity of players with and without a nickname.

c. Conduct a one-tailed test at a 5% level to determine if players with a nickname live longer.

11. FILE The SAT has gone through many revisions over the years. In 2005, a new writing section was introduced that includes a direct writing measure in the form of an essay. People argue that female students generally do worse on math tests but better on writing tests. Therefore, the new section may help reduce the usual male lead on the overall average SAT score (*Washington Post*, August 30, 2006). Consider the following portion of data on 20 students who took the SAT test last year; the entire data set, labeled **SATdummy**, can be found on the text website. Information includes each student's score on the writing and math sections of the exam. Also included

are the student's GPA and the values of a Gender dummy variable with 1 for females and 0 for males.

Writing	Math	GPA	Gender
620	600	3.44	0
570	550	3.04	0
⋮	⋮	⋮	⋮
540	520	2.84	0

a. Estimate a linear regression model with Writing as the response variable and GPA and Gender as the explanatory variables.

b. Compute the predicted writing score for a male student with a GPA of 3.5. Repeat the computation for a female student.

c. Perform a test to determine if there is a statistically significant gender difference in writing scores at a 5% level.

12. FILE Use the data described in Exercise 11 to estimate a linear regression model with Math as the response variable and GPA and Gender as the explanatory variables.

a. Compute the predicted math score for a male student with a GPA of 3.5. Repeat the computation for a female student.

b. Perform a test to determine if there is a statistically significant gender difference in math scores at the 5% level.

13. FILE A manager at an ice cream store is trying to determine how many customers to expect on any given day. Overall business has been relatively steady over the past several years, but the customer count seems to have ups and downs. He collects data over 30 days and records the number of customers, the high temperature (degrees Fahrenheit), and whether the day fell on a weekend (1 equals weekend, 0 otherwise). A portion of the data is shown in the accompanying table; the entire data set, labeled **Ice_Cream**, can be found on the text website.

Customers	Temperature	Weekend
376	75	0
433	78	0
⋮	⋮	⋮
401	68	0

a. Estimate: Customers $= \beta_0 + \beta_1$Temperature $+ \beta_2$Weekend $+ \varepsilon$.

b. How many customers should the manager expect on a Sunday with a forecasted high temperature of 80°?

c. Interpret the estimated coefficient for Weekend. Is it significant at the 5% level? How might this affect the store's staffing needs?

14. FILE A researcher wonders whether males get paid more, on average, than females at a large firm. She interviews 50 employees and collects data on each employee's hourly wage (Wage), years of higher education (EDUC), experience (EXPER), age (AGE), and gender. The GENDER dummy

variable equals 1 if male, 0 if female. A portion of the data is shown in the accompanying table; the entire data set, labeled **Hourly_Wage**, can be found on the text website.

Wage	EDUC	EXPER	AGE	GENDER
$37.85	11	2	40	1
21.72	4	1	39	0
⋮	⋮	⋮	⋮	⋮
24.18	8	11	64	0

a. Estimate: Wage $= \beta_0 + \beta_1 EDUC + \beta_2 EXPER + \beta_3 AGE + \beta_4 GENDER + \varepsilon$.

b. Predict the hourly wage of a 40-year-old male employee with 10 years of higher education and 5 years experience. Predict the hourly wage of a 40-year-old female employee with the same qualifications.

c. Interpret the estimated coefficient for GENDER. Is the variable GENDER significant at the 5% level? Do the data suggest that gender discrimination exists at this firm?

15. FILE A government researcher is analyzing the relationship between retail sales and the gross national product (GNP). He also wonders whether there are significant differences in retail sales related to the quarters of the year. He collects 10 years of quarterly data. A portion is shown in the accompanying table; the entire data set, labeled **Retail_Sales**, can be found on the text website.

Year	Quarter	Retail Sales (in $ millions)	GNP (in $ billions)	d_1	d_2	d_3	d_4
2001	1	696,048	9,740.5	1	0	0	0
	2	753,211	9,983.5	0	1	0	0
⋮	⋮	⋮		⋮	⋮	⋮	⋮
2009	4	985,649	14,442.8	0	0	0	1

Source: Retail sales obtained from http://www.census.gov; GNP obtained from http://research.stlouisfed.org.

a. Estimate $y = \beta_0 + \beta_1 x + \beta_2 d_1 + \beta_3 d_2 + \beta_4 d_3 + \varepsilon$ where y is retail sales, x is GNP, d_1 is a dummy variable that equals 1 if quarter 1 and 0 otherwise, d_2 is a dummy variable that equals 1 if quarter 2 and 0 otherwise, and d_3 is a dummy variable that equals 1 if quarter 3 and 0 otherwise. Here the reference category is quarter 4.

b. Predict retail sales in quarters 2 and 4 if GNP equals $13,000 billion.

c. Which of the quarterly sales are significantly different from those of the 4th quarter at the 5% level?

d. Reformulate the model to determine, at the 5% significance level, if sales differ between quarter 2 and quarter 3. Your model must account for all quarters.

16. FILE The issues regarding executive compensation have received extensive media attention. The government is even considering a cap on high-flying salaries for executives (*New York Times*, February 9, 2009). Consider a regression model that links executive compensation with the total assets of the firm and the firm's industry. Dummy variables are used to represent four industries: Manufacturing Technology d_1, Manufacturing Other d_2, Financial Services d_3, and Nonfinancial Services d_4. A portion of the data for the 455 highest-paid CEOs in 2006 is given in the accompanying table; the entire data set, labeled **Industry_Compensation**, can be found on the text website.

Compensation (in $ million)	Assets (in $ millions)	d_1	d_2	d_3	d_4
16.58	20,917.5	1	0	0	0
26.92	32,659.5	1	0	0	0
⋮	⋮	⋮	⋮	⋮	⋮
2.30	44,875.0	0	0	1	0

Source: SEC website and Compustat.

a. Estimate the model: $y = \beta_0 + \beta_1 x + \beta_2 d_1 + \beta_3 d_2 + \beta_4 d_3 + \varepsilon$, where y and x denote compensation and total assets, respectively. Here the reference category is nonfinancial services industry.

b. Interpret the estimated coefficients.

c. Use a 5% level of significance to determine which industries, relative to the nonfinancial services industry, have a different executive compensation.

d. Reformulate the model to determine, at the 5% significance level, if compensation is higher in Manufacturing Other than in Manufacturing Technology. Your model must account for assets and all industry types.

13.2 Interval Estimates for the Response Variable

In the last section, we selected Model 2 for making predictions regarding a professor's salary. Recall that this model uses experience and a gender dummy variable as the two explanatory variables. In particular, we estimated the model as $\hat{y} = 39.43 + 1.24x + 13.89d$ where y denotes salary, x denotes experience, and d is a gender dummy variable that takes a value of 1 for male and 0 otherwise (here we use d instead of d_1). Suppose we want to predict the

LO **13.3**

Calculate and interpret confidence intervals and prediction intervals.

salary of a male professor with 10 years of experience. We can easily use the above estimated model with $x = 10$ and $d = 1$ to derive the predicted salary as

$$\hat{y} = 39.43 + 1.24 \times 10 + 13.89 \times 1 = 65.72, \text{ or } \$65,720.$$

Predictions, such as the one above, are certainly useful, but we need to be aware that such predictions are subject to sampling variations. In other words, the prediction will change if we use a different sample to estimate the regression model. Recall from Chapter 8 that the point estimate along with the margin of error is used to construct the relevant interval estimate. In the above example, $\$65,720$ represents the point estimate.

In this section we will make a distinction between the interval estimate for the mean (expected value) of y and the interval estimate for the individual value of y. It is common to refer to the former as the **confidence interval** and the latter as the **prediction interval**. For given values of the explanatory variables, we can think of the confidence interval as the range that contains the mean of y and the prediction interval as the range that contains the individual value of y. We use the same point estimate for constructing both interval estimates. In the context of the above example, $\$65,720$ is the point estimate for the mean salary as well as the individual salary of a male professor with 10 years of experience. Due to the added uncertainty in predicting the individual value of y, the prediction interval is always wider than the corresponding confidence interval, for given values of the explanatory variables.

CONFIDENCE INTERVAL AND PREDICTION INTERVAL

We construct two types of interval estimates regarding the response variable y for given values of the explanatory variables. The interval estimate for the mean (expected value) of y is referred to as the **confidence interval**. It is common to refer to the interval estimate for an individual value of y as the **prediction interval**. The prediction interval is always wider than the corresponding confidence interval.

We will now describe the general procedure for constructing the confidence interval and the prediction interval. For the sake of simplicity, we let x's denote all explanatory variables, including dummy variables. In the context of the above salary example, we let x_1 and x_2 represent experience and a gender dummy variable, respectively.

Consider a multiple regression model $y = \beta_0 + \beta_1 x_1 + \beta_2 x_2 + \cdots + \beta_k x_k + \varepsilon$ with k explanatory variables, $x_1, x_2, \ldots, x_k$.

Moreover, let

$$y^0 = \beta_0 + \beta_1 x_1^0 + \beta_2 x_2^0 + \cdots + \beta_k x_k^0 + \varepsilon^0,$$

where $x_1^0, x_2^0, \ldots, x_k^0$ denote specific values for $x_1, x_2, \ldots, x_k$ at which y^0 is evaluated and ε^0 is the (unobserved) random error term. In the salary example, we used $x_1^0 = 10$ and $x_2^0 = 1$. Alternatively, we can evaluate the expected value of the response variable at $x_1^0, x_2^0, \ldots, x_k^0$ as

$$E(y^0) = \beta_0 + \beta_1 x_1^0 + \beta_2 x_2^0 + \cdots + \beta_k x_k^0.$$

The expected value equation uses the fact that the expected value of the random error term is assumed to be zero, that is, $E(\varepsilon^0) = 0$; we discuss this assumption in the next section. Note that the prediction interval is wider than the confidence interval because it also incorporates the additional uncertainty due to ε^0. We first derive a confidence interval for $E(y^0)$, followed by a prediction interval for y^0.

The predicted value, $\hat{y}^0 = b_0 + b_1 x_1^0 + b_2 x_2^0 + \cdots + b_k x_k^0$, is the point estimate for $E(y^0)$. In our earlier example, 65.72 is the point estimate of $E(y^0)$ when $x_1^0 = 10$ and $x_2^0 = 1$. We form a $100(1 - \alpha)\%$ confidence interval for $E(y^0)$ as $\hat{y}^0 \pm t_{\alpha/2,df} se(\hat{y}^0)$, where $se(\hat{y}^0)$ is the estimated standard error of the predicted value. While there is a simple formula to compute the standard error $se(\hat{y}^0)$ for a simple linear regression model, it is very cumbersome to do so for a multiple linear regression model. We describe a relatively easy way to construct a confidence interval that works for both simple and multiple linear regression models.

CONFIDENCE INTERVAL FOR THE EXPECTED VALUE OF y

For specific values of $x_1, x_2, \ldots, x_k$, denoted by $x_1^0, x_2^0, \ldots, x_k^0$, the $100(1 - \alpha)\%$ confidence interval of the expected value of y is computed as

$$\hat{y}^0 \pm t_{\alpha/2, df} se(\hat{y}^0),$$

where $\hat{y}^0 = b_0 + b_1 x_1^0 + b_2 x_2^0 + \cdots + b_k x_k^0$, $se(\hat{y}^0)$ is the standard error of $\hat{y}^0$, and $df = n - k - 1$.

To derive $\hat{y}^0$ together with $se(\hat{y}^0)$ we first estimate a modified regression model where y is the response variable and the explanatory variables are defined as $x_1^* = x_1 - x_1^0$, $x_2^* = x_2 - x_2^0, \ldots, x_k^* = x_k - x_k^0$. The resulting estimate of the intercept and its standard error equal $\hat{y}^0$ and $se(\hat{y}^0)$, respectively.

EXAMPLE 13.5

We again reference the data from Table 13.1 and the regression model $y = \beta_0 + \beta_1 x_1 + \beta_2 x_2 + \varepsilon$ where y, x_1, and x_2 represent salary, experience, and a gender dummy variable, respectively. Recall that the gender dummy variable equals 1 if male and 0 if female. Construct the 95% confidence interval for the mean salary of a male professor with 10 years of experience.

SOLUTION: In order to construct a confidence interval for $E(y^0)$, we follow the above-mentioned procedure to derive $\hat{y}^0$ and $se(\hat{y}^0)$. First, given $x_1^0 = 10$ and $x_2^0 = 1$, we define two modified explanatory variables as $x_1^* = x_1 - 10$ and $x_2^* = x_2 - 1$. Table 13.8 shows the computations of their values.

TABLE 13.8 Computing the Values of Modified Explanatory Variables (Example 13.5)

y	x_1	x_2	$x_1^* = x_1 - 10$	$x_2^* = x_2 - 1$
67.50	14	1	$14 - 10 = 4$	$1 - 1 = 0$
53.51	6	1	$6 - 10 = -4$	$1 - 1 = 0$
⋮	⋮	⋮	⋮	⋮
73.06	35	0	$35 - 10 = 25$	$0 - 1 = -1$

The regression output for a multiple linear regression model that uses y as the response variable and x_1^* and x_2^* as the explanatory variables is presented in Table 13.9.

TABLE 13.9 Regression Results with Modified Explanatory Variables (Example 13.5)

Regression Statistics						
Multiple R	0.8471					
R Square	0.7176					
Adjusted R Square	0.7031					
Standard Error	**9.1326**					
Observations	42					

ANOVA						
	df	SS	MS	F	Significance F	
Regression	2	8266.1526	4133.0763	49.5546	0.0000	
Residual	39	3252.7766	83.4045			
Total	41	11518.9292				

	Coefficients	Standard Error	t Stat	p-value	Lower 95%	Upper 95%
Intercept	**65.7151**	**2.1572**	30.4636	0.0000	**61.3518**	**70.0784**
x_1^*	1.2396	0.1332	9.3067	0.0000	0.9702	1.5090
x_2^*	13.8857	2.8617	4.8522	0.0000	8.0973	19.6741

We note that this modified regression output is identical to the original regression output (see the summarized results for Model 2 in Table 13.4) except for the estimates of the intercept term. The boldface intercept estimate is 65.7151 and its standard error is 2.1572. Therefore, we use $\hat{y}^0 = 65.7151$ and $se(\hat{y}^0) = 2.1572$ in constructing the confidence interval. Note that Excel's calculation for $\hat{y}^0$ is the same as our earlier estimate, $\hat{y}^0 = 39.43 + 1.24 \times 10 + 13.89 \times 1 = 65.72$, except for rounding.

For a 95% confidence level and $df = n - k - 1 = 42 - 2 - 1 = 39$, we find $t_{\alpha/2,df} = t_{0.025,39} = 2.023$. The 95% confidence interval for $E(y^0)$ is

$$\hat{y}^0 \pm t_{\alpha/2,df} se(\hat{y}^0) = 65.7151 \pm 2.023 \times 2.1572 = 65.7151 \pm 4.3640.$$

Or, with 95% confidence,

$$61.35 \le E(y^0) \le 70.08.$$

With 95% confidence, we can state that the mean salary of all male professors with 10 years of experience falls between \$61,350 and \$70,080. Note that these limits are also provided in the boldface Lower 95% and Upper 95% values of Table 13.9.

As mentioned earlier, the prediction interval pertains to the individual value of the response variable defined for specific explanatory variables as $y^0 = \beta_0 + \beta_1 x_1^0 + \beta_2 x_2^0 + \cdots + \beta_k x_k^0 + \varepsilon^0$. The prediction interval is wider than the confidence interval because it incorporates the variability of the random error term ε^0.

PREDICTION INTERVAL FOR AN INDIVIDUAL VALUE OF *y*

For specific values of $x_1, x_2, \ldots, x_k$, denoted by $x_1^0, x_2^0, \ldots, x_k^0$, the $100(1 - \alpha)\%$ prediction interval for an individual value of y is computed as

$$\hat{y}^0 \pm t_{\alpha/2,df} \sqrt{(se(\hat{y}^0))^2 + s_e^2},$$

where $df = n - k - 1$, $se(\hat{y}^0)$ is the standard error of $\hat{y}^0$ and s_e is the standard error of the estimate.

Note that the standard error of the estimate s_e captures the variability of the random error term ε^0.

EXAMPLE 13.6

Reconsider the estimated model $\hat{y} = 39.43 + 1.24x_1 + 13.89x_2$ where y, x_1, and x_2 represent salary, experience, and a gender dummy variable, respectively.

a. Construct the 95% prediction interval for the salary of a male professor with 10 years of experience.

b. Comment on the differences between this prediction interval and the confidence interval reported in Example 13.5.

SOLUTION:

a. As in the calculation of the confidence interval, we find $\hat{y}^0 = 65.7151$, $se(\hat{y}^0) = 2.1572$, and $t_{\alpha/2,df} = t_{0.025,39} = 2.023$. The only thing missing from the prediction interval formula is the standard error of the estimate s_e. From Table 13.9, we extract the boldface value, $s_e = 9.1326$. The 95% prediction interval is then

$$\hat{y} \pm t_{\alpha/2,df} \sqrt{(se(\hat{y}^0))^2 + s_e^2} = 65.7151 \pm 2.023\sqrt{2.1572^2 + 9.1326^2}$$
$$= 65.7151 \pm 18.9837.$$

Or, with 95% confidence,

$$46.73 \le y^0 \le 84.70.$$

b. Using this 95% prediction interval, we can state that the salary of a male professor with 10 years of experience falls between \$46,730 and \$84,700. In the previous example, we used a 95% confidence interval to state that the mean salary of a male professor with 10 years of experience falls between $61,350 and $70,080. As expected, the prediction interval is wider than the corresponding confidence interval. In forming the prediction interval, we also have to account for a very important source of variability caused by the (unobserved) random error term. This is captured by the standard error of the estimate s_e in the prediction interval formula. The higher variability makes it more difficult to predict accurately, thus necessitating a wider interval. In the above examples, we have less uncertainty about the mean salary of a professor than about the salary of an individual professor.

Mechanics

17. In a simple linear regression based on 30 observations, the following information is provided: $\hat{y} = -6.92 + 1.35x$ and $s_e = 2.78$. Also, $se(\hat{y}^0)$ evaluated at $x = 30$ is 1.02.
    a. Construct the 95% confidence interval for $E(y)$ if $x = 30$.
    b. Construct the 95% prediction interval for y if x equals 30.
    c. Which interval is narrower? Explain.

18. In a multiple regression with 40 observations, the following sample regression equation is obtained: $\hat{y} = 12.8 + 2.6x_1 - 1.2x_2$ with $s_e = 5.84$. Also, when x_1 equals 15 and x_2 equals 6, $se(\hat{y}^0) = 2.20$.
    a. Construct the 95% confidence interval for $E(y)$ if x_1 equals 15 and x_2 equals 6.
    b. Construct the 95% prediction interval for y if x_1 equals 15 and x_2 equals 6.
    c. Which interval is wider? Explain.

19. Consider the following sample data:

x	12	23	11	23	14	21	18	16
y	28	43	21	40	33	41	37	32

    a. Find the sample regression line, $\hat{y} = b_0 + b_1x$.
    b. Construct the 95% confidence interval for $E(y)$ if $x = 15$.
    c. Construct the 95% prediction interval for y if $x = 15$.

20. Consider the following sample data:

y	46	51	28	55	29	53	47	36
x_1	40	48	29	44	30	58	60	29
x_2	13	28	24	11	28	28	29	14

    a. Find the sample regression equation, $\hat{y} = b_0 + b_1x_1 + b_2x_2$.
    b. Construct the 95% confidence interval for $E(y)$ if x_1 equals 50 and x_2 equals 20.
    c. Construct the 95% prediction interval for y if x_1 equals 50 and x_2 equals 20.

Applications

21. Using the data in the accompanying table, estimate the model: Salary $= \beta_0 + \beta_1$Education $+ \varepsilon$, where Salary is measured in $1,000s and Education refers to years of higher education.

Education	3	4	6	2	5	4	8	0
Salary	40	53	80	42	70	50	110	38

    a. Construct the 90% confidence interval for the expected salary for an individual who completed 6 years of higher education.
    b. Construct the 90% prediction interval for salary for an individual who completed 6 years of higher education.
    c. Comment on the difference in the widths of these intervals.

22. With the data in the accompanying table, estimate GPA $= \beta_0 + \beta_1$GRE $+ \varepsilon$, where GRE is a student's score on the math portion of the Graduate Record Examination and GPA is the student's grade point average in graduate school.

GRE	700	720	650	750	680	730	740	780
GPA	3.0	3.5	3.2	3.7	3.1	3.9	3.3	3.5

    a. Construct the 90% confidence interval for the expected GPA for an individual who scored 710 on the math portion of the GRE.
    b. Construct the 90% prediction interval for GPA for an individual who scored 710 on the math portion of the GRE.

23. FILE Access the data labeled **Debt_Payments** from the text website and estimate Debt $= \beta_0 + \beta_1$Income $+ \varepsilon$, where Debt is the average debt payments for a household in a particular city (in $) and Income is the city's median income (in $1,000s).
    a. Construct the 95% confidence interval for expected debt payments if a city's median income is $80,000.
    b. Construct the 95% prediction interval for debt payments if a city's median income is $80,000.

24. FILE Access the data labeled **Arlington_Homes** from the text website and estimate: Price $= \beta_0 + \beta_1$Sqft $+ \beta_2$Beds $+ \beta_3$Baths $+ \varepsilon$, where Price, Sqft, Beds, and Baths refer to home price, square footage, number of bedrooms, and number of bathrooms, respectively. Construct the 95% confidence interval for the expected price of a 2,500-square-foot home in Arlington, Massachusetts, with three bedrooms and two bathrooms. Construct the corresponding prediction interval for an individual home. Interpret both intervals.

25. FILE Access the data, labeled **BMI_Salary**, from the text website to estimate a regression model using the salary of a

college-educated worker as the response variable and BMI and Race as the two explanatory variables. Race is a dummy variable that equals 1 if white and 0 if non-white.

a. Construct and interpret the 90% confidence interval for the mean salary of a white, college-educated worker with a BMI of 30.

b. Construct and interpret the 90% prediction interval for the individual salary of a white, college-educated worker with a BMI of 30.

26. FILE Access the data, labeled **Urban_Rural**, from the text website to estimate a regression model using consumption as the response variable. The explanatory variables include income and a dummy variable that equals 1 for urban, 0 otherwise.

a. Construct and interpret the 99% confidence interval for the average consumption of an urban family with an income of $80,000.

b. Construct and interpret the 99% confidence interval for the average consumption of a rural family with an income of $80,000.

c. Comment on the width of the above confidence intervals.

27. FILE Access the data, labeled **Professor_Salary**, from the text website. These data were used in the introductory case of this chapter. Recall that we estimated our preferred model as $\hat{y} = 39.43 + 1.24x + 13.89d$, where y represents salary (in $1,000s), x represents experience (in years), and d is a gender dummy variable that equals 1 for male and 0 for female.

a. Use the preferred model to construct the 90% prediction interval for the salary of a male professor with 20 years of experience.

b. Use the preferred model to construct the 95% prediction interval for the salary of a male professor with 20 years of experience.

c. Comment on the width of the above prediction intervals.

28. FILE Access the data, labeled **Retail_Sales**, from the text website. Estimate the model $y = \beta_0 + \beta_1 x + \beta_2 d_1 + \beta_3 d_2 + \beta_4 d_3 + \varepsilon$, where y is Retail Sales, x is GNP, d_1 is a dummy variable that equals 1 for quarter 1, d_2 is a dummy variable that equals 1 for quarter 2, and d_3 is a dummy variable that equals 1 for quarter 3. Compare the 95% confidence intervals for expected sales (in $ millions) in quarter 2 and quarter 4 with GNP equal to $13,000 billion.

13.3 Model Assumptions and Common Violations

LO **13.4**

Explain the role of the assumptions on the OLS estimators.

So far we have focused on the estimation and the assessment of simple and multiple linear regression models. It is important to understand that the statistical properties of the OLS estimator, as well as the validity of the testing procedures, depend on the assumptions of the classical linear regression model. In this section we discuss these assumptions. We also address common violations to the assumptions, discuss the consequences when the assumptions are violated, and, where possible, offer some remedies.

REQUIRED ASSUMPTIONS OF REGRESSION ANALYSIS

1. The regression model given by $y = \beta_0 + \beta_1 x_1 + \beta_2 x_2 + \cdots + \beta_k x_k + \varepsilon$ is *linear in the parameters,* $\beta_0, \beta_1, \ldots, \beta_k$.

2. Conditional on $x_1, x_2, \ldots, x_k$, the error term has a an *expected value of zero*, or $E(\varepsilon) = 0$. This implies that $E(y) = \beta_0 + \beta_1 x_1 + \beta_2 x_2 + \cdots + \beta_k x_k$.

3. There is no exact linear relationship among the explanatory variables; or in statistical terminology, there is *no perfect multicollinearity*.

4. Conditional on $x_1, x_2, \ldots, x_k$, the variance of the error term ε is the same for all observations; or in statistical terminology, there is *no heteroskedasticity*. The assumption is violated if observations have a *changing variability*.

5. Conditional on $x_1, x_2, \ldots, x_k$, the error term ε is uncorrelated across observations; or in statistical terminology, there is *no serial correlation*. The assumption is violated if *observations are correlated*.

6. The error term ε is not correlated with any of the explanatory variables $x_1, x_2, \ldots, x_k$; or in statistical terminology, there is *no endogeneity*. In general, this assumption is violated if important *explanatory variables are excluded*.

7. Conditional on $x_1, x_2, \ldots, x_k$, the error term ε is *normally distributed*. This assumption allows us to construct interval estimates and conduct the tests of significance. If ε is not normally distributed, the interval estimates and the hypothesis tests are valid only for large sample sizes.

Under the assumptions of the classical linear regression model, the OLS estimators have all desired properties. In particular, the OLS estimators of the regression coefficients β_j are unbiased, that is, $E(b_j) = \beta_j$. Moreover, among all linear unbiased estimators, they have minimum variations among samples. These desirable properties of the OLS estimators become compromised as one or more model assumptions are violated. Aside from coefficient estimates, the validity of the significance tests is also impacted by the assumptions. For certain violations, the estimated standard errors of the OLS estimators are inappropriate; in these cases it is not possible to make meaningful inferences from the t and the F test results.

The assumptions of the classical linear regression model are, for the most part, based on the error term ε. Since the residuals, or the observed error term, $e = y - \hat{y}$, contain useful information regarding ε, it is common to use the residuals to investigate the assumptions. In this section, we will rely on **residual plots** to detect some of the common violations to the assumptions. These graphical plots are easy to use and provide informal analysis of the estimated regression models. Formal tests are beyond the scope of this book.

RESIDUAL PLOTS

For the regression model, $y = \beta_0 + \beta_1 x_1 + \beta_2 x_2 + \cdots + \beta_k x_k + \varepsilon$, the residuals are computed as $e = y - \hat{y}$, where $\hat{y} = b_0 + b_1 x_1 + b_2 x_2 + \cdots + b_k x_k$. These residuals can be plotted sequentially or against an explanatory variable x_j to look for model inadequacies.

It is common to plot the residuals e on the vertical axis and the explanatory variable x_j on the horizontal axis. Such plots are useful for detecting deviations from linearity as well as constant variability. If the regression is based on time series data, we can plot the residuals sequentially to detect if the observations are correlated.

Residual plots can also be used to detect outliers. Recall that outliers are observations that stand out from the rest of the data. For an outlier observation, the resulting residual will appear distinct in a plot; it will stand out from the rest. While outliers can greatly impact the estimates, it is not always clear what to do with them. As mentioned in Chapter 3, outliers may indicate bad data due to incorrectly recorded (or included) observations in the data set. In such cases, the relevant observation should be corrected or simply deleted. Alternatively, outliers may just be due to random variations, in which case the relevant observations should remain. In any event, residual plots help us identify potential outliers so that we can take corrective actions, if needed.

In Figure 13.2, we present a residual plot when none of the assumptions has been violated. (Excel computes the residuals and also plots them against all explanatory variables. After choosing **Data** > **Data Analysis** > **Regression**, we select *Residuals* and *Residual Plots* in the *Regression* dialog box.)

FIGURE 13.2 Residual plot of a correctly specified model

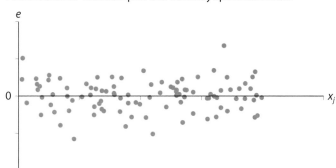

Note that all the points are randomly dispersed around the zero value of the residuals. Also, there is no evidence of outliers since no residual stands out from the rest. As we will see next, any discernible pattern of the residuals indicates that one or more assumptions have been violated.

Common Violation 1: Nonlinear Patterns

Linear regression models are often justified on the basis of their computational simplicity. A simple linear regression model $y = \beta_0 + \beta_1 x + \varepsilon$ implies that if x goes up by one unit, we expect y to change by β_1, irrespective of the value of x. However, in many applications, the relationship cannot be represented by a straight line and, therefore, must be captured by an appropriate curve. It is always good to rely on economic theory to determine if the linearity assumption is appropriate. We confirm our intuition by analyzing scatterplots or residual plots. The OLS estimates can be quite misleading if there are obvious nonlinear patterns in the data.

Detection

We can use residual plots to identify nonlinear patterns. Linearity is justified if the residuals are randomly dispersed across the values of an explanatory variable. A discernible trend in the residuals is indicative of nonlinear patterns.

EXAMPLE 13.7 FILE

A sociologist wishes to study the relationship between age and happiness. He interviews 24 individuals and collects data on age and happiness, measured on a scale from 0 to 100. A portion of the data is shown in Table 13.10; the entire data set, labeled ***Happiness_Age***, can be found on the text website. Examine the linearity assumption in the regression model, Happiness = $\beta_0 + \beta_1$Age + ε.

TABLE 13.10 Happiness and Age

Age	Happiness
49	62
51	66
⋮	⋮
69	72

SOLUTION: We start the analysis with a scatterplot of Happiness against Age. Figure 13.3 shows the scatterplot and the superimposed trend line, which is based on the sample regression equation, Happiness = 56.18 + 0.28Age. It is fairly clear from Figure 13.3 that the linear regression model does not appropriately capture the relationship between Happiness and Age. In other words, the prediction that, every year, happiness of a person increases by 0.28 units is misleading.

FIGURE 13.3 Scatterplot and the superimposed trend line
(Example 13.7)

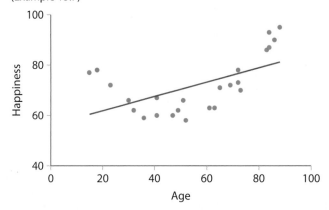

A residual plot, shown in Figure 13.4, further explores the linearity assumption of the regression model.

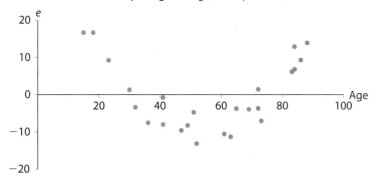

FIGURE 13.4 Residual plot against Age (Example 13.7)

The above residual plot shows that there is an obvious trend with the residuals decreasing until the age of 50 and steadily increasing thereafter. The linear regression model is inappropriate as it underestimates at lower and higher age levels and overestimates in the middle. This result is consistent with a report that shows that happiness initially decreases with age and then increases with age (*The Economist*, December 16, 2010).

Remedy

Linear regression models are often used as a first pass for most empirical work. In many instances they provide a very good approximation for the actual relationship. However, if residual plots exhibit strong nonlinear patterns, the inferences made by a linear regression model can be quite misleading. In such instances, we should employ nonlinear regression methods based on simple transformations of the response and the explanatory variables; these methods are outside the scope of this text.

Common Violation 2: Multicollinearity

Perfect multicollinearity exists when two or more explanatory variables have an exact linear relationship. Consider the model $y = \beta_0 + \beta_1 x_1 + \beta_2 x_2 + \varepsilon$, where y is bonus, x_1 is the number of cars sold, and x_2 is the number of cars remaining in the lot. If all car salesmen started with the same inventory, we have a case of *perfect* multicollinearity ($x_2 = $ Constant $- x_1$) and the model cannot be estimated. However, if x_2 represents the proportion of positive reviews from customers, we have *some* multicollinearity since the number of cars sold and the proportion of positive reviews are likely to be correlated. In most applications, some degree of correlation exists between the explanatory variables.

Multicollinearity makes it difficult to disentangle the separate influences of the explanatory variables on the response variable. If multicollinearity is severe, we may find insignificance of important explanatory variables; some coefficient estimates may even have wrong signs.

Detection

The detection methods for multicollinearity are mostly informal. The presence of a high R^2 coupled with individually insignificant explanatory variables can be indicative of multicollinearity. Sometimes researchers examine the correlations between the explanatory variables to detect severe multicollinearity. One such guideline suggests that multicollinearity is severe if the sample correlation coefficient between any two explanatory variables is more than 0.80 or less than -0.80. Seemingly wrong signs of the estimated regression coefficients may also be indicative of multicollinearity.

EXAMPLE 13.8 FILE

Examine the multicollinearity issue in a linear regression model that uses median home values as the response variable and median household incomes, per capita incomes, and the proportion of owner-occupied homes as the explanatory variables. A portion of 2010 data for all states in the United States is shown in Table 13.11; the entire data set, labeled ***Home_Values***, can be found on the text website.

TABLE 13.11 Home Values and Other Factors

State	Home Value	HH Income	Per Cap Inc	Pct Owner Occ
Alabama	$117,600	$42,081	$22,984	71.1%
Alaska	229,100	66,521	30,726	64.7
⋮	⋮	⋮	⋮	⋮
Wyoming	174,000	53,802	27,860	70.2

Source: 2010 U.S. Census.

SOLUTION: We estimate three models to examine the multicollinearity issue; Table 13.12 presents the regression results.

TABLE 13.12 Summary of Model Estimates (Example 13.8)

Variable	Model 1	Model 2	Model 3
Intercept	417892.04*	348187.14*	285604.08
	(0.00)	(0.00)	(0.08)
HH Income	9.04*	7.74*	NA
	(0.00)	(0.00)	
Per Cap Inc	−3.27	NA	13.21*
	(0.31)		(0.00)
Pct Owner Occ	−8744.30*	−8027.90*	−6454.08*
	(0.00)	(0.00)	(0.36)
Adjusted R^2	0.8071	0.8069	0.6621

Notes: The table contains parameter estimates with p-values in parentheses; NA denotes not applicable; * represents significance at the 5% level; Adjusted R^2, reported in the last row, is used for model selection.

Model 1 uses all three explanatory variables. Surprisingly, the per capita income variable has a negative estimated coefficient of −3.27 and, with a p-value of 0.31, is not even statistically significant at the 5% level. Multicollinearity might be the reason for this surprising result since household income and per capita income are likely to be correlated. We compute the sample correlation coefficient between these two variables as 0.8582, which suggests that multicollinearity is severe. We estimate two more models where one of these collinear variables is removed; Model 2 removes per capita income and Model 3 removes household income. Note that per capita income in Model 3 now exerts a positive and significant influence on home values. Between these two models, Model 2 is preferred to Model 3 because of its higher adjusted R^2 (0.8069 > 0.6621). The choice between Model 1 and Model 2 is a little unclear. In general, Model 1, with the highest adjusted R^2 value of 0.8071, is preferred. This is especially so if the purpose of the analysis is to make predictions. However, if the coefficient estimates need to be evaluated, then Model 2 may be the preferred choice.

Remedy

Inexperienced researchers tend to include too many explanatory variables in their quest not to omit anything important and in doing so may include redundant variables that essentially measure the same thing. When confronted with multicollinearity, a good remedy is to drop one of the collinear variables if we can justify its redundancy. Another option is to obtain more data, since the sample correlation may get weaker as we include more observations. Sometimes it helps to express the explanatory variables differently so that they are not collinear. At times, the best approach may be to *do nothing*, especially if the estimated model yields a high R^2, which implies that the estimated model is good for prediction as is.

Common Violation 3: Changing Variability

The assumption of constant variability of observations often breaks down in studies with cross-sectional data. Consider the model $y = \beta_0 + \beta_1 x + \varepsilon$, where y is a household's consumption expenditure and x is its disposable income. It may be unreasonable to assume that the variability of consumption is the same across a cross-section of household incomes. For example, we would expect higher-income households to have a higher variability in consumption as compared to lower-income households. Similarly, home prices tend to vary more as homes get larger and sales tend to vary more as firm size increases.

In the presence of changing variability, the OLS estimators are still unbiased. However, the estimated standard errors of the OLS estimators are inappropriate. Consequently, we cannot put much faith in the standard t or F tests since they are based on these estimated standard errors.

Detection

We can use residual plots to gauge changing variability. The residuals are generally plotted against each explanatory variable x_j; for a multiple regression model, we can also plot them against the predicted value $\hat{y}$. There is no violation if the residuals are randomly dispersed across the values of x_j. On the other hand, there is a violation if the variability increases or decreases over the values of x_j.

EXAMPLE 13.9

Consider a simple regression model that relates monthly sales (Sales) from a chain of convenience stores with the square footage (Sqft) of the store. A portion of the data used for the analysis is shown in Table 13.13; the complete data, labeled **Convenience_Stores**, are available on the text website. Estimate the model and use a residual plot to determine if the observations have a changing variability.

TABLE 13.13 Sales and Square Footage of Convenience Stores

Sales (in $1,000s)	Sqft
140	1810
160	2500
⋮	⋮
110	1470

SOLUTION: The sample regression is given by $\widehat{\text{Sales}} = 22.08 + 0.06\text{Sqft}$. A residual plot of the estimated model is shown in Figure 13.5.

FIGURE 13.5 Residual plot against square footage (Example 13.9)

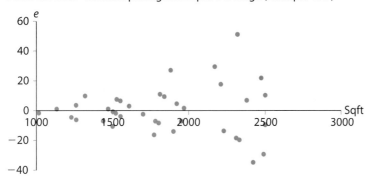

Note that the residuals seem to fan out across the horizontal axis. Therefore, we conclude that changing variability is a likely problem in our application relating sales to square footage. This result is not surprising, since you would expect sales to vary more as square footage increases. For instance, a small convenience store is likely to include only bare essentials for which there is a fairly stable demand. A larger store, on the other hand, may include specialty items, resulting in more fluctuation in sales.

Remedy

As mentioned earlier, in the presence of changing variability, the OLS estimators are unbiased but their estimated standard errors are inappropriate. Therefore, OLS still provides reasonable coefficient estimates, but the t and the F tests are no longer valid. This has prompted some researchers to use the OLS estimates along with a correction for the standard errors, called White's correction. Many statistical computer packages routinely make this correction, thus enabling researchers to perform legitimate t and F tests. Unfortunately, the current version of Excel does not have the ability to make this correction.

Common Violation 4: Correlated Observations

When obtaining the OLS estimators, we assume that the observations are uncorrelated. This assumption often breaks down in studies with time series data. Variables such as GDP, employment, and asset returns exhibit business cycles. As a consequence, successive observations are likely to be correlated.

In the presence of correlated observations, the OLS estimators are unbiased, but their estimated standard errors are inappropriate. Generally, these standard errors are distorted downwards, making the model look better than it really is with a spuriously high R^2. Furthermore, the t and F tests may suggest that the explanatory variables are individually and jointly significant when this is not true.

Detection

We can plot the residuals sequentially over time to look for correlated observations. If there is no violation, then the residuals should show no pattern around the horizontal axis. A violation is indicated when a positive residual in one period is followed by positive residuals in the next few periods, followed by negative residuals for a few periods, then positive residuals, and so on. Although not as common, a violation is also indicated when a positive residual is followed by a negative residual, then a positive residual, and so on.

EXAMPLE 13.10

Consider $y = \beta_0 + \beta_1 x_1 + \beta_2 x_2 + \varepsilon$ where y represents sales at a sushi restaurant and x_1 and x_2 represent advertising costs and the unemployment rate, respectively. A portion of monthly data from January 2008 to June 2009 is given in Table 13.14; the entire data set, labeled **Sushi_Restaurant**, can be found on the text website. Inspect the behavior of the residuals in order to comment on serial correlation.

TABLE 13.14 Sales, Advertising Costs, and Unemployment Data for Example 13.10

Month	Year	Sales (in $1,000s)	Advertising Costs (in $)	Unemployment Rate (in percent)
January	2008	27.0	550	4.6
February	2008	24.2	425	4.3
⋮	⋮	⋮	⋮	⋮
May	2009	27.4	550	9.1

SOURCE FOR THE UNEMPLOYMENT RATE DATA: Development Department, State of California, June 2009.

SOLUTION: The model is estimated as $\hat{y} = 17.5060 + 0.0266x_1 - 0.6879x_2$. In order to detect serial correlation, we plot the residuals sequentially against time t, where t is given by 1, 2, ..., 17 for the 17 months of time series data. (In order to construct this residual plot with Excel, we first estimate the model and choose *Residuals* from Excel's *Regression* dialog box. Given the regression output, we select the residual data and choose **Insert > Scatter**; choose the option on the top left.)

Figure 13.6 shows a wavelike movement in the residuals over time, first cluster-ing below the horizontal axis, then above the horizontal axis, etc. Given this pattern around the horizontal axis, we conclude that the observations are correlated.

FIGURE 13.6 Scatterplot of residuals against time t

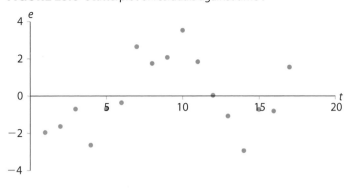

Remedy

As mentioned earlier, in the presence of correlated observations, the OLS estimators are unbiased but their standard errors are inappropriate and generally distorted downwards, making the model look better than it really is. Therefore, OLS still provides reasonable coefficient estimates, but the t and the F tests are no longer valid. This has prompted some researchers to use the OLS estimates but correct the standard errors using the Newey-West procedure. As in the case of changing variability, many statistical computer pack-ages have the capacity to make this correction; unfortunately, the current version of Excel does not have this capability. We can perform legitimate t and F tests once the standard errors have been corrected.

Common Violation 5: Excluded Variables

Another crucial assumption in a linear regression model is that the error term is not cor-related with the explanatory variables. In general, this assumption breaks down when important explanatory variables are excluded. If one or more of the relevant explanatory variables are excluded, then the resulting OLS estimators are biased. The extent of the bias depends on the degree of the correlation between the included and the excluded explanatory variables.

Suppose we want to estimate $y = \beta_0 + \beta_1 x + \varepsilon$, where y is salary and x is years of education. This model excludes innate ability, which is an important ingredient for sal-ary. Since ability is omitted, it gets incorporated in the error term and the resulting error term is likely to be correlated with years of education. Now consider someone who is highly educated and also commands a high salary. The model will associate high salary with education, when, in fact, it may be the person's unobserved high level of ability that has raised both education and salary. In sum, this violation leads to unreliable coefficient estimates; some estimates may even have the wrong signs.

Remedy

It is important that we include all relevant explanatory variables in the regression model. An important first step before running a regression model is to compile a comprehensive list of potential explanatory variables. We can then build down to perhaps a smaller list of explanatory variables using the adjusted R^2 criterion. Sometimes due to data limitations, we are unable to include all relevant variables. For example, innate ability may be an im-portant explanatory variable for a model that explains salary, but we are unable to include it since innate ability is not observable. In such instances, we use a technique called the instrumental variable technique, which is outside the scope of this text.

Summary

Regression models are an integral part of business statistics. It takes practice to become an effective user of the regression methodology. We should think of regression modeling as an iterative process. We start with a clear understanding of what the regression model is supposed to do. We define the relevant response variable and compile a comprehensive list of potential explanatory variables. The emphasis should be to pick a model that makes economic and intuitive sense and avoid explanatory variables that more or less measure the same thing, thus causing multicollinearity. We then apply this model to data and refine and improve its fit. Specifically, from the comprehensive list, we build down to perhaps a smaller list of explanatory variables using significance tests and goodness-of-fit measures such as the standard error of the estimate and the adjusted R^2. It is important that we explore residual plots to look for signs of changing variability and correlated observations in cross-sectional and time series studies, respectively. If we identify any of these two violations, we can still trust the point estimates of the regression coefficients. However, we cannot place much faith in the standard t or F tests of significance unless we employ the necessary correction.

EXERCISES 13.3

Mechanics

29. Using 20 observations, the multiple regression model
$y = \beta_0 + \beta_1 x_1 + \beta_2 x_2 + \varepsilon$ was estimated. Excel produced the following relevant results.

	df	SS	MS	F	Significance F
Regression	2	2.12E+12	1.06E+12	56.5561	3.07E-08
Residual	17	3.19E+11	1.88E+10		
Total	19	2.44E+12			

	Coefficients	Standard Error	t Stat	p-value	Lower 95%	Upper 95%
Intercept	−987557	131583	−7.5052	0.0000	−1265173	−709941
x_1	29233	32653	0.8952	0.3832	−39660	98125
x_2	30283	32645	0.9276	0.3666	−38592	99158

a. At the 5% significance level, are the explanatory variables jointly significant?

b. At the 5% significance level, is each explanatory variable individually significant?

c. What is the likely problem with this model?

30. A simple linear regression, $y = \beta_0 + \beta_1 x + \varepsilon$, is estimated with cross-sectional data. The resulting residuals e along with the values of the explanatory variable x are shown in the accompanying table.

x	1	2	5	7	10	14	15	20	24	30
e	−2	1	−3	2	4	−5	−6	8	11	−10

a. Graph the residuals e against the values of the explanatory variable x and look for any discernible pattern.

b. Which assumption is being violated? Discuss its consequences and suggest a possible remedy.

31. A simple linear regression, $y = \beta_0 + \beta_1 x + \varepsilon$, is estimated with time series data. The resulting residuals e and the time variable t are shown in the accompanying table.

t	1	2	3	4	5	6	7	8	9	10
e	−5	−4	−2	3	6	8	4	−5	−3	−2

a. Graph the residuals against time and look for any discernible pattern.

b. Which assumption is being violated? Discuss its consequences and suggest a possible remedy.

Applications

32. **FILE** Numerous studies have shown that watching too much television hurts school grades. Others have argued that television is not necessarily a bad thing for children (*Mail Online*, July 18, 2009). Like books and stories, television not only entertains, it also exposes a child to new information about the world. While watching too much TV is harmful, a little bit may actually help. Researcher Matt Castle gathers information on the grade point average (GPA) of 28 middle-school children and the number of hours of TV they watched per week. The data set, labeled **Television**, can be found on the text website. Examine the linearity assumption in the regression model, GPA $= \beta_0 + \beta_1$Hours $+ \varepsilon$.

33. **FILE** Access the data labeled **Work_Experience** from the text website. The data contain information on salary (in $) and work experience (in years) of 100 employees in a marketing firm. Estimate a model $y = \beta_0 + \beta_1 x + \varepsilon$, where y is salary and x is work experience.

a. Explain why you would be concerned about changing variability in this application.

b. Use a residual plot to confirm your economic intuition.

34. Consider the results of a survey where students were asked about their GPA and also to break down their typical 24-hour day into study, leisure (including work), and sleep. Consider the model GPA $= \beta_0 + \beta_1$Study $+ \beta_2$Leisure $+ \beta_3$Sleep $+ \varepsilon$.

a. What is wrong with this model?

b. Suggest a simple way to reformulate the model.

35. [FILE] Consider the monthly rent (Rent) of a home in Ann Arbor, Michigan, as a function of the number of bedrooms (Beds), the number of bathrooms (Baths), and square footage (Sqft).

   a. Access the data labeled **AnnArbor_Rental** from the text website and estimate Rent = $\beta_0 + \beta_1$Beds + β_2Baths + β_3Sqft + ε.

   b. Which of the explanatory variables might cause changing variability? Explain.

   c. Use residual plots to verify your economic intuition.

36. [FILE] Healthy living has always been an important goal for any society. In a recent ad campaign for Walt Disney, First Lady Michelle Obama shows parents and children that eating well and exercising can also be fun (*USA TODAY*, September 30, 2010). Consider a regression model that conjectures that fruits and vegetables and regular exercising have a positive effect on health and smoking has a negative effect on health. The sample consists of the percentage of these variables observed in various states in the United States in 2009. A portion of the data is shown in the accompanying table; the entire data set, labeled **Healthy_Living**, can be found on the text website.

State	Healthy (%)	Fruits/Vegetables (%)	Exercise (%)	Smoke (%)
AK	88.7	23.3	60.6	14.6
AL	78.3	20.3	41	16.4
⋮	⋮	⋮	⋮	⋮
WY	87.5	23.3	57.2	15.2

Source: Centers for Disease Control and Prevention.

   a. Estimate the model Healthy = $\beta_0 + \beta_1$Fruits/Vegetables + β_2Exercise + β_3Smoke + ε.

   b. Analyze the data to determine if multicollinearity and changing variability are present.

37. [FILE] A capital asset pricing model (CAPM) for Johnson & Johnson (J&J) was discussed in Example 12.10 in Chapter 12. The model uses the risk-adjusted stock return $R - R_f$ for J&J as the response variable and the risk-adjusted market return $R_M - R_f$ as the explanatory variable. The data for the model, labeled **Johnson_Johnson**, can be found on the text website. Since serial correlation may occur with time series data, it is prudent to inspect the behavior of the residuals. Construct a scatterplot of the residuals against time to comment on correlated observations.

38. [FILE] In August 2010, the Department of Commerce reported that economic weakness persists across the country with consumer spending continuing to stagnate. The government is considering various tax benefits to stimulate consumer spending through increased disposable income. The consumption function is one of the key relationships in economics, where consumption *y* depends on disposable income *x*. Consider the quarterly data for these seasonally adjusted variables, measured in billions of dollars. A portion of the data is shown in the accompanying table; the entire data set, labeled **Consumption_Quarterly**, can be found on the text website.

Date	Consumption ($ billions)	Disposable Income ($ billions)
2006:01	9148.2	9705.2
2006:02	9266.6	9863.8
⋮	⋮	⋮
2010:04	10525.2	11514.7

Source: U.S. Department of Commerce.

   a. Estimate Consumption = $\beta_0 + \beta_1$Disposable Income + ε. Plot the residuals against time to determine if there is a possibility of correlated observations.

   b. Discuss the consequences of correlated observations and suggest a possible remedy.

WRITING WITH STATISTICS

Ben Leach is a statistician for a Major League Baseball (MLB) team. One aspect of his job is to assess the value of various players. At the moment, Ben's team is in dire need of an outfielder. Management is ready to make an offer to a certain prospect but asks Ben for some input concerning salary. Management believes that a player's batting average (BA), runs batted in (RBI), and years of experience playing professional baseball (Experience) are the most important factors that influence a player's salary. Management is focusing on a player who has played professional baseball for seven years and whose average BA and RBI over this time have been 266 and 50, respectively. Ben collects data on salary (in $1,000s), BA, RBI, and Experience for 138 outfielders in 2008. Table 13.15 shows a portion of the data; the entire data set, labeled **MLB_Salary**, can be found on the text website.

TABLE 13.15 Major League Baseball Outfielder Data, $n = 138$

FILE

Player	Salary (in $1,000s)	BA	RBI	Experience
1. Nick Markakis	455	299	87	3
2. Adam Jones	390	261	23	3
⋮	⋮	⋮	⋮	⋮
138. Randy Winn	8,875	288	53	11

NOTES: All data collected from http://usatoday.com or http://espn.com; BA and RBI are averages over the player's professional life through 2008. For exposition, BA has been multiplied by 1000.

Ben would like to use information in Table 13.15 to:

1. Summarize Salaries, BAs, RBIs, and Experience of current outfielders. Examine the potential multicollinearity problem.

2. Address management's claim that BA, RBI, and Experience have a statistically significant influence on salary.

3. Evaluate the expected salary for the prospective player, given his values for BA, RBI, and Experience.

Sample Report— Baseball Salaries

In an attempt to assess the factors that influence an outfielder's salary in Major League Baseball (MLB), data were collected from 138 current players. Management believes that an outfielder's salary is best predicted using the outfielder's overall batting average (BA), runs batted in (RBI), and years of experience (Experience) as an MLB player. Table 13.A provides some descriptive statistics on these relevant variables.

TABLE 13.A Descriptive Statistics on Salary, BA, RBI, and Experience, $n = 138$

	Salary (in $1,000s)	BA	RBI	Experience
Mean	3,459	271	43	6
Minimum	390	152	1	1
Maximum	18,623	331	102	20

The average salary of an MLB outfielder in 2008 is a staggering $3,459,000; however, the minimum salary of $390,000 and the maximum salary of $18,623,000 suggest quite a bit of variability in salary. The average outfielder has a BA of 271 with 43 RBIs in a season. Experience of outfielders in 2008 varied from only 1 year to 20 years, with an average of 6 years.

Table 13.B provides regression results from estimating a model where BA, RBI, and Experience are the explanatory variables and Salary is the response variable. All sample correlation coefficients (not reported), between explanatory variables, are less than 0.50, indicating that multicollinearity is not a serious problem in this application.

TABLE 13.B Analysis of Salary of Baseball Players

Variable	Coefficient
Intercept	−4769.40 (0.1301)
BA	4.76 (0.6984)
RBI	80.44* (0.0000)
Experience	539.67* (0.0000)
$R^2 = 0.58$	
$F_{(3,133)} = 61.54$ (associated p-value = 0.0000)	

NOTES: p-values are in parentheses; *denotes significance at the 5% level.

The slope coefficients suggest that BA, RBI, and Experience exert a positive influence on Salary. For instance, the slope coefficient of Experience indicates that if an outfielder stays in the major leagues for one additional year, then, on average, his salary will increase by $539,670, holding BA and RBI constant. The p-value associated with the value of the $F_{(3,133)}$ test statistic shows that the explanatory variables are jointly significant at the 5% level. Upon testing the explanatory variables individually, the extremely small p-values associated with RBI and Experience reveal that these variables have a significant linear relationship with Salary; surprisingly, BA is not significant at the 5% level. The coefficient of determination R^2 shows that 58% of Salary is explained by the estimated regression model, leaving 42% of the variability in Salary unexplained.

Lastly, for an MLB player with seven years' experience and an average BA and RBI of 266 and 50, respectively, the model predicts a salary of $4,295,320. With 95% confidence, expected salary will lie between $3,731,360 and $4,859,280. Perhaps before management makes an offer to the player, the model should consider including other factors that may significantly influence a player's salary. One possible explanatory variable for inclusion is a player's on-base percentage.

Conceptual Review

LO 13.1 | Use dummy variables to represent qualitative explanatory variables.

A **dummy variable** d is defined as a variable that takes on values of 1 or 0. Dummy variables are used to represent categories of a qualitative variable. The number of dummy variables needed should be one less than the number of categories of the variable.

A regression model with a quantitative variable x and a dummy variable d is specified as $y = \beta_0 + \beta_1 x + \beta_2 d + \varepsilon$. We estimate this model to make predictions as $\hat{y} = (b_0 + b_2) + b_1 x$ for $d = 1$ and as $\hat{y} = b_0 + b_1 x$ for $d = 0$.

LO 13.2 | Test for differences between the categories of a qualitative variable.

Using $y = \beta_0 + \beta_1 x + \beta_2 d + \varepsilon$, we can perform a standard t test to determine whether differences exist between two categories.

LO 13.3 | Calculate and interpret confidence intervals and prediction intervals.

For specific values of $x_1, x_2, \ldots, x_k$, denoted by $x_1^0, x_2^0, \ldots, x_k^0$, the $100(1 - \alpha)\%$ **confidence interval of the expected value of** y is given by $\hat{y}^0 \pm t_{\alpha/2,df} se(\hat{y}^0)$ where $df = n - k - 1$ and $se(\hat{y}^0)$ is the standard error of $\hat{y}^0$. To derive $\hat{y}^0$ together with $se(\hat{y}^0)$ we first estimate a modified regression model where y is the response variable and the explanatory variables are defined as $x_1^* = x_1 - x_1^0, x_2^* = x_2 - x_2^0, \ldots, x_k^* = x_k - x_k^0$. The resulting estimate of the intercept and its standard error equal $\hat{y}^0$ and $se(\hat{y}^0)$, respectively.

For specific values of $x_1, x_2, \ldots, x_k$, denoted by $x_1^0, x_2^0, \ldots, x_k^0$, the $100(1 - \alpha)\%$ **prediction interval for an individual value of** y is given by $\hat{y} \pm t_{\alpha/2,df}\sqrt{(se(\hat{y}^0))^2 + s_e^2}$, where $df = n - k - 1$, $se(\hat{y}^0)$ is the standard error of $\hat{y}^0$, and s_e is the standard error of the estimate.

LO 13.4 | Explain the role of the assumptions on the OLS estimators.

Under the assumptions of the classical linear regression model, OLS provides the best estimates. However, the desirable properties of the OLS estimators become compromised as one or more model assumptions are violated. In addition, for certain violations, it is not possible to make meaningful inferences from the t and F test results.

Residual plots are used to identify model inadequacies; they also help identify outliers. The model is adequate if the residuals are randomly dispersed around the zero value.

Some degree of **multicollinearity** is present in most applications. A high R^2 coupled with insignificant explanatory variables is often indicative of multicollinearity. Multicollinearity is considered serious if the sample correlation coefficient between any two explanatory variables is more than 0.80 or less than -0.80. We can drop one of the collinear variables if its omission can be justified. We can obtain more data, as that may weaken the correlation. Another option is to express the explanatory variables differently. At times the best approach may be to do nothing, especially if the estimated model yields a high R^2.

The assumption of **constant variability** often breaks down in cross-sectional studies. The resulting OLS estimators are unbiased but the standard errors of the OLS estimators are inappropriate, making the standard t or F tests invalid. This assumption is violated if the variability of the residuals increases or decreases over the value of an explanatory variable. Researchers often use the OLS estimates along with a correction for the standard errors, called White's correction.

The assumption of **uncorrelated observations** often breaks down in time series studies. The resulting OLS estimators are unbiased but their standard errors are inappropriate. In general, correlated observations make the model look better than it really is with a spuriously high R^2. Furthermore, the t and the F test results may incorrectly suggest significance of the explanatory variables. This assumption is violated if the residuals show a pattern around the horizontal time axis. Researchers often use the OLS estimates along with a correction for the standard errors, using the Newey-West procedure.

It is important that the regression model incorporates all relevant explanatory variables. In the case of **excluded variables**, the OLS estimators are generally biased.

Additional Exercises and Case Studies

39. FILE A financial analyst would like to determine whether the return on Fidelity's Magellan mutual fund varies depending on the quarter; that is, if there is a seasonal component describing return. He collects 10 years of quarterly return data. A portion is shown in the accompanying table; the entire data set, labeled **Magellan_dummy**, can be found on the text website.

Year	Quarter	Return	d_1	d_2	d_3
2000	1	4.85	1	0	0
2000	2	−3.96	0	1	0
⋮	⋮	⋮	⋮	⋮	⋮
2009	4	4.06	0	0	0

Source: http://finance.yahoo.com.

a. Estimate $y = \beta_0 + \beta_1 d_1 + \beta_2 d_2 + \beta_3 d_3 + \varepsilon$, where y is Magellan's quarterly return, d_1 is a dummy variable that equals 1 if quarter 1 and 0 otherwise, d_2 is a dummy variable that equals 1 if quarter 2 and 0 otherwise, and d_3 is a dummy variable that equals 1 if quarter 3 and 0 otherwise.

b. At the 10% significance level, can we conclude that Magellan's stock return varies by season? Explain.

40. FILE In a seminal study, researchers documented race-based hiring in the Boston and Chicago labor markets (*American Economic Review*, September 2004). They sent out identical resumes to employers, half with traditionally African-American names and the other half with traditionally Caucasian names. Interestingly, there was a 53% difference in call-back rates between the two groups of people. A research fellow at an institute in Santa Barbara decides to repeat the same experiment with names along with age in the Los Angeles labor market. She repeatedly sends out resumes for sales positions in the city that are identical except for the difference in the names and ages of the applicants. She also records the call-back rate for each candidate. The accompanying table shows a portion of the data on call-back rate (%), age, and a dummy variable Caucasian that equals 1 for a Caucasian-sounding name; the entire data set, labeled **Hiring**, can be found on the text website.

Call-back	Age	Caucasian
12	60	1
9	56	0
⋮	⋮	⋮
15	38	0

a. Estimate a linear regression model with Call-back as the response variable, and Age and Caucasian as the explanatory variables.

b. Conduct a test for race discrimination at the 5% significance level.

c. Construct the 95% confidence interval for the mean call-back rate for a 30-year-old applicant with a Caucasian-sounding name. Find the corresponding confidence interval for the applicant without a Caucasian-sounding name.

41. An analyst uses quarterly data to study the relationship between retail sales (y, in $ millions), gross national product (x, in $ billions), and a dummy variable d that equals 1 if the sales are for the 4th quarter; 0 otherwise. He estimates the model $y = \beta_0 + \beta_1 x + \beta_2 d + \varepsilon$. Relevant regression results are shown in the accompanying table.

	Coefficients	Standard Error	t Stat	p-value
Intercept	186553.3	56421.1	3.31	0.0021
x	55.0	4.6	12.08	0.0000
d	112605.8	117053.0	0.96	0.3424

Interpret the dummy variable d. Is it significant at the 5% level?

42. **FILE** According to the U.S. Department of Health and Human Services, African-American women have the highest rates of being overweight compared to other groups in the United States. Individuals are considered overweight if their body mass index (BMI) is 25 or greater. Consider the following data on BMI of 120 individuals and dummy variables Female and Black corresponding to gender and race. The entire data set, labeled **Overweight**, can be found on the text website.

BMI	Female	Black
28.70	0	1
28.31	0	0
⋮	⋮	⋮
24.90	0	1

Note: Female = 1 for females and 0 for males; Black = 1 for African Americans and 0 otherwise.

a. Estimate the model, BMI $= \beta_0 + \beta_1$Female $+ \beta_2$Black $+ \varepsilon$, to predict the BMI for white males, white females, black males, and black females.

b. Is the difference between the BMIs of females and males statistically significant at the 5% level?

c. Is the difference between the BMIs of whites and blacks statistically significant at the 5% level?

d. Construct and interpret the 90% prediction intervals for the BMI of a white male and a black female.

43. **FILE** According to the Centers for Disease Control and Prevention, life expectancy at age 65 in America is about 18.7 years. Medical researchers have argued that while excessive drinking is detrimental to health, drinking a little alcohol every day, especially wine, may be associated with an increase in life expectancy. Others have also linked longevity with income and gender. The accompanying table shows a portion of data relating to the length of life after 65, average income (in $1,000s) at a retirement age of 65, a dummy variable

Woman that equals 1 if woman, and the average number of alcoholic drinks consumed per day. The entire data set, labeled **Longevity**, can be found on the text website.

Life	Income (in $1,000)	Woman	Drinks
19.00	64	0	1
19.30	43	1	3
⋮	⋮	⋮	⋮
20.24	36	1	0

a. Use the data to model life expectancy at 65 on the basis of Income, Woman, and Drinks.

b. Conduct a one-tailed test at $\alpha = 0.01$ to determine if women live longer than men.

c. Estimate the life expectancy at 65 of a man with an income of $40,000 and an alcoholic consumption of two drinks per day; repeat the prediction for a woman.

44. **FILE** The homeownership rate in the United States was 67.4% in 2009. In order to determine if homeownership is linked with income, 2009 state level data on the homeownership rate (Ownership) and median household income (Income) were collected. A portion of the data is shown below; the entire data set, labeled **Home_Ownership**, can be found on the text website.

State	Income	Ownership
Alabama	$39,980	74.1%
Alaska	$61,604	66.8%
⋮	⋮	⋮
Wyoming	$52,470	73.8%

Source: http://www.census.gov.

a. Estimate: Ownership $= \beta_0 + \beta_1$Income $+ \varepsilon$.

b. At the 5% significance level, is Income linearly related to Ownership?

c. Construct a 95% confidence interval for the expected value of Ownership if Income is $50,000.

d. Compare the above confidence interval with a 95% prediction interval for Ownership.

45. **FILE** A researcher studies the relationship between SAT scores, the test-taker's family income (Income), and his/her grade point average (GPA). Data are collected from 24 students. A portion of the data is shown; the entire data set, labeled **SAT**, can be found on the text website.

SAT	Income	GPA
1651	47,000	2.79
1581	34,000	2.97
⋮	⋮	⋮
1940	113,000	3.96

Estimate: SAT $= \beta_0 + \beta_1$Income $+ \beta_2$GPA $+ \varepsilon$.

a. At the 5% significance level, are Income and GPA jointly and individually significant? Show the relevant steps of each test, using the critical value approach.

b. Predict SAT if Income is $80,000 and GPA is 3.5. Use these values for the explanatory variables to construct the 95% prediction interval for the individual SAT score.

46. **FILE** The manager of a diner wants to reevaluate his staffing needs depending on variations in customer traffic during the day. He collects data on the number of customers served along with four dummy variables representing the morning, afternoon, evening, and night shifts. The dummy variable Morning equals 1 if the information was from the morning shift and 0 otherwise; other dummy variables are defined similarly. The accompanying table shows a portion of the data; the entire data set, labeled **Diner_Shifts**, are available on the text website.

Customers	Morning	Afternoon	Evening	Night
99	0	0	0	1
148	0	1	0	0
⋮	⋮	⋮	⋮	⋮
111	0	1	0	0

a. Estimate a regression model using the number of customers as the response variable and the shift dummies as the explanatory variables.
b. What is the predicted number of customers served during the morning, afternoon, evening, and night shifts?
c. Estimate the appropriate model to determine, at the 5% significance level, if the diner is busier in the afternoon than at other times.

47. **FILE** A researcher in the education department wants to determine if the number of hours that business students study per week at a state university varies by quarter. He conducts a survey where business students are asked how much they study per week in each of the three quarters. He defines a dummy variable Fall that equals 1 if the survey was conducted in the fall quarter and 0 otherwise. The dummy variables Winter and Spring are defined similarly. The accompanying table shows a portion of the data for 120 students; the entire data set, labeled **Study_Quarter**, can be found on the text website.

Study Hours	Fall	Winter	Spring
15	0	0	1
16	0	1	0
⋮	⋮	⋮	⋮
14	0	0	1

a. Estimate the appropriate model to determine, at the 5% significance level, if students study the least in the spring quarter.
b. Find the predicted number of hours that students study per week in the fall and spring quarters.
c. Construct the 95% confidence interval for the expected number of hours that students study per week in the fall and spring quarters.

48. **FILE** Consider a regression model for per capita income y. The explanatory variables consist of the percentage of the population in the United States that is (a) without a high school diploma x_1, (b) foreign born x_2, and (c) non-English speaking x_3. The accompanying table shows a portion of the data; the entire data set, labeled **PerCapita**, can be found on the text website.

State	Per Capita Income	No High School	Foreign Born	No English
Alabama	$22,984	18.6%	3.4%	4.9%
Alaska	30726	9.3	7.2	16.5
⋮	⋮	⋮	⋮	⋮
Wyoming	27860	8.7	3.1	6.7

Source: 2010 U.S. Census.

a. Estimate and interpret the regression model,
$y = \beta_0 + \beta_1 x_1 + \beta_2 x_2 + \beta_3 x_3 + \varepsilon.$
b. Do you suspect multicollinearity in the model? Use sample data to confirm.

49. **FILE** George believes that returns of mutual funds are influenced by annual turnover rates and annual expense ratios. In order to substantiate his claim, he randomly selects eight mutual funds and collects data on each fund's five-year annual return (Return), its annual holding turnover rate (Turnover), and its annual expense ratio (Expense). The entire data set, labeled **Turnover_Expense**, can be found on the text website.

	Return (%)	Turnover (%)	Expense (%)
American Funds EuroPacific	6.06	41	0.83
Artisan International	2.94	54	1.22
⋮	⋮	⋮	⋮
Royce Value Plus	1.48	42	1.48

Source: All data as of July 31, 2009 from http://finance.yahoo.com.

a. Estimate Return $= \beta_0 + \beta_1$ Turnover $+ \beta_2$ Expense $+ \varepsilon$. Conduct appropriate tests to verify George's theory at the 5% significance level.
b. Discuss the potential problems of multicollinearity and changing variability.

50. **FILE** A government researcher examines the factors that influence a city's crime rate. For 41 cities, she collects the crime rate (crimes per 100,000 residents), the poverty rate (in %), the median income (in $1,000s), the percent of residents younger than 18, and the percent of residents older than 65. A portion of the data is shown; the entire data set, labeled **Crime**, can be found on the text website.

Crime	Poverty	Income	Under 18	Over 65
710.6	3.8	58.422	18.3	23.4
1317.7	16.7	48.729	19.0	10.3
⋮	⋮	⋮	⋮	⋮
139.7	3.9	59.445	19.7	16

a. Estimate Crime $= \beta_0 + \beta_1$Poverty $+ \beta_2$Income $+ \beta_3$Under 18 $+ \beta_4$Over 65 $+ \varepsilon$. Discuss the individual and joint significance of the explanatory variables at the 5% significance level.

b. Which explanatory variables are likely to be collinear? Find their sample correlation coefficients to confirm.

51. FILE A research analyst is trying to determine whether a firm's price-earnings (P/E) and price-sales (P/S) ratios can explain the firm's stock performance over the past year. Generally, a high P/E ratio suggests that investors are expecting higher earnings growth in the future compared to companies with a lower P/E ratio. Investors use the P/S ratio to determine how much they are paying for a dollar of the firm's sales rather than a dollar of its earnings (P/E ratio). In short, the higher the P/E ratio and the lower the P/S ratio, the more attractive the investment. The accompanying table shows a portion of the 2010 annual returns, the P/E ratios, and the P/S ratios for the 30 firms included in the Dow Jones Industrial Average. The entire data set, labeled **Dow_2010**, can be found on the text website.

DOW Components	Return (in %)	P/E ratio	P/S ratio
3M Co.	4.4	14.37	2.41
Alcoa Inc.	−4.5	11.01	0.78
⋮	⋮	⋮	⋮
Walt Disney Company	16.3	13.94	1.94

Source: The 2010 returns (January 1, 2010–December 31, 2010) were obtained from *The Wall Street Journal*, January 3, 2011; the P/E ratios and the P/S ratios were obtained from http://finance.yahoo.com on January 20, 2011.

a. Estimate: Return $= \beta_0 + \beta_1$P/E $+ \beta_2$P/S $+ \varepsilon$. Show the regression results in a well-formatted table.

b. Determine whether P/E and P/S are jointly significant at the 5% significance level.

c. Establish whether the explanatory variables are individually significant at the 5% significance level.

d. What is the predicted return for a firm with a P/E ratio of 10 and a P/S ratio of 2? Use this value to construct the 95% confidence interval for the expected return.

52. FILE A nutritionist wants to understand the influence of income and healthy food on the incidence of smoking. He collects 2009 data on the percentage of smokers in each state in the United States and the corresponding median income and the percentage of the population that regularly eats fruits and vegetables. A portion of the data is shown in the accompanying table; the entire data set, labeled **Smoking**, can be found on the text website.

State	Smoke (%)	Fruits/Vegetables (%)	Median Income
AK	14.6	23.3	61,604
AL	16.4	20.3	39,980
⋮	⋮	⋮	⋮
WY	15.2	23.3	52,470

Source: Centers for Disease Control and Prevention and U.S. Census Bureau.

a. Estimate: Smoke $= \beta_0 + \beta_1$Fruits/Vegetables $+ \beta_2$Median Income $+ \varepsilon$.

b. At the 5% level of significance, are the explanatory variables individually and jointly significant? Explain.

c. Use the sample correlation coefficients to evaluate the potential problem of multicollinearity.

53. FILE A researcher examines the factors that influence student performance. She gathers data on 224 school districts in Massachusetts. The response variable is the students' mean score on a standardized test (Score). She uses four explanatory variables in her analysis: the student-to-teacher ratio (STR), the average teacher's salary (TSAL), the median household income (INC), and the percentage of single family households (SGL). A portion of the data is shown in the accompanying table; the entire data set, labeled **MCAS**, can be found on the text website.

Score	STR (%)	TSAL (in $1,000s)	INC (in $1,000s)	SGL (%)
227.00	19.00	44.01	48.89	4.70
230.67	17.90	40.17	43.91	4.60
⋮	⋮	⋮	⋮	⋮
230.67	19.20	44.79	47.64	5.10

Source: Massachusetts Department of Education and the Census of Population and Housing.

a. Estimate: Score $= \beta_0 + \beta_1$STR $+ \beta_2$TSAL $+ \beta_3$INC $+ \beta_4$SGL $+ \varepsilon$ and show the regression results in a well-formatted table.

b. Evaluate the potential problems of multicollinearity and changing variability in this regression model.

CASE STUDIES

Case Study 13.1

A recent study examined "sidewalk rage" in an attempt to find insight into anger's origins and offer suggestions for anger-management treatments (*The Wall Street Journal*, February 15, 2011). "Sidewalk ragers" tend to believe that pedestrians should behave in a certain way. For instance, slower pedestrians should keep to the right or should step aside to take a picture. If pedestrians violate these "norms," then ragers feel that the "violaters" are breaking the rules of civility. Since anger is associated with a host of negative health consequences, psychologists suggest developing strategies to quell the rage. One possible strategy is to avoid slow walkers. A portion of the study looked at the average speed of walkers (feet per second) in Lower Manhattan and found that average speeds differ when the pedestrian is distracted by other activities (smoking, talking on a cell phone, tourism, etc.) or exhibits other traits (elderly, obese, etc.). Sample data were obtained from 50 pedestrians in Lower Manhattan. Each pedestrian's speed was calculated (feet per second). In addition, it was noted if the pedestrian was smoking (equaled 1 if smoking, 0 otherwise), was a tourist (equaled 1 if tourist, 0 otherwise), was elderly (equaled 1 if over 65 years old, 0 otherwise), or was obese (equaled 1 if obese, 0 otherwise). Each pedestrian is associated with no more than one of these four characteristics/traits. The accompanying table shows a portion of the data; the entire data set, labeled *Pedestrian_Speeds*, can be found on the text website.

Data for Case Study 13.1 Pedestrian Speeds with Defining Characteristics/Traits

FILE

Speed	Smoking	Tourist	Elderly	Obese
3.76	0	1	0	0
3.82	0	1	0	0
⋮	⋮	⋮	⋮	⋮
5.02	0	0	0	0

In a report, use the sample information to:

1. Estimate Speed $= \beta_0 + \beta_1 \text{Smoking} + \beta_2 \text{Tourist} + \beta_3 \text{Elderly} + \beta_4 \text{Obese} + \varepsilon$.
2. Interpret the slope coefficient of Tourist. Interpret the intercept. Predict the speed of an elderly pedestrian. Predict the speed of an obese pedestrian.
3. Are the explanatory variables jointly significant in explaining speed at the 5% significance level? Are all explanatory variables individually significant at the 5% level? What type of pedestrian should a "sidewalk rager" avoid?

Case Study 13.2

Jack Sprague is the relocation specialist for a real estate firm in the town of Arlington, Massachusetts. He has been working with a client who wishes to purchase a single-family home in Arlington. After seeing the information that Jack provided, the client is perplexed by the variability of home prices in Arlington. She is especially puzzled by the premium that a colonial house commands. (A colonial house is a style dating back to the time of the American colonies, with a simple rectangular structure and a peaked roof.) Despite Jack's eloquent explanations, it seems that the client will not be satisfied until she understands the quantitative relationship between house prices and house characteristics. Jack decides to use a multiple regression model to provide the client with the necessary information. He collects data on the prices for 36 single-family homes in Arlington sold in the first quarter of 2009. Also included in the data is the information on square footage, the number of bedrooms, the number of bathrooms, and whether or not the house is a colonial (1 for colonial; 0 otherwise). A portion of the data is shown in the accompanying table; the entire data set, labeled *Arlington_Homes*, can be found on the text website.

Data for Case Study 13.2 Sales Information of Single-Family Homes in Arlington, MA

FILE

Price	Square feet	Bedrooms	Baths	Colonial
$840,000	2768	4	3.5	1
822,000	2500	4	2.5	1
⋮	⋮	⋮	⋮	⋮
307,500	850	1	1	0

Source: http://NewEnglandMoves.com.

In a report, use the sample information to:

1. Explain why we must include a colonial dummy variable to the list of explanatory variables for explaining home price.
2. Use your preferred model to make predictions for a colonial home versus other styles, given the average values of the explanatory variables.
3. Evaluate the potential problem of changing variability in this model.

Case Study 13.3

American football is the highest-paying sport on a per-game basis. Given that the quarterback is considered the most important player on the team, he is typically well-compensated. A sports statistician examines the factors that influence a quarterback's salary (Salary). He believes that a quarterback's pass completion rate (PC) is the most important variable affecting Salary. The statistician also wonders how total touchdowns scored (TD) and a quarterback's age (Age) might impact Salary. The statistician collects 2009 data on Salary, PC, TD, and Age. A portion of the data is shown in the accompanying table; the entire data set, labeled *Quarterback_Salaries*, can be found on the text website.

Data for Case Study 13.3 Quarterback Salary Data, 2009

Name	Salary (in $ millions)	PC	TD	Age
Philip Rivers	25.5566	65.2	28	27
Jay Cutler	22.0441	60.5	27	26
⋮	⋮	⋮	⋮	⋮
Tony Romo	0.6260	63.1	26	29

Source: *USA TODAY* database for salaries; http://NFL.com for other data.

In a report, use the sample information to:

1. Estimate and interpret the model: Salary $= \beta_0 + \beta_1 PC + \beta_2 TD + \beta_3 Age + \varepsilon$.
2. Construct and interpret the 95% confidence interval for the expected salary of a quarterback with average values of PCT, TD, and Age.
3. Construct and interpret the 95% prediction interval for the individual salary of a quarterback with average values of PCT, TD, and Age.

Case Study 13.4

According to a recent report by the government, new home construction fell to an 18-month low in October 2010 (http://CNNMoney.com, November 17, 2010). Housing starts, or the number of new homes being built, experienced an 11.7% drop in its seasonally adjusted annual rate. Urmil Singh works for a mortgage company in Madison, Wisconsin. She wants to better understand the quantitative relationship between housing starts, the mortgage rate, and the unemployment rate. She gathers seasonally adjusted monthly data on these variables from 2006:01–2010:12. A portion of the data is shown in the accompanying table; the entire data set, labeled *Housing_Starts*, can be found on the text website.

Data for Case Study 13.4 Housing Starts and Other Factors, $n = 60$

Date	Housing Starts (in 1000s)	Mortgage Rate (%)	Unemployment Rate (%)
2006–01	2273	6.15	4.7
2006–02	2119	6.25	4.8
⋮	⋮	⋮	⋮
2010–12	520	4.71	9.4

Source: Census Bureau and Board of Governors.

In a report, use the sample information to:

1. Estimate a multiple regression model for housing starts using the mortgage rate and the unemployment rate as the explanatory variables.
2. At the 5% significance level, evaluate the individual and joint significance of the explanatory variables.
3. Discuss the potential problems of multicollinearity and correlated observations in this time series data application.

Appendix 13.1 Guidelines for Other Software Packages

The following section provides brief commands for specific software packages: Minitab, SPSS, and JMP. More detailed instructions can be found on the text website.

MINITAB

Residual Plots

(Replicating Figure 13.5) From the menu choose **Stat** > **Regression** > **Regression**. Select Sales as **Response** and Sqft as **Predictors**. Choose **Graphs**. Under **Residual Plots**, choose **Four in one**. In order to obtain a plot of the residuals against the explanatory variable(s), under **Residual versus the variables**, select Sqft.

Assessing Multicollinearity with a Correlation Matrix

(Replicating Example 13.8) From the menu choose **Stat** > **Basic Statistics** > **Correlation**. Under **Variables**, select x_1, x_2, and x_3.

SPSS

Residual Plots

(Replicating Figure 13.5) From the menu choose **Analyze** > **Regression** > **Linear**. Select Sales as **Dependent** and Sqft as **Independents**. Choose **Plots**. In order to check the linearity assumption as well as whether the observations have a changing variability, select **ZRESID** as **Y** and **ZPRED** as **X**, where ZRESID and ZPRED are the standardized residuals and standardized predicted values, respectively. In order to check whether the observations are correlated, choose **Save** and under **Residuals** select **Unstandardized**. After estimating the model, plot these residuals (RES_1) against time.

Assessing Multicollinearity with a Correlation Matrix

(Replicating Example 13.8) From the menu choose **Analyze** > **Correlate** > **Bivariate**. Under **Variables**, select x_1, x_2, and x_3.

JMP

Residual Plots

(Replicating Figure 13.5) From the menu choose **Analyze** > **Fit Y by X**. Select Sales as **Y, Response** and Sqft as **X, Factor**. Click on the red triangle next to the header **Bivariate Fit of Sales by Sqft** and select **Fit line**. Click on the red triangle next to the header **Linear Fit** and select **Plot Residuals**.

Assessing Multicollinearity with a Correlation Matrix

(Replicating Example 13.8) From the menu choose **Analyze** > **Multivariate Methods** > **Multivariate**. Click **Y, Columns** in order to insert the response variable and all explanatory variables. If you do not see the correlation matrix, click the red triangle at the top next to **Multivariate** and select **Correlations Multivariate**.

APPENDIX A

Tables

TABLE 1 Standard Normal Curve Areas

Entries in this table provide the area under the curve to the left of −z. For example, $P(Z \leq -1.52) = 0.0643$.

$P(Z \leq -z)$

z	0.00	0.01	0.02	0.03	0.04	0.05	0.06	0.07	0.08	0.09
−3.9	0.0000	0.0000	0.0000	0.0000	0.0000	0.0000	0.0000	0.0000	0.0000	0.0000
−3.8	0.0001	0.0001	0.0001	0.0001	0.0001	0.0001	0.0001	0.0001	0.0001	0.0001
−3.7	0.0001	0.0001	0.0001	0.0001	0.0001	0.0001	0.0001	0.0001	0.0001	0.0001
−3.6	0.0002	0.0002	0.0001	0.0001	0.0001	0.0001	0.0001	0.0001	0.0001	0.0001
−3.5	0.0002	0.0002	0.0002	0.0002	0.0002	0.0002	0.0002	0.0002	0.0002	0.0002
−3.4	0.0003	0.0003	0.0003	0.0003	0.0003	0.0003	0.0003	0.0003	0.0003	0.0002
−3.3	0.0005	0.0005	0.0005	0.0004	0.0004	0.0004	0.0004	0.0004	0.0004	0.0003
−3.2	0.0007	0.0007	0.0006	0.0006	0.0006	0.0006	0.0006	0.0005	0.0005	0.0005
−3.1	0.0010	0.0009	0.0009	0.0009	0.0008	0.0008	0.0008	0.0008	0.0007	0.0007
−3.0	0.0013	0.0013	0.0013	0.0012	0.0012	0.0011	0.0011	0.0011	0.0010	0.0010
−2.9	0.0019	0.0018	0.0018	0.0017	0.0016	0.0016	0.0015	0.0015	0.0014	0.0014
−2.8	0.0026	0.0025	0.0024	0.0023	0.0023	0.0022	0.0021	0.0021	0.0020	0.0019
−2.7	0.0035	0.0034	0.0033	0.0032	0.0031	0.0030	0.0029	0.0028	0.0027	0.0026
−2.6	0.0047	0.0045	0.0044	0.0043	0.0041	0.0040	0.0039	0.0038	0.0037	0.0036
−2.5	0.0062	0.0060	0.0059	0.0057	0.0055	0.0054	0.0052	0.0051	0.0049	0.0048
−2.4	0.0082	0.0080	0.0078	0.0075	0.0073	0.0071	0.0069	0.0068	0.0066	0.0064
−2.3	0.0107	0.0104	0.0102	0.0099	0.0096	0.0094	0.0091	0.0089	0.0087	0.0084
−2.2	0.0139	0.0136	0.0132	0.0129	0.0125	0.0122	0.0119	0.0116	0.0113	0.0110
−2.1	0.0179	0.0174	0.0170	0.0166	0.0162	0.0158	0.0154	0.0150	0.0146	0.0143
−2.0	0.0228	0.0222	0.0217	0.0212	0.0207	0.0202	0.0197	0.0192	0.0188	0.0183
−1.9	0.0287	0.0281	0.0274	0.0268	0.0262	0.0256	0.0250	0.0244	0.0239	0.0233
−1.8	0.0359	0.0351	0.0344	0.0336	0.0329	0.0322	0.0314	0.0307	0.0301	0.0294
−1.7	0.0446	0.0436	0.0427	0.0418	0.0409	0.0401	0.0392	0.0384	0.0375	0.0367
−1.6	0.0548	0.0537	0.0526	0.0516	0.0505	0.0495	0.0485	0.0475	0.0465	0.0455
−1.5	0.0668	0.0655	0.0643	0.0630	0.0618	0.0606	0.0594	0.0582	0.0571	0.0559
−1.4	0.0808	0.0793	0.0778	0.0764	0.0749	0.0735	0.0721	0.0708	0.0694	0.0681
−1.3	0.0968	0.0951	0.0934	0.0918	0.0901	0.0885	0.0869	0.0853	0.0838	0.0823
−1.2	0.1151	0.1131	0.1112	0.1093	0.1075	0.1056	0.1038	0.1020	0.1003	0.0985
−1.1	0.1357	0.1335	0.1314	0.1292	0.1271	0.1251	0.1230	0.1210	0.1190	0.1170
−1.0	0.1587	0.1562	0.1539	0.1515	0.1492	0.1469	0.1446	0.1423	0.1401	0.1379
−0.9	0.1841	0.1814	0.1788	0.1762	0.1736	0.1711	0.1685	0.1660	0.1635	0.1611
−0.8	0.2119	0.2090	0.2061	0.2033	0.2005	0.1977	0.1949	0.1922	0.1894	0.1867
−0.7	0.2420	0.2389	0.2358	0.2327	0.2296	0.2266	0.2236	0.2206	0.2177	0.2148
−0.6	0.2743	0.2709	0.2676	0.2643	0.2611	0.2578	0.2546	0.2514	0.2483	0.2451
−0.5	0.3085	0.3050	0.3015	0.2981	0.2946	0.2912	0.2877	0.2843	0.2810	0.2776
−0.4	0.3446	0.3409	0.3372	0.3336	0.3300	0.3264	0.3228	0.3192	0.3156	0.3121
−0.3	0.3821	0.3783	0.3745	0.3707	0.3669	0.3632	0.3594	0.3557	0.3520	0.3483
−0.2	0.4207	0.4168	0.4129	0.4090	0.4052	0.4013	0.3974	0.3936	0.3897	0.3859
−0.1	0.4602	0.4562	0.4522	0.4483	0.4443	0.4404	0.4364	0.4325	0.4286	0.4247
−0.0	0.5000	0.4960	0.4920	0.4880	0.4840	0.4801	0.4761	0.4721	0.4681	0.4641

Source: Probabilities calculated with Excel.

TABLE 1 (*Continued*)

Entries in this table provide the area under the curve to the left of z. For example, $P(Z \le 1.52) = 0.9357$.

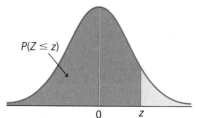

$P(Z \le z)$

z	0.00	0.01	0.02	0.03	0.04	0.05	0.06	0.07	0.08	0.09
0.0	0.5000	0.5040	0.5080	0.5120	0.5160	0.5199	0.5239	0.5279	0.5319	0.5359
0.1	0.5398	0.5438	0.5478	0.5517	0.5557	0.5596	0.5636	0.5675	0.5714	0.5753
0.2	0.5793	0.5832	0.5871	0.5910	0.5948	0.5987	0.6026	0.6064	0.6103	0.6141
0.3	0.6179	0.6217	0.6255	0.6293	0.6331	0.6368	0.6406	0.6443	0.6480	0.6517
0.4	0.6554	0.6591	0.6628	0.6664	0.6700	0.6736	0.6772	0.6808	0.6844	0.6879
0.5	0.6915	0.6950	0.6985	0.7019	0.7054	0.7088	0.7123	0.7157	0.7190	0.7224
0.6	0.7257	0.7291	0.7324	0.7357	0.7389	0.7422	0.7454	0.7486	0.7517	0.7549
0.7	0.7580	0.7611	0.7642	0.7673	0.7704	0.7734	0.7764	0.7794	0.7823	0.7852
0.8	0.7881	0.7910	0.7939	0.7967	0.7995	0.8023	0.8051	0.8078	0.8106	0.8133
0.9	0.8159	0.8186	0.8212	0.8238	0.8264	0.8289	0.8315	0.8340	0.8365	0.8389
1.0	0.8413	0.8438	0.8461	0.8485	0.8508	0.8531	0.8554	0.8577	0.8599	0.8621
1.1	0.8643	0.8665	0.8686	0.8708	0.8729	0.8749	0.8770	0.8790	0.8810	0.8830
1.2	0.8849	0.8869	0.8888	0.8907	0.8925	0.8944	0.8962	0.8980	0.8997	0.9015
1.3	0.9032	0.9049	0.9066	0.9082	0.9099	0.9115	0.9131	0.9147	0.9162	0.9177
1.4	0.9192	0.9207	0.9222	0.9236	0.9251	0.9265	0.9279	0.9292	0.9306	0.9319
1.5	0.9332	0.9345	0.9357	0.9370	0.9382	0.9394	0.9406	0.9418	0.9429	0.9441
1.6	0.9452	0.9463	0.9474	0.9484	0.9495	0.9505	0.9515	0.9525	0.9535	0.9545
1.7	0.9554	0.9564	0.9573	0.9582	0.9591	0.9599	0.9608	0.9616	0.9625	0.9633
1.8	0.9641	0.9649	0.9656	0.9664	0.9671	0.9678	0.9686	0.9693	0.9699	0.9706
1.9	0.9713	0.9719	0.9726	0.9732	0.9738	0.9744	0.9750	0.9756	0.9761	0.9767
2.0	0.9772	0.9778	0.9783	0.9788	0.9793	0.9798	0.9803	0.9808	0.9812	0.9817
2.1	0.9821	0.9826	0.9830	0.9834	0.9838	0.9842	0.9846	0.9850	0.9854	0.9857
2.2	0.9861	0.9864	0.9868	0.9871	0.9875	0.9878	0.9881	0.9884	0.9887	0.9890
2.3	0.9893	0.9896	0.9898	0.9901	0.9904	0.9906	0.9909	0.9911	0.9913	0.9916
2.4	0.9918	0.9920	0.9922	0.9925	0.9927	0.9929	0.9931	0.9932	0.9934	0.9936
2.5	0.9938	0.9940	0.9941	0.9943	0.9945	0.9946	0.9948	0.9949	0.9951	0.9952
2.6	0.9953	0.9955	0.9956	0.9957	0.9959	0.9960	0.9961	0.9962	0.9963	0.9964
2.7	0.9965	0.9966	0.9967	0.9968	0.9969	0.9970	0.9971	0.9972	0.9973	0.9974
2.8	0.9974	0.9975	0.9976	0.9977	0.9977	0.9978	0.9979	0.9979	0.9980	0.9981
2.9	0.9981	0.9982	0.9982	0.9983	0.9984	0.9984	0.9985	0.9985	0.9986	0.9986
3.0	0.9987	0.9987	0.9987	0.9988	0.9988	0.9989	0.9989	0.9989	0.9990	0.9990
3.1	0.9990	0.9991	0.9991	0.9991	0.9992	0.9992	0.9992	0.9992	0.9993	0.9993
3.2	0.9993	0.9993	0.9994	0.9994	0.9994	0.9994	0.9994	0.9995	0.9995	0.9995
3.3	0.9995	0.9995	0.9995	0.9996	0.9996	0.9996	0.9996	0.9996	0.9996	0.9997
3.4	0.9997	0.9997	0.9997	0.9997	0.9997	0.9997	0.9997	0.9997	0.9997	0.9998
3.5	0.9998	0.9998	0.9998	0.9998	0.9998	0.9998	0.9998	0.9998	0.9998	0.9998
3.6	0.9998	0.9998	0.9999	0.9999	0.9999	0.9999	0.9999	0.9999	0.9999	0.9999
3.7	0.9999	0.9999	0.9999	0.9999	0.9999	0.9999	0.9999	0.9999	0.9999	0.9999
3.8	0.9999	0.9999	0.9999	0.9999	0.9999	0.9999	0.9999	0.9999	0.9999	0.9999
3.9	1.0000	1.0000	1.0000	1.0000	1.0000	1.0000	1.0000	1.0000	1.0000	1.0000

Source: Probabilities calculated with Excel.

TABLE 2 Student's *t* Distribution

Entries in this table provide the values of $t_{\alpha,df}$ that correspond to a given upper-tail area α and a specified number of degrees of freedom *df*. For example, for $\alpha = 0.05$ and $df = 10$, $P(T_{10} \geq 1.812) = 0.05$.

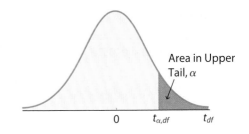

Area in Upper Tail, α

			α			
df	0.20	0.10	0.05	0.025	0.01	0.005
1	1.376	3.078	6.314	12.706	31.821	63.657
2	1.061	1.886	2.920	4.303	6.965	9.925
3	0.978	1.638	2.353	3.182	4.541	5.841
4	0.941	1.533	2.132	2.776	3.747	4.604
5	0.920	1.476	2.015	2.571	3.365	4.032
6	0.906	1.440	1.943	2.447	3.143	3.707
7	0.896	1.415	1.895	2.365	2.998	3.499
8	0.889	1.397	1.860	2.306	2.896	3.355
9	0.883	1.383	1.833	2.262	2.821	3.250
10	0.879	1.372	1.812	2.228	2.764	3.169
11	0.876	1.363	1.796	2.201	2.718	3.106
12	0.873	1.356	1.782	2.179	2.681	3.055
13	0.870	1.350	1.771	2.160	2.650	3.012
14	0.868	1.345	1.761	2.145	2.624	2.977
15	0.866	1.341	1.753	2.131	2.602	2.947
16	0.865	1.337	1.746	2.120	2.583	2.921
17	0.863	1.333	1.740	2.110	2.567	2.898
18	0.862	1.330	1.734	2.101	2.552	2.878
19	0.861	1.328	1.729	2.093	2.539	2.861
20	0.860	1.325	1.725	2.086	2.528	2.845
21	0.859	1.323	1.721	2.080	2.518	2.831
22	0.858	1.321	1.717	2.074	2.508	2.819
23	0.858	1.319	1.714	2.069	2.500	2.807
24	0.857	1.318	1.711	2.064	2.492	2.797
25	0.856	1.316	1.708	2.060	2.485	2.787
26	0.856	1.315	1.706	2.056	2.479	2.779
27	0.855	1.314	1.703	2.052	2.473	2.771
28	0.855	1.313	1.701	2.048	2.467	2.763
29	0.854	1.311	1.699	2.045	2.462	2.756
30	0.854	1.310	1.697	2.042	2.457	2.750

TABLE 2 (*Continued*)

df	α					
	0.20	0.10	0.05	0.025	0.01	0.005
31	0.853	1.309	1.696	2.040	2.453	2.744
32	0.853	1.309	1.694	2.037	2.449	2.738
33	0.853	1.308	1.692	2.035	2.445	2.733
34	0.852	1.307	1.691	2.032	2.441	2.728
35	0.852	1.306	1.690	2.030	2.438	2.724
36	0.852	1.306	1.688	2.028	2.434	2.719
37	0.851	1.305	1.687	2.026	2.431	2.715
38	0.851	1.304	1.686	2.024	2.429	2.712
39	0.851	1.304	1.685	2.023	2.426	2.708
40	0.851	1.303	1.684	2.021	2.423	2.704
41	0.850	1.303	1.683	2.020	2.421	2.701
42	0.850	1.302	1.682	2.018	2.418	2.698
43	0.850	1.302	1.681	2.017	2.416	2.695
44	0.850	1.301	1.680	2.015	2.414	2.692
45	0.850	1.301	1.679	2.014	2.412	2.690
46	0.850	1.300	1.679	2.013	2.410	2.687
47	0.849	1.300	1.678	2.012	2.408	2.685
48	0.849	1.299	1.677	2.011	2.407	2.682
49	0.849	1.299	1.677	2.010	2.405	2.680
50	0.849	1.299	1.676	2.009	2.403	2.678
51	0.849	1.298	1.675	2.008	2.402	2.676
52	0.849	1.298	1.675	2.007	2.400	2.674
53	0.848	1.298	1.674	2.006	2.399	2.672
54	0.848	1.297	1.674	2.005	2.397	2.670
55	0.848	1.297	1.673	2.004	2.396	2.668
56	0.848	1.297	1.673	2.003	2.395	2.667
57	0.848	1.297	1.672	2.002	2.394	2.665
58	0.848	1.296	1.672	2.002	2.392	2.663
59	0.848	1.296	1.671	2.001	2.391	2.662
60	0.848	1.296	1.671	2.000	2.390	2.660
80	0.846	1.292	1.664	1.990	2.374	2.639
100	0.845	1.290	1.660	1.984	2.364	2.626
150	0.844	1.287	1.655	1.976	2.351	2.609
200	0.843	1.286	1.653	1.972	2.345	2.601
500	0.842	1.283	1.648	1.965	2.334	2.586
1000	0.842	1.282	1.646	1.962	2.330	2.581
∞	0.842	1.282	1.645	1.960	2.326	2.576

Source: *t* values calculated with Excel.

TABLE 3 χ^2 (Chi-Square) Distribution

Entries in this table provide the values of $\chi^2_{\alpha,df}$ that correspond to a given upper-tail area α and a specified number of degrees of freedom df. For example, for $\alpha = 0.05$ and $df = 10$, $P(\chi^2_{10} \geq 18.307) = 0.05$.

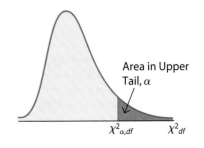

Area in Upper Tail, α

$\chi^2_{\alpha,df}$ χ^2_{df}

df	α									
	0.995	0.990	0.975	0.950	0.900	0.100	0.050	0.025	0.010	0.005
1	0.000	0.000	0.001	0.004	0.016	2.706	3.841	5.024	6.635	7.879
2	0.010	0.020	0.051	0.103	0.211	4.605	5.991	7.378	9.210	10.597
3	0.072	0.115	0.216	0.352	0.584	6.251	7.815	9.348	11.345	12.838
4	0.207	0.297	0.484	0.711	1.064	7.779	9.488	11.143	13.277	14.860
5	0.412	0.554	0.831	1.145	1.610	9.236	11.070	12.833	15.086	16.750
6	0.676	0.872	1.237	1.635	2.204	10.645	12.592	14.449	16.812	18.548
7	0.989	1.239	1.690	2.167	2.833	12.017	14.067	16.013	18.475	20.278
8	1.344	1.646	2.180	2.733	3.490	13.362	15.507	17.535	20.090	21.955
9	1.735	2.088	2.700	3.325	4.168	14.684	16.919	19.023	21.666	23.589
10	2.156	2.558	3.247	3.940	4.865	15.987	18.307	20.483	23.209	25.188
11	2.603	3.053	3.816	4.575	5.578	17.275	19.675	21.920	24.725	26.757
12	3.074	3.571	4.404	5.226	6.304	18.549	21.026	23.337	26.217	28.300
13	3.565	4.107	5.009	5.892	7.042	19.812	22.362	24.736	27.688	29.819
14	4.075	4.660	5.629	6.571	7.790	21.064	23.685	26.119	29.141	31.319
15	4.601	5.229	6.262	7.261	8.547	22.307	24.996	27.488	30.578	32.801
16	5.142	5.812	6.908	7.962	9.312	23.542	26.296	28.845	32.000	34.267
17	5.697	6.408	7.564	8.672	10.085	24.769	27.587	30.191	33.409	35.718
18	6.265	7.015	8.231	9.390	10.865	25.989	28.869	31.526	34.805	37.156
19	6.844	7.633	8.907	10.117	11.651	27.204	30.144	32.852	36.191	38.582
20	7.434	8.260	9.591	10.851	12.443	28.412	31.410	34.170	37.566	39.997
21	8.034	8.897	10.283	11.591	13.240	29.615	32.671	35.479	38.932	41.401
22	8.643	9.542	10.982	12.338	14.041	30.813	33.924	36.781	40.289	42.796
23	9.260	10.196	11.689	13.091	14.848	32.007	35.172	38.076	41.638	44.181
24	9.886	10.856	12.401	13.848	15.659	33.196	36.415	39.364	42.980	45.559
25	10.520	11.524	13.120	14.611	16.473	34.382	37.652	40.646	44.314	46.928
26	11.160	12.198	13.844	15.379	17.292	35.563	38.885	41.923	45.642	48.290
27	11.808	12.879	14.573	16.151	18.114	36.741	40.113	43.195	46.963	49.645
28	12.461	13.565	15.308	16.928	18.939	37.916	41.337	44.461	48.278	50.993
29	13.121	14.256	16.047	17.708	19.768	39.087	42.557	45.722	49.588	52.336
30	13.787	14.953	16.791	18.493	20.599	40.256	43.773	46.979	50.892	53.672

TABLE 3 (*Continued*)

					α					
df	0.995	0.990	0.975	0.950	0.900	0.100	0.050	0.025	0.010	0.005
31	14.458	15.655	17.539	19.281	21.434	41.422	44.985	48.232	52.191	55.003
32	15.134	16.362	18.291	20.072	22.271	42.585	46.194	49.480	53.486	56.328
33	15.815	17.074	19.047	20.867	23.110	43.745	47.400	50.725	54.776	57.648
34	16.501	17.789	19.806	21.664	23.952	44.903	48.602	51.966	56.061	58.964
35	17.192	18.509	20.569	22.465	24.797	46.059	49.802	53.203	57.342	60.275
36	17.887	19.233	21.336	23.269	25.643	47.212	50.998	54.437	58.619	61.581
37	18.586	19.960	22.106	24.075	26.492	48.363	52.192	55.668	59.893	62.883
38	19.289	20.691	22.878	24.884	27.343	49.513	53.384	56.896	61.162	64.181
39	19.996	21.426	23.654	25.695	28.196	50.660	54.572	58.120	62.428	65.476
40	20.707	22.164	24.433	26.509	29.051	51.805	55.758	59.342	63.691	66.766
41	21.421	22.906	25.215	27.326	29.907	52.949	56.942	60.561	64.950	68.053
42	22.138	23.650	25.999	28.144	30.765	54.090	58.124	61.777	66.206	69.336
43	22.859	24.398	26.785	28.965	31.625	55.230	59.304	62.990	67.459	70.616
44	23.584	25.148	27.575	29.787	32.487	56.369	60.481	64.201	68.710	71.893
45	24.311	25.901	28.366	30.612	33.350	57.505	61.656	65.410	69.957	73.166
46	25.041	26.657	29.160	31.439	34.215	58.641	62.830	66.617	71.201	74.437
47	25.775	27.416	29.956	32.268	35.081	59.774	64.001	67.821	72.443	75.704
48	26.511	28.177	30.755	33.098	35.949	60.907	65.171	69.023	73.683	76.969
49	27.249	28.941	31.555	33.930	36.818	62.038	66.339	70.222	74.919	78.231
50	27.991	29.707	32.357	34.764	37.689	63.167	67.505	71.420	76.154	79.490
55	31.735	33.570	36.398	38.958	42.060	68.796	73.311	77.380	82.292	85.749
60	35.534	37.485	40.482	43.188	46.459	74.397	79.082	83.298	88.379	91.952
65	39.383	41.444	44.603	47.450	50.883	79.973	84.821	89.177	94.422	98.105
70	43.275	45.442	48.758	51.739	55.329	85.527	90.531	95.023	100.425	104.215
75	47.206	49.475	52.942	56.054	59.795	91.061	96.217	100.839	106.393	110.286
80	51.172	53.540	57.153	60.391	64.278	96.578	101.879	106.629	112.329	116.321
85	55.170	57.634	61.389	64.749	68.777	102.079	107.522	112.393	118.236	122.325
90	59.196	61.754	65.647	69.126	73.291	107.565	113.145	118.136	124.116	128.299
95	63.250	65.898	69.925	73.520	77.818	113.038	118.752	123.858	129.973	134.247
100	67.328	70.065	74.222	77.929	82.358	118.498	124.342	129.561	135.807	140.169

SOURCE: χ^2 values calculated with Excel.

TABLE 4 F Distribution

Entries in this table provide the values of $F_{\alpha,(df_1,df_2)}$ that correspond to a given upper-tail area α and a specified number of degrees of freedom in the numerator df_1 and degrees of freedom in the denominator df_2. For example, for $\alpha = 0.05$, $df_1 = 8$, and $df_2 = 6$, $P(F_{(8,6)} \geq 4.15) = 0.05$.

Area in Upper Tail, α

$F_{\alpha,(df_1,df_2)}$

df_2	α	1	2	3	4	5	6	7	8	9	10	15	25	50	100	500
1	0.10	39.86	49.5	53.59	55.83	57.24	58.2	58.91	59.44	59.86	60.19	61.22	62.05	62.69	63.01	63.26
	0.05	161.45	199.50	215.71	224.58	230.16	233.99	236.77	238.88	240.54	241.88	245.95	249.26	251.77	253.04	254.06
	0.025	647.79	799.50	864.16	899.58	921.85	937.11	948.22	956.66	963.28	968.63	984.87	998.08	1008.12	1013.17	1017.24
	0.01	4052.18	4999.50	5403.35	5624.58	5763.65	5858.99	5928.36	5981.07	6022.47	6055.85	6157.28	6239.83	6302.52	6334.11	6359.50
2	0.10	8.53	9.00	9.16	9.24	9.29	9.33	9.35	9.37	9.38	9.39	9.42	9.45	9.47	9.48	9.49
	0.05	18.51	19.00	19.16	19.25	19.30	19.33	19.35	19.37	19.38	19.40	19.43	19.46	19.48	19.49	19.49
	0.025	38.51	39.00	39.17	39.25	39.30	39.33	39.36	39.37	39.39	39.40	39.43	39.46	39.48	39.49	39.50
	0.01	98.50	99.00	99.17	99.25	99.33	99.33	99.36	99.37	99.39	99.40	99.43	99.46	99.48	99.49	99.50
3	0.10	5.54	5.46	5.39	5.34	5.31	5.28	5.27	5.25	5.24	5.23	5.20	5.17	5.15	5.14	5.14
	0.05	10.13	9.55	9.28	9.12	9.01	8.94	8.89	8.85	8.81	8.79	8.70	8.63	8.58	8.55	8.53
	0.025	17.44	16.04	15.44	15.10	14.88	14.73	14.62	14.54	14.47	14.42	14.25	14.12	14.01	13.96	13.91
	0.01	34.12	30.82	29.46	28.71	28.24	27.91	27.67	27.49	27.35	27.23	26.87	26.58	26.35	26.24	26.15
4	0.10	4.54	4.32	4.19	4.11	4.05	4.01	3.98	3.95	3.94	3.92	3.87	3.83	3.80	3.78	3.76
	0.05	7.71	6.94	6.59	6.39	6.26	6.16	6.09	6.04	6.00	5.96	5.86	5.77	5.70	5.66	5.64
	0.025	12.22	10.65	9.98	9.60	9.36	9.20	9.07	8.98	8.90	8.84	8.66	8.5	8.38	8.32	8.27
	0.01	21.20	18.00	16.69	15.98	15.52	15.21	14.98	14.80	14.66	14.55	14.20	13.91	13.69	13.58	13.49
5	0.10	4.06	3.78	3.62	3.52	3.45	3.4	3.37	3.34	3.32	3.30	3.24	3.19	3.15	3.13	3.11
	0.05	6.61	5.79	5.41	5.19	5.05	4.95	4.88	4.82	4.77	4.74	4.62	4.52	4.44	4.41	4.37
	0.025	10.01	8.43	7.76	7.39	7.15	6.98	6.85	6.76	6.68	6.62	6.43	6.27	6.14	6.08	6.03
	0.01	16.26	13.27	12.06	11.39	10.97	10.67	10.46	10.29	10.16	10.05	9.72	9.45	9.24	9.13	9.04
6	0.10	3.78	3.46	3.29	3.18	3.11	3.05	3.01	2.98	2.96	2.94	2.87	2.81	2.77	2.75	2.73
	0.05	5.99	5.14	4.76	4.53	4.39	4.28	4.21	4.15	4.10	4.06	3.94	3.83	3.75	3.71	3.68
	0.025	8.81	7.26	6.60	6.23	5.99	5.82	5.70	5.6	5.52	5.46	5.27	5.11	4.98	4.92	4.86
	0.01	13.75	10.92	9.78	9.15	8.75	8.47	8.26	8.10	7.98	7.87	7.56	7.30	7.09	6.99	6.90
7	0.10	3.59	3.26	3.07	2.96	2.88	2.83	2.78	2.75	2.72	2.70	2.63	2.57	2.52	2.50	2.48
	0.05	5.59	4.74	4.35	4.12	3.97	3.87	3.79	3.73	3.68	3.64	3.51	3.4	3.32	3.27	3.24
	0.025	8.07	6.54	5.89	5.52	5.29	5.12	4.99	4.90	4.82	4.76	4.57	4.4	4.28	4.21	4.16
	0.01	12.25	9.55	8.45	7.85	7.46	7.19	6.99	6.84	6.72	6.62	6.31	6.06	5.86	5.75	5.67

df_1

df_2	α	1	2	3	4	5	6	7	8	9	10	15	25	50	100	500
8	0.10	3.46	3.11	2.92	2.81	2.73	2.67	2.62	2.59	2.56	2.54	2.46	2.40	2.35	2.32	2.30
	0.05	5.32	4.46	4.07	3.84	3.69	3.58	3.50	3.44	3.39	3.35	3.22	3.11	3.02	2.97	2.94
	0.025	7.57	6.06	5.42	5.05	4.82	4.65	4.53	4.43	4.36	4.30	4.1	3.94	3.81	3.74	3.68
	0.01	11.26	8.65	7.59	7.01	6.63	6.37	6.18	6.03	5.91	5.81	5.52	5.26	5.07	4.96	4.88
9	0.10	3.36	3.01	2.81	2.69	2.61	2.55	2.51	2.47	2.44	2.42	2.34	2.27	2.22	2.19	2.17
	0.05	5.12	4.26	3.86	3.63	3.48	3.37	3.29	3.23	3.18	3.14	3.01	2.89	2.80	2.76	2.72
	0.025	7.21	5.71	5.08	4.72	4.48	4.32	4.20	4.10	4.03	3.96	3.77	3.6	3.47	3.40	3.35
	0.01	10.56	8.02	6.99	6.42	6.06	5.8	5.61	5.47	5.35	5.26	4.96	4.71	4.52	4.41	4.33
10	0.10	3.29	2.92	2.73	2.61	2.52	2.46	2.41	2.38	2.35	2.32	2.24	2.17	2.12	2.09	2.06
	0.05	4.96	4.1	3.71	3.48	3.33	3.22	3.14	3.07	3.02	2.98	2.85	2.73	2.64	2.59	2.55
	0.025	6.94	5.46	4.83	4.47	4.24	4.07	3.95	3.85	3.78	3.72	3.52	3.35	3.22	3.15	3.09
	0.01	10.04	7.56	6.55	5.99	5.64	5.39	5.20	5.06	4.94	4.85	4.56	4.31	4.12	4.01	3.93
11	0.10	3.23	2.86	2.66	2.54	2.45	2.39	2.34	2.30	2.27	2.25	2.17	2.10	2.04	2.01	1.98
	0.05	4.84	3.98	3.59	3.36	3.20	3.09	3.01	2.95	2.90	2.85	2.72	2.60	2.51	2.46	2.42
	0.025	6.72	5.26	4.63	4.28	4.04	3.88	3.76	3.66	3.59	3.53	3.33	3.16	3.03	2.96	2.90
	0.01	9.65	7.21	6.22	5.67	5.32	5.07	4.89	4.74	4.63	4.54	4.25	4.01	3.81	3.71	3.62
12	0.10	3.18	2.81	2.61	2.48	2.39	2.33	2.28	2.24	2.21	2.19	2.10	2.03	1.97	1.94	1.91
	0.05	4.75	3.89	3.49	3.26	3.11	3.00	2.91	2.85	2.80	2.75	2.62	2.50	2.40	2.35	2.31
	0.025	6.55	5.10	4.47	4.12	3.89	3.73	3.61	3.51	3.44	3.37	3.18	3.01	2.87	2.80	2.74
	0.01	9.33	6.93	5.95	5.41	5.06	4.82	4.64	4.50	4.39	4.30	4.01	3.76	3.57	3.47	3.38
13	0.10	3.14	2.76	2.56	2.43	2.35	2.28	2.23	2.20	2.16	2.14	2.05	1.98	1.92	1.88	1.85
	0.05	4.67	3.81	3.41	3.18	3.03	2.92	2.83	2.77	2.71	2.67	2.53	2.41	2.31	2.26	2.22
	0.025	6.41	4.97	4.35	4.00	3.77	3.60	3.48	3.39	3.31	3.25	3.05	2.88	2.74	2.67	2.61
	0.01	9.07	6.70	5.74	5.21	4.86	4.62	4.44	4.30	4.19	4.10	3.82	3.57	3.38	3.27	3.19
14	0.10	3.10	2.73	2.52	2.39	2.31	2.24	2.19	2.15	2.12	2.10	2.01	1.93	1.87	1.83	1.80
	0.05	4.60	3.74	3.34	3.11	2.96	2.85	2.76	2.70	2.65	2.60	2.46	2.34	2.24	2.19	2.14
	0.025	6.30	4.86	4.24	3.89	3.66	3.50	3.38	3.29	3.21	3.15	2.95	2.78	2.64	2.56	2.50
	0.01	8.86	6.51	5.56	5.04	4.69	4.46	4.28	4.14	4.03	3.94	3.66	3.41	3.22	3.11	3.03
15	0.10	3.07	2.7	2.49	2.36	2.27	2.21	2.16	2.12	2.09	2.06	1.97	1.89	1.83	1.79	1.76
	0.05	4.54	3.68	3.29	3.06	2.90	2.79	2.71	2.64	2.59	2.54	2.40	2.28	2.18	2.12	2.08
	0.025	6.20	4.77	4.15	3.80	3.58	3.41	3.29	3.20	3.12	3.06	2.86	2.69	2.55	2.47	2.41
	0.01	8.68	6.36	5.42	4.89	4.56	4.32	4.14	4.00	3.89	3.80	3.52	3.28	3.08	2.98	2.89
16	0.10	3.05	2.67	2.46	2.33	2.24	2.18	2.13	2.09	2.06	2.03	1.94	1.86	1.79	1.76	1.73
	0.05	4.49	3.63	3.24	3.01	2.85	2.74	2.66	2.59	2.54	2.49	2.35	2.23	2.12	2.07	2.02
	0.025	6.12	4.69	4.08	3.73	3.50	3.34	3.22	3.12	3.05	2.99	2.79	2.61	2.47	2.40	2.33
	0.01	8.53	6.23	5.29	4.77	4.44	4.20	4.03	3.89	3.78	3.69	3.41	3.16	2.97	2.86	2.78

df_1

TABLE 4 (Continued)

		df_1														
df_2	α	1	2	3	4	5	6	7	8	9	10	15	25	50	100	500
17	0.10	3.03	2.64	2.44	2.31	2.22	2.15	2.10	2.06	2.03	2.00	1.91	1.83	1.76	1.73	1.69
	0.05	4.45	3.59	3.20	2.96	2.81	2.70	2.61	2.55	2.49	2.45	2.31	2.18	2.08	2.02	1.97
	0.025	6.04	4.62	4.01	3.66	3.44	3.28	3.16	3.06	2.98	2.92	2.72	2.55	2.41	2.33	2.26
	0.01	8.40	6.11	5.18	4.67	4.34	4.10	3.93	3.79	3.68	3.59	3.31	3.07	2.87	2.76	2.68
18	0.10	3.01	2.62	2.42	2.29	2.20	2.13	2.08	2.04	2.00	1.98	1.89	1.80	1.74	1.70	1.67
	0.05	4.41	3.55	3.16	2.93	2.77	2.66	2.58	2.51	2.46	2.41	2.27	2.14	2.04	1.98	1.93
	0.025	5.98	4.56	3.95	3.61	3.38	3.22	3.10	3.01	2.93	2.87	2.67	2.49	2.35	2.27	2.20
	0.01	8.29	6.01	5.09	4.58	4.25	4.01	3.84	3.71	3.60	3.51	3.23	2.98	2.78	2.68	2.59
19	0.10	2.99	2.61	2.40	2.27	2.18	2.11	2.06	2.02	1.98	1.96	1.86	1.78	1.71	1.67	1.64
	0.05	4.38	3.52	3.13	2.90	2.74	2.63	2.54	2.48	2.42	2.38	2.23	2.11	2.00	1.94	1.89
	0.025	5.92	4.51	3.90	3.56	3.33	3.17	3.05	2.96	2.88	2.82	2.62	2.44	2.30	2.22	2.15
	0.01	8.18	5.93	5.01	4.50	4.17	3.94	3.77	3.63	3.52	3.43	3.15	2.91	2.71	2.60	2.51
20	0.10	2.97	2.59	2.38	2.25	2.16	2.09	2.04	2.00	1.96	1.94	1.84	1.76	1.69	1.65	1.62
	0.05	4.35	3.49	3.10	2.87	2.71	2.60	2.51	2.45	2.39	2.35	2.20	2.07	1.97	1.91	1.86
	0.025	5.87	4.46	3.86	3.51	3.29	3.13	3.01	2.91	2.84	2.77	2.57	2.40	2.25	2.17	2.10
	0.01	8.10	5.85	4.94	4.43	4.10	3.87	3.70	3.56	3.46	3.37	3.09	2.84	2.64	2.54	2.44
21	0.10	2.96	2.57	2.36	2.23	2.14	2.08	2.02	1.98	1.95	1.92	1.83	1.74	1.67	1.63	1.60
	0.05	4.32	3.47	3.07	2.84	2.68	2.57	2.49	2.42	2.37	2.32	2.18	2.05	1.94	1.88	1.83
	0.025	5.83	4.42	3.82	3.48	3.25	3.09	2.97	2.87	2.80	2.73	2.53	2.36	2.21	2.13	2.06
	0.01	8.02	5.78	4.87	4.37	4.04	3.81	3.64	3.51	3.40	3.31	3.03	2.79	2.58	2.48	2.38
22	0.10	2.95	2.56	2.35	2.22	2.13	2.06	2.01	1.97	1.93	1.90	1.81	1.73	1.65	1.61	1.58
	0.05	4.30	3.44	3.05	2.82	2.66	2.55	2.46	2.40	2.34	2.30	2.15	2.02	1.91	1.85	1.80
	0.025	5.79	4.38	3.78	3.44	3.22	3.05	2.93	2.84	2.76	2.70	2.50	2.32	2.17	2.09	2.02
	0.01	7.95	5.72	4.82	4.31	3.99	3.76	3.59	3.45	3.35	3.26	2.98	2.73	2.53	2.42	2.33
23	0.10	2.94	2.55	2.34	2.21	2.11	2.05	1.99	1.95	1.92	1.89	1.80	1.71	1.64	1.59	1.56
	0.05	4.28	3.42	3.03	2.80	2.64	2.53	2.44	2.37	2.32	2.27	2.13	2.00	1.88	1.82	1.77
	0.025	5.75	4.35	3.75	3.41	3.18	3.02	2.90	2.81	2.73	2.67	2.47	2.29	2.14	2.06	1.99
	0.01	7.88	5.66	4.76	4.26	3.94	3.71	3.54	3.41	3.30	3.21	2.93	2.69	2.48	2.37	2.28
24	0.10	2.93	2.54	2.33	2.19	2.10	2.04	1.98	1.94	1.91	1.88	1.78	1.70	1.62	1.58	1.54
	0.05	4.26	3.40	3.01	2.78	2.62	2.51	2.42	2.36	2.30	2.25	2.11	1.97	1.86	1.80	1.75
	0.025	5.72	4.32	3.72	3.38	3.15	2.99	2.87	2.78	2.70	2.64	2.44	2.26	2.11	2.02	1.95
	0.01	7.82	5.61	4.72	4.22	3.90	3.67	3.50	3.36	3.26	3.17	2.89	2.64	2.44	2.33	2.24

df_2	α	df_1														
		1	2	3	4	5	6	7	8	9	10	15	25	50	100	500
25	0.10	2.92	2.53	2.32	2.18	2.09	2.02	1.97	1.93	1.89	1.87	1.77	1.68	1.61	1.56	1.53
	0.05	4.24	3.39	2.99	2.76	2.60	2.49	2.40	2.34	2.28	2.24	2.09	1.96	1.84	1.78	1.73
	0.025	5.69	4.29	3.69	3.35	3.13	2.97	2.85	2.75	2.68	2.61	2.41	2.23	2.08	2.00	1.92
	0.01	7.77	5.57	4.68	4.18	3.85	3.63	3.46	3.32	3.22	3.13	2.85	2.60	2.40	2.29	2.19
26	0.10	2.91	2.52	2.31	2.17	2.08	2.01	1.96	1.92	1.88	1.86	1.76	1.67	1.59	1.55	1.51
	0.05	4.23	3.37	2.98	2.74	2.59	2.47	2.39	2.32	2.27	2.22	2.07	1.94	1.82	1.76	1.71
	0.025	5.66	4.27	3.67	3.33	3.10	2.94	2.82	2.73	2.65	2.59	2.39	2.21	2.05	1.97	1.90
	0.01	7.72	5.53	4.64	4.14	3.82	3.59	3.42	3.29	3.18	3.09	2.81	2.57	2.36	2.25	2.16
27	0.10	2.90	2.51	2.30	2.17	2.07	2.00	1.95	1.91	1.87	1.85	1.75	1.66	1.58	1.54	1.50
	0.05	4.21	3.35	2.96	2.73	2.57	2.46	2.37	2.31	2.25	2.20	2.06	1.92	1.81	1.74	1.69
	0.025	5.63	4.24	3.65	3.31	3.08	2.92	2.80	2.71	2.63	2.57	2.36	2.18	2.03	1.94	1.87
	0.01	7.68	5.49	4.60	4.11	3.78	3.56	3.39	3.26	3.15	3.06	2.78	2.54	2.33	2.22	2.12
28	0.10	2.89	2.50	2.29	2.16	2.06	2.00	1.94	1.90	1.87	1.84	1.74	1.65	1.57	1.53	1.49
	0.05	4.20	3.34	2.95	2.71	2.56	2.45	2.36	2.29	2.24	2.19	2.04	1.91	1.79	1.73	1.67
	0.025	5.61	4.22	3.63	3.29	3.06	2.90	2.78	2.69	2.61	2.55	2.34	2.16	2.01	1.92	1.85
	0.01	7.64	5.45	4.57	4.07	3.75	3.53	3.36	3.23	3.12	3.03	2.75	2.51	2.30	2.19	2.09
29	0.10	2.89	2.50	2.28	2.15	2.06	1.99	1.93	1.89	1.86	1.83	1.73	1.64	1.56	1.52	1.48
	0.05	4.18	3.33	2.93	2.70	2.55	2.43	2.35	2.28	2.22	2.18	2.03	1.89	1.77	1.71	1.65
	0.025	5.59	4.20	3.61	3.27	3.04	2.88	2.76	2.67	2.59	2.53	2.32	2.14	1.99	1.90	1.83
	0.01	7.60	5.42	4.54	4.04	3.73	3.50	3.33	3.20	3.09	3.00	2.73	2.48	2.27	2.16	2.06
30	0.10	2.88	2.49	2.28	2.14	2.05	1.98	1.93	1.88	1.85	1.82	1.72	1.63	1.55	1.51	1.47
	0.05	4.17	3.32	2.92	2.69	2.53	2.42	2.33	2.27	2.21	2.16	2.01	1.88	1.76	1.70	1.64
	0.025	5.57	4.18	3.59	3.25	3.03	2.87	2.75	2.65	2.57	2.51	2.31	2.12	1.97	1.88	1.81
	0.01	7.56	5.39	4.51	4.02	3.70	3.47	3.30	3.17	3.07	2.98	2.70	2.45	2.25	2.13	2.03
50	0.10	2.81	2.41	2.20	2.06	1.97	1.90	1.84	1.80	1.76	1.73	1.63	1.53	1.44	1.39	1.34
	0.05	4.03	3.18	2.79	2.56	2.40	2.29	2.20	2.13	2.07	2.03	1.87	1.73	1.60	1.52	1.46
	0.025	5.34	3.97	3.39	3.05	2.83	2.67	2.55	2.46	2.38	2.32	2.11	1.92	1.75	1.66	1.57
	0.01	7.17	5.06	4.20	3.72	3.41	3.19	3.02	2.89	2.78	2.70	2.42	2.17	1.95	1.82	1.71
100	0.10	2.76	2.36	2.14	2.00	1.91	1.83	1.78	1.73	1.69	1.66	1.56	1.45	1.35	1.29	1.23
	0.05	3.94	3.09	2.70	2.46	2.31	2.19	2.10	2.03	1.97	1.93	1.77	1.62	1.48	1.39	1.31
	0.025	5.18	3.83	3.25	2.92	2.70	2.54	2.42	2.32	2.24	2.18	1.97	1.77	1.59	1.48	1.38
	0.01	6.90	4.82	3.98	3.51	3.21	2.99	2.82	2.69	2.59	2.50	2.22	1.97	1.74	1.60	1.47
500	0.10	2.72	2.31	2.09	1.96	1.86	1.79	1.73	1.68	1.64	1.61	1.5	1.39	1.28	1.21	1.12
	0.05	3.86	3.01	2.62	2.39	2.23	2.12	2.03	1.96	1.9	1.85	1.69	1.53	1.38	1.28	1.16
	0.025	5.05	3.72	3.14	2.81	2.59	2.43	2.31	2.22	2.14	2.07	1.86	1.65	1.46	1.34	1.19
	0.01	6.69	4.65	3.82	3.36	3.05	2.84	2.68	2.55	2.44	2.36	2.07	1.81	1.57	1.41	1.23

Source: *F*-values calculated with Excel.

Chapter 1

1.2   35 is likely the estimated average age. It is both costly and time consuming (likely impossible) to reach all video game players.

1.4   a. The population is all marketing managers.

   b. No, the average salary is a sample statistic computed from a sample, not the population.

1.6   Answers will vary depending on when data are retrieved. The numbers represent time series data.

1.8   Answers will vary depending on when data are retrieved. The numbers represent cross-sectional data.

1.10 Answers will vary depending on when data are retrieved. The numbers represent cross-sectional data.

1.12 a. Qualitative

   b. Quantitative, continuous

   c. Quantitative, discrete

1.14 a. Ratio

   b. Ordinal

   c. Nominal

1.16 a. Nominal

   b.

Major	Number of Students
Accounting	5
Economics	7
Finance	5
Marketing	3
Management	6
Undecided	4

   c. Economics (Marketing) has the highest (lowest) number of students.

Chapter 2

2.2   a.

Rating	Frequency	Relative Frequency
Excellent	5	0.208
Good	12	0.500
Fair	4	0.167
Poor	3	0.125

   b. The most common response is Good. Over 70 percent of the patients reveal that they are in either good or excellent health, suggesting overall health of first-time patients is strong.

2.4   a.

Delays	Frequency	Relative Frequency
PM Delays	1	0.056
All Day Delays	6	0.333
AM Delays	4	0.222
None	7	0.389

   b.

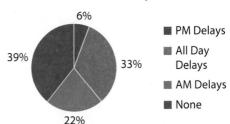

Air Travel Delays

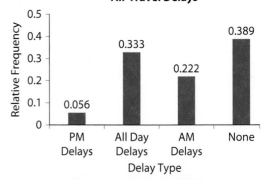

Air Travel Delays

2.6   a.

Response	Frequency
Good jobs	1970
Affordable homes	799
Top schools	586
Low crime	1225
Things to do	745

   b.

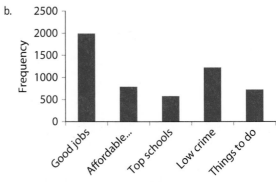

2.8   a.

Company	Relative Frequency
Enterprise	0.489
Hertz	0.215
Avis Budget	0.183
Dollar Thrifty	0.068
Other	0.046

b. Hertz accounted for 21.5% of sales.

c.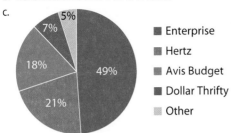

2.10 a. 5584

b. 0.052

c.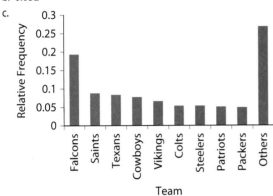

2.12 a. Football player (martial arts athlete) was most (least) likely to sustain an injury with lifelong consequences.

b. Approximately 79 ($= 992 \times 0.08$)

2.14 This graph does not correctly depict the data. The vertical axis has been stretched so that the increase in sales appears more pronounced than warranted.

2.16

Class	Frequency	Relative Frequency	Cumulative Relative Frequency
−10 up to 0	9	0.129	0.129
0 up to 10	31	0.443	0.572
10 up to 20	19	0.271	0.843
20 up to 30	8	0.114	0.957
30 up to 40	3	0.043	1

a. 19 observations

b. 27.1%; 84.3%

c.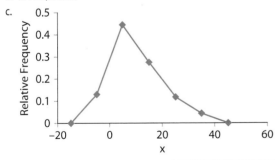

2.18 a.

Class	Relative Frequency
1000 up to 1100	0.1250
1100 up to 1200	0.4375
1200 up to 1300	0.1875
1300 up to 1400	0.2500

43.75% of observations are at least 1100 but less than 1200.

b.

Class	Cumulative Frequency	Cumulative Relative Frequency
1000 up to 1100	2	0.125
1100 up to 1200	9	0.562
1200 up to 1300	12	0.750
1300 up to 1400	16	1

12 observations are less than 1300.

c.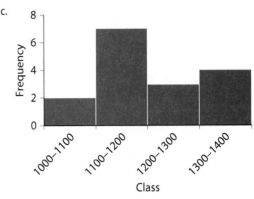

2.20 a.

Class	Frequency
−20 up to −10	2
−10 up to 0	14
0 up to 10	13
10 up to 20	11
20 up to 30	10

14 observations are at least −10 but less than 0.

b.

Class	Cumulative Frequency
−20 up to −10	2
−10 up to 0	16
0 up to 10	29
10 up to 20	40
20 up to 30	50

40 observations are less than 20.

c.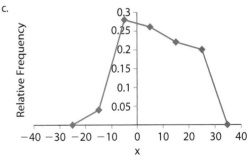

2.22 a.

Assets (in billions USD)	Frequency
40 up to 70	9
70 up to 100	8
100 up to 130	2
130 up to 160	0
160 up to 190	1

b.

Assets (in billions USD)	Relative Frequency	Cumulative Frequency	Cumulative Relative Frequency
40 up to 70	0.45	9	0.45
70 up to 100	0.40	17	0.85
100 up to 130	0.10	19	0.95
130 up to 160	0	19	0.95
160 up to 190	0.05	20	1

c. 2 funds; 19 funds

d. 40%; 95%

e.

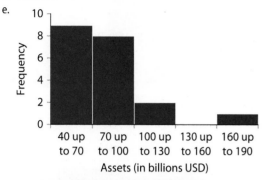

2.24 a.

Temperature (°F)	Frequency
60 up to 70	2
70 up to 80	7
80 up to 90	14
90 up to 100	10

b.

Temperature (°F)	Relative Frequency	Cumulative Frequency	Cumulative Relative Frequency
60 up to 70	0.061	2	0.061
70 up to 80	0.212	9	0.273
80 up to 90	0.424	23	0.697
90 up to 100	0.303	33	1

c. 9 cities

d. 42.4%; 69.7%

e.

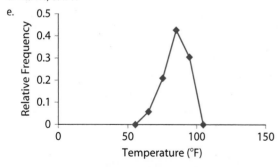

The distribution is slightly negatively skewed.

2.26 a.

Age	Frequency	Cumulative Frequency	Cumulative Relative Frequency
15 up to 20	0.10(2000) = 200	200	0.1
20 up to 25	0.25(2000) = 500	200 + 500 = 700	0.10 + 0.25 = 0.35
25 up to 30	0.28(2000) = 560	700 + 560 = 1260	0.35 + 0.28 = 0.63
30 up to 35	0.24(2000) = 480	1260 + 480 = 1740	0.63 + 0.24 = 0.87
35 up to 40	0.11(2000) = 220	1740 + 220 = 1960	0.87 + 0.11 = 0.98
40 up to 45	0.02(2000) = 40	1960 + 40 = 2000	0.98 + 0.02 = 1
	Total = 2000		

b. 28%; 87%

c.

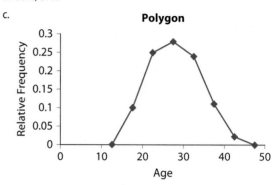

The distribution appears to be relatively symmetric with possibly a slight positive skew.

d.

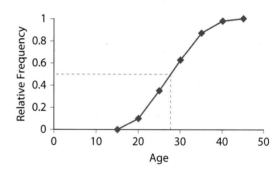

If we draw a horizontal line that corresponds to the 0.5 value on the vertical axis, it will intersect the ogive at the age of approximately 28 years old.

2.28 a. No. The distribution is positively skewed.

b. 44%

c. 66%

2.30 a. No. The distribution is positively skewed.

b. 50, 450.

c. The $150–$250 class has the highest relative frequency, which is about 0.3.

2.32 a. About 65%.

b. About 75%.

2.34 a.

House Value	Frequency
0 up to 100,000	2
100,000 up to 200,000	26
200,000 up to 300,000	16
300,000 up to 400,000	4
400,000 up to 500,000	1
500,000 up to 600,000	1
	Total = 50

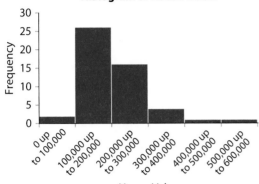

Histogram of House Value

b. No. The distribution is positively skewed.

c. The class "$100,000 up to $200,000" has the highest frequency.

d. 8%

e. 44

2.36 a.

DJIA Price Index	Frequency
12,250 up to 12,500	10
12,500 up to 12,750	11
12,750 up to 13,000	26
13,000 up to 13,250	14
13,250 up to 13,500	1
	Total = 62

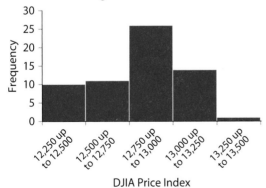

Histogram for DJIA Price Index

The DJIA was less than 12,500 on 10 days during this quarter.

b.

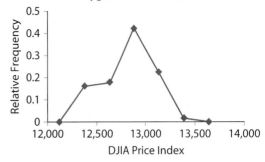

Polygon for DJIA Price Index

The distribution is positively skewed.

c.

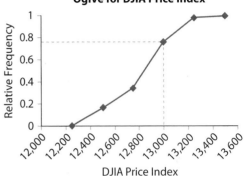

Ogive for DJIA Price Index

On approximately 75% of the days, the DJIA was less than 13,000.

2.38

Stem	Leaf
−8	7 5 5 3 2 0 0 0
−7	9 7 5 3 3 2 1
−6	5 5 4
−5	2 0

The distribution is not symmetric.

2.40

Stem	Leaf
7	3 4 6 7 8 8
8	0 1 2 3 4 4 4 4 7 8
9	0 0 0 1 1 2 2 2 3 3 4 4 4 4 4 5 6 6 6 8 8 9
10	6 7

Temperatures ranged from 73 to 107. Temperatures in the 90s were most frequent.

2.42 Spain

Stem	Leaf
2	1 1 1 2 3 3 4 4 5 5 5 6 7 8 9 9 9
3	0 0 2

Netherlands

Stem	Leaf
2	2 3 3 4 5 5 5 6 6 6 7 7 7 7 9
3	0 3 5 5 9

Spain has a relatively younger team. Spain's ages range from 21 to 32 while the Netherlands' ages range from 22 to 39. Most players on both teams are in their 20s.

2.44

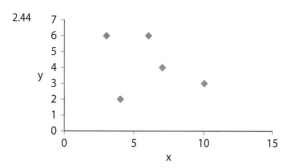

There is no clear relationship between x and y.

2.46

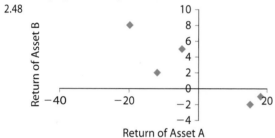

There is a positive relationship; as the number of hours spent studying increases, grades tend to increase.

2.48

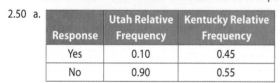

There is a negative relationship between the two assets; it would be wise for the investor to include them in her portfolio.

2.50 a.

Response	Utah Relative Frequency	Kentucky Relative Frequency
Yes	0.10	0.45
No	0.90	0.55

45% of households in Kentucky allow smoking at home whereas only 10% do in Utah.

b.

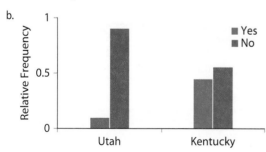

The bar chart shows that smoking at home is much more common in Kentucky.

2.52 a.

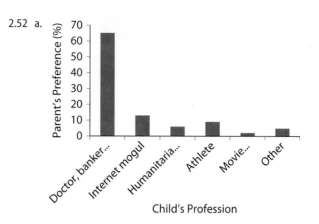

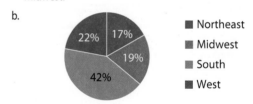

b. $(0.09)(550) \approx 50$ parents.

2.54 a.

Region	Relative Frequency
Northeast	0.165
Midwest	0.194
South	0.416
West	0.225

19.4% of people living below the poverty line live in the Midwest.

b.

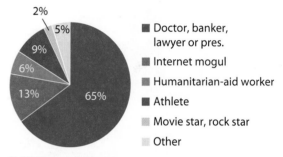

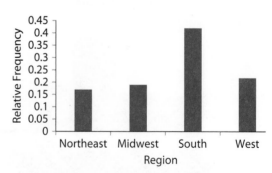

2.56 a.

Response	Frequency
A few days	642
A few long weekends	550
One week	1101
Two weeks	764

b.

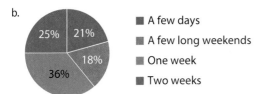

- A few days
- A few long weekends
- One week
- Two weeks

2.58 a.

Drug	Relative Frequency
Topamax	0.319
Lamictal	0.295
Depakote	0.135
Lyrica	0.127
Keppra	0.124

b. Lamictal accounted for 29.5% of sales.

c.

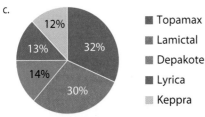

- Topamax
- Lamictal
- Depakote
- Lyrica
- Keppra

2.60 a.

Average MPG	Relative Frequency	Cumulative Frequency	Cumulative Relative Frequency
15 up to 20	0.1875	15	0.1875
20 up to 25	0.3750	45	0.5625
25 up to 30	0.1875	60	0.75
30 up to 35	0.1250	70	0.875
35 up to 40	0.0875	77	0.9625
40 up to 45	0.0375	80	1

b. 60 cars; 37.5%; 87.5%; 12.5%

c.

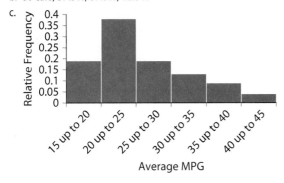

2.62 a. 16%

b. 76%

c.

Stem	Leaf
3	6 6
4	4 7
5	3 3 4 6
6	0 1 5 5 6 7 7 9
7	0 1 3 3 3 7 8 9 9

The distribution is negatively skewed.

2.64 a.

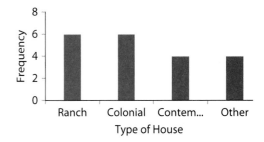

- Ranch
- Colonial
- Contemporary
- Other

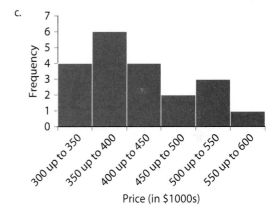

60% of homes sold are either Ranch or Colonial; remaining 40% split between Contemporary and Other.

b.

Price ($)	Frequency
300,000 up to 350,000	4
350,000 up to 400,000	6
400,000 up to 450,000	4
450,000 up to 500,000	2
500,000 up to 550,000	3
550,000 up to 600,000	1

c.

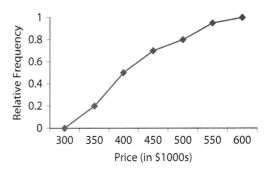

2.66

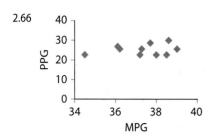

No clear relationship between PPG and MPG.

Chapter 3

3.2 Mean $= -2.67$; Median $= -3.5$; Mode $= -4$

3.4 Mean $= 18.33$; Median $= 20$; Mode $= 15, 20$

3.6 a. $\bar{x} = 3.7$; Median $= 3.5$; Mode $= 3$

b. Since we are describing the typical number of bedrooms in a home, the best measure of central location is the mode.

3.8 Average price per share $= 23.862$.

3.10 a. Average price per share $= 12.17$.

b. Average price per share $= 13.27$.

3.12 a. Mean$_{Yankees} = 4.70$; Median$_{Yankees} = 4.68$

b. Mean$_{Orioles} = 6.05$; Median$_{Orioles} = 5.23$

c. The Yankees

3.14 Mean $= 3.90$; Median $= 3.87$; Mode $= 3.89$

3.16 $P_{20} = 160.2$; $P_{50} = 215$; $P_{80} = 324.4$

3.18 a. The asterisk (*) on the left indicates the presence of an outlier.

b. Negatively skewed

3.20 a. $P_{25} = 13.5$; $P_{50} = 22$; $P_{75} = 33.5$

b. No outliers

3.22 a. $P_{25} = 66.25$; $P_{50} = 75$; $P_{75} = 85.75$

b. 25 is an outlier

c. Negatively skewed

3.24 a. $P_{25} = 11.5$; $P_{50} = 15$; $P_{75} = 19$

b. The PE values of 44 and 49 are outliers; positively skewed

3.26 a. Range $= 32$

b. $\mu = 24$; MAD $= 11.2$

c. $\sigma^2 = 153.6$

d. $\sigma = 12.39$

3.28 a. Range $= 20$

b. $\bar{x} = 42$; MAD $= 7.33$

c. $s^2 = 51.2$

d. $s = 7.16$

3.30 a. Range $= 11.78$

b. $\bar{x} = 8.34$; Median $= 8.84$

c. $s^2 = 15.74$; $s = 3.97$

3.32 a. Monthly rent: $\bar{x} = 1222.93$; $s = 424.80$

b. Square footage: $\bar{x} = 1286.03$; $s = 645.81$

c. Monthly rent: $CV = 0.35$

d. Square footage: $CV = 0.50$; there is greater relative dispersion in square footage than in monthly rent.

3.34 a. Range of household income $= 32,766$;

Range of house value $= 442,900$.

b. $\bar{x}_{Income} = 51,641.4$;

MAD$_{Income} = 6834.68$;

$s^2_{Income} = 70,323,534$;

$s_{Income} = 8385.91$

$\bar{x}_{Value} = 199,324$;

MAD$_{Value} = 71,738.88$;

$s^2_{Value} = 8,758,919,820$;

$s_{Value} = 93,589.10$

c. The coefficient of variation is the recommended measure.

3.36 a. Investment B; Investment A

b. Sharpe$_A = \dfrac{\bar{x}_I - \bar{R}_f}{S_I} = \dfrac{10 - 1.4}{5} = 1.72$; Sharpe$_B = \dfrac{\bar{x}_I - \bar{R}_f}{S_I} =$

$\dfrac{15 - 1.4}{10} = 1.36$;

Investment A; hence it provides a higher reward per unit of risk.

3.38 a. Energy fund

b. Energy fund

c. Sharpe$_{Energy} = \dfrac{19.35 - 3}{35.99} = 0.45$; Sharpe$_{Health} = \dfrac{6.64 - 3}{15.28} =$

0.24; the Energy fund

3.40 a. $\bar{x}_{Technology} = 3.89$; $s_{Technology} = 41.16$; $\bar{x}_{Service} = 15.45$; $s_{Service} = 32.29$

The Service fund has a higher mean annual return and a lower sample standard deviation than the Technology fund.

b. Sharpe$_{Technology} = (3.89 - 2)/41.16 = 0.046$; Sharpe$_{Service} = (15.45 - 2)/32.29 = 0.417$

The Service fund has a much higher Sharpe ratio than the Technology fund, suggesting that the Fidelity Select Service Fund has more reward per unit of risk.

3.42 a. At least 75%

b. At least 94%

3.44 a. 68%

b. 95%

c. 2.5%

3.46 a. 95% + 2.5% = 97.5%

b. 975

3.48 Approximately 6 observations

3.50 The z-scores for the smallest and largest observations are $z = -1.14$ and $z = 2.01$, respectively; hence, not outliers.

3.52 a. 16% (32%/2) of the observations are greater than 20%.

b. 2.5% (5%/2) of the observations are less than -16%.

3.54 a. 68%

b. 16%

c. 2.5%

3.56 a. The z-scores for the smallest and largest observations are $z = -1.13$ and $z = 1.83$, respectively; hence, no outliers.

b. The z-scores for the smallest and largest observations are $z = -1.97$ and $z = 1.71$, respectively; hence, no outliers.

3.58 a. $\mu = \dfrac{\Sigma m_i f_i}{N} = \dfrac{1100}{180} = 6.11$

b. $\sigma^2 = \dfrac{\Sigma (m_i - \mu)^2 f_i}{N} = \dfrac{497.78}{180} = 2.76$; $\sigma = \sqrt{\sigma^2} = 1.67$

3.60 $\mu = \dfrac{\Sigma m_i f_i}{N} = \dfrac{-700}{200} = -3.5$; $\sigma^2 = \dfrac{\Sigma (m_i - \mu)^2 f_i}{N} = \dfrac{18,550}{200}$

$= 92.75$;

$\sigma = \sqrt{\sigma^2} = 9.63$

3.62 a. $\bar{x} = \dfrac{\Sigma m_i f_i}{n} = \dfrac{450}{50} = 9$

b. $s^2 = \dfrac{\Sigma (m_i - \bar{x})^2 f_i}{n - 1} = \dfrac{652.50}{49} = 13.32$; $s = \sqrt{s^2} = 3.65$

3.64 a. $\bar{x} = \dfrac{\Sigma m_i f_i}{n} = \dfrac{2065}{80} = 25.81$

b. $s^2 = \dfrac{\Sigma (m_i - \bar{x})^2 f_i}{n - 1} = \dfrac{3647.19}{79} = 46.17$; $s = \sqrt{s^2} = 6.79$

3.66 a. $\bar{x} = \dfrac{\Sigma m_i f_i}{n} = \dfrac{3767}{100} = 37.67$

b. $s^2 = \dfrac{\Sigma(m_i - \bar{x})^2 f_i}{n - 1} = \dfrac{46{,}386.61}{99} = 468.55; s = \sqrt{s^2} = 21.65$

3.68 a. $s_{xy} = \dfrac{\Sigma(x_i - \bar{x})(y_i - \bar{y})}{n - 1} = \dfrac{-49.21}{4} = -12.3$; negative linear relationship

b. $r_{xy} = \dfrac{s_{xy}}{s_x s_y} = -0.96$; negative and strong linear relationship

3.70 a. $s_{\text{Price,Days}} = \dfrac{\Sigma(x_i - \bar{x})(y_i - \bar{y})}{n - 1} = \dfrac{4419.75}{7} = 631.39$; positive linear relationship

b. $r_{\text{Price,Days}} = \dfrac{s_{\text{Price,Days}}}{s_{\text{Price}} s_{\text{Days}}} = 0.45$; positive and moderate relationship

3.72 a. $s_{\text{Educ,Sal}} = \dfrac{\Sigma(x_i - \bar{x})(y_i - \bar{y})}{n - 1} = \dfrac{245}{7} = 35$; positive linear relationship

b. $r_{\text{Educ,Sal}} = \dfrac{s_{\text{Educ,Sal}}}{s_{\text{Educ}} s_{\text{Sal}}} = 0.95$; positive and strong relationship

3.74 a. $r_{\text{Age,Happiness}} = 0.57$; positive and moderate linear relationship

b.

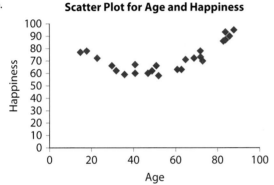

Scatter Plot for Age and Happiness

The scatterplot indicates a nonlinear relationship between Happiness and Age.

3.76 Mean = 809.14; Median = 366; Mode = *not available*. The median best reflects the typical sales as the value 3,300 is clearly an outlier that pulls the mean up.

3.78 a.

	Firm A	Firm B
Mean	31.33	23.50
Variance	8.67	6.70
Standard Deviation	2.94	2.59
Coefficient of Variation	0.09	0.11

b. Firm A

c. Firm A: greater standard deviation (2.94 > 2.59). Firm B: greater relative dispersion with a coefficient of variation of 0.11 against 0.09 for Firm A.

3.80 a. $\bar{x} = \dfrac{\Sigma m_i f_i}{n} = \dfrac{3262}{200} = 16.31$

b. $s^2 = \dfrac{\Sigma(m_i - \bar{x})^2 f_i}{n - 1} = \dfrac{12{,}111.78}{199} = 60.86; s = \sqrt{s^2} = 7.80$

3.82 a. $\bar{x}_{\text{Ad}} = 25$ and $\bar{x}_{\text{Sales}} = 18$

b. $s_{\text{Ad}} = 3.58$ and $s_{\text{Sales}} = 2.10$

c. $s_{xy} = \dfrac{\Sigma(x_i - \bar{x})(y_i - \bar{y})}{n - 1} = \dfrac{35}{5} = 7$; positive linear relationship

d. $r_{xy} = \dfrac{s_{xy}}{s_x s_y} = 0.93$; positive and strong linear relationship

3.84

	Income
Mean	8.86
Median	7.96
Standard Deviation	6.71
Range	24.93

There is a great deal of variability in salaries. The difference between the highest-and lowest-paid quarterback is $24.93 million. The sample standard deviation of salaries is $6.71 million.

3.86 a. There are two outliers in the gasoline price data: Alaska and Hawaii prices.

b. $\bar{x} = 3.90; s = 0.18$. Since the z-score, $z = 3.92$, for Hawaii is greater than 3, there are outliers in the data. This is consistent with the box plot.

Chapter 4

4.2 a. $P(D) = 0.20$ (the events are equally likely).

b. $P(B^c) = 0.80$

c. $P(A \cup C \cup E) = P(A) + P(C) + P(E) = 0.60$

4.4 a. $P(D) = 1 - [P(A) + P(B) + P(C)] = 0.30$

b. $P(C^c) = 1 - P(C) = 0.75$

c. $P(A \cup B) = P(A) + P(B) = 0.45$

4.6 Empirical probability

4.8 a. A union

b. An intersection

4.10 a. $P(\{\text{overweight}\} \cup \{\text{obese}\}) = 0.688$

b. $P((\{\text{overweight}\} \cup \{\text{obese}\})^c) = 1 - P(\{\text{overweight}\} \cup \{\text{obese}\}) = 0.312$

c. The events {overweight} and {obese} are not exhaustive.

d. Mutually exclusive

4.12 a. $P(\{\text{Mild}\}) = 0.215$

b. $P(\{\text{No Depression}\}) = 0.568$

c. $P(\{\text{Moderately Severe}\} \cup \{\text{Severe}\}) = 0.115$

d. Cape Cod has a higher level of moderately severe to severe depression with 11.5% of its residents compared to 6.7% at the national level.

4.14 $P(A) = 0.55; P(B) = 0.30; P(A \cap B) = 0.10$

a. $P(A \mid B) = \dfrac{P(A \cap B)}{P(B)} = 0.33$

b. $P(A \cup B) = P(A) + P(B) - P(A \cap B) = 0.75$

c. $P((A \cup B)^c) = 1 - P(A \cup B) = 0.25$

4.16 $P(A) = 0.40; P(B) = 0.50$

a. $P(A \cap B) = P(A)P(B) = (0.40)(0.50) = 0.20$

b. $P((A \cup B)^c) = 1 - P(A \cup B) = 1 - 0.70 = 0.30$

c. $P(A \mid B) = \dfrac{P(A \cap B)}{P(B)} = 0.40$

4.18 $P(A) = 0.15, P(B) = 0.10$, and $P(A \cap B) = 0.05$

a. A and B are not independent events since $P(A \mid B) = 0.50 \neq 0.15 = P(A)$.

b. A and B are not mutually exclusive events since $P(A \cap B) \neq 0$.

c. $P((A \cup B)^c) = 1 - P(A \cup B) = 0.80$

4.20 $P(A^c) = 0.30, P(B) = 0.60$, and $P(A \cap B^c) = 0.24$

a. $P(A \mid B^c) = \dfrac{P(A \cap B^c)}{P(B^c)} = 0.60$

b. $P(B^c|A) = \dfrac{P(A \cap B^c)}{P(A)} = 0.343$

c. A and B are not independent events since A and B^c are not independent events: $P(A|B^c) = 0.60 \neq 0.70 = P(A)$.

4.22 Let events SM, W, and M correspond to "Mobile phone subscribers who use smartphones," "Women," and "Men," respectively.

$P(SM) = 0.44$, $P(W|SM) = 0.51$

a. $P(W \cap SM) = P(W|SM)P(SM) = (0.51)(0.44) = 0.2244$

b. $P(M \cap SM) = P(SM) - P(W \cap SM) = 0.2856$

4.24 $P(A) = 0.40$, $P(B) = 0.60$, $P(A|B) = 0.80$

a. $P(A \cup B) = P(A) + P(B) - P(A \cap B) = 0.52$

b. Events A and B are not mutually exclusive since $P(A \cap B) = 0.48 \neq 0$.

c. Events A and B are not independent since $P(A|B) = 0.80 \neq 0.40 = P(A)$.

4.26 Let events H and P correspond to "Do homework regularly" and "Pass the course," respectively.

$P(H) = 0.60$, $P(P|H) = 0.95$, $P(P) = 0.85$

a. $P(H \cap P) = P(P|H)P(H) = (0.95)(0.60) = 0.57$

b. $P((H \cup P)^c) = 1 - P(H \cup P) = 0.12$

c. No, because $P(H \cap P) = 0.57 \neq 0$

d. No, because $P(P|H) = 0.95 \neq 0.85 = P(P)$.

4.28 Let event A be "Default on a seven-year AA bond" and B be "Default on a seven-year A bond."

$P(A) = 0.06$, $P(B) = 0.13$, and $P(A \cap B) = 0.04$

a. $P(A \cup B) = P(A) + P(B) - P(A \cap B) = 0.15$

b. $P((A \cup B)^c) = 1 - P(A \cup B) = 0.85$

c. $P(B|A) = \dfrac{P(A \cap B)}{P(A)} = 0.67$

4.30 a. $P(A) = 0.40$, $P(A^c) = 1 - P(A) = 0.60$, $P(B) = 0.50$

b. Events A and B are not exhaustive since $P(A \cup B) < 1$.

c. Mike's preference is described by the event $A \cap B$. It is the intersection of the events of getting both a "white or blue" and "size L" shirt.

4.32 For $i = 1,2$, let event A_i be "the i-th selected member is in favor of the bonus."

a. $P(A_1 \cap A_2) = \dfrac{10}{15} \times \dfrac{9}{14} = 0.4286$

b. $P(A_1^c \cap A_2^c) = \dfrac{5}{15} \times \dfrac{4}{14} = 0.0952$

4.34 Let event A correspond to "Asians," B to "black," W to "white," H to be "Hispanic," and T to be "both parents at home."

$P(T|A) = 0.85$, $P(T|W) = 0.78$, $P(T|H) = 0.70$, $P(T|B) = 0.38$

a. $A \cap B = \varnothing$ (empty set). Events corresponding to "Asians" and "black" are mutually exclusive.

$P(A) + P(B) < 1$. Events corresponding to "Asians" and "black" are not exhaustive.

b. $P(W^c) = 1 - P(W) = 1 - \dfrac{280}{500} = 0.44$

c. $P(W \cap T) = P(T|W)P(W) = (0.78)(0.56) = 0.4368$

d. $P(A \cap T) = P(T|A)P(A) = (0.85)(0.10) = 0.085$

4.36 S = Women face sexual harassment; T = Women use public transportation

a. $P(S \cap T) = P(S|T)P(T) = 0.23$

b. $P(T|S) = P(S \cap T)/P(S) = 0.34$

4.38 F = Foreclosed; H = centered in Arizona, California, Florida, or Nevada; since $P(F) = 0.0079$ and $P(H|F) = 0.62$:

$P(F \cap H) = P(H|F)P(F) = 0.0049$

4.40 a.

	B	B^c	Total
A	0.26	0.34	0.60
A^c	0.14	0.26	0.40
Total	0.40	0.60	1.00

b. $P(A) = 0.60$

c. $P(A \cap B) = 0.26$

d. $P(A|B) = P(A \cap B)/P(B) = 0.65$

e. $P(B|A^c) = P(A^c \cap B)/P(A^c) = 0.35$

f. No, since $P(A \cap B) = 0.26 \neq 0$.

g. No, since $P(A|B) = 0.65 \neq 0.60 = P(A)$.

4.42 a.

	IT	G	Total
Yes	0.2214	0.3657	0.5871
No	0.2071	0.2057	0.4129
Total	0.4286	0.5714	1

b. $P(IT) = 0.4286$

c. $P(Yes) = 0.5871$

d. $P(IT|Yes) = P(Yes \cap IT)/P(Yes) = 0.3771$

e. $P(Yes|G) = P(Yes \cap G)/P(G) = 0.64$

f. No, since $P(IT|Yes) \neq P(IT)$.

4.44 a.

	Study Hard		
Major	Yes	No	Total
Business	20	100	120
Nonbusiness	48	102	150
Total	68	202	270

b. $P(B \cap No) = \dfrac{100}{270} = 0.3704$

c. $P(Yes) = \dfrac{68}{270} = 0.2519$

d. $P(B|Yes) = \dfrac{20}{68} = 0.2941$; $P(B^c|Yes) = \dfrac{48}{68} = 0.7059$

4.46 a.

	Vaccinated (V)	Dummy Shot (D)	Total
Infected (I)	0.016	0.014	0.030
Not Infected	0.477	0.493	0.970
Total	0.493	0.507	1

b. $P(V) = 0.493$

c. $P(I) = 0.03$

d. $P(I|V) = 0.03$

e. Yes, since $P(I|V) = P(I) = 0.03$.

4.48 L = Like it, M = man, W = woman, A = American, B = European, C = Asian

a. $P(L|M) = 480/(480 + 520) = 0.48$

b. $P(L|C) = (120 + 180)/500 = 0.60$

c. BW = European woman; $P(L^c|BW) = 190/(310 + 190) = 0.38$

d. AM = American man; $P(L^c|AM) = 290/(210 + 290) = 0.58$

e. i. America: $P(L|M) = 210/(210 + 290) = 0.42 \neq P(L) = (210 + 370)/1200 = 0.48$; not independent

ii. Europe: $P(L|M) = 150/(150 + 150) = 0.50 \neq P(L) = (150 + 310)/800 = 0.58$; not independent

iii. Asia: $P(L|M) = 120/(120 + 80) = 0.60 = P(L) = (120 + 180)/500$; independent

f. $P(L|M) = 480/(480 + 520) = 0.48 \neq P(L) =$ (480 + 860)/2500 = 0.54; not independent

4.50 a. $P(B^C) = 0.40$

b. $P(A \cap B) = P(A|B)P(B) = 0.48$
$P(A \cap B^C) = P(A|B^C)P(B^C) = 0.04$

c. $P(A) = P(A \cap B) + P(A \cap B^C) = 0.52$

d. $P(B|A) = P(A \cap B)/P(A) = 0.9231$

4.52

Prior Probabilities	Conditional Probabilities	Joint Probabilities	Posterior Probabilities
$P(B_1) = 0.1$	$P(A|B_1) = 0.4$	$P(A \cap B_1) = 0.04$	$P(B_1|A) = 0.06$
$P(B_2) = 0.6$	$P(A|B_2) = 0.6$	$P(A \cap B_2) = 0.36$	$P(B_2|A) = 0.56$
$P(B_3) = 0.3$	$P(A|B_3) = 0.8$	$P(A \cap B_3) = 0.24$	$P(B_3|A) = 0.38$
Total = 1		$P(A) = 0.64$	Total = 1

4.54 D = Experience a decline; N = Ratio is negative
$P(N) = P(N \cap D) + P(N \cap D^C) = P(N|D)P(D) + P(N|D^C)P(D^C) = 0.26$. Then, $P(D|N) = P(N \cap D)/P(N) = 0.54$

4.56 Let event O be "Teen owns a cell phone" and event T correspond to "Older teens." We have $P(O|T) = 0.90, P(O|T^C) = 0.60$, and $P(T) = 0.70$.

a. $P(O) = P(O|T)P(T) + P(O|T^C)P(T^C) = (0.90)(.70) + (.60)(1 - .70) = 0.81$

b. $P(T|O) = \dfrac{P(O \cap T)}{P(O)} = \dfrac{P(O|T)P(T)}{P(O|T)P(T) + P(O|T^C)P(T^C)} = \dfrac{0.63}{0.81} = 0.7778$

c. $P(T^C|O) = \dfrac{P(O \cap T^C)}{P(O)} = \dfrac{P(O|T^C)P(T^C)}{P(O|T)P(T) + P(O|T^C)P(T^C)} = \dfrac{0.18}{0.81} = 0.2222$

4.58 Let F = "Player is fully fit to play," S = "Player is somewhat fit to play," N = "Player is not able to play," and W = "The Lakers win the game."

a. Consider the following table:

Prior Probabilities	Conditional Probabilities	Joint Probabilities
$P(F) = 0.40$	$P(W|F) = 0.80$	$P(W \cap F) = 0.40(0.80) = 0.32$
$P(S) = 0.30$	$P(W|S) = 0.60$	$P(W \cap S) = 0.60(0.30) = 0.18$
$P(N) = 0.30$	$P(W|N) = 0.40$	$P(W \cap N) = 0.30(0.40) = 0.12$
Total = 1.00		$P(W) = 0.32 + 0.18 + 0.12 = 0.62$

The Lakers have a 62% chance of winning the game.

b. $P(F|W) = \dfrac{P(W \cap F)}{P(W)} = \dfrac{0.32}{0.62} = 0.52$

4.60 a. The given probabilities are $P(A) = 0.10, P(B) = 0.44$, and $P(B|A) = 0.60$. The probability $P(A) = 0.10$ is subjective because it is based on judgment. The other two probabilities are empirical because they are based on survey data.

b. $P(A \cap B) = P(B|A)P(A) = 0.60(0.10) = 0.06 > 0$. Thus, the events A and B are not mutually exclusive. Since $P(A \cup B) = P(A) + P(B) - P(A \cap B) = 0.10 + 0.44 - 0.06 = 0.48 < 1$, these events are not exhaustive.

c. Since $P(B|A) = 0.60 \neq 0.44 = P(B)$, the events A and B are not independent.

d. $P(A|B) = \dfrac{P(A \cap B)}{P(B)} = \dfrac{0.06}{0.44} \approx 0.136$.

4.62 Let event U correspond to "US equity" and F to "Foreign equity"; $P(U) = 0.70, P(F) = 0.50$, and $P(U \cap F) = 0.40$.

a. $P(U|F) = \dfrac{P(U \cap F)}{P(F)} = \dfrac{0.40}{0.50} = 0.80$

b. $P((U \cup F)^C) = 1 - P(U \cup F) = 1 - 0.80 = 0.20$.

4.64 $P(A) = 0.40, P(B) = 0.25$

a. Using the independence, $P(A \cup B) = P(A) + P(B) - P(A \cap B) = P(A) + P(B) - P(A)P(B) = 0.40 + 0.25 - 0.40(0.25) = 0.55$

b. $P((A \cup B)^C) = 1 - P(A \cup B) = 1 - 0.55 = 0.45$

4.66 Let event S correspond to "Biggest smilers," F to "Biggest frowners," and D to "Divorced"; $P(D|S) = 0.11$ and $P(D|F) = 0.31$.

a. Since $P(S \cap D) = 0.02$, we use $P(S \cap D) = P(D|S)P(S)$ to solve for $P(S)$:

$$P(S) = \dfrac{P(S \cap D)}{P(D|S)} = \dfrac{0.02}{0.11} = 0.1818, \text{ or } 18.18\%.$$

b. Since $P(F) = 0.25, P(F \cap D) = P(D|F)P(F) = 0.31(0.25) = 0.0775$, or 7.75%.

4.68 For i = 1,2, let event D_i be "the i-th selected mango is damaged."

a. $P(D_1^C) = \dfrac{17}{20} = 0.85$

b. $P(D_1^C \cap D_2^C) = \dfrac{17}{20} \times \dfrac{16}{19} = 0.7158$

c. $P(D_1 \cap D_2) = \dfrac{3}{20} \times \dfrac{2}{19} = 0.0158$

4.70 a.

	Gender		
Drink Choice	Male (M)	Female (F)	Total
Beer (B)	150	38	188
Wine (W)	40	20	60
Soft Drinks (D)	20	12	32
Total	210	70	280

b. $P(W) = \dfrac{60}{280} = 0.2143$

c. $P(W|M) = \dfrac{40}{210} = 0.1905$

d. Since $P(W) = 0.2143 \neq 0.1905 = P(W|M)$, gender and drink choice are not independent.

4.72

	Survived for Discharge (S)	Did Not Survive for Discharge (S^C)	Total
Day or Evening Shift (D)	0.1338	0.5417	0.6755
Graveyard Shift (G)	0.0477	0.2768	0.3245
Total	0.1815	0.8185	1.00

a. $P(G) = 0.3245$

b. $P(S) = 0.1815$

c. $P(S|G) = \dfrac{P(G \cap S)}{P(G)} = \dfrac{0.0477}{0.3245} = 0.1470$

d. $P(G|S) = \dfrac{P(G \cap S)}{P(S)} = \dfrac{0.0477}{0.1815} = 0.2628$

e. $P(S|G) = 0.1470 \neq 0.1815 = P(S)$. Also, $P(G|S) = 0.2628 \neq 0.3245 = P(G)$.) Therefore, the events are not independent.

4.74 Let A = "U.S. economy performs well" and B = "Asian countries perform well." We have $P(A) = 0.40, P(B|A) = 0.80$, and $P(B|A^C) = 0.30$.

a. $P(A \cap B) = P(B|A)P(A) = 0.80(0.40) = 0.32$

b. $P(B) = P(B \cap A) + P(B \cap A^C) = P(B|A)P(A) + P(B|A^C)P(A^C) = 0.32 + 0.30(1 - 0.40) = 0.32 + 0.18 = 0.50$

c. $P(A|B) = \dfrac{P(A \cap B)}{P(B)} = \dfrac{0.32}{0.50} = 0.64$

4.76 Let event M correspond to "Men," F to "Women," and H to "Healthy weight." Then $P(H|W) = 0.365$, $P(H|M) = 0.266$, and $P(W) = 0.5052$.

a. $P(H) = P(H \cap W) + P(H \cap M) = P(H|W)P(W) + P(H|M)P(M) = 0.365(0.5052) + 0.266(1 - 0.5052) = 0.3160$

b. $P(W|H) = \dfrac{P(H \cap W)}{P(H)} = \dfrac{0.365(0.5052)}{0.3160} = 0.5835$

c. $P(M|H) = \dfrac{P(H \cap M)}{P(H)} = \dfrac{0.266(1 - 0.5052)}{0.3160} = 0.4165$

4.78 Let event A correspond to "Asians," B to "black," W to "white," H to "Hispanic," and T to "Both parents at home." It is known that $P(T|A) = 0.85$, $P(T|W) = 0.78$, $P(T|H) = 0.70$, $P(T|B) = 0.38$. Also, $P(A) = \dfrac{50}{500} = 0.10$, and similarly $P(W) = 0.56$, $P(H) = 0.20$, and $P(B) = 0.14$.

a. $P(T) = P(T|A)P(A) + P(T|W)P(W) + P(T|H)P(H) + P(T|B)P(B) = 0.85(0.10) + 0.78(0.56) + 0.70(0.20) + 0.38(0.14) = 0.7150$

b. $P(A|T) = \dfrac{P(A \cap T)}{P(T)} = \dfrac{0.85(0.10)}{0.7150} = 0.1189$

c. $P(B|T) = \dfrac{P(B \cap T)}{P(T)} = \dfrac{0.38(0.14)}{0.7150} = 0.0744$

Chapter 5

5.2 a. $P(X = 10) = 0.45$

b.
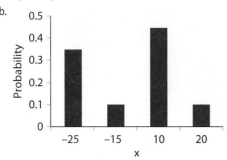

The distribution is not symmetric.

c. $P(X < 0) = 0.45$

d. $P(X > -20) = 0.65$

e. $P(X < 20) = 0.90$

5.4 a. $P(X \le 0) = 0.5$

b. $P(X = 50) = 0.25$

c. Yes. The distribution is symmetric, has a finite number of values, and each value has an equal probability of occurring.

5.6 a. $X \in \{10, 12, 14, 16\}$; X is discrete.

b. $X \in [8, 20]$; X is not discrete.

c. $X \in [0, 1, 2, \ldots]$; X is discrete.

d. $X \in [0, \infty)$; X is continuous.

5.8 a.
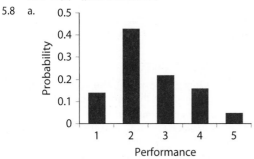

The analyst has a somewhat pessimistic view based on the positively skewed distribution.

b.

Performance	Cumulative Probability
1 (Very poor)	0.14
2 (Poor)	0.57
3 (Neutral)	0.79
4 (Good)	0.95
5 (Very good)	1

c. $P(X \ge 4) = P(X = 4) + P(X = 5) = 0.21$

5.10 a. 0.40

b. 0.65

5.12 a. $P(X = 1) = 1 - P(X = 0) - P(X = 2) = 0.15$

b. Let the random variable X represent the number of students that Jane will be able to fund.

X	$P(X \le x)$
0	0.05
1	0.20
2	1

5.14 $\mu = \Sigma x_i P(X = x_i) = 10.75$;
$\sigma^2 = \Sigma (x_i - \mu)^2 P(X = x_i) = 28.19$;
$\sigma = \sqrt{28.19} = 5.31$

5.16 a. $E(X) = \Sigma x_i P(X = x_i) = 0.95$

b. $\sigma^2 = \Sigma (x_i - \mu)^2 P(X = x_i) = 0.65$
$\sigma = \sqrt{0.65} = 0.81$

5.18 a. $E(X) = \Sigma x_i P(X = x_i) = 1\%$

b. $\sigma^2 = \Sigma (x_i - \mu)^2 P(X = x_i) = 31.5$;
$\sigma = \sqrt{31.5} = 5.61$

5.20 $E(X) = \Sigma x_i P(X = x_i) = 2.2$

5.22 $E(X) = \$8$; $E(Y) = 120E(X) = \$960$

5.24 a. $E(X) = \Sigma x_i P(X = x_i) = \$3,150$

b. If Victor is risk neutral, he should not buy the warranty. The decision is not clear-cut if he is risk averse.

5.26 a. $E(R) = \Sigma x_i P(X = x_i) = 6\%$;
$\sigma^2 = \Sigma (x_i - \mu)^2 P(X = x_i) = 124$; $\sigma = \sqrt{124} = 11.14$

b. $E(R) = \Sigma x_i P(X = x_i) = 6\%$;
$\sigma^2 = \Sigma (x_i - \mu)^2 P(X = x_i) = 964$; $\sigma = \sqrt{964} = 31.05$

c. Pick Fund 1; while both have the same expected return, Fund 1 has a smaller standard deviation.

5.28 a. $P(X = 0) = \dfrac{5!}{0!5!} (0.35)^0 (0.65)^5 = 0.1160$

b. $P(X = 1) = \dfrac{5!}{1!4!} (0.35)^1 (0.65)^4 = 0.3124$

c. $P(X \le 1) = P(X = 0) + P(X = 1) = 0.4284$

5.30 a. $P(X = 4) = \dfrac{8!}{4!4!} (0.32)^4 (0.68)^4 = 0.1569$

b. $P(3 < X \le 5) = P(X = 4) + P(X = 5) = 0.2160$

c. $P(3 \le X \le 5) = P(X = 3) + P(X = 4) + P(X = 5) = 0.4828$

5.32 a. $P(X \le 50) = 0.2776$; Excel command: =BINOM.DIST(50, 150, 0.36, 1)

b. $P(X = 40) = 0.0038$; Excel command: =BINOM.DIST(40, 150, 0.36, 0)

c. $P(X > 60) = 0.1348$; Excel command: =1 − BINOM.DIST(60, 150, 0.36, 1)

d. $P(X \ge 55) = 0.4630$; Excel command: 1 − BINOM.DIST(54, 150, 0.36, 1)

5.34 a. $P(X = 0) = \frac{8!}{0!8!}(0.20)^0(0.80)^8 = 0.1678$

b. $P(X \le 2) = P(X = 0) + P(X = 1) + P(X = 2) = 0.7969$

c. $P(X \ge 7) = P(X = 7) + P(X = 8) = 0.0001$

d. $E(X) = np = 1.6$

e. $\sigma^2 = npq = 1.28; \sigma = 1.13$

5.36 a. $P(X < 5) = 0.9431$

b. $P(X < 5) = 0.6078$

5.38 a. $P(X = 1) = \frac{6!}{1!5!}(0.76)^1(0.24)^5 = 0.0036$

b. $P(X \ge 5) = P(X = 5) + P(X = 6) = 0.5578$

c. $P(X < 2) = P(X = 0) + P(X = 1) = 0.0038$

d. $E(X) = np = 4.56; P(X > 4.56) = 0.5578$ (from b.)

5.40 a. $p = 0.50; P(X > 2) = 0.3125$

b. $p = 0.63; P(X > 2) = 0.5276$

c. $p = 0.36; P(X > 2) = 0.1362$

5.42 a. $P(X \ge 1) = 1 - P(X = 0) = 0.4375 < 0.50$; the statement she made would not be correct.

b. $P(X \ge 1) = 1 - P(X = 0) = 0.5781 > 0.50$; the statement she made would be correct.

5.44 a. $P(X = 10) = 0.1171$; Excel command: =BINOM.DIST(10, 20, 0.40, 0)

b. $P(X \le 10) = 0.8725$; Excel command: =BINOM.DIST(10, 20, 0.40, 1)

c. $P(X \ge 15) = 0.0016$; Excel command: =1 − BINOM.DIST(14, 20, 0.40, 1)

5.46 a. $P(X = 1) = \frac{e^{-1.5}1.5^1}{1!} = 0.3347$

b. $P(X = 2) = \frac{e^{-1.5}1.5^2}{2!} = 0.2510$

c. $P(X \ge 2) = 1 - [P(X = 0) + P(X = 1)] = 0.4422$

5.48 a. $\mu = \frac{8}{2} = 4$

b. $P(X \ge 2) = 1 - [P(X = 0) + P(X = 1)] = 0.9084$

c. $\mu = 16$

d. $P(X = 10) = 0.0341$

5.50 a. $P(X < 14) = 0.0661$; Excel command: POISSON.DIST(13, 20, 1)

b. $P(X \ge 20) = 0.5297$; Excel command: 1 − POISSON.DIST(19, 20, 1)

c. $P(X = 25) = 0.0446$; Excel command: POISSON.DIST(25, 20, 0)

d. $P(18 \le X \le 23) = 0.4905$; Excel command: POISSON.DIST(23, 20, 1) − POISSON.DIST(17, 20, 1)

5.52 Statements a and c can be represented using Poisson random variables.

5.54 a. $P(X = 2) = \frac{e^{-2}2^2}{2!} = 0.2707$

b. $P(X \le 2) = P(X = 0) + P(X = 1) + P(X = 2) = \frac{e^{-2}2^0}{0!} + \frac{e^{-2}2^1}{1!} + \frac{e^{-2}2^2}{2!} = 0.6767$

c. $\mu_{25} = \frac{2}{2} = 1, P(X = 0) = \frac{e^{-1}1^0}{0!} = 0.3679$

5.56 a. $\mu_{60} = \frac{400}{16} = 25$ calls per hour

$\mu_{30} = \frac{25}{2} = 12.5$ calls per 30-minute period

$\mu_{15} = \frac{25}{4} = 6.25$ calls per 15-minute period

b. $P(X = 6) = \frac{e^{-6.25}6.25^6}{6!} = 0.1598$

c. $P(X = 0) = \frac{e^{-6.25}6.25^0}{0!} = 0.0019$

d. $P(X \ge 2) = 1 - [P(X = 0) + P(X = 1)] = 0.986$

5.58 a. $\mu_{month} = 4/12 = 1/3$

$\sigma = \sqrt{1/3} = 0.5774$

b. $P(X = 0) = \frac{e^{-1/3}(1/3)^0}{0!} = 0.7165$

c. $P(X \ge 1) = 1 - P(X = 0) = 0.2835$

5.60 a. $\mu_1 = \frac{24,584}{260} = 94.55$

b. $P(X = 100) = 0.0342$; Excel command: =POISSON.DIST(100, 94.55, 0)

c. $P(X \le 100) = 0.7332$; Excel command: =POISSON.DIST(100, 94.55, 1)

5.62 a. $P(X = 0) = \frac{\frac{3!}{0!3!} \times \frac{22!}{4!18!}}{\frac{25!}{4!21!}} = 0.5783$

b. $P(X = 1) = \frac{\frac{3!}{1!2!} \times \frac{22!}{3!19!}}{\frac{25!}{4!21!}} = 0.3652$

c. $P(X \le 1) = P(X = 0) + P(X = 1) = 0.9435$

5.64 $P(X = 0) = \frac{\frac{2!}{0!2!} \times \frac{10!}{3!7!}}{\frac{12!}{3!9!}} = 0.5455; \mu = 0.5; \sigma = 0.5839$

5.66 $P(X \ge 8) = 0.0777$; Excel command: =1 − HYPGEOM.DIST(7, 20, 25, 100, 1); $\mu = 5; \sigma = 1.74$

5.68 a. $P(X = 0) = \frac{\frac{8!}{0!(8 - 0)!} \times \frac{32!}{3!(32 - 3)!}}{\frac{40!}{3!(40 - 3)!}} = 0.5020$

b. $P(X \ge 1) = 1 - P(X = 0) = 0.4980$

5.70 a. $P(X = 3) = \frac{\frac{12!}{3!9!} \times \frac{6!}{0!6!}}{\frac{18!}{3!15!}} = 0.2696$

b. $P(X \ge 2) = 1 - [P(X = 0) + P(X = 1)] = 0.7549$

5.72 $P(X = 2) = \frac{\frac{4!}{2!2!} \times \frac{16!}{0!16!}}{\frac{20!}{2!18!}} = 0.0316$

5.74 a. $P(X = 2) = 0.0495$; Excel command: =HYPGEOM.DIST(2, 5, 5, 59, 0)

b. $P(X = 5) = 0.0000002$; Excel command: HYPGEOM.DIST(5, 5, 5, 59, 0)

c. $P(X = 1) = 0.0256$; Excel command: HYPGEOM.DIST (1, 1, 1, 39, 0)

d. 0.00000000512

5.76 a. $E(R) = \Sigma x_i P(X = x_i) = 2$

b. $\sigma^2 = \Sigma(x_i - \mu)^2 P(X = x_i) = 101; \sigma = 10.05$

5.78 a. $P(X = 1) = P(X < 2) - P(X = 0) = 0.13$

$P(X = 3) = 1 - P(X = 4) - P(X = 2) - P(X < 2) = 0.02$

$E(X) = \Sigma x_i P(X = x_i) = (4)(0.50) + (3)(0.02) + (2)(0.30) + (1)(0.13) = 2.79$

$\sigma^2 = \Sigma(x_i - \mu)^2 P(X = x_i) = (4 - 2.79)^2(0.50) + (3 - 2.79)^2(0.02) + (2 - 2.79)^2(0.30) + (1 - 2.79)^2(0.13) + (0 - 2.79)^2(0.05) = 1.7259$

$\sigma = \sqrt{1.7259} = 1.3137$

b. $E(R) = 15E(X) = 15 \times 2.79 = 41.85$

$E(120R) = 120E(R) = 120 \times 41.85 = 5022$

5.80 a. $P(X = 4) = \dfrac{4!}{(4!)(0!)}(0.44)^4(0.56)^0 = 0.0375$

b. $P(X < 2) = P(X = 0) + P(X = 1) = \left[\dfrac{4!}{(0!)(4!)}(0.44)^0(0.56)^4\right] +$

$\left[\dfrac{4!}{(1!)(3!)}(0.44)^1(0.56)^3\right] = 0.4074$

c. $E(X) = 4(0.44) = 1.76$
$\sigma^2 = 4(0.44)(0.56) = 0.9856$
$\sigma = \sqrt{0.9856} = 0.9928$

5.82 a. $P(X = 2) = \dfrac{4!}{(2!)(2!)}(0.51)^2(0.49)^2 = 0.3747$

b. $P(X = 4) = \dfrac{4!}{(4!)(0!)}(0.51)^4(0.49)^0 = 0.0677$

$E(X) = 100 \times 0.51 = 51$
$\sigma^2 = 100(0.51)(0.49) = 24.99$
$\sigma = \sqrt{24.99} = 4.999$

5.84 a. $P(X = 10) = 0.0272$; Excel command: =BINOM.DIST(10, 30, 0.19, 0)

b. $P(10 \le X \le 20) = 0.0451$; Excel command: =BINOM.DIST(20, 30, 0.19, 1) − BINOM.DIST(9, 30, 0.19, 1)

c. $P(X \le 8) = 0.8996$; Excel command: =BINOM.DIST(8, 30, 0.19, 1)

5.86 a. $P(X \ge 5) = 0.5595$; Excel command: =1 − POISSON.DIST(4, 5, 1)

b. $P(X < 5) = P(X \le 4) = 0.4405$; Excel command: =POISSON.DIST(4, 5, 1)

5.88 a. $P(X = 3) = \dfrac{\dfrac{13!}{3!(13 - 3)!}}{\dfrac{52!}{3!(52 - 3)!}} = 0.0099$

b. $P(X \le 2) = P(X = 0) + P(X = 1) + P(X = 2) =$

$\dfrac{\dfrac{39!}{3!(39 - 3!)}}{\dfrac{52!}{3!(52 - 3)!}} + \dfrac{\dfrac{39!}{2!(39 - 2!)}\dfrac{13!}{1!(13 - 1)!}}{\dfrac{52!}{3!(52 - 3)!}} +$

$\dfrac{\dfrac{39!}{1!(39 - 1!)}\dfrac{13!}{2!(13 - 2)!}}{\dfrac{52!}{3!(52 - 3)!}} = 0.8724$

c. $2P(X = 3) = 0.0198$

5.90 a. $P(X = 6) = 0.0115$; Excel command: =HYPGEOM.DIST(6, 10, 20, 80, 0)

b. $P(X \ge 5) = 0.0647$; Excel command: =1 − HYPGEOM.DIST(4, 10, 20, 80, 1)

c. $P(X \le 2) = 0.5206$; Excel command: =HYPGEOM.DIST(2, 10, 20, 80, 1)

d. $E(X) = 2.5$

Chapter 6

6.2 a. $P(X < 0) = 0.30$
b. $P(X > 2.5) = 0.16$
c. $P(0 \le X \le 4) = 0.70$

6.4 a. $f(x) = 0.0333$ for $5 \le x \le 35$
b. $\mu = 20; \sigma^2 = 75; \sigma = 8.66$
c. $P(X > 10) = 0.8325$

6.6 a. $\mu = 20; \sigma^2 = 33.33; \sigma = 5.77$
b. $f(x) = 0.05$ for $10 \le x \le 30; P(X > 22) = 0.4$
c. $P(15 \le X \le 23) = 0.4$

6.8 a. $\mu = 16$
b. $f(x) = 0.125; 0.125$ for $12 \le x \le 20; P(X < 15.5) = 0.4375$
c. $P(X > 14) = 0.75$

6.10 $f(x) \approx 0.11$ for $7 \le x \le 16; P(X > 10) = 0.67$

6.12 $f(x) = \dfrac{1}{30 - 18} = 0.0833$

a. $P(X > 25) = (30 - 25)(0.0833) = 0.4167$
b. $P(X < 20) = (20 - 18)(0.0833) = 0.1667$

6.14 a. $P(Z > 1.32) = 0.0934$
b. $P(Z \le -1.32) = 0.0934$
c. $P(1.32 \le Z \le 2.37) = 0.9911 - 0.9066 = 0.0845$
d. $P(-1.32 \le Z \le 2.37) = 0.9911 - 0.0934 = 0.8977$

6.16 a. $P(-0.67 \le Z \le -0.23) = 0.4090 - 0.2514 = 0.1576$
b. $P(0 \le Z \le 1.96) = 0.9750 - 0.5 = 0.4750$
c. $P(-1.28 \le Z \le 0) = 0.5 - 0.1003 = 0.3997$
d. $P(Z > 4.2) \approx 1 - 1 = 0$

6.18 a. $z = -1.27$
b. $z = -0.46$
c. $z = -2.45$
d. $z = 2.42$

6.20 a. About 68.26%
b. About 2.28%

6.22 a. About 95.44%
b. About 2.28%; $(82)(0.0228) = 1.87$; approx. 2 games

6.24 a. $P(X \le 0) = P(Z \le -2.5) = 0.0062$
b. $P(X > 2) = P(Z > -2) = 1 - 0.0228 = 0.9772$
c. $P(4 \le X \le 10) = P(-1.5 \le Z \le 0) = 0.5 - 0.0668 = 0.4332$
d. $P(6 \le X \le 14) = P(-1 \le Z \le 1) = 0.8413 - 0.1587 = 0.6826$

6.26 a. $P(X > 7.6) = P(Z > 2.55) = 1 - 0.9946 = 0.0054$
b. $P(7.4 \le X \le 10.6) = P(2.45 \le Z \le 4.05) = 1 - 0.9929 = 0.0071$
c. $z = 1.96; x = 6.42$
d. $P(X < x) = 0.0057; z = -2.53; x = -2.56$

6.28 a. $z = 1.28; \mu = 130.8$
b. $\mu = 118$
c. $\sigma = 10.94$
d. $\sigma = 17.19$

6.30 a. $P(X > -12) = 1 - P(X < -12) = 0.3694$; Excel command: =1 − NORM.DIST(−12, −15,9,1)
b. $P(0 \le X \le 5) = P(X \le 5) - P(X \le 0) = 0.0347$; Excel command: =NORM.DIST(5, −15,9,1) − NORM.DIST(0, −15,9,1)
c. $P(X \le x) = 0.25; x = -21.0704$; Excel command: =NORM.INV(0.25, −15,9)
d. $P(X > x) = 0.25; P(X \le x) = 1 - 0.25; x = -8.9296$; Excel command: =NORM.INV(0.75, −15,9)

6.32 a. $P(X > 8) = P(Z > 1.5) = 0.0668$
b. $P(X < 6) = P(Z < -0.17) = 0.4325$
c. $P(6 \le X \le 8) = P(-0.17 \le Z \le 1.5) = 0.5007$

6.34 a. $P(X \ge 40) = P(Z \ge 1.77) = 0.0384$
b. $P(30 \le X \le 35) = P\left(\dfrac{30 - 33.8}{3.5} \le Z \le \dfrac{35 - 33.8}{3.5}\right) =$
$P(-1.09 \le Z \le 0.34) = 0.4952$
c. Given $P(Z \le z) = 0.99$, we find $z = 2.33$. Therefore, $x = 33.8 + 2.33(3.5) = 41.96$.

6.36 $P(X < 0) = P\left(Z < \dfrac{0 - 8}{12}\right) = P(Z < -0.67) = 0.2514 \approx 0.25$;

$P(X > 16) = P\left(Z > \dfrac{16 - 8}{12}\right) = P(Z > 0.67) = 0.2514 \neq 0.15$;

thus, it is not reasonable to assume the distribution is normal.

6.38 a. $P(X > 19) = P(Z > -1.5) = 1 - 0.0668 = 0.9332$
   b. $P(X > 19) = P(Z > 1.5) = 1 - 0.9332 = 0.0668$
   c. $P(23 \leq X \leq 25) = P(0.5 \leq Z \leq 1.5) = 0.9332 - 0.6915$
       $= 0.2417$
   d. $P(23 \leq X \leq 25) = P(3.5 \leq Z \leq 4.5) \approx 1 - 0.9998 = 0.0002$

6.40 a. $P(10 \leq X \leq 20) = P(-0.75 \leq Z \leq 0.5) = 0.6915 - 0.2266$
       $= 0.4649$
   b. $P(X > 24) + P(X < 6) = P(Z > 1) + P(Z < -1.25)$
       $= 0.1587 + 0.1056 = 0.2643$

6.42 $P(X \leq 28) = P(Z \leq z) = 0.975; z = 1.96; \sigma = 1.53$

6.44 a. $P(50 \leq X \leq 80) = P(-0.5 \leq Z \leq 1) = 0.8413 - 0.3085$
       $= 0.5328$
   b. $P(20 \leq X \leq 40) = P(-2 \leq Z \leq -1) = 0.1587 - 0.0228$
       $= 0.1359$
   c. $P(X < x) = 0.85; z = 1.04; x = 80.8$
   d. $P(X < x) = 0.10; z = -1.28; x = 34.4$

6.46 $P(X \leq 0) = 0.10; z = -1.28; \sigma = 4.375$

6.48 a. Risky fund: $P(X < 0) = P(Z < -0.57) = 0.2843$; Less risky
       fund: $P(X < 0) = P(Z < -0.8) = 0.2119$; pick the less risky
       fund.
   b. Risky fund: $P(X > 8) = P(Z > 0) = 0.5$; Less risky fund:
       $P(X > 8) = P(Z > 0.8) = 1 - 0.7881 = 0.2119$; pick the
       riskier fund.

6.50 a. $P(X < 24) = P(Z < -1) = 0.1587$
   b. $P(X > 24) = 1 - P(X \leq 24) = 1 - 0.1587 = 0.8413$
       $E(X) = (-10)(0.1587) + (20)(0.8413) = 15.239$
   c. $E(500X) = 500E(X) = 500(15.239) = 7619.5$

6.52 a. $P(X < 6.5) = 0.00001$; Excel command: $=$NORM.DIST
       $(6.5, 15, 2, 1)$
   b. $P(X > 23) = 1 - P(X \leq 23) = 1 - 0.9999 = 0.0001$;
       Excel command: $=1 - $ NORM.DIST$(23, 15, 2, 1)$
   c. $P(X < x) = 1 - 0.03 = 0.97, x = 18.7$; Excel command:
       $=$NORM.INV$(0.97, 15, 2)$

6.54 a. $\mu_{Poisson} = 4; \mu_{Exponential} = \dfrac{10}{4} = 2.5$
   b. $\lambda = \dfrac{1}{\mu} = \dfrac{1}{2.5} = 0.4$
   c. $P(1 \leq X \leq 2) = P(X \leq 2) - P(X < 1) = e^{-0.4(1)} - e^{-0.4(2)}$
       $= 0.2310$

6.56 a. $\lambda = \dfrac{1}{E(X)} = \dfrac{1}{25} = 0.04; SD(X) = E(X) = 25$
   b. $P(20 \leq X \leq 30) = P(X \leq 30) - P(X < 20) =$
       $(1 - e^{-0.04(30)}) - (1 - e^{-0.04(20)}) = 0.1481$
   c. $P(15 \leq X \leq 35) = P(X \leq 35) - P(X < 15) =$
       $(1 - e^{-0.04(35)}) - (1 - e^{-0.04(15)}) = 0.3022$

6.58 a. $P(X \leq 1) = 0.3935$; Excel command: $=$EXPON.DIST$(1, 0.5, 1)$
   b. $P(2 < X < 4) = P(X < 4) - P(X \leq 2) = 0.2326$;
       Excel command: $=$EXPON.DIST$(4, 0.5, 1) - $ EXPON.DIST$(2, 0.5, 1)$
   c. $P(X > 10) = 1 - P(X \leq 10) = 0.0067$;
       Excel command: $=1 - $ EXPON.DIST$(10, 0.5, 1)$

6.60 a. $\mu_{Poisson} = 10; \mu_{Exponential} = \dfrac{60}{10} = 6$
   b. $\lambda = \dfrac{1}{\mu} = \dfrac{1}{6} = 0.1667; P(X < 15) = 1 - e^{-0.1667(15)} = 0.9179$

   c. $P(15 \leq X \leq 20) = P(X \leq 20) - P(X < 15) =$
       $e^{-0.1667(15)} - e^{-0.1667(20)} = 0.0464$.

6.62 a. $\mu_{Exponential} = \dfrac{1}{360}$
   b. $\lambda = \dfrac{1}{\mu} = \dfrac{1}{360} = 0.0028$
   c. $P\left(X < \dfrac{10}{3600}\right) = 1 - e^{-360\left(\frac{1}{360}\right)} = 0.6321$

6.64 a. $\lambda = 0.2; E(X) = \dfrac{1}{\lambda} = \dfrac{1}{0.2} = 5$, which is the average waiting
       time.
   b. $P(X > 5) = 1 - P(X \leq 5) = 0.3679$
   c. $P(X > 10) = 1 - P(X \leq 10) = 0.1353$
   d. $P(4 \leq X \leq 6) = P(X \leq 6) - P(X < 4) = 0.1481$

6.66 a. $\mu_{Poisson} = 8; \mu_{Exponential} = 7.5; \lambda = 0.1333; P(X < 10) = 0.7364$;
       Excel command: $=$EXPON.DIST$(10, 0.1333, 1)$
   b. $P(15 \leq X \leq 20) = P(X \leq 20) - P(X < 15) = 0.0659$; Excel
       command: $=$EXPON.DIST$(20, 0.1333, 1) - $ EXPON.DIST
       $(15, 0.1333, 1)$
   c. $P(X > 25) = 1 - P(X \leq 25) = 0.0357$; Excel command:
       $=1 - $ EXPON.DIST$(25, 0.1333, 1)$

6.68 a. $\mu = \dfrac{1 + 5}{2} = 3; Var(X) = \dfrac{(5 - 1)^2}{12} = \dfrac{16}{12} = 1.33$
   b. $f(x) = \dfrac{1}{5 - 1} = 0.25; P(X > 4) = (5 - 4)(0.25) = 0.25$
   c. $P(X < 2.5) = (2.5 - 1)(0.25) = 0.375$

6.70 a. $P(80 \leq X \leq 90) = P(0.1 \leq Z \leq 1.1) = 0.8643 - 0.5398$
       $= 0.3245$
   b. $P(120 \leq X \leq 139) = P(-0.29 \leq Z \leq 0.82) = 0.7939$
       $- 0.3859 = 0.4080$

6.72 a. $P(X > 50) = P(Z > 2.04) = 1 - 0.9793 = 0.0207$
   b. $P(X > 50) = P(Z > 1.86) = 1 - 0.9686 = 0.0314$
   c. Women are slightly more likely to spend over $50, with a
       3.14% likelihood as opposed to 2.07% likelihood for men.

6.74 Given $P(Z < z) = 1 - 0.03 = 0.97; z = 1.88$. Therefore,
       $x = 72 + 1.88(15) = 100.2$.

6.76 Given $P(Z < z) = 0.25; z = -0.67; Q1 = 6 + (-0.67)(0.02)$
       $= 5.9866$.

   Given $P(Z < z) = 0.50; z = 0; Q2 = 6$.

   Given $P(Z < z) = 0.75; z = 0.67; Q3 = 6 + 0.67(0.02) = 6.0134$.

6.78 a. $P(X < 10) = P(Z < -1.2) = 0.1151$
   b. The expected profit per one system is: $300(1 - 0.1151) +$
       $50(0.1151) = 271.225$; therefore, the total expected profit
       is 271,225.

6.80 a. $P(50{,}000 \leq X \leq 65{,}000) = P(X \leq 65{,}000) - P(X < 50{,}000) =$
       0.8536

       Excel command: $=$NORM.DIST$(65{,}000, 55{,}000, 4{,}500, 1) -$
       NORM.DIST$(50{,}000, 55{,}000, 4{,}500, 1)$
   b. $P(X > 70{,}000) = 1 - P(X \leq 70{,}000) = 1 - 0.9996 = 0.0004$
       Excel command: $=1 - $ NORM.DIST$(70{,}000, 55{,}000, 4{,}500, 1)$
   c. $P(X < x) = 1 - 0.05 = 0.95; x = 62{,}401.84$; Excel
       command: $=$NORM.INV$(0.95, 55{,}000, 4{,}500)$
   d. $P(X < x) = 0.40; x = 53{,}859.94$; Excel command:
       $=$NORM.INV$(0.40, 55{,}000, 4{,}500)$

6.82 a. $\lambda = \dfrac{1}{22} = 0.0455; P(X < 60) = 1 - e^{-0.0455(60)} = 0.9348$
   b. The probability will be the same.

6.84 a. $\mu = \dfrac{365}{1000} = 0.365$

b. $\lambda = \frac{1}{\mu} = \frac{1}{0.365} = 2.7397$

c. $P(X \leq 1) = 1 - e^{-2.7397(1)} = 0.9354$

6.86 $\lambda = \frac{1}{E(X)} = \frac{1}{50} = 0.02$

a. $P(X \leq 40) = 0.5507$; Excel command: =EXPON.DIST (40, 0.02, 1)

b. $P(X \geq 65) = 1 - P(X < 65) = 0.2775$; Excel command: =1 $-$ EXPON.DIST(65, 0.02, 1)

c. $P(70 \leq X \leq 80) = P(X \leq 80) - P(X < 70) = 0.0447$; Excel command: =EXPON.DIST(80, 0.02, 1) $-$ EXPON.DIST(70, 0.02, 1).

Chapter 7

7.2 Nonresponse bias if some people are less likely to stop at the booth. Selection bias since the booth is only open on the weekend.

7.4 a. Nonresponse bias if the people who respond are systematically different from those who do not respond.

b. Selection bias since those who frequent the store in the morning are likely to prefer an earlier opening time.

c. Selection bias since not everyone reads a newspaper. Nonresponse bias since people who respond may be systematically different.

7.6 a. Both sample means will be normally distributed since the population is normally distributed.

b. Yes

c. $n = 20$: $P(\bar{X} < 12.5) = P(Z < 1.49) = 0.9319$

$n = 40$: $P(\bar{X} < 12.5) = P(Z < 2.11) = 0.9826$

7.8 a. $E(\bar{X}) = 80$; $se(\bar{X}) = \frac{14}{\sqrt{100}} = 1.4$

b. $P(77 \leq \bar{X} \leq 85) = P(-2.14 \leq Z \leq 3.57) = 0.9998 - 0.0162 = 0.9836$

c. $P(\bar{X} > 84) = P(Z > 2.86) = 1 - 0.9979 = 0.0021$

7.10 a. $P(\bar{X} > 105) = P(Z > 1.77) = 1 - 0.9616 = 0.0384$

b. $P(\bar{X} < 95) = P(Z < -1.77) = 0.0384$

c. $P(95 \leq \bar{X} \leq 105) = P(-1.77 \leq Z \leq 1.77) = 0.9616 - 0.0384 = 0.9232$

7.12 a. $P(\bar{X} \geq 18) = P(Z \geq 1.85) = 1 - 0.9678 = 0.0322$

b. $P(\bar{X} \geq 17.5) = P(Z \geq 2.03) = 1 - 0.9788 = 0.0212$

c. Janice; her findings are more likely if a representative sample is used.

7.14. a. The sample mean has a normal distribution because the population is normally distributed.

b. $P(\bar{X} > 25) = P(Z > 2.4) = 1 - 0.9918 = 0.0082$

c. $P(18 \leq \bar{X} \leq 24) = P(-3.20 \leq Z \leq 1.60) = 0.9452 - 0.0007 = 0.9445$

7.16 a. $P(\bar{X} > 25{,}000) = P(Z > -0.63) = 0.7357$

b. $P(\bar{X} > 30{,}000) = P(Z > 0.80) = 0.2119$

7.18 a. $P(X > 1{,}000{,}000) = P(Z > 0.80) = 0.2119$

b. $P(\Sigma X_i > 4{,}000{,}000) = P(\bar{X} > 1{,}000{,}000) = P(Z > 1.60) = 0.0548$

7.20 a. $P(X < 90) = P(Z < -0.63) = 0.2643$

b. $P(\bar{X} < 90) = P(Z < -1.25) = 0.1056$

c. $(P(X < 90))^4 = 0.2643^4 = 0.0049$

7.22 a. With $n = 20$, $E(\bar{P}) = 0.12$ and $se(\bar{P}) = \sqrt{\frac{0.12(1 - 0.12)}{20}}$ $= 0.0727$. With $n = 50$, $E(\bar{P}) = 0.12$ and $se(\bar{P}) = 0.0460$.

The sampling distribution of the sample proportion is approximately normal when $n = 50$ but not when $n = 20$.

b. As shown in part a, we can use the normal approximation for $n = 50$. For $n = 20$, we cannot assume that $\bar{P}$ is approximately normally distributed.

c. $P(0.10 \leq \bar{P} \leq 0.12) = P(-0.44 \leq Z \leq 0) = 0.1700$

7.24 a. The sampling distribution of $\bar{P}$ has $E(\bar{P}) = 0.82$ and $se(\bar{P}) = 0.038$; it is approximately normal.

b. $P(\bar{P} < 0.80) = P(Z < -0.52) = 0.3015$

c. $P(0.80 \leq \bar{P} \leq 0.84) = P(-0.52 \leq Z \leq 0.52) = 0.3970$

7.26 a. $P(0.55 \leq \bar{P} \leq 0.65) = P(-2.07 \leq Z \leq -0.67) = 0.2259$, so there is a 22.59% chance of getting fined.

b. $P(\bar{P} < 0.55) = P(Z < -2.07) = 0.0192$, so there is a 1.92% chance of getting dissolved.

7.28 50 balls because with larger sample sizes the standard deviation of $\bar{P}$ is *reduced*; to confirm calculate $P(\bar{P} > 0.70)$ with $n = 50$ and $n = 100$; higher likelihood with $n = 50$.

7.30 a. $E(\bar{X}) = \mu = -45$; $se(\bar{X}) = \sqrt{\frac{81}{100}} = 0.90$. It is not necessary to apply the finite population correction because the sample constitutes less than 5 percent of the population: $n = 100 < 125 = 2500(0.05)$.

b. $P(-47 \leq \bar{X} \leq -43) = P(-2.22 \leq Z \leq 2.22) = 0.9736$

c. $P(\bar{X} > -44) = P(Z > 1.11) = 0.1335$

7.32 a. $E(\bar{P}) = p = 0.34$; $se(\bar{P}) = \sqrt{\frac{0.34(1 - 0.34)}{100}} = 0.047$; there is no need to apply the finite population correction factor because the sample size does not account for 5 percent of the population size: $n = 100 < 150 = 0.05(3{,}000)$.

b. $P(\bar{P} > 0.37) = P(Z > 0.63) = 1 - 0.7357 = 0.2643$

7.34 a. Yes, it is necessary because the sample size is greater than 5 percent of the population size: $n = 32 > 25 = 0.05(500)$.

b. The sampling distribution of the sample mean is approximately normal because the sample size is greater than 30.

c. $E(\bar{X}) = 10.32$; $se(\bar{X}) = \frac{9.78}{\sqrt{32}} \sqrt{\frac{500 - 32}{500 - 1}} = 1.6743$

d. $P(\bar{X} > 12) = P(Z > 1.00) = 1 - 0.8413 = 0.1587$

7.36 a. $np = 20(0.60) = 12$ and $n(1 - p) = 20(1 - 0.60) = 8$. Therefore, the sampling distribution of the sample proportion is approximately normal. Since the sample accounts for more than 5 percent of the population size ($n = 20 > 12.5 = 0.05(250)$, we need to apply the finite population correction;

$E(\bar{P}) = 0.46$ and $se(\bar{P}) = \sqrt{\frac{0.60(1 - 0.60)}{20}} \sqrt{\frac{250 - 20}{250 - 1}} = 0.1053$.

b. $P(\bar{P} < 0.50) = P(Z < -0.95) = 0.1711$

7.38 a.

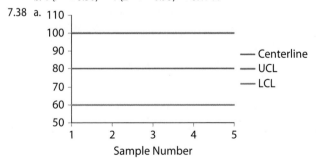

Centerline: $\mu = 80$

$$UCL = 80 + 3\left(\frac{14}{\sqrt{5}}\right) = 98.78$$

$$LCL = 80 - 3\left(\frac{14}{\sqrt{5}}\right) = 61.22$$

b.

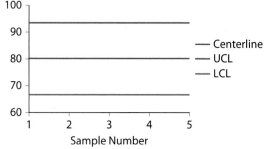

Sample Number

Centerline: $\mu = 80$

$$UCL = 80 + 3\left(\frac{14}{\sqrt{10}}\right) = 80 + 13.28 = 93.28$$

$$LCL = 80 - 3\left(\frac{14}{\sqrt{10}}\right) = 80 - 13.28 = 66.72$$

c. The larger sample size gives narrower control limits due to the smaller standard deviation.

7.40 a.

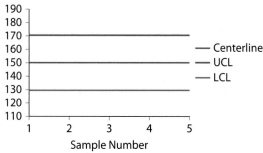

Sample Number

Centerline: $\mu = 150$

$$UCL = 150 + 3\left(\frac{42}{\sqrt{36}}\right) = 150 + 21 = 171$$

$$LCL = 150 - 3\left(\frac{42}{\sqrt{36}}\right) = 150 - 21 = 129$$

b.

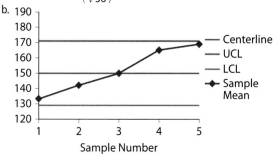

Sample Number

c. There are no points outside of the control limits. However, there is a positive trend, suggesting that the process may soon have a mean outside of the upper control limit if it is not adjusted.

7.42 a.

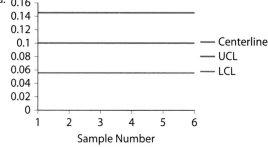

Sample Number

Centerline: $p = 0.10$

$$UCL = 0.10 + 3\sqrt{\frac{0.10(1 - 0.10)}{400}} = 0.10 + 0.045 = 0.145$$

$$LCL = 0.10 - 3\sqrt{\frac{0.10(1 - 0.10)}{400}} = 0.10 - 0.045 = 0.055$$

b.

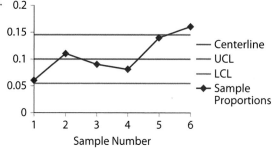

Sample Number

c. No, the production process seems to be out of control due to the 6th sample proportion, which is above the upper control limit.

7.44 a.

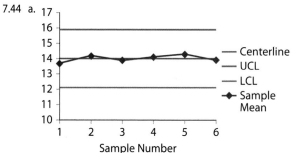

Sample Number

Centerline: $\mu = 14$

$$UCL = 14 + 3\left(\frac{2}{\sqrt{10}}\right) = 14 + 1.897 = 15.897$$

$$LCL = 14 - 3\left(\frac{2}{\sqrt{10}}\right) = 14 - 1.897 = 12.103$$

b. All the sample means randomly lie within the control limits. Therefore, we can conclude that the production process is in control and operating properly.

7.46 a.

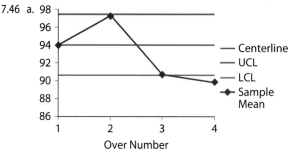

Over Number

Centerline: $\mu = 94$

$$UCL = 94 + 3\left(\frac{2.8}{\sqrt{6}}\right) = 94 + 3(1.14) = 97.43$$

$$LCL = 94 - 3\left(\frac{2.8}{\sqrt{6}}\right) = 94 - 3(1.14) = 90.57$$

To plot the average speed, take the average of each over:

$$\text{Over 1: } \bar{x} = \frac{96.8 + 99.5 + 88.8 + 81.9 + 100.1 + 96.8}{6}$$

$$= 93.98.$$

Similarly, Over 2: $\bar{x} = 97.23$, Over 3: $\bar{x} = 90.70$, Over 4: $\bar{x} = 89.85$.

b. Kalwant's average speed is out of the control limits on 1 out of 4 of his overs, which rather justifies his coach's concern that he is not very consistent.

7.48 a.

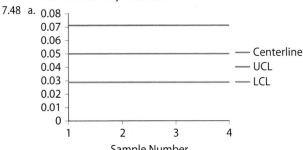

Centerline: $p = 0.05$

$$UCL = 0.05 + 3\sqrt{\frac{0.05(1 - 0.05)}{1000}} = 0.05 + 3(0.007) = 0.071$$

$$LCL = 0.05 - 3\sqrt{\frac{0.05(1 - 0.05)}{1000}} = 0.05 - 3(0.007) = 0.029$$

b. Since 0.062 is within the control limits, the process is in control.

7.50 a.

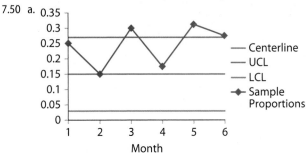

Centerline: $p = 0.15$

$$UCL = 0.15 + 3\sqrt{\frac{0.15(1 - 0.15)}{80}} = 0.15 + 0.12 = 0.27$$

$$LCL = 0.15 - 3\sqrt{\frac{0.15(1 - 0.15)}{80}} = 0.15 - 0.12 = 0.03$$

b. Find the proportion of complaints each month:

Month	Sample Proportion
1	20/80 = 0.25
2	12/80 = 0.15
3	24/80 = 0.30
4	14/80 = 0.175
5	25/80 = 0.3125
6	22/80 = 0.275

See control chart in part a; 3 out of 6 months were out of the control limits, which is a good justification for why Dell chose to direct customers away from India call centers.

7.52 a. As one example, use a random number table or a random number generator (in Excel, for instance) to randomly select individuals into the sample from the list of all residents of Miami. Then conduct the survey by contacting those selected.

b. To get a stratified random sample, you could create strata based on ethnicity—for example, white, black, Hispanic, Asian—and then randomly select adults in each group and ask whether or not they walk regularly.

c. To get a cluster sample, you could choose a number of representative neighborhoods in Miami and randomly

select adults within these neighborhoods and ask whether or not they walk regularly.

7.54 a. $P(\bar{X} > 52,000) = P(Z > 2.66) = 1 - 0.9961 = 0.0039$

b. $P(\bar{X} > 52,000) = P(Z > 2.30) = 1 - 0.9893 = 0.0107$

c. Even though finance graduates have a lower mean starting salary than accounting graduates, there is a greater standard deviation for the salary for finance graduates. Therefore, 100 finance graduates have a slightly higher probability (1.07% compared to 0.39%) of earning an average salary of more than $52,000.

7.56 a. The sampling distribution of the sample mean will be approximately normal for any sample size because the population is normally distributed; in addition, $E(\bar{X}) = \mu$; $se(\bar{X}) = \frac{\sigma}{\sqrt{n}}$.

b. $P(\bar{X} < 16) = P(Z < -0.56) = 0.2877$

c. $\bar{x} = \frac{48}{3} = 16; P(\bar{X} \geq 16) = P(Z \geq -0.22) = 0.5871$

7.58 a. $P(\bar{X} > 200) = P(Z > -2.08) = 0.9812$

b. $P(\bar{X} > 600) = P(Z > -0.61) = 0.7291$

7.60 a. $P(\bar{P} > 0.40) = P(Z > 1.05) = 0.1469$

b. $P(\bar{P} > 0.40) = P(Z > 1.48) = 0.0694$

c. There is a smaller probability that more than 40 percent have pushed back their retirement date with the larger sample size of 200 adults (0.0694 compared to 0.1469 with a sample size of 100). This is because with larger sample sizes, the standard deviation of $\bar{P}$ is reduced; $\bar{P}$ is more likely to be closer to the population proportion of 0.35 and therefore has less probability of being greater than 0.40.

7.62 a.

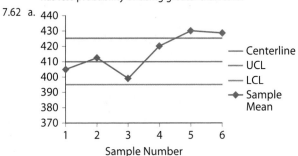

Centerline: $\mu = 410$

$$UCL = 410 + 3\left(\frac{25}{\sqrt{25}}\right) = 410 + 15 = 425$$

$$LCL = 410 - 3\left(\frac{25}{\sqrt{25}}\right) = 410 - 15 = 395$$

b. Two of the sample means are above the upper control limit, indicating that the advertised amount of sodium content is not accurate.

7.64 a. $P(\bar{P} > 0.15) = P(Z > 1.18) = 0.1190$

b. $P(\bar{P} > 0.15) = P(Z > 1.67) = 0.0475$

Chapter 8

8.2 a. $\alpha/2 = 0.055; z_{0.055} = 1.598$

b. $\alpha/2 = 0.04; z_{0.04} = 1.751$

c. $\alpha/2 = 0.02; z_{0.02} = 2.054$

8.4 a. Yes, $n = 64 > 30$.

b. $1.96\frac{26.8}{\sqrt{64}} = 6.57$

c. $1.96\frac{26.8}{\sqrt{225}} = 3.50$

d. The one with the smaller sample size.

8.6 a. $\bar{x} = 78.1$

b. $1.645\dfrac{4.5}{\sqrt{50}} = 1.05$

c. 78.1 ± 1.05

8.8 a. The 95% confidence interval is $6.4 \pm 1.96\dfrac{1.8}{\sqrt{80}}$

b. Yes, because the value 7 does not fall in the interval.

8.10 a. $2.576\left(\dfrac{500}{\sqrt{100}}\right) = 128.80$

b. The 99% confidence interval is 7790 ± 128.80

8.12 a. $\bar{x} = \dfrac{14.355 + 17.645}{2} = 16$

b. $\alpha = 0.10$. The confidence level used for the analysis is 90%.

8.14 $n = 50, \sigma = 6, \bar{x} = 20.21$; Excel command: $=$AVERAGE(A2:A51)

At 90% confidence level, $z_{\alpha/2} = z_{0.05} = 1.645$ (Excel command: $=$NORM.S.INV(0.95)).

$\bar{x} \pm z_{\alpha/2}\dfrac{\sigma}{\sqrt{n}} = 20.21 \pm 1.40$

At 99% confidence level, $z_{\alpha/2} = z_{0.005} = 2.576$ (Excel command: $=$NORM.S.INV(0.995)).

$\bar{x} \pm z_{\alpha/2}\dfrac{\sigma}{\sqrt{n}} = 20.21 \pm 2.19$

8.16 a. $t_{0.025,12} = 2.179$

b. $t_{0.10,12} = 1.356$

c. $t_{0.025,25} = 2.060$

d. $t_{0.10,25} = 1.316$

8.18 $\bar{x} = 104.6, n = 24, s = 28.8$

a. $t_{0.05,23} = 1.714$; 104.6 ± 10.08

b. $t_{0.005,23} = 2.807$; 104.6 ± 16.50

c. As the confidence level increases, the interval becomes wider.

8.20 $n = 8$

a. $\bar{x} = 20, s^2 = 24, s = 4.90$

b. $t_{0.10,7} = 1.415$; 20 ± 2.45

c. $t_{0.05,7} = 1.895$; 20 ± 3.28

d. As the confidence level increases, the interval becomes wider.

8.22 a. $\bar{x} = 6.6; s^2 = 5.42; s = 2.33; t_{0.025,6} = 2.447$. The margin of

error for the 95% confidence interval is $2.447\dfrac{2.33}{\sqrt{7}} = 2.15$.

b. We can reduce the margin of error by decreasing the confidence level.

8.24 $n = 6; \bar{x} = 160; s^2 = 2470; s = \sqrt{s^2} = 49.70; t_{0.05,5} = 2.015$

The 90% confidence interval is 160 ± 40.88

8.26 $\bar{x} = 158,000, n = 36, s = 36,000; t_{0.025,35} = 2.03$

The 95% confidence interval is $158,000 \pm 12,180$

8.28 a. $\bar{x} = 5.35; s = 2.07; t_{0.05,5} = 2.015$; the 90% confidence interval is 5.35 ± 1.70

b. Sara must assume that CEO compensations have a normal distribution since n is smaller than 30.

c. In order to reduce the margin of error of a 90% confidence interval, Sarah has to increase her sample size n.

8.30 a. $\bar{x} = 75.67; s^2 = 12.67; s = 3.56; t_{0.05,5} = 2.015$

b. The 90% confidence interval is 75.67 ± 2.93

c. The margin of error increases as the confidence level increases, and therefore the confidence interval becomes wider.

8.32 $n = 25$. The 90% confidence interval is $[1690, 1810]$. Therefore,

$\bar{x} = 1250$; find s from $1750 + 2.064\dfrac{s}{\sqrt{n}} = 1810$;

so $s = 145.35$.

8.34 $\bar{x} = 1080; n = 35; s = 260; t_{0.025,34} = 2.032$. The 95% confidence interval is: 1080 ± 90.61.

The manager is wrong with the new strategy.

8.36 $n = 40$

a. Microeconomics: $\bar{x} = 71.83$; Excel command: $=$AVERAGE(B2:B41)

$s = 9.65$; Excel command: $=$STDEV.S(B2:B41)

The 95% confidence interval is 71.83 ± 3.09.

Macroeconomics: $\bar{x} = 70.40$; Excel command: $=$AVERAGE(C2:C41)

$s = 13.26$; Excel command: $=$STDEV.S(C2:C41)

The 95% confidence interval is 70.40 ± 4.24.

b. The sample standard deviations of microeconomics and macroeconomics are different. Therefore, the widths of these two intervals are different.

8.38 $t_{0.05,25} = 1.708$

Debt payments: $\bar{x} = 983.46$; Excel command: $=$AVERAGE(D2:D27)

$s = 124.61$; Excel command: $=$STDEV.S(D2:D27)

The 90% confidence interval is 983.46 ± 41.74.

The 95% confidence interval is 983.46 ± 50.34.

The 95% confidence interval is wider because its confidence level is higher.

8.40 a. $z_{0.025} = 1.96$; the 95% confidence interval is 0.625 ± 0.106

b. Since the proportion of successes $= 0.625$, the proportion of failures $= 1 - 0.625 = 0.375$. The margin of error remains the same, so the 95% confidence interval for the proportion of failures is 0.375 ± 0.106.

8.42 a. $\bar{p} = \dfrac{30}{80} = 0.375$

b. $z_{0.05} = 1.645$; the 90% interval is 0.375 ± 0.089.
$z_{0.005} = 2.576$; the 99% interval is 0.375 ± 0.139.

c. Yes, with 90% confidence, we can conclude that the population proportion differs from 0.5 because the value 0.5 does not fall within the interval.

d. No, since the value 0.5 falls within the interval, we cannot conclude with 99% confidence that the population proportion differs from 0.5.

8.44 a. $z_{0.025} = 1.960$; the margin of error is 0.031.

b. 0.47 ± 0.031

8.46 a. $z_{0.05} = 1.645$; 0.467 ± 0.024

b. With 90% confidence, we can conclude that the population proportion is not 0.50%.

8.48 $z_{0.05} = 1.645$; the 90% confidence interval is 0.20 ± 0.024

8.50 a. $z_{0.05} = 1.645$; the 90% confidence interval is 0.275 ± 0.037

b. No, we cannot conclude that the adult obesity rate in the United States is not 30% because the value 0.30 falls in the interval.

8.52 a. The margin of error is $1.960\sqrt{\dfrac{0.23(1 - 0.23)}{5324}} = 0.011$.

b. The margin of error is $1.960\sqrt{\dfrac{0.52(1 - 0.52)}{5324}} = 0.013$.

c. The margin of error in parts a and b are different because the population proportions in parts a and b are different.

8.54 a. $\bar{p} = \dfrac{20}{80} = 0.25$

b. $z_{0.025} = 1.960$; 0.25 ± 0.095

c. No, the mayor's claim cannot be justified with 95% confidence since the national average value 0.20 $(= 1/5)$ falls within the interval.

8.56 $\hat{\sigma} = \dfrac{range}{4} = \dfrac{80-20}{4} = 15; n = \left(\dfrac{1.282 \times 15}{2.6}\right)^2 = 54.70,$ which is rounded up to 55.

With 95% confidence, $z_{\alpha/2} = z_{0.025} = 1.96$. Thus, $n = \left(\dfrac{1.96 \times 15}{2.6}\right)^2 = 127.86$, which is rounded up to 128.

8.58 $n = \left(\dfrac{2.576 \times 6}{1.2}\right)^2 = 165.89$, which is rounded up to 166

8.60 Given $E = 0.12$, $\hat{p} = 0.80$, with 99% confidence, $z_{\alpha/2} = z_{0.005} = 2.576$. Thus, $n = 73.73$, which is rounded up to 74.

With 90% confidence, $z_{\alpha/2} = z_{0.05} = 1.645$. Thus, $n = \left(\dfrac{1.645}{0.12}\right)^2 \times 0.80(1 - 0.80) = 30.07$, which is rounded up to 31.

8.62 $n = \left(\dfrac{2.576 \times 0.32}{0.06}\right)^2 = 188.75$, which is rounded up to 189

8.64 $n = \left(\dfrac{1.96 \times 1.8}{0.5}\right)^2 = 49.79$, which is rounded up to 50

8.66 a. $n = \left(\dfrac{1.96 \times 18}{5}\right)^2 = 49.79$, which is rounded up to 50

b. $n = \left(\dfrac{1.96 \times 18}{3}\right)^2 = 138.30$, which is rounded up to 139

8.68 $n = \left(\dfrac{1.645}{0.02}\right)^2 \times 0.46(1 - 0.46) = 1680.44$, which is rounded up to 1,681

8.70 $n = \left(\dfrac{1.96}{0.06}\right)^2 \times 0.40(1 - 0.40) = 256.11$, which is rounded up to 257.

8.72 $t_{0.025,9} = 2.062$; the 95% confidence interval is 10 ± 10.73

8.74 a. $t_{0.025,5} = 2.571$; 580 ± 94.66

b. We assume that the prices of single-family homes in San Luis Obispo follow a normal distribution.

8.76 a. The parameter of interest is the average filling weight of all cereal packages. The margin of error is 0.02.

b. The confidence interval is 1.22 ± 0.02, which means that with 95% confidence we can conclude that the machine is operating properly because the interval contains the target filling weight of 1.20 pounds.

c. $n = \left(\dfrac{1.96 \times 0.06}{0.01}\right)^2 = 138.3$, which is rounded up to 139.

Thus, the sample size should be at least 139 in order to get a margin of error below 0.01.

8.78 a. $z_{0.005} = 2.576$; the 99% confidence interval is 0.82 ± 0.14

b. The 99% margin of error is 0.14.

8.80 $\bar{x} = 27{,}500$, $n = 40$, $s = 9{,}120$; $t_{0.05,39} = 1.685$; the 90% confidence interval is $27{,}500 \pm 2429.77$.

With 90% confidence we can conclude that the average debt has not changed because the interval contains the target average debt of $25,250.

8.82 a. $n = 50$, $\sigma = 5$, $\bar{x} = 78.4$. Excel command: =AVERAGE(A2:A51) $z_{0.025} = 1.96$; Excel command: =NORM.S.INV(0.975); 78.4 ± 1.39

b. With 95% confidence, we can conclude that the mean life expectancy of Michigan residents differs from that for Hawaii residents.

8.84 a. Monday: $s = 21.12$. Excel command: =STDEV.S(A2:A31) The margin of error of tickets sold for Monday is 7.89. Tuesday: $s = 11.82$. Excel command: =STDEV.S(B2:B31) The margin of error of tickets sold for Tuesday is 4.41.

b. Monday: $\bar{x} = 222.37$. Excel command: =AVERAGE(A2:A31). Tuesday: $\bar{x} = 190.07$. Excel command: =AVERAGE(B2:B31). The 95% confidence intervals for tickets sold for Monday and Tuesday are 222.37 ± 7.89, and 190.07 ± 4.41, respectively.

c. For both Monday and Tuesday, the population mean differs from 200 because 200 does not belong to either of the two confidence intervals.

8.86 a. $z_{0.025} = 1.96$; the margin of error is 0.018.

b. 0.121 ± 0.018.

8.88 $n = \left(\dfrac{1.645}{0.05}\right)^2 \times 0.20(1 - 0.20) = 173.19$, which is rounded up to 174. This is assuming that $\hat{p} = 0.20$, based on prior studies, is a reasonable estimate of p in the planning stage.

8.90 a. $z_{0.025} = 1.96$; 0.20 ± 0.111. With 95% confidence, we can conclude that the percentage of pedestrians in Lower Manhattan who smoke while walking is between 8.9% and 31.1%.

b. $z_{0.025} = 1.96$; 0.40 ± 0.136. With 95% confidence, we can conclude that the percentage of pedestrians in Lower Manhattan who are tourists is between 26.4% and 53.6%.

8.92 $n = 259.35$, which is rounded up to 260.

Chapter 9

9.2 a. Invalid. The test is about the population parameter μ.

b. Valid

c. Valid

d. Invalid. The null hypothesis must include some form of the equality sign.

9.4 a. Incorrect. It is not correct to conclude "accept the null hypothesis" because while the sample data may not be inconsistent with the null hypothesis, they do not necessarily prove that the null hypothesis is true.

b. Correct.

c. Incorrect. We cannot establish a claim because the null hypothesis is not rejected.

d. Correct.

9.6 a. Type I error is to incorrectly conclude the mean weight is different from 18 ounces. Type II error is to incorrectly conclude the mean weight does not differ from 18 ounces.

b. Type I error is to incorrectly conclude that the stock price increases on more than 60 percent of trading days. Type II error is to incorrectly conclude that the price does not increase on more than 60 percent of trading days.

c. Type I error is to incorrectly conclude that Americans sleep less than 7 hours a day. Type II error is to incorrectly conclude that Americans do not sleep less than 7 hours a day.

9.8 a. Type I error is to incorrectly conclude that the majority of voters support the candidate. Type II error is to incorrectly conclude that the majority of the voters do not support the candidate.

b. Type I error is to incorrectly conclude that the average pizza is less than 10 inches. Type II error is to incorrectly conclude that the average pizza is not less than 10 inches.

c. Type I error is to incorrectly conclude that the average ibuprofen contents differ from 250 mg. Type II error is to incorrectly conclude that the average ibuprofen contents do not differ from 250 mg.

9.10 a. 0.03

b. 0.02

c. Type I error is to incorrectly conclude that an individual has the disease. Type II error is to incorrectly conclude that an individual does not have the disease.

d. We do not prove that the individual is free of disease if we do not reject the null hypothesis.

9.12. a. H_0: The new software does not significantly reduce assembly costs; H_A: The new software significantly reduces assembly costs. The manager of the restaurant is more concerned about Type I error. The consequence of a Type I error is to conclude that the restaurant uses higher fat content, when the restaurant does not.

   b. The consumer group should be more concerned about Type II error. Type II error is to fail to reject the null hypothesis that the restaurant uses higher fat content, when the restaurant does use higher fat content.

9.14 a and b. $z = \dfrac{13.4 - 12.6}{3.2/\sqrt{25}} = 1.25$; $1.25 < 1.28 = z_{0.10}$; do not reject H_0

   c and d. $z = \dfrac{13.4 - 12.6}{3.2/\sqrt{100}} = 2.5$; $2.5 > 1.28 = z_{0.10}$; reject H_0

9.16 a and b. $z = \dfrac{144 - 150}{28/\sqrt{80}} = -1.92$; $p\text{-value} = 0.0274 > 0.01 = \alpha$; do not reject H_0

   c. $0.0274 < 0.05 = \alpha$; reject H_0

9.18 a. $-z_{0.025} = -1.96$ and $z_{0.025} = 1.96$

   b. $z = \dfrac{132 - 120}{46/\sqrt{50}} = 1.84$; do not reject H_0 since $-1.96 < 1.84 < 1.96$

   c. $-z_{0.05} = -1.645$ and $z_{0.05} = 1.645$

   d. Reject H_0 since $1.84 > 1.645$

9.20 $z = \dfrac{80 - 75}{30/\sqrt{100}} = 1.67$; for this left-tailed test, the $p\text{-value} = P(Z \le 1.67) = 0.9525$. Since $\alpha = 0.10$, we do not reject H_0 because the $p\text{-value} = 0.9525 > 0.10 = \alpha$. Note: We really do not need formal testing here since there is no discrepancy between the sample mean ($\bar{x} = 80$) and the hypothesized mean ($\mu \ge 75$).

9.22 a. H_0: $\mu \le 130$; H_A: $\mu > 130$

   b. $p\text{-value} = P(Z \ge 2.50) = 1 - 0.9938 = 0.0062$

   c. Since the $p\text{-value} = 0.0062 < 0.05 = \alpha$, we reject H_0. At the 5% significance level, average spending is more than $130.

   d. With $\alpha = 0.05$, the critical value is $z_{0.05} = 1.645$; the decision rule is to reject H_0 if $z > 1.645$. Since $2.50 > 1.645$, we reject H_0.

9.24 a. H_0: $\mu \ge 7$; H_A: $\mu < 7$; $z = \dfrac{6.7 - 7}{2.1/\sqrt{150}} = -1.75$. The $p\text{-value} = P(Z \le -1.75) = 0.0401$. Since the $p\text{-value} = 0.0401 > 0.01 = \alpha$, we do not reject H_0. At the 1% significance level, we cannot conclude that average sleep time is less than 7 hours.

   b. With $\alpha = 0.01$, the critical value is $-z_{0.01} = -2.33$; the decision rule is to reject H_0 if $z < -2.33$. Since $z = -1.75 > -2.33$, we do not reject H_0.

9.26 a. H_0: $\mu = 16$; H_A: $\mu \ne 16$

   b. $z = \dfrac{15.80 - 16}{0.8/\sqrt{48}} = -1.73$. With $\alpha = 0.05$, the critical values are -1.96 and 1.96. Since $z = 1.73$ falls between -1.96 and 1.96, we do not reject H_0.

   c. Based on the sample data, the average content of bottles is not significantly different from 16 ounces at the 5% significance level. Thus, the accuracy of the bottling process is not compromised.

9.28 a. H_0: $\mu \ge 22$; H_A: $\mu < 22$

   b. Excel command: =Z.TEST(A2: A51, 22, 6) = 0.9825; the $p\text{-value} = P(Z \le z) = 1 - 0.9825 = 0.0175$.

   c. Since the $p\text{-value} = 0.0175 < 0.05 = \alpha$, we reject H_0. At the 5% significance level, we conclude that the average hourly wage is less than $22.

9.30 a. H_0: $\mu \le 27{,}200$; H_A: $\mu > 27{,}200$

   b. With $\alpha = 0.10$, $z_{\alpha/2} = z_{0.05} = 1.645$; the critical values are -1.645 and 1.645; Excel command: =NORM.S.INV(0.95)

   c. Excel command: =Z.TEST(B2: B27, 27200, 5000) = 0.9857

   d. The $p\text{-value} = 1 - P(Z \le z) = 1 - 0.9857 = 0.0143$. Since the $p\text{-value} = 0.0143 < 0.10 = \alpha$, we reject H_0. At the 10% significance level, the debt of recent undergraduates from Connecticut is, on average, higher than the national average debt.

9.32 a. Reject H_0 at $\alpha = 0.10$; do not reject H_0 at $\alpha = 0.01$

   b. Reject H_0 at $\alpha = 0.10$; do not reject H_0 at $\alpha = 0.01$

   c. Reject H_0 at $\alpha = 0.10$; do not reject H_0 at $\alpha = 0.01$

   d. Reject H_0 at $\alpha = 0.10$; do not reject H_0 at $\alpha = 0.01$

9.34 a. Reject H_0 at $\alpha = 0.10$; do not reject H_0 at $\alpha = 0.01$

   b. Reject H_0 at $\alpha = 0.10$; do not reject H_0 at $\alpha = 0.01$

   c. Reject H_0 at $\alpha = 0.10$; do not reject H_0 at $\alpha = 0.01$

   d. Reject H_0 at $\alpha = 0.10$; do not reject H_0 at $\alpha = 0.01$

9.36 a. $t_{23} = \dfrac{4.8 - 4.5}{0.8/\sqrt{24}} = 1.84$; $0.025 < p\text{-value} < 0.05$; since the $p\text{-value} < \alpha = 0.05$, reject H_0

   b. $t_{23} = 1.84$; $0.05 < p\text{-value} < 0.10$; since the $p\text{-value} > \alpha = 0.05$, do not reject H_0

9.38 H_0: $\mu = 16$; H_A: $\mu \ne 16$; $t_{31} = \dfrac{15.2 - 16}{0.6/\sqrt{32}} = -7.54$

   a. $p\text{-value} < \alpha = 0.01$; reject H_0. The sample data suggest that the population mean is different from 16.

   b. $t_{31} = 7.54 > t_{0.005,31} = 2.744$; reject H_0.

9.40 $t_5 = \dfrac{92.33 - 100}{7.89/\sqrt{6}} = -2.38 > -3.365 = -t_{0.01,5}$; do not reject H_0.

9.42 a. H_0: $\mu \le 5$; H_A: $\mu > 5$

   b. $t_6 = \dfrac{5.53 - 5}{2.18/\sqrt{7}} = 0.64$; normal population

   c. $t_6 = 0.64 < 1.440 = t_{0.10,6}$; do not reject H_0. Do not hire another employee.

   d. $p\text{-value} > \alpha = 0.10$; do not reject H_0.

9.44 a. H_0: $\mu = 12$; H_A: $\mu \ne 12$

   b. No, $n = 48 > 30$.

   c. $t_{0.025,47} = 2.012$; reject H_0 if $t_{47} < -2.012$ or $t_{47} > 2.012$

   d. $t_{47} = \dfrac{11.8 - 12}{0.8/\sqrt{48}} = -1.73$; do not reject H_0. No adjustment is necessary.

9.46 H_0: $\mu \ge 6$; H_A: $\mu < 6$; $t_{11} = \dfrac{5.92 - 6}{0.09/\sqrt{12}} = -3.08$; $0.005 < p\text{-value} < 0.001$; since the $p\text{-value} < \alpha = 0.05$, reject H_0. The carmaker's goal has been achieved.

9.48 H_0: $\mu \le 4.2$; H_A: $\mu > 4.2$; $t_6 = \dfrac{4.38 - 4.20}{0.20/\sqrt{7}} = 2.38$

   a. The $p\text{-value} = P(T_6 \ge 2.38)$; $0.025 < p\text{-value} < 0.05$. Since the $p\text{-value} < \alpha = 0.10$, we reject H_0. The mean mortgage rate for the population is higher than 4.2%.

   b. With $\alpha = 0.10$, the critical value is $t_{0.10,6} = 1.440$; the decision rule is to reject H_0 if $t_6 > 1.440$. Since $t_6 = 2.38 > 1.440$, we reject H_0.

9.50 a. H_0: $\mu = 95$; H_A: $\mu \ne 95$

   b. $t_{24} = \dfrac{96.52 - 95}{10.70/\sqrt{25}} = 0.71$; use Excel to compute the $p\text{-value}$ as '=T.DIST.2T(0.71,24)' = 0.48.

   c. Since the $p\text{-value} = 0.48 > 0.05 = \alpha$, we do not reject H_0. The average MPG is not significantly different from 95.

9.52 a. $H_0: \mu = 65; H_A: \mu \neq 65$

b. $t_{0.005,39} = 2.708$; the critical values are -2.708 and 2.708. The decision rule is to reject H_0 if $t_{39} > 2.708$ or $t_{39} < -2.708$.

c. $t_{39} = \dfrac{66 - 65}{3/\sqrt{40}} = 2.108$

d. Since $t_{39} = 2.108$ falls between -2.708 and 2.708, we do not reject H_0. At the 1% significant level, we cannot conclude that the average speed differs from the speed limit.

9.54 a. $z = \dfrac{0.3 - 0.38}{\sqrt{\dfrac{0.38(1 - 0.38)}{74}}} = -1.42; p\text{-value} = 0.0778$

b. $z = \dfrac{0.37 - 0.38}{\sqrt{\dfrac{0.38(1 - 0.38)}{300}}} = -0.36; p\text{-value} = 0.3594$

c. $z = \dfrac{0.34 - 0.38}{\sqrt{\dfrac{0.38(1 - 0.38)}{50}}} = -0.58; p\text{-value} = 0.2810$

d. $z = \dfrac{0.34 - 0.38}{\sqrt{\dfrac{0.38(1 - 0.38)}{400}}} = -1.65; p\text{-value} = 0.0495$

9.56 a. $z = \dfrac{0.3 - 0.32}{\sqrt{\dfrac{0.32(1 - 0.32)}{66}}} = -0.35; p\text{-value} = 0.7264$

b. $z = \dfrac{0.38 - 0.32}{\sqrt{\dfrac{0.32(1 - 0.32)}{264}}} = 2.09; p\text{-value} = 0.0366$

c. $z = \dfrac{0.40 - 0.32}{\sqrt{\dfrac{0.32(1 - 0.32)}{40}}} = 1.08; p\text{-value} = 0.2802$

d. $z = \dfrac{0.38 - 0.32}{\sqrt{\dfrac{0.32(1 - 0.32)}{180}}} = 1.73; p\text{-value} = 0.0836$

9.58 a. $z_{0.05} = 1.645$

b. $-z_{0.025} = -1.96$ and $z_{0.025} = 1.96$

c. $-z_{0.05} = -1.645$

9.60 a. $z = \dfrac{0.4 - 0.45}{\sqrt{\dfrac{0.45(1 - 0.45)}{320}}} = -1.80 > -2.33 = -z_{0.01};$ do not reject H_0.

b. $-2.576 < z = -1.80 < 2.576$; do not reject H_0.

9.62 $H_0: p \leq 0.5; H_A: p > 0.5; z = \dfrac{0.65 - 0.5}{\sqrt{\dfrac{0.5(1 - 0.5)}{20}}} = 1.34;$
$p\text{-value} = 0.0901 > 0.05 = \alpha;$ do not reject H_0. Cannot conclude that more than 50% of the observations in the population are below 10.

9.64 a. $H_0: p \leq 0.2; H_A: p > 0.2$

b. $z = \dfrac{0.263 - 0.2}{\sqrt{\dfrac{0.2(1 - 0.2)}{190}}} = 2.17$

c. $p\text{-value} = 0.015 < 0.05 = \alpha;$ reject H_0. The concern is supported.

9.66 a. $H_0: p \leq 0.3; H_A: p > 0.3; z = \dfrac{0.34 - 0.3}{\sqrt{\dfrac{0.3(1 - 0.3)}{200}}} = 1.23;$
$p\text{-value} = 0.1093 > 0.05 = \alpha.$ Do not reject H_0.

b. $p\text{-value} = 0.1093 > 0.10 = \alpha.$ Do not reject H_0.

c. Cannot conclude that more than 30% of moviegoers return to see movie for a second time.

9.68 $H_0: p \leq 0.5; H_A: p > 0.5; z = \dfrac{0.6 - 0.5}{\sqrt{\dfrac{0.5(1 - 0.5)}{40}}} = 1.26;$
$p\text{-value} = 0.1038 > 0.05 = \alpha;$ do not reject H_0. The claim is not justified.

9.70 $H_0: p \leq 0.6; H_A: p > 0.6; z = \dfrac{0.64 - 0.6}{\sqrt{\dfrac{0.6(1 - 0.6)}{140}}} = 0.97; p\text{-value} =$
$0.166 > 0.01 = \alpha;$ do not reject H_0. The claim is not supported.

9.72 H_0: The drug does not raise the blood pressure of its users; H_A: The drug raises the blood pressure of its users. The manager of the pharmaceutical company is more concerned about a Type I error. The consequence of a Type I error is to conclude that the drug raises the blood pressure of its users when it does not.

9.74 a. $H_0: \mu \leq 10; H_A: \mu > 10$

b. $t_{44} = \dfrac{10.5 - 10}{1.8/\sqrt{45}} = 1.86$

c. $t_{0.05,44} = 1.680$; the decision rule is to reject H_0 if $t_{44} > 1.680$. Since $t_{44} = 1.86 > 1.680$, reject H_0. The sample evidence supports the manufacturer's claim that the battery life is more than 10 hours.

d. $0.025 < p\text{-value} < 0.05$. Since the p-value $< \alpha = 0.05$, reject H_0.

9.76 $H_0: \mu \leq 20; H_A: \mu > 20; t_{31} = \dfrac{22.08 - 20}{5.42/\sqrt{32}} = 2.17$
$t_{0.01,31} = 2.453$; the decision rule is to reject H_0 if $t_{31} > 2.453$. Since $t_{31} = 2.17 < 2.453$, do not reject H_0. At the 1% significance level, we cannot conclude that drivers' waiting time exceeds 20 minutes. Thus, there is no need for the city council to spend additional money to reduce the amount of traffic.

9.78 a. $H_0: \mu \leq 12; H_A: \mu > 12$

b. Use Excel to find the p-value as '=Z.TEST(B2:B26,12,30)' = 0.2966.

c. Since the p-value $= 0.7879 > 0.05 = \alpha$, do not reject H_0. At the 5% significance level, the sample evidence does not support that the mean return is greater than 12%.

9.80 a. $H_0: \mu = 13,500; H_A: \mu \neq 13,500$

b. $t_{49} = \dfrac{14,562 - 13,500}{2895.66/\sqrt{50}} = 2.59$. Use Excel to find the p-value as '=T.DIST.2T(2.59,49)' = 0.013.

c. Since the p-value $= 0.013 < 0.10 = \alpha$, reject H_0. The average number of miles driven annually by Midwesterners is different from the U.S. average at the 10% significance level.

9.82 a. $H_0: p \geq 0.90; H_A: p < 0.90$

b. $\bar{p} = \dfrac{1068}{1200} = 0.89; z = \dfrac{0.89 - 0.90}{\sqrt{0.90(1 - 0.90)/1200}} = -1.15$

c. The p-value $= P(Z \leq -1.15) = 0.1251$.

d. Since the p-value $= 0.1251 > 0.05 = \alpha$, do not reject H_0. Based on the sample evidence, there is no need for the retailer to improve its services at the 5% significance level.

9.84 a. $H_0: p \leq 0.50; H_A: p > 0.50$

b. $\bar{p} = \dfrac{428}{827} = 0.52; z = \dfrac{0.52 - 0.50}{\sqrt{0.50(1 - 0.50)/827}} = 1.15$

c. $z_{0.01} = 2.33$. The decision rule is to reject H_0 if $z > 2.33$.

d. Since $z = 1.15 < 2.33$, do not reject H_0. At the 1% significance level, the percentage of individuals who want to watch the new show is not more than 50%. As a result, the television network should keep its current lineup.

9.86 a. $H_0: p \le 0.33$; $H_A: p > 0.33$

b. $\bar{p} = 0.42$; $z = \dfrac{0.42 - 0.33}{\sqrt{0.33(1 - 0.33)/100}} = 1.91$

c. $z_{0.01} = 2.33$. The decision rule is to reject H_0 if $z > 2.33$.

d. Since $z = 1.91 < 2.33$, we do not reject H_0. At the 1% significance level, the Massachusetts teens do not engage in this behavior at a rate greater than the national rate.

Chapter 10

10.2 a. $t_{0.025,33} = 2.035$;

$s_p^2 = \dfrac{(15 - 1)7.9 + (20 - 1)9.3}{15 + 20 - 2} = 8.71$;

$(-10.5 + 16.8) \pm 2.035\sqrt{8.71\left(\dfrac{1}{15} + \dfrac{1}{20}\right)} = 6.3 \pm 2.05$

b. $H_0: \mu_1 - \mu_2 = 0$; $H_A: \mu_1 - \mu_2 \ne 0$

c. Since the interval [4.25, 8.35] does not contain 0, the value hypothesized under the null hypothesis, reject H_0. At the 5% significance level, the population means differ.

10.4 a. $s_p^2 = \dfrac{(10 - 1)2.5^2 + (12 - 1)4.4^2}{10 + 12 - 2} = 13.46$;

$t_{20} = \dfrac{(20.2 - 17.5) - 0}{\sqrt{13.46\left(\dfrac{1}{10} + \dfrac{1}{12}\right)}} = 1.72$; $t_{0.05,20} = 1.725$.

Since $t_{20} = 1.72 < 1.725 = t_{0.05,20}$, we do not reject H_0; at the 5% significance level, μ_1 is not greater than μ_2.

b. $t_{0.10,20} = 1.356$. Since $t_{20} = 1.72 > 1.356 = t_{0.10,20}$, we reject H_0; at the 10% significance level, μ_1 is greater than μ_2.

10.6 a. $s_p^2 = \dfrac{(22 - 1)21.5^2 + (18 - 1)15.2^2}{22 + 18 - 2} = 358.81$;

$t_{38} = \dfrac{(57 - 43) - 5}{\sqrt{358.81\left(\dfrac{1}{22} + \dfrac{1}{18}\right)}} = 1.49$.

The p-value $= 2P(T_{38} \ge 1.49)$; $0.10 < p$-value < 0.20. Since the p-value $> \alpha = 0.05$, do not reject H_0. At the 5% significance level, we cannot conclude that the difference between the means differs from 5.

b. $t_{0.025,38} = 2.024$. Since $t_{38} = 1.49 < 2.024 = t_{0.025,38}$, do not reject H_0.

10.8 a. $H_0: \mu_1 - \mu_2 = 0$; $H_A: \mu_1 - \mu_2 \ne 0$

b. $t_{df} = \dfrac{(98.33 - 111.67) - 0}{\sqrt{\dfrac{16.27^2}{6} + \dfrac{10.91^2}{6}}} = -1.67$

c. $df = \dfrac{\left(\dfrac{16.27^2}{6} + \dfrac{10.91^2}{6}\right)^2}{\dfrac{\left(\dfrac{16.27^2}{6}\right)^2}{6 - 1} + \dfrac{\left(\dfrac{10.91^2}{6}\right)^2}{6 - 1}} = 8.74$, which is rounded

down to 8.

$t_8 = -1.67$, and its corresponding p-value $= 2P(T_8 \le -1.67)$; $0.10 < p$-value < 0.20.

d. Since the p-value $> \alpha = 0.10$, do not reject H_0. At the 10% significance level, we cannot conclude that the population means differ.

10.10 a. $H_0: \mu_1 - \mu_2 \ge 0$; $H_A: \mu_1 - \mu_2 < 0$

b. $z = \dfrac{52{,}000 - 54{,}700}{\sqrt{\dfrac{4400^2}{100} + \dfrac{1500^2}{100}}} = -5.81$; the p-value $=$

$P(Z \le -5.81) \approx 0$.

c. Since the p-value $\approx 0 < 0.05 = \alpha$, reject H_0. The sample data indicate that $\mu_1 < \mu_2$ at the 5% significance level. The "community college penalty" seems to apply to Lucille's university as well.

10.12 Sample 1 consists of students in the first section and Sample 2 represents students in the second section.

a. $H_0: \mu_1 - \mu_2 \le 0$; $H_A: \mu_1 - \mu_2 > 0$

b. $t_{df} = \dfrac{(77.40 - 74.10) - 0}{\sqrt{\dfrac{10.80^2}{18} + \dfrac{12.20^2}{14}}} = 0.80$.

It is necessary to assume that each population is normally distributed as the sample sizes are not sufficiently large to use the Central Limit Theorem. Also, following Mark's remark, the population standard deviations are not equal.

c. There is no need to calculate the degrees of freedom because the value of the test statistic $t_{df} = 0.80$ is so small. Regardless of the value of the degrees of freedom, H_0 will not be rejected. There is no evidence that the first class outperforms the second class.

10.14 Let Sample 1 be the sample of SUVs and Sample 2 be the sample of small cars.

a. $H_0: \mu_1 - \mu_2 = 30$; $H_A: \mu_1 - \mu_2 \ne 30$

b. $s_p^2 = \dfrac{(18 - 1)32.00^2 + (38 - 1)24.00^2}{18 + 38 - 2} = 717.04$;

$t_{54} = \dfrac{(95.00 - 48.00) - 30}{\sqrt{717.04\left(\dfrac{1}{18} + \dfrac{1}{38}\right)}} = 2.22$

c. $t_{0.05,54} = 1.674$. The decision rule is to reject H_0 if $t_{54} > 1.674$ or $t_{54} < -1.674$. Since $t_{54} = 2.22 > 1.674$, reject H_0. The sample data support the claim that it takes 30 days longer to sell SUVs compared to smaller cars at the 10% significance level.

10.16 a. $H_0: \mu_1 - \mu_2 \le 0$; $H_A: \mu_1 - \mu_2 > 0$

b. Excel output:

t-Test: Two-Sample Assuming Equal Variances		
	Low-Carb/Mediterranean Diets	Low-Fat Diet
Mean	9.7733	6.2833
Variance	3.1979	3.1607
Observations	30	30
Pooled Variance	3.1793	
Hypothesized Mean Difference	0	
df	58	
t Stat	7.5806	
P(T < =t) one-tail	0.0000	
t Critical one-tail	1.6716	
P(T < =t) two-tail	0.0000	
t Critical two-tail	2.0017	

$t_{0.05,58} = 1.672$. The decision rule is to reject H_0 if $t_{58} > t_{0.05,58} = 1.672$.

c. Since $t_{58} = 7.58 > 1.672 = t_{0.05,58}$, reject H_0. At the 5% significance level, the sample data suggest that overweight individuals on a low-carbohydrate or the Mediterranean diet lose more weight than their counterparts on a low-fat diet.

10.18 $H_0: \mu_1 - \mu_2 \le 0; H_A: \mu_1 - \mu_2 > 0$

Excel output:

t-Test: Two-Sample Assuming Unequal Variances		
	Salary 2008	**Salary 2010**
Mean	48700	46825
Variance	68574359	2.25E + 08
Observations	40	40
Hypothesized Mean Difference	0	
df	61	
t Stat	**0.691961**	
P(T < =t) one-tail	**0.245794**	
t Critical one-tail	1.670219	
P(T < =t) two-tail	0.491587	
t Critical two-tail	1.999624	

Since the p-value $= 0.2458 > 0.05 = \alpha$, we do not reject H_0. At the 5% significance level, we cannot conclude that the starting salary has declined from 2008 to 2010.

10.20 a. $t_{0.05,19} = 1.729$;

$$\bar{d} \pm t_{\alpha/2,df} \frac{s_D}{\sqrt{n}} = 1.3 \pm 1.729 \frac{1.61}{\sqrt{20}} = 1.3 \pm 0.62,$$

or [0.68, 1.92]

b. Since the value zero is not included in the [0.68, 1.92] interval, we reject H_0. At the 10% significance level, we can conclude that the mean difference is not zero.

10.22 a. $-t_{0.05,11} = -1.796$

b. $t_{df} = -1.702$.

$$t_{11} = \frac{-2.8 - 0}{\frac{5.7}{\sqrt{12}}} = -1.702$$

c. Since $t_{11} = -1.702 > -1.796 = -t_{0.05,11}$, we do not reject H_0. At the 5% significance level, we cannot conclude that the mean difference is less than 0.

10.24 a. $H_0: \mu_D \le 0; H_A: \mu_D > 0$

b. $t_{34} = \frac{1.2 - 0}{\frac{3.8}{\sqrt{35}}} = 1.87$. The p-value $= P(T_{34} \ge 1.87)$;

$0.025 < p$-value < 0.05.

c. Since the p-value $< \alpha = 0.05$, we reject H_0. At the 5% significance level, we can conclude that the mean difference is greater than 0.

d. $t_{\alpha,df} = t_{0.05,34} = 1.691$. Since $t_{34} = 1.87 > 1.691 = t_{0.05,34}$, we reject H_0.

10.26 a. $H_0: \mu_D = 0; H_A: \mu_D \ne 0$

b. $\bar{d} = -1.86; s_D = \sqrt{\frac{32.8571}{6}} = 2.34$;

$$t_6 = \frac{-1.86 - 0}{\frac{2.34}{\sqrt{7}}} = -2.10$$

c. $t_{0.05,6} = 1.943$. The decision rule is to reject H_0 if $t_6 > 1.943$ or $t_6 < -1.943$.

d. Since $t_6 = -2.10 < -1.943$, we reject H_0. The manager's assertion is supported by the data at the 5% significance level.

10.28 a. $H_0: \mu_D = 0; H_A: \mu_D \ne 0$

b. $t_{0.025,5} = 2.571$

c. $\bar{d} = -2166.67; s_D = 6177.92; t_5 = \frac{-2166.67 - 0}{\frac{6177.92}{\sqrt{6}}} = -0.86$

d. Since $t_5 = -0.86$ falls between -2.571 and 2.571, we do not reject H_0. We cannot conclude that the appraisers are inconsistent in their estimates.

10.30 a. $H_0: \mu_D = 0; H_A: \mu_D \ne 0$

b.

t-Test: Paired Two Sample for Means		
	Electronic	**Utilities**
Mean	5.905555556	3.812222222
Variance	2210.948853	672.6680694
Observations	9	9
Pearson Correlation	0.673056959	
Hypothesized Mean Difference	0	
df	8	
t Stat	**0.178196299**	
P(T < =t) one-tail	0.431499266	
t Critical one-tail	1.859548038	
P(T < =t) two-tail	**0.862998531**	

$t_8 = 0.18$; p-value $= 0.8630$. Since the p-value $= 0.8630 > 0.05 = \alpha$, we do not reject H_0. We cannot conclude that the mean returns on Electronics and Utilities differ at the 5% significance level.

10.32 a. $H_0: \mu_D \ge 0; H_A: \mu_D < 0$

b.

t-Test: Paired Two Sample for Means		
	Average when Shift	**Average when No Shift**
Mean	0.2129	0.2391
Variance	0.002540322	0.0016361
Observations	10	10
Pearson Correlation	-0.079839194	
Hypothesized Mean Difference	0	
df	9	
t Stat	**-1.234811569**	
P(T < =t) one-tail	**0.124083054**	
t Critical one-tail	1.833112933	
P(T < =t) two-tail	0.248166109	
t Critical two-tail	2.262157163	

$t_9 = -1.235$ and the p-value $= 0.1241$.

c. Since the p-value $= 0.1241 > 0.05 = \alpha$, we do not reject H_0. We cannot conclude that the defensive shift is effective in lowering a power hitter's batting average at the 5% significance level.

10.34 a. $\bar{\bar{x}} = \frac{-174}{15} = -11.6$

b. $SSTR = 3(-11.3 - (-11.6))^2 + 4(-12 - (-11.6))^2 + 5(-10.4 - (-11.6))^2 + 3(-13.3 - (-11.6))^2 = 16.78$

$MSTR = \frac{16.78}{4 - 1} = 5.59$

c. $SSE = (3 - 1)2.33 + (4 - 1)8.7 + (5 - 1)6.3 + (3 - 1)2.3 = 60.56$

$MSE = \frac{60.56}{15 - 4} = 5.51$

d. $H_0: \mu_A = \mu_B = \mu_C = \mu_D$; H_A: Not all population means are equal

e. $F_{(3,11)} = \frac{5.59}{5.51} = 1.01$

f. $F_{(3,11)} = 1.01$, so the p-value $= P(F_{(3,11)} \geq 1.01)$; using the F table, the p-value > 0.10.

g. Since the p-value $> 0.10 = \alpha$, we do not reject H_0. At the 10% significance level, we cannot conclude that the population means are not all equal.

10.36

Source of Variation	SS	df	MS	F	F crit at 5%
Between Groups	11.34	3	3.78	3.58	2.77
Within Groups	59.13	56	1.06		
Total	70.47	59			

Note: F critical is obtained from Excel using '=F.INV.RT (0.05, 3, 56)'.
Since $F_{(3,56)} = 3.58 > 2.77$, we reject H_0. At the 5% significance level, we can conclude that the population means are not all equal.

10.38 a.

Source of Variation	SS	df	MS	F	p-Value	F crit
Between Groups	548.37	5	109.67	1.37	0.250	1.96
Within Groups	4,321.11	54	80.02			
Total	4,869.48	59				

Note: The p-value is obtained from Excel using '=F.DIST.RT(1.37, 5, 54)'; F critical is obtained from Excel using '=F.INV.RT(0.05, 5, 54)'.

b. $H_0: \mu_1 = \mu_2 = \mu_3 = \mu_4 = \mu_5 = \mu_6$; H_A: Not all population means are equal

c. Since the p-value $= 0.250 > 0.10 = \alpha$, we do not reject H_0. At the 10% significance level, we cannot conclude that the population means differ.

10.40 a. $SSTR = 8(86.3 - 82.5)^2 + 8(80.3 - 82.5)^2 + 8(80.9 - 82.5)^2 = 174.72$; $MSTR = \frac{174.72}{3 - 1} = 87.36$;

$SSE = (8 - 1)20.8 + (8 - 1)45.1 + (8 - 1)27.3 = 652.40$;

$MSE = \frac{652.40}{24 - 3} = 31.07$

Source of Variation	SS	df	MS	F	p-Value	F crit at 5%
Between Groups	174.72	2	87.36	2.81	0.083	3.47
Within Groups	652.40	21	31.07			
Total	827.12	23				

Note: The p-value is obtained from Excel using '=F.DIST.RT(2.81, 2, 21)'.

b. $H_0: \mu_1 = \mu_2 = \mu_3$
H_A: Not all population means are equal

c. Since the p-value $= 0.083 > 0.05 = \alpha$, we do not reject H_0. At the 5% significance level, we cannot conclude that significant differences exist in the average whitening effectiveness of the three detergents.

10.42 a. $H_0: \mu_{Snorkeling} = \mu_{Sailing} = \mu_{NBoarding/Windsurfing} = \mu_{Bowling} = \mu_{On - road\ triathlon} = \mu_{Off - road\ triathlon}$
H_A: Not all population mean incomes are equal

b. $SSTR = 5(93.5 - 76.6)^2 + 5(89.4 - 76.6)^2 + 5(77.9 - 76.6)^2 + 5(77.3 - 76.6)^2 + 5(64.0 - 76.6)^2 + 5(57.4 - 76.6)^2 = 4895.15$

$MSTR = \frac{4895.15}{6 - 1} = 979.03$

$SSE = (5 - 1)28.8 + (5 - 1)28.5 + (5 - 1)13.8 + (5 - 1)7.4 + (5 - 1)10.3 + (5 - 1)66.4 = 620.80$

Source of Variation	SS	df	MS	F	p-Value	F crit at 5%
Between Groups	4895.15	5	979.03	37.85	0.000	2.62
Within Groups	620.80	24	25.87			
Total	5515.95	29				

Note: The p-value is obtained from Excel using '=F.DIST.RT (37.85, 5, 24)'.

c. $F_{0.05,(5,24)} = 2.62$. We reject H_0 if $F_{(5,24)} > 2.62$.

d. Since $F_{(5,24)} = 37.85 > 2.62$, we reject H_0. At the 5% significance level, we can conclude that average incomes differ depending on the recreational sport.

10.44 a.

Source of Variation	SS	df	MS	F	p-Value
Between Groups	7,531,769.00	3	2,510,589.67	69.01	0.000
Within Groups	3,492,385.00	96	36,379.01		
Total	11,024,154.00	99			

b. Since the p-value $\approx 0 < 0.01 = \alpha$, we reject H_0. At the 1% significance level, we can conclude that the average annual energy bills vary by region.

10.46

SUMMARY				
Groups	Count	Sum	Average	Variance
Section 1	10	728	72.8	142.84
Section 2	10	787	78.7	104.01
Section 3	10	694	69.4	70.71

ANOVA						
Source of Variation	SS	df	MS	F	p-Value	F crit
Between Groups	442.87	2	221.43	2.09	0.143	3.35
Within Groups	2858.10	27	105.86			
Total	3300.97	29				

$F_{0.05,(2,27)} = 3.35$. Since $F_{(2,27)} = 2.09 < 3.35$, we do not reject H_0. At the 5% significance level, we cannot conclude that average final exam scores are not equal among the instructor's three sections.

10.48

SUMMARY				
Groups	Count	Sum	Average	Variance
Field 1	30	2438	81.26667	35.16782
Field 2	30	2249	74.96667	36.44713
Field 3	30	2400	80	15.44828

ANOVA						
Source of Variation	SS	df	MS	F	p-Value	F crit
Between Groups	666.2889	2	333.1444	11.4794	3.76E − 05	2.364616
Within Groups	2524.833	87	29.02107			
Total	3191.122	89				

H_0: $\mu_1 = \mu_2 = \mu_3$; H_A: Not all population means are equal
Since $F_{(2,87)} = 11.479 > 2.365$, reject H_0. At the 10% significance level, we can conclude that the average job satisfaction differs by field.

10.50 a. H_0: $\mu_1 - \mu_2 \leq 0$; H_A: $\mu_1 - \mu_2 > 0$

b. $s_p^2 = 16.43$, $t_{58} = \dfrac{(30 - 24) - 0}{\sqrt{16.43\left(\frac{1}{30} + \frac{1}{30}\right)}} = 5.73$

c. p-value $= P(T_{58} \geq 5.73) < 0.005$

d. p-value $= 0.005 < 0.05 = \alpha$; thus reject H_0; relative to the 1981 levels, 6- to 12-year-old children spend less time today on household chores.

e. $t_{0.05,58} = 1.672$. Since $t_{58} = 5.73 > 1.672 = t_{0.05,58}$, we reject H_0.

10.52 H_0: $\mu_{Men} - \mu_{Women} = 0$; H_A: $\mu_{Men} - \mu_{Women} \neq 0$

t-Test: Two-Sample Assuming Equal Variances		
	Men	Women
Mean	194.48	188.88
Variance	68.70367347	76.55673469
Observations	50	50
Pooled Variance	72.63020408	
Hypothesized Mean Difference	0	
df	98	
t Stat	3.285484322	
P(T < =t) one-tail	0.000706557	
t Critical one-tail	2.36500241	
P(T < =t) two-tail	0.001413114	
t Critical two-tail	2.626931096	

Since $t_{98} = 3.285 > 2.627 = t_{0.005,98}$, we reject H_0. At the 1% significance level, we conclude that the mean cholesterol levels for men and women are different.

10.54 a. H_0: $\mu_D = 0$; H_A: $\mu_D \neq 0$

b. $\bar{d} = -0.67$; $s_D = 1.63$; $t_5 = \dfrac{-0.67 - 0}{\frac{1.63}{\sqrt{6}}} = -1.01$

c. $t_{0.025,5} = 2.571$. The decision rule is to reject H_0 if $t_5 > 2.571$ or $t_5 < -2.571$.

d. Since $t_5 = -1.01$ falls between -2.571 and 2.571, we do not reject H_0. At the 5% significance level, the crop yield with the new fertilizer is not significantly different from the crop yield with the old fertilizer. There is no need for the farmer to be concerned.

10.56 a. H_0: $\mu_{Males} - \mu_{Females} \geq 0$; H_A: $\mu_{Males} - \mu_{Females} < 0$

b.

t-Test: Two-Sample Assuming Unequal Variances (at $\alpha = 0.01$)		
	Males	Females
Mean	572.5	601.25
Variance	2078.5714	1669.6429
Observations	8	8
Hypothesized Mean Difference	0	
df	14	
t Stat	−1.32822	
P(T < =t) one-tail	0.10268	
t Critical one-tail	2.62449	
P(T < =t) two-tail	0.20535	
t Critical two-tail	2.97684	

$t_{14} = -1.3282$

c. Since the p-value $= 0.1027 > 0.01 = \alpha$, we do not reject H_0. The sample data do not support the claim that females outscore males on the writing test at the 1% significance level.

10.58 a.

Source of Variation	SS	df	MS	F	p-Value	F crit
Between Groups	2011.33	3	670.4433	429.7714	0.00	3.24
Within Groups	24.96	16	1.56			
Total	2036.29	19				

b. H_0: $\mu_{Locomotive\ Engineer} = \mu_{Truck\ Driver} = \mu_{Bus\ Driver} = \mu_{Taxi\ and\ Limousine\ Driver}$
H_A: Not all population means are equal

c. p-value $\approx 0 < 0.05 = \alpha$; reject H_0; at the 5% significance level, we can conclude that the average salaries of the four different transportation operators differ.

10.60 H_0: $\mu_{Route\ 1} = \mu_{Route\ 2} = \mu_{Route\ 3}$; H_A: Not all population means are equal.
p-value $= 0.0059 < 0.01 = \alpha$; reject H_0; at the 1% significance level, we can conclude that the average commute times differ between the three routes.

10.62 a.

Source of Variation	SS	df	MS	F	p-Value	F crit
Between Groups	57.39	2	28.70	1.08	0.3461	3.159
Within Groups	1512.80	57	26.54			
Total	1570.19	59				

b. H_0: $\mu_{Section\ 1} = \mu_{Section\ 2} = \mu_{Section\ 3}$; H_A: Not all population means are equal
Since the p-value $= 0.3461 > 0.05 = \alpha$, we do not reject H_0. At the 5% significance level, we cannot conclude that the average grades differ between the instructor's accounting sections.

10.64

SUMMARY				
Groups	**Count**	**Sum**	**Average**	**Variance**
Glue 1	20	756	37.8	31.74737
Glue 2	20	821	41.05	24.26053
Glue 3	20	839	41.95	12.47105

ANOVA						
Source of Variation	**SS**	**df**	**MS**	**F**	**p-Value**	**F crit**
Between Groups	190.6333	2	95.31667	4.175736	0.020307	3.158843
Within Groups	1301.1	57	22.82632			
Total	1491.733	59				

$H_0: \mu_1 = \mu_2 = \mu_3$; H_A: Not all population means are equal
Since $F_{(2,57)} = 4.176 > 3.159$, we reject H_0. At the 5% significance level, we can conclude that the average strength of the plywood boards differs by the type of glue used.

Chapter 11

11.2 $(0.85 - 0.90) \pm 1.645\sqrt{\dfrac{0.85(1 - 0.85)}{400} + \dfrac{0.90(1 - 0.90)}{350}} =$

-0.05 ± 0.0395 or $[-0.0895, -0.0105]$

With 90% confidence, the difference in the proportion is in the $[-0.0895, -0.0105]$ interval. Since the interval does not contain the value 0, we can conclude that there is a difference between the population proportions at the 10% significance level.

11.4 a. $-z_{0.05} = -1.645$

b. $\bar{p}_1 = \dfrac{250}{400} = 0.6250; \bar{p}_2 = \dfrac{275}{400} = 0.6875;$

$\bar{p} = \dfrac{x_1 + x_2}{n_1 + n_2} = \dfrac{525}{800} = 0.6563;$

$z = \dfrac{0.6250 - 0.6875}{\sqrt{0.6563(1 - 0.6563)\left(\dfrac{1}{400} + \dfrac{1}{400}\right)}} = -1.86$

c. Since $z = -1.86 < -1.645 = -z_{0.05}$, we reject H_0; p_1 is significantly less than p_2 at the 5% significance level.

11.6 a. $\bar{p}_1 = \dfrac{150}{250} = 0.60; \bar{p}_2 = \dfrac{130}{400} = 0.325;$

$z = \dfrac{(0.600 - 0.325) - 0.20}{\sqrt{\dfrac{0.600(1 - 0.600)}{250} + \dfrac{0.325(1 - 0.325)}{400}}} = 1.93$

b. The p-value $= 2P(Z \geq 1.93) = 2(0.0268) = 0.0536.$

c. Since the p-value $= 0.0536 > 0.05 = \alpha$, we do not reject H_0. The difference between population proportions does not differ from 0.20 at the 5% significance level.

d. $z_{0.025} = 1.96$. The decision rule is to reject H_0 if $z > 1.96$ or $z < -1.96$. Since $z = 1.93$ falls between -1.96 and 1.96, we do not reject H_0.

11.8 Let p_1 represent the population proportion in 2008 and p_2 the population proportion in 1980.

a. $H_0: p_1 - p_2 \leq 0; H_A: p_1 - p_2 > 0$

b. $\bar{p}_1 = 0.146, n_1 = 120;$

$\bar{p}_2 = 0.068, n_2 = 120;$

$\bar{p} = \dfrac{120(0.146) + 120(0.068)}{120 + 120} = 0.107;$

$z = \dfrac{0.146 - 0.068}{\sqrt{0.107(1 - 0.107)\left(\dfrac{1}{120} + \dfrac{1}{120}\right)}} = 1.95$; the p-value

$= P(Z \geq 1.95) = 1 - 0.9744 = 0.0256$. Since the p-value $= 0.0256 < 0.05 = \alpha$, we reject H_0. There has been an increase in the proportion of individuals marrying outside their race or ethnicity.

11.10 Let p_1 represent the population proportion of recent jobseekers and p_2 the population proportion of job seekers three years ago.

$H_0: p_1 - p_2 \leq 0; H_A: p_1 - p_2 > 0$

$\bar{p}_1 = \dfrac{67}{150} = 0.4467; \bar{p}_2 = \dfrac{58}{140} = 0.4143;$

$\bar{p} = \dfrac{67 + 58}{290} = 0.4310;$

$z = \dfrac{0.4467 - 0.4143}{\sqrt{0.4310(1 - 0.4310)\left(\dfrac{1}{150} + \dfrac{1}{140}\right)}} = 0.56.$

Since $z = 0.56 < 1.645 = z_{0.05}$, we do not reject H_0. We cannot conclude that the proportion of recent workers finding jobs on LinkedIn is more than the proportion three years ago, at the 5% significance level.

11.12 Let p_1 represent the population proportion of satisfied accounting majors and p_2 the population proportion of satisfied psychology majors.

a. $H_0: p_1 - p_2 \leq 0.20; H_A: p_1 - p_2 > 0.20$

b. $\bar{p}_1 = 0.50, n_1 = 350; \bar{p}_2 = 0.26, n_2 = 300;$

$z = \dfrac{(0.50 - 0.26) - 0.20}{\sqrt{\dfrac{0.50(1 - 0.50)}{350} + \dfrac{0.26(1 - 0.26)}{300}}} = 1.09.$

The p-value $= P(Z \geq 1.09) = 0.1379.$

c. Since the p-value $= 0.1379 > 0.05 = \alpha$, we do not reject H_0. The proportion of accounting majors satisfied with their career path does not differ from that of psychology majors by more than 20%.

11.14 Let p_1 represent the proportion of all male students who think men and women are not feasible to be just friends and p_2, the proportion of all female students who think men and women are not feasible to be just friends.

$H_0: p_1 - p_2 \leq 0.10; H_A: p_1 - p_2 > 0.10$

$\bar{p}_1 = 0.57, n_1 = 86; \bar{p}_2 = 0.32, n_2 = 100;$

$z = \dfrac{(0.57 - 0.32) - 0.10}{\sqrt{\dfrac{0.57(1 - 0.57)}{86} + \dfrac{0.32(1 - 0.32)}{100}}} = 2.12.$

The p-value $= P(Z \geq 2.12) = 0.017$. Since the p-value $= 0.017 < 0.05 = \alpha$, we reject H_0. There is a greater than 10 percentage point difference between the proportion of male and female students who think that men and women are not feasible to be just friends.

11.16 a. H_A: Not all $p_i (i = 1, 2, 3)$ equal their hypothesized values

b.

Category	o_i	e_i	$o_i - e_i$	$(o_i - e_i)^2$	$(o_i - e_i)^2/e_i$
1	250	240.0	10	100	0.417
2	94	100.0	-6	36	0.360
3	56	60.0	-4	16	0.267
Total	400	400.0			1.043

$\chi_2^2 = 1.043$; the p-value is more than 0.10.

c. Since the p-value $> 0.05 = \alpha$, we do not reject H_0. At the 5% significance level, we cannot conclude that at least one of the $p_i(i = 1, 2, 3)$ is different from its hypothesized value.

11.18 We use the *p*-value approach.

H_A: Not all $p_i(i = 1, 2, 3)$ equal their hypothesized values

Category	o_i	e_i	$o_i - e_i$	$(o_i - e_i)^2$	$(o_i - e_i)^2/e_i$
1	128	120.0	8	64	0.533
2	87	80.0	7	49	0.613
3	185	200.0	−15	225	1.125
Total	400	400.0			2.271

$\chi_2^2 = 2.271$; the *p*-value is more than 0.10. Since the *p*-value > $0.01 = \alpha$, we do not reject H_0. At the 1% significance level, we cannot conclude that not all $p_i(i = 1, 2, 3)$ equal their hypothesized values.

11.20 Let p_1 be the population proportion of employers who will "definitely hire," p_2 be the proportion who are "likely to hire," p_3 be the proportion with "hire uncertain," and p_4 be the proportion who "will not hire."

a. H_0: $p_1 = 0.37, p_2 = 0.17, p_3 = 0.28, p_4 = 0.18$

H_A: Not all $p_i(i = 1, 2, 3, 4)$ equal their hypothesized values

b. $\chi_{0.05,3}^2 = 7.815$; reject H_0 if $\chi_3^2 > 7.815$

c.

Responses	o_i	e_i	$o_i - e_i$	$(o_i - e_i)^2$	$(o_i - e_i)^2/e_i$
Definitely hire	170	185	−15	225	1.216
Likely to hire	100	85	15	225	2.647
Hire uncertain	120	140	−20	400	2.857
Will not hire	110	90	20	400	4.444
Total	500	500			11.16

$\chi_3^2 = 11.16$

d. Since $\chi_3^2 = 11.16 > 7.815$, we reject H_0. At the 5% significance level, we can conclude that the proportions from the initial study have changed.

11.22 Let $p_1, p_2,$ and p_3 represent the population proportion of tourists from Europe, North America, and the rest of the world, respectively.

a. H_0: $p_1 = p_2 = p_3 = 1/3$; H_A: Not all population proportions are equal to 1/3

b.

Region	o_i	e_i	$o_i - e_i$	$(o_i - e_i)^2$	$(o_i - e_i)^2/e_i$
Europe	135	126.67	8.333	69.444	0.548
North America	126	126.67	−0.667	0.444	0.004
Rest of the world	119	126.67	−7.667	58.778	0.464
Total	380	380.0			1.016

$\chi_2^2 = 1.02$; $\chi_{0.05,2}^2 = 5.991$; since $\chi_2^2 = 1.02 < 5.991 = \chi_{0.05,2}^2$, we do not reject H_0 at the 5% significance level. We cannot conclude that Zimbabwe visitors are not equally represented by Europe, North America, and the rest of the world. The visitor's claim is not supported by the sample data.

c. Given $\chi_2^2 = 1.02$, the *p*-value is greater than 0.10. Since the *p*-value > $0.05 = \alpha$, we do not reject H_0.

11.24 Let $p_1, p_2,$ and p_3 represent the population proportion of American drivers who favor U.S. cars, Asian cars, and other foreign cars, respectively.

H_0: $p_1 = 0.38, p_2 = 0.33, p_3 = 0.29$;

H_A: Not all $p_i(i = 1, 2, 3)$ equal their hypothesized values

Car Preference	o_i	e_i	$o_i - e_i$	$(o_i - e_i)^2$	$(o_i - e_i)^2/e_i$
American	66	76	−10	100	1.316
Asian	70	66	4	16	0.242
Other foreign	64	58	6	36	0.621
Total	200	200			2.179

$\chi_2^2 = 2.18$. The *p*-value is greater than 0.10. Since the *p*-value > $\alpha = 0.05$, we do not reject H_0. At the 5% significance level, the researcher cannot conclude that car preferences have changed since the Associated Press-GfK Poll.

11.26 a. $df = (5 - 1)(2 - 1) = 4$; $\chi_{0.025,4}^2 = 11.143$

b. $df = (3 - 1)(5 - 1) = 8$; $\chi_{0.01,8}^2 = 20.090$

11.28 H_0: The two variables are independent

H_A: The two variables are dependent

o_{ij}	e_{ij}	$o_{ij} - e_{ij}$	$(o_{ij} - e_{ij})^2$	$(o_{ij} - e_{ij})^2/e_{ij}$
120	115.65	4.35	18.933	0.164
112	108.36	3.64	13.240	0.122
100	104.56	−4.56	20.786	0.199
110	113.43	−3.43	11.771	0.104
127	127.16	−0.16	0.026	0.000
115	119.15	−4.15	17.209	0.144
120	114.97	5.03	25.324	0.220
124	124.72	−0.72	0.522	0.004
118	122.19	−4.19	17.556	0.144
115	114.49	0.51	0.260	0.002
110	110.47	−0.47	0.224	0.002
124	119.85	4.15	17.251	0.144
Total				1.25

$\chi_6^2 = 1.25$

a. The *p*-value is more than 0.95. Since the *p*-value > $0.01 = \alpha$, we do not reject H_0. At the 1% significance level, we cannot conclude that Variable 1 and Variable 2 are dependent.

b. $\chi_{0.01,6}^2 = 16.812$. Since $\chi_6^2 = 1.25 < 16.812$, we do not reject H_0.

11.30 a. H_0: Color preference is independent of gender

H_A: Color preference is dependent on gender

b. $\chi_{\alpha,df}^2 = \chi_{0.01,2}^2 = 9.210$. Reject H_0 if $\chi_2^2 > 9.210$.

c.

o_{ij}	e_{ij}	$o_{ij} - e_{ij}$	$(o_{ij} - e_{ij})^2$	$(o_{ij} - e_{ij})^2/e_{ij}$
470	465.84	4.16	17.318	0.037
280	284.16	−4.16	17.318	0.061
535	509.32	25.68	659.628	1.295
285	310.68	−25.68	659.628	2.123
495	524.84	−29.84	890.707	1.697
350	320.16	29.84	890.707	2.782
Total				8.00

$\chi_2^2 = 8.00$

d. Since $\chi_2^2 = 8.00 < 9.210 = \chi_{0.01,2}^2$, we do not reject H_0. At the 1% significance level, we cannot conclude that color preference is dependent on gender. Thus, there is no need for gender-targeted advertisement.

11.32 a. H_0: Optimism in China and age are independent

b. H_A: Optimism in China and age are dependent

o_{ij}	e_{ij}	$o_{ij} - e_{ij}$	$(o_{ij} - e_{ij})^2$	$(o_{ij} - e_{ij})^2/e_{ij}$
23	30.23	−7.23	52.201	1.727
50	43.23	6.78	45.901	1.062
18	17.55	0.45	0.202	0.012
51	34.88	16.13	260.016	7.456
38	49.88	−11.88	141.016	2.827
16	20.25	−4.25	18.063	0.892
19	27.90	−8.90	79.210	2.839
45	39.90	5.10	26.010	0.652
20	16.20	3.80	14.440	0.891
Total				18.36

$\chi_4^2 = 18.36$. We use the Excel function '=CHISQ.DIST.RT (18.36,4)' to find the p-value as 0.001.

c. Since the p-value is less than $\alpha(0.001 < 0.01)$, we reject H_0. At the 1% significance level, we can conclude that optimism among Chinese is dependent on age.

11.34 H_0: Breakup reasons and gender are independent

H_A: Breakup reasons and gender are dependent

o_{ij}	e_{ij}	$o_{ij} - e_{ij}$	$(o_{ij} - e_{ij})^2$	$(o_{ij} - e_{ij})^2/e_{ij}$
54	61.20	−7.20	51.840	0.847
48	40.80	7.20	51.840	1.271
378	342.00	36.00	1296.000	3.789
192	228.00	−36.00	1296.000	5.684
324	352.80	−28.80	829.440	2.351
264	235.20	28.80	829.440	3.527
504	489.60	14.40	207.360	0.424
312	326.40	−14.40	207.360	0.635
540	554.40	−14.40	207.360	0.374
384	369.60	14.40	207.360	0.561
Total				19.46

$\chi_4^2 = 19.46$; $\chi_{0.01,4}^2 = 13.277$. We reject H_0 since $\chi_4^2 = 19.46 > 13.277 = \chi_{0.01,4}^2$. At the 1% significance level, we conclude that breakup reason is dependent on gender.

11.36 Let p_1 represent the population proportion of young adults (18–24) with depression and p_2 the population proportion of older adults (65+) with depression.

a. $H_0: p_1 - p_2 \le 0$; $H_A: p_1 - p_2 > 0$

b. $\bar{p}_1 = 0.109$, $n_1 = 250$; $\bar{p}_2 = 0.068$, $n_2 = 200$;

$$\bar{p} = \frac{250(0.109) + 200(0.068)}{250 + 200} = 0.0908;$$

$$z = \frac{0.109 - 0.068}{\sqrt{0.0908(1 - 0.0908)\left(\frac{1}{250} + \frac{1}{200}\right)}} = 1.50.$$

The p-value $= 0.0668$.

c. Since the p-value $= 0.0668 > 0.05 = \alpha$, we do not reject H_0. The proportion of young adults suffering from depression is not significantly greater than that of older adults, at the 5% significance level.

11.38 a. $H_0: p_1 = 0.40, p_2 = 0.30, p_3 = 0.20, p_4 = 0.10$

H_A: Not all $p_i (i = 1, 2, 3, 4)$ equal their hypothesized values

b. $\chi_{0.01,3}^2 = 11.345$. Reject H_0 if $\chi_3^2 > 11.345$.

c.

Firm	o_i	e_i	$o_i - e_i$	$(o_i - e_i)^2$	$(o_i - e_i)^2/e_i$
1	200	220.00	−20.00	400.00	1.818
2	180	165.00	15.00	225.00	1.364
3	100	110.00	−10.00	100.00	0.909
4	70	55.00	15.00	225.00	4.091
Total	550	550.00			8.182

$\chi_3^2 = 8.182$

d. Since $\chi_3^2 = 8.18 < 11.345$, we do not reject H_0. At the 1% significance level we cannot conclude that at least one p_i is different from its hypothesized value. In other words, the market shares in 2011 have not changed from what they were in 2010.

11.40 a. $H_0: p_A = 0.60, p_B = 0.30, p_C = 0.10$

$H_A: p_A \ne 0.60$ or $p_B \ne 0.30$ or $p_C \ne 0.10$

b.

Candidate	o_i	e_i	$o_i - e_i$	$(o_i - e_i)^2$	$(o_i - e_i)^2/e_i$
A	350	300.00	50.00	2500.00	8.333
B	125	150.00	−25.00	625.00	4.167
C	25	50.00	−25.00	625.00	12.500
Total	500	500.00			25.000

$\chi_2^2 = 25.0$. The p-value $= P(\chi_2^2 \ge 25.0)$ is almost zero. Since the p-value $< 0.01 = \alpha$, we reject H_0. At the 1% significance level we conclude that not all population proportions equal their hypothesized values. This suggests that, contrary to the TV station's claim, voter preference has changed.

11.42 a. H_0: Surviving for discharge is independent of the time of the cardiac arrest

H_A: Surviving for discharge is dependent of the time of the cardiac arrest

b. $\chi_{0.01,1}^2 = 6.635$. Reject H_0 if $\chi_1^2 > 6.635$.

c.

o_{ij}	e_{ij}	$o_{ij} - e_{ij}$	$(o_{ij} - e_{ij})^2$	$(o_{ij} - e_{ij})^2/e_{ij}$
11,604	10,633.44	970.56	941,987.925	88.587
46,989	47,959.56	−970.56	941,987.925	19.641
4139	5109.56	−970.56	941,987.925	184.358
24,016	23,045.44	970.56	941,987.925	40.875
Total				333.46

$\chi_1^2 = 333.46$.

d. Since $\chi_1^2 = 333.46 > 6.635$, we reject H_0. At the 1% significance level, the sample data suggest that a patient's surviving a cardiac arrest is dependent on the time that it happens. Given that patients do not have control over the timing of cardiac arrest, hospitals need to put in place resources that ensure that patients have equal chances of surviving a cardiac arrest, regardless of when it happens.

11.44 H_0: Effect on ADHD is independent of the treatment

H_A: Effect on ADHD is dependent on the treatment

o_{ij}	e_{ij}	$o_{ij} - e_{ij}$	$(o_{ij} - e_{ij})^2$	$(o_{ij} - e_{ij})^2/e_{ij}$
12	13	−1	1	0.077
15	14	1	1	0.071
14	13	1	1	0.077
13	14	−1	1	0.071
Total				0.297

$\chi_1^2 = 0.297$; $\chi_{0.05,1}^2 = 3.841$. Since $\chi_1^2 = 0.297 < 3.841 = \chi_{0.05,1}^2$, we do not reject H_0. At the 5% significance level, we cannot conclude that the effect of ADHD depends on the treatment by St. John's wort.

11.46 H_0: A household's delinquency in payment is independent of the type of heating

H_A: A household's delinquency in payment is dependent on the type of heating

o_{ij}	e_{ij}	$o_{ij} - e_{ij}$	$(o_{ij} - e_{ij})^2$	$(o_{ij} - e_{ij})^2/e_{ij}$
50	55.10	−5.10	26.010	0.472
20	28.50	−8.50	72.250	2.535
15	6.65	8.35	69.723	10.485
10	4.75	5.25	27.563	5.803
240	234.90	5.10	26.010	0.111
130	121.50	8.50	72.250	0.595
20	28.35	−8.35	69.723	2.459
15	20.25	−5.25	27.563	1.361
Total				23.820

$\chi_3^2 = 23.82$; $\chi_{0.05,3}^2 = 7.815$. Since $\chi_3^2 = 23.82 > 7.815 = \chi_{0.05,3}^2$, we reject H_0. At the 5% significance level, we conclude that the type of heating that a household uses is dependent on whether or not the household is delinquent on its bill payment.

Chapter 12

12.2 a. $b_1 = \dfrac{\Sigma(x - \bar{x})(y - \bar{y})}{\Sigma(x - \bar{x})^2} = \dfrac{-866}{711} = -1.22$

b. $b_0 = \bar{y} - b_1\bar{x} = 56 - (-1.22)(-25) = 25.50$

c. $\hat{y} = 25.50 - 1.22x$; if $x = -20$, $\hat{y} = 25.50 - 1.22(-20) = 49.90$

12.4 a. As x increases by 1 unit, the predicted y decreases by 17 units.

b. $\hat{y} = 436 - 17(-15) = 691$

12.6 a.

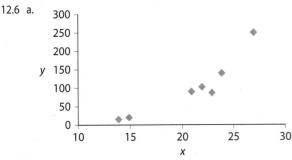

There appears to be a positive relationship between x and y, so estimating a simple linear regression model is appropriate.

b. $b_1 = \dfrac{\Sigma(x - \bar{x})(y - \bar{y})}{\Sigma(x - \bar{x})^2} = \dfrac{2577}{176} = 14.64$

$b_0 = \bar{y} - b_1\bar{x} = 89.375 - (14.64)(20) = -203.43$

The sample regression equation is $\hat{y} = -203.43 + 14.64x$

c. If $x = 15$, $\hat{y} = -203.43 + 14.64(15) = 16.17$

If $x = 20$, $\hat{y} = -203.43 + 14.64(20) = 89.37$

If $x = 25$, $\hat{y} = -203.43 + 14.64(25) = 162.57$

12.8 a. As x increases by 1 unit, the predicted y decreases by 0.16 unit.

b. $\hat{y} = 2.25 - 0.16x$

c. If $x = 2$, $\hat{y} = 2.25 - 0.16(2) = 1.93$

If $x = -2$, $\hat{y} = 2.25 - 0.16(-2) = 2.57$

12.10 a. $b_1 = \dfrac{\Sigma(x - \bar{x})(y - \bar{y})}{\Sigma(x - \bar{x})^2} = \dfrac{394}{42} = 9.38$

$b_0 = \bar{y} - b_1\bar{x} = 60.375 - (9.38)(4) = 22.85$

The sample regression equation is $\widehat{Salary} = 22.85 + 9.38$ Education.

b. As Education increases by 1 unit (1 additional year of higher education), an individual's predicted annual salary (measured in thousands of dollars) increases by 9.38, or by $9,380.

c. $\widehat{Salary} = 22.85 + 9.38(7) = 88.51$, or $88,510

12.12 a. The estimate of β_1 is $b_1 = 0.42$, which is positive. Thus, the sign of the slope is as expected. As x increases by 1 unit, the predicted y increases by 0.42 unit.

b. $\hat{y} = -7.42 + 0.42x$

c. If $x = 50$, $\hat{y} = -7.42 + 0.42(50) = 13.58$

12.14 a. $\widehat{Salary} = 18.43 - 3.82$ ERA; for a one-unit increase in ERA, predicted salary decreases by $3.82 million

b and c.

	Predicted Salary $\hat{y}$	Actual Salary y	Residual $e = y - \hat{y}$
J. Santana	8.76	17.0	8.24
C. Lee	8.73	4.0	−4.73
T. Lincecum	8.42	0.4	−8.02
C. Sabathia	8.12	11.0	2.88
R. Halladay	7.81	10.0	2.19
J. Peavy	7.54	6.5	−1.04
D. Matsuzaka	7.35	8.3	0.95
R. Dempster	7.12	7.3	0.18
B. Sheets	6.63	12.1	5.48
C. Hamels	6.63	0.5	−6.12

There might be factors other than ERA that contribute to the pitchers' salaries. This model only considers ERA and, given high residuals, is not a very good model for predicting salary.

12.16 a. The estimated model is $\widehat{Final} = 27.58 + 0.68$ Midterm.

b. If Midterm = 80, then $\widehat{Final} = 27.58 + 0.68(80) = 81.98$.

12.18 a. If $x_1 = 20$ and $x_2 = 35$, $\hat{y} = 152 + 12.9(20) + 2.7(35) = 504.5$

b. As x_1 increases by one unit, the predicted y increases by 12.9 units, holding x_2 constant.

12.20 a. $b_1 = 30$; as x_1 increases by 1 unit, the predicted y increases by 30 units, holding x_2 constant.

b. $\hat{y} = 21.97 + 30x_1 - 1.88x_2$

c. If $x_1 = 30$ and $x_2 = 20$, $\hat{y} = 21.97 + 30(30) - 1.88(20) = 884.37$

12.22 a. 4.85

b. $\hat{y} = 40.55 + 0.25$ Math $+ 4.85$ Hours

c. If Math $= 70$ and Hours $= 4$, $\hat{y} = 40.55 + 0.25(70) + 4.85(4) = 77.45$

12.24 a. $\widehat{\text{Sales}} = 10.35 + 8.47$ Population $+ 7.62$ Income

b. The slope coefficient of 8.47 suggests that as the number of women over the age of 60 increases by 1 million, the predicted sales of StrongBones increase by $8.47 million, holding Income constant. Similarly, the slope coefficient of 7.62 suggests that as the average income of women over the age of 60 increases by $1,000, the predicted sales of StrongBones increase by $7.62 million, holding Population constant.

c. If Population $= 1.5$ and Income $= 44$, then $\widehat{\text{Sales}} = 10.35 + 8.47(1.5) + 7.62(44) = 358.34$ ($ million)

12.26 a. $\widehat{\text{Price}} = 153,348.27 + 95.86$ Sqft $+ 556.89$ Beds $+ 92,022.91$ Baths

b. The slope coefficient of 95.86 suggests that for every additional square foot, the predicted price of a home increases by $95.86, holding number of bedrooms and bathrooms constant. The slope coefficient of 556.89 suggests that for every additional bedroom, the predicted price of a home increases by $556.89, holding square footage and number of baths constant. The slope coefficient of 92,022.91 suggests that for every additional bathroom, the predicted price of a home increases by 92,022.91, holding square footage and number of bedrooms constant.

c. If Sqft $= 2500$, Beds $= 3$, and Baths $= 2$, then $\widehat{\text{Price}} = 153,348.27 + 95.86(2500) + 556.89(3) + 92,022.91(2) = $578,714.76$

12.28 a. $\widehat{\text{Salary}} = 32.79 - 0.83$ PCT $+ 0.79$ TD $+ 0.39$ Age

b. Yes, the estimated coefficient of -0.83 is surprising. This coefficient suggests that as a quarterback's pass completion percentage increases by 1 percent, his predicted salary decreases by $0.83 million holding other variables constant.

c. $\widehat{\text{Salary}} = 32.79 - 0.83(70.6) + 0.79(34) + 0.39(30) = 12.75$

d. $\widehat{\text{Salary}} = 32.79 - 0.83(65.7) + 0.79(28) + 0.39(32) = 12.86$

e. Drew Brees' residual is $12.9895 - 12.75 = 0.2395$; Tom Brady's residual is $8.0073 - 12.86 = -4.8527$. The estimated model implies that Drew Brees is slightly overpaid whereas Tom Brady is grossly underpaid. Perhaps there are other important factors impacting salary that were not included in the model.

12.30 a. $\widehat{\text{Rent}} = 300.41 + 225.81$ Bed $+ 89.27$ Bath $+ 0.21$ Sqft

b. The slope coefficient of Bath is 89.27, which suggests that for every additional bathroom, the predicted rent increases by $89.27, holding number of bedrooms and square feet constant.

c. $\widehat{\text{Rent}} = 300.41 + 225.81(2) + 89.27(1) + 0.21(1500) = 1,156.3$

12.32 a. $s_e^2 = \dfrac{SSE}{n - k - 1} = \dfrac{2540}{30 - 1 - 1} = 90.71$;

$s_e = \sqrt{90.71} = 9.52$

b. $R^2 = 1 - \dfrac{2540}{13,870} = 0.8169$

12.34 a. $s_e = \sqrt{\dfrac{SSE}{n - k - 1}} = \sqrt{\dfrac{2.87}{100 - 4 - 1}} = \sqrt{0.03} = 0.17$

b. $R^2 = 1 - \dfrac{SSE}{SST} = 1 - \dfrac{2.87}{7.62} = 0.6234$.

c. Adjusted $R^2 = 1 - (1 - R^2)\left(\dfrac{n - 1}{n - k - 1}\right) =$

$1 - (1 - 0.6234)\left(\dfrac{100 - 1}{100 - 4 - 1}\right) = 0.6075$

12.36 a. $s_e = \sqrt{MSE} = \sqrt{0.42} = 0.65$

b. $R^2 = \dfrac{SSR}{SST} = \dfrac{75.92}{87.81} = 0.8646$; 86.46% of the sample variation in y is explained by the estimated regression model.

12.38 a. $s_e = \sqrt{s_e^2} = \sqrt{MSE} = \sqrt{2,673.96} = 51.71$

b. $R^2 = \dfrac{SSR}{SST} = \dfrac{188,246.8}{233,704.1} = 0.8055$; 80.55% of the sample variation in y is explained by the estimated regression model.

c. From the ANOVA table we get $k = 2$ and $n = 19 + 1 = 20$. Thus, adjusted $R^2 = 1 - (1 - R^2)\left(\dfrac{n - 1}{n - k - 1}\right) =$

$1 - (1 - 0.8055)\left(\dfrac{20 - 1}{20 - 2 - 1}\right) = 0.7826$.

12.40 a. $R^2 = \dfrac{SSR}{SST} = \dfrac{199.93}{240.92} = 0.8299$; 82.99% of the variability in sales is explained by advertising expenditures.

b. $1 - R^2 = 1 - 0.8299 = 0.1701$; 17.01% of the variability in sales is unexplained by advertising expenditures.

12.42 a. $s_e = \sqrt{MSE} = \sqrt{110,070.1} = 331.77$

b. The proportion that is explained is $R^2 = \dfrac{SSR}{SST} = \dfrac{3,549,788}{7,732,451} = 0.4591$. The proportion that is unexplained is $1 - R^2 = 1 - 0.4591 = 0.5409$.

12.44 a. The sample regression equation is $\widehat{\text{Final}} = 27.5818 + 0.6774$ Midterm.

b. $s_e = 14.95$

c. $R^2 = 0.3045$; 30.45% of the sample variation in Final grades is explained by the sample regression equation.

12.46 This table reports the regression results from each model:

Variable	Model 1	Model 2	Model 3
Intercept	−79.0342	151.0092	−30.6198
Yards made	0.3860	NA	0.3501
Yards allowed	NA	−0.3003	−0.1085
s_e	13.0472	18.0975	12.8867
R^2	0.5931	0.2171	0.6163
Adjusted R^2	0.5795	0.1910	0.5898

Notes: Parameter estimates are in the top half of the table. The lower part of the table contains goodness-of-fit measures.

a. Model 1 has a lower standard error of the estimate and a higher R^2; thus, Model 1 appears to be the better model for prediction.

b. Since the number of explanatory variables, k, is not the same between Model 3 and Models 1 and 2, we must use adjusted R^2 to compare these models. Model 3 has an adjusted R^2 of 0.5898, compared to 0.5795 and 0.1910 for Model 1 and Model 2, respectively. Therefore, with the highest adjusted R^2, Model 3 is an improvement over the other two models. Model 3 also has the lowest standard error.

12.48 a. $t_{28} = \dfrac{b_1 - \beta_{10}}{se(b_1)} = \dfrac{3.25 - 0}{1.36} = 2.39$

b. With $df = 28$, the p-value for the two-tailed test is $2P(T_{28} \geq 2.39)$. Therefore, $2(0.01) < p\text{-value} < 2(0.025)$, that is, $0.02 < p\text{-value} < 0.05$.

c. Since the p-value $< \alpha = 0.05$, we reject. H_0. At the 5% significance level, we can conclude that the explanatory variable is significant.

12.50 a. $t_{\alpha,df} = t_{0.05,28} = 1.701$. Since it is a left-tailed test, the critical value is -1.701; thus, reject H_0 if $t_{28} < -1.701$.

b. $t_{28} = \dfrac{b_1 - \beta_{10}}{se(b_1)} = \dfrac{7.2 - 10}{1.8} = -1.56$

c. Since $-1.56 > -1.701$, we do not reject H_0. At the 5% significance level, we cannot conclude that β_1 is less than 10.

12.52 a. $H_0: \beta_1 = -1$

   $H_A: \beta_1 \neq -1$

b. $t_{0.025,38} = 2.024$. For a two-tailed test the critical values are 2.024 and -2.024. The decision rule is to reject H_0 if $t_{38} > 2.024$ or $t_{38} < -2.024$.

c. $t_{38} = \dfrac{b_1 - \beta_{10}}{se(b_1)} = \dfrac{0.9178 - (-1)}{0.9350} = 2.05$

d. Since $2.05 > 2.024$, we reject H_0. At the 5% significance level, we can conclude that the slope differs from -1.

12.54 a. Here $k = 2$ and $n = 20$; the degrees of freedom for total sum of squares equals $df = n - 1 = 19$.

b. $H_0: \beta_1 = \beta_2 = 0$

   $H_A:$ At least one $\beta_j \neq 0$

c. $F_{(2,17)} = \dfrac{MSR}{MSE} = \dfrac{11,008.38}{2310.996} = 4.76$

d. Since the p-value $= 0.0228 < 0.05 = \alpha$, we reject H_0. At the 5% significance level, the explanatory variables are jointly significant in explaining y.

12.56 a. $H_0: \beta_1 \leq 0$

   $H_A: \beta_1 > 0$

b. $t_{18} = \dfrac{b_1 - \beta_{10}}{se(b_1)} = \dfrac{0.42 - 0}{0.05} = 8.40$. The p-value for this one-tailed test is $3.63 \times 10^{-8} \approx 0$.

c. Since the p-value $< \alpha = 0.05$, we reject H_0. At the 5% significance level, we can conclude that advertising expenditures and sales have a positive linear relationship.

12.58 $H_0: \beta_1 = 0$

   $H_A: \beta_1 \neq 0$

Since the reported p-value $= 0.0067 < 0.05 = \alpha$, we reject H_0. At the 5% significance level, the economist's claim that changes in short-term rates are significant in explaining long-term rates is supported.

12.60 a. $\widehat{Return} = -12.0243 + 0.1459\,(P/E) + 5.4417\,(P/S)$

b. $H_0: \beta_1 = \beta_2 = 0$

   $H_A:$ At least one $\beta_j \neq 0$

   $F_{(2,27)} = \dfrac{MSR}{MSE} = \dfrac{459.3728}{163.0661} = 2.8171$

   Since the p-value $= 0.0774 < 0.10 = \alpha$, we reject H_0. At the 10% significance level, the two explanatory variables are jointly significant.

c. For the first explanatory variable, P/E, the hypotheses are

   $H_0: \beta_1 = 0$

   $H_A: \beta_1 \neq 0$

   The test statistic value and its p-value are 0.1459 and 0.7383, respectively. Thus, since the p-value is greater than $\alpha = 0.10$, we do not reject H_0. At the 10% significance level, we cannot conclude that P/E is significant in explaining Return.

   For the second explanatory variable, P/S, we state the hypotheses as

   $H_0: \beta_2 = 0$

$H_A: \beta_2 \neq 0$

   The reported p-value associated with P/S is equal to 0.0250. Thus, since the p-value is less than $\alpha = 0.10$, we reject H_0. At the 10% significance level, we can conclude that P/S is significant in explaining Return.

12.62 The sample regression equation is $\widehat{Final} = 27.5818 + 0.6774$ Midterm .

   $H_0: \beta_1 = 0$ and $H_A: \beta_1 \neq 0$

   Since the p-value $= 2P(T_{30} \geq 3.62) = 0.0011 < 0.01 = \alpha$, we reject H_0. At the 1% significance level, a student's midterm grade is significant in explaining a student's final grade.

12.64 a. The sample regression equation is $\widehat{R - R_f} = 1.5804 + 1.7584(R_M - R_f)$. A portion of the regression results is shown in the accompanying table.

	Coefficients	Standard Error	t Stat	p-Value
Intercept	1.5804	0.9296	1.7002	0.0945
$R_M - R_f$	1.7584	0.1843	9.5412	0.0000

b. $H_0: \beta \leq 1$

   $H_A: \beta > 1$

   $t_{58} = \dfrac{b - \beta_0}{se(b)} = \dfrac{1.7584 - 1}{0.1843} = 4.1150;$

   $t_{0.05,58} = 1.672$. Since $t_{58} = 4.1150 > 1.672 = t_{0.05,58}$, we reject H_0. At the 5% significance level, we conclude that investment in Caterpillar is riskier than the market.

c. $H_0: \alpha = 0$

   $H_A: \alpha \neq 0$

   Since $0.0945 > 0.05$, we do not reject H_0. Thus, at the 5% significance level, we cannot conclude that there are abnormal returns.

12.66 a. The sample regression equation is $\widehat{Final} = 40.55 + 0.25$ Math $+ 4.85$ Hours.

b. $H_0: \beta_1 = \beta_2 = 0$

   $H_A:$ At least one $\beta_j \neq 0$

   $F_{(2,57)} = 55.019$

   Since the p-value $= P(F_{(2,57)} \geq 55.019) \approx 0 < 0.05 = \alpha$, we reject H_0. At the 5% significance level, the explanatory variables are jointly significant.

c. The hypotheses for each test of individual significance would be

   $H_0: \beta_j = 0$ and $H_A: \beta_j \neq 0$

   For Math, the p-value $= 2P(T_{57} \geq 6.06) \approx 0 < 0.05 = \alpha$; thus, we reject H_0. Math score has a significant influence on Final score at the 5% significance level.

   For Hours, the p-value $= 2P(T_{57} \geq 8.53) \approx 0 < 0.05 = \alpha$; thus, we reject H_0. Number of hours studied per week has a significant influence on Final score at the 5% significance level.

12.68 a. The sample regression equation is $\widehat{Happiness} = 56.18 + 0.28$ Age.

b. When Age $= 45$, $\widehat{Happiness} = 56.18 + 0.28(45) = 68.78$.

c. $R^2 = 0.3267$. This means that 32.67% of the sample variation in Happiness is explained by the estimated model.

d. $H_0: \beta_1 = 0$

   $H_A: \beta_1 \neq 0$

   For Age, the p-value $= 2P(T_{22} \geq 2.27) = 0.0035 < 0.01 = \alpha$; thus, we reject H_0. Age has a significant influence on Happiness at the 1% significance level.

12.70 a. The sample regression equation is $\widehat{\text{Ownership}} = 78.9791 - 0.0002\text{Income}$. For a \$1,000 increase in income, the predicted homeownership rate decreases by 2%. This negative relationship is surprising. Note, however, that this model ignores home affordability. For example, homes are very affordable in Alabama and as a result their homeownership rate is 74.1% despite a low median household income of \$39,980. By contrast, California has only a 57% homeownership rate even though its median household income is \$56,134.

b. $s_e = 5.77$

c. $R^2 = 0.0618$; 6.18% of the sample variation in y is explained by the sample regression equation.

12.72 a. The sample regression equation is $\widehat{\text{Return}} = -33.40 + 3.97(\text{P/E}) - 3.37(\text{P/S})$. The signs are as expected. Holding the other variable constant, as P/E increases, the predicted returns increase, and as P/S increases, the predicted returns decrease.

b. As the P/S ratio increases by 1 unit, the predicted return of the firm decreases by 3.37%, holding P/E constant.

c. $\widehat{\text{Return}} = -33.40 + 3.97(10) - 3.37(2) = -0.44\%$

d. $s_e = 13.64$

e. $R^2 = 0.4028$; 40.28% of the sample variation in y is explained by the sample regression equation.

f. $H_0: \beta_1 = \beta_2 = 0$

H_A: At least one $\beta_j \neq 0$

$F_{(2,27)} = 9.10$ and the p-value $= P(F_{(2,27)} \geq 9.10) \approx 0 < 0.05 = \alpha$. Thus, we reject H_0. At the 5% significance level, the explanatory variables are jointly significant.

g. The hypotheses for each test of individual significance would be

$H_0: \beta_j = 0$

$H_A: \beta_j \neq 0$

For P/E, the p-value $= 2P(T_{27} \geq 4.14) = 0.0003 < 0.05 = \alpha$; thus, we reject H_0. The P/E ratio has a significant influence on the expected returns at the 5% level.

For P/S, the p-value $= 2P(T_{27} \leq -1.28) = 0.2111 > 0.05 = \alpha$; thus, we do not reject H_0. We cannot conclude that the P/S ratio has a significant influence on the expected returns at the 5% level.

12.74 a. $\widehat{\text{Startups}} = 0.4190 + 0.0087 \text{ Research} + 0.0517 \text{ Patents} - 0.0194 \text{ Duration}$

b. $\widehat{\text{Startups}} = 0.4190 + 0.0087(120) + 0.0517(8) - 0.0194(20) = 1.49$ startups

c. A \$1 million increase in research expenditure results in a predicted increase in the number of startups by 0.0087, holding everything else constant. Thus, approximately $\$114.94 \text{ million} \left(\frac{1}{0.0087} = 114.94 \right)$ in additional research expenditures would be needed to have 1 additional predicted startup, everything else being the same.

12.76 a. The sample regression equation is $\widehat{\text{Rent}} = 300.41 + 225.81 \text{ Bed} + 89.27 \text{ Bath} + 0.21 \text{ Sqft}$.

b. $R^2 = 0.8091$; 80.91% of the sample variation in Rent is explained by the sample regression equation; 19.09% of the sample variation in Rent is unexplained by the sample regression equation.

c. $H_0: \beta_1 = \beta_2 = \beta_3 = 0$

H_A: At least one $\beta_j \neq 0$

$F_{(3,36)} = 50.88$ and the p-value $= P(F_{(3,36)} \geq 50.88) \approx 0 < 0.05 = \alpha$; thus, we reject H_0. At the 5% level, the explanatory variables are jointly significant.

d. The hypotheses for each test of individual significance would be

$H_0: \beta_j = 0$

$H_A: \beta_j \neq 0$

For Bed, the p-value $= 2P(T_{36} \geq 3.74) = 0.0006 < 0.05 = \alpha$; thus, we reject H_0. The number of bedrooms has a significant influence on Rent at the 5% level. For Bath, the p-value $= 2P(T_{36} \geq 1.60) = 0.1195 > 0.05 = \alpha$; thus, we do not reject H_0. The number of bathrooms does not have a significant influence on Rent at the 5% level. For Sqft, the p-value $= 2P(T_{36} \geq 2.30) = 0.0276 < 0.05 = \alpha$; thus, we reject H_0. The square footage has a significant influence on Rent at the 5% level.

Chapter 13

13.2 a. $\hat{y} = 160 + 15(1) + 32(1) = 207$

b. $\hat{y} = 160 + 15(0) + 32(0) = 160$

13.4 a. The reference group for Model 1 is the employees who are female.

b. The reference group for Model 2 is the employees who are female and without an MBA.

c. The inference would not change if we set $d_1 = 1$ for female employees.

13.6 a. For an urban family with income of \$80,000,

$\widehat{\text{Expenditure}} = 13,007.26 + 0.44(80,000) + 6544.43(1) = 55,102.09$.

For a rural family with income of \$80,000,

$\widehat{\text{Expenditure}} = 13,007.26 + 0.44(80,000) + 6544.43(0) = 48,557.66$.

b. For an urban family with income of \$80,000,

$\widehat{\text{Expenditure}} = 19,551.68 + 0.44(80,000) - 6544.43(0) = 55,102.09$.

For a rural family with income of \$80,000,

$\widehat{\text{Expenditure}} = 19,551.68 + 0.44(80,000) - 6544.43(1) = 48,557.66$.

c. The two models produce the same results because it does not matter how we assign 0 and 1 to two categories of a qualitative variable.

13.8 a. The sample regression equation is $\widehat{\text{Salary}} = 62.34 - 0.96 \text{ BMI} + 4.49 \text{ White}$. Using the hypotheses $H_0: \beta_1 = 0$, $H_A: \beta_1 \neq 0$, the p-value $= 2P(T_{27} \leq -7.60) \approx 0 < 0.05 = \alpha$. Therefore, we reject H_0 and conclude that BMI influences salary significantly at the 5% level.

b. For a white college-educated worker with BMI $= 30$, $\widehat{\text{Salary}} = 62.34 - 0.96(30) + 4.49(1) = 38.01$.

c. For a nonwhite college-educated worker with BMI $= 30$, $\widehat{\text{Salary}} = 62.34 - 0.96(30) + 4.49(0) = 33.52$.

13.10 a. The average lifespan for players with nicknames is 68.05 years. Without nicknames, the average lifespan is 64.08 years. The difference in lifespan for players with and without nicknames is $68.05 - 64.08 = 3.97$.

b. For the players with a nickname, $\widehat{\text{Years}} = 64.08 + 3.97(1) = 68.05$. For the players without a nickname, $\widehat{\text{Years}} = 64.08 + 3.97(0) = 64.08$. Thus, the difference $68.05 - 64.08 = 3.97$ is the same as in part a.

c. The hypotheses are

$H_0: \beta_1 \leq 0$

$H_A: \beta_1 > 0$

For this one-tailed test, the p-value $= P(T_{27} \geq 1.71) = 0.0989/2 = 0.0494$. Since $0.0494 < 0.05 = \alpha$, we reject H_0. At the 5% significance level, we conclude that players with a nickname do live longer than players without a nickname.

13.12 a. $\widehat{\text{Math}} = 274.12 + 98.71\text{GPA} - 21.10\text{Gender}$. For a male student with a GPA of 3.5, $\widehat{\text{Math}} = 274.12 + 98.71(3.5) - 21.10(0) = 619.60$. For a female student with a GPA of 3.5, $\widehat{\text{Math}} = 274.12 + 98.71(3.5) - 21.10(1) = 598.50$.

b. For the hypotheses $H_0: \beta_2 = 0$, $H_A: \beta_2 \neq 0$, the p-value $= 2P(T_{17} \leq -1.999) = 0.0618 > 0.05 = \alpha$, so we do not reject H_0. Therefore, we cannot conclude that there is a statistically significant gender difference in math scores at the 5% level.

13.14 a. $\widehat{\text{Wage}} = 8.68 + 1.23\text{ EDUC} + 0.42\text{ EXPER} - 0.02\text{ AGE} + 2.29\text{ GENDER}$

b. For a 40-year-old male with 10 years of education and 5 years of experience, $\widehat{\text{Wage}} = 8.68 + 1.23(10) + 0.42(5) - 0.02(40) + 2.29(1) = \$24.57/\text{hour}$.
For a female with the same qualifications, $\widehat{\text{Wage}} = 8.68 + 1.23(10) + 0.42(5) - 0.02(40) + 2.29(0) = \$22.28/\text{hour}$.

c. The coefficient of 2.29 for GENDER suggests that for the same age, years of education, and experience, males earn \$2.29 per hour more than females. However, for the hypotheses $H_0: \beta_4 \leq 0$, $H_A: \beta_4 > 0$, the p-value $= P(T_{45} \geq 1.37) = 0.1787/2 > 0.05 = \alpha$, so we cannot reject H_0. It means that at the 5% significance level we cannot conclude that gender discrimination exists at the firm.

13.16 a. $\widehat{\text{Comp}} = 8.09 + 0.000028\text{ Assets} + 1.49d_1 + 2.01d_2 - 0.57d_3$

b. The coefficient 0.000028 of Assets suggests that in any industry, for a 1% increase in assets, the predicted compensation increases by about 0.0028%. The coefficient 1.49 of d_1 suggests that compensation in Manufacturing Technology is predicted to be about 149% ($= 1.49 \times 100\%$) higher than that of Nonfinancial Services, holding total assets the same. The coefficient 2.01 of d_2 suggests that compensation in Manufacturing Other is predicted to be about 201% ($= 2.01 \times 100\%$) higher than that of Nonfinancial Services, holding total assets the same. The coefficient -0.57 of d_3 suggests that compensation for Financial Services is predicted to be about 57% ($= 0.57 \times 100\%$) lower than that of Nonfinancial Services, holding total assets the same.

c. Since the p-values corresponding to d_1, d_2, and d_3 are greater than 0.05, we conclude at the 5% level that executive compensation in Manufacturing Technology, Manufacturing Other, and Financial Services firms is not significantly different from that in Nonfinancial Services firms.

d. Replace d_1 with d_4 and the relevant regression results for Compensation $= \beta_0 + \beta_1\text{ Assets} + \beta_2 d_2 + \beta_3 d_3 + \beta_4 d_4 + \varepsilon$ are

	Coefficients	Standard Error	t Stat	p-Value
Intercept	9.579574	0.861431	11.12054	1.51E-25
Assets	2.83E-05	3.02E-06	9.364637	3.68E-19
d_2	0.523026	1.084728	0.482172	0.629918
d_3	-2.05893	1.232231	-1.6709	0.095437
d_4	-1.49089	1.542738	-0.96639	0.334368

For the hypotheses $H_0: \beta_2 \leq 0$, and $H_A: \beta_2 > 0$, the p-value $\approx 0.6300/2 = 0.315 > 0.05 = \alpha$, so we cannot conclude, at the 5% level, that executive compensation in Manufacturing Other is significantly higher than in Manufacturing Technology.

13.18 a. $t_{0.025,37} = 2.026$; $\hat{y}^0 = 12.8 + 2.6(15) - 1.2(6) = 44.6$. The 95% confidence interval is $44.6 \pm 2.026(2.20) = 44.6 \pm 4.4572$. Or, with 95% confidence, $40.14 \leq E(y^0) \leq 49.06$.

b. $44.6 \pm 2.026\sqrt{2.20^2 + 5.84^2} = 44.6 \pm 12.6435$. Or, with 95% confidence, $31.96 \leq y^0 \leq 57.24$.

c. The confidence interval is narrower because it assumes that the expected value of the error term is zero, whereas the prediction interval incorporates the nonzero error term.

13.20 a. The estimated regression equation is $\hat{y} = 22.81 + 0.85x_1 - 0.71x_2$.

b. The relevant portion of the regression output with y as the response variable and $x_1^* = x_1 - 50$ and $x_2^* = x_2 - 20$ as the explanatory variables is

Regression Statistics	
Multiple R	0.9291
R Square	0.8632
Adjusted R Square	0.8085
Standard Error	**4.6868**
Observations	8

	Coefficients	Standard Error	t Stat	p-Value	Lower 95%	Upper 95%
Intercept	**51.0041**	**2.1821**	23.3742	0.0000	**45.3949**	**56.6133**
x_1^*	0.8460	0.1523	5.5546	0.0026	0.4545	1.2376
x_2^*	-0.7053	0.2451	-2.8773	0.0347	-1.3353	-0.0752

Therefore, $\hat{y}^0 = 51.0041$ and $se(\hat{y}^0) = 2.1821$.
$t_{0.025,5} = 2.571$. The 95% confidence interval is $51.0041 \pm 2.571(2.1821) = 51.0041 \pm 5.6102$. Or, with 95% confidence, $45.39 \leq E(y^0) \leq 56.61$.

c. The 95% prediction interval is $51.0041 \pm 2.571\sqrt{2.1821^2 + 4.6868^2} = 51.0041 \pm 13.2918$. Or, with 95% confidence, $37.71 \leq y^0 \leq 64.30$.

13.22 a. The relevant portion of the regression output with y as the response variable, $x^* = x - 710$ as the explanatory variable, and the 90% confidence level is

Regression Statistics	
Multiple R	0.5871
R Square	0.3446
Adjusted R Square	0.2354
Standard Error	**0.2685**
Observations	8

	Coefficients	Standard Error	t Stat	p-Value	Lower 90%	Upper 90%
Intercept	**3.3617**	**0.0973**	34.5353	0.0000	**3.1726**	**3.5509**
x^*	0.0044	0.0025	1.7763	0.1260	-0.0004	0.0092

$t_{0.05,6} = 1.943$. The 90% confidence interval is $3.3617 \pm 1.943(0.0973) = 3.3617 \pm 0.1891$. Or, with 90% confidence, $3.17 \leq E(y^0) \leq 3.55$.

b. The 90% prediction interval is $3.3617 \pm$
$1.943\sqrt{0.0973^2 + 0.2685^2} = 3.3617 \pm 0.5549$.
Or, with 90% confidence, $2.81 \leq y^0 \leq 3.92$.

13.24 Using y for Price and x_1, x_2, and x_3 for Sqft, Beds, and Baths, respectively, the estimated model is: $\hat{y} = 153348.27 + 95.86x_1 + 556.89x_2 + 92022.91x_3$. The relevant portion of the regression output with y as the response variable and $x_1^* = x_1 - 2500$, $x_2^* = x_2 - 3$, and $x_3^* = x_3 - 2$ as the explanatory variables is

Regression Statistics	
Multiple R	0.8507
R Square	0.7237
Adjusted R Square	0.6978
Standard Error	**74984.9842**
Observations	36

	Coefficients	Standard Error	t Stat	p-Value	Lower 95%	Upper 95%
Intercept	578704.6200	24653.7674	23.4733	0.0000	528486.5392	628922.7008
x_1^*	95.8559	35.3997	2.7078	0.0108	23.7490	167.9629
x_2^*	556.8907	20280.3128	0.0275	0.9783	−40752.7546	41866.5360
x_3^*	92022.9126	25012.2976	3.6791	0.0009	41074.5297	142971.2955

$t_{0.025,32} = 2.037$; the 95% confidence interval is $578,704.62 \pm 2.037(24,653.7674) = 578,704.62 \pm 50,219.72$. Or, with 95% confidence, $528,484.90 \leq E(y^0) \leq 628,924.34$. The 95% prediction interval is $578,704.62 \pm 2.037$ $\sqrt{24,653.7674^2 + 74,984.9842^2} = 578,704.62 \pm 160,788.2967$. Or, with 95% confidence, $417,916.32 \leq y^0 \leq 739,492.92$.

Given a 2500-square-foot house with 3 bedrooms and 2 bathrooms, we have 95% confidence that the *average* price will be between $528,484.90 and $628,924.34. Also, given a 2500-square-foot house with 3 bedrooms and 2 bathrooms, we have 95% confidence that the *individual* price will be between $417,916.32 and $739,492.92.

13.26 a. Using y for Consumption and x_1 and x_2 for Income and the dummy variable Urban, respectively, the estimated model is: $\hat{y} = 13007.26 + 0.44x_1 + 6544.43x_2$. The relevant portion of the regression output with y as the response variable, $x_1^* = x_1 - 80,000$ and $x_2^* = x_2 - 1$ as the explanatory variables, and the assumed 99% confidence level is

	Coefficients	Standard Error	t Stat	p-Value	Lower 99.0%	Upper 99.0%
Intercept	55102.05	2128.574	25.88683	1.84E-29	49387.78	60816.33
x_1^*	0.44438	0.085772	5.180936	4.55E-06	0.21412	0.67464
x_2^*	6544.426	3551.267	1.842843	0.071664	−2989.15	16078

$t_{0.005,47} = 2.685$; the 99% confidence interval is $55,102.05 \pm 2.685(2128.57) = 55,102.05 \pm 5714.28$. Or, with 99% confidence, $49,387.78 \leq E(y^0) \leq 60,816.33$. Given an urban family with an income of $80,000, we have 99% confidence that their average consumption will be between $49,387.78 and $60,816.33.

b. The relevant portion of the regression output with y as the response variable, $x_1^* = x_1 - 80,000$ and $x_2^* = x_2 - 0$ as the explanatory variables, and the assumed 99% confidence level is

	Coefficients	Standard Error	t Stat	p-Value	Lower 99.0%	Upper 99.0%
Intercept	48557.63	2313.48	20.9890	1.62E-25	42346.97	54768.29
x_1^*	0.44438	0.08577	5.18094	4.55E-06	0.21412	0.67464
x_2^*	6544.426	3551.27	1.84284	0.071664	−2989.15	16078

The 99% confidence interval is $48,557.63 \pm 2.685(2313.48) = 48,557.63 \pm 6210.66$. Or, with 99% confidence, $42,346.97 \leq E(y^0) \leq 54,768.29$. Given a rural family with an income of $80,000, we have 99% confidence that their average consumption will be between $42,346.97 and $54,768.29.

c. The confidence interval for the urban family is narrower because the standard error $se(\hat{y}^0) = 2128.57$ found for the urban family is less than the standard error $se(\hat{y}^0) = 2313.48$ found for the rural family.

13.28 The estimated model is: $\hat{y} = 263995.07 + 53.13x - 98646.08d_1 - 26350.62d_2 - 38084.93d_3$. The relevant portion of the regression output with y as the response variable and $x^* = x - 13,000$, $d_1^* = d_1 - 0$, $d_2^* = d_2 - 1$, and $d_3^* = d_3 - 0$ as the explanatory variables is

	Coefficients	Standard Error	t Stat	p-Value	Lower 95%	Upper 95%
Intercept	928374.9	9832.84	94.4157	9.83E-44	908413.2	948336.6
x^*	53.13311	2.915002	18.22747	1.91E-19	47.21534	59.05088
d_1^*	−98646.1	13631.46	−7.23665	1.9E-08	−126319	−70972.7
d_2^*	−26350.6	13605.46	−1.93677	0.06088	−53971.2	1269.933
d_3^*	−38084.9	13592.18	−2.80197	0.008221	−65678.5	−10491.3

$t_{0.05,35} = 2.030$; the 95% confidence interval is $928,374.9 \pm 2.030(9832.84) = 928,374.9 \pm 19,961.73$. Or, with 95% confidence, $908,413.15 \leq E(y^0) \leq 948,336.62$.

The relevant portion of the regression output with y as the response variable and $x^* = x - 13,000$, $d_1^* = d_1 - 0$, $d_2^* = d_2 - 0$, and $d_3^* = d_3 - 0$ as the explanatory variables is

	Coefficients	Standard Error	t Stat	p-Value	Lower 95%	Upper 95%
Intercept	263995.1	37720.51	6.998714	3.84E-08	187418.4	340571.8
x^*	53.13311	2.915002	18.22747	1.91E-19	47.21534	59.05088
d_1^*	−60561.2	13611.64	−4.44922	8.36E-05	−88194.3	−32928
d_2^*	11734.31	13594.3	0.863179	0.393916	−15863.6	39332.21
d_3^*	38084.93	13592.18	2.801973	0.008221	10491.34	65678.52

The 95% confidence interval is $263,995.1 \pm 2.030(37,720.51) = 263,995.1 \pm 76,572.64$. Or, with 95% confidence, $187,422.4 \leq E(y^0) \leq 340,567.8$.

The confidence interval for expected sales in quarter 2 is narrower because the standard error $se(\hat{y}^0) = 9832.84$ found for quarter 2 is less than the standard error $se(\hat{y}^0) = 37,720.51$ found for quarter 4.

13.30 a.

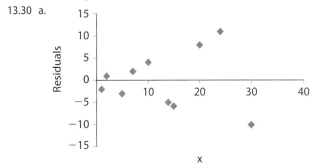

b. Since the residuals are getting larger as x increases, this suggests changing variability. This means that the estimators are unbiased but not efficient. Another problem is that the t tests and F test are not valid because the standard errors are inappropriate. A common correction for the standard errors is White's procedure.

13.32 A scatterplot of GPA against Hours suggests that a simple linear regression model may not be the most appropriate model because of nonlinearities.

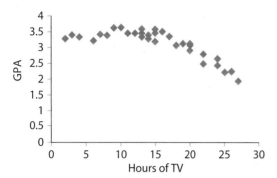

13.34 a. This is a case of perfect multicollinearity (Study + Sleep + Leisure = 24). With perfect multicollinearity we cannot even estimate the proposed model.

b. To fix the model, we might drop the variable Sleep, as the correlation between Study and Leisure is not perfect.

13.36 a. The estimated model is $\widehat{\text{Healthy}} = 75.94 - 0.10$ Fruits/Veggies $+ 0.36$ Exercise $- 0.50$ Smoke.

b. Using the CORREL function in Excel, the sample correlation coefficients between variables are all below 0.80, which suggests that multicollinearity is not serious.

Variables	Correlation
Fruits/Veggies & Exercise	0.5767
Fruits/Veggies & Smoke	−0.6349
Exercise & Smoke	−0.5661

The plots of residuals against explanatory variables suggest that the residuals are more or less randomly dispersed across their values. So the problem of changing variability does not seem to be serious.

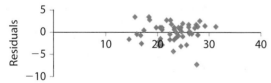

Fruits/Vegetables

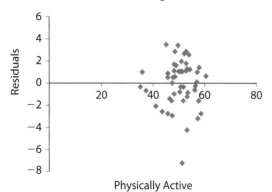

Physically Active

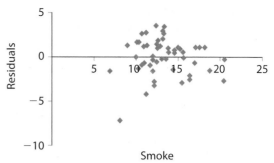

Smoke

13.38 a.

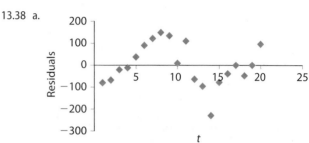

t

There is a definite pattern in the residuals over time with clustering above the horizontal axis, then below, showing positively correlated observations.

b. With correlated obervations, the estimators are unbiased but not efficient. Also, the standard errors are spuriously small, making the model look better than it really is. A common correction for the standard errors is the Newey-West procedure.

13.40 a. Relevant regression results for Callback $= \beta_0 + \beta_1$Age $+ \beta_2$Caucasian $+ \epsilon$:

	Coefficients	Standard Error	t Stat	p-Value
Intercept	25.1466	1.84	13.70	0.0000
Age	−0.3196	0.04	−7.31	0.0000
Caucasian	9.4504	1.01	9.36	0.0000

b. $H_0: \beta_2 = 0; H_A: \beta_2 \neq 0$. With a p-value of approximately zero, we reject H_0 and conclude that the dummy variable Caucasian is significant at the 5% level. Therefore, the data suggest that there is race discrimination.

c. The relevant portion of the regression output with $y =$ Callback as the response variable and Age* = Age − 30 and Caucasian* = Caucasian − 1 as the explanatory variables is

	Coefficients	Standard Error	t Stat	p-Value	Lower 95%	Upper 95%
Intercept	25.0090	0.94340	26.5097	7.02E-22	23.0796	26.9385
Age*	−0.3196	0.04370	−7.3133	4.69E-08	−0.40898	−0.23022
Caucasian*	9.4505	1.00984	9.35842	2.91E-10	7.38512	11.5158

$t_{0.025,29} = 2.045$. The 95% confidence interval is $25.01 \pm 2.045(0.94) = 25.01 \pm 1.929$. Or, with 95% confidence, $23.08 \leq E(y^0) \leq 26.94$.

The relevant portion of the regression output with $y =$ Callback as the response variable and Age* = Age − 30 and Caucasian as the explanatory variables is

	Coefficients	Standard Error	t Stat	p-Value	Lower 95%	Upper 95%
Intercept	**15.5585**	**0.77153**	20.1658	1.31E-18	**13.9806**	**17.1365**
Age*	−0.3196	0.043701	−7.3133	4.69E-08	−0.40898	−0.23022
Caucasian	9.45047	1.009844	9.35842	2.91E-10	7.385124	11.51582

The 95% confidence interval is $15.56 \pm 2.045(0.77) = 15.56 \pm 1.578$. Or, with 95% confidence, $13.98 \le E(y^0) \le 17.14$.

13.42 a. Relevant regression results for $BMI = \beta_0 + \beta_1 Female + \beta_2 Black + \epsilon$:

Regression Statistics	
Multiple R	0.090675
R Square	0.008222
Adjusted R Square	−0.00873
Standard Error	**2.495101**
Observations	120

	Coefficients	Standard Error	t Stat	p-Value
Intercept	**27.60108**	**0.328376**	84.05332	1.9E-106
Female	−0.48951	0.545453	−0.89744	0.371326
Black	0.187295	0.458675	0.40834	0.683771

The predicted BMI for white males is $\widehat{BMI} = 27.60 - 0.49(0) + 0.19(0) = 27.60$.

The predicted BMI for white females is $\widehat{BMI} = 27.60 - 0.49(1) + 0.19(0) = 26.57$.

The predicted BMI for black males is $\widehat{BMI} = 27.60 - 0.49(0) + 0.19(1) = 27.79$.

The predicted BMI for black females is $\widehat{BMI} = 27.60 - 0.49(1) + 0.19(1) = 27.30$.

b. The corresponding p-value for Female $\approx 0.37 > 0.05 = \alpha$, so we cannot conclude that Female is significant. Therefore, at the 5% level, we cannot conclude that there is a significant difference between BMIs of black females and black males, as well as between BMIs of white females and white males.

c. The p-value corresponding to Black $\approx 0.68 > 0.05 = \alpha$, so we cannot conclude that Black is significant. Therefore, at the 5% level, we cannot conclude that there is a significant difference between BMIs of black and white females, as well as between BMIs of black and white males.

d. To find the 90% prediction interval for the BMI of a white male, we first observe that the modified explanatory variables Female* = Female − 0 and Black* = Black − 0 are the same as the original explanatory variables. Therefore, from the output shown in part a, the 90% confidence interval is $27.60 \pm 1.658\sqrt{0.33^2 + 2.50^2} = 27.60 \pm 4.17$. Or, with 90% confidence, $23.43 \le y^0 \le 31.77$.

The relevant portion of the regression output with $y = $ BMI as the response variable, Female* = Female − 1 and Black* = Black − 1 as the explanatory variables, and the entered confidence level of 90% is

Regression Statistics	
Multiple R	0.090675
R Square	0.008222
Adjusted R Square	−0.00873
Standard Error	**2.495101**
Observations	120

	Coefficients	Standard Error	t Stat	p-Value
Intercept	**27.29887**	**0.543607**	50.21806	5.16E-81
Female*	−0.48951	0.545453	−0.89744	0.371326
Black*	0.187295	0.458675	0.40834	0.683771

The 90% prediction interval is $27.30 \pm 1.658\sqrt{0.54^2 + 2.50^2} = 27.30 \pm 4.23$. Or, with 90% confidence, $23.06 \le y^0 \le 31.53$.

13.44 a. The estimated equation is $\widehat{Ownership} = 78.98 - 0.0002\,Income$.

b. The hypotheses are
$H_0: \beta_1 = 0$
$H_A: \beta_1 \ne 0$
$t_{0.025,49} = 2.010$; the decision rule is to reject H_0 if $t_{49} > 2.010$ or $t_{49} < -2.010$. Since $-2.010 < t_{49} = -1.7973 < 2.010$, we do not reject H_0. At the 5% significance level, we cannot conclude that Ownership is linearly related to Income.

c. The relevant regression output with $y = $ Ownership as the response variable and Income* = Income − 50,000 as the explanatory variable is

Regression Statistics	
Multiple R	0.2487
R Square	0.0618
Adjusted R Square	0.0427
Standard Error	**5.7685**
Observations	51

	Coefficients	Standard Error	t Stat	p-Value
Intercept	**69.1995**	**0.8079**	85.6533	0.0000
Income*	−0.0002	0.0001	−1.7973	0.0785

$t_{0.025,49} = 2.010$; the 95% confidence interval is $69.1995 \pm 2.010(0.8079) = 69.1995 \pm 1.6239$. Or, with 95% confidence, $67.58 \le E(y^0) \le 70.82$.

d. The 95% prediction interval is $69.1995 \pm 2.010\sqrt{0.8079^2 + 5.7685^2} = 69.1995 \pm 11.7078$. Or, with 95% confidence, $57.49 \le y^0 \le 80.91$. The prediction interval is wider than the confidence interval since it accounts for the nonzero random error term.

13.46 a. $\widehat{Customers} = 103.96 - 1.92\,Morning + 18.27\,Afternoon - 39.68\,Evening$

b. Morning: $\widehat{Customers} = 103.96 - 1.92 = 102.04$

Afternoon: $\widehat{Customers} = 103.96 + 18.27 = 122.23$

Evening: $\widehat{Customers} = 103.96 - 39.68 = 64.28$

Night: $\widehat{Customers} = 103.96$

c. To test the difference between the afternoon and night shifts, we test $H_0: \beta_{Afternoon} = 0$ against $H_A: \beta_{Afternoon} \ne 0$. The value of the corresponding test statistic is $t_{96} = 3.49$ and the p-value $= 2P(T_{96} \ge 3.49) \approx 0 < 0.05 = \alpha$. Thus, at the 5% level, there is a significant difference between the afternoon and night shifts. To test for a difference between afternoon and other shifts, we look at d_2. With a p-value ≈ 0, we can conclude that the afternoon dummy is significant and therefore there is a significant difference between the afternoon and other shifts at the 5% level, holding all other variables constant.

13.48 a. The regression equation is Per capita income = 30,561.89 − 519.69NoHighSchool + 814.36ForeignBorn − 258.78NoEnglish.

b. The explanatory variables Foreign Born and No English are likely to be positively correlated. The coefficient of correlation between Foreign Born and No English found by Excel function CORREL is 0.9179, which is greater than 0.80, suggesting a potential problem with multicollinearity.

13.50 a.

Variables	
Intercept	−610.0517
	(0.4497)
Poverty	56.1349*
	(0.0046)
Income	6.0517
	(0.5119)
Under 18	3.3515
	(0.8520)
Over 65	11.6092
	(0.6168)
S_e	339.46
R^2	0.4635
F	7.7753*
(p-value)	(0.0001)

The p-values given in the table (shown in parentheses) suggest that Poverty is the only explanatory variable that is significant in the model at the 5% level. Also, the value of the F test statistic with a p-value of 0.0001 suggests that the explanatory variables are jointly significant at the 5% significance level.

b. The sample correlation coefficient between Poverty and Income found using Excel's function CORREL is −0.8180. Since its absolute value is greater than 0.80, multicollinearity is likely to be a problem.

13.52 a. The estimated model is Smoke = 27.41 − 0.35Fruits/Vegetable − 0.0001Income

Variables	
Intercept	27.4116*
	(0.0000)
Fruits/Vegetable (%)	−0.3547*
	(0.0012)
Income	−0.0001*
	(0.0272)
S_e	2.1941
R^2	0.4613
F	20.5489
(p-value)	(0.0000)

b. The p-values for testing the individual significance of Fruits/Vegetable and Income and the p-value for testing their joint significance are less than 0.05 (see values in parentheses). Therefore, we can conclude at the 5% significance level that all the explanatory variables are individually and jointly significant.

c. The sample correlation coefficient between Fruits/Vegetable and Income found by Excel's function CORREL is 0.5993. Since it is not greater than 0.80, multicollinearity is not likely to be a problem.

Addition rule   The probability that A or B occurs, or that at least one of these events occurs, is equal to the probability that A occurs, plus the probability that B occurs, minus the probability that both A and B occur, that is, $P(A \cup B) = P(A) + P(B) - P(A \cap B)$.

Adjusted R^2   A modification of the coefficient of determination that imposes a penalty for using additional explanatory variables in the linear regression model. It is used to compare models with different numbers of explanatory variables; the higher the adjusted R^2, the better the model.

Alternative hypothesis (H_A)   In a hypothesis text, the alternative hypothesis contradicts the default state or status quo specified in the null hypothesis. Generally, whatever we wish to establish is placed in the alternative hypothesis.

Analysis of variance (ANOVA)   A statistical technique used to determine if differences exist between three or more population means.

Assignable variation   In a production process, the variation that is caused by specific events or factors that can usually be identified and eliminated.

Bar chart   A graph that depicts the frequency or relative frequency of each category of qualitative data as a series of horizontal or vertical bars, the lengths of which are proportional to the values that are to be depicted.

Bayes' theorem   The rule for updating probabilities is
$$P(B|A) = \frac{P(A|B)P(B)}{P(A|B)P(B) + P(A|B^c)P(B^c)}, \text{ where } P(B) \text{ is the}$$
prior probability and $P(B|A)$ is the posterior probability.

Bernoulli process   A series of n independent and identical trials of an experiment such that each trial has only two possible outcomes, conventionally labeled success and failure, and each time the trial is repeated, the probabilities of success and failure remain the same.

Between-treatments variance   In ANOVA, a measure of the variability between sample means.

Bias   The tendency of a sample statistic to systematically overestimate or underestimate a population parameter.

Binomial distribution   A description of the probabilities associated with the possible values of a binomial random variable.

Binomial random variable   The number of successes achieved in the n trials of a Bernoulli process.

Box plot   A graphical display of the minimum value, quartiles, and the maximum value of a data set.

Central limit theorem (CLT)   The CLT states that the sum or mean of a large number of independent observations from the same underlying distribution has an approximate normal distribution. The approximation steadily improves as the number of observations increases.

Chance variation   In a production process, the variation that is caused by a number of randomly occurring events that are part of the production process.

Chebyshev's theorem   For any data set, the proportion of observations that lie within k standard deviations from the mean will be at least $1 - 1/k^2$, where k is any number greater than 1.

Chi-square (χ^2) distribution   A family of distributions where each distribution depends on its particular degrees of freedom

df. It is positively skewed, with values ranging from zero to infinity, but becomes increasingly symmetric as *df* increase.

Classes   Intervals for a frequency distribution of quantitative data.

Classical probability   A probability often used in games of chance. It is based on the assumption that all outcomes are equally likely.

Cluster sampling   A population is first divided up into mutually exclusive and collectively exhaustive groups of observations, called clusters. A cluster sample includes observations from randomly selected clusters.

Coefficient of determination (R^2)   The proportion of the sample variation in the response variable that is explained by the sample regression equation; used as a goodness-of-fit measure in regression analysis.

Coefficient of variation (CV)   The ratio of the standard deviation of a data set to its mean; a relative measure of dispersion.

Complement rule   The probability of the complement of an event is one minus the probability of the event, that is, $P(A^c) = 1 - P(A)$.

Conditional probability   The probability of an event given that another event has already occurred.

Confidence coefficient   The probability that a given confidence interval will contain the population parameter of interest.

Confidence interval   A range of values that, with a certain level of confidence, contains the population parameter of interest.

Changing variability   In regression analysis, a violation of the assumption that the variance of the error term is the same for all observations. It is also referred to as heteroskedasticity.

Contingency table   A table that shows frequencies for two qualitative (categorical) variables, x and y, where each cell represents a mutually exclusive combination of the pair of x and y values.

Continuous (random) variable   A variable that assumes uncountable values in an interval.

Continuous uniform distribution   A distribution describing a continuous random variable that has an equally likely chance of assuming a value within a specified range.

Control chart   A plot of statistics of a production process over time. If the statistics randomly fall in an expected range, then the production process is in control. If the statistics reveal an undesirable trend, then adjustment of the production process is likely necessary.

Correlated observations   In regression analysis, a violation of the assumption that the observations are uncorrelated. It is also referred to as serial correlation.

Correlation coefficient   A measure that describes the direction and strength of the linear relationship between two variables.

Covariance   A measure that reveals the direction of the linear relationship between two variables.

Critical value   In a hypothesis test, the critical value is a point that separates the rejection region from the non-rejection region.

Cross-sectional data   Values of a characteristic of many subjects at the same point in time or approximately the same point in time.

Cumulative distribution function A probability that the value of a random variable X is less than or equal to a particular value x, $P(X \leq x)$.

Cumulative frequency distribution A distribution of quantitative data recording the number of observations that falls below the upper limit of each class.

Cumulative relative frequency distribution A distribution of quantitative data recording the fraction (proportion) of observations that falls below the upper limit of each class.

Degrees of freedom The number of independent pieces of information that go into the calculation of a given statistic. Many probability distributions are identified by the degrees of freedom.

Dependent events The occurrence of one event is related to the probability of the occurrence of the other event.

Descriptive statistics The summary of a data set in the form of tables, graphs, or numerical measures.

Deterministic relationship A relationship in which the value of the response variable is uniquely determined by the values of the explanatory variables.

Discrete (random) variable A variable that assumes a countable number of values.

Discrete uniform distribution A symmetric distribution where the random variable assumes a finite number of values and each value is equally likely.

Dummy variable A variable that takes on values of 0 or 1. It is commonly used to describe a qualitative variable with two categories.

Dummy variable trap A linear regression model where the number of dummy variables equals the number of categories of a qualitative variable. In a correctly specified model, the number of dummy variables is one less than the number of categories.

Empirical probability A probability value based on observing the relative frequency with which an event occurs.

Empirical rule Given a sample mean $\bar{x}$, a sample standard deviation s, and a relatively symmetric and bell-shaped distribution, approximately 68% of all observations fall in the interval $\bar{x} \pm s$; approximately 95% of all observations fall in the interval $\bar{x} \pm 2s$; and almost all observations fall in the interval $\bar{x} \pm 3s$.

Estimate A particular value of an estimator.

Estimator A statistic used to estimate a population parameter.

Event A subset of the sample space.

Excluded variables In regression analysis, a situation where important explanatory variables are excluded from the regression. It often leads to the violation of the assumption that the error is uncorrelated with the (included) explanatory variables.

Exhaustive events When all possible outcomes of an experiment are included in the events.

Expected value A weighted average of all possible values of a random variable.

Experiment A process that leads to one of several possible outcomes.

Explanatory variables In regression analysis, the variables that we assume influence the response variable. They are also called the independent variables, predictor variables, control variables, or regressors.

Exponential distribution A continuous, nonsymmetric probability distribution used to model lifetimes or failure times. It is based on one parameter that is referred to as the rate parameter.

F distribution A family of distributions where each distribution depends on two degrees of freedom: the numerator degrees of freedom df_1 and the denominator degrees of freedom df_2. It is positively skewed, with values ranging from zero to infinity, but becomes increasingly symmetric as df_1 and df_2 increase.

Finite population correction factor A correction factor that accounts for the added precision gained by sampling a larger percentage of the population. It is recommended when the sample constitutes at least 5% of the population.

Frequency distribution A table that groups qualitative data into categories, or quantitative data into intervals called classes, where the number of observations that fall into each category or class is recorded.

Goodness-of-fit test A test, using the chi-square statistic, to determine if the sample proportions resulting from a multinomial experiment differ from the hypothesized population proportions specified in the null hypothesis.

Grand mean In ANOVA, the sum of all observations in a data set divided by the total number of observations.

Heteroskedasticity See *Changing variability*.

Histogram A graphical depiction of a frequency or relative frequency distribution; it is a series of rectangles where the width and height of each rectangle represent the class width and frequency (or relative frequency) of the respective class.

Hypergeometric distribution A description of the probabilities associated with the possible values of a hypergeometric random variable.

Hypergeometric random variable The number of successes achieved in the n trials, each with two outcomes, of an experiment where the trials cannot be assumed to be independent.

Hypothesis test A statistical procedure to resolve conflicts between two competing claims (hypotheses) on a particular population parameter of interest.

Independent events The occurrence of one event does not affect the probability of the occurrence of the other event.

Independent random samples Two (or more) random samples are considered independent if the process that generates one sample is completely separate from the process that generates the other sample.

Inexact relationship In regression analysis, a relationship in which the explanatory variables do not exactly predict the response variable.

Inferential statistics The practice of extracting useful information from a sample to draw conclusions about a population.

Interquartile range (IQR) The difference between the third and first quartiles.

Interval data Values of a quantitative variable that can be categorized and ranked, and in which differences between values are meaningful.

Interval estimate See *Confidence interval*.

Inverse transformation A standard normal variable Z can be transformed to the normally distributed random variable X with mean μ and standard deviation σ as $X = \mu + Z\sigma$.

Joint probability table A contingency table whose frequencies have been converted to relative frequencies.

Law of large numbers In probability theory, if an experiment is repeated a large number of times, its empirical probability approaches its classical probability.

Margin of error A value that accounts for the standard error of the estimator and the desired confidence level of the interval.

Matched-pairs sample When samples are matched or paired in some way. They are commonly employed in "before" and "after" studies.

Mean The average value of a data set; the most commonly used measure of central location.

Mean absolute deviation (MAD) The average of the absolute differences between the observations and the mean.

Mean square error (MSE) The average of the sum of squares due to error (residual), where residual is the difference between the observed and the predicted value of a variable.

Mean-variance analysis The idea that the performance of an asset is measured by its rate of return, and this rate of return is evaluated in terms of its reward (mean) and risk (variance).

Median The middle value of a data set.

Mode The most frequently occurring value in a data set.

Multicollinearity In regression analysis, a situation where two or more explanatory variables are linearly related.

Multinomial experiment A series of n independent and identical trials, such that on each trial: there are k possible outcomes, called categories; the probability p_i associated with the ith category remains the same; and, the sum of the probabilities is one.

Multiple linear regression model In regression analysis, more than one explanatory variable is used to explain the variability in the response variable.

Multiplication rule The probability that A and B both occur is equal to the probability that A occurs given that B has occurred times the probability that B occurs, that is, $P(A \cap B) = P(A|B)P(B)$.

Mutually exclusive events Events that do not share any common outcome of an experiment.

Negatively skewed (left-skewed) distribution A distribution in which extreme values are concentrated in the left tail of the distribution.

Nominal data Values of a qualitative variable that differ merely by name or label.

Nonresponse bias A systematic difference in preferences between respondents and nonrespondents of a survey or a poll.

Normal curve A graph depicting the normal probability density function; also referred to as the bell curve.

Normal distribution The most extensively used probability distribution in statistical work and the cornerstone of statistical inference. It is symmetric and bell-shaped and is completely described by the mean and the variance.

Null hypothesis (H_0) In a hypothesis test, the null hypothesis corresponds to a presumed default state of nature or status quo.

Ogive A graph of the cumulative frequency or cumulative relative frequency distribution in which lines connect a series of neighboring points, where each point represents the upper limit of each class and its corresponding cumulative frequency or cumulative relative frequency.

One-tailed hypothesis test A test in which the null hypothesis is rejected only on one side of the hypothesized value of the population parameter.

One-way ANOVA A statistical technique that analyzes the effect of one categorical variable (factor) on the mean.

Ordinal data Values of a qualitative variable that can be categorized and ranked.

Ordinary least squares (OLS) A regression technique for fitting a straight line that is "closest" to the data. Also known as the method of least squares. It chooses the line whereby the sum of squares due to error (residual) is minimized.

Outliers Extreme small or large data values.

$\bar{p}$ chart A control chart that monitors the proportion of defectives (or some other characteristic) of a production process.

p-value In a hypothesis test, the likelihood of observing a sample mean that is at least as extreme as the one derived from the given sample, under the assumption that the null hypothesis is true.

Parameter See *Population parameter*.

Percentile The pth percentile divides a data set into two parts: approximately p percent of the observations have values less than the pth percentile and approximately $(100 - p)$ percent of the observations have values greater than the pth percentile.

Pie chart A segmented circle portraying the categories and relative sizes of some qualitative variable.

Point estimate The value of the point estimator derived from a given sample.

Point estimator A function of the random sample used to make inferences about the value of an unknown population parameter.

Poisson distribution A description of the probabilities associated with the possible values of a Poisson random variable.

Poisson process An experiment in which the number of successes within a specified time or space interval equals any integer between zero and infinity; the numbers of successes counted in nonoverlapping intervals are independent from one another; and the probability that success occurs in any interval is the same for all intervals of equal size and is proportional to the size of the interval.

Poisson random variable The number of successes over a given interval of time or space in a Poisson process.

Polygon A graph of a frequency or relative frequency distribution in which lines connect a series of neighboring points, where each point represents the midpoint of a particular class and its associated frequency or relative frequency.

Population The complete collection of items of interest in a statistical problem.

Population parameter A characteristic of a population.

Positively skewed (right-skewed) distribution A distribution in which extreme values are concentrated in the right tail of the distribution.

Prediction interval In regression analysis, an interval that pertains to the individual value of the response variable defined for specific explanatory variables.

Probability A numerical value between 0 and 1 that measures the likelihood that an event occurs.

Probability distribution Every random variable is associated with a probability distribution that describes the variable completely. It is used to compute probabilities associated with a random variable.

Qualitative variable A variable that uses labels or names to identify the distinguishing characteristics of observations.

Quantitative variable A variable that assumes meaningful numerical values for observations.

Quartiles Any of the three values that divide the ordered data into four equal parts, where the first, second, and third quartiles refer to the 25th, 50th, and 75th percentiles, respectively.

Random variable A function that assigns numerical values to the outcomes of an experiment.

Range The difference between the maximum and the minimum values in a data set.

Ratio data Values of a quantitative variable that can be categorized and ranked, and in which differences between values are meaningful; in addition, a true zero point (origin) exists.

Regression analysis A statistical method for analyzing the relationship between variables. The method assumes that one variable, called the response variable, is influenced by other variables, called the explanatory variables.

Rejection region In a hypothesis test, a range of values such that if the value of the test statistic falls into this range, then the decision is to reject the null hypothesis.

Relative frequency distribution A frequency distribution that shows the fraction (proportion) of observations in each category of qualitative data or class of quantitative data.

Residual (e) In regression analysis, the difference between the observed and the predicted of the response variable value, that is, $e = y - \hat{y}$.

Residual plots In regression analysis, the residuals are plotted sequentially or against an explanatory variable to identify model inadequacies. The model is adequate if the residuals are randomly dispersed around the zero value.

Response variable In regression analysis, the variable that we assume is influenced by the explanatory variable(s). It is also called the dependent variable, the explained variable, the predicted variable, or the regressand.

Risk-averse consumer Someone who takes risk only if it entails a suitable compensation and may decline a risky prospect even if it offers a positive expected gain.

Risk-loving consumer Someone who may accept a risky prospect even if the expected gain is negative.

Risk-neutral consumer Someone who is indifferent to risk and makes his/her decisions solely on the basis of the expected gain.

Sample A subset of a population of interest.

Sample space A record of all possible outcomes of an experiment.

Sample statistic A random variable used to estimate the unknown population parameter of interest.

Sampling distribution The probability distribution of an estimator.

Scatterplot A graphical tool that helps in determining whether or not two variables are related in some systematic way. Each point in the diagram represents a pair of known or observed values of the two variables.

Selection bias A systematic underrepresentation of certain groups from consideration for a sample.

Serial correlation See *Correlated observations*.

Sharpe ratio A ratio calculated by dividing the difference of the mean return from the risk-free rate by the asset's standard deviation.

Simple linear regression model In regression analysis, one explanatory variable is used to explain the variability in the response variable.

Simple random sample A sample of n observations that has the same probability of being selected from the population as any other sample of n observations. Most statistical methods presume simple random samples.

Skewness coefficient A measure that determines if the data are symmetric about the mean. Symmetric data have a skewness coefficient of zero.

Standard deviation The positive square root of the variance; a common measure of dispersion.

Standard error The standard deviation of an estimator.

Standard error of the estimate The standard deviation of the residual; used as a goodness-of-fit measure for regression analysis.

Standard normal distribution A special case of the normal distribution with a mean equal to zero and a standard deviation (or variance) equal to one.

Standard normal table See z table.

Standard transformation A normally distributed random variable X with mean μ and standard deviation σ can be transformed into the standard normal random variable Z as $Z = (X - \mu)/\sigma$.

Statistic See *Sample statistic*.

Statistical quality control Statistical techniques used to develop and maintain a firm's ability to produce high-quality goods and services.

Stem-and-leaf diagram A visual method of displaying quantitative data where each value of a data set is separated into two parts: a stem, which consists of the leftmost digits, and a leaf, which consists of the last digit.

Stratified random sampling A population is first divided up into mutually exclusive and collectively exhaustive groups, called strata. A stratified sample includes randomly selected observations from each stratum. The number of observations per stratum is proportional to the stratum's size in the population. The data for each stratum are eventually pooled.

Subjective probability A probability value based on personal and subjective judgment.

Sum of squares due to error (*SSE*) In ANOVA, a measure of the degree of variability that exists even if all population means are the same. Also known as within-sample variance. In regression analysis, it measures the unexplained variation in the response variable.

Sum of squares due to regression (*SSR*) In regression analysis, it measures the explained variation in the response variable.

Symmetric distribution A distribution where one side of the mean is just the mirror image of the other side.

***t* distribution** A family of distributions that are similar to the z distribution except that they have broader tails. They are identified by their degrees of freedom df; as df increase, the t distribution resembles the z distribution.

Test of independence A goodness-of-fit test analyzing the relationship between two qualitative variables. Also called a chi-square test of a contingency table.

Test of individual significance In regression analysis, a test that determines whether an explanatory variable has an individual statistical influence on the response variable.

Test of joint significance In regression analysis, a test to determine whether the explanatory variables have a joint statistical influence on the response variable; it is often regarded as a test of the overall usefulness of a regression model.

Time series data Values of a characteristic of a subject over time.

Total probability rule A rule that expresses the unconditional probability of an event, $P(A)$, in terms of probabilities conditional on various mutually exclusive and exhaustive events. The total probability rule conditional on two events B and B^c is $P(A) = P(A \cap B) + P(A \cap B^c) = P(A|B)P(B) + P(A|B^c)P(B^c)$.

Total sum of squares (*SST*) In regression analysis, it measures the total variation in the response variable. It can be decomposed into explained and unexplained variations.

Two-tailed hypothesis test A test in which the null hypothesis can be rejected on either side of the hypothesized value of the population parameter.

Type I error In a hypothesis test, this error occurs when the decision is to reject the null hypothesis when the null hypothesis is actually true.

Type II error In a hypothesis test, this error occurs when the decision is to not reject the null hypothesis when the null hypothesis is actually false.

Unbiased An estimator is unbiased if its expected value equals the unknown population parameter being estimated.

Unconditional probability The probability of an event without any restriction.

Variable A general characteristic being observed on a set of people, objects, or events, where each observation varies in kind or degree.

Variance The average of the squared differences from the mean; a common measure of dispersion.

Within-treatments variance In ANOVA, a measure of the variability within each sample.

$\bar{x}$ chart A control chart that monitors the central tendency of a production process.

***z*-score** The relative position of a value within a data set; it is also used to detect outliers.

***z* table** A table providing cumulative probabilities for positive or negative values of the standard normal random variable Z.

PHOTO CREDITS

Chapter 1
Page 3: © Michael Schmitt/Workbook Stock/ Getty Images; page 7: © Digital Vision/ PunchStock RF; page 9: © Ed Young/ Agstockusa/age fotostock, America, Inc.; page 13: © Dennis Welsh/UpperCut Images/Getty Images RF

Chapter 2
Page 17: © A. Ramey/PhotoEdit Inc.; page 18: © sbk_20d pictures/Flickr/Getty Images RF; page 37: © Brand X Pictures RF; page 47: © Rubberball/Getty Images RF

Chapter 3
Page 59: © Jose Luis Pelaez, Inc./Getty Images RF; page 64: © Sebastian Pfuetze/ Taxi/Getty Images; page 77: © Ingram Publishing RF; page 92: © Mike Watson Images/PunchStock RF

Chapter 4
Page 101: © Smith Collection/Iconica/Getty Images; page 121: © Digital Vision/Punch-Stock RF; page 130: © Rolf Bruderer/ Blend Images/Getty Images RF

Chapter 5
Page 139: © AP Photo/Kevin P. Casey; page 161: © Bubbles Photolibrary/Alamy; page 166: © Image Source/Alamy RF

Chapter 6
Page 175: © QxQ IMAGES/Datacraft/ Getty Images RF; page 194: © Mewes, K./ Healthy Food Images/age fotostock, America, Inc.; page 201: © Image Source/ Getty Images RF

Chapter 7
Page 211: © Melanie Conner/Getty Images; page 227: © Joe Raedle/Getty Images; page 237: © Ryan McVay/Photodisc/Getty Images RF

Chapter 8
Page 247: © Car Culture/Corbis; page 267: © The McGraw-Hill Companies, Inc./ Mark A. Dierker, photographer RF; page 269 (left): © The McGraw-Hill Companies, Inc./Andrew Resek, photographer, (right): © AP Photo/Paul Sakuma

Chapter 9
Page 279: © Fotosearch/age fotostock, America, Inc. RF; page 300: © Asia Images Group/Getty Images RF; page 308: © Ariel Skelley/Blend Images LLC, RF

Chapter 10
Page 317: © Robin Nelson/PhotoEdit, Inc.; page 332: © Chris Hondros/Getty Images;

page 344: © Mitchell Funk/Photographer's Choice/Getty Images

Chapter 11
Page 353: © Liu Jin/AFP/Getty Images; page 370: © Jean Baptiste Lacroix/WireImage/ Getty Images; page 372 (top): © JGI/Blend Images LLC, RF, (bottom): © Banana-Stock/JupiterImages RF

Chapter 12
Page 381: © Digital Vision/Getty Images RF; page 408: © AP Photo/David J. Phillip; page 412: © Scott Boehm/Getty Images

Chapter 13
Page 421: © Jose Luis Pelaez, Inc./Blend Images/Corbis; page 428: © Tom Stewart/ Corbis; page 445: © Elsa/Getty Images

A

Acceptance sampling, 231
Addition rule, 110–111, 132
Adidas Group, 19–20, 101, 118–121, 353, 367, 370
Adjusted R^2, 398–399, 414, 425
Alpha, of stock, 405
Alstead, Troy, 4
Alternative hypothesis, 280, 281–283, 309
Analysis of variance (ANOVA) test, 334–335
    for coefficient of determination, 396–398
    F distribution and, 335–336, 346
    one-way, 336–341, 346
        between-treatments estimate of σ^2, 338
        one-way ANOVA table, 340
        software solutions, 340–341, 351
        test statistic, 339, 346
        within-treatments estimate of σ^2, 338–339
        written report using, 344–345
Arithmetic mean. See Mean
Assignable variation, 232
Associated Press, 308
Asymptotic distribution, 180
Average. See Mean

B

Bar charts, 21–24, 49, 54–56
Bayes, Rev. Thomas, 126
Bayes' theorem, 123, 126–128, 132
Bell curve, 180–181
Bell-shaped distribution. See Normal distribution
Bell Telephone Laboratories, 232
Bernoulli, James, 150
Bernoulli process, 150–156, 168
Beta, of stock, 405
Between-treatments estimate of σ^2, 338
Between-treatments variance (MSTR), 338
Bias, in sampling, 212–213, 215–216, 239
Bimodal data, 63
Binomial distribution, 150–156
    normal approximation of, 193
    software solutions, 155–156, 172, 173
Binomial random variables, 150–155, 168
Bloomberg Businessweek, 227
Boston Globe, 4, 215
Box-and-whisker plots. See Box plots
Box plots, 70–72, 93
Brady, Tom, 370
Brown, Scott, 4, 215
Bureau of Economic Analysis (BEA), 7
Bureau of Labor Statistics (BLS), 6, 7

C

c charts, 232
Categorical variables. See Qualitative variables
Centerline, 232
Central limit theorem (CLT), 240
    for sample mean, 220–222
    for sample proportion, 225–227
Central location, measures of, 60–67
    mean. See Mean
    median, 62–63, 65–66, 93

mode, 63–64, 65–66, 93
sample mean, 60–61, 85–87, 93
software solutions, 64–67, 98–99
weighted mean, 66–67, 86
written report using, 92–93
Chance variation, 231–232
Charts. See Graphical displays
Chebyshev, Pavroty, 81
Chebyshev's Theorem, 81–82, 83, 94
Chi-square (χ^2) distribution, 359–360, 373
    goodness-of-fit tests, 361–365, 374
    test of a contingency table, 366–370, 374, 378–379
    test of independence, 366–370, 374, 378–379
Chi-square (χ^2) tables, 460–461
Classes, 26, 27–28, 29, 49
Classical probability, 105, 107, 131
Clinton, Hillary, 215
Cluster sampling, 215–216, 239
Coakley, Martha, 4, 215
Coefficient of determination (R^2), 396–398, 414, 439
Coefficient of variation (CV), 76, 94
Column charts, 21–22
Complement, of an event, 104
Complement rule, 109, 132
Conditional probability, 112–113, 132
Confidence coefficient, 250
Confidence intervals, 248–263, 270
    for expected value of y, 432–434, 447
    margin of error and, 248–249, 271
    for mean difference, 328, 346
    95 percent, 249–250, 403–404
    for population mean (μ), 249–259, 271, 276, 277
    for population proportion (p), 262–263, 271
    precision of, 252–253, 271
    for regression coefficients, 403–404
    for response variable, 431–435
    sample size requirements, 265–267, 271
    t distribution, 255–258, 271
    for two population means ($\mu_1 - \mu_2$), 318–320, 345
    for two population proportions ($p_1 - p_2$), 354–355, 373
    two-tailed hypothesis tests and, 293–294
    using Excel to construct, 253, 259
    width of, 251–253, 271
    written reports using, 269–270
Constant, 217
Consumer risk tolerance, 147–148
Contingency tables, 118–121, 132
    chi-square test of, 366–370, 374, 378–379
Continuous probability distributions, 174–209
    exponential distribution, 197–199, 203, 207, 208, 209
    normal distribution. See Normal distribution
    software solutions, 207–209
    uniform, 177–178, 203, 207, 208
    written report using, 201–202
Continuous random variables, 140, 141, 168, 176, 202
    cumulative distribution function, 176, 202

probability density function, 176, 202.
    See also Continuous probability distributions
Continuous uniform distributions, 177–178, 203, 207, 208
Continuous variables, 9, 15
Control charts, 232–235, 240
Correlation coefficient, 89–90, 95
Correlation-to-causation fallacy, 5
Covariance, 88–90, 95
Critical value, 290
Critical value approach, 310
    testing population mean (μ), 290–293, 297–298
    testing population proportion (p), 305–306
    testing two population proportions ($p_1 - p_2$), 356–357
Cross-sectional data, 6, 7, 15
Cumulative distribution function
    of continuous random variables, 176, 202
    of discrete random variables, 141, 142, 168
    for exponential distribution, 197, 203
Cumulative frequency distribution, 29–30, 49
Cumulative probabilities, 197, 203
Cumulative relative frequency distribution, 30, 49
Curvilinear relationships, 44

D

Data
    bimodal, 63
    cross-sectional, 6, 7, 15
    grouped, 85–87, 94
    Internet sources of, 7
    qualitative. See Qualitative data
    quantitative. See Quantitative data
    time series, 6–7, 15
    unimodal, 63
De Moivre, Abraham, 180n
Decision rule, 293
Degrees of freedom (df), 256, 271, 359
Dependent events, 113–114, 132
Descriptive statistics, 5, 15
Detection approach, 231
Deterministic relationships, 382
Discrete probability distributions, 138–173
    algebraic formulas for, 142
    binomial distribution. See Binomial distribution
    described, 141–144
    graphical representations of, 142–143
    hypergeometric distribution. See Hypergeometric distribution
    key properties of, 142
    random variables and, 140–141
    tabular forms, 141–142
    uniform, 143
    written report using, 166–167
Discrete random variables, 138, 140–141, 168
    cumulative distribution function, 141, 142, 168
    expected value of, 145–146, 168
    probability mass function, 141. See also Discrete probability distributions
    standard deviation of, 146–147, 168
    variance of, 146–147, 168

Discrete uniform distributions, 143
Discrete variables, 8–9, 15
Dispersion, measures of, 73–77
    coefficient of variation (CV), 76, 94
    mean absolute deviation (MAD), 74, 76, 94
    range, 73–74, 76, 94
    software solutions, 76–77, 98–99
    standard deviation. See Standard deviation
    variance, 74–75, 94
    written report using, 92–93
Dow Jones Industrial Average (DJIA), 5,
    9–10
Dummy variable trap, 426
Dummy variables, 422–428, 447
    with multiple categories, 425–428
    testing significance of, 424–425
    with two categories, 422–425
Dunkin' Donuts, 211
Duracell, 6

E

The Economist, 7
Empirical probability, 105, 106, 131
Empirical rule, 82–83, 94, 186–188
Error sum of squares (*SSE*), 338–339
espn.com, 7
Estimates, 217, 239
Estimators, 217, 239. See also OLS estimators
Events, 102–105, 131
    complement of an event, 104
    dependent, 113–114, 132
    exhaustive, 103, 131
    independent, 113–114, 115, 132
    intersection of two events, 103–104
    mutually exclusive, 103, 111, 131
    simple, 102–103
    union of two events, 103, 104
Excel software
    bar charts, 21–22
    binomial probabilities, 155–156
    central location measures, 64–67
    chi-square (χ^2) distribution, 363–365
    confidence intervals, 253, 259
    control charts, 235
    correlation coefficient, 90
    covariance, 90
    data analysis toolpak option, 65–67, 77
    dispersion measures, 76–77
    exponential distribution, 199
    formula option, 64, 76
    goodness-of-fit test statistic, 363–365
    histograms, 32–34
    hypergeometric probabilities, 165
    hypothesis testing
        for μ, σ is known, 294–295
        for μ, σ is unknown, 299–300
        multinomial experiments, 363–365
        p-value approach, 294–295, 299–300,
            363–365
        for two population means ($\mu_1 - \mu_2$),
            322–324
    inverse transformation, 193
    ogives, 37
    pie charts, 21
    Poisson probabilities, 160–161
    polygons, 35
    random sample generation, 214
    sample regression equation, 386–387

scatterplots, 45–46, 384
    standard transformation, 193
    trendlines, 384
Exhaustive events, 103, 131
Expected frequencies, 367–368
Expected value. See also Population mean (μ)
    of binomial random variable, 153–155, 168
    consumer risk tolerance and, 147–148
    of discrete random variable, 145–146, 168
    of hypergeometric random variable,
        164, 169
    of Poisson random variable, 159, 168
    of the sample mean, 218–219, 239
    of the sample proportion, 224–225, 240
    of *y*, confidence interval for, 432–434, 447
Experiments, 102, 131, 359–365, 374
Explained variation, 396
Explanatory variables, 382, 413, 422–428
Exponential distribution, 197–199, 203,
    207, 208, 209

F

F distribution, 335–336, 346
F tables, 336, 462–465
Federal Reserve Economic Data (FRED), 7
Fidelity Investments, 59, 77
finance.yahoo.com, 7
Finite population correction factor,
    228–230, 240
Fisher, Sir Ronald, 335n
Fortune, 7
Frequency distributions, 49
    cumulative, 29–30, 49
    cumulative relative, 30, 49
    guidelines for constructing, 27–30
    mean calculation for, 85–87
    for qualitative data, 18–24, 49
    for quantitative data, 26–37, 49
    relative, 18–19, 29–30, 49, 87
    skewed, 32, 66
    symmetric, 32, 66
    variance calculation for, 85–87

G

Gallup, George, 213
Gallup Organization, 213
Gallup Poll, 5
Gauss, Carl Friedrich, 180n
Gaussian distribution. See Normal distribution
Goodness-of-fit measures
    adjusted R^2, 398–399, 414
    coefficient of determination (R^2),
        396–398, 414, 439
    for multinomial experiments, 359–365, 374
    for sample regression equations, 393–399
    software solutions, 378
    standard error of the estimate, 394–396,
        413–414
Google, Inc., 7
Gossett, William S., 255n
Grand mean, 338
Graphical displays
    bar charts, 21–24, 49, 54–56
    box plots, 70–72, 93
    control charts, 232–235, 240
    discrete probability distributions, 142–143
    guidelines for, 23–24
    histograms, 31–34, 49, 54–56
    normal (bell) curve, 180–181

ogives, 36–37, 49, 55–57
pie charts, 20–21, 49, 54–56
Poisson distribution, 160
polygons, 31, 34–35, 49, 54–57
    for qualitative data, 20–24
    for quantitative data, 31–37, 42–43
    residual plots. See Residual plots
    scatterplots. See Scatterplots
    stem-and-leaf diagrams, 42–43, 49
    written report using, 47–48
Grouped data, summarizing, 85–87, 94
Guinness Brewery, 255n

H

Histograms, 31–34, 49, 54–56
Home Depot, 269–270
Hoover, Herbert, 212
Horizontal bar charts, 22–23
Hypergeometric distribution, 163–165,
    168–169, 172–173
Hypergeometric random variables, 163–164,
    168–169
Hypothesis testing, 278–315
    alternative hypothesis, 280, 281–283, 309
    ANOVA test. See Analysis of variance
        (ANOVA) test
    chi-square (χ^2) tests
        for goodness-of-fit, 361–365, 374
        of independence, 366–370, 374,
            378–379
    critical value approach. See Critical value
        approach
    for mean difference, 329–332, 346, 351
    for multinomial experiments, 359–365
    null hypothesis, 280–283, 309
    one-tailed tests, 281–283, 309
    p-value approach. See *p*-value approach
    for population mean (μ), 285–295,
        297–300, 310–311
    for population proportion (*p*), 303–306,
        311, 315
    reject/not reject decision, 280,
        287, 309
    software solutions, 294–295,
        299–300, 315
    test statistics. See Test statistics
    tests of significance, 401–408
    for two population means ($\mu_1 - \mu_2$),
        320–324, 345
    for two population proportions ($p_1 - p_2$),
        355–357, 373
    two-tailed tests, 281–283, 293–294, 309
    Type I/Type II errors, 283–284, 309
    written report using, 308–309

I

IBM, 6
Independent events, 113–114, 115, 132
Independent random samples, 318, 345
Indicator variables. See Dummy variables
Inexact relationships, 382
Inferential statistics, 5, 15
The Internet, 7
Interquartile range (IQR), 71
Intersection, of two events, 103–104
Interval estimation, 246–277
    confidence intervals. See Confidence
        intervals

of population mean (μ)
   sample size requirements, 265–266, 271
   when σ is known, 249–253, 271,
     276, 277
   when σ is unknown, 255–259, 271,
     276, 277
   written report using, 269–270
Interval scale, 12, 15
Intervals, 248
Inverse transformation, 191–193, 207, 208, 209

J

JMP software
   bar charts, 56
   binomial distribution, 173
   box plots, 99
   correlation coefficient, 99
   covariance, 99
   estimating population mean (μ), 277
   exponential distribution, 209
   histograms, 56
   hypergeometric distribution, 173
   hypothesis testing
     for mean difference, 351
     one-way ANOVA, 351
     test of independence, 379
     for two population means ($\mu_1 - \mu_2$), 351
   inverse transformation, 209
   multicollinearity assessment, 455
   multiple regression, 419
   normal (standard) transformation, 208–209
   ogives, 57
   pie charts, 56
   Poisson distribution, 173
   polygons, 57
   random sample generation, 245
   residual plots, 454
   scatterplots, 57, 419
   simple linear regression, 419
   summary measures, 99
   testing population mean (μ), 315
   trendline, 419
   $\bar{x}$ chart construction, 245
Johnson & Johnson, 23, 405–406
Joint probabilities, 120
Joint probability tables, 119–120, 130–131

K

Kennedy, Ted, 4, 215

L

Landon, Alf, 212
Law of large numbers, 107
Linear regression. *See* Regression analysis
Linear relationship, quantifying, 44, 88–90
Literary Digest, 212–213, 215
Lower control limit (LCL), 232–233
Lowe's, 269–270

M

Margin of error, 248–249, 271
Marginal probabilities, 120
Matched-pairs sampling, 327–328, 346
McDonald's, 211
Mean, 60–61, 64–67, 93
   grand, 338
   for grouped data, 85–87, 94

population. *See* Population mean (μ)
sample. *See* Sample mean ($\bar{x}$)
weakness of, 61
weighted, 66–67, 86
Mean absolute deviation (MAD), 74, 76, 94
Mean square (due to) error (*MSE*),
   338–339, 394
Mean square (due to) regression (*MSR*), 406
Mean square for treatments (*MSTR*), 338
Mean-variance analysis, 79–80, 94
Mean ($\bar{x}$) charts, 232, 233–234, 240, 245
Measurement, scales of. *See* Scales of
   measurement
Median, 62–63, 65–66, 93
Method of least squares. *See* OLS estimators
Minitab software
   bar charts, 54
   binomial distribution, 172
   box plots, 99
   correlation coefficient, 99
   covariance, 99
   estimating population mean (μ), 276
   exponential distribution, 207
   histograms, 54
   hypergeometric distribution, 172
   hypothesis testing
     goodness-of-fit test, 378
     for mean difference, 351
     one-way ANOVA, 351
     for population mean (μ), 315
     for population proportion (p), 315
     test of independence, 378
     for two population means ($\mu_1 - \mu_2$),
      350, 378
   inverse transformation, 207
   multicollinearity assessment, 454
   multiple regression, 419
   normal (standard) transformation, 207
   ogives, 55
   pie charts, 54
   Poisson distribution, 172
   polygons, 54–55
   random sample generation, 244
   residual plots, 454
   scatterplots, 55, 418
   simple linear regression, 419
   summary measures, 98–99
   trendlines, 418
   uniform distribution, 207
   $\bar{x}$ chart construction, 245
Mode, 63–64, 65–66, 93
Multicollinearity, 439–440, 448, 454, 455
Multimodal data, 63
Multinomial experiments, 359–365, 374. *See
   also* Chi-square (χ^2) distribution
Multiple linear regression model. *See*
   Regression analysis
Multiplication rule, 114–115, 132
Mutually exclusive events, 103, 111, 131

N

Nasdaq (National Association of Securities
   Dealers Automated Quotations), 9–10
New York Stock Exchange (NYSE), 9–10
The New York Times, 7
Newey-West procedure, 443
Nike, Inc., 101, 118–121, 353, 367, 370
95% confidence interval, 249–250, 403–404

Nominal scale, 9–10, 15
Nonresponse bias, 213, 239
Normal curve, 180–181
Normal distribution, 180–193, 203
   binomial distribution approximation, 193
   characteristics of, 180–181
   empirical rule and, 186–188
   problem solving with, 189–193
   exponential distribution, 209
     inverse transformation, 191–193, 207,
      208, 209
     software solutions, 193, 207–209
     standard transformation, 83, 189–191,
      193, 207, 208–209
   standard. *See* Standard normal
     distribution
Normal probability distribution. *See* Normal
   distribution
Normal transformation. *See* Standardizing
   data
Null hypothesis, 280–283, 309
Numerical descriptive measures, 58–99
   box plots, 70–72, 93
   central location. *See* Central location,
     measures of
   Chebyshev's Theorem, 81–82, 83, 94
   correlation coefficient, 89–90, 95
   covariance, 88–90, 95
   dispersion. *See* Dispersion, measures of
   empirical rule, 82–83, 94
   grouped data, summarizing, 85–87, 94
   mean-variance analysis, 79–80, 94
   percentiles, 69–72, 93
   relative location analysis, 81–84
   Sharpe ratio, 79–80, 94
   written report using, 92–93
   z-scores, 83–84, 94

O

Obama, Barack, 5, 215
Ogives, 36–37, 49, 55–57
The Ohio State University, 5, 6
OLS estimators, 384, 413, 436–443,
   447–448
One-tailed hypothesis tests, 281–283, 309
One-way ANOVA test. *See* Analysis of
   variance (ANOVA) test
Ordinal scale, 10–12, 15
Ordinary least squares (OLS). *See* OLS
   estimators
Outliers, 61, 93

P

$\bar{p}$ charts, 232, 234–235, 240
p-value approach, 286–290, 309–310
   testing population mean (μ), 286–290,
     298–300
   testing population proportion (p),
     304–305
   testing two population proportions
     ($p_1 - p_2$), 357
   using Excel, 294–295, 299–300, 363–365
Parameters, 5, 6, 61, 212, 217, 239
Percent frequency, 19
Percentiles, 69–72, 93
Pie charts, 20–21, 49, 54–56
Point estimates, 217
Point estimator, 217

Poisson, Simeon, 158
Poisson distribution, 158–161
  exponential distribution and, 197
  software solutions, 160–161, 172, 173
Poisson process, 158
Poisson random variables, 158–160, 168
Polygons, 31, 34–35, 49, 54–57
Population, 5, 6, 15, 212
Population coefficient of variation, 76
Population correlation coefficient, 89
Population covariance, 88, 90
Population MAD, 74
Population mean (μ), 60–61, 85–87, 93. *See also* Expected value
  difference between two means ($\mu_1 - \mu_2$), 318–324
    confidence interval, 318–320, 345
    hypothesis testing, 320–324, 345
    software solutions, 322–324, 350–351
    test statistic, 321–322, 345
  differences among many means, 334–341
    between-treatments estimate of σ^2, 338
    F distribution, 335–336, 346
    one-way ANOVA test, 336–341, 346
    test statistic, 339, 346
    within-treatments estimate of σ^2, 338–339
  estimating
    sample size requirements, 265–266, 271
    when σ is known, 249–253, 271, 276, 277
    when σ is unknown, 255–259, 271, 276, 277
  hypothesis testing
    for mean difference, 329–332, 346
    for two population means ($\mu_1 - \mu_2$), 320–324, 345
    when σ is known, 285–295, 310, 315
    when σ is unknown, 297–300, 310–311, 315
  mean difference (μ_D), 327–332
    confidence interval, 328, 346
    hypothesis testing, 329–332, 346
    software solutions, 330–332, 351
    test statistic, 329–330, 346
Population parameters, 5, 6, 212
Population proportion (p)
  comparisons of proportions, 352–379
    confidence interval for $p_1 - p_2$, 354–357, 373
    expected frequencies, calculating, 367–368
    goodness-of-fit test, 359–365, 374
    hypothesis test for $p_1 - p_2$, 355–357, 373
    multinomial experiment conditions, 361, 374
    software solutions, 363–365, 378–379
    test of independence, 366–370, 374
    test statistic, 373
    written reports using, 372–373
  confidence intervals, 262–263, 271
  estimating, 266–267, 271
  hypothesis testing, 303–306, 311, 315
  test statistic, 304, 311
Population standard deviation (σ), 75, 76, 94
Population variance (σ^2), 75, 76, 85–87, 94

Posterior probability, 126–128
Prediction interval, 432–435, 447
Prior probability, 126
Probability
  assigning probabilities, 105–107
  classical, 105, 107, 131
  conditional, 112–113, 132
  contingency tables, 118–121, 132
  defined, 102, 131
  empirical, 105, 106, 131
  events. *See* Events
  fundamental concepts, 102–107
  law of large numbers, 107
  properties of a probability, defining, 105, 131
  rules of, 109–115
    addition rule, 110–111, 132
    Bayes' theorem, 123, 126–128, 132
    complement rule, 109, 132
    conditional probability, 112–113, 132
    independent vs. dependent events, 113–114, 132
    multiplication rule, 114–115, 132
    total probability rule, 123–128, 132
  subjective, 105, 131
  tabular method for computing, 125–126
  unconditional, 112, 132
  Venn diagrams, 103–104, 110–112
Probability density function, 176, 202. *See also* Continuous probability distributions
Probability distributions
  chi-square (χ^2) distribution. *See* Chi-square (χ^2) distribution
  for continuous random variables. *See* Continuous probability distributions
  for discrete random variables. *See* Discrete probability distributions
  normal. *See* Normal distribution
Probability mass function, 141. *See also* Discrete probability distributions
Probability trees, 124–125, 151–152

Q

Qualitative data
  bar charts, 21–24, 49
  control charts, 232, 234–235
  frequency distributions, 18–24, 49
  graphical displays, 20–24
  mode, 63–64, 65–66, 93
  pie charts, 20–21, 49, 54–56
  population proportion. *See* Population proportion (p)
  summarizing, 18–24, 49
Qualitative variables, 8, 9, 15
  contingency tables, 118–121, 132
  nominal scale, 9–10, 12
  ordinal scale, 10–12
  in regression analysis
    with multiple categories, 425–428
    vs. quantitative variables, 422
    with two categories, 422–425
Quality control. *See* Statistical quality control
Quantitative data
  control charts, 232, 233–234
  frequency distributions, 26–37, 49

  graphical displays, 31–37, 42–43
  histograms, 31–34, 49, 54–56
  ogives, 36–37, 49, 55–57
  polygons, 31, 34–35, 49, 54–57
  stem-and-leaf diagrams, 42–43
  summarizing, 26–37, 49
Quantitative variables, 8–9, 15, 422
Quartiles, 70–72

R

R charts, 232
Random variables, 140–141, 168, 217, 239
  binomial, 150–155, 168
  continuous. *See* Continuous random variables
  discrete. *See* Discrete random variables
  exponential distribution, 209
  hypergeometric, 163–164, 168–169
  inverse transformation of, 191–193, 207, 208, 209
  Poisson, 158–160
  standard normal, 182, 219–220, 225–227, 240
  standard transformation of, 189–191, 193, 207, 208–209
Range, 73–74, 76, 94
Rate parameter, 197
Ratio scale, 12, 15
Raw data, 32–34, 54
Regression analysis, 380–455
  assumptions of, 436–437
  defined, 382, 413
  dummy variables, 422–428, 447
  explanatory variables, 382, 413, 422–428
  goodness-of-fit measures, 393–399
    adjusted R^2, 398–399, 414, 425
    coefficient of determination (R^2), 396–398, 414, 439
    standard error of the estimate, 394–396, 413–414
  interval estimates, 431–435
  multiple linear regression model, 382, 389–391, 413
    sample regression equation, 390–391
    software solutions, 419
  OLS estimators, 384, 413, 436–443, 447–448
  quantitative vs. qualitative variables in, 422
  reporting results from, 407–408, 412–413, 445–447
  response variable (y), 382, 413, 431–435
  simple linear regression model, 382–387
    defined, 383, 413
    deterministic vs. inexact relationships, 382
    sample regression equation, 383–384, 386–387
    scatterplots, 383–386
    software solutions, 384, 386–387, 419
  tests of significance, 401–408
    computer-generated, 404
    for dummy variables, 424–425
    for individual significance, 401–406, 414
    for joint significance, 406–407, 414
    for nonzero slope coefficient, 404–406

using confidence intervals, 403–404
using standard *t* test, 424–425
violations of assumptions
changing variability, 440–442, 448
correlated observations, 442–443, 448
excluded variables, 443, 448
multicollinearity, 439–440, 448, 454,
455
nonlinear patterns, 438–439
Rejection region, 290
Relative frequency distributions, 18–19,
29–30, 49
cumulative, 30, 49
mean and variance for, 87
Relative location analysis, 81–84
Chebyshev's Theorem, 81–82, 83, 94
empirical rule, 82–83, 94
z-scores, 83–84, 94
Representative sample, 212
Residual, 383
Residual plots, 437
changing variability, 441
correlated observations, 442–443
nonlinear patterns, 438–439
software solutions, 454
Response variable (*y*), 382, 413, 431–435
Risk-averse consumers, 147–148, 168
Risk-loving consumers, 148, 168
Risk-neutral consumers, 147–148, 168
Roosevelt, Franklin Delano, 212

S

s charts, 232
Sample, 5, 6, 15, 212. *See also* Sampling
Sample coefficient of variation, 76
Sample correlation coefficient, 89
Sample covariance, 88, 90
Sample MAD, 74
Sample mean ($\bar{x}$), 60–61, 85–87, 93
derivation of properties of, 244
finite population correction factor, 229
sampling distribution of, 217–222
Sample proportion ($\bar{P}$)
derivation of properties of, 244
finite population correction factor, 229–230
sampling distribution of, 224–227, 240
Sample regression equation, 383–384,
386–387, 390–391
Sample space, 102, 131
Sample standard deviation (*s*), 75, 76, 94
Sample statistic, 5, 6, 212
Sample variance (s^2), 75, 76, 85–87, 94
Sampling, 210–216
biases in, 212–213, 215–216, 239
cluster samples, 215–216, 239
finite population correction factor,
228–230, 240
independent random samples, 318, 345
matched-pairs samples, 327–328, 346
methodology, 213–216
need for, 6
precision vs. costs, 215, 239
random sample generation, 214, 244, 245
without replacement, 163, 169
sample size requirements, 265–267
simple random samples, 213–214, 239,
244, 245

statistical quality control, 231–235,
237–239, 240
stratified random samples, 214–215, 239
Sampling distributions
of the sample mean, 217–222
central limit theorem, 220–222
expected value, 218–219
sampling from a normal population,
219–220
standard error, 218–219
of the sample proportion, 224–227, 240
central limit theorem, 225–227
expected value, 224–225
standard error, 224–225
variance, 224–225
Scales of measurement, 9–13, 15
interval scale, 12, 15
nominal scale, 9–10, 15
ordinal scale, 10–12, 15
ratio scale, 12, 15
Scatterplots, 44–46, 49
simple linear regression model, 383–386
software solutions, 45–46, 55–57, 384
Selection bias, 213, 215–216, 239
Seton Hall University, 421, 428
Sharpe, William, 79
Sharpe ratio, 79–80, 94
Shewhart, Walter A., 232
Significance level, 287
Significance tests. *See* Regression analysis
Simple events, 102–103
Simple linear regression model. *See*
Regression analysis
Simple random samples, 213–214, 239,
244, 245
Skewness, 32, 66, 71–72
Software. *See* Excel software; JMP software;
Minitab software; SPSS software
SPSS software
bar charts, 55
binomial distribution, 172
correlation coefficient, 99
covariance, 99
estimating population mean (μ), 276
exponential distribution, 208
histograms, 55
hypergeometric distribution, 173
hypothesis testing
goodness-of-fit test, 378
for mean difference, 351
one-way ANOVA, 351
for population (μ), 315
test of independence, 378
for two population means ($\mu_1 - \mu_2$), 351
inverse transformation, 208
multicollinearity assessment, 454
multiple regression, 419
normal (standard) transformation, 208
ogives, 56
pie charts, 55
Poisson distribution, 172
polygons, 55–56
residual plots, 454
scatterplots, 56
simple linear regression, 419
summary measures, 99
uniform distribution, 208

$\bar{x}$ chart construction, 245
Spurious correlation, 5
Standard deviation, 74–75, 94
of binomial random variable, 153–155,
168
of discrete random variable, 146–147,
168
of hypergeometric random variable, 164,
169
of Poisson random variable, 159, 168
population standard deviation (σ), 75,
76, 94
of the sample mean, 218–219, 239
sample standard deviation (*s*), 75, 76, 94
Standard error
of the estimate, 394–396, 413–414
of the sample mean, 218–219, 239
of the sample proportion, 224–225, 240
Standard normal distribution, 182–188, 203
exponential distribution, 209
finding probability for given *z* value,
182–184
finding *z* value for given probability,
185–186
inverse transformation, 191–193, 207,
208, 209
standard transformation, 83, 189–191,
193, 207, 208–209
z tables, 182–186, 203, 456–457
Standard normal random variables, 182,
219–220, 225–227, 240
Standard normal tables, 182–186, 203,
456–457
Standardizing data, 83, 189–191, 193, 207,
208–209
Starbucks Corp., 4, 139, 161, 211, 227
Statistic, 61, 212, 217, 239
Statistical quality control, 231–235,
237–239, 240
Statistics, 5–7
descriptive, 5, 15
importance of, 4–5, 14–15
inferential, 5, 15
Stem-and-leaf diagrams, 42–43, 49
Strata, 214
Stratified random sampling, 214–215, 239
Student's *t* distribution, 255–258
Student's *t* tables, 458–459
Subjective probability, 105, 131
Suffolk University, 215–216
Sum of squares due to error (residual) (*SSE*),
384
Sum of squares due to regression (*SSR*), 397
Sum of squares due to treatments (*SSTR*), 338
Symmetric distributions, 32, 66, 180
Symmetry, 66

T

t distribution, 255–258, 271
t tables, 256–257, 458–459
Tabular methods
contingency tables. *See* Contingency
tables
discrete probability distributions,
141–142
frequency distributions. *See* Frequency
distributions

Tabular methods (*Cont.*)
  joint probability tables, 119–120, 130–131
  regression results, 407–408
  representation of probabilities, 125–126
  written report using, 47–48
Test of independence, 366–370, 374, 378–379
Test statistics
  goodness-of-fit, 362–365, 374
  for $\mu_1 - \mu_2$, 321–322, 345
  for mean difference, 329–330, 346
  for one-way ANOVA test, 339, 346
  for $p_1 - p_2$, 356–357, 373
  for population mean (μ), 286, 297, 310–311
  for population proportion (p), 304, 311
  for test of independence, 369–370, 374
  for test of individual significance, 402–403
  for test of joint significance, 406–407
Texas Transportation Institute, 344
Time series data, 6–7, 15
Total probability rule, 123–128, 132
Total sum of squares (*SST*), 340, 396
Total variation, 396
True zero point, 12
Tukey, John, 42
Two-tailed hypothesis tests, 281–283, 293–294, 309
Type I errors, 283–284, 309
Type II errors, 283–284, 309

U

Unconditional probability, 112, 132
Under Armour, Inc., 101, 118–121, 353, 367, 370

Unexplained variation, 396
Unimodal data, 63
Union, of two events, 103, 104
U.S. Census Bureau, 7
University of New Hampshire, 215
University of Pennsylvania Medical Center, 4
University of Utah, 130
Upper control limit (UCL), 232–233
USA Today, 5, 7, 372

V

The Vanguard Group, 59, 77
Variables, 8–9, 15
  continuous, 9, 15
  discrete, 8–9, 15
  dummy, 422–428, 447
  explanatory, 382, 413, 422–428
  qualitative. *See* Qualitative variables
  quantitative. *See* Quantitative variables
  random. *See* Random variables
  response, 382, 413, 431–435
  standard normal. *See* Standard normal random variables
Variance, 74–75, 94
  of binomial random variable, 153–155, 168
  of discrete random variable, 146–147, 168
  for grouped data, 85–87, 94
  of hypergeometric random variable, 164, 169
  of Poisson random variable, 159, 168
  population variance (σ^2), 75, 76, 85–87, 94
  of the sample mean, 218

of the sample proportion, 224–225
  sample variance (s^2), 75, 76, 85–87, 94
Venn, John, 103
Venn diagrams, 103–104, 110–112
Vertical axes, misleading scales on, 23–24
Vertical bar charts, 21–22

W

The Wall Street Journal, 7
Weighted mean, 66–67, 86
White's correction, 442
Within-treatments estimate of σ^2, 338–339
Within-treatments variance (*MSE*), 338–339

X

$\bar{x}$ charts, 232, 233–234, 240, 245

Y

Yahoo!, 7

Z

z distribution. *See* Standard normal distribution
z-scores, 83–84, 94, 182
z tables, 182–186, 203, 456–457
Zero point, 12
zillow.com, 7

Standard Normal Curve Areas

Entries in this table provide the area under the curve to the left of $-z$.
For example, $P(Z \leq -1.52) = 0.0643$.

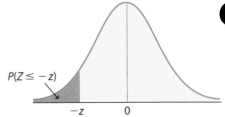

$P(Z \leq -z)$

$-z$ 0

z	0.00	0.01	0.02	0.03	0.04	0.05	0.06	0.07	0.08	0.09
−3.9	0.0000	0.0000	0.0000	0.0000	0.0000	0.0000	0.0000	0.0000	0.0000	0.0000
−3.8	0.0001	0.0001	0.0001	0.0001	0.0001	0.0001	0.0001	0.0001	0.0001	0.0001
−3.7	0.0001	0.0001	0.0001	0.0001	0.0001	0.0001	0.0001	0.0001	0.0001	0.0001
−3.6	0.0002	0.0002	0.0001	0.0001	0.0001	0.0001	0.0001	0.0001	0.0001	0.0001
−3.5	0.0002	0.0002	0.0002	0.0002	0.0002	0.0002	0.0002	0.0002	0.0002	0.0002
−3.4	0.0003	0.0003	0.0003	0.0003	0.0003	0.0003	0.0003	0.0003	0.0003	0.0002
−3.3	0.0005	0.0005	0.0005	0.0004	0.0004	0.0004	0.0004	0.0004	0.0004	0.0003
−3.2	0.0007	0.0007	0.0006	0.0006	0.0006	0.0006	0.0006	0.0005	0.0005	0.0005
−3.1	0.0010	0.0009	0.0009	0.0009	0.0008	0.0008	0.0008	0.0008	0.0007	0.0007
−3.0	0.0013	0.0013	0.0013	0.0012	0.0012	0.0011	0.0011	0.0011	0.0010	0.0010
−2.9	0.0019	0.0018	0.0018	0.0017	0.0016	0.0016	0.0015	0.0015	0.0014	0.0014
−2.8	0.0026	0.0025	0.0024	0.0023	0.0023	0.0022	0.0021	0.0021	0.0020	0.0019
−2.7	0.0035	0.0034	0.0033	0.0032	0.0031	0.0030	0.0029	0.0028	0.0027	0.0026
−2.6	0.0047	0.0045	0.0044	0.0043	0.0041	0.0040	0.0039	0.0038	0.0037	0.0036
−2.5	0.0062	0.0060	0.0059	0.0057	0.0055	0.0054	0.0052	0.0051	0.0049	0.0048
−2.4	0.0082	0.0080	0.0078	0.0075	0.0073	0.0071	0.0069	0.0068	0.0066	0.0064
−2.3	0.0107	0.0104	0.0102	0.0099	0.0096	0.0094	0.0091	0.0089	0.0087	0.0084
−2.2	0.0139	0.0136	0.0132	0.0129	0.0125	0.0122	0.0119	0.0116	0.0113	0.0110
−2.1	0.0179	0.0174	0.0170	0.0166	0.0162	0.0158	0.0154	0.0150	0.0146	0.0143
−2.0	0.0228	0.0222	0.0217	0.0212	0.0207	0.0202	0.0197	0.0192	0.0188	0.0183
−1.9	0.0287	0.0281	0.0274	0.0268	0.0262	0.0256	0.0250	0.0244	0.0239	0.0233
−1.8	0.0359	0.0351	0.0344	0.0336	0.0329	0.0322	0.0314	0.0307	0.0301	0.0294
−1.7	0.0446	0.0436	0.0427	0.0418	0.0409	0.0401	0.0392	0.0384	0.0375	0.0367
−1.6	0.0548	0.0537	0.0526	0.0516	0.0505	0.0495	0.0485	0.0475	0.0465	0.0455
−1.5	0.0668	0.0655	0.0643	0.0630	0.0618	0.0606	0.0594	0.0582	0.0571	0.0559
−1.4	0.0808	0.0793	0.0778	0.0764	0.0749	0.0735	0.0721	0.0708	0.0694	0.0681
−1.3	0.0968	0.0951	0.0934	0.0918	0.0901	0.0885	0.0869	0.0853	0.0838	0.0823
−1.2	0.1151	0.1131	0.1112	0.1093	0.1075	0.1056	0.1038	0.1020	0.1003	0.0985
−1.1	0.1357	0.1335	0.1314	0.1292	0.1271	0.1251	0.1230	0.1210	0.1190	0.1170
−1.0	0.1587	0.1562	0.1539	0.1515	0.1492	0.1469	0.1446	0.1423	0.1401	0.1379
−0.9	0.1841	0.1814	0.1788	0.1762	0.1736	0.1711	0.1685	0.1660	0.1635	0.1611
−0.8	0.2119	0.2090	0.2061	0.2033	0.2005	0.1977	0.1949	0.1922	0.1894	0.1867
−0.7	0.2420	0.2389	0.2358	0.2327	0.2296	0.2266	0.2236	0.2206	0.2177	0.2148
−0.6	0.2743	0.2709	0.2676	0.2643	0.2611	0.2578	0.2546	0.2514	0.2483	0.2451
−0.5	0.3085	0.3050	0.3015	0.2981	0.2946	0.2912	0.2877	0.2843	0.2810	0.2776
−0.4	0.3446	0.3409	0.3372	0.3336	0.3300	0.3264	0.3228	0.3192	0.3156	0.3121
−0.3	0.3821	0.3783	0.3745	0.3707	0.3669	0.3632	0.3594	0.3557	0.3520	0.3483
−0.2	0.4207	0.4168	0.4129	0.4090	0.4052	0.4013	0.3974	0.3936	0.3897	0.3859
−0.1	0.4602	0.4562	0.4522	0.4483	0.4443	0.4404	0.4364	0.4325	0.4286	0.4247
−0.0	0.5000	0.4960	0.4920	0.4880	0.4840	0.4801	0.4761	0.4721	0.4681	0.4641

Source: Probabilities calculated with Excel.

Standard Normal Curve Areas (cont'd)

Entries in this table provide the area under the curve to the left of z.
For example, $P(Z \leq 1.52) = 0.9357$.

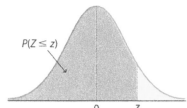

$P(Z \leq z)$

z	0.00	0.01	0.02	0.03	0.04	0.05	0.06	0.07	0.08	0.09
0.0	0.5000	0.5040	0.5080	0.5120	0.5160	0.5199	0.5239	0.5279	0.5319	0.5359
0.1	0.5398	0.5438	0.5478	0.5517	0.5557	0.5596	0.5636	0.5675	0.5714	0.5753
0.2	0.5793	0.5832	0.5871	0.5910	0.5948	0.5987	0.6026	0.6064	0.6103	0.6141
0.3	0.6179	0.6217	0.6255	0.6293	0.6331	0.6368	0.6406	0.6443	0.6480	0.6517
0.4	0.6554	0.6591	0.6628	0.6664	0.6700	0.6736	0.6772	0.6808	0.6844	0.6879
0.5	0.6915	0.6950	0.6985	0.7019	0.7054	0.7088	0.7123	0.7157	0.7190	0.7224
0.6	0.7257	0.7291	0.7324	0.7357	0.7389	0.7422	0.7454	0.7486	0.7517	0.7549
0.7	0.7580	0.7611	0.7642	0.7673	0.7704	0.7734	0.7764	0.7794	0.7823	0.7852
0.8	0.7881	0.7910	0.7939	0.7967	0.7995	0.8023	0.8051	0.8078	0.8106	0.8133
0.9	0.8159	0.8186	0.8212	0.8238	0.8264	0.8289	0.8315	0.8340	0.8365	0.8389
1.0	0.8413	0.8438	0.8461	0.8485	0.8508	0.8531	0.8554	0.8577	0.8599	0.8621
1.1	0.8643	0.8665	0.8686	0.8708	0.8729	0.8749	0.8770	0.8790	0.8810	0.8830
1.2	0.8849	0.8869	0.8888	0.8907	0.8925	0.8944	0.8962	0.8980	0.8997	0.9015
1.3	0.9032	0.9049	0.9066	0.9082	0.9099	0.9115	0.9131	0.9147	0.9162	0.9177
1.4	0.9192	0.9207	0.9222	0.9236	0.9251	0.9265	0.9279	0.9292	0.9306	0.9319
1.5	0.9332	0.9345	0.9357	0.9370	0.9382	0.9394	0.9406	0.9418	0.9429	0.9441
1.6	0.9452	0.9463	0.9474	0.9484	0.9495	0.9505	0.9515	0.9525	0.9535	0.9545
1.7	0.9554	0.9564	0.9573	0.9582	0.9591	0.9599	0.9608	0.9616	0.9625	0.9633
1.8	0.9641	0.9649	0.9656	0.9664	0.9671	0.9678	0.9686	0.9693	0.9699	0.9706
1.9	0.9713	0.9719	0.9726	0.9732	0.9738	0.9744	0.9750	0.9756	0.9761	0.9767
2.0	0.9772	0.9778	0.9783	0.9788	0.9793	0.9798	0.9803	0.9808	0.9812	0.9817
2.1	0.9821	0.9826	0.9830	0.9834	0.9838	0.9842	0.9846	0.9850	0.9854	0.9857
2.2	0.9861	0.9864	0.9868	0.9871	0.9875	0.9878	0.9881	0.9884	0.9887	0.9890
2.3	0.9893	0.9896	0.9898	0.9901	0.9904	0.9906	0.9909	0.9911	0.9913	0.9916
2.4	0.9918	0.9920	0.9922	0.9925	0.9927	0.9929	0.9931	0.9932	0.9934	0.9936
2.5	0.9938	0.9940	0.9941	0.9943	0.9945	0.9946	0.9948	0.9949	0.9951	0.9952
2.6	0.9953	0.9955	0.9956	0.9957	0.9959	0.9960	0.9961	0.9962	0.9963	0.9964
2.7	0.9965	0.9966	0.9967	0.9968	0.9969	0.9970	0.9971	0.9972	0.9973	0.9974
2.8	0.9974	0.9975	0.9976	0.9977	0.9977	0.9978	0.9979	0.9979	0.9980	0.9981
2.9	0.9981	0.9982	0.9982	0.9983	0.9984	0.9984	0.9985	0.9985	0.9986	0.9986
3.0	0.9987	0.9987	0.9987	0.9988	0.9988	0.9989	0.9989	0.9989	0.9990	0.9990
3.1	0.9990	0.9991	0.9991	0.9991	0.9992	0.9992	0.9992	0.9992	0.9993	0.9993
3.2	0.9993	0.9993	0.9994	0.9994	0.9994	0.9994	0.9994	0.9995	0.9995	0.9995
3.3	0.9995	0.9995	0.9995	0.9996	0.9996	0.9996	0.9996	0.9996	0.9996	0.9997
3.4	0.9997	0.9997	0.9997	0.9997	0.9997	0.9997	0.9997	0.9997	0.9997	0.9998
3.5	0.9998	0.9998	0.9998	0.9998	0.9998	0.9998	0.9998	0.9998	0.9998	0.9998
3.6	0.9998	0.9998	0.9999	0.9999	0.9999	0.9999	0.9999	0.9999	0.9999	0.9999
3.7	0.9999	0.9999	0.9999	0.9999	0.9999	0.9999	0.9999	0.9999	0.9999	0.9999
3.8	0.9999	0.9999	0.9999	0.9999	0.9999	0.9999	0.9999	0.9999	0.9999	0.9999
3.9	1.0000	1.0000	1.0000	1.0000	1.0000	1.0000	1.0000	1.0000	1.0000	1.0000

SOURCE: Probabilities calculated with Excel.